A
History of
American
Life

PAUL LAUNE

A HISTORY OF AMERICAN LIFE

IN

TWELVE VOLUMES

ARTHUR M. SCHLESINGER
DIXON RYAN FOX

Editors

ASHLEY H. THORNDIKE   CARL BECKER
Consulting Editors

The Lure of the City

A HISTORY OF AMERICAN LIFE
Volume X

THE RISE
OF THE CITY
1878-1898

BY
ARTHUR MEIER SCHLESINGER
PROFESSOR OF HISTORY, HARVARD UNIVERSITY

THE MACMILLAN COMPANY

We are now a nation of cities.

> W. H. TOLMAN, *Municipal Reform Move-
> ment in the United States* (N. Y., 1895), 35.

*What shall we do with our great cities? What will
our great cities do with us? These are the two problems which confront every thoughtful American.
For the question involved in these two questions does
not concern the city alone. The whole country is
affected, if indeed its character and history are not
determined, by the condition of its great cities. . . .
The city is not all bad nor all good. It is humanity
compressed, the best and the worst combined, in a
strangely composite community.*

> LYMAN ABBOTT, "Introduction," HELEN
> CAMPBELL AND OTHERS, *Darkness and
> Daylight* (Hartford, 1891), 40, 42.

CONTENTS

ILLUSTRATIONS

(By the Editors)

From the frontispiece of Will Carleton, *City Ballads* (N. Y., 1885), a book of poems designed "to reproduce some of the effects of city scenes and character upon the intellect of two people from the country," page v. The drawing is by the Anglo-American artist Harry Fenn (1838-1911), though by no means one of his best.

(a) Electioneering in upland Georgia. This unsigned drawing in *Harper's Weekly*, XXXII, 696 (Sept. 15, 1888), 9 x 7 inches, illustrates the new importance of the mountaineer's vote as the old hierarchies were being vanquished. Note the boy outside off to shoot a meal.

(b) The Highland Gingham Mills, near Charlotte, N. C. This plant with 500 gingham looms cost $150,000 and was paid for within two years at a rate of $1.00 per week per share. From D. A. Tompkins, *Cotton Mill, Commercial Features* (Charlotte, N. C., 1899).

(a) Pueblo, Colorado. From a full page of drawings by Charles Graham in *Harper's Weekly*, XXXII, 332 (May 12, 1888). Founded in 1858 and at first slow in development, Pueblo had 20,000 population in 1888 and, with its extensive steel works, was already known as the "Pittsburgh of the West." The highest tower is on the high school and the long building somewhat to the left is the insane asylum.

(b) Using Graham's borders we have substituted a figure from a drawing by Frederic Remington, entitled "Dragging a Bull's Hide over a Prairie Fire," in the same periodical, XXXII, Oct. 27, 1888, supplement. After studying art Remington (1861-1909) went west for actual experience as a cowboy and became the most famous delineator of life on the ranches and of the western Indian wars.

A map of the United States "corrected" to show the importance of states with respect to population rather than area, prepared for this volume by Margaret Hilferty and Jane Worcester of the statistical staff of the School of Public Health, Harvard University. Locating where the Mississippi River would be, note the comparative importance of

EDITORS' FOREWORD

American civilization in the 1880's and 1890's offers a study in contrasts. Different in many respects from anything that had preceded it, different too from what would follow, it was itself marked by diversities and contradictions which give distinctive color and tone to the era. The South, emerging from the deep shadows of Reconstruction, was troubled by strange new stirrings, by a pressing sense that it must modernize its economic order, by a growing apprehension that it must treat as full-fledged human beings both the Negroes and the mass of white commoners. The Great West had its own variety and interest, but it too was undergoing rapid change as the old glamour of mystery and bold adventure gave way before the myriad husbandmen, brought in by the railroads, with their women and children and their prosaic round of unremitting toil. Even in the older agricultural districts to the eastward, contrasts abounded, the emaciated farmer on his bleak New England hillside forming a curious foil for the sturdy yeoman of the Mid-Western prairies. This varied rural scene the author paints with broad strokes clearly limning the main masses of the changing picture, while with reflected lights he indicates relationships in different parts and animates the whole with vivid instance. It is, indeed, replete with incident and illustration, for he is, above all, concerned with the human consequences of what are oftentimes depicted as large impersonal movements.

But Professor Schlesinger's purpose is not merely to make live again a phase of American life that has half faded from memory. His account is strongly charged with meaning. The United States in the eighties and nineties was trembling between two worlds, one rural and agricultural, the other urban and industrial. In this span of years the fateful decision was made. Traditional America gave way to a new America, one more akin to Western Europe than to its own former self, yet retaining an authentic New World quality. The author recognizes that Americans formed a part of the larger human family and had behind them the general history of mankind; their achievements, therefore, are measured by world standards—a procedure rare among American historians. Such writers, too, gazing eastward toward the Atlantic Seaboard, have been accustomed to emphasize the long-time influence of the frontier upon American civilization and the disastrous effects of the passing of free fertile lands. The present volume is devoted, rather, to describing and appraising the new social force which waxed and throve while driving the pioneer culture before it: the city.

In the ever widening reach of its influence the author finds the key to an understanding of the most multifarious developments. The city, in Josiah Strong's phrase, was "the mighty heart of the body politic, sending its streams of life pulsating to the very finger-tips of the whole land." Aside from the part played by urban leadership in building a new structure of industry and trade—a theme treated in a companion volume—the city is envisaged as the dominant force of all those impulses and movements which made for a finer, more humane civilization. Education, literature, science, invention, the fine arts, social reform, public hygiene, the use of leisure, the "good life"—all these were given lift and direction by those who lived in urban centers. As rumor of the city's fascination and its opportunity reached the far-flung countryside, a townward trek set in, which in magnitude recalls the hosts who once had sought a larger life in the unpeopled wilderness. The author investigates the rich cultural record of these years, the so-called "buried renaissance," and makes clear its contributions toward the achievements of the twentieth century.

But the city was also a center of evil as well as of good; the children of darkness as well as of light congregated there. Crime, vice and graft, deeply rooted in the slum and the saloon, offered problems which this generation solved as best it could. Dense populations also presented new difficulties of transit, lighting, sewerage, fire protection and sanitation. American childhood rapidly lost its rural heritage of outdoor life, necessitating a larger measure of social concern for the welfare of the growing generation. The status of women was vitally affected, not always for the better, while the presence of hordes of immigrants, sharply different in their cultural types from those who had made America throughout the previous three hundred years, raised grave questions as to the effective working of the "melting pot." Religion itself was confronted with the need for adapting its teaching and methods to an urban rather than to a rural constituency.

There is incident, as in the rush into Oklahoma, and color, as in the magnificent World's Fair; interesting individuals appear, like Burbank, Tillman, Gladden, Riis, Howells, Saint-Gaudens, Pulitzer, Booker T. Washington, each with his aspirations and accomplishments. We learn, too, what such observant foreigners as Kipling, Bryce and Robert Louis Stevenson thought of the changing American scene. But all these come not for their own sake. Significance is emphasized and the large averages of life are accounted of greater consequence than the unusual and the picturesque. There is high respect throughout for definite, concrete facts, but these, with a logic too rare in social history, build forward to support a major thesis, that suggested in the title. It is this which integrates the book. Modern America had emerged by 1878, as Professor Nevins has pointed out in another volume, but the rise of the city, together with the nationalizing of the economic order, brought it very much nearer to the America we know today.

These chapters deal with times not yet the stock of many general histories. The sources indicated as their basis, so various and abundant, suggest innumerable inquiries useful and rewarding. At least, it may be hoped that a reading of this book will help win for these two decades an appreciation of their rightful place in the history of American life.

D. R. F.

THE RISE
OF THE CITY
1878-1898

THE RISE OF THE CITY

CHAPTER I

THE NEW SOUTH

AMERICAN civilization in 1878 was, in one essential respect, like that of earlier times: it rested upon the farms and country towns of the nation. An American Sully of that day might truly have remarked, "Tillage and pasture are the two breasts of the state." His observation would have applied no less to the sources of material prosperity than to those subtler currents of thought and aspiration which from the beginning had given tone and color to American life. The generation destined to dominate the scene during the next twenty years was to be responsible for turning the needle of national interest from the country to the city, but as the period opened there was little to show that so momentous a change impended. Of the fifty million people counted in the census of 1880, three fourths, or nearly forty million, lived on the open land or in villages of less than four thousand inhabitants.

The term, "rural," was a cloak covering all types of country life from the meager existence eked out on the tiny breakneck farms of northern New England to the far-flung activities of the great bonanza farms of the West. Without leaving the national borders the student of social development could have discovered ample contemporary evidence of the historic evolution of agriculture from the use of primitive soil-scratching implements, as in the Kentucky hill country, to the puffing, snorting black monsters that threshed the grain of the

1

prairie farmers. Had he wished, he could have unrolled
the scroll further and have found great patches of country in which mankind had not yet passed beyond the
hunting or the pastoral stage. One traveler in 1878
found men in a secluded valley of southwestern Virginia
hunting squirrels and rabbits with the English short
bow, the arrows hefted in the ancient manner.[1]

Only in a few Atlantic states—Massachusetts, Rhode
Island, Connecticut, New York and New Jersey—were
the rural inhabitants outnumbered by the urban in
1878, though throughout the region north of the Potomac and the Ohio the city was unmistakably gaining
at the expense of the country. The stamp of ruralism
lay heaviest upon the remaining sections of the nation—
on the South, stretching in a broad belt along the Atlantic and the Gulf from the Potomac to the Rio Grande,
and the Great West, spreading its imperial expanse over
plain and mountain from Minnesota and the Missouri
River to the rim of the Pacific. One was a region, long
occupied and much tilled, still in process of readjust-
ment to the profound changes wrought by the Civil War
and its aftermath. The other was a section so recently
taken over by the whites that in 1878 its chief characteristic continued to be unsettlement rather than settlement.

As of old, the vast majority of Southerners were
farmers and the typical farmer was addicted to the
staple-crop system.[2] If he lived in the Lower South he
cultivated cotton, or perhaps rice or sugar cane. If he
lived in the Upper South he was apt to make tobacco

---

[1] N. S. Shaler, "The Transplantation of a Race," *Pop. Sci. Mo.*, LVI
(1899-1900), 519.

[2] R. H. Edmonds, *Facts about the South* (Balt., 1902), 14-33, gives
a good summary of Southern economic progress, 1880-1900. See also
P. A. Bruce, *The Rise of the New South* (G. C. Lee and F. N. Thorpe,
eds., *The History of North America*, Phila., 1903-1907, XVII), 17-306,
and J. A. C. Chandler and others, *The South in the Building of the
Nation* (Richmond, 1909), VI, *passim*.

his main reliance. Yet every year showed that the people were learning the unwisdom of pivoting their prosperity on one or two staple crops. Corn, hay, wheat, potatoes and other products began to count in the Southern agricultural list during the 1880's. The demand of the swiftly growing urban centers of the North for a greater abundance and variety of fruits and vegetables led to the rapid spread of orcharding and trucking in the lands along the Atlantic from Maryland to the Gulf. The Albemarle pippin of the Virginia piedmont and the peanut of the tidewater, the Scuppernong wine grape of North Carolina, the luscious watermelon of Georgia, soon commanded a nation-wide patronage. Stimulated by the example of California, Florida awoke to the golden possibilities of developing her subtropical fruits; and her oranges, lemons and pineapples began to vie on Northern fruit stands with those of the Coast and far-off Sicily.[1] These years demonstrated the ability of the South to raise almost any crop that could be grown in the United States.

Equally striking was the continuance of the postwar trend toward smaller units of cultivation. The attempt to resume agriculture on a large-scale basis had generally broken down after the war because of the heavy taxes, lack of operating capital and the irresponsible character of the Negro workers.[2] The impoverished aristocrat eagerly seized the opportunity to sell or lease "parcels" or "cuts" of ground to Negroes or landless whites. Already in 1880 there were one and a half million farms of all kinds in the South, more than double the number when the war broke out. By 1890 three hundred thousand additional ones had come into existence and the

[1] A. K. McClure, *The South: Its Industrial, Financial, and Political Condition* (Phila., 1886), 149-162.
[2] See Allan Nevins, *The Emergence of Modern America* (*A History of American Life*, VIII), 20-21, 24-25.

process was far from halted.[1] Some of the new holdings
resulted from clearing the forest from land that had
never known hoe and plow, or had known them so
long since that a new growth of pine or hickory had
replenished the worn-out soil. But most of them represented further subdivision of the great plantations. A
marked decline in average acreage resulted. The Georgia
farmer who in 1880 tilled 188 acres held but 147 ten
years later. In Mississippi in the same decade the typical
holding shrank from 156 to 122 acres, and in Tennessee
and Kentucky from 127 to about 118.

The effects of this democratizing process were far-
reaching both economically and socially. In increasing
number the patrician families which had traditionally
dominated Southern life and politics fled the countryside for the towns. Cut off from the expansive life on
their great estates, the members of the younger generation gave their attention to the professions or, in continuance of an old tradition, to politics. The pursuit of
agriculture, once a badge of social distinction, suffered
a serious loss of prestige.

On the other hand, the partition of land offered a
new footing to the unprivileged folk, not only to the
former slaves but also to the mass of white people. A
minority of the latter consisted of a sturdy yeomanry
who for generations had tilled their small farms in the
fertile backcountry valleys, usually without the help of
slaves and always without the social and political rewards that accrued to the large planters. In sharp contrast to them stood the poor whites of the black belt,
a numerous folk who had always formed the very dregs

---

[1] From 1880 to 1900 over a million new farms were added. See *U. S.
Twelfth Census* (1900), V, 688-689, 692-693, for these and later
statistics. The census definition of farm refers to operation, not ownership; thus a tract of a thousand acres divided among a dozen tenants
is reported as twelve farms.

of Southern white society. Lacking both capital and ambition, they had in early times allowed themselves to be crowded off into waste lands, like the pine barrens of south-central Georgia and the sand hills of northern Alabama and eastern Mississippi. There, rearing great litters of children, they had fallen into a squalid, ignorant, shiftless way of living hardly superior to that of the swine that ran half wild about their rude cabins.[1]

They seemed to be of a debased, if not vicious, strain, the local contempt for them being reflected in the names by which they were best known—"crackers" and "clay eaters" in Georgia, "hill billies" in Mississippi and "po' white trash" everywhere. Yet their stock had originally been as sound as any; and their customs, speech and ballads, like those of the isolated mountain folk of the South, preserved much of the Elizabethan flavor that their ancestors had brought with them to America. That they labored under a very special handicap was not revealed until a later day when it was discovered that a tiny intestinal parasite, the hookworm, had for generations been sapping the vital energies of many of them and thus thwarting every impulse to enterprise.[2]

The plight of the former planter class gave all who would a chance to share in a new partition of the kingdom. While the yeoman farmers, able to outbid their poorer rivals, succeeded in securing the choicest cuts, in the long run the poor whites were the chief beneficiaries. For the first time since their forebears ventured into the

[1] S. A. Hamilton, "The New Race Question in the South," *Arena*, XXVII (1902), 352-358, is one of few articles on the poor whites of the Lower South.

[2] The morbid appetites of the clay eaters were, it is believed, due to the hookworm infection. On this whole subject, see C. W. Stiles, *Report upon the Prevalence and Geographic Distribution of the Hookworm Disease in the United States* (U. S. Treas. Dept., Hygienic Lab., *Bull.*, no. 10, 1903), and H. U. Faulkner, *The Quest for Social Justice* (*A History of American Life*, XI), 233-234.

section they were able to escape their piney-woods
solitudes and take a self-respecting part in the life of
the countryside. Normal social relations became theirs;
schools began to touch the lives of their children; glass
panes in the windows and carpets on the floors evidenced
an increasing sense of pride and taste.

The road to economic independence, however, was a
steep and rocky one, conditions in the eighties showing
little improvement over those which had prevailed in
Reconstruction days.[1] The aspiring but poverty-stricken
husbandman must first become a "cropper" or share
tenant, obtaining tools, seed and draft animals from the
landlord and usually giving him half of the crop grown.
To safeguard his interests the landlord often retained a
measure of centralized control. Sometimes, as on the
D. C. Barrow plantation near Oglethorpe in central
Georgia, the oversight was loose and general;[2] but more
typical was the arrangement whereby the landlord or
his manager planned and directed the work, kept the
implements and mules at a central barn and controlled
the marketing of the crop.[3] This system, while lending
itself to many abuses, had the advantage of providing a
period of apprenticeship for the unskilled and protecting
them from destitution in times of low prices or crop
failure. It also preserved the benefits, enjoyed under
slavery, of large-scale operation. The plan was more
characteristic of the Lower South than of other parts
and more workable with the ex-slaves than with the
white toilers.

[1] See Nevins, *Emergence of Modern America*, 18-20.
[2] Anon., "A Georgia Plantation," *Scribner's Mo.*, XXI (1880-1881),
830-836.
[3] L. C. Gray and others, "Farm Ownership and Tenancy," U. S.
Dept. of Agr., *Yearbook for 1923*, esp. 529-532; Bureau of the Census,
Plantation Farming in the United States (*Special Rep.*, 1916), 7, 13;
R. P. Brooks, *The Agrarian Revolution in Georgia, 1865-1912* (Univ.
of Wis., *Bull.*, no. 639), 48-49. 65-68.

Given favorable conditions and the exercise of thrift, the cropper might advance to the position of renter or cash tenant and, in time perhaps, to full ownership. The chief obstacle in his path was the vicious credit system which constantly tempted him to borrow from the local merchant or banker at excessive rates of interest in anticipation of his harvest. This "lazy 'descent into hell,' " as Ben Tillman called it, plunged him into a bog of debt-peonage from which extrication was heartbreakingly difficult.[1] It was also an important deterrent to the rapid development of mixed farming, for the money lender insisted upon the one-crop routine—cotton or tobacco—with which he had always been familiar. Perhaps eighty or ninety per cent of the cotton growers— tenants and proprietors, whites and blacks—were normally enmeshed in the crop-lien system.[2] Despite all discouragements, however, the number of farmers who graduated from share tenancy to cash renting, as well as those who became freeholders, grew steadily through these years.[3]

The credit system also added to the difficulties of farmers of yeoman strain. Of this class Ben Tillman was typical in many respects. He had at first been able to make money on his upcountry farm in South Carolina, enlarging his holdings from time to time and buying more mules. In 1881, according to his own account, "I ran thirty plows, bought guano, rations, etc., as usual,

[1] G. K. Holmes, "The Peons of the South," Am. Acad. of Polit. and Social Sci., *Annals*, IV (1893-1894), 265-274; C. H. Otken, *The Ills of the South* (N. Y., 1894); M. B. Hammond, *The Cotton Industry* (Am. Econ. Assoc., *Publs.*, n.s., no. 1), chap. v; B. B. Kendrick, "Agrarian Discontent in the South, 1880-1900," Am. Hist. Assoc., *Rep. for 1920*, 270-272.

[2] A. M. Arnett, *The Populist Movement in Georgia* (Columbia Univ., *Studies*, CIV, no. 1), 57-58. *Cf.* Hammond, *Cotton Industry*, 155.

[3] The figures for the years 1880-1900 are given in *U. S. Twelfth Census*, V, 688-689; the two races are not separated. See also Brooks, *Agrarian Revolution*, chap. iv.

and the devil tempted me to buy a steam engine and other machinery, amounting to two thousand dollars, all on credit." Quickly the situation changed. Drought and crop failures, the usurious exactions of his creditors, extortionate prices paid to country storekeepers, forced him to sell much of his land.[1] Others found themselves in a similar dilemma. Not all were as ready as the fiery South Carolinian to "do something about it," but they shared his resentment that, with the mass of the people engaged in agriculture, the Southern state governments seemed so indifferent to their welfare.

This indifference was due in some quarters to a conviction that the South might more profitably devote its chief energies to the development of factory industry. The idea appealed to a variety of motives. How better to retaliate on the late enemy than to fight the devil with fire? "If we have lost the victory on the field of fight," declared the *Columbia Register* in 1881, "we can win it back in the work shop, in the factory, in an improved agriculture and horticulture, in our mines and in our schoolhouses." [2] More important, however, was the belief that economic salvation rested upon the exploitation of the raw materials, water power and cheap white labor which lay immediately at hand. The South, relieved of the incubus of slavery, had at last a chance to take its place in modern industrial society. Efforts in that direction were urged forward by the doubling of the Southern railway net in the twelve years after 1878. But many were not ready for the change; much inertia had to be overcome. The enemies of progress, asserted the *Register* in the same editorial, "are the prejudices of

[1] F. B. Simkins, *The Tillman Movement in South Carolina* (Duke Univ., *Publs.;* Durham, 1926), esp. 51-52.
[2] Quoted in the *Charleston News and Courier*, March 18, 1881, and cited by Broadus Mitchell, *The Rise of Cotton Mills in the South* (Johns Hopkins Univ., *Studies*, XXXIX, no. 2), 90.

the past, the instincts of isolation, the brutal indifference and harmful social infidelity which stands up in
our day with the old slave arguments . . . on its lips,
'I object' and 'You can't do it.' "

As a matter of fact, the South, even during slavery
times, had engaged in a considerable amount of manufacturing activity. Most of this effort, however, centered
in the mechanical trades which every well-equipped
plantation maintained, production being only for local
use. One of the natural, though unanticipated, effects
of subdivision of the great estates was the dispersion or
destruction of these local industries. Though a few of
the largest plantations continued to support a carpenter,
a blacksmith, a saddler, a shoemaker and a weaver, such
workmen generally were obliged to move to the nearest
crossroads where their little establishments served a whole
circle of small farms. Spinning and weaving vanished
as household occupations, and the people learned to depend increasingly upon the cheap fabrics bought at the
country stores, goods supplied from the manufacturing
districts of the North.

While this unobtrusive economic revolution was
going on, nascent industrialists were cheered by the success which greeted tobacco manufacturing in the Upper
South. From humble beginnings shortly after the war
the industry had already by 1878 reached a position of
importance. The new decade brought fresh enterprise,
more economical production, improved methods of
marketing.[1] Through skillful advertising, brands like
Bull Durham and Duke's Mixture, made at Durham,
North Carolina, became known throughout the world.
Across the Atlantic Tennyson was a devotee of Bull

---

[1] W. K. Boyd, *The Story of Durham* (Duke Univ., *Publs.*; Durham,
1925), chaps. iv-v; Meyer Jacobstein, *The Tobacco Industry in the
United States* (Columbia Univ., *Studies*, XXVI, no. 3), pt. ii, chap. iii.

Durham, to which he had been introduced by James Russell Lowell. Thomas Carlyle likewise found its pungent aroma congenial to his taste. For a time misguided zeal even caused the taurine lineaments of its trademark to decorate the pyramids of Egypt. The Dukes' business was based upon the making of smoking tobacco, snuff, chewing tobacco and cigars, but they saw interesting possibilities also in the cigarette, which prior to 1867 had been produced exclusively in Europe. Early in the 1880's, when they effected a satisfactory means of making the white tubes by machinery and invented a sliding pasteboard box for their sale to smokers, the cigarette trade began to add materially to their revenues. In the three states of North Carolina, Virginia and Kentucky the value of tobacco manufactures rose from about twenty-one million dollars in 1880 to nearly thirty-one million in 1890.[1]

The enthusiasm for manufacturing was even more strikingly shown in the so-called cotton-mill campaign of the eighties. Only a feeble start had been made at cotton manufacturing before 1878. Now something akin to a religious fervor swept over the seaboard states, directed toward the establishment of local factories for utilizing the basic Southern crop. Newspapers, large and small, helped propagate the new gospel, none more effectively than the *Charleston News and Courier* under the editorship of the brilliant Anglo-American F. W. Dawson.[2] Soon the rallying cry, "Bring the mills to the cotton!" was echoed from village to village and from hamlet to hamlet. Money for launching the enter-

---

[1] If Maryland and Missouri be included as part of the Upper South the totals would be $30,765,441 and $54,372,568. Florida also became important in tobacco manufacturing, producing over eight million dollars' worth of cigars and cigarettes by 1890. *U. S. Tenth Census* (1880), II, 78, 79; *U. S. Twelfth Census*, IX, 647, 649, 661.

[2] Mitchell, *Rise of Cotton Mills*, 112-115.

prises was not to be had from the North where, for example, such a man as Edward Atkinson, biased perhaps by his Massachusetts mill connections, publicly counseled his Southern friends against the new departure.[1] Capital had to be raised from the people of the neighborhood out of their meager savings. While a few upcountry mills such as Piedmont, Pacolet, Clifton and Pelzer were financed in part by Charleston investors, this was the exception rather than the rule.[2] The zeal often outran prudent business considerations, but everywhere it evidenced a heartening spirit of enterprise and a resolve to rescue the community from the slough of agricultural distress.

If a town could not set up a large factory, it set up a small one; if not a sheeting, then a spinning mill. Merchants, doctors, bankers, preachers, teachers—men outstanding in their neighbors' eyes—were at the forefront of such efforts. Thus Charles Estes, well known to his fellow townsmen because of his success in the drygoods and grocery businesses, was made president of a mill in Augusta, Georgia, at the urging of a local judge who backed his opinion by taking one hundred thousand dollars' worth of stock. At Salisbury, a down-at-the-heels North Carolina town, a gaunt, fiery-eyed Tennessee evangelist conducted a month's revival in 1887, driving home with such force the thought that the wickedness and misery of the poor came from idleness that three local ministers promptly joined with other citizens in organizing a highly successful factory.[3] In general, the great natural advantages of locating along the fall line of the rivers in the Carolinas and Georgia

[1] Edward Atkinson, *Address Given in Atlanta* (Boston, 1881).

[2] Mitchell, *Rise of Cotton Mills*, chap. iv; Holland Thompson, *From the Cotton Field to the Cotton Mill* (N. Y., 1906), 59 ff., 81; Edmonds, *Facts about the South*, 25.

[3] Mitchell, *Rise of Cotton Mills*, 108, 135-136.

appealed strongly to the mill promoters and there, with
the aid of cheap water power, the most flourishing factories were apt to be found.

While a few men like Daniel A. Tompkins of
Charlotte had the proper technical training for cotton
manufacturing, many more succeeded because their native
shrewdness carried them through a period when close
figuring was not necessary.[1] Others were plain incom-
petents, chosen for social reasons, and the enterprises
they headed quickly languished. The success of the
cotton-mill campaign is attested by the fact that from
1880 to 1890 the number of spindles and looms nearly
trebled. Before the close of another decade the production of coarse cottons would be virtually monopolized
by the South. Even the cottonseed, generally neglected
before 1878 as valueless, was discovered to have commercial possibilities in its various uses as fertilizer, cattle
food, salad oil, etc. The forty-five cottonseed mills of
1880 grew into one hundred and fourteen in 1890 with
a capital of twelve million dollars.[2]

Less spectacular in its development than the cotton
industry, the manufacture of iron made almost as notable
an advance.[3] Not only were new beds discovered, but
they were found in close proximity to deposits of coal
and limestone, as if nature had designedly associated
the necessary ingredients for reducing the ore. Between
1880 and 1890 fifty new blast furnaces were erected in
the three states of Alabama, Tennessee and Virginia,

[1] Tompkins's chief services were as a builder and distributor of mill
machinery and supplies, as adviser to other manufacturers, as a promoter
of industrial and technical education and, in general, as an apostle of
Southern industrialization. G. T. Winston, *A Builder of the New South*
(Garden City, 1920), chaps. vii-xii.

[2] Bruce, *Rise of New South*, 206-209.

[3] Bruce, *Rise of New South*, 112-113, 210-217; R. H. Edmonds,
The South's Redemption (Balt., 1890), 12-24; Ethel Armes, *The
Story of Coal and Iron in Alabama* (Birmingham, 1910), chaps. xvii-
xix, xxi-xxv.

the sites so well chosen that most of them continued in operation well into the twentieth century. Though other manufactures made less progress, yet many a local community did what it could in its straitened circumstances to utilize such raw materials as lay within reach. A Northern visitor to Southern cities in the eighties reported the section "wide awake to business, excited and even astonished at the development of its own immense resources in metals, marbles, coal, timber, fertilizers . . . ." [1] He hardly needed to add that "the nonsense that it is beneath the dignity of any man or woman to work for a living is pretty much eliminated from the Southern mind." [2]

Leading cities like New Orleans and Louisville were the natural centers of the new industrial development. Other places such as Atlanta, Memphis and Chattanooga forged rapidly ahead in population and manufacturing importance, though without attaining a size that would have been considered large according to Northern standards.[3] No champion of Southern industry failed to take pride in the meteoric rise of Birmingham. Without existence until 1871, its location in the heart of the Alabama iron and coal district had by 1890 caused it to become a bustling town of twenty-six thousand, the center of rolling mills, foundries, iron furnaces and machine shops.

Generally speaking, however, Southern manufactur-

[1] C. D. Warner, *Studies in the South and West* (N. Y., 1889), 111.

[2] Warner, *Studies*, 112-113. See also W. P. Trent, "Dominant Forces in Southern Life," *Atlantic Mo.*, LXXIX (1897), 49-50. Compare F. L. Olmsted's prewar comment: "To work industriously . . . is, in the Southern tongue, to 'work like a nigger.' " *The Cotton Kingdom* (N. Y., 1861), I, 22.

[3] The population of the principal cities in 1890 was: New Orleans, 242,039; Louisville, 161,129; Richmond, 81,388; Atlanta, 65,533; and Memphis, 64,495. Chattanooga, like Birmingham an iron center, grew from 12,892 in 1880 to 29,100 in 1890. *U. S. Twelfth Census*, I, 430-433.

ing was conducted on too small a scale to breed important urban communities. Even Durham had less than six thousand residents as late as 1890. The typical mill village possessed but a few hundred people, mostly laborers and their families gathered for the purpose of working in a particular factory and living in unpainted shanties along a single street ankle-deep with dust. The entire South in 1880 contained only ten cities of twenty-five thousand or more inhabitants and this number had grown to but nineteen in 1890. Historic old cities like Charleston and Mobile showed little sign of new life, resting tranquilly in the autumnal glory of their past renown.

In emulating the industrial course of the North, the South had never been more truly Southern. Unlike New England or Great Britain she depended for her basic supplies entirely upon the tobacco produced in her own fields, the cotton grown on her own lands, the coal and iron mined in her own hills, the timber cut in her own forests. Not a dollar's worth of raw materials did she need to buy from outside her own borders. Moreover, apart from the railways, the new undertakings were nourished largely by her own capital, usually in the form of an aggregation of petty savings. It was only after the path had been blazed and the certainty of profits demonstrated that Northern investors began to show an active interest. The turning point perhaps came in the mid-eighties when the important Thomas Iron Company of Pennsylvania constructed a million-dollar branch plant in Alabama, one of the finest in America.[1] In 1889 a large party of Northern capitalists and bankers, including Andrew Carnegie and the two leading partners of Cooper, Hewitt & Company, toured the South and brought back glowing reports. Soon an in-

[1] Edmonds, *South's Redemption*, 5-6, 14.

creasing stream of Northern capital began to flow southward.

What was true of financial support was even truer of
the human energies devoted to the new developments.
Northern promotion played a negligible part. The editor
of the *Manufacturers' Record* could well say in 1890:
"Southern energy and enterprise mainly are entitled to
the credit for what has been accomplished." [1] In the
South itself the drive toward industrialization came
chiefly from the former nonslaveholding class, for, as
we have seen, the members of the old landed gentry
turned to the professions rather than to manufacturing.
The typical *entrepreneur*, as he may be generalized from
a few hundred random instances, was the son of a
country merchant.[2] Beginning as a clerk with perhaps a
common-school education, he rose in time to storekeeper and petty money lender, laid by his profits and,
with his savings, aided in starting a local factory or mine
which he headed as president. When it is recalled how
much of the leadership and financial strength of the
prewar South was monopolized by the slavocracy, this
change may be regarded as little short of revolutionary.

Similarly the manual labor was supplied by the South.
This was not wholly a matter of choice, for ever since
the close of the war an active campaign had been waged
to make the section attractive to foreign immigrants.
Most of the states had passed laws to encourage their

[1] R. H. Edmonds in issue of Dec. 21, 1889, and in his *South's Redemption*, 47. See also F. W. Moore, "The Condition of the Southern
Farmer," *Yale Rev.*, III (1894-1895), 63.

[2] This generalization is based on a manuscript study of the background of three hundred postwar industrialists of Virginia, North and
South Carolina, Georgia, Alabama and Tennessee, made in 1928 by
G. W. Adams of the Harvard Graduate School. Of a total of two
hundred and fifty-four, about eighty per cent came of nonslaveholding
parentage; of the entire three hundred, only thirteen per cent were
born in the North, about half of them having gone South before the
war.

coming, boom literature was circulated under official auspices, and recruiting agents were dispatched to European countries, Virginia, it is said, sending several hundred to Great Britain and Germany in 1870.[1] Not discouraged by the negligible results, renewed efforts were made in the eighties as the industrial possibilities of the section were disclosed. State immigration bureaus were reëstablished or given enlarged powers; and official endeavors were supplemented by the activities of popular conventions, land companies, boards of trade and, most important of all, the new railways eager to build up their satellite territories. In 1883 a Southern Immigration Association was formed for the purpose of redoubling such exertions and to press for the opening of direct steam communication between Southern ports and Europe.[2]

Immigrant wage-earners, however, continued to prefer the North and the West where their countrymen had long been accustomed to go and where they need fear no competition from cheap native labor. Thus Southern manufacturing development had to rest on the brawn of the poor whites. By the same token it opened a fresh road of escape for this submerged element. The new industrialism did for the unprivileged commoners of

[1] *American Annual Cyclopedia*, X (1870), 749. Of course, the South sought farmers as well as factory hands. See 61 Cong., 3 sess., *Senate Docs.*, XXI, *passim*, for abstracts of Southern laws relating to immigration. Coolie labor was envisaged as a solution of the Southern economic problem in A. P. Merrill, "Southern Labor," *De Bow's Rev.*, VI (1869), 586-592; in refutation, see W. M. Burwell, "Science and the Mechanic Arts against Coolies," same issue, 557-571. An English visitor reported having seen six or seven hundred Chinese digging ditches alongside Negroes on the Alabama & Chattanooga Railway in 1870; but this was exceptional. Robert Somers, *The Southern States since the War* (London, 1871), 163-164, 225.

[2] Southern Immigration Association, *Proceedings* (Nashville, 1884). See also W. M. Barrows, *The New South* (N. Y., 1884), 4-5, and U. S. Industrial Commission, *Reports* (Wash., 1900-1902), XV, 550-575.

the upland South what the break-up of the great plantations was doing for those of the lowland districts. As
fast as factories were set up, labor was drawn from the
foothill and mountain country to operate them. Employers, somewhat to their surprise, discovered that as
workers they were industrious, self-improving and reliable, thus giving color to the belief that the highlanders
were not degenerate but simply unstarted.[1] Machine
shops, the cotton industry and furniture factories were
wholly dependent upon their labor. Only in the saw-
mills, tobacco factories and a few other less skilled employments did they find it necessary to compete with
Negroes for jobs. With every factory owner a law unto
himself, the workday was long, wages were low, conditions wretched. Yet, even so, the new job in the
busy mill village, with its opportunities for human
fellowship, held more attraction than the bleak life in
a distant mountain cove.

Since the whole family had worked together on the
farm, it seemed natural to comply with the wishes of
the mill proprietor to have the family as the working
unit in the factory. So arose the evil of child labor—not
the healthful outdoor choring of the farm, but the
steady, benumbing toil of the ill-ventilated, ill-lighted
mill—and its concomitant evil, the idle father living off
the working child. By 1890 twenty-three thousand
children were employed in industry in the thirteen
states.[2] A distinct "factory people" was in process of

[1] D. A. Tompkins, "The Mountain Whites as an Industrial Labor
Factor," Chandler and others, *South in Building of Nation*, VI, 58-61;
W. G. Frost, "Our Contemporary Ancestors in the Southern Moun-
tains," *Atlantic Mo.*, LXXXIII (1899), 311-319. For a discussion
of the various mountaineer groups, see S. T. Wilson, *The Southern
Mountaineers* (N. Y., 1906), chaps. ii, iv-vi.

[2] The census definition of child laborer is a boy of sixteen or under
and a girl of fifteen or under. E. G. Murphy, *Problems of the Present
South* (N. Y., 1904), 96-125; *U. S. Eleventh Census* (1890), IV, 89.

creation—a folk whose life was shaped by a common origin and a social experience not reaching beyond the sound of the factory whistle. When all was said and done, however, the mill hand was a part of the pulsing world; he had gained a real foothold in the struggle for existence. A few became superintendents of the new instrumentalities that had called them from their long sleep. Even the most wretched of them were unwilling to return to their mountain solitudes.

Though far fewer in numbers than the tenant farmers of the lowlands, the mill workers were like them in constituting a new economic and social class in Southern life. Together, these two sections of the poor-white population formed a Third Estate of which the earlier South offered no counterpart. The mill people were too new to their situation and too scattered to be alert to their grievances—the "damn factory class," Tillman impatiently called them—but each year marked increasing restiveness among the small-farmer contingent.[1] Politically untrained, they had, since the overthrow of the Carpetbaggers, accepted the leadership of the old gentry. This leadership, however, little heeded the critical conditions which beset the rural majority, such as the nefarious credit system, "landlordism," high transportation costs and low crop prices.

The decade after 1878 saw a rapid spread of farmers' clubs and societies where the ills and needs of agriculture were hotly debated and new men fresh from the people trained for leadership. Enough pressure was exerted upon the ruling class in various states to secure the establishment of departments of agriculture, state agricultural

---

[1] A. D. Mayo, "The Third Estate of the South," *Journ. of Social Sci.*, XXVII (1890), xx-xlii; Simkins, *Tillman Movement*, 176-177. See also a speech by E. A. Alderman before the National Congress of Education, Oct. 25, 1895. U. S. Commissioner of Education, *Report for 1894-95*, II, 1748.

Politics sought the votes of the poor whites

of the South and manufacturing their labor.

The New South

experiment stations and agricultural and mechanical colleges. But the more acute grievances remained unsolved, and the farmers themselves came to doubt whether measures which looked to increased production were what the situation called for.

Throughout the lean hard years of the eighties, in state after state, discontent with the rule of the well-born flickered and flared. The pretext for the Readjuster movement, which captured the Virginia legislature in 1879, was the resolve to scale down the prewar state debt, but the real animus was supplied by "men of the people" determined to cast off the leadership of the upper classes and the towns.[1] In South Carolina the "wool-hat boys" had a tribune of great promise in Martin Gary, demagogic foe of the "aristocratic oligarchy," but his premature death, in 1881, occurred before he had had time to mobilize the forces he had helped to rouse.[2] What he failed to accomplish Tillman, one of his lieutenants, eventually succeeded in bringing about, being swept into the governorship in 1890 by a popular demand for reform.[3] The same year an agrarian upheaval in Texas catapulted into the executive mansion "Jim" Hogg, a man of crude force, whose very name endeared him to the horny-handed sons of the soil.[4] In other states like forces were pushing from below. Everywhere the new leaders made political capital out of arraying the rural white masses against the railways, business

[1] C. C. Pearson, *The Readjuster Movement in Virginia* (*Yale Hist. Publs. Miscellany*, IV), esp. chap. ix.

[2] Simkins, *Tillman Movement*, 20-22, 49.

[3] Though the factory vote had played little part in his success, Governor Tillman secured the passage in 1893 of a law limiting the hours of labor to sixty-six a week. Simkins, *Tillman Movement*, 103-134, 164, 176-177.

[4] Herbert Gambrell, "James Stephen Hogg: Statesman or Demagogue?," *Southwest Rev.*, XIII (1928), 338-366. For similar movements in other states, see J. D. Hicks, *The Populist Revolt* (Minneapolis, 1931), 170-179.

men, bankers and aristocrats of the towns. Everywhere, too, their opponents sought to checkmate them with warnings of the danger of black supremacy if they pushed their insurgency to the point of splitting the ranks of the "white man's party."

A time of economic distress and political upheaval, the decade of the eighties was pivotal in the history of the postwar South. While the brave attempts at factory industry foreshadowed the future, the section retained its predominantly rural character. Agriculture passed through a period of storm and stress which aroused the agrarian masses to organized activity and eventually to political triumph. For better or for worse the Third Estate mounted the saddle. Southern politics was no longer to be merely government of the people and for the people but also by the people.[1] But it was equally clear that the people must be white people, for, as we shall see, legal disfranchisement of the Negro was one of the first fruits of the new dispensation.[2] Though the farmers' difficulties were largely of local origin, they were similar in kind to those of the other great agricultural region of the nation, the Great West. Thus, as the decade ended, the Southern agrarian leaders were ripe for coöperation with their Western brethren in demands upon the federal government for remedial action.

If the changes which the section underwent during this critical decade made its way of life more nearly like that of the remainder of the United States, the responsibility rested squarely upon the South itself. The homogeneity which characterized the white population in slavery times continued unaltered. The dominant race in the thirteen states advanced in the ten years from nine

[1] J. W. Johnston, *The Emancipation of the Southern Whites and Its Effects on Both Races* (Balt., 1887), argued that the whites had derived greater benefit from emancipation than the blacks.

[2] See later, 383-384.

and a half million to nearly twelve.[1] The number of Americans born outside the section who lived in the South in 1880 was four hundred and fifty thousand and the total had increased to probably not more than six hundred thousand in 1890. As for foreign infusions, at no time during the decade did aliens number more than one in fifty of the entire population. In 1890 fully seven eighths of the white inhabitants were of Southern nativity. On the other hand, the section contributed to the upbuilding of other parts of the nation a wealth of human material that it could ill afford to lose. The Negroes, while increasing at a slower rate than the former master class, advanced from five and a half million to six and a half.

In view of the frantic efforts made to attract immigrants an incident at the close of the decade caused many Southerners to question the wisdom of such endeavors and rejoice at their lack of success. Sometime during the 1880's a compact colony of Sicilians settled in New Orleans where they worked mainly as longshoremen, forming a turbulent and lawless element. The bloody clashes of their secret oath-bound societies led finally to the assassination of the Irish chief of police. When a trial of three of those accused of the crime resulted in their acquittal, a mob of citizens formed on the morning of March 14, 1891, and strung up all eleven.[2] The affair precipitated an international crisis, caused the withdrawal of the Italian minister and even-

[1] For population data, see *U. S. Eleventh Census*, I, xcviii, 560-563; *U. S. Tenth Census*, I, 480-483; *U. S. Twelfth Census*, I, 485.

[2] None of the mob was ever indicted or brought to trial. *U. S. Foreign Relations for 1891*, 665-667, 671-672, 674-686, 712-713; J. B. Moore, *A Digest of International Law* (Wash., 1906), VI, 837-841. Later mob outbreaks occurred against the Italians elsewhere in Louisiana: at Hahnville in 1896 when three held on a charge of homicide met violent death; and at Tallulah in 1899 when five others were taken from jail and lynched. Moore, *Digest*, VI, 843-845.

tually brought the payment of an indemnity by the Washington government. Though the Southern people might in many ways have benefited from a more varied racial make-up, they were at least saved the possibility of adding to their own inherited race problem one which they had no experience to meet.

Within the section itself there was considerable shifting of population during the decade, notably toward the rich farming country of the Gulf region and particularly into the half-developed state of Texas.[1] Railroads were penetrating the Texan interior; the great ranches in the western section were slowly crumbling before the farmer advance; cotton was asserting its primacy among agricultural crops. As heavy beef cattle and dairy cows crowded out the longhorns, so Merinos and Shropshires replaced the old Mexican sheep, and stocky, quickly grown hogs the lean and voracious razorbacks. Despite the great drought of 1886, which lasted twenty-three months and affected thirty-seven western counties, the total number of people in Texas increased by three quarters of a million, reaching two and a quarter million in 1890 drawn from many parts of the country as well as other portions of the world. What had been a thinly inhabited region ten years before had become well populated and the edge of settlement had reached the escarpment of the Staked Plains. This phenomenal growth, however, betrayed the essential kinship of Texas with the Great West rather than with the South.

[1] W. B. Bizzell, *Rural Texas* (L. H. Bailey, ed., *Rural State and Province Series;* N. Y., 1924), 123-136, 155-232; W. C. Holden, "West Texas Drouths," *Southwestern Hist. Quar.,* XXXII, 103-123.

CHAPTER II

THE GREAT WEST

MOST of the Great West in 1878 lay as yet beyond
the pale of statehood.[1] Five states had indeed been
formed as a result of mining rushes, partisan exigency at
Washington or other fortuitous circumstance. The bulk
of this vast region, however, consisted of eight great
territories—Dakota, Montana, Idaho, Wyoming, Washington, Utah, New Mexico and Arizona—and of a
special reserve, Indian Territory, set aside for the red
men. These eight territories embraced nearly a third of
the total national area and already contained six hundred
thousand white inhabitants—the vanguard of the restless, dusty army of civilization moving westward. As the
1880's began, the main body came into view, their advent hastened by the taming of the wild Indians and the
completion of the transcontinental railways. Over twice
as many settlers scattered through this region in the years
from 1880 to 1890 as in the two picturesque decades
preceding. Wealth, adventure, health, *Wanderlust,* the
desire for an easier living, all played their part in swelling
the tide of migrants.

The results as recorded by the census delighted the
heart of the Westerner with his love of bigness and
quick results, while furnishing some excuse for the saying
of skeptical Easterners that it was impossible to tell the
truth about the West without lying. By 1890 the popu-

[1] By the Great West is meant that section of the country lying between the Pacific and the first tier of states west of the Mississippi River,
exclusive of Texas.

lation of Utah had grown nearly one half beyond that
of 1880, Idaho held two and a half times as many
people, Wyoming almost three times as many. Aided
by silver and copper discoveries near Butte, Montana
more than tripled its population by 1890, while in
Dakota, where farming was the chief lodestone, the
numbers grew quite as rapidly notwithstanding the
shortage of rainfall toward the close of the decade.[1] The
progress of Washington was even more remarkable.
There the farmer could count not only on a fertile soil
but on ample rainfall, and the rush of settlement enlarged the population nearly fivefold. The number of
whites in the eight territories exceeded one and a half
million in 1890.[2]

The states of the Great West did nearly as well as
the territories in their rate of growth and achieved an
even greater increment of population.[3] Though thousands of families were forced by the drought late in
the eighties to abandon their farms, Nebraska doubled
her population by 1890, passing the million mark and
reducing her unoccupied domain to a third of what it
had been in 1880, while Kansas, adding a half-million
people to the million she possessed at the outset, had
settlers strewn through her entire area. In Colorado and
California the decline of the mining fever might have
had disastrous results but for the growth of their agricultural districts and towns. The former state numbered
four hundred thousand inhabitants in 1890, a gain of
one hundred per cent, and California grew from eight

[1] H. E. Briggs, "The Great Dakota Boom, 1879-1886," *N. D. Hist.
Quar.*, IV, 78-108.

[2] *U. S. Twelfth Census* (1900), I, xxii-xxv. These figures should
be read in the light of a gloomy prediction recorded in the *Washington*
(D. C.) *Star,* June 14, 1877, that the Great West could never develop
into populous and prosperous communities.

[3] *U. S. Compendium of Eleventh Census* (1890), I, xlvii; *U. S.
Statistical Atlas* (U. S. Twelfth Census), plates 11 and 12.

hundred thousand to one million two hundred thousand. Nevada alone could not recover from the blow and in the ten-year period lost a third of her citizens.

Except in early colonial times Western growth had always been a drain on the older American communities from which the migrants came. The familiar story was repeated once more, and for the last time, as the trans-Missouri country passed under the hand of the settler. Broadly speaking, the Middle West was the motherland of the newer states and territories. Her children fared forth to face the hardships and hazards of life in strange parts with the same dauntless spirit that their fathers and mothers had once set forth from the still older lands to the east. To their ranks were added many from those counties of New York and Pennsylvania bordering on the Ohio Valley. It is significant that these colonizing areas were also the parts of the North where the white population was breeding its largest families and which, according to the standards dictated by a simple rural economy, were threatened with overpopulation.[1]

The restless Middle Westerners were at home in all parts of the region.[2] They flocked into Kansas in such numbers that by 1890 one fifth of the inhabitants consisted of natives of Illinois and Ohio. Farther to the west, the major strains in the population of Colorado and California derived from Iowa, Missouri, Illinois, Ohio, New York and Pennsylvania; and a similar situation prevailed elsewhere. From Illinois alone a third of a million persons settled in the newer commonwealths. This was a "wandering of the nations" that was none the less notable because confined within the boundaries of a single country. It involved a transplantation, not

[1] *U. S. Eleventh Census* (1890), I, 914.
[2] For the data in this paragraph, see *U. S. Eleventh Census,* I, cxii-cxv, cxxiv.

only of men and material possessions but also of
ideas and institutions, which, in spite of different conditions of geography and climate, were, after the initial
shock of adjustment, to shape the lives of Westerners
along traditional American lines.

In making the journey westward the "prairie
schooner" was rapidly giving way to swifter means of
travel. Many, however, clung to the time-tried mode.
But the old-fashioned ox team had now been supplanted
by horses or mules, the necessity for carrying large stores
of food no longer existed, and few or no cattle were
driven along. Mr. and Mrs. C. D. Ide and a large party
from Mondovi, Wisconsin, made such a journey in the
spring of 1878, reaching their destination at Dayton in
Washington territory four and a half months later.
Despite the better trails and other ameliorations of travel
Mrs. Ide's diary shows that hardship and excitement
remained a-plenty.[1]

The number who went in this way, however, steadily
diminished. Railways advertised their advantages, offered
special rates and sometimes, as in the case of the Northern
Pacific Railroad, temporarily gave free transportation
to persons intending to settle upon railway land.[2] "Without the railroad," declared a prominent Dakotan in
1884, "it would have required a century to accomplish
what has been done in five years under its powerful
influence." [3] The Ide party made such a strange appearance while moving through southern Minnesota as to

[1] Mrs. Lucy A. Ide's diary of this journey has been edited by J. O.
Oliphant under the title, "In a Prairie Schooner, 1878," *Wash. Hist.
Quar.*, XVIII, 122-131, 191-198, 277-288.

[2] J. B. Hedges, "The Colonization Work of the Northern Pacific
Railroad," *Miss. Valley Hist. Rev.*, XIII, 320-321, 327, 332-333;
same author, "Promotion of Immigration to the Pacific Northwest by
the Railroads," same mag., XV, 183-203; G. D. Bradley, *The Story
of the Santa Fé* (Boston, 1920), chap. v. The emigrant guidebooks of
the 1880's ignored the possibility of traveling by wagon.

[3] Briggs, "Great Dakota Boom," 80.

cause people in a passing train to mistake them for a circus. The space-conquering locomotive inevitably rang the death knell of the covered wagon.[1]

The spell of the Great West was felt not only within the national borders but across the seas as well. Though a majority of the alien newcomers to America stopped in the industrial centers to the east, others sought the farming life with which they were familiar in their home lands, and special immigrant trains distributed them by the thousands through the remote trans-Missouri country. In a single week in the spring of 1882, according to the *Chicago Tribune*, nine thousand foreigners arrived in Chicago, most of them destined for Dakota.[2] Robert Louis Stevenson, short of funds and in search of health and a bride, boarded a transcontinental immigrant train in 1879, carrying with him a minimum of luggage and Bancroft's *History of the United States*.[3] The trip was marked by greater discomfort than the passage by immigrant ship from the Clyde to New York.[4] After many stops and transfers he and his bewildered polyglot companions reached the Pacific Transfer Station, near Council Bluffs, where they exchanged to the Union and Central Pacific railways for their ten days' trip to the Coast.

Every passenger was sold a board and three straw cushions; when darkness fell, the seats were rearranged

[1] But travelers must complain however they ride! See Helen Hunt Jackson's amusing account of her trip by Pullman from Chicago to San Francisco in 1878 in H. H. (*pseud.*), *Bits of Travel at Home* (Boston, 1878), 3-40.

[2] Briggs, "Great Dakota Boom," 86.

[3] R. L. Stevenson, *Across the Plains* (N. Y., 1892), esp. 26-39. See also Rosaline Masson, *The Life of Robert Louis Stevenson* (N. Y., 1923), 147-153, 168-169, 178-181.

[4] Described in R. L. Stevenson, *The Amateur Emigrant* (Chicago, 1895). For a detailed account of a steerage passage made by a Swedish immigrant in 1891, see A. G. Carlson, *En Emigrants Resa* (Chicago, 1894).

and the distance between each pair bridged with the boards, thus forming a perilous couch for two sleepers in a cramped position. For food and comforts the travelers relied chiefly upon the newsboys who noisily peddled fruit, canned beans and bacon, coffee, soap and tin basins. A single flat-topped stove at the end of the car provided cooking facilities. Stevenson good-naturedly took part in the rough camaraderie of the train. He even succeeded in attaining the democratic distinction of a nickname, no less a one than "Shakespeare," bestowed perhaps because of his accent and the erudition implied by the six volumes of Bancroft. None too robust when he began the adventure, Stevenson reached his destination "feverish and sick," looking "like a man at death's door."

The business of transporting immigrants was eagerly sought by the railroads, not so much because of the immediate returns of the passenger traffic as because of their desire to hasten settlement, develop a shipping business and enhance the value of their land holdings. After a period of relative quiet during the five hard years following the Panic of 1873 the railway immigration departments in the Atlantic ports and Europe resumed their activities with redoubled energy.[1] In 1883, for instance, the Northern Pacific had one hundred and twenty-four agents stationed on the Continent and eight hundred and thirty-one in the British Isles. Over half a million copies of its publications, printed in five languages, issued from its Liverpool office within the year.

By 1890 one in every five persons in the Great West was foreign-born. The total number of immigrant settlers had increased three quarters of a million in ten

[1] For accounts of such activities, see Hedges, "Northern Pacific Railroad," 315-319, 322-325, 329-330, and Bradley, *Santa Fé*, 113 ff. The state governments also carried on similar work. See, for example, Briggs, "Great Dakota Boom," 105-108.

years. In particular places, as in Dakota, Montana or Nevada, every third or fourth person might be of alien birth.[1] No other section of the country contained so high a percentage except the North Atlantic states where the proportion was about the same. To an Eastern student of Western conditions it seemed that "No such experiment in the blending of the different races of men into one homogeneous nation, has ever been attempted, on a scale so grand and extensive." [2] Yet, despite the strong foreign admixture, the West impressed Bryce as "the most distinctively American part of America." [3] He, of course, was thinking not of racial origins but of qualities of character, conduct and ideals. In all these respects, though it is often forgotten, the immigrant on the frontier had, from earliest times, contributed significantly to a genuine Americanism.

As in the nation at large, the Germans were the most numerous of any alien strain.[4] Nearly two hundred and seventy thousand of them had spread over the Great West by 1890, settling most densely in the river valleys of Nebraska, Kansas and California where they earned a living mainly as farmers and miners. Next came the Scandinavians, about two hundred and twenty-five thousand in all, overflowing from the Middle West into the wheat lands of Dakota and Nebraska, with strong contingents in the Pacific states. The settlers from England, one hundred and forty-five thousand strong, were attracted by the opportunities of mining, ranching and agriculture. Thickest in central California, they were also to be found about Puget Sound, in the Salt Lake area, eastern Kansas and Nebraska, and the mining districts

[1] U. S. Eleventh Census, I, lxxxii, lxxxvii, 395.
[2] L. P. Brockett, Our Western Empire (Phila., 1884), 71.
[3] James Bryce, The American Commonwealth (London, 1888), III, 86.
[4] U. S. Eleventh Census, I, 606-609, and maps 10-14.

of Denver, Leadville and Pueblo, Colorado. The Canadians, though not quite so numerous, shared fully in the varied economic activities of the West, being especially important in the life of the Pacific Coast. The one hundred and thirty thousand Irish, for the most part, continued to cling to the rims of the Great West, half of them being found in the more settled parts of California and most of the others in Kansas and Nebraska.

Many of these racial groups came in family clans; sometimes whole neighborhoods in Norway or Prussia emptied themselves onto the prairies and plains. At least one migration, that of the German Russians, was a genuine folk migration. Something like an Old Testament flavor attaches to their story. In the half-century after 1763 nearly one hundred thousand German peasants—Catholic, Lutheran and Mennonite—had been induced by the czarist government to flock over the border into south Russia. There, exempt from military service and allowed to preserve their German language and religious customs, they dwelt in distinct settlements along the Volga and the north shore of the Black Sea.[1] By thrift and hard work they made their section the granary of Russia. All went well until Alexander II in 1871 announced his intention of withdrawing their special privileges. Thoroughly alarmed, the German Russians sent small bands to the western parts of North America to spy out the land for a new haven of refuge. Everywhere the agents met with a cordial reception. The Canadian government offered them large tracts of cheap land; on the American side of the border the land-grant railways made similar inducements, the Santa Fé even

---

[1] Konrad Keller, *Die Deutschen Kolonien in Süd-Russland* (Odessa, 1905); Gottlieb Bauer, *Geschichte der Deutschen Ansiedler an der Wolga* (Saratow, 1908).

sending a special representative for that purpose to the Russian Mennonite districts.[1]

The organized movement began in the mid-seventies. Though many arrived with insufficient funds, one group of four hundred families brought with them over two million dollars and purchased sixty thousand acres in Marion, McPherson, Harvey and Reno counties in Kansas.[2] By 1880 twenty thousand German Russians had taken up their abode in that state, Dakota, Nebraska and Minnesota, nearly half of them in the Arkansas Valley in Kansas. During the eighties an equal number came, and colonies of Volga Germans, mostly railway laborers, were started in the Pacific states and Colorado. Their numbers would have been much greater if the czar, fearful of losing more such valuable subjects, had not restored most of the canceled privileges in 1883. Despite this concession more than fifty thousand German Russians were to be found in the West by the end of the century.[3]

By dint of thrift, enterprise and the labor of all members of the family they made themselves the most successful farming group in the Western states.[4] The hot winds and clouds of locusts created great fear in their hearts at first; yet, unlike the thousands of native-born farmers

[1] For a first-hand account of his experiences, see C. B. Schmidt, "Reminiscences of Foreign Immigration Work for Kansas," Kan. State Hist. Soc., *Colls.*, IX, 485-497. See also Bradley, *Santa Fé*, 113-134.

[2] Schmidt, "Reminiscences," 495.

[3] The census figures, which do not distinguish German Russians from Slavic or Jewish Russians, have been checked against other data for these estimates. At least an equal number of German Russians settled in western Canada. *U. S. Tenth Census* (1880), I, 494-495; *U. S. Eleventh Census*, I, 608; *U. S. Twelfth Census*, I, 734.

[4] The two standard general treatments are C. H. Smith, *The Coming of the Russian Mennonites* (Berne, Ind., 1927), and Richard Sallet, *Ruszlanddeutsche Siedlungen in den Vereinigten Staaten von Amerika* (reprinted from Deutsch-Amerikanischen Historischen Gesellschaft von Illinois, *Jahrbuch*, Chicago, 1931), which deals with the Lutheran and Catholic groups.

who fled the region, they held stubbornly on.[1] Fifty-five Lutheran families, who had colonized in Clay County, Nebraska, about ten years before, owned property valued at a half-million dollars in 1882. It was a Black Sea Mennonite, Bernhard Warkentin, who a few years later introduced into Kansas the justly famed hard (or Turkey) wheat, an improved Russian variety which soon made that commonwealth the greatest wheat-producing state in the Union. Though, as in Russia, the settlers strove to live their life apart, Americanizing influences crept into the communities and imperceptibly altered many of their manners and customs.[2] Even their names began to bear testimony to the forces making for change, for in the hands of ignorant public officials and careless school teachers Grünwald became Greenwalt, Jost became Yost, Junk Young, etc.

While the racial make-up of the Great West seems sufficiently varied, in most respects the ethnic pattern would not have appeared fantastic to an American of older stock. The Teutonic and Celtic strains had, from earliest times, formed the basis of the American breed. But two other elements gave a touch of the exotic to the scene: the seventy-five thousand Spanish-speaking, adobe-dwelling Mexicans along the southern border (in-

[1] This was partly because their experience in Russia had taught them some knowledge of dry farming. M. A. Carleton, "Successful Wheat Growing in Semiarid Districts," U. S. Dept. of Agr., *Yearbook for 1900*, 531-532, 539 ff.

[2] Judge J. C. Ruppenthal made a study of the German speech used by the Kansas colonists, first, as modified by their long stay in Russia, and, secondly, as affected by their residence in America (to 1913). In the latter instance, the number of non-German words absorbed was "many times as great." See his "The German Element in Central Kansas," Kan. State Hist. Soc., *Colls.*, XIII, esp. 524-525. Striking evidence of rapid adjustment may be found in first-hand observations made of the Mennonite settlements near Newton, Kansas, in 1875 and 1882. See N. L. Prentis, *Kansas Miscellanies* (Topeka, 1889), 162-184. C. C. Regier studies the process in even more intimate terms in "An Immigrant Family of 1876," *Social Science*, VII, 250-266.

cluding Texas); and a somewhat larger body of
Orientals in flapping pantaloons, basket hats and ebony
queues on the Pacific Slope. Neither group, however,
was sufficiently numerous or widely enough scattered to
alter the general character of Western civilization.

In no part of the Great West were the contrasts of
race and culture more striking than in California. Ranking next to Kansas in total population, she exceeded
every other state of this section in the bewildering variety
and sheer numbers of her immigrant elements. At Monterey, where the Scotchman Stevenson remained for a
time, his daily companions at the little restaurant were
a Frenchman, an Italian, a Mexican and two Portuguese,
who were occasionally joined by a Middle Westerner,
an Indian, a Chinese, a Switzer and a German.[1] But the
common life of the town remained strongly Mexican in
tinge. Spanish was the language of the streets; the people,
dressed in gaudy colors, went about their business with
true Latin leisureliness; serenaders added charm to the
lingering dusks. Underneath the surface, however, this
tranquil world was vibrant with new life. Not only
were all the great estates of the vicinity held by Americans, but the new county seat, Salinas City, was a hustling town of pure American stamp. As for the original
sovereigns of the region, the Indians, they eked out a
miserable existence as hired hands on the near-by estates.

Though the Mexican coloration faded as one went
north, racial heterogeneity reached its height in San Francisco, the metropolis of the state, a city which reminded
Helen Hunt Jackson of New York—"a little lower of
story, narrower of street, and stiller, perhaps." [2] It surpassed New York, however, as the American capital of
the Chinese. Thousands of these Orientals huddled to-

[1] Stevenson, *Across the Plains*, 97-98.
[2] H. H., *Bits of Travel*, 77.

gether in the sunless rooms and alleys of Kearny, Du-
pont, Jackson and Sacramento streets, outrivaling the St.
Giles of London or its American counterpart, the old
Five Points of New York. There, in the heart of the
city, they lived, worshiped strange gods and smoked
opium; while in ill-ventilated quarters, screened from the
street with long scrolls of red paper, they carried on all
the trades of Canton and Hong Kong.[1] Their presence
was a visible reminder of a "problem" whose reverberations were still ringing through the nation. Farther to
the north, the state retained its frontier characteristics
and alien newcomers were relatively few. All told, there
were in California about three hundred and seventy
thousand foreign-born residents in 1890, a gain of
nearly seventy-five thousand in the decade.[2]

Economically, the Great West at the close of the
seventies was passing out of one era into another. The
older industries, mining and ranching, were being obliged
to assume new forms and agriculture was about to take
its dominant place in Western economy. Just as the
period opened, a silver rush to Leadville, Colorado,
transformed that place in three years from an unnamed
settlement of six log cabins in April, 1877, to a busy
hive of thirty thousand inhabitants.[3] Such stampedes,
however, occurred with rapidly diminishing violence and
frequency. Indeed, mining was losing its earlier spirit of

[1] For contemporaneous descriptions of Chinatown, see H. H., *Bits
of Travel*, 62-76; Willard Glazier, *Peculiarities of American Cities*
(Phila., 1883), 464-471; G. A. Sala, *America Revisited* (3d edn.,
London, 1883), II, chaps. xvi-xix; W. H. Barneby, *Life and Labour
in the Far Far West* (London, 1884), 40-41; C. A. Stoddard, *Beyond
the Rockies* (N. Y., 1894), 175-179.

[2] Besides 70,000 Asiatics, the total included more than 60,000 each
of Irish and Germans, about 50,000 natives of Great Britain, and
substantial contingents of Canadians, Italians, French, Swedes, Portuguese, Swiss and Danes. *U. S. Eleventh Census*, I, 608.

[3] Brockett, *Western Empire*, 671-673; Allan Nevins, *The Emergence
of Modern America* (*A History of American Life*, VIII), 374-375.

individualistic adventure. That picturesque nomad, the prospector, was giving way to the trained metallurgist employed by a mining company; the rocker, the sluice and other primitive devices for obtaining ore were yielding to the hydraulic process and great rock-crushing and smelting machines.

The new system required large investments of capital and the formation of mining corporations. Already by 1880 groups of capitalists controlled not only the Leadville district, but also the richest mines in Nevada. One gigantic California company owned all the best mines near Deadwood in the Black Hills, while similar conditions prevailed in Utah and Montana.[1] Emigrant guidebooks cautioned the tenderfoot against the hardships, risks and almost certain losses of seeking precious metals by rule-of-thumb methods, pointing out that most of the mining kings had had comfortable fortunes to begin with.[2] Such advice did not go unheeded. So far as mineral wealth was concerned, the typical American of the 1880's preferred to get his thrills vicariously, risking his money (rather than his life) by buying stock in mining corporations which, alas, too often defaulted their dividends. One hundred and forty such companies, located at San Francisco in 1880, had already assessed their stockholders forty-seven million dollars in addition to their original investment and had paid a total of but six million in dividends.[3]

No less notable was the change that took place in the conduct of the cattle industry. As the decade began, stock raising seemed to be at the noontide of its prosperity. The northerly push of longhorns along the trails

---

[1] Brockett, *Western Empire*, 118.
[2] L. P. Brockett, *Handbook of the United States of America* (N. Y., 1883), 120-127; F. V. Hayden, *The Great West* (Bloomington, Ill., 1880), 221-224, 247, 283-291.
[3] Brockett, *Handbook*, 116.

from Texas was as great as ever while on the northwestern ranges the herds increased in size and value.
Huge cattle companies were formed, often with English
and Scotch capital, and in many sections of the Western
range the cowboy began to receive his orders from a boss
appointed by a board of directors in New York or London—a man who kept ledgers and gave serious study to
cattle breeding and market conditions. As ranching
sobered down to a businesslike basis, the position of the
cowboy became steadily less that of a romantic hero and
more that of a plain hired hand.

The abounding prosperity, however, was doomed
from the outset, for it rested upon the rancher's possession of unfenced and unsettled public domain—obviously a temporary condition.[1] As the homesteader or
"nester" advanced into the open range and the prairie
was "cleft by skirmish lines of fence," the zone of free
pasturage steadily dwindled. An angry desultory warfare occurred between the upholders of two types of
civilization, the herdsman and the husbandman, with all
history tilting the balance in favor of the husbandman.
Each spring saw new homesteads marking the plains like
a checkerboard and erecting prickly barriers against the
free movement of the herds. Each year, too, the Long
Drive from Texas was being slowly blotted out of existence, an event hastened by the cattle quarantines laid
in 1885 by Kansas and Colorado. The federal government also sided with the farmer. Thus the tortoise once
more defeated the hare. The last half of the decade witnessed the collapse of the old range industry. In order
to survive, the stock raiser was obliged to reorganize his

---

[1] F. L. Paxson, "The Cow Country," *Am. Hist. Rev.*, XXII, 71-82;
W. P. Webb, *The Great Plains* (Boston, 1931), 227-244; E. E. Dale,
The Range Cattle Industry (Norman, Okla., 1930), chap. v; E. S.
Osgood, *The Day of the Cattleman* (Minneapolis, 1929), chaps. iv-vii.

ing new cities such as Pueblo, Colorado, soon called the "Pittsburgh of the West."

The cowboy of the open range was riding out of the western scene, making way for thriv-

The Wild West Passes

business on a new basis—own his grazing grounds, fence them, provide winter feed and breed better and fewer cattle.[1]

As the mining and cattle industries settled down to an orderly routine the social disorders characteristic of the rawer early days subsided. To be sure, Leadville in the first flush of the boom reproduced all the elements of a tumultuous mining town—saloons, dance halls, gambling hells; ruffians, prostitutes, criminals. But the advent of the railway in 1880 quickly and quietly gave the forces of civilization the upper hand, and the citizens presently began to boast of their schools, churches, newspapers and banks.[2] A similar fate befell Dodge City, Kansas, last of the border "cow towns" and magnet of a turbulent, bird-of-passage population.[3] The settlement of a hinterland of farming communities and the effects of the state quarantine in keeping away the cattle drives caused this "Bibulous Babylon of the Frontier" to lose the chief source both of its prosperity and its wickedness.

Sporadic flare-ups of criminality continued to occur, but generally at points remote from the centers of law and order. The chief breeding ground was central and eastern New Mexico, a region less accessible and less known than Africa is today. Here in 1879 the Lincoln County cattle war dragged to a weary and gory close after the intervention of federal troops, though the principal killer, Billy the Kid, escaped a violent death for two years more.[4] Other bad men—Joel Fowler,

[1] Overstocking of the ranges and a succession of severe winters hastened the end. Twelve great companies which in 1883 had been in a flourishing condition passed their dividends in 1887. R. A. Clemen, *The American Livestock and Meat Industry* (N. Y., 1923), 186.

[2] C. C. Davis, *Olden Times in Colorado* (Los Angeles, 1916), 114-304.

[3] R. M. Wright, *Dodge City, the Cowboy Capital* (n.p., n.d.), chaps. vii-xvii.

[4] He died at the age of twenty-one with the reputation of having

Jesse Evans, Billy Wilson—had their day of truculence and death-dealing before they themselves became victims of their own system of private justice or else, surprisingly enough, changed their names and localities and settled down to become respected and useful citizens.[1] Undoubtedly much of the old border wildness—the "desperado complex"—was a result of social sanction. When times changed men changed with them. A full meed of credit, however, belongs to the frontier sheriff, the good man who terrified bad men and made the country safe for law-abiding citizens.

The plague of banditry also came to an end in that part of the Mississippi Valley most exposed to lawless influences.[2] Though temporarily disorganized by their bloody repulse three years before when trying to rob the Northfield (Minnesota) bank, the most notorious gang, the James Boys, resumed their depredations in 1879 in Missouri, holding up trains and robbing or shooting the passengers. Public opinion was so aroused that in September, 1881, the governor of the state joined with various railway and express companies in setting a price on the heads of Jesse and Frank James. Tempted by the heavy reward, a member of the gang treacherously killed Jesse several months later. Frank voluntarily gave himself up and, after several futile attempts to convict him, quietly lived out the rest of his life as a decent member of society.[3]

killed one man for each of his years. Emerson Hough, *The Story of the Outlaw* (N. Y., 1907), 196-226, 256-273, 300-312; W. N. Burns, *The Saga of Billy the Kid* (Garden City, 1926), 53-289.

[1] Hough, *Story of the Outlaw*, chap. xvi.

[2] Robertus Love, *The Rise and Fall of Jesse James* (N. Y., 1926), 300-399.

[3] A recrudescence of brigandage, inspired by the example of the James Boys, occurred in Oklahoma territory in 1891-1892 when the Dalton Brothers' gang ran their swift and bloody course as train and bank robbers. Hough, *Story of the Outlaw*, 375-391.

The evil that the old West had done continued to live after it, highly romanticized in song, dime novel and cheap melodrama. The substance, however, was gone. This satisfactory condition had been hastened by the spread of agricultural life through most parts of the Great West—by the coming of people who built houses and lived in them and were not content with a blanket for a bed and the sky for a roof. The typical miner or cowboy was a bachelor and a rover, but with the farmer came his women folk, home makers, supplying the Great West for the first time with the "right kind of girls" in sufficient quantities. There were twice as many women there in 1890 as in 1880. In certain parts, such as Wyoming, Idaho and Oregon, their number tripled and, in the cases of Washington and Montana, quadrupled.[1] Quickly the family hearth took the place of the ranch house or the camp saloon as the social center of Western life. It was a change which, however much for the better, involved for men a lessening of desirable simplicities and freedoms as well as of moral laxities. We can at least spare a transient tear for the last surviving longhorn who, in the cowboy lay, declaimed with his dying breath:

> I little dreamed what would happen
>   Some twenty summers hence,
> When the nester came with his wife, his kids,
>   His dogs and his barbed-wire fence.[2]

Though by 1878 the technique of farming in the well-watered sections had been mastered by the old timers, the fresh arrivals, especially those from the wooded belts, had to learn the lessons anew.[3] Lacking

[1] In every case the rate of growth exceeded that of the population in general. *U. S. Eleventh Census*, I, 398.

[2] "The Last Longhorn," J. A. Lomax, comp., *Cowboy Songs and Other Frontier Ballads* (N. Y., 1910), 198.

[3] Finlay Dun, *American Farming and Food* (London, 1881), 424-

timber for buildings and fences, they usually had to
spend their first years in dugouts or sod houses, while
strands of barbed wire were made to take the place of
the familiar zigzag log fences of the Middle West. As
protection from the winter winds, the thrifty pioneer
set about at once planting trees, selecting those which
grew most rapidly, such as willows, cottonwoods, soft
maples or Lombardy poplars. The thick, tough prairie
sod, beaten down for ages by wind and rain and the
hoofs of buffaloes, presented another problem, making
deep plowing—fifteen inches or more—a necessity. It
took hard work, skill and patience to "get the Indian out
of the soil." Fortunately the new and constantly improving farm implements of these years came to the aid of the
pioneer. Many a homestead was mortgaged to secure
more efficient work tools. Without them Western agriculture must have advanced at a much slower pace.

As the better and more accessible lands were occupied, the tidal wave of migration in the early eighties
pushed great numbers of prospective farmers into districts which a few years before would have been avoided.
Thus the zone of settlement spread into western
Nebraska, Kansas and Dakota and eastern Colorado and
Wyoming, places where the soil was fertile but the rainfall uncertain and the rivers shallow and inconstant. A
wet season meant smiling crops and reduction of the
farmer's mortgage; but the dice of nature were loaded
against him and what was won one year was wiped out
the next. Harried by droughts and other afflictions and
ignorant of the possibilities of dry farming, thousands
abandoned their hard-earned homes in the late eighties
and returned East. It was this uneven duel with nature

426; Brockett, *Western Empire*, 138-142. For descriptions of dugouts
and sod houses, see anon., "Kansas Farmers and Illinois Dairymen,"
Atlantic Mo., XLIV (1879), 718.

which injected much bitterness into the farmer's soul and helped goad him into movements of protest.

Though the small farm was everywhere the typical unit of cultivation, this accustomed American system was for a time threatened by a spectacular new development in agricultural management. This was the bonanza farm, which had first appeared when Jay Cooke's failure in 1873 dumped large quantities of Northern Pacific land on the security holders. By the early eighties scores of great tracts of from five thousand to a hundred thousand acres in Kansas, Dakota, Minnesota, Texas and California had gravitated into the hands of individuals or companies, many of them absentee owners.[1] On one such farm near Colusa in the Sacramento Valley, California, nearly ninety square miles were under cultivation, principally in wheat, most of the laborers being Chinese. One of the famous Red River farms at Casselton in Dakota, managed by Oliver Dalrymple, half-owner in partnership with some directors of the Northern Pacific, spread over one hundred and fifteen square miles. It was conducted with the efficiency of a railway. The principal buildings were connected by telephone, a central clerical staff kept accounts, and free medical service was maintained for the workers. Though only a third of the area was as yet under the plow, an army of six hundred were employed during the harvest. A formidable line of one hundred and fifteen self-binding reapers attacked the ripe wheat, cutting a swath of one fifth of a mile; then the grain, after passing through seventy-one steam threshers, was loaded into waiting trains that

[1] Three excellent accounts are Dun, *American Farming*, 199-212; W. G. Moody, *Land and Labor in the United States* (N. Y., 1883), chaps. ii-iii; and H. E. Briggs, "Early Bonanza Farming in the Red River Valley of the North," *Agricultural History*, VI, 26-37. See also Brockett, *Western Empire*, 78-79, 740-745 n., and Paul de Rousiers, *American Life* (A. J. Herbertson, tr., Paris, 1892), chap. iv.

every night puffed away toward Duluth. With land
bought at from forty cents to five dollars an acre yielding
an average of fifteen or twenty bushels, and with the
wheat grown at a minimum cost and commanding special
shipping rates, the profits were enormous.

The bonanza farm was a revival, under unexpected
conditions, of a type of agriculture reminiscent of the
plantation system of the prewar South but really allied
to the mass-production methods that were transforming
the Eastern factory system. Alarmed by the new development, students of the social trend did not hesitate to
predict that rural America was approaching the condition to which Europe had been reduced by "a thousand
years of feudal robbery and tyranny of wealth—with
the lands concentrated . . . in the hands of the few and
cultivated by a people who are dependent upon the
rich." [1] Such fears, however, proved premature. The
same decade that saw the greatest efflorescence of large-
scale farming saw its fading. After the riches were once
skimmed from the soil by the staple-crop system and
when land values began to rise, the large holders inevitably yielded to the pressure to sell their farms in
units small enough for more intensive cultivation. The
census of 1890 showed everywhere, except in the grazing
sections, a marked tendency to return to medium-sized
holdings. [2]

While the westward extension of the wheat and corn
belts was the most striking development in Western
agriculture, almost equally significant was the increasing
diversification of farming through most parts of the
region. California, for example, was in 1878 not only

[1] [W. G. Moody], "The Bonanza Farms of the West," *Atlantic Mo.*,
XLV (1880), 42-44.
[2] U. S. Dept. of Agr., *Yearbook for 1899*, 323; *U. S. Twelfth
Census*, V, xxi, xliv-xlvi, cxxv, 688; C. D. Warner, *Studies in the
South and West* (N. Y., 1889), 124-125.

the greatest wheat-growing state in the Union, but also the banner state in wool production.[1] Sheep raising, however, waned in importance as new settlers appeared, eager to invest in more intensive agriculture. Orange groves, peach farms, prune orchards, vineyards, chicken ranches, bee farms and similar undertakings attested the diverse interests of the later comers. Although fruit culture had been tried earlier, it was the decade after 1878 which, by means of irrigation and better marketing facilities, changed it from a highly speculative venture to a settled business. Through "citrus fairs," held first at Riverside in 1879, and fruit-growers' conventions, beginning a year or so later in southern California, the motley crowd of ex-sheepmen, teachers, health seekers and tired business men were taught the basic principles of scientific culture and correct standards of judging fruit. Citrus settlements or "colonies" sprang up at Redlands, Riverside, Pasadena and Pomona, organized not on any fanciful utopian principles but as the best practical way of sharing the expense of irrigation works. Irrigation colonies were also formed in the Fresno district of the San Joaquin Valley and there laid the permanent foundations for the raisin industry.

Into the midst of this varied activity there came, in 1875, a young man of Massachusetts birth named Luther Burbank, who established a nursery at Santa Rosa. From the outset he displayed an astounding wizardry in developing new forms of plant life through selection, grafting and cross fertilization. The improved varieties of fruits, berries, vegetables, grains and grasses which

---

[1] D. S. Jordan, "California and the Californians," *Atlantic Mo.*, LXXXII (1898), 793-801; E. J. Wickson, *Rural California* (L. H. Bailey, ed., *Rural State and Province Series;* N. Y., 1923), 79-82, 169-176, 292-297; Osgood Hardy, "Agricultural Changes in California, 1860-1900," Pacific Coast Branch, Am. Hist. Assoc., *Proceeds. for 1929*, 216-230.

Burbank produced, each involving the patient handling of countless seedlings, contributed greatly to the wealth of the state, and added variety and flavor to the diet of people the world over.[1] In fruit growing California found a Golconda which yielded greater wealth than the gold deposits Sutter first laid bare.

In other Western commonwealths, also, economic life showed a similar tendency toward greater diversity. The people of Washington, for example, turned their energies to vegetables and fruits as well as to grain growing and grazing. Alongside of these, lumbering and the fisheries with their satellite industries every year grew in importance. Even a state like Kansas, though clinging to the cultivation of corn, wheat and oats as its mainstay, devoted increasing attention to the raising of swine and domestic fowls, meat packing and the growing of flax and potatoes.

Over the broad and sometimes wrinkled face of the Great West there were two spots which, though in many respects peculiar to themselves, were nevertheless profoundly affected by the new economic forces at work. One was the religious commonwealth of Utah, which by 1878 the Mormons had transformed from a sand-girt solitude into a cultivated domain rich in flocks, herds, farms and orchards and threaded with highways and railroads.[2] The fanatical ardor which had fired the original colonists already showed signs of cooling as Brigham Young passed from the scene in 1877 and a

[1] In 1893 Burbank gave up his nursery business and devoted himself solely to the work in which he had already won an international reputation. W. S. Harwood, *New Creations in Plant Life* (N. Y., 1905); John Wilson, Robert John and H. S. Williams, eds., *Luther Burbank, His Methods and Discoveries and Their Practical Application* (N. Y., 1914-1915), prepared from Burbank's notes covering more than one hundred thousand experiments.

[2] Nevins tells the story of the Mormons from 1865 to 1878 in *Emergence of Modern America* 141-146. 366-367.

new generation came into control. Thanks to its ready access by rail, Salt Lake City exhibited a lusty growth —from twenty thousand in 1880 to nearly forty-five thousand in 1890. While some of the newcomers were Mormon converts from Great Britain and the Scandinavian countries, many more were "Gentiles" utterly at variance with the Mormon creed and seeking their share of this world's goods. Under the circumstances the contagion of new ideas was not to be avoided. The *Deseret News*, the church organ, dating from 1850, now had rivals in the independent *Salt Lake Herald* and the anti-Mormon *Tribune*. Even in the religious field proper the Latter-day Saints, as they called themselves, were challenged by the efforts of other sects, notably the Presbyterians, Methodists and Congregationalists.[1]

Looked at apart from their peculiar religious beliefs, the Mormons were a canny practical folk, hard working, temperate and clannish.[2] The plague of saloons, brothels and gambling dens was apparently introduced by the non-Mormons, though the latter insisted that the Saints were the sinners.[3] How many Mormon marriages were polygamous it is difficult to ascertain, but the Mormon figure of about three per cent is probably nearer the truth than the feverish guesses of their opponents.[4] The church, however, did not recede from its earlier attitude

[1] *Appletons' Annual Cyclopaedia*, XXI (1881), 860; D. L. Leonard, "Six Years in Utah," *Missionary Rev.*, IX (1896), 807-813; Sala, *America Revisited*, II, 316 n.

[2] R. T. Ely, "Economic Aspects of Mormonism," *Harper's Mag.*, CVI (1903), 667-678, is an unusually discriminating account.

[3] H. H. Bancroft, *History of the Pacific States* (San Fran., 1882-1890), XXI, 686-687. *Cf.* E. H. Murray, "The Crisis in Utah," *N. Am. Rev.*, CXXXIV (1882), 340-342; Sala, *America Revisited*, II, 291-292.

[4] Compare, for example, C. W. Penrose, "Church Rule in Utah," *Forum*, V (1888), 673, with the charges of anti-Mormon critics: G. E. Edmunds, "Political Aspects of Mormonism," *Harper's Mag.*, LXIV (1882), 286, and Theodore Schroeder, "Polygamy and the Constitution," *Arena*, XXXVI (1906), 493-495.

that polygamy was a divine institution, designed by the Hebrew patriarchs to produce a eugenically superior race. It was this stubborn contention which, more than anything else, hindered the growing friendliness between Mormon and Gentile, sharpened the long-standing antagonism of the rest of America, and for many years kept Utah from statehood.

Though Congress in 1862 had prescribed fine and imprisonment as penalties for polygamy and twelve years later had strengthened the enforcement provisions, the legislation had remained virtually a dead letter. Prior to 1882, when a more drastic act was passed, only three final convictions had been secured by the government, largely because of the difficulty of obtaining proper testimony. The Edmunds law of that year aimed to cure the defects of earlier legislation and at the same time destroy the temporal power of the church.[1] While legitimating children born in polygamy before 1883, it threw safeguards about the jury system and the testimony of witnesses, and added to the previous penalties for polygamy the loss of the right to vote and hold office. An even more direct blow at the Mormon theocracy was the provision for placing the conduct of Utah elections under a federal commission. Though this stringent measure brought gratifying results—there were over a thousand convictions by 1888 [2]—public opinion was not yet appeased. As a result the Edmunds-Tucker law in 1887 empowered the United States to take over all the property of the church except such as was used for exclusively religious purposes.[3]

[1] U. S. Statutes at Large, XXII, 30-32.
[2] According to the "Report" of the Utah Commission, 50 Cong., 1 sess., House Exec. Doc., no. 447. See also Deseret News, July 8, 1888; Latter-day Saints' Millennial Star, L (1888), 568-570; W. A. Linn, The Story of the Mormons (N. Y., 1902), 599-600.
[3] U. S. Statutes at Large, XXIV, 635-641.

The resentment of the Mormon leaders knew no bounds. Despite Supreme Court decisions to the contrary they rang all the changes on the charge that they were being denied their constitutional right of freedom of worship.[1] They faced a crisis of national proportions, however, which could no longer be met either by open defiance or by passive evasion. Some of them went into hiding temporarily rather than submit; but this was a gesture of futility. It was clear that the days of polygamy were numbered and that the church must soon take the necessary steps to bring itself into harmony with the spirit of the age.

The region now known as Oklahoma presented a different kind of problem. All of it but the narrow strip, "No Man's Land," north of the Texas panhandle had been set aside as a protected area for the Indians in the period before the Civil War. The original colonizing tribes—the Cherokee, Creek, Chickasaw, Choctaw and Seminole—had developed an orderly and prosperous farming life and, by establishing schools, churches and governmental institutions, had done much to justify their name of the Five Civilized Tribes.[2] As a result of choosing the losing side in the Civil War, however, they had been forced to give up the western half of their lands. The ceded region was in part assigned to newly conquered bands of the plains and mountains, such as the Kiowa, Apache, Cheyenne and Ponca Sioux, but a great district near the heart of the present state, known to the

[1] For example, see *Latter-day Saints' Millennial Star*, XLIV (1882), 267-269, 284-286; XLIX (1887), 648-649, 809-811.

[2] Such periodicals as the *Democrat* and the *Republican* of St. Louis, *Harper's Magazine* and territorial newspapers were to be found in many Cherokee homes in the eighties. Commissioner of Indian Affairs, *Report for 1886*, 148. See also W. P. Adair, "The Indian Territory in 1878," and V. A. Travis, "Life in the Cherokee Nation," *Chronicles of Oklahoma*, IV, 255-274, and 16-30; and Brockett, *Western Empire*, 797-813.

Indians as Oklahoma ("the beautiful land") and two thirds as large as the state of Connecticut, remained unoccupied.

The existence of this vacant central tract was a constant source of irritation and temptation to land-hungry Westerners; and shrewd railway promoters, eager to hasten white occupation, helped to keep this irritation at the boiling point. Moreover, since federal laws did not apply to the Indian country and the tribal authorities lacked jurisdiction over vagrant whites, the territory had become a threat to the peace of the older Western communities by the use horse thieves and other desperate characters made of it. The Indians, on the other hand, suspicious of any move to tamper with their existing status, preferred to bear the ills they had than to fly to others they knew not of. In this position they found ardent allies in the cattlemen to whom they had leased vast unused acres for grazing purposes.[1]

In 1879 began a stubborn ten years' struggle by squatters to seize choice sites in the Oklahoma district in defiance of all the forces of law and order.[2] The early raids were led by Captain David L. Payne, a veteran of the Civil War and a former border fighter. About twice each year he and a party of "boomers," after eluding the soldiery, would squat on desirable ground, be removed by United States cavalry, and then be vainly prosecuted under a faulty federal statute. Payne had made no less than eight attempts at colonization when he suddenly died in November, 1884, under circumstances which excited ugly suspicions of poisoning by

[1] Dale, *Range Cattle Industry*, chap. vii.
[2] The best accounts are S. J. Buck, "The Settlement of Oklahoma," Wis. Acad., *Trans.*, XV, 335-342; J. B. Thoburn and I. M. Holcomb, *A History of Oklahoma* (San Fran., 1908), 148-170; and Roy Gittinger, *The Formation of the State of Oklahoma* (Univ. of Calif., *Publs.*, VI), chaps. vii-ix.

cattlemen. His work was promptly taken up by William L. Couch, who led two boomers' forays in 1885.

Meantime whites steadily sifted into the eastern half of the territory where the Five Civilized Tribes held sway. In ten years the number of whites who had not been adopted as tribal citizens grew from six thousand in 1879 to perhaps more than a hundred thousand.[1] While most of these were in the employ of the Indians or the government, one third of them were plain intruders who persistently returned when shooed off by the military. The situation was equally unsatisfactory in No Man's Land, adjoining the northwest corner of Indian Territory. Though the strip was open to legal settlement, Congress had left the five or six thousand inhabitants without a government. After resorting to vigilance committees and unofficial claims courts, the settlers assembled a convention at Beaver, the chief town, in 1887 and boldly proclaimed the formation of the territory of Cimarron. This improvisation, however, Congress refused to recognize.[2]

Each year of the decade emphasized increasingly the need of a different handling of the problem by the government at Washington. A first and very important step was taken in 1889 when President Harrison, acting under congressional authorization, gave public notice that the Oklahoma district would be thrown open to home seekers at high noon on April 22. A week or so before the appointed time eager throngs began to gather along the border until finally twenty thousand boomers awaited the signal to cross the line. "Every man was armed like a walking arsenal," declared a participant, "and many also constituted themselves walking com-

---

[1] The total population at the end of the ten-year period was 175,000. Gittinger, *Formation of State of Oklahoma*, 176-177.

[2] E. E. Brown, "No Man's Land," *Chronicles of Oklahoma*, IV, 89-99.

missaries." [1] At exactly twelve a shrill bugle blast rent
the air, the troops stood aside, and the impatient hosts—
by horseback and rail, in buggies and buckboards, even
on foot—began the mad race for claims and homes.

Into a few hours of intense drama was packed the
whole story of American pioneering. Guthrie, which
had been scarcely more than a town site six hours before,
was by nightfall a tented city of more than ten thousand
inhabitants. Its chief rival, Oklahoma City, thirty miles
to the south, held a population of perhaps half as many.
Everywhere over the countryside flickered the camp
fires of the scattered homesteaders. One hundred days
later Guthrie presented the appearance of a typical
Western city, with banks, hotels, stores, newspapers,
parks and an electric-light plant. By the end of 1889
the Oklahoma district had a population of about sixty
thousand. Through some ineptitude of Congress the settlers, like those in No Man's Land, were left without
any law or organized government save that established
by common consent. It was clear, however, that formal
territorial status could not long be withheld.

As in the South, so in the Great West the decade of
the eighties was significant as marking the end of one
cycle and the beginning of another. The trans-Missouri
country was like a well-favored woman who, having
given her adolescent years to an exciting and somewhat
dubious round of gayety, decides while the conventions
still permit to settle down to a life of sober respectability. The West looked back over its shoulder toward
a glamorous and romantic past, cherishing memories
which have become a part of the national folklore, but

---

[1] H. S. Wicks, "The Opening of Oklahoma," *Cosmopolitan*, VII
(1889), 460-470, reprinted in *Chronicles of Oklahoma*, IV, 129-142.
Good accounts may also be found in M. T. Rock, *Illustrated History of
Oklahoma* (Topeka, 1890), 20-78; Buck, "Settlement of Oklahoma,"
344-351; and Gittinger, *Formation of State of Oklahoma*, chap. x.

bent its energies to the rewards of a life of steady habits and prosaic toil. It was no mere coincidence that border heroes like Buffalo Bill, Texas Jack Omohundro and Wild Bill Hickok forsook the rapidly paling drama of Western life to take part in blood-curdling frontier melodramas on the mimic stage.[1]

Yet the eighties also taught the Westerner that hard work was not enough. Like his Southern brother, he was caught in the toils of an economic transition which too frequently denied him the legitimate fruits of his labors. Low crop prices, grinding debts, high freight rates, droughts and insect visitations made him feel that the hand of both man and nature was raised against him. Thus the settling down of the Great West was, paradoxically enough, attended by multiplying evidences of agrarian unrest. Just as in the South, the farmers, despite their traditional individualism, turned increasingly to organized action. The Farmers' Alliances by 1890 controlled many of the legislatures and even had spokesmen in both houses of Congress.[2]

These loudly declaimed grievances, however, did little to halt the movement of settlers into the region. As the population enlarged, demands for statehood were made with ever greater vehemence. Only the inevitable jockeying for party advantage delayed appropriate action by Congress. In the summer and fall of 1889 conventions in North and South Dakota, Washington, Idaho, Montana and Wyoming drew up constitutions reflecting the agrarian dislike of railroads and other corporations and

---

[1] M. B. Leavitt, *Fifty Years of Theatrical Management* (N. Y., 1911), chap. xi; F. J. Wilstach, *Wild Bill Hickok* (Garden City, 1926), chap. xiii. When Wild Bill took to the stage, he had behind him a record of perhaps eighty-one homicides, not all of them performed in the interests of public justice though all his victims fell in fair fight. Hough, *Story of the Outlaw*, 182-185.

[2] J. D. Hicks, *The Populist Revolt* (Minneapolis, 1931), 153-170, 179-181.

embodying sundry demands for reform.[1] In 1889 and 1890 the six new states were admitted to the Union. The economic ills of the people remained, but the Great West was now in a position to join with the South and other discontented groups in pressing for relief through national action.

[1] J. D. Hicks, *The Constitutions of the Northwest States* (Univ. of Neb., *Studies*, XXIII, nos. 1-2).

CHAPTER III

THE LURE OF THE CITY

IN the Middle West and the North Atlantic states rural America, like a stag at bay, was making its last stand. The clash between the two cultures—one static, individualistic, agricultural, the other dynamic, collectivistic, urban—was most clearly exhibited in the former section, for the march of events had already decided the outcome in the East. Agriculturally the Middle West, unlike the Great West, was beyond its period of growing pains. Farming was no longer pioneering and speculative; save in some of the newer districts the tendency everywhere was toward stabilization and a settled routine. Though the corn belt cut a wide swath through the lower tier of states and wheat predominated in the colder climes, the individual farmer was apt to supplement his main product with hay, orchard fruits and vegetables and to raise horses, cattle and hogs as well as crops, meantime guarding his soil resources through systematic rotation and the use of fertilizers.

The maturity of agriculture was mirrored in the physical appearance of the farms, particularly in the older regions. Neat frame dwellings housed the owners. Barns of increasing size and solidity, built of trimmed painted boards and perhaps protected below the ground line by stonework, sheltered the livestock and crops in place of the pioneer's slender framework of poles covered with straw. Instead of the old-time zigzag fences of split logs now appeared orderly rail fences or the new-fashioned wire variety. One observant Old World visitor formed a distinctly favorable impression of Middle America as it flashed by his car window. "The tall corn pleased the eye;" he wrote afterwards, "the trees were graceful in themselves, and framed the plain into long, aërial vistas; and the clean, bright, gardened townships spoke of country fare and pleasant summer evenings on the stoop." That this "flat paradise" was "not unfrequented by the devil" was suggested to him only by the billboards along the car tracks advertising cures for the ague.[1]

Economic stabilization bred political caution. Though the Granger agitation and the Greenback propaganda of earlier years had centered largely in the Middle West, the agrarian unrest which shook the trans-Missouri country and the South in the 1880's won little response. Already in the preceding decade the growth of a prosperous dairying interest in Wisconsin and Iowa had caused opposition to the demands of the wheat growers for greenback inflation.[2] Even more notable results appeared in the eighties as mixed farming became the rule and agricultural products found a ready market in near-by cities. Urban sentiment, always hostile to agrarian panaceas, also colored the farmers' thinking in countless imperceptible ways and helped confirm their new-found conservatism. In 1893 the states from Ohio to Iowa and Minnesota would vote more than seven to one in both houses of Congress for Cleveland's proposal to repeal the silver-purchase act, while the Solid South and the Great West would plump heavily in the other direction.[3]

[1] R. L. Stevenson, *Across the Plains* (N. Y., 1892), 15-17.
[2] C. O. Ruggles, "The Economic Basis of the Greenback Movement in Iowa and Wisconsin," Miss. Valley Hist. Assoc., *Proceeds.*, VI, 142-165.
[3] The Populist vote, both in 1892 and 1894, failed to reach one twelfth of the total in any Mid-Western state except Minnesota. H. C.

It should further be noted that the migration of many sons of the Middle West into the trans-Missouri farming country and into the cities did much to relieve the pressure on the means of rural livelihood. As we have seen, the Far West, like another Eve, was formed out of a rib taken from the side of Middle America. By 1890 a million native Mid-Westerners lived in Kansas, Nebraska and the Dakotas and six hundred thousand more in the region beyond.[1] Still others were trying their luck in the newer parts of Texas and Arkansas. This great exodus drew off many restless and adventurous souls whose staying might have given the politics of the home states a distinctly radical cast. Professor Turner has pointed out that the agrarian leadership in the new Western commonwealths came chiefly from the ranks of natives of the Middle West.[2]

While great numbers of immigrant farmers settled in the section, they generally shunned the older agricultural regions, flocking rather into Minnesota, Michigan and other of the less developed parts. Though the promise of an easier living beckoned them farther westward, they preferred to consort with fellow countrymen who had already firmly established themselves and were well satisfied with the returns of their toil. State immigration boards in Minnesota, Wisconsin, Michigan and Missouri exerted themselves to attract alien newcomers,[3] but with

Nixon, "The Cleavage within the Farmers' Alliance Movement," *Miss. Valley Hist. Rev.*, XV, 31, 33.

[1] *U. S. Eleventh Census* (1890), I, 560-563.

[2] F. J. Turner, "Dominant Forces in American Life," *Atlantic Mo.*, LXXIX (1897), 440-441, reprinted in his *The Frontier in American History* (N. Y., 1920), chap. xii.

[3] T. C. Blegen, "The Competition of the Northwestern States for Immigrants," *Wis. Mag. of History*, III, 20-29; M. L. Hansen, "Official Encouragement of Immigration to Iowa," *Iowa Journ. of History and Politics*, XIX, 185-195; Kate A. Everest, "How Wisconsin Came by Its Large German Element," State Hist. Soc. of Wis., *Colls.*, XII, 327-330.

diminishing energy as the decade advanced. In 1884 Iowa frankly discontinued all official efforts, no longer desiring people "merely to count up in the census."

Norwegians, Swedes and Danes, following the well-worn tracks of their countrymen in earlier years, came in such numbers as to make of Minnesota and Wisconsin a New Scandinavia.[1] Industrious, thrifty, law-abiding, highly literate, these descendants of the Vikings contributed materially to the prosperity and civic advancement of their adopted states. The whole family—ten children were common, twenty not unknown—toiled in the fields, at least until comparison with Yankee ways planted seeds of revolt in the daughters' breasts.[2] There were two hundred and sixty-five thousand more Scandinavians in the Middle West in 1890 than a decade before. Most of them became agriculturists, a third settling in the single state of Minnesota.

Like the Scandinavians, a majority of the four hundred thousand Germans who came in the 1880's turned farmer. But they were less imbued with the true pioneer spirit and generally bought the partly worked farms of Americans who were itching to be up and doing elsewhere. As thrifty and hard working as the Scandinavians, they were also deeply interested in education and quite as easily assimilated.[3] They were not, however, such stern Protestants, many indeed being Catholics, and they brought to rural life a *Gemüthlichkeit*, a sociability, which set them apart from all other racial elements. On

[1] K. C. Babcock, "The Scandinavian Contingent," *Atlantic Mo.*, LXXVII (1896), 660-670. See his fuller treatment, *The Scandinavian Element in the United States* (Univ. of Ill., *Studies*, III, no. 3), chaps. vii-xiii, and also G. T. Flom, "The Scandinavian Factor in the American Population," *Iowa Journ. of History and Politics*, III, 57-91.

[2] Hamlin Garland treats this theme in "Among the Corn Rows," *Main-Travelled Roads* (Cambridge, Mass., 1893), 139-174.

[3] A. B. Faust, *The German Element in the United States* (Boston, 1909), II, chaps. ii-iii, v, viii.

local political issues the two north European peoples were often divided, particularly when the Teutonic bias in regard to "blue laws" and the liquor traffic entered as a factor. By 1890 more than half the Germans and Scandinavians resided in the Middle West, about the same proportion of the Swiss and Poles and nearly two thirds of the Dutch and Bohemians.[1]

A traveler familiar with the great stretches of country toward the Pacific and the Gulf would have been immediately aware that in the Middle West the traditional rural culture of America was rapidly dissolving and a new form rising in its stead. Though occasional cities, some of them populous and wealthy, were to be found in the Great West and the South, their existence merely accented the general rural character of the civilization which encompassed them. But in the great triangular central region, extending from Ohio to Missouri and Minnesota and containing nearly one third of all the people of the nation, the migration from the country districts had attained a momentum that was fast giving the city a dominant position in the social organism. In 1880 one out of every five Middle Westerners lived in urban communities of four thousand or more inhabitants, ten years later one out of every three.[2] In the single decade the number dwelling in such centers doubled, attaining a total of six and a quarter million. Illinois and Ohio boasted nearly one hundred and twenty towns and cities, including some of the largest in the land, while even in Minnesota and Missouri three out of every ten persons in 1890 were townsfolk.

[1] The Dutch immigrant is given special attention in G. F. Huizinga, *What the Dutch Have Done in the West of the United States* (Phila., 1909).

[2] *U. S. Twelfth Census* (1900), I, lxvi, lxxxiv-lxxxv. For the same census years, the percentage of people living in cities of eight thousand or more inhabitants was 18.5 and 27.6. *U. S. Eleventh Census,* I, lxviii; *U. S. Twelfth Census,* I, lxxxii.

The drawbacks of life on the farm had, of course, been felt by earlier generations, but never before with such compelling force.[1] At least since the adoption of a national land policy in 1785, isolation and loneliness had been the almost inescapable conditions of country existence, for by the ordinance of that year the government rejected the New England system of farmer communities and provided for large, scattered, individual holdings. These tendencies were confirmed and strengthened by the homestead law of 1862. Thus in the less developed parts of the Middle West such as Minnesota and Wisconsin, or in the near-by territory of Dakota, country neighbors dwelt too far apart for friendly intercourse, being but four to the square mile when land was held in quarter sections and even farther away if the homesteads were larger or tracts remained unoccupied.[2] Even in the older farming districts families generally lived out of sight of other habitations; they had no mail deliveries; and the balm of a telephone was denied to all but a tiny minority.

As urban communities increased in number and importance, the farmer's feeling of isolation was deepened by a knowledge of the pleasant town life not many miles away. The craving for solitudes is not as natural as the craving for multitudes; and the companionable sense of rubbing elbows, even if anonymously, with one's fellows compensates for many of life's repulses and frustrations. If the chief historian of the Scandinavian

[1] N. H. Egleston, *Villages and Village Life* (N. Y., 1878), chaps. iv-v; same author, *The Home and Its Surroundings* (rev. edn., N. Y., 1883), chaps. i-vi, xxv; J. G. Holland, *Every-Day Topics* (N. Y., 1882), 303-309; W. L. Anderson, *The Country Town* (N. Y., 1906), esp. chap. xii.

[2] "In no civilized country have the cultivators of the soil adapted their home life so badly to the conditions of nature as have the people of our great Northwestern prairies," according to E. V. Smalley, "The Isolation of Life on Prairie Farms," *Atlantic Mo.*, LXXII (1893), 378-382.

Americans is correct, the cheerlessness and hardships of
farm life accounted for the uncommonly high proportion of insanity among the Norwegians and Swedes in
the Middle West.[1] Certainly where families of different
nationalities occupied the same neighborhood social intercourse was at a minimum, though a homogeneous
immigrant community sometimes succeeded for a time in
keeping alive the friendly social customs of the home
land.[2]

Despite such drawbacks many farmers valued the free
open country life above all else and would not willingly
have exchanged it for any other type of existence. Rural
life, too, had its occasional cherished diversions for both
young and old: its picnics and its gatherings at the
swimming hole in summer, its nutting and hunting expeditions in the fall, its annual county fair and horse
races, its family reunions at Thanksgiving, its bob-sled
parties of merrymakers in winter, its country dances in
all seasons of the year.[3] Even its religious revivals might
be so regarded. Funerals, too, were as much social events
as solemn obsequies, attracting people from miles around
and affording a treasured opportunity for brushing
shoulders and exchanging gossip on the doorstep of the
church or under the horse sheds. For those with eyes
to see, nature itself in its vagrant moods and infinite
variety was a never ending source of pleasure. A field
of growing wheat—"deep as the breast of a man, wide
as a sea, heavy-headed, supple-stalked, many-voiced,

[1] Babcock, *Scandinavian Element*, 136-137.
[2] For example, see F. S. Laing, "German-Russian Settlements in Ellis
County, Kansas," Kan. State Hist. Soc., *Colls.*, XI, 518-522.
[3] For such pleasures in Iowa and Dakota, see Hamlin Garland, *Boy
Life on the Prairie* (N. Y., 1899); in Kansas, J. E. House, "A Boy's
Job in the Eighties," *Sat. Eve. Post*, CXCVII, 10 ff. (May 16, 1925);
in Wisconsin, Grant Showerman, *A Country Chronicle* (N. Y., 1916)
—fictional autobiography—and Joseph Schafer, *A History of Agriculture in Wisconsin* (*Wis. Domesday Book, General Studies*, I), 172-178.

full of multitudinous, secretive, whispered colloquies"—
was to the æsthetic "a meeting-place of winds and of
magic." [1]

But such pastimes and diversions paled before the
bright attractions of the city, for, after the manner of
human nature, the country dweller was apt to compare
the worst features of his own lot with the best aspects
of urban life. Nor, in the thinking of many, especially
the younger folk, did these occasional pleasures repay
for the drudgery and monotony which attended much
of the daily toil, only to yield in the end a modest living. Farm work in former days had been spiced with
greater variety. Now the advent of railroads and the
lowered cost of manufactures led the farmer to buy
over the store counter or through the mail-order catalogue multifarious articles which he had once made for
himself. With no apparent reduction in the amount of
labor, the kinds of tasks were fewer and often less appealing to his special interests and aptitudes. In contrast
the city offered both better business openings and a
greater chance for congenial work.

The parents of Hamlin Garland, after a taste of Iowa
village life, returned to the farm, to the resentful disappointment of their two sons (one of whom had clerked
in an "ice-cream parlor"), who compared unfavorably
the "ugly little farmhouse" and the "filthy drudgery of
the farm-yard" with the "care-free companionable existence" of the town. Herbert Quick's mother pleaded
in vain with her husband to leave their Iowa homestead
for a place where their children might attend better
schools. About the same time in Wisconsin Grant
Showerman's farmer father told him, "I hope you won't

[1] Garland, *Boy Life*, 273. For further expressions of this lyric mood,
see his *Prairie Songs* (Cambridge, Mass., 1893) and Herbert Quick,
One Man's Life (Indianapolis, 1925), chaps. ix-x.

have to drudge the way I've had to . . . . I want you to be a lawyer. I might have been a lawyer if I'd only had an education." [1] Men and boys, however, were probably less sensitive to the shortcomings of rustic life than the women who, as Herbert Quick recorded in after years, "in many, many cases . . . were pining for neighbors, for domestic help, for pretty clothes, for schools, music, art, and the things tasted when the magazines came in." [2] It was the city rather than the unpeopled wilderness that was beginning to dazzle the imagination of the nation. The farmer, once the pride of America, was descending from his lofty estate, too readily accepting the city's scornful estimate of him as a "rube" and a "hayseed." [3]

Different from Australia, where a few great centers gathered in the city-wending throng, the tendency was to move from the countryside to the nearest hamlet, from the hamlet to the town, and from the town to the city.[4] The reasons that impelled a person to leave the farm to go to a crossroads village were likely to cause the ambitious or maladjusted villager to remove to a larger place, or might in time spur the transplanted farmer lad himself to try his fortunes in a broader sphere. The results were seen in the records of city growth. The pyramid of urban population enlarged at every point from base to peak, and the countryside found itself encroached upon by hamlet, town and city.

---

[1] Hamlin Garland, *A Son of the Middle Border* (N. Y., 1917), 204-206; Quick, *One Man's Life*, 240-241; Showerman, *Country Chronicle*, 148-149.

[2] "The 'drift to the cities,'" Quick added, "has been largely a woman movement." "Women on the Farms," *Good Housekeeping*, LVII (1913), 426-436.

[3] Eugene Davenport, "The Exodus from the Farm," U. S. Dept. of Agr., *Experiment Station Bull.*, no. 41 (1897), 84-86.

[4] H. J. Fletcher, "The Drift of Population to Cities," *Forum*, XIX (1895), 737-745.

The typical Mid-Western urban community was a small town varying in size from a few thousand to ten or fifteen thousand people.[1] Amidst such surroundings, it may be noted, youths like George Ade, Charles A. Beard, Meredith Nicholson and Charles H. Mayo grew up and had their first taste of life's sweets and bitters with no foreknowledge of that greater world where their names were to gain repute.[2]

Such a town, for instance, was Xenia with its seven or eight thousand inhabitants, the county seat of a rich agricultural community in southwestern Ohio. The well-shaded dirt streets, running at right angles, were lined with trim two-story houses set well back from the brick sidewalk behind neat picket fences and looking out on the world from under the screen of pleasant, if over-ornate, porches. Deep backyards with a stable and other outhouses and an occasional fruit tree allowed ample space for children's play and, through a back gate, opened onto a highway of dust and dark adventure known to matter-of-fact grown-ups as "th' alley."

Except for a ropewalk, paper mill and lumber yard on the outskirts, the chief business activity centered at the intersection of Main and Detroit streets. Here within a few minutes' walk were situated the only shops of the town: the "notion" store, a hardware store, two or three groceries, the drug store displaying great bottles of colored liquid in its windows, the odorous harness shop fronted with a huge dapple-gray wooden Percheron, the cigar store with its undersized wooden Indian on guard. Here the Little Miami train came puffing through two or three times a day, the shrill whistle of the "eight-

---

[1] There were 1028 towns ranging in population from 1000 to 8000 in the year 1890, 102 cities of from 8000 to 25,000 and 32 of 25,000 or over. *U. S. Twelfth Census*, I, lxvi.

[2] Ade recalls his childhood in "The Dark Ages," *Hearst's International and Cosmopolitan*, LXXXI (1926), 80 ff.

thirty" serving as a sort of curfew for the youngsters. Here, too, overlooked by the upstairs offices of the lawyers along Main Street, the stone courthouse reared its bulk, surrounded by trees and lawn, with a band stand and commodious hitching rails in the rear. Behind the courthouse grounds, around the corner from the Y. M. C. A. quarters and the *Gazette* office, stood the only other civic building—a barnlike brick structure sheltering the jail, the mayor's office and an auditorium and stage. The "op'ry house" it was called by official decree.

Signs abounded of the important place the horse occupied in the doings of the town. A hitching block or post hospitably reposed in front of nearly every store or house, while at important street corners municipal watering troughs offered refreshment. For the accommodation of the citizen who lacked his own horse and buggy a half-dozen livery stables plied a brisk trade. Blacksmith shops—dark caverns of enchantment to passing juveniles—replaced the horses' worn or cast shoes. For six days of the week life was uneventful enough; but on Saturday the streets took on an unwonted stir and bustle, for then the country people hitched up Nelly or Dobbin and invaded the town— whiskered adults self-conscious in their Sunday "best," young swains beauing bashful sweethearts, thin-chested mothers herding restless broods. It was a gala occasion for the farmers and their families, a day of hard work and many sales for the merchants.

The morals of the townspeople were safeguarded less by the single blue-clad policeman or the lively concern signified by the six or eight steepled churches than by the intimate knowledge which everyone had of everyone else's affairs. City sophistication was conspicuous for its absence; yet the people enjoyed advantages of education

and social commingling which made them the envy of
their country cousins. For many a young man, however, Xenia was not a spacious enough world, and there
was a constant drift of the young people to larger
places.

The extraordinary growth of its bigger cities was one
of the marvels of Middle Western life in the eighties.
Chicago, which best represented the will power and
titanic energy of the section, leaped from a half million
in 1880 to more than a million ten years later, establishing its place as the second city of the nation. The Twin
Cities trebled in size; places like Detroit, Milwaukee,
Columbus and Cleveland increased by from sixty to
eighty per cent.[1] Of the fifty principal American cities
in 1890 twelve were in the Middle West.

The rapid urbanization was, of course, accelerated by
the swarming of foreigners into the section. During the
eighties the immigrant population of Middle America
increased nearly nine hundred thousand, reaching a total
at the close of the decade of three and a half million.[2]
Every fifth or sixth person in 1890 was of alien birth.
Though the Scandinavians, as we have seen, generally
preferred the farm to the city, seventy thousand of them
were working in Chicago in 1890, the men as mechanics
or factory hands, the daughters usually as domestic servants. Fifty thousand more dwelt in the Twin Cities.
The Germans also divided their allegiance. James Bryce
heard German commonly spoken on the streets of Milwaukee; the Teutonic element in Chicago, while thrice
as numerous, was less conspicuous because of the babel
of other tongues. As skilled workers the newcomers
from the *Vaterland* were generally found in such trades

---

[1] *U. S. Eleventh Census*, I, lxvii.
[2] *U. S. Eleventh Census*, I, lxxxiii, lxxxvii-lxxxviii, xc, cxxxviii-
cxxxix.

as photography, tailoring, baking, locksmithing and lithography.[1] The nationalities which most thoroughly identified themselves with city life, however, were the Irish and particularly the increasing stream of Russian and Polish Jews and Italians who constituted the "new immigration."

So great was the influx of all races into Chicago that its foreign-born inhabitants in 1890 numbered nearly as many as its entire population in 1880. A writer in the nineties, analyzing its school census, pointed out that "only two cities in the German Empire, Berlin and Hamburg, have a greater German population than Chicago; only two in Sweden, Stockholm and Göteborg, have more Swedes; and only two in Norway, Christiania and Bergen, more Norwegians."[2] If the "seacoast of Bohemia" was a figment of the poet's imagination, the third largest city of Bohemians in the world could at least boast an extended lake front.

These and other immigrant groups huddled together in dense colonies like islands in a sea of humanity. They jealously maintained their own business institutions, churches, beneficial societies, foreign-language newspapers and often their own parochial schools. In the small district about Hull House on South Halsted Street eighteen nations were represented. As individuals ventured forth from these racial fastnesses into the bewildering world outside, they generally found it their lot to perform the disagreeable or arduous work which Americans of older stock disdained. The sweatshops in the garment industry were recruited largely from Bohe-

---

[1] J. F. Willard (Josiah Flynt, *pseud.*), "The German and the German-American," *Atlantic Mo.*, LXXVIII (1896), 655-664.
[2] Quoted by Turner, "Dominant Forces in American Life," 438. See also G. W. Steevens, *The Land of the Dollar* (N. Y., 1897), 144, and J. C. Ridpath, "The Mixed Populations of Chicago," *Chautauquan*, XII (1891), 483-493.

mians and Russian Jews; the rough unskilled jobs in
the building trades fell chiefly to Irish and Italians;
while the business of peddling became a specialty of
Jews.

Assimilation went on at an uneven pace, being
notably slow in the case of the new arrivals from southern Europe and Russia. Timidity and ignorance on the
part of the immigrant, suspicion and contempt on the
part of the native-born, constantly retarded the process.
Even the American-born children, if reared in an Old
World atmosphere and taught their school lessons in an
alien tongue, were more apt to be second-generation immigrants than first-generation Americans. But sooner or
later the influences of the new land began to penetrate.
Perhaps unusual business success or the liberalizing effect
of membership in a labor union helped break down the
barriers. More often, however, the change reflected the
influence of the public school carried into the immigrant
home by the children. Though a regrettable breach
sometimes resulted between the older and younger generations, the democratic school system was a major force
for rapid Americanization. The number of American-
born immigrant children in Chicago in 1890 nearly
equaled that of the total alien-born, thus increasing,
though not by that proportion, the foreign character of
her population.[1]

As was Chicago, so in a measure were Cleveland,
Minneapolis and Detroit. Yet Chicago's four hundred
and fifty thousand foreign-born, Cleveland's one hundred thousand, Detroit's eighty thousand and Minneapolis's sixty thousand formed only two fifths of all
the people in those cities in 1890. In places like Columbus and Indianapolis seven eighths of the population
continued to be of American nativity. Many of the

[1] *U. S. Eleventh Census*, I, clxii-clxiii.

native-born, however, were of alien parentage and still in the process of learning American ways.

In so far as the swiftly growing urban localities drew population away from the countryside, the effects were severe enough to threaten many rural districts with paralysis. A map of the Middle West, shading the counties which suffered the chief losses between 1880 and 1890, would have been blackest across central Missouri and in the eastern half of Iowa, northern and western Illinois, central and southeastern Indiana, southern Michigan and central and southern Ohio.[1] Though some of the depletion, particularly in Iowa and western Illinois, was connected with the building up of the agricultural country to the west, much of it was due to the cityward flight. In Ohio 755 townships out of 1316 declined in population; in Illinois 800 out of 1424. Yet during the same decade every Middle Western state gained substantially in total number of inhabitants— Ohio about one seventh and Illinois nearly a quarter— an advance only in part to be accounted for by immigrant additions and the natural increase of population.

Such indications of rural decay, however, were mild as compared with conditions in the North Atlantic states. In this great seaboard section stretching from the Potomac to the St. Croix the city had completed its conquest. Already in 1880 about half the people—seven and a half million—lived in towns and cities of four thousand or more inhabitants; within a decade the proportion grew to nearly three fifths or eleven million.[2]

[1] For this purpose the Census Bureau classifies as urban any compact community of one thousand or more. *U. S. Eleventh Census*, I, lxix-lxxi. See also E. W. Miller, "The Abandoned Farms of Michigan," *Nation* (N. Y.), XLIX (1889), 498; H. J. Fletcher, "The Doom of the Small Town," *Forum*, XIX (1895), 214-223; anon., "The City in Modern Life," *Atlantic Mo.*, LXXV (1895), 552-556.

[2] *U. S. Twelfth Census*, I, lxxxiv-lxxxv. In terms of cities of eight

In 1890 about two out of every three persons in New
York and Connecticut were townsfolk, four out of every
five in Massachusetts and nine out of every ten in Rhode
Island. Only the states of northern New England preserved their essentially rural character. In the East, too,
most of the nation's great cities were to be found. New
York City, with already more than a million people in
1880, reached a million and a half in 1890 without the
help of Brooklyn which contained eight hundred thousand more. Philadelphia attained a million in 1890,
though since the previous census Chicago had supplanted
her as the second city of the United States. Boston, Baltimore and Washington had about half a million each,
Buffalo and Pittsburgh a quarter million each. Countless
smaller places spotted the landscape and gave to the
entire region a strongly urban cast.

   In striking contrast were the rural backwaters.
"Sloven farms alternate with vast areas of territory,
half forest, half pasturage;" an observant foreign traveler wrote of Pennsylvania and New England, "farm
buildings, partly in ruins, testify at once to the former
prosperity of the agricultural industry and to its present
collapse." Then, "all at once, on rounding a hill, one
comes upon a busy valley, its slopes dotted with charming cottages, while at the further end rise the immense
blocks of buildings and chimneys that tell of the factory." [1]

   The census of 1890 first revealed the extent of the
rural exodus.[2] Two fifths of Pennsylvania, a good quar-

thousand or more inhabitants the urban percentages for the two years
were 43.1 and 51.8. *U. S. Eleventh Census*, I, lxviii.

   [1] Paul de Rousiers, *American Life* (A. J. Herbertson, tr., Paris,
1892), 189.

   [2] *U. S. Eleventh Census*, I, lxviii-lxxi. See also M. A. Veeder, "Deserted
Farms in New York," *Nation*, XLIX (1889), 431; Clarence Gordon,
"The Revival of Agriculture," same vol., 498-499; J. R. Elliott, *American Farms* (*Questions of the Day Series*, LXII, 2d edn., N. Y., 1890),
46.

ter of New Jersey, nearly five sixths of New York state and much of New England had fallen off in population during the decade. The eclipse of the Eastern countryside had, of course, been long in process, indeed ever since the old farming districts of the Atlantic states first felt the competition of the virgin lands of the interior.[1] After the Civil War the pressure became even greater, for the opening of new railway lines enabled the prairie farmers, with the aid of favoring freight rates, to undersell Eastern farmers in their own natural markets. The normal drain on the older agricultural districts was intensified by the drift of country boys and girls to the towns and cities as industry boomed and the lure of the near-by metropolis captured their imaginations. Far removed from the free lands of the Great West, the rural youth was now less inclined to ask "Where is the fittest farm?" than "Where is the fitter vocation?"

New England was hardest hit of all, especially those parts in which agricultural retrogression was not offset by corresponding urban development. Three fifths of Connecticut, three fourths of Vermont and nearly two thirds of New Hampshire and Maine declined in population. Out of 1502 townships in all New England 932 had fewer people in 1890 than at the start of the decade.[2] Cellar holes choked with lilac and woodbine, tumble-down buildings, scrubby orchards, pastures bristling with new forest growths, perhaps a lone rosebush—these mute, pathetic memorials of once busy farming communities attested the reversal of a familiar

[1] Thus in 1857 Professor J. W. Patterson estimated that that very season had seen an exodus to the West of 300,000 "from the impoverished hillsides and valleys of New England." *Address before the Grafton County Agricultural Society* (Hanover, N. H., 1857), 7.

[2] Josiah Strong, *The New Era* (N. Y., 1893), 167. See also J. D. Long and others, "The Future of the New England Country," *New England Mag.*, n.s., III (1890-1891), 661-673.

historic process, with civilization retreating before the advancing wilderness.

Official inquiries at the end of the eighties revealed more than a thousand farms in Vermont abandoned for agricultural purposes, over thirteen hundred in New Hampshire, nearly fifteen hundred in Massachusetts and more than thirty-three hundred in Maine.[1] Vermont farms with good buildings went begging at five dollars or less an acre. Nor did the upland villages escape the general *debâcle*. "The proportion of abandoned wagon-shops, shoeshops, saw-mills and other mechanical businesses has far outstripped the abandonment of farms," wrote one contemporary.[2] Judge Nott of Washington, D. C., happening upon a stricken village in southern Vermont, found that

> the church was abandoned, the academy dismantled, the village deserted. The farmer who owned the farm on the north of the village lived on one side of the broad street, and he who owned the farm on the south lived on the other, and they were the only inhabitants.

All others had fled—"to the manufacturing villages, to the great cities, to the West." Where once had dwelt "industry, education, religion, comfort, and contentment," there remained "only a drear solitude of forsaken homes." [3]

[1] F. H. Fowler, "Abandoned Farms," L. H. Bailey, ed., *Cyclopedia of American Agriculture* (N. Y., 1909), IV, 102-106; Anderson, *Country Town*, 66-69; Elliott, *American Farms*, 42-43, 60-64.

[2] G. F. Wells, "The Status of Rural Vermont," *Twenty-Third Ann. Vt. Agricultural Rep.*, 621.

[3] C. C. Nott, "A Good Farm for Nothing," *Nation*, XLIX (1889), 406. A. F. Sanborn, "The Future of Rural New England," *Atlantic Mo.*, LXXX (1897), 74-83, also presents a striking picture of a decayed town—its outward dilapidation and the emptiness of its inner life. Even more lugubrious is R. L. Hartt, "A New England Hill Town," *Atlantic Mo.*, LXXXIII (1899), 561-574, 712-720.

Generally the people of push and initiative migrated while the less enterprising stayed at home. Thus Yankee energy, though continuing to contribute vitally to the upbuilding of America, did so at a terrible cost to the stock it left behind. Ministers and humanitarian workers in the country districts were appalled by the extent of inbreeding, the prevalence of drunkenness, bastardy and idiocy, the lack of wholesome amusements and the almost universal poverty. In nearly the same words two Congregational preachers reported, "My people are degenerates; the people all through my district are degenerates." [1] It may well be believed that such characterizations applied to the most neglected communities rather than to typical ones. Yet everywhere the process of folk depletion was going on at an alarming rate, lending color to the assertion that New England's woods and templed hills were breeding their own race of poor whites.

Dismayed by the trend of the times, the close of the eighties saw the several state governments engaged in frantic efforts to promote a back-to-the-country movement. Few literate Americans were allowed to remain ignorant of the bargains in land and farm buildings that might be found in New England's rustic parts. Vermont even tried the expedient of colonizing three small groups of Swedish immigrants on deserted tracts. The situation, however, had to grow worse before it could become better. Once the nation-wide agricultural sickness of the early nineties had run its course, rural New England would discover sources of new wealth in dairying, truck gardening, the expansion of wood-working industries

[1] Comments quoted in R. L. Hartt, "Our Rural Degeneracy," *Boston Transcript*, May 17, 1899. On this subject, see also R. L. Hartt, "The Regeneration of Rural New England: Social," *Outlook*, LXIV (1900), 577-583, the article by A. F. Sanborn already cited, Anderson, *Country Town*, chaps. v-vi, and Strong, *New Era*, chap. viii.

based on second forest growths and, last but not least, the rapid development of the summer-boarder business.[1]

Despite the decline of rural population in New England and other parts of the East the attractions of city life were so great that from 1880 to 1890 the section in general gained twenty per cent in number of inhabitants. By the latter year nineteen million, or somewhat less than a third of all the nation, lived there. Urban growth, even more than in Middle America, was nourished by foreign immigration.[2] A larger proportion of the alien arrivals settled in the East and fewer of them took up farming as a livelihood. The census of 1890 disclosed a million more immigrants than a decade earlier. In the section as a whole one out of every five persons was foreign-born.

Nor could one assume, as ten years before, that any immigrant he met was likely to belong to the older racial strains that had fused into the historic American stock. The Eastern commonwealths with their great ports and thriving industries were the first to feel the impact of the new human tide that was setting in from southern and eastern Europe. While in 1890 they contained more Irish and Britons than did any other section—a total of two and a third million—and with nine hundred thousand Germans ranked in that respect next to the Middle West, they also embraced more Italians, Russians and Hungarians than any other section, to the number of a quarter million.

A fourth of the people of Philadelphia and a third

[1] F. H. Chase, "Is Agriculture Declining in New England?," *New England Mag.*, n.s., II (1890), 449-452; J. W. Sanborn, "Comparison of Eastern and Western Farming," Mass. State Bd. of Agr., *Forty-Second Ann. Rep., 1894*, 161-218; G. W. Atherton, "The Future of New England Agriculture," Mass. State Bd. of Agr., *Forty-Fourth Ann. Rep., 1896*, 118; Anderson, *Country Town*, 83-85; U. S. Industrial Commission, *Reports* (Wash., 1900-1902), XIX, 116-120.

[2] *U. S. Eleventh Census*, I, cxviii-cxix, clv, 606-609.

of the Bostonians were in 1890 of alien birth. New York-Brooklyn was the greatest center of immigrants in the world, having half as many Italians as Naples, as many Germans as Hamburg, twice as many Irish as Dublin and two and a half times as many Jews as Warsaw.[1] Four out of every five residents of Greater New York were foreigners or of foreign parentage. Different from Boston and Philadelphia, the newer type of immigrant had become a considerable element in the city's population though the Germans and Irish still greatly predominated.

These latest arrivals, ignorant, clannish, inured to wretched living conditions, gravitated naturally to the poorest quarters of the city toward the tip of Manhattan and gradually pushed the older occupants into the better sections to the north.[2] Lower New York was like a human palimpsest, the writings of earlier peoples being dimmed, though not entirely effaced, by the heavier print of the newest comers. Through the eighties the Italians crowded into the old Irish neighborhoods west of Broadway, while the Russian and Polish Jews took possession of the German districts to the east with the tenth ward as their center.[3] The Hungarians settled thickly east of Avenue B, about Houston Street, and

[1] Compared with Chicago, Greater New York in 1890 possessed more Irish, English, Germans, Russians and Italians, but Chicago had a larger number of Scandinavians, Bohemians, Poles and Canadians. Thirty-nine per cent of the population of New York-Brooklyn was foreign-born in 1890.

[2] Kate H. Claghorn, "The Foreign Immigrant in New York City," U. S. Industrial Comn., *Reports*, XV, 465-492. See also J. A. Riis, *How the Other Half Lives* (N. Y., 1890), chap. iii.

[3] The specialized character of Italian clannishness is shown by the fact that Neapolitans and Calabrians clung to the Mulberry Bend district, a colony of Genoese lived in Baxter Street, a Sicilian colony in Elizabeth Street, between Houston and Spring, while north Italians predominated in the eighth and fifteenth wards west of Broadway, and south Italians in "Little Italy" between 110th and 115th streets in Harlem.

the Bohemians near the river on the upper East Side
from about Fiftieth to Seventy-sixth Street. Smaller
groups like the Greeks and Syrians also had their special
precincts where picturesque Old World customs and
trades prevailed; and in the heart of the lower East Side
grew up a small replica of San Francisco's Chinatown.

Quite as strange to Americans as the south Europeans
were the French Canadians who began their mass invasion of New England shortly after 1878. For over
two centuries these descendants of the pioneers of New
France had tilled the soil of the province of Quebec
where, intensely race-conscious and devoted to Catholicism, they had stubbornly maintained their identity and
language apart from the conquering English. Harried,
however, by hard times from the 1860's on and tempted
by better opportunities elsewhere, many of them sought
escape in migration.[1] Some moved westward to set up
farm colonies in Ontario and Manitoba. Others, feeling
the pull of the busy mill towns across the international
border, succumbed to *le mal des États-Unis*. Presently
the trickle of population into New England became a
flooding stream. About fourteen thousand had removed
to Rhode Island by 1875, sixty-four thousand to Massachusetts ten years later. Northern New England made
less appeal though occasional settlements of farmers and
lumberjacks were to be found. By 1890 the French
Canadians, then numbering two hundred thousand,
formed approximately a sixth of the entire immigrant
population of New England.[2] Nearly half of them were
in Massachusetts.

[1] D. M. A. Magnan, *Histoire de la Race Française aux États-Unis*
(Paris, 1912), 250; Alexandre Beslisle, *Histoire de la Presse Franco-
Américaine* (Worcester, 1911), 4-9.

[2] Before 1890, when the federal enumerators (*Eleventh Census*, I,
clxxiii-clxxv) first took cognizance of French Canadians as distinguished
from Anglo-Canadians, statistics of settlement must be based on state
census reports.

Hiving in the manufacturing towns, they were eagerly welcomed by employers who found them not only hard workers but also slow to give trouble even when conditions were galling. The opprobrium of being the "Chinese of the Eastern states," however, they scarcely deserved, although their ready acceptance of low living standards naturally roused the ire of organized labor.[1] Religiously, too, they were viewed askance by the older elements. Added to the already large Irish Catholic contingent, their presence seemed to threaten the traditional Puritan and Protestant character of the section. "Protestant New England will soon have within itself, a Roman Catholic New France, as large as, if not larger than itself," cried one alarmist.[2] As a matter of fact, the language barrier and the desire of the new-comers to import their own priests caused more friction than friendship between them and the resident Irish-American clergy.[3] It was said that French-Canadian support of the Republican party at the polls was due to no reason so good as that the Irish preferred the Democrats.

A race so resistant could hardly be expected to adopt new ways of life overnight. Yet, scattered in a hundred different communities and obliged constantly to rub elbows with people unlike themselves, the chemistry of Americanization worked as quickly with them as with most other alien groups. Intermarriage, while not com-

---

[1] Massachusetts Bureau of Labor Statistics, *Twelfth Annual Report* (1881), 469. This document should be read in the light of the record of the public hearings held in 1882. See *Thirteenth Ann. Rep.* (1882), 3-92.

[2] C. E. Amaron, *Your Heritage; or New England Threatened* (Springfield, Mass., 1891), 116.

[3] Édouard Hamon, *Les Canadiens-Français de la Nouvelle-Angleterre* (Quebec, 1891), 57, 60, 175; Magnan, *Histoire*, 255-261, 266, 273-274, 296-297; Prosper Bender, "A New France in New England," *Mag. of Am. History*, XX (1888), 391.

mon, took place most readily with Anglo-Canadians.[1]
Less adept politically than the Irish, they nevertheless
gradually found their way into local offices and by 1890
thirteen French Canadians were members of New England legislatures.[2] Different from other immigrant peoples, however, they massed themselves in New England,
few of them going into the Middle West or even into
other parts of the East.

As a lodestone for both immigrant and native-born
the city had decisively placed the East under thrall. Its
hand already lay heavily upon the Middle West. Even
in the farther West and the South its power and distant
allure were strongly felt though society as yet lingered
in an agricultural state. Through the nation in general
every third American in 1890 was an urban dweller,
living in a town of four thousand or more inhabitants.[3]
Cities of from twelve to twenty thousand people had
since 1880 increased in number from 76 to 107; cities
of from twenty to forty thousand from 55 to 91;
larger places up to seventy-five thousand inhabitants
from 21 to 35; cities of yet greater size from 23 to 39.[4]

Moreover, the concentration of population had been
attended by a significant concentration of wealth. This
latter circumstance furnished ample basis for the agrarian contention that the rural districts were not sharing
proportionately in the advancing national wealth. In
1880, according to the census, the value of farms was
equal to that of urban real estate, about ten billion dollars for each. In 1890 the value of farms was returned
as thirteen billion while other real estate—mostly urban

[1] U. S. Eleventh Census, I, 698-701; U. S. Twelfth Census, I, 850-
853; Mass. Census of 1895, III, 152-154.
[2] Adélard Desrosiers and P. A. Fournet, La Race Française en Amérique
(Montreal, 1910), 240.
[3] U. S. Twelfth Census, I, lxxxiv-lxxxv.
[4] U. S. Eleventh Census, I, lxvii.

MAP OF THE UNITED STATES IN 1890
ACCORDING TO POPULATION.

The size of each state and city is
based on population.

A space this size represents
50,000 people.

All cities of 50,000 population
or more are shown.

The Populous States in 1890

—was listed at twenty-six billion. Nor did the people on the farms and in the rural hamlets of the East fare better than those of the West and South. On the contrary, the farms in the Eastern states declined in absolute value during the decade.

If personalty were included, the contrast between city and country became even sharper, particularly since the tangible personalty on the farms was in considerable degree offset by mortgages held in the towns and cities. The most careful contemporary student of the subject estimated that in 1890 the average wealth of families in the rural districts did not exceed $3250 while the average wealth of city families was over $9000.[1] The wider implications of urban growth, however, reached far beyond exigent considerations of wealth and income. These, as they affected the character of American civilization for good or ill, remain yet to be examined.

[1] The data for the above discussion are derived from C. B. Spahr, *An Essay on the Present Distribution of Wealth in the United States* (N. Y., 1896), 46-49, which concludes the passage with the observation: "When American political parties shall again divide upon issues vitally affecting the distribution of wealth, the clearly marked line of division will not be between East and West, but between city and country."

CHAPTER IV

THE URBAN WORLD

THE clash of country and city was not a phenomenon peculiar to America. All over the civilized globe the rural regions lay under a cloud—in Great Britain, France, Germany, Russia, Italy, Belgium.[1] The introduction of farm machinery and the opening up of virgin fields in the Argentine and Australia, added to those of the new American West, rendered unprofitable much of the agricultural labor of the Old World, stirred rural conservatism into fierce discontent and enhanced the attractions of the near-by city for the peasant toilers. Everywhere there was an exodus from the soil while the trading and industrial centers waxed by leaps and bounds. Between 1881 and 1891 Prussia added two million to her cities while her countryside barely increased a half million; rural France lost a half million at the same time that her urban places gained well over a million; the rural population of England and Wales declined over two hundred thousand while the towns and cities advanced by three and a quarter million.[2] By 1891 London and Paris had doubled their population of mid-century and Berlin had more than quadrupled hers.

From earliest times the painful, upward march of mankind had beaten a path through the streets of the town. The cities, not the country districts, had been—

[1] See the authorities cited by A. F. Weber, *The Growth of Cities in the Nineteenth Century* (Columbia Univ., *Studies*, XI), 210-211 *n*.
[2] Weber, *Growth of Cities*, 46, 68, 73, 82, 84.

in Theodore Parker's phrase—"the fireplaces of civilization whence light and heat radiated out into the dark cold world." Memphis, Thebes, Nineveh, Babylon, were the great capitals of early civilized man. In Greek and Roman times the city was the state itself. The revival of a vigorous urban life in the eleventh century, along the shores of the Mediterranean and in northern Germany, hastened the breakdown of feudalism and paved the way for the Renaissance and modern times. Unregarded by all but etymologists, the age-long contrast between city and country survives in the very language we speak—that language which townsmen coined with such glib facility. The well-mannered *civis* living in *urbs* was, for that reason, civil and urbane as well as civic and urban; his manner of life was epitomized in the very word, civilization. His rude rural neighbor, on the other hand, was a pagan or a rustic (from the Latin words, *paganus* and *rusticus,* for peasant), a boor (from the Dutch *boer,* a farmer), or a heathen (that is, a dweller on the heaths).

In America in the eighties urbanization for the first time became a controlling factor in national life.[1] Just as the plantation was the typical product of the *antebellum* Southern system and the small farm of the Northern agricultural order, so the city was the supreme achievement of the new industrialism. In its confines were focused all the new economic forces: the vast accumulations of capital, the business and financial institutions, the spreading railway yards, the gaunt smoky mills, the white-collar middle classes, the motley wage-earning population. By the same token the city inevitably became the generating center for social and

[1] For a contemporary appreciation of the dynamic rôle of the city, see F. J. Kingsbury, "The Tendency of Men to Live in Cities," *Journ. of Social Sci.,* XXXIII (1895), 1-19.

intellectual progress. To dwell in the midst of great affairs is stimulating and broadening; it is the source of a discontent which, if not divine, is at least energizing. In a populous urban community like could find like; the person of ability, starved in his rural isolation, might by going there find sympathy, encouragement and that criticism which often refines talent into genius.

Moreover the new social needs created by crowded living stimulated inventors to devise mechanical remedies—appliances for better lighting, for faster communication and transit, for higher buildings—which reacted in a thousand ways on the life of urban folk. Density of population plus wealth concentration also facilitated organized effort for cultivating the life of mind and spirit.[1] In the city were to be found the best schools, the best churches, the best newspapers, and virtually all the bookstores, libraries, art galleries, museums, theaters and opera houses. It is not surprising that the great cultural advances of the time came out of the city, or that its influence should ramify to the farthest countryside.

As the cradle of progress the city, in some manner or other, seemed to favor persons born within its walls over those born on the farm. One investigator, basing his conclusions on *Who's Who in America,* found that towns of eight thousand and more people produced nearly twice as many men of distinction as their numerical importance warranted.[2] A study of the antecedents

[1] U. S. Commissioner of Education, *Report for 1894-95,* I, 3-8.
[2] The names under the first five letters of the alphabet in *Who's Who* for 1908-1909 were analyzed. F. A. Woods, "City Boys versus Country Boys," *Science,* n.s., XXIX, 577-579. For similar conclusions, see S. S. Visher, *Geography of American Notables* (Indiana Univ., *Studies,* XV, no. 79), esp. pt. v; and R. H. Holmes, "A Study in the Origins of Distinguished Living Americans," *Am. Journ. of Sociology,* XXXIV, 670-685. Alfred Odin, *Genèse des Grands Hommes* (Paris, 1895), made a study of over six thousand French men of letters during five centuries

of leading American scientific men disclosed that a disproportionate number of these were likewise of city birth. "The main factors in producing scientific and other forms of intellectual performance," concluded the investigator, "seem to be density of population, wealth, opportunity, and institutions and social traditions and ideals." [1]

But the heirs of the older American tradition did not yield the field without a struggle. To them, as to Jefferson, cities were "ulcers on the body politic." In their eyes the city spiritual was offset by the city sinister, civic splendor by civic squalor, urban virtues by urban vices, the city of light by the city of darkness. In politics they sought to preserve or restore their birthright of equality by stoutly belaboring their capitalistic foe embattled in his city fortress; but against the pervasive lure of metropolitan life, felt by their sons and daughters, they could do no better than invent sensational variations of the nursery tale of the country mouse and the city mouse. Urban growth evoked a voluminous literature of bucolic fear, typified by such titles as *The Spider and the Fly; or, Tricks, Traps, and Pitfalls of City Life by One Who Knows* (N. Y., 1873) and J. W. Buel's *Metropolitan Life Unveiled; or the Mysteries and Miseries of America's Great Cities* (St. Louis, 1882). It may be questioned, however, whether such exciting accounts with their smudgy but realistic pictures did more to repel than entice their breathless readers to partake of the life they depicted.

To traveled persons familiar with the distinctive personalities of European centers American cities presented

and found that the cities produced thirteen times as many in proportion to population as the rural districts.

[1] J. M. Cattell, "A Statistical Study of American Men of Science: III. The Distribution of American Men of Science," *Science*, n.s., XXIV, esp. 735.

a monotonous sameness. Apart from New York, Boston, Washington, New Orleans and a few other places Bryce believed that "American cities differ from one another only herein, that some of them are built more with brick than with wood, and others more with wood than brick." [1] Most places possessed the same checkerboard arrangement of streets lined with shade trees, the same shops grouped in much the same way, the same middle-class folk hurrying about their business, the same succession of unsightly telegraph poles, the same hotels with seedy men lounging in the dreary lobbies. Few foreign visitors stopped to think, however, that American cities were the handiwork not of many national states but of a fairly uniform continent-wide culture. If they lacked the colorful variety of ancient European foundations, they also lacked the physical inconveniences and discomforts which picturesqueness was apt to entail. But it could not be gainsaid that a tendency toward standardization, as well as toward higher standards, was one of the fruits of American urban development.

While in the European sense there was no single dominant city in America—no city both metropolis and capital—yet all agreed in according the foremost position to New York. Nowhere else were there such fine buildings, such imposing financial houses, such unusual opportunities for business and recreation. No other place had such an air of rush and bustle, the streets constantly being torn up, dug up or blown up. To New York an unending stream of visitors discovered some pretext to go each year; in it many foreign travelers, going no further, found material for pithy, if ill-informed, com-

[1] James Bryce, *The American Commonwealth* (London, 1888), III, 621. See also E. Catherine Bates, *A Year in the Great Republic* (London, 1887), I, 248, and Paul Blouët (Max O'Rell, *pseud.*), *A Frenchman in America* (N. Y., 1891), 244-245.

ments on the whole American scene. "The streets are narrow," wrote one observer in 1883, "and overshadowed as they are by edifices six or more stories in height, seem to be dwarfed into mere alley-ways." [1] At that time the well-populated district did not extend much beyond Fifty-ninth Street; and Madison Square at the intersection of Broadway and Fifth Avenue had recently supplanted Union Square as the nerve center of New York life. But the period of growth and expansion was at hand. The corporate limits, which before 1874 had not reached beyond Manhattan Island, spread rapidly until in 1898, as Greater New York, they embraced Bronx County, Kings County (Brooklyn), Richmond County (Staten Island), and a portion of Queens County (on Long Island).

As earlier, Broadway was the main artery of New York life, lending itself successively to wholesale trade, newspaper and magazine publishing, retail shopping, hotels and theaters, as it wended its way northward from the Battery. Manhattan's other famous thoroughfare, Fifth Avenue, offered a continuous pageant of "palatial hotels, gorgeous club-houses, brownstone mansions and magnificent churches." [2] Different from most American cities, the finest residences stood side by side without relief of lawn or shrubbery; only on the striking but as yet unfinished Riverside Drive, with its noble view of the Hudson, was architecture assisted by nature.

[1] Willard Glazier, *Peculiarities of American Cities* (Phila., 1883), 290. On New York, see also Paul de Rousiers, *American Life* (A. J. Herbertson, tr., Paris, 1892), chap. xiii; W. G. Marshall, *Through America* (London, 1881), chap. i; G. J. Holyoake, *Among the Americans* (Chicago, 1881), chap. ii; G. A. Sala, *America Revisited* (London, 1883), I, chaps. ii-vi; S. R. Hole, *A Little Tour in America* (N. Y., 1895), chaps. iv-vi.

[2] Glazier, *Peculiarities of American Cities*, 301; J. F. Muirhead, *The Land of Contrasts* (N. Y., 1898), 193-197; H. C. Brown, *In the Golden Nineties* (*Valentine's Manual of Old New York*, XII, Hastings-on-Hudson, 1927), 25-48.

Merchant princes and Wall Street millionaires vied with one another to sustain Fifth Avenue's reputation of being the most splendid thoroughfare in America, "a very alderman among streets." During the 1880's a dark brown tide swept up the avenue. The late A. T. Stewart's marble palace at the corner of Thirty-fourth Street, long a magnet for sightseers, was eclipsed by the newer brownstone mansions of the Vanderbilts and others farther up the avenue, inclosed by forbidding iron fences. In the late afternoon Fifth Avenue churned with "a torrent of equipages, returning from the races or the park: broughams, landaus, clarences, phætons, . . . equestrians in boots and corduroys, slim-waisted equestriennes with blue veils floating from tall silk hats." [1]

Yet New York was a city of contradictions, reminding one visitor of "a lady in ball costume, with diamonds in her ears, and her toes out at her boots." [2] Against the splendors of Fifth Avenue and the show places of the metropolis had to be set the rocky wastes of Shantytown, extending during the 1880's along the East Side from Forty-second to One Hundred and Tenth Street and inhabited by Irish squatters, goats and pigs living promiscuously together. Contrasting with the pillared citadels of wealth in Wall Street was the near-by slum section, a festering spot of poverty and immorality, finding a tawdry outlet for its life in the notorious Bowery. [3]

The New Yorker was already famed for his provincialism: his proud ignorance of the rest of the nation

[1] Raymond Westbrook, "Open Letters from New York," *Atlantic Mo.*, XLI (1878), 92.

[2] Muirhead, *Land of Contrasts*, 193.

[3] H. C. Brown, *New York in the Elegant Eighties* (*Valentine's Manual of Old New York*, XI, Hastings-on-Hudson, 1926), 11-16; anon., "Along the Bowery, When Vice Stalked Openly," *Police Gazette*, Nov. 29, 1930.

and lofty condescension toward cities of lesser note.[1] Yet foreign tourists found much to interest and detain them in these other centers, and at least one felt a native New Yorker to be "less American than many Westerners born on the banks of the Oder or on the shores of some Scandinavian *fjord*." [2] Boston charmed with the quiet tenor of her life, her atmosphere of intellectuality, her generally English appearance.[3] With the reclamation of the Back Bay, a great engineering project completed in 1881, the city acquired over a hundred acres of filled land which made possible its expansion southward and the development of straight, wide thoroughfares to Copley Square and beyond.

Even more than Boston, Philadelphia impressed her visitors as a city of homes, with row upon row of prim brick houses with white wooden shutters, owned by their occupants. "If there are few notable buildings, there are few slums." [4] In Washington the traveler found America's most beautiful city, "one of the most singularly handsome cities on the globe." [5] Its parks and wide shaded avenues, its spacious vistas, the dazzling white of its public edifices, were reminiscent of great European capitals. In the absence of an army of factory

[1] This attitude was one of the certain symptoms of *Newyorkitis*, a malady amusingly described by J. H. Girdner in a small volume so titled (N. Y., 1901).

[2] Rousiers, *American Life*, 242.

[3] See Emily Faithfull, *Three Visits to America* (Edinburgh, 1884), chap. viii; G. W. Steevens, *The Land of the Dollar* (N. Y., 1897), 50-53; O'Rell, *Frenchman in America*, chaps. xvi-xvii.

[4] Steevens, *Land of the Dollar*, 115-116. See also Rousiers, *American Life*, 209-214, and Ephraim Turland, *Notes on a Visit to America* (Manchester, 1877), 21.

[5] Muirhead, *Land of Contrasts*, 218. See also H. L. Nelson, "Social Washington," *Atlantic Mo.*, LII (1883), 818-825; Hole, *Tour in America*, chap. xxi; Paul Blouët (Max O'Rell, *pseud.*) and Jack Allyn, *Jonathan and His Continent* (Madame Paul Blouët, tr., N. Y., 1889), 39-42; A. M. Low, "Washington: the City of Leisure," *Atlantic Mo.*, LXXXVI (1900), 767-778.

workers the general tone was one of dignified ease in pleasing contrast to the feverish anxiety typical of other cities. "The inhabitants do not rush onward as though they were late for the train . . . or as though the dinner-hour being past they were anxious to appease an irritable wife . . . ." [1]

Farther to the west lay Chicago, "the most American of American cities, and yet the most mongrel," a miracle city risen Phœnix-like from its great fire of 1871. [2] Its business and shopping district, rivaling New York's in high buildings, noise and impressiveness, was fringed by three residential areas: the north side, its broad streets lined with handsome abodes, churches and club houses overlooking the lake; the south side, a newer and hardly less aristocratic section, studded with stately mansions and spacious parks; and the vast west side, more populous than the other two combined, where dwelt the immigrants and laboring folk. Like every other great city, Chicago offered a study in contrasts: squalor matching splendor, municipal boodle contending with civic spirit; the very air now reeking with the foul stench of the stockyards, now fresh-blown from prairie or lake. A "splendid chaos" indeed, causing the roving Kipling to exclaim, "Having seen it, I urgently desire never to see it again." [3]

No better example could be found of what one contemporary called "urban imperialism." The surrounding prairie was for miles laced with railroads, and a

[1] Hole, *Tour in America*, 246.

[2] Steevens, *Land of the Dollar*, 144-145. See also Finlay Dun, *American Farming and Food* (London, 1881), chap. xii; William Archer, *America To-day* (N. Y., 1899), chap. ix; Hole, *Tour in America*, chap. xviii; Marshall, *Through America*, chap. iv; Sala, *America Revisited*, II, chap. ix; C. D. Warner, *Studies in the South and West* (N. Y., 1889), 184-186, 200-201; Glazier, *Peculiarities of American Cities*, chap. ix.

[3] Rudyard Kipling, *American Notes* (Boston, 1899), esp. 91.

large portion of the city and its suburbs was made up of a series of huge stations, car yards, grain elevators, cattle pens and storehouses. As the world's greatest corn, cattle and timber market Chicago completely dominated the Mississippi Valley and, to some degree, the farther West as well. Other places like Milwaukee, Kansas City, Detroit and the Twin Cities rose and flourished largely by its sufferance or favor. Even the older *entrepôts*— Cincinnati, St. Louis, New Orleans—lay under tribute to the Lake city, and Denver and San Francisco were not too remote to escape its influence.[1] Yet these and other cities had their own economic and cultural spheres of influence, and astonished Europeans found in them a level of material comfort typical only of the principal foreign centers.

Certain problems growing out of crowded living conditions vexed all municipalities, differing among them in degree rather than in kind. None was more important in 1878 than that of adequate traffic facilities. Even in the major cities streets were ill paved, if paved at all, and in the business sections were apt to be choked with rushing, jostling humanity. "The visitor is kept dodging, halting and shuffling to avoid the passing throng . . . ," asserted one timid contemporary. "The confusing rattle of 'busses and wagons over the granite pavement in Broadway almost drowns his own thoughts, and if he should desire to cross the street a thousand misgivings will assail him . . . although he sees scores of men and women constantly passing through the moving line of vehicles . . . ."[2] Cobblestones and

[1] A Chicagoan of these times, being asked his opinion of New York, which he had just visited, replied, "Wal, I guess it's too far away from Chicago to do any partic'lar amount of business!" Marshall, *Through America*, 103.

[2] J. W. Buel, *Metropolitan Life Unveiled* (St. Louis, 1882), 26. For similar reactions, see Rousiers, *American Life*, 240; Hole, *Tour in America*, 43-45; Marshall, *Through America*, 7.

granite blocks were the favorite paving materials in the
East because of their local availability, just as wood
blocks were in the Middle West.

But streets so constructed soon wore rough and uneven, and the eighties marked an era of experimentation
with more satisfactory types of surfacing.[1] The discovery of natural beds of pitch on the Island of Trinidad
directed attention to asphalt, already widely used in
Paris and London. When Washington laid four hundred
thousand square yards of it between 1878 and 1882,
that city set a pace soon followed by Buffalo, Philadelphia and other places. By 1898 the United States possessed nearly thirty million square yards of asphalt
paving. The imported material, however, was rivaled
by a native product, brick. Charleston, West Virginia,
and Bloomington, Illinois, had tried it in the previous
decade, but it was not until the mid-eighties that it came
into general use, notably in the Middle West. By 1898
Des Moines, Columbus and Cleveland stood first in the
proportion of brick paving to population, though Philadelphia with its two million square yards had more than
any other one city. In most cities macadam, a much
cheaper material, was deemed sufficiently durable for
residential and suburban roadways. Smaller towns contented themselves with dirt or gravel.

In the twenty years the streets of America were
greatly improved, though the civic conscience did not
regard it essential that good streets should be kept clean.[2]

[1] G. W. Tillson, *Street Pavements and Paving Materials* (N. Y.,
1900), chaps. ix-x; N. P. Lewis, "Modern City Roadways," *Pop. Sci.
Mo.*, LVI (1899-1900), 524-539.

[2] European cities were far ahead in the cleanliness of their streets.
Emmons Clark, "Street-Cleaning in Large Cities," *Pop. Sci. Mo.*,
XXXVIII (1890-1891), 748-755. However, in 1895-1898, when
Colonel Waring was commissioner of street cleaning in New York under
the anti-Tammany administration, he actually kept the streets clean and
set an example for other American cities. Among other things, he dressed
the street sweepers in white, from which the term, "white wings,"

By the end of the century Washington and Buffalo had become the best-paved cities in the world while Boston and the borough of Manhattan in New York were not far behind.[1] Chicago remained the Cinderella of great American municipalities, closely rivaled by Baltimore. In 1890 only 629 of Chicago's 2048 miles of streets were paved at all, about half with wood block, the rest with macadam, gravel, stone block, asphalt, cinders or cobblestones. Despite the civic lift given by the World's Fair of 1893 the situation was but little better at the close of the decade.

Since most large cities were intersected by waterways, the needs of rapidly growing municipalities required an adequate system of bridges. The problem appeared in its most acute form in New York where hordes of people must cross over each day to their places of work on Manhattan Island. After thirteen years in course of construction, a great bridge connecting New York with Brooklyn was completed in 1883. Its designer, John A. Roebling, had died from an injury before the work had more than started, leaving the actual construction to be directed by his son, Colonel Washington A. Roebling, who worked out the details as the enterprise proceeded.[2] All the riveting of steel in the structure was done by hand, pneumatic tools and compressed air being as yet unknown. Falling ill from overwork in December, 1872, Colonel Roebling supervised the operations from a wheel chair on the roof of his home, directing the progress with field glasses as a general might a battle.

When finished, Brooklyn Bridge was the longest suspension bridge in the world. The formal opening on

derives. G. E. Waring, *Street-Cleaning* (N. Y., 1897), chaps. i-v; Charles Zueblin, *American Municipal Progress* (N. Y., 1902), 78-81.

[1] J. A. Fairlie, *Municipal Administration* (N. Y., 1901), 234-235.

[2] Allan Nevins, *The Emergence of Modern America* (*A History of American Life*, VIII), 80; *N. Y. Times*, May 24, 1883.

May 24 was attended by President Arthur and his cabinet, the governors of near-by states and many other
distinguished persons. The only discordant note in the
chorus of rejoicing came from Hibernian New Yorkers
who denounced the choice of Queen Victoria's birthday
for the grand occasion. Majestic in the sweep of its
great cables from tower to tower, the completed structure was over a mile long, with a central river span of
nearly sixteen hundred feet and a passageway wide
enough for two rail lines, two double carriage lanes and
a footpath.

Though the traffic relief was considerable it was not
sufficient. Between 1886 and 1889 Washington Bridge
was built over the Harlem River, its two great steel
arches each over five hundred feet in span. and in 1896
a second bridge, the Williamsburg, was begun to link
Brooklyn and New York.[1] Other cities wrestled with
the same problem. Thus Pittsburgh built the Seventh
Street suspension bridge over the Allegheny River in
1884, Philadelphia completed a cantilever bridge carrying Market Street over the Schuylkill two years later,
and Richmond, Indiana, spanned the Whitewater River
with a suspension bridge in 1889.[2]

Horse cars, omnibuses, cabs and other similar vehicles
had suited the needs of simpler days, but the age of the
great city called for swifter conveyance. The old "bob-
tail" cars, modeled on the stagecoach and pulled by
horses or mules, did not suffice for moving an enormous
mass of people to and from their places of work at
about the same hours of the day. Already New York
had shown the utility of an overhead railway, four-car
trains being drawn by diminutive steam locomotives

[1] Anon., "The New East River Bridge," *Scientific Am.*, LXXV
(1896), 213, 218.
[2] For these and many other examples, see H. G. Tyrrell, *History of
Bridge Engineering* (Chicago, 1911), chaps. xii-xiii.

which scattered oil and live ashes on the heads of unwary pedestrians.[1] In 1878 a second unit, the Sixth Avenue Elevated, extending nearly the length of the island, was added to the original line. The "L" three years later was transporting one hundred and seventy-five thousand passengers daily or, if you prefer, "12,000 tons of human flesh, averaging each person at 140 lbs."[2] Under the spur of faster transit population spread rapidly northward. New lines were projected and built, reaching beyond the Harlem River into the northern suburban districts.[3] Kansas City also elevated some of her tracks in the mid-eighties and Brooklyn built an extensive system the same decade. But Chicago did not open her first line until 1892, and Boston, which meantime had begun to burrow underground, not until 1901.

The slow adoption of the overhead system was due partly to its ugliness and noise, but even more to the initial cost of construction. Of greater popularity in the eighties was the cable car, first contrived by a Scotch immigrant, Andrew S. Hallidie, in 1873 to solve the problem of transit over the hilly streets of San Francisco. The car moved by means of a grappling device which descended from the floor to an endless steel cable moving in a slotted trench between the tracks.[4] After a few years the system was taken over by cities which lacked San Francisco's peculiar need. In 1882 Charles T. Yerkes laid a cable road in Chicago, achieving not only a success for the city but a fortune for himself. Philadelphia followed the next year and New York in 1886.

[1] Nevins, *Emergence of Modern America*, 82.

[2] Marshall, *Through America*, 26. At the formal opening the trip from Trinity Church to Central Park took twenty-two minutes. *N. Y. Tribune*, May 1, 1878.

[3] Bureau of the Census, *Street and Electric Railways, 1902* (*Special Rep.*), 36.

[4] *Appletons' Annual Cyclopaedia*, XXVI (1886), 122-125, gives a technical description.

By the mid-nineties Eastern cities had one hundred and
fifty-seven miles in operation, the Middle West two hundred and fifty-two, the Far West two hundred and
seventeen and the South six.[1]

While the cable system was yet in its heyday, this
generation made its most substantial contribution toward
solving the problem of urban transit. For many years—
at least since 1835—inventors in America and abroad
had been working on the idea of an electrical railway.
Until the development of a practicable dynamo in the
1870's, however, they had been baffled by the lack of
an adequate supply of cheap current. The 1880's saw
the launching of trial lines at points as far removed as
Boston and Denver,[2] but the credit for the first American
electric railway successfully operated for profit over city
streets belongs to Lieutenant Frank J. Sprague. In 1887-
1888 he installed two and a half miles of track in Richmond, Virginia, the cars securing their current from an
overhead trolley wire fed from a central power house.

Its instant success started a veritable revolution in
urban transit. Not only were electric-propelled cars fast
and comfortable but they were relatively cheap to con-
struct and maintain. Fifty-one cities installed the new
system by 1890, and five years later eight hundred and
fifty lines were in operation, mostly in the East and
Middle West, with a total mileage of ten thousand.[3]

[1] H. H. Vreeland, "The Street Railways of America," C. M. Depew,
ed., *One Hundred Years of American Commerce* (N. Y., 1895), I,
141-143.

[2] By T. A. Edison at Menlo Park, C. J. Van Depoele in Chicago
and elsewhere, Leo Daft in Boston and elsewhere, E. M. Bentley and
W. H. Knight in Cleveland, J. C. Henry in Kansas City (where the
term, trolley, probably originated), S. H. Short in Denver, and by
others. Germany really led the way, Berlin having constructed a line in
1867 on the third-rail principle. T. C. Martin, "History and Development of Electric Traction," *Street and Electric Railways, 1902*, 160-167.

[3] Anon., "A Retrospect of the Year 1895," *Scientific Am.*, LXXIV
(1896), 2; Vreeland, "Street Railways," 144. Steps were also taken

Though horse and cable cars lingered on many streets, their doom was sealed. European cities lagged far behind those of America in adopting electric transit. At the close of the century Germany, with a trackage as great as all other European countries combined, possessed only one ninth the mileage of the United States.[1]

Traffic congestion, however, kept even pace with the new facilities for dealing with it. The tangled situation in down-town Boston, whose narrow crooked streets exemplified the old adage that one good turn deserves another, led to the final effort of this generation. Taking a leaf from the experience of London and Budapest, Boston between 1895 and 1897 constructed a subway line a mile and a half long under Tremont Street.[2] It was a notable engineering feat costing the city four and a quarter million dollars. Plans were at once made for extensions, and New York, as was fitting, projected a much more ambitious tunnel system which, however, did not open to the public until 1904.[3] Except for these last two instances, the varied and heroic endeavors made during these twenty years to clear the city streets were all carried out under private auspices.

Hardly less urgent than the need for better transit was the need for readier communication. In 1878 the recently invented telephone was hardly more than a scientific toy.[4] To use it a person, after briskly turning a crank, screamed into a crude mouthpiece and then, if

to electrify the elevated systems, though New York did not do so until 1901-1903. For an explanation, see Brown, *New York in Elegant Eighties,* 16-17.

[1] Fairlie, *Municipal Administration,* 296.

[2] *Street and Electric Railways, 1902,* 37-39.

[3] J. B. Walker, *Fifty Years of Rapid Transit* (N. Y., 1918), chaps. xii-xiii.

[4] Nevins, *Emergence of Modern America,* 88-89; G. M. Shaw, "The Telephone and How It Works," *Pop. Sci. Mo.,* XII (1877-1878), 559-569.

the satanic screechings and groanings of static permitted, faintly heard the return message. There was no central exchange station, telephone users being directly connected with one another by separate wires. Besides these disadvantages the sheer novelty of Bell's miracle made it unpopular. People felt "a sense of oddity, almost of foolishness," in using the instrument. "The dignity of talking consists in having a listener and there seems a kind of absurdity in addressing a piece of iron . . . ." [1] For a number of years Bell traveled about the country exhibiting his invention. On one such trip he offered Mark Twain stock in the enterprise at twenty-five, but that usually gullible humorist "didn't want it at any price," though before the year was out he put up the first telephone wire in Hartford, Connecticut, connecting his home with the *Courant* office. [2]

As population centers grew, social and business needs caused the telephone to be perfected rapidly and made the public forget its earlier prejudices. An important obstacle to success was removed in 1879 when the Western Union Telegraph Company, which had bitterly fought the Bell group by fair means and foul, came to terms and sold out its own telephone interests to the Bell Company. [3] Had the Western Union been able to invalidate Bell's claims as prior inventor before the courts, it is almost certain that the development of the telephone would have been sacrificed to that of the telegraph and hence its extension greatly retarded. Under the circumstances, however, mechanical improvements

[1] Edit., "Some Teachings of the Telephone," *Pop. Sci. Mo.*, XII (1877-1878), 626.

[2] He believed it was "the *first* one that was ever used in a private house in the world." A. B. Paine, *Mark Twain* (N. Y., 1912), II, 726.

[3] A. B. Paine, *In One Man's Life* (N. Y., 1921), chap. xxiii; Bureau of the Census, *Telephones and Telegraphs, 1902 (Special Rep.)*, 66-67; J. W. Stehman, *The Financial History of the American Telephone and Telegraph Company* (Boston, 1925), 13-18.

quickly ensued.[1] Francis Blake's invention of a carbon transmitter in 1878, an advance over Emile Berliner's and Edison's devices of the year before, greatly improved the carrying qualities of the voice. Five years later another young man, J. J. Carty, exorcised the mysterious noises of the wires by a simple mechanical arrangement known as the metallic-circuit system.

Hardly less important was the contriving of a central switchboard, the work principally of George W. Coy who installed the first commercial board at New Haven, Connecticut, in January, 1878, for the use of twenty-one subscribers.[2] When L. B. Firman followed in 1879 with the invention of a multiple switchboard, the nerve center of the telephone was complete. At first boys were employed at "central," but being addicted to fighting one another and swearing at their unseen customers, they were soon superseded by girls who thus found a new vocation.[3]

The rapid expansion of the Bell system owed much to the business genius of Theodore N. Vail, general manager of the company from 1878 to 1885. Grand-nephew of Stephen Vail, who had built the engines for the first transatlantic steamship, and a cousin of Alfred Vail, who had worked with Morse on the telegraph, young Vail came naturally by his interest in the latest mechanical marvel. He threw himself into the work with boundless enthusiasm, overcoming innumerable obstacles

[1] H. N. Casson, *The History of the Telephone* (Chicago, 1910), 118-125; E. W. Byrn, *The Progress of Invention in the Nineteenth Century* (N. Y., 1900), 82-85; Paine, *One Man's Life*, 161-162.

[2] Other exchanges, established the same year, were Meriden, Connecticut, San Francisco, Albany, Chicago, Wilmington, Delaware, St. Louis, Detroit and Philadelphia. Casson, *History of the Telephone*, 143-147; anon., *Things Worth Knowing about the Telephone* (N. Y., 1929), 43.

[3] Casson, *History of the Telephone*, 153-155; Katherine M. Schmitt, "I Was Your Old 'Hello' Girl," *Sat. Eve. Post*, CCV, 18 ff. (July 12, 1930).

and in the end making the telephone an indispensable adjunct to every business house.[1] By insisting that equipment should be uniform and leased, not sold, to the subscriber, he saved the United States from the chaos which exists in certain other countries, notably France, where each customer buys his own instrument from a selection of about forty different varieties.

In 1880 eighty-five towns had telephone exchanges with nearly fifty thousand subscribers and about thirty-five thousand miles of wire. Ten years later the number of subscribers had grown fivefold and the wire mileage sevenfold.[2] From the first intercity line joining Boston and Lowell in 1879, the reach of the telephone grew constantly greater until by 1892 Boston and New York were talking with Washington, Pittsburgh, Chicago and Milwaukee and a few years later with Omaha.[3] As presidential candidate McKinley sat in his home at Canton, Ohio, and talked with his campaign managers in thirty-eight states. When in 1893 the patents owned by the Bell Company expired, many independent companies sprang up, especially in the smaller towns of the Middle West where the Bell system had not found it worth while to extend its service.[4]

Nearly eight hundred thousand phones were in use by 1900, one for every ninety-five persons as compared with one for every nine hundred and twenty-three twenty years before; the United States had twice as many telephones as all Europe. In two decades Bell's invention had, from a mechanical curiosity, become a

[1] Paine, *One Man's Life*, chaps. xx-xxviii.
[2] Anon., "The Telephonic Exchange in the United States," *Nature*, XXIV (1880), 495; *Telephones and Telegraphs*, 1902, 5.
[3] Anon., "Progress of the Bell Telephone," *Scientific Am.*, LXX (1894), 250.
[4] K. B. Miller, "Merits of Independent and Industrial Telephone Systems," *Engineering Mag.*, XVIII (1900), 550-557; *Telephones and Telegraphs*, 1902, 9-11, 67.

necessity of American life. That it added to the speed of living and the breaking down of personal privacy cannot be doubted. That it helped make the American people the most talkative nation in the world is likewise clear. On the credit side of the ledger, however, must be put the enormous gains resulting from the facilitation of social and business intercourse and from the extension of urban influences into areas of rural isolation.

Largely because of the greater utility of the telephone the telegraph expanded slowly during these years. In 1874 Edison had doubled the carrying capacity of the wires by his invention of quadruplex telegraphy, which allowed two messages to be sent simultaneously from opposite ends of the same line.[1] Actual wire mileage, however, grew but fourfold between 1878 and 1898. By the mid-nineties only one telegram per person per year was being sent in the United States while the people were using the telephone ten times as much.[2] The telephone far outstripped its elder sister even for long-distance use; only in submarine communication did the telegraph continue to reign unchallenged. In the closing years of the decade, however, new vistas opened for it in a field in which it was thought the telephone could never compete. This was wireless telegraphy, the invention in 1896 of Guglielmo Marconi, an Italian engineer. Still in the experimental stage, the chief use of "wireless" before the coming of the new century was for ocean vessels.[3]

[1] F. L. Dyer and T. C. Martin, *Edison* (N. Y., 1910), I, 154-160; *Telephones and Telegraphs, 1902*, 99-105, 115.

[2] T. C. Martin, "Electrical Manufacturing Interests," Depew, *American Commerce*, II, 377-378.

[3] J. A. Fleming, "Scientific History and Future Uses of Wireless Telegraphy," *N. Am. Rev.*, CLXVIII (1899), 630-640; P. B. Delaney, "The Development of Wireless Telegraphy," *Engineering Mag.*, XVIII (1900), 747-754; Guglielmo Marconi, "Origin and Develop-

Meantime the slower communication afforded by the postal service had shown steady improvement as city populations thickened.[1] In 1883 the rate for single letters was cut from three to two cents a half-ounce and, two years later, to two cents an ounce, with a provision for special-delivery service to secure swifter transmission. In 1887 free delivery was extended to towns with as few as ten thousand people, increasing the number of places so served by one hundred and sixty-nine.[2] The sale of ordinary postage stamps leaped from seven hundred and forty-two million in 1878 to nearly two billion in 1888 and to three billion ten years later.[3] Despite the quickened pace of American life the post office with its cheaper rates remained the basic means of intercommunication, being supplemented by the faster services of the telephone and telegraph.

Improved lighting was almost as great a necessity as improved communication, for the new conditions of city life required something better than the dim rays shed from gas lamp-posts on the streets and the yellow glow of kerosene lamps or open-flame gas jets indoors. For years inventors in many countries had been seeking to harness electricity to the service of illumination, but success, as in the case of the trolley car, had to await the development of the modern dynamo.[4] Though the Rus-

ment of Wireless Telegraphy," N. Am. Rev., CLXVIII (1899), 625-629; anon., "Recent Development of Wireless Telegraphy," Nature, LXI (1899), 78.

[1] D. C. Roper, The United States Post Office (N. Y., 1917), 75, 141-142, 178, 206, 371-372.

[2] Eighty-seven cities had free-carrier service in 1877-1878; 358 in 1887-1888; and 688 in 1897-1898. In the same years the number of mail carriers increased from 2275 to 6346 to 13,696. Postmaster-General, Report for 1900, 108-109.

[3] Postmaster-General, Report for 1878, 6; for 1888-89, 704; for 1899, 30.

[4] Bureau of the Census, Central Electric Light and Power Stations, 1902 (Special Rep.), 86-92.

sian engineer, Paul Jablochkoff, in 1876 devised an arc
lamp which was used with some success to light the
boulevards of Paris, his achievement was quickly eclipsed
by the ingenuity of Charles F. Brush, a young Ohio
engineer, who in 1879 illuminated the public squares of
Cleveland, Ohio, by means of a system which could
maintain sixteen arc lamps on a single wire.[1] The
superiority of the new device won immediate public
favor. Soon the hissing, sputtering noise of the carbons
and the brilliant glare of the lamp were familiar sights
on American city streets, San Francisco leading the way
by setting up a central power plant the same year as the
Cleveland trial. The Brush system quickly spread across
the Atlantic and presently, too, to the cities of Japan and
China.

Satisfactory as was the arc lamp for outdoors it proved
of little use for interior illumination. For this purpose
some method had to be found of minutely subdividing
the electric current so as to produce lights corresponding
to gas jets in size and cheapness. Inventors on both sides
of the Atlantic labored at the problem;[2] but success
came first to Thomas A. Edison, whose wizardry in the
domain of electricity was already presaged by his improvements on the telegraph and the telephone. Edison
was at this time thirty-two years old, "a pleasant looking man, of average size . . . with dark hair slightly
silvered, and wonderfully piercing gray eyes," who was
apt to be found "with acid-stained garments, dusty eyebrows, discolored hands and dishevelled hair."[3] Since

[1] Brush has a number of American rivals in the invention of arc lighting. See Henry Schroeder, *History of the Electric Light* (*Smithsonian
Miscel. Colls.*, LXXVI, no. 2), 33-41.

[2] Notably Swan, Lane-Fox and Crookes in England and Edison,
W. E. Sawyer, M. G. Farmer, Edward Weston and H. E. Maxim in
the United States. *Central Electric Light and Power Stations, 1902*,
92-94; Schroeder, *Electric Light*, 42.

[3] J. B. McClure, ed., *Edison and His Inventions* (Chicago, 1879),

1876 he had been conducting his experiments in a great laboratory at Menlo Park, New Jersey; but this establishment had been acquired only after years as a tramp telegrapher and mechanical tinker had led him by devious paths from his native town of Milan, Ohio, to Boston and New York, where his inventions won generous financial backing.

The problem of incandescent lighting quickly reduced itself, in Edison's mind, to finding a suitable filament which, when sealed in a vacuum bulb, would burn more than a few hours.[1] After patiently trying many substances he succeeded in October, 1879, in getting a carbonized cotton thread to last forty-five hours. Soon after, he attained even better results from a bamboo strip torn from a palm-leaf fan. Now began a search of the world for the most suitable fiber. One of his agents made his way to the Malay Peninsula, Burma and south China; others tried Ceylon, India, the West Indies and South America. Out of six thousand specimens Edison found three varieties of bamboo and one of cane exactly suited to his purpose. His incandescent lamp was patented on January 27, 1880. It not only gave a steadier, cooler and brighter light than gas, but he had also solved the problem of switching lamps off without affecting others on the same circuit.[2]

The public gazed with wonder at the new illuminant

15-16. See also W. H. Bishop, "A Night with Edison," *Scribner's Mo.*, XVII (1878-1879), 88-99, and F. A. Jones, *Thomas Alva Edison* (N. Y., 1908), chaps. i-vii. From 1878 to 1898 inclusive Edison took out 613 patents. Dyer and Martin, *Edison*, II, 947-965.

[1] Jones, *Edison*, chap. viii; Schroeder, *Electric Light*, 43-50; Dyer and Martin, *Edison*, I, chaps. xi-xv.

[2] By 1894 manufacturers were substituting cellulose for bamboo or vegetable-fiber filaments. The price of globes fell from one dollar or more apiece in the early eighties to eighteen cents in 1900. For these and other improvements, see *Central Electric Light and Power Stations, 1902*, 94-95; Byrn, *Progress of Invention*, 73; Schroeder, *Electric Light*, 50-62, 93-94.

in Edison's showroom at 65 Fifth Avenue. In 1882 central lighting stations were erected in London and New York. Perhaps no mechanical invention ever spread so swiftly over the world.[1] The new light first entered American homes at the residence of J. Hood Wright in New York; it began to burn in American hotels at the Blue Mountain House in the Adirondacks; it first appeared in a theater when six hundred and fifty bulbs lighted up a performance of Gilbert and Sullivan's opera "Iolanthe" at the Bijou in Boston on December 12, 1882. The number of central electric stations for all purposes—incandescent and arc lighting, traction power, etc.—rose from thirty-eight in 1882 to nearly six hundred in 1888 and to approximately three thousand in 1898.

The greater convenience and safety of incandescent lighting put gas-light producers at a serious disadvantage, but they did what they could to meet the competition by lowering the cost of their product, at the same time improving its quality.[2] Gas made from coal was supplemented in Pennsylvania and other parts of the country by natural gas drawn from underground reservoirs. An even greater advance came in 1875 when T. S. C. Lowe discovered that a successful illuminant could be made at extremely low cost by decomposing steam and mixing it with carbonic acid and other gases. In less than a dozen years one hundred and fifty cities were using water gas, as it was called, and soon it prevailed over the other varieties. The need of achieving a steady white flame comparable to the Edison lamp was also met when Carl Auer von Welsbach of Vienna in 1885 invented a net-like conical mantle which gave forth an intense incan-

[1] Dyer and Martin, *Edison*, chaps. xvi-xvii; *Central Electric Light and Power Stations, 1902*, 7, 106-107.
[2] Byrn, *Progress of Invention*, chap. xxvi.

descent light. After the United States patent was granted in 1890, Americans developed a new skill in adjusting the fragile Welsbach mantles without breaking them. The gas-light industry, though steadily losing ground, achieved a new lease of life. Only in the field of heating, however, was it as yet able to breast electricity without fear of failure.

Improved lighting not only dispelled much of the darkness of urban night life but also many of its dangers. By helping erase the difference between day and night it lengthened the working hours for intellectual toilers, made possible continuous operation of factories and, at the same time, gave an enormous stimulus to after-dark amusements and the theater. Better illumination also meant less eye strain, though this advantage may have been offset by the constant temptation to overwork on the part of the studious. The vastly increased productivity of mind and mill in this period owes more than has ever been recognized to the services of Brush, Edison and Welsbach.

Municipalities were less successful in coping with the problem of waste elimination. Since the middle of the century and earlier, places like New York, Boston and Chicago had had public underground conduits for discharging sewage into near-by bodies of water. But their facilities lagged behind the growth of population and most other cities employed village methods of surface-draining their streets and of using private vaults and cesspools for family wastes. In 1877 Philadelphia had eighty-two thousand such vaults and cesspools, Washington fifty-six thousand and Chicago, despite its sewerage system, thirty thousand.[1] Two years later a noted sanitary engineer called proper sewage disposal "the

[1] Azel Ames, "Removal of Domestic Excreta," Am. Public Health Assoc., *Public Health*, IV (1877), 74.

great unanswered question of the day." [1] Its solution involved grave problems of community health, for dense populations made private uncleanliness increasingly a public concern.

In the two decades following, however, sewerage facilities were greatly extended, while important improvements were effected in sewer construction and in methods of ultimate disposal. [2] This last problem was an especially difficult one. Cities with water fronts usually discharged their sewage into sea or river with always a danger of water pollution, especially where there was a tidal backwash; elsewhere filter beds and farm irrigation systems were commonly used. Progress was very uneven. While Boston and Washington spent millions in improving their sewerage works during these years, Philadelphia and St. Louis had at the close of the period little more than half as great a mileage of sewers as of streets, and Baltimore, New Orleans and Mobile continued to rely for drainage mainly on open gutters. [3] The allied problem of garbage disposal was taken care of hardly better. [4] In New York, Boston and other ports such matter was carried in scows and barges several miles out to sea and discharged upon an outgoing tide. A common practice in inland towns was to contract for its collection by farmers who fed it to swine. Since animals so fed were subject to trichinæ, with a consequent danger to meat eaters, after 1885 furnaces began to be intro-

[1] G. E. Waring, "Recent Modifications in Sanitary Drainage," *Atlantic Mo.*, XLIV (1879), 62.

[2] G. E. Waring, *Modern Methods of Sewage Disposal* (N. Y., 1894); G. W. Rafter and M. N. Baker, *Sewage Disposal in the United States* (N. Y., 1894).

[3] Zueblin, *American Municipal Progress*, 120-126; Fairlie, *Municipal Administration*, 250-251.

[4] N. S. Shaler, ed., *The United States of America* (N. Y., 1894), III, 1235-1237; M. N. Baker, *Municipal Engineering and Sanitation* (R. T. Ely, ed., *The Citizen's Library of Economics, Politics, and Sociology*; N. Y., 1901), chap. xx.

duced, especially in Middle Western cities, for the reduction of garbage by fire.[1]

The growing volume of urban wastes complicated the problem of a potable water system. This generation, however, gave less heed to the quality of the water than to its quantity. Only about six hundred cities had public waterworks in 1878, but in the next two decades their number grew nearly sixfold. At the same time some of the greater cities enlarged their existing facilities.[2] Thus between 1885 and 1892 New York, at a cost of twenty-four million dollars, constructed the New Croton Aqueduct with a carrying capacity of nearly three hundred million gallons a day.

Gradually, however, as a result of European example and the advance of the germ theory of disease, attention was also given to the purity of the water. The Massachusetts board of health in 1886 was granted by law general oversight of all inland waters of the state with power to advise municipal authorities in regard to water supply, sewage disposal and methods of preventing pollution.[3] Within the next few years careful investigations were also made by the state health boards of Connecticut, Minnesota, New Jersey, New York, Ohio and Rhode Island.[4] Cities differed greatly as to the purity of their water supplies, and public-health guardians were not slow in pointing out corresponding differences as to mortality from typhoid fever. Between 1880 and 1890 about half as many people proportion-

---

[1] About ninety cities had installed furnaces by the end of 1898. W. F. Morse, *The Collection and Disposal of Municipal Waste* (N. Y., 1908), 99-116.

[2] Zueblin, *American Municipal Progress*, chap. iv.

[3] W. T. Sedgwick, "Notable Sanitary Experiments in Massachusetts," *Forum*, XX (1895-1896), 752-756; G. C. Whipple, *State Sanitation* (Cambridge, Mass., 1917), I, 125-128.

[4] C. V. Chapin, *Municipal Sanitation in the United States* (Providence, 1901), 298.

ately died of typhoid fever in New York and Boston, where the water was comparatively pure, as in Philadelphia and Chicago, where the supply was contaminated.[1] Pollution by sewage and manufacturers' wastes was especially serious in the case of cities drawing their water from rivers or other natural sources.

The activity in developing municipal water plants was in part caused by the greatly increased fire risks which resulted from the crowding together of buildings and the extensive use of electric wiring. This generation was resolved to have no such conflagrations as those of Chicago and Boston in the early seventies.[2] Though they succeeded in this aim, scarcely a year passed without one or more million-dollar fires and the waste of thousands of lives. The estimated total fire losses in 1878 were over sixty-four million dollars. In 1883 they passed permanently beyond the hundred-million-dollar mark and in 1892 and 1893 rose above one hundred and fifty million.[3]

That the situation was no worse was due to the new methods devised for combating the danger. While small towns and the more backward cities still clung to the volunteer system of fire fighting, with sometimes a nucleus of professional firemen, the large places possessed full-time paid·departments, though Philadelphia's

[1] The death rate per ten thousand inhabitants was: New York 3.36; Boston 3.5; Chicago 6.25; Philadelphia 6.8. Shaler, *United States,* III, 1230.

[2] See Nevins, *Emergence of Modern America,* 84-85.

[3] *World Almanac for 1929,* 375. A letter of Dec. 3, 1925, from R. S. Moulton of the National Fire Protection Association, Boston, says: "During the period 1875 to 1900, while there were no large conflagrations, the total amount of the fire loss was larger in proportion to the then national wealth than it is today, being variously estimated at from three to four dollars per thousand dollars of burnable wealth as compared with from one dollar and a half to two dollars today." See also Clifford Thomson, "The Waste by Fire," *Forum,* II (1886-1887), 27-39.

dated only from 1871 and St. Paul did not have one until ten years later.[1] With more efficient organization appeared improved apparatus and equipment.[2] Swinging harness for hitching the horses to the fire wagons came into use in the seventies, as did also the fire boat, the fire-alarm signal box and the water tower. In the next decade chemical engines were introduced in Chicago, Milwaukee, Springfield, Ohio, and elsewhere. The invention of the Grinnell automatic fire sprinkler in 1877, added to the widening use of fire-resistant building materials—concrete, terra cotta, brick, steel, asbestos— helped further to reduce fire hazards, particularly in factories and office buildings. Though wide differences continued to exist among cities, the fire departments in general compared favorably with those of any other country. Chicago, for example, had twice as many men and horses and half again as many steam fire engines as London, a city three times as populous.

Conditions of lodging varied as widely as types of people and differences in income. For well-to-do transients the great cities offered hotels constantly increasing in number, size and sumptuousness.[3] Already famous in the eighties were such hostelries as the Grand Union, Park Avenue and Murray Hill in New York, the Stratford and the Lafayette in Philadelphia, Young's and the Vendôme in Boston, the Grand Pacific, Palmer

---

[1] Scranton was the only city in the hundred-thousand class which at the close of the century still relied mainly upon call men. Fairlie, *Municipal Administration*, 154-155; Zueblin, *American Municipal Progress*, 65-66.

[2] Fairlie, *Municipal Administration*, 152-154; Zueblin, *American Municipal Progress*, 68; Helen Campbell and others, *Darkness and Daylight* (Hartford, 1891), chap. xxvii; P. J. McKeon, *Fire Prevention* (N. Y., 1912), esp. 6-7; C. J. H. Woodbury, "Conflagrations in Cities," Franklin Inst., *Journ.*, CXXXII (1891), 209-223.

[3] Hiram Hitchcock, "The Hotels of America," Depew, *American Commerce*, I, 153-155; Alexander Craib, *America and the Americans* (London, 1892), chap. xxvii; Brown, *Golden Nineties*, 311-323.

House and Auditorium in Chicago, the Brown Palace Hotel in Denver and Baldwin's in San Francisco. Among the new ones in the last decade of the century were the Plaza, Savoy and Waldorf-Astoria in New York, the Jefferson in Richmond, Virginia, and the Raleigh in Washington.

Such hotels, gorgeously decorated and furnished, with a steadily diminishing emphasis on the "steamboat style," made a special appeal with their private baths, electric elevators, electric-call service and other up-to-the-minute conveniences. Though the incessant "tinkle, tinkle, tinkle of the ice-pitcher" proved "positively nauseous" to the British compiler of *Baedeker*, he otherwise thought well of the American institution and had even a word of praise and commiseration for that "mannerless despot," the hotel clerk.[1] Every large city also had hotels of second and third class or of no class at all, falling as low in New York as lodging places in Chatham Street (now Park Row) and the Bowery where one could secure sleeping space for a few pennies a night.[2] In general, hotels in the South were apt to be poorer than in any other section, while in the West, even in the newer towns, they were unexpectedly good.

If the traveler did not wish to patronize his own hotel dining room, he could usually find in the larger cities excellent restaurants at hand. In Delmonico's at Fifth Avenue and Twenty-sixth Street he could eat the best meals in America, at the highest prices. There important political conferences were held, college societies celebrated their reunions and distinguished foreigners

[1] Muirhead, *Land of Contrasts*, 255-257. See also [J. F. Muirhead], *The United States* (Karl Baedeker, ed., *Handbook for Travellers;* 2d rev. edn., Leipsic, 1899), xxvi-xxvii.

[2] Over four and a half million cheap lodgings were provided in such houses in the single year 1888 in New York.   H. L. Myrick, *The Importance of the Scientific and Practical Study of Crime* (N. Y., 1895), 25; J. A. Riis, *How the Other Half Lives* (N. Y., 1890), chap. viii.

were fêted. The Brunswick and the Brevoort were hardly less fashionable, the former receiving its summer patrons in an attractive garden in the rear. While other centers were not as well served as New York, Chicago boasted of the Richelieu and Kingsley's, and the French restaurants in New Orleans—Moreau's, Mme. Venn's, Flêche's, Victor's—were justly famed the country over.

City dwellers who wished to escape the drudgery and responsibility of housekeeping usually lived in boarding houses. With the opening of the Buckingham Hotel in New York in 1877, however, an increasing number of attractive apartment hotels for private families made their appearance. At the same time the swifter means of transit and communication caused a flow of population into suburban districts where shaded streets, ample lawns and neighborly friendliness gave everyday living something of a bucolic flavor. This dispersion was particularly noticeable in the last ten years of the period, far outdistancing the rapid extension of official municipal limits.[1] By the end of the nineties New York's suburbs held over a million people, one third as many as the city proper, while more people actually lived on Boston's outskirts than within her corporate confines. Pittsburgh, Providence and Cincinnati had similarly acquired strong satellite colonies.

In contrast to this agreeable picture must be placed another, that of the living conditions of the less prosperous classes and particularly of the immigrants. Of the great cities of the land Philadelphia and Chicago were least scarred by slums. Boston, Cincinnati, Jersey City and Hartford had badly diseased spots, but the evil was most deeply rooted in New York City, where land rentals

---

[1] *U. S. Thirteenth Census* (1910), I, 73-75; *Street and Electric Railways, 1902*, 26-29; Brown, *New York in Elegant Eighties*, 69-73; A. F. Weber, "Suburban Annexations," *N. Am. Rev.*, CLXVI (1898), 612-617.

were highest and the pressure of immigrants strongest.[1] In all Europe only one city district, in Prague, was half as congested as certain parts of Manhattan. Bad as conditions had been earlier in New York, they became worse in 1879 with the advent of a new type of slum, the "dumb-bell" tenement, so called because of the outline of the floor plan. This became virtually the only kind erected there in the next two decades.

Five or six stories high, the bleak narrow structure ran ninety feet back from the street, being pierced through the center by a stygian hallway less than three feet wide.[2] Each floor was honeycombed with rooms, many without direct light or air and most of them sheltering one or more families. Almost at once such barracks became foul and grimy, infested with vermin and lacking privacy and proper sanitary conveniences. The sunless, ill-smelling air shafts at the sides of the building proved a positive menace during fires by insuring the rapid spread of flames. In rooms and hallways, on stairs and fire escapes, in the narrow streets, dirty half-clad children roamed at will, imbibing soiled thoughts from their soiled surroundings. The dense slum district bounded by Cherry, Catherine, Hamilton and Market streets was known as "lung block" because of the many deaths from tuberculosis. No wonder such rookeries were nurseries of immorality, drunkenness, disease and crime. The real surprise is, as the state tenement-house commission pointed out in 1900, that so many of the children grew up to be decent, self-respecting citizens.

[1] R. W. De Forest and Lawrence Veiller, eds., *The Tenement House Problem* (N. Y., 1903), I, 57, 131-170. For the situation earlier, see Nevins, *Emergence of Modern America*, 319-320.

[2] A New York invention, the dumb-bell tenement was unknown in any European city. De Forest and Veiller, *Tenement House Problem*, I, 8-14, 100-102; Riis, *How the Other Half Lives*, 18-19.

In 1879 the total number of tenements in New York was estimated at twenty-one thousand, their inhabitants at more than half a million. A census taken in 1888 showed over thirty-two thousand tenements with a population exceeding a million. By 1900 the number of buildings had grown to nearly forty-three thousand and their occupants to over one and a half million.[1] From time to time philanthropic citizens like Ellen Collins and Alfred T. White built model tenements in New York and Brooklyn to demonstrate that decent lodgings for the poor comported with fair profits for the landlord. Organizations like the State Charities Association and the Association for Improving the Condition of the Poor insistently agitated for stricter housing laws. To their aid came a young Danish American, Jacob A. Riis. As police reporter on the *Sun* he had gained a first-hand knowledge of slum conditions, which he used with great literary effect in a series of newspaper and magazine articles beginning in the eighties. His first book, *How the Other Half Lives,* published in 1890, came to Theodore Roosevelt as "an enlightenment and an inspiration for which . . . I could never be too grateful."[2]

Remedial legislation, following the first tenement-house statute of 1867, was passed in 1879, 1887 and 1895.[3] But in spite of the reformers the laws contained loopholes and enforcement was sporadic. The tenement-house commission of 1900 felt that, on the whole, conditions were worse than they had been fifty years before. Yet one year later a comprehensive statute was adopted

[1] For various estimates, see Riis, *How the Other Half Lives,* 275, 300; De Forest and Veiller, *Tenement House Problem,* I, 5, 37; II, 78.
[2] Theodore Roosevelt, *An Autobiography* (N. Y., 1919), 169. Riis's *The Battle with the Slum* (N. Y., 1902) is autobiographical.
[3] De Forest and Veiller, *Tenement House Problem,* I, 5, 95-115; II, 207-345.

which showed that the humanitarian energies of this generation had not been spent in vain. The act of 1901 not only insured real housing reform in New York, but prompted other states and municipalities to a fundamental attack on the evil.[1]

The problem of urban lawlessness and crime was deeply rooted in that of the slums. Vile places like "Misery Row," "Poverty Lane" and "Murderers' Alley" were both continuous recruiting grounds for juvenile delinquents and hiding places for criminal bands. Lacking normal outlets for play, the tenement waifs naturally drifted into gangs in which what might have been a laudable spirit of group loyalty was twisted into an ambition to emulate the lawless exploits of their elders. Beginning as beggars, sneak thieves and pickpockets, they graduated all too quickly into the ranks of shoplifters, robbers and thugs.[2] The foreign origin of many of the slum dwellers made this transition all the easier because of prior unfamiliarity with American traditions and laws. In particular, the Irish and Italians contributed more than their proportionate share of the country's prison population, though it was the American-born immigrant children, lacking proper parental guidance and wholesome surroundings, who turned most readily to underworld life.[3] One student of the problem, observing that most of the men, women and children in the jails and penitentiaries he had visited were native-born, concluded: "We have ourselves evolved as cruel and cunning

[1] H. U. Faulkner, *The Quest for Social Justice* (*A History of American Life*, XI), 158-159.

[2] W. F. Howe and A. H. Hummel, *Danger!* (Buffalo, 1886), chap. iii; Campbell and others, *Darkness and Daylight*, chap. vi; Herbert Asbury, *The Gangs of New York* (N. Y., 1927), 238-246.

[3] W. M. F. Round, "Immigration and Crime," *Forum*, VIII (1889-1890), 428-440; S. G. Fisher, "Immigration and Crime," *Pop. Sci. Mo.*, XLIX (1896), 625-630; F. H. Wines, *Report on Crime, Pauperism, and Benevolence in the United States* (*U. S. Eleventh Census, 1890,* XXII), I, 23-43, 131-133.

criminals as any that Europe may have foisted upon us." [1]

Other than New York the great criminal centers of the nation were Chicago, Boston, Philadelphia, Pittsburgh, Buffalo, Detroit, Cleveland, Cincinnati, St. Louis and San Francisco.[2] The freemasonry of crookdom made it possible for evildoers to pass quickly from city to city as self-preservation required, or to congregate like birds of prey when crowds gathered for such occasions as the Philadelphia Centennial or the Chicago World's Fair of 1893. In San Francisco lawlessness in the 1880's still possessed a strong frontier flavor, being characterized by the depredations of youthful hoodlums who brandished large knives and six-shooters and did not hesitate to use them.[3] In the older American centers crime for profit had fallen into the hands of professionals who constantly devised new traps for the unwary. Pickpockets, badger-game experts, knock-out-drop artists, green-goods men (who circulated worthless money), bunco steerers (swindlers), gamblers, hold-up men—all these prospered in such a hotbed of evil as New York's Tenderloin, bounded by Twenty-fourth and Fortieth streets and Fifth and Seventh avenues.[4]

In particular, New York was the national base for bank robbers. One band led by George L. Leslie was credited by Chief of Police Walling with being responsible for four fifths of the bank burglaries in Amer-

[1] J. F. Willard (Josiah Flynt, *pseud.*), *Notes of an Itinerant Policeman* (Boston, 1900), 10.

[2] Flynt, *Notes*, 33.

[3] Marshall, *Through America*, 269-272.

[4] The very name, Tenderloin, is a product of these turbulent years. Being in 1876 transferred from an obscure precinct to West Thirtieth Street, Police Captain A. S. Williams exclaimed, "I've been having chuck steak ever since I've been on the force, and now I'm going to have a bit of tenderloin." H. L. Mencken, *The American Language* (N. Y., 1919), 163, *n.* 64. Taken up by the newspapers, the term was soon applied to gay, wicked districts in any city.

Broadway and John Street, New York City, in 1890.

A farmer's bitter memory of his visit to the city: a "green goods" swindle on the Bowery

In the Metropolis

ica until "Western George's" murder in 1884. His greatest coup was the looting of the Manhattan Savings Institution in New York on October 27, 1878, to the extent of nearly three million dollars, the result of three years' careful planning.[1] In order to protect the financial district from other similar maraudings Inspector Thomas Byrnes established his famous Dead Line on March 12, 1880, at Fulton Street, south of which a known criminal would be arrested on sight. While not usually of the professional ilk, absconding bank cashiers were perhaps the most elegant culprits of the time, though this form of law breaking became less frequent with the conclusion of extradition arrangements with Canada in 1889. Of the new swindles contrived during these years probably the most successful was the gold brick, introduced into New York in 1880 by Reed Waddell, a native of Springfield, Illinois. In ten years' time he is believed to have made more than two hundred and fifty thousand dollars from the sale of his gilded lead bricks and from green goods.[2]

Organized crime was the special product of the slum districts where such bands as the Hartley Mob, the Molasses Gang, the Dutch Mob, the Potashes and the Stable Gang flourished in the dives along the Bowery and its sordid byways.[3] The Whyos, the most powerful gang of all, had their principal base in Mulberry Bend whence they sallied forth on their missions of pillage and death

[1] Two of his accomplices were sentenced to long prison terms, but the police could not find enough evidence against Leslie to bring him to trial. G. W. Walling, *Recollections of a New York Chief of Police* (N. Y., 1887), chap. xix; Asbury, *Gangs of New York*, 203-211; T. F. Byrnes, *Professional Criminals of America* (N. Y., 1886), 81-82.

[2] Waddell met a violent death in 1895 as a result of a thieves' quarrel. Asbury, *Gangs of New York*, 194-197.

[3] Riis, *How the Other Half Lives*, chap. xix; Asbury, *Gangs of New York*, chaps. xi-xii; Howe and Hummel, *Danger!*, chap. ii; Walling, *Recollections*, chap. xxxv; Campbell and others, *Darkness and Daylight*, chap. xxiv.

until their own destruction in the early nineties. Fortunately for the general safety these bands spent a part of their murderous energy in fighting one another.

Criminologists and publicists pointed with alarm to the portentous increase of lawlessness in the United States. A census inquiry disclosed a fifty-per-cent rise in the number of prison inmates from 1880 to 1890.[1] Statistics collected by the *Chicago Tribune* revealed a growth of murders and homicides from 1266 during the year 1881 (24.7 to a million people) to 4290 in 1890 (or 68.5 to the million) and to 7840 in 1898 (or 107.2 to the million).[2] Such figures were all the more startling since most other civilized countries showed a declining homicide rate, the ratio in England and Germany being less than half that of the United States. Students of the subject were agreed in placing the fundamental blame on unhealthy urban growth, unrestricted immigration, the saloon and the maladjusted Negro.[3] In addition, Lombroso pointed to the lingering habits of frontier lawlessness even in the more settled states, the new opportunities for crime afforded by discoveries in chemistry and toxicology, and the evil effects of sensation-mongering newspapers. Another writer stressed the

[1] Wines, *Report*, I, 11, 124. In general, crime statistics need to be used with considerable caution because of lack of registration in most states, divergent legal definitions of crime in the United States and abroad, differences in law enforcement as between states and from time to time within the same state, and other similar circumstances.

[2] Figures cited in S. S. McClure, "The Increase of Lawlessness in the United States," *McClure's*, XXIV (1904), 168. For the same years suicides numbered 605, 2640 and 5920.

[3] See, for example, H. M. Boies, *Prisoners and Paupers* (N. Y., 1893), chaps. i, vi-xi; I. C. Parker, "How to Arrest the Increase of Homicides in America," *N. Am. Rev.*, CLXII (1896), 667-673; W. D. Morrison, *Juvenile Offenders* (N. Y., 1897), esp. chap. ii; Cesare Lombroso, "Why Homicide Has Increased in the United States," *N. Am. Rev.*, CLXV (1897), 641-648; CLXVI (1898), 1-11; James O'Meara, "Concealed Weapons and Crimes," *Overland Mo.*, XVI (1890), 11-16.

undoubted fact that violence and criminality had come to be regarded "as a sort of natural and inevitable concomitant" of every great labor disturbance.[1]

Yet it seemed to an acute observer like James Bryce that the Americans were at bottom a law-abiding people.[2] Indeed, in the absence of adequate data for earlier periods, it is possible that crime, being mainly concentrated in the cities, had become merely more conspicuous rather than greater in volume. However this may be, all agreed that the evil was accentuated by lax law enforcement. The official guardians of society only too often were in league with the antisocial elements, passively or actively. In most large centers a crook could secure police "protection" provided he agreed to hunt his prey elsewhere or, if operating locally, to share his profits with the authorities.[3] It was the opinion of the widely experienced Josiah Flynt that, from Maine to California, the aim of police departments was merely "to keep a city superficially clean, and to keep everything quiet that is likely to arouse the public to an investigation." [4] Beyond that point they felt no genuine concern.

Yet now and then conditions became intolerable, and official inquests laid bare a state of affairs almost too vile for belief. Such was the outcome of the courageous war against vice waged by the Reverend Charles H. Parkhurst, of the Madison Square Presbyterian Church in New York, with the help of the New York Society for the Prevention of Crime. The ensuing legislative inquiry, conducted in 1894 under Senator Clarence Lexow as chairman, caused the overturn of the Tammany gov-

---

[1] G. C. Holt, "Lynching and Mobs," *Journ. of Social Sci.*, XXXII (1894), 76-81.

[2] Bryce, *American Commonwealth*, III, 312.

[3] Flynt, *Notes*, chaps. iv, vi; J. F. Willard (Josiah Flynt, *pseud.*), *The World of Graft* (N. Y., 1901), *passim*.

[4] Flynt, *Notes*, 101.

ernment the following year and the appointment of Theodore Roosevelt to a strenuous administration as main police commissioner.[1] Among other things the Lexow investigation revealed that appointments and promotions in the police force were for sale and that police officials, besides collecting monthly blackmail from gamblers, saloonists and bawdyhouse keepers, exacted percentages of the profits of "street walkers," pickpockets and gun men.[2]

In various states efforts were made from time to time to divorce police administration from corrupt municipal politics, the favorite scheme being to head the city forces with officials appointed by the governor. This plan was tried in cities as widely separated as Boston, Charleston, South Carolina, Cincinnati, Detroit, Minneapolis, Omaha and Denver. But in most cases it resulted merely in transferring political control from one group of self-seeking overlords to another, without real improvement from the standpoint of the public.[3] The judiciary also shared responsibility for the bad conditions. In the opinion of one judge at least, "the greatest cause of the increase of crime is the action of the appellate courts, which . . . make the most strenuous efforts, as a rule, to see not when they can affirm but when they can reverse a case."[4]

Discouraging as was the situation, it was less so than it seemed. Individual police chiefs and officers were noted

[1] C. H. Parkhurst, *Our Fight with Tammany* (N. Y., 1895); Roosevelt, *Autobiography,* chap. vi.

[2] One woman who owned a chain of brothels testified that she paid $30,000 annually for protection. For a summary of the findings, see N. Y. State Committee Appointed to Investigate the Police Department of the City of New York, *Report and Proceedings* (Albany, 1895), I, 3-61. The commission paid by criminals in Chicago was ten per cent of their earnings, according to L. W. Moore, a reformed bank robber, in *His Own Story* (Boston, 1892), chap. xl.

[3] R. B. Fosdick, *American Police Systems* (N. Y., 1920), 90-102.

[4] Parker, "How to Arrest Increase of Homicides," 670.

for their bravery and rectitude; and every city now and then, under reform pressure, treated its wrongdoers with Draconian severity. Moreover the path of the wicked was rendered increasingly thorny by by-products of American inventive genius.[1] To overcome the difficulties presented by improvements in vault and safe construction and the constantly spreading use of Yale locks, burglars had to be ever on the alert. Likewise, electricity aided the law-abiding citizen not only by means of better-lighted streets but also through its application to burglar-alarm wiring and to emergency street boxes for summoning police help. The utility of the "rogues' gallery," in limited use since mid-century, was also greatly extended by a free exchange of photographs with other cities; and beginning in 1887 the whole method of identifying criminals was revolutionized by the introduction, first in Illinois, then in Massachusetts and elsewhere, of the Bertillon system of the Paris police, whereby detailed measurements of the culprit's body were taken and recorded.

Unfortunately urban delinquency had its repercussions on the countryside, most notoriously in the case of the "tramp evil," which had first appeared in America in the hard years following 1873.[2] While the return of prosperity after 1878 somewhat diminished the number of such vagrants, habit, uncertainties of work, difficulties of personal adjustment, *Wanderlust* and the ease of stealing rides on the railroads caused many to continue in their old ways. Pitiful caricatures of the restless hardy pioneers of earlier times, these aimless wanderers were freely spawned by the great urban centers, particularly in years of unemployment and industrial con-

[1] B. P. Eldridge and W. B. Watts, *Our Rival, the Rascal* (Boston, 1896), chap. xviii; *Telephones and Telegraphs, 1902,* 146-148.
[2] See Nevins, *Emergence of Modern America,* 301-302.

flict like 1885-1886 and 1892-1894.[1] An unofficial tramp census taken in the year 1893 indicated that three out of five were between twenty and fifty years of age, about the same proportion were native-born and trained to skilled trades, five out of six enjoyed good health, and nearly all were literate and unmarried.[2] If, as the investigator estimated, the total number of tramps then in the nation was 45,845, they represented an army larger than Wellington's at Waterloo and their vagabondage involved the withdrawal of a quarter of one per cent of the male population from productive work, not to mention the burdens thrown on the public in the form of alms, police supervision and hospital care.

These nomads developed a manner of living, a culture, peculiar to themselves. A well-marked caste system distinguished between the hobo, forced temporarily "on the road" by lack of work, and the habitual tramp in his ascending social scale from "gay-cat" (tenderfoot) and harmless wanderer to expert criminal.[3] By cabalistic chalk marks on gate posts the elect were informed as to chances for a "hand-out"; a rigid code of ethics governed their conduct toward one another; and an argot, characterized by such expressions as doss (sleep), elbow (detective), mooch (beg) and shack (brakeman), marked their common speech.[4]

[1] For the marching columns of the jobless in 1894, see D. L. McMurry, Coxey's Army (Boston, 1929).

[2] J. J. McCook, "A Tramp Census and Its Revelations," Forum, XV (1893), 753-766. 1349 tramps were interviewed. Their ages averaged younger than those of tramps in England and Germany. Nearly half of them said they had taken to the road within a week of losing their last real job. Of immigrant elements the Irish were the most prominent, accounting for one fifth of all the tramps.

[3] E. L. Bailey (an ex-tramp), "Tramps and Hoboes," Forum, XXVI (1898-1899), 217-221; Flynt, Notes, 49-53, 118-140; Jack London, The Road (N. Y., 1907).

[4] J. F. Willard (Josiah Flynt, pseud.), Tramping with Tramps (N. Y., 1899), 381-398, contains a glossary with comments. This student of trampdom estimated that at least three thousand distinctive

In the 1880's a gang of itinerant criminals, known as the Lake Shore Push, working out of Cleveland, forcibly monopolized the "empties" of the Lake Shore line to the exclusion of other wanderers; and in 1886 bands, numbering a hundred or more, seized trains for temporary use in Mississippi and Tennessee. But, for the most part, tramps went about alone or by twos and threes, their occasional presence and overindulgence in drink increasing the hazards of solitary rural living. Beginning with New Jersey in 1876, a wave of anti-tramp legislation swept over the nation so that by 1893 twenty-one or more states had passed such acts.[1] Varying in severity—from a short jail sentence to public whipping or even (in two Southern states) sale into temporary servitude—these laws varied even more greatly in the degree of their enforcement. Local communities often found it necessary to improvise their own remedies; town authorities in Massachusetts attained the desired object by exacting manual work from vagrants.[2] The nuisance showed no abatement during the life of this generation; there were probably more tramps abroad at the close of the period than at its beginning.[3] Improvement awaited a better adjustment of wages and employment to available labor supply and a less indulgent attitude on the part of railroads toward the unbidden occupants of "side-door Pullmans."[4]

expressions had been in vogue in the previous twenty years. *Cf.* Flynt's glossary in *World of Graft*, 219-221.

[1] Samuel Leavitt, "The Tramps and the Law," *Forum*, II (1886-1887), 190-200; McCook, "Tramp Census," 764-765.

[2] Committee of the Massachusetts Association of Relief Officers, "Tramps and Wayfarers," Am. Stat. Assoc., *Publs.*, n.s., VII (1900), 74-84—a report on the practices of 184 Massachusetts towns and cities.

[3] Flynt in *Tramping with Tramps*, 304, estimated their number in 1898 as sixty thousand; Bailey's guess in "Tramps and Hoboes," 220, was one hundred thousand.

[4] The lenience of the railroads was considered by Flynt a major factor in the situation. See *Tramping with Tramps*, 291-314, 355.

If we consider only the sordid aspects of urban life the American city of the period seems a cancerous growth. But the record as a whole was distinctly creditable to a generation which found itself confronted with the phenomenon of a great population everywhere clotting into towns. No other people had ever met such an emergency so promptly or, on the whole, so successfully. The basic facilities of urban living—transit, lighting and communication—were well taken care of by an outburst of native mechanical genius which helped make these years the Golden Age of Invention. Some places moved forward faster than others, of course, and all lagged in some respects while advancing in others. If the rural spirit of neighborliness was submerged in the anonymity of city life, there developed in its place a spirit of impersonal social responsibility which devoted itself, with varying earnestness and success, to questions of pure water, sewage disposal and decent housing for the poor, sometimes taking the extreme form of municipal ownership. Moreover, what the great cities felt obliged to do under the whip of necessity, smaller towns undertook in a spirit of imitation, so that the new standards affected urban life everywhere. What most impresses the historical student is the lack of unity, balance, planfulness, in the advances that were made. Urban progress was experimental, uneven, often accidental: the people were, as yet, groping in the dark. A later generation, taking stock of the past and profiting by its mistakes, would explore the possibilities of ordered city planning, not only in the interests of material welfare and community health but also with an eye to beautification.[1]

[1] See P. W. Slosson, *The Great Crusade and After* (*A History of American Life*, XII), 407-408.

CHAPTER V

THE AMERICAN WOMAN

THE American woman reigned if she did not govern. She was in transition—as she always has been—and while the American man was too gallant to regard her as a "problem," her unusual restlessness in the eighties and nineties proved a constant source of worry to the old-fashioned of both sexes. It was as mistress of the home and dispenser of its hospitality that she was most favorably known; and in this rôle she inspired masculine visitors from Europe to a catalogue of such adjectives as vivacious, fascinating, candid, unaffected, intelligent, self-reliant. With an effort at statistical restraint the musician Offenbach at the opening of the era declared, "Out of a hundred women, ninety are perfectly ravishing"; while another artist, Soissons, observing America twenty years later, could agree that the "modern American woman is charming and almost superior to the majority of European women." [1] Even Matthew Arnold, who saw little to relieve the drab monotony of the transatlantic scene, accounted the unusual measure of feminine charm as an authentic touch of civilization. [2]

Nothing more sharply set off the American woman from her sisters abroad than the deference paid her by men and the unaffected social relations between the

[1] Jacques Offenbach, *America and the Americans* (London, 1876), 43-44; S. C. de Soissons, *A Parisian in America* (Boston, 1896), 8.
[2] Matthew Arnold, *Civilization in the United States* (Boston, 1888), 168-169.

sexes. "It is the pride of Americans," noted one foreign observer, "that a woman, unaccompanied, can travel from one end of their country to the other without being subjected to any unpleasantness or to a vestige of impertinence." [1] This attitude, of course, had long been a national characteristic; but as a product of frontier and rural influences it was subjected during these years to a new and unexpected strain as greater numbers of people came to live under urban conditions and women entered the world of men as breadwinners.

In correct social circles of the Eastern cities the practice of chaperonage took root during the 1880's, stimulated by the example of the Old World with which an increasing number of traveled Americans had become acquainted. "The duties of a chaperon are very hard and unremitting, and sometimes very disagreeable," wrote an editor of *Harper's Bazar* in 1884.

> She must accompany her young lady everywhere; she must sit in the parlor when she receives gentlemen; she must go with her to the skating rink, the ball, the party, the races, the dinners, and especially to theater parties; she must preside at the table, and act the part of a mother, so far as she can; she must watch the characters of the men who approach her charge, and endeavor to save the inexperienced girl from the dangers of a bad marriage, if possible. [2]

Three years later another authority noted that the chaperon was "slowly but surely extending her sway," and in 1898 it was announced that the practice was so generally observed in the East that "a girl of the

[1] William Saunders, *Through the Light Continent* (London, 1879), 401. See also Emily Faithfull, *Three Visits to America* (Edinburgh, 1884), 323, and E. Catherine Bates, *A Year in the Great Republic* (London, 1887), II, 281-283.

[2] Mrs. John Sherwood, *Manners and Social Usages* (N. Y., 1884), 147.

present generation would not venture to combat it without the risk of sharp criticism from alien tongues." [1]

Despite the undoubted spread of the new custom its well-wishers overstated the facts. As Mrs. Sherwood ruefully acknowledged, the "vivacious American girl, with all her inherited hatred of authority, is a troublesome charge. All young folks are rebels." Not appreciating "what Hesperidean fruit they are," they "dislike being watched and guarded." [2] And the young lady found an ally in her young man who, besides sharing her libertarianism, objected to the extra drain on his purse which the presence of a third party at dinner or the theater entailed. In the smaller towns and rustic parts of the nation the two sexes continued to mingle socially, go buggy riding in the moonlight and pay court unvexed by the attentions of a duenna. Even in the cities spinsters or "elderly girls" of twenty-five years or more were generally regarded as exempt from the requirement, for "with the assumption of years" had they not safely left behind them "the wild grace of a giddy girlhood"? Yet an "elderly girl," though of thirty-five, was deemed to act unwisely if she visited an artist's studio alone, even though "there is in art an ennobling and purifying influence which should be a protection." [3]

On none did the yoke of Victorian convention lie so heavily or so unreasonably as on affianced lovers.

A chaperon is indispensable to an engaged girl. . . . Nothing is more vulgar in the eyes of our modern society than for an engaged couple to travel together or

---

[1] Florence H. Hall, *Social Customs* (Boston, 1887), 177; Mrs. Burton Harrison, *The Well-Bred Girl in Society* (N. Y., 1898), 39. See also Mrs. Burton Kingsland, "A Daughter at Sixteen," *Ladies' Home Journ.*, XI (1894), no. 10, 10.

[2] Sherwood, *Manners and Social Usages*, 147 (rev. edn., 1900, 196).

[3] Sherwood, *Manners and Social Usages*, 153-154 (rev. edn., 1900, 202-203).

to go to the theatre unaccompanied, as was the primitive custom. . . . Society allows an engaged girl to drive with her *fiancé* in an open carriage, but it does not approve of his taking her in a close carriage to an evening party.[1]

While the young lady was not expected to abstain entirely from social contacts, she must be extremely circumspect in her relations with the other sex, for even the "shadow of a flirtation" constituted a breach both of manners and morals.[2] Once the wedding cards were issued, it was *"de rigueur"* for the bride-to-be to withdraw from the public gaze, allowing herself only the occasional privilege of a quiet walk with her future husband during the day.[3]

Despite new social and economic conditions marriage continued to be the cherished goal of the majority of women, all the more so as the numerical excess of females over males steadily climbed in the urban parts of America.[4] Nevertheless the growing practice of seeking matrimonial mates through the advertising columns of the newspapers was generally frowned upon as betraying an unmaidenly zeal. Though in a few Eastern cities the "woman bachelor," as she called herself, gained steadily in standing and public respect, in most parts of the country the "elderly girl" was looked upon as a

[1] Sherwood, *Manners and Social Usages*, 148-149 (rev. edn., 1900, 197-198). See also Hall, *Social Customs*, 171.

[2] Clara S. J. Moore (Mrs. H. O. Ward, *pseud.*), *Sensible Etiquette* (16th rev. edn., Phila., 1878), 334-335; A Lounger in Society (*pseud.*), *The Glass of Fashion* (N. Y., 1881), 43; Frances Stevens, *The Usages of the Best Society* (N. Y., 1884), 175; J. H. Young, *Our Deportment* (Springfield, Mass., 1881), 190.

[3] Ward, *Sensible Etiquette*, 337. One regrets to note, however, that on one occasion "A young lady at the sea-shore greatly shocked public opinion by going down to the surf beach and bathing on the morning of her wedding day." Hall, *Social Customs*, 171.

[4] *Supplementary Analysis and Derivative Tables* (U. S. Twelfth Census, *Special Rep.*), 86, 89.

creature of frustrated purpose.[1] A fragile clinging vine was the ideal of an age which little dreamed a later generation would prefer the rambler.

The Americans were, in fact, one of the most married peoples in the world, being surpassed in Western Europe only by the French. There was a difference, however, between city and country. Matrimony generally took place earlier in the rural districts, was likely to endure longer and, whether ended by death or divorce, was more often followed by fresh nuptials.[2] In the cities the higher cost of living, together with the greater economic independence of women and the many substitutes for the sociability of the fireside, served to delay marriage or to prevent it entirely. Higher education also proved a deterrent, at least so far as women were concerned. It was widely noted that fewer college-bred girls married proportionately than did their less educated sisters, though the graduates of coeducational institutions showed less reluctance in this respect than those of women's colleges.[3]

From the later marriages of middle-class urban folk came smaller families, due partly to an increasing resort to the practice of birth control. One medical authority dared assert openly that such conduct was "not only not in itself sinful" but even "under certain circumstances commendable." [4] The result, as Bryce and others pointed

[1] Mary G. Humphreys, "Women Bachelors in New York," *Scribner's Mag.*, XX (1896), 626-636. See also anon., "The Old Maid," *Harper's Bazar*, XII (1879), 251; anon., "Old Maids," *Harper's Bazar*, XV (1882), 434. Mrs. Burton Harrison's novel, *A Bachelor Maid* (N. Y., 1894), is a gentle satire on the "new woman."

[2] *Supplementary Analysis and Derivative Tables*, 386, 395-402.

[3] Milicent W. Shinn, "The Marriage Rate of College Women," *Century*, L (1895), 946-948; Horace Davis, "Collegiate Education of Women," *Overland Mo.*, XVI (1890), 337-344; Mary R. Smith, "Statistics of College and Non-College Women," *Am. Stat. Assoc., Publs.*, n.s., VII, 1-26.

[4] J. S. Billings, "The Diminishing Birth Rate in the United States,"

out, seemed a reversal of the principle of natural selection, for the progeny of poor and undernourished parents multiplied while the better-nurtured classes barely held their own. In general, the membership of the average household steadily shrank. In 1890 the most usual size was four members; in 1900 three.[1]

All the moral preachments of the time pointed to the wife and mother as the one upon whom rested the chief responsibility for connubial bliss. Hers it was "to embellish the home, and to make happy the lives of the near and dear ones who dwell within it." [2] Addressing her in the *Christian Herald,* the Reverend T. DeWitt Talmage declared:

> Whether in professional, or commercial, or artistic, or mechanical life, your husband from morning to night is in a Solferino, if not a Sedan. It is a wonder that your husband has any nerves or patience or suavity left. . . . If he come home and sit down preoccupied, you ought to excuse him. If he do not feel like going out that night . . . , remember he has been out all day. . . . Remember, he is not overworking so much for himself as . . . for you and the children.[3]

Nevertheless the law, more charitable, it would seem, than the pulpit, accorded married women larger rights than they had ever before enjoyed in America. The

Forum, XV (1893), esp. 475-477. Contraceptive information and devices had been excluded from the mails under heavy penalties by a federal act of 1873. Anthony Comstock, *Frauds Exposed* (N. Y., 1880), 401.

[1] James Bryce, *The American Commonwealth* (London, 1888), III, 676; *Supplementary Analysis and Derivative Tables,* 376, 379, 408-409.

[2] Ward, *Sensible Etiquette,* 353.

[3] That a husband with a slatternly wife "stays at home as little as possible is no wonder," he added. "It is a wonder that such a man does not go on a whaling voyage of three years, and in a leaky ship." Reprinted in T. DeW. Talmage, *The Wedding Ring* (N. Y., 1896), 80-81, 83.

old common-law discriminations, already beginning to crumble prior to the Civil War,[1] continued to fall before the assaults of new legislation. By 1898 the special disabilities of wives had been wholly removed in Mississippi, Oregon and Washington; and in most other states they could own and control their property, retain their earnings, make contracts, sue and be sued.[2] Here and there, however, inequalities of civil status remained. Thus in Georgia, Louisiana, New Mexico, the Dakotas and California the law still expressly designated the husband as head of the family and the wife subject to him. Furthermore, in all but seven states, the father continued to enjoy prior authority in the guardianship of minor children; and a few commonwealths—North Carolina, Kentucky and Texas—ordinarily permitted divorce for adultery only when the wife was the offender. So widely was the principle of civil equality recognized, however, that only time was required to remove the few remaining discriminations from the statute books.

If woman's chief sphere were the home, complaint was general that she had failed badly in one department of her duties, that of training her children. European visitors invariably described them as "pert and disrespectful," one Frenchman maintaining that a composite photograph of American youth would reveal *"le plus terrible de tous les enfants terribles."* [3] Even American

[1] See C. R. Fish, *The Rise of the Common Man* (*A History of American Life*, VI), 271.

[2] Annie N. Meyer, ed., *Woman's Work in America* (N. Y., 1891), 271-274, 446-448; H. C. Whitney, *Marriage and Divorce, the Effect of Each on Personal Status and Property Rights* (Phila., 1894); G. J. Bayles, *Woman and the Law* (N. Y., 1901).

[3] Anon., *America and the Americans* (N. Y., 1897), 222. See also Bates, *Year in Great Republic*, I, 52; Hugo Münsterberg, *American Traits from the Point of View of a German* (Boston, 1902), 129; Paul de Rousiers, *American Life* (A. J. Herbertson, tr., Paris, 1892) 254-260; edit., *Ladies' Home Journ.*, IX (1892), no. 7, 12.

writers admitted that filial irreverence was "the greatest blemish that exists on the childhood of this country today," and one suggested that "the present problem of the children is the painless extinction of their elders." [1] Nevertheless the gradual disappearance of corporal punishment from the home was regarded even by such critics as a sign of increasing civilization. [2] Whether the slump in manners was due to parental indulgence, or to a desire to give children a freer and more self-reliant start in life, the experts were not agreed, though doubtless both elements entered into the situation. One thoughtful European was obliged to confess that "the fruit does not by any means correspond to the seed. . . . The unendurable child does not necessarily become an intolerable man." [3]

Perhaps no factor affected child life more than the growth of cities. In the rural districts boys and girls continued to live in the customary manner, close to nature's bosom; but not so in the urban centers. An investigation conducted in 1880 by G. Stanley Hall, then a lecturer in psychology at Harvard, showed that over half the children entering Boston's primary schools had never seen a plow or spade, a robin, squirrel, snail or sheep; they had never observed peaches on a tree or growing grain and could not distinguish an oak tree from a willow or poplar. [4] In place of these traditional

---

[1] Martha B. Mosher, *Child Culture in the Home* (N. Y., 1898), 168; Kate Douglas Wiggin, *Children's Rights* (Boston, 1892), 3. See also Hall, *Social Customs*, chap. xi; Mary V. Terhune (Marian Harland, *pseud.*), *The Secret of a Happy Home* (N. Y., 1896), chaps. xxi, xxiii; anon., "The Next Generation," *Harper's Bazar*, XV (1882), 754; E. W. Bok, "The Blot on Our American Life," *Ladies' Home Journ.*, XII (1895), no. 8, 14.

[2] Edit., *Ladies' Home Journ.*, X (1893), no. 8, 12.

[3] J. F. Muirhead, *The Land of Contrasts* (Boston, 1898), 70.

[4] G. S. Hall, "The Contents of Children's Minds on Entering School," *Pedagogical Seminary*, I (1891), 139-173. See also C. D. Kellogg, "Child-Life in City and Country," *Journ. of Social Sci.*, XXI (1885),

experiences of American childhood the city youth must arrange his play with reference to paved streets, telegraph poles and iron lamp-posts. Instead of collecting birds' eggs he collected the small picture cards of burlesque queens and prize fighters, which came in cigarette packages. His greatest thrills centered in the clang and clatter of the passing patrol wagon, fire engine or ambulance.

While the swift panorama of the streets more or less colored the manners and outlook of all city children, it was, of course, the center of existence for the waifs of the tenement districts. With such homes particularly in mind, many cities in the 1880's followed New York's earlier example by forming societies for the prevention of cruelty to children. It was due to the activity of such bodies, for instance, that the vicious practice of selling Italian children into the slavery of *padroni*, who compelled them to become beggars or strolling musicians, was stamped out or driven under cover.[1]

Less successful were humanitarians in coping with the growing evil of child labor in factories and sweatshops. Though the census undoubtedly understated the facts, the number of boys and girls from ten to fifteen years old engaged in gainful work was recorded as having increased from a million in 1880 to a million and three quarters in 1900. They were employed mostly in the textile industry, and in the new Southern mill towns often began work as young as seven or eight. In Northern cities children also thronged the streets as newsboys and, with their mothers, formed the mainstay of the

207-223; Stewart Culin, "Street Games of Boys in Brooklyn, N. Y.," *Journ. of Am. Folk-Lore,* IV (1891), 221-237; R. A. Woods, ed., *The City Wilderness* (Boston, 1898), 198.

[1] U. S. Commissioner of Education, *Report for 1879,* ccxi-ccxii; *for 1882-83,* ccvi; Helen Campbell and others, *Darkness and Daylight* (Hartford, 1892), 398-400.

sweating trades. In Chicago large numbers of them
toiled as meat packers in the stockyards. State legislation, somewhat more restrictive than in the previous
generation, ordinarily forbade child labor under the
ages of twelve or fourteen; but even such laws were
lacking in most Southern states and in few parts of
the Union were they effectively enforced.[1]

In an effort to recover for childhood a part of its
natural heritage of outdoor recreation, a Boston society
in 1885 tried the experiment of providing sand gardens
for youngsters. The success of the undertaking led to an
ampler provision of public playgrounds there and to
imitation on the part of other municipalities. By the end
of 1898, however, the movement had spread to but thirteen cities, mostly in the East.[2] As a special provision for
poor and invalid children, the Reverend Willard Parsons of Sherman, Pennsylvania, devised the scheme of
"country week" in 1877 to secure a blessed respite of
blue sky and pure air during the stifling hot season—a
plan quickly taken up by charitable organizations in
leading cities and assisted by the "fresh-air funds" of
enterprising newspapers.[3] For sons of the well-to-do,
summer camps began to be established where city-bred
boys were taught the ways of the woods under skilled
instruction. The success of the first camp, at Squam
Lake, New Hampshire, in 1881, caused others to be set
up in New England, New York, Pennsylvania and elsewhere until by the close of the period nearly a score
were in operation.[4] If this generation did little more than

[1] Bureau of the Census, *Occupations at the Twelfth Census* (*Special Rep.*), lxvi-lxviii; U. S. Industrial Commission, *Reports* (Wash., 1900-1902), XIX, 917, 922; Campbell, *Darkness and Daylight*, chaps. iv-v.

[2] C. E. Rainwater, *The Play Movement in the United States* (Chicago, 1921), chap. ii.

[3] Campbell, *Darkness and Daylight*, 313-317; R. A. Woods and others, *The Poor in Great Cities* (N. Y., 1895), 131-150.

[4] Porter Sargent, *A Handbook of Summer Camps* (Boston, 1925),

glimpse the problem of conserving childhood under the new conditions of American life, at least it laid foundations upon which its successors were to build more soundly.

One pleasure the city could give young America which the country could not rival. This consisted in the variety and savoriness of the comestibles at hand.[1] Nor was the child specialist yet come to judgment, intent on turning into Dead Sea fruit the dainties most appetizing to juvenile palates. On the Northern farm the long winter usually meant an uninterrupted routine of heavy foods without fresh fruit or green vegetables, followed by a general "spring sickness" which sent the people helter-skelter to the village druggist for tonics and "molasses 'n' sulphur." The city, on the other hand, with its concentration of wealth and population, supplied a market for the ready sale of myriad food products brought from all parts of the world by means of ever swifter transportation and improved methods of refrigeration.[2]

Moreover, the sedentary habits of many urban dwellers, calling for a diet less burdened with meat, made them eager to diversify their fare and caused them to rely more on vegetables, salads, fish and fruit. In the mid-century fresh fish had been available only to persons living near bodies of water; but in the eighties and nineties fish, caught in the Northern Pacific and transported several thousand miles, was daily supplied fresh to the markets of the Middle West and the Atlantic

17-31; Louis Rouillon, "Summer Camps for Boys," *Am. Rev. of Revs.*, XXI (1900), 697-703.

[1] "No other people existing, or that ever did exist, could command such a variety of edible products for daily consumption as the mass of the American people habitually use to-day." C. D. Warner, *The Relation of Literature to Life* (N. Y., 1897), 264. See also N. S. Shaler, ed., *The United States of America* (N. Y., 1894), III, 1243.

[2] W. A. Taylor, "The Influence of Refrigeration on the Fruit Industry," U. S. Dept. of Agr., *Yearbook for 1900*, 561-580.

Coast.[1] Most tropical fruits—oranges, lemons, red-skinned bananas—were as abundant and cheap in the city as domestic fruits, sometimes cheaper, and their consumption increased greatly throughout the period.[2] After the attractive exhibit of grapefruit at the Chicago World's Fair epicures began tentatively to add that dish to their breakfast menu.

Steadily the factory invaded the precincts of the city kitchen, lightening the drudgery of the home and enriching the family dietary. Quaker Oats, Wheatena and other package cereals began to take the place of corn-meal mush and similar concoctions at the breakfast table. The prejudice against baker's bread as the mark of a lazy housewife waned in face of the greater convenience of commercially prepared loaves, though even town women usually continued to make their own cakes and cookies. Factory-canned foods also came, for the first time, to occupy an important place in the housewife's activities. After 1878 canning factories multiplied in the East and the Middle West while improved machinery cheapened the cost and increased the variety of the foods packed.[3] By the mid-nineties the principal canned goods, in the order of their importance, were tomatoes, corn, milk, oysters, corned beef, salmon, sardines, peaches, peas and beans. "Housekeeping is getting to be ready made, as well as clothing," rejoiced one

[1] C. M. Depew, ed., *One Hundred Years of American Commerce* (N. Y., 1895), II, 390, 393; D. A. Wells, *Recent Economic Changes* (N. Y., 1889), 340.

[2] For instance, from 1880 to 1887 the importation of bananas into the United States grew fortyfold. Wells, *Recent Economic Changes,* 339; anon., "Bananas," *Good Housekeeping,* VIII (1889), 112. See also Depew, *American Commerce,* II, 603-605, and Arnold, *Civilization in United States,* 165.

[3] Depew, *American Commerce,* II, 398-399; J. H. Collins, *The Story of Canned Goods* (N. Y., 1924), esp. 38, 80-82, 126-127, 155, 166, 187; anon., "Canned Goods," *Good Housekeeping,* X (1890), 105 ff.

woman, who predicted that "Even the cook book may yet be obsolete, for every can of prepared food has a label with directions how to cook." [1] At the same time synthetic food products made their appearance. The rapid spread of the use of oleomargarine in place of butter threatened a serious rift in the ranks of the Farmers' Alliance movement in the 1880's, with the dairy farmers opposing the cattle raisers and the Southern cottonseed crushers. [2] Not content with the restrictive measures adopted by nearly twenty states, the dairy interests induced Congress in 1886 to pass a law taxing oleo and regulating its sale. [3]

Though the antagonism to oleo was based on economic rather than sanitary grounds, the increasing part played by outside agencies in preparing food for the home made governmental supervision important as a health measure. The Supreme Court's decision in the Slaughter House cases (1873) breathed new life into the efforts of states and municipalities to regulate the slaughtering of meat. Thanks to agitation by medical and health associations, pure-food laws were passed in 1881 by New York, New Jersey, Michigan and Illinois, and before the end of 1895 twenty-three other states had followed their lead. [4] Milk came in for special attention because of its relation to infant mortality. Not only did

[1] Anon., "Ready-made Housekeeping," *Good Housekeeping*, V (1887), 266.

[2] H. C. Nixon, "The Cleavage within the Farmers' Alliance Movement," *Miss. Valley Hist. Rev.*, XV, esp. 25-26. For the similar strife over compound lard and vegetable shortening, see 26-31.

[3] R. A. Clemen, *By-Products in the Packing Industry* (Chicago, 1927), 170-180.

[4] Modeled on the English laws of 1875 and 1879. W. M. Ravenel, ed., *A Half Century of Public Health* (N. Y., 1921), 213-214; W. K. Newton, "The Sanitary Control of the Food Supply," Am. Public Health Assoc., *Public Health*, IV, 151-154; Shaler, *United States*, III, 1232; C. O. Bates, "Pure Food Laws," Iowa Acad. of Sci., *Proceeds.*, VIII, 206 ff.

the principal cities provide for systematic inspection of their sources of supply, but by 1900 twenty-nine states had pure-milk laws on their statute books. Aside from milk inspection, such laws were usually not well enforced, though Wisconsin, Michigan, Ohio and Connecticut stand out as shining exceptions.

American cooking was not favorably regarded by foreign travelers though their opinion may have been influenced by national prejudices. The worst conditions prevailed in the country where the frying pan remained the mainstay of all cooking. But even in the cities the ordinary American family cared more about the quantity than the quality of the food set before them. In such centers, however, inherited frontier culinary habits were becoming modified by contact with foreign peoples. Italian spaghetti and olives, Hungarian goulash and Chinese chop suey (unknown in China) were gastronomic contributions of the newer immigrant stocks as surely as the white potato and sauerkraut had been of earlier ones. More important was the attention which Americans began to give to the subtleties of seasoning. In the five years following the removal of the tariff on unground spices in 1883 the amount of pepper, pimento, cloves and nutmegs imported into America doubled.[1]

That cooking was a subject worthy of scientific study was recognized when the New York Cooking School was opened in 1874 and the Boston Cooking School three years later. The former had twelve hundred students enrolled in the winter of 1877-1878.[2] Other schools were established in Philadelphia, Washington and elsewhere and courses were even introduced into the high schools. At the same time dietary studies were

[1] Wells, *Recent Economic Changes*, 384-385.
[2] U. S. Comr. of Educ., *Rep. for 1878*, cxcv.

undertaken by official and private agencies and the printing press groaned with the production of new and improved manuals and cookbooks.[1]

Nor did the pleasures of between-meal eating escape attention, especially on the part of commercial caterers to the popular palate. The simple candies of yore— peppermint sticks, gum drops, candy hearts inscribed with sentimental mottoes—were supplemented by boxed confections such as Gunther's (Chicago) and Lowney's (Boston). Chewing gum won an army of addicts, notably among children and the vulgar classes.[2] Ginger beer, pop and other "soft" drinks acquired a new popularity, partly as a result of discoveries which made the artificial production of ice a commercial success.[3] Soda fountains, introduced by the previous generation, grew rapidly in number until, at the close of the period, perhaps sixty thousand were in use.[4] Constructed imposingly of marble, onyx and various decorative metals, some of them cost as much as ten thousand dollars. Few courtships lacked the odorous adjunct of the soda fountain. The young lady and her escort, having made their choice of syrups, waited in palpitant ecstasy while the attendant pulled the faucet first this way for the broad,

---

[1] See A. P. Bryant, "Some Results of Dietary Studies in the United States," U. S. Dept. of Agr., *Yearbook for 1898*, 439-452, and A. C. True and R. D. Milner, "Development of the Nutrition Investigations of the Department of Agriculture," U. S. Dept. of Agr., *Yearbook for 1899*, 403-414. Fannie Merritt Farmer's *The Boston Cooking-School Cook Book*, which quickly became standard, was first published in 1896.

[2] In *As We Were Saying* (N. Y., 1891), 80-85, C. D. Warner amusingly deplores the wasted energy resulting from the "gum habit" of "the last ten years."

[3] Ice-making plants first appeared in the South in the 1870's and, after the failure of the natural-ice crop in the two mild winters of 1888-1890, spread rapidly through the North. T. M. Prudden, "Our Ice Supply," *Pop. Sci. Mo.*, XXXII (1888), 668-682; F. A. Fernald, "Ice-Making and Machine Refrigeration," *Pop. Sci. Mo.*, XXXIX (1891), 19-20.

[4] Depew, *American Commerce*, II, 470-474.

silvery, foaming stream of soda and then that for the sharp hissing spurt which crowned the glass with iridescent bubbles.

As the cost of manufactured tobacco steadily declined and its quality improved, the tobacco habit affected an ever greater proportion of people. Red-blooded men smoked cigars and pipes and chewed tobacco, the latter habit being shared by men otherwise so dissimilar as James Whitcomb Riley, President Cleveland and the eminent zoologist, Professor W. K. Brooks of Johns Hopkins. The new-fangled cigarette, on the other hand, bore the taint of the dude, the sissy and the underworld. Notwithstanding this stigma and the belief that the "insane asylums . . . are being constantly recruited from excessive smokers of the cigarette," its use grew nearly nine times as fast as that of the cigar during the period.[1] Perhaps as a quick nervous smoke it accorded better with the increasing tension of urban life. In the world of fashion smoking in any form was frowned upon as a reprehensible masculine habit not to be practised in the presence of the other sex. It was even "bad form for a gentleman to smoke on streets . . . at the hours at which he will be likely to meet many ladies."[2] At the dinner parties of the 1890's, however, an increasing number of hostesses permitted their male guests to smoke, though any woman who ventured to join them would at once have placed herself beyond the pale.

The interior of the home showed signs of emerging from the reign of terror which had afflicted it in the preceding generation.[3] In the early 1880's the typical

[1] Mosher, *Child Culture*, 202-203; Depew, *American Commerce*, II, 420-421; Meyer Jacobstein, *The Tobacco Industry in the United States* (Columbia Univ., *Studies*, XXVI, no. 3), 45-52.

[2] Hall, *Social Customs*, 290-291.

[3] See Allan Nevins, *The Emergence of Modern America* (*A History of American Life*, VIII), 205-208.

middle-class abode was still likely to be a museum of æsthetic horrors, the choicest rooms cluttered up with easels, bamboo stands, gilded rams' horns, hand-painted rolling pins, and inverted glass domes sheltering wax flowers and china statuettes. To complete the chaos, Japanese lanterns often hung from the ceiling and a painted iron heron stood one-legged amidst cat-tails beside the marble mantel. Such a home, for example, the Marches in Howells's *A Hazard of New Fortunes* found themselves obliged to take after six weary chapters of house hunting in New York.[1] But better things portended. While Mrs. John A. Logan, writing from Washington in the decorous traditions of senatorial conservatism, continued to hymn the advantages of turning cupid-decorated tambourines into photograph frames, another widely read authority, the sister of President Cleveland, was announcing that "every room in the house should be arranged for occupancy, having nothing too good for use," and no room should be overcrowded.[2]

American taste was steadily improving as Americans traveled more widely, as art museums and art schools multiplied, and as women's magazines like the *Ladies' Home Journal,* founded in 1883, and *Good Housekeeping,* dating from 1885, devoted increasing space to sanity in household decoration. The Philadelphia Centennial in 1876 gave an important stimulus to better standards of home furnishing, particularly in the East, equaled only by the influence of the far superior exhibits of the World's Fair of 1893 on the minds of countless

[1] W. D. Howells, *A Hazard of New Fortunes* (N. Y., 1889), I, 58-60. For other descriptions, see anon., "Forty Years Ago, and Now," *Harper's Bazar,* XIII (1880), 514, and anon., "N. Y. Fashions: House-Furnishing," *Harper's Bazar,* XV (1882), 323.

[2] Mrs. J. A. Logan, *The Home Manual* (Boston, 1889), 267-268; Rose E. Cleveland, ed., *The Social Mirror* (St. Louis, 1888), 345, 348.

thousands of Middle Westerners.[1] At the same time the æsthetic doctrines of the Englishmen Charles L. Eastlake and William Morris swept like a fresh breeze through American drawing rooms, helping to clean out much of the débris; and the efforts—not always successful—of manufacturers in Grand Rapids, Chicago and New York to duplicate the superior furniture at lower cost brought better-designed pieces into the homes of the masses.

Undoubtedly, too, the servant problem—"the great unsolved American Question," according to one domestic authority—had a wholesome effect on the situation.[2] Whether, as some maintained, the arrogant mistress was the problem rather than the impertinent maid, servants were hard to get and harder to keep despite the enormous immigration of these years.[3] Accordingly, common sense dictated greater simplicity in furnishings and the adoption of labor-saving devices to lighten housework. The introduction of courses in domestic science in high schools and universities helped also to raise housekeeping from a traditional folk exercise to somewhat the dignity of a profession. Whatever the causes, the results were so marked that Judge Robert Grant described the typical American home of the mid-nineties as

[1] See, for example, J. L. Ford, *Forty-Odd Years in the Literary Shop* (N. Y., 1921), 75-77; C. D. Warner, *Studies in the South and West* (N. Y., 1889), 153; F. A. Fernald, "Household Arts at the World's Fair," *Pop. Sci. Mo.*, XLIII (1893), 803-812.

[2] M. E. W. Sherwood, *The Art of Entertaining* (N. Y., 1892), 206-220. See also Julia M. Wright, *The Complete Home* (Phila., 1879), chap. xviii; Helen Campbell, *Household Economics* (N. Y., 1897), chap. xi; Lucy M. Salmon, *Domestic Service* (N. Y., 1897), esp. chaps. vi-ix.

[3] Among the Cleveland Papers in the Library of Congress are protests against the proposed literacy test of 1897 on the ground that thereby the incoming stream of domestic servants would be seriously reduced. Mr. J. L. Norton has called my attention especially to letters of J. H. Semmes to J. G. Carlisle, Feb. 18, 1897, and C. S. Hamlin to H. T. Thurber, Feb. 23, 1897.

"intended for every-day use by rational beings." [1] He was referring, of course, primarily to city abodes because in smaller towns and in the country the older customs still held sway.

The changes can be followed in greater detail. Nothing was more revolutionary, perhaps, than the widespread abolition of the parlor, a ceremonial room which, darkened with drawn shades and closed doors, had hitherto served as a sort of mortuary chapel for the reception of guests. As the normal life of the family reached into all parts of the house other improvements were inaugurated. More and larger windows made the home cheerier, as did also the replacement of dark gloomy wallpaper with pale tints and simple chintz designs, and the substitution of lighter furniture for ponderous mahogany and black walnut. Upholstery of glossy black horsehair, once the pride of every middle-class household though always a mortification to the flesh, gave way rapidly to rep coverings or even to cretonne and plush. [2] In many homes metal bedsteads, for better or worse, replaced the old top-heavy wooden ones with their elaborately carved headboards reaching almost to the ceiling. Carpets continued to stretch from wall to wall in the average house, but as the rough board floors were succeeded by evenly joined, polished ones, rugs became increasingly popular, commending themselves by reason of greater cleanliness and the possibility of more artistic effects. [3]

At the same time better arrangements for plumbing

[1] Robert Grant, "The Art of Living," *Scribner's Mag.*, XVII (1895), esp. 308 (later printed in book form under the same title). See also Florence R. Simmons, "Superannuated Trash," *Good Housekeeping*, XII (1891), 41.

[2] Campbell, *Household Economics*, 113-114.

[3] Mrs. M. J. Plumstead, "Sweeping Day," *Good Housekeeping*, III (1886), 51; Sarah B. Thayer, "A Reconstructed Household," same mag., XII (1891), 11.

and heating enhanced both comfort and safety. The primitive plumbing of the 1870's, by conveying noxious odors into the rooms, was often a threat to the family health,[1] but with the introduction of improved methods and appliances, adopted under the prod of state and municipal inspection laws, a great change resulted in domestic sanitary equipment in the 1880's.[2] Plumbing could no longer be installed in a first-class dwelling for about two hundred and fifty dollars, as in Civil War times, but was more apt to cost from two to four thousand dollars. Nowhere was the change more welcome than in the bathroom, which at the beginning of the period was usually small and gloomy, its atmosphere tainted with sewer gas. As plumbing fixtures became more tasteful and the bath tub shed its zinc lining for white enamel or porcelain, the mistress of the house began to take a special delight in keeping this room spotless and airy.

Less alteration occurred in methods of heating. The base burner, with funereal urns on top and mica windows showing the blaze within, continued to be the chief resort of most homes; and any woman considered herself fortunate who owned a Crown Jewel, a Hub or an Art Garland. Yet well-to-do families usually aspired to a hot-air furnace and, as the price of steam-heating and hot-water systems fell with the expiration of the basic patents, there was a notable expansion in the use of such furnaces as well.

[1] Clarence Cook, "Beds and Tables, Stools and Candlesticks," *Scribner's Mo.*, XIII (1876-1877), 86; C. F. Wingate, "The Unsanitary Homes of the Rich," *N. Am. Rev.*, CXXXVII (1883), 172; Campbell, *Household Economics*, 75-77.

[2] G. E. Waring, jr., "Recent Modifications in Sanitary Drainage," *Atlantic Mo.*, XLIV (1879), 56-62; W. P. Trowbridge, "Modern Sanitary Engineering," *Harper's Mag.*, LXVIII (1884), 761; W. T. (*pseud.*), "Some Common Facts about Plumbing," *Architectural Record*, I (1891), 97-108.

In the kitchen the housewife learned to rely increasingly upon a wide assortment of new conveniences, such as the steam cooker, double boiler, Dover egg beater, gas toaster, asbestos stove mat, triple saucepans and cake tins with removable bottoms. More important perhaps was the introduction of aluminum ware shortly after 1890 in place of the iron or tin or granite variety. New metallurgical processes had made the metal almost as cheap as tin, and it won quick favor by reason of its lightness, durability and freedom from poisonous alloys.[1] Improved makes of washing machines also appeared and, thanks to the genius of Mrs. Potts, a practicable flatiron with a detachable handle was added to the equipment of the laundry. Even greater relief was promised by the enlarging patronage of commercial laundries by private families.[2] One form of drudgery, however, resisted all efforts at abatement: the washing of dishes.

The progressive liberation from household routine left the middle-class woman with more leisure on her hands than ever before and opened the way for a wider participation in the world that lay beyond domestic walls. The wives and daughters of the poor had long been swelling the ranks of industry, and the five-year depression following 1873 had shown that women even of the comfortable classes might unexpectedly be obliged to supplement the family income. At the same time the colleges and universities were training increasing numbers for pursuits hitherto followed chiefly by men, while the new conditions of American life were opening employments to them wholly unknown to previous generations.

Though the old prejudice against self-support for

[1] J. W. Richards, "Recent Progress in the Aluminum Industry," Franklin Inst., *Journ.*, CXLIX, 451, 454.
[2] Edith Minister, "Ironing Day," *Good Housekeeping*, XVII (1893), 20.

women lingered, its doom was rendered more certain
with the passage of each year. "We have reached a new
era," declared a women's magazine in 1883. "Slowly as
woman has come to her inheritance, it stretches before
her now into illimitable distance, and the question of
the hour is rather whether she is ready for her trust than
whether that trust is hampered by conditions." [1] Never
before had such attractive and multifarious occupations
been within reach. Women who would have shrunk
from factory work and domestic service or even from
teaching trooped forth with a sense of adventure to
become typists, telephone girls, typesetters, bookkeep-
ers, nurses, librarians, journalists, lecturers, social workers, doctors, lawyers, artists. Even in the realm of
mechanical invention, a time-honored monopoly of
men, they were displaying surprising capacity in a
variety of fields. [2] Miss Faithfull reported that in Massachusetts alone there were in 1882 nearly three hundred
branches of business and industry in which women could
earn from one hundred to three thousand dollars a year. [3]
It is not surprising that the number of feminine bread-
winners in the United States rose from two and a half
million in 1880 to four million in 1890 and to five and
a third million in 1900, or that legislatures in the chief
industrial states began in the 1880's to give serious attention to acts for regulating factory conditions of female
toil. [4]

[1] Anon., "The Promise of the Dawn," *Harper's Bazar*, XVI (1883),
18. See also Robert Burdette, "Woman Yesterday and Today," *Ladies'
Home Journ.*, IX (1892), no. 2, 11.
[2] Anon., "Women as Inventors," *Good Housekeeping*, VIII (1889),
119.
[3] Faithfull, *Three Visits to America*, 275. See also Mary P. Jacobi,
"Common Sense" Applied to Woman Suffrage (N. Y., 1894), 16,
118-119, 201.
[4] *Occupations at the Twelfth Census*, lxxxvi; Bayles, *Woman and
the Law*, 257-260; F. J. Stimson, *Handbook to the Labor Law of the
United States* (N. Y., 1896), 55, 71, 79-80.

THE LADIES HOME JOURNAL

*The woman in
business, a new
phenomenon.*

The New Woman

Nowhere was the change in the position of the sex more striking than in the old Confederacy. There the "nobility of helplessness in woman" was still cherished as an ideal by many survivors of the old régime; but postwar realities—the goad of poverty, the opportunities of city life, the shiftlessness of hired help—caused the younger generation to discover the ideal of self-reliance and self-support. "The crowning glory of the present age is that every woman is free to develop her own personality," proclaimed one daughter of Dixie in the early 1890's. In contrast to former times, "a woman is respected and honored in the South for earning her own living, and would lose respect if . . . she settled herself as a burden on a brother" or hard-working father.[1] It was noted that a larger proportion of girls, even of the poorer classes, were going to college than formerly and that more of them stayed on to take their degrees.

Not all American women used their new-found time in bread-winning pursuits: many of them, especially of the upper middle class, found an outlet in club activities. "We have art clubs, book clubs, dramatic clubs, pottery clubs. We have sewing circles, philanthropic associations, scientific, literary, religious, athletic, musical, and decorative art societies," testified one writer.[2] "The absence of men," observed a visiting French woman, "would make French women feel . . . as if they were eating bread without butter."[3] But such extramural contacts were the best means the average housewife had of learning about the complex world in which circumstances were forcing her to play a part; and

[1] W. F. Tillett, "Southern Womanhood as Affected by the War," Century, XLIII (1891-1892), 9-16.
[2] "Contributors' Club," Atlantic Mo., XLVI (1880), 724-725.
[3] Thérèse Blanc, The Condition of Woman in the United States (Abby L. Alger, tr., Boston, 1895), 107.

though the clubs often served as mere excuses for evading domestic responsibility, they proved to be an indispensable training school for countless women who became active civic and humanitarian leaders in their respective communities. By 1889 the clubs were so numerous and influential that they became linked together in a great national system under the name of the General Federation of Women's Clubs.[1]

Conservative folk were not at all certain that the widening range of feminine activity denoted progress. "What is this curious product of to-day, the American girl or woman?" asked one woman writer. ". . . is it possible for any novel, within the next fifty years, truly to depict her as a finality, when she is still emerging from new conditions . . . , when she does not yet understand herself . . . ?" She added, "The face of to-day is stamped with restlessness, wandering purpose, and self-consciousness." [2] As the years passed the note of disapprobation was sounded more and more frequently. "The great fault of the girl of to-day," declared another member of the sex in 1890, "is discontent. She calls it by the more magnificent sounding name of ambition, but in reality she is absolutely restless and dissatisfied with whatever may be her position in life." [3]

Nothing more excited both male and female disapproval than the energetic attempts of certain women to claim for their sex equal political rights with men. In the opening years of the period even the historian Park-

[1] By 1896 the membership consisted of 495 individual clubs and 20 state federations. Ellen M. Henrotin, "The General Federation of Women's Clubs," *Outlook*, LX (1897), 443-444.

[2] Kate G. Wells, "The Transitional American Woman," *Atlantic Mo.*, XLVI (1880), 817-818 (reprinted in her *About People*, Boston, 1885).

[3] Ruth Ashmore, "Side-Talks with Girls," *Ladies' Home Journ.*, VII (1890), no. 4, 10. See also her "The Restlessness of the Age" in same mag., XII (1895), no. 2, 16; and editorials in VII (1890), no. 11, 10; X (1893), no. 5, 18.

man was tempted away from his cloisters long enough to deliver some smashing blows against this effort to overleap "Nature's limitations," disrupt the home and give women excitements and cares "too much for their strength." Especially in the "crowded cities," he pointed out, woman suffrage would be "madness," a certain means of making bad government worse.[1] Five leading feminists joined in a powerful counterblast: Julia Ward Howe, Thomas Wentworth Higginson, Lucy Stone (Blackwell), Elizabeth Cady Stanton and Wendell Phillips.[2] Reaffirming the principles of the Declaration of Independence, they declared that women as well as men had contributions to make to public life and denounced the failure to accept the consequences of woman's altered position as an effort to "put the bird back into the egg." "One of two things is true:" asserted the forthright Phillips, "either woman is like man—and if she is, then a ballot based on brains belongs to her as well as to him; or she is different, and then man does not know how to vote for her as well as she herself does."

This widely read debate marked the lines on which the great battle over the ballot was fought in periodicals, public gatherings, legislative halls and constitutional conventions. While the majority of women remained somewhat indifferent spectators, the militant "antis" did not feel that their disapproval of feminine political activity precluded them from organizing committees and societies in opposition. In effectiveness of organization, however, they were completely outdone by their antagonists, many of whom had been trained in the old

[1] Francis Parkman, "The Woman Question," *N. Am. Rev.*, CXXIX (1879), 303-321. See also his reply to his critics, "The Woman Question Again," in same mag., CXXX (1880), 16-30.

[2] Anon., "The Other Side of the Woman Question," *N. Am. Rev.*, CXXIX (1879), 413-446.

days of the antislavery struggle and the Sanitary Commission. Already two strong woman-suffrage associations were in the field, the American and the National, one seeking the ballot through state action, the other through a federal amendment.[1] New branches of these bodies were organized in the various states; and in 1890, when it became clear that the parent societies were but two blades of the same scissors, they united under the name of the National American Woman Suffrage Association.

Meantime campaigns were being hotly waged on every front and with many weapons. As Colonel Higginson pointed out, "Mrs. Stowe helps to free Uncle Tom in his cabin, and then strikes for the freedom of women in her own 'Hearth and Home.' Mrs. Howe writes the 'Battle Hymn of the Republic,' and keeps on writing more battle-hymns in behalf of her own sex. Miss Alcott not only delineates 'Little Women,' but wishes to emancipate them." [2] Prominent men lent their pens and voices to the cause: George W. Curtis, Senator G. F. Hoar, the venerated Whittier and others. Both the Knights of Labor and the American Federation of Labor rallied to the banner. In 1878 Senator A. A. Sargent of California introduced into Congress an equal-suffrage amendment, drafted by Susan B. Anthony in the very language which forty-two years later was to find lodgment in the Constitution.[3] In the next two decades Senate committees reported five times and House committees twice in favor of the proposal, but action went no further. The platforms of the major parties ignored the issue, and the Prohibitionists perhaps hurt

[1] See Nevins, *Emergence of Modern America*, 340.
[2] T. W. Higginson, *Common Sense about Women* (Boston, 1881), 329.
[3] Susan B. Anthony and others, *History of Woman Suffrage* (Rochester and N. Y., 1881-1926), V, 623.

it by associating it in the public mind with their battle against rum. In 1884 a group of suffragists launched a political party of their own, the Equal Rights party, defiantly nominating for president a woman lawyer, Mrs. Belva A. Lockwood of Washington, D. C. Though the outcome scarcely justified it, she was put forward in the next election as well.[1]

The policy of divide-and-conquer brought more encouraging results. Campaign after campaign was conducted in state after state under the inspiration of veteran leaders like the angular Miss Anthony and the motherly Mrs. Stanton, aided by such new recruits as Dr. Anna Howard Shaw and Mrs. Carrie Chapman Catt.[2] The initial gains, as in Britain and the Scandinavian countries during these same years, took the form of obtaining the vote in school elections and sometimes also in regard to municipal or taxation questions. Thus in 1878 New Hampshire and Oregon, following the earlier example of a few other states, authorized school suffrage. Massachusetts, New York and Vermont acted in the next two years, and by the close of 1898 thirteen additional states and territories, representing all parts of the Union but the old Confederacy, had fallen into line.[3]

The cause of full equality in voting, on the other hand, showed signs of losing ground when Congress by the Edmunds law of 1887 deprived the women of Utah territory of the ballot as a means of destroying polygamy and when, two years later, the voters of

[1] T. H. McKee, ed., *The National Conventions and Platforms of All Political Parties* (3d edn., Balt., 1900), 226-228, 256.

[2] Ida H. Harper, *The Life and Work of Susan B. Anthony* (Indianapolis, 1898-1908), II, *passim*.

[3] Montana, Iowa and Louisiana established a form of taxation suffrage, respectively in 1887, 1894 and 1898; Kansas municipal suffrage in 1887 and Michigan in 1893 (declared unconstitutional). E. A. Hecker, *A Short History of Women's Rights* (N. Y., 1910), 167.

Washington refused to authorize the reëstablishment of equal suffrage at the election for adopting a state constitution.[1] The next year, however, Wyoming was admitted into the Union with the universal suffrage she had practised since 1869; and three of her neighbors after achieving statehood—Colorado in 1893 and Utah and Idaho in 1896—ranged themselves by her side. Nevertheless the closing years of the decade showed an apparent decline of interest in the movement. For some years to come most Americans were to regard "ballots for both" as an aberration of the wild and woolly West.

Feminism, with considerably less success, sought to play a rôle in the reform of women's clothing. In this domain Paris ruled supreme, and the law and the prophets required that the human figure be used to display clothes, not clothes the figure. Most American women in the late 1870's, tightly imprisoned in wasplike waists, reveled in flounces and frills, their long, trailing skirts, drawn in at the bottom, making a quick gait impossible. The "street-cleaning-department style" it was called by a writer in *Harper's Bazar*.[2] Underneath they were stuffed out with layers of garments known collectively as "unmentionables." Young women dressed like their elders and, by a natural law of descent, even the children were clad to look like premature grownups.[3] About 1880 began the vogue of the pannier, an overskirt draped up at the hips or back by means of a bustle. With each season pannier draperies grew more "bouffant," dress extenders or cushion bustles with

[1] Mary A. Greene, "Results of the Woman-Suffrage Movement," *Forum*, XVII (1894), esp. 414-416.

[2] Anon., "Clothed and in Her Right Mind," *Harper's Bazar*, XIV (1881), 562.

[3] See, for example, anon., "Childish Children," *Harper's Bazar*, XIV (1881), 663; Isabel A. Mallon, "Dressing a Growing Girl," *Ladies' Home Journ.*, X (1893), no. 9, 21.

steel springs being used to produce the desired effect. A walking costume, described in the *Cosmopolitan* for October, 1887, called for fifteen and a half yards of material twenty-two inches wide; a stylish frock for eighteen and a half yards. But at the close of the decade the pannier was on the decline, while the skirt was worn wider at the bottom and the sleeves, hitherto tight, had become high and full.[1] The new mode reached its climax in 1896 in the leg-o'-mutton sleeve, puffed out balloonlike from a tight band below the elbow and projecting beyond the shoulder.

Recurrent protests against the tyranny of fashion were based partly upon considerations of cost,[2] but much more on the presumed unhealthful effects of long, heavy skirts, tight, high-heeled shoes and, worst of all, the breath-taking, steel-reënforced corsets. "Woman by her injurious style of dress," asserted one physician, "is doing as much to destroy the race as is man by alcoholism." "Niggardly waists and niggardly brains go together," agreed Miss Frances Willard.[3] In the 1870's the New England Women's Club, led by Elizabeth Stuart Phelps, had raised the banner of revolt, declaring war in particular against the corset, and had even opened

[1] Modish skirts in 1890 were from four and a half to five yards wide at the bottom. *Ladies' Home Journ.*, VII (1890), no. 7, 15.

[2] One well-known pulpiteer, calling attention to the fact that "Arnold of the Revolution proposed to sell his country in order to get money to support his home wardrobe," announced that a similar cause had "sent prominent business men to the watering of stocks, and life insurance presidents to perjured statements about their assets, and some of them to the penitentiary, and has completely upset our American finances." Talmage, *Wedding Ring*, 103-104.

[3] Dr. R. L. Dickinson of Brooklyn estimated the pressure exerted by corsets as varying, in given cases, from 21 to 88 pounds. Helen G. Ecob, *The Well-Dressed Woman* (N. Y., 1892), 27-29, 34-35. See also B. W. Richardson, "Dress in Relation to Health," *Pop. Sci. Mo.*, XVII (1880), 182-199. But Mrs. Terhune declared: "Women will wear corsets; they always have and they always will. We may as well consider this a settled fact." Mary V. Terhune (Marion Harland, *pseud.*), *Talks upon Practical Subjects* (N. Y., 1895), 119.

a shop for the sale of "dress-reform garments." [1] Though a limited number of women, presumably in the vicinity of Boston, adopted the new "health waists," evidence is overwhelming that, in general, the corset continued to hold its own.

Yet each year, by emphasizing anew the cramping effects of the prevailing styles upon the enlarging activities of women, prepared the way for a new rebellion. In 1891 the National Council of Women of the United States, meeting in Washington, gave the matter of rational attire particular consideration. Its committee reported the following year in favor of a model based upon the "Syrian costume adopted by the English Society for Rational Dress, the short-skirted gown with leggins, and the new gymnastic suit." [2] While no change so radical could hope for adoption, a wider vogue of "mannish styles" such as tailored suits and shirt waists, an increasing use of discreetly shorter skirts for business and even, in some cases, the wearing of divided skirts for bicycling gave promise of a better day. [3]

By none were the caprices of fashion more hypnotically followed than by the leaders of society. But this generation remained more or less puzzled as to who were the leaders and just what was Society. Culture, wealth, family—no single criterion was conclusive. In Boston, it was said, the question was, "How much do you know?"; in New York, "How much are you worth?"; in Philadelphia, "Who was your grandfather?" In Chicago, social life remained "more fluid and undetermined

---

[1] Julia A. Sprague, *History of the New England Women's Club* (N. Y., 1894), 19-20; Julia Ward Howe, "Dress and Undress," *Forum*, III (1887), esp. 315; Ecob, *Well-Dressed Woman*, 130-132.

[2] Ecob, *Well-Dressed Woman*, 143-146. A series of articles favorable to the movement appeared in the *Arena*, VI-VIII (1892-1893).

[3] May R. Kern, "Dressing without the Corset," *Ladies' Home Journ.*, X (1893), no. 8, 17; C. H. Crandall, "What Men Think of Women's Dress," *N. Am. Rev.*, CLXI (1895), 251-254.

than in Eastern large cities," with the newly rich aspiring to inherit the kingdom.[1] San Francisco was noted for its "terribly fast so-called society set, engrossed by the emptiest and most trivial pleasures . . . ."[2] Yet even in Boston and Philadelphia the forward thrust of postwar millionaires, merchant princes and railway barons was upsetting established values and introducing the gold standard. Throughout the country in fact, even in the urban parts of the South, social gradations were rapidly taking the form expressed by the Englishman who said that "all humanity is divided into pounds, shillings and pence."

The aspirations of social climbers were reflected in the appearance of a plethora of etiquette books, bearing such titles as *The Social Etiquette of New York* (1878), *The P. G., or, Perfect Gentleman* (1887) and *Success in Society* (1888).[3] How should socially inexperienced but well-to-do nobodies manipulate a fork, wear a dress coat, know when and on whom to leave cards?[4] How could they attain that lofty distinction of manner which would permit them to be ill-bred in a well-bred way? Invited to dine at the Coreys' on the water side of Beacon Street, the ladies of Silas Lapham's household consulted not one but several etiquette books to prepare for the great occasion. The social game usually was played by the deft hands of women who often developed a skill of strategy and execution which exceeded that of their husbands on the Rialto. Palatial mansions and liveried retinues helped obscure the rise from humble origins; liberal patronage of fashionable

[1] Warner, *Studies*, 196.
[2] Faithfull, *Three Visits to America*, 216-217.
[3] Many others are referred to in footnotes earlier in this chapter.
[4] See the frank recognition of this situation in the preface of Mrs. John Sherwood, *Manners and Social Usages* (N. Y., 1884; rev., 1887, 1897).

charities might provide the magic key; a busy guild of genealogists stood ready to furnish "ancestors." Even Mrs. Mary Baker Eddy for a time paraded a coat of arms until her right to it was protested by the representative of the family in Scotland.[1] If such measures failed, there was always the possibility of a brilliant international marriage.

To upholders of a more genteel tradition American society seemed to smack too much of the marriage mart. "The parents launch their offspring as well as possible, and display their wares to the greatest advantage, but the business of the market is carried on chiefly by the young girls themselves, instead of by their mothers as in England and Europe."[2] "Care should be taken in presenting foreigners to young ladies," cautioned one authority on etiquette, for "sometimes titles are dubious."[3] Yet a surprising number of the sensationally rich families which came to the fore in the 1870's and 1880's succeeded in annexing a genuine foreign title by marriage.[4] It was estimated toward the end of the century that over two hundred million dollars had by this means been exported to replenish the coffers of impoverished European nobility. The year 1895 was especially glamorous in New York social annals by reason of three such alliances: the Paget-Whitney, the Castellane-Gould and the Marlborough-Vanderbilt. When it was learned that the Duke of Marlborough and his new American duchess would attend the horse show, a frantic mob early choked the entrances, eager to render that uproar-

---

[1] J. D. Champlin, jr., "The Manufacture of Ancestors," *Forum*, X (1890-1891), 565-572; Sibyl Wilbur (O'Brien), *The Life of Mary Baker Eddy* (N. Y., 1908), 4-5 n.

[2] Unsigned comment in *Atlantic Mo.*, LI (1883), 558.

[3] Sherwood, *Manners and Social Usages* (1884), 45.

[4] See the imposing list in W. T. Stead, *The Americanization of the World* (N. Y., 1902), 318-329.

ious acclaim which only a democracy can accord the hereditary distinctions of effete monarchy.

In every great city the citadels of exclusiveness were being assailed by the gold rush. The Vanderbilt fancy-dress ball of March 26, 1883, the most sumptuous entertainment that had yet been given in America, marked the entry into New York society of the William K. Vanderbilts, whose grand-uncle, the "Commodore," had begun his career as a ferryboat master.[1] Yet society, in the high and holy sense of the word, could not survive if the wife of every successful captain of industry should gain a place within the sacred portals. In order to maintain a judicious blend of patrician and parvenu, Ward McAllister, self-styled "Autocrat of the Drawing-Rooms," organized in 1872 the Patriarchs, a group of twenty-five socially impeccable men who assumed the function of censoring the guest lists at select gatherings.[2]

A chance remark of McAllister in 1890 that about four hundred people in New York comprised the inner circle gave coinage to an expression which became synonymous the country over for the smart set. Every considerable city soon had its "Four Hundred," and local newspapers vied with their New York contemporaries in giving prominence to society news. As a matter of fact, the moneyed element was definitely setting the tone of New York society by the 1890's.[3] A ten-thousand-dollar dinner for seventy-two guests at Delmonico's no longer excited comment; pretentious winter residences in the city must be supplemented by

[1] Harold Seton, "How the Vanderbilts Crashed Society Gates," *Boston Herald*, Feb. 12, 1928.

[2] Ward McAllister, *Society as I Found It* (N. Y., 1890), esp. 214-252. See also Moran Tudury, "Ward McAllister," *Am. Mercury*, VIII (1926), 138-143; and Arthur Train, "The Perfect Goldfish," *Sat. Eve. Post*, CCII, 25 ff. (Sept. 28, 1929).

[3] Mrs. John K. Van Rensselaer and Frederick Van de Water, *The Social Ladder* (N. Y., 1924), chaps. v-viii.

luxurious summer homes at Newport, Bar Harbor, Lenox or Tuxedo; the courtly Knickerbocker strain had lost most of its influence. Even Ward McAllister himself had become a butt of ridicule—"Would Make All-a-stir," as someone derisively called him.

The growing absorption of women in interests outside the home, whether as social butterflies or as breadwinners or reformers, seemed to some a sufficient explanation of the waning sanctity of the marriage relation. Whatever the reason there could be no doubt as to the fact. With sixteen thousand divorces granted in 1878, the number rose to nearly twenty-nine thousand in the year 1888 and to almost forty-eight thousand in 1898. The rate of increase was far greater than the rate of population growth—indeed, in the last decade of the century, three times as great—and the proportion of divorces granted in the United States far exceeded that of any foreign country except Japan.[1] In 1890 one divorce was granted for every sixteen marriages solemnized, in 1900 one for every twelve. Since the practice was forbidden Roman Catholics, the frequency of divorce among those not of that faith was even greater than these figures indicate.

The situation excited the widespread alarm of press and pulpit. As a result of the activity of the National Divorce Reform League, formed in 1881, the federal government undertook in 1887-1888 a comprehensive collection of data concerning marriage and divorce. The findings confirmed a cherished notion of the reformers that one fruitful source of the evil was the diversity of state legislation. In some states marriage was permitted as early as twelve or fourteen years; in most a civil cere-

[1] The divorce rate in Switzerland, which was the highest of any European country, was about three sevenths that of the United States at the close of the century. Bureau of the Census, *Marriage and Divorce, 1867-1906 (Special Rep.)*, pt. i, 12-13, 19, 54-55, 62-64.

mony would suffice; and, in perhaps half, a ceremony
could be dispensed with altogether under the general
principles of the "Scotch law of marriage," which
required merely mutual consent.[1]

Divorce might be made an equally simple matter
provided the proper jurisdiction were sought. South
Carolina denied divorce on any ground whatever; but
elsewhere the causes varied from the single one of adultery, in the case of New York, to a list of ten or more,
including, in the case of Washington, "any other cause
deemed by the court sufficient"—the so-called "omnibus
clause." While residence of a year or more was usually
necessary to secure a divorce in most states, in Nevada
and Wyoming only six months were demanded and in
the Dakotas but ninety days. As a result "large divorce
colonies" were to be found in the Dakotas, and in all
four commonwealths a majority of the defendants were
residents of other states.[2] The fruits of such a system
were scandalous and demoralizing. As one writer expressed it, "a husband who has obtained a divorce in
one State on trivial grounds . . . may marry again, and
with his new wife and children travel through the
United States, and in some places his new relations will
be considered legal and proper, while in others he will
be a bigamist, his new wife a paramour, and their children illegitimate."[3]

The lax standards of the law were largely an inheri-

[1] E. H. Bennett, "National Divorce Legislation," *Forum*, II (1886-
1887), 429-438; same author, "Marriage Laws," *Forum*, III (1887),
219-229; E. J. Phelps, "Divorce in the United States," *Forum*, VIII
(1889-1890), 349-364; Duncan Convers, *Marriage and Divorce in
the United States* (Phila., 1889); Whitney, *Marriage and Divorce*,
chaps. iii-iv, xxix-xlv; Bayles, *Woman and the Law*, 55-119; *Marriage
and Divorce, 1867-1906*, pt. i, chaps. ii-iii.

[2] South Dakota changed her residence requirement to one year in
1893. *Marriage and Divorce, 1867-1906*, pt. i, 33, 305, 312, 318, 327.

[3] Bennett, "National Divorce Legislation," 434.

tance from a rural age when early and easy marriage was desired for population growth and community disapproval prevented reckless recourse to the divorce courts. The phenomenal increase of divorce was largely an outgrowth of urban conditions: the anonymity of city life, its distractions and temptations, the growing practice of living in boarding houses and flats, the harsh struggle for existence, the opportunities for self-support afforded women.[1] Not only was the divorce rate higher in large cities than in small ones and country districts, but the rate of increase was also greater there than elsewhere.[2] Since twice as many divorces in the period 1878-1898 were granted upon the wife's complaint as on the husband's, it is likely that the increase reflected, in part, a greater self-respect among women and an unwillingness to put up with conditions which their mothers would have accepted in silence.[3] Legislative changes during the period were in the direction of greater strictness, Connecticut leading the way in 1878 by repealing her "omnibus clause." But the gains were not impressive, and no headway was made toward the reformers' goal: a uniform divorce law for all the states.[4] The more thoughtful perceived that what was needed was not so much a change of legislation as of ethical attitudes.

Even more shocking to most people was the growth of commercialized immorality. Primarily an urban phenomenon, it throve most extensively in the great pop-

---

[1] Whitney, *Marriage and Divorce*, 10-12; S. G. Fisher, *The Cause of the Increase of Divorce* (Phila., 1890), esp. 19-20.

[2] *Marriage and Divorce, 1867-1906*, pt. i, 19.

[3] In the South, where cities were fewer and women less accustomed to the idea of earning their own living, wives were less active in seeking to sever the marriage tie. In four Southern states, indeed, more divorces were granted to husbands than to wives. *Marriage and Divorce, 1867-1906*, pt. i, 24-25, 94-95.

[4] S. E. Dike, *A Review of Fifteen Years* (Natl. Divorce Reform League, *Rep. for 1895*), esp. 11-12.

ulation centers where unmarried men congregated in largest numbers and out-of-town visitors were numerous. In New York, for example, vice catered to all tastes and purses—in "palatial bagnios" as well as in widely scattered medium-class houses and places of assignation, not to mention basement dives on the Bowery where, we may well believe, the business was "divested of the gaslight glare and tinsel of the high-toned seraglios."[1] As in the seaboard metropolis, "sporting houses" existed in all parts of Chicago, though the traffic was most boldly carried on in the district between Harrison and Polk and between Clark and Dearborn streets.[2] There, as in the red-light districts of other cities, the male passer-by after dark was almost certain to be hailed from curtained windows or accosted on the street by pert sauntering women.

The number of such wretched females cannot be known, but the circumstances which brought them to their life of shame and eventual disease are not difficult to understand.[3] As one brothel keeper in Chicago told W. T. Stead, the English journalist, "Prostitution is an effect, not a careless, voluntary choice on the part of the fallen." Some of them were country newcomers to

[1] W. F. Howe and A. H. Hummel, *Danger!* (Buffalo, 1886), chap. xii. See also Herbert Asbury, *The Gangs of New York* (N. Y., 1927), chap. ix.

[2] See frontispiece map and first appendix of W. T. Stead, *If Christ Came to Chicago!* (Chicago, 1894). For Boston, see Woods, *City Wilderness*, 159-173, and F. A. Bushee, *Ethnic Factors in the Population of Boston* (Am. Econ. Assoc., *Publs.*, IV, no. 2), 107-116.

[3] Police Inspector Thomas Byrnes in 1893 believed there were forty thousand prostitutes in New York City. National Purity Congress, *Papers* (N. Y., 1896), 113. Stead's estimate for Chicago about the same time was ten thousand. *If Christ Came to Chicago*, 35. The census figures possess even less reliability; thus in 1890 Indianapolis was credited with nearly as many brothels as New York, and Baltimore with three times as many as either Philadelphia or Washington. *U. S. Eleventh Census* (1890), XXIII, 1024-1035. For the 1880 figures, see *U. S. Tenth Census* (1880), XXI, 566.

the city, starved for companionship and lacking the wholesome restraining influence of neighborhood opinion. Others were shopgirls or housemaids eager for the pretty clothes and good times which their meager wages denied them. Many more perhaps were the hapless victims of evil youthful surroundings in the slums, while still others were girls of feeble mentality who in a better-ordered society would have been under institutional care. In the opinion of Stead's informant, "the real cause lies not in the girls who fall, but in the social conditions that make the fall easy and the men who tempt to the step . . . ." [1] The situation was made worse by the growth of an organized traffic in "white slaves," intercity in character, which often involved forcible induction into a life of vice.

Everywhere in the nation the law placed a ban on prostitution; but while municipalities outlawed the evil to prove themselves respectable, they condoned lax enforcement to prove themselves liberal. [2] In some places the authorities raided the vice resorts every month or so, imposing fines that amounted to an irregular license fee. Elsewhere the police were apt to be in collusion with the keepers of disorderly houses, levying blackmail on them for their private gain. As we have seen, the Lexow investigation revealed such a system at work in New York, and Stead exposed a similar situation in Chicago. Though without warrant in law, segregation was permitted or required in many cities; and in a few isolated cases, like that of Cleveland, the experiment was briefly tried of introducing the Continental European system

[1] Stead, If Christ Came to Chicago, 252. Cf. W. F. Garrison, "The Relation of Poverty to Purity," Natl. Purity Congress, Papers, 398-405.

[2] D. F. Wilcox, The American City (N. Y., 1904), 127-133; Stead, If Christ Came to Chicago, 37, 382; G. W. Hale, ed., Police and Prison Cyclopaedia (rev. edn., Boston, 1893), 189 ff. See also a series of articles on "Official Complicity with Vice" in six different cities, in Christian Union, XLVI (1892).

of police registration and medical inspection. The recurrent upheavals of civic reform generally disclosed the alliance of commercialized vice with corrupt politics and the liquor interests, and brought about a temporary improvement of conditions. In general, community sentiment upheld the time-honored double standard of morality, which conceived of sexual promiscuity as permissible only for the male. Few reform officials were willing to emulate Police Commissioner Roosevelt in treating the men taken in vice raids precisely as their female companions, so far as the law allowed him to do so.[1]

Serious as was the social evil, there was little spread of licentiousness upward through society; and foreign observers were justified in rating American standards of sexual morality as superior to those of most European countries. Indeed, in spite of the whips and buffetings of circumstance, the American woman had substantial cause for pride in the advances made by her sex. Though, as the writer in the *Atlantic Monthly* had said, she might not yet understand herself, she was responding to her highest instincts in struggling toward an easier, more self-respecting and self-reliant footing in American society. Her failures, though disheartening at the time, were not irreparable, while her successes formed a lasting heritage to those who were to follow.

[1] Theodore Roosevelt, *An Autobiography* (N. Y., 1919), esp. 196.

CHAPTER VI

THE EDUCATIONAL REVIVAL

THE closing decades of the century saw an educational renaissance comparable in many respects to the great days of Horace Mann and Henry Barnard.[1] While the cities were the chief beneficiaries, the country also shared in the movement and the South for the first time became a part of the national educational order. Nor was the awakening one of the schools alone, for countless other agencies of a less formal sort began to play a significant rôle in shaping popular culture. Lewis Miller, Frederick W. Poole, S. S. McClure, Joseph Pulitzer and Edward W. Bok, no less than the professional educators, helped instruct the people and mold their outlook on life.

The ideal of free tax-supported elementary schools had been accepted in the North already by mid-century, but even there practice had lagged behind theory while in the South such facilities hardly existed at all. In the dozen years after the Civil War, though enrollments grew, operating expenses were generally held down in the North, school buildings kept simple, and few new features added to the curriculum. The South, obliged by the Reconstruction constitutions to set up public-school systems, was handicapped by poverty, Carpetbag exploitation and the very magnitude of the task.[2] But

[1] See C. R. Fish, *The Rise of the Common Man* (*A History of American Life*, VI), 216-224.

[2] E. P. Cubberley, *Public Education in the United States* (Boston, 1919), 252-253; E. W. Knight, *The Influence of Reconstruction on Education in the South* (Teachers College, *Contribs. to Educ.*, no. 60), esp. 99.

with the widespread economic recovery following 1878 and the end of Republican meddling in Southern affairs, a new era opened for both sections. Though the North and West now faced the duty of caring for hordes of immigrant children, the vast accumulation of taxable wealth and the growth of cities facilitated accomplishment. If the visible progress was less spectacular in the old slave states, the difficulties overcome were even greater.

Taking the nation as a whole, improvement of the educational system occurred at every point from top to bottom. Congress had evidenced its interest in 1867 by creating a special department (later bureau) of education which, under able leadership, served as a national clearing house, gathering statistics, disseminating information and holding up the torch for the more backward commonwealths. After 1870 compulsory-attendance laws began to spread over the North and West, nineteen states and territories taking this step by 1881, and twelve more by 1898.[1] Rhode Island, for example, had been notorious as a haven for immigrant parents who preferred their children's wages to their education, but this condition was corrected in 1883.[2] The typical statute required children from eight to fourteen years old to attend school from twelve to sixteen weeks a year; as late as 1890 Connecticut was the only state to exact attendance for the full session. Enforcement, however, was another thing. With notable exceptions it was only the older, well-established communities which compelled parents and children to observe the law.[3] Elsewhere so-

[1] Though such laws were to be found in Massachusetts (enacted in 1852), Vermont and the District of Columbia before 1870, they were of a crude and unsatisfactory character. For their spread after 1870, see *Reports* of the U. S. Commissioner of Education: for *1882-83*, xxx-xxxvi; for *1886-87*, 56; for *1888-89*, I, 15-16, 475-531; for *1894-95*, I, 1118-1121; for *1896-97*, II, 1525.

[2] U. S. Comr. of Educ., *Rep. for 1888-89*, I, 501.

[3] U. S. Comr. of Educ., *Rep. for 1897-98*, II, 1695.

cial custom and parental pride were more influential than legal coercion in keeping youngsters at their tasks.

The number of pupils in the common schools of the nation rose from nine and a half million in 1878 to twelve million a decade later and to fifteen in 1898, somewhat outstripping the growth of population. Kindergartens, public and private, increased from less than two hundred in 1878 to nearly three thousand at the close of the period when perhaps two hundred thousand children were tasting the delights of learning through play-activities.[1] Even more remarkable was the growth of high schools from less than eight hundred in 1878 to fifty-five hundred in 1898. For the first time, the American public, at least in the North and West, squarely accepted the responsibility of extending the benefits of free education upward from the elementary grades. With less than one hundred thousand pupils in the secondary schools in 1878, over half a million were so accommodated in 1898.[2]

Educational development, of course, varied from section to section and even more between country and city. The concentration of wealth and population in urban centers and the greater spirit of progress insured higher salaries for teachers, longer school terms, better buildings and, in general, superior organization and methods of instruction. It was the cities which promoted the kindergarten movement and were most active in providing high schools. Some places like St. Louis under the superintendency of William T. Harris (1867-1880) became the generating centers of ideas that helped revolutionize the theory and practice of teaching throughout the land.

[1] U. S. Comr. of Educ., *Rep. for 1897-98*, II, 2537; E. G. Dexter, *A History of Education in the United States* (N. Y., 1904), 166-169.
[2] U. S. Comr. of Educ., *Rep. for 1898-99*, II, 1842, 1844.

In the rural districts, on the other hand, ungraded schools were the rule. The single schoolmaster shepherded students of all ages and degrees of advancement and, in intervals between chastising unruly charges, listened to the halting recitations of individual pupils whenever they were ready. The rural schoolmaster in his value to the community might be compared to the country doctor, but he seldom enjoyed the same neighborhood respect and, if opportunity offered, he fled his employment for something more rewarding. The school year also ended sooner than in the cities and large towns, where in 1891 the typical session lasted from one hundred and eighty to two hundred days as compared with from seventy to one hundred and fifty in the country.[1]

In the North and West the rural school situation was the subject of constant recommendation by state commissioners of instruction. A basic difficulty was the dissipation of meager resources among many small, independent school districts. Under a Massachusetts law of 1882 abolishing the district system, such schools began to be consolidated, the scattered pupils being daily carried by wagon to a centrally located, graded school. Before 1898 the idea made some headway elsewhere—in Ohio, New York, New Jersey and a few other places— but, in general, rural conservatism was slow to yield and the country schools remained in an unsatisfactory condition.[2]

The rural school problem in the South was, in a sense, the problem of the entire section. With relatively few cities and a country population more thinly distributed than in most parts of the North, the South had

[1] U. S. Comr. of Educ., *Rep. for 1890-91*, I, x. "The increase in urban population is accompanied by increase in the length of the school year," remarked the commissioner. *Rep. for 1898-99*, I, x.

[2] U. S. Comr. of Educ., *Rep. for 1883-84*, xxxiv; *for 1899-1900*, I, x-xi.

also a greater number of children in proportion to adults than did the North and a net taxable wealth considerably less.[1] The burden of educational support on adults in such a state as Mississippi was about twice as heavy as in Vermont. The situation was further complicated by the lingering financial effects of Reconstruction and the fact that the cost of maintaining separate racial schools rested almost wholly on the whites. For these and other reasons, little or no trace of a state school system existed in Virginia, South Carolina, Georgia, Mississippi and Texas until 1870 or 1871. In several other commonwealths public schools were confined chiefly to the larger towns.

To get the new system under way, women of the impoverished gentry helped by promptly enlisting as teachers.[2] Northern philanthropy, notably the fund of $3,500,000 established by George Peabody in 1867 and 1869, quickened the spread of town and city schools and also made provision for systematic teacher training.[3] Between 1881 and 1889 repeated appeals were made to Congress for aid in bearing the burden. A proposal by Senator Henry W. Blair of New Hampshire, himself a victim of poor rural schools, to distribute federal funds among the states in proportion to their illiteracy passed the Senate on three different occasions. But the measure

[1] In 1880 the eighteen Northern states had 909 minors for every thousand adults; the sixteen ex-slave states 1242. The net wealth per capita of minors in the North was $2225; in the South $851. U. S. Comr. of Educ., *Rep. for 1887-88*, 22-29.

[2] A. D. Mayo, "Southern Women in the Recent Educational Movement in the South," U. S. Bur. of Educ., *Circular of Information for 1892*, no. 1.

[3] There was not a normal school in the entire South in 1868. For the work of the Peabody Fund, see E. W. Knight, *Public Education in the South* (Boston, 1922), chap. xi; E. A. Alderman and A. C. Gordon, *J. L. M. Curry* (N. Y., 1911), chaps. xv, xvii; and J. L. M. Curry, *A Brief Sketch of George Peabody and a History of the Peabody Education Fund* (Cambridge, Mass., 1898).

died in the House because of opposition from members who were unwilling to have the lion's share of the money go to the South.[1]

Despite the failure of this badly needed assistance and notwithstanding the many other handicaps, the expansion of the common-school system in the South was characterized by the federal commissioner of education in 1890 as probably "without a parallel." The enrollment grew from two million seven hundred thousand in 1878—less than one quarter Negroes—to nearly four and a half million in 1888, including a somewhat larger proportion of Negroes. "At present," the commissioner asserted, "the schools of the South, taken as whole, enroll a larger percentage of the population than those of the older States of the North, and furnish to every child an opportunity to acquire at least the essential rudiments of a school education."[2] The rise of the agrarian elements to political power in the late eighties and the nineties gave added momentum to the cause of free education, especially in the rural districts. By 1898 the total enrollment had risen to more than five million.[3]

However bright the picture may appear against the former darkness, the South throughout the period lagged behind the rest of the nation. Its chief energies were necessarily absorbed in the basic task of abolishing illiteracy, the curse of the white masses as well as of the colored race. In many rural districts schoolhouses were often mere log shacks without windows, desks, maps

[1] *What is the Blair Bill?* (Charleston, 1887), a pamphlet reprinting articles from the *News and Courier;* P. B. Plumb, *The Blair Education Bill* (Wash., 1890), esp. 4.

[2] U. S. Comr. of Educ., *Rep. for 1889-90*, I, xviii, 11-12. This statement needs to be read in light of the fact that, though enrolling a larger proportion of the whole population, the South did not enroll a larger proportion of the population of school-going age. Also, the school term was much shorter. *Rep. for 1886-87*, 89.

[3] U. S. Comr. of Educ., *Rep. for 1898-99*, I, xiv.

or blackboards. The school term averaged about a hundred days in 1890 as compared with one hundred and fifty in the Middle West and one hundred and seventy-four in the North Atlantic states. When the assertion might still be heard that "it is robbery to tax one man to educate another man's children,"[1] the time was not yet ripe for a forward thrust along all lines as in the North. At most, education was regarded in the South as an opportunity for the individual child and not as a civic obligation, for not one of the states of the former Confederacy applied the principle of compulsion to attendance.

Even in the North teachers were often badly underpaid, the worst conditions prevailing in the rural regions and among women. The state superintendent of Iowa reported in 1883 that teachers of ungraded schools did not average a hundred and fifty dollars a year, though an ordinary farmhand with no obligation to dress well or pay institute fees received two hundred with board.[2] For the country as a whole the average monthly salary for a male teacher in 1888-1889 was $42.43, for a woman $34.27; by 1898-1899 these amounts had advanced to $45.25 and $38.14.[3] The displacement of men by women teachers, already marked in Civil War days, continued at an accelerating rate, partly because of the

[1] Cited from report of the North Carolina superintendent of education, by U. S. Comr. of Educ., *Rep. for 1887-88*, 161. In a somewhat similar spirit Governor F. W. M. Holliday of Virginia declared to the legislature in 1878, "Public free schools are not a necessity. The world, for hundreds of years, grew in wealth, culture, and refinement, without them." Knight, *Public Education in the South*, 347-348.

[2] U. S. Comr. of Educ., *Rep. for 1882-83*, xxix.

[3] The wide variation among sections is indicated by the average monthly salary of $136.23 paid in 1898-1899 to men teachers in Massachusetts as contrasted with $50.00 in Ohio and $25.07 in North Carolina. In these same states women were paid $51.41, $40.00 and $22.24 respectively. U. S. Comr. of Educ., *Rep. for 1888-89*, I, 8; *for 1898-99*, I. lxxix-lxxx.

lower price at which women would work and partly because of the higher rewards for men in the business world. In 1878 about three out of every five teachers were women; in 1898 two out of three.[1] Women won recognition also as educational administrators. By 1897 over two hundred were county superintendents, while twelve were city superintendents and two were state commissioners of instruction.[2] For better or for worse—and educational writers were not certain which—the youth of the nation were receiving their instruction increasingly from that sex which hitherto had had least contact with the world of affairs.

For both men and women, teaching was too apt to be a mere stepping-stone to something more congenial or profitable. The federal commissioner of education, noting in 1887 that twenty-six changes occurred yearly in every one hundred positions, estimated the average term of service at less than four years.[3] Such conditions militated against the conception of teaching as a life career, a profession to be cultivated as was law or medicine. Another deterrent to the attainment of professional standards was the active meddling, not only of politicians but also of schoolbook publishers, in teaching appointments and the selection of textbooks.[4]

Nevertheless, the increase of normal schools, the

[1] U. S. Comr. of Educ., *Rep. for 1888-89*, I, 23, 319, 327-328; for *1891-92*, II, 669; for *1898-99*, I, lxxviii.

[2] The state superintendents were Grace E. Patton in Colorado and Estelle Reel in Wyoming. U. S. Comr. of Educ., *Rep. for 1896-97*, II, 1528-1533.

[3] In the Middle West the changes ran as high as sixty-five. J. T. Prince, "American and German Schools," *Atlantic Mo.*, LXVI (1890), esp. 415.

[4] G. S. Hall, "The Case of the Public Schools," *Atlantic Mo.*, LXXVII (1896), esp. 405-407; anon., "Confessions of Public School Teachers," *Atlantic Mo.*, LXXVIII (1896), 97-110. The extent of the corrupt activities of schoolbook publishers will never be known, but the fact was generally admitted. In the case of Washington in 1890 a

progressiveness of city systems and the waxing strength
of teachers' associations helped offset some of these bane-
ful influences. As public schools grew nation-wide in
their reach, the American people were exalted by a lyric
faith in education which rivaled an earlier generation's
zeal for democracy. In a time of low political morality
it was expected to be the solvent of all governmental
ills. Indeed, reformers urged that its precepts be directly
applied to officeholders through the examination system of appointment.

The period was marked not only by a physical expansion of the school system, but also by a spread of
new ideas, the addition of fresh subjects to the curriculum
and a marked improvement in textbooks. In the late
1880's a number of young Americans who had studied
under Professor William Rein at the University of Jena
brought back with them the Herbartian conception of
instruction.[1] Charles De Garmo's *Essentials of Method*
(1889) and C. A. McMurry's *General Method* (1892),
by popularizing the new ideas for American educators,
did much to change the teacher from a mere drillmaster
and disciplinarian to a person charged with the responsibility of interesting his pupils through an effective
presentation of subject matter.

Due less to Herbartianism perhaps than to humanitarianism, a setback was given to those pedagogues who,
as a wag put it, thought of the hickory stick as the chief
board of education. Many city systems—in New York,
Albany, Cleveland, Chicago and elsewhere—forbade
corporal punishment, New Jersey going so far as to

member of the state board of education exposed a prominent book concern (which he named) which had paid him $5000 in the expectation
of receiving help in securing state-wide adoptions. *Publishers' Wkly.*,
XXXVII, 793 (June 14, 1890).

[1] S. C. Parker, *History of Modern Elementary Education* (Boston,
1912), chap. xvii.

forbid it by state law.[1] New studies—drawing, nature lore, sewing, cooking, manual training—were introduced here and there into city elementary schools, while high-school courses were broadened to include sciences, commercial subjects and the manual and household arts. As the new offerings multiplied, it became necessary to add a fourth year to the high school (common everywhere by 1890 except in the South), and the curriculum was often arranged in alternative four-year courses.

Though the new studies and methods were designed to fit children better for the life of the new America, educational "advance" impressed some critics as a mere succession of "crazes—the method craze, the object-lesson craze, the illustration craze, the 'memory-gem' craze, the civics craze . . . , the phonics craze, the word-method craze, the drawing and music craze," not to mention the "craze" for "business forms, picture study, and physics."[2] In a somewhat similar fashion the federal commissioner of education in 1885 felt obliged to combat the charge of "communism" leveled against the growing practice of providing free textbooks for pupils. Begun by New York City some years before, the plan spread to other centers in the 1880's and was made obligatory throughout Massachusetts by a law of 1884. By 1898 free textbooks were provided for by state action in ten Northern and Western commonwealths while ten other states empowered local communities to decide the question for themselves.[3]

Though the complex racial situation raised many difficulties for educators, German communities could gen-

[1] U. S. Comr. of Educ., *Rep. for 1886-87*, 228; *for 1896-97*, II, 1537; *for 1897-98*, II, 1701-1702.

[2] *N. Y. Eve. Post*, quoted by U. S. Comr. of Educ., *Rep. for 1888-89*, I, 597.

[3] U. S. Comr. of Educ., *Rep. for 1884-85*, cix-cx; *for 1896-97*, II, 1538; *for 1897-98*, I, 894.

erally be counted on as sturdy champions of better schools. The Swedes, Danes and Norwegians, accustomed to popular education at home, also gave them hearty support. The language question, however, caused trouble in the late 1880's, particularly in the case of the more recent Scandinavian arrivals. In Dakota territory they openly defied the law requiring the teaching of English. When in 1889 Wisconsin and Illinois declined by statute to recognize schools in which English was not the language of instruction, the Scandinavians successfully united with other racial groups to force through a repeal.[1]

The Catholic parochial schools, relatively few and poorly equipped at the opening of the period, were ill prepared to take care of the many immigrant children who sought their doors. To remedy this lack the third plenary council of Catholic bishops in Baltimore in 1884 laid down detailed regulations for the management of such schools, requiring their establishment wherever possible and directing Catholic parents to send their children to them. From this action dated the rapid growth of the parochial system, especially notable in New England and only less so in the Middle Atlantic states and the newly formed dioceses of the West.[2]

It is easier to record the outer aspects of educational development than to appraise its results. Like religion, the influence of education cannot be gauged by a count of buildings, the amount of capital invested or the sheer number of persons reached. European visitors were deeply interested in the unfolding American experiment, and no less a person than James Bryce believed that, due

[1] Board of Education of Dakota, *First Biennial Report* (1888), xxxvi; K. C. Babcock, *The Scandinavian Element in the United States* (Univ. of Ill., *Studies*, III, no. 3), 166-169.
[2] M. M. Sheedy, "The Catholic Parochial Schools of the United States," U. S. Comr. of Educ., *Rep. for 1903*, I, esp. 1083-1089.

to its effects, "the average of knowledge is higher, the habit of reading and thinking more generally diffused, than in any other country."[1] Of course, many members of this generation owed their formal training to the schools of an earlier time and, by the same token, the schoolrooms of the 1880's and 1890's were cradling the intellectual life of the early twentieth century.

Certainly, in accomplishing their primary task, the schools made an impressive record, for the proportion of illiteracy in the nation declined from seventeen per cent in 1880 to thirteen in 1890 and to less than eleven in 1900.[2] The large cities made a better showing than the small towns and country districts, the North and West better than the South, and the children of immigrants better than their parents. Indeed, the American-born children of the European newcomers were more literate than the white children of native parentage, chiefly perhaps because of their concentration in cities. If the ability to read and write may be supposed to have any relationship to political intelligence, conservative folk must have been dismayed to observe that, of the nine states that stood highest in literacy, all but one voted for Bryan and free silver in the notable "campaign of education" of 1896.

Despite the remarkable growth of educational facilities since the 1830's, the comparative newness of the system in many parts of the country left vast numbers of adults with a pitifully inadequate share of systematic instruction. In 1880 the total amount of schooling received by the average person in his entire lifetime was less than

[1] James Bryce, *The American Commonwealth* (London, 1888), III, 52. See also Emily Faithfull, *Three Visits to America* (Edinburgh, 1884), 219-220.

[2] The corresponding figures for native-born whites were: 8.7%, 6.2% and 4.6%; for foreign-born whites: 11.9%, 13% and 12.8%. J. A. Hill, "Illiteracy," *Supplementary Analysis and Derivative Tables* (U. S. Twelfth Census, *Special Rep.*), 328-375.

four years; in 1898 it amounted to exactly five.[1] In other words, the average American had not advanced, in his formal training, beyond the attainments of the fourth or fifth grade of the elementary school. As we shall see, the varied literary aspirations and attainments of the time were conditioned by this fundamental fact. Fortunately the constant tendency to pull literature down to the level of the half-educated masses was somewhat offset by the fact that more people than ever before were pouring from the halls of the high schools and colleges.

If the schools were primarily concerned with the instruction of children, their elders had a special opportunity of their own in the contagious spread of the Chautauqua movement. This novel institution gave countless middle-class folk a chance to make up for the deficiencies of their youthful education. Founded in 1874 by an Ohio manufacturer, Lewis Miller, and a Methodist minister, John H. Vincent, as a sort of camp meeting for the training of Sunday-school teachers, the annual summer gatherings on the forested shores of Lake Chautauqua, New York, quickly developed broader educational functions whose influence ramified to many parts of the country.[2] "Any man who loves knowledge and his native land," observed Professor G. H. Palmer of Harvard,

> must be glad at heart when he visits a summer assembly of Chautauqua: there . . . attends the swiftly

[1] All kinds of schooling, whether in public or private schools or colleges, are included. These statistical years consist of ten months of twenty school days each. U. S. Comr. of Educ., *Rep. for 1899-1900*, I, xvi.

[2] H. B. Adams, "Chautauqua: a Social and Educational Study," U. S. Comr. of Educ., *Rep. for 1894-95*, I, 977-1077; J. H. Vincent, *The Chautauqua Movement* (Boston, 1886); Ellwood Hendrick, *Lewis Miller* (N. Y., 1925), chaps. xxi-xxiii; L. H. Vincent, *John Heyl Vincent* (N. Y., 1925), chaps. xi-xiii; J. L. Hurlbut, *The Story of Chautauqua* (N. Y., 1921).

successive Round Tables upon Milton, Temperance, Geology, the American Constitution, the Relations of Science and Religion, and the Doctrine of Rent; perhaps assists at the Cooking School, the Prayer Meeting, the Concert, and the Gymnastic Drill; or wanders under the trees among the piazzaed cottages, and sees the Hall of Philosophy and the wooden Doric Temple shining on their little eminences.[1]

At the annual assemblies the best scholars of this and other countries gave courses, and for many years Professor William Rainey Harper of Yale, later president of the University of Chicago, served as director of instruction. To supplement the summer offerings the Literary and Scientific Circle was formed in 1878, involving a plan of reading and study lasting four years and carried on in books most of which were especially written for the purpose. By 1892 one hundred thousand students were enrolled in the Circle, half of them between thirty and forty years of age. These and innumerable others were reached also by the *Chautauquan,* a monthly magazine established in 1880. For more ambitious students the Chautauqua College of Liberal Arts was organized in 1888 to afford an opportunity to secure a bachelor's degree by means of a four-year combination of resident, extension and correspondence study.

The parent Chautauqua proved to be a prolific mother. Led by Petoskey, Michigan, and Clear Lake, Iowa, in 1877, outdoor assemblies of one or two weeks' duration were conducted in various localities until about seventy were in operation at the close of the century, representing nearly every state in the Union. "To find a popular movement so composite and aspiring," declared Professor Palmer, "we must go back to the mediaeval

1 G. H. Palmer, "Doubts about University Extension," *Atlantic Mo.,* LXIX (1892), esp. 369-370.

Crusades or the Greek mysteries." [1] If these minor Chautauquas presented somewhat less serious programs than their progenitor, they nevertheless served as yeast to small-town intellectual life and inspired many a parent to "pathetic sacrifices . . . in the next generation to send the boys and girls to a real college." [2]

During the winter "star courses" or lecture series—survivals of the once powerful lyceum movement—were offered in most small and many large towns, featuring a wide variety of inspirational speakers, authors, politicians and entertainers. [3] On such programs no one was more welcome than John L. Stoddard whose "travel talks" afforded fascinating glimpses of foreign peoples and customs and whose colored lantern slides were rivaled only by the lecturer's splendor of diction. Stoddard it was who introduced the now familiar double stereopticon by which each picture dissolves magically into the one succeeding. Other favorites were the humorists Mark Twain, Edgar Wilson ("Bill") Nye and James Whitcomb Riley; George W. Cable who interspersed his Creole tales with haunting Creole melodies; the Norwegian violinist Ole Bull; and the Reverend Russell H. Conwell of Philadelphia, whose fame was inseparably identified in the public mind with his lecture, "Acres of Diamonds." [4]

[1] These supplementary Chautauquas are listed, with brief historical accounts, in U. S. Comr. of Educ., *Rep. for 1891-92*, II, 937-945. See also Vincent, *Chautauqua Movement*, 289-301; Hurlbut, *Story of Chautauqua*, chap. xxiv; H. A. Orchard, *Fifty Years of Chautauqua* (Cedar Rapids, 1923), chaps. iii-iv.

[2] Palmer, "Doubts about University Extension," 370.

[3] C. F. Horner, *The Life of James Redpath and the Development of the Modern Lyceum* (N. Y., 1926), chap. xv; W. M. Emery, "John L. Stoddard of Yesterday and Today," *Boston Transcript*, Feb. 5, 1927.

[4] The theme of "Acres of Diamonds" was that people listening to tales of "easy money" to be had far away are apt to neglect the opportunities at their very door. Between 1861 and 1913 it was delivered five thousand times. Says his admiring biographer, "Little did he foresee how it would affect the lives of thousands upon thousands of people;

Of more lasting value for the diffusion of culture was the multiplication of public libraries. Though dating back to mid-century, tax-supported free libraries had remained few in number outside of certain Eastern cities. Neither in these nor in college and society libraries did proper catalogues exist to indicate the contents of the collections, and the tired ex-teacher or ex-preacher who served as librarian was usually more interested in hoarding books than in having them used. But all this was forced to change as an eager public stormed the reading rooms and demanded untrammeled access to the republic of the printed word. In 1876 a group of progressive librarians, meeting in Philadelphia, formed the American Library Association, which thereafter proceeded aggressively to foster the ideal of providing "the best reading for the largest number at the least expense."[1] Leaders in this body—such as Justin Winsor of the Harvard Library, F. W. Poole of the Chicago Public, Charles Cutter of the Boston Athenaeum and Melvil Dewey, librarian at Columbia—were responsible for developing those ingenious methods of cataloguing, shelf classification and book circulation, which have helped make the American library the most efficient in the world.

At the same time the establishment of new libraries was promoted by both public and private agencies. Between 1878 and 1898 eighteen commonwealths authorized the use of taxation for such purposes, and in 1895 New Hampshire went so far as to make its permissive law obligatory.[2] Private munificence for library

nor the influence it would have upon the industries of this country." Agnes R. Burr, *Russell H. Conwell and His Work* (Phila., 1917), chaps. xxxi-xxxiv, 405-438.

[1] Melvil Dewey, "The American Library Association," *Library Journ.* (N. Y.), I (1876-1877), 247.

[2] Sixteen states already had permissive laws before 1878, most of them enacted after 1871. Dexter, *History of Education*, 484-485.

construction is inseparably connected with the name of
the steel magnate, Andrew Carnegie, whose first benefactions went in 1881 to the city of Pittsburgh and near-
by towns. Widening his field of activity, he presently
paid for the erection of buildings in many parts of the
country, stipulating only that a site be furnished and
maintenance provided by taxation. By the end of 1898
he had given nearly six million dollars to the cause, a
mere hint, however, of what was to follow.[1] Carnegie,
though the greatest giver, was not the only one. During
the two decades a total of not less than thirty-six million
dollars was contributed for library purposes. Some
donors, like Enoch Pratt who gave a million to Baltimore and Samuel J. Tilden who in 1886 bequeathed
most of his estate to New York City, helped create new
foundations. Others, like Mrs. John M. Reid who presented the German historian Leopold von Ranke's
library of twenty thousand books and manuscripts to
Syracuse University, greatly enriched existing collections.[2]

The climax of this age of unexampled library expansion came in the closing years. In 1895 the Astor,
Lenox and Tilden libraries—each the product of private
bounty—united to form the great New York Public
Library and plans were made for adequate housing of
the collections. The same year Boston opened its new
two-million-dollar building to the public, a pleasing
edifice in Roman Renaissance style facing Richardson's
noble Trinity Church across Copley Square. Chicago
followed in 1897 with an impressive building in the
classical mode, erected on the lake front at a cost of two

[1] T. W. Koch, *A Book of Carnegie Libraries* (White Plains, 1917);
H. U. Faulkner, *The Quest for Social Justice* (*A History of American
Life*, XI), 279-280.
[2] Adolph Rein, "Nachricht über Rankes Bibliothek," *Historische Vier-
teljahrsschrift*, XXIV (1928), 253-254.

million. The same year the Library of Congress was removed from its cramped quarters in the Capitol to a splendid new structure built in Italian Renaissance style, costing over six million dollars and possessing a floor space of over thirteen acres.[1] It was the largest and costliest library building in the world—a generous, if somewhat belated, recognition by the federal government of the central importance of books in American culture.

By 1900 the total number of free circulating libraries of all kinds, possessing three hundred or more volumes, had grown to over nine thousand, more than half of them being located in the Middle and Far West.[2] The number of volumes in these collections had increased in twenty-five years from twelve million to nearly forty-seven. A Massachusetts inquiry revealed that library patrons, especially in rural towns, were generally young people, and that in such places the taste ran more strongly to "books of a high class" than in large centers.[3] When Luther Burbank in 1868, at the age of nineteen, read a book by Darwin, which he had discovered at the Lancaster, Massachusetts, public library, he received an impulse which, he tells us, was "probably the turning point of my career in fixing my life work in the production of new species and varieties of plant life." [4] Thirty years later there was scarcely an American community, save in parts of the South, in which the library did not stand ready to perform a similar service for eager and talented youths. It had "come to be recognized as no less im-

[1] Herbert Putnam, "The Library of Congress," *Atlantic Mo.,* LXXXV (1900), 145-158.

[2] U. S. Comr. of Educ., *Rep. for 1899-1900,* I, 939.

[3] E. B. Tillinghast, "Books and Readers in Public Libraries," *Forum,* XVI (1893-1894), 61.

[4] Emma B. Beeson, *The Early Life and Letters of Luther Burbank* (San Fran., 1927), 74.

portant than the schoolhouse in the system of popular education." [1]

Although libraries spread the habit of reading books, most people did not freely patronize bookstores. This situation was ascribed by publishers to lack of enterprise on the part of retailers, but a more important cause was the antiquated system of distributing books to the trade. Semiannual auctions were held in New York where large purchasers were able to buy their supplies from publishers at extremely low figures and subsequently sell the volumes to the public at cut-rate prices. This system was a special boon to department stores whose practice of "book butchering" caused a running fire of complaint throughout these years in the pages of the *Publishers' Weekly,* the main trade organ. [2] Such stores often sold books at an actual loss in order to attract customers for other articles. In smaller places like Madison, Wisconsin, and Los Angeles people had no choice but to buy their books at shops dealing mainly in other wares. In the latter city a drygoods store in 1885 announced that every purchaser of six pair of lisle hose might, for ten cents additional, have his selection of their stock of novels. [3]

Bad methods of distribution accounted also for the continued vogue of subscription selling by house-to-house canvassers. The largest of such firms was Baird & Dillon of Chicago whose sales in 1883 amounted to over a million dollars. [4] They employed fifteen hundred canvassers and had agents in fifteen thousand towns

[1] R. G. Thwaites, "Ten Years of American Library Progress," *Library Journ.,* XXV (1900), no. 8, 3. In 1875 there were in libraries twenty-five volumes per hundred of population; in 1900, fifty-nine.

[2] See also J. H. Dingman, "American Bookselling and Booksellers," *Dial,* XXVIII (1900), 345-346.

[3] C. D. Warner, *Studies in the South and West* (N. Y., 1889), 173-175; *Publishers' Wkly.,* XXVII, 733 (June 27, 1885).

[4] *Publishers' Wkly.,* XXVI, 33 (July 12, 1884).

and cities. While the business was ordinarily confined to standard sets, dictionaries and encyclopedias, Mark Twain had found the method paid so well in the case of his earlier books that in 1884 he organized his own subscription house. His first offering, *The Adventures of Huckleberry Finn*, had forty thousand orders before it was ready for delivery. His greatest coup, U. S. Grant's *Memoirs*, written or dictated by the old warrior as he lay slowly dying, sold more than three hundred thousand sets of two volumes each, and netted the ex-president's widow around four hundred and twenty-five thousand dollars.[1]

Both subscription selling and book auctions declined in importance in the last years of the century. As the trade became better organized through a system of fixed discounts, retailers developed the habit of ordering from traveling salesmen or through one of the great jobbing houses, such as A. C. McClurg & Company of Chicago or the Baker & Taylor Company in New York. While the department store continued to hamper an extensive development of independent bookshops, on the other hand, by its hustling salesmanship, it accustomed this generation to think of literature as ordinary merchandise —something within the reach of all—and thus greatly stimulated book buying.

Though book knowledge had never before constituted so large a part of the common intellectual stock, the mental world of the average man continued in large measure to consist of a *mélange* of information, lore and gossip culled from the periodical press. Even the magazines catered to the most diverse tastes. If the score of years from 1878 to 1898 did little to increase their

[1] "The first check of $200,000, drawn Feb. 27, 1886, remains the largest single royalty check in history." For Clemens's publishing activities and the eventual failure of the firm in 1894, see A. B. Paine, *Mark Twain* (N. Y., 1912), II, chaps. cxlix, cliii-clvi, clix, clxiv.

variety, it added to their number and adapted their manner and matter better to the stratified reading public. Monthly periodicals increased from about twelve hundred to eighteen hundred, while their more sedate quarterly contemporaries grew from about one hundred to well over two hundred.[1] The chief gains occurred in periodicals devoted to transportation, business (including trade journals) and fraternal organizations. Magazines for general readers were less remarkable for their growth in number than, as we shall see, for their greatly expanded circulations.

Of the better-class periodicals this generation could hardly improve upon those it had inherited from earlier years: *Harper's Monthly,* the *Atlantic* and *Scribner's Monthly* (changed to the *Century* in 1881 when the Scribner interests withdrew). An enlarging clientèle, however, made it possible for Charles Scribner's Sons to launch in 1887 a new monthly of similar appeal, *Scribner's Magazine.* Distinguished in typography, dignified in tone, careful in diction, these journals, the *Atlantic* excepted, also took special pride in their illustrations. Indeed, the triangular rivalry was responsible for important improvements in the art of engraving and the technique of printing pictures. On the literary side they were aided by continuity of editorial policy, Richard Watson Gilder serving throughout these years as editor of the *Century,* as did H. M. Alden and E. L. Burlingame respectively of *Harper's* and *Scribner's Magazine.*[2] A citizen attained a certain prestige merely by having one of these periodicals on his library table.

---

[1] W. S. Rossiter, "Printing and Publishing," *U. S. Twelfth Census* (1900), IX, 1045, gives these and other data cited.

[2] Though the *Atlantic* had three editors—W. D. Howells (1871-1881), T. B. Aldrich (1881-1890) and H. E. Scudder (1890-1898) —an examination of its files reveals no change in editorial policy or standards.

Though clearly partial to long serialized biographies and heavy descriptive articles, the editors were yet ever on the alert for new writers and fresh themes. George W. Cable, Frank R. Stockton, Charles Egbert Craddock (Mary N. Murfree), W. D. Howells, F. Marion Crawford, Joel Chandler Harris, Henry James, Thomas Nelson Page, Ruth McEnery Stuart, Richard Harding Davis and, among foreign contributors, Rudyard Kipling, Joseph Conrad and Gilbert Parker—such a list suggests the throng of authors whose fictional wares were retailed to the public by these journals. All contributors, however, were required to conform to certain canons of "good taste," difficult to define but natural to persons of fastidious breeding; editorial lapses in this regard brought prompt reprisals from indignant subscribers.[1] Even the manuscripts of Howells, James and Edmund C. Stedman, and of course those of the irrepressible Mark Twain, were subjected to such treatment, usually without protest from the authors. When, however, Gilder cut out certain dubious passages in "Pudd'nhead Wilson," the long-suffering author burst into a torrent of wrath.

A sudden access of prosperity came to the *Century* when in November, 1884, it began the publication of a succession of Civil War narratives by leading commanders on the two sides, a feat which required two

---

[1] On this whole subject, see L. F. Tooker, *The Joys and Tribulations of an Editor* (N. Y., 1924), chap. vi, 180-188; R. U. Johnson, *Remembered Yesterdays* (N. Y., 1923), 124-131; Richard Watson Gilder, *Letters* (Rosamond Gilder, ed., Boston, 1916), chap. xi; Algernon Tassin, *The Magazine in America* (N. Y., 1916), 321-336; J. L. Ford, *Forty-Odd Years in the Literary Shop* (N. Y., 1921), 118-121; Bernard DeVoto, "Mark Twain and the Genteel Tradition," *Harvard Graduates' Mag.*, XL (1931), 155-163. Once when Gilder wrote a commencement poem for Smith College, some wags in the *Century* office gave him an uncomfortable half-hour by sending him a telegram, purporting to come from a Smith professor, which read: "Faculty doubt morality of fourth stanza. Can it be changed?" Johnson, *Remembered Yesterdays,* 93-94.

years for completion. Whether due to the appeal to half-forgotten memories, the fame of the contributors or the curiosity of a new generation grown old since Appomattox, the series was a spectacular success, swelling the circulation from one hundred and twenty-five thousand to two hundred and fifty. But in the fall of 1886, when the elated editors sought to repeat the coup with the first installment of Nicolay and Hay's monumental life of Lincoln—paying fifty thousand dollars for the full serial rights—the subscription list steadily shrank as the ponderous narrative, "apparently facing eternity," clogged its pages for nearly three and a half years.[1]

Magazines for special constituencies were legion. For critical literary appraisals the reader found one of his ablest mentors in a Chicago publication, the *Dial*, founded in 1880 under the editorship of Francis F. Browne. The *Overland Monthly*, revived in 1882 after six years' suspension, served the wide reaches of the Pacific West with reading matter of a robust type. *Outing*, begun the same year, performed a similar function for lovers of sport. For those seeking a longer-range view of current events than that afforded by the newspapers, four well-conducted magazines appeared: *Public Opinion* in 1886, *Current Literature* two years later, and in 1890 the *Literary Digest* and the *American Review of Reviews*, the last an American version of a British journal. Older weeklies like the *Nation*, *Independent* and *Outlook* (known until 1893 as the *Christian Union*) continued to survey analytically the passing scene, the two latter from a religious angle.[2] But in impatience and crusading zeal they were outstripped by two new monthlies, the

---

[1] Tooker, *Joys and Tribulations*, 45-46, 77-79, 255-257, 304-308; Johnson, *Remembered Yesterdays*, 189-208.

[2] J. F. Muirhead considered these three weeklies superior to any of a similar kind in England. *The Land of Contrasts* (N. Y., 1898), 159.

Forum (1886) and the *Arena* (1889), whose ardent course prepared the way for the Muckrakers of the twentieth century. A flock of new publications bespoke the widening interests of women who no longer needed to content themselves with old-fashioned journals of the *Godey* type. Of such magazines none was so influential as the *Ladies' Home Journal*. Established in 1883 by Cyrus H. K. Curtis, it began its astonishing success six years later when Edward W. Bok, an aggressive journalist of Dutch birth, took the editorial helm.[1] Bok, without neglecting familiar household concerns, introduced many fresh features: fiction by the best writers, articles on interesting personalities of the world, attractive illustrations, inexpensive house plans, and special departments like "Ruth Ashmore's Side Talks with Girls" which brought an average of ten thousand letters a year from maidens troubled with affairs of the heart. And for such riches the reader paid but ten cents a copy. A feminine rather than a feminist magazine, the *Ladies' Home Journal* not only kept in stride with the intelligent middle-class woman, but walked several paces ahead.

Bok's success called attention to the existence of a mass of readers, suckled largely on newspapers, whom fiction magazines selling at twenty-five and thirty-five cents had never been able to reach. What Bok had done to interest women, might not others do for this greater public of both sexes? New manufacturing processes, large-scale production and the possibility of unusual advertising revenues suggested the means of accomplishment. Armed with this bold idea and savings of seventy-three hundred dollars, Samuel S. McClure in 1893 launched a new periodical, *McClure's*, which sold for

[1] E. W. Bok, *The Americanization of Edward Bok* (N. Y., 1920), chaps. xv-xviii.

but fifteen cents a copy. Within a few months *Munsey's* and the *Cosmopolitan* went him one better, lowering their rates to ten cents.[1] The great popularity which all of them achieved rested almost as much on their ability to attract able authors and illustrators and on the crisp manner of writing as on the low cost to readers. Ida M. Tarbell's careful articles on Napoleon and Abraham Lincoln in 1894 and 1895 helped increase the circulation of *McClure's* by the tens of thousands. By 1898 the popular-priced magazine had enlarged the number of magazine buyers from about five hundred thousand to nearly three million.[2]

The cheap periodical emphasized a tendency noticeable in the more expensive journals, a trend away from pedantic prose and literary attitudinizing toward a warmly human treatment of life and its interests. A review of magazine literature for the two decades reveals a marked decline of the polite essay and of the old-fashioned travel sketch, a gain in the number of timely articles, and a notable increase of short stories.[3] To magazines was largely due the rise of the short story to its significant place in American letters. Moreover, there was hardly an important novel which did not first find publication in their pages. By this means the author not only reached a wider audience but also assured himself a competence. As Howells and others pointed out, literary earnings came mainly from serialization, and "the prosperity of the magazines has given

---

[1] S. S. McClure, *My Autobiography* (N. Y., 1914), chap. vii; same author, "An Open Letter," *Haldeman-Julius Wkly.*, no. 1475, 4 (March 8, 1924). The *Cosmopolitan* had been founded by John Brisben Walker in 1886; *Munsey's* by Frank A. Munsey in 1891.

[2] F. A. Munsey, "Advertising in Some of Its Phases," *Munsey's*, XX (1898-1899), 480.

[3] See A. R. Kimball, "The Invasion of Journalism," *Atlantic Mo.*, LXXXVI (1900), esp. 123-124; W. D. Howells, *Literature and Life* (N. Y., 1902), 26-27; also later, 199, 201.

a whole class existence which, as a class, was wholly un-known" in America before the Civil War. The return from book sales was merely "so much money found in the road."[1] Just as more people read magazines than books, so a greater number read newspapers than magazines. The nineteenth-century American had long since come to regard the newspaper as second only to the church and the school in importance; indeed, in many a pioneer settlement it leaped into lusty manhood while the other two were still gasping for birth. The sweep of population into the Great West, the gargantuan growth of cities and the increasing literacy of the masses now afforded newspapers new areas for conquest. The result was seen in a multiplication of papers, tremendous competition in news gathering and a growing vulgarization of the press. Between 1880 and 1900 the number of dailies advanced from 971 to 2226, and the weeklies and semiweeklies—published chiefly in rural towns—from less than nine thousand to nearly fourteen thousand. At the latter date the United States was fathering more than half the newspapers in the world. Yet the growth of subscribers outstripped even the increase of journals.[2]

While the newspapers clustered most thickly in the states possessing large cities, the two new commonwealths carved out of Dakota contained twenty-five dailies and three hundred and fifteen weeklies at the close of the

[1] Toward the close of the period magazine remuneration to authors varied from five or six dollars a thousand words for beginners to $150 for veterans. Howells, *Literature and Life*, 7-9, 11. See also edit., "Authors' Incomes," *Publishers' Wkly.*, XXVII, 732 (June 27, 1885); and G. P. Lathrop, "Reward of Authorship in America," same mag., XXX, 523-524 (Oct. 9, 1886).

[2] In 1880 there were two copies of a newspaper issued for every three persons; twenty years later there were two copies for each individual. For these and other data cited in the text, see Rossiter, "Printing and Publishing," 1037-1119.

century, and even Oklahoma territory could boast of
nine daily papers and nearly a hundred weeklies. Indeed
it is worth recalling that, though the dynamic forces in
journalism emanated from the cities, the average American remained addicted to a weekly or semiweekly journal. As late as 1900 forty-two and a half million took
such papers as compared with fifteen million who bought
dailies.[1] The country weekly of 1900 was, however, a
far different sheet from its counterpart of twenty years
before.

The character of metropolitan journalism was determined in part by the rapid pace and high tension everywhere manifest in city life and in part by the presence
of vast multitudes who had but freshly mastered the art
of reading. To command a large circulation the presentation of news must be terse, colorful, entertaining,
dramatic. It must interest, but not too long detain, and,
withal, afford the reader a romantic respite from the
daily grind. Equally important was the discovery that, as
a source of revenue, subscribers were less important than
advertisers. At the opening of the period income from
subscriptions and sales still provided well over half the
total; but with the tremendous growth of retail stores
and nation-wide merchandising, advertising had by the
early 1890's come to provide the major share.[2] Not that
the newspapers could afford to neglect subscribers, but
big circulations were more important as a means
of prying up advertising rates than for their own
sake.

As vast business undertakings the larger papers grew
more and more to reflect the opinions of the intrenched
interests represented by their owners and leading ad-

[1] The figures for 1880 were sixteen and a half million for weeklies
and semiweeklies and three and a half million for dailies. Rossiter,
"Printing and Publishing," 1046.
[2] Rossiter, "Printing and Publishing," 1042, 1044.

vertisers. The journalism of these two decades thus presents the apparent paradox of an editorial policy tending to become spineless or conservative while the treatment of day-by-day news became increasingly sensational. No generalization, however, could fit so diversified a world. Organs like the *New York Evening Post* and the *Boston Transcript* made few concessions to the moronic mentality of the enlarged reading public, journals like the *Chicago Daily News* and the *Kansas City Star* battled for the common weal without regard to advertising revenue, while the advent of persons like Pulitzer, Hearst and Melville E. Stone showed it was still possible for vigorous men to imprint their personalities on even mammoth newspaper enterprises.

Of the new generation of editors Joseph Pulitzer occupied the center of the stage for most of the period. His career illustrates some of the best as well as some of the worst phases of journalistic practice.[1] Born in Hungary, Pulitzer had come to America in 1864 at the age of seventeen, penniless and friendless. Going soon after to St. Louis, he quickly made himself a force in the community, doing newspaper work for Carl Schurz, mixing in politics and being ever active for civic betterment. In 1878 he acquired the *Post-Dispatch* which under his militant direction became the principal evening paper of the city and earned him the money with which to try his fortunes in a wider field. In 1883 he bought the rundown *New York World* from Jay Gould—an event from which dates the rise of modern American journalism.

Declaring in the first issue that his efforts would be "dedicated to the cause of the people rather than that of

[1] D. C. Seitz, *Joseph Pulitzer* (N. Y., 1924), chaps. iv-x; J. L. Heaton, *The Story of a Page* (N. Y., 1913), chaps. i-xii; Alleyne Ireland, *Joseph Pulitzer* (N. Y., 1914)—a personal portrait by his secretary.

purse-potentates," [1] he frankly directed his appeal to the toiling masses, shrewdly suiting the form and content of his paper to their mental capacity and tastes. "Human interest" was emphasized in the day's news; illustrations, including diagrams showing "X—where the body was found," lent variety; headlines such as "Death Rides the Blast" and "Baptized in Blood" arrested attention. An ardent supporter of Cleveland in 1884, he published the first series of political cartoons ever appearing in an American newspaper, "picturized editorials" four or five columns wide, drawn by Walt McDougall and Valerian Gribayédoff.

He plunged with crusading zeal into every manner of humanitarian cause. In the years 1885 and 1886, for instance, the World exposed the bribery of New York aldermen in connection with the Broadway street-car franchise, it bared the white-slave traffic carried on by a self-styled astrologer and, when Congress failed to make an appropriation, it induced one hundred and twenty thousand persons to subscribe a hundred thousand dollars for a pedestal for Bartholdi's colossal Statue of Liberty in New York Harbor. [2] His addition of a colored supplement to the Sunday edition in 1893 caused another leap in sales and, by means of R. F. Outcault's portrayal of "The Yellow Kid" and child

[1] Signed statement in N. Y. World, May 11, 1883. His platform of reform, announced on May 17, called for taxation of luxuries, inheritances, large incomes and privileged corporations; reform of the tariff and of the civil service; and the punishment of corrupt officials, vote buyers and employers who coerced employees in elections.

[2] Pulitzer also set a new pace for journalism in the grand manner when he commissioned a reporter "Nellie Bly" (Elizabeth Cochrane) to outdo Jules Verne's hero in Around the World in Eighty Days. Leaving Hoboken on Nov. 14, 1889, she girdled the globe in 72 days, 6 hours, 11 minutes and 14 seconds, her return on Jan. 25 being greeted by the screeching of sirens and the booming of cannon. She lost one day by stopping to interview Verne at his home in Amiens. See Elizabeth Cochrane, Nellie Bly's Book: Around the World in Seventy-Two Days (N. Y., 1890).

life in "Hogan's Alley," paved the way for the coming of colored comics. It was largely due to Pulitzer that the Sunday newspaper became the remarkable cyclopedia of fact, fiction, fun and folly so characteristic of our own era.[1] Even when ill health and increasing blindness forced him to spend much time abroad, he nevertheless continued aggressively to direct the *World's* policies.

When Pulitzer acquired the *World* it had à daily circulation of fifteen thousand. Within a year this number grew to more than sixty thousand, and by 1898 it passed the million mark.[2] Pulitzer's course was a beacon light to newspapers in all parts of the country. In Detroit the *Evening News,* launched in 1873 by James E. Scripps, found sensational methods so effective that between 1878 and 1881 his brother, E. W. Scripps, set up journals of the same type in Cleveland, St. Louis and Cincinnati. By somewhat similar means the *Chicago Daily News,* established in 1875, advanced its circulation from fifty thousand in 1881 to one hundred and thirty thousand in 1890. As evening papers, moreover, such journals were able to make a special appeal to office workers and wage-earners when the long day's work was done, thus opening up a fresh field for newspaper enterprise.

Meanwhile a wealthy young Californian, enrolled at Harvard from 1883 to 1885, had been so captivated by the success of Pulitzer's methods that on his return home he induced his father to buy him the *San Francisco Examiner.* Emboldened by the results, he invaded

[1] The credit, or responsibility, really belonged to Morrill Goddard, Pulitzer's Sunday editor. Anon., "The Man Who Invented the Sunday Newspaper," *Am. Rev. of Revs.,* XXII (1900), 619.

[2] In September, 1886, when the circulation went beyond 250,000, a silver medal was struck off to commemorate "the largest circulation ever attained by an American newspaper."

the New York field in 1895 with the purchase of the
Morning Journal. William Randolph Hearst, this latest
gale out of the West to agitate Eastern journalism, there
set himself to outdo Pulitzer at his own game.[1] As
Pulitzer's *World* marked an advance in sensational methods over Charles A. Dana's *Sun*,[2] so Hearst's sensationalism now surpassed Pulitzer's in spite of all efforts of
the latter to keep pace. The struggle of the giants over
the publication rights of "The Yellow Kid"—resulting
in two series by different cartoonists being run simultaneously—gave coinage to the term by which their brand
of newspaper enterprise has ever since been known,
"yellow journalism."

The battle royal raged fiercely through the campaign
of 1896, Pulitzer condemning free silver while Hearst's
cartoonist, Homer Davenport, inflamed popular prejudice against the Republicans by portraying Mark Hanna,
McKinley's chief backer, as an ogrelike figure plastered
over with dollar signs. Their efforts reached a feverish
pitch as the Spanish-American War approached.[3] The
mysterious destruction of the *Maine* in Havana Harbor
caused the rival papers to break out in a rash of inch-
high type, page-wide streamer headlines, and blood-
curdling full-page pictures showing alleged Spanish
atrocities in Cuba. In the second week following the
explosion the *World's* circulation passed five million.
Hearst insistently called for armed intervention; and
though Pulitzer earlier had rebuked Cleveland for jingo-

[1] J. K. Winkler, *William Randolph Hearst* (N. Y., 1928), chaps.
iii-vii; Faulkner, *Quest for Social Justice*, 251-252.

[2] See Allan Nevins, *The Emergence of Modern America* (*A History
of American Life*, VIII), 240-241.

[3] In 1897 a party organized by the *Journal* effected the escape from
a Havana prison of Evangelina Cisneros, a young Cuban girl convicted
of treason. Winkler, *Hearst*, 147-151. The incident of the De Lôme
letter, published by the *Journal*, is too well known to require further
comment here. See J. F. Rhodes, *The McKinley and Roosevelt Administrations* (N. Y., 1922), 48-49.

HOW "DO YOU LIKE THE JOURNAL'S" WAR?

NEW YORK JOURNAL
AND ADVERTISER.

HOW DO YOU LIKE THE JOURNAL'S WAR?

NO. 3,852.   NEW YORK, SUNDAY, MAY 8, 1898.—64 PAGES.—Copyright, 1898, by W. R. Hearst.   PRICE FIVE CENTS

OUR VICTORIOUS FLEET

TWO DETAILED AMERICAN ACCOUNTS OF THE
GREAT BATTLE AT MANILA.---
FROM JOURNAL CORRESPONDENT JOHN T. M'CUTCH
ON BOARD THE UNITED STATES GUNBOAT M'CU
FROM JOURNAL CORRESPONDENT HENRY C. LADD,
OF HONG KONG, ALSO ON THE M'CUL

(Copyright, 1898, by W. R. Hearst.)
Special Cable to the New York Journal.
By *John T. McCutcheon, Journal Correspondent with Admiral Dewey's Squadron.*

HONG KONG, May 7.—This is the result of the great fight in Manila Bay:
Eleven Spanish ships destroyed.
Eight Spanish ships captured.
Four shore batteries at Cavite demolished.
Three forts on Corregidor Island reduced.
Four hundred Spaniards killed.
Six hundred Spaniards wounded.
Spanish supplies lost and captured to the amount of $5,000,000.
American loss:
Eight men slightly wounded.
One thousand dollars damage.
Those are the figures of victory. The story of the battle will live forever. The
its heroes can never die.
The fighting began at 5 o'clock in the morning.
...ship surrendered at 12:40 in ...afternoon.

New Journalism

ism at the time of the Venezuela boundary crisis, he now also demanded a "short and sharp" war.[1] "Nothing so disgraceful as the behavior" of these two papers, commented E. L. Godkin, "has been known in the history of American journalism."[2] Undoubtedly such melodramatic tactics, pursued primarily to boost sales, pushed the peace-loving McKinley into a war for objects which were already on the point of being gained untheatrically through the channels of diplomacy.

Enormous circulations with frequent editions and "extras" could not have been achieved without great improvements in the mechanics of manufacture. These years saw the introduction of larger and ever faster presses, color printing, quicker and cheaper methods of reproducing pictures (photolithography, the line-cut and half-tone processes), and a sharp reduction in the cost of print paper. By 1878 the typewriter was perfected, equipped at last to print both small and large letters,[3] and six years later L. E. Waterman placed on the market the first successful fountain pen—two conveniences which the new generation of reporters quickly adapted to their uses. Newspaper composition was transformed from a hand to a machine process in 1885 through Ottmar Mergenthaler's invention of the linotype, a mechanical marvel which, under the fingers of a skilled operator, cast from molten lead solid lines

[1] Signed edit. in *N. Y. World*, April 10, 1898.

[2] W. M. Bleyer, *Main Currents in the History of American Journalism* (Boston, 1927), 377. Pulitzer's sober second thought is revealed by instructions given to his editors in 1907 when President Roosevelt proposed to send battleships into the Pacific to impress Japan: "Show that Spain had granted to Cuba all that we demanded, but passion in Spain and here forced the hands of government. . . . Give further details of jingoism causing Cuban War after Spain had virtually granted everything . . . ." Seitz, *Pulitzer*, 312-313.

[3] This improvement was devised by Byron A. Brooks, a public-school teacher in New York City, and was at once bought by the Remingtons who incorporated it in a new model, Remington No. 2.

of type ready for printing, thus shortening the time required to put news into type.[1]

To secure greater efficiency and economy in "covering" the world's happenings newspapers found it advantageous to pool their resources. Though the New York Associated Press, which sold its service also to out-of-town papers, was already in the field, several news-gathering agencies arose and waged hot war with one another. One of these, the Western Associated Press, after a temporary alliance with the Eastern body, broke away in 1892, forming the Associated Press of Illinois. With Melville E. Stone as general manager it soon established its dominance in the national news-distributing field, driving its chief rival to the wall five years later.[2] Newspaper chains, foreshadowed by the activities of Pulitzer, took definite form when a league of Mid-Western papers was organized in the 1880's by the Scripps brothers.[3] The establishment of the Scripps-McRae Press Association in 1897 marked the entry of a new competitor of the Associated Press.

Hardly less important was the growth in the amount of syndicated material used by the press, a practice begun in 1884 when S. S. McClure, then on the *Century Magazine,* formed the first American agency for the purpose. By the early nineties the "S. S. McClure Newspaper Features" consisted of novels and short stories, articles on current topics by men in the public eye, a woman's page and a juvenile department; and there were rival syndicates in the field, notably one belonging to Edward

[1] Rossiter, "Printing and Publishing," 1092-1097; G. E. Barnett, "The Introduction of the Linotype," *Yale Rev.,* XIII (1904-1905), 251-273.

[2] The present-day Associated Press dates from a reorganization in 1900 under a New York charter. M. E. Stone, *Fifty Years a Journalist* (Garden City, 1921), 207-218, 235.

[3] M. A. McRae, *Forty Years in Newspaperdom* (N. Y., 1924), 21-79.

Bok.[1] Politicians were not slow to take the hint. In the
campaign of 1896 it is estimated that the Republican
national committee, by organizing its own syndicate
service, reached five million families every week with
arguments and caricatures against Bryanism and bi-
metallism.[2]

As a result of these various developments, newspaper
readers were kept abreast the passing show as never
before in American history. If a fifty-mile radius represented the approximate distance to which a city daily
had a general sale, there were twenty-one principal
newspaper-distribution areas in the United States, embracing a population of nearly nineteen and a half million or about a third of all the people in the nation.
Here were found three fourths of the dailies with the
greatest circulation.[3] At the same time the country press
moved closer into the orbit of metropolitan journalism,
and, seconded by the magazines, city standards and interests were ceaselessly dinned into the ears of the rural
audience—a telling example of urban imperialism in the
cultural sphere and indirectly the source of much rustic
unhappiness.

To foreigners the new journalism seemed a peculiarly
American phenomenon. "The whole character of the nation is there: spirit of enterprise, liveliness, childishness,
inquisitiveness, deep interest in everything that is human,
fun and humor, indiscretion, love of gossip, brightness,"
wrote Paul Blouët.[4] A more thoughtful European ob-

[1] McClure, *Autobiography*, 164-206; Rossiter, "Printing and Publishing," 1103-1104.
[2] W. B. Shaw, "Methods and Tactics of the Campaign," *Am. Rev.
of Revs.*, XIV (1896), esp. 555.
[3] Based on the census of 1890. See D. F. Wilcox, "The American
Newspaper," Am. Acad. of Polit. and Social Sci., *Annals*, XVI (1900),
59-61.
[4] Paul Blouët (Max O'Rell, *pseud.*), *A Frenchman in America*
(N. Y., 1891), 110.

server, however, deemed the ordinary journal fit only for the servants' hall.[1] Undoubtedly prying sensationalism robbed American life of much of its privacy to the gain chiefly of morbid curiosity. As an American journalist charged, from dieting on the press the "mind loses the power of discrimination, the taste is lowered, and the appetite becomes diseased."[2] Such sweeping appraisals, however, left out of account the enormous additions to the newspaper-reading public. Fifty years earlier the only literate class was that which in the 1880's and 1890's read papers like the *New York Times* and the *Boston Transcript;* the audience corresponding to that addressed by the yellow press did not read at all.

Nor was sensation-mongering without advantages to civic welfare. Pulitzer's zeal in exposing corruption and jarring public complacency was matched by the efforts of editors in scores of other cities. Bryce himself testified that in the war against boodling politicians "the newspapers of New York, Boston, Philadelphia and Chicago have been one of the most effective battalions."[3] Journalism, moreover, for the first time began to provide an important training school for authors. In the last two decades of the century the *New York Sun,* for example, numbered among its reporters Julian Ralph, David Graham Phillips, Will Irwin, Samuel Hopkins Adams, Jacob Riis and Richard Harding Davis.[4] These and many other young men in all parts of the country

---

[1] Herbert Spencer, *Civilization in the United States* (6th edn., Boston, 1900), 177-180. See Muirhead's similar verdict in *Land of Contrasts,* chap. ix.

[2] C. D. Warner, *The Relation of Literature to Life* (N. Y., 1897), 268-269 (an essay first published in 1890).

[3] Bryce, *American Commonwealth,* III, 41.

[4] On the staff of the *Chicago News* were George Harvey, George Ade, Slason Thompson, Finley Peter Dunne, Eugene Field, James Whitcomb Riley, Henry Guy Carleton and others. Stone, *Fifty Years,* 111-112.

climbed the first rungs of the literary ladder while grubbing for the day's news.

If income from advertising was one of the prime factors in remaking the periodical press, advertising also deserves notice for its own sake as a potent influence in American culture. Hitherto, outdoor signs and billboards had been the chief means of catching the eye of a people, many of whom did not regularly read newspapers.[1] "America is daubed from one end of the country to the other with huge white-paint notices of favorite articles of manufacture," wrote one observer.[2] The great cities were plastered and painted and papered with blaring notices, while the rural landscape where "every prospect pleases and only man is vile" suffered from the same misguided zeal. Bret Harte in 1876 wrote of one energetic concern:

> One Sabbath morn, as heavenward
> White Mountain tourists slowly spurred,
> On every rock, to their dismay,
> They read the legend all the way—
> SAPOLIO.[3]

Outdoor publicity showed no decline in the 1880's and 1890's, but advertisers centered their energies on reaching the hordes of newspaper and magazine readers.[4] Between 1880 and 1900 the amount of newspaper advertising increased from about forty million dollars

[1] Frank Presbrey, *The History and Development of Advertising* (Garden City, 1929), 366.

[2] G. W. Steevens, *The Land of the Dollar* (N. Y., 1897), 49-50. Similar comments may be found in O'Rell, *Frenchman in America*, 263; W. G. Marshall, *Through America* (London, 1882), 111-113; Muirhead, *Land of Contrasts*, 136.

[3] In a booklet designed to explain to dealers the unflagging enterprise of this particular soap company. Bret Harte's name did not appear. Presbrey, *Advertising*, 374.

[4] Other avenues were not neglected, however, such as mail-order catalogues, street-car signs, gas and electric signs and the use of novelties.

to nearly ninety-six.[1] An analysis of an ordinary week-day issue of ten leading dailies in different sections of the country in the mid-nineties showed that advertising occupied from twenty-five to seventy per cent of the space, or an average of forty per cent.[2] From the start the *Century* was an active advertising medium; and in 1882 *Harper's Magazine*, yielding its earlier compunctions, swung into line. By October, 1888, *Harper's* was carrying one hundred and ninety-three ads—a total of fifty-four pages—and by October, 1898, three hundred and thirty ads filling eighty-three pages.[3] The new *Scribner's* was one of the first to entice readers into the vast hinterland of its advertising section by spreading the disjected members of an illustrated comic through its length. Strangely enough, the several hundred religious journals found their most profitable source of revenue in the space devoted to patent medicines.

On the part of merchants and manufacturers, the new age entailed unprecedented and ever mounting expenditures of money and brains to capture and retain the fickle public. The makers of Sapolio, for instance, while content with an appropriation of fifteen thousand dollars in 1871, were spending seventy in 1885 and four hundred by 1896.[4] The old bill-posting traditions taught advertisers the importance of a crisp, striking phrase to

---

[1] Rossiter, "Printing and Publishing," 1042. In the early 1890's about a fourth of all advertising expenditure was still going into outdoor display. Presbrey, *Advertising*, 366, 394.

[2] F. W. Ayer, "Advertising in America," C. M. Depew, ed., *One Hundred Years of American Commerce* (N. Y., 1895), I, 78.

[3] See tables in S. A. Sherman, "Advertising in the United States," Am. Stat. Assoc., *Publs.*, n.s., VII, 122, 142-143. Sherman also analyzes periodical advertising in 1898 from the standpoint of number and distribution of general advertisers.

[4] Presbrey, *Advertising*, 394. It is to be noted, however, that the increase of advertising was attended by a decline in the number of drummers or traveling salesmen, though this was partly a result of the merger of competing companies. Sherman, "Advertising," 129, 157-158.

impale the fleeting attention of possible patrons. Even people who professed never to look at ads knew of Ivory Soap that "It Floats," of Castoria that "Children Cry for It," of the Eastman Kodak that "You Press the Button; We Do the Rest," and that Schlitz was "The Beer that Made Milwaukee Famous." The lineaments and fame of Dr. Munyon—"I Am for Men"—were familiar to many an illiterate mountaineer or foreign immigrant who might have fumbled at naming the chief executive of the nation.[1]

For the most part, both the advertising agencies and the publications in which the announcements appeared assumed the attitude of *caveat emptor*. This was frankly the position, for instance, of George P. Rowell & Company, a leading New York agency, though a certain measure of discretion resulted when they inadvertently inserted a notice of H. R. Stiles's *Bundling, Its Origin, Progress and Decline* in the pages of the *Churchman*.[2] A few men like John E. Powers, who in the 1880's directed publicity for Wanamaker's in Philadelphia, discovered that honesty in advertising pays. But the fact was not so evident to a periodical which derived its heaviest revenues from patent-medicine sources—and as late as 1898 such firms still comprised the most important group of general advertisers.[3] A different attitude, however, was evinced by the *Farm Journal*, founded at Philadelphia in 1877, which from the outset declined "quack medical advertisements at any price" and, three years later, inaugurated the first known guarantee against

---

[1] The devices of the advertiser were endless. When a canning establishment found that its salmon would not sell because of the whitish color, it reversed its fortunes by advertising: "Positively Guaranteed Not to Turn Pink."

[2] G. P. Rowell, *Forty Years an Advertising Agent* (N. Y., 1906), 382-383, and *passim*.

[3] Presbrey, *Advertising*, 295, 303-310, 363-364.

fraudulent representations.[1] After the *Ladies' Home Journal* in 1892 banned such ads, others of its contemporaries adopted the same policy. But no widespread benefit resulted until the early years of the next century when the Muckrakers began their career of pitiless exposure.[2]

Partly for weal and partly for woe, the new age of commercial publicity made a deep impress on American life. With advertising "playing upon the brain of man like a musician does upon a piano,"[3] the average citizen learned the blessings of frequent applications of soap and dentifrice, his dietary habits were influenced, and his standards of home decoration improved. He learned, in fact, what merchants with wares to sell thought should constitute the American standard of living. At the same time he was constantly being inveigled into ill-advised expenditures, when not actually gulled by misrepresentations, and his notions of personal therapy were violently distorted by the extravagant claims made for worthless or injurious medicines.

The American of the period could not escape being educated whether by the school or the multifarious other instrumentalities seeking to woo his thought and mold his will. What, then, was the content of the average American's mind in the 1880's and 1890's? What subjects excited his attention and what shifts of interest took place? In so far as a highest common denominator existed, it was probably implied by the way the newspaper press divided its space among various categories of news. This may be assumed whether one argues that newspapers reflect or seek to direct public opinion.

The accompanying table, though confined to an

[1] Wilmer Atkinson, *An Autobiography* (Phila., 1920), 161, 180.

[2] See Faulkner, *Quest for Social Justice*, 237-238, 255-256.

[3] Jacques Offenbach, *America and the Americans* (London, 1876), 51-52.

A testimonial advertisement.

The Hall of Philosophy—Chautauqua—The Golden Gate.

A great public library, Boston, Massachusetts.

Influencing the American Mind

ANALYSIS OF CONTENT OF SELECTED METROPOLITAN
DAILIES, 1878-1898 [1]

SHOWING THE ORDER OF IMPORTANCE AND PERCENTAGE OF SPACE
DEVOTED TO VARIOUS CATEGORIES OF NEWS

1878	%	1888	%	1898	%
1. Advertising	21.5	1. Advertising	29.8	1. Advertising	28.2
2. Government and politics	14.8	2. Government and politics	19.2	2. Government and politics	18.5
3. Foreign affairs	10.0	3. Business and finance	8.7	3. Business and finance	11.2
4. Business and finance	9.6	4. Editorials	6.1	4. Foreign affairs	6.5
5. Editorials	8.5	5. Transportation	4.7	5. Cultural interests	6.2
6. Cultural interests	7.9	6. Cultural interests	4.4	6. Editorials	5.0
7. Crimes and disasters	5.2	7. Crimes and disasters	4.1	7. Sports	4.2
8. Transportation	5.1	8. Foreign affairs	3.5	8. Women	3.2
9. Religion	2.5	9. Sports	3.2	9. Transportation	3.1
10. Education	2.1	10. Religion	3.1	10. Education	2.6
11. "Society"	1.8	11. Social welfare	2.2	11. Crimes and disasters	2.0
12. Labor	1.3	12. "Society"	2.1	12. Religion	1.6
13. Social welfare	1.1	13. Education	1.6	13. Social welfare	1.4
14. Agriculture	0.8	14. Labor	1.3	14. "Society"	1.2
15. Sports	0.6	15. Agriculture	0.8	15. Labor	0.4
16. Women	0.6	16. Women	0.3	16. Agriculture	.2

[1] Based upon an unpublished study made by Mr B. B Bouton of
Howe School, Howe, Indiana. The issues of the *New York Tribune*,
Chicago Tribune and *Boston Transcript* for Jan. 1, April 1, July 1
and Oct. 1 were examined for each of the years 1878, 1888 and 1898.
When articles belonged to more than one category an appropriate division was made. Cultural interests include the fine arts, literary items,
poetry and theatrical notices. In general, allowance needs to be made for
the fact that hard times directed unusual attention to business and
finance in 1878, that 1888 was a presidential-election year, and that war
news (the Balkans in 1878 and Cuba in 1898) temporarily increased
the space given to foreign affairs.

analysis of metropolitan dailies, reveals certain well-marked trends.[1] Through the two decades business and finance bulked ever larger in the common consciousness. Along with governmental and partisan interests these items accounted for from a fourth to almost a third of the time which the ordinary person gave to extramural concerns.[2] Foreign affairs were of small import save in times of war and rumors of war. Religion retreated before the rush of other interests, as did also the attention given labor questions, though the latter circumstance was probably due to the growing alliance of the press with the employing class. Urban cerebration in regard to agriculture sank almost to the vanishing point. On the contrary, consideration of women's concerns increased fourfold and of sports sevenfold. In general, the mental universe of the newspaper-reading citizen seemed more and more occupied with matters of material welfare, comfort and pleasure; and it is clear that the great energy which special groups were devoting to humanitarian reform, education, science, literature and the fine arts had as yet made relatively little dent on the mass mind.

These impressions are in large measure supported by the tendencies displayed in the better magazines. Designed for leisure-time perusal and for a more restricted clientèle, such periodicals, of course, gave their lion's share of space to fiction, poetry, literary criticism,

[1] If allowance is made for differences of classification, much the same conclusions are sustained by certain content studies made at the time: H. R. Elliot, "The Ratio of News," *Forum*, V (1888), 99-107, which analyzes issues of current newspapers in selected cities; J. G. Speed, "Do Newspapers Give the News?," *Forum*, XV (1893), 705-711, which compares Sunday editions of four New York dailies in 1881 and 1893; Wilcox, "American Newspaper," 56-92, an elaborate sampling analysis of the content of 240 different dailies in 1898 and 1899.

[2] From a third to over two fifths, if the space occupied by advertisements be disregarded.

history and travel.[1] Where their subject matter over-
lapped that of the newspaper press, however, similar
drifts of reader interest appear: an increasing absorption in current business and political affairs and in feminine welfare, variability in regard to foreign affairs, and
a declining curiosity as to religion, cultural subjects
(fine arts, music and the drama) and agriculture. Education, labor, science and invention, on the other hand,
fared somewhat better than in the dailies, while the vicarious excitement afforded by fiction may perhaps account
for the relative neglect of sports.

Despite all setbacks and shortcomings the educational
advance during the 1880's and 1890's was astonishing.
All parts of the country and all classes of society were
affected. Through the spread of schools, bookstores,
libraries, magazines and newspapers America had become, in Freeman's phrase, "the land of the general
reader," the home of the greatest reading public hitherto known in the history of the world.[2] If cultural
progress in a democracy depends upon a continuous
process of recruitment from the ranks of the many,
never before had America so ample an opportunity for
a forward push along all lines of intellectual endeavor.

[1] These categories account for about seventy per cent of the contents
in 1878 and 1888 and a little more than sixty per cent in 1898. This
analysis is based on an unpublished study of all issues of *Harper's Mo.*,
Atlantic Mo., *N. Am. Rev.*, *Lippincott's Mag.*, *Scribner's Mo.-Century*
and the *Overland Mo.* for the years 1878, 1888 and 1898, made by
Dr. R. L. Welty of Texas Christian University.

[2] E. A. Freeman, *Some Impressions of the United States* (N. Y.,
1883), 184-185.

CHAPTER VII

INCREASING THE WORLD'S KNOWLEDGE

NEW forces were at work in the colleges and universities as well as in the wider reaches of popular education. Not only did institutions of higher learning grow in number, endowment and quality of instruction, but for the first time they began to take seriously their obligation to enrich the world's store of knowledge. "Nothing more strikes a stranger who visits the American universities," declared an English scholar familiar with Oxford and Cambridge, "than the ardour with which the younger generation has thrown itself into study, even kinds of study which will never win the applause of the multitude." [1] By way of historical parallel observers were reminded of the brilliant days of the Italian Renaissance.

Colleges and universities increased from three hundred and fifty-odd in 1878 to nearly five hundred in 1898, the combined student body from about fifty-eight thousand to approximately one hundred thousand. [2] Mere growth in number of institutions, however, did not necessarily denote progress except on the theory of the misguided patriot who exulted, "There are two universities in England, four in France, ten in

[1] James Bryce, *The American Commonwealth* (London, 1888), III, 571. See also anon., "The American College," *Atlantic Mo.*, LXXV (1895), esp. 703.

[2] This was a more rapid growth of enrollment than of total population. U. S. Commissioner of Education, *Report for 1887-88*, 632, and later *Reports, passim.*

Prussia and thirty-seven in Ohio." Particularly in the rural South and the Middle West, the country was wretchedly overstocked with institutions making pretensions to the name of college or university, at a time when higher standards of instruction and research called for a concentration of funds. In 1881 the total income of all the colleges and universities in Ohio fell considerably short of that of Harvard alone.[1] Most institutions of this kind had been planted by denominational zeal, and catered to local rural constituencies. Once pioneers in the westward march of higher culture, they were now fallen on bitter times, for the state universities, with constantly increasing legislative support, superior equipment and richer curricula, were drawing away their students and undermining their position of influence. In many a Western and Southern state legislature the tax-maintained university won its appropriations only in the teeth of hardy opposition from those who decried its "godless" character.

But in an age of the glorification of public education such die-hards contended against the spirit of the times. Between 1885 and 1895 the number of students in eight representative state universities—Michigan, Illinois, Wisconsin, Minnesota, Iowa, Kansas, Nebraska and California—trebled, while the gain in eight equally reputable church schools of the Middle West was scarcely fifteen per cent. In the latter year there were more Presbyterian students in seventeen state universities than in the thirty-seven best Presbyterian colleges.[2]

[1] C. F. Smith, "Southern Colleges and Schools," *Atlantic Mo.*, LIV (1884), 544-547. Ohio was not the only sinner: Illinois had 25 colleges, Iowa 18, Indiana 16, Michigan 10. U. S. Comr. of Educ., *Rep. for 1887-88*, 1040-1041.

[2] F. W. Kelsey, "State Universities and Church Colleges," *Atlantic Mo.*, LXXX (1897), 826-832. See also A. A. Johnson, "The State Universities and Denominational Colleges," *Educ.*, XVI (1895-1896), 435-437.

Moreover, ten commonwealths of the West and South which, for one reason or another, had not earlier seen fit to set up their own universities now proceeded to do so.[1] To the University of Michigan more than any other was due the constant improvement in state-university standards during these years. One of the first to free herself from the hampering influence of politics, she vied with Eastern institutions in introducing new educational methods and was the first to link the public schools with the university by admitting graduates of accredited high schools without examination.[2]

When Emily Faithfull, the English social worker, visited the University of Michigan in 1883, she was told by President J. B. Angell that, though coeducation was still on trial in the East, the question was definitely settled in the West. Moreover, he assured her, "none of the ladies had found the curriculum too heavy for their physical endurance . . . ."[3] All the new state universities in the West and South, as a matter of course, were coeducational and the strength of the tide was such that most of the Southern state institutions which had hitherto held aloof now succumbed.[4] While the practice continued to be less common in the older parts of the nation than in the West, the proportion of mixed colleges in the United States grew from fifty-one per cent

[1] South Dakota, 1882; North Dakota and Texas, 1883; Nevada and Wyoming, 1886; Idaho, 1889; Arizona and New Mexico, 1891; Oklahoma, 1892; and Montana, 1895.

[2] G. E. Howard, "The State University in America," *Atlantic Mo.*, LXVII (1891), esp. 340; Sara A. Burstall, *The Education of Girls in the United States* (London, 1894), chap. vi.

[3] Emily Faithfull, *Three Visits to America* (Edinburgh, 1884), 56-58. Thomas Woody, *A History of Women's Education in the United States* (J. M. Cattell, ed., *Science and Education*, IV, N. Y., 1929), bk. ii, chaps. iv-vi, is the fullest treatment of the subject.

[4] Only the state universities of Virginia, Georgia and Louisiana declined to change. E. G. Dexter, *A History of Education in the United States* (N. Y., 1904), 446-447.

in 1880 to seventy per cent in 1898, and the number of women students from twenty-seven hundred and fifty to more than twenty-five thousand.[1] To meet the challenge of coeducation the East established new women's colleges of high rank and improved existing ones. Thus Bryn Mawr, near Philadelphia, was opened in 1885 with ample resources and excellent scientific equipment, while three years later Mount Holyoke Seminary was converted into a college with degree-granting powers. Most interesting of all was the grudging compromise by certain men's institutions, of setting up affiliated colleges for the other sex—coöperation without entanglement—after the manner of Oxford and Cambridge. Starting in 1879 with twenty-seven students, an organization, informally known as the Harvard Annex, enrolled studious young women who, under the guidance of such professors as William James, John Knowles Paine and Ephraim Emerton, were enabled to take the same courses as the men at Harvard, though not in their company. By the time this undertaking ripened into Radcliffe College (1894), Tulane University, Western Reserve and Columbia had created coördinate women's colleges and Brown University was in the course of so doing. By 1898 four out of every five colleges, universities and professional schools in the United States admitted women. Their right to as complete and diversified an education as men was no longer seriously questioned.

Meanwhile the old-fashioned, hard-and-fast college course was everywhere rapidly crumbling under the hammering blows inflicted by President Charles W. Eliot of Harvard and his like. However valid were the

[1] In calculating the proportions, separate women's colleges were not included. U. S. Comr. of Educ., Rep. for 1889-90, II, 764; for 1900-01, I, xlix.

pedagogical reasons for the elective system, the reform was in any case inevitable because of the great advances in science and scholarship and the sheer impossibility of a student's taking in four years all the courses offered. The world had changed; and as life itself became more diverse, more complex, it was fitting that education, as a preparation for life, should take on greater richness and variety. The elective system, moreover, was the practice of German universities where many American professors had studied. At Harvard freedom of election went farthest; in most other places the principle of liberty in the choice of subjects was introduced gradually, the first two years being largely prescribed with options thereafter.[1]

Under the new plan the college curriculum offered a variety of appeal which accounts in part for the swelling stream of students.[2] The time-honored courses in Latin, Greek and mathematics lost favor in competition with such newer subjects as English literature, certain laboratory sciences, modern languages, history, economics and political science.[3] While critics deplored an irrational scattering of choices by students and a tendency to concentrate on "snap" courses, Dean LeB. R. Briggs maintained, after many years' experience, that, "as a body, the students of Harvard College use the elective system with some sense of responsibility and with reasonable

[1] U. S. Comr. of Educ., *Rep. for 1883-84*, clviii; D. R. Phillips, "The Elective System in American Education," *Pedagogical Seminary*, VIII (1901), 206-230.

[2] The elective system took the curse off coeducation for many parents who would have been unwilling to let their daughters take the traditional prescribed course for men. Annie N. Meyer, ed., *Woman's Work in America* (N. Y., 1891), 76-77. A synoptic view of courses of study in over a hundred colleges is given in U. S. Comr. of Educ., *Rep. for 1888-89*, II, 1224-1361.

[3] C. F. Thwing, *A History of Higher Education in America* (N. Y., 1906), 439-445; same author, *A History of Education in the United States since the Civil War* (Boston, 1910), chap. v.

intelligence." [1] The system had one unanticipated result: by making possible greater specialization of teaching by the faculty, the diversity of offerings contributed indirectly to the increase of productive scholarship. Further flexibility was given higher education by the development of summer schools and extension work. Though Harvard had initiated summer courses a few years earlier, the success of the New York Chautauqua and the needs of school teachers prompted a fuller development of the plan both there and elsewhere. [2] Under President Harper's leadership the University of Chicago in 1892 made the summer session an integral part of the academic year. In a somewhat similar fashion the example of Chautauqua, fortified by English experience, led universities in the 1890's to offer off-campus courses to special audiences, sometimes in other cities. [3] Less popular than summer study in residence, nevertheless certain institutions like Rutgers, Chicago, Wisconsin and Kansas succeeded in developing extension work as an important phase of their educational contribution.

Curricular changes were attended by changes in student life and conduct. While hazing continued to make the first months of the Freshman year a rough apprenticeship, in other respects there was greater soberness, a less excitable class spirit, fewer outbreaks of rowdyism and violence, than in former times. [4] The effect of the

[1] President and Treasurer of Harvard College, *Annual Report for 1899-1900*, esp. 120.

[2] W. W. Willoughby, "The History of Summer Schools in the United States," U. S. Comr. of Educ., *Rep. for 1891-92*, II, 893-959. See also U. S. Comr. of Educ., *Rep. for 1894-95*, II, 1483-1503; for *1899-1900*, I, 303-313.

[3] U. S. Comr. of Educ., *Rep. for 1891-92*, II, 945-55; for *1894-95*, II, 1483-1484; J. E. Russell, *The Extension of University Teaching in England and America* (Univ. of State of N. Y., *Extension Bull.*, no. 10, 1895), 176-184.

[4] H. D. Sheldon, *Student Life and Customs* (W. T. Harris, ed., *International Education Series*, LI, N. Y., 1901), chap. v.

elective system in destroying class unity, together with the greater age at which students were entering college, was partly responsible.[1] Equally important was the increasing absorption in intercollegiate athletics. The ancient loyalty to one's class was supplanted by loyalty to the college as a whole. Typical displays of undergraduate spirit thus took the form of mass meetings, athletic celebrations, rooting on the side lines and perhaps pitched battles after the game with supporters of the other team. The growing sense of responsibility encouraged colleges to experiment with plans of student self-government. At the University of Illinois such a scheme prevailed from 1868 to 1883, only to be abandoned by vote of the undergraduates themselves. The student senate at Amherst, continuing from 1883 to 1894, might have lasted longer but for the opposition of the incoming college administration. Elsewhere the attempts ran a fluctuating course, being usually most successful in small homogeneous institutions.[2]

Next to athletics, the chief focus of undergraduate interest was to be found in the clubs and fraternities. The older institutions in the East had their exclusive local societies of long standing, while throughout the West and generally in the South the Greek-letter fraternity system dominated student social life and, to a considerable extent, campus politics as well. To meet the needs of ever expanding enrollments the national fraternities increased the number of their chapters from four hun-

[1] The average age at Harvard rose from 18 years 9 months in 1878 to 19 years 6 months in 1889; during the years 1856-1860 it had been 17 years 11 months. See U. S. Comr. of Educ., *Rep. for 1889-90,* II, 799-803, for various colleges.

[2] See J. M. Gregory, "An Experiment in College Government," *International Rev.,* X (1881), 510-518 (for Illinois); John Bigham, "An Instructive Experiment in College Government," *Educational Rev.,* III (1892), 162-167 (for Amherst); Sheldon, *Student Life,* 256-271 (for a variety of experiments, including the honor system in examinations).

dred and sixty-two in 1879 to seven hundred and eighty-one in 1898 and their total membership from about sixty-three thousand to over one hundred and thirty thousand.[1] Ex-President White of Cornell defended the Greek-letter system as a means of developing group responsibility and higher personal standards, but others deplored its snobbish tendency and objected to the brutality of the initiation ceremonies.[2] The intrenched position of the fraternities is indicated by the fact that the efforts of the University of California in 1879 and of Purdue in 1881 to ban them were thwarted by an appeal to the courts. On the whole, it seems fair to say that, while fraternities generally exalted social above intellectual attainments, leadership in undergraduate activities usually came from their ranks, and their worst features were accentuated where college authorities were hostile.[3]

Virtually every institution also had a numerous array of literary, oratorical, debating, musical and dramatic societies, often, like the fraternities, bearing Greek names though lacking their exclusiveness. Student publications multiplied, the advent of the *Daily Illini* at the University of Illinois in 1871 and of the *Lampoon* at Harvard in 1876 marking the appearance respectively of the first undergraduate daily and the first humorous

[1] W. R. Baird, *American College Fraternities* (N. Y., 1879), 160-161; (5th edn., 1898), 424-431. See also J. A. Porter, "College Fraternities," *Century*, XXXVI (1888), 749-760; E. H. L. Randolph, "Greek-Letter Societies in American Colleges," *New England Mag.*, n.s., XVII (1897), 70-82; P. F. Piper, "College Fraternities," *Cosmopolitan*, XXII (1897), 641-648.

[2] A. D. White, "College Fraternities," *Forum*, III (1887), 243-253.

[3] According to Baird, writing in 1898, within the past twenty years "the Universities of California, Missouri, Alabama, North Carolina, Georgia, Iowa, Harvard and Vanderbilt have either repealed their anti-fraternity laws or allowed them to drop into disuse." In 1897, however, the South Carolina legislature succeeded in driving fraternities from the state university. Baird, *American College Fraternities* (5th edn.), 410, 415.

sheet. Oratory assumed an intercollegiate aspect with the formation of the Northwestern Interstate Collegiate Association in 1875; it was perhaps not without significance to the future of American politics that the contest at Iowa City in 1879 was won by a youth from the University of Wisconsin named Robert M. La Follette.[1] Interest in debating also took on new life with the beginning of intercollegiate rivalry. Harvard sent the first challenge to Yale in 1889; soon regional leagues sprang up in many parts of the country.

Denominational institutions were pervaded with an intense evangelical fervor; and everywhere the college Y. M. C. A. grew lustily, increasing its branches from twenty-six in 1877 to four hundred and seventy-five in 1895. While the drinking habit was on the wane, especially in the West, in the East high-spirited colts like the Harvard youths Bertie and Billy in *Philosophy Four* sought occasional bibulous adventure in near-by taverns. Seldom, however, it may be presumed, did such roisterers succeed in minting their experiences into satisfactory grades in the next day's examination, like those obtained by Owen Wister's heroes. Where girls attended classes with men, their presence had a refining influence on masculine manners and apparel; but the college authorities, alert to anticipate hostile outside criticism, saw to it that co-education did not become co-recreation. A quasi-inquisitorial discipline usually prevailed. In the first decade of the University of North Dakota (opened in 1884), dancing with the other sex was forbidden, chaperonage strictly enforced, and not a dress suit or evening gown was to be found in the whole student body.[2] Though in mixed colleges annual class "proms"

[1] Pauline Grahame, "La Follette Wins," *Palimpsest*, XII (1931), 179-188.
[2] Mattie G. Massee, "Student Life during the First Decade of the

and cotillions came gradually into favor, the "coeds" continued to find their chief social outlet in sororities, Greek-letter societies patterned after those of the men. Beginning with Kappa Alpha Theta founded at De Pauw in 1870, seven were in existence by the early 1880's, with a membership in 1898 totaling nearly twelve thousand scattered among one hundred and twenty-two chapters.

Only a relatively few college graduates went on to more advanced study. Postgraduate instruction represented the culmination of the Teutonic influence in higher education. The graduate school was the American counterpart of the *philosophische Facultät*. Its quick and firm rooting in the national soil attested the missionary zeal of hundreds of young scholars who, returning home with German doctorates, resolved to replace American superficiality with the Teutonic ideal of patient thoroughness. During the 1880's over two thousand Americans were studying in German universities, twice as many as in the preceding ten years and considerably more than in the next decade.[1] Berlin, Leipzig, Heidelberg, Jena, Halle—these were the chief academic springs at which their thirsty young minds drank deep of the learning of such great masters as Bluntschli, Ranke, Wagner, Schmoller, Wolf, Weismann, Johannes Müller, Ehrlich, Koch, Gauss, Helmholtz and Bunsen.

It was not hope of material reward that fired these youthful pilgrims, for the highest salary they could hope

University of North Dakota," Univ. of N. Dak., *Quar. Journ.*, XIII, esp. 373-374.

[1] C. F. Thwing, *The American and the German University* (N. Y., 1928), 42. Much smaller numbers of students were to be found in Austria, Switzerland and the University of Paris. U. S. Comr. of Educ., *Rep. for 1897-98*, II, 1702-1703; *for 1902*, I, 617. See also Samuel Sheldon, "Why Our Science Students Go to Germany," *Atlantic Mo.*, LXIII (1889), 463-466.

to attain was two thousand dollars in a small college, in a large one perhaps three or four.[1] It was something different, something which never before had had so ample an expression in American life: a passion for truth born of knowledge; an eagerness to do a few things supremely well instead of many things well enough; perhaps also an unconscious withdrawal of sensitive spirits from the soiling materialism which characterized the ethics of the great captains of industry and colored the whole business world. Moreover, the broad diffusion of worldly goods made it possible for middle-class sons to take advantage of opportunities which an earlier day had restricted to the wealthy few.

These returning Americans made their influence felt in faculties far and wide.[2] The Johns Hopkins University, which had opened in Baltimore in 1876 primarily for the promotion of graduate study in the Teutonic sense, had scarcely anyone on its staff of fifty-three in 1887 who had not studied in Germany. To this bracing center went troops of youths who in turn were to help spread the new ideals to all corners of the land: Josiah Royce, John Dewey, Joseph Jastrow, in philosophy and psychology; Henry C. Adams, Davis R. Dewey, John R. Commons, in political economy; Charles H. Haskins, J. Franklin Jameson, Woodrow Wilson, Frederick J. Turner, Charles M. Andrews, in history and political science; Albion W. Small and E. A.

[1] Even college presidents received only from two to six thousand dollars. Bryce, *American Commonwealth*, III, 437; W. R. Harper, "The Pay of American College Professors," *Forum*, XVI (1893-1894), 96-109; One of Them (*pseud.*), "The Status of the American Professor," *Educational Rev.*, XVI (1898), 417-434.

[2] In some instances, Germans themselves were translated to American faculties, notably in the case of the historian Hermann von Holst and the neurologist Adolf Meyer at the new University of Chicago and of Kuno Francke at Harvard.

A worried artist's vision of a future Commencement.

A great teaching hospital, Johns Hopkins University.

The Higher Learning

Ross in sociology; Edmund B. Wilson, T. H. Morgan, E. G. Conklin, in biology; and Edwin H. Hall, Joseph S. Ames and A. L. Kimball in chemistry.[1]

Spurred by the example of Johns Hopkins, the older foundations of the East placed their graduate work on a stronger basis.[2] Not a few state universities made starts in the same direction, the interest in research there usually spreading outward from the department of agriculture. Assisted by an increasing provision of fellowships, the number of students pursuing nonprofessional graduate work in American universities rose from a little over four hundred in 1878 to nearly five thousand in 1898. So rapid and sound was the development that before the end of the eighties the primacy of Hopkins was already seriously challenged and by the mid-nineties she was outstripped in number of registrants by Chicago, Harvard and Yale. It was no longer necessary for talented young men to seek their higher specialized training across the sea, for a dozen American institutions now offered as rich opportunities as could be found anywhere in the world.

Of the newly established universities three emulated Johns Hopkins by stressing graduate work. One of these, the Catholic University of America, which received its apostolic constitution from Leo XIII, threw open its doors in Washington, D. C., in 1889, offering instruc-

[1] Of the first holders of fellowships at Hopkins, one became professor of political economy at Michigan, another of natural history at Williams, a third of physics in New York University, a fourth of Greek at the University of Virginia, a fifth of political science at Middlebury College; two were called to chairs at Harvard; and three were retained on the Hopkins faculty. Other American graduate centers were, of course, performing a similar service. Between 1870 and 1890 the Cornell graduate school furnished fourteen college professors and twenty-four college presidents.

[2] In recognition of its transformed character Yale College assumed the name of Yale University in 1887, Columbia did likewise in 1896, and in the same year the College of New Jersey changed to Princeton University.

tion in divers fields.[1] Clark University, founded by a million-dollar gift of Jonas G. Clark, was launched the same year under the presidency of G. Stanley Hall, formerly a Hopkins professor. Gathering a small but choice faculty about him, Hall limited instruction to psychology and a few closely related subjects. Though but the "torso of a university," in Von Holst's famous phrase, the band of scholars at Worcester, Massachusetts, came to wield an influence altogether incommensurate to their number. As administrator, however, Hall had to face many difficulties: inadequate funds, the idiosyncrasies of a living donor and, on one memorable occasion, the larceny of a majority of his faculty by a still newer and much wealthier institution, the University of Chicago.

Though bearing the name of an older foundation, the University of Chicago was virtually a fresh creation. Backed by the Rockefeller millions and Chicago's hustling enterprise, and headed by William Rainey Harper of Yale, a former captain of the Chautauqua movement, the new university at its opening in 1892 stood already at a point which it had taken the old Eastern institutions generations to reach.[2] Its faculty was distinguished not only for erudition but also for the fact that Chicago salaries greatly overtopped any paid elsewhere. One can understand President Hall's bitterness in characterizing President Harper's surreptitious raid on his faculty "an act of wreckage . . . comparable to anything that the worst trust had ever attempted against its competitors," but Hall could hardly blame his colleagues for welcom-

[1] A. S. Will, *Life of Cardinal Gibbons* (N. Y., 1922), I, 254-257, 447-452.

[2] The original faculty contained eight members who had formerly been presidents of other colleges and universities. H. P. Judson, "The University of Chicago," *Educ.*, XVI (1895-1896), 278-289; T. W. Goodspeed, *William Rainey Harper* (Chicago, 1928), chap. iv; same author, *A History of the University of Chicago* (Chicago, 1916), chaps. i-x.

ing salaries twice as high as he could offer.[1] While vigorously developing graduate instruction, Harper was almost equally interested in all other phases of education, undergraduate and professional.

Whatever other elements entered into Chicago's success its location in a great and growing city was an important factor. Its sensational rise was a tribute to the cultural power of population centers and served to emphasize the fact that, save for one or two state universities, all the large, progressive, prosperous institutions of higher learning were to be found in or near urban districts.[2] The closing years of the century found Columbia and New York University crowded beyond capacity and obliged to acquire, at extraordinary expense, new and larger sites.

Fortunately the new forces shaking the academic world were felt also in the departments devoted to technological and professional training. Already well established when the period opened, progress in technical education during these two decades consisted chiefly in its extension and in improved standards of instruction.[3] The East emphasized engineering; the Far West mining and metallurgy; the South and Middle West agriculture and horticulture. Agricultural education underwent the greatest expansion, due partly to the formation of additional land-grant colleges under the Morrill act of 1862 and partly to new federal bounties.[4] In 1887 the Hatch

[1] G. S. Hall, *Life and Confessions of a Psychologist* (N. Y., 1923), 295-297.

[2] C. F. Thwing, *The American College in American Life* (N. Y., 1897), 203-207; W. R. Harper, *The Trend in Higher Education* (Chicago, 1905), 156-160.

[3] T. C. Mendenhall, "Scientific, Technical and Engineering Education," and C. W. Dabney, "Agricultural Education," N. M. Butler, ed., *Education in the United States* (Albany, 1900), II, 551-592, 593-652.

[4] A. C. True, "Agricultural Education in the United States," and "Agricultural Experiment Stations in the United States," U. S. Dept. of Agr., *Yearbook for 1899*, 157-190, 513-548.

law dispensed financial aid for agricultural research through the establishment of experiment stations in connection with land-grant institutions; and three years later a second Morrill act provided annual subsidies for instruction. The law of 1890 was badly needed because of the improvidence of many colleges in wasting their original patrimony, and was designed to enable them to improve both their faculties and their equipment.

Notwithstanding the reforms introduced at Harvard and a few other places, professional education in 1878 still lingered in the dark ages.[1] Diploma selling was a regular business in several large cities. In 1880 John Norris, a Philadelphia newspaper editor, publicly exposed one nest of offenders after he had obtained, with no effort but that of loosening his purse, two M.D. degrees, two doctorates in law, one "master in electrotherapeutics" and a doctorate of sacred theology from a half-dozen duly incorporated institutions.[2] The traffic could not be easily downed, however. Despite an increasingly watchful professional censorship such fraudulent practices survived in certain states to the end of the century and after.[3]

More serious, of course, were the lax standards prevailing in reputable universities. At most institutions in 1878 a medical student, after absorbing atmosphere in a doctor's office for a time and taking a lecture course of four or five months, repeating it the second year, could obtain his degree and start practising on the innocent

[1] See Allan Nevins, *The Emergence of Modern America* (*A History of American Life*, VIII), 276-279.

[2] U. S. Comr. of Educ., *Rep. for 1880*, clx-clxv; for *1882-83*, clxxiii.

[3] The Illinois state board of health was particularly active in the work of exposure in the 1890's. When in 1899 the state supreme court revoked the charter of the Independent Medical College of Chicago, it was discovered that in one Michigan town twenty-three physicians held its diplomas. U. S. Comr. of Educ., *Rep. for 1892-93*, II, 1622-1623; for *1898-99*, II, 1681-1683.

public. Before 1898, however, pressure from without the profession and leadership from within wrought a gratifying change. For the protection of the community, state after state set up boards of medical examiners, empowered to license properly qualified candidates.[1] At the same time medical schools, partly to meet the new legal standards, tightened their entrance requirements and added graded subjects and laboratory and clinical instruction, while lengthening their course to three or even four years.[2] The medical school at Johns Hopkins set an even higher standard by requiring a college degree for admission, but Harvard was the only one to follow its lead before the period ended.

Legal education, unhappily, was a different story. Throughout these years the law continued to be, as a contemporary ruefully remarked, "a learned profession which requires little learning."[3] With a few praiseworthy exceptions like Columbia and Harvard, law schools had virtually no entrance conditions. The great majority required two years rather than three for the degree, the work of instruction being left to busy practitioners who preferred sonorous lectures to a laborious use of the case method. Nor did many states have effective regulations for admission to the bar. If a speaker before the American Bar Association may be believed, "an inundation of incompetency . . . has in recent years

[1] By 1895 twenty-one commonwealths had the examination system, and fourteen others allowed only graduates of accredited medical schools to practise. U. S. Comr. of Educ., *Rep. for 1885-86*, 561-569; for *1892-93*, II, 1617-1619; for *1894-95*, II, 1230-1232. After 1878 there was an astonishing increase of dental schools and dental students, due to the action of many states in requiring graduation from a dental school as a condition for license. J. R. Parsons, "Professional Education," Butler, *Education*, II, 527, 531-533.

[2] Parsons, "Professional Education," 506-525; Dexter, *History of Education*, 327-340; C. F. Thwing, "Better Training for Law and Medicine," *Educational Rev.*, XVI (1898), 49-60.

[3] U. S. Comr. of Educ., *Rep. for 1894-95*, II, 1248.

deluged our profession." [1] Yet in public esteem the law
continued to rank as one of the most honorable of the
professions, and Bryce was told of individuals whose
incomes were quite as large as those of leaders of the
English bar. [2]

Theological training was on a sounder basis, maintaining good standards and experiencing little change
except as new religious conceptions penetrated the classroom and caused trouble for those who harbored them.
While business had not yet taken on the pretensions of
a profession, later times were foreshadowed by the establishment of the Wharton School of Finance and Economy in 1881 at the University of Pennsylvania. Of all
the professions medicine attracted the most students,
with theology second until the early 1890's when it was
overtaken by law. It is worth noting that the number
of professional students grew faster than did the population in general. Despite the tempting opportunities
offered by business and finance, despite the thornier path
which confronted the neophyte, the lure to professional
service increased rather than diminished its hold on
American youth.

If to the moralist the educational achievements of the
1880's and 1890's seem to offset the sinister practices of
the world of big business, it should not be forgotten
that, without the wealth made possible by the latter,
such progress could hardly have been accomplished.
Cornelius Vanderbilt's death in 1877 had revealed to
an amazed public the unprecedented private fortune of
one hundred million dollars, while the next two decades

---

[1] U. S. Comr. of Educ., *Rep. for 1894-95*, II, 1247. For a description of conditions, see *Rep. for 1880*, cl-clii; *for 1890-91*, I, 383-385,
414-433; *for 1893-94*, I, 997; *for 1896-97*, II, 1191; Dexter, *History of Education*, 316-327; Parsons, "Professional Education," 495-
505.

[2] Bryce, *American Commonwealth*, III, 380.

produced at least two score others who were rated as multimillionaires and, if shrewd guesses may be credited, some three thousand millionaires.[1] Without inquiring here into the noxious effects of such a huge concentration of riches, suffice it to say that from sources like these and from men of lesser means a golden stream flowed into the coffers of colleges and universities and turned what would otherwise have been fantastic dreams into attainable realities. By critics of the social order this largess was cynically attributed to a frantic love of display, an anxiety for social approval or perhaps a sedative to an uneasy conscience.[2] Yet, since most of the money came in the form of bequests, there is evidence also of a developing sense of *richesse oblige,* an altruistic desire of those who had, to share with those who had not.

Between 1878 and 1898 private benefaction added no less than one hundred and forty million dollars to the revenues for higher education, affecting all its branches, undergraduate, graduate, professional and technical.[3] Scientific apparatus was improved, professorships were established, dormitories provided, libraries enlarged, fellowships endowed, additional buildings constructed. Most spectacular of all was the out-of-hand

---

[1] See M. C. Stevens, "Great Fortunes in New England," E. F. Gay and A. A. Young, eds., *The New England Economic Situation* (Chicago, 1927), 17-24, and authorities cited. The average annual income of the one hundred richest Americans was estimated as $1,200,000 by T. G. Shearman, "The Owners of the United States," *Forum,* VIII (1889-1890), 262-273.

[2] There is little indication that college authorities hesitated to accept "tainted money"—a phrase which Washington Gladden was to coin in 1905. In 1899, when John D. Rockefeller offered $100,000 to Wellesley, eighteen professors demanded a prior investigation of his business methods. But the money was accepted without an investigation and with gratitude. *New International Year Book for 1900,* 911.

[3] This is a conservative estimate based on U. S. Comr. of Educ., *Reps.,* esp. for *1899-1900,* II, 2596, and on J. B. Sears, *Philanthropy in the History of American Higher Education* (U. S. Bur. of Educ., *Bull. for 1922,* no. 26), 55-56, 62.

creation of a series of new institutions by princely gifts from single donors. Besides Clark and the new University of Chicago, their number included the Case School of Applied Science (1880), Leland Stanford Junior University (1885), Drexel Institute (1891) and the Armour Institute of Technology (1893).

Amply equipped for the first time with tools of research—laboratories, instruments of precision, libraries, museums, observatories, hospitals—scholars and scientists in the United States were enabled to make a contribution to the world's learning fully comparable to that of the first nations of Europe. Minute specialization was the investigator's aim and his achievement. Only at rare intervals has a great genius appeared in the history of intellectual advance—a Newton, a Linnæus, a Comte. Rather, science and learning, especially in modern times, have been carried forward by myriad workers, each of whom, in President Eliot's phrase, has sought to "pierce with his own little search-light, if only by a hand's-breadth, the mysterious gloom which surrounds on every side the area of ascertained truth." [1] Withdrawn from the marketplace and the forum, closeted with the idea, brooding and moiling in monkish seclusion, the specialist wedded a skeleton bride whose osseous kiss and rattling embrace rewarded him with an ecstasy beyond Helen's.

Conversant with the trends and methods of investigation abroad, the research experts faced their greatest peril in a loss of contact with their fellow workers at home. In order to overcome this difficulty, and affected no doubt also by the human desire for comradeship with one's kind, the leading men brought about the formation of nation-wide associations in all the principal branches of research endeavor. America had never before

[1] C. W. Eliot, *Educational Reform* (N. Y., 1898), esp. 233.

witnessed such a banding together for the advancement
of knowledge.[1] Though the American Social Science
Association had been actively cultivating its broad field
since 1865, the demands of specialists led to the organ-
ization of the Archaeological Institute of America in
1879, the American Historical Association and the
American Catholic Historical Society in 1884, the
American Economic Association in 1885, the American
Society of Church History in 1888 and the American
Academy of Political and Social Science in 1889, along
with a vast array of local or more specialized societies.
Though the all-inclusive American Association for the
Advancement of Science dated from 1848, the new re-
quirements of scientific work brought into being the
American Chemical Society (1876), the American Soci-
ety of Mechanical Engineers (1880), the American
Forestry Association (1882), the American Ornitholo-
gists' Union (1883), the American Society of Naturalists (1883), the American Climatological Society
(1884), the American Institute of Electrical Engineers
(1884), the Geological Society of America (1888), the
National Statistical Association (1888), the American
Mathematical Society (1888), the American Physical
Society (1889), the Association of Economic Ento-
mologists (1890) and the American Psychological
Association (1892), not to mention countless regional
and local bodies. Similarly, the Modern Language Association, founded in 1883, began at once to yield off-

[1] S. B. Weeks, comp., "A Preliminary List of American Learned and
Educational Societies," U. S. Comr. of Educ., *Rep. for 1893-94,* II,
1493-1661; J. M. Cattell, "Scientific Societies and Associations," Butler,
Education, II, 865-892; H. R. Steeves, *Learned Societies and English
Literary Scholarship in Great Britain and the United States* (Columbia
Univ., *Studies in English and Comparative Literature,* 1913), chap. vii.
An incomplete enumeration shows that 79 learned societies, national
and local but excluding teachers' associations, were formed in the 1870's,
121 in the 1880's and 45 in the 1890's. Dexter, *History of Education,*
552.

shoots in the American Folklore Society (1888), the American Dialect Society (1889) and the American Dante Society (1890). The tendency went so far in medicine as to bring about a union of the various specialized groups under the name of a congress.

Such organizations through their annual gatherings not only provided mutual stimulus but, by means of their publications and printed proceedings, made possible ready intercommunication among widely scattered students.[1] Including the numerous research series conducted by Johns Hopkins, Columbia and other graduate centers, nearly fifty thousand printed pages were being produced annually in the 1890's by men who, as Eliot said, cared to be known "not to millions of people, but to five or six students of the Latin dative case, . . . or of fossil beetles, or of meteorites, or of starfish." [2] If mere pedantry or antiquarian curiosity marred some of this enormous output, the gain to society was still beyond computation.

In history the seminar was the characteristic ordeal of training, the monograph the typical product. So much had been left undone or misunderstood by earlier writers, so much conceived in a spirit of partisanship or treated primarily for literary effect, that the professionally trained student had virtually a free field for applying his canons of thorough and accurate research and rigorous objectivity. History, if not a science, at least became consciously scientific. Even those who, not trained in historical seminars, essayed the broader canvas, were imbued with the new spirit; and the breadth and excellence of their work helped make this the Augustan age of American historiography.

[1] R. R. Bowker, comp., *Publications of Societies* (N. Y., 1899); E. D. Perry, "The American University," Butler, *Education*, I, 298-300; Cattell, "Scientific Societies and Associations," 880-884.
[2] Eliot, *Educational Reform*, 233.

In 1880 the legal scholar James Schouler inaugurated his seven-volume survey of American public life from 1783 to 1865. About the same time Richard Hildreth and George Bancroft revised their long-standard histories in the light of new evidence, and Francis Parkman added *Montcalm and Wolfe* (1884), the great historian's greatest achievement, to his saga of the American forest. Influenced by the example of the Englishman J. R. Green, the clergyman-novelist Edward Eggleston in 1880 projected his unfinished *History of Life in the United States,* and J. B. McMaster, then an instructor in civil engineering at Princeton, produced in 1883 the initial volume of his vast *History of the People of the United States from the Revolution to the Civil War,* based mainly on newspapers, pamphlets and other hitherto neglected sources. The next decade brought the first volumes of James Ford Rhodes's *History of the United States from the Compromise of 1850,* a sober, scholarly narrative written by an ex-captain of industry and marked by measured judgments which won ready acceptance from a generation tired of the warmed-over controversies of the Civil War.[1]

More characteristic of the scientific school were the large-scale histories constructed by piecing together the contributions of specialists. The most significant undertaking of this sort was Justin Winsor's coöperative *Narrative and Critical History of America* (published from 1884 to 1889), in eight mastodontic volumes covering the period from 1000 to 1850, a massive feat of erudition, enduring in value because of its critical bibliographical notes. An interesting variant was Hubert Howe Bancroft's *History of the Pacific States* in thirty-four

---

[1] Hermann von Holst's *The Constitutional and Political History of the United States* (J. J. Lalor and Paul Shorey, trs., Chicago, 1876-1892), an able work but marred by a strong antislavery bias, was written before the author became an American professor.

volumes (1882-1890). The self-styled author, a San Francisco publisher who had amassed a remarkable collection of books and manuscripts bearing on the past of the region, employed a staff of copyists, note takers, cataloguers and research workers to organize the material for publication under his general direction.[1] Despite a method smacking more of the business than the academic world, the mountainous product contained much scholarly merit.

Of more particularized works Henry Adams's nine-volume *History of the United States* was widely influential, partly because of its detailed treatment of the years 1800-1817 in the light of European high politics and even more so because of its rare literary charm. The pioneer efforts of McMaster and Eggleston, reënforced by the example of the German Ratzel, meantime had a quickening effect on the minds of brilliant young students like Frederick J. Turner and Ellen C. Semple who in the 1890's started to extend the outposts of historical inquiry to areas beyond the Freemanesque confines of statecraft, war and diplomacy.[2] No longer could it fairly be said that American history was written "as if Plymouth Rock underlay the whole geological formation of the United States," for students from all sections contributed to the new illumination.[3] Outside the

[1] See H. H. Bancroft, *Literary Industries* (same author, *Works*, San Fran., 1883-1890, XXXIX), chap. xxiv. This account, however, needs to be checked with *"Literary Industries" in a New Light* (San Fran., 1893) by H. L. Oak, who wrote seven or more volumes of the history, and with W. A. Morris, "The Origin and Authorship of the Bancroft Pacific States Publications," *Ore. Hist. Quar.*, IV, 287-364.

[2] The clarion note of the new departure was sounded in Turner's "The Significance of the Frontier in American History," an address before the American Historical Association, printed in its *Annual Report for 1893*, 199-227, and elsewhere. See also H. U. Faulkner, *The Quest for Social Justice* (*A History of American Life*, XI), 247.

[3] Anon., "The Dutch Influence in America," *Atlantic Mo.*, LXX (1892), 698.

sphere of national history the activity, though less notable, was not without significance. Thus, Charles Gross, whose Göttingen dissertation (1883) on the gild merchant demolished prevailing theories, prepared a monumental critical bibliography of English history. The chief large-scale work was a series of studies of ecclesiastical institutions, culminating in a *History of the Inquisition in the Middle Ages* (1888), made by Henry C. Lea, a retired Philadelphia book publisher.

The evolutionary concept, so momentous in its influence upon the natural sciences, was reflected in the historians' emphasis on continuity and growth as the key to understanding human development. Few writers, however, went so far as John Fiske, that skillful popularizer of other men's researches, who commenced his narrative of the *Beginnings of New England* with the year 476 A.D. In the related social sciences the Darwinian hypothesis had equally salient consequences— Stanley Hall called it "the greatest intellectual stimulus of the modern age." [1] The umbilical cord connecting history and political science, while retarding the latter's growth as a separate discipline, insured a knowledge of the historical and comparative development of institutions. Systematic theoretical treatises like John W. Burgess's *Political Science and Comparative Constitutional Law* (1890) and W. W. Willoughby's *An Examination of the Nature of the State* (1896) scorned the easy rationalizations of earlier native writers. Deeply influenced by the German historico-juristic approach, these men broke boldly with their American past by throwing overboard the whole cargo of natural rights' philosophy and declaring for an active employment of governmental powers for the common weal. Of descriptive and analytical studies the most important were Woodrow

[1] Hall, *Life and Confessions*, 362.

Wilson's *Congressional Government* (1885), a realistic inquiry into the system of checks and balances, written while the author was yet a student at Hopkins; and F. J. Goodnow's *Comparative Administrative Law* (1893), the first work of its kind in English.

Sociological writing, though largely in the hands of amateurs and sentimentalists in the opening years, found its master in 1883 when Lester F. Ward, turning aside from his studies in paleobotany, published his *Dynamic Sociology*.[1] This seminal work, strongly Comtean in its antecedents, formulated a complete system of cosmic philosophy. Sharply opposed to Herbert Spencer's fatalism, Ward called for a conscious direction of the forces of social evolution; and his great deliverance stimulated and colored the studies of young men like F. H. Giddings, Albion W. Small and E. A. Ross who would in the future be leaders in the field. Meantime the collection of basic data on primitive life was being advanced by the bureau of American ethnology, set up by the government in 1879. The foremost field investigator perhaps was A. F. A. Bandelier, of Swiss birth, who explored aboriginal sites and studied ways of life in the American Southwest, Mexico and South America. By shattering many ancient fables he did much to substitute critical investigation for romantic preconceptions.[2]

Imbued with the German spirit, returning students of economics took sharp issue with the abstract doctrinaire teachings of the so-called classical school. One of the avowed objects of the newly formed American Economic Association was to foster historical and statistical investigation of economic phenomena. Only less manifest was the ardent desire of certain founders like Rich-

[1] A. W. Small, "Fifty Years of Sociology in the United States," *Am. Journ. of Sociology*, XXI, 721-864.
[2] F. W. Hodge, "A. F. A. Bandelier," *Am. Anthropologist*, n.s., XVI, 349-358.

ard T. Ely, E. J. James and H. C. Adams to employ the powers of the state to convert the "dismal science," with its emphasis upon untrammeled individualism, into an active agency for general economic welfare. The rapid success of the new ideals owed much to the weighty support of President Francis A. Walker of the Massachusetts Institute of Technology, the foremost economist and statistician of the day. Though not himself German-trained, his acute and catholic intelligence cast him inevitably for the rôle of "champion and emancipator"—Ely's phrase—and his treatise *Political Economy,* published in 1883, marked the transition from the old to the new.[1] Unless it be history, no other branch of the social sciences attracted so many able minds; and the multitudinous treatises they produced illuminated all phases of the subject, particularly those to which the increasing complexity of the economic order called attention. Not of least importance was the fact that the professionally trained, academic students of society performed an essential service in providing a philosophical sanction for the strivings of reformers and humanitarians.[2]

In the effort to lift the study of social relations to the dignity of a science, scholars and teachers offended many cherished notions of the comfortable classes and excited the disapproval of powerful beneficiaries of the *status quo.* Tariff protectionists repeatedly tried to oust W. G. Sumner from Yale, almost worrying him into a resig-

[1] J. P. Munroe, *A Life of Francis Amasa Walker* (N. Y., 1923), chaps. xiv, xvi. On the new economics, see also L. L. Price, "The Present Condition of Economic Science," *Forum,* XXIV (1897-1898), 422-431; R. T. Ely, "The American Economic Association, 1885-1909," Am. Econ. Assoc., *Publs.,* ser. 3, XI, 47-111; L. H. Haney, *History of Economic Thought* (rev. edn., N. Y., 1920), 612-629.

[2] A brilliant exception to the rule was Professor William G. Sumner of Yale, who continued a champion of extreme *laissez-fairism.* See, for example, his pungent essay *What Social Classes Owe to Each Other* (N. Y., 1883).

nation in 1880 on the charge of using Spencer's textbook of sociology. Six years later H. C. Adams was
forced out of Cornell because of a frank expression of
his views on the Gould strike. In 1894 Ely was haled
before the regents of the University of Wisconsin on
charges of economic heresy, and the following year
brought E. W. Bemis's resignation from the University
of Chicago as a result of criticizing certain public-utility
corporations.

In 1897 the entire faculty of the Kansas Agricultural
College was dismissed for their failure to subscribe to
Populist tenets, while J. A. Smith was driven from
Marietta College because of antimonopoly utterances.
The same year, when E. Benjamin Andrews tendered
his resignation as president of Brown rather than yield
his free-silver convictions, the editor of the *St. Louis
Globe-Democrat* (July 30) spoke for most Americans
in declaring: "He was only a servant; and a servant
must do as his employers wish, or quit their service."
But the Brown faculty and alumni, seconded by college
presidents and professors elsewhere, rallied to the cause
of academic freedom and secured Andrews's vindica-
tion.[1] History professors were not in so exposed a position; but if or when their new findings got into school
textbooks, the authors were likely to find themselves
subjected to a cross fire, on the one hand, between the
Grand Army of the Republic and the United Confederate Veterans and, on the other, between militant Catholics and Protestants. In the popular mind propaganda
was still the main function of history, and textbook

[1] The other signal victory for academic freedom was the action of
the Wisconsin regents in asserting Ely's right "to follow the indications
of the truth wherever they may lead." An incomplete list in T. E.
Will, "A Menace to Freedom: The College Trust," *Arena*, XXVI
(1901), 244-257, names fifteen professors who by that time had lost
positions because of unorthodox social or economic views. See also
Encyclopaedia of the Social Sciences, I, 348.

publishers solved the dilemma by broad-mindedly issuing versions to suit all tastes.[1]

Humanistic scholarship was strongly colored by the
German preoccupation with the scientific study of philology. Americans, thought Bryce, showed an almost
excessive anxiety to master all that had been written
even by third-rate German scholars, and he noted also
a tendency to imitate the Teutonic fault of neglecting
form and style.[2] In Greek studies Basil L. Gildersleeve
was the foremost leader, his seminar at Johns Hopkins
being a training school for a multitude of coworkers.
A great stimulus resulted from the establishment of the
American School of Classical Studies at Athens in 1882;
and the manifold benefits to students from making
excavations and carrying on research in a classical land
led to the founding of a similar center at Rome in
1895.[3] Minton Warren's seminar in Latin at Johns
Hopkins was second only to Gildersleeve's in its influence on classical scholarship. Equally significant in
ancient philology were the thoroughgoing studies of
William Dwight Whitney of Yale and his followers in
Sanskrit and Indo-European linguistics.

Whitney also made important contributions to general
linguistics, while A. M. Elliott at Hopkins was the
pioneer in organizing the scientific study of modern languages and literatures. Literary scholarship was further
enriched by achievements like the *New Variorum*

[1] Bessie L. Pierce, *Public Opinion and the Teaching of History* (N.
Y., 1926), 146-170, 175-176; anon., "The Anti-Catholic Spirit of
Certain Writers," *Catholic World*, XXXVI (1883), 658-667; G. W.
Cooke, "How the Catholic Church Teaches History," *Unitarian*, IV
(1889), 156-161.

[2] Bryce, *American Commonwealth*, III, 568-569. See also H. E. Shep-
herd, "English Philology and English Literature in American Universities," *Sewanee Rev.*, I (1893), 153-159.

[3] B. L. Gildersleeve, "Classical Studies in America," *Atlantic Mo.*,
LXXVIII (1896), 728-737; J. E. Sandys, *A History of Classical*

Shakespeare, edited by H. H. Furness, which had begun publication in 1871; Charles Eliot Norton's critical writings on the fine arts and Dante; and F. J. Child's definitive collection of *English and Scottish Popular Ballads* (1883-1898). If most of such work little touched the common life, the new erudition made contact with the lay world through the production of three great dictionaries: a thorough revision of Webster's, entitled, in disregard of the original author's uncompromising Americanism, the *International* (1890); the *Century* (1889-1891); and the *Standard* (1890-1895). These enterprises, involving years of painstaking labor by myriad experts, set a new standard for dictionary making.

In recording the growth of the language these lexicons incidentally paid impressive tribute to the advance of the pure and applied sciences. "The prominence given to . . . scientific, technological and zoölogical terms," said the editor of *Webster's International,* "will attract the attention of every critic." Even the few years between the appearance of the *Century* and the *Standard* made it possible for the latter to include terms like appendicitis and antitoxin, unknown to the former. The extraordinary progress of science owed much to generous governmental support, especially for geology, meteorology and agriculture, much also to private beneficence, and a very great deal to the immediate practical value which a considerable amount of the research possessed for the country's industrial life. Though the general public esteemed science chiefly for its utilitarian results, the specialists themselves strove to uphold the German academic ideal of science pursued for its own sake. Yet,

Scholarship (Cambridge, Eng., 1908), III, chap. xli; T. D. Seymour, *The First Twenty Years of the American School of Classical Studies at Athens* (School of Classical Studies at Athens, *Bull.,* V, 1902).

Americans under the skin, it was seldom they failed to assert in almost the same breath that without pure science applied science would not be possible.[1]

The echoes of the evolution controversy lingered but faintly in scientific halls in the 1880's. In all branches the hypothesis served as a salient working principle and the scientist's mind remained unruffled save when he ventured to tilt lances with orthodox religionists.[2] Broadly speaking, American science in this new era was less concerned with the mere collection of data and more with the determination of relations. The zoologist Spencer F. Baird became secretary of the Smithsonian Institution in 1878 and, under his direction and that of S. P. Langley, who followed him in 1887, that agency strengthened its leadership in the scientific world.[3]

Contributions to pure mathematics were not numerous. With a few notable exceptions like J. J. Sylvester and E. H. Moore, those capable of pursuing this difficult and abstract subject soon turned their attention to physics, astronomy, engineering and other branches where mathematical laws were applied to visible realities. In physics three Americans won international fame. J. Willard Gibbs of Yale, whom Henry Adams esteemed "the greatest of Americans, judged by his rank in science," was a classic example of the unassuming, self-sacrificing seeker for truth. Devoting himself to research in thermodynamics, he extended the fundamental laws of heat and energy to the most varied departments of

[1] See, for example, J. J. Stevenson, "The Debt of the World to Pure Science," R. M. La Follette, ed., *The Making of America* (Chicago, 1906), VII, 24-39; and Addison Brown, "Endowment for Scientific Research," Smithsonian Inst., *Ann. Rep. for 1892*, 621-638.

[2] See, for example, Asa Gray, *Natural Science and Religion* (N. Y., 1880), and W. N. Rice, *Twenty-Five Years of Scientific Progress* (N. Y., 1894). Nevins, *Emergence of Modern America*, 286-288, describes the earlier attitude of American scientists.

[3] Baird was father of the great National Museum which Congress housed in a fine new building in 1882.

physics and provided the theoretical basis for the new science of physical chemistry, which Europeans quickly proceeded to cultivate.[1] Wrote a former student in 1931, "The scientific world has been and still is writing the biography of Gibbs's mind in expounding, amplifying, and applying his ideas."[2] H. A. Rowland at Johns Hopkins performed basic experiments on the formation of magnetic fields by the rotation of static charges and, in another phase of his work, revolutionized spectroscopy by his exquisitely delicate diffraction gratings and his ingenious mechanism for producing them. Younger than either of these, A. A. Michelson of Case, Clark and Chicago was already well launched on his brilliant career, inventing the inferential refractometer and, in 1879 and 1882, measuring the velocity of light.[3]

Simon Newcomb, attaining the summit of his achievements in the 1880's and 1890's, gained recognition as the world's foremost astronomer, preëminent for his researches in mathematical astronomy. Dividing his time between the government *Nautical Almanac* office and Johns Hopkins, he made a recomputation of the elements

---

[1] For his contributions to physical chemistry, see particularly his epoch-making paper, "On the Equilibrium of Heterogeneous Substances," published obscurely in the *Transactions* of the Connecticut Academy of Arts and Sciences in 1876 and 1878. It consisted of three hundred pages with over seven hundred equations. The best known of the formulas is his famous phase rule, which served to classify and explain in a logical manner experimental facts of much apparent complexity.

[2] E. B. Wilson, "Josiah Willard Gibbs," *Dict. of Am. Biog.*, VII, esp. 251.

[3] Apart from invention and applied mechanics, the life of the masses was most vitally touched by physics in its application to the study of weather, the special branch known as meteorology. The federal weather bureau, founded in 1870, rapidly expanded until it became the largest and best equipped in the world. Carrying on scientific studies, it also elaborated its system of warning farmer, shipper and navigator against the hazards of storm, flood and sudden climatic change, saving millions of dollars annually for the public. F. H. Bigelow, "Work of the Meteorologist for the Benefit of Agriculture, Commerce and Navigation," U. S. Dept. of Agr., *Yearbook for 1899*, 71-92.

of the solar system, which marked an epoch. In the words of a fellow scientist, "the sun and moon and planets have been weighed as exactly as sugar and tea at the grocer's and their paths measured as precisely as silks and woolens at the draper's." [1] His contributions won him membership in nearly all the national academies of science in the world.

Yet he was only one among a brilliant group of American astronomers. At the Harvard Observatory E. C. Pickering and his staff, drafting photography into the service of science, mapped the heavens from the north to the south pole by means of thirty thousand glass plates, taken partly in Cambridge and partly in Peru. S. C. Chandler at Harvard reconciled the discrepancies in latitude records of European and American observatories and elucidated a new law of planetary motion expressed in the periodic wandering of the terrestrial poles. In 1877 Asaph Hill at the Naval Observatory in Washington detected the two satellites of Mars, the most remarkable event since the discovery of Neptune in 1846, but one exceeded in 1892 by the announcement of a fifth satellite of Jupiter, observed by E. E. Barnard at the Lick Observatory.[2] America's achievements were facilitated by the establishment of observatories such as Lick in California in 1887 and the Yerkes Observatory of the University of Chicago in 1895, possessing the most powerful refracting telescopes in the world.

[1] W. H. McGee, "Fifty Years of American Science," *Atlantic Mo.*, LXXXII (1898), 309. See also Marcus Benjamin, "Simon Newcomb," D. S. Jordan, ed., *Leading American Men of Science* (N. Y., 1910), 363-390; and R. C. Archibald, "Simon Newcomb," *Science*, n.s., XLIV, 871-878. Newcomb's versatile genius is indicated by the fact that he also made significant contributions to economic theory.

[2] C. A. Young, "The Latest Astronomical News," *Forum*, X (1890-1891), 83-93; E. S. Holden, "America's Achievements in Astronomy," *Forum*, XIII (1893), 744-752; Simon Newcomb, "Recent Astronomical Progress," *Forum*, XXV (1898), 109-119.

Chemistry remained a monument chiefly to European genius. In the absence of laboratories comparable to the great observatories and natural-history museums, little theoretical work of import was done in America save for Willard Gibbs's contributions from the standpoint of thermodynamics and perhaps Wolcott Gibbs's researches upon complex inorganic acids.[1] Applied chemistry, on the other hand, had never before been so central to the national effort in industry and agriculture.[2] Where earlier only a few dye houses and steel mills had employed chemical experts, the practice now became general. To meet increasing competition, their aid was indispensable in oil refineries, soap and candle works, glass factories, paint works and metallurgical plants. Many such concerns maintained their own laboratories. Yet, even in this respect, the United States lagged behind older industrial countries, especially Germany. It was only in agricultural chemistry—concerned with soil analysis, the use of plant foods, principles of animal nutrition, etc.—that America set the pace for the world. For this, the importance of farming in the national economy, together with the scientific competence of the newly established experiment stations, was largely responsible.

Geology likewise was closely identified with the nation's material development. Most of the principal advances stemmed from the work of a score of state geological surveys and particularly of the United States survey created in 1879. Besides disclosing and describing natural resources, progress was made in unlocking

[1] E. F. Smith, *Chemistry in America* (N. Y., 1914), 264-272, 343-349.

[2] F. W. Clarke, "Chemistry in the United States," La Follette, *Making of America*, VII, 84-90; H. W. Wiley, "The Relation of Chemistry to the Progress of Agriculture," and Milton Whitney, "Soil Investigations in the United States," U. S. Dept. of Agr., *Yearbook for 1899*, 201-258, 335-346.

the secrets of earth history by applying the evolutionary principle to the study both of land forms and fossil life.[1] T. C. Chamberlin, N. S. Shaler, W. M. Davis, R. D. Salisbury and others, using America's incomparable drift plains, drumlins and moraines as their library, solved the riddle of loess and shed new light upon the glacial period. Instead of a single great ice sheet, as had been supposed, they established the existence of five definite glacial epochs.

Meantime other geologists, notably O. C. Marsh and E. D. Cope, enriched the world's knowledge of paleontology.[2] As a result of excavations of vast fossil beds in Kansas, Dakota, Colorado and Wyoming, a glow of antique romance was cast over the sobering West. In scientific eyes at least, grasshoppers and chinch bugs paled into insignificance beside the discovery of leviathan remains of the reptilian and mammalian ages: great flesh-eating lizards, flying serpents eighty feet long, and enormous, ungainly beasts, with swaying necks, whose fearsome aspect may be sufficiently suggested to the layman by the scientific name *elasmosaurus platyurus*. Many of the finds supplied visible evidence of the transitional stages in the evolution of animal life, notably in the case of the winged beast which scientists accept as the ancestor of all hoofed animals.[3] If America continued to follow after Europe in mineralogy and petrography, the relation was reversed in other branches of geology and in its underlying principles. More and more European

[1] Geological progress is summarized in G. P. Merrill, *The First One Hundred Years of American Geology* (New Haven, 1924), chaps. viii-xiii, and E. S. Dana and others, *A Century of Science in America* (New Haven, 1918), chaps. ii-viii.

[2] G. B. Grinnell, "Othniel Charles Marsh," and Marcus Benjamin, "Edward Drinker Cope," Jordan, *Leading American Men of Science,* 283-340; Merrill, *American Geology,* 528-530.

[3] See E. D. Cope, *The Primary Factors of Organic Evolution* (Chicago, 1896); also R. T. Young, *Biology in America* (Boston, 1922), chap. iv.

geologists found it desirable to take field lessons on this side of the Atlantic.

In no phase of science was the evolutionary doctrine of such essential importance as in biology. American botanists did much to reconstruct the older system of plant classification in accordance with the principle of descent; and in zoology interest turned strongly to embryological and morphological studies, branches in which W. K. Brooks, Edmund B. Wilson, E. L. Mark, C. S. Minot and C. O. Whitman were leading figures.[1] Biological research was greatly aided by the setting up of study centers like the Arnold Arboretum (1872) in Boston, the Marine Laboratory (1887) at Wood's Hole and the New York Aquarium (1896) on Manhattan. The chief progress, however, was made in the applied aspects of biology, especially as regards farming, for here the state and national governments lent generous support and the agricultural experiment stations were powerful allies. For the first time, systematic attempts were made to throw light on crop diseases, while scientific methods were devised to combat fungi, bacteria and other organisms which lived on food-producing plants.[2]

Equally efficacious were the means employed to protect fields and orchards from the ever present menace of injurious insects and birds.[3] When, for instance, the white scale threatened to ruin the citrus crops of California in 1889, they were saved only by the importation

[1] W. R. Coe, "A Century of Zoology," and G. L. Goodale, "The Development of Botany," Dana and others, *Science in America,* esp. 411-412, 453-454.

[2] The work of T. J. Burrill of the University of Illinois, W. J. Farlow of Harvard, J. C. Arthur of the Geneva (N. Y.) experiment station and B. T. Galloway of the U. S. department of agriculture was particularly important. See B. T. Galloway, "Progress in the Treatment of Plant Diseases," U. S. Dept. of Agr., *Yearbook for 1899,* 191-200.

[3] L. O. Howard, "Progress in Economic Entomology," and T. S. Palmer, "A Review of Economic Ornithology," U. S. Dept. of Agr., *Yearbook for 1899,* esp. 153-154, 259-292.

of its enemy, the Australian ladybird beetle. At the same time systematic measures were taken to conserve useful native birds whose existence was menaced by the inroads of game markets, the egg trade and the millinery business. States were induced to repeal ill-advised laws and to protect beneficial species, New Hampshire and Ohio beginning with eagles, Rhode Island with fishhawks and New York and Minnesota with owls.[1] The federal government coöperated by establishing great national parks such as Yellowstone in 1872 and Sequoia and Yosemite in 1890. There an unmatched natural scenery provided an appropriate setting for the survivors of a brute creation which had once covered most of the continent.[2] Important advances were also made in methods of plant and animal breeding and in scientific forestry.[3] Though farmers still had to gamble with the weather, which might be forecast but could not be controlled, in other respects some of their worst enemies had been routed by science.

Psychology had traditionally been an appendage of philosophy, but the rapid developments in biological science hastened the end of the ancient connection. No longer could a psychologist deem his own important self a sufficient basis for generalizations respecting all mankind; he must forsake his armchair for the laboratory. Experimental psychology—the study of mental processes

[1] Following the passage of a Pennsylvania act in 1885 placing bounties on hawks and owls, ornithologists proved by examining the stomachs of twenty-seven hundred that only six of the seventy-five varieties were harmful. By 1898 Pennsylvania was actively protecting all birds except six genuinely injurious species. Palmer, "Economic Ornithology," 265-266.

[2] John Muir gives a delightful account in *Our National Parks* (Boston, 1902).

[3] Gifford Pinchot, "Progress of Forestry," H. J. Webber and E. A. Bessey, "Progress of Plant Breeding," and John Clay, "Work of the Breeder in Improving Live Stock," U. S. Dept. of Agr., *Yearbook for 1899*, 293-306, 465-490, 627-644.

by exact, objective, experimental methods—became the
new gospel. For this trend G. Stanley Hall, a former
student of Wilhelm Wundt, and particularly William
James of Harvard, also German-trained, were largely
responsible.[1] With James the chief emphasis was on the
discovery of physiological changes in the nervous system which might explain psychic processes. His *Principles
of Psychology* (1890), clothed in an irresistible magic
of words, had a wide and deep influence, and furnished
a point of departure for the behaviorists in the next
century.[2]

Meantime philosophy itself could not remain indifferent to the scientific temper. Both here and abroad it
tentatively reconsidered its technique and concepts in
the light particularly of the Darwinian hypothesis and
the new psychology. Within these limits, however, many
winds of doctrine blew across the scene.[3] From 1879
to 1888 popular interest in the subject was keen enough
to bring together each summer at Concord, Massachusetts, a band of men and women to hear philosophical
discussions presented both by amateurs and professionals.
The long-suffering daughter of Bronson Alcott, the
picturesque genius who presided over the gatherings,
wrote of the "budding philosophers" who "roost on
our steps like hens waiting for corn."[4]

[1] G. T. Ladd of Yale contributed to the movement though in a less
important way. E. G. Boring, *A History of Experimental Psychology*
(N. Y., 1929), chap. xx; W. B. Pillsbury, *The History of Psychology*
(N. Y., 1929), chap. xiv; Josiah Royce, "The New Psychology,"
Forum, XXVI (1898-1899), 80-96.

[2] See P. W. Slosson, *The Great Crusade and After* (*A History of
American Life*, XII), 382-383.

[3] The main trends are considered by Woodbridge Riley, *American
Thought* (rev. edn., N. Y., 1923), chaps. vii-ix; A. K. Rogers, *English
and American Philosophy since 1800* (N. Y., 1922), 283-296, 359-
387; and M. R. Cohen, "Later Philosophy," W. P. Trent and others,
eds., *Cambridge History of American Literature* (N. Y., 1921), III,
226-265; IV, 751-760.

[4] Louisa spoke for most of her fellow countrymen when she added:

The Concord School of Philosophy provided a meeting place for many minds. Such success as it met was due largely to the organizing talent of William T. Harris, an ardent Hegelian, long editor of the *Journal of Speculative Philosophy*. His appointment as federal commissioner of education, though bringing the meetings to a close, did not end his battles for his philosophic creed, which he renewed in a series of provocative treatises. Hegelianism had its opponents, notably in James McCosh, leader of the Scottish school of common-sense realism. But the doughty president of Princeton felt obliged to give his chief attention to rendering the new evolutionary philosophy, which John Fiske had done so much to champion, harmless to the cause of religious orthodoxy.

The impact of scientific thought was best represented by Charles S. Peirce, son of the mathematician Benjamin Peirce, and a man thoroughly familiar with laboratory method by reason of his own achievements in science. While he never constructed a finished system, his restless mind was fertile in new insights of seminal importance. Not least to his credit is the deep influence he exerted upon two of the most powerful thinkers of the time, who, save for being friends and colleagues at Harvard, had otherwise little in common: Josiah Royce and William James. Royce was a full-fledged metaphysical idealist who united moral energy with wide historical learning, command of scientific method and an intense interest in logical technique. James, on the other hand, sought to humanize philosophy and, through his mastery

"Speculation seems a waste of time when there is so much real work to be done." E. D. Cheney, *Louisa May Alcott* (Boston, 1889), 321. See also T. W. Brown, *Alcott and the Concord School of Philosophy* (Concord, 1926); Austin Warren, "The Concord School of Philosophy," *New England Quar.*, II (1929), 199-233; U. S. Comr. of Educ., *Rep. for 1891-92*, II, 909-917.

of psychology, bring it to terms with everyday living. He cared less for cosmic purpose than for individual achievement and was frankly scornful of dialectical legerdemain.

Throughout these years James's mind was growing toward a theory of method which, first clearly formulated in his University of California address in 1898, was to be widely influential under the name of pragmatism. His emphasis on individualism and his concern with the immediate results of conduct brought him nearer the dominant temper of America than any of his fellow philosophers. His "philosophy of practicality" made a profound impression abroad as well. It was left, however, to his great successor, John Dewey, to show in later years that pragmatism might become an instrument for social amelioration as well as for the attainment of individual satisfactions.[1]

To the average American the beneficent effects of the scientific revolution were brought home most forcibly in the domain of medicine. The phrase, science and health, was a potent formula even for the new religious sect which rejected medicine as the science of health. For the man on the street the words implied fresh safeguards against the ravages of sickness and greater certainty of recovery. This new posture of affairs was, in large measure, the result of an epochal discovery as to the cause of communicable diseases. First worked out by the Frenchman Louis Pasteur in the 1860's and 1870's, the germ theory in the early 1880's was rapidly widened in its application to human ills by the German Robert Koch's invention of improved methods and his isolation of the microbes of tuberculosis and Asiatic cholera. Then in 1884 G. T. A. Gaffsky introduced a better knowledge of the typhoid bacillus and Friedrich Loeffler discovered

[1] See Faulkner, *Quest for Social Justice*, 189, 245.

the diphtheria bacillus.[1] Americans also made primary contributions to medical bacteriology, notably in the work of Theobald Smith and F. L. Kilborne on Texas fever, a plague which was decimating Western cattle herds.[2] With the development of the serum treatment of infectious diseases, so strikingly exemplified by the use of antitoxin in diphtheria, the healing art attained possibilities undreamed of a few years before. Medical practice in the United States was profoundly affected as respects both the diagnosis and treatment of sickness and also, as we shall see, as regards the science of epidemiology.[3]

America's original contributions to medical science were perhaps better represented by the attention given to the nervous ailments which tightened their hold on the people as the social order became more urban and complex. In this field George M. Beard of New York, who coined the term, neurasthenia, was a pioneer.[4] His researches, however, were less influential than those of S. Weir Mitchell of Philadelphia, who originated the familiar "rest cure," and of William A. Hammond in New York City. At the same time the practice of psychiatry was enriched by the work of Shobal V. Clevenger in Illinois, his treatise *Spinal Concussion* (1889) gaining international repute. The new science

---

[1] Other significant contributors to medical bacteriology were Roux, Strauss, Metchnikoff and Bouchard of Paris, Fränkel, Behring and Klebs in Germany, and Kitasato of Japan.

[2] D. E. Salmon, "Some Examples of the Development of Knowledge Concerning Animal Diseases," U. S. Dept. of Agr., *Yearbook for 1899*, esp. 124-134; Paul de Kruif, *Microbe Hunters* (N. Y., 1926), chap. viii.

[3] G. F. Shrady, "Recent Triumphs in Medicine and Surgery," *Forum*, XXIII (1897), 33-41. Dr. Henry Gradle of Chicago, a former student of Koch, published in 1883 *Bacteria and the Germ Theory of Disease*, the first book in the English language on the subject.

[4] See his readable volume, *American Nervousness* (N. Y., 1881), with its provocative sociological explanation of the disorder.

of laryngology was similarly advanced by the efforts of
F. H. Bosworth of New York and J. Solis Cohen of
Philadelphia, whose publications on throat and nose
diseases also had a deep influence abroad. In a related
field A. H. Buck's *Diagnosis and Treatment of Ear
Diseases* (1880) was for many years the *vade-mecum*
of otologists.

Among general practitioners and the public at large
medical sects continued to thrive. Besides "regulars,"
homeopaths and eclectics, there was a profusion of magnetic healers, physiomedicalists (who prescribed only
botanical remedies), vitapaths, hydropaths, electropaths,
sun curists and the like. Some states explicitly banned
nonmedical healing, but others, like Illinois and most of
the New England states, were on much the same footing as the Cherokee Nation in Indian Territory which
permitted "enchantments in any form." Of the new sects
osteopathy, whose principles were first formulated in
1874 by Dr. Andrew T. Still of Baldwin, Kansas, possessed the greatest vitality. By the close of the century
its practice had express legal sanction in the Dakotas,
Iowa, Missouri, Michigan, Tennessee and Vermont.[1]

Many people preferred self-dosing in the form of pills,
tablets and liquids, obtained as proprietary medicines
from drug stores.[2] While some of these nostrums were
harmless, others were habit-forming opiates or thinly
disguised alcoholic stimulants. The enormous demand
for "cures" for "lost manhood" and alleged remedies
for venereal diseases sheds an interesting, if somewhat
puzzling, light on the moral conditions of the time. The
use of patent medicines, stimulated, as we have seen, by

[1] J. R. Parsons, "Professional Education," Butler, *Education*, II,
513-515.
[2] Anthony Comstock, *Frauds Exposed* (N. Y., 1880), chap. xix;
G. P. Rowell, *Forty Years an Advertising Agent* (N. Y., 1906), chaps.
xlv-xlvi.

high-pressure advertising,[1] was also assisted, especially in rural towns, by traveling medicine shows. These reached their greatest vogue in the 1880's and 1890's. Gathered about the medicine wagon in a circle dimly lighted by a flickering kerosene torch, the gaping crowd listened approvingly to the banjoist's vocal rendition of such ditties as "The Animal Fair," and then, as the long-haired, self-styled doctor harrowed their feelings with tales of the fatal results of certain symptoms common to all, showered the boards with coins for his famous "Indian" remedy.[2] The addiction of untold numbers to fantastic "cures" forms a splendid testimonial to the basic robustness of the American stock.

As in medical science, so in surgery the germ theory wrought a transformation, largely through the efforts of the Englishman Joseph Lister, a follower of Pasteur, who about 1865 established the principle of cleanliness in wound treatment. By opening up new opportunities for operative skill, antiseptic surgery, as it was called, gave American practitioners for the first time ample scope for their manual dexterity.[3] Intestinal operations had seldom been attempted earlier because even accidental wounds of internal tissues might cause destructive inflammations; but now the whole domain of abdominal

[1] See earlier, 196-198.

[2] The Kickapoo Indian Medicine Company, organized in 1881, for a time hired about a thousand Indians as "atmosphere" for its wagon shows. N. T. Oliver (Nevada Ned) and Wesley Stout, "Med Show," *Sat. Eve. Post*, CCII, 12 ff. (Sept. 14, 1929). T. J. Le Blanc, "The Medicine Show," *Am. Mercury*, V (1925), 232-237, is a veracious sketch. Both James Whitcomb Riley and Paul Dresser, future composer of "On the Banks of the Wabash," traveled with such shows in the 1870's. Marcus Dickey, *The Youth of James Whitcomb Riley* (Indianapolis, 1919), chap. v, and Theodore Dreiser, *The Songs of Paul Dresser* (N. Y., 1927), v.

[3] Shrady, "Recent Triumphs in Medicine and Surgery," 28-33; same author, "American Achievements in Surgery," *Forum*, XVII (1894), 167-178; Frederick Peterson, "Recent Progress in Medicine and Surgery," *Journ. of Social Sci.*, XXXI (1894), 1-lx.

surgery was explored and conquered, in large part by Americans. Appendicitis was robbed of most of its terrors, and the removal of the appendix reduced to almost a minor operation, as a result of the researches of Reginald H. Fitz at Harvard.[1] Great advances were also made in the surgery of eye, ear and brain.

At one critical turn in the history of these years the surgeon's hand proved more effective than the statesman's in holding to a steady course the ship of state. In July, 1893, at the crest of the financial panic, the knife of Dr. J. D. Bryant of New York saved President Cleveland's life from a malignant growth (sarcoma) of the upper left jaw. The principal operation occurred on a yacht in New York Harbor and, because of the precarious state of public affairs, all knowledge of the president's desperate plight as well as of his convalescence was withheld from Congress and the nation.[2] When the closing years of the period brought to America Roentgen's discovery of the X-ray, satisfaction at this new boon to surgery was alloyed only by the reflection that, had the knowledge been possessed twenty years before, the assassin's bullet in Garfield's body would have been correctly located and the life of another president probably saved.

The germ theory registered its greatest triumph in the new direction given to community efforts for health conservation. Recurrent epidemics had caused most of the large cities and fifteen of the states to set up boards of health prior to 1878.[3] In 1878-1879 yellow fever swept

[1] In his classic paper, "Perforating Inflammation of the Vermiform Appendix; with Special Reference to Its Early Diagnosis and Treatment," published in the first volume of the *Transactions* of the Association of American Physicians in 1886, he named the disease appendicitis, traced its origin to the appendix and, in defiance of existing practice, advocated radical surgical intervention for its cure.

[2] W. W. Keen, *The Surgical Operations on President Cleveland in 1893* (Phila., 1928), chap. i.

[3] See Nevins, *Emergence of Modern America*, 322-323.

through the Gulf states, Tennessee and, in some measure, Kentucky and Missouri, exacting a toll of sixteen thousand lives out of about seventy-four thousand afflicted.[1] At Memphis, where the scourge raged most fiercely, over five thousand died while twenty thousand others, fleeing in terror before an effective quarantine could be established, helped spread the plague to other communities. Although the transmitting cause of the disease continued to elude scientists, Memphis hastened to repair its criminal neglect of the past by laying out many miles of sewers and drainage tiles; and the nation-wide horror was reflected in the prompt creation of additional state boards of health. Twelve commonwealths acted before 1882 and fifteen others followed by the close of 1898.[2]

To the service of public-health agencies medical bacteriology brought a rational or scientific knowledge of disease prevention in place of the older empirical methods.[3] Early and definite diagnosis of infectious ailments became possible; new and effective systems of control were devised. Quarantine was extended to other ills than the traditional ones of smallpox and yellow fever, and port cities were barred against the admission of dangerous imported plagues like cholera and typhus. Progress was made also in providing special hospitals for the isolation and treatment of infectious cases. Equally important was the fact that, through a well-sustained publicity, the average citizen came to accept

[1] *Appletons' Annual Cyclopaedia*, XVIII (1878), 315-322; XIX (1879), 359-364.

[2] A national board was also created in 1879, but unfortunately was allowed to lapse four years later. In addition, the new interest led to the holding of an international sanitary conference at Washington in 1881. S. W. Abbott, *The Past and Present Condition of Public Hygiene and State Medicine in the United States* (H. B. Adams, ed., *Monographs on American Social Economics*, XIX, Boston, 1900), 11, 14-16.

[3] F. P. Gorham, "Bacteriology and Its Relation to Public Health Work," M. P. Ravenel, ed., *A Half Century of Public Health* (N. Y., 1921), 76-90.

personal cleanliness as an ally of health as well as of godliness. Smooth-shaven jowls began to emerge from behind the unhygienic whiskers of Civil War times; and the constant drive against tuberculosis led to a steady banishment of the national vice of spitting, noted by foreign travelers since colonial times.

Such efforts, it will be recalled, were supplemented by the enterprise of municipalities in constructing water and drainage systems, inspecting milk supplies, undertaking pure-food measures, and the like.[1] Sanitary engineering, though it had its own reasons for being, was an indispensable arm of the public-health movement. The war against disease, of course, was hampered by the limited knowledge of the age, especially in regard to methods of immunization, and sometimes also by the interference of time-serving politicians. Yet, despite these handicaps and the further difficulty presented by the herding of immigrants in the worst quarters of the cities, the mortality rate in the United States fell nearly ten per cent from 1890 to 1900, and the average age at death rose from thirty-one years to thirty-five.[2] This gain was due largely to the lessening mortality from tuberculosis, diphtheria and children's diseases. The benefits of public-health efforts fell chiefly to the cities where, of course, the need was greatest. It was a fortunate conjunction of circumstances for America that, when the age of large cities arrived, medical science made it possible to protect the dense population centers from the terrible scourges which for so many centuries had ravaged Europe.

[1] See earlier, 102-105, 110-111, 133-134.

[2] In the absence of reliable vital statistics for most of the country, these figures, strictly interpreted, apply only to the registration area. See *U. S. Twelfth Census* (1900), III, lvii, lxxxvi-lxxxvii, and *Supplementary Analysis and Derivative Tables* (U. S. Twelfth Census, *Special Rep.*), 495, 504-507.

CHAPTER VIII

THE RENAISSANCE IN LETTERS AND ARTS

SUPERFICIALLY, America presented such an appearance of bustle and clatter that Bryce did not understand how anyone could "withdraw his mind from the endless variety of external impressions" long enough for the "repose and meditation which art and philosophy need." "The noise of living drowns the celestial harmonies," agreed a French visitor.[1] Yet, just as American life was being channeled by science and scholarship, so amidst the turmoil of everyday living significant changes were occurring in literature and the fine arts. Noise need not drown celestial harmonies if one's ear be attuned to stiller voices. Specialization of sense function seemed, indeed, a price of survival in the strange new complexity of life.

In the great cities writers and artists were quickly drawn into comradeship with persons like themselves, while in the nearness of publishers, art dealers and wealthy patrons they possessed a potential market for their wares. Hearkening to the siren call of Boston in the early 1880's, Hamlin Garland, having mortgaged his newly won Dakota homestead for the purpose, spent a bleak but glorious winter living in an attic room on Boylston Place. "My mental diaphragm creaked with the pressure of inrushing ideas," he wrote in later years. Shortly he discovered himself freely communing with

[1] James Bryce, *The American Commonwealth* (London, 1888), III, 559; S. C. de Soissons, *A Parisian in America* (Boston, 1896), 182.

247

fellow craftsmen like Mary E. Wilkins (Freeman) and
Sylvester Baxter and even with the great Mr. Howells
himself.[1] About the same time the youthful James L.
Ford in New York found intellectual oases on every
hand—in newspaper rooms and magazine offices, in the
convivial gatherings at cheap *table d'hôte* restaurants, in
the homes of established literary friends.[2] The early
1890's saw the first migration of artists and writers to
Greenwich Village in the heart of lower Manhattan.
There, in old dwellings reclaimed from wretchedly poor
tenants, they would in time evolve a colorful life somewhat like that of the Latin Quarter in Paris. While no
Western city could rival the older cultural centers, yet
Cincinnati, St. Louis, San Francisco and notably Chicago
had their own colonies of literary and artistic folk,
which did for their localities what New York and, in
lesser degree, Boston and Philadelphia did for the
nation.

Many influences help account for the character and
variety of literary production. In greater or less measure
both author and publisher must bow to "the tyranny
exercised by the taste of the common-schooled millions
who have been taught to read, but have never learned to
discriminate."[3] The republic of letters had reached its
period of Jacksonian democracy. But if the number of
undiscriminating readers had never before been so large,
the same was also true of the number of cultivated
readers. "The conscientious publisher," wrote Charles
Dudley Warner, "asks two questions: Is the book good?
and Will it sell? The publisher without a conscience asks

[1] Hamlin Garland, *A Son of the Middle Border* (N. Y., 1917),
chaps. xxv-xxix.

[2] J. L. Ford, *Forty-Odd Years in the Literary Shop* (N. Y., 1921),
passim.

[3] Paul Shorey, "Present Conditions of Literary Production," *Atlantic
Mo.*, LXXVIII (1896), 156. See also James Bryce, *Studies in History
and Jurisprudence* (N. Y., 1901), I, 200.

only one question: Will the book sell?"[1] The author, too, had to make his choice, though compunctions of conscience probably played a lesser part with him than financial need or his particular literary flair.

A special characteristic of the enlarged reading public was the arbitrament exercised by women. Apart from newspaper humorists, who might safely cater to crude masculine tastes, no writer of fiction could hope to get far without the favor of that sex which, generally speaking, had both greater leisure and liking for literary cultivation.[2] And women were stalwart upholders of the genteel tradition, being averse to vulgarity or frank discussion of sex, and partial to sentiment, especially moral and domestic sentiment. To a literary rebel like H. H. Boyesen the woman reader was "the Iron Madonna who strangles in her fond embrace the American novelist."[3] It seems likely that the feminine influence had much to do with preventing the local-color school from achieving the stark realism of Continental European portraiture. Besides, women themselves were prolific and successful as fictionists, especially in New England and the South, and thus, by direct intervention, helped buttress that attitude toward literature which Gilder of the *Century* called "good taste."

To meet the increased demand for books publishing houses grew in number and size. The *Dial*, which contained notices of just ten firms in its first issue in 1880, twenty years later carried advertisements of nearly a

---

[1] C. D. Warner, "The Novel and the Common School" (1890), reprinted in *The Relation of Literature to Life* (N. Y., 1897), 272.

[2] W. D. Howells, *Literature and Life* (N. Y., 1902), 21-22; Bryce, *American Commonwealth*, III, 521-522; R. W. Gilder, "Certain Tendencies in Current Literature," *New Princeton Rev.*, IV (1887), 7-10; O. B. Bunce, "Literature for Women," *Critic*, n.s., XII (1889), 67-68.

[3] H. H. Boyesen, "Why We Have No Great Novelists," *Forum*, II (1886-1887), esp. 619.

hundred.[1] Publishing houses sprang up in New York like mushrooms after a spring rain. Besides important new concerns like the Century Company, the Frederick A. Stokes Company and the Macmillan Company, a migration of publishers set in from other cities. Yet Boston, Philadelphia and other places continued to be centers of consequence.[2] Chicagoans were not slow to point out that in sheer volume of output their city outranked even New York, their presses emitting tons of German and Scandinavian Bibles for the farmhouses of the Northwest and enormous quantities of school-books, not to mention unnumbered cheap editions of trashy novels and "pirated" works.[3]

So keen was the popular appetite for books that the publishers' annual lists contained an ever increasing number of new titles in nearly every department of reading matter. While fiction consistently led every other class, at no time did it represent more than a minority of the total. In the first few years religious works and children's stories contended for second position, but both were presently outstripped by legal publications.

[1] F. F. Browne, "American Publishing and Publishers," Dial, XXVIII (1900), 340-343. The total number of publishers was actually much larger, for in 1894 Harper listed 617, of which 187 were in New York, 60 in Philadelphia, 52 in Boston, 51 in Chicago and 12 in San Francisco. Most of these, however, published only a few books annually. J. W. Harper, "American Publishing," C. M. Depew, ed., One Hundred Years of American Commerce (N. Y., 1895), I, 309.

[2] In Boston the historic firm of Houghton, Osgood & Company split into Houghton Mifflin & Company and J. R. Osgood & Company. Similarly, Ginn, Heath & Company divided into Ginn & Company and D. C. Heath & Company.

[3] H. B. Fuller, "The Upward Movement in Chicago," Atlantic Mo., LXXX (1897), esp. 544. Because of the character of much of this output E. W. Bok denominated Chicago "something akin to a literary sewer," but others thought it no worse than other great cities. Publishers' Wkly., XLVII, 460-461, 537 (March 16, 30, 1895). Of course, Chicago possessed firms like A. C. McClurg & Company and the Fleming H. Revell Company which vied with those of the East in the quality of their publications.

During the economic unrest of the mid-nineties books on history, government and social questions forged into second place, with works on law and religion ranking third and fourth.[1]

In fiction the interest of readers is more clearly indicated by library-circulation figures. These show a strong persistence of past preferences with but a cautious adoption of new ones. Judged by a canvass of leading libraries in 1893, *David Copperfield* was the most popular novel, then *Ivanhoe*, followed by *The Scarlet Letter, Uncle Tom's Cabin, Ben Hur, Adam Bede, Vanity Fair, Jane Eyre* and *The Last Days of Pompeii*.[2] Dickens was the most widely read novelist, with Louisa May Alcott, Walter Scott, E. P. Roe, James Fenimore Cooper, George Eliot, Nathaniel Hawthorne, O. W. Holmes, Bulwer Lytton and Thackeray as his chief rivals— evidence a-plenty of the existence, not of one but of a gradation of reading publics. Mark Twain, F. Marion Crawford, Frank R. Stockton and W. D. Howells appeared respectively as thirteenth, fifteenth, eighteenth and twenty-sixth on the list. Their relatively low ranking, together with the absence of the leaders of the American local-color school, probably indicates merely that the public was content as yet to read them in the current magazines. On the other hand, the omission of the younger English novelists like Hardy, Meredith and Stevenson and of contemporary Russian and French fictionists suggests the restricted horizon of the average reader.

For both publisher and author, the chaos resulting

[1] Classified data appear in annual summaries published in the *Publishers' Wkly.*, starting in Jan., 1880; and the totals of copyrighted works may be found in the annual reports of the Librarian of Congress. The discrepancies between the two sets of figures are too great to justify any but the most general conclusions.

[2] H. W. Mabie, "The Most Popular Novels in America," *Forum*, XVI (1893-1894), 508-516.

from the lack of international copyright arrangements was fast becoming intolerable. It would be difficult to exaggerate the hampering effect which this anomalous situation had had for many years on the growth of an autochthonous literature.[1] So long as publishers and magazine editors could reprint, or pirate, popular English authors without payment of royalty, and so long as readers could buy such volumes far cheaper than books written by Americans, native authorship remained at a marked disadvantage.[2] As early as 1837 petitions signed by prominent authors on both sides of the Atlantic had been presented to Congress on behalf of an international copyright; but to this and later appeals that body had remained uniformly cold. Publishers, for the most part, were satisfied with the existing situation, while many other persons, lacking a selfish motive, deemed low-priced books essential for a rapid diffusion of culture among the mass of the people. Even Mark Twain wrote Howells in 1880:

> My notions have mightily changed lately. I can buy *Macaulay's History*, three vols., bound, for $1.25; *Chambers's Cyclopaedia*, ten vols., cloth, for $7.25 (we paid $60), and other English copyrights in proportion; I can buy a lot of the great copyright classics, in paper, at from three to thirty cents apiece. These things must find their way into the very kitchens and hovels of the country.[3]

[1] For the consequences in an earlier period, see C. R. Fish, *The Rise of the Common Man* (*A History of American Life*, VI), 248-249.

[2] "A volume of Carlyle," said the *Hour* (N. Y.), April 21, 1883, "may be bought at the price of a glass of whiskey, but a volume of Emerson . . . is as costly as a pint bottle of champagne."

[3] A. B. Paine, *Mark Twain* (N. Y., 1912), II, 687. In another and soberer mood he pointed out that the "cheap alien books" contained "an ounce of wholesome literature to a hundred tons of noxious." G. H. Putnam, comp., *The Question of Copyright* (N. Y., 1891), 343; "Mark Twain on Copyright," *Publishers' Wkly.*, XXXIII, 77 (Jan. 21, 1888).

This attitude, which Twain swiftly repented, ignored, of course, other aspects of the matter, notably the question of common honesty involved in the international theft of literary property.

Among the better publishers a "courtesy of the trade" had gradually developed whereby, if one of them bought the advance sheets or made other payment to a foreign author or publisher, the rest refrained from issuing reprints. But the practice collapsed with the crowding in of many new book concerns in the 1870's and 1880's and the sharp competition offered by their endless "libraries" of cheap paper-back reprints. Disreputable piracy was ruining the business of respectable piracy. At the same time American publishers discovered that their own books were being increasingly pirated abroad. By 1878 one in every ten works issued in England was an American reprint.[1] Longfellow ruefully admitted having twenty-two unsought publishers there. By a process perhaps more appropriately called kidnaping than piracy, John Habberton's *Helen's Babies* appeared in nine British editions besides four in the colonies. The serial publication of his next book precipitated such a scramble that one British firm issued it without the final chapter and another with the conclusion furnished by an English hand.[2] The prime recipients of the dubious compliment, however, were Hawthorne, Mrs. Stowe, Miss Alcott and Roe. Meanwhile, across the Canadian border, enterprising dealers not only marketed reprinted American novels locally, but sold them in the United States by mail in

[1] Putnam, *Question of Copyright*, 92. Brander Matthews, "American Authors and British Pirates," *New Princeton Rev.*, IV (1887), 201-212, and V (1888), 54-65, cites many specific instances of British literary piracy.

[2] G. H. Putnam, "International Copyright," *Publishers' Wkly.*, XV, 350 (March 22, 1879). James Russell Lowell's ministership to England (1880-1885) was the occasion for the unauthorized reprinting of his many writings in countless cheap "libraries."

competition with the authorized editions. Mark Twain believed that Canadian piracy cost him an average of five thousand dollars a year.[1]

As a result of these developments the more reputable American publishers became as clamorous as the united authors for an international copyright. In 1878 Harper & Brothers, long in opposition, proposed to the state department a draft treaty on the subject with Great Britain, but the slow negotiations were brought to a close by the death of President Garfield.[2] His successor, Chester A. Arthur, recommended legislative action instead. At the same time public opinion, energized by the American Copyright League, founded by leading authors and magazine editors in 1883, and the American Publishers' Copyright League (1887), exerted increasing pressure upon Congress. The chief resistance came from organizations representing typographers, binders and employing printers. When their objections were met by a provision requiring separate manufacture of the foreign book in America, the international-copyright law was finally enacted by Congress on March 4, 1891.[3]

Under this act authors belonging to foreign countries willing to make reciprocal arrangements were granted the privilege of copyright on virtually the same terms as native authors. France, Great Britain, Germany and other governments speedily made the required arrangements with the United States. While the law, particu-

[1] Paine, Mark Twain, II, 687.

[2] J. H. Harper, The House of Harper (N. Y., 1928), 425-428; R. R. Bowker, Copyright: Its History and Its Law (Boston, 1912), 354-356.

[3] Putnam, Question of Copyright, 142-185, 380-410. The law also applied to works of art and musical compositions without, however, requiring American manufacture. In the case of the latter this made possible a continuance of "song piracy," greatly to the discontent of reputable music publishers. Publishers' Wkly., XL, 141-142 (July 25, 1891); LI, 997 (June 19, 1897); LIII, 489 (March 12, 1898).

larly in its manufacturing clause, fell short of the standard set by leading powers in the Berne copyright convention of 1887,[1] it had the important effect of stabilizing the book market at home and abroad for both publisher and author. By the same token it removed a stain from the national honor. Whether aspiring young authors found it easier thereafter to secure publishers it would be difficult to know; but it is at least suggestive that the year 1894 saw, for the first time, more novels published in the United States from American pens than from European.[2]

Never before had writers been more authentically children of their own era. Responding instinctively to the sharpening conflict between urban and rural culture, their sensitive artistry mirrored the varying and inconsistent moods evoked by the new orientation of society. Some sought to preserve in their pages idyllic glimpses of a civilization fast passing: a new South recalled the old South. Some, symbolizing their own removal to the city, viewed the traditional culture with acute distaste. Others perceived in the city itself an unanticipated source of gathering ills. And amidst this confusion of tongues flourished still others who, turning their backs on what they did not care to see, sounded the clarion call to romance and forgetfulness.

Literary preoccupation with the West, so pronounced in the 1870's,[3] was eclipsed by the new attention given the South. The West still spoke, but with feebler voice

[1] All the signatory nations agreed, as among themselves, to treat foreigners and citizens identically alike in the matter of copyright; there was no manufacturing clause. Putnam, *Question of Copyright*, 297-323.

[2] *Publishers' Wkly.*, XLVII, 170 (Jan. 26, 1895). See also A. R. Spofford, "Directions and Volume of Our Literary Activities," and G. H. Putnam, "Results of the Copyright Law," *Forum*, XVI (1893-1894), 602-604, 616-623.

[3] Allan Nevins, *The Emergence of Modern America* (*A History of American Life*, VIII), 247-254; F. L. Pattee, *A History of American Literature since 1870* (N. Y., 1915), chap. xiv.

and usually to less eager listeners. In 1878 Bret Harte left America to spend the rest of his life abroad, writing year after year new volumes of highly colored stories of California life without regaining his earlier American following. Edward Eggleston, while publishing several novels concerned with his favorite theme of primitive society in Hoosierland, gave himself by preference to magazine editing and historical research. Mark Twain, however, succeeded in adding Huckleberry Finn (1884) and Pudd'nhead Wilson (1894) to his notable gallery of Mid-Western characters, and Helen Hunt Jackson, an Easterner by birth, scored a brilliant success in *Ramona* (1884), a romance of the passing of the old Spanish order in California.

By contrast, the fictional world veritably swarmed with decayed Southern gentlemen, ladies of the old régime, Virginia darkies, Georgia crackers, Tennessee mountaineers and Louisiana Creoles, limned by brushes that blended a nice attention to dialect and local color with a mellow glow of sentiment. It was as though Dixie, long negligent of her literary riches and freed from the palsying effects of slavery, had commissioned her sons and daughters to take their rightful place in the world of letters. Virtually all the important writers, Harris being a notable exception, were children of the prewar planter aristocracy. Thomas Nelson Page and F. Hopkinson Smith portrayed with tender feeling the life of the old Virginia gentry. In finely wrought sketches George W. Cable, Grace King and Kate Chopin introduced a wondering America to the exotic orange-scented atmosphere of Creole life among the Louisiana bayous. Charles Egbert Craddock's *In the Tennessee Mountains* (1884) and many later volumes wove tales about the humble folk living amid the grandeur of the interior highlands, while James Lane Allen wrote with careful artistry of human passion and conflict against a Kentucky background.

None of these literary creations, however, seems so certain of lasting fame as the folk stories retold by a young Georgia reporter writing against time to fill up space in his newspaper, the *Atlanta Constitution*. When Joel Chandler Harris in 1880 published his first volume of Uncle Remus tales, he at once gained a wide audience —among lovers of humor, among children, among students of folklore—which he was never to relinquish. Quite apart from their literary charm, these Negro animal legends, recounted so faithfully by Harris through Uncle Remus, are of interest to the social historian, for they are an unconscious revelation of the soul of a people —their wisdom, their fun, their pathos. Br'er Rabbit, most timid of forest creatures, was none other than the black race itself. Br'er Rabbit's versatile use of roguery and deceit to outwit Br'er Fox and Br'er Wolf betokened a helpless people's sole defense against major force and vested oppression.

While New England also had its sectional spokesmen, they wrote not of a glamorous past but of the gray realities of the present. How had the drift to the cities affected the inner life of the men and women who continued to dwell in the stagnant villages and on the deserted countryside? Their pages abound in acute but sympathetic portrayals of narrow, repressed, introspective lives. Authors like Sarah Orne Jewett, Mary E. Wilkins and Rose Terry Cooke made themselves authentic chroniclers of New England's rural decline.

In general, the local colorists of all sections erred upon the side of *genre* painting, their art failing to make vital and convincing the part their regional characters played in the situations in which Fate had entangled them. The

limits of realistic treatment were so sharply marked
among the new Southern school that in 1879 Cable
changed his residence to Northampton, Massachusetts,
in order to be able to write without constraint on Southern themes, particularly the Negro question. Likewise
Walter Hines Page, thwarted in his ardent efforts as a
North Carolina newspaper editor to lay those foes of
progress, "the Ghost of the Confederate dead, the Ghost
of religious orthodoxy, the Ghost of Negro domination,"
removed in 1885 to the North, where his literary abilities
soon won him recognition, first as staff writer on the
New York Evening Post, and then as editor successively
of the *Forum* and of the *Atlantic.*[1]

The local colorists, for the most part, wrote in innocence of the school of mordant realism which had its
exemplars in Europe in such masters as Flaubert,
Maupassant, Zola, Tolstoy, Gogol, Turgeniev, Dostoi-
evski and Björnson.[2] For traces of this powerful movement one must look, rather, to the writings of William
Dean Howells and Henry James who worked more consciously in the world stream of literature. Their realism,
however, was less of the sordid and ugly aspects of life
than a faithful reporting of the foibles and trials of
middle-class folk living on the same general plane of
existence as themselves. As a wit phrased it, "the present
realism in fiction is in France a discovery of the un-
clean, and in America a discovery of the unimportant."[3]
Howells was a Middle Westerner who had deserted his
native heath for the cultured atmosphere of Boston;
James an Easterner who, sensitive to the crudenesses of

[1] B. J. Hendrick, *The Life and Letters of Walter H. Page* (Garden
City, 1921), I, 42-63, 72-83; W. H. Page (Nicholas Worth, *pseud.*),
The Southerner (N. Y., 1909), chaps. xi-xxxi.

[2] The great activity in publishing translations from the Russian began
in 1886. *Publishers' Wkly.,* XXXIII, 319 (Feb. 11, 1888).

[3] Quoted by Gilder, "Certain Tendencies in Current Literature," 2.

even literary Boston, fled American shores for the older, riper civilization of Europe.

Both were expert craftsmen; but Howells tempered his acute observation of everyday mankind with kindly and tolerant understanding, while James, impaling his human creatures as an entomologist his insects, subjected them to a relentless dissection which made his pages more minutely psychological than those of his brother William, the professional psychologist. Howells dealt characteristically with American life and American materials, and never perhaps rose to greater artistic heights than in *A Modern Instance* (1882) and *The Rise of Silas Lapham* (1884), both unforgettable transcripts of Boston life. James displayed his unique powers to best advantage in tales like *Daisy Miller* (1878), *An International Episode* (1879) and *The Portrait of a Lady* (1881), dealing with the clash of Old World culture upon Americans abroad. Along with the local colorists, these men did much to mold the short story into a finished work of art, a form characterized by compactness and singleness of impression.

The grimmer realism lacking in Howells and James found expression in a younger group of writers. Their work, however, reflected less the current European mode than it did a sharp dissent from the romantic notions of pioneer life prevalent among Easterners. To Western youths ambitious of the intellectual opportunities afforded by the city, the rural life of the 1880's seemed, by contrast, a barren, drear, soul-starving existence. They were less impressed by the pleasures of communing with nature than by "the grime and the mud and the sweat"; "the working farmer . . . must pitch manure as well as clover." [1]

The note of disillusionment was first powerfully

[1] Garland, *Son of the Middle Border,* 377. See also earlier, 60-61.

sounded in E. W. Howe's *The Story of a Country Town* (1884), a morbid, strongly etched tale of the constricted life of Atchison, Kansas, written by a local newspaper editor.[1] Two years later Joseph Kirkland added to the indictment *Zury; the Meanest Man in Spring County,* and Harold Frederic wrote *Seth's Brother's Wife.* Then in 1891 Hamlin Garland published his first of a series of harsh, acrid sketches dealing with Mid-Western rural life. For it the author sardonically chose the title *Main-Travelled Roads* because, as he explained in a foreword, in a farming region the main road "is long and wearyful and has a dull town at one end and a home of toil at the other."[2]

Other fictionists, however, were discovering that even the city was not all sweetness and light; that it had drab and sordid aspects, its way of thwarting human hopes; that the industrial system upon which it fed was a prolific womb of man's inhumanity to man. Such writers as John Hay, the anonymous author of *The Bread-Winners* (1883), and Robert Barr in *The Mutable Many* (1896) dealt trenchantly with the labor problem. In *The Mammon of Unrighteousness* (1891) Boyesen exposed the brutalizing effects of ill-gotten wealth. Paul Leicester Ford's *The Honorable Peter Stirling* (1894) presented a striking study of ward politics in New York with Grover Cleveland supposedly as its central figure. The youthful Stephen Crane, after the manner of Zola,

---

[1] A reviewer thought it "not true to Western life, which is the most cheerful and rollicking life in the world; but it is true to Mr. Howe's disgust for its limitations, its lack of sympathy with art, its rawness, and its uninspiring air of mere bigness." "Contributors' Club," *Atlantic Mo.,* LVI (1885), 715.

[2] Garland was execrated in the West as "a bird willing to foul his own nest." Statistics were discovered to show "that pianos and Brussels carpets adorned almost every Iowa farmhouse." Garland, *Son of the Middle Border,* esp. 415. *Prairie Folks* (Chicago, 1892) and *A Little Norsk* (N. Y., 1892) repeated the essential qualities of the first book. He set forth his literary creed in *Crumbling Idols* (Chicago, 1894).

contributed a somber picture of slum degeneracy in *Maggie, a Girl of the Streets* (1892).[1] Even Howells, confronted by "the hideousness of a competitive metropolis" when he removed to New York in the late eighties, and deeply disquieted by the Haymarket riot and other portents of threatening class war, turned his deft pen to criticism of the existing social order.[2] "What I object to," he makes Basil March say in *A Hazard of New Fortunes,*

> is this economic chance-world in which we live. . . . It ought to be law as inflexible in human affairs as the order of day and night in the physical world, that if a man will work he shall both rest and eat, and shall not be harassed with any question as to how his repose and provision shall come.[3]

What "ought to be law" was magically made law by a group of novelists who dreamed worlds in which chaos and self-seeking were replaced by a society of millennial perfection. Under different circumstances America might have experienced another epidemic of socialistic communities like those of the thirties and forties.[4] But with desirable cheap lands difficult to get and the growing disrepute of rural life, the heat vented itself through the exhaust pipe of fiction. Over two score writers indulged

[1] In his best-known work *The Red Badge of Courage* (N. Y., 1895) Crane recreated out of his imagination a story of the Civil War, stocked with repulsive details of army life and the battle-field.

[2] The quoted phrase is taken from a striking passage attributed to a character in *The World of Chance* (N. Y., 1893), 297. Howells's recent discovery of Tolstoy undoubtedly facilitated the transition. See D. G. Cooke, *William Dean Howells* (N. Y., 1922), chap. vii; W. F. Taylor, "On the Origin of Howells' Interest in Economic Reform," *Am. Literature*, II, 3-14; and A. L. Bass, "The Social Consciousness of William Dean Howells," *New Republic*, XXVI (1921), 192-194.

[3] W. D. Howells, *A Hazard of New Fortunes* (N. Y., 1889), II, 252. See also his *Annie Kilburn* (N. Y., 1888), *The Quality of Mercy* (N. Y., 1892) and *The World of Chance.*

[4] See Fish, *Rise of the Common Man,* 189-190, 252-253.

themselves in such fine-spun fancies; and while few of their efforts ranked high as *belles-lettres,* there can be no doubt that they ministered to an inarticulate yearning of the public.[1] The most widely read, though not the earliest, of these homespun utopias was Edward Bellamy's *Looking Backward, 2000-1887,* published in 1888. The author visioned a society in which the mighty trust development of the 1880's had fruited in one great all-embracing trust, owned and operated by the people in their own interest. Everyone was obliged to work, hence everyone had leisure. Poverty and its attendant evil, crime, were unknown; hospitals served in the place of prisons; and the creative energies of humanity were released for an unparalleled intellectual and technological advance. With minor variations the same theme recurred in most of the other novels. Howells made his contribution in *A Traveller from Altruria* (1894), while in the Middle West the Populist *littérateur* Ignatius Donnelly, skillfully reversing the formula in *Caesar's Column* (1890), pictured the climax of current economic tendencies in a stupendous social cataclysm. More than any of its competitors, Bellamy's fantasy captured the popular imagination, nearly four hundred thousand copies being sold in ten years in the United States alone. His system of "Nationalism" seemed so far from visionary that it led to a short-lived organized movement in its support.[2]

Romance, however, did not need to be flavored with purpose in order to win a large audience. Lew Wallace's

[1] A. B. Forbes, "The Literary Quest for Utopia, 1880-1900," *Social Forces,* VI, 179-189, includes a list of these writings. The absence of the terms, socialism and communism, from these volumes suggests that the authors' inspiration came wholly, or chiefly, from their American environment.

[2] See later, 426. While writing the book Bellamy became so convinced of its early practicability that he shifted the date of his commonwealth from the year 3000 to 2000. *Nationalist* (Boston), I (1889), 1-4.

Ben Hur, published in 1880, was probably more widely read than any other American novel of equal merit produced during these years. The most brilliant romancer of the era, however, and a much more fecund author, was F. Marion Crawford, son of the sculptor Thomas Crawford, whose long residence abroad fitted him in an unusual degree to deal with Old World themes. To read him gave the public a sense of cosmopolitan breadth and an intimate familiarity with aristocratic society in many lands. Beginning with *Mr. Isaacs* (1882)—which anticipated Kipling by five years in its Indian *locale*—nearly every year saw one or more volumes from his pen. By the close of 1896 his American sales alone totaled nearly half a million copies.[1] Mark Twain also entered the lists but with tongue in cheek. His *The Prince and the Pauper* (1881) and *A Connecticut Yankee in King Arthur's Court* (1889), designed to rob the past of its spurious claims to high romance, were vastly enjoyed by countless readers.

For the semiliterate masses nothing less would suffice than the sentimental unrealities of writers like Mary J. Holmes, Bertha M. Clay and Laura Jean Libbey.[2] Such novels as *Parted at the Altar* and *Fancy Free Yet Linked for Life* injected a welcome glow of romance into drab lives and enabled factory girls and kitchen maids to see themselves as beautiful, suffering heroines courted by knightly and quite impossible heroes. The death of the Reverend E. P. Roe in 1888 revealed the fact that his

[1] *Publishers' Wkly.,* LI, 83 (Jan. 23, 1897). His Italian cycle: *Saracinesca, Sant' Ilario, Don Orsino* and *Corleone* (1887-1896), reveal his work at its best. For the outburst of historical romances at the end of the nineties, see H. U. Faulkner, *The Quest for Social Justice* (*A History of American Life,* XI), 261-262.

[2] Bertha M. Clay was the pen name at various times of Frederick Van Rensselaer Dey and J. R. Coryell who were also expert dime novelists. Miss Libbey was known to her acquaintances as Mrs. Van Mater Stilwell, the prosperous wife of a Brooklyn lawyer. J. E. Pember, "Laura Jean Libbey's 'Happy Endings,'" *Boston Herald,* Nov. 2, 1924.

unnumbered moralistic tales had been earning him an
annual royalty of fifteen thousand dollars.[1]

No department of fiction showed more varied currents or, on the whole, greater progress than that for
children. Where parental rule was firm and watchful,
the older type of didactic story was apt to prevail—
tales of saintly candidates for early graves. This persistence of goody-goody literature, for example, brought
almost yearly additions to the *Elsie* series, in which the
author, Martha F. Finley, painstakingly followed the
career of her exemplary heroine, Elsie Dinsmore, from
infancy to old age. Where parents were less vigilant the
dime novel made its inroads. Youthful imagination,
sated with "moral sugar-plums," [2] was naturally attracted by legendary feats of valor on the Western plains
and the exciting exploits of criminal bands in the great
cities. "Stories for children," remarked a newspaper
humorist, "used to begin, 'Once upon a time there lived
—.' Now they begin, 'Vengeance, blood, sdeath,
shouted Rattlesnake Jim,' or words to that effect." [3]
Among the favorite characters were Deadwood Dick,
Mustang Sam, Denver Dan and the superdetectives, Old
Cap Collier and Old Sleuth, all heroes of a succession of
gory and breathless adventures illustrated by luridly
colored paper covers.

Harlan P. Halsey, author of the *Old Sleuth* series,
wrote nearly six hundred and fifty dime novels before
his death in 1898 and is said to have amassed nearly half
a million dollars from his trade.[4] Like his fellow crafts-

[1] *Publishers' Wkly.*, XXXIV, 140 (July 28, 1888). See also Matthew Arnold, *Civilization in the United States* (Boston, 1888), 184.
[2] Julian Hawthorne's characterization in *Confessions and Criticisms*
(Boston, 1886), 125.
[3] "Phunnygraphs," *Exeter* (N. H.) *News-Letter*, May 5, 1882.
[4] *Publishers' Wkly.*, LIV, 1137 (Dec. 24, 1898); anon., "Harlan
Page Halsey," *Current Literature*, XXV (1899), 114-115; Edmund
Pearson, *Dime Novels* (Boston, 1929), 191-197.

Old Sleuth Library

OLD IRONSIDES IN NEW YORK; OR, THE DAUGHTER OF THE G. A. R.
By OLD SLEUTH

A SERIES OF THE MOST THRILLING DETECTIVE STORIES EVER PUBLISHED.

| No. 54. | SINGLE NUMBER. | GEORGE MUNRO'S SONS, PUBLISHERS, 17 to 27 VANDEWATER ST., NEW YORK. | PRICE 5 CENTS. | Vol. III. |

Old Sleuth Library, Issued Quarterly.—By Subscription, 25 cents per Annum. Entered at the Post Office at New York at Second Class Rates.—September 26, 1891. Copyrighted in 1886, by George Munro.

Old Ironsides in New York;

OR,

The Daughter of the G. A. R.

BY OLD SLEUTH.

NEW YORK: GEORGE MUNRO'S SONS, PUBLISHERS, 17 TO 27 VANDEWATER STREET.

A "Dime Novel"

men he could dash off a book in a single day. George Munro, his publisher, engaged in a series of law suits to restrain rival firms from using the word, sleuth, which Halsey had coined as a synonym for detective; but in the end the New York supreme court decided against him and a new word, or at least a word with a new meaning, found its way into the American language.[1] Halsey served for ten years as a member of the New York board of education, much to the consternation of those who regarded his literary effusions as " 'hurrah-for-hades' publications" and incitements to juvenile criminality.[2] As a matter of fact, dime novels, though crudely written and replete with sensational incidents, pictured a world of immaculate morality in which villains always met their just deserts and virtue ever triumphed.

Of a somewhat higher degree of respectability were the boys' books written by Horatio Alger, Jr., and William T. Adams (Oliver Optic). Avoiding blood-and-thunder plots, these men wrote volume after volume to glorify the theme of worldly success, telling with mild variations of the poor but honest lad who, through pluck and perseverance, battled his way against seemingly impossible obstacles to fame and fortune. But even these books were banned by most librarians as presenting a false picture of life.

Luckily, children possessed the thumb-worn volumes of an earlier day: *Robinson Crusoe, Gulliver's Travels, The Swiss Family Robinson, Hans Brinker* and the

[1] *Publishers' Wkly.*, XXXV, 24-25 (Jan. 12, 1889); XXXVII, 253-254, 718 (Feb. 8, May 31, 1890).

[2] For stern disapproval of such "boy and girl devil-traps" and instances of their alleged responsibility for juvenile crime, see Anthony Comstock, *Traps for the Young* (N. Y., 1883), chap. iii, and *Library Journal* (N. Y.), VIII (1883), 36-37. For a more sympathetic attitude, read W. H. Bishop, "Story-Paper Literature," *Atlantic Mo.*, XLIV (1879), 383-389, and Pearson, *Dime Novels*, 90-103.

delightful girls' stories of Miss Alcott.[1] Luckily, too, their stock of reading was greatly enriched during these years by some of the most eminent writers of the time. Unwilling to leave the field to catch-penny sensationalists, such authors wrote books which combined honesty, virility and an understanding of American youth with good literary style. Two editors of the *Atlantic*— Howells and H. E. Scudder—entered the lists, Mark Twain, Harris and Stockton appealed to the spirit of youth in readers of all ages, while J. O. Kaler (James Otis) scored a merited success with his child classic of circus life, *Toby Tyler* (1881).

Soon young America was busily discovering new treasures in a stream of books flowing from the pens of Kaler, Kirk Munroe, Howard Pyle, Kate Douglas Wiggin, Hezekiah Butterworth and C. C. Coffin.[2] At the same time the very little ones found delight in Palmer Cox's drawings and stories of the inimitable "Brownies" —the Brownie Wheelman, the Brownie Policeman and other roly-poly reflections of the life of grown-ups. Much of the new juvenile fiction was purveyed through the pages of *St. Nicholas,* founded in 1873 with Mary Mapes Dodge as editor, its enterprise being rivaled by that of *Harper's Young People,* begun in 1879, and by a change of policy on the part of the older *Youth's Companion.* Two books by American authors scored sensational successes. One, Frances Hodgson Burnett's *Little Lord Fauntleroy* (1886), pictured the model child which every mother in her secret heart wants her boy to be; the other, *Peck's Bad Boy and His Pa*

[1] C. B. Tillinghast, "Books and Readers in Public Libraries," *Forum,* XVI (1893-1894), 64-65; Constance C. Harrison, "Some Favorites, Old and New," *Critic,* n.s., IV (1885), 253-254.

[2] Almost as popular were the pseudoscientific romances of the Frenchman Jules Verne, the historical novels of Anglo-Saxon valor written by the Englishman G. A. Henty, and Robert Louis Stevenson's tales of high adventure.

(1883) by George W. Peck, narrated the pranks of the kind of child every normal boy aspires to be. Though classed by most parents with dime novels, *Peck's Bad Boy* had already sold half a million copies by 1885.[1]

Every branch of literature was pervaded by humor—from Henry James's keen-edged satire and James Whitcomb Riley's wistful poems of childhood to the droll exaggerations of Bill Nye and Mark Twain.[2] Country folk had never before seemed so funny, particularly when they ventured out of their rustic environment. The experiences of the bucolic up-state New Yorker Samantha Allen at Saratoga, the Chicago World's Fair and elsewhere, as told by Marietta Holley, kept the nation in gales of laughter. The polyglot city had its own ludicrous characters. Charles Follen Adams wrote in rhyme of *Leedle Yawcob Strauss* (1877), while E. W. Townsend brought the slangy Bowery youth *Chimmie Fadden* (1895) to national attention. If misspelled words no longer seemed amusing for their own sake, dialect differences continued to delight a public rapidly becoming standardized in speech.

The typical humorists were trained in newspaper offices and, under pressure of the daily grind, their writings tended to be crisp, racy and ephemeral. Newspaper wags like the *"Danbury News* Man" (J. M. Bailey) and "M. Quad" (C. B. Lewis) commanded a delighted following, and prepared the way for the coming of Eugene Field and his many successors of a later day.[3]

[1] *Publishers' Wkly.*, XXVIII, 919-920 (Dec. 12, 1885).

[2] Although Mark Twain's humor marked an advance over that of his Western predecessors, it is unlikely that he would ever have become the force he was in American letters if Mrs. Clemens, Howells and other friendly critics had not helped turn him from the hoaxes and rollicking burlesque of his earlier work to the fields where his real talents lay. He seemed particularly lacking in the faculty of self-criticism.

[3] See P. W. Slosson, *The Great Crusade and After* (*A History of American Life*, XII), 355-356.

Perhaps the greatest of all "colyumists," Field from
1883 until his death in 1895 contributed a daily column
of "Sharps and Flats" to the *Chicago News*. His personal life was a ceaseless round of hoaxes and practical
jokes, and into his column he distilled the essence of a
brilliant and incorrigible wit.[1] If most American humor
lacked delicacy, composure and literary charm, the balance was in some measure redressed by the prolific writings of Frank R. Stockton. *Rudder Grange* (1879) and
The Casting Away of Mrs. Lecks and Mrs. Aleshine
(1886) illustrate his calmly ingenious manner of entangling matter-of-fact people in absurdly whimsical
situations. One of his short stories, "The Lady or the
Tiger?" (1884), though somewhat less characteristic
of his drollery, divided the reading public into two factions in a vain attempt to answer the question which
the author had artfully refrained from solving.

In poetry this generation fared less well. The great
masters of mid-century—Emerson, Whittier, Whitman
and the rest—dropped quietly from the scene burdened
with years, their places being taken by lesser figures. R.
H. Stoddard, T. B. Aldrich, E. C. Stedman, R. W.
Gilder, Richard Hovey, Madison Cawein—men like
these wrote with neatness, delicacy and faultless technique, but they were essentially romantic, seldom, if
ever, coming to grips with the throbbing life of their
times. Emily Dickinson, "small like the wren" and living secluded in her Berkshire village, composed brief
breathless poems which stabbed and startled by their
deftness of thought and phrase.[2] One of her fellow

---

[1] Cullings from his column were given book form in *A Little Book
of Western Verse* (N. Y., 1889), *A Little Book of Profitable Tales*
(N. Y., 1889) and other volumes.
[2] The first volume of her poems appeared in 1890, four years after
her death. For a critical appraisal of her work, see Conrad Aiken, ed.,
Selected Poems of Emily Dickinson (London, 1929), 5-22.

bards, Joaquin Miller, more bird of paradise than wren, sang the beauties of the mountain ranges from Alaska to Nicaragua—the poet preëminent of the untamed West. It was left, however, to two versifiers of lesser merit, both Middle Westerners, to tune their lyres to the heart of average humanity. Riley wrote wistfully tender dialect poems about rustic life—about "home," "old times," the "old swimmin' hole." His rival in popular favor, Will Carleton, had anticipated him with *Farm Ballads* (1873) and *Farm Legends* (1875); then, joining the trek to the city, discovered new play for his talents in *City Ballads* (1885), *City Legends* (1889) and *City Festivals* (1892).

While essayists addressed a more limited circle, these years showed that the number of such writers might be legion. None, however, displayed so rich or undisciplined a genius as Lafcadio Hearn.[1] The nature essay won increasing favor as outdoor life receded before the advance of the city. Thoreau, neglected earlier, came finally into his own, and the prose form which he did so much to perfect was further developed by John Burroughs and John Muir. Literary criticism flourished in the pages of the *Nation,* the *Dial* and the *Critic;* and never before in America had the art of book reviewing reached so high a plane. Yet professional criticism did less to mold literature than the standards imposed by publishers and editors intent on sales' possibilities and by the popular aversion to plain talk about the physical aspects of sex.[2]

When Mark Twain wrote his *Fireside Conversation in the Time of Queen Elizabeth,* a Rabelaisian effusion,

[1] Half Greek, half Celt, a wanderer in many lands, Hearn stands out of relation to his American environment—exotic, intensely individualistic, yet a dealer in fragments of imperishable beauty.

[2] As Gilder remarked in "Certain Tendencies in Current Literature," 8, "There are many who believe that America has the purest society in the world. Is not this purity worth paying for with a little prudery?"

it was hotly rejected by a magazine editor and, though privately printed by John Hay, its circulation was carefully restricted to a few friends.[1] When the Chicago merchant prince John Crerar in 1889 bequeathed two and a half million dollars for founding the great library which bears his name, he expressly excluded from the proposed collection "dirty French novels" and "works of questionable moral tone."[2] To nearly everyone Gallic frankness was a thorn in the flesh. Funk & Wagnalls wrathily declined to publish Daudet's *Sappho*, and when another firm issued Zola's *La Terre*, two booksellers in Nashville were fined for selling it.[3] The *American Medico-Surgical Journal* in 1895, after descanting on the moral poison administered by such works, added sarcastically, "As yet there exists no novel of the ear, no drama of the digestive organs, no romance of the kidneys, no pastels of the intestines."[4]

Victorian reticence found sanction in a federal law of 1873, which had been passed at the instigation of Anthony Comstock, a reformer whose nature embodied the passionate propriety of a long line of Puritan ancestors. As amended in 1876, the act inflicted heavy penalties for sending through the mails printed material or pictures of "an indecent character," the indecency to be adjudged by a federal court and jury. Although its repeal was demanded in 1878 by a two-thousand-foot petition containing fifty thousand names, the law not only remained on the statute books but was supplemented by state legislation as well. Moreover, Com-

[1] The pamphlet was retitled *1601*. Paine, *Mark Twain*, II, 580-581.
[2] J. D. Wade, "John Crerar," *Dict. of Am. Biog.*, IV, 537.
[3] *N. Y. Eve. Post*, July 10, 1884; *Publishers' Wkly.*, XXXIV, 184 (Aug. 11, 1888). For further evidence of a similar attitude, see Herbert Edwards, "Zola and the American Critics," *Am. Literature*, IV, 114-129.
[4] Quoted by *Publishers' Wkly.*, XLVII, 630 (April 13, 1895).

stock's Society for the Suppression of Vice in New York and similar groups in Boston, Cincinnati, Chicago, St. Louis and elsewhere undertook energetic enforcement. Thus, from 1873 to 1882, Comstock confiscated fourteen tons of books and sheet stock and a million and a half obscene circulars, poems and pictures.[1] While his efforts lessened improper newspaper advertising and reduced the amount of erotic matter in circulation among school youth, he unfortunately failed to distinguish between pornography on the one hand and literary classics and medical treatises on the other. His square, stocky figure, bald head and ginger-tinted side whiskers became for many the symbol of a licensed bigotry destructive of much that was choice in art and letters.

Despite deterrent influences these years stand forth as a new creative epoch in American letters, backed by a popular appreciation and support without earlier parallel in the country's history.[2] The true distinction of the eighties, however, appears in the fact that the renaissance in *belles-lettres* was attended by an equally significant renaissance in the arts of line, color and form. Aesthetic appreciation had been greatly stimulated by the Centennial Exhibition of 1876. Not only was the general taste in domestic decoration raised, not only did American workmanship in glass, tableware, pottery and fabric designing improve, but courses in art appreciation began to creep into the universities.[3] Meanwhile new mechani-

[1] He also waged war against gambling, dishonest advertising, birth control and nudity in art. Heywood Broun and Margaret Leech, *Anthony Comstock* (N. Y., 1927), chaps. ix-xv, is a balanced treatment. Comstock defended his militant course in *Frauds Exposed* (N. Y., 1880) and *Traps for the Young* (N. Y., 1883).

[2] "The decade 1880-1890 produced more good novels than any other American decade," says Carl Van Doren, *The American Novel* (N. Y., 1921), 221, citing an amplitude of evidence.

[3] For the rising interest in art, see S. G. W. Benjamin, "American Art since the Centennial," *New Princeton Rev.*, IV (1887), 14-30; E. A. Barber, "Recent Advances in the Pottery Industry," *Pop. Sci.*

cal processes, by simplifying the reproduction of art works in magazines and books, helped further to familiarize the public with better standards.[1] The new interest effloresced in a trebling of the number of art training schools and, at the same time, the spread of art schools, art societies and galleries to inland cities like Chicago, St. Louis, Detroit, Milwaukee and Minneapolis.[2] Frank Duveneck, who earlier had taught a notable group of younger painters at his studios in Munich and Florence, was content to spend the years after 1888 in Cincinnati, where for the next quarter of a century he continued to exert a fruitful influence on American art as dean of the Cincinnati Academy.[3]

Among the painters themselves there appeared a so-called New School.[4] In the late 1870's the first of a throng of young artists returned to New York after study in Munich and particularly in Paris. Trained in the careful draftsmanship of European studios, they were scornful of older American traditions. The "Younger Men," though sometimes affecting eccentric mannerisms, sought in general to render nature naturally rather than in accordance with certain arbitrary principles. Their advent was like a fresh breeze on a sultry day. "There are new ideas afloat,—dash, breadth, free-

Mo., XL (1891-1892), 289-322; Ford, *Forty-Odd Years,* 75-77; I. E. Clarke, "Art and Industrial Education," N. M. Butler, ed., *Education in the United States* (Albany, 1900), II, 707-767.

[1] Illustrations which once cost $100 and a month's labor could, by means of photoengraving, be reproduced for one tenth the price and sometimes in a single day. T. L. De Vinne, "American Printing," Depew, *American Commerce,* I, 318-319.

[2] Anon., "The Field of Art," *Scribner's Mag.,* XX (1896), 649-652.

[3] Norbert Heermann, *Frank Duveneck* (Boston, 1918), chap. vi.

[4] Sadikichi Hartmann, *A History of American Art* (Boston, 1901), I, chap. iv; Samuel Isham, *The History of American Painting* (N. Y., 1905), chaps. xix-xx; C. H. Caffin, *The Story of American Painting* (N. Y., 1907), chaps. ix-xi; Suzanne La Follette, *Art in America* (N. Y., 1929), chaps. vi-vii.

dom, originality," wrote a contemporary.[1] Snubbed by the leaders of the National Academy of Design, they founded in 1877 their own Society of American Artists, drawing into their ranks some of the more progressive older artists like John La Farge and W. M. Chase. The leaders of the new body included such men of later distinction as J. Alden Weir, A. H. Thayer, E. H. Blashfield, Kenyon Cox and F. D. Millet. The clash of the old and new schools and the rivalry excited by their annual exhibitions had a healthful effect on both, and ushered in a period of American art which in quantity and quality surpassed any earlier era.

From such an embarrassment of riches it is difficult to make a selection, a difficulty increased by the fact that most artists displayed versatile talents, trying all things from landscape to miniature, from mural decoration to illustration, from etching to water color. Professor Münsterberg, reporting to his German compatriots on the state of American art shortly after the close of the period, rated James A. McNeill Whistler and John S. Sargent as the most noted painters. Though, as we know, neither had yet reached the summit of his powers, Sargent was already well established as a brilliant portraitist of "elegant ladies, prosperous men, and interesting children," while Whistler, like Henry James in a kindred field, "reproduced his human victims with positively uncanny perspicacity."[2] One of the latter's early masterpieces, "Portrait of the Artist's Mother," a study in rich twilight tones, was bought in 1891 by the French government after failing of a purchaser in America at an absurdly low price.

As Münsterberg was well aware, however, portraiture

[1] Raymond Westbrook, "Open Letters from New York," *Atlantic Mo.*, XLI (1878), 95. See also W. C. Brownell, "The Younger Painters of America," *Scribner's Mo.*, XX (1880), 1-15, 321-335.
[2] Hugo Münsterberg, *The Americans* (N. Y., 1904), 480-483.

was less characteristic of American effort than landscape painting. The increasing popularity of photography, especially after the improvements introduced by George Eastman in the 1880's, undermined portrait painting as a profession. The photograph supplied every commemorative need of the average household, and only the very wealthy continued to indulge in the luxury of oil likenesses. On the other hand, landscape painting reflected the revived interest in nature which pervaded much American poetry and essay writing. Among the productions in this mode Münsterberg particularly noted those of George Inness, "who has seen American landscapes more individually than anyone else," the bold seascapes of Winslow Homer, Childe Hassam's street scenes, the autumn forests of J. J. Enneking, the blossoming apple trees of J. Appleton Brown and the delicate landscapes of Weir and D. W. Tryon. The temptation to add to this list indicates the richness and variety of the work which the generation produced.[1]

Though less significant than other phases, mural art became for the first time an important branch of American painting, thanks to the opportunities afforded by imposing public edifices and pretentious private dwellings and to a technical proficiency hitherto lacking among native artists. In 1878 William Morris Hunt decorated the vaulted ceiling of the new Albany capitol, and later years saw R. F. Blum's panels for Mendelssohn Hall in New York, the wall paintings of Blashfield and W. H. Low in the Waldorf-Astoria ballroom and the notable murals of the Library of Congress by John W. Alexander, H. O. Walker, Elihu Vedder and others. La Farge, besides his memorable decorations of Trinity

[1] Thus, a recent critic esteems Thomas Eakins and A. P. Ryder superior to any of the painters mentioned above. See Lewis Mumford, *The Brown Decades* (N. Y., 1931), 210-231.

Church in Boston, added to the richness of artistic interiors by his invention of opalescent for stained glass in decorated windows. The new windows, distinguished by subtlety of color, recalled the ancient glories of medieval glass work.

Some of the painters, discouraged by slow recognition at home, followed the example of Whistler, Sargent and Mary Cassatt by pursuing their careers amidst more congenial surroundings in London or Paris. Others from lack of sufficient patronage were obliged to devote their chief energies to art instruction rather than to creative work. Still others found a useful and profitable outlet for their talents in illustration.[1] While most artists did occasional work in this medium, with some it was their principal claim to fame. At a time when magazine and book illustration was reaching untold numbers of people, men like Howard Pyle, E. A. Abbey and Joseph Pennell lifted the art to a dignity and distinction never before attained in America. Pyle was at his best in picturing the life of pirates and buccaneers, the traffic at colonial waterfronts, the fanciful world of Sherwood Forest. Perhaps more characteristic were the illustrators who spoke the idiom of their own times: M. A. Woolf and W. A. Rogers when they portrayed immigrant types and ragged slum youngsters, A. B. Frost in his humorous delineations of rustic life, E. W. Kemble in his sprightly pictures of Negroes and Frederic Remington in his spirited sketches of cowboy and Indian.

Meanwhile political caricature throve as never before.[2]

[1] Frank Weitenkampf, *American Graphic Art* (rev. edn., N. Y., 1912), chaps. xi, xiii; Hartmann, *American Art*, II, chap. ii.

[2] J. A. Mitchell, "Contemporary American Caricature," *Scribner's Mag.*, VI (1889), 728-745; anon., "Historical Campaign Caricature," *World's Work*, I (1900), 73-77; La T. Hancock, "American Caricature and Comic Art," *Bookman*, XVI (1902-1903), 120-131, 263-274; R. R. Wilson, "Caricature in America," *New England Mag.*, n.s., XXXI (1904-1905), 95-104; and esp. A. B. Maurice and F. T.

Thomas Nast's assaults on the Tweed Ring in the early 1870's had taught politicians the power of the cartoon as a partisan weapon; and, with the restoration of genuine party rivalry after the Hayes-Tilden contest, two weeklies devoted exclusively to humor were founded: *Puck* (1877), representing the Democratic point of view, and *Judge* (1881), representing the Republican.[1] Bernhard Gillam's forceful series in *Puck* in 1884, presenting James G. Blaine as the "Tattooed Man," did much to convince the voters that the Republican candidate had too checkered a political past to warrant their support.

The leading cartoonists, like Gillam himself, were of European birth and worked in the tradition of the *Fliegende Blätter*. From these weeklies the cruder form of comic art which became general in the newspapers of the 1890's was a logical development.[2] Of a somewhat different cast was *Life,* founded in 1883. Though Democratic in bias, it devoted its energies chiefly to social caricature, for which the growing urbanization, the life of the summer resorts and the manifold discomforts involved in being fashionable gave ample scope. One of its artists, Charles Dana Gibson, developed such skill in portraying the smart set that in the 1890's his black-and-white drawings of the "Gibson girl" and the "Gibson man," immaculately groomed and exultantly self-reliant, excited emulation among the younger generation throughout the land.

In sculpture, too, new forces were astir. Vulgar taste was typified by the civic monuments which began to dot

Cooper, *The History of the Nineteenth Century in Caricature* (N. Y., 1904), chaps. xxvi-xxxi.

[1] *Puck,* founded by the Austrian-American Joseph Keppler in 1876 as a German-language weekly, became English the next year. For Nast's cartoons of the Tweed Ring, see Nevins, *Emergence of Modern America,* 184, 311 and plate vii.

[2] See earlier, 188-190.

American towns in the late 1870's—statuary pieces of a pronounced foundry type intended to commemorate the heroic achievements of the late war.[1] Washington, commented an observer in 1884, is "in the military phase. Its statues represent warriors on horseback and on foot, some of them—most of them, in fact—wonderful to behold." [2] Except for Joseph Henry in front of the Smithsonian Institution no image of a scientist or artist or humanitarian was to be found anywhere in the nation's capital. Nor does the history of the times record the instance of a single general who, like Cato, preferred to have posterity ask why there was no statue of him rather than why there was. In the average household the acme of taste was represented by the plaster statuettes of John Rogers, illustrating such themes as "The Slave Auction," "One More Shot" and "The Emancipation Proclamation."

To stem this flood of mediocrity a high order of creative talent was needful; and fortunately this generation was able to supply it. Returning from Paris in the 1870's were sculptors as well as painters—young men bored with the cold neoclassicism of the Italian school which had hitherto dominated American sculpture, and skilled in the superior technique and greater naturalism of the French school. They endeavored to translate form into fresh and spirited compositions, often of a pictorial tendency, and they succeeded in stamping their art with an individuality which made it something more than derivative.[3]

[1] Factories were said to keep on hand a stock of military statues, complete in every detail except the number of the regiment, which was riveted on to suit the requirements. C. H. Caffin, *American Masters of Sculpture* (N. Y., 1903), 136.

[2] O. B. Frothingham, "Washington as It Should Be," *Atlantic Mo.*, LIII (1884), 841.

[3] Lorado Taft, *The History of American Sculpture* (J. C. Van Dyke, ed., *The History of American Art*, I, N. Y., 1903), pt. iii;

When the statue of Admiral Farragut was unveiled in
1881 in Madison Square, New York, its young author
Augustus Saint-Gaudens at once took his place at the
forefront of the new group. Of Irish birth, he had been
identified with his adopted country since infancy, and
his conception of Farragut, as well as his Lincoln Park
statue of Lincoln (1887) in Chicago, revealed him as an
accurate and forceful interpreter of the American spirit.
His "Peace of God" (1891), erected at the grave of
Mrs. Henry Adams in Rock Creek Cemetery, Washington, is generally accounted the greatest sculpture America
has yet produced. A shrouded figure, the proud face expressing the majesty of despair, is made to symbolize
the universality of grief while posing the eternal question: to what end? In these and other compositions his
influence was profound. More than anyone else, he
demonstrated the value of dignity and repose in sculptured figures and taught the importance of a proper
setting.

To say that Saint-Gaudens stood first need not obscure the merits of his fellow artists. Less prolific than
some, Olin L. Warner displayed an almost Greek sensi-
tiveness to form, while Saint-Gaudens's pupil F. W.
MacMonnies did his most distinctive work in the rendering of exuberant movement. One of MacMonnies's
masterpieces, the bronze "Bacchante" (1894), became
a moral issue in Puritan Boston. Rejected for the court
of the public library, the "nude, drunken woman" was
obliged to find sanctuary in the Metropolitan Museum
of Art in New York.[1] Daniel Chester French, though
almost wholly without foreign training, revealed equally

Hartmann, *American Art*, II, chap. i; La Follette, *Art in America*,
221-239; P. W. Bartlett, "American Sculpture and French Influence
on Its Development," *N. Y. Times*, Feb. 9, 1913.
[1] In 1910 a replica was admitted to a rear hallway of the Museum of
Fine Arts in Boston.

strongly the effects of transatlantic influence. His statue of John Harvard (1884), with its thoughtful face and sensitive hands, and his bronze allegory, "Death Staying the Hand of the Sculptor" (1892), in the Forest Hills Cemetery, Boston, were among the notable productions of the age.

A fuller and more unconventional talent found expression in the work of George Grey Barnard. Of Mid-Western rearing, Barnard's natural robustness of temper was accentuated by his studies with Rodin in Paris. Scorning mere decorative beauty, he devoted himself to subjects of crude and elemental strength. This is evidenced by one of his early symbolic pieces, "Brotherly Love" (1887), a strangely moving sculpture composed of a massive rough-hewn block in which two powerful nude figures are shown with groping hands, their faces half submerged in the marble. Though nothing less than an earthquake could have cleared away the monumental excrescences of American cities, yet the increasing public patronage accorded the newer sculptors and the excellence and variety of their work evinced a marked improvement in general taste. Their acceptance prefigured an epoch of even greater achievement in the years just ahead.[1]

While civic pride provided new opportunities for sculpture, the sheer growth of cities afforded new possibilities for architecture. Unfortunately the architectural traditions and practices inherited from the mid-century were unsafe guides.[2] Unfortunately, too, the ease with which factories could turn out iron ornaments and jigsaw wood into fantastic shapes proved a constant temptation to a people just learning to distinguish between pretentiousness and art. When city streets did not dis-

[1] See Faulkner, *Quest for Social Justice*, 274-276.
[2] See Nevins, *Emergence of Modern America*, 203-205.

play a monotonous regularity, they were apt to present
an array of shrieking, discordant individualities which
Bill Nye called the "mental hallucination and morbid
delirium tremens peculiar to recent architecture." [1]

Yet already in 1878 this vernacular style showed signs
of yielding to better standards. [2] Henry Hobson Richardson, fresh from his triumph of Trinity Church in Boston, trained in the best methods of the École des Beaux
Arts, proceeded in the short years left him to sow Eastern
cities with public and private structures in the Romanesque style of southern France. These sturdily built stone
or brick edifices, marked by short massive columns, low
arches, wide-spreading gables and heavy balconies, were
imitated by architects and builders throughout the land.
A recent critic has said that Richardson's houses were
not defensible except in a military sense; but their very
ruggedness and large simplicity was a needful object lesson to a nation which had run architecturally amuck.
His deeper influence was reflected in the work of craftsmen who realized that the vigor of his treatment was
independent of the detail he employed or of his style.

Like Richardson, most of the leading architects had
had the benefit of Parisian training. In the 1880's Richard Morris Hunt, his senior in years, built the magnificent mansions of W. K. Vanderbilt and John Jacob
Astor on Fifth Avenue in New York as well as summer
"cottages" of equal splendor at Newport and elsewhere.
Two of Richardson's pupils, C. F. McKim and Stanford
White, associated in the New York firm of McKim,
Mead and White, made their chief contributions in the

[1] Quoted in anon., "Crazy Quilt Architecture," *Scientific Am.*, LIII
(1885), 49.
[2] For the new era in architecture, see T. E. Tallmadge, *The Story of
Architecture in America* (N. Y., 1927), chaps. vii-x; Fiske Kimball,
American Architecture (Indianapolis, 1928), chaps. x-xiii; G. H. Edgell,
The American Architecture of To-day (N. Y., 1928), *passim;* La Follette, *Art in America*, 262-272.

classical style or some of its Renaissance derivatives, among their more notable edifices being the new buildings of Columbia University on Morningside Heights and the Boston Public Library.

Such architectural achievements denoted the growing acceptance of sound canons of design and construction, the substitution of harmony and beauty for eclecticism and ostentation. Nor were the improved standards confined to a few great cities or to the Atlantic Seaboard. "Some of the new residential streets of places as recent as Chicago or St. Paul," attested the editor of the American *Baedeker,* "more than hold their own . . . with any contemporaneous thoroughfares of their own class in Europe." [1] While the average abode continued to be contrived by carpenter or contractor, even at this level improvement appeared as a result of the better taste fostered by widely read magazines like *Scribner's, Harper's Bazar* and the *Ladies' Home Journal.* Domestic architecture, however, refused to be regimented. One of the features of these years was the unceasing warfare of styles: Romanesque, Queen Anne, Eastlake, Colonial, Victorian Gothic and nondescript blends of each and all of them.

The advances in domestic and public architecture were less distinctive of the age than the efforts to solve the problems created by the concentration of business in the down-town districts of cities. The need to economize ground area, coupled with the invention of the hydraulic (and later the electric) elevator, suggested great perpendicular buildings as the answer. If built of masonry, however, the supporting piers would be so huge as to devour the space in the lower floors most desirable for office use; Richardson's tallest structure, the Marshall Field Wholesale Building in Chicago, rose but seven

[1] J. F. Muirhead, *The Land of Contrasts* (Boston, 1898), 192.

stories from the street. Moreover, unlike the greatly admired builders of medieval times, the architect had to cope with countless difficulties as a result of modern systems of heating, lighting, plumbing and ventilation.[1]

Less bound by tradition than Boston or even New York, it was Chicago, only recently risen from its ashes, which discovered the solution. This was the use of iron or steel for the support of floors and walls, thus reducing the masonry to a mere veneer resting on a vast metal framework solidly riveted together and braced to resist stresses and strains. The first of all skyscrapers was the Home Insurance Building in Chicago in 1885, contrived by William LeB. Jenney and rising ten stories.[2] Soon, with constant structural improvements, followed the twelve-story Rookery Building, designed by the firm of Burnham & Root, the fourteen-story Tacoma Building, by Holabird & Roche, and in 1891 the Masonic Temple, one of Burnham's creations, which soared skyward for twenty-one stories. The challenging opportunities afforded by this marriage of art and engineering brought to the fore a trio of great leaders: Daniel Burnham, John W. Root and, most individual of the three, Louis Sullivan, who "had the analytical mind of a scientist, the soul of a dreamer and artist."[3] A skyscraper, said Mait-

[1] Henry Van Brunt, "On the Present Condition and Prospects of Architecture," *Atlantic Mo.*, LVII (1886), esp. 381-382, and his "Architecture in the West," same mag., LXIV (1889), esp. 778.

[2] W. A. Starrett, *Skyscrapers and the Men Who Build Them* (N. Y., 1928), chaps. i-iii; Francisco Mujica, *History of the Skyscraper* (Paris, 1929), chaps. i-ii. The credit for designing, rather than building, the first example of the new structural form has been claimed for the Minneapolis architect, L. S. Buffington, who finished the plans for a twenty-eight-story structure in 1883. H. W. Corbett, "America's Great Gift to Architecture," *N. Y. Times Mag.*, March 18, 1928; Starrett, *Skyscrapers*, 27-28.

[3] Kimball, *American Architecture*, 153. The Wainwright Building (1890) in St. Louis and the Transportation Building at the Chicago World's Fair, the latter of course not a skyscraper, were in Sullivan's best vein.

land's *American Slang Dictionary* (1891) in the earliest
known definition, is "a very tall building such as now
are being built in Chicago."

But New York was already entering the race and,
spurred by her narrow insular limits, her office structures soon began to overtop those of Chicago. Her
loftiest achievement came in the final year of the period
with the completion of the twenty-nine-story Ivins
Syndicate Building. The soar and sweep of the great
vertical structures stirred the imagination of the average
man. They emphasized the new elements in modern life
rather than its continuity with the past. As one contemporary said, "I admire the daring, wisdom, and
genius of the men who designed and erected them without reference—in the jargon of politics—to any other
nation on earth." [1] Many æsthetic critics, however, seeing in the skyscraper only an elongated boxlike structure, perceived in it neither beauty nor the possibilities
of beauty.

All the aspiring artistic tendencies of the period
reached a brilliant climax in the World's Columbian
Exposition, held at Chicago from May 1 to October 26,
1893.[2] As early as 1889 New York, Washington, St.
Louis and Chicago had begun to urge upon Congress
their respective claims as the appropriate place for cele-
brating the four-hundredth anniversary of the discovery
of America. But the great midland metropolis, conscious
of her waxing power, eager for notice, heady with
ambition, was not to be denied. When the matter came
up for decision in the spring of 1890, she carried Con-

---

[1] O. L. Triggs, "Democratic Art," *Forum*, XXVI (1898-1899), 75.
See also A. L. A. Himmelwright, "High Buildings," *N. Am. Rev.*,
CLXIII (1896), 580-586.

[2] The exposition was a year late in being held. *History of the World's
Fair* (n.p., 1893), by B. C. Truman and others prominently connected with the exposition, recites the main facts.

gress by storm. At once a national commission was appointed, particularly for intercourse with foreign nations, and a local corporation was formed for planning and conducting the enterprise.

A skeptical East, blind to the recent cultural progress of the Middle West, visioned a colossal but tasteless display of the nation's economic resources as the outcome. Chicago's answer was decisive. America's most noted landscape architect, F. L. Olmsted, was called into consultation, and with him were associated the principal architects, sculptors, painters and engineers of the nation under Burnham's general supervision. "Look here," cried Saint-Gaudens as the leaders gathered to consider their tentative plans, "do you realize that this is the greatest meeting of artists since the fifteenth century!" [1] Coming from many different parts of the country, representing many different points of view, these men worked with a zeal and concert of purpose which made their finished product a landmark in the history of American artistic achievement.[2] The classical rather than the Romanesque style was adopted as the prevailing architectural mode.

On the shore of Lake Michigan a rough, tangled stretch of bog and dune was transformed into a dream of loveliness. No one who set foot within the Court of Honor, the crowning glory of the whole, could fail to be thrilled by the beauty of the spectacle—the splashing fountains, the snowy colonnades, the graceful arches, the gleaming domes, the clustered sculptures, all set off with greenery and interlaced by lagoons of tranquil water. Within, the principal buildings were decorated

---

[1] Charles Moore, *Daniel H. Burnham* (Boston, 1921), I, 47.

[2] Edgell, *American Architecture of To-day*, 42-49, 68; Tallmadge, *Story of Architecture*, chap. viii; Moore, *Burnham*, I, chaps. iv-vi; Henry Van Brunt, "The Columbian Exposition and American Civilization," *Atlantic Mo.*, LXXI (1893), 577-588.

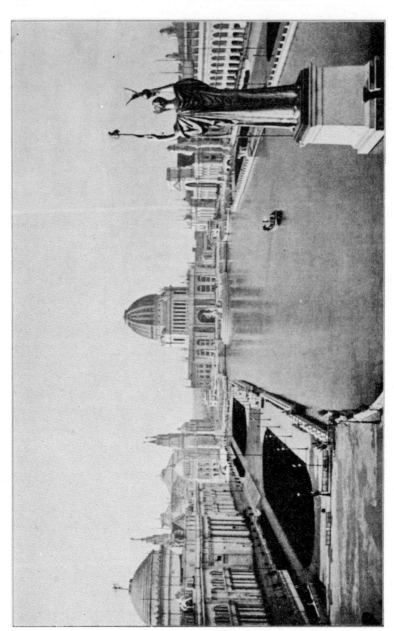

The World's Columbian Exposition

by the foremost mural painters of the nation, while in the regal Palace of Fine Arts there was spread before the visitor an array of the products of pen, brush and chisel in which American artists easily held their own with their European contemporaries. Like other international expositions, the fair was also a mammoth ledger on which were recorded the nation's material achievements. Foreign countries, too, displayed their distinctive wares; and the Midway Plaisance, with its great Ferris Wheel, its Streets of Cairo and other exotic attractions, provided a playground for the twelve million visitors.[1] The event, moreover, was made the occasion for holding important congresses of scientists, scholars and students of affairs.

But it was the sheer splendor of the ensemble, rather than any special feature, that made the "White City" so significant in its impress on American civilization. The bad business conditions resulting from the Panic of 1893 seemed to have little effect upon attendance. The exposition was visited, in great part, by average men and women, particularly from the Middle West, whose lives had hitherto been colorless and narrow, many of whom indeed had never before seen a large city. "Sell the cook stove if necessary and come," wrote Hamlin Garland to his aged parents on their Dakota farm. "You *must* see this fair." [2] They came, saw and, like countless other rural folk, were moved to tears by the compelling power of its beauty. Even sophisticated Easterners like Charles Eliot Norton and Henry Adams were poignantly stirred.[3]

Only seventeen years had elapsed since the Centennial

[1] This is the official estimate. The admissions totaled 27,500,000. Truman and others, *World's Fair*, 609.

[2] Garland, *Son of the Middle Border*, 458-461.

[3] Norton was moved to say to William James that if he were a younger man he would like to cast his lot with a city like Chicago. Moore, *Burnham*, I, 78-79; Henry Adams, *The Education of Henry Adams* (Boston, 1918), 339-343.

Exposition in Philadelphia but, in terms of artistic accomplishment, a whole age had passed. Just as the earlier event had awakened the nation somewhat from its preoccupation with commercial gain, so the World's Fair quickened and strengthened all the new forces making for æsthetic appreciation in American life. While Chicago and Middle America were most directly affected, no part of the country remained untouched.[1] If rural families began to demand better taste in their surroundings, it was no less true that creative artists everywhere worked with renewed inspiration, and that municipal authorities for the first time began seriously to plan cities made beautiful with boulevards and wooded stretches and vistas. The Chicago exposition was both the visual evidence and the promise of a new stage in American civilization.

[1] Alice F. Palmer, "Some Lasting Results of the World's Fair," *Forum*, XVI (1893-1894), 517-523; M. C. Robbins, "The Art of Public Improvement," *Atlantic Mo.*, LXXVIII (1896), esp. 751; H. B. Fuller, "The Upward Movement in Chicago," *Atlantic Mo.*, LXXX (1897), esp. 534.

CHAPTER IX

THE PURSUIT OF HAPPINESS

JAMES A. GARFIELD, pausing at Lake Chautauqua for a nonpartisan address during his presidential campaign in 1880, declared: "We may divide the whole struggle of the human race into two chapters; first, the fight to get leisure; and then the second fight of civilization—what shall we do with our leisure when we get it." [1] There can be no doubt that the closing decades of the century marked a great advance on the part of the American people in gaining freedom from bread-winning toil. Nearly all classes were affected: the extremely rich whose idle wives and children knew so well how to "make amusement into a business"; [2] the wage-earners who benefited from the gradual shortening of the workday; the salaried workers who were coming to consider a two weeks' summer vacation part of the normal conditions of employment. Only the tillers of the soil continued to live very much as of yore. To the farmers, more toil, rather than less, seemed necessary to pull them out of their slough; and constant contrast with the frivolous aspects of urban life deepened the conviction of the older generation that leisure was a polite name for laziness.

It was, indeed, in the city that the people were squarely engaged in "the second fight of civilization." With more leisure at their command than so large a

[1] J. L. Hurlbut, *The Story of Chautauqua* (N. Y., 1921), 184.
[2] James Bryce's phrase in *The American Commonwealth* (London, 1888), III, 559. See earlier, 151-154.

287

body of mankind had ever before enjoyed, their use or abuse of its opportunities would give at least a provisional answer to the question as to the capacity of the masses to achieve the arts and graces of living. Certainly the new freedom caught many methodically ordered lives in a state of dishabille. Life under American conditions had taught them how to work but not how to relax.[1] They were inclined to pursue their avocations with the same feverish intensity that had won success in their other undertakings. As Matthew Arnold remarked in 1883 while in New York, "Old Froissart, who said of the English of his day, that 'they take their pleasures sadly, after their fashion,' would, doubtless, if he lived now, say of the Americans, that they take their pleasures hurriedly, after their fashion." [2]

For the average person no use of leisure so well suited his taste as that afforded by the ubiquitous fraternal orders which sprang up during the last quarter of the century. Earlier organizations of this character had been few in number and usually imported from abroad.[3] Now Americans turned with furious zeal to the creation of secret societies cut to their own pattern. In the large cities some form of organized social commingling seemed called for to replace the spontaneous friendliness of small rural towns. Liberty and equality this generation was willing to take for granted, but fraternity filled a compelling human need. Moreover, the romantic opportunity to posture before a mystic brotherhood in

[1] For a contemporaneous appreciation of this fact, see C. D. Warner, "Aspects of American Life," *Atlantic Mo.*, XLIII (1879), 1-9.

[2] Quoted by W. G. Moody, *Land and Labor in the United States* (N. Y., 1883), 279.

[3] Such as the Freemasons (1730) and the Odd Fellows (1819), introduced from England, the Ancient Order of Hibernians (1836) from Ireland, the German Turnerbund (1850) and the Bohemian Sokol (1865). For the earlier antagonism to secret societies, see C. R. Fish, *The Rise of the Common Man* (*A History of American Life*, VI), 39-40.

all the glory of robe, plume and sword restored a sense of self-importance bruised by the anonymity of life amidst great crowds.[1] If further inducement were needed, it was supplied by the provision made by most lodges for sickness and death benefits for their members.[2]

Though some important indigenous orders like the Knights of Pythias and the Elks had appeared in the sixties, in the two decades after 1880 their number became legion. At least one hundred and twenty-four new secret societies were founded between 1880 and 1890, one hundred and thirty-six between 1890 and 1895, and two hundred and thirty more by 1901.[3] The nomenclature of fraternalism will doubtless some day offer interesting material for the student of suppressed desires and wishful thinking, but to one of less imaginative endowment there seems little enough in common among such names as the Knights and Ladies of the Golden Rule, the Royal Society of Good Fellows, the Modern Woodmen of America, the American Order of Druids, the Owls, the Prudent Patricians of Pompeii and the Concatenated Order of Hoo-Hoo.

As was to be expected, membership was greatest in the urbanized sections of the country notwithstanding the energy with which the Negroes of the South aped their white brethren and the increasing interest of Western farmers in lodge activities. By the end of the period there were over six million names on the rosters of

[1] H. C. Merwin, "A National Vice," *Atlantic Mo.,* LXXI (1893), esp. 769; W. B. Hill, "The Great American Safety-Valve," *Century,* XLIV (1892), 383-384.

[2] Walter Basye, *History and Operation of Fraternal Insurance* (Rochester, 1919), chaps. i, iv-v.

[3] These data are taken from H. B. Meyer, "Fraternal Beneficiary Societies in the United States," *Am. Journ. of Sociology,* VI, 655-656. According to this enumeration, which seems more reliable than the somewhat different estimates in A. C. Stevens, comp., *Cyclopaedia of Fraternities* (N. Y., 1899), only seventy-eight fraternal orders antedated 1880.

fraternal bodies.[1] America possessed more secret societies
and a larger number of "joiners" than all other nations.
The "big four" were the Odd Fellows, the Freemasons,
the Knights of Pythias and the Ancient Order of United
Workmen which collectively embraced more than one
third of the entire lodge membership. Nor did students
of religion fail to note that in all the large cities the
lodges outnumbered the churches, Brooklyn and Boston
each having twice and St. Louis and Chicago three times
as many.[2]

The great increase of city dwellers also provided wider
patronage for the theater. As the nation's metropolis
New York was the chief producing center; its supremacy
in matters histrionic was unquestioned.[3] There money
could be found for new theatrical ventures, there actors'
reputations were won or lost, there aspiring playwrights
flocked to offer their wares. There, too, in the field of
the polite drama, were to be found the three greatest
producing managers of the 1880's: J. Lester Wallack,
Augustin Daly and A. M. Palmer. At their theaters they
maintained stock companies which gave the best performances of the era and included such finished players
as Fanny Davenport, Ada Rehan, Stuart Robson,
Charles Coghlan, James O'Neil and Annie Russell.

Throughout the decade, however, the resident stock-
company type of production was losing ground to the

---

[1] Stevens, *Cyclopaedia*, v, 114; W. S. Harwood, "Secret Societies in
the United States," *N. Am. Rev.*, CLXIV (1897), 617-624; J. M.
Foster, "Secret Societies and the State," *Arena*, XIX (1898), 229-239.

[2] Josiah Strong, *The New Era* (N. Y., 1893), 128 *n*.

[3] Anon., "New York Theatres," *Atlantic Mo.*, XLIII (1879), 452-
455. For general treatments of the drama during the period, see L. C.
Strang, *Players and Plays of the Last Quarter Century* (Boston, 1902),
II; M. J. Moses, *The American Dramatist* (Boston, 1926), chaps. v-xi;
Arthur Hornblow, *A History of the Theatre in America* (Phila., 1919),
chaps. xxiii-xxix; Mary C. Crawford, *The Romance of the American
Theatre* (Boston, 1913), chaps. xii-xiv; A. H. Quinn, *A History of
the American Drama from the Civil War* (N. Y., 1927), I.

traveling company and the "star" system.[1] Easier and cheaper means of transportation led newer producers to reach out for the patronage that awaited in the cities of the hinterland. With this in view it was more profitable to employ a featured actor, supported by nonentities, than to maintain the standards of performance which a sophisticated New York audience expected at a place like Daly's or Palmer's Madison Square Theatre. The new system also benefited local managers by relieving them of the greater financial risks of a stock company.

As road companies multiplied, the supply of actor talent could not keep up with the demand.[2] Some of the pathetic or ludicrous mishaps which befell the roving Thespians were less attributable to the arrested mental development of their audiences than to their own histrionic deficiencies. A performance of a perennially popular play was dismissed by a Minnesota paper in the 1890's with the laconic comment: "Thompson's Uncle Tom's Cabin company appeared at the opera house last night. The dogs were poorly supported."[3] A favorite subject with cartoonists in *Puck* and *Judge* was the hollow-cheeked actor attired in a mangy fur-collared overcoat and straw hat, indulging in delusions of grandeur before a group of his fellow artists similarly arrayed. "We notice of late," said the *New York Dramatic News* of March 29, 1884, "that professionals

[1] The *N. Y. Dramatic Mirror* in 1879 listed the routes of forty-nine traveling companies; twenty years later the list was nearly ten times as great.

[2] Difficulties of booking also increased, leading by gradual stages to the formation of a theatrical syndicate or trust in 1896. See M. B. Leavitt, *Fifty Years in Theatrical Management* (N. Y., 1912), 265-272; J. L. Ford, *Forty-Odd Years in the Literary Shop* (N. Y., 1921), chap. xii; Norman Hapgood, *The Stage in America, 1897-1900* (N. Y., 1901), chap. i; and H. U. Faulkner, *The Quest for Social Justice* (*A History of American Life*, XI), 300.

[3] Cited by W. W. Stout, "Little Eva Is Seventy-Five," *Sat. Eve. Post*, CC, 10 ff. (Oct. 8, 1927).

returning by rail to New York after the company has 'busted up' have got past complaining of this mode of travel. . . . They admit, however, that it is exceedingly annoying to have to get off the track so often to allow the trains to pass up and down." Yet so great was the lure of the footlights that between 1880 and 1900 the number of actors increased from less than five thousand to nearly fifteen thousand.[1]

To satisfy the miscellaneous public which now went to plays, the theater had to spread a fare pleasing to many palates and all pocketbooks. While some persons attended, or imagined they did, to enjoy the drama as a form of art, the vast majority frankly sought amusement, forgetfulness or the thrill of vicarious romance or adventure. Yet the serious drama has perhaps never been better presented in America than in the 1880's and 1890's. To see Edwin Booth or John McCullough as Hamlet; Mary Anderson portray Galatea or Juliet; Lawrence Barrett, Cassius; or Clara Morris, Camille, was an experience no theatergoer was ever likely to forget.

One of the versatile and successful actresses of the time was Louisa Lane Drew whose theatrical career went back to her first stage appearance in 1827. During her seventy years before the footlights she played with nearly every noted actor from Edwin Forrest to Joseph Jefferson. What was of even greater consequence was the fact that she was the founder of America's most famous actor family.[2] In the 1870's two of her children, John and Georgiana, began to establish themselves as players in their own right, the former as an accomplished member

[1] These figures include performers in musical plays as well as the legitimate drama. *U. S. Tenth Census* (1880), I, 744; *U. S. Twelfth Census* (1900), II, cxliv.

[2] M. J. Moses, *Famous Actor-Families in America* (N. Y., 1906), chap. vii.

of Augustin Daly's troupe. In 1876 Georgiana Drew, then in "The Princess Royal," married a fellow performer, a handsome young Oxford graduate named Maurice Barrymore. In 1878-1879 a road company, headed by the Barrymores and John Drew, started on tour, and subsequent years often found two or more of the Drew-Barrymore connection acting together. The three Barrymore children, Lionel, Ethel and John, could hardly escape their destiny. Lionel made his début in 1893 in "The Rivals," in which his grandmother, Louisa Lane Drew, was playing the part of Mrs. Malaprop; three years later Ethel began her stage career as a member of her uncle John Drew's company.

Native performers, however, had to look to their laurels as the promise of unusual profits attracted to American shores the foremost artists of the European stage. Players like Sarah Bernhardt, Tommaso Salvini, Henry Irving, Helena Modjeska, Adelaide Ristori and Eleanora Duse could always count on an enthusiastic welcome.[1] On the other hand, American actors—Booth, Barrett, Ada Rehan and others—met with a cordial response in England and on the Continent when they betook themselves thence.

Just as the reading public demanded fictional treatments of American life, so theatergoers were increasingly eager to see plays about themselves—plays depicting American types, American backgrounds, and humorous or exciting situations compatible with American conditions.[2] Departing from the custom of older producers like Daly and Wallack, venturesome young managers—

[1] Ford, *Forty-Odd Years*, 137-143, 249-251; Crawford, *Romance of American Theatre*, chap. xii; Leavitt, *Fifty Years*, 488-502; H. A. Clapp, *Reminiscences of a Dramatic Critic* (Boston, 1902), chaps. xvi-xvii, xx.

[2] Strang, *Players and Plays*, II, chap. vii. The lack of an international copyright provision until 1891 was a discouragement to the native playwright as well as to the native *littérateur*. See earlier, 252-255.

David Belasco, Charles and Daniel Frohman and others —perceived the box-office possibilities of the native drama and used it as a means of climbing to a position of financial stability and eventual theatrical dominance. Though some of the plays like "Pudd'nhead Wilson" and "Editha's Burglar" were dramatizations of popular novels, every year saw a greater number prepared in first instance for the stage. "Hazel Kirke," written by Steele MacKaye, had a New York run of four hundred and eighty-six nights, beginning on February 4, 1880. This record was exceeded only by another play of native authorship, Charles Hoyt's "A Trip to Chinatown," which started its career of six hundred and fifty nights on November 9, 1891. The successive offerings of Bronson Howard, the foremost American dramatist of the time, were also usually certain of a cordial reception. "The Young Mrs. Winthrop," produced in 1882, continued uninterruptedly in New York for more than one hundred and fifty nights, while three years later "One of Our Girls" held the boards for two hundred nights. "The Henrietta," produced in 1887, ran for sixty-eight weeks, earning admission receipts of nearly half a million dollars.

Though MacKaye's greatest success and some of Howard's pieces had a European setting, native playwrights turned more and more to purely American themes and materials. Like the local-color novel, the drama of rural life made a special appeal to nostalgic city dwellers desirous of renewing their childhood memories. A prime favorite was "Joshua Whitcomb" (later renamed "The Old Homestead") which toured the country almost continuously with Denman Thompson, who had helped write it, in the title rôle of the simple, lovable old farmer. Two other popular hits were "The County Fair," by Charles Barnard and Neil Burgess, first staged in 1889, and Lottie Blair Parker's "Way Down East," produced early in 1898, each of which enjoyed an initial New York run of more than a year. Thickly buttered with sentimentality and rural heroics, such offerings suffered artistically beside James A. Herne's "Shore Acres," first performed in Chicago in 1892. Herne was an apostle of realism in the drama in much the same sense that his friends, Howells and Garland, were of realism in literature.[1] "Shore Acres," though largely devoid of theatricalism and dealing primarily with the fundamentals of human character, was nevertheless long in demand.

In general, however, the public did not care to see real life on the stage. One could hardly have guessed from the serious drama, as he might from the serious fiction, that industrialism and the growth of cities were thrusting forward acute problems to plague society. For purposes of stage presentation all such matters had to be given a comic turn. By exploiting humorous possibilities of immigrant life, Edward Harrigan succeeded in writing a series of hilarious comedies about the relations of the embattled Mulligans with their friendly enemies, the Lochmüllers—pieces which incidentally shed much light on the feudal character of New York machine politics.[2] Other aspects of the passing scene were caricatured by Charles Hoyt who turned off a succession of rapid-fire farces which reached their climax in "A Texas Steer" (1890) and "A Trip to Chinatown" (1891), already

[1] His more important play "Margaret Fleming," produced in 1890, proved quite too bold in its realism, according to the standards of the time, to win public favor. Herne's confession of faith, "Art for Truth's Sake in the Drama," *Arena*, XVII (1897), 361-370, is a significant document in the history of the American drama.

[2] Among Harrigan's chief comedies were "The Mulligan Guard Ball" (1879), "The Mulligan Guard Nominee" (1880) and "Cordelia's Aspirations" (1883). Harrigan also acted in the plays; and the team name of Harrigan and Hart was considered by theatergoers a guarantee of an evening of unmitigated fun.

mentioned. Profiting by his experience as paragrapher on the *Boston Post*, he paraded before his delighted audiences all the stock characters of comic journalism: the temperance crank, the mannish feminist, the social climber, the chronic joiner, the spiritualist, the baseball hero and their like.

The comedy of contemporary manners was also cultivated with notable facility by Howard, Belasco and, starting in the 1890's, by the youthful Clyde Fitch. But as the generation which had fought the Civil War died off, such dramatists turned to romantic plays based on the sectional struggle and its outcome. William Gillette's "Held by the Enemy" (1886), Howard's "Shenandoah" (1888), Augustus Thomas's "Alabama" (1891) and Belasco's "The Heart of Maryland" (1895) proved to be among the most popular offerings of the closing years.

A great many playgoers, however, demanded stronger meat than the polite drama offered. Nourished on the dime novel and the yellow press, they saw life in terms of startling contrasts and swift sensational action. "Uncle Tom's Cabin," greatest of all native melodramas, retained its accustomed following only by introducing novel features.[1] A half-dozen or more troupes, in the eighties and later, gave performances featured by two Toms, two Evas, two Topsys and two Simon Legrees. In the nineties the colored pugilist, Peter Jackson, played Uncle Tom in one company, sparring three friendly rounds with Joe Choynski who played George Shelby. A rival company presented John L. Sullivan in the part of Simon Legree. Meantime "East Lynne" retained its earlier vogue; and "The Two Orphans," a French adaptation first produced in 1874 with Kate

---

[1] J. F. Davis, "Tom Shows," *Scribner's Mag.*, LXXVII (1925), 350-360.

Claxton as the blind orphan, reached its twenty-five-hundredth performance at Dayton, Ohio, on May 6, 1884.[1]

More distinctive of the changing national scene were the gun-and-gore dramas of Western life in which, it will be remembered, Buffalo Bill and other actual frontier Bills strode the boards.[2] These presently gave way to a plethora of melodramas depicting the dangers and wickedness of metropolitan life, endless variants of the theme of honest Nell and the city slicker. Although the better dramatists occasionally indulged, such pieces were ordinarily concocted by specialists in the *genre* like Charles Gayler, C. H. Foster and Bartley Campbell. Foster was responsible for more than seventy-five thrillers, including "Bertha, the Sewing-Machine Girl," "The Gunmaker's Bride" and "The Turf Digger's Doom." Campbell, before he went insane in 1886, produced "The Galley Slave," "The White Slave" and other smashing hits, besides composing the deathless line, "Rags are royal raiment when worn for virtue's sake."[3] On Campbell's letterhead were displayed portraits of himself and Shakespeare with the legend, "A friendly rivalry." Any lack of plausibility in such effusions was compensated for by the scenic effects: snowstorms, raging fires, shipwrecks, the thundering approach of the fast mail. The standard admission price was ten, twenty and thirty cents, and the plays proved quite as popular in the great cities as in the country villages where they were often presented, with nightly changes, under canvas.

The principal attraction in the rural towns, however, was the circus, which reached the zenith of its popular-

[1] *N. Y. Dramatic Mirror*, XLI, no. 1043, 40 (Dec. 24, 1898).
[2] See earlier, 51.
[3] Quinn, *American Drama from the Civil War*, I, 118-124.

ity in the last quarter of the century with nearly forty organizations annually on tour.[1] Traveling by train or wagon during the warm seasons, the human freaks and exotic animals were exhibited in the ubiquitous dime museums during the winter while the acrobats dispersed into the vaudeville circuits. When the two principal circus magnates, P. T. Barnum and J. A. Bailey, combined their shows in 1881, they set a new pace for their competitors, signalized further by acquisition of the elephant Jumbo from the Royal Zoological Gardens, a piece of Yankee enterprise loudly resented by the London populace. Intense rivalry with the Adam Forepaugh circus led in 1882 to a short-lived agreement for a division of routes between them and later to the purchase of the Forepaugh outfit. American circuses, notably Barnum & Bailey's, also met with great favor abroad, and one, W. W. Cole's Colossal Circus, in 1880-1881 made a thirty-thousand-mile tour to Australia and New Zealand.

While circuses grew bigger, it is doubtful whether the Toby Tylers of the time thought they grew better, for the increasing size of the "big top" diminished the importance of the clowns whose fun making under the new conditions was reduced mainly to broad pantomime and slapstick acrobatics. The chief new development in tent entertainment was the advent of Buffalo Bill's Wild West Show in 1883, a truly autochthonous circus exhibiting to the descendants of pioneers stirring glimpses of vanishing frontier life, including real cowboys, Indian attacks, bronco busting and stagecoach holdups.[2]

---

[1] Leavitt, *Fifty Years*, chaps. x-xi; M. R. Werner, *Barnum* (N. Y., 1923), chap. xiii.

[2] In the second season Sitting Bull and other Sioux who had participated in the Custer massacre joined the company. W. F. Cody (Buffalo Bill, *pseud.*), *Story of the Wild West and Camp Fire Chats* (Chicago, 1902), 693-700, and Leavitt, *Fifty Years*, esp. 143.

Horsemanship Delights All Classes

When Buffalo Bill took his show to England in 1887, the tour netted seven hundred thousand dollars and it is said that Gladstone witnessed the performance no less than six times.

It was the production of the Gilbert and Sullivan operas in America, beginning with "Pinafore" in 1878, that brought music into general favor as a form of light entertainment. The delightful nonsense of these two British masters of the art not only set a high standard, but also helped break down a popular disapproval based on the supposed naughtiness of musical shows of the "Black Crook" type.[1] A veritable "Pinafore" craze ensued, with amateur productions galore, an endless number of hastily assembled road companies and at one time, in 1881, five simultaneous New York presentations. The chief home of comic opera was the New York Casino, opened in 1882 under the direction of Rudolph Aronson.[2] His presentation in 1886 of "Erminie," an English operetta with Pauline Hall and Francis Wilson in the leading rôles, enjoyed a phenomenal run of twelve hundred and fifty-six performances. It was the Casino stage which established the reputation of such favorites as Lillian Russell, Fay Templeton, De Wolf Hopper and David Warfield, making it possible for them in time to go forth as stars heading their own companies.

In Boston the best standards of light opera were maintained by a company first known as the Boston Ideals and then the Bostonians. H. C. Barnabee, Marie Stone,

---

[1] See Allan Nevins, *The Emergence of Modern America* (*A History of American Life*, VIII), 93. The staid *Philadelphia Public Ledger* editorially gave "Pinafore" a clean bill of health and invited the attendance of the pure-minded. J. P. Sousa, *Marching Along* (Boston, 1928), 62.

[2] T. A. Brown, *A History of the New York Stage* (N. Y., 1903), III, 485-506; Rudolph Aronson, *Theatrical and Musical Memoirs* (N. Y., 1913), chaps. iv-viii; same author, "Most Successful Operetta Ever Heard Here," *Theatre*, XVIII (1913), 17 ff.

Eugene Cowles and Jessie Bartlett Davis were their bright particular stars. In 1890 they presented in Chicago Reginald de Koven's "Robin Hood," one of the most melodious and certainly the most popular American operetta ever written.[1] This striking success led to almost yearly scores from De Koven's pen and made easier the path of other composers such as John Philip Sousa and the Irish American, Victor Herbert. Among the most successful operas of the closing years were Sousa's "El Capitan" and Herbert's "The Wizard of the Nile."

Musical extravaganza after the English fashion also enjoyed wide popularity. One of the most famous, "Evangeline," first presented in 1875, was frequently revived, being played over five thousand times.[2] At its vulgarest, musical entertainment took the form of burlesque—performances patronized by males who were more intent on nature's lines than on the author's and in which music served as a pretext for suggestive posing.[3] Meantime the old-fashioned black-face minstrel show, confronted with competition on every hand, became constantly bigger and more pretentious, but thereby lost

[1] H. B. Smith, *First Nights and First Editions* (Boston, 1931), esp. chap. xviii; C. B. Palmer, "As the Bostonians Caroled a Half Century Ago," *Boston Transcript*, Dec. 27, 1930; H. C. Barnabee, *Reminiscences* (Boston, 1913), chaps. xxvii-xxxvii.

[2] "Adonis" (1884) in which Henry E. Dixey starred and "1492," first produced in Chicago during the World's Fair, were other successes of a similar kind under E. E. Rice's direction. Leavitt, *Fifty Years*, 315-316; L. C. Strang, *Celebrated Comedians of Light Opera and Musical Comedy* (Boston, 1901), 195-202.

[3] M. J. O'Neill, *How He Does It. Sam T. Jack* (Chicago, 1895), is a highly colored, press agent's account of the "King of Burlesque," who at the date of publication was proprietor of Lilly Clay's Colossal Gaiety Company, the Ada Richmond Folly Company, the Creole Burlesque Company, the Big Burlesque Company, the Big Brazilian Company, the Mazeppa Company and other similar troupes which were advertised by such descriptions as: "50—Pairs of Rounded Limbs, Ruby Lips, Tantalizing Torsos—50." Everyone, of course, understood that the "limbs" and "torsos" would be clothed in tights, usually of cotton.

its distinctive flavor and eventually its grip on the public.[1] The thirty-odd touring minstrel companies of the early 1880's dwindled to perhaps ten in the late nineties. In place of the minstrel show there sprang up a type of theatrical *mélange* better adapted to the restlessness of city life and the urban dwellers' craving for novelty.[2] Like megalopolis itself, vaudeville was of hybrid origin, tracing its paternity variously to the dime museum (in which the youthful Weber and Fields got their start), the cheap variety hall with its rude stage and loose women, the circus and the minstrel show. Following the Civil War Tony Pastor in New York strove valiantly to purvey variety without vulgarity, but it was not until the early 1880's that modern "refined vaudeville" really established itself.[3] When B. F. Keith in 1885 introduced into Boston the continuous performance, he added a feature so popular that it was presently adopted by his rivals.[4] Keith, F. F. Proctor, J. W. Considine and other managers vigorously exploited the new field, acquiring more theaters, developing circuits and improving the quality of their offerings. Legitimate actors were tempted by fancy salaries to try the "con-

[1] Carl Wittke, *Tambo and Bones* (Durham, 1930), esp. chap. iii.

[2] "The vaudeville theatre belongs to the era of the department store and the short story," wrote E. M. Royle in "The Vaudeville Theatre," *Scribner's Mag.*, XXVI (1899), 495.

[3] Leavitt claims he was the first to adopt the word, vaudeville, for a variety show, in 1880. *Fifty Years*, 189, 382. But C. P. Sawyer, "Mirrors of Variety," *Boston Transcript*, Oct. 2, 1926, found the term used in America as early as 1852; and a handbill in the Boston Public Library shows that in 1840 there was a "Vaudeville Saloon" in Boston which presented variety. On the rise of modern vaudeville, see anon., "Twenty Years of Vaudeville," *N. Y. Dramatic Mirror*, XLI, 90-95 (Dec. 24, 1898); and W. J. Kingsley, "Thirty Years of Vaudeville," same mag., LXX, 4-5 (Nov. 26, 1913).

[4] B. F. Keith, "The Origin of Continuous Vaudeville," *N. Y. Dramatic Mirror*, XLI, 95-96 (Dec. 24, 1898). Proctor introduced the innovation into New York in 1893. Keith two years later showed the first motion pictures in connection with vaudeville. Leavitt, *Fifty Years*, 205-206.

tinuous" from time to time, and the vaudeville stage in
turn proved a training ground for musical-comedy talent. Vaudeville accounted for the attendance of perhaps
half the theatergoers in the 1890's. Keith's circuit alone,
though embracing but four theaters and not showing on
Sundays, entertained over five million annually.[1]

People living or visiting in the cities could hardly
escape the contagion of the latest popular tune. If they
avoided the theater and the amusement park, the strains
assailed their ears from the Italian organ grinder or the
roving German street band. Each year, too, saw improvements in the phonograph, first put upon the market by Edison in 1877-1878. The original instrument,
consisting of a tin-foil cylinder record turned by a hand
crank, emitted loud, scarcely recognizable sounds; but
further experimentation by Edison, C. A. Bell, C. S.
Tainter, Emile Berliner and others led to the use of flat
waxlike disks operated by spring or battery motors and
resulting in much clearer tone reproduction.[2] How many
of these contrivances invaded American homes in the
1880's and 1890's it is impossible to say, but in the
single year 1900 over one hundred and fifty thousand
machines and nearly three million records were sold.

The rage for popular music was without precedent
in the earlier history of America. Chosen by a spontaneous universal suffrage, these melodies were subject to
the proverbial fickleness of democracy. Most of them
were composed by self-made bards who did not venture
beyond the average person's singing range of eight notes
or less. However trivial or trite the words, they are of
continuing interest to the student of American life as
current memoranda of manners, emotions, morals and

[1] Royle, "Vaudeville Theatre," 485.
[2] *U. S. Twelfth Census*, X, 181-184; P. G. Hubert, "The New
Talking Machines," *Atlantic Mo.*, LXIII (1889), 256-261.

absurdities. The same thick vein of sentimentality mined by the yellow press and the writers of sentimental romances and melodrama found musical outlet in an endless succession of moralistic ballads, characterized by such "hits" as Jennie Lindsay's "Always Take Mother's Advice" (1884) —

> To you in this world she is dearest,
> At your downfall her grief is severest;

Charles Graham's "The Picture That Is Turned to the Wall" (1891) —the story of why one girl left home; Charles K. Harris's "After the Ball" (1892) —

> Many a heart is aching,
> If you could read them all;
> Many the hopes that have vanish'd
> After the ball;

Gussie L. Davis's "The Fatal Wedding" (1893) — "Just another fatal wedding, Just another broken heart"; James Thornton's "She May Have Seen Better Days" (1894) ; Joe Stern's "My Mother Was a Lady" (1896) —

> I've come to this great city
> To find a brother dear,
> And you wouldn't dare insult me, Sir,
> If Jack were only here;

and Paul Dresser's "On the Banks of the Wabash" (1896).[1] Few of such songs, however, attained the musical distinction of De Koven's "O Promise Me" which, popularized by Jessie Bartlett Davis in "Robin

[1] In every case above the composer's name is given. Many popular songs of the period have been reprinted by Sigmund Spaeth in *Read 'Em and Weep* (Garden City, 1926) and *Weep Some More, My Lady* (Garden City, 1927). See also E. C. May, "Words with Music," *Sat. Eve. Post*, CXCVII, 11 ff. (Oct. 18, 1924), and Isaac Goldberg, *Tin Pan Alley* (N. Y., 1930), chaps. v-vi.

Hood," soon became a melodic accompaniment of every well-conducted American wedding.

Hardly less popular than the theme of misplaced affections was the spirited balladry which centered about life in the city tenements—such songs as "The Mulligan Braves" (1879) and "The Widow Nolan's Goat" (1881), from the Harrigan and Hart comedies; J. J. Sullivan's "Where Did You Get That Hat?" (1888); Joseph Flynn's "Down Went McGinty" (1889); Frank Harding's "Throw Him Down, McCloskey" (1890)—

And future generations, with wonder and delight,
Will read on hist'ry's pages of this great McCloskey fight;

and C. B. Lawler's "The Sidewalks of New York" (1894). While the Negro continued to be a subject of the white man's compositions, the slow-paced, wistful melodies of the plantation type gave way to the sprightly "coon song," written in syncopated time to suit the quicker tempo of urban life and designed to stir people's feet instead of their hearts. The first genuine "ragtime" pieces were Barney Fagan's "My Gal Is a High-Born Lady" and C. E. Trevathan's "The Bully," both written in 1896. Their appeal was so great that they set a fashion which lasted into the second decade of the next century.

It remains an open question whether music of the lighter and more ephemeral sort debases the public taste or whether it breeds an appreciation of the nobler forms. The relationship between the two in the eighties and nineties may have been wholly fortuitous, but there can be no doubt that the craze for popular songs was attended by a remarkable growth of interest in serious music. The public schools helped by imparting a knowledge of the rudiments of music; by 1885 seven out of every eight pupils were being taught singing and the ability to read notation.[1] Private teachers also abounded in almost every locality; and piano playing was an ordeal which fond parents customarily imposed upon their offspring, musical and unmusical alike. "There is no country where there are so many pianos and players on them," commented Soissons with not entire approval.[2] A traveler observed a Chickering piano in a miner's tent at Leadville, Colorado, in 1878,[3] and no self-respecting home in the more settled sections was without an instrument of some make or other.

In nearly every important city one or more conservatories of music were to be found. The largest and most distinguished, the New England Conservatory, established at Boston in 1867, closely approached the best European schools in the excellence of its curriculum. After 1896 it was under the direction of George W. Chadwick who had long been a member of its faculty. The Cincinnati College of Music, dating from 1878, maintained artistic standards that leavened the musical culture of the entire West. From the start most women's colleges had special instruction, while men's institutions began to follow in 1875 when Harvard made music a regular part of the curriculum with John Knowles Paine in charge.[4] Though the older musicians had felt obliged

[1] U. S. Bureau of Education, *Circular of Information for 1886*, no. 1.

[2] S. C. de Soissons, *A Parisian in America* (Boston, 1896), 186. From 1880 to 1900 the number of establishments making pianos and materials increased from 174 to 263, their products from more than twelve million dollars to well over thirty-five. While before 1866 nearly all the pianos made were square pianos, by 1900 nearly all of them were uprights, an indication perhaps of the more crowded conditions of living. *U. S. Twelfth Census*, X, 448, 454.

[3] L. P. Brockett, *Our Western Empire* (Phila., 1882), 198-199.

[4] Yale and Columbia established chairs in 1894 and 1896 with Horatio Parker and Edward A. MacDowell respectively as the incumbents. L. C. Elson, *The History of American Music* (J. C. Van Dyke, ed., *The History of American Art*, II, N. Y., 1904), 339-358.

to get their training in Germany, the younger men were finding it increasingly possible to secure adequate instruction without leaving American shores.

In the matter of artists' concerts the leading cities could be sure of hearing some of the best native performers every season, as well as distinguished European visitors like Adelina Patti, Ignace Jan Paderewski and Fritz Kreisler. Where the German element was strong, choral societies also flourished. The May musical festivals at Cincinnati, beginning in 1873 and long directed by Theodore Thomas, had a chorus of nearly a thousand, drawn in part from the singing societies of near-by cities. In addition, almost every town possessed a brass band, usually made up of self-taught players. A few bands, notably Patrick S. Gilmore's in New York and John Philip Sousa's United States Marine Band, commanded a nation-wide reputation. When Sousa organized his own troupe in 1892, he went on to new and greater triumphs. Besides being a conductor, he was a composer of merit, and his stirring martial airs—"The Washington Post," "The Liberty Bell," "The Stars and Stripes Forever" and others—quickly won him the title of the "March King." "The Washington Post" (1889) was probably the best-known instrumental piece in the world at the time, and in America its lively rhythm established the vogue of the two-step as successor to the old-time waltz.[1]

Similarly, orchestral music finally became naturalized in America during this period. The year 1878 saw the founding of the New York Symphony Orchestra, conducted at first by Leopold Damrosch and from 1885 by his son Walter. Meantime, in 1881, the Boston Symphony Orchestra was established with a guarantee of

[1] In England and Germany the new dance was known generically as the "Washington Post." See Sousa, *Marching Along*, chaps. iv-ix.

financial independence provided by the public-spirited banker Henry Lee Higginson. Along with the older New York Philharmonic and Theodore Thomas's Chicago Orchestra (1891), these orchestras presented to American audiences in many parts of the country musical masterpieces with something akin to European technique and ensemble. The conductors and most of the performers, however, were of European birth and training, a condition which also held true of grand opera.[1]

Though remaining an exotic, grand opera was placed upon a firmer footing with the opening in New York in 1883 of the Metropolitan Opera House, an edifice costing nearly two million dollars. The most eminent singers from all over the world were attracted to its stage and, under the conductorships of the elder Damrosch and Anton Seidl (1884-1892), Wagnerian and other German opera won favor with audiences hitherto habituated to the Italian school.[2] But, apart from New Orleans where good French troupes had long held forth, no other American city felt able to indulge in the luxury of a resident company.

If the record of these years is mainly one of the growth of musical appreciation, yet America began in a modest way to repay a part of its debt for the rich stores of melody which it had derived from Europe.[3] Paine, Chadwick and Horatio Parker all achieved a transatlantic reputation for their orchestral and choral scores, setting a high standard for the next generation to emulate. Similarly, the compositions of Dudley Buck

[1] America in this period, however, contributed to the grand-opera stage two prima donnas in Emma Eames and Lillian Nordica.

[2] H. E. Krehbiel, *Chapters of Opera* (N. Y., 1908), chaps. viii-xix.

[3] For the composers mentioned in the text and others, see J. T. Howard, *Our American Music* (N. Y., 1931), 315-403, and Rupert Hughes, *Contemporary American Composers* (Boston, 1900), chaps. ii-v.

exerted a profound influence for good on American choir music. Ethelbert Nevin and Edward A. Mac-Dowell, on the other hand, devoted their talents to art-songs and piano selections. The latter was the most original composer America had yet produced. He had a genius for catching the moods of forest, field and ocean and expressing them in a musical idiom exquisitely his own. "To a Wild Rose" and "To a Water Lily," published in 1896 as a part of his *Woodland Sketches,* quickly became a precious folk possession of America.

While music and the drama were extending their dominion over men's leisure time, open-air recreations attained a new and stronger hold upon the public. "The disappearance of the backwoods and the growth of large centres of population have created the demand for an artificial outlet," wrote a contemporary, "and the games are the natural successors of the youthful activities of a pioneer period."[1] Indeed, with an increasing proportion of mankind cooped up for long hours in factory and office, working a single set of muscles or benumbing their minds with columns of figures, some form of outdoor diversion was indispensable. But the pioneer inheritance unfortunately did not ordinarily include pioneer biceps. Most people were therefore content to take their more strenuous forms of exercise by proxy, a tendency zealously stimulated by sport promoters who coveted the gate receipts which gladiatorial contests made possible. The audience habit, cultivated by the theater, thus came to infect sport lovers as well.

Much of this new play life reflected the athletic revival which had been taking place in England since the

---

[1] I. N. Hollis, "Intercollegiate Athletics," *Atlantic Mo.,* XC (1902), esp. 534. See also D. A. Sargent, "The Physical State of the American People," N. S. Shaler, ed., *The United States of America* (N. Y., 1894), III, 1135-1136.

middle of the century. In the United States, however, the new games were not deemed a special perquisite of the upper classes but rather a boon to be enjoyed by all. Nor did the Americans hesitate to modify the rules when it suited their pleasure so to do. In only one instance did they invent a sport of their own; yet that effort was conspicuously successful. Basketball, an indoor game devised by James Naismith in 1891 at the Y. M. C. A. Training College in Springfield, Massachusetts, quickly spread to other countries.[1]

Of the older sports thoroughbred racing enjoyed an era of unparalleled prosperity.[2] Capital was lavishly invested in new club houses and courses, faster tracks were built at the county and state fairs, stakes were increased in size and the great stables sent horses to meets in all parts of the country. In 1876 the record for the mile was set by Ten Broeck at one minute thirty-nine and three-quarters seconds, where it remained until Salvator in 1890 brought the crowd to their feet at Long Branch by clipping the time by four and a quarter seconds. One of the noted racing horses, Hanover, sired by Hindoo, also a great racer of the 1880's, won thirty-two events and finished second thirteen times, earning for his owners, Philip and Michael Dwyer, over one hundred and twenty thousand dollars in a four years' turf career. Despite its wide popularity, however, racing failed of universal favor because of the evils of betting and fraud which ordinarily attended it and which neither the true friends of the sport nor the enactments of legislatures could suppress.

[1] By 1894 it had encircled the globe and had ardent advocates in such extremes as Paris and Melbourne. J. P. Paret, "Basketball," *Outing*, XXXI (1897), 224.

[2] S. C. Hildreth and J. R. Crowell, *The Spell of the Turf* (Phila., 1926), chaps. ii-vii. On all phases of sport, J. A. Krout, *Annals of American Sport* (R. H. Gabriel, ed., *The Pageant of America*, New Haven, 1926-1929, XIV), is valuable.

Even more was professional pugilism viewed askance by the respectable elements. Generally banned by law, the fighting was usually with bare fists, the bouts often lasting forty or fifty rounds. In 1882 John L. Sullivan, a slugging fighter of great power, won the heavyweight championship from Paddy Ryan in a battle marked by hitting, wrestling, scratching and biting. Five years later, while fighting Patsy Cardiff at Minneapolis, he broke his right arm in the third round, but continued to a six-round draw. In 1889,

> Nigh New Orleans
> Upon an emerald plain
> John L. Sullivan
> The strong boy
> Of Boston
> Fought seventy-five red rounds with Jake Kilrain,

winning twenty thousand dollars and a diamond belt offered by the *Police Gazette*.[1] His admirers now talked of running him for Congress; but he undertook a boxing tour to Australia instead, coming back only to lose his title in a twenty-one-round bout to the young Californian, James J. Corbett. "Gentleman Jim's" victory in 1892 marked a turning point in the sport, for it demonstrated the superiority of scientific boxing over sheer brute strength. His reign, however, was ended in 1897 when, in the fourteenth round of a match with "Bob" Fitzsimmons at Carson City, his Cornish opponent in less than three seconds "accomplished three epochal feats: he had knocked out an Irishman on Saint Patrick's Day, he had won the heavyweight champion-

---

[1] This was the last bare-knuckle championship fight. The quotation is from Vachel Lindsay's rhythmic commemoration of the event in *Collected Poems* (N. Y., 1925), 93-95. For pugilistic development in general, see Alexander Johnston, *Ten—and Out* (N. Y., 1927), chaps. vi-xi.

ship of the world, and he had invented the terrible 'solar plexus punch' " that is always associated with his name.[1]

Baseball reached far larger numbers of people than either racing or pugilism. Though everywhere a vacant-lots sport, it was in its professionalized aspects that it took on the dimensions of "the national game." [2] Alert to stamp out gambling and dishonesty, the National League, formed in 1876 by teams representing four Eastern and four Western cities, made professional baseball respectable at the same time that it offered the most expert playing that could be witnessed anywhere in the country. Minor or "bush" leagues also existed in profusion and in 1882 a rival to the National League appeared in the American Association.

As competition between nines and leagues grew keener, constant modifications of the rules gave greater scope for both individual skill and team play. Following 1875 the umpire was given power to call strikes and balls, three of the former and four of the latter being made the limit for the batsman. The removal in 1884 of all restrictions on pitching led to the rapid development of the outcurve, incurve, drop and fadeaway, aspects of the game of which J. B. Clarkson of Chicago and Boston and Timothy Keefe of New York were the particular masters. Protective equipment was also adopted such as the catcher's mask, breastpad and mitt. In demonstrating the possibilities of team strategy and coördinated play no nine equaled the Baltimore Orioles which, under Ned Hanlon's leadership, won the

[1] R. F. Dibble, "Robert Prometheus Fitzsimmons," *Dict. of Am. Biog.*, VI, 443.
[2] A. G. Spalding, *America's National Game* (N. Y., 1911), chaps. xiv-xx, xxxiv; G. L. Moreland, *Balldom* (N. Y., 1914), 16-133; Bozeman Bulger, "What Made Great Ball Players Great," *Des Moines Register*, March 14-April 11, 1924, *passim*.

National League pennant for three successive years after 1893.

Rivalry between the major leagues led in 1884 to the inauguration of postseason battles between the pennant-winning teams, an annual event which continued until the collapse of the American Association in 1891.[1] Beginning with Providence's triumph over the New York Metropolitans, victory in the World Series, as it was called, usually rested with the National League. That the world whose championship was yearly at stake might actually learn of America's premier sport, A. G. Spalding in 1888 arranged a series of exhibition matches around the globe between "Pop" (A. C.) Anson's Chicago White Sox and an all-American team. At Kensington Oval grounds the Prince of Wales (later Edward VII) was an excited, if somewhat uncomprehending, spectator, while in Egypt a game was played on the desert close enough to one of the pyramids for it to serve as a backstop. At home ever greater throngs found the baseball season the most zestful period of the year. The unprecedented number of forty thousand paid admission to the four games between New York and Chicago in 1885 at the Chicago Club grounds. The World Series in 1887 between Detroit and St. Louis had a total attendance of over fifty-one thousand.

In the closing years of the period another sport threatened the supremacy of the national game. As long as bicycling was confined to gymnasts whose courage was not daunted by an occasional header from the lofty perch over the high front wheel, it tended to remain in the hands of professionals.[2] Nevertheless, as early as 1880, the League of American Wheelmen was formed

[1] The World Series was revived in 1903 between the winners of the National League and the newly formed American League.

[2] See Nevins, *Emergence of Modern America*, 223-224, for the earlier form of bicycle.

with a steadily enlarging membership, and in 1883 a California amateur, Thomas Stevens, undertook a four-year cycling tour of the globe.[1] The real vogue of the sport, however, began a few years later with the introduction of the "safety" bicycle—possessing low wheels of equal size—and the substitution of pneumatic tires for solid rubber ones. At the same time a drop frame was designed for the sake of the gentler sex who could, if they wished, reassure themselves further by attaching a folded screen to the front of the bicycle "to protect the feet and ankles from view when mounting or riding."[2]

By 1893 a million bicycles were in use.[3] It seemed as though all America had taken to wheels. Frances E. Willard, the temperance leader, fell prey to the craze, announcing her conversion in a book *A Wheel within a Wheel: How I Learned to Ride the Bicycle* (1895). By physicians the therapeutic benefits were declared to be beyond compare, while dress reformers welcomed cycling as an aid to more rational fashions.[4] The new means of locomotion carried people to and from their work; it sped mail carriers and physicians on their rounds; for countless thousands it renewed the forgotten pleasures of open road and countryside. The historian Claude H. Van Tyne, while an undergraduate at the University of Michigan, made a thirty-five-hundred-

[1] Thomas Stevens, *Around the World on a Bicycle* (N. Y., 1887-1888).

[2] Anon., "Skirt Protecting Screen for Bicycles," *Scientific Am.*, LXXIV (1896), 261.

[3] In the single year 1895, over half a million were manufactured; in 1900, well over a million. A. A. Pope, "The Bicycle Industry," C. M. Depew, ed., *One Hundred Years of American Commerce* (N. Y., 1895), II, 551; *U. S. Twelfth Census*, X, 328.

[4] Not only skirts of short walking length, but even bloomers, it was urged, might be worn without offense to "feminine dignity and modesty." L. H. Porter, *Cycling for Health and Pleasure* (N. Y., 1895), 3-22, 106-117, 177-195.

mile trip from Ann Arbor over the Rockies in 1894.
Meantime, bicycle clubs were formed which pedaled
together in a body for pleasure, or conducted meets in
which professional riders strove to set new records for
speed or endurance.

From the outset the League of American Wheelmen
carried on a vigorous propaganda for good roads, which
finally bore fruit in the nineties. Starting with New
Jersey in 1891, the last decade saw new and improved
highway legislation in over half the states.[1] "It is safe
to say," declared an expert of the census bureau in 1900,
"that few articles ever used by man have created so great
a revolution in social conditions as the bicycle."[2] Only
a person of fevered imagination could have guessed that
the noisy, puffing "horseless carriages," which now and
then ventured forth upon the roads, would within a few
years spell the doom of the universally popular "bike."[3]

Other forms of physical recreation, while attracting
fewer devotees, resembled cycling in their essentially amateur character. Roller skating was an epidemic which
raged intermittently and affected all ages; in 1885 skating rinks represented an investment of over twenty million dollars. Croquet made a wide appeal by reason of
its simplicity and leisurely pace, though it was objected
to by some because of the opportunity it afforded for
flirtation.[4] With the hope of converting the game into
an exhibition of skill the National Croquet Association
was formed in 1882 and held annual tournaments.
Lawn tennis, introduced from England in 1875, was

[1] M. O. Eldridge, "Progress of Road Building," U. S. Dept. of Agr.,
Yearbook for 1899, 377-380; N. S. Shaler, American Highways (N. Y.,
1896), chap. vi.
[2] U. S. Twelfth Census, X, 329. See also J. B. Bishop, "Social and
Economic Influence of the Bicycle," Forum, XXI (1896), 680-689.
[3] See Faulkner, Quest for Social Justice, 132-133.
[4] G. B. Bartlett, "The Recreations of the People," Journ. of Social
Sci., XII (1880), 141.

at first also regarded merely as a pleasant pastime; but with the formation of a national association six years later, uniform rules were adopted and the annual tournaments at Newport and elsewhere quickly brought to the fore such masters of the racquet as R. D. Sears, James Dwight and H. W. Slocum. Meanwhile the formation of the American Canoe Association in 1880 popularized this water sport. Within a dozen years there were some sixty canoe clubs in the East with over five thousand members.[1] Skiing was a contribution of Norwegian Americans, who organized the first ski club at Red Wing, Minnesota, in 1883, and held the first tournament the following year.[2]

Rifle shooting also had its addicts, and since 1874 international matches had been held with picked teams from Ireland, England, Australia and other lands. Fishing and hunting, which belonged to the older American tradition, had now to be carried on with due regard to the laws for preserving wild life.[3] In the last quarter of the century anglers' associations and sportmen's clubs appeared everywhere; in the East the members were usually city dwellers who journeyed long distances to find their pleasure. To discourage the indiscriminate slaughter of game birds George B. Grinnell brought about the formation in 1886 of the Audubon Society, which soon had fifty thousand members; and the following year Theodore Roosevelt, an expert hunter, helped organize the Boone and Crockett Club for the protection of big game. Though less adventurous, trap shooting also enjoyed considerable vogue, the first national tournament being held in 1886 at New Orleans.

Certain sports—trap shooting, archery, polo, golf—

[1] J. H. Mandigo, "Outdoor Sports," *Chautauquan*, XIX (1894), 393.
[2] *Daily Eagle* (Red Wing, Minn.), Feb. 2, 1928.
[3] See earlier, 237.

were largely monopolized by the fashionable few.[1] This was notably true, of course, of international yacht racing in which vessels sponsored by the New York Yacht Club continued successfully to defend the *America's* cup against all challengers.[2] It was the wealthy, too, who fostered the growth of country clubs where, amidst the lovely verdure of hill and dale, such pleasures as polo and golf might be pursued under the best obtainable conditions.[3] In the nineties country clubs could be found in well-to-do communities from Palm Beach to Puget Sound.

The new gospel of physical well-being led everywhere also to an extension of indoor facilities for exercise. Gymnasiums were proliferated by the Y. M. C. A. and Y. W. C. A., while the rapid spread of city athletic clubs provided additional opportunities, especially for track sports.[4] Beginning in cities like Milwaukee (1877) and Kansas City (1885), where the German Turner influence was strong, physical training was also introduced into the schools.[5] At the university level the erection of the Hemenway Gymnasium at Harvard in 1878 and the effective work of its director, Dr. D. A. Sargent, set new standards which other colleges quickly followed.

[1] The growth of interest in such games is indicated by the formation of the National Archery Association in 1879, the United States Polo Association in 1890, and the United States Golf Association in 1894. Polo had been introduced from Great Britain in 1873 or 1874, golf in 1878.

[2] Against a Canadian sloop in 1881, and British cutters in 1885, 1886, 1887, 1893 and 1895.

[3] The Brookline Country Club, founded in 1882 near Boston, was apparently the first. Caspar Whitney, "Evolution of the Country Club," *Harper's Mag.*, XC (1894), 16-33; Robert Dunn, "The Country Club: A National Expression," *Outing*, XLVII (1905), 160-174.

[4] Samuel Crowther and Arthur Ruhl, *Rowing and Track Athletics* (Caspar Whitney, ed., *The American Sportsman's Library*; N. Y., 1905), pt. ii, chap. iii.

[5] U. S. Commissioner of Education, *Report for 1891-92*, I, 518-521; for *1897-98*, I, 549-557; C. F. Thwing, *A History of Education in the United States since the Civil War* (Boston, 1910), chap. x.

Yet, despite the interest lent indoor exercise by the new apparatus which Sargent and his disciples introduced, college youths continued to find greater zest in open-air contests.[1] Few of these did they wholly neglect, and there was one, football, in which they admittedly excelled. As played in the late seventies the sport still bore a strong family resemblance to the English game of Rugby; but under the influence of innovators, notably Walter Camp at Yale, constant changes were made until the game became thoroughly Americanized.[2] The number of players was reduced from fifteen to eleven; the free-for-all scramble for the ball was replaced by having one side put it in play; the quarter-back, thus promoted to a key position, introduced numerical signals; and new rules were adopted as regards downs, tackling and interference. For many years the best teams were in the East and, when Walter Camp selected his first "All-American" eleven in 1889, he did not need to look beyond the "Big Three": Yale, Harvard and Princeton. The appointment of A. A. Stagg as coach at the University of Chicago in 1892 began a new era for the sport in the Middle West. Most institutions, however, could not afford to employ regular coaches. At Connecticut Wesleyan Professor Woodrow Wilson, in his hours away from the classroom, helped train a team that in 1889 defeated Pennsylvania, Amherst, Williams, Rutgers and Trinity.

The intensity of intercollegiate rivalry aroused sharp criticism of the game both on and off the campus in the early 1890's. The absorbing interest of undergraduates

[1] A. M. F. Davis, "College Athletics," *Atlantic Mo.*, LI (1883), 677-684; N. S. Shaler, "The Athletic Problem in Education," same mag., LXIII (1889), 79-88; A. B. Hart, "Status of Athletics in American Colleges," same mag., LXVI (1890), 63-71.

[2] Walter Camp and L. F. Deland, *Football* (Boston, 1896), chap. vii; P. H. Davis, *Football* (N. Y., 1911), 65-105; A. M. Weyand, *American Football* (N. Y., 1926), chaps. i-ii.

made one college president fear lest the degree of B.A. would come to stand for "Bachelor of Athletics." [1] As mass tactics and momentum plays became the common practice under the new regulations, parents grew increasingly alarmed at the annual toll of injuries. [2] Moreover, the contests, constantly more expensive and elaborate, took on the aspect of shows conducted primarily for the pleasure of alumni and the general public. Over fifty thousand watched the annual Yale-Princeton game on Thanksgiving Day, 1893, while telegraphic bulletins acquainted the country with the fortunes of the battle. Some light is shed on the prevalent laxness of standards by the fact that seven members of the University of Michigan squad in 1893 were not even enrolled as students. From time to time the Eastern colleges took measures to improve conditions, while the Western Conference of seven leading institutions was formed in 1896 for a similar purpose. But the problem was far from solved when the period closed.

The athletic awakening of the 1880's and 1890's added a new dimension to American life. Though primarily of concern to men, outdoor play increasingly enlisted the interest of the gentler sex, and in sports like tennis and archery they established excellent records for skill. Sometimes it seemed as if the mass of people could take a serious interest in nothing else. F. B. Opper, the *Puck* cartoonist, drew a phrenological chart, dividing Uncle Sam's cranium among such interests as football, bicycling, tennis and golf with the biggest bump of all assigned to baseball. [3] That Uncle Sam did have sport

[1] U. S. Comr. of Educ., *Rep. for 1896-97*, I, 705. The chief objections to football are summarized in H. D. Sheldon, *Student Life and Customs* (W. T. Harris, ed., *International Education Series*, LI, N. Y., 1901), 235-245.

[2] E. G. Dexter, "Accidents from College Football," *Educational Rev.*, XXV (1903), 415-428.

[3] *Puck*, XXI, 236 (June 1, 1887).

on the brain seemed conclusive to the English visitor who found that, of two events occurring on September 7, 1892, his American newspaper gave one column to the death of John Greenleaf Whittier and nearly a dozen to the Corbett-Sullivan prize fight.[1]

If the generation did not solve the problem of leisure, it at least succeeded in dodging it. The "second battle of civilization," as Garfield called it, found the average citizen in an attitude of nonresistance toward the forces that rushed in on him from every side. He did as others did and hence discovered himself without leisure. The pursuit of happiness tended to become a breathless chase, the provision of recreation an organized traffic. Yet such is not the whole story. Human beings, even when regimented for purposes of historians' generalizations, have a way of remaining annoyingly individualistic and self-willed. It is important to recall that the deeper values of leisure were also explored and by an ever larger number of people. Only in this way can one understand some of the most striking developments of the time: the longer years spent in school and university, the phenomenal growth of the reading habit, the increased enjoyment of good music, the deepened interest in works of mercy, the growth of transatlantic travel, the wider appreciation of the rôle of art and beauty in life. And these were enduring gains of which any age might be proud.

[1] J. F. Muirhead, *The Land of Contrasts* (Boston, 1898), 158.

CHAPTER X

THE CHANGING CHURCH

DESPITE the multiplying demands on their leisure hours a majority of the people, at least in the rural sections, continued to find time to go to church each Sunday and many of them also to mid-week prayer meeting. Judging not only from this habit but also from other indications—the sale of theological works, the general respect paid to Christian precepts and ministers, the lively interest in doctrinal questions, the religious coloration of so much philanthropic effort—Bryce considered the influence of the church deeper and stronger than in any European nation.[1] Most professed Christians accepted unhesitatingly what the Reformation had handed down, provided it bore a Protestant label, whether the Nicene doctrine of the Trinity, the Augustinian theory of man's fall, Calvin's insistence upon God's arbitrary will, or less exacting modern variants of these traditional dogmas. With over one hundred and fifty denominations from which to choose, no country in the world so well exemplified Frederick the Great's principle that everyone should be allowed to go to heaven in his own way. Save in rural neighborhoods and particularly in the South, differences within Protestantdom, however, had lost their ancient fierceness. Religious attendance and church work were often hardly more than "a kind of sacred amusement," a social rather

[1] James Bryce, *The American Commonwealth* (London, 1888), III, 483.

than a spiritual fellowship.[1] In the new communities of the Great West the dearth of churches eased the passage from one denomination into another, a trait characteristic also of the great cities.

A disposition to distinguish sharply between the sacred and the secular tended to divorce religion from everyday thought and conduct. So far as the mass of churchgoers were concerned, this made possible the survival, into a critical and scientific age, of theological ideas which the more progressive clerics were questioning or had already rejected. After the feverish labors of the week Americans generally displayed a "docile acquiescence" in any teachings which freed them from mental disturbance and satisfied their emotional need of belief.[2] The theological cosmos of the average man is probably mirrored in a census of the religious opinions of a thousand California children in the early 1890's.[3] God was generally conceived as an old man with a long beard and flowing white garments, benevolent rather than stern of mien, but possessing power to "have an earthquake at any time." Heaven, suspended "in the clouds," had houses and streets of gold where angels flew about and strummed on harps. For Satan the conventional figure in *Faust* was the prototype, though two pupils derived their impressions more immediately from the labels on deviled-ham cans. If such views show little change from those of colonial times, they were, for the godly at least, an anchor of faith and the source of abiding comfort.

Yet above these quiet depths the winds of contro-

[1] [J. B. Harrison], *Certain Dangerous Tendencies in American Life* (Boston, 1880), 10-11.

[2] See comments of the French psychologist Gabriel Compayré, quoted in U. S. Commissioner of Education, *Report for 1895-96*, II, 1165.

[3] Earl Barnes, "Theological Life of a California Child," *Pedagogical Seminary*, II, 442-448, which summarizes the views expressed by 1091 school children of from six to twenty years of age. Nine different religious groups, including the Catholic, were represented.

versy were chopping the theological seas and affrighting conservatives as to the eventual survival of revealed religion. The new findings of science and scholarship impelled intellectual people to reconsider their traditional attitude toward the Bible, while the devout were driven to blind resistance or a new apologetics. Religion, in other words, was engaged in one of those recurrent conflicts between orthodoxy and heterodoxy, between fundamentalism and modernism, which have formed a law of its growth. In the eyes of stalwart believers the foundations of faith were imperiled by three grave heresies: the doctrine of Darwinism, the science of Biblical criticism, and the new interest in comparative religion.

The religious controversy over biological evolution reached its most critical stage in the 1880's, for by that time American scientists stood a solid phalanx in its support and many of the thoughtful public had been won over by the persuasive writings of Spencer, Huxley and Fiske.[1] It no longer sufficed for theological disputants to castigate Darwinism with such epithets as materialistic and atheistic. If evolution was the "bestial hypothesis" of man's origin, it was only too easy to retort in kind that the Biblical account was the "mudman theory" of creation. Reason must be appealed to as well as inherited belief.[2] An analysis of the turbid flood of argument which poured from the press during the decade reveals a steady advance—or retreat—from a position of pure emotional obscurantism to one of concession and accommodation. Some found the way out

[1] See earlier, 231. Allan Nevins, *The Emergence of Modern America* (*A History of American Life*, VIII), 286-289, treats the initial stages of the dispute.

[2] The antievolutionists made the most of the internal strife among naturalists, which, however, did not question the fact of evolution but rather the particular mode set forth by Darwin. See *Nation* (N. Y.), XLIV, 121-123 (Feb. 10, 1887), and LX, 31 (Jan. 10, 1895).

by asserting that religion and science belonged to mutually exclusive spheres; that the Bible was a rule of conduct and a guide to faith, not a scientific cyclopedia.[1] Others held that the account in Genesis, when allegorically construed, really anticipated and supported Darwin's thesis.[2] Still others contended that genuine religion remained unaffected by what was, at most, a conflict between science and theology.[3]

Gradually, an increasing number of ministers, influenced by the example of Henry Ward Beecher in his Brooklyn pulpit and by Lyman Abbott's sermons and writings in the *Christian Union* and elsewhere, came to embrace evolution as a new and grander revelation of the mysterious way God moves his wonders to perform.[4] Mark Twain's facetious proposal, early in the eighties, of a monument to Adam before that great progenitor of mankind should be wholly supplanted by Darwin's simian, was decidedly premature. But unmistakable evidence of a sweeping change of sentiment among thoughtful religionists appeared when, after another decade of discussion, the great New York Chautauqua gave over its platform in 1893 to a series of lectures by the well-known Scotch evolutionist Henry Drummond. "It is a sign of the times which no observer can neglect," commented the *Nation*.[5]

Like the doctrine of natural selection, textual criti-

[1] Henry Calderwood, *The Relations of Science and Religion* (N. Y., 1881), esp. 298, 308; C. B. Warring, *Miracle, Law and Evolution* (N. Y., 1887), esp. 8; review of Arnold Guyot's *Creation, Am. Catholic Quar.*, IX (1884), 374.

[2] S. B. Goodenow, "Primeval Man," *Bibliotheca Sacra*, LI (1894), esp. 159.

[3] T. T. Munger, "Religion's Gain from Science," *Forum*, VI (1888), 45-54.

[4] Beecher introduced evolution into his sermons as early as 1880. Lyman Abbott, *Henry Ward Beecher* (Boston, 1903), 317-324.

[5] A. B. Paine, *Mark Twain* (N. Y., 1912), II, 707-709; edit., *Nation*, LVII, 21 (July 13, 1893).

cism of the Bible also called into question the infallibility of the Scriptures. Imported from German university centers, the higher criticism, as it was known, subjected the Holy Writ to rigorous historical analysis. According to the new findings, the sixty-six books, far from being all of one piece and inspired throughout, comprised a storehouse of history, folklore, discourses, poetry and prophecy brought together over a period of a thousand years.[1] Acceptance of the new point of view was somewhat facilitated by the appearance of a revised version of the King James Bible in 1881 and 1885, a laborious enterprise carried through by a group of English and American scholars.[2] So great was the public interest that two hundred thousand copies of the New Testament were sold in New York alone within less than a week, and the *Chicago Times* and the *Chicago Tribune* printed the text entire.

While ministers and churchgoers accustomed themselves to changed readings and often changed meanings of treasured passages, liberal theologians wrote books and articles to disseminate the teachings of the higher critics. President Orello Cone of Buchtel College, for example, published in 1891 his *Gospel Criticism and Historical Christianity,* the ablest work in its field from an American pen. All was not smooth sailing, of course. Dwight L. Moody, the famous evangelist, venting contempt on those who found inconsistencies and contradictions in the Scriptures, shouted to vast audiences with

[1] George Harris, *A Century's Change in Religion* (Boston, 1914), chap. iv; C. A. Briggs, *Whither?* (N. Y., 1889), 277-285; A. D. White, *A History of the Warfare of Science with Theology in Christendom* (N. Y., 1896), II, chap. xx.

[2] The first installment, in 1881, consisted of the New Testament. Philip Schaff was chairman of the American revisers. D. S. Schaff, *The Life of Philip Schaff* (N. Y., 1897), 354-363, 382-388; anon., "The New and Old Versions," *Nation,* XXXII, 401-402 (June 9, 1881).

all the force of his two hundred and eighty pounds: "The Bible was not made to understand." [1] Professor W. H. Green of Princeton Seminary stoutly defended the orthodox position in a notable debate with President Harper of Chicago, and many a household and congregation continued to find solace in an unquestioning acceptance of the King James version. Yet the reception accorded Washington Gladden's *Who Wrote the Bible?*, published in 1891, indicates the broad appeal of the more advanced attitude. A summary and popularization of the newer studies, it not only enjoyed the largest sale of any of his widely read books, but became a manual for Bible classes and Young Men's Christian Associations. [2] Sober reflection was convincing even many of the earlier objectors that, if critical analysis stripped the Bible of its vesture of infallibility, it revealed it as a work of literary, spiritual and ethical power, a veritable book among books. [3]

The crumbling of orthodoxy was furthered by certain by-products of American missionary enterprise in the Orient. Thousands of Christian workers, brought into contact with the great faiths of Asia, learned that Christianity and religion were not coextensive, that all good was not monopolized by their own system of belief. At the same time the work of secular scholars in the realms of mythology, folklore, psychology and anthropology suggested points of departure for an understanding of religious phenomena. James Freeman Clarke's sympathetic portrayal of *Ten Great Religions* made such an impression upon the public that in the

[1] E. J. Goodspeed, *A Full History of the Wonderful Career of Moody and Sankey in Great Britain and America* (Ashland, Ohio, 1877), 315.

[2] Washington Gladden, *Recollections* (Boston, 1909), 320-321.

[3] Lyman Abbott, *Reminiscences* (Boston, 1915), 460-462; C. W. Shields, "Does the Bible Contain Scientific Errors?," *Century*, XLV (1892-1893), 126-134; C. A. Briggs, "Works of the Imagination in the Old Testament," *N. Am. Rev.*, CLXIV (1897), 356-373.

fifteen years after 1871 it passed through twenty-one editions. Comparative religion became not only a pre-occupation of scholars but a new measuring rod for Christianity. As dramatic evidence of the widened horizon, a World's Parliament of Religions, the first of its kind, was convened during the Columbian Exposition of 1893. More than one hundred and fifty thousand people attended. While all was not harmony, the animating spirit of the great assemblage was expressed in the words of Malachi, which served as its motto: "Have we not all one Father? hath not one God created us?" [1] In the light of fuller knowledge the old misunderstanding and intolerance once accorded non-Christian faiths was beginning to wane.

If these new intellectual currents little touched the average mind, they deeply affected the thinking of the more intelligent. In 1881 the American Institute of Christian Philosophy was formed in New York state for the purpose of producing and distributing literature upon the relations of science and the Bible. Magazines, both religious and secular, gave generous space to appraisals of the new learning. Even more significant was the discussion of theological issues in certain notable works of fiction. The best sellers of the year 1888 were Margaret Deland's *John Ward, Preacher,* described by a contemporary as "a profound outcry against the intolerance of the creeds," and Mrs. Humphry Ward's *Robert Elsmere,* an English novel of similar import which sold more copies in America than in the author's own country.[2] Here and there theological schools intro-

[1] F. H. Stead, "The Story of the World's Parliament of Religions," *Am. Rev. of Revs.,* IX (1894), 299-310.

[2] Anon., "The Books of 1888," *Publishers' Wkly.,* XXXV, 205, 208 (Feb. 9, 1889) ; anon., "The Influence of the Religious Novel," *Nation,* XLVII, 329-330 (Oct. 25, 1888). Sarah B. Elliott's novel *The Felmeres,* published in 1879, was of the same *genre,* as was also

duced courses dealing with the relations of science and religion and with the study of comparative religion.[1]

Traditionalism, however, maintained a stubborn front where it could. In 1878 the geologist Alexander Winchell was dismissed from the Methodist-controlled Vanderbilt University, with the exultant pronouncement of the Tennessee Methodist conference—anticipating the state of mind behind the Dayton "monkey trial" of 1925—that "our university alone has had the courage to lay its young but vigorous hand upon the mane of untamed Speculation and say, 'We will have no more of this.' " [2] Not to be outdone in good works, the Southern Baptist Seminary at Louisville followed Vanderbilt's example within a year by forcing Professor C. H. Toy's resignation because of his attempts to interpret the Old Testament from the viewpoint of modern science. Five years later Dr. James Woodrow was driven from his post in the Presbyterian Theological Seminary at Columbia, South Carolina, for avowing the truth of evolution, and in 1891 W. J. Alexander was dropped from the chair of philosophy at the state university because of unorthodox views regarding the divinity of Christ.[3]

Such bigotry, however, was not confined to the South or to three denominations. In 1882 Dr. E. P. Gould was obliged to resign from Newton Theological Insti-

the widely discussed *The Damnation of Theron Ware* (1896) by Harold Frederic.

[1] U. S. Comr. of Educ., *Rep. for 1889-90*, II, 942-943.

[2] White, *Warfare of Science with Theology*, I, 313-316. Winchell's views are set forth in *The Doctrine of Evolution* (N. Y., 1874) and *Adamites and Pre-Adamites* (Syracuse, 1878). For the Dayton trial, see P. W. Slosson, *The Great Crusade and After* (*A History of American Life*, XII), 431-432.

[3] G. F. Moore, "An Appreciation of Professor Toy," *Am. Journ. of Semitic Languages and Literatures*, XXXVI, 3-5; White, *Warfare of Science with Theology*, I, 316-318; F. B. Simkins, *The Tillman Movement in South Carolina* (Duke Univ., *Publs.*; Durham, 1926), 142, 144.

tution (Baptist) in Massachusetts as a result of doctrinal differences with the president.[1] The next year the
Reverend R. Heber Newton of All Souls' Protestant
Episcopal Church, New York City, was charged with
heresy at the instance of Bishop H. C. Potter and other
divines, the case later being allowed to drop.[2] In 1886
a fire that for several years had been smoldering at
Andover Theological Seminary (Congregational) in
Massachusetts burst into flame when the board of visitors tried five professors for theological liberalism and
declared one of them guilty.[3]

Even more rancorous than the "Andover controversy" was the storm that rose in 1891 within Presbyterian ranks over the transfer of Professor Charles A.
Briggs, a distinguished exponent of the higher criticism
and long an ornament of Union Theological Seminary,
to the new chair of Biblical theology. More than seventy
presbyteries protested the appointment. Although the
New York Presbytery recommended that in the interests of "the peace . . . of the Church" no action be
taken, the General Assembly in 1893 suspended Briggs
from the ministry for heresy. The peace of the church
was indeed involved. In Albany a clergyman resigned
because of the decision, while Professor H. P. Smith was
suspended from Lane Theological Seminary in Cincinnati for supporting Briggs's views.[4]

---

[1] Edit., *Nation*, XXXV, 279 (Oct. 5, 1882).

[2] Edit., *Nation*, XXXVIII, 179 (Feb. 28, 1884).

[3] The professors were J. W. Churchill, George Harris, E. Y. Hincks,
W. J. Tucker and E. C. Smyth, the last for some reason being the only
one adjudged guilty. The case was taken before the state supreme court
and in 1893 a decision handed down against the board. W. J. Tucker,
My Generation (Boston, 1919), chap. vii.

[4] The incident caused Union Seminary to sever its affiliation with the
General Assembly and Briggs continued in his professorship, subsequently
becoming an Episcopal clergyman. Philip Schaff, "Other Heresy Trials
and the Briggs Case," *Forum*, XII (1891-1892), 621-633; *Nation*,
LVI, 412, 414-415 (June 8, 1893).

The harm to the cause of religion inflicted by such incidents was greater than that to the cause of science and learning. Yet the wayward religious tendencies of the times help explain the fears of the pious that, once old moorings were cut, the people would drift into uncharted seas. Untold thousands listened receptively to the eloquent and pungent discourses of Robert G. Ingersoll, the "notorious infidel"; many a village Jaques won his reputation for bold speculation by filching the doughty Colonel's iconoclastic shafts. Himself a minister's son in lifelong revolt against his father's extreme Calvinism, Ingersoll was an agnostic, not an atheist: "I do not deny. I do not know—but I do not believe." [1] A relentless foe of dogmatism and illiberalism, he inveighed against Old Testament terrors and New Testament miracles, finding good in all the great religious systems and extolling science as "the only true religion, . . . the only Savior of the world." Starting from much the same position, Dr. Felix Adler, like Ingersoll a clergyman's son though of the Jewish faith, rejected Ingersoll's negative attitude and sought to erect ethical purpose as the vital principle of living without reference to any kind of theological doctrine.[2] With this as his aim he founded in 1876 the Society for Ethical Culture, which presently attracted small bands of intellectuals, usually of Hebrew extraction, in the great cities of the East and Middle West.

Whatever Ethical Culture lacked in mysticism was supplied in full measure by another sect which sought disciples during these years. Originated by Helena P. Blavatsky, an obese Russian woman of somewhat un-

---

[1] For a summary of his views, see R. G. Ingersoll, "Why Am I an Agnostic?," *N. Am. Rev.*, CXLIX (1889), 741-749; CL (1890), 330-338.

[2] His work *Creed and Deed* (N. Y., 1877) sets forth his view that the essence of religion is "fervent devotion to the highest moral ends."

savory antecedents, Theosophy was a curious blend of
spiritualism and certain occult doctrines derived from
the Brahmanic and Vedic literatures of India.[1] The The-
osophical Society, formed in New York in 1875, was
to be the spearhead of the new movement, but, converts
remaining few, Madame Blavatsky three years later
transferred her colorful activities to India and Europe.
Meantime the cult managed to maintain a tenuous existence in America and was temporarily stirred to a
flurry of activity in the 1890's by the arrival of numerous swamis at the time of the World's Fair.

If these new systems lacked warmth of appeal, their
plight was shared to some extent by the older, Protestant
sects whose ministers, immersed in intellectual controversy, often failed to satisfy deeper spiritual needs.[2]
Even more harmful was the failure of the church to
adjust itself to the unprecedented conditions created by
rapid urban and industrial growth.[3] American Protestantism, the product of a rural, middle-class society,
faced a range of problems for which it had neither
experience nor aptitude. In the cities the building of
church edifices lagged behind the advance of population,
while the shifting of residential districts left once pros-

[1] For her exposition of the tenets of Theosophy, see *Isis Unveiled*
(N. Y., 1877) and *The Secret Doctrine* (London, 1888).

[2] [Harrison], *Certain Dangerous Tendencies*, 206-213; F. H. Hedge,
The Church in Modern Society (n.p., 1882), 266-267; C. F. Thwing,
"Young Men and the Preaching They Want," *Century*, XLIX (1894-
1895), 637-639.

[3] Awareness of this failure is expressed in books like Washington
Gladden, *Applied Christianity* (Boston, 1886), 146-179; S. L. Loomis,
Modern Cities and Their Religious Problems (N. Y., 1887), esp. chap.
iii; Josiah Strong, *The New Era* (N. Y., 1893), chap. x; and W. T.
Stead, *If Christ Came to Chicago!* (Chicago, 1894), 389-405; as well
as in an abundant periodical literature, including O. F. Adams, "Aristo-
cratic Drift of American Protestantism," *N. Am. Rev.*, CXLII (1886),
194-199; C. M. Morse, "The Church and the Working Man," *Forum*,
VI (1888), 653-661; T. B. Wakeman, "Our Unchurched Millions,"
Arena, II (1890), 604-613; and C. A. Briggs, "The Alienation of
Church and People," *Forum*, XVI (1893-1894), esp. 375-377.

perous houses of worship stranded and abandoned on the bleak shores of factory and slum neighborhoods. In the twenty years preceding 1888 seventeen Protestant churches moved out of the district below Fourteenth Street, New York, though two hundred thousand more people crowded into it.[1] In the decade after 1878 twenty-two thousand residents in the thirteenth ward of Boston were without a single Protestant church, and it was said that in the heart of Chicago sixty thousand people had no church either Protestant or Catholic. It was generally true of large cities that those parts which needed most religious attention got least.

When better accommodations existed, the working class commonly regarded the church—with its fine upholstery, stained-glass windows and expensive choirs— as an institution where ill-clad worshipers were unwelcome and the Nazarene himself would have been rebuffed. As someone has observed, in religion nothing fails like success. The pulpit, increasingly beholden to contributions from the rich, ordinarily ignored or condoned the terrible injustices from which the wage-earning multitude were suffering. In one instance, reported by Professor Ely, when the bakers' union petitioned five hundred clergymen of New York and Brooklyn to preach sermons against compulsory Sunday labor, all but half a dozen ignored the appeal.[2] Even popular sects like the Baptists abandoned their contempt for wealth. In 1890 the Indiana state Baptist convention "thankfully recognized the rich blessing of the Great

[1] Data in regard to the distribution of churches in urban centers are summarized in Loomis, *Modern Cities*, 7-9, 88-89, and Strong, *New Era*, 197-201.

[2] R. T. Ely, *Social Aspects of Christianity* (rev. edn., N. Y., 1889), 44-45. In at least one case on record, that of a Lutheran congregation in Oshkosh, Wis., in Feb., 1894, trade unionists were excluded from the church on the ground that membership in a labor organization violated the law of God. Stead, *If Christ Came to Chicago*, 394-395 *n*.

Head of the Church in the recent gift of Brother John
D. Rockefeller to the Baptist Seminary in Chicago." [1]
To laborites religion seemed a sort of capitalistic sooth-
ing-syrup. Samuel Gompers bluntly charged that the intellect and talent of the ministry had been suborned by
the plutocratic oppressors of the poor.[2]

While few religious bodies, like Trinity Church in
New York City, actually owned slum properties, too
many congregations imbibed their Sabbath teachings at
the hands of preachers such as the one Kipling heard
in Chicago in 1891.[3] "With a voice of silver and imagery borrowed from the auction-room," the minister
exultantly portrayed

> a heaven on the lines of the Palmer House (but with
> all the gilding real gold, and all the plate-glass dia-
> mond), and set in the centre of it a loud-voiced, argu-
> mentative, very shrewd creation that he called God.
> One sentence . . . caught my delighted ear. It was
> apropos of some question of the Judgment, and ran:—
> "No! I tell you God doesn't do business that way."

"Go into an ordinary church on Sunday morning,"
declared a Protestant clergyman in 1887, "and you see
lawyers, physicians, merchants, and business men with
their families . . . but the workingman and his household are not there." [4] Of the older faiths the Roman
Catholic and the Jewish alone knew how to attract and
hold the laborer and the immigrant newcomer. Evan-

---

[1] R. H. Johnson, "American Baptists in the Age of Big Business,"
Journ. of Religion, XI, esp. 72.

[2] H. F. Perry, "The Workingman's Alienation from the Church,"
Am. Journ. of Sociology, IV (1898-1899), esp. 622.

[3] Rudyard Kipling, *American Notes* (Boston, 1899), 97-98. For the
public exposure of Trinity's connection with slum properties, see H. U.
Faulkner, *The Quest for Social Justice* (*A History of American Life*,
XI), 221-222.

[4] Loomis, *Modern Cities*, 82.

gelistic endeavors might temporarily bridge the chasm in the case of Protestants; but even such ardent harvesters of souls as Dwight L. Moody and Ira D. Sankey found their chief work among laggard members of existing congregations and did little to reach the unchurched masses.[1] The Catholic Church, on the other hand, reared its edifices where humanity was densest and thronged its pews three or four times each Sunday with worshipers whose hands and clothing plainly betrayed their humble station.

Another token of alienation from the church appeared in the growing secularization of the Sabbath. This, too, was largely a city phenomenon, for in rural communities, and notably in the South, the people continued to regard the day as one set aside for religious observance and rest.[2] In urban centers, on the other hand, the pressure of life turned the toiling masses to thoughts of pleasure on their one free day while, to satisfy their desire, thousands of their fellows needs must operate trains and street cars and provide the means of recreation.[3] The altered attitude owed much to the practices of immigrant groups unfamiliar with the strait-laced American Lord's Day—the Germans with their Continental Sabbath, the Irish and other aliens with their Catholic Sunday and the Jews who observed Saturday as their holy day. "Where is the city in which the Sabbath day is not losing ground?" asked one sad voice. "To the mass of the workingmen Sunday . . . is a

---

[1] Gamaliel Bradford, D. L. Moody (Garden City, 1927), 115-118.

[2] W. R. Crafts, "Impressions of a Transcontinental Tour," Our Day (Boston), IV (1889), 543; Bryce, American Commonwealth, III, 488; B. J. Ramage, "Sunday Legislation," Sewanee Rev., IV (1895), 121.

[3] J. H. Ward, "The New Sunday," Atlantic Mo., XLVII (1881), 526-538; C. W. Clark, "The Day of Rest," Atlantic Mo., LXIV (1889), 366-375. For the Catholic attitude, see anon., "The Catholic Sunday and the Puritan Sabbath," Catholic World, XXIII (1876), 550-565.

day for labor meetings, for excursions, for saloons, beer-
gardens, base-ball games and carousals." [1]

The change in Sabbath habits had little relation to
Sabbath legislation. Such laws existed in almost every
state and were usually very strict, forbidding all labor
except works of necessity and charity and, in many
cases, banning also travel and nearly every kind of
amusement.[2] As late as 1885 Vermont and South Carolina required church attendance on Sunday and in Pennsylvania the stay-at-home was liable to the penalty of
sitting in the stocks. But if rural majorities in the legislatures insisted on retaining the laws, they seemed
strangely indifferent to lax law enforcement in the
cities. Indeed, certain strongly urban states like New
York (1883) and Massachusetts (1887) markedly
relaxed their statutes; and in California in 1883, after
a thorough public discussion of the issue, the legislature
repealed all the Sabbath blue laws.[3] The running of
passenger trains was a particular affront to sabbatarians
who, however, saw each year an increasing number on
the tracks.

The portentous spread of Sabbath desecration
brought a revival of militant efforts to restore its sanctity. In 1884 the W. C. T. U. established a department
of Sabbath observance, and four years later the American Sabbath Union, formed by several evangelical
churches, began organizing local branches to arouse
opinion. In addition, the International Sabbath Association and the Sunday League of America were in the
field. But even such bodies reflected a changed attitude

[1] Loomis, *Modern Cities*, 104.

[2] Bryce, *American Commonwealth*, III, 488-489; W. F. Crafts, *The Sabbath for Man* (N. Y., 1885), 111; J. G. Woerner, "Sunday and Sunday Laws," *Am. Law Rev.*, XVIII (1884), 778-800.

[3] *Laws of New York for 1883*, chap. ccclviii; *Acts and Resolves of Massachusetts for 1887*, chap. cccxci; W. A. Blakely, ed., *American State Papers Bearing on Sunday Legislation* (N. Y., 1891), 275 n.

on the subject. Their main plea was less a religious than a humanitarian one: Sabbath breaking was condemned not so much as an offense against God as against man.[1] In other words, a rational regard for a secular day of rest was supplanting the old idea of a day exclusively for religious consecration. For this reason their efforts often won support from powerful labor groups like the Knights of Labor, the Brotherhood of Locomotive Engineers and the American Federation of Labor.

It was a union of these forces which bombarded Congress from 1887 to 1889 with memorials, said to represent fourteen million people, for a cessation of dispensable Sunday labor in interstate commerce and the postal and military services and also in the territories and the District of Columbia. The desired measure was introduced by Senator H. W. Blair on May 21, 1888; hearings were held, but the bill mysteriously never came to a vote.[2] On the matter of Sabbath recreation, however, laborites parted company with the professional sabbatarians. The question of opening the World's Fair on Sunday proved the occasion for a pitched battle. The management vacillated and, when finally it opened the gates but with incomplete exhibits, the attendance was so poor that after a few weeks it shut them again.[3]

Whether or not a more vibrant religious message would have kept more people within bounds on the

[1] See, for example, W. R. Crafts, "Valid Grounds for Sabbath Observance," *Our Day*, II (1888), 262-275.

[2] "Sunday Observance," 50 Cong., 1 sess., *Miscel. Senate Doc.*, no. 108; "Sunday Rest Bill," 50 Cong., 2 sess., *Miscel. Senate Doc.*, no. 43; *Our Day*, III (1889), 51-53, 192, 310.

[3] W. R. Crafts, "Sunday Closing of the Columbian World's Fair," *Our Day*, VIII (1891), 259-267; edit., "Jesus, the Church, and the World's Fair," *Arena*, VI (1892), 250-260; Elizabeth C. Stanton, "Sunday at the World's Fair," *N. Am. Rev.*, CLIV (1892), 254-256; J. W. Chadwick, "Why the Fair Must Be Open on Sunday," *Forum*, XIV (1892-1893), 541-550; edit., *Nation*, LVII, 39 (July 20, 1893).

Lord's Day, the older Protestant churches, as we have seen, were not prepared to give it. To help the common man rekindle the altar fires of his faith two new religions, however, made their appearance. One was a British importation, the other an authentic American creation. The Salvation Army had been organized in London by William Booth in an effort to adapt the Methodist revivalistic technique to the needs of the city wilderness. Extended to America in 1879, it grew by leaps and bounds in the next two decades.[1] Its uniformed bands, parading the down-town districts with bass drum and trombone, gathered knots of the curious at the street corners and preached to "rumdom, slumdom and bumdom" the exciting gospel of repentance and reform. After 1889 the Army added social service to its evangelism. By means of its employment bureaus, "slum brigades" to work with tenement families, cheap lodgings for vagrants and rescue homes for fallen women, it carried on an essential work of Christian service.[2]

The rise of Christian Science is inseparably bound up with the life and personality of its founder, Mrs. Mary Baker Glover Patterson Eddy.[3] Of New England Puritan descent and a prey from childhood to ill health and recurrent hysteria, she had dabbled in mesmerism, spiritualism and hydropathy until she found relief from a distressing spinal malady at the hands of P. P. Quimby, a mental healer of Portland, Maine. Upon his

[1] F. W. Farrar, "The Salvation Army," *Harper's Mag.*, LXXXII (1891), 897-906; C. A. Briggs, "The Salvation Army," *N. Am. Rev.*, CLIX (1894), 697-710.

[2] A schism within the ranks led in 1896 to the establishment of the Volunteers of America which had less military autocracy in its form of organization but was otherwise devoted to a similar mission. Anon., "Ballington Booth and the Salvation Army," *Public Opinion*, XX (1896), 304-305.

[3] Two recent biographies are E. F. Dakin, *Mrs. Eddy* (rev. edn., N. Y., 1930), a critical study, and L. P. Powell, *Mary Baker Eddy* (N. Y., 1930), a work commended by Mrs. Eddy's followers.

death in 1866 she presently set up as a practitioner in her own right. At first an avowed Quimbyite, using one of his manuscripts as the fount of her teachings, she gradually evolved a system which she came to regard as wholly her own and which she put into print in 1875 under the title of *Science and Health*.[1] "Disease is caused by mind alone" and matter is an illusion—this was the essence of the newly proclaimed Christian Science. "You can prevent or cure scrofula, hereditary disease, etc., in just the ratio you expel from mind a belief in the transmission of disease" by working in harmony with the Eternal Mind as revealed through Jesus Christ.[2]

The founder gathered about her a small band of adherents in Lynn, Massachusetts, consisting mostly of factory workers and other artisans, "their hands stained with the leather and tools of the day's occupation."[3] She also provided for the training of healers by setting up the Massachusetts Metaphysical College in 1881, with herself as the faculty. Converts coming too slowly to suit her, she next changed her base of operations to Boston eight miles away. Though the period of struggle was not yet over, the removal to a large population center proved the turning point. Attacked by foes both within and without the church and harried by delusions

[1] There were many later editions and revisions. Though in retrospect Mrs. Eddy denied any indebtedness to Quimby, Powell in *Mary Baker Eddy*, 103, admits he played an important part in shaping her thinking. Incidentally, the exact term, Christian Science, had occasionally been used by Quimby. P. P. Quimby, *The Quimby Manuscripts* (H. W. Dresser, ed., 2d edn., N. Y., 1921), 388. Unadulterated Quimbyism became the basis of the New Thought movement which began to emerge toward the end of the century. See Faulkner, *Quest for Social Justice*, 215.

[2] Moreover, "Healing the sick through mind instead of matter, enables us to heal the absent as well as the present." Edn. of 1875, 334, 348, 398. Conversely, vindictive persons, through malicious animal magnetism ("M.A.M."), can produce disease or misfortune in others— a doctrine which first appeared in the edition of 1878.

[3] Sibyl Wilbur (O'Brien), *The Life of Mary Baker Eddy* (N. Y., 1907), 198.

of persecution, this frail, spectacled, ill-educated woman, already past sixty, proceeded to build up a solid support in Boston and to spread her doctrines afar. As a philosophy Christian Science would probably have had little appeal, but as a system of therapeutics it assured nerve-racked urban dwellers of the immediate cure of their bodies as well as the ultimate cure of their souls.

By 1890 there were over two hundred Christian Science groups with nearly nine thousand members, a majority of them in the larger cities of the Middle West. The number of local bodies doubled in the next decade while the membership perhaps quadrupled.[1] Meanwhile, as Mrs. Eddy became increasingly well-to-do and many of her practitioners acquired economic security, the cult sloughed off its working-class origins, directing its chief appeal to members of other denominations at higher income levels. This transition to a religion of the comfortable may be said to have been completed in 1895 when the First Church of Christ, Scientist, built at a cost of two hundred thousand dollars, opened in Boston as the "Mother Church" of the faith.[2]

Unlike the Salvation Army, the Christian Scientists did not develop social work as one of their interests, since poverty, like disease, was regarded as an illusion of mortal mind. Meantime, however, leaders in some of the older Protestant sects were awakening to a sense of responsibility for the world about them. Those most active in the effort to liberalize religious thought were

---

[1] *U. S. Eleventh Census* (1890), XVI, 297-298; *Christian Science Journal*, XVIII (1900), 202. From a scrutiny of the advertisements in the *Journal* it appears that the number of practitioners rose from fourteen in April, 1883, to two hundred in April, 1890, and to nine hundred and sixty-three in April, 1896.

[2] *Christian Science Journal*, XII (1894), 90-93, 451-454; *Boston Herald*, Jan. 7, 1895. Edward Eggleston's novel *The Faith Doctor* (N. Y., 1891) satirized the growing enthusiasm for Christian Science among the socially ambitious of New York.

usually also at the forefront of the effort to socialize religious practice. Notable among them were Lyman Abbott, Beecher's successor at the Plymouth Church in 1888; his neighbor on Manhattan, R. Heber Newton; and Francis G. Peabody, who from 1886 occupied the chair of Christian morals at the Harvard Divinity School. Particularly influential were Josiah Strong, general secretary of the Evangelical Alliance from 1886, and author of an eloquent book on social religion, *Our Country* (1885), which sold a half-million copies in twenty years; and Washington Gladden, Congregational minister in Columbus, Ohio, whose voice and example made him perhaps the great outstanding leader.[1] The more liberal theological schools responded by introducing courses in economics and sociology and even in some cases, as at Andover Seminary and the Chicago Theological Seminary, encouraging their students to get practical experience in social work. In the last years of the century it was possible to say that the "theological seminary of today . . . is a totally different institution from that of a generation ago."[2]

At the same time efforts began to be made by Protestant bodies to minister to the religious and practical needs of immigrants when they landed in the great Atlantic ports. In 1883 the interdenominational American Home Missionary Society organized German, Scandinavian and Slavic departments for this purpose. Of single sects the Lutherans in particular vied with the Catholics and the Jews in watching over the alien newcomer.[3] More significant was the steady tendency of

[1] Professor R. T. Ely, though not a cleric, also wielded great influence, especially through his volume *Social Aspects of Christianity.*

[2] John Tunis, "Social Science in the Theological Seminaries," *Lend-a-Hand*, XVI (1896), 3-10; anon., "Sociology and the Church," *Nation*, LIII, 114 (Aug. 13, 1891).

[3] Helen M. Sweeney, "Handling the Immigrant," *Catholic World*, LXIII (1896), 497-508. Early in the eighties Jewish charitable agen-

Protestant churches in down-town districts to develop "institutional" features, that is, conduct organized philanthropic and educational work among the poor and unchurched.[1] Thus, St. George's Episcopal Church in New York, the People's Temple (Congregational) in Denver and Russell H. Conwell's Baptist Temple in Philadelphia began in the eighties to provide reading rooms, gymnasiums, social clubs, day nurseries, sewing classes and manual-training courses which, along with religious instruction, were available throughout the week to all comers. By 1894 the number of institutional churches was sufficiently large to justify the organization of an Open and Institutional Church League on an intercity and interdenominational basis. The success of the new methods was attested by phenomenal increases in religious membership.[2] St. George's Episcopal Church, which had but seventy-five communicants in 1882 when it started institutional work, numbered over four thousand in 1897; Berkeley Temple (Congregational) in Boston grew in seven years from three hundred to eleven hundred; and the Ninth Street Baptist Church of Cincinnati added nearly nine hundred members in four years. It was reported in 1900 that over a period of six years Congregational churches employing institutional methods had increased six times as fast as those which did not.

cies began to look after the needs of their Russian coreligionists; Baron de Hirsch in 1890 established a fund of $2,400,000 for this and allied uses. E. J. James and others, *The Immigrant Jew in America* (N. Y., 1906), 64-66, 79, 84-85.

[1] C. S. Mills, "The Institutional Church," *Bibliotheca Sacra*, XLIX (1892), 453-470; G. W. Cooke, "The Institutional Church," *New England Mag.*, n.s., XIV (1896), 645-660; Josiah Strong, *Religious Movements for Social Betterment* (H. B. Adams, ed., *Monographs on American Social Economics*, XIV, N. Y., 1900), 15-34.

[2] G. W. Mead, *Modern Methods of Church Work* (N. Y., 1897), 337-339; Strong, *New Era*, 245, and *Religious Movements*, 31-33.

Moody

Sankey

Though still flanked by "old-time religion," the institutional church was emerging.

Protestant Christianity.

To give the new social tendencies a wider backing various organizations were formed, one of the most influential being the Church Organization for the Advancement of the Interests of Labor in 1887 among the Episcopal clergy. Two years later some of the more radical religionists of Boston, following an English example and inspired by the Reverend W. D. P. Bliss of Grace Church (Episcopal), founded the Society of Christian Socialists in order "to awaken members of the Christian churches to the fact that the teachings of Jesus Christ lead directly to some specific form or forms of Socialism." [1] Though the movement did not prosper widely, the Congregationalists and Baptists in the early nineties formed national agencies to direct attention to social and economic problems, and two interdenominational societies, the Christian Social Union in 1891 and the American Institute of Christian Sociology in 1894, gave further impetus to the cause. In the latter year, too, the Evangelical Alliance of the United States, largely as a result of Josiah Strong's efforts, turned definitely to a social program. [2]

These attempts to socialize Christian thought and practice, of course, represented the efforts of energetic minorities. "We were few and we shouted in the wilderness," a pioneer of the social gospel later wrote of this time. [3] Yet that a rich harvest awaited beyond the turn of the century was plainly indicated by the extraordinary interest excited among the lay public by the ap-

[1] *The Dawn* (Boston), I (1889), no. 1, 3. R. Heber Newton became president of the New York branch.

[2] As further evidence of the socializing trend, the United Society of Christian Endeavor, composed of young people, began to take an active interest in civic and social reform after 1893. J. W. Baer, "The Work of Christian Endeavor Societies in Behalf of Better Citizenship," Natl. Conf. for Good City Government, *Proceeds. for 1895*, 517-523.

[3] Walter Rauschenbusch, *Christianizing the Social Order* (N. Y., 1912), 9.

pearance of *In His Steps,* a book written by the Reverend C. M. Sheldon of Topeka in 1896. It told the story of a congregation which resolved to live for a year, regardless of consequences, in accordance with the teachings of Jesus. Its wider message was inescapable: "If the church members were all doing as Jesus would do, could it remain true that armies of men would walk the streets for jobs, and hundreds of them curse the church, and thousands of them find in the saloon their best friend?" [1] Within a year sixteen different publishers were issuing the book to meet a demand that showed no sign of appeasement.

Since early colonial times clergymen had often lifted their voices at critical public junctures, but never before had religious ethics been so sharply challenged by the practices of the business order or the ministry so apparently helpless before the economic masters of society. Yet, despite Gompers's sweeping denunciation of churchmen, individuals stood forth who, not content with "making faces at the devil from behind the pulpit" or with treating symptoms rather than the disease itself, strove to cope with the deeper forces responsible for the conditions. Few went so far as Bliss when he became a Master Workman of the Knights of Labor and candidate for lieutenant governor of Massachusetts on the Labor ticket; nor were many willing to risk the obloquy which befell the Methodist pastor, W. H. Cawardine of Pullman, Illinois, when he flayed the Pullman corporation for precipitating the strike of 1894.

Washington Gladden, on the other hand, showed how actively a minister might concern himself with indus-

---

[1] Edn. of 1899 (Street & Smith, N. Y.), 261. In 1925 it was estimated that over eight million copies had been sold in the United States and twelve million more in the British Empire. The author received little financial return because of a defective copyright. C. M. Sheldon, *His Life Story* (N. Y., 1925), chap. iv.

trial relations without forfeiting the confidence of even a well-to-do congregation. During the Hocking Valley coal strike of 1884 he preached the "right and necessity of labor organizations" to a congregation which included high officers of the corporation involved. Two years later, while a fierce street-car strike raged in Cleveland, he journeyed thither from Columbus and spoke to a great meeting of employers and employees on "Is It Peace or War?" again declaring the right of wage-earners to organize. A little later he headed a committee of Ohio Congregationalists to investigate employment conditions in the state in an effort to promote better understanding between capital and labor. He visioned the solution of the difficulties in an "industrial partnership" in which the toilers would receive "a fixed share of the profits of production."[1]

The attitude of the Roman Catholic clergy toward the labor problem was greatly influenced by the course of Cardinal Gibbons of Baltimore. Thoroughly American in outlook and deeply sympathetic with the workingmen who composed the great bulk of his church, he made an eloquent plea to Rome in 1886 which saved the Knights of Labor from papal condemnation and ultimately secured the reversal of an edict against the organization in Canada.[2] He also resisted the recommendation of Archbishop Corrigan of New York that Henry George's *Progress and Poverty* be put upon the Index, again winning his point in Rome.[3] Of other

[1] Gladden, *Recollections*, 291-293, 300-305; same author, *Applied Christianity*, 1-37, 102-145. For the Reverend C. H. Parkhurst's effective battle against Tammany and organized vice, see earlier, 115-116.

[2] A. S. Will, *Life of Cardinal Gibbons* (N. Y., 1922), I, chaps. xviii-xx.

[3] In 1887 Archbishop Corrigan removed Father Edward McGlynn from his pastorate in New York City because of activity on behalf of Henry George's candidacy for mayor. When Dr. McGlynn declined to go to Rome to make submission to the pope, he was excommunicated. He was, however, reinstated as a priest in 1892. There was the closely

Catholic ecclesiastics Archbishop Ireland of St. Paul was notable for the pacificatory part he took in two great railway strikes in 1894 in the Northwest.[1] Catholic liberalism received high sanction in 1891 from the encyclical *Rerum Novarum* in which the pope, while denouncing socialism, defended the dignity of labor and declared that the problem could be solved only through the application of religious ethics.

Despite the many difficulties, theological and practical, which beset the path of religion, the last two decades of the century witnessed a substantial gain in church membership. Protestant communicants increased from ten million to nearly eighteen; the Roman Catholic population from well over six million to more than ten; the number of Jews from less than a quarter million to approximately a million. It was a striking testimonial to the vitality of organized religion that the growth was proportionately greater than the general advance of population, though, as was to be expected, less than the rate of increase of the urban wage-earning class.[2] Of the Protestant communicants the Methodist bodies repre-

similar case of Father R. L. Burtsell, also a follower of George. F. J. Zwierlein, *The Life and Letters of Bishop McQuaid* (Rochester, 1927), III, chap. xxix; Will, *Cardinal Gibbons*, I, chap. xxi; J. R. Commons and others, *History of Labour in the United States* (N. Y., 1918), II, 453-461.

[1] *Appletons' Annual Cyclopaedia*, XXXIV (1894), 699.

[2] The religious statistics of the period, unhappily, have to be used with great caution. The statements in the text must therefore be regarded as only rough approximations. The principal sources of information are Philip Schaff, "Progress of Christianity in the United States," *Princeton Rev.*, LV (1879), esp. 217-219; Bryce, *American Commonwealth*, III, 476, giving figures for 1887; H. K. Carroll, *Report on Statistics of Churches* (U. S. *Eleventh Census*, XVI); same author, *The Religious Forces of the United States* (Philip Schaff and others, eds., *The American Church History Series*, I, N. Y., 1893); Daniel Dorchester, *Christianity in the United States* (rev. edn., N. Y., 1895), pt. iii; David Sulzberger, "Growth of Jewish Population in the United States," Am. Jewish Hist. Soc., *Publs.*, no. 6 (1897), 144-145, 149; Daniel Dorchester, "The Evangelical Churches at the Close of the Nineteenth Century," *Christian Advocate*, LXXVI, 52-53 (Jan. 10, 1901).

sented a third of the total throughout the period, followed in order by the Baptists, Presbyterians, Lutherans and Congregationalists. At all times, however, the Catholics greatly outnumbered any Protestant group. The geographic distribution of the sects remained substantially as before. The East continued to be the seat of Catholicism, Congregationalism and Episcopalianism with a strong infusion of Presbyterianism, while the Methodists and Baptists, numerous everywhere, dominated the religious life of the South. In the Middle West all faiths flourished—Chicago was the most Catholic of American cities—and in that section, too, the Lutherans had their principal stronghold. The most conspicuous religious feature of the Great West was the Mormon community in Utah.[1] As might be expected, the great Scandinavian influx swelled the number of Lutherans, while it was the anti-Semitic persecutions in Russia, Austria-Hungary and Roumania that made the Jewish faith for the first time important in America.[2]

Roman Catholicism, however, garnered the richest harvest from among the immigrant newcomers, notably those from Ireland, Germany, Austria-Hungary, Italy, Poland and French Canada.[3] The heightened importance of the American Church was signally recognized not only, as we have seen, by the creation of a pontifical university, but also by the appointment of an American cardinal and, in 1893, the sending of an apostolic delegate to Washington.[4] On the other hand, many Americans, particularly in the Middle West,/ viewed with

[1] See earlier, 44-46.

[2] Samuel Joseph, *Jewish Immigration to the United States* (Columbia Univ., *Studies*, LIX, no. 4), pt. i, chap. iv; pt. ii.

[3] Gerald Shaughnessy, *Has the Immigrant Kept the Faith?* (N. Y., 1925), 162-172.

[4] See earlier, 213. The first American cardinal, John McCloskey, was appointed in 1875; James Gibbons, his successor, was elevated in 1886.

mounting alarm the rapid accretion of Catholic power. They took amiss the agitation to secure public funds for parochial schools and regarded even the labor encyclical of 1891 as a sinister move by the Vatican to gain American working-class support.

As in the 1830's and 1840's, the fear and misunderstanding took the form of organized bigotry, embodied this time principally in the American Protective Association, a secret oath-bound order founded in 1887 by H. F. Bowers, a sixty-year-old lawyer of Clinton, Iowa.[1] Cradled in the heart of agricultural America, the anti-Catholic animus was vaguely mingled with the long-standing rural antagonism toward the great cities where, of course, the citadels of Romanism were to be found. The A. P. A. gained adherents slowly at first, having only seventy thousand members in 1893. Then, spurred by fear of immigrant competition for jobs during the hard times and a sudden flaming resentment on the part of urban dwellers against Irish machine politicians, the movement had a mushroom growth in the cities, probably commanding a million members in 1896.[2]

All the familiar phenomena of the earlier Know-Nothing movement were reproduced. The members of the order swore not to vote for or employ Catholics. "Escaped nuns" and "converted priests" told their harrowing tales to any who would listen. Forged documents

[1] H. J. Desmond, The A. P. A. Movement (Wash., 1912). For the earlier anti-Catholic movement, see C. R. Fish, The Rise of the Common Man (A History of American Life, VI), 115.

[2] In Chicago in 1894 the mayor, chief of police, fire chief, city attorney, a number of judges, forty-five aldermen, nine out of ten policemen, four fifths of the fire department and two thirds of the school teachers were said to be Catholics. Stead, If Christ Came to Chicago, 265. It was alleged that the municipal offices of New York, St. Louis, New Orleans, San Francisco and other important cities were also largely under Catholic control. W. H. J. Traynor, "The Aims and Methods of the A. P. A.," N. Am. Rev., CLIX (1894), 69. Traynor, the national president, claimed a membership of two and a half million for the A. P. A.

were circulated to expose the designs of Rome against
free America, one of them, an alleged papal encyclical,
ordering the faithful to "exterminate all heretics" at the
time of the feast of Ignatius Loyola (July 31) in
1893.[1] In a similar spirit stories were whispered of the
gathering of arms in the basements of Catholic churches;
and in at least one instance, that of the Toledo council
of the A. P. A., a quantity of Winchester rifles was
purchased as a measure of self-defense—a fact revealed
by the dealer's suit for nonpayment.[2] At Dallas, Keokuk
and elsewhere mob outrages occurred, the riot in East
Boston on July 4, 1895, causing the death of one man
and the injury of forty others.

As the movement turned to political action, its stronghold was shown to be a zone extending through northern
Ohio, eastern Michigan and northern and central Illinois
into the southern half of Iowa, northern Missouri and
eastern Kansas and Nebraska, an area originally peopled
largely by religionists of New England Puritan background.[3] The anti-Catholic groups held the balance of
power in many local elections, controlled the Ohio
legislature and helped pile up a triumphant majority for
William McKinley in 1893 when he ran for governor.[4]
By 1896, however, free silver and Bryanism made the
Catholic menace seem the veriest specter. Both major

---

[1] Washington Gladden, "The Anti-Catholic Crusade," *Century*, XLVII
(1893-1894), 789-795; T. J. Jenkins, "The A. P. A. Conspirators,"
Catholic World, LVII (1893), 685-693.

[2] Anon., "The Purchase of Guns by the A. P. A.," *Public Opinion*,
XVI (1893-1894), 621.

[3] The movement also possessed strength in Massachusetts and Rhode
Island and in parts of the remoter West. Desmond, *A. P. A. Movement*,
chaps. iii, vii.

[4] McKinley kept his peace while his Democratic opponent denounced
the A. P. A. As late as October, 1894, Governor McKinley, when
asked by a heckler, "What is the matter with the A. P. A.?" replied
blandly, "The question with us is: What is the matter with the country?" "The A. P. A. in Politics," *Public Opinion*, XVII (1894-1895),
615; Desmond, *A. P. A. Movement*, 34.

parties snubbed the A. P. A., and the movement withered
as suddenly as it had grown. By bringing to the defense
of Catholicism and fair play such respected figures as
Gladden, Roosevelt and Senator Hoar, the church issued
from the conflict in a stronger position before the public
than when the attack began.[1] Within a few years it
could be written, "Old feuds between Protestant and
Catholic have ceased to be as important as their united
battles against moral decay."[2] Organized religion had
made great strides in the two decades, not the least of
which was an enhanced appreciation of the common
spiritual ideals for which all faiths stood.

[1] Gladden, *Recollections*, 359-365; Theodore Roosevelt, "What
Americanism Means," *Forum*, XVII (1894), 196; G. F. Hoar, *Autobiography of Seventy Years* (N. Y., 1903), II, 278-293.

[2] H. D. Sedgwick, jr., "The United States and Rome," *Atlantic Mo.*,
LXXXIV (1899), 445-458.

CHAPTER XI

SOCIETY'S WARDS

IF the church as such was slow to engage in works of social amelioration, the humanitarian leaders of the day were deeply imbued with the Christian spirit and most of them were loyal church members. The zeal to serve afflicted humanity, receiving impetus from the prolonged depression following 1873, was intensified by the hardship and misery which, even in normal times, befell the lot of many city dwellers. To Professor Sumner, the uncompromising individualist, there seemed "an unlimited supply of reformers, philanthropists, humanitarians, and would-be managers-in-general of society." Bryce with kindlier intent opined that no other country equaled the United States either in the sums spent or the personal effort devoted to beneficence.[1] Megalopolis, having crushed the human spirit with its million iron hoofs, became suddenly sorry, wept from its innumerable eyes and strove ardently to make up for its carelessness and greed. The driving force behind much of this effort came from women and the personnel which carried on the work was drawn increasingly from them.[2]

America in 1878 did not so much lack agencies of social welfare as a knowledge of how most wisely to use them. For many years the state and even some local governments had provided almshouses, orphanages, hos-

[1] W. G. Sumner, *What Social Classes Owe to Each Other* (N. Y., 1883), 112; James Bryce, *The American Commonwealth* (London, 1888), III, 498.
[2] Annie N. Meyer, ed., *Woman's Work in America* (N. Y., 1891), chaps. xii-xv, xvii-xviii.

pitals, homes for inebriates, insane asylums and institutions for the deaf, the dumb and the blind; but their administration was often marred by incompetent or wasteful methods. Such instrumentalities were supplemented by the work of church societies, individual charity and philanthropic organizations of widely diverse origins. In the single city of Philadelphia in 1878 there were more than eight hundred agencies engaged in aiding the poor and unfortunate.[1] It was typical of the situation generally that these bodies, lacking knowledge of each other's activities, often worked at cross purposes, duplicating almsgiving and thus indirectly encouraging duplicity and chronic improvidence on the part of applicants.

Because of the need to bring order out of the chaos, the example of Massachusetts in 1864 in setting up a state board of charities prompted other commonwealths to do likewise, until by 1893 nineteen states had established central boards to oversee and coördinate their tax-supported relief institutions.[2] The highly individualistic field of private philanthropy presented a more difficult problem; yet the Reverend S. H. Gurteen, an English migrant who had been active in a similar body in London, pointed the way to a solution when he brought about the establishment of the Charity Organization Society at Buffalo in 1877.[3] Its purpose was to serve as a clearing house for all existing agencies, public as well as private, and through concerted action to curtail the

[1] D. O. Kellogg, "On the Organization of Charity in Philadelphia," *Penn Mo.*, IX (1878), 707-723.

[2] Allan Nevins, *The Emergence of Modern America* (*A History of American Life*, VIII), 329-330; A. G. Warner, *American Charities* (R. T. Ely, ed., *Library of Economics and Politics*, IV, N. Y., 1894), chap. xviii.

[3] Earlier attempts of a somewhat similar but more limited character had been made in a Philadelphia ward (1873), New York City (1873) and Boston (1876). F. D. Watson, *The Charity Organization Movement in the United States* (N. Y., 1922), chaps. vi-vii.

abuses of indiscriminate charity while at the same time fostering constructive methods of dealing with poverty. The new ideal was the use of temporary aid to help the needy help themselves. By 1880 New Haven, Philadelphia, Brooklyn, Syracuse, Newport, Boston, Indianapolis, Cincinnati and Detroit had formed similar bodies under various names, and by the close of the century a total of one hundred and thirty-eight cities had followed their example. Though handicapped by a dearth of trained workers and often by jealousy among the associated charities, the plan richly justified itself by the results.

The newer trend was even more strikingly exemplified by the migration of resident colonies of social workers to the worst quarters of the larger cities. Anticipated in part by the institutional church, the social settlement was more immediately indebted to the example of Toynbee Hall in East London, which many American pioneer workers knew at first hand.[1] The initial settlement to open its doors was the Neighborhood Guild, started in New York in 1886 by Dr. Stanton Coit, an Amherst graduate, but the most famous one was Hull House, founded three years later in Chicago by Jane Addams and her coworker Ellen G. Starr.[2] Reared under Quaker influences, Miss Addams while yet a student at Rockford College had evinced an ardent interest in social questions. A trip to Europe during which she was irresistibly drawn to Toynbee Hall deepened her concern

---

[1] Among the more noted settlement workers who visited for a time at Toynbee Hall, besides Jane Addams, were Stanton Coit, Ellen G. Starr, Charles Zueblin and Robert A. Woods.

[2] Jane Addams, *Twenty Years at Hull House* (N. Y., 1910), chaps. iv-xi; Dorothea Moore, "A Day at Hull House," *Am. Journ. of Sociology*, II (1897), 629-642; Thérèse Blanc, *The Condition of Woman in the United States* (Abby L. Alger, tr., Boston, 1895), 67-87; Jane Addams and others, *Philanthropy and Social Progress* (N. Y., 1893), chap. ii.

for the plight of the poor and made her resolve to set up a similar institution in the metropolis of her native state.

Hull House was planted on South Halsted Street amidst a factory and tenement district swarming with Russian and Polish Jews, Italians, Bohemians, Germans and Irish, and containing nine churches and missions along with two hundred and fifty-five saloons. At first the founders contented themselves with inviting the street waifs and strays to take part in clubs and kindergartens. But as relations of mutual confidence were established they branched out into myriad activities such as men's clubs, a day nursery for working mothers, courses in arts and crafts, a gymnasium, a penny savings bank, an employment bureau and an orchestra.

Though only four settlements were established before 1890, they increased rapidly in the years thereafter, particularly in the train of the Panic of 1893. By 1895 over fifty were to be found in the principal Northern and Western cities and by the close of the century their number had perhaps doubled.[1] Not every one of these, of course, was equipped to perform the varied services of a Hull House or a South End House (Boston), but all of them, within the limits of their resources and opportunities, gave convincing demonstration of the truth of the adage that a fence at the top of a precipice is better than an ambulance at the bottom. The settlement movement appealed strongly to the idealism of young college men and women. Everywhere they were active in the work. The New York College Settlement on Rivington Street, begun the same year as Hull House, was initiated by Smith College students, while enterprises

[1] A chronological table of the more important ones is given in C. R. Henderson, *Social Settlements* (N. Y., 1899), 43-46; a complete list in R. A. Woods and A. J. Kennedy, eds., *Handbook of Settlements* (N. Y., 1911).

Recruiting poor children among city tenements to be sent for outings on "Fresh Air" farms.

The Social Worker

under similar auspices were launched in Boston, Philadelphia and Chicago.

Whether engaged in putting up fences or providing ambulances, humanitarian workers could not avoid seeing that the social maladjustments with which they dealt were often conditioned by forces and influences of which the individual was a hapless victim. Their aggressive altruism thus caused them to support all movements for uplift—better working conditions, abolition of child labor, sanitary housing, public-health reform, penal reform, campaigns against municipal corruption.[1] In particular, they perceived in the ubiquitous saloon a relentless foe; and without caring whether poverty caused intemperance or intemperance poverty, they coöperated with those groups in American society which had long been battling against the evil.

The mainspring of the temperance movement had always been rural sentiment.[2] When the period opened it was four rural states—Maine, New Hampshire, Vermont and Kansas—which had state-wide prohibition. Likewise, it was the churches most deeply rooted in the farming regions—the Methodist, Baptist and Presbyterian—that furnished the shock troops for the "dry" assault. Most important of all was the Women's Christian Temperance Union, founded in 1874 by women dwelling mainly in country towns. When Frances E. Willard became president in 1879, she changed its emphasis from moral suasion to an insistence upon outright legal proscription. The W. C. T. U. under

[1] See, for example, Addams, *Twenty Years*, chaps. vii, ix-x, xiii-xiv; Eleanor H. Woods, *Robert A. Woods* (Boston, 1929), chaps. xi, xiii; R. A. Woods and A. J. Kennedy, *The Settlement Horizon* (N. Y., 1922), chaps. xvi-xvii; Julia C. Lathrop and others, "Social Settlements and the Labor Question," Natl. Conf. of Charities and Correction, *Proceeds. for 1896*, pt. iii.

[2] On this point, see J. R. Elliott, *American Farms* (*Questions of the Day Series*, LXII, 2d edn., N. Y., 1890), 236-239.

her energetic direction became the leading force in the antiliquor movement.[1] Soon no community in the land was without its corps of "white ribboners," ready at a moment's notice to join battle for the cause.

Shrewder than any other reform group of the time, the W. C. T. U. seized upon the public schools as a means of attaining in the future what might not be accomplished at once. Systematic pressure caused state after state to require "scientific temperance instruction" as part of the school curriculum. With Vermont leading the way in 1882, within five years thirty-one states and territories had followed suit, and by 1898 only two states held off. The textbooks used, according to two well-qualified medical authorities, "fairly bristle with statements of a character to work upon the fears of the reader, and remind one in this respect of patent medicine advertisements." After analyzing a number of the books they concluded that such teaching was "neither scientific, nor temperate, nor instructive." [2] But that it was effective as propaganda the future was to disclose.

The principal battlements of the "wet" interests were in the cities. There the strains and stresses of existence made the ordinary man seek solace in the flowing cup after a hard workday. There the immigrant horde found no reason to surrender cherished folk customs in a land of freedom. There the saloon with its free lunch and rough sociability took the place which the lodge and the club filled in the lives of those higher up in the social

[1] Frances E. Willard, *Glimpses of Fifty Years* (Boston, 1889), 368-478.

[2] H. P. Bowditch and C. F. Hodge, "Report," W. O. Atwater and others, eds., *Physiological Aspects of the Liquor Problem* (Boston, 1903), I, 33, 44. The main facts concerning temperance instruction may be found in the same vol., 21-45, 95-136; U. S. Commissioner of Education, *Report for 1889-90*, II, 695-742; edit., "Temperance Text-Books," *Outlook*, LXVI (1900), 706-709, 974-975, with a reply by the W. C. T. U., 996-999.

scale.[1] New York in 1890 possessed seventy-five hundred saloons, or one to every two hundred people. Chicago was proportionately well supplied, while smaller places like Albany, San Francisco and Cincinnati had an even greater relative number.[2] In the cities, too, the liquor industry was firmly intrenched, representing millions of capital and employing countless persons not only in the retail traffic but at every stage of manufacture and distribution. Besides, the liquor interests had their state and national organizations, formidable by reason of their funds. With the formation of the National Protective Association in 1886 these forces were enabled to present a united front to the common enemy.

Yet some counteracting influences were at work in the cities. As the trade unions waxed in strength, their policy opposed the abuse, if not the use, of alcoholic beverages.[3] A few, like the Order of Railroad Conductors and the Brotherhood of Locomotive Firemen, refused membership to persons connected with the sale of intoxicants. The International Typographical Union in 1894 even demanded "the state and national destruction of the liquor traffic." Had the Knights of Labor, instead of their rival, the American Federation of Labor, inherited the kingdom, the labor movement might have become a militant force for temperance. The Knights in 1878 denied admission to liquor employees; and in 1886, the year that marked the crest of their strength, Terence V. Powderly, head of the order, secured a hun-

---

[1] S. L. Loomis, *Modern Cities and Their Religious Problems* (N. Y., 1887), 101-102; Raymond Calkins, *Substitutes for the Saloon* (Boston, 1901), chap. i; John Koren, *Economic Aspects of the Liquor Problem* (Boston, 1899), chap. viii.

[2] J. S. Billings, comp., *Report on the Social Statistics of Cities* (*U. S. Eleventh Census*, 1890), 109-117.

[3] Koren, *Economic Aspects of Liquor Problem*, 35-37; Calkins, *Substitutes for Saloon*, 303-313; T. V. Powderly, *Thirty Years of Labor* (Columbus, 1889), 580-626; *Cyclopaedia of Temperance and Prohibition* (N. Y., 1891), 264-266.

dred thousand signatures to a five-year teetotal pledge. Business leaders here and there also began to sense the advantages of a sober working force. George Pullman in establishing his model industrial town in 1880 banned the drink traffic through his control of the title deeds to the land. Before the decade ended, the Philadelphia and Reading, the Lake Erie and Western, the Northern Pacific and the Missouri Pacific railways had forbidden the use of intoxicants by men on duty. An inquiry by the federal commissioner of labor in 1897 disclosed that fifty-three hundred employers out of seven thousand customarily inquired into the bibulous habits of job seekers, while eighteen hundred "prohibited, more or less strictly, drinking."[1]

Most urban Protestant churches maintained total-abstinence societies. To the efforts of the Catholic Total Abstinence Union were added the weighty words of the third plenary council of Baltimore in 1884-1885, instructing priests to induce all Catholic liquor dealers to "choose a more honorable way of making a living."[2] Though the sentiment for legal prohibition was not the same as that for self-abstinence, the drys received aid and comfort from such sources, as well as from persons who favored prohibition for others if not for themselves. They could also count ordinarily upon the support of good citizens outraged by the lawlessness of the saloon power and its evident relationship to corruption, vice and crime.[3]

[1] Koren, *Economic Aspects of Liquor Problem*, 37-38; *Economic Aspects of the Liquor Problem* (U. S. Comr. of Labor, *Ann. Rep. for 1897*), chap. vii.

[2] *Cyclopaedia of Temperance and Prohibition*, 536, 597-600, 632 *n.* Bishop John A. Watterson of Columbus, Ohio, in 1894 went so far as to deny liquor dealers the right of joining any Catholic society in the diocese. *Nation* (N. Y.), LIX, 73, 113 (Aug. 2, 16, 1894).

[3] G. F. Parsons, "The Saloon in Politics," *Atlantic Mo.*, LVIII (1886), 404-414; Josiah Strong, *Our Country* (rev. edn., N. Y.,

As the record of accomplishment shows, the embattled drys were able to wrest few lasting gains from the forces arrayed against them. The question of state-wide prohibition was submitted to popular vote in eighteen states between 1878 and 1898, but only one commonwealth, North Dakota from 1889, continued long with the four which had already taken that stand.[1] The restrictionists, however, had other strings to their bow. For a time they saw in high-license laws—imposing annual fees of perhaps five hundred or a thousand dollars for the saloon privilege—a means of lessening in wet states the number of liquor resorts and hence of reducing liquor consumption. Though, following the example of Nebraska in 1881, thirty-two states and territories had gone over to this system by 1889, high-license laws unexpectedly resulted everywhere in handsomer and more commodious saloons, many of them maintained as retail establishments of great breweries and distilleries.[2]

The drys therefore turned with redoubled zeal to that method of divide-and-conquer known as local option—local prohibitory enactments by popular vote. Centering their efforts first upon rural counties and villages, they pressed forward a policy of encirclement of

1891), 131-137; H. M. Boies, *Prisoners and Paupers* (N. Y., 1893), chap. xi; H. G. Wadlin, "Relation of the Liquor Traffic to Pauperism, Crime and Insanity," Mass. Bur. of Labor Stat., *Twenty-Sixth Ann. Rep.* (1895), pt. i; D. L. Colvin, *Prohibition in the United States* (N. Y., 1926), 209-211, 216-217, 555-574.

[1] Rhode Island from 1886 to 1889, and South Dakota from 1889 to 1896, had prohibition by constitutional amendment. Kansas in 1880, Maine in 1884 and North Dakota in 1889 made prohibition a constitutional requirement. E. H. Cherrington, *The Evolution of Prohibition in the United States* (Westerville, 1920), 202-266; Colvin, *Prohibition*, 137-144, 177-183, 202-216.

[2] *Cyclopaedia of Temperance and Prohibition*, 207-220; E. L. Fanshawe, *Liquor Legislation in the United States and Canada* (London, 1893), chap. v; J. G. Woolley and W. E. Johnson, *Temperance Progress of the Century* (Justin McCarthy, ed., *The Nineteenth Century Series;* Toronto, 1903), chap. x.

the larger towns and cities. But beyond this point they were seldom able to get. From year to year the saloon-less area expanded or shrank as the fortunes of battle veered. The most notable progress under local option was made in the South and the Middle West. Sometimes it seemed as though communities changed merely for change's sake, but even in such cases the recurrent public discussions kept voters primed as to the merits of the issue.[1]

The chief difficulties of enforcing liquor restrictions occurred in places where public sentiment was hostile or sharply divided. Local prohibition was often tolerated merely because of the accessibility of near-by city dram-shops. In states dry by state-wide enactment it was constantly necessary to make the enforcement provisions more drastic. Maine, the vaunted Eden of prohibitionists, found it impossible to keep applejack produced in local cider mills away from rural tipplers. In Portland, her chief city, "blind tigers" and "pocket peddlers" (boot-leggers) plied a brisk trade alongside of saloons, hotel bars, apothecary shops and bottling establishments where, as a result of collusion with the police, "customers lounged about, smoking and drinking, with an apparent sense of freedom and security." In 1893 no less than one hundred and sixty-one dealers paid federal liquor taxes in that city.[2]

[1] Fanshawe, *Liquor Legislation*, chap. iv. As a variant from the usual methods of dealing with the liquor problem, South Carolina in 1893, under prod of Governor Tillman, set up exclusive government dispensaries, a system which remained in force until 1907. Its dual purpose was to garner larger revenues for the state and reduce the private-profit motive in the sale of drinks. Though modeled upon a municipal system in Athens, Ga., the plan gained no favor elsewhere; for once prohibitionists and private saloonists saw eye to eye. F. H. Wines and John Koren, *The Liquor Problem in Its Legislative Aspects* (2d edn., Boston, 1898), 141-180 b; F. B. Simkins, *The Tillman Movement in South Carolina* (Duke Univ., Publs.; Durham, 1926), chap. viii; Gallus Thomann, *The South Carolina Dispensary* (N. Y., 1905).

[2] This view of the situation is based upon evidence presented in Wines

The ever present problem of alcoholic shipments into dry territory directed attention to the need for federal action. Since 1876 proposals for a national prohibition amendment had vainly been offered in Congress. The two great parties refrained from committing themselves on the question, fearing either the disruptive effects of a new and uncertain issue or the loss of campaign contributions from the liquor magnates. Nor did the Prohibition party, despite temporary gains in the elections of 1888 and 1892, succeed in winning an electoral vote. Nevertheless Congress in 1890, in order to offset certain adverse judicial decisions, provided that liquor shipments into any state or territory should, upon arrival, be subject to the laws there in effect. The Supreme Court interpreted the law to mean, however, that importations for private consumption were not affected.[1] In response to the need for more vigorous action upon all fronts the Anti-Saloon League of America was born in 1895. It frowned upon the third-party effort and used its energies to bore from within both major parties. Of great future significance, it was still operating chiefly in local politics when the period closed.[2]

To the observer in 1898 the temperance forces appeared to have been fighting a losing battle. The growth of cities and the increasing tension of living constantly raised up new adherents of the doctrine of "personal liberty." Moreover, though both the W. C. T. U. and the Prohibition party favored woman suffrage, none of

and Koren, *Liquor Problem*, 22-95, and Fanshawe, *Liquor Legislation*, chap. vii. These authors also review enforcement difficulties in Massachusetts, New York, Pennsylvania, Ohio, Indiana, Iowa, Missouri, South Carolina and elsewhere.

[1] *U. S. Statutes at Large*, XXVI, 313; Fanshawe, *Liquor Legislation*, 21-24; Wines and Koren, *Liquor Problem*, 119-122, 180.

[2] E. H. Cherrington, *History of the Anti-Saloon League* (Westerville, 1906), chaps. i-ii; H. U. Faulkner, *The Quest for Social Justice* (*A History of American Life*, XI), 225-226.

the equal-suffrage states took the dry side. The two
decades saw an enormous increase in alcoholic consumption, from three hundred and eighty-six million gallons
in 1878 to one and a quarter billion in 1898. The
annual consumption per capita rose from a little over
eight gallons to more than seventeen.[1] Since there was
also probably a larger proportion of teetotalers at the
end than at the beginning of the period, it is clear that
the habit of drinking to excess had greatly increased. Yet,
in spite of the dark outlook, Miss Willard spoke truly
when she said, "While the enemy has brewed beer, they
[the drys] have brewed public opinion." [2]

If the efforts of temperance reformers and humanitarian workers were designed in part to check the impulse
to crime, others made it their main concern to look after
the welfare of those who had run afoul of the law. The
condition of jails and prisons in the late seventies remained as bad as in the years immediately following the
Civil War.[3] The structures were generally antiquated
and unsanitary, the officials in charge politicians ignorant
of penal science, and the discipline stupid or brutal. Of
the Kentucky state prison Governor L. P. Blackburn
asserted, "The Black Hole of Calcutta, so abhorred in
history, was not much worse than this." [4] Through the
South generally the practice prevailed of leasing convicts,

[1] If ten-per-cent reduction be allowed for use in manufactures and
the arts, the increase in personal consumption still remains startling.
The capital investment in liquor grew from $118,000,000 to $458,-
000,000. *U. S. Statistical Abstract for 1906*, 687; *U. S. Twelfth
Census* (1900), IX, 599, 612, 624.

[2] Meyer, *Woman's Work in America*, 404.

[3] See Nevins, *Emergence of Modern America*, 330-331.

[4] *Appletons' Annual Cyclopaedia*, XIX (1879), 539-540. As for
lesser prisons, according to a leading penal authority, "the American
jails of today are, with here and there an exception, substantially what
Howard in the eighteenth century found jails to be." Z. R. Brockway,
"Needed Reforms in Prison Management," *N. Am. Rev.*, CXXXVII
(1883), esp. 40.

usually Negroes, to railways, lumber camps and mines where they were subjected to conditions often worse than those of prewar slavery.[1] Counties and even states operated their own chain gangs for road construction and repair.

The progress of prison reform owed much to the activities of the state boards of charities and correction, much also to the work of educating public opinion carried on by leaders of the National Prison Association, notably the Reverend E. C. Wines, Dr. Theodore Dwight, Franklin B. Sanborn and Zebulon R. Brockway. In line with the best European penological thought these men stressed reformation, rather than retribution, as the prime object of imprisonment as well as the best guarantee of future law observance. Make the convict good, they said, and make him good for something. Such ideas, while too far in advance of the times in respect to habitual criminals, appealed strongly as a means of reclaiming juvenile offenders of twenty years or younger, a class which in 1880 formed over a fifth of the prison population.

The new program was first put into effect with the opening of the New York State Reformatory at Elmira in 1877 under Brockway's superintendency.[2] Young men of from fifteen to thirty years of age who had been convicted of a first offense were admitted under indeter-

[1] G. W. Cable gives a harrowing account of the system in *The Silent South* (N. Y., 1885), 111-180. In *The American Siberia* (Phila., 1891) J. C. Powell describes vividly his fourteen years as manager of a Florida convict camp.

[2] The Elmira plan was drawn very largely from the Irish prison system established by Sir Walter Crofton in the middle of the century. For the Elmira system in operation, see Alexander Winter, *The New York State Reformatory at Elmira* (London, 1891); F. H. Wines, *Punishment and Reformation* (Crowell's Library of Economics and Politics, VI, N. Y., 1895), chap. x; Z. R. Brockway, *Fifty Years of Prison Service* (N. Y., 1912), pt. ii; and F. B. Sanborn, "The Elmira Reformatory," S. J. Barrows, ed., *The Reformatory System in the United States* (Wash., 1900), 28-47.

minate sentence. There, free from association with hardened criminals, the length of their stay (up to the maximum period set by the statute) depended largely upon their good conduct and their earnest application to means of self-improvement. When released they were sent to places of employment previously arranged, and continued under parole until their discharge was made absolute. It was claimed after ten years' trial that four out of every five Elmira graduates showed complete reformation.[1] The merits of the system commended themselves so strongly that before 1898 it was adopted, in more or less modified form, by Massachusetts, Pennsylvania, Ohio, Michigan, Illinois, Minnesota, Kansas, South Dakota and Indiana. Reformatories for girls apart from older women developed less rapidly, New York again leading the way with the Western House of Refuge at Albion in 1893.

Improvement, though less radical, was also introduced into the treatment of older criminals. Beginning in the 1870's Massachusetts experimented with the plan of placing reformable offenders, immediately upon conviction, on probation without physical confinement.[2] The parole system, another form of conditional liberation, spread to Ohio's prisons in 1884 and by 1898 was in effect in twenty-five states.[3] New and larger prisons were constructed, most of them upon approved sanitary principles, while Massachusetts and other states made a trial of state farms worked by convict labor. In the South the benighted situation showed signs of abate-

[1] *Appletons' Annual Cyclopaedia*, XXVII (1887), 703; Brockway, *Fifty Years*, 325.

[2] First tried out in Suffolk County, the scheme was made permissive for the entire state in 1891. No state followed Massachusetts till Rhode Island acted in 1899. L. N. Robinson, *Penology in the United States* (Phila., 1921), 194-196.

[3] E. H. Sutherland, *Criminology* (E. C. Hayes, ed., *Lippincott Sociological Series*; Phila., 1924), 525.

ment when Mississippi in 1890 abolished the lease system.

Agitation against the death penalty added but one state, Colorado in 1897, to the four—Michigan, Rhode Island, Wisconsin and Maine—which had abolished it before the period opened.[1] The worst conditions obtained within the United States civil jurisdiction in which eighteen crimes were capital, in Georgia where ten offenses were so classified, and in Alabama, Louisiana and Maryland which specified seven each. In 1892, however, the number of capital crimes in the federal code was reduced to three (murder, rape and treason). In a spirit of reform New York in 1888 first provided for electrocution in place of hanging, and two years later this new mode of death was inflicted upon the murderer William Kemmler.

In other respects the situation was less encouraging. Glaring contrasts in the sentences inflicted for the same offense in different states, or in the same state in different courts, or in the same court on different days, rendered the administration of justice chaotic.[2] Political pull determined the appointment of too many judges and prison officials. Moreover, plans for the self-support of inmates were badly disorganized by the success of trade unions in securing laws against prison contract labor. Finally, the county jails and city lock-ups, ill planned and worse managed, jumbled together young and old in such a fashion as to make these minor prisons a veritable "public school of crime."[3] Progress had been made dur-

[1] Maine, which had acted in 1876, restored the death penalty in 1883 only to abolish it again in 1887. In Colorado it was restored in 1901. S. J. Barrows, "Legislative Tendencies as to Capital Punishment," Am. Acad. of Polit. and Social Sci., *Annals*, XXIX, 619-620; "Capital Crimes," 54 Cong., 1 sess., *House Rep.*, no. 108, 4-7.
[2] Wines, *Punishment and Reformation*, 212-213; *U. S. Eleventh Census*, XXII, 373-411.
[3] W. F. Spalding, "The Progress of Prison Reform," Natl. Conf. of

ing the two decades, however, and the foundations laid for the notable advances which impended in the years ahead.[1]

One class of unfortunates, the temporary sufferers from public disasters, lacked regular provision for relief until the formation of the American Red Cross Society in 1881. This event was due largely to the persistent efforts of Clara Barton of Massachusetts, who, from comparing her experiences as nurse in the Civil War with those in the Franco-Prussian War, was strongly convinced of the superior advantages of the Red Cross type of organization in caring for the sick and wounded. Haunted by the specter of entangling alliances, the United States delayed ratifying the Geneva international pact until 1882, being then the thirty-second nation (in Miss Barton's phrase) to take itself "out of the roll of barbarians."[2] From the first the American leaders thought primarily in terms of disaster relief, for in their far-flung country recurrent public calamities were unavoidable while war seemed a remote and odious contingency. Even before the official ratification, the preliminary Red Cross organization carried succor to refugees from the Michigan forest fires of 1881. Miss Barton succeeded three years later in having the Geneva pact amended to provide for similar humanitarian activities in all the signatory nations.

From 1881 to 1898 the American Red Cross dispensed relief to fifteen scenes of fire, cyclone, flood and pestilence,

Charities and Correction, Proceeds. for 1896, esp. 409; J. F. Willard (Josiah Flynt, pseud.), Notes of an Itinerant Policeman (Boston, 1900), 86-92; Wines, Punishment and Reformation, 313-315.

[1] See Faulkner, Quest for Social Justice, 182-183, and P. W. Slosson, The Great Crusade and After (A History of American Life, XII), 103-104, 357-358.

[2] Helen H. S. Thompson, "The Red Cross," Atlantic Mo., LX (1887), 646-654; W. E. Barton, The Life of Clara Barton (Boston, 1922), II, chaps. i-x.

three of them in lands across the sea. Nearly one million dollars in money and supplies were handled at a total cost of less than two per cent.[1] One of the worst catastrophes was the memorable flood at Johnstown, Pennsylvania, in 1889.[2] On Friday afternoon, May 31, an enormous wall of water released from a broken mountain dam roared down the narrow Conemaugh Valley, catching the inhabitants as unready as the people of Pompeii. With incredible swiftness the swirling torrent uprooted a city of twenty-eight thousand inhabitants, snuffed out several thousand lives and jammed a huge fantastic mass of blazing wreckage against the stone railroad bridge below the town. Red Cross workers arrived by the first train from the east and for five weary months labored amid scenes of want and woe. Over twenty thousand persons were reached by their ministrations.

While the Red Cross strove to mitigate the horrors of peace, other humanitarians busied themselves with plans to preclude the possibility of future war. Discredited by the Civil War and outrivaled by the veterans' organizations, the once promising pacifist movement had much lost ground to regain. The old American Peace Society, however, found fresh allies in the Universal Peace Union, arrayed since 1866 against defensive as well as offensive war, the National Arbitration League (1881), and various bodies representing religious groups, such as the Peace Association of the Friends (1869), the Christian Arbitration and Peace Society (1886) and the Peace Department of the W. C. T. U. (1887). Ceaselessly active, these bodies diversified their attack from opposition to the use of toy soldiers and the erection of military statues, to the sending of a protest of

---

[1] Clara Barton, *The Red Cross* (Wash., 1898), 101, 104-358.
[2] *N. Y. Tribune*, June 1, 1889, and later; *Appletons' Annual Cyclopaedia*, XXIX (1889), 476-482; Barton, *Red Cross*, 155-171; W. F. Johnson, *History of the Johnstown Flood* (Edgewood, 1889).

five hundred thousand women to Washington at the
time of the Chilean crisis in 1891.[1] Their main purpose,
however, was to secure the negotiation of arbitration
treaties and, beyond that, the establishment of a permanent arbitral court.

So far as arbitration was concerned, they were in-
vesting in a rising market.[2] In the afterglow of the
settlement of the *Alabama* claims the House and Senate
adopted resolutions in 1874 indorsing the plan. Moreover, the state department repeatedly used its good offices
to quiet the turbid waters of Latin-American international relations, and the Pan-American Congress,
which the United States called into being at Washington in 1889, drew up a thoroughgoing scheme of arbitration for submission to the several governments. Two
years earlier some two hundred members of the British
House of Commons had memorialized the president and
Congress in behalf of a general arbitration treaty between the two English-speaking powers. Congress in
1890 responded with a unanimous reaffirmation of its
attachment to the principle, and in 1892 the government
agreed with Great Britain to arbitrate the Bering Sea
controversy.

Three years later, however, this structure of good
will was imperiled by President Cleveland's blunt threat
to go to war in defense of the Monroe Doctrine if
Britain declined to arbitrate her boundary differences
with Venezuela. Important elements of public opinion

[1] B. F. Trueblood, "History and Work of Peace Societies in America," *Am. Advocate of Peace*, LV (1893), 219-222; Frances E. Willard, "Peace and International Arbitration," *Am. Advocate of Peace*,
LVI (1894), 271; Devere Allen, *The Fight for Peace* (N. Y., 1930),
465-497; H. L. Boyle, *History of Peace* (Grand Rapids, 1902),
chap. viii.

[2] *Arbitration and the United States* (World Peace Found., *Pamphlets,*
X, nos. 6-7), 463-467, 492-513; E. L. Whitney, *The American
Peace Society* (Wash., 1928), chaps. xx-xxvi; A. C. F. Beales, *The
History of Peace* (N. Y., 1931), chaps. viii-ix.

PUCK.

TWO KINDS OF FOOL AMERICANS.

in both countries recoiled in horror; but Congress accorded the executive unanimous support, while Roosevelt, bespeaking still a different point of view, wrote privately to his friend Senator Lodge, "The clamor of the peace faction has convinced me that this country needs a war."[1] Fortunately the British government, for its own reasons, gracefully yielded the point. Events in 1897 and 1898 showed further how little the will to peace had penetrated responsible government circles. In the former year the Senate refused to ratify a general arbitration treaty which had been negotiated with Great Britain. In the latter, the same president who in his inaugural address had declared that "peace is preferable to war in almost every contingency" was rushed into war with Spain by the sound and fury of the sensational press joined to the vociferations of the jingoes in Congress.[2] Even the churches, hitherto the mainstay of the organized peace movement, promptly set their seal of approval upon this war "for humanity's sake."

The operations in Cuba gave the Red Cross its first opportunity to mobilize for war service. A few months before the American intervention Miss Barton and a staff had gone to Havana to carry on work among the sick and starving *reconcentrados*. After the declaration of war on April 25 their activities expanded to all parts of Cuba as well as to the mobilization camps in southern United States and eventually to the Philippines and Porto Rico.[3] Local branches to the number of two thousand

[1] *Selections from the Correspondence of Theodore Roosevelt and Henry Cabot Lodge* (N. Y., 1925), I, 205.

[2] The experienced diplomat John W. Foster wrote in 1910 that if McKinley had kept his head "the war might have been averted." Cleveland shared this opinion during the event and later. J. F. Rhodes, *The McKinley and Roosevelt Administrations* (N. Y., 1922), 63-64; Robert McElroy, *Grover Cleveland* (N. Y., 1923), II, 271-274.

[3] Margherita A. Hamm, "The Red Cross in the Spanish War," *Am. Rev. of Revs.*, XIX (1899), 56-59; Barton, *Red Cross*, 359-665; American National Red Cross Relief Committee, *Report* (N. Y., 1899).

were formed throughout the nation to collect money and provide supplies. The Pacific states alone raised over one hundred thousand dollars and the grand total exceeded half a million. The camps and hospitals served by the Red Cross in the field were often located in places accessible only by difficult mountain passes or long sea voyages, but the organization proved equal to every emergency. Though the soldiers were repeatedly subject to an almost criminal mismanagement, the responsibility fell solely upon the war department, not on this volunteer army of humanitarians whose initial proffer of coöperation had been rebuffed by army officials.

The Red Cross issued from its first baptism of fire with fresh claims upon the gratitude of the American people. To the peace leaders, on the other hand, it seemed that the labors of a generation had gone for naught.[1] Little could they guess in their hour of gloom that forces already at work in European chancelleries were paving the way for the speedy attainment of their cherished objective, the establishment of a permanent international arbitration tribunal.[2]

Not all the social questions confronting this generation stemmed from the maladjustments of city living or the perversity of nature or nations. Two far-reaching problems, heritages from America's rural past, were localized in the two great agricultural sections of the country. One concerned the civilizing of the American aborigine, the other the assimilation of the ex-slave to conditions of freedom. By 1878 Indian outbreaks had become the exception rather than the rule. The fierce Apache in the Southwest fought desperately from 1882 to 1886 to resist being penned up in reservations; in 1889-1890 the unregenerate Sitting Bull, conqueror of

---

[1] Whitney, *American Peace Society*, chap. xxvii.
[2] See Faulkner, *Quest for Social Justice*, 327-328.

General Custer, helped propagate the Messiah craze among the Dakota Sioux, culminating in the battle of Wounded Knee and a loss of over five hundred lives; and as late as 1898 a Chippewa band in Minnesota were stung to warlike reprisals.[1] But every mile of Western railroad enhanced the military effectiveness of the United States, while the spreading zone of settlement reduced the savage's chances of living solely by the chase. The typical red man of the 1880's was a pensioner of the government, living a tribal life within the narrow limits of a reservation, his health impaired by the white man's contagious diseases and his self-reliance sapped by annuities and rations provided by the Great White Father.

At the beginning of the eighties there were a quarter of a million Indians in the United States, the vast majority west of the Mississippi, dwelling on one hundred and twenty different reservations aggregating an area as large as Texas. Many of the government agents to whose care they were confided were deplorably inefficient when not outright corrupt, and the savages were further victimized by unscrupulous licensed traders who grossly overcharged or otherwise duped them. The remnants of about thirty tribes had been herded in Indian Territory, often by methods violating every dictate of humanity. The removal thence of the peaceable Cheyenne of the Upper Missouri is a story of the ill-deserved sufferings of a band taken from an invigorating northern climate to a fever-infested district where the rascality of the agent exposed them to slow starvation. When in the fall of 1878 three hundred of the Indians, men, women and children, escaped in an at-

[1] Flora W. Seymour, *The Story of the Red Man* (N. Y., 1929), chap. xvii; L. H. Roddis, "The Last Indian Uprising in the United States," *Minn. History*, III, 273-290.

tempted flight to their old home, the fugitives after a desperate resistance surrendered upon condition of being restored to their former reservation. Confined in midwinter in a Nebraska fort without food or fuel, they broke prison only to be shot down by the troops until but sixty remained.[1]

Equally shocking was the treatment accorded the Ponca whose story, told to audiences throughout the East in 1879 by Standing Bear and an educated girl Bright Eyes, appalled the humane.[2] Their pathetic recountal prompted Helen Hunt Jackson to write her widely influential *A Century of Dishonor* (1881), a passionate indictment of long-continued Indian mistreatment based upon a study of official records. Shortly afterward Eastern humanitarians formed two organizations—the Indian Rights Association in 1882 and the annual Lake Mohonk Conference of Friends of the Indians in 1883—to influence public opinion and official action for reform. In the next few years the legislatures of Maine, Connecticut, New York, Pennsylvania, Delaware and Michigan memorialized Congress on behalf of a peaceable and constructive solution.[3]

In reality, the government had not been wholly remiss in its duty to the red man, but its efforts had been halfhearted, vacillating and of limited application. For many years it had aided missionary schools, and in 1878 four thousand Indian children were attending schools which the government itself had provided. Something had been

[1] "The Report of the Senate Committee on the Removal of the Northern Cheyennes to Indian Territory," 46 Cong., 2 sess., *Senate Rep.*, no. 708 (June 8, 1880).

[2] The Ponca episode is described in "The Report of the Senate Committee on the Removal of the Poncas to Indian Territory," 46 Cong., 2 sess., *Senate Rep.*, no. 670 (May 31, 1880).

[3] Women's National Indian Association, *Report for 1885*, 26. This body, formed in 1879 under Protestant auspices, had seventy branches in leading centers in 1886.

done also to encourage the use of domestic animals and farm implements. By special treaties and other enactments certain tribes had even been authorized to abandon the communal system of land ownership (though few did so), and at least three thousand individuals before 1887 had attained citizenship status.[1] Congress, however, had resisted the repeated recommendations of presidents, secretaries of the interior and Indian commissioners, over a long space of years, to provide a normal and general means by which capable individuals wherever found might attain to the white man's way of life. All students of the question, in the government and out, were agreed that no amount of education, or even the gift of citizenship, would civilize the red man so long as he remained enmeshed in tribal and reservation life. Nor could he be expected to turn earnestly to farming when, like the Ponca, he might at any time be robbed of his improved lands. Indian sloth and improvidence, in the opinion of thoughtful agents on the spot, were the fruits of a system for which the government, not the savage, was to blame.[2]

President Cleveland, whose sympathies had been deeply stirred by Mrs. Jackson's volume, actively interested himself in the problem.[3] Moreover, the philanthropic incentive to reform was now reënforced by a growing Western demand for the break-up of reservations in order to open virgin tracts for white occupancy.[4]

[1] *Congressional Record*, XI, pt. ii, 1060-1061; Commissioner of Indian Affairs, *Report for 1891*, I, 21.

[2] See, for example, Comr. of Indian Affairs, *Rep. for 1877*, 114, 119, 165; *for 1878*, vii, 5, 31, 84, 128, 140.

[3] G. F. Parker, "Grover Cleveland's First Administration," *Sat. Eve. Post*, CLXCV, esp. 52, 54 (April 7, 1923). Cleveland's private papers reveal that he also received much unsolicited advice from the spirit world through the Indian "controls" of self-avowed mediums. McElroy, *Cleveland*, I, 226.

[4] Secretary of Interior, *Rep. for 1879*, 4; *for 1884*, xi; Mohonk Conference, *Proceeds. for 1886*, 34; *for 1887*, 68.

The humanitarians sought rights for the Indians, the Westerners lands for themselves. This combination of forces resulted on February 8, 1887, in the adoption of a general allotment law, sponsored by Henry L. Dawes of Massachusetts, Charles Sumner's successor in the Senate and a leading spirit in the Mohonk Conference. By its provisions the president was authorized, whenever time and circumstances seemed ripe, to end the tribal government and parcel out the lands of any reservation among individual owners according to certain fixed amounts.[1] The private owners were thereupon to become American citizens though, in order to protect them from white avarice, they were denied the right to sell or mortgage their holdings for twenty-five years. The land remaining undivided might be bought by the government for sale to actual settlers, the money to be held as a trust fund for educating and civilizing the Indians concerned. Although the Five Civilized Tribes in Indian Territory preferred to remain outside the scope of the statute, systematic pressure was exerted to get them to accept its underlying principles, an end finally attained in 1898.[2]

As the benefits of the Dawes law were extended to an increasing number of tribes, the results attested the wisdom of the policy. An official inquiry five years after

[1] One hundred and sixty acres for each head of family, smaller allotments for others, the amounts to be doubled in the case of grazing lands. *U. S. Statutes at Large,* XXIV, 388-391. Because of the discrimination against the younger and more educable tribesmen a supplementary act of 1891 provided for tracts of eighty acres share and share alike. *U. S. Statutes at Large,* XXVI, 794-796. Eleven tribes were, for various reasons, exempted from the operation of these laws.

[2] *U. S. Statutes at Large,* XXX, 495-519. This antagonistic attitude was due to many causes, chiefly perhaps to the position of power and profit held in the semiautonomous Indian states by mixed bloods and to the influence of cattle magnates who were benefiting from a cheap rental of the rich pasture lands. In 1901 the Five Tribes were brought specifically under the terms of the Dawes law. *U. S. Statutes at Large,* XXXI, 848, 861.

its passage showed that a large proportion of the favored Indians were tilling the soil or raising stock.[1] While the older generation often clung tenaciously to tribal traditions and customs, the younger men tended to break away from the chief's influence and adopt civilized ways. This tendency grew markedly with the extension of educational facilities.[2] Some of the children attended neighborhood day schools, but the majority were taken from home influences and placed in reservation boarding schools, or in training schools outside the reservation as at Carlisle, Pennsylvania, or at Haskell Institute in Lawrence, Kansas. Everywhere stress was placed upon vocational training and an appreciation of the values of civilization. The young buck who graduated from Carlisle was not likely to return to the blanket of his forefathers or prefer a squalid tepee to a livable frame house.

Though school accommodations lagged behind the need, nearly twenty thousand youths were enrolled as pupils in 1898. Between 1878 and that year the annual government appropriations rose from thirty thousand dollars to well over two and a half million. Meantime the break-up of the reservations had been proceeding apace. Between 1887 and 1906, when important changes were made in the Dawes act, seventy-five million acres, or nearly three fifths of the total, were disposed of. About seven million acres were allotted to fifty-eight thousand Indians, and over fifty million were acquired by the government for sale to white settlers.[3] In addi-

---

[1] Comr. of Indian Affairs, Rep. for 1892, 185-195.

[2] W. N. Hailmann, "Education of the Indian," N. M. Butler, ed., Education in the United States (Albany, 1900), II, 941-972; H. L. Dawes, "Have We Failed with the Indian?," Atlantic Mo., LXXXIV (1899), 280-283.

[3] The government reserved relatively small tracts for religious and educational purposes and as timber preserves. Detailed figures as regards allotments may be found in Esther F. Cooper, The Genesis and Application

tion, before 1906 ninety-two thousand members of the Five Civilized Tribes received allotments aggregating fourteen and a half million acres.

Despite this gratifying progress certain evils attended the application of the law. Allotments were sometimes made before the red men were ready for the responsibility. In other instances, capable and self-reliant individuals chafed at the inflexible twenty-five-year restriction. Cases were also numerous in which well-meaning Indians were induced to enter illegal leasing arrangements with powerful cattle interests.[1] As voters, moreover, the adult males were preyed upon by unscrupulous politicians who taught too many of them to regard the franchise as a "merchantable article to be disposed of in the best market." [2]

From their new status as citizens came also the right to buy liquor at will. The startling increase in drunkenness, resulting often in immorality and crime, caused Congress somewhat belatedly, in 1897, to ban the traffic among Indians during the probationary period.[3] The reversal of this law by the Supreme Court in 1905, as a denial of the equal rights of citizens, would hasten the passage of the Burke act (1906), designed to cure this as well as other defects in the original statute.[4] Even without these remedial provisions no one doubted that this oldest of American race problems was in a fair way to solution. The "Emancipation Act of the Indians,"

of the Dawes Act (M.A. thesis, Univ. of Iowa, 1924), 111-112, and app. C. See also Dawes, "Have We Failed with the Indian?," 283.

[1] The original statute was amended from time to time to permit leasing but under strict conditions. *U. S. Statutes at Large*, XXVI, 794; XXVIII, 305; XXX, 85.

[2] Comr. of Indian Affairs, *Rep. for 1892*, 139, 186, 192; *for 1893*, 335.

[3] *U. S. Statutes at Large*, XXIX, 506; Koren, *Economic Aspects of Liquor Problem*, chap. vii.

[4] U. S. *v.* Heff, 197 U. S., 488; Faulkner, *Quest for Social Justice*, 13-14.

as the Dawes law was called, may be rated as perhaps the generation's most notable humanitarian venture. Without any regard to consistency, the Americans of the eighties and nineties were resolved that the Negro question was one for the South to solve, not for the politicians in Washington.[1] President Hayes's recall of the last garrisons in 1877, after a decade of ceaseless governmental activity on behalf of Negro equality, was a tacit admission of the South's right to manage its own race relations, as well as a symbol of the North's increasing absorption in the exigent problems arising from its new industrial order. When a belated flare-up of Radical fervor in 1890 secured from the House of Representatives the passage of a "force bill" for facilitating federal intervention in congressional elections, party leaders in the Senate quietly quashed the measure mainly because of their greater concern for the enactment of a new tariff law.[2]

Partly in response to the Republican party's desertion of their cause, a mass movement of Negroes set in toward the North and West in the spring and summer of 1879, directed chiefly toward Kansas.[3] For several years Benjamin ("Pap") Singleton, a Tennessee ex-slave, and Henry Adams of Louisiana, a colored veteran of the late war, had been sowing seeds of unrest, and the agents of

[1] See, for example, edit., "Political Rights of Negroes," *Andover Rev.*, XIII (1890), 305; R. P. Hollowell, *The Southern Question Past and Present* (Boston, 1890), 21-26. The policy of noninterference was facilitated by the fact that until 1889 the Republicans were at no time in effective control of both the presidency and the two houses of Congress.

[2] J. F. Rhodes, *History of the United States from Hayes to McKinley* (N. Y., 1919), 358-364.

[3] W. L. Fleming, " 'Pap' Singleton, the Moses of the Colored Exodus," *Am. Journ. of Sociology*, XV, 61-82; J. C. Hartzell, "The Negro Exodus," *Methodist Quar. Rev.*, LXI (1879), 722-748; F. R. Guernsey, "The Negro Exodus," *International Rev.*, VII (1879), 373-390; J. B. Runnion, "The Negro Exodus," *Atlantic Mo.*, XLIV (1879), 222-230; *Appletons' Annual Cyclopaedia*, XIX (1879), 354-358; XX (1880), 417.

Western railway and land companies, for their own reasons, vigorously seconded their efforts. Crop failures and low cotton prices in 1879, added to the usurious credit system and increasing election brutalities, brought matters to a head. By the thousands Negroes, ill clad and often penniless, threw down their hoes in Louisiana, Mississippi, Tennessee, Texas and elsewhere, crowded toward the river wharves and, by hook or crook, made their way to the new Canaan. Some of them were turned back at St. Louis or Kansas City; others, upon arrival at their destination, were saved only by the exertions of emergency relief societies.

But the great majority, perhaps twenty or twenty-five thousand in all, remained in Kansas, winning the respect of their white neighbors by their diligence and self-denial.[1] Meantime the Southern planting interests, fearful of losing their principal labor supply, sought by argument and force to stay the exodus. A biracial convention at Vicksburg on May 6 discussed ways and means of improving the lot of the Negro in the South.[2] In many localities would-be migrants were dealt with by violence, defrauded of their money or jailed on false charges. But the movement ended mainly for other reasons, chiefly, perhaps, a better understanding by the credulous blacks of the difficulties and hardships which the northward trek involved.

For the remainder of the century the bulk of Afro-Americans stayed in Dixie, content to work out their destiny in the land where slavery had originally planted

[1] Successful examples of Negro colonies were Nicodemus, Baxter Springs, Morton City and Singleton. F. H. Fletcher, *Negro Exodus* (n.p., 1879); Henry King, "A Year of the Exodus in Kansas," *Scribner's Mo.*, XX (1880), 211-218; anon., "The Administration of Governor John P. St. John," Kan. Hist. Soc., *Colls.*, IX, 378-395.

[2] "The Proceedings of a Migration Convention and Congressional Action Respecting the Exodus of 1879," *Journ. of Negro History*, IV, 41-92.

them. Migration, however, occurred within the area, notably a steady southwesterly trend from the old border states into the Gulf region, where their dense numbers along the river courses and in the rich alluvial plains made the black belt still blacker. While the vast majority clung to the rural districts, local centripetal movements resulted in straggling colonies in the alley ways and poorer quarters of the cities. The total colored population of the ex-slave states advanced from six million in 1880 to eight in 1900, a rate of growth which should not have caused (though it did) fears of impending Africanization, for the whites meantime increased from eleven million to nearly twenty.[1] Though the Negro birth rate was higher than the Caucasian, it was greatly offset by excessive infant mortality and the inroads of diseases from which the paternalistic life of the plantation had in large degree protected the race in slavery.[2] In 1880 they made up a third of all the people of the section and at no time did they form less than a quarter of the total. In certain states of the Lower South—Georgia, Alabama and Florida—the two races were about evenly divided, while in South Carolina, Mississippi and Louisiana the Negroes actually outnumbered the whites.

While Pap Singleton was still exhorting tumultuous crowds to flee the land of their oppressor, Frederick Douglass, the Nestor of his race, sounded a solemn note of warning. "The exodus the colored people want," he affirmed, "is the exodus from ignorance, vice and lack of thrift."[3] The history of the years that fol-

[1] Negroes in the United States (Bur. of the Census, Bull., no. 129, 1915), 12-13, 57-58.

[2] F. L. Hoffman, Race Traits and Tendencies of the American Negro (N. Y., 1896), chaps. i-ii; T. N. Chase, ed., Mortality among Negroes in Cities (Atlanta Univ., Publs., no. 1), passim.

[3] Appletons' Annual Cyclopaedia, XX (1880), 585. See also Frederick Douglass, "The Negro Exodus," Journ. of Social Sci., IX (1880), esp. 12-21.

lowed is an impressive commentary on his words. For the Negro it was a time of painful awakening from the fool's paradise of Reconstruction days—of sordid, unremitting struggle with ignorance and poverty. The statesman of this new emancipation was Booker T. Washington, an ex-slave who, as a result of youthful schooling at Hampton Institute, Virginia, was inspired, as he later said, to go into the Lower South and "give my life to providing the same kind of opportunity for self-reliance and self-awakening that I had found provided for me at Hampton." [1] Starting at Tuskegee, Alabama, in 1881 with one teacher, thirty students and a borrowed log shanty, he succeeded, with state aid and Northern benefactions, in building up his Normal and Industrial Institute until by 1898 it had about ninety instructors, nearly a thousand students, twenty-three hundred acres of land, and forty buildings erected largely by student labor.

Believing that his people must begin at the bottom and that it was to their best interest to perfect the mechanical skills which they had been taught in slavery, he provided training in all the trades and occupations necessary for securing a footing in Southern economic life. Along this path too, he maintained, lay the best hope for the recovery of legal equality, for "No race that has anything to contribute to the markets of the world is long in any degree ostracized." His reply to those who beat their breasts for immediate recognition of Negro rights was: "The opportunity to earn a dollar in a factory just now is worth infinitely more than the opportunity to spend a dollar in an opera-house." [2]

[1] B. T. Washington, "The Awakening of the Negro," *Atlantic Mo.*, LXXVIII (1896), esp. 322. See also same author, *Up from Slavery* (N. Y., 1901), chaps. vii-xii, and M. B. Thrasher, *Tuskegee* (Boston, 1900).

[2] The quotations are taken from his noted speech in 1895 at the

The scarcely perceptible emphasis on the words, "just now," was missed by Southern whites who, thinking it his purpose to breed a race of robots, acclaimed his wisdom and leadership.

Washington's teachings, backed by the visible success of the work carried on at Hampton and Tuskegee and the ever widening influence of their graduates, made a deep impress on Negro education everywhere.[1] As we have already seen, the South was too poor to provide enough schools for the scattered inhabitants of the great rural areas and especially so under the policy of separate instruction for the two races.[2] This, perhaps more than white indifference or antagonism, impeded the development of adequate instructional facilities.[3]

Fortunately Northern philanthropy did something to relieve the situation. A small part of the Peabody Fund was used for training colored teachers, while two new benefactions exclusively for Negroes—the John F. Slater Fund of a million dollars in 1882 and Daniel Hand's gift of one and a half million to the American Missionary Association in 1888—stimulated educational effort in every department. Though about half the Afro-American children had no schools of any kind to attend,

opening of the Atlanta Exposition, reprinted in *Up from Slavery*, 218-225, and elsewhere.

[1] U. S. Comr. of Educ., *Reps.*, 1878-1901, *passim*; esp. J. L. M. Curry, "The Slater Fund and the Education of the Negro," *Rep. for 1894-95*, II, 1367-1424; Kelley Miller, "The Education of the Negro," *Rep. for 1900-01*, I, 731-859; and A. D. Mayo, "The Work of Certain Northern Churches in the Education of the Freedmen, 1861-1900," *Rep. for 1901-02*, I, 285-314.

[2] See earlier, 163-166.

[3] Miller estimates that the per-capita school expenditure in the ex-slave states was in 1878-1879 $2.60 for whites and $1.00 for blacks, the comparable figures for 1897-1898 being $4.25 and $2.27. "Education of the Negro," 753. If his estimates are accurate, it is probable that the disparity may be, in considerable degree, accounted for by the difference in the per-capita expenditure on education in the cities, where Negroes were few, and in the rural districts where the vast bulk of them dwelt.

the total number of those who did attend rose from six hundred and eighty-five thousand in 1878 to a million and a half in 1898.[1] A serious lack was the dearth of secondary schools in which more intensive instruction in manual training and industrial education could be given. The score or more of Negro colleges and universities, however, were of hardly better than high-school rank and they usually stressed courses of the vocational type. Howard University at Washington was about the only one whose standards of admission approximated those of the better Northern colleges.

As farmers the race continued to be handicapped, on the one hand, by the shiftless habits learned in slavery and, on the other, by the vicious crop-lien system.[2] All through the black belt they lived in wretched single-room cabins, tilling "one-mule" cotton farms of from twenty-five to thirty acres, and managing to pay their rent and buy supplies only by mortgaging their unharvested crops at exorbitant interest rates. For many it was an economic serfdom from which there was no release. Their diet rarely included much more than hominy, corn bread, rank fat "sidemeat" and coffee, while half their clothing was begged from the whites. In Tennessee, Kentucky and Virginia the situation was somewhat more hopeful, and a higher proportion of tenants were emerging into the class of farm owners and householders.

In 1890 six out of every ten Negroes gainfully em-

---

[1] U. S. Comr. of Educ., *Rep. for 1898-99*, II, 2202. The rural school term usually lasted about two months, and Negro parents were not able to lengthen it by voluntary contributions as was often done by the whites for their own schools.

[2] S. J. Barrows, "What the Southern Negro Is Doing for Himself," *Atlantic Mo.*, LXVII (1891), 805-815; P. A. Bruce, *The Plantation Negro as a Freeman* (*Questions of the Day Series*, LVII, N. Y., 1889), chaps. xiii-xiv; L. J. Greene and C. J. Woodson, *The Negro Wage Earner* (Wash.. 1930), chap. ii.

ployed were husbandmen, while three out of the remaining four were in domestic and personal service, mostly in the towns.[1] Cartmen and porters were ordinarily Negroes, and many were doing well as carpenters, barbers, bricklayers, blacksmiths and mechanics. There were individual cases of conspicuous affluence. Several Negroes in Baltimore were reputed to be worth fifteen thousand dollars, and three or four from forty to sixty thousand. A few doctors and lawyers were also to be found in the larger Southern cities, though their livelihood suffered because of the preference of their own race for white men in the same lines. Of the older professions the ministry was the only one in which an Afro-American could count upon an enthusiastic following of his own color, but success here depended less upon training than upon a sonorous eloquence.

Race antipathy hampered economic progress only when blacks competed with poor whites for the same jobs, particularly in the skilled trades. Although both the Knights of Labor and the American Federation of Labor were willing to have them as members, and white employers valued them as a docile labor force, local working-class sentiment often managed to block their employment.[2] The antagonism sometimes took the form of strikes; yet in thirty-nine recorded instances from 1882 to 1898 only seven strikes had the desired outcome of excluding Negro workers.

The color line was most rigidly drawn at points where the association of the two peoples might suggest social equality. While white persons might cheerfully work side by side with colored employees or be attended in public places by their ebon-hued nurse maids, they

[1] Barrows, "What the Southern Negro Is Doing," 807, 810; C. H. Wesley, *Negro Labor in the United States* (N. Y., 1927), 226-235; Greene and Woodson, *Negro Wage Earner*, chap. iii.
[2] Wesley, *Negro Labor*, 236-237, 254-263.

did not voluntarily tolerate such proximity when the Negroes were not in a menial relationship.[1] Blacks and whites even worshiped their common God in different churches. Though the law throughout the South prohibited intermarriage, few states expressly forbade irregular sex relations. Yet Philip A. Bruce, a Virginian of the former master class, writing in 1888, deemed it a "remarkable evidence of the social antipathy of the white people" that since abolition "illicit sexual commerce between the two races has diminished so far as to have almost ceased, outside the cities and towns." The reason, he believed, was that since the woman was no longer a slave the relationship implied a kind of temporary social recognition.[2]

While the census reveals a growing proportion of mixed strains in the South, it is possible that the enumeration was inaccurate or that the increase derived from the intermarriage of mulattoes with others having more or less Negro blood. At any rate, the figures for 1890 indicate that the greatest admixture existed outside the ex-slave states and that within that section the race grew generally blacker as it approached the Gulf.[3] A single drop of Negro blood, if it could be detected, everywhere stigmatized the individual as a "person of color." Nothing more strikingly evinced the difference in the Caucasian's attitude toward the two major race problems of the time than that men of the standing of

[1] Bruce, *Plantation Negro*, 48-53; G. W. Cable, *The Negro Question* (N. Y., 1890), 21-24.

[2] Bruce, *Plantation Negro*, 53-55, 243. See also same author, "The Negro Population of the South," *Conservative Rev.*, II (1899), 276.

[3] The percentage of mulattoes in the Negro population of the nation, as determined by the census enumerators, was 12 in 1870, 15.2 in 1890 and 20.9 in 1910. No data are available for the intermediate census years. In Bruce's own state of Virginia the official count reveals a growth from 14.1 per cent in 1870 to 33.2 per cent in 1910. *Negroes in United States*, 15, 60. See also E. B. Reuter, *The Mulatto in the United States* (Boston, 1918), esp. 118-126.

Senator Matthew S. Quay took pride in the Indian blood in their veins.[1] Apart from the denial of intermarriage and the provision for separate schools, Southern legislatures moved cautiously in applying the color test to race relations. As early as 1881 Tennessee passed a "Jim Crow" law requiring different coaches or compartments on trains, but it was not until the Supreme Court two years later emasculated the federal civil-rights act of 1875 that her sister commonwealths generally followed her example.[2] On the other hand, Negroes could at no time and in no place secure accommodations in hotels, restaurants and amusement places conducted by whites, though such discrimination seldom had statutory sanction. Opinions differed as to whether colored citizens received equal treatment before the courts, but their treatment at the hands of self-appointed enforcers of the law was a reproach to Anglo-Saxon ideas of justice. In the period 1882-1898 over sixteen hundred recorded lynchings, mainly of blacks, took place in the former slave states, the most tragic years falling in the early nineties.[3] Though these outrages were supposed to represent a species of degenerate chivalry, the victims suspected of rape or attempted rape formed but a minority of the whole number murdered.

In the matter of voting the South allowed the guarantees in the Reconstruction state constitutions to stand for a time. Meanwhile, however, the dominant race actually disfranchised most Afro-Americans by "bull-dozing" and other terroristic methods, by fantastic gerry-

[1] Theodore Roosevelt, An Autobiography (N. Y., 1919), 156.

[2] 109 U. S. (1883), 1; Franklin Johnson, The Development of State Legislation Concerning the Negro (N. Y., 1919), 14-19, and passim.

[3] Nearly four fifths of the victims were Negroes. J. E. Cutler, Lynch-Law (N. Y., 1905), chap. vi; Ida B. Wells, A Red Record (Chicago, ca. 1895); Walter White, Rope and Faggot (N. Y., 1929), app.

mandering arrangements and by unfair manipulation of electoral regulations.[1] In South Carolina after 1882, for instance, the voter must deposit each of his various ballots correctly in the eight or more boxes before him, a test which the untutored darky seldom found it possible to meet. When the rising agrarianism of the late eighties split the white electorate into two fairly balanced parties, however, deep-grained prejudices against the Negro in politics temporarily disappeared, particularly when victory depended upon which side could poll the colored vote. Thoughtful Southerners, fearing the remoter consequences of such tactics, believed the time had come to disfranchise the race by constitutional mandate provided, of course, that the step could be taken without infringing the letter of the Fifteenth Amendment.

The three states in which Negroes outnumbered the whites were the first to act. Mississippi in 1890 pointed the way by limiting the ballot to paid-up male taxpayers who were able to read a passage from the state constitution or understand it when read to them or give "a reasonable interpretation thereof." The flexible clause was confessedly designed to enable election officials to reject illiterate blacks without rejecting illiterate whites. Five years later South Carolina followed with a somewhat similar provision and then, in 1898, Louisiana found a means of exempting whites from the property and educational tests by placing on the voting list all male applicants whose fathers or grandfathers had been eligible to vote prior to 1867. Other states were presently to devise ingenious variants of these restrictions. Thus the postwar political importance of the Negro

[1] S. B. Weeks, "History of Negro Suffrage," *Polit. Sci. Quar.*, IX, 671-703; W. A. Dunning, *Essays on the Civil War and Reconstruction* (N. Y., 1904), 363-385; W. C. Hamm, "The Three Phases of Colored Suffrage," *N. Am. Rev.*, CLXVIII (1899), 285-296; Paul Lewinson, *Race, Class, & Party* (London, 1932), chaps. iv-v.

vanished almost as quickly as it had come. He became once more a negligible factor in Southern public life. Notwithstanding these many onerous restrictions, even George W. Cable conceded that the Afro-American enjoyed "a larger share of private, public, religious and political liberty than falls to the lot of any but a few peoples . . . ." [1] The most salient rights of all—to accumulate property, establish a home and acquire some measure of schooling—remained unobstructed by legal barriers. Nor could any disinterested observer deny that the race had taken excellent advantage of its opportunities. By 1900 one Negro in every five owned his home, and the total value of the farms they operated reached nearly half a billion dollars. About two hundred thousand owned their farms while over half a million more worked as tenants.[2] Fifty-six per cent were literate as compared with thirty per cent twenty years before, and with the advance of education had gone a slow but steady improvement in morals and family relations. One-room cabins were everywhere beginning to give way to two or even three-room houses, with an occasional parlor organ and some attention to the decencies and comforts of living. If one test of racial capacity is the ability to breed leaders, the Negroes could evidence not only Booker T. Washington, but also Paul Laurence Dunbar, the lyric poet, Henry O. Tanner whose painting "The Raising of Lazarus" was bought by the French government, the novelist C. W. Chesnutt, the electrical inventor Granville T. Woods, as well as others equally distinguished in their fields.[3] We may agree with the

[1] Cable, Negro Question, 66.
[2] Negroes in United States, 29, 158-160.
[3] C. G. Woodson, The Negro in Our History (Wash., 1922), 291-304. Four of the five named above were of hybrid descent. Reuter, Mulatto in United States, chap. viii, presents long lists of names which show, at least at this transitional stage of the race's development, that mixed bloods greatly predominated among the more gifted individu-

contemporary judgment of a young Negro intellectual that thirty years of struggle and privation had "changed the child of emancipation to the youth with dawning self-consciousness, self-realization, self-respect." [1]

als. Benjamin Brawley, himself a mulatto, briefly denies the advantage of an infusion of white blood in *A Social History of the American Negro* (N. Y., 1921), 330-332.

[1] W. E. B. Du Bois, "Strivings of the Negro People," *Atlantic Mo.*, LXXX (1897), 196.

CHAPTER XII

POLITICAL FACTORS AND FORCES

THE average American in the 1880's accepted democracy as he accepted the telephone, sanitary plumbing and the electric light, expecting someone to furnish him with as much of them as he needed, or could afford, and keep them in good running order. Though the party managers usually succeeded in getting him to the polls on election day, he saved himself the vexation of thinking about candidates and issues by voting the straight party ticket. Nor did the epoch possess its due proportion of political leaders of the first rank. Henry Adams declared in retrospect: "No period so thoroughly ordinary had been known in American politics since Christopher Columbus first disturbed the balance of American society." [1] Apparently the men of creative vision and constructive ability were attracted into fresher and more challenging fields. Bryce was impressed, for example, by the "splendid practical capacity" of the great railway builders, whose scope of activities required "administrative rulers, generals, diplomatists, financiers, of the finest gifts," talents which in the Old World would have gone into parliamentary management and civil administration. [2]

Surprisingly enough, the extraordinary educational opportunities which the generation boasted did little to increase the participation of the "better classes" in poli-

[1] Henry Adams, *The Education of Henry Adams* (Boston, 1918), 355.
[2] James Bryce, *The American Commonwealth* (London, 1888), II, 407.

tics. To be sure, Henry Cabot Lodge, one of Harvard's first Ph.D.'s, deserted teaching for public life, but as early as 1883 it was observed that he was "the gentleman and scholar in politics without the guilelessness and squeamishness of the said gentleman and scholar."[1] When Roosevelt fresh from Harvard in 1881 decided to run for the New York legislature, his lawyer and business friends sought to dissuade him from a career which, they pointed out, was controlled not by "gentlemen" but by "saloon-keepers, horse-car conductors, and the like."[2]

The opinion that "politics were low," so forcibly conveyed to young Roosevelt, caused most men of cultivation and scholarly training, including such gifted students of public affairs as Woodrow Wilson and F. J. Goodnow, to prefer the rôle of observer and critic. A few like George W. Curtis and Dorman B. Eaton, whose emotions were too strong to permit inactivity, compromised by indulging in that form of nonpartisan organized effort which it is now fashionable to call "pressure politics." As a result, political management, like other phases of man's activities, fell increasingly into the hands of specialists, of professional practitioners, known to the public as bosses and machine politicians. Roosevelt quickly discovered that his district in New York City was run by Jake Hess and "his captains of tens and of

[1] Clement's weekly Boston letter to the *N. Y. Tribune*, quoted by S. E. Morison, "Memoir of Edward Henry Clement," Mass. Hist. Soc., *Proceeds.*, LVI, 64.

[2] Theodore Roosevelt, *An Autobiography* (N. Y., 1919), 56. Henry Adams wrote Lodge, rather sourly, the same year: "I have never known a young man go into politics who was not the worse for it . . . from my two brothers, John and Brooks, down to Willy Astor, Ham Fish, and Robert Ray Hamilton." Henry Adams, *Letters (1858-1891)* (W. C. Ford, ed., Boston, 1930), 331. English travelers were naturally much struck by "the divorce between politics and . . . the higher culture." See, for example, E. A. Freeman, *Some Impressions of the United States* (N. Y., 1883), 202-204, and Emily Faithfull, *Three Visits to America* (Edinburgh, 1884), 10-12.

hundreds"; but Jake himself was but a tiny cog in a well-integrated Republican organization which reached upward through the state into all parts of the nation. At no point was the political mettle of the generation so sorely tried as in the government of cities. From long experience Americans had learned how to rule populations scattered over large areas, but they had had little or no training in the management of densely packed urban centers. Yet every year a larger proportion of the people hived in cities, rendering all human relations more complex, creating new social maladjustments and requiring governmental services and safeguards unknown to the earlier and simpler days of the republic.[1] If conscientious municipal officials floundered in the effort to administer their unruly charges, all too frequently those in the seats of power were not actuated by upright motives. Lax enforcement of the law commanded a price which the liquor interests and the purveyors of commercialized vice were ever ready to pay. Even more serious was the corruption and fraud involved in the letting of municipal contracts and in the sale of the social values created by the rapid growth of population.

Some of the shrewdest and most unscrupulous men of the time specialized in the exploitation of municipal utilities (water, fuel, light and rapid transit), their activities often embracing a network of cities.[2] One group of six capitalists—C. T. Yerkes, W. L. Elkins, P. A. B. Widener, W. C. Whitney, T. F. Ryan and Thomas Dolan—combined the street railways of New York City, Philadelphia, Chicago, Pittsburgh and at

[1] G. W. Julian, "The Pending Ordeals of Democracy," *International Rev.*, V (1878), 737-738; W. R. Martin, "Cities as Units in Our Polity," *N. Am. Rev.*, CXXVIII (1879), esp. 21; Josiah Strong, *The Twentieth Century City* (N. Y., 1898), 60-61.

[2] B. J. Hendrick, *The Age of Big Business* (Allen Johnson, ed., *The Chronicles of America Series*, New Haven, 1918-1921, XXXIX), chap. v.

least a hundred other places in New England, Pennsylvania, Ohio and Indiana. Either jointly or severally they also controlled the gas and electric-light facilities of eighty-some communities as far apart as Philadelphia, St. Augustine, Vicksburg, Kansas City, Minneapolis and Syracuse. A single corporation developed most of the trolley and lighting companies of the cities of New Jersey; another managed similar utilities in San Francisco and other places on the Pacific Coast.

The full story of the graft and dishonor involved in the traffic in franchises will never be known. From indirect evidence as well as from occasional court testimony it seems clear that there was a cesspool under nearly every city hall, dug secretly by politicians in the pay of respectable, or at least respected, business men. Hazen S. Pingree of Detroit, one of the few reform mayors, was offered a bribe of fifty thousand dollars by one company and a trip around the world by another if he would refrain from vetoing certain franchises.[1] "Keep the newspapers on your staff" as well as the city officials, advised a speaker before the Ohio Gas-Light Association in 1896, and proceeded to explain how a friendly press could be nurtured by a judicious distribution of stock.[2] Moreover, if the public-utility interests failed to take the initiative, they were likely to be held up by venal aldermen with the threat of ordinances —"strike bills"—hostile to them. In Pingree's opinion, "Good municipal government is an impossibility while valuable franchises are to be had and can be obtained by corrupt use of money in bribing public servants."[3]

[1] E. W. Bemis, ed., *Municipal Monopolies* (R. T. Ely, ed., *Library of Economics and Politics;* 4th edn., N. Y., 1904), 657.

[2] Just a month before, court testimony had disclosed the secret financial control of the *Minneapolis Tribune* by the president of the street railways of the Twin Cities. Bemis, *Municipal Monopolies*, 658-660.

[3] Quoted in Bemis, *Municipal Monopolies*, 658.

The evil fruit of this unholy alliance of big business and bad politics was the worst city government the country had ever known. The voters themselves were in part responsible because of their habit, in municipal as well as national elections, of dividing along national party lines. Wrongdoers also found many advantages in the cumbersome form of government which, in faulty analogy to the state government, ordinarily consisted of a mayor and a two-chambered council. In New York the Tammany organization, recovering quickly from the shock of the Tweed Ring exposure, resumed its career of systematic looting of the city's wealth.[1] After an investigation in 1884 three aldermen were sentenced to prison, six fled to Canada, three turned state's evidence and ten others were indicted but not brought to trial. According to the *New York Evening Post*, April 3, 1890, the Tammany executive committee at that time consisted of twenty-seven "professional politicians," including

> convicted murderer, 1; acquitted of murder, 1; convicted of felonious assault, 1; professional gamblers, 4; former dive-keepers, 5; liquor dealers, 4; former liquor dealers, 5; sons of liquor dealers, 3; former pugilists, 3; former toughs, 4; members of Tweed gang, 6; officeholders, 17.

Richard Croker, Irish immigrant, former prize fighter and gang leader, who had reigned as boss since 1886, had already justified his early training under Tweed by becoming the possessor of untold wealth.

But New York City did not stand alone. The "gas ring" in Philadelphia, the "real-estate ring" in the

[1] Allan Nevins, *The Evening Post* (N. Y., 1922), chap. xxii; Gustavus Myers, *The History of Tammany Hall* (rev. edn., N. Y., 1917), chaps. xxvii-xxix; Lothrop Stoddard, *Master of Manhattan: The Life of Richard Croker* (N. Y., 1931).

nation's capital, George B. Cox's strangle hold on Cincinnati's political life, Colonel "Ed" Butler's organized traffic in the franchises and contracts of St. Louis, the malodorous Ames régime in Minneapolis, the systematic exploitation of San Francisco by "Blind Boss" (Christopher A.) Buckley—these provided hardly less glaring instances of what Bryce called "the one conspicuous failure" of American democracy.[1] Echoing Bryce's sentiment, Andrew D. White asserted that, "with very few exceptions, the city governments of the United States are the worst in Christendom—the most expensive, the most inefficient, and the most corrupt."[2] Audiences might more profitably have been stirred to wrath instead of laughter by a famous sally in one of the Harrigan and Hart comedies. When the municipal fathers fell asleep at the Mulligan home from too much entertainment, "Will I wake them?" asked Mrs. Mulligan. "Lave thim be," replied her spouse. "While they sleep the city's safe."[3] The immigrant was often blamed for the sorry condition of affairs, but outside New York City the bosses and grafting politicians were usually of native stock. Moreover municipal misrule was as rampant in "American" cities like Philadelphia and Portland, Oregon, as in those which had a far larger proportion of foreign-born voters.[4]

[1] Bryce considered these cities along with Chicago, Brooklyn, Baltimore and New Orleans as the places where "Ring-and-bossdom" throve most luxuriantly. Bryce, *American Commonwealth*, II, 281, 468-473.

[2] A. D. White, "The Government of American Cities," *Forum*, X (1890-1891), 357.

[3] J. L. Ford, *Forty-Odd Years in the Literary Shop* (N. Y., 1921), 98.

[4] C. W. Eliot, "One Remedy for Municipal Misgovernment," *Forum*, XII (1891-1892), 153-168; C. R. Woodruff, "Cleveland Conference for Good City Government," *Am. Mag. of Civics*, VII (1895), 169; T. N. Strong, "Municipal Condition of Portland," Natl. Conf. for Good City Government, *Proceeds. for 1895*, 432-438; edit., "Redemption of our Cities," *Nation* (N. Y.), LXIII, 359-360 (Nov. 12, 1896).

The commanding position of the city in cultural life made its failure as a political organism all the more tragic. From time to time the citizens, stung beyond endurance, banded together to "turn the rascals out." Sometimes they were betrayed by their own officials; more often they were so spent by their exertion of virtue that at the next election the machine romped back into power. Philadelphia chose a reform mayor against the gas-ring candidate in 1881, only to sink back into its shame two years later. Buffalo similarly secured a respite in 1881 by electing Grover Cleveland who, by his defiance of a corrupt council, quickly won the name of "the veto mayor." The famous revolt against Tammany in 1894, of which the preacher Parkhurst was the particular hero, was followed three years later by the triumph of the Tammany henchman Robert A. Van Wyck.

Few cities, unfortunately, emulated the example of Detroit which, from 1889 to his elevation seven years later to the governorship, continued to reëlect the militant reformer Pingree as mayor. During his lease of power Pingree exposed grafting members of the council, wrung important concessions from the street-railway and gas companies and, against the most ruthless opposition, secured the establishment of a municipal electric-lighting plant.[1] He was the forerunner of a series of local executives who in the early years of the next century were to bring about a civic renaissance.[2]

For the most part, reform interludes left few enduring gains. More significant was the improvement which came from state legislation requiring secret, uniform and officially printed ballots. Until Kentucky in February,

[1] G. B. Catlin, *The Story of Detroit* (Detroit, 1923), chaps. ci-cvi.
[2] See H. U. Faulkner, *The Quest for Social Justice* (*A History of American Life*, XI), 93-104.

1888, imposed this plan upon the city of Louisville, it had everywhere been the practice of party organizations to print and distribute their own lists to voters who, with or without help, marked them before going to deposit them in the plain view of any who cared to see. Massachusetts, acting the same year as Kentucky, gave the system state-wide application.[1] So keenly was the need for reform felt that within a decade the new plan, in complete or partial form, prevailed throughout the country save in Georgia, the two Carolinas and New Mexico. Though the results were not miraculous, vote buyers thereafter were obliged to take a sporting chance, intimidation and rioting at the polls tended to disappear, and municipal politics was freed from one of the most blatant aspects of public disregard of the citizens' rights.

Less successful were the efforts to better the method of appointing city officeholders. The National Civil Service Reform League, formed in 1881, from the start included municipal offices as a part of its program. In 1883 and 1884 the New York and Massachusetts legislatures prescribed the merit system for the larger cities, though local politicians often managed to circumvent it in practice. By 1898 laws providing for the new method were also operative in Philadelphia, Chicago, New Orleans and elsewhere.[2] While ballot and civil-service laws im-

---

[1] The original proponents of the influential Massachusetts statute were in touch with English experience, but did not learn until at a later stage of the Australian law, which antedated the English one and which provided the popular tag for the reform in America. R. H. Dana, "Sir William Vernon Harcourt and the Australian Ballot Law," Mass. Hist. Soc., *Proceeds.*, LVIII, 401-418. For the quick spread of the reform, see J. B. Bishop, "The Secret Ballot in Thirty-Three States," *Forum*, XII (1891-1892), 589-598.

[2] F. M. Stewart, *The National Civil Service Reform League: History, Activities, and Problems* (Austin, 1929), 34-37; T. C. Devlin, *Municipal Reform in the United States* (*Questions of the Day Series*, XC, N. Y., 1896), 89, 99.

proved the municipal system at certain points, few of the reformers saw as clearly as Seth Low and Andrew D. White that a more drastic reconstruction was required— that American cities with their vastly expanded functions were "not so much little states as large corporations." [1] The bitter lessons learned during these years, however, did much to clear the way for that experimentation in new governmental forms which was to signalize the opening decades of the next century.

Because of the close control wielded by legislatures over cities, municipal bosses and their henchmen took up their residence in the state capital when the law makers were in session. Particularly in urbanized states like New York and Pennsylvania, ways could be found of inducing the legislature to oblige the city to buy property, undertake costly construction and create lucrative municipal offices. [2] The chief threat to legislative purity, apart from this fecund source of infection, came from privilege-seeking corporations. By 1890, however, so many states had enacted statutes against conspiracies and agreements in restraint of trade that corporation lobbyists centered their efforts chiefly on maintaining the lax laws effective in a few places like New Jersey, Delaware and West Virginia. From any one of these as a base, big business could, under a guarantee in the federal Constitution, trade unmolested across state lines.

Laws were also enacted in an attempt to regulate the expenditure of money in elections. Beginning with New

---

[1] Seth Low, "An American View of Municipal Government," Bryce, *American Commonwealth*, II, esp. 303; White, "Government of American Cities," 368-369.

[2] In the 1880's the New York legislature passed 390 acts amending the laws governing New York City and 189 relating to Brooklyn. Bryce in 1888 rated the New York and Pennsylvania legislatures as lowest in political morality while accounting those of Massachusetts, Vermont and several Mid-Western states as substantially "pure." *American Commonwealth*, II, 191, 519.

York in 1890, seventeen states adopted corrupt-practices
acts before the close of the century, and in 1897 three
states—Nebraska, Tennessee and Florida—expressly
prohibited contributions by corporations.[1] When all is
said and done, legislative corruption was the exception
rather than the rule. In the country as a whole, and notably in the new South, the political life of the states
had risen high above the moral ebb tide of postwar
years. The outpouring of legislation for educational and
humanitarian welfare attested a reassuring devotion on
the part of law makers to the public weal.

Even more so than the states, the national government had purged itself of the bribery and wrongdoing
which had come with the moral backwash of the Civil
War.[2] Though United States senators were still occasionally elected with a taint of corruption, as in the case
of Henry B. Payne of Ohio in 1884, the only major
scandal involving high federal officials was the belated
exposé of the Star Route frauds in the post-office department, dating from the Grant era. These cases, involving
among others the Republican ex-Senator S. W. Dorsey
of Arkansas, dragged through the courts from 1881 to
1884. While the principal rascals in some mysterious
way escaped prison, in Attorney-General B. H. Brew-
ster's opinion they might better have taken their punishment than face an aroused public opinion, the "objects
of scorn and aversion."[3]

The sharpened insistence upon public probity in the
nation's rulers was dramatically exemplified in the presi-

[1] Four states—Kansas, Nevada, Michigan and Ohio—quickly repealed
their laws. G. L. Fox, "Corrupt Practices and Election Laws in the
United States since 1890," Am. Polit. Sci. Assoc., Proceeds., II, 171-
172.
[2] See Allan Nevins, The Emergence of Modern America (A History
of American Life, VIII), chap. vii.
[3] E. P. Oberholtzer, A History of the United States since the Civil
War (N. Y., 1917, in progress), IV, 115-119, 132-140.

dential election of 1884.[1] The Republican candidate, James G. Blaine, nominated over the protests of the progressive members of his party, had a congressional record scarred by such dubious relations with privilege-seeking railway corporations that even his rare personal magnetism had not erased the memory of them. The Democrats, on the other hand, chose as their leader Grover Cleveland who, since leaving the mayoralty of Buffalo, had shown the same stubborn devotion to reform as governor of the state. By the precedents of earlier campaigns (that of 1876 excepted), the Democrats, still popularly tainted with Copperheadism and rebellion, had small chance for success. Party loyalty was a religion; and even Roosevelt and Lodge, who in the convention had fought Blaine's nomination to the last ditch, yielded him their support, though Roosevelt only after sulking for a time on his Dakota ranch.

Nevertheless an influential group of so-called Independents bolted the ticket and began an electioneering campaign which eventually covered most of the Northern states. The name of Cleveland, they declared in a public pronunciamento, "is the synonym of political courage and honesty and of administrative reform," while Blaine was "a representative of men, methods, and conduct which the public conscience condemns." [2] Stigmatized by the regulars as "Mugwumps," "dudes" and "assistant Democrats," the group included such highminded publicists as Carl Schurz, George W. Curtis, Francis A. Walker, E. L. Godkin and T. W. Higginson, and attracted the support of Republican newspapers in

[1] H. C. Thomas, *The Return of the Democratic Party to Power in 1884* (Columbia Univ., *Studies*, LXXXIX, no. 2), chaps. vi-x; Oberholtzer, *United States*, IV, 159-212; A. A. Lawrence, jr., Aspects of the Whispering Campaign of 1884 (unpublished seminar report, Harvard Univ.).

[2] *N. Y. Times*, July 23, 1884.

many of the leading cities. The Democrats, on their part, made their campaign slogan: "Public office is a public trust"—a precept which gained fresh cogency from the disclosure of additional letters bearing upon Blaine's tortuous financial dealings while speaker of the House.

Alarmed by such tactics, the Republican managers tried desperately to divert attention to other matters. Party orators resorted to the customary emotional appeal of "waving the bloody shirt." Meantime, efforts made to draw Irish Catholics from their Democratic allegiance—Cleveland being, it was said, a "Presbyterian bigot" while Blaine's mother was a Romanist—succeeded at least to the point of winning the fiery support of the *Irish World*, American organ of the Irish Land League.[1] "Agonize more and more on the tariff," Blaine implored his campaign associates, regardless of the fact that not on this or any other concrete policy did the opposing platforms present real differences.[2]

In their dilemma the Republicans gladly seized upon the whispers concerning Cleveland's personal character, which began to circulate shortly after his nomination. These rumors were first categorically spread before the public by the *Buffalo Evening Telegraph* on July 21. On the authority of the Reverend G. H. Ball, a Baptist minister of that city, Cleveland was charged with the "grossest licentiousness" and specifically with being the father of a seven-year-old bastard son whose mother he had tried vainly to keep locked up in an insane asylum. The friends of reform were struck with consternation. A group of Independent Republicans in Buffalo, after an investigation, admitted the fact of the liaison stripped of the embellishments of seduction and abduction, but

---

[1] Blaine was also supposed to have been notably active as secretary of state in safeguarding the interests of Irish Americans imprisoned in England.

[2] Royal Cortissoz, *The Life of Whitelaw Reid* (N. Y., 1921), II, 83.

repudiated the general charges of libertinism and drunkenness.[1] The Buffalo Association of Ministers divided, some asserting and others denying that the circumstances evinced Cleveland's unfitness for the presidency. The candidate himself, importuned by anxious friends, replied tersely, "Whatever you say, tell the truth." [2]

By this unexpected turn of events the conscientious citizen was confronted with a perplexing choice. The ultra-Republican *New York Tribune* felt confident the voters were not yet "so degraded" as to "care nothing for home, nothing for the attractiveness of domestic life, nothing for the offenses which the religious press so strongly censures." [3] So sure was the pious P. T. Barnum that no decent man could now vote for Cleveland that he offered a high price for the *rara avis* "provided I could make the people believe that the monster was real flesh and blood and not another humbug." [4] Under the impact of the "sickening disclosures" the *Independent*, a magazine under denominational auspices, hastily repented of its earlier advocacy, though later, in good conscience, it felt obliged to demand the withdrawal of both candidates. The religious press generally joined in the hue and cry against Cleveland while clergymen in all parts of the North ardently carried the "moral issue" into the pulpit. Even so staunch a Mugwump as Henry

[1] Committee of Independent Republicans of Buffalo, *The Charges Swept Away* (n.p., 1884). The Reverend Kinsley Twining of New York, quoted in the same pamphlet, commended Cleveland for "showing no attempt to evade responsibility, and doing all he could to meet the duties involved, of which marriage was certainly not one."

[2] There are grounds for believing that Cleveland's reply was more cryptic than candid. The child was apparently of doubtful paternity; it may or may not be significant that he was given the name of one of Cleveland's close friends, a married man. See edit., "What We Think About It Now," *Nation*, XXXIX, 106 (Aug. 7, 1884); Oberholtzer, *United States*, IV, 191, and citations; H. T. Peck, *Twenty Years of the Republic* (N. Y., 1906), 36.

[3] *Semi-Weekly Tribune*, Aug. 26, 1884.

[4] *Springfield Republican*, Aug. 7, 1884.

Ward Beecher wavered for a time, made wary perhaps by alleged sexual irregularities in his own past.[1]

With redoubled zeal the pro-Cleveland hosts insisted that the issue remained unchanged; that the test of public, not private, morality should be applied to the candidates. Asked why it was backing the Democrat, the *New York World* replied: "(1) He is an honest man. (2) He is an honest man. (3) He is an honest man. (4) He is an honest man . . . ."[2] The outcome of the election was very close. Cleveland carried the ordinarily doubtful states of Connecticut, New Jersey and Indiana by a few thousand votes each, and the pivotal state of New York by but 1149 out of a total of over a million votes. If he had lost New York, or if he had lost New Jersey and either of the other two states, Blaine would have won a majority in the electoral college and hence the presidency.

Many factors helped tip the scale for Cleveland: the current business depression, the lukewarmness of the old Republican Stalwart faction toward Blaine, the deflection of Republican votes into the Prohibition party, the estrangement of Irish Catholics by the "Rum, Romanism and Rebellion" remark made at an important Blaine rally.[3] But, in last analysis, the chief credit belongs to the reform hosts whose strength was greatest in those

[1] See Nevins, *Emergence of Modern America*, 227; Carl Schurz, *Speeches, Correspondence and Public Papers* (Frederic Bancroft, ed., N. Y., 1913), IV, 222; *Boston Transcript*, Aug. 6, 7, 1884. Washington Gladden and Felix Adler could not bring themselves to vote for either candidate. Gladden, *Recollections* (Boston, 1909), 316, 378; Adler, *The Ethics of the Political Situation* (n.p., 1884).

[2] *N. Y. World*, Sept. 22, 1884. The text of sexual morality, Godkin believed, "would have prevented Washington, Franklin, Jefferson, Hamilton, not to go any further, from taking any prominent part in the foundation of the American Republic." *Nation*, XXXIX, 106 (Aug. 7, 1884).

[3] This characterization of the Democracy was uttered by a Presbyterian clergyman in introducing Blaine. W. C. Hudson, *Random Recollections of an Old Political Reporter* (N. Y., 1911), 205-212; F. W. Mack,

states where the Republicans could least afford to lose support. Through their persistent campaign of education they had clarified the "moral issue" and induced a sufficient number of voters, as one of their leaders said, to "elect Mr. Cleveland to the public office which he is so admirably qualified to fill and remand Mr. Blaine to the private life which he is so eminently fitted to adorn."[1] The lesson of 1884 was not learned in vain. At no election later in the period did the leading parties present presidential candidates whose official rectitude was open to question.

Meantime the sentiment for governmental purity was waging war against another form of political vice, one which long-continued practice had endowed with a certain halo of respectability: the federal spoils system. In the course of time the spoils system had come to exhibit two glaring evils: first, the prostitution of the civil service to purely party ends and, second, the systematic exploitation of officeholders for campaign funds. Flagrant instances of incompetence and dishonesty in the public service since the Civil War, together with the high-pressure methods of Republican managers in raising a hundred thousand dollars from federal employees in 1878 and again in 1880, would in themselves have been enough to alarm the friends of good government. In addition, the assumption by the federal departments of a wide variety of new scientific and technical work emphasized the importance of safeguards such as had

"Rum, Romanism and Rebellion," *Harper's Wkly.*, XLVIII, 1140-1142 (July 23, 1904).

[1] Quoted in M. A. DeW. Howe, *Portrait of an Independent: Moorfield Storey* (Boston, 1932), 151. When the voters of Nebraska in the gubernatorial election of 1891 were presented with a somewhat similar option, they too elected the candidate of reform leanings, though his opponents had revealed his paternity of an illegitimate child. J. D. Barnhart, The History of the Farmers' Alliance and of the People's Party in Nebraska (unpublished Ph.D. thesis, Harvard Univ., 1930), 282-285.

recently been introduced so successfully into the English civil service.

The half-hearted attempts of Grant and the zealous devotion of President Hayes had done little to improve the situation, thanks to the bitter hostility of the pro-fessional politicians in Congress. Starting in 1877, civil-service-reform societies sprang up in many cities. *Harper's Weekly* and the *Nation* helped keep the issue alive, and the National Civil Service Reform League came into existence with George W. Curtis as president. But it was the assassination of President Garfield by a disap-pointed office seeker that shocked the public into an awareness of the real gravity of the evil.[1]

The new president, Chester A. Arthur, himself a notorious spoilsman before entering office, promptly championed the reform and Congress acceded in 1883 with the passage of the Pendleton act. Drafted by Dor-man B. Eaton of the Civil Service Reform League, this law provided for the creation of a bipartisan commission which should set up and administer a system of com-petitive examinations as a test of fitness for appointment to office. The new plan applied at once only to the ex-ecutive departments in Washington, the customhouses and the larger post offices,. and there only in the case of future vacancies. But the president was given dis-cretion to extend the "classified list," as it was called, to other groups of federal employees.[2]

Because of this elastic provision the act has rightly been termed the "Magna Charta of civil-service reform." When Arthur left the presidency nearly 16,000 offices out of a total of about 110,000 had been transferred to

---

[1] C. R. Fish, *The Civil Service and the Patronage* (*Harvard Historical Studies*, XI), chap. x; W. D. Foulke, *Fighting the Spoilsmen* (N. Y., 1919), chaps. iii-ix; Stewart, *National Civil Service Reform League*, 8-64.

[2] *U. S. Statutes at Large*, XXII, 403-407.

the classified list; and, influenced by the example of Washington, the New York and Massachusetts legislatures had adopted the plan for state positions. The accession of the job-hungry Democrats put an enormous pressure upon Cleveland to take a backward step. While appeasing "the d——d everlasting clatter for offices" mainly from the unclassified service, he quietly extended the merit system to nearly twelve thousand more places.[1] Later presidents followed more or less falteringly in his footsteps.[2] As a member of the civil-service commission from 1889 to 1895 Roosevelt kept alive public interest in the cause and made his name a source of real terror to the politicians of both parties. Curiously enough, the alternating party control of the presidency during these years had the effect of helping rather than hurting the reform since an outgoing administration might, through an eleventh-hour enlargement of the classified list, hope to continue its followers longer in office. This practice gave coinage to the saying, "To the vanquished belong the spoils."

The Pendleton act also sought to scotch the evil of campaign assessments. Federal officeholders were forbidden to solicit or receive, directly or indirectly, political contributions or assessments from one another, or to make such payments to other federal employees. Though an improvement over an earlier statute of 1876, the provision still contained too many loopholes to do away with the practice entirely and, of course, the prohibitions did not extend to state and local officeholders, whose salaries continued to furnish the main source of

[1] Robert McElroy, *Grover Cleveland* (N. Y., 1923), esp. I, 149; Thomas, *Return of Democratic Party*, 237-246.

[2] According to D. M. Matteson's figures in J. F. Rhodes, *History of the United States from Hayes to McKinley* (N. Y., 1919), 166 *n.*, Harrison added 10,535 places, Cleveland in his second term 38,961, and McKinley 3261.

funds in the lesser elections. But political requisitions in national politics after 1883 had to be managed in a manner not to offend public opinion, and the yield therefore was doubtless proportionately less.[1] Definite figures unfortunately are not available.

One untoward result of the statutory limitation upon assessments was the increasing dependence of the major parties upon business and banking interests for financial support.[2] This might have come about in any case, however, thanks to the high cost of reaching an electorate which was rapidly expanding in numbers and geographic extent. Moreover, the waning effectiveness of bloody-shirt tactics convinced Republican managers that a more elaborate presentation of issues must be undertaken, while the injection of economic questions into national politics suggested the sources from which the golden stream might be made to gush. Already well established as the party of conservative business, the Republicans took prompt advantage of the opening afforded by President Cleveland's message of 1887 in which he squarely committed his hitherto wabbling party to a low-tariff system.

In the ensuing presidential canvass, while spellbinders vaunted the "American system of protection" from every stump, the Philadelphia merchant John Wanamaker, who had had wide experience in raising money for the Y. M. C. A., quietly bestirred himself on behalf

---

[1] Yet, almost a quarter-century after the Pendleton law, the Civil Service Reform League asserted that during the campaign of 1904 "there is no possible doubt but that assessments have been levied on federal employees all over the country." John Carr, "Campaign Funds and Campaign Scandals," Outlook, LXXXI, 549 (Nov. 4, 1905).

[2] The size of the campaign funds in the successive elections is given in anon., "Cost of National Campaigns," World's Work, I (1900-1901), 77-80, and in the World Almanac for 1925, 185, citing the Wall Street Journal. The two lists differ in vital respects and, in view of the secrecy which cloaked such transactions, neither list may be correct.

of the party to collect the sinews of war from leading industrialists. "If you were confronted," he asked each of them, "with from one to three years of general depression by a change in our revenue and protective methods . . . , what would you pay to be insured for a better year?" [1] Funds rolled in to an amount variously estimated at from over $200,000 to $1,350,000. Though most of the money was doubtless devoted to legitimate campaign uses, the corruption of voters in Indiana, Connecticut, West Virginia and certain other close states was so bold and undisguised as to make the campaign of 1888 probably the most venal in American history.[2] Wanamaker himself was rewarded for his services with an office in President Harrison's cabinet.

While the Australian ballot system, adopted in most states before the next presidential contest, placed a curb upon direct bribery, the size of party war chests steadily grew as elections continued to turn upon questions of vital economic policy. Adult education directed by political schoolmasters, though expensive, proved increasingly important. As Republican manager in the free-silver campaign of 1896, the Ohio capitalist Marcus A. Hanna secured contributions of unprecedented size from business corporations, insurance companies and men of wealth and actually levied an assessment of one fourth of one per cent on the capital and surplus of leading banks.[3] The audited account shows that the national committee collected no less than $3,500,000, thus making the election of William McKinley the costliest yet

[1] Herbert Welsh, "Publicity as a Cure for Corruption," *Forum*, XIV (1892-1893), 29-30.

[2] F. A. Ogg, "The Dollars behind the Ballots," *World To-Day*, XV (1908), 947-948. Harrison was "the first American President who has obtained his office by open venality," declared a *Nation* editorial, LV, 252 (Oct. 6, 1892).

[3] Herbert Croly, *Marcus Alonzo Hanna* (N. Y., 1912), 218-221; *Congressional Record*, XL, pt. vi, 5366 ff.

held. Oddly enough, the efforts of Bryan to destroy the gold standard brought the Democratic party capitalistic support also, in the form of several hundred thousand contributed by silver-mining interests.[1] Though, as we have seen, the states were beginning to regulate expenditures in their own elections, similar action by Congress had to await the prod of the progressive movement early in the next century.[2]

While these years are generally envisaged as years of Republican supremacy, a glance beneath the surface discloses how slender was that party's hold upon the electorate. Not only did the Republicans after 1880 fail to occupy the White House for longer than a single term at a stretch, but neither they nor the Democrats controlled both the presidency and the two legislative branches for more than two years at a time. Harrison in 1888, under the curious workings of the electoral-college system, attained victory with a smaller popular support than that accorded Cleveland. Of all the successful aspirants, Republican or Democratic, McKinley alone, in the last election of the period, commanded a clear majority of the popular ballots.

The restoration of the two-party system, foreshadowed by the contest of 1876, was due partly to the growing up of a new generation of voters in the North, partly also to the unwavering support given the Democrats by the ex-Confederate states after the restoration of white supremacy. The "Solid South" in the election of 1880, for instance, cast a bloc of ninety-five electoral votes out of a total of three hundred and sixty-nine. To this irreducible minimum might ordinarily be added the

[1] According to the *N. Y. Herald*, Sept. 7, Oct. 21, 1896, Moffat of Denver gave $100,000, Straton of Helena $50,000, and Clark of Montana $70,000.

[2] See acts of 1907, 1910 and 1911. *U. S. Statutes at Large*, XXXV, 1103-1104; XXXVI, 822-824; XXXVII, 25-29.

electoral votes of the former border slave states—Missouri, Kentucky, Maryland and Delaware—amounting in that year to thirty-five.

The nice poise of parties explains both the strategic importance of the Independent movement in the eighties and the spleen of faithful party men against its leaders. The Mugwumps were, even to Roosevelt, "perverse lunatics," while Godkin of the *Nation,* their most distinguished spokesman, was nothing less than a "malignant and dishonest liar." [1] This situation, too, proved a constant spur to the formation of minor parties which, if they could not hope to sweep the nation, might at least aspire to seize the balance of power. No presidential canvass occurred without at least three of them in the field. In 1892 the People's party, by uniting the malcontents of countryside and city, actually cast a large enough vote to frighten the Democratic convention into vital concessions in the next campaign.

In the hectic scramble for votes Republican spellbinders fought the Civil War over in election after election, exhorting their Northern audiences to vote as they had shot. Every presidential candidate of the party was a war veteran except Blaine, and Blaine's running mate possessed the requisite qualification. What was even more to the point, when in power they dispensed pensions with lordly extravagance and thus consolidated the old-soldier vote of the North in their support.

While the Democrats could not hope to equal this aspect of the Republican record and Cleveland's many pension vetoes counted heavily against them, they enjoyed a decided advantage in dealing with the naturalized voters, particularly the Irish who were traditionally of their fold and politically effective in the great urban

---

[1] *Selections from the Correspondence of Theodore Roosevelt and Henry Cabot Lodge* (N. Y., 1925), I, 39, 74.

centers.[1] Blaine's efforts to break this alliance, though a failure in 1884, caused Republican managers as the years passed to give less attention to "waving the bloody shirt" and more to "twisting the lion's tail," the latter a sure bid for Hibernian favor. In the next two campaigns the Republicans disparaged the Democrats as "British free traders," and in 1888 gave wide publicity to a letter, which the British minister at Washington had been tricked into writing, advising a supposed former fellow countryman to vote for Cleveland as the better president for Great Britain.[2] In both campaigns the two parties blithely disregarded the three-mile limit by adopting platform declarations for home rule for Ireland. Nor were more recent racial accessions overlooked, as is indicated by the planks in 1892 condemning anti-Semitic persecution in Russia.

With the parties so evenly matched, political managers left no stone unturned to poll their full voting strength. Much of the increased campaign expenditures went into providing meetings, bands, parades, picnics, barbecues and other means of rekindling old party loyalties. Particularly in the rural regions, politics accordingly took the place of "the opera-house, the theatre, the club, . . . the foreign tour, the summer sport, the dinner-party, the institute, and one may almost say the church."[3] In the poorer quarters of the great cities a similar method was employed by machine politicians to solidify their following. Among Alfred E. Smith's most cherished youthful memories were the holiday parades, the prize shooting contests and summer out-

[1] Anon., "Power of the Irish in American Cities," *Littell's Living Age*, CLXXI (1886), 382-384; Patrick Ford, "The Irish Vote in the Presidential Election," *N. Am. Rev.*, CXLVII (1888), 185-190; H. C. Merwin, "The Irish in American Life," *Atlantic Mo.*, LXXVII (1896), esp. 296-298.

[2] *Appletons' Annual Cyclopaedia*, XXVIII (1888), 269.

[3] Anon., "Two Journalists," *Atlantic Mo.*, LII (1883), 415.

ings provided for East Side families by "Big Tim" Sullivan and other Tammany henchmen.[1]

Thanks to the hot competition for electoral support,
four out of every five eligible voters cast their ballots in
each presidential election of the period, and this in spite
of the steady decline of the Negro vote in the South.[2]
Never since has so large a proportion of the electorate
taken part. European visitors were constantly surprised
at the good-natured acquiescence in the outcome of
fiercely fought contests. Muirhead believed that the
American sense of humor provided the necessary safety
valve.[3] Even more ingenious was the suggestion that the
passion for competitive sport was teaching the people
to be good losers and to abide by the rules of the game.[4]
But probably much more influential was a deep-rooted
habit reaching back to the beginnings of the republic and
violated but once—in 1860—then to the irreparable
injury of all concerned.

The most striking political phenomenon of the times,
the exaltation of national at the expense of state power,
had little relation to the fortunes of party. It was due,
rather, to a new sentiment of national unity which
began to tide through American life as soon as Lee's
surrender determined that the United States was to
remain a geographic entity. Its force was increased by
the notable growth of business and capital across state
borders and the multiplying contacts resulting from im-

[1] A. E. Smith, *Up to Now* (N. Y., 1929), 29-33. See also H. C.
Brown, *New York in the Elegant Eighties* (*Valentine's Manual of Old
New York*, XI, Hastings-on-Hudson, 1926), 243-249; same author,
In the Golden Nineties (same ser., XII, Hastings-on-Hudson, 1927),
300-305.

[2] A. M. Schlesinger and E. M. Eriksson, "The Vanishing Voter,"
New Republic, XL, 162-167 (Oct. 15, 1924).

[3] J. F. Muirhead, *The Land of Contrasts* (Boston, 1898), 140-141.

[4] L. S. Bryce, "A Plea for Sport," *N. Am. Rev.*, CXXVIII (1879),
esp. 523-524. See also W. J. Shepard, "The Psychology of the Bi-Party
System," *Social Forces*, IV, 795-804.

proved means of travel and communication.[1] By the
1880's it was rushing at full torrent through all the
channels of American thought and action. One of the
most impressive spontaneous manifestations of the new
spirit was the Vesuvian energy which went into the
formation of voluntary nation-wide bodies, not only of
trade unionists and business men but also, as we have
seen, of scholars, scientists, artists, professional men,
social and political reformers, sport lovers and members
of secret fraternal orders. Nothing equaling it had been
known before in America or anywhere else in the world.
In a quite different way the fading of local loyalties led
in 1883 to the adoption of a scheme of standard time
for the entire country. Without awaiting action by the
general government the railways took the initiative and
local communities and states fell quickly into step.[2]

The heightened sense of national pride was nourished
by the succession of patriotic celebrations which clustered about the opening of a second century of Independence. Beginning with the centenary of Concord and
Lexington in 1875, no year passed without one or more
such jubilees, until in 1889 and 1890 the inauguration
of President Washington and the setting up of the
Supreme Court were commemorated with due pomp and
circumstance. Everybody was "centennializing himself,
and looking over his shoulder to catch a glimpse of the
century behind him in the mirror which he held." [3]
Those who were in a position to do so sought to garner
the unearned increment of ancestral reputations by banding together in patriotic-hereditary societies. Among the

[1] For contemporary comment on the new nationalism, see anon., "The
Strong Government Idea," *Atlantic Mo.*, XLV (1880), 273-277; and
Bryce, *American Commonwealth*, II, 188-190; III, 649-650, 652.

[2] R. E. Riegel, "Standard Time in the United States," *Am. Hist. Rev.*,
XXXIII, 84-89.

[3] R. Fellow, "American History on the Stage," *Atlantic Mo.*, L
(1882), 309.

more influential of such bodies, dating from the late eighties and the nineties, were the Sons of the American Revolution, the Daughters of the American Revolution, the Colonial Dames, the Society of Colonial Wars, the Society of the War of 1812, the Society of Mayflower Descendants and the Order of Indian Wars.

But no phase of the nationalizing process so clearly revealed the deep spiritual wells which fed it as the change effected in the attitude of South and North toward each other. Crushed on the battle-field, only to be subjected to the searing humiliation of Reconstruction, the Southern people were never allowed to forget their past acts either by their own partisan zealots or by Republican demagogues in the North. Yet forces beyond the politicians' ken were steadily obliterating old rancors and misunderstandings and weaving the once broken strands into a new and firmer fabric of nationality. A fresh generation was coming of age that had no memory of the Civil War. The recurrent centennial celebrations helped by focusing attention upon that remoter past when South and North had fought as brethren in a common cause. At the centenary of Bunker Hill, for example, General Fitzhugh Lee spoke from the same platform as General W. T. Sherman and both sounded the same note of patriotism and reconciliation.[1] The Yorktown celebration in 1881 called forth the eloquent plea of James Barron Hope:

> Give us back the ties of Yorktown!
> Perish all the modern hates!
> Let us stand together, brothers,
> In defiance of the Fates;
> For the safety of the Union
> Is the safety of the States![2]

[1] *Boston Transcript*, June 16-18, 1875.

[2] J. B. Hope, *Arms and the Man* (Norfolk, Va., 1882), 70. For James Whitcomb Riley's poems on the reconciliation theme, see *Com-*

In the same year veterans' organizations of both armies met together, for the first time, for the express purpose of rejoicing that they were no longer foes. Such occasions, repeated with increasing frequency, reached a happy climax in 1888 in the great spectacle commemorating the twenty-fifth anniversary of the battle of Gettysburg.[1] Three years earlier both Union and Confederate soldiers had joined at Grant's funeral in a notable tribute to their military brother.

Other circumstances conspired to the same end. As the Northern manufacturing system extended southward, fundamental economic antagonisms began to disappear, new ties of interest emerge. Atlanta, Chattanooga and Durham were the outposts of a new nationalism as well as of a new industrialism. Northern willingness to let the South manage its own race relations, another important factor in healing the breach, rested in final analysis upon the nationalization of the Southern economic order. Senator Don Cameron of Pennsylvania spoke for the dominant group of his party when he denounced the proposed force bill of 1890 as certain to disturb the "community of commercial interests" resulting from the flow of Northern capital into Dixie and the growth of manufactures there.[2] Nor did the turn of Southern agriculture toward small farming and the growth of agrarian unrest fail to create new bonds with the rest of the country. Such influences were strengthened by Northern migrants settling in the South for business or health reasons, and by the increasing number of young Southerners frequenting Northern educational institutions or finding employment in that section.[3]

plete Works (Indianapolis, 1913), II, 466-467; IV, 25-26.
[1] G. L. Kilmer, "A Note of Peace: Reunions of 'the Blue and the Gray,'" *Century*, XXXVI (1888), 440-442.
[2] *Public Opinion*, IX (1890), 428.
[3] Florida had so many Northern health seekers that already by 1889

Northern opinion was perhaps even more greatly mollified by the novel and somewhat romantic view of Southern character and ideals afforded by the local-color writers. To untold numbers of fiction readers Hopkinson Smith's Colonel Carter became a more credible bit of portraiture than Mrs. Stowe's Simon Legree, while even Uncle Tom was eclipsed by the loving regard accorded Uncle Remus. In the theater few plays aroused greater enthusiasm than those which, like "Shenandoah" and "The Heart of Maryland," gave dramatic form to the theme of love triumphant over sectional barriers. Of great importance, too, particularly in Dixie, was the influence exerted by certain Southern editors and publicists who, in season and out, kept exhorting their people to look forward, not backward—such men as the educator J. L. M. Curry, A. G. Haygood of Emory College, Henry Watterson of the *Louisville Courier-Journal* and Henry W. Grady of the *Atlanta Constitution*. Yet Watterson felt, after seeing Augustus Thomas's play "Alabama" in 1891, that it "had done more to reconcile the two sections . . . than his editorials had accomplished in twenty years." [1]

Southerners could not be denied the privilege of dwelling fondly upon the "lost cause," but nearly every year brought fresh evidence of their satisfaction that the cause was indeed lost. In a Thanksgiving Day address in 1880 President Haygood declared he spoke for the "vast majority of our people" in saying, "I, for one, thank

it was "scarcely a Southern State except in climate." C. D. Warner, *Studies in the South and West* (N. Y., 1889), 37. On the other hand, according to the *St. Paul Pioneer Press*, Sept. 1, 1879, Southerners were beginning again to crowd Minnesota summer resorts. In 1890-1891 nearly 700 Southern students were attending Northern colleges. U. S. Commissioner of Education, *Report for 1890-91*, II, 822-826.

[1] A. H. Quinn, *A History of the American Drama from the Civil War* (N. Y., 1927), I, 245. See also F. P. Gaines, *The Southern Plantation* (Columbia Univ., *Studies in English and Comparative Literature*; N. Y., 1924), 113-114, 117-119, 122-125.

God that there is no longer slavery in these United
States!" [1] The following year Jefferson Davis, former
president of the Confederacy, concluded his two-volume
apologia with the earnest wish that "there may be written on the arch of the Union, *Esto perpetua.*" [2] The
election of a president in 1884, backed by the solid vote
of the South, reassured that section of its political equality in the Union, while the character of Cleveland's
administration reassured the country as to the loyalty
and national outlook of the former rebel party.[3]

The coming of the war with Spain drowned the last
faint notes of discord in an exultant chorus of patriotism. The well-known ex-Confederate cavalry leader,
General Joseph Wheeler, promptly proffered his sword,
and a song bard, catching the spirit of the hour, set the
nation to singing, "He laid away a suit of gray to wear
the Union blue." [4] In the surge of sentiment Congress
expunged from the statute books the remaining disabilities imposed upon Confederate leaders by the Fourteenth
Amendment.[5] The lightning flash of war had made the
people suddenly aware of the miracle that had been hap-

[1] A. G. Haygood, *The New South* (Oxford, Ga., 1880), 11. See also
his *Our Brother in Black* (Oxford, 1881), chap. v; J. B. Gordon and
C. C. Jones, jr., *The Old South. Addresses Delivered before the Confederate Survivors' Association* (Augusta, Ga., 1887), 9; Warner,
Studies, 101; W. F. Tillett, "Southern Womanhood as Affected by
the War," *Century,* XLIII (1891-1892), 13-15; J. L. M. Curry,
Address before the Association of Confederate Veterans (Richmond, Va.,
1896), 23; J. S. Wise, *The End of an Era* (Boston, 1899), 88.

[2] Jefferson Davis, *The Rise and Fall of the Confederate Government*
(N. Y., 1881), II, 774.

[3] A. K. McClure, *The South: Its Industrial, Financial, and Political
Condition* (Phila., 1886), 53-54; Warner, *Studies,* 3-4; B. J. Hen-
drick, *The Life and Letters of Walter H. Page* (Garden City, 1922),
I, 41.

[4] It was rivaled by Paul Dresser's "The Blue and the Gray," first
copyrighted in 1890 but not accorded popular favor until reissued in
1898 with appropriate references to the Cuban war. Brown, *Golden
Nineties,* 174; J. T. Howard, *Our American Music* (N. Y., 1931), 582.

[5] *U. S. Statutes at Large,* XXX, 432.

"YANKEE DOODLE!!"

In the Spanish War President McKinley found hearty support in North and South alike.

The Blue and Gray United

pening under their very eyes. As one newspaper rhyme-
ster wrote,

One thing'd make this war wuth while, 'f we hed no other
    reason,
An' to yer Uncle Sam, I swaow, th' fac' is mighty pleasin';
It's good ter free th' Cubans; it's good ter lick the Spanish;
It's better far ter make th' hate 'twixt North an' Saouth ter
    vanish.[1]

Within the span of a single generation the foemen of
1861 had become comrades in spirit as well as in name.

New horizons, new attachments of interest, new
views, new men—these account for the strong centripetal trend in government, which shaped the policies of
both major parties. Extreme tariff protection, lavish
grants for river and harbor improvement, increasing
restrictions upon immigration and the Sherman law
against trusts were Republican contributions toward
national consolidation. Nor did the Democrats, who
when out of power liked to complain of "Cæsarism"
and "centralizationism," show by their conduct in office
any considerable regard for the once hallowed state
rights. The interstate-commerce act of 1887, which
Cleveland signed, embodied a startling assumption of
national authority. When later he defied the traditional
reading of the Constitution by sending troops to Chicago during the Pullman strike of 1894, Governor J. P.
Altgeld of Illinois felt obliged to remind him that "the
principle of local self-government is just as fundamental
in our institutions as is that of Federal supremacy."[2]

---

[1] C. B. Loomis, "When North and South Unite," taken from a scrapbook of the Spanish-American War compiled by F. D. Stiles of South
Hanson, Mass. Similar rhymed rejoicings may be found in S. A. Wither-
bee, comp., *Spanish-American War Songs* (Detroit, 1898), 8-9.

[2] Cleveland later alluded to Altgeld's "rather dreary discussion of the
importance of preserving the rights of the States." McElroy, *Cleveland*,
II, 158-162.

Political conflicts no longer turned upon the constitutional question as to how much authority the general government possessed, but rather upon the alternative uses to which the expanded powers should be put. If certain minor parties had had their way, centralization would have been carried to the point of the national ownership of railways and telegraphs and a national ban upon the drink habit. Indeed, sectional and class demands usually took the form of a purpose to interpose federal authority for the protection of minority rights. The judiciary mirrored the same tendency. Under a law of 1875 the volume of federal business was greatly augmented at the cost of the state courts, while, in a series of decisions qualifying the judgment in Munn *v.* Illinois (1876), the Supreme Court gradually assumed the high function of reviewing all state legislation regulating the use of property and labor.[1] As a thoughtful contemporary admitted, "the general government now exercises authority which the stoutest Federalist of 1789 would have shuddered to foresee, yet does this with the approval of all." [2]

With the enhanced nationalism at home came a corresponding change of attitude toward internationalism. Traditional taboos continued to be mouthed by statesmen, but in countless respects the old hermitlike fear of Europe began to wane. A confident sense of national strength and well-being, of national fulfillment in scholarship, art and technology, made it possible for Americans to meet the gaze of the world with steadier nerves, to speak less often in tones edged with that boastfulness which in the past had so frequently cloaked

[1] Felix Frankfurter and J. M. Landis, *The Business of the Supreme Court* (N. Y., 1928), chap. ii; Charles Warren, *The Supreme Court in United States History* (Boston, 1922), III, esp. 344-429.

[2] E. B. Andrews, "Money as an International Question," *Atlantic Mo.,* LXXI (1893), 543.

an inner feeling of deficiency.[1] As the United States became more urbanized, American political and social problems became more and more like those of Western Europe, and civic leaders turned increasingly to the Old World for guidance in coping with conditions unprecedented in their own experience.

The cosmopolitan spirit was most deeply implanted in the intellectual classes, for many of the foremost men in education and the arts had spent their adolescent years in European centers of study. Nevertheless all sections of society were touched with a new sense of world community if only as a backwash from the growth of missionary activities in the remoter regions of the globe.[2] When the Russian people faced a terrible famine in 1891, the farmers of Iowa and other Western states supported the efforts of the Red Cross by sending carloads of corn, and the fraternal order of the Elks defrayed a large part of the cost of transportation. Five years later Miss Barton was directing relief work in Armenia, a labor of mercy made possible by the subscription of over one hundred thousand American dollars.[3]

Meantime, the business classes were looking beyond the national borders for new openings for trade and investment. The industrial progress of the country was beginning to produce a surplus of goods and capital which, by an imperious law of business enterprise, must be made to produce more goods and more capital. With increasing frequency from the 1880's on, American consuls in far parts of the world reported the capture of new trophies by Yankee *entrepreneurs:* now the launch-

[1] The decline of the national habit of bragging was noted, among others, by Bryce, *American Commonwealth*, III, 540, 573, 659, and Muirhead, *Land of Contrasts*, 78-79.
[2] J. S. Dennis, *Centennial Survey of Foreign Missions* (N. Y., 1902), 9-16, 279-293.
[3] Corra Bacon-Foster, *Clara Barton, Humanitarian* (Wash., 1918), 37, 48.

ing of a telephone company in Rio de Janeiro; now the construction of a railroad in Colombia; now mining enterprises in Honduras; now the establishment of branch insurance agencies in New Zealand or the ownership of sugar plantations in Hawaii or Cuba.[1] By the close of the period the chief of the United States bureau of foreign commerce asserted: "The 'international isolation' of the United States so far as industry and commerce are concerned, has, in fact, been made a thing of the past by the logic of the change in our economic requirements, and we can no longer afford to disregard international rivalries, now that we ourselves have become a competitor in the world-wide struggle for trade." [2]

It is not surprising therefore that the American government found itself drawn increasingly into the world stream of affairs. The nation was officially represented in a succession of foreign expositions and, as a matter of course, coöperated in various international scientific inquiries, such as the polar expeditions of 1882-1883 and the simultaneous observation of basic weather phenomena conducted during the late seventies and early eighties throughout the northern hemisphere.[3] Following the general adoption of standard time in America,

[1] *U. S. Commercial Relations for 1880-1881*, 612; *for 1885-1886*, II, 1124; *for 1884-1885*, II, 918; *for 1882-1883*, II, 799; *Hawaiian Almanac and Annual for 1894*, 40-41; Perfecto Lacoste, *Opportunities in the Colonies and Cuba* (N. Y., 1902), 268. These citations were kindly supplied by Mr. H. R. Bartlett of the Massachusetts Institute of Technology.

[2] *Review of the World's Commerce for 1896-1897*, 22. At about that date America's foreign investments totaled more than half a billion dollars, an amount considerably less, of course, than that of European investments in the United States. R. W. Dunn, *American Foreign Investments* (N. Y., 1926), 2.

[3] Six foreign expositions and many international scientific conferences, 1878-1898, are listed in *Check List of United States Documents, 1789-1909* (Wash., 1911), I, 944-953. See also J. C. Faries, *The Rise of Internationalism* (N. Y., 1915), chaps. iii-v.

the state department in 1884 called a conference of twenty-seven nations to recommend a universal prime meridian for the reckoning of both longitude and time. Upon at least four other occasions the United States initiated international conferences to consider the bimetallic standard.

Even more indicative perhaps were the commitments involved in the signing of various multilateral treaties and pacts. In the two decades eight were ratified as compared with one in all the years before. They dealt with a wide range of nonpolitical interests of growing world concern.[1] Besides accepting the Geneva convention for establishing the Red Cross, the United States agreed to common action in such matters as weights and measures, patents and trademarks, suppression of the African slave trade and the interchange of official and learned publications. Tentative ventures were also made in the troubled waters of international politics. The United States not only joined with European powers in a treaty with Morocco in 1880, but nine years later found herself somewhat unexpectedly involved with Great Britain and Germany in a tripartite protectorate over Samoa—an "entangling alliance" in whatever sense that phrase be understood.[2]

Meanwhile America's expanding interests were fruiting in the acquisition of a few score guano islands in two oceans, the modernization of the navy and the securing of strategic naval stations in the Pacific. In 1893 a revolution in Hawaii, fomented by American interests, would have resulted in prompt annexation but for the grim refusal of Cleveland, which, however, merely delayed the final outcome. Nationalism, crossed

[1] W. M. Malloy, comp., *Treaties, Conventions, International Acts, Protocols and Agreements* (Wash., 1910), II, 1903-2005.

[2] J. B. Henderson, *American Diplomatic Questions* (N. Y., 1901), pt. iii.

by a sort of bastard internationalism, was begetting an American counterpart of the much decried European imperialism. The Spanish war merely hastened a process already well under way. The annexation of insular dependencies was less a new departure than a consummation.[1]

In reviewing the multifarious trends in government one is impressed by the close correlation of political action with social, economic and intellectual forces. The imposing façade of party hid more realities than it disclosed. Nor is it possible to arrive at any satisfactory balance of profit and loss in the political life of the day. The leaders of the time did, indeed, succeed in curing some of the worst evils which had been visited upon them by the sins of their fathers, but they permitted others to arise which were to make their successors despair of the safety of the republic.

[1] See Faulkner, *Quest for Social Justice*, 308-314.

CHAPTER XIII

FIN DE SIÈCLE

THROUGHOUT the 1890's the people of the United States were deeply imbued with the feeling that the greatest of centuries was drawing to a close. Nor was this feeling confined to the American side of the Atlantic. In France the sense of destiny fulfilling itself was compacted into the phrase *fin de siècle*. Early in the nineties the expression found its way into English newspapers and, by this channel, quickly reached the United States where, as Henry Adams tells us, "during this last decade every one talked, and seemed to feel *fin-de-siècle*." [1] To the fashionable and the light-minded the phrase denoted ultramodernism—an anticipation of the latest mode in artistic decoration and personal adornment, a new orgy of extravagance in manners and social entertainment. [2] To the humanitarians and reformers in general it meant a final opportunity to cure the abuses and injustices which a heedless society had permitted to appear. To the toilers these closing years afforded fresh hope and a desperate purpose to solve the staggering problems which beset them both in factory and on farm.

[1] Henry Adams, *The Education of Henry Adams* (Boston, 1918), 331. After accounting for the origin of the phrase a contemporary writer says: "Everywhere we are treated to dissertations on fin-de-siècle literature, fin-de-siècle statesmanship, fin-de-siècle morality." "Contributors' Club," *Atlantic Mo.*, LXVII (1891), 859-860.

[2] The philosophy of fashionable boredom is amusingly depicted in Edmund Vance Cooke's poem, "Fin de Siècle," which was set to music and introduced into Hoyt's farce, "A Night in New York." E. V. Cooke, *Rimes to Be Read* (rev. edn., N. Y., 1905), 67-69.

Life in America had never before been so complex.
An introverted personality like Henry Adams's, out of
key with the times, continually sought escape by flight—
to the South Seas, Cuba, the Yellowstone, Mexico, Russia, Egypt, Normandy—only to be drawn back each
time, fascinated and repelled by a sense of new energies
astir in human fate, comparable in his own day to the
will exerted on an earlier mankind by the Virgin. "We
call ourselves the masters of machinery: are we quite
sure that machinery is not mastering us?" wondered
Josiah Strong.[1] "Our industry is a fight of every man
for himself," warned Henry Demarest Lloyd, who saw
the vaunted American gospel of equality yielding "incalculable power and pleasure for a few, and partial existence for the many who are the fountains of these
powers and pleasures." [2] "The huge, rushing, aggregate
life of a great city," complained another, ". . . cur-
tails man of his wholeness, specializes him, quickens
some powers, stunts others . . . ." [3] A cloistered scholar
deplored the increasing demands placed upon the educated man: "He must be familiar with magnetism as well
as mythology, with evolution as well as elegiacs, with
geology as well as genesis." [4] Once it had been easy to
be human, Professor Wilson observed, but now "haste,
anxiety, preoccupation, the need to specialize and make
machines of ourselves have transformed the once simple
world . . . ." [5] "Do you really think the 'game pays for
the candle'?" queried a publicist. "I get yearly more

[1] Josiah Strong, *Expansion under New World Conditions* (N. Y.,
1900), 72-73.
[2] H. D. Lloyd, *Wealth against Commonwealth* (N. Y., 1894), 7,
494.
[3] Woodrow Wilson, "On Being Human," *Atlantic Mo.*, LXXX
(1897), 322.
[4] J. J. Greenough, "The Basis of Our Educational System," *Atlantic
Mo.*, LXXV (1895), 530.
[5] Wilson, "On Being Human," 321.

tired of what we call civilization. It seems to me a preposterous fraud." [1]

The attrition of town on country continued with un-
abated force. The unbroken frontier was gone and, as
Professor Turner pointed out in his memorable address
of 1893, "with its going has closed the first period of
American history." [2] Yet the impetus to Western settlement was not yet spent, and a seventh state now joined
the six admitted to the Union in 1889 and 1890. Utah
had been denied the privilege for more than a decade
because of the continuance of polygamy. By 1890, however, Mormons and non-Mormons had become about
equal in numbers, mutual business advantage was dissolving religious prejudices, and the nation through
recent acts of Congress had announced its implacable
purpose to stamp out the hated practice. [3] Making a virtue of necessity, Wilford Woodruff, head of the church,
on September 30 openly pledged his personal influence
in behalf of enforcing the antipolygamy statutes, while
the general conference of the church a few weeks later
unanimously indorsed his stand. [4]

The sincerity of this action was widely questioned;
but aside from evidence showing the unwillingness of
husbands to abandon family obligations already contracted, there could be no doubt that polygamy had been
dealt a death blow. [5] In local politics the People's or

[1] Quoted by D. A. Wells, *Recent Economic Changes* (N. Y., 1889),
325.

[2] F. J. Turner, *The Frontier in American History* (N. Y., 1920), 38.

[3] See earlier, 46.

[4] *Latter-day Saints' Millennial Star*, LII (1890), 648, 721-725, 737-
741, 744-745, 753-757.

[5] Glen Miller, "Will Polygamists Control the New State of Utah?,"
Forum, XVIII (1894-1895), 466-467; anon., "Is Polygamy Prac-
tised?," *Home Mission Mo.*, XV (1901), 279-280; W. M. Raine and
A. W. Dunn, "Mormon or Patriot," *Leslie's*, LIX (1905), 537-547;
Theodore Schroeder, "Polygamy and the Constitution," *Arena*, XXXVI
(1906), 492-497.

Mormon party and the Liberal or Gentile party disbanded to reorganize along national political lines. In 1893 President Harrison granted amnesty to such violators of the Edmunds law as had since November 1, 1890, abstained from unlawful cohabitation, while Congress restored the escheated property and funds to the church.[1] Nothing now stood in the way of statehood but the jockeying of the politicians in Washington for party advantage. In 1896 Utah was admitted into the Union upon the "irrevocable" condition that "polygamy or plural marriages are forever prohibited."[2]

In another part of the West the status of Oklahoma continued somewhat uncertain as the decade began. Opened under spectacular circumstances to homesteaders in 1889, the district lay entirely surrounded by Indian country and the people remained without proper governmental provision. In 1890, however, Congress authorized the formation of the territory of Oklahoma to include, besides the original district, No Man's Land and such additional lands as the tribes might be induced to part with.[3] New tracts were opened from time to time, attended, as in 1889, by frantic rushes of settlers. By 1898 virtually all the region outside of the area held by the Five Civilized Tribes was occupied.[4] The population had grown meantime from sixty-two thousand in 1890 to three hundred and eleven thousand in 1898. The achievement of statehood awaited the coming of the new century.

[1] *U. S. Statutes at Large*, XXVII, 1058; XXVIII, 980, 1257; XXIX, 758.

[2] *U. S. Statutes at Large*, XXVIII, 107-112; XXIX, 461, 876-877.

[3] *U. S. Statutes at Large*, XXVI, 80-100. See also earlier, 47-50.

[4] S. J. Buck, "The Settlement of Oklahoma," Wis. Acad., *Trans.*, XV, 355-366; Helen C. Candee, "Social Conditions in Our Newest Territory," *Forum*, XXV (1898), 426-437; F. E. Sutton and A. B. Macdonald, "Hands Up!," *Sat. Eve. Post*, CXCVIII, 32 ff. (April 24, 1926).

The West in the *fin de siècle,* however, was less concerned with attracting new settlers than with the problem of adjusting its life to a national political and social order regulated by the people of the Eastern cities. Agrarian leaders, zealous in treating symptoms, talked cheap money, lower transportation rates, the curbing of Wall Street and big business; but behind their bill of particulars lay something less tangible and often unacknowledged: a deepening sense of frustration and defeat. The men, women and children who gathered in ten thousand schoolhouses to debate the farmers' grievances in the early 1890's had only vague notions about the intricacies of the free-silver question and its relation to prices and prosperity, but they were grimly aware that mysterious new forces in American life were robbing them of their traditional rural heritage of freedom and spiritual and material well-being.

During the decade the western and central parts of Kansas, Nebraska and South Dakota declined in population, as did also eastern Colorado, a third of the state of Nevada and eleven counties of California. Similar losses occurred in northern New England and in the backward agricultural parts of New York, Pennsylvania, Ohio and Michigan.[1] The land of promise was no longer the land of performance unless one joined the backward trail toward the East, as more and more of the ambitious youth of the countryside were doing each year. As the decade proceeded, the nation grew steadily more urbanized, the number of cities with four thousand or more inhabitants advancing from less than nine thousand to nearly twelve and the proportion of urban dwellers from one third of the total to approximately two fifths.[2]

[1] *Supplementary Analysis and Derivative Tables* (U. S. Twelfth Census, *Special Rep.*), 44-45, 277.
[2] *U. S. Twelfth Census* (1900), I, lxxxiv-lxxxv.

In a Farmers' Alliance campaign song a rural youth
pleads with his father, before it is too late, to cast his
ballot for farmers' rights:

> Free land will be gone and naught else can I do
> But be to the rich man a slave.

When the father accedes the lad rejoices:

> I'll have clothes like the rich boys in town.[1]

Yet the bulk of city wage-earners were equally irked
by their lot. While millionaires raised up their gaudy
palaces and Ward McAllister led society into ever more
extravagant revels, the masses toiled long hours in factory and office, returning at length to their frugal abodes
embittered or benumbed. Industrial outbreaks occurred
with increasing frequency and destructiveness. The Panic
of 1893 cast a deep black shadow across their lives.
Presently began the tramp of the unemployed from all
parts of the country upon Washington, a veritable petition in boots whose inglorious ending did not hide the
gravity of the conditions which had given it rise.[2] James
Whitcomb Riley's friend, Eugene V. Debs, jailed in Chicago in 1894 for his activities during the Pullman strike,
read socialist tracts in his enforced leisure and dedicated
himself to the gospel of the abolition of capitalism.
Meanwhile Hamlin Garland and other intellectuals
pinned their faith to Henry George's panacea of the single tax. Still others, lingering fondly over Bellamy's
utopian dream, banded together in so-called Nationalist
Clubs.[3]

[1] Luna E. Kellie, "Vote for Me," *Farmers' Alliance* (Lincoln, Neb.),
Sept. 6, 1890, quoted by J. D. Barnhart, History of the Farmers' Al-
liance and of the People's Party in Nebraska (unpublished Ph.D. thesis,
Harvard Univ., 1930), 124.

[2] D. L. McMurry, *Coxey's Army* (Boston, 1929).

[3] Such societies to the number of 163 were active in 1891 from
coast to coast. *Nationalist* (Boston), III (1891), 505.

The air was full of revolt against things as they were. Howells, deploring the increasing resort to violence and murder by the unprosperous, feared lest a "blood-mist" would screen the real issues from the thoughtful.[1] Even the usually mild-spoken Thomas Bailey Aldrich predicted: "We shall have bloody work in this country some of these days, when the lazy *canaille* get organized."[2] What a vision of *fin de siècle,* cried a magazine poet:

Strange vision! The land is filled full with the harvest—
Hungry men look for the morrow with dread;
Our hearts swell with pride of our civilization—
God! hear that piteous crying for bread![3]

The campaign of 1896 provided vent for an expression of class antagonisms such as the country had never before known. Perhaps, like the new device employed in surgical operations, the occasion gave drainage to pent-up poisons which might have prostrated the body politic. Though embattled conservatism won the election, it could never again ignore questions that vitally concerned the average man and woman or, in Populist parlance, "drown the outcries of a plundered people with the uproar of a sham battle over the tariff."[4]

Nor, as the sequel showed, were politicians and statesmen properly accountable for all the ills to which society had fallen heir. In so far as these distresses stemmed from an insufficient circulating medium, they were, as Miss Tarbell points out, soon ameliorated by the dis-

[1] W. D. Howells, *Life in Letters* (Mildred Howells, ed., Garden City, 1928), II, 26.

[2] Ferris Greenslet, *Life of Thomas Bailey Aldrich* (Boston, 1908), 168-169.

[3] Margaret S. Sibley, "A 'Fin-de-Siècle' Vision," *Arena,* XI (1894-1895), 99.

[4] Platform of 1892, quoted in T. H. McKee, *The National Conventions and Platforms of All Political Parties* (Balt., 1900), 281.

covery of fresh sources of gold supply together with a
return of prosperity and an expansion of credit facilities. As opportunities for work multiplied, the acerbities
of the industrial struggle lessened: within a few years
Mark Hanna and Samuel Gompers would join hands in
a constructive effort to harmonize the interests of employer, employee and consumer.[1] In the South manufactures, recovering from the blow of 1893, actually
overtopped that section's agricultural yield by nearly
$200,000,000 in 1898.[2] Birmingham could boast of
being the third largest iron-shipping point in the world,
the first in America. The farmer in West and South
shared in the general well-being, facing an era of better
crops and higher prices with the discipline of much
needed lessons in thrift and prudent management,
learned in the lean hard years that had gone before.
At the same time the introduction of rural free delivery,
the springing up of mutual telephone companies, the
advent of interurban electric railways, the building of
good roads, and better provision for schools promised
for the countryside advantages which earlier had belonged only to the urban dweller.[3] Parity with the city,
of course, was not attained—perhaps never could
be attained—but rural inferiority was becoming less
flagrant, less a source of hopelessness and despair.

In reality, the mists and shadows that gathered over
America in the beginning years of the *fin de siècle* had
always been streaked with light for those with eyes to

[1] See H. U. Faulkner, *The Quest for Social Justice* (*A History of
American Life*, XI), 53-54.
[2] E. G. Murphy, *Problems of the Present South* (N. Y., 1904), 102.
[3] Sylvester Baxter, "The Trolley in Rural Parts," and C. M. Harger,
"The New Era in the Middle West," *Harper's Mag.*, XCVII (1898),
60-69, 276-282; W. L. Anderson, *The Country Town* (N. Y., 1906),
chap. xiii. For the introduction of rural free delivery in 1896 and its
development, see Postmaster-General, *Report for 1899*, 16-18; for *1900*,
113-146.

see. One needed only to look about him to appreciate the justice of Muirhead's characterization of the United States as the "Land of Contrasts." Howells makes a character in one of his books assert that the passion of Americans for doing things on a large scale extended even to their inconsistencies.[1] Thus, while capitalistic greed ground the faces of the poor under its iron heel, individual potentates of wealth lavished millions upon hospitals, libraries, colleges, churches, museums and art galleries for the good of all. While the Panic palsied the country's industrial energies and turned hordes of the jobless into the streets, an extraordinary outburst of philanthropic relief effort attested the essential humaneness of the American character,[2] and the Columbian Exposition on the south shore of Lake Michigan revealed to a wondering world the summit of American accomplishment in the fine arts and the graces of life.

The year 1897 not only brought the turn to prosperity, but touched American life once more with that sense of romance and adventure which had seemed forever gone.[3] In the middle of June two steamships arrived respectively at San Francisco and Seattle with prospectors from Alaska carrying with them one and a half million dollars' worth of gold dust. In this startling fashion the world learned of the fabulously rich placer deposits discovered the preceding year along Klondike Creek in the Yukon country, mostly in British territory. The

[1] W. D. Howells, *A Traveller from Altruria* (N. Y., 1894), 50.

[2] Anon., "The Relief of the Unemployed during the Winter of 1893-94," *Journ. of Social Sci.*, XXXII (1894), 1-51; C. C. Closson, jr., "The Unemployed in American Cities," *Quar. Journ. of Econ.*, VIII (1894), 168-217; F. D. Watson, *The Charity Organization Movement in the United States* (N. Y., 1922), 248-265.

[3] W. B. Haskell, *Two Years in the Klondike and Alaskan Gold-Fields* (Hartford, 1898); Tappan Adney, *The Klondike Stampede of 1897-98* (N. Y., 1899); Charmian London, *Jack London* (London, 1921), I, chaps. xv-xvi; H. W. Clark, *History of Alaska* (N. Y., 1930), 100-107.

gold fever ran through all parts of the United States and attracted adventurers from remote corners of the globe. Taxing all available means of water transport northward, the argonauts braved incredible hardships presented by a frozen and forbidding country in order to reach the new El Dorado.

Between two and three hundred thousand set forth on the journey. Many turned back or died on the way, not more than fifty thousand reaching the interior fastnesses. In the late autumn of 1897 the carcasses of nearly four thousand horses strewed the difficult White Pass Trail. The camps, picturesque and lively, were yet more orderly than those of the forty-niners in California. From 1898 to 1904 the annual yield of the Yukon territory alone was never less than ten million dollars. Meantime gold deposits were discovered on American soil along the Yukon River and even around the head of Cook Inlet and about Nome, near Bering Strait. The richest finds were made by veteran miners. The bulk of the fortune hunters had to be content with the satisfaction of novel adventures; few of them possessed young Jack London's or Rex Beach's talent for coining their experiences into authors' royalties.

The stampede might have been the greatest in history had not the Spanish war intervened to divert popular attention to other scenes of derring-do. Whatever self-interested motives may have colored the government's decision to enter the conflict, and however much credit or blame may attach to the enterprise of Hearst, Pulitzer and company, the populace answered the call to arms in the spirit of schoolboys off for a picnic.[1] "There'll Be a Hot Time in the Old Town Tonight" inevitably outrivaled all other popular ditties that sought to capture the spirit of the moment. Thus the *fin de siècle* which

[1] Walter Millis, *The Martial Spirit* (Boston, 1931), 160-167.

had begun in a vale of gloom and foreboding had, by an unexpected turn of events, suddenly issued forth into the sunshine of prosperity, optimism and high emprise.

It was in a mellow mood that Americans in 1898 could look backward and appraise the developments of the two decades just past. Impatient young men might mutter that the deeper economic conflict had only been postponed; that a truce, not a term, had stilled the popular outcry for social justice. But their elders could reply that, while wealth and economic power had tended to concentrate at a faster rate than they would have wished, the general condition of the masses had not been materially affected for the worse. If one eighth of the families of the United States possessed seven eighths of the country's property,[1] the enormous growth in aggregate national wealth still afforded ample elbow room for the less favored classes. In support of this contention a leading statistician pointed out that the number of persons in the higher and more skilled walks of life had increased faster relatively than the population, that the laborers' workday was lessening, and that the general tendency of wages was upward and of prices downward. Admitting that the toilers had not got their due share of the enlarged aggregate wealth, he nevertheless concluded that, though the rich were growing richer, "many more people than formerly are growing rich, and the poor are better off."[2]

The improved position of the common man, however, owed far more to the multifold mechanical inventions which these years brought forth and to the enlarged

[1] C. B. Spahr, *An Essay on the Present Distribution of Wealth in the United States* (R. T. Ely, ed., *Library of Economics and Politics*, XII, N. Y., 1896), esp. 69.

[2] C. D. Wright, "Are the Rich Growing Richer and the Poor Poorer?," *Atlantic Mo.*, LXXX (1897), 300-309.

rôle of public and private agencies in fostering better
living standards. Labor-saving devices in the home, improved methods of plumbing, better lighting indoors
and out, the commercial development of the telephone,
the advent of the safety bicycle, the new conveniences of
rapid transit in city and suburbs, showered blessings
upon the many as well as the few, though urban dwellers were, of course, the chief gainers. In like manner
ordinary folk benefited from the energetic attention
given by municipalities to water purification, sewerage,
street paving, parks, fire protection and public hygiene.
Both in country and city, schools showed steady progress during the twenty years and, in the *fin de siècle,* a
high-school education was becoming the normal expectation of most city youths. Poverty continued to exist,
but it was treated by the new profession of social workers as a malady that was functional rather than organic.
Even the churches began to take a hand in the exigent
work of human rehabilitation.

Laymen and physicians alike testified to the altered
physical appearance of the people. While the change was
most marked in those rural parts once noted for lean-
ness, angularity and sallowness of complexion, fifty
years' familiarity with the streets of New York and
Boston caused a careful observer to declare that there,
also, "The men are more robust and more erect, the
women have greatly improved both in feature and carriage; and in the care and condition of the teeth in both
sexes a surprising change has taken place." [1] During the
1880's dealers in ready-made clothing were obliged to
adopt a larger scale of sizes and many more extra sizes,
in width as well as in length, than had been needed ten

[1] F. J. Kingsbury, "The Tendency of Men to Live in Cities," *Journ.
of Social Sci.,* XXXIII (1895), 15. See also C. D. Warner, *The Relation
of Literature to Life* (N. Y., 1897), 263-264, and S. Weir Mitchell,
Wear and Tear (5th edn., Phila., 1887), 3-4.

years before.[1] Nor did the reasons for the improvement
in physique baffle the inquirer. Apart from the advances
in medical science and an ampler provision of physicians, it was generally ascribed to greater leisure, a lessening anxiety by a larger number of people concerning
food and shelter, the growing cult of physical exercise
and, not least of all, the varied and better-prepared diet
which the generation enjoyed.

On the other hand, the restless energy bottled up in
the urban centers, and constantly excited by noises, jars
and the rush of crowds, tended more and more to make
nervousness the national disease that medical writers
were prone to call it.[2] Neurasthenia (to use Dr. Beard's
term) and insanity were as characteristically city phenomena as feeble-mindedness and impaired physical
vigor were rural complaints.[3] In its milder effects the
high strain of urban living robbed American life of
much of the repose which increasing leisure should have
afforded it and often betrayed artists and writers into
giving the world something less than their best.

If, as was widely asserted, women were the particular
victims of the national disease,[4] it was doubtless the price
they paid for their steadily enlarging share in activities
outside the home—in the world of fashion, clubs, industry, the professions, literature and the arts. In educa-

[1] In the case of the Southern trade the increase was fully one inch
around the chest and waist. Edward Atkinson, "The American Physique," Science, X (1887), 239-240, 276.

[2] G. M. Beard, American Nervousness (N. Y., 1881), chaps. ii-v;
Mitchell, Wear and Tear, 7-10, 22-30; Grace Peckham, "The Nervous-
ness of Americans," Journ. of Social Sci., XXII (1887), 37-49; W. B.
Platt, "Certain Injurious Influences of City Life," Journ. of Social Sci.,
XXIV (1888), 24-30; Edward Wakefield, "Nervousness: The National
Disease of America," McClure's, II (1894), 302-307.

[3] A. F. Weber, The Growth of Cities in the Nineteenth Century
(Columbia Univ., Studies, XI), 392.

[4] Mitchell, Wear and Tear, 30-55; edit., Ladies' Home Journ., X
(1893), no. 9, 14.

tion and in enterprises of social uplift they were often the mainstay. Old notions of family integrity were rudely jarred by the centrifugal forces at work in the home. Outside agencies assumed an ever greater responsibility for the welfare of city children and the nation was startled by the leap in the divorce rate. Yet no finite intelligence could know whether even such changes implied a rise or decline in general ethical standards. Though in the large cities commercialized vice flaunted itself as never before and many would have agreed that "human life is rather more secure in Arizona than in the streets of New York," it was Bryce's considered judgment that, taking the country as a whole, "the average of temperance, chastity, truthfulness, and general probity is somewhat higher than in any of the great nations of Europe." [1] Nor is it to be overlooked that organized religion, after a period of doubt and confusion, attained a numerical and relative strength in the *fin de siècle* greater than at any preceding time in the twenty-year period.

By posterity the generation will be remembered less for the way it managed the retail traffic of life than for its more permanent contributions to American civilization. While every generation is born with its hands tied by the generation which went before, the constructive work of the 1880's and 1890's was less a fulfillment of the past than a starting point for the future. Apart from the impressive feat of forging a national economic order,[2] the men and women of the time laid the firm foundations for continuing achievement in all the elements of intellectual and æsthetic culture. The spread of

[1] W. E. Smythe, "Real Utopias in the Arid West," *Atlantic Mo.*, LXXIX (1897), 609; James Bryce, *The American Commonwealth* (London, 1888), III, 54.
[2] See *A History of American Life*, IX, by Ida M. Tarbell.

graduate schools, with their goal far beyond the reach
of the college, evidenced the new emphasis upon the
value of pure knowledge. In an age of supposed dominant materialism a larger proportion of Americans con-
secrated themselves to the cause of science and learning
than ever before in history and a greater number of
them attained an eminence that compelled the attention
of the world. Literature and the arts had an equal drawing power, with results hardly less fruitful. A Gibbs, a
Newcomb, a Ward, a James, a Mark Twain, a Whistler,
a MacDowell, a Saint-Gaudens, stand out not as unexpected flowers along a scrubby roadside, but as among
the most perfect blossoms in a well-tended field.

Cultural achievement, moreover, was bottomed upon
a broadening popular appreciation of creative effort. So
diversified a population reflected a multiplicity of standards and tastes, and popular culture contained much
that was transitory and cheap. But the steady leavening
of the mass was revealed in the unexampled patronage
accorded public libraries, art galleries and the more
serious dramatic and musical performances, as well as
by the multiplication of literary periodicals and the
greatly increased production of books. For the first time
in the national annals, creative workers might count
upon a receptive public and ample financial reward at
home. The few who preferred a foreign abode usually
did so because their work was more European than
American in spirit.

Underlying all the varied developments that made up
American life was the momentous shift of the center of
national equilibrium from the countryside to the city.
Long foreshadowed, it had at last become an actuality.
A civilization traditionally rural was obliged to learn
how to come to terms with a civilization predominantly
urban. The process was painful and confusing to those

who clung to the older mores and even to many who joined the cityward flight. But to untold numbers of others it meant the attainment of a new Promised Land, the release of energies and ambitions which the constricted opportunities of the farm had always denied. The city had come and, it was clear to all, it had come to stay. Was its mission to be that of a new Jerusalem or of ancient Babylon? The answer to this question was the chief unfinished business of the departing generation.

CHAPTER XIV

CRITICAL ESSAY ON AUTHORITIES

PHYSICAL SURVIVALS

MEMORIALS of the life of these years may be found at every hand, though time, abetted by real-estate enterprise, has done considerable damage to architectural achievements. Most of the edifices listed in chapter viii are still standing, but it is to be regretted that the first skyscraper, the Home Insurance Building (1885) in Chicago, has recently been razed. Among the many bridges that survive is the greatest of them all, Brooklyn Bridge (1883), a structure remarkable both as an engineering feat and as an artistic creation. Several monuments of national interest date from the period: the Washington Monument at the national capital, left unfinished from 1854 but completed during 1880-1884; the Statue of Liberty (1886) in New York Harbor, executed by the French sculptor F. A. Bartholdi and presented by his countrymen to the United States; and Grant's Tomb (1897) overlooking the Hudson at One Hundred and Twenty-third Street, designed by J. H. Duncan and built by popular subscription.

Samples of pictorial art can be found in any public gallery, as well as in the form of mural paintings in the Library of Congress, Bowdoin College, the Boston Public Library and elsewhere. Sculptures also abound in the larger cities (see earlier, chap. viii), while in Cornish, New Hampshire, at Saint-Gaudens's former home, are preserved the original models of many of that genius's masterpieces. As a well-rounded representation of the work of an unusually versatile artist, the Frank Duveneck collection in the Cincinnati Museum (founded in 1881), comprising about a hundred paintings besides etchings and sculptures, is unique. Good collections of "Rogers groups" of plaster statuettes are on display at the New York Historical Society, the Albany Institute, the Essex Institute, Salem, Massachusetts, and the Harrison Gray Otis House, Boston. The ebb and flow of women's fashions is illustrated by costumes in the Essex Institute, the Minnesota Historical Society and elsewhere and by a collection of dressed wax miniatures in the Chicago Historical Society.

The United States National Museum in Washington contains the original patent-office models of the more important dynamos and arc lamps and a large collection of incandescent lights illustrating chronologically the improvements of the Edison bulb from its inception. Especially interesting is a unit of the equipment installed for the incandescent-lighting system of a New York engraving establishment in 1881. Many aspects of technological development are depicted by models in the Museum of Science and Industry in New York and in the institution of the same name in Chicago. In the British Museum, London, is preserved a "dummy-and-trailer" cable car of the original Clay Street line in San Francisco.

Most significant of all for the social historian are the results already fruiting from the recent movement to preserve aspects of American culture in their appropriate context. Following the example of great European centers, America's chief metropolis formed in 1931 the Museum of the City of New York, dedicated to the object of tracing the evolution of its civic life from earliest times by means of material remains and the use of group models. Of broader scope is the Edison Institute of Technology, founded by Henry Ford on a two-hundred-acre tract next to his experimental laboratories at Dearborn, Michigan. Here, in a vast exhibition hall and in the adjoining Greenfield Village of some two hundred and fifty historic houses, may be seen many and varied evidences of general conditions of living in different periods and sections. Phonographs, hurdy-gurdies, typewriters, kerosene lamps, barber chairs, horse vehicles, along with blacksmith shops, domestic interiors and a steam manufacturing plant in the 1880's, suggest the ramifications of the collection. Included, also, are the original Edison laboratory at Menlo Park and the office in Santa Rosa, California, where Luther Burbank did his writing. A third repository of interest is maintained by the Norwegian-American Historical Society at Luther College, Decorah, Iowa. Its collection consists of exhibits and log cabins illustrative of the life of the immigrants both before their departure from Norway and during the process of their adjustment to American life. It is earnestly to be hoped that other racial groups will follow this excellent example.

The *Handbook of American Museums* (Wash., 1932), issued by the American Association of Museums, contains information in regard to about fourteen hundred institutions in the United States and Canada, including art galleries. R. C. Smith, comp., *A Bibliography of Museums and Museum Work* (Wash., 1928), lists books and articles concerned with such interests. For nearly all phases of American civilization the fine group of pictures brought together in R. H. Gabriel, ed., *The Pageant of America* (15 vols., New Haven, 1926-1929), is helpful.

GENERAL TREATMENTS

HISTORICAL ACCOUNTS: In the bibliography that follows, no attempt is made to cite again all the sources that have been named in the footnotes. Typical examples have to suffice, a completer enumeration being precluded by limitations of space. Until recently, historians have been so preoccupied with the details of party struggles and the sensational aspects of economic strife that Edmund Wilson doubtless expressed a widely held opinion when he declared in the *New Republic,* January 2, 1924: "The eighties and nineties in America appear . . . perhaps the most provincial and uninspired moment in the history of American society." The older historical convention is upheld by E. P. Oberholtzer, *A History of the United States since the Civil War* (5 vols., N. Y.,

1917, in progress), whose fourth volume (1931) gives an encyclopedestrian treatment of political happenings during the years 1878-1888, with an occasional squint at economic events. Other general writers, however, have ventured beyond these narrow limits, with results most interesting. In C. A. and Mary R. Beard, *The Rise of American Civilization* (2 vols., N. Y., 1927), may be found a swift but brilliant characterization of varied developments. Mark Sullivan, *Our Times* (5 vols., N. Y., 1926, in progress), dipping back occasionally into the period before 1900, has all the fascination of an old newspaper file. Lewis Mumford, *The Brown Decades* (N. Y., 1931), is a suggestive essay on the state of the arts from 1865 to 1895, while Thomas Beer, *The Mauve Decade* (N. Y., 1926), gives a sparkling, impressionistic account of certain phases of life in the 1890's. Certain volumes of Allen Johnson, ed., *The Chronicles of America Series* (50 vols., New Haven, 1918-1921), also attest that man does not live by politics alone. Despite the growing number of such works, many matters important for an understanding of intellectual currents and social growth have been omitted or insufficiently considered; nor, in many cases, have such topics had adequate monographic study.[1]

CONTEMPORANEOUS AMERICAN ANALYSES: The most important descriptive works of the period seeking to summarize salient trends in American life are D. A. Wells, *Recent Economic Changes* (N. Y., 1889); N. S. Shaler, ed., *The United States of America* (3 vols., N. Y., 1894); and C. M. Depew, ed., *One Hundred Years of American Commerce* (2 vols., N. Y., 1895), the last having a wider sweep than the title suggests. Among reminiscent personal records Henry Adams, *The Education of Henry Adams* (Boston, 1918),

[1] In helping fill up some of these gaps and for other assistance the author of the present volume is indebted to his wife, Elizabeth Bancroft, his secretary, Elizabeth F. Hoxie, Professor E. F. Gay and Dr. E. A. Darling of Cambridge, Mr. Stewart Mitchell of the Massachusetts Historical Society, and former members of his seminar, particularly G. P. Bauer, W. J. Bender, Ruth Jones Bowersox, Frances M. Camp, H. W. Cary, N. H. Dawes, B. J. Loewenberg, R. W. Logan, B. F. McKelvey, N. O. Mason, J. L. Norris, John O'Brien, J. F. Onthank, C. W. Upton and H. F. Wilson.

belongs in a niche by itself as an aloof but highly subjective commentary by an acute observer.

The chief general source of statistical information is, of course, the successive census inquiries. The *Tenth Census* (1880), directed by Francis A. Walker after training as superintendent of the *Ninth,* is the first to be a genuine national inventory. In 1890, through the use of the electric tabulating machine, demographic data are presented with minuter statistical analysis than had before been feasible. While the *Twelfth Census* (1900) covers a narrower field than either of the two preceding, its value in other respects is enhanced by the series of special supplementary reports prepared after the decennial work was completed and often containing valuable historical introductions. In using census data students would do well first to consult C. D. Wright, "The Limitations and Difficulties of Statistics," *Yale Rev.,* III (1894-1895), 121-143.

The best guide to social and economic materials in official state publications is Adelaide R. Hasse, comp., *Index of Economic Material in Documents of the States of the United States* (Carnegie Inst., *Publs.,* no. 85, 1907-1922), covering thirteen states down to the year 1904. There is great need of a systematic study of state legislation and court decisions for the light they can shed on social history. Very little progress has been made since G. J. Bayles wrote in *Woman and the Law* (N. Y., 1901), vi, "Within these dreary-looking books . . . is written a large portion of the life history of the nation. Read into the laws the efforts and hopes of generations of earnest men and women, and the study becomes one of living organism—human society." For a guide to the most important *corpus* of unprinted sources dealing with the period, see C. W. Garrison, comp., "List of Manuscript Collections in the Library of Congress to July, 1931," Am. Hist. Assoc., *Ann. Rep. for 1930,* I, esp. 215-227.

FOREIGN VIEWS: The most complete list of the books written by British visitors to America appears in Allan Nevins, ed., *American Social History as Recorded by British Travellers* (rev. edn., N. Y., 1931), which also contains generous excerpts from the more important volumes. While such works must be used with caution, none can be safely neglected. Perhaps the most useful accounts from British pens are E. A. Freeman, *Some Impressions of the United States* (N. Y., 1883) ; Herbert Spencer, "The Americans" [1883], *Essays, Scientific, Political and Speculative* (3 vols., N. Y., 1891), III, 471-492; Emily Faithfull, *Three Visits to America* (Edinburgh, 1884) ; Matthew Arnold, *Civilization in the United States* (Boston, 1888) ; James Bryce, *The American Commonwealth* (3 vols., London, 1888), valuable for the author's insight into social and intellectual as well as political conditions; and J. F. Muirhead, *The Land of Contrasts* (N. Y., 1898). The last is of special interest not only as a penetrating analysis, but also because the writer was the principal author of *The United States* (Karl Baedeker, ed., *Handbook for Travellers;* Leipsic, 1893; 2d rev. edn., 1899), a detailed descriptive guide to cities, traveling accommodations and sight-seeing excursions.

Though travel accounts by non-British visitors are less numerous, their variety is indicated by the following: K. T. Broberg, *Iakttagelser under en Pedagogisk Resa i Nord Amerika* (Helsingfors, 1889), observations in regard to American education by a Finlander; Paul de Rousiers, *American Life* (A. J. Herbertson, tr., Paris, 1892), an acute commentary by a French artist; Friedrich Ratzel, *Politische Geographie der Vereinigten Staaten von Amerika* (2d edn., München, 1893), an anthropogeographic interpretation of American life and problems; P. A. Tverskoi, *Ocherki Severo-Amerikanskich So-edinennich Shtatov* (St. Petersburg, 1895), based on ten years' experience in America; Marie Dugard, *La Société Américaine; Moeurs et Caractère—la Famille—Rôle de la Femme—Écoles et Universités* (Paris, 1896), a work crowned by the French Academy; and Manuel de Oliveira Lima, *Nos Estados Unidos. Impressões Politicas e Sociaes* (Leipzig, 1899), a friendly critique by a Brazilian. In later sections are cited foreign appraisals of special aspects of American culture, such as temperance reform and the status of women.

PERSONAL MATERIAL: GENERAL

While political biography is better represented than any other kind, lives of leaders in other fields of American civilization are appearing in increasing number. Of particular interest are the following series: M. A. DeW. Howe, ed., *The Beacon Biographies* (31 vols., Boston, 1899-1910), including authors, inventors and actors; C. D. Warner, ed., *American Men of Letters* (Boston, 1881-1906) ; W. D. Lewis, ed., *Great American Lawyers* (8 vols., Phila., 1907-1909) ; Carlos Martyn, ed., *American Reformers* (N. Y., 1890-1896) ; and Laurence Hutton, ed., *American Actor Series* (Boston, 1881-1882). Frequently, however, a better life may be found outside any of the standard series. Particular biographies are cited later in the present chapter in appropriate contexts. An invaluable aid to the social historian is the *Dictionary of American Biography* (20 vols., N. Y., 1928, in progress), edited by Allen Johnson and Dumas Malone. It covers the whole range of American culture in crisp sketches, often written by specialists, and, in addition, presents a brief, well-selected bibliography in connection with each memoir.

GENERAL PERIODICAL SOURCES

NEWSPAPERS: The multiplicity of newspapers in the 1880's and 1890's offers an embarrassment of riches. Their vast number and distribution are indicated by N. W. Ayer & Son, comp., *American Newspaper Annual and Directory* (Phila., from 1880), and presented analytically in W. S. Rossiter, "Printing and Publishing," *U. S. Twelfth Census* (1900), IX, 1037-1119—which also includes magazines. The leading journals are characterized in chapter vi of the present volume. The latest and best general historical survey is W. G. Bleyer, *Main Currents in the History of American Journalism* (Boston, 1927). Unfortunately the only newspapers of the period to be indexed are the *New York Tribune*, Republican, for the years 1875-1906; and the *Brooklyn Daily Eagle*, Democratic, for the years 1891-1902. Summaries of editorial opinion appear, however, in *Public Opinion* (Wash., 1886-1906) and the *Literary Digest* (N. Y., from 1890).

Particular newspapers are treated historically in a rapidly swelling literature, including Elmer Davis, *History of the New York Times, 1851-1921* (N. Y., 1921); Allan Nevins, *The Evening Post* (N. Y., 1922); D. C. Seitz, *The James Gordon Bennetts; Father and Son* (Indianapolis, 1928), dealing with the *New York Herald;* F. M. O'Brien, *The Story of the Sun* (N. Y., 1918); Royal Cortissoz, *The New York Tribune* (N. Y., 1923); J. E. Chamberlin, *The Boston Transcript* (Boston, 1930); Richard Hooker, *The Story of an Independent Newspaper* (N. Y., 1924)—the *Springfield Republican;* and anon., *William Rockhill Nelson* (Cambridge, Mass., 1915), concerned with the *Kansas City Star*. The fathers of yellow journalism are dealt with in Alleyne Ireland, *An Adventure with a Genius* (N. Y., 1920), and D. C. Seitz, *Joseph Pulitzer* (N. Y., 1924)—concerned with the proprietor of the *New York World*—and J. K. Winkler, *W. R. Hearst* (N. Y., 1928). The "Fiftieth Anniversary Number" of the *St. Louis Post-Dispatch,* December 9, 1928, reviews Pulitzer's career in that city and at the same time gives a swift panorama of St. Louis social history. Progress in coöperative journalism is traced in Victor Rosewater, *History of Coöperative News-Gathering in the United States* (N. Y., 1930).

MAGAZINES: The utility of magazine literature for the social historian is perhaps amply indicated by the footnotes of the present work. Even the humorous weeklies—*Puck* (N. Y., 1877-1918), *Judge* (N. Y., from 1881) and *Life* (N. Y., from 1883)—are valuable for the indirect evidence they afford as to social customs, moral standards, manners and foibles. Winifred Gregory, comp., *Union List of Serials in Libraries of the United States and Canada* (N. Y., 1927), offers the most complete list of magazines, with place and period of issue, while *Poole's Index to Periodical Literature* (various compilers, Boston and N. Y., 1882-1907), supplies a subject guide to the contents of the more important ones. A general critique of leading magazines appears in chapter vi of the present volume. Unlike the instance of newspapers, secondary historical accounts, even of leading magazines, are almost wholly lacking. Algernon Tassin, *The Magazine in America* (N. Y., 1916), is a readable but highly notional conspectus of magazine development. For information in regard to the conduct of the *Century Magazine* (N. Y., from 1881), which Paul Blouët called "that most successful of all magazines in the world," the following books by its editors are essential: R. W. Gilder, *Letters* (Rosamond Gilder, ed., Boston, 1916); L. F. Tooker, *The Joys and Tribulations of an Editor* (N. Y., 1924); and R. U. Johnson, *Remembered Yesterdays* (Boston, 1923). Another important periodical is sketched in M. A. DeW. Howe, *The Atlantic Monthly and Its Makers* (Boston, 1919). The *Dial* (Chicago, from 1880), XXVIII (1900), no. 333, reviews the first twenty years of its career as an organ of literary criticism. Two weekly journals of opinion are dealt with in W. H. Ward, "Fifty Years of *The Independent*," *Independent*, L (1898), 1642-1646; and in Rollo Ogden, *Life and Letters of Edwin Lawrence Godkin* (2 vols., N. Y., 1907), and Gustav Pollak, ed., *Fifty Years of American Idealism* (N. Y., 1920), the latter a reprint of *Nation* articles and editorials. An understanding of the spirit animating the *Arena* (Boston, from 1889) is afforded by B. O. Flower, *Progressive Men, Women and Movements of the Past Twenty-Five Years* (Boston, 1914). Light is shed on the new crop of low-priced periodicals by anon., "The Cosmopolitan," *Cosmopolitan*, XXIII (1897), 465-482, a ten years' retrospect; F. A. Munsey, "Getting On in Journalism," and "The Making and Marketing of Munsey's Magazine," *Munsey's*, XIX (1898), 214-224; XXII (1899), 323-343; and S. S. McClure, *My Autobiography* (N. Y., 1914). The editor of the *Ladies' Home Journal* explains its special preëminence in *The Americanization of Edward Bok* (N. Y., 1922). Magazines of a more particularized character are mentioned later in the present chapter in appropriate connections.

RURAL LIFE

GENERAL: Many articles in L. H. Bailey, ed., *Cyclopedia of American Agriculture* (4 vols., N. Y., 1907-1909), shed light on social conditions in the farming regions. E. E. Edwards, comp., *A Bibliography of the History of Agriculture in the United States* (Dept. of Agr., *Miscel. Publs.*, no. 84, 1930), touches on many phases of the subject while emphasizing economic and political developments. J. D. Hicks, *The Populist Revolt* (Minneapolis, 1931), sets forth the economic causes for agrarian unrest in South and West. Varied reasons for the cityward trend are discussed in two studies by N. H. Egleston: *Villages and Village Life* (N. Y., 1878), and *The Home and Its Surroundings* (rev. edn., N. Y., 1883). W. G. Moody, *Land and Labor in the United States* (N. Y., 1883), and J. R. Elliott, *American Farms* (*Questions of the Day Series*, LXII, 2d edn., N. Y., 1890), paint a gloomy picture of the farmers' decline, to which W. L. Anderson, *The Country Town* (N. Y., 1906), written when the rural situation had taken a turn for the better, forms a useful corrective. The plague of tramps, with particular reference to rural neighborhoods, receives first-hand study by Jack London in *The Road* (N. Y., 1907), based on his hobo wanderings from 1892 to 1897; by W. A. Wyckoff in *The Workers* (2 vols., N. Y., 1897-1898), derived from his experiences in 1891-1892; and most notably by J. F. Willard (Josiah Flynt, *pseud.*) who sets forth material collected over a period of ten years in *Tramping with Tramps* (N. Y., 1899), *Notes of an Itinerant Policeman* (Boston, 1900) and *The World of Graft* (N. Y., 1901).

THE SOUTH: General surveys covering the period include P. A. Bruce, *The Rise of the New South* (G. C. Lee and F. N. Thorpe, eds., *The History of North America*, 20 vols., Phila., 1903-1907, XVII); and J. A. C. Chandler and others, *The South in the Building of the Nation* (12 vols., Richmond, 1909-1910). L. J. Cappon, comp., *Bibliography of Virginia History since 1865* (Univ. of Va. Inst. for Research in the Social Sciences, *Monograph*, V, 1930), not only is indispensable for its own particular subject, but should serve as a beacon light for other states to follow. Contemporaneous accounts, stressing economic change, are A. K. McClure, *The South: Its Industrial, Financial, and Political Condition* (Phila., 1886); W. D. Kelley, *The Old South and the New* (N. Y., 1887); R. H. Edmonds, *The South's Redemption* (Balt., 1890), reprinted from the *Manufacturers' Record* (Balt., from 1882) of which Edmonds was editor; and same author, *Facts about the South* (Balt., 1902).

The emergence of the white masses in economic and political life has received much study in recent years, the principal articles and monographs being listed in Edwards, *Bibliography*, and Hicks, *Populist Revolt*, both cited previously. The cultural aspects of this transformation have scarcely been noted, however. The secluded mountain population has received considerable attention in such works as S. T. Wilson, *The Southern Mountaineers* (N. Y., 1906); Horace Kephart, *Our Southern Highlanders* (N. Y., 1913); and A. W. Spaulding, *The Men of the Mountains* (Nashville, 1915). The turn to manufacturing development is considered in Broadus Mitchell, *The Rise of Cotton Mills in the South* (Johns Hopkins Univ., *Studies*, XXXIX, no. 2, 1921); Holland Thompson, *From the Cotton Field to the Cotton Mill* (N. Y., 1906), with special reference to North Carolina; Meyer Jacobstein, *The Tobacco Industry in the United States* (Columbia Univ., *Studies*, XXVI, no. 3, 1907); and Ethel Armes, *The Story of Coal and Iron in Alabama* (Birmingham, 1910). For the changing fortunes of the Afro-American, see later, Race Relations.

THE WEST: Comprehensive and authoritative descriptions at the beginning of the period are L. P. Brockett, *Our Western Empire* (Phila., 1880), prepared primarily for prospective settlers; and F. V. Hayden, *The Great West* (Bloomington, 1880), written from experiences gained while a member of the geological survey. From a group of studies, most of them quite recent, emerges a vivid picture of the cattleman and his economic and social significance. Notable among such works are P. A. Rollins, *The Cowboy* (N. Y., 1922); Douglas Branch, *The Cowboy and His Interpreters* (N. Y., 1926); E. S. Osgood, *The Day of the Cattleman* (Minneapolis, 1929); E. E. Dale, *The Range Cattle Industry* (Norman, Okla., 1930); and W. P. Webb, *The Great Plains* (Boston, 1931). William French, *Some Recollections of a Western Ranchman* (N. Y., 1928), affords a graphic picture of life in the Southwest as experienced by an Englishman from 1883 to 1899. Frontier lawlessness provides the theme for Emerson Hough, *The Story of the Outlaw* (N. Y., 1907); F. J. Wilstach, *Wild Bill Hickok* (Garden City, 1926); Robertus Love, *The Rise and Fall of Jesse James* (N. Y., 1926); W. N. Burns, *The Saga of Billy the Kid* (Garden City, 1926); and Emmett Dalton and Jack Jungmeyer, *When the Daltons Rode* (Garden City, 1931). For the Indian problem, see later, Race Relations.

Agricultural conditions and methods are ably discussed by the Britisher, Finlay Dun, in *American Farming and Food* (London, 1881) from first-hand observations in 1879. While many special studies canvass the economic sources of the farmers' difficulties, insight may be gained into the much neglected subject of psychological causes in such works as E. W. Howe, *The Story of a Country Town* (N. Y., 1883), semifictional; Hamlin Garland, *A Son of the Middle Border* (N. Y., 1917); Grant Showerman, *A Country Chronicle* (N. Y., 1916); and Herbert Quick, *One Man's Life* (Indianapolis, 1925).

URBAN LIFE

The American city has not yet been studied generically, nor do there exist any adequate social histories of particular cities. Basic data for many aspects of urban development can be gleaned from *Social Statistics of Cities: 1880* (*U. S. Tenth Census*, XVIII-XIX); J. S. Billings, comp., *Report on the Social Statistics of Cities* (*U. S. Eleventh Census, 1890*); and *Statistics of Cities Having a Population of Over 25,000: 1902 and 1903*, and *Statistics of Cities Having a*

Population of 8,000 to 25,000: 1903 (Bur. of the Census, *Bulls.,* nos. 20, 45). A. F. Weber, *The Growth of Cities in the Nineteenth Century* (Columbia Univ., *Studies,* XI, 1899), is an excellent comparative study covering various countries, with some reference to social implications. The expansion of municipal functions in the United States and Europe is traced in J. A. Fairlie, *Municipal Administration* (N. Y., 1901). Josiah Strong, *The Twentieth Century City* (N. Y., 1898), offers a sociological analysis of the impact of the city on American life, while W. H. Tolman, *Municipal Reform Movements in the United States* (N. Y., 1897), and C. M. Robinson, "Improvement in City Life," a series of articles in the *Atlantic Mo.,* LXXXIII (1899), set forth remedial tendencies. Willard Glazier, *Peculiarities of American Cities* (Phila., 1883), discusses the principal features of thirty-nine centers. Picturesque and amusing aspects of Manhattan life are presented in something akin to scrapbook fashion by H. C. Brown in *The Last Fifty Years in New York, New York in the Elegant Eighties* and *In the Golden Nineties* (*Valentine's Manual of Old New York,* X-XII, Hastings-on-Hudson, 1925-1927). M. M. Quaife, ed., *The Development of Chicago, 1674-1914* (Chicago, 1916), comprises a series of contemporary original narratives.

The literature on living conditions of the urban poor is voluminous. New York state commissions, especially appointed for the purpose, issued elaborate reports in 1885 and 1894. The important work edited by R. W. De Forest and Lawrence Veiller, *The Tenement House Problem* (2 vols., N. Y., 1903), reviews earlier conditions and submits the findings and recommendations of the state commission of 1900. Such inquiries should be supplemented by the personal experiences of Jacob A. Riis, embodied in *How the Other Half Lives* (N. Y., 1890), *The Battle with the Slum* (N. Y., 1902), *The Children of the Poor* (N. Y., 1892) and *The Making of an American* (N. Y., 1901), his autobiography. Equally enlightening for Chicago is *Hull-House Maps and Papers* (N. Y., 1895) by the Residents of that settlement; and for Boston, R. A. Woods, ed., *The City Wilder-*

ness (Boston, 1898), a collaborative study by the members of South End House. The U. S. commissioner of labor submits the results of federal investigations in C. D. Wright, *The Slums of Baltimore, Chicago, New York, and Philadelphia* (*Seventh Special Rep.*, 1894), and E. R. L. Gould, *The Housing of the Working People* (*Eighth Special Rep.*, 1895).

The chief statistical study of criminality is F. H. Wines, *Report on Crime, Pauperism, and Benevolence in the United States* (2 vols., *U. S. Eleventh Census*, 1890, XXII-XXIII), which should be scrutinized in the light of R. P. Falkner's critique, *Crime and the Census* (Am. Acad. of Polit. and Social Sci., *Publs.*, no. 190, 1897). Herbert Asbury, *The Gangs of New York* (N. Y., 1928), is a lively and reliable narrative. Contemporary accounts dealing with criminal conditions in New York include A. E. Costello, *Our Police Protectors* (N. Y., 1884) ; T. F. Byrnes, *Professional Criminals of America* (N. Y., 1886) ; W. F. Howe and A. H. Hummel, *Danger! A True History of a Great City's Wiles and Temptations* (Buffalo, 1886) ; and G. W. Walling, *Recollections of a New York Chief of Police* (N. Y., 1887). Alexander Gardiner, *Canfield* (N. Y., 1930), tells the story of the notorious gambler whose sumptuous Saratoga Club in New York became in the 1890's the Monte Carlo of America. Sensational accounts of notorious crimes and high scandals, originally appearing in the *Police Gazette* (N. Y., from 1845), are reprinted in S. A. MacKeever, *Glimpses of Gotham and City Characters* (N. Y., 1880), and Edward Van Every, *Sins of New York as "Exposed" by the Police Gazette* (N. Y., 1931). C. H. Parkhurst recounts his experiences as a crusader against vice and crime in *Our Fight with Tammany* (N. Y., 1895), while the findings of the Lexow Committee are embodied in *Report and Proceedings of the Senate Committee Appointed to Investigate the Police Department of the City of New York* (5 vols., Albany, 1895). B. P. Eldridge and W. B. Watts, *Our Rival, the Rascal* (Boston, 1896), is an account by two Boston police officials. The leading detective agency is the subject of R. W.

Rowan, *The Pinkertons* (Boston, 1931), while L. W. Moore, *His Own Story of His Eventful Life* (Boston, 1892), presents the authentic life story of a safe blower active in divers cities.

The many mechanical inventions that helped transform urban life are discussed in E. W. Byrn, *Progress of Invention in the Nineteenth Century* (N. Y., 1900); a group of articles in the "50th Anniversary Number" of the *Scientific American*, July 25, 1896; and Waldemar Kaempffert, ed., *A Popular History of American Invention* (2 vols., N. Y., 1924). More specialized treatments are T. C. Martin and S. L. Coles, *The Story of Electricity* (2 vols., N. Y., 1919-1922); Henry Schroeder, *History of Electric Light* (*Smithsonian Miscel. Colls.*, LXXVI, no. 2, 1923), a technical account; and H. N. Casson, *The History of the Telephone* (Chicago, 1910). Other aspects of urban life are touched upon in later sections of this bibliography.

THE WOMAN'S WORLD

Annie N. Meyer, ed., *Woman's Work in America* (N. Y., 1891), is a coöperative work illuminating many aspects of the sex's increasing participation in American life. C. V. C. de Varigny, *La Femme aux États-Unis* (Paris, 1893), and Thérèse Blanc, *The Condition of Woman in the United States* (Abby L. Alger, tr., Boston, 1895), attest French interest in the subject. The position of the average middle-class woman is best understood, however, from a reading of the magazines which affected and reflected her outlook, notably *Harper's Bazar* (N. Y., from 1867)', the *Delineator* (N. Y., from 1873), *Ladies' Home Companion* (Springfield, Ohio, from 1873, titled *Woman's Home Companion* from 1895), *Ladies' Home Journal*, (Phila., from 1883) and *Good Housekeeping* (Holyoke and N. Y., from 1885).

All aspects of the quest for women's rights are the concern of the *History of Woman Suffrage* (6 vols., N. Y. and Rochester, 1881-1922), written by Elizabeth Cady Stanton, Susan B. Anthony and others. For intimate views of these two leaders of the movement, Ida H. Harper, *The Life and Work of Susan B. Anthony* (3 vols., Indianapolis, 1898-1908), and Elizabeth Cady Stanton, *Elizabeth Cady Stanton as Revealed in Her Letters, Diary and Reminiscences* (Theodore Stanton and Harriot S. Blatch, eds., 2 vols., N. Y., 1922), are important. A suffragist of different stamp is charmingly portrayed by her daughter, Alice Stone Blackwell, in *Lucy Stone* (Boston, 1930). Material of interest also appears in E. A. Hecker, *A Short History of Women's Rights* (N. Y., 1911); Bertha A. Rembaugh, *The Political Status of Women in the United States* (N. Y., 1911); and Jennie L. Wilson, *The Legal and Political Status of Women in the United States* (N. Y., 1911).

G. E. Howard, *A History of Matrimonial Institutions* (3 vols., Chicago, 1904), includes an account of the American family, while A. W. Calhoun, *A Social History of the American Family* (3 vols., Cleveland, 1919), though somewhat resembling a notebook on the subject, is valuable as the first attempt at a comprehensive study. For cross-sectional summaries of the legal status of married women, consult J. P. Bishop, *Commentaries on the Law of Married Women* (2 vols., Boston, 1875); James Schouler, *A Treatise on the Law of Domestic Relations* (Boston, 1889); H. C. Whitney, *Marriage and Divorce* (Phila., 1894); and G. J. Bayles, *Woman and the Law* (N. Y., 1901). *Marriage and Divorce, 1867-1906* (Bur. of the Census, *Special Rep.*, 1909, 2 pts.) is an indispensable compilation of statistical and legislative data. Additional information may be gathered from the *Reports* (dating from 1885) and the numerous special *Publications* of the National Divorce Reform League (founded in 1881; name changed in 1897 to National League for the Protection of the Family).

Contemporaneous studies of family budgets exist in profusion, representing every part of the country and all classes of people. They were usually made by state bureaus of labor statistics and published in their annual reports. Besides other details these studies show the distribution of family income among such items as food, clothing, rent, fuel, furnishings, medical care, education and reading. Lucy M. Salmon, *Domestic Service* (rev. edn., N. Y., 1901), the first comprehensive inquiry into the servant problem, emphasizes conditions as found in 1889 and 1890. Standard manuals of household management in the nineties are Helen Campbell, *Household Economics* (N. Y., 1896), and *Home Economics* (N. Y., 1898) by Maria Parloa, founder of the popular Boston Cooking School.

HUMANITARIAN STRIVING

CHARITY AND SOCIAL WORK: The growth of scientific methods in the administration of charity can be followed in Sophonisba P. Breckenridge, ed., *Public Welfare Administration in the United States, Select Documents* (Chicago, 1927); National Conference of Charities and Correction, *Proceedings for 1893*, which contains historical papers on the new methods in charity, prison reform, and the care of the insane and feeble-minded; A. G. Warner, *American Charities* (R. T. Ely, ed., *Library of Economics and Politics*, IV, N. Y., 1894; rev. 1908, 1919); and F. D. Watson, *The Charity Organization Movement in the United States* (N. Y., 1922). Such works should be supplemented by examining the *Annual Reports* of the Charities Aid Association of New York State (from 1873), of the National Conference of Charities and Correction (from 1874) and of local bodies. *Lend-a-Hand* (Boston), founded in 1886 by Edward Everett Hale, is valuable as "a record of progress and journal of organized charity"; in 1897 it was merged with the *Charities Review* (N. Y., 1891-1901).

The movement for the prevention of cruelty to animals and children is traced in R. C. McCrae, *The Humane Movement* (N. Y., 1910), and S. H. Coleman, *Humane Society Leaders in America* (Albany, 1924), with special reference to the work of the American Humane Association, formed in 1877. *The Brother of Girls* (Chicago, 1910) is the autobiography of C. N. Crittenton, founder of the Florence Crittenton Missions for fallen women, the first one, in New York City, dating from 1883. Caroline W. Montgomery, ed., *Bibliography of College, Social, University and Church Settlements* (5th edn., Chicago, 1905), is an excellent guide to the earlier literature on the subject, while R. A. Woods and A. J. Kennedy, *The Settlement Horizon* (N. Y., 1922), gives the best general account. The career of four trail blazers can be followed in Jane Addams, *Twenty Years at Hull House* (N. Y., 1910); Eleanor H. Woods, *Robert A. Woods* (Boston, 1929), dealing with the founder of South End House in Boston (1892); Lillian D. Wald, *The House on Henry Street* (N. Y., 1915), written by the organizer of the Nurses' Settlement (1893); and H. E. Wilson, *Mary Mc-Dowell, Neighbor* (Chicago, 1928), relating the history of the early years and achievements of the University of Chicago Settlement House (1894).

TEMPERANCE: The bulk of the material on the temperance question is highly explosive. For the student the most valuable volumes are the reports of the investigations carried on from 1893 to 1903 by the Committee of Fifty consisting of prominent educators, clergymen, scientists and publicists: F. H. Wines and John Koren, *The Liquor Problem in Its Legislative Aspects* (Boston, 1897; rev. edn., 1898); John Koren, *Economic Aspects of the Liquor Problem* (Boston, 1899); Raymond Calkins, *Substitutes for the Saloon* (Boston, 1901); J. S. Billings, ed., *The Physiological Aspects of the Liquor Problem* (2 vols., Boston, 1903); and J. S. Billings and others, *The Liquor Problem* (Boston, 1905), a summary of the results. Very serviceable, too, are E. L. Fanshawe, *Liquor Legislation in the United States and Canada* (London, 1893), a disinterested inquiry by a foreigner including twenty-odd American states; and *Economic Aspects of the Liquor Problem* (U. S. Comr. of Labor, *Twelfth Ann. Rep.*, 1897), the most comprehensive official investigation. Historical sketches with a temperance bias include J. G. Woolley and W. E. Johnson, *Temperance Progress of the Century* (Justin McCarthy, ed., *The Nineteenth Century Series;* Toronto, 1903); A. F. Fehlandt, *A Century of Drink Reform in the United States* (Cincinnati, 1904); E. H. Cherrington, *The Evolution of Prohibition in the United*

States (Westerville, 1920); and D. L. Colvin, *Prohibition in the United States* (N. Y., 1926).

PRISON REFORM: The situation is summarized at the beginning of the period in E. C. Wines, *The State of Prisons and of Child Saving Institutions* (Cambridge, Mass., 1880), and at its end by F. H. Wines, *Punishment and Reformation* (*Crowell's Library of Economics and Politics,* VI, N. Y., 1895; also later edns.), and by S. J. Barrows, ed., *The Reformatory System in the United States* (56th Cong., 1 sess., *House Doc.,* no. 459, 1900), a volume consisting of articles by officers of leading reformatories and prisons. For all phases the *Annual Reports* and *Proceedings* of the National Prison Association (from 1881) are of the utmost value, while much that is useful can also be found in C. R. Henderson, ed., *Correction and Prevention* (4 vols., N. Y., 1910), a collection of authoritative articles, historical and descriptive, on prison reform, preventive agencies and allied topics.

PEACE MOVEMENT AND RED CROSS: The best general account of the peace movement in the eighties and nineties is given by A. C. F. Beales, *The History of Peace* (N. Y., 1931), while further information of interest appears in Devere Allen, *The Fight for Peace* (N. Y., 1930), and E. L. Whitney, *The American Peace Society, A Centennial History* (Wash., 1928). Sarah E. Pickett, *The American National Red Cross* (N. Y., 1923), sketches the history of that organization. The story of its founder is related by her kinsman W. E. Barton in *The Life of Clara Barton* (2 vols., Boston, 1922).

RACE RELATIONS

THE IMMIGRANT: There is an extensive literature in respect to immigration in general and as regards special racial groups, but, unhappily, there are few studies of immigrant acculturation in a particular community. Important exceptions are Kate H. Claghorn, "The Foreign Immigrant in New York City," U. S. Indus. Commission, *Reports* (Wash., 1900-1902), XV, 449-492; in the case of Chi-

cago, *Hull-House Papers,* previously cited; and in the case
of Boston, two volumes edited by R. A. Woods: *The City
Wilderness,* mentioned earlier, and *Americans in Process*
(Boston, 1902). Supplementary material for Boston appears
in F. A. Bushee, *Ethnic Factors in the Population of Boston*
(Am. Econ. Assoc., *Publs.,* ser. 3, IV, no. 2, 1903).

Kate H. Claghorn, "Agricultural Distribution of Immigrants," U. S. Indus. Comn., *Reports,* XV, 492-646, is
extremely useful, while many Mid-Western state historical
societies, and especially the Swedish Historical Society of
America and the Norwegian-American Historical Association,
have published noteworthy articles dealing with particular
immigrant elements in the rural sections. A circumstantial
account of the German-Russian colonies is given in a series
of articles, based on personal observation and interviews,
contributed by Richard Sallet to the *Dakota Freie Presse*
(New Ulm, Minn.), 1924-1927. The historical setting of
this unusual folk migration is given more fully in Sallet,
Ruszlanddeutsche Siedlungen in den Vereinigten Staaten (reprinted from Deutsch-Amerikanischen Historischen Gesellschaft von Illinois, *Jahrbuch,* Chicago, 1931), except for the
Mennonites who are separately treated in C. H. Smith, *The
Coming of the Russian Mennonites* (Berne, Ind., 1927). Of
the more general works G. M. Stephenson, *A History of
American Immigration* (Boston, 1926), is perhaps the best
attempt at an historical synthesis. In his "Select Bibliography" will be found the titles of the principal books dealing
with particular nationalities; a shorter list appears in H. U.
Faulkner, *The Quest for Social Justice (A History of American Life,* XI), 254-255.

THE NEGRO: The most comprehensive bibliography is
M. N. Work, comp., *A Bibliography of the Negro in Africa
and America* (N. Y., 1928). Essential statistical information
in regard to the race, 1880-1900, is brought together in *Supplementary Analysis and Derivative Tables* (U. S. Twelfth
Census, *Special Rep.*), 185-272. In the same volume, 511-
579, appears an analytical survey of "The Negro Farmer"
by W. E. B. Du Bois, while Carl Kelsey sums up conditions

at the end of the century in *The Negro Farmer* (Chicago, 1903). The growing industrialization of the race is examined in C. H. Wesley, *Negro Labor in the United States* (N. Y., 1927). C. G. Woodson, *A Century of Negro Migration* (Wash., 1918), contains a valuable chapter on the exodus of 1879. The official investigation of the exodus, with majority and minority reports as to the causes therefor, may be found in Select Committee of the U. S. Senate to Investigate the Causes of the Removal of the Negroes from the Southern States to the Northern States, *Report and Testimony* (46 Cong., 2 sess., *Senate Rep.*, no. 693, 3 pts., 1880). Franklin Johnson, *The Development of State Legislation Concerning the Free Negro* (N. Y., 1919), is a pioneer attempt at an objective study of race discrimination in law. J. E. Cutler, *Lynch-Law* (N. Y., 1905), is the best study of mob murder. Paul Lewinson, *Race, Class, & Party* (London, 1932), deals with the problem of voting.

A "Bibliography of Negro Education" appears in U. S. Comr. of Educ., *Rep. for 1893-94*, I, 1038-1061. Important phases of the subject are canvassed in J. L. M. Curry, *Education of the Negroes since 1860* (John F. Slater Fund, *Occasional Papers*, no. 3, 1894) ; J. L. M. Curry and others, "The Slater Fund and the Education of the Negro," U. S. Comr. of Educ., *Rep. for 1894-95*, II, 1367-1424; Kelly Miller, "The Education of the Negro," *Rep. for 1900-01*, I, 731-859; A. D. Mayo, "The Work of Certain Northern Churches in the Education of the Freedmen, 1861-1900," *Rep. for 1901-02*, I, 285-314; and W. E. B. Du Bois, ed., *The Negro Common School* (Atlanta Univ., *Publs.*, no. 6, 1901). An enlightening symposium on "Education for the Negro," participated in by Southern colored educational and religious leaders, may be found in the *New Orleans Times-Democrat*, January 24, 1897. The Moses of his people, Booker T. Washington, has left two autobiographies: *The Story of My Life and Work* (Toronto, 1900), and *Up from Slavery* (N. Y., 1901), presenting somewhat different material. M. B. Thrasher, *Tuskegee* (Boston, 1900), is a good brief account of its subject.

THE INDIAN: Useful general sketches include W. C. Macleod, *The American Indian Frontier* (C. K. Ogden, ed., *The History of Civilization;* London, 1928); Flora W. Seymour, *The Story of the Red Man* (N. Y., 1929); and W. K. Moorehead, *The American Indian in the United States* (Andover, 1914), the last being more concerned than the others with social aspects. C. J. Kappler in *Indian Affairs. Laws and Treaties* (2 vols., Wash., 1903) has compiled the official enactments relating to Indian affairs. Of basic importance, also, are the *Annual Reports* (from 1877) of the Commissioner of Indian Affairs and a similar series (from 1877) issued by the Board of Indian Commissioners. The administration of Indian relations is surveyed historically in an able monograph *The Office of Indian Affairs* (Inst. for Government Research, *Service Monographs*, no. 48, 1927) by L. F. Schmeckebier.

The attitude of the reformers is revealed by the *Annual Reports* (Phila., from 1882) of the Indian Rights Association and the *Proceedings* (Lake Mohonk, from 1883) of the Lake Mohonk Conference of the Friends of the Indians. Among the more reliable contemporary accounts of conditions are E. S. Otis, *The Indian Question* (N. Y., 1878); J. B. Harrison, *The Latest Studies on Indian Reservations* (Phila., 1887); G. B. Grinnell, *The Indians of Today* (N. Y., 1900); and F. E. Leupp, *The Indian and His Problem* (N. Y., 1910), based upon twenty-five years' experience with the red man.

EDUCATION

GENERAL: Of paramount importance are the *Reports* (dating from 1867) of the U. S. Commissioner of Education. An index to the bureau's publications for the years 1867-1890 is included in U. S. Comr. of Educ., *Rep. for 1888-89*, II, 1453-1551. In 1900 there were nearly three hundred periodicals of one type or another devoted primarily to educational matters. The *Addresses and Proceedings* (from 1871; title varies) of the National Educational Association contain papers by leading educators. The annual reports of state and city superintendents are a virtually unexploited source. The most valuable single secondary work is N. M. Butler, ed., *Education in the United States* (2 vols., Albany, 1900), comprising a series of monographs prepared for the Paris Exposition of 1900 and covering all phases of educational effort. E. G. Dexter, *A History of Education in the United States* (N. Y., 1904), is broadly conceived and still useful. Thomas Woody, *A History of Women's Education in the United States* (2 vols., J. M. Cattell, ed., *Science and Education*, IV, bks. i-ii, N. Y., 1929), also treats all levels of education.

COMMON SCHOOLS: R. G. Boone, *Education in the United States* (W. T. Harris, ed., *International Education Series*, XI, N. Y., 1894), and E. P. Cubberley, *Public Education in the United States* (Boston, 1919), deal briefly with elementary and secondary-school education in the period. Caroline D. Aborn and others, eds., *Pioneers of the Kindergarten in America* (N. Y., 1924), contains short biographical sketches, while S. C. Parker, *History of Modern Elementary Education* (Boston, 1912), is the standard treatise in its field. One phase of private education is carefully explored in J. A. Burns, *The Growth and Development of the Catholic School System in the United States* (N. Y., 1912).

E. W. Knight, *Public Education in the South* (Boston, 1922), gives a somewhat darker picture of educational development than that in the present volume. A. D. Mayo has made valuable contributions to the subject in various articles in U. S. Comr. of Educ., *Reports,* including "The Final Establishment of the American Common School System in West Virginia, Maryland, Virginia and Delaware, 1863-1900," *Rep. for 1903*, I, 391-462; and "The Final Establishment of the American Common School System in North Carolina, South Carolina and Georgia, 1863-1900," *Rep. for 1904*, I, 999-1090. The best systematic account of the work of the Peabody Education Fund is *A Brief Sketch of George Peabody and a History of the Public Education Fund through Thirty Years* (Cambridge, Mass., 1898) by J. L.

M. Curry, who served as general agent after the death of Dr.
Barnas Sears in 1880. For Negro education, see earlier, Race
Relations.
COLLEGES AND UNIVERSITIES: C. F. Thwing has helped
illuminate the history of higher education in many studies,
including *The American College in American Life* (N. Y.,
1897) ; *College Administration* (N. Y., 1900), the earliest
treatment of the subject; *A History of Higher Education in
America* (N. Y., 1906), the only general account; *A History
of Education in the United States since the Civil War* (Boston, 1910), which emphasizes university instruction; and
The American and the German University (N. Y., 1928),
showing the importance of Teutonic influences in American
higher education. Historical sketches have been published of
nearly every important college and university. There is also
an abundant literature by and about the great university
presidents, including D. C. Gilman, *The Launching of a
University* (N. Y., 1906), written by the founder of Johns
Hopkins; T. W. Goodspeed, *William Rainey Harper, First
President of the University of Chicago* (Chicago, 1928) ;
and Henry James, *Charles W. Eliot* (2 vols., Boston, 1930).
Two able contemporaneous appraisals of higher education by
foreigners are Gabriel Compayré, *L'Enseignement Supérieur
aux États-Unis* (Paris, 1896), and Athanasius Zimmer-
mann, *Die Universitäten in den Vereinigten Staaten Amerikas*
(Freiburg, 1896).
    H. D. Sheldon, *Student Life and Customs* (W. T. Harris,
ed., *International Education Series*, LI, N. Y., 1901), is a
valuable descriptive study. G. Stanley Hall offers a psychological interpretation of Sheldon's facts in "Student Customs," Am. Antiquarian Soc., *Proceeds.*, n. s., XIV, 83-124.
Further information concerning undergraduate life may be
gleaned from C. F. Thwing, *American Colleges: Their Students and Their Work* (N. Y., 1878) ; C. H. Patton and
W. T. Field, *Eight O'Clock Chapel* (Boston, 1927), describing New England college life in the eighties; a series of
articles by various authors on "Social Life in American Colleges" in *Lippincott's Mag.*, XXXIX-XL (1887-1888) ;

and a similar series entitled "Undergraduate Life in American Universities" in *Scribner's Mag.*, XXI-XXII (1897).

LIBRARIES: H. B. Adams, *Public Libraries and Popular Education* (Home Educ. Dept., Univ. of State of N. Y., *Bull.*, no. 31, 1900), contains a full bibliography. American Library Association, *Papers and Proceedings* (from 1876), and the *Library Journal* (from 1876) throw light on the progress of the movement, while S. S. Green treats the movement as a whole in *The Public Library Movement in the United States, 1853-1893* (Boston, 1913). One important influence is discussed in T. W. Koch, *A Book of Carnegie Libraries* (White Plains, 1917).

THE ADVANCE OF KNOWLEDGE

For learned and scientific societies the chief source of information is to be found in their periodical publications and annual reports. J. D. Thompson, comp., *Handbook of Learned Societies* (Carnegie Inst., *Publs.*, no. 39, 1908), contains a brief history of each. Among longer historical sketches are F. B. Sanborn, "The Work of Twenty-Five Years," *Journ. of Social Sci.*, XXVII, xliii-xlix, reviewing the American Social Science Association to 1890; J. F. Jameson, "The American Historical Association, 1884-1909," *Am. Hist. Rev.*, XV, 1-20; R. T. Ely, "The American Economic Association, 1885-1909," Am. Econ. Assoc., *Publs.*, ser. 3, XI, 47-111; S. W. Fernberger, "The American Psychological Association," *Psychol. Bull.*, XXIX, 1-89; D. S. Martin, "The First Half Century of the American Association," *Pop. Sci. Mo.*, LIII (1898), 822-835, dealing with the American Association for the Advancement of Science; and F. R. Hutton, *A History of the American Society of Mechanical Engineers* (N. Y., 1915). G. B. Goode, *The Smithsonian Institution, 1846-1896* (Wash., 1897), treats the chief independent research agency.

L. H. Haney, *History of Economic Thought* (rev. edn., N. Y., 1920), has a chapter on American economic theory in the late nineteenth century. Two important figures in economics are delineated in J. P. Munroe, *A Life of Francis Amasa Walker* (N. Y., 1923), and H. E. Starr, *William Graham Sumner* (N. Y., 1925). The natal years of sociology in America are explored by A. W. Small in "Fifty Years of Sociology in the United States," *Am. Journ. of Sociology*, XXI, 721-864; "Evolution of Sociological Consciousness in the United States," same mag., XXVII, 226-231; and *Origins of Sociology* (Chicago, 1924), chap. xix; while the foremost contributor is portrayed in Emily P. Cape, *Lester F. Ward* (N. Y., 1922). For a summary of the chief developments in political science, see two works by C. E. Merriam: *American Political Ideas, 1865-1917* (N. Y., 1920), and *New Aspects of Politics* (Chicago, 1925), chap. ii. In *The New History and the Social Studies* (N. Y., 1925) and other works H. E. Barnes explicates the major trends in American historiography. More particularly concerned with the eighties and nineties are W. A. Dunning, "A Generation of American Historiography," Am. Hist. Assoc., *Rep. for 1917*, 345-354; and J. A. Woodburn, "The Promotion of Historical Study in America Following the Civil War," Ill. Hist. Soc., *Trans. for 1922*, 37-50. Full-length biographies of leading historians have also been published, such as J. S. Clark, *John Fiske* (2 vols., Boston, 1917); E. S. Bradley, *Henry Charles Lea* (Phila., 1931); and M. A. DeW. Howe, *James Ford Rhodes* (N. Y., 1929).

J. E. Sandys, *A History of Classical Scholarship* (3 vols., Cambridge, Eng., 1908), summarizes the American contributions of the period, while H. N. Fowler sketches the first forty years of "The American School of Classical Studies at Athens" in *Art and Archaeology*, XIV, 171-260. American advances in philosophy are considered in A. K. Rogers, *English and American Philosophy since 1800* (N. Y., 1922), and Woodbridge Riley, *American Thought* (rev. edn., N. Y., 1923). The share of Americans in helping to develop another field is adequately set forth in E. G. Boring, *A History of Experimental Psychology* (R. M. Elliott, ed., *The Century Psychology Series*; N. Y., 1929), and Gardner Murphy, *An Historical Introduction to Modern Psychology*

(C. K. Ogden, ed., *International Library of Psychology, Philosophy and Scientific Method;* London, 1929). G. Stanley Hall, *Life and Confessions of a Psychologist* (N. Y., 1923), an important source for both the man and his subject, should be read in the light of E. D. Starbuck, "Some Notes on the Psychology of Genius," *Journ. of Philosophy,* XXI, 141-154, an interesting psychological analysis based on the above work.

L. L. Woodruff, ed., *The Development of the Sciences* (New Haven, 1923), contains brief historical sketches of six branches of science in their international development. American contributions are more particularly considered in W. J. McGee, "Fifty Years of American Science," *Atlantic Mo.,* LXXXII (1898), 307-320; D. S. Jordan, ed., *Leading American Men of Science* (W. P. Trent, ed., *Biographies of Leading Americans;* N. Y., 1910); and E. S. Dana and others, *A Century of Science in America* (New Haven, 1918), chiefly as reflected in the pages of the *American Journal of Science.* Fuller treatments of particular branches include E. F. Smith, *Chemistry in America* (N. Y., 1914); C. A. Browne, ed., *A Half-Century of Chemistry in America, 1876-1926* (Am. Chemical Soc., *Journ.,* XLVIII, no. 8A, 1926); R. H. Chittenden, *The Development of Physiological Chemistry in the United States* (Am. Chemical Soc., *Monograph Series;* N. Y., 1930); G. P. Merrill, *The First One Hundred Years of American Geology* (New Haven, 1924); and R. T. Young, *Biology in America* (Boston, 1922), which stresses zoology. Henry Crew, *The Rise of Modern Physics* (Balt., 1928), and D. E. Smith, *History of Mathematics* (2 vols., Boston, 1923), shed light upon American developments in those fields. U. S. Dept. of Agr., *Yearbook for 1899,* contains a notable series of articles showing the transformation of agriculture into a science.

The state of astronomical knowledge at the beginning and end of the period is set forth in two manuals by Simon Newcomb: *Popular Astronomy* (N. Y., 1878), and *The Stars* (J. M. Cattell and others, eds., *The Science Series;* N. Y., 1901), while the author's own intellectual rôle may be sensed from his *The Reminiscences of an Astronomer* (Boston, 1903), an engaging human record. Among biographical treatments are W. H. Dall, *Spencer Fullerton Baird* (Phila., 1915); H. F. Osborn, *Cope: Master Naturalist* (Princeton, 1931); and D. C. Gilman, *The Life of James Dwight Dana* (N. Y., 1899). For medical progress see the next section; and for mechanical invention consult earlier, Urban Life.

MEDICAL PROGRESS

A great medical scientist is portrayed in Harvey Cushing, *The Life of Sir William Osler* (2 vols., Oxford, 1925), which devotes fourteen chapters to Osler's American career, 1884-1905. Ruth Putnam, *The Life and Letters of Mary Putnam Jacobi* (N. Y., 1925), deals with the foremost woman physician of the time. A special branch in which Americans achieved greatly is discussed in J. A. Taylor, *History of Dentistry* (Phila., 1922). Investigators of the public-hygiene movement will get valuable help from American Public Health Association, *Public Health, Reports and Papers* (1873-1895; titled thereafter *Journal*). Much of this material is utilized in M. P. Ravenel, ed., *A Half Century of Public Health* (N. Y., 1921). H. I. Bowditch, *Public Hygiene in America* (Boston, 1877), presents the lamentable state of affairs when the period began, while S. W. Abbott, *The Past and Present Condition of Public Hygiene and State Medicine in the United States* (H. B. Adams, ed., *Monographs on American Social Economics*, XIX, Boston, 1900), summarizes the situation at its close. G. C. Whipple, *State Sanitation* (3 vols., Cambridge, Mass., 1917), is an excellent historical sketch of the activities of the influential Massachusetts state board of health. The father of medical and vital statistics in America is depicted in F. H. Garrison, *John Shaw Billings* (N. Y., 1915).

LITERARY PRODUCTION

AUTHORSHIP: Of the innumerable histories of American letters *The Cambridge History of American Literature* (4 vols., N. Y., 1917-1921), edited by W. P. Trent and others, is outstanding as a pioneer effort to envisage literature as something broader than *belles-lettres*, while V. L. Parrington's uncompleted *The Beginnings of Critical Realism in America* (*Main Currents in American Thought*, N. Y., 1927-1930, III), is equally notable as a bold and provocative attempt at an economic and social interpretation. Surveys showing unusual perspicuity include Carl Van Doren, *The American Novel* (N. Y., 1921), and F. L. Pattee, *A History of American Literature since 1870* (N. Y., 1915), which is continued and amplified in his *The New American Literature, 1890-1930* (N. Y., 1930). Constance Rourke, *American Humor* (N. Y., 1931), is by far the best work on its subject. Among contemporaneous appraisals of American letters H. C. Vedder, *American Writers of To-day* (N. Y., 1894), and Robert Ford, *American Humourists* (London, 1897), are still of interest.

No second-hand acquaintance with literature, however, can take the place of personal familiarity with the contents of the books. Thanks to the vogue of local-color writing and realistic fiction, the delver into social history will find a rich mine of hitherto neglected ore in many of the novels and short stories, or, to adopt Paul Shorey's scornful phrase, "these laborious inventories of unconcerning things." Howells, for example, in a score or so of novels gives posterity a picture of middle-class life and thought which the most relentless scrutiny of official documents will fail to disclose. An intimate insight into current literary conditions can be gained from such books as Hamlin Garland, *Roadside Meetings* (N. Y., 1930); C. D. Warner, *The Relation of Literature to Life* (N. Y., 1897); W. D. Howells, *My Literary Passions* (N. Y., 1895), and *Literature and Life* (N. Y., 1902); and Henry James, *Letters* (Percy Lubbock, ed., 2 vols., N. Y., 1920). Representative biographies of major contributors are A. B. Paine, *Mark Twain* (3 vols., N. Y., 1912); D. G. Cooke, *William Dean Howells* (N. Y., 1922); Julia C. Harris, *The Life and Letters of Joel Chandler Harris* (Boston, 1918); F. O. Matthiessen, *Sarah Orne Jewett* (Boston,

1929); and C. H. Dennis, *Eugene Field's Creative Years* (N. Y., 1924). Two lesser figures are pictured in Mary A. Roe, *E. P. Roe* (N. Y., 1899), and H. R. Mayes, *Alger* (N. Y., 1928). Juvenile "thrillers" are described and sympathetically assessed in Edmund Pearson, *Dime Novels* (Boston, 1929).

PUBLISHING: The *Publishers' Weekly* (N. Y., from 1872) is the principal source of information. Its last issue in January each year contains a summary of all the important books of the preceding year, often with critical comments. The *Dial*, XXVIII, no. 333 (May 1, 1900), gives a "Twenty Years' Retrospect" of publishing, book selling and allied interests. No adequate history of an American publishing house has yet appeared, though for three firms pertinent material can be found in J. H. Harper, *The House of Harper* (N. Y., 1912); G. H. Putnam, *Memories of a Publisher* (N. Y., 1915); and Henry Holt, *Garrulities of an Octogenarian Editor* (Boston, 1923). One knotty problem of publishers is thoroughly canvassed in G. H. Putnam, comp., *The Question of Copyright* (N. Y., 1891), and R. R. Bowker, *Copyright: Its History and Its Law* (Boston, 1912). For magazine publishing, see earlier, General Periodical Sources.

RELIGIOUS CURRENTS

S. M. Jackson, comp., "A Bibliography of American Church History, 1820-1893," Philip Schaff and others, eds., *The American Church History Series* (13 vols., N. Y., 1893-1897), XII, 441-513, is the first systematic attempt to bring together the titles of books and pamphlets on the subject. P. G. Mode, comp., *Source Book and Bibliographical Guide for American Church History* (Menasha, Wis., 1921), besides printing certain key documents, gives a select list of books and articles. H. K. Rowe, *The History of Religion in the United States* (N. Y., 1924), is an interpretation of religious trends, marked by insight and a full appreciation of diverse conditioning factors. Other general surveys of religious development, of which the latest is W. W. Sweet, *The*

Story of Religions in America (N. Y., 1930), are sketchy and unsatisfactory for the period since Reconstruction. Much the same is true of most denominational histories, including those in the *American Church History Series* except H. K. Carroll, *The Religious Forces of the United States* (I, rev. edn., N. Y., 1912), which is valuable for statistical analyses. Daniel Dorchester, *Christianity in the United States* (N. Y., 1887; rev. edn., 1895), also contains data on church growth.

Emotional methods and experiences are discussed in F. G. Beardsley, *A History of American Revivals* (N. Y., 1912); G. C. Loud, *Evangelized America* (N. Y., 1928); and H. C. Weber, *Evangelism* (N. Y., 1929), an attempt at graphic presentation; while the foremost revivalist is understandingly portrayed in Gamaliel Bradford, *D. L. Moody* (N. Y., 1927). For the Christian Endeavor Society, founded in 1881, and other similar organizations, the best general sketch is F. O. Erb, *The Development of the Young People's Movement* (Chicago, 1917). Three useful works on foreign missionary activity are D. L. Leonard, *Missionary Annals of the Nineteenth Century* (Cleveland, 1899); J. S. Dennis, *Christian Missions and Social Progress* (3 vols., N. Y., 1897-1906); and same author, *Centennial Survey of Christian Missions* (N. Y., 1902).

Among the influential books written by those whom Walter Rauschenbusch later called the "pioneers of Christian social thought in America" are R. H. Newton, *Social Studies* (N. Y., 1886); S. L. Loomis, *Modern Cities and Their Religious Problems* (N. Y., 1887); Josiah Strong, *Our Country* (N. Y., 1885; rev. edn., 1891), and *The New Era* (N. Y., 1893); R. T. Ely, *Social Aspects of Christianity* (N. Y., 1889); Lyman Abbott, *Christianity and Social Problems* (Boston, 1896); and Washington Gladden's volumes: *Workingmen and Their Employers* (Boston, 1876), *Applied Christianity* (Boston, 1886), *Tools and the Man* (Boston, 1893) and *Social Salvation* (Boston, 1902). Two of the leaders tell their life stories in Lyman Abbott, *Reminiscences* (Boston, 1915), and Washington Gladden, *Recollections* (Boston, 1909).

A. D. White, *A History of the Warfare of Science with Theology in Christendom* (2 vols., N. Y., 1896), is interesting as the product of a period when the issues discussed were acute and ever present. George Harris, *A Century's Change in Religion* (Boston, 1914), is valuable as a dispassionate discussion of theological reconstruction by one of the participants in the "Andover controversy." J. H. Barrows, ed., *The World's Parliament of Religions* (2 vols., Chicago, 1893), offers the best account of that notable gathering. Phillips Brooks of Trinity Church, Boston, the subject of a biography by A. V. G. Allen entitled *Life and Letters of Phillips Brooks* (N. Y., 1900), is the best example of a forceful and influential churchman who remained indifferent, though not antagonistic, to the scientific and social forces that were remaking religion.

James MacCaffrey, *History of the Catholic Church in the Nineteenth Century* (2 vols., 2d edn., Dublin, 1910), sketches briefly the history of the American Church in its international setting. Gerald Shaughnessy, *Has the Immigrant Kept the Faith?* (N. Y., 1925), is a statistical demonstration showing that the American Church assimilated and retained the vast Catholic influx from Europe. Of indispensable importance are A. S. Will, *Life of Cardinal Gibbons* (2 vols., N. Y., 1922), and F. J. Zwierlein, *The Life and Letters of Bishop McQuaid* (3 vols., Rochester, 1927). The best treatment of anti-Catholic sentiment is H. J. Desmond, *The A. P. A. Movement* (Wash., 1912). Another religion heavily indebted to immigration is dealt with historically in Joseph Leiser, *American Judaism* (N. Y., 1925).

The American history of the Salvation Army is traced in three works by its leaders: Maud Ballington Booth, *Beneath Two Flags* (N. Y., 1890); Ballington Booth, *From Ocean to Ocean* (N. Y., 1891); and F. de L. Booth-Tucker, *The Salvation Army in the United States* (N. Y., 1891). No historical account of the Christian Science movement as such has been written, but many lives of its progenitor are available. Sibyl Wilbur (O'Brien), *The Life of Mary Baker Eddy* (rev. edn., Boston, 1913), and L. P. Powell, *Mary Baker*

Eddy (N. Y., 1930), are biographies acceptable to Christian Scientists. Of a more critical character are Georgine Milmine, *The Life of Mary Baker G. Eddy and the History of Christian Science* (N. Y., 1909), containing valuable documents, and E. F. Dakin, *Mrs. Eddy* (rev. edn., N. Y., 1930). Mrs. Eddy's version of her life work is presented in the various editions of *Science and Health*, in *Retrospection and Introspection* (Boston, 1891) and in *Miscellaneous Writings* (Boston, 1896), the last embracing many of her contributions to the *Christian Science Journal* (Boston, from 1883), the files of which should be examined for accounts of cures claimed by healers. For Mormonism it is important to consult the *Millennial Star* (Liverpool and Salt Lake City, from 1840), which contains exegetical articles from the Mormon point of view and official resolutions and proceedings.

THE FINE ARTS

GRAPHIC ART: Sadakichi Hartmann, *A History of American Art* (2 vols., Boston, 1901), includes, besides painting, a discussion of sculpture, while Suzanne La Follette in *Art in America* (N. Y., 1929) extends her treatment to architecture. Standard historical manuals are Eugen Neuhaus, *The History and Ideals of American Art* (Stanford, 1931); Samuel Isham, *The History of American Painting* (J. C. Van Dyke, ed., *The History of American Art*, III, rev. edn., N. Y., 1927); C. H. Caffin, *The Story of American Painting* (N. Y., 1907); Pauline King, *American Mural Painting* (Boston, 1902); and Frank Weitenkampf, *American Graphic Art* (rev. edn., N. Y., 1924), which covers the various forms of illustrative art. The monthly reviews of "The Field of Art" in *Scribner's Magazine* during the period give a "close-up" of developments. Royal Cortissoz, *American Artists* (N. Y., 1923), brilliantly characterizes a number of the painters of the eighties and nineties, while among the larger biographical studies are Alfred Trumble, *George Inness* (N. Y., 1904); W. H. Downes, *John Singer Sargent* (Boston, 1925); Cecilia Waern, *John La Farge* (*Portfolio*

Monographs, XXVI, N. Y., 1896); Frank Rutter, *James McNeill Whistler* (N. Y., 1911); and C. H. Abbott, *Howard Pyle* (N. Y., 1925).

A. B. Maurice and F. T. Cooper, *The History of the Nineteenth Century in Caricature* (N. Y., 1904), is perhaps the best work on the evolution of the cartoon. Contemporary collections of drawings include F. B. Opper, *The Tariff Question* (N. Y., 1888), selected from his contributions to *Puck;* C. D. Gibson, *Drawings* (N. Y., 1894), and *Sketches and Cartoons* (N. Y., 1898), taken from *Life;* Charles Nelan, *Cartoons of Our War with Spain* (N. Y., 1898), which originally appeared in the *New York Herald;* C. L. Bartholomew, *Cartoons of the Spanish-American War* (Minneapolis, 1899), drawn by "Bart" for the *Minneapolis Journal;* F. G. Attwood, *Attwood's Pictures: an Artist's History of the Last Ten Years of the Nineteenth Century* (N. Y., 1900), first contributed to *Life;* and Homer Davenport, *Cartoons* (N. Y., 1898), drawn for the *New York Journal.*

SCULPTURE AND ARCHITECTURE: The chief general discussions of plastic art are Lorado Taft, *The History of American Sculpture* (J. C. Van Dyke, ed., *The History of American Art,* I, rev. edn., N. Y., 1924); C. H. Caffin, *American Masters of Sculpture* (N. Y., 1903); and J. W. McSpadden, *Famous Sculptors of America* (rev. edn., N. Y., 1927). The greatest American sculptor tells of his life in *The Reminiscences of Augustus Saint-Gaudens* (Homer Saint-Gaudens, ed., 2 vols., N. Y., 1913).

J. W. Dow, *American Renaissance* (N. Y., 1904), is a badly jumbled history of American architecture, which has been superseded by such surveys as T. E. Tallmadge, *The Story of American Architecture* (N. Y., 1927); Fiske Kimball, *American Architecture* (Indianapolis, 1928); and G. H. Edgell, *The American Architecture of To-day* (N. Y., 1928). W. A. Starrett, *Skyscrapers and the Men Who Build Them* (N. Y., 1928), gives the best account of the origins of what the author calls "the most distinctively American thing in the world." Popular taste is mirrored in manuals

*Augustus Saint-Gaudens' statue
of "The Puritan."*

John W. Alexander's portrait of President McCosh of Princeton.

Art

like S. B. Reed, *House-Plans for Everybody* (N. Y., 1878),
L. H. Gibson, *Convenient Houses* (N. Y., 1889), and same
author, *Beautiful Houses* (N. Y., 1895). Outstanding architects receive biographical treatment in Mrs. Schuyler Van
Rensselaer, *Henry Hobson Richardson and His Works* (Boston, 1888); Harriet Monroe, *The Life of John Wellborn
Root* (Boston, 1896); Charles Moore, *Daniel H. Burnham*
(2 vols., N. Y., 1921); same author, *The Life and Times
of Charles Follen McKim* (Boston, 1929); and C. C. Baldwin, *Stanford White* (N. Y., 1931).

MUSIC: Four comprehensive surveys of American music
are L. C. Elson, *The History of American Music* (J. C. Van
Dyke, ed., *The History of American Art*, II, N. Y., 1904;
rev. by Arthur Elson, N. Y., 1925); W. L. Hubbard, ed.,
History of American Music (same ed., *The American History
and Encyclopedia of Music;* N. Y., 1910); Arthur Farwell
and W. D. Darby, eds., *Music in America* (D. G. Mason, ed.,
The Art of Music, 14 vols., N. Y., 1915-1917, IV); and
J. T. Howard, *Our American Music* (N. Y., 1931), the
latest and best. H. C. Lahee, *Annals of Music in America*
(Boston, 1920), supplies a chronological record of significant
musical events. Important periodicals for historical reference
are the *Musical Courier* (N. Y., from 1880); the *Musical
Year-Book of the United States* (Boston, 1886-1893); and
the *Etude* (Phila., from 1883).

For orchestral music the following works are particularly
helpful: Theodore Thomas, *A Musical Autobiography* (G.
P. Upton, ed., 2 vols., Chicago, 1905); C. E. Russell, *The
American Orchestra and Theodore Thomas* (N. Y., 1927);
M. A. DeW. Howe, *The Boston Symphony Orchestra* (rev.
edn., Boston, 1931); and Walter Damrosch, *My Musical
Life* (N. Y., 1923). The best general account of grand opera
during the period is H. C. Lahee, *Grand Opera in America*
(*Music Lovers' Series;* Boston, 1902). The lives and work
of leading composers are sympathetically appraised in Rupert
Hughes, *Contemporary American Composers* (Boston,
1900). Separate biographies and memoirs of importance include W. H. Humiston, *MacDowell* (N. Y., 1921); Vance

Thompson, *The Life of Ethelbert Nevin* (Boston, 1913);
Joseph Kaye, *Victor Herbert* (N. Y., 1931); Mrs. Reginald
de Koven, *A Musician and His Wife* (N. Y., 1926); and
J. P. Sousa, *Marching Along* (Boston, 1928).

Julius Mattfeld, comp., *The Folk Music of the Western
Hemisphere* (N. Y., 1925), lists much material on the folk
music of Negroes, cowboys, lumberjacks, mountaineers,
sailors, miners, etc. Two volumes by Sigmund Spaeth recall
the vogue of popular songs: *Read 'Em and Weep* (Garden
City, 1926); and *Weep Some More, My Lady* (Garden City,
1927). On the personal side, such books should be supplemented by C. K. Harris, *After the Ball* (N. Y., 1926), and
Theodore Dreiser, *Twelve Men* (N. Y., 1919), which contains an account of the author's brother, Paul Dresser.

SPORTS AND RECREATIONS

SPORTS: Compiled by C. M. Van Sockum, *Sport* (N. Y.,
1914) is an "attempt at a bibliography of books and periodi-
cals published during 1890-1912" on that subject in the
United States and other countries. Of periodicals, *Outing*
(N. Y., from 1882) is particularly useful as it deals exclu-
sively with sports and was itself an outgrowth of the sports
movement. Important reference works for baseball are A. G.
Spalding, *America's National Game* (N. Y., 1911); G. L.
Moreland, *Balldom* (N. Y., 1914); F. C. Richter, *Richter's
History and Records of Baseball* (Phila., 1914); and E. J.
Lanigan, ed., *Baseball Cyclopedia* (N. Y., 1922). The A. G.
Spalding Baseball Collection, consisting of manuscripts,
books and pamphlets, is in the New York Public Library.
Developments in the chief college sport are traced in Walter
Camp and L. F. Deland, *Football* (N. Y., 1896); P. H.
Davis, *Football* (N. Y., 1911); and A. M. Weyand, *Ameri-
can Football* (N. Y., 1926), while the rôle of two masters of
strategy is set forth in Harford Powel, jr., *Walter Camp*
(Boston, 1926), and A. A. Stagg and W. W. Stout, *Touch-
down!* (N. Y., 1927).

Besides the general accounts of professional boxing in

Alexander Johnston, *Ten—and Out* (N. Y., 1927), and Jeffery Farnol, *Famous Prize Fights* (Boston, 1928), the careers of three heavyweight champions are elucidated in R. F. Dibble, *John L. Sullivan* (Boston, 1925), J. J. Corbett, *The Roar of the Crowd* (N. Y., 1925), and R. H. Davis, *Bob Fitzsimmons* (N. Y., 1926). For other sports, see J. P. Paret, *Lawn Tennis* (N. Y., 1912); J. D. Travers and J. R. Crowell, *The Fifth Estate* (N. Y., 1926), dealing with golf; R. P. Elmer, *Archery* (Phila., 1926); Samuel Crowther and Arthur Ruhl, *Rowing and Track Athletics* (Caspar Whitney, ed., *The American Sportsman's Library;* N. Y., 1905); R. F. Kelley, *American Rowing* (N. Y., 1932); W. P. Stephens, *American Yachting* (N. Y., 1904); and Nigel Lindsay, *The America's Cup* (London, 1930).

THE THEATER: Varied aspects of theatrical development are treated in A. H. Quinn, *A History of American Drama from the Civil War to the Present Day* (2 vols., N. Y., 1927); Arthur Hornblow, *A History of the Theatre in America* (2 vols., Phila., 1919); Mary C. Crawford, *The Romance of the American Theatre* (rev. edn., Boston, 1925); M. J. Moses, *The American Dramatist* (rev. edn., Boston, 1926); and same author, *Famous Actor-Families in America* (N. Y., 1906). T. A. Brown, *A History of the New York Stage* (3 vols., N. Y., 1903), traces theatrical development in one city, while Eugene Tompkins and Quincy Kilby, *The History of the Boston Theatre, 1854-1901* (Boston, 1908), reviews the situation in another. Indispensable sources are the *New York Clipper* (N. Y., from 1853) and the *New York Dramatic Mirror* (N. Y., from 1879), the leading journals of the theatrical profession. Special collections of playbills, clippings and the like can be found in the Library of Congress, the public libraries of New York and Boston, and at the Harvard and University of Chicago libraries.

The intense popular interest in the theater led to the production of a number of books, usually journalistic in character but valuable as reflecting contemporary taste: F. E. McKay and C. E. L. Wingate, eds., *Famous American Actors of To-day* (N. Y., 1896); J. B. Clapp and E. F. Edgett,

Players of the Present (3 vols., Dunlap Soc., *Publs.*, n. s., nos. 9, 11, 13, 1899-1901) ; Norman Hapgood, *The Stage in America, 1897-1900* (N. Y., 1901) ; L. C. Strang, *Players and Plays of the Last Quarter Century* (2 vols., Boston, 1902) ; and the volumes contributed by L. C. Strang to the *Stage Lovers' Series* (Boston, 1899-1902). Leading figures in the legitimate drama are pictured at greater length in such works as Lester Wallack, *Memories of Fifty Years* (N. Y., 1889) ; J. F. Daly, *The Life of Augustin Daly* (N. Y., 1917) ; Percy MacKaye, *Epoch* (2 vols., N. Y., 1927), a biography of Steele MacKaye; and William Winter, *The Life and Art of Joseph Jefferson* (N. Y., 1914). Reminiscent writings by important dramatic critics include Henry A. Clapp, *Reminiscences of a Dramatic Critic* (Boston, 1902) ; J. R. Towse, *Sixty Years of the Theater* (N. Y., 1916) ; and William Winter, *The Wallet of Time* (2 vols., N. Y., 1913).

M. B. Leavitt, *Fifty Years in Theatrical Management* (N. Y., 1912), is valuable as a hodgepodge of information in regard to musical, burlesque, minstrel, vaudeville and circus attractions. H. B. Smith, *First Nights and First Editions* (Boston, 1931), written by a prolific librettist, and Rudolph Aronson, *Theatrical and Musical Memoirs* (N. Y., 1913), by a leading manager, throw light on the evolution of light opera, while Robert Grau, *Forty Years Observation of Music and the Drama* (N. Y., 1909), is a repository of theatrical gossip with particular reference to vaudeville. Comic-opera stars have their innings in H. C. Barnaby, *Reminiscences* (G. L. Varney, ed., Boston, 1913) ; Felix Isman, *Weber and Fields* (N. Y., 1924) ; De Wolf Hopper, *Once a Clown, Always a Clown* (Boston, 1927) ; and Francis Wilson, *Life of Himself* (Boston, 1924). The one-hundred-per-cent-American minstrel show is discussed from different angles in Carl Wittke, *Tambo and Bones* (Durham, 1930), and Dailey Paskman and Sigmund Spaeth, *"Gentlemen, Be Seated!"* (Garden City, 1928). The burlesque stage is treated in Bernard Sobel, *Burleycue* (N. Y., 1931).

INDEX

ABBOTT, Lyman, and social religion, 323, 339.

Academic freedom, and social-science instruction, 227-228; and theological instruction, 327-328.

Adams, Henry, as historian, 224; on Gibbs, 231; at World's Fair, 285; on politics, 387, 388 *n.*; and *fin de siècle*, 421, 422.

Adams, W. T., as juvenile author, 265.

Addams, Jane, and settlement movement, 351-352.

Adler, Felix, and Ethical Culture, 329; in campaign of 1884, 400 *n.*

Advertising, tobacco, 9-10; billboard, 54, 195; newspaper, 186-187, 195-196; influence of, 195, 198; magazine, 196-198, 338 *n.*; expenditure, 196; patent-medicine, 196, 197-198, 243.

Agrarianism, in South, 19-20, 54, 165, 384, 412; in West, 51-52, 54, 55, 425, 426; in election of 1892, 54-55 *n.*, 407, 427.

Agriculture, in South, 1-8, 412, 428; growth of scientific, 18-19, 215-216, 234, 236-237; in Great West, 24, 31-32, 39-44, 428; in Middle West, 53-58, 428; in East, 68-71. *See also* Agrarianism.

Alabama, poor whites in, 5; manufacturing in, 12-13, 14; capital crimes in, 363; mixed population of, 377; Negro education in, 378.

Alaska, gold rush to, 429-430.

Alcott, Louisa M., as feminist, 146; and Concord School, 238; as author, 251, 253, 266.

Aldrich, T. B., as poet, 268; on social dangers, 427.

Alexander, J. W., as painter, 274.

Alger, Horatio, as juvenile author, 265.

Allen, J. L., as author, 256-257.

Altgeld, J. P., on state rights, 415.

American Federation of Labor, for woman suffrage, 146; and Sabbath movement, 335; admits Negroes, 381.

American Library Association, founded, 175.

American Peace Society, work of, 365-366.

American Protective Association, career of, 346-348.

American Red Cross Society, formed, 364; at work, 364-365, 367-368, 417.

American School of Classical Studies, established, 229.

Amusements, rural, 59; for children, 128-129, 130; of wealthy, 153; theatrical, 290-297, 300-302; circus, 297-299; opera, 299-300, 307; athletic, 308-319; Sunday, 333-334; as political aid, 408-409. *See also* Fraternal orders. Music.

Anderson, Mary, as actress, 292.

Andover Theological Seminary, controversy in, 328; social science in, 339.

Andrews, E. B., accused of economic heresy, 228; on national consolidation, 416.

Angell, J. B., as university president, 204.

Anthony, Susan B., in suffrage movement, 146, 147.

Anti-Saloon League, formed, 359.

Appendicitis, new treatment for, 244.

475

incomes, 184-185; as social critic, 261, 262, 427; as Herne's friend, 295; on national inconsistencies, 429.

Hoyt, Charles, as playwright, 294, 295-296.

Hull House, work of, 65, 352; founded, 351.

Humanitarianism, and children, 129, 130, 168-169; aided by press, 188, 194; and social work, 336, 339-340, 349-353; and Indian, 370-375; and internationalism, 417; bibliography of, 453-455. *See also* American Red Cross Society, Peace movement, Prisons, Temperance.

Humor, pictorial, 188, 190, 275, 291, 318, 444; in literature, 267-268; on stage, 295-296, 299, 300-301; as safety valve, 409.

Hungarians, in East, 72, 73.

Hunt, R. M., as architect, 280.

Hunt, W. M., as artist, 274.

IDAHO, population changes in, 24, 39; enters Union, 51-52; suffrage in, 148; education in, 204 *n.*

Illinois, population changes in, 57, 67; passes pure-food laws, 133; education in, 170; University of, 203, 208, 209; fraudulent degrees exposed in, 216 *n.*; penal reform in, 362.

Illiteracy, as immigration test, 138 *n.*; and Blair bill, 164; in South, 165, 384, 385; declines, 171.

Immigrants, in South, 15-16, 21; aided by railroads, 16, 26, 28; in Great West, 27-34; in Middle West, 55-57, 59, 64-66; religion of, 56, 333, 339, 345; in politics, 57, 75, 76, 392; education of, 66, 169-170, 171; in East, 71, 72-76; affect social conditions, 111, 114, 354; in literature and song, 267, 295, 304; bibliography of, 455-456. *See also* nationalities by name.

In His Steps, published, 342.

Independent movement, supports Cleveland, 397-400, 407.

Indian Territory, formed, 369-370.

Indiana, population changes in, 67; education in, 203 *n.*; penal reform in, 362; in national politics, 400, 405.

Indians, in Oklahoma, 47-49; as entertainers, 243 *n.*, 298; as art subjects, 275; rebel, 368-370; reform efforts for, 370-375; bibliography of, 458.

Industry, manufacturing, 8-18, 100 *n.*, 138; mining, 34-35; cattle, 35-37; lumber, 44; fishing, 44, 131; canning, 132-133; women in, 141-143; liquor, 355; international aspects of, 417-418. *See also* Agriculture, Labor.

Ingersoll, R. G., as agnostic, 329.

Inness, George, as artist, 274.

Institutional church, promoted, 339-340.

Intellectual life, influence of city on, 80-81, 247-248; Negro in, 378-380, 385-386; international influence on, 417. *See also* Colleges and universities, Education, Literature, Scholarship, Science.

International copyright, sought, 251-255, 293 *n.*

International influences, on etiquette, 122; on diet, 133 *n.*, 134; through marriage, 152-153; on control of prostitution, 158-159; on education, 168, 206, 207, 211-212; on scholarship, 223, 224, 225-226, 229; on science, 230, 235-236, 238, 240-244; on literature, 258-259, 270; on painting, 272-273, 275; on cartooning, 276; on sculpture, 277-279; on architecture, 280-281; at World's Fair, 285; on theater, 293, 294; on music, 305-307; on sport, 308-309, 315-316; on religion, 324-326, 336, 341; on social work, 350-351, 364; on penology, 361; on peace

Playgrounds, begun, 130.
Plumbing, improved, 139-140.
Poetry, characterized, 268-269.
Police, corruption, 115-116, 158, 358; efforts to reform, 116, 159; aided by inventions, 117.
Political science, advances in, 225-226.
Polygamy, legislation against, 45-47, 423-424.
Ponca, maltreated, 370.
Poole, F. W., as librarian, 160, 175.
Poor whites, changed status of, 4-6, 16-18.
Population, of South, 20-21, 22, 377; of Great West, 23-25, 28-31; of Middle West, 56, 67; of East, 67-72; of cities: in general, 1, 76, 425; in South, 13-14; in Middle West, 57, 62, 64; in East, 68, 72-73.
Postal service, improvement in, 98.
Presidential elections of
1880: Solid South in, 406-407.
1884: suffragists in, 147; cartooning in, 276; in general, 396-401; Solid South in, 414.
1888: suffragists in, 147; Prohibitionists in, 359; corruption in, 405; outcome of, 406; trickery in, 408.
1892: Prohibitionists in, 359; Populism in, 407, 427; racial appeals in, 408.
1896: affected by phone, 96; affected by literacy, 171; yellow press and, 190; syndicated material in, 193; A. P. A. in, 347-348; campaign funds in, 405-406; characterized, 427.
Prisons, inmates of, 111, 114, 361; movement to reform, 360-364; bibliography of, 455.
Prohibition. *See* Temperance.
Prohibition party, and woman suffrage, 146-147; gains, 359, 400.

Prostitution, and police collusion, 116; extent of, 156-159; combated by religious workers, 336, 453.
Psychology, advances in, 237-238.
Public-health movement, 244-246. *See also* Health, Medicine, Sanitation.
Publishing, corrupt methods in, 167; standards, 248-249, 270; expansion in, 249-250; copyright affects, 251-255; bibliography of, 466.
Pugilism, 310-311.
Pulitzer, Joseph, as journalist, 160, 187-191, 194, 430.
Pullman, George, bans drink traffic, 356.

QUAY, M. S., Indian heritage of, 383.
Quick, Herbert, and rural maladjustment, 60, 61.
Quimby, P. P., as magnetic healer, 336-337.

RACING, popularity of, 309.
Radcliffe College, founded, 205.
Railroads, increase, 8, 22; aid settlers, 26-27, 28; ban drinking, 356; aid standard time, 410. *See also* Rapid transit.
Ranching, transformed, 35-37.
Rapid transit, elevated, 90-91; cable, 91-92; electrical, 92-93; underground, 93; lines consolidated, 389-390. *See also* Bridges, Railroads, Roads, Streets.
Realism, in literature, 257-261; in theater, 293-295.
Red Cross. *See* American Red Cross Society.
Reform, labor, 19 n., 129-130, 431; humanitarian, 110-111, 336, 349-353; in police department, 115-116; dress, 148-150, 313; in divorce legislation, 154-156; in moral standards, 158-159, 197-198, 270-271; efforts for Sabbath, 334-335; temperance, 353-360; prison, 360-364; in treatment of Indians, 370-375; in city gov-

The THIRTIES
A TIME TO REMEMBER

edited by *DON CONGDON*

SIMON AND SCHUSTER • NEW YORK • 1962

ACKNOWLEDGMENTS

"I Remember the Thirties"—Copyright 1960 by John Steinbeck; reprinted by permission of McIntosh & Otis, Inc.

"From Riches to Rags" and other selections from *The Age of the Great Depression*—Copyright 1948 by The Macmillan Company; reprinted by permission of the Publisher.

"How to Solve the Traffic Situation"—Copyright 1930 by Condé Nast Publications Inc.; reprinted by permission of Harold Ober Associates, Inc.

"New England's Tragic Towns"—Copyright 1938 by Louis Adamic; reprinted by permission of Harper & Brothers.

"Catastrophe in Coal"—Copyright 1960 by Irving Bernstein; reprinted by permission of Houghton Mifflin Company.

Selections from *Only Yesterday*—Copyright 1931 by Frederick Lewis Allen; reprinted by permission of Harper & Brothers.

"Pepper Martin—The Happiest Hooligan"—Copyright 1959 by W. C. Heinz; reprinted by permission of William Morris Agency, Inc.

"The Gashouse Gang, the Deans, and Other Heroes," from *Baseball*—Copyright 1947 by Robert Smith; reprinted by permission of Simon and Schuster.

"The Texas Babe"—Copyright 1932 by Condé Nast Publications Inc.; reprinted by permission of Harold Ober Associates, Inc.

"The *Akron* and Three Who Came Back"—Copyright 1957 by John Toland; reprinted by permission of Holt, Rinehart and Winston, Inc.

"Hitchhiker"—Copyright 1946 by Eric Sevareid; reprinted by permission of Alfred A. Knopf, Inc.

"The Flight of the Bonus Army"—Copyright 1932 by The New Republic, Inc.; reprinted by permission of the Author and *The New Republic*.

"The Inaugural"—Copyright 1957 by Arthur M. Schlesinger, Jr.; reprinted by permission of Houghton Mifflin Company.

"The Great Bank Holiday"—Copyright 1960 by Curtis Publishing Company; reprinted by permission of Harold Matson Company.

"The Rise of Federal Relief" and "More on the Rise of Federal Relief"—Copyright 1958 by Arthur M. Schlesinger, Jr.; reprinted by permission of Houghton Mifflin Company.

"How to Relieve Everybody"—Copyright 1933 by Condé Nast Publications Inc.; reprinted by permission of Harold Ober Associates, Inc.

"Weary Willie"—Copyright 1939 by The University of North Carolina; reprinted by permission of University of North Carolina Press.

Material in "Scottsboro Boys" abstracted from *They Shall Be Free*—Copyright 1951 by Allan K. Chalmers; used by permission of Doubleday & Company, Inc.

"Life with Fiorello"—Copyright 1955 by Ernest Cuneo; reprinted by permission of The Macmillan Company.

"Repeal" and other selections from *Since Yesterday*—Copyright 1939, 1940 by Harper & Brothers; reprinted by permission of the Publisher.

"The Judging of Hauptmann" and "*Morro Castle* Aftermath"—Copyright 1935 by Stanley Walker; reprinted by permission of the Author.

"Dillinger"—Copyright 1956 by Fawcett Publications, Inc.; reprinted by permission of the Author.

"The Great Nickel Panic"—Copyright 1931 by Condé Nast Publications Inc.; reprinted by permission of the Author.

"The Almost-Assassination of Thomas E. Dewey"—Copyright 1951 by Burton B. Turkus and Sid Feder; reprinted by permission of Farrar, Straus and Cudahy, Inc.

"The *Morro Castle* Fire"—Copyright 1949 by Simon and Schuster; reprinted by permission of the Author.

"Rescue at Sea"—Copyright 1934 by The New Republic, Inc.; reprinted by permission of *The New Republic*.

"Boulder Dam"—Copyright 1935 by The New Republic, Inc.; reprinted by permission of *The New Republic*.

"In Search of America"—Copyright 1937 by W. W. Norton, Inc.; reprinted by permission of the Author.

Table of Contents

7

Table of Contents

8

Table of Contents

Table of Contents

Table of Contents

stand it. They'd hang onto the cage and ride back up on the first trip and quit right there."   *—Boulder Dam spectator*

Table of Contents

13

Table of Contents

15

Table of Contents

16

17

Table of Contents

FOREWORD

RECENTLY I have been urging friends to look back at the Nineteen Thirties as a time of unprecedented social reform, artistic ferment and imaginative leadership (qualities found in very small measure in the "Fabulous Fifties"). I believe that a portrait of the period would remind us of its particular vitality—and entertain readers, too.

The Thirties gave us social security and unemployment insurance, hospitalization plans, the first cyclotron, sulfa drugs and the artificial lung, insulin-shock therapy, television, the five-day week and frozen foods. But it was hardly a golden age. In the first three years of the decade the country seemed to be wallowing in a sea of turmoil, without leadership. A new political administration in 1933 suddenly galvanized the nation, supplied new hope for the future, and released dormant energies with which Americans began to deal with the tremendous problems before them. The change seemed almost miraculous.

To high-school students, such as I was then, the adventures of the Gashouse Gang in the National League seemed more important, or scraping together the fifteen dollars necessary for a trip aboard the Ford Company excursion train special to the Chicago World's Fair. But the year I was graduated from high school the banks took over the small hotel my family managed, and my father and I signed up with the WPA. Before I could be handed a shovel, I heard of a possible job in New York City, where two days later, with eight dollars in my pocket, I arrived by Greyhound bus.

My first day on the job was my last. I was sent out for Scotch Tape, needed in a hurry for an advertising layout, and came back with black electrician's tape: Scotch Tape—also an innovation of the Thirties—was unknown to this country boy.

Eventually I landed another job. It paid twelve dollars a week. Out of this, six dollars went for rent, and, while I longingly eyed the belt-backed suits in Crawford's windows, I managed to squeak by on cheap meals at places like Nedick's, where a breakfast of two doughnuts, orange drink and coffee cost ten cents. My rooming-house landlady, who claimed she had been swindled by Samuel Insull, often tried to bully me into paying an advance on next week's rent—showing that if she hadn't learned much about financial operations she had at least learned to look sharp for the angles.

I would not say I look back on the Thirties with pleasure, but rather with an appreciation of the air of excitement that pervaded the country. People spoke out freely and were quick to fight for what they believed in. I remember how, as young people, we often argued hotly over the social and political issues of the day. When I was nineteen, a skillful persuader sold me Communism for about three days, until with the help of a wise friend I learned better. The week after, I remember debating before a large group the right of assembly for Fritz Kuhn and his Nazis, who wanted to meet in Madison Square Garden. Thus I sampled the ideas of the day, testing myself against them and developing confidence in my own judgment.

Then the war years intervened. For a long time afterward no one seemed moved to recall the Thirties, and today many people—particularly the younger generation—don't bother to look beyond the label "Depression" and perceive one of America's great victories, in the face of unprecedented domestic crisis. To them, and to those Americans who are heel-draggers and nay-sayers when faced with social reform today, this book is addressed.

The Thirties is, of course, about much more than social reform and politics.

It is also about:

The lively arts of radio, movies, theater, books and popular music; sports figures Joe Louis, Dizzy Dean and Babe Didrikson; the Lindbergh kidnaping, and bankbusting John Dillinger; dust storms, the Ohio River flood of 1936, and the New England hurricane of 1938; the *Morro Castle* fire; Americans fighting in the Spanish Civil War; the last flight of the dirigible *Akron;* the construction of the great dams at Boulder, Grand Coulee and in the Tennessee River Valley; Marian Anderson and the DAR; and "invasion" by Martians.

These were all a part of the Thirties. John Steinbeck says he knows of "no other decade in history when so much happened in so many directions." His "I Remember the Thirties" serves as a fine prologue to the unfolding story of those years.

Prologue

JOHN STEINBECK

I REMEMBER THE THIRTIES*

SURE I remember the Nineteen Thirties, the terrible, troubled, triumphant, surging Thirties. I can't think of any decade in history when so much happened in so many directions. Violent changes took place. Our country was modeled, our lives remolded, our government rebuilt, forced to functions, duties and responsibilities it never had before and can never relinquish. The most rabid, hysterical Roosevelt-hater would not dare to suggest removing the reforms, the safeguards and the new concept that the government is responsible for all its citizens.

Looking back, the decade seems to have been as carefully designed as a play. It had beginning, middle and end, even a prologue—1929 gave contrast and tragic stature to the ensuing ten years.

I remember '29 very well. We had it made (I didn't, but most people did). I remember the drugged and happy faces of people who built paper fortunes on stocks they couldn't possibly have paid for. "I made ten grand in ten minutes today. Let's see—that's eighty thousand for the week."

In our little town, bank presidents and trackworkers rushed to pay phones to call brokers. Everyone was a broker, more or less. At lunch hour, store clerks and stenographers munched sandwiches while they watched the stock boards and calculated their pyramiding fortunes. Their eyes had the look you see around the roulette table.

I saw it sharply because I was on the outside, writing books no one would buy. I didn't have even the margin to start my fortune. I saw the wild spending, the champagne and caviar through windows, smelled the heady perfumes on fur-draped ladies when they came warm and shining out of the theaters.

Then the bottom dropped out, and I could see that clearly too, because I had been practicing for the Depression a long time. I wasn't involved with loss. I didn't have money to lose, but in common with millions I did

* Condensed from *Esquire*, June 1960.

dislike hunger and cold. I had two assets. My father owned a tiny three-room cottage in Pacific Grove in California, and he let me live in it without rent. That was the first safety. Pacific Grove is on the sea. That was the second. People in inland cities or in the closed and shuttered industrial cemeteries had greater problems than I. Given the sea, a man must be very stupid to starve. That great reservoir of food is always available. I took a large part of my protein food from the ocean. Firewood to keep warm floated on the beach daily, needing only handsaw and ax. A small garden of black soil came with the cottage. In northern California you can raise vegetables of some kind all year long. I never peeled a potato without planting the skins. Kale, lettuce, chard, turnips, carrots and onions rotated in the little garden. In the tide pools of the bay, mussels were available and crabs and abalones and that shiny kelp called sea lettuce. With a line and pole, blue cod, rock cod, perch, sea trout, sculpin could be caught.

I must drop the "I" for "we" now, for there was a fairly large group of us poor kids, all living alike. We pooled our troubles, our money when we had some, our inventiveness and our pleasures. I remember it as a warm and friendly time. Only illness frightened us. You have to have money to be sick—or did then. And dentistry also was out of the question, with the result that my teeth went badly to pieces. Without dough you couldn't have a tooth filled.

It seems odd now to say that we rarely had a job. There just weren't any jobs. One girl of our group had a job in the Woman's Exchange. She wasn't paid, but the cakes that had passed their salable prime she got to take home, and of course she shared so that we were rarely without dry but delicious cakes. Being without a job, I went on writing—books, essays, short stories. Regularly they went out and just as regularly came back. Even if they had been good, they would have come back because publishers were hardest hit of all. When people are broke, the first things they give up are books. I couldn't even afford postage on the manuscripts. My agents, McIntosh & Otis, paid it, although they couldn't sell my work. Needless to say, they are still my agents, and most of the work written at that time has since been published.

Given the sea and the gardens, we did pretty well with a minimum of theft. We didn't have to steal much. Farmers and orchardists in the nearby countryside couldn't sell their crops. They gave us all the fruit and truck we could carry home. We used to go on walking trips carrying our gunny sacks. If we had a dollar, we could buy a live sheep, for two dollars a pig, but we had to slaughter them and carry them home on our backs, or camp beside them and eat them there. We even did that.

Keeping clean was a problem because soap cost money. For a time we washed our laundry with a soap made of pork fat, wood ashes and salt. It worked, but it took a lot of sunning to get the smell out of the sheets.

For entertainment we had the public library, endless talk, long walks, any number of games. We played music, sang and made love. Enormous invention went into our pleasures. Anything at all was an excuse for a party: all holidays, birthdays called for celebration. When we felt the need to celebrate and the calendar was blank, we simply proclaimed a Jacks-Are-Wild Day.

It's not easy to go on writing constantly with little hope that anything will come of it. But I do remember it as a time of warmth and mutual caring. If one of us got hurt or ill or in trouble, the others rallied with what they had. Everyone shared bad fortune as well as good.

In Pacific Grove we heard that business was improving but that hadn't much emphasis for us. One of the indices of improvement was that the men who had begged the Administration to take over and tell them what to do were now howling against government control and calling Mr. Roosevelt highly colored names. This proved that they were on their feet again and was perfectly natural. You only tolerate help when you need it.

By 1936 the country must have been on the upgrade. When a writer does well, the rest of the country is doing fine. A book of mine which had been trudging wearily from publisher to publisher was finally bought and brought out by Pat Covici. It sold well enough so that it was bought for motion pictures for $3,000. I had no conception of this kind of dough. It was like thinking in terms of light years. You can't.

The subsequent history of that book is a kind of index of the change that was going on. The studio spent a quarter of a million dollars having my book rewritten before they abandoned it. Then they fired the man who had bought it in the first place. He bought it back for three thousand and later sold it for $90,000. It shows how values change. But I still think of that original $3,000 as about as much money as there is in the world. I gave a lot of it away because it seemed like too much to be in private hands. I guess I wasn't cut out for a capitalist. I even remained a Democrat.

My books were beginning to sell better than I had ever hoped or expected and while this was pleasing it also frightened me. I knew it couldn't last and I was afraid my standard of living would go up and leave me stranded when the next collapse came. We were much more accustomed to collapse than to prosperity. Also I had an archaic angry-gods feeling that made me give a great lot of my earnings away. I was a pushover for anyone or any organization asking for money. I guess it was a kind of propitiation. It didn't make sense that a book, a humble, hat-in-hand, rejected book, was now eagerly bought—even begged for. I didn't trust it. But I did begin to get around more.

I met Mr. Roosevelt and for some reason made him laugh. To the end of his life, when occasionally he felt sad and burdened, he used to ask me to come in. We would talk for half an hour and I remember how he would rock back in his chair behind his littered desk and I can still hear his roars of laughter.

A few weeks ago I called on a friend in a great office building in midtown New York. On our way out to lunch he said, "I want to show you something."

And he led me into a broker's office. One whole wall was a stock-exchange trading board. Two young men moved back and forth swiftly filling in changes, rises, falls, buying, selling. Behind an oaken rail was a tight-packed, standing audience—clerks, stenographers, small businessmen. Most of them munched sandwiches as they spent their lunch hour watching the trading. Now and then they made notations on envelopes. And their eyes had the rapt, glazed look one sees around a roulette table.

THE THIRTIES

THE THIRTIES

THE THIRTIES

DIXON WECTER

FROM RICHES TO RAGS*

In mid-October 1929 the average middle-class American saw ahead of him an illimitable vista of prosperity. Herbert Hoover had announced soberly in the previous year that the conquest of poverty was no longer a mirage: "We have not yet reached the goal, but given a chance to go forward with the policies of the last eight years, we shall soon with the help of God be within sight of the day when poverty will be banished from this nation."

The aftermath of America's latest war had seen the arrival in strength of mass production, to compound the wonders of the new technology. Even now, in this third week of October 1929, with the President and other notables in attendance, Henry Ford was sponsoring the "Golden Jubilee of Light," honoring Edison and the fiftieth birthday of the incandescent lamp. Motorcars, bathtubs, electric refrigerators, radios, were the touchstones of progress. Keeping up with the Joneses, under the spur of fashion and advertisement, demanded nothing less than the latest model. Pressures of salesmanship urged even the duplication of luxuries—two cars in every garage—in a consumer's market already displaying symptoms of surfeit, not because all Americans were gorged with worldly goods, but because buying power was unevenly distributed.

Time Magazine, in January 1929, had hailed Walter P. Chrysler as Man of the Year, because during the past twelve months he had introduced the public to Plymouth and DeSoto cars, bought out Dodge Brothers for 160 million dollars and begun to build "the world's tallest skyscraper, a 68-story colossus." Now, on the cover of *Time* for October 14, 1929, appeared the face of William Wrigley, Jr., to be followed in successive weeks by Harry Guggenheim, Ivar Kreuger, Samuel Insull and T. W. Lamont— heroes all. They represented the stimuli which beat incessantly upon the mind of the average magazine reader.

Masses of Americans who bought their first bonds in the Liberty Loans of 1918 had lately turned to more speculative issues. Advertisements flaunting high prices instead of bargains—$2.50 lipsticks, and razor blades at

* From Dixon Wecter's *The Age of the Great Depression* (New York, Macmillan, 1948).

three for fifty cents—set the sumptuary scale for a generation of easy money. To keep abreast of the traffic in this climb to the highlands of permanent prosperity, the stock market was the obvious vehicle. In 1920 there had been 29,609 stockbrokers in the country; within ten years they had jumped to 70,950. It was commonly observed that a great many citizens no longer read the front page of their newspaper, but turned hurriedly to the financial columns.

If a man saves $15 a week, and invests in good common stocks, and allows the dividends and rights to accumulate, at the end of twenty years he will have at least $80,000 and an income from investments of around $400 a month. He will be rich. And because income can do that, I am firm in my belief that anyone not only can be rich, but ought to be rich.

So declared J. J. Raskob, chairman of the Democratic National Committee, in the summer of 1929. Employees were encouraged to invest in the stocks and bonds of their employers—a system regarded somewhat vaguely as the American equivalent of profit sharing, or perhaps social security.

Much of this buying of stocks was on margin, which meant that investors, including the small fry with little cash but big hopes, put up about a fourth of the price. The broker advanced the rest by borrowing from banks. This precarious credit structure of brokers' loans had trembled in February 1929, when the Federal Reserve Board ordered member banks not to lend money for such speculative purposes. But private bankers, led by Charles E. Mitchell, had promptly unlocked their millions for speculation and given a further fillip to the great bull market and the age of confidence upon which it was built. This caused another spasm of activity, unwarranted by any such tangibles as consumer demand, gains in productive efficiency or real earning of the stocks in question. While the rich were growing richer, several million citizens with small incomes were raiding their savings, reducing their immediate purchasing power and mortgaging their future in order to speculate. Ninety per cent of these market transactions in the Twenties, it has been estimated, were gambling ventures rather than permanent investments.

The overexpansion of credit was a prime cause of the disasters that followed 1929. The First World War began a process which reckless financing continued to accelerate. In the background loomed the huge structure of long-term debt in the United States—a public debt, federal, state and municipal, of 33 billion dollars, and corporate and individual debts of 100 billion—which demanded expanding markets and world prosperity for successful carrying. A relatively small reduction in buying power, or backsliding of prices, could send tremors along the whole length of the chain. The grand operations of credit, a new force of such power that one economist likened it to the prime movers of physics, were still imperfectly understood and recklessly abused.

The common man knew more about overexpansion of credit in such homely shapes as installment buying. Intensive campaigns to break down "sales resistance"—often sheer insufficient purchasing power among small citizens—led to new extensions of the time-payment plan for cars, clothes, washers, etc. In effect it was a loan from producer to consumer, because the latter lacked cash, and the former, with his urgent need for sales, preferred this method to that of increasing mass purchasing power by cutting prices and boosting wages.

Meanwhile important business enterprises were being concentrated in fewer hands. The forging of chain stores all over the nation was no less significant than recent big mergers in the automotive industry. Centralized industry made every metropolis the center of a regional web, and each of these networks fitted into a national pattern for making, selling and distributing commodities. The economy of a continent had never been so highly integrated, nor its equilibrium so sensitive. The frontier, the farm, the village and Middletown had at last been engulfed by the rise of the city.

These sweeping changes had hardly entered the consciousness of the average citizen. In his own mind he was never more loyal than in 1929 to the doctrine of individualism and unhampered private enterprise. Clashes between theory and practice, like the potential friction of capital and labor, remained almost inaudible so long as the nation's economic mechanism ran with the oil of prosperity.

Yet beyond question the major shortcomings of the American economy lay not in production but in consumption. Already in the early autumn of 1929 financial pages gloomed over "heaviness" in automobiles and radios, slackening of the building trades, disappointment along the new frontiers of aviation. Much of America's productive effort and income had lately gone into luxuries and durable goods, whose purchase could be postponed without affecting daily needs. At the first storm warnings these goods would pile up in warehouses, causing wheels to stop turning and huge areas of joblessness to appear. This was one reason why the Depression following 1929 was unparalleled for severity and duration.

Two thirds of the country's savings were made by families with incomes over $10,000 a year. Those with less than $1,500, comprising 40 per cent of the population, actually paid out more than they earned. Mass buying

31

power was unable to absorb the nation's output, not alone because wages had advanced comparatively little but because retail prices took virtually no cut between 1922 and 1929. Savings achieved by improved technologies were not being handed on to the consumer in the form of lower prices. They were diverted into dividends, reserves, bigger salaries and bonuses. Various shapes of monopoly, like trusts in disguise, mergers, et cetera, helped keep prices up, even while new machinery, better production methods and services of "efficiency experts" increased the over-all output of American labor by more than a third in the decade after the First World War. In some trades, like automobiles, productive efficiency was reported to have tripled. But from this plenitude the average consumer gathered only the crumbs, and even the producer reaped merely a shortsighted advantage.

Upon this world of uneasy prosperity the first blow fell in late October. Like the sound of gunshot which starts an Alpine avalanche, a minor panic on the New York Stock Exchange began on the twenty-third among stocks that speculators had pushed to fantastic heights. The next day, "Black Thursday," saw hysteria rampant. Brokers wept and tore off their collars trying to keep abreast of selling orders; sight-seers jammed the Wall Street district, ogled the arrival of great bankers in the limousines before the House of Morgan, and under the rumor of mass suicide gathered to watch an ordinary workman on a scaffolding in morbid expectation of his plunge.

At first it appeared that the magicians of finance had arrested disaster, but just as the public cheered them and breathed more easily, another sickening lurch sent the market to new depths, spreading conviction that these wizards had merely propped the falling timbers long enough to get out from under. At the month's close 15 billion dollars in market value had been wiped out, and before the end of the year losses reached an estimated 40 billion.

The solvent of American humor began early to attack the crisis. Grim jokes arose about the complimentary revolver given with every share of Goldman Sachs, or the room clerk's query of every registrant, "For sleeping or jumping?" A little later, when mass unemployment began to steal the headlines from Wall Street, bravado succeeded flippancy. Billboards began to ask, "Wasn't the Depression terrible?" The departing owner of a ruined shop scrawled upon the door "Opened by mistake." Trained in the cult of the stiff upper lip, of singing in the rain, Americans hated to admit that things were not as they had always been. The International Association of Lions Clubs observed the week of October 19, 1930, as Business Confidence Week. Prosperity was just around the corner.

32

SUNDAY DRIVERS

In 1930, although the Depression had begun to make itself widely felt, a few of Prosperity's problems remained. One of them was traffic congestion on our highways. More than 31 million passenger automobiles had been manufactured from 1920 through 1929, and to at least one observer it seemed that every one of them was out on the road every Sunday.

Since 1930, our federal, state and county governments have employed thousands of experts and have spent billions of dollars to alleviate the problem, but the problem remains, apparently never to be completely solved. It may be that our experts have not approached the problem as sweepingly, or as radically, as Corey Ford, who in the following piece presents his view of the situation and his ideas for remedying it; and it may be that Corey Ford was, and still is, just too far ahead of his time.

COREY FORD

HOW TO SOLVE THE
TRAFFIC SITUATION*

THE SCENE is practically any well-traveled Motor Highway in America. It is Sunday afternoon.

And what a pleasant scene it is, to be sure! The broad highway, lined with the gay autumn colors of red and yellow! The smooth concrete road, unwinding like a magic carpet, who knows whither? The hum of myriad bees, the lowing of contented cattle, the gentle Sabbath breezes! The long line of pleasure cars, extending up and down the road as far as the eye can reach, filled with fortunate American families who have left the hot stuffy city behind them and driven out here into the peaceful countryside for a breath of fresh air.

Let us draw nearer. Let us examine this pleasant scene a little more closely. Things, it appears, are not quite as they seemed. The gay autumn colors of red and yellow still line the broad highway, it is true; but they

* From *Vanity Fair,* October 1930.

are contributed by the red and yellow gasoline pumps in front of Ye Olde Hotte Dog Fyllynge Statione. The smooth concrete road unwinds like a magic carpet for five hundred feet, and then terminates abruptly in a deep morass of muddy ruts, red lanterns, steam shovels and a gloating sign: "Construction Ahead: Proceed at Your Own Risk." What we took for the hum of bees is the grinding of myriad gears; the lowing of cattle is the honk of discontented horns; and the gentle breezes are laden with our standard Sabbath mixture of two parts gasoline, one part burning brakes and the rest fresh tar.

And what of the long line of pleasure cars, extending up and down the road as far as the eye can reach? Here, too, something appears to be wrong. The cars extend up and down the road, to be sure; but they are not moving. They are, in fact, standing perfectly still. They have been standing still for the past three quarters of an hour; and they are filled with as sour a lot of American families as ever deserted their comfortable rocking chairs and paper-strewn sofas to spend their Sunday afternoon sitting out here in the broiling sun, waiting for the line to start forward again.

But stay! A ray of hope! Something is moving at last along the interminable file of halted cars. It is a motorcycle; and on the motorcycle, my pet, is seated a curious individual in a blue uniform with brass buttons, whose heart apparently was removed when he was very, very young. And what word of cheer does this lone messenger bring? His greeting is brief, but to the point; to each car in turn, as he chugs past, he tosses over his shoulder a single sunny message, squeezed out between his clenched teeth like sausage meat through a grinder: "Keep in line! Keep in line! Keep in line!"

And the driver of each car sinks a little lower behind the wheel, his eyes glazed, his cigar drooping despondently, his gaze fixed stolidly ahead. He is humming to himself. He is humming a forgotten refrain. It is the Song of the Open Road. . . .

As matters stand, he hasn't got a prayer. On every thoroughfare and country lane, on highway and byway, up and down the length and breadth of our native land, America is spending its Sabbath day on wheels. If all the automobiles purchased in 1930 were placed end to end along the Boston Post Road on a single Sunday afternoon, experts state, it would be just like any other Sunday. Bumper to bumper, fender to fender, they edge forward patiently three feet at a time, radiators pressed to spare tires like an interminable file of circus elephants with their tails in their trunks. Roadsters and sedans, touring cars and trucks, limousines and coupés extend from horizon to horizon in a solid and immovable queue, hour after hour, mile upon weary mile. Gears grind, horns honk, brakes squeak, the sun mounts higher and higher, the spirits sink lower and lower. The drivers stare ahead. As a form of Sunday relaxation, they decide, the automobile is not all it is cranked up to be.

In order to settle the whole question a Traffic Commission was recently appointed to study the traffic situation in America. Its suggestions were:

1. Enforce the speed limit. This plan was later discovered to be impracticable, owing to the fact that the cars were already standing still.

2. Establish One-Way Streets. By means of this unique system, all the cars on the odd-numbered streets would move steadily east, and all the cars on the even-numbered streets would move steadily west, the idea being that with two lines of cars advancing continuously in either direction, one would eventually fall with a splash into the Atlantic Ocean and the other would fall with a splash into the Pacific Ocean, thus disposing of hundreds of cars every Sunday.

3. Build cars with runways up the back, so that other cars could drive up on top of them and park.

4. Invent a portable road.

5. Walk.

But the Sunday driver still sits patiently in line, hour after hour, his hands clutching the steering wheel at the very top, his head lowered, bowed but not yet beaten. There is still a faint glow of hope in his weary eyes.

He is waiting, as a matter of fact, for the traffic problem in America to settle itself. Sooner or later, he knows, the roads will grow more and more congested, and the cars will move slower and slower, until that time is not so far distant when they will stop moving altogether. Then we can simply fill in the chinks between them with cement, pave the hoods, and start life all over again on top.

WHERE WOULD IT STOP?

BEGINNING in 1929 the national income dropped from 87 billion dollars to a low in 1933 of 40 billion. This collapse was so extreme as to mark 1929 as a frontier between an old and a new world. In the words of Angel Gabriel in *Green Pastures,* "Everything nailed down is comin' loose."

Even so, some industrial projects were brought to completion, and a few begun, in the early Depression years. In 1931, the new Waldorf-Astoria, world's finest luxury hotel, was opened to the public; the Empire State Building, tallest skyscraper in the world, was completed, although many of its floors, as in other Manhattan office buildings, would remain vacant; and architects' plans for Rockefeller Center were published. As Dixon Wecter says in his *The Age of the Great Depression,* "some critics of architecture prophesied that these would be the last dinosaurs of America's metropolitan era, convinced that such vainglory had overreached itself, promoting little save congested traffic, overcrowding and colossal debts. Like many other vanities of the century, perhaps the skyscraper too was bankrupt. At any rate, the nation's outlay for new construction fell 60 per cent between 1931 and 1932 as the momentum of prosperity ground to a dead stop. By 1933 architects were doing less than a seventh of the business they had enjoyed in 1928."

Behind the statistics measuring unemployment and the ever-shrinking wage levels were stories of bitter privation among the employed, as well as among the idle. "Many industries and small businesses," wrote Wecter, "denied even lip service to the Administration's plea for maintenance of wage rates. A growing backwater of unemployment led department stores to pay clerks as little as five or ten dollars weekly. Investigation of a group of working girls in Chicago showed the great majority toiling for less than twenty-five cents an hour, a fourth for less than ten cents. Makers of ready-to-wear dresses, confectionery employees and cannery workers were among the classes exploited most callously. Domestic servants were obliged to labor for room and board plus ten dollars a month. As usual, unskilled workers had been the shock troops, followed by white-collar workers and technicians. Professional classes felt the jar a little later, as teachers' and ministers' salaries were cut or fell into arrears, and the practice of other groups declined, with fees increasingly hard to collect."

In the mill towns of New England the Depression had begun somewhat earlier than in most of the rest of the nation. Due largely to the short-sightedness of the millowners, the people there in 1930 were in their fourth and fifth years of deprivation. One of the hardest-hit communities was Lowell, Massachusetts; its story has an unusual historical irony.

Back in 1820, according to a *Fortune* Magazine account, "women's first experience in large-scale industry in this country had begun with the 'Lowell factory system.' It combined the advantages of a humanely run workshop and a seminary for young ladies. The mill girls were never driven and were always paid for extra work. Their hours would today seem long—from five in the morning to seven at night—and the wages, low—$2.25 to $4 a week (men got about twice that). But such working hours were considered only normal then, and such wages extremely high.

"There were nonmonetary perquisites attached to working at Lowell. For two decades, from the 1820s on, girls such as now go to colleges went to Lowell for its educational advantages. The mill girls' 'Improvement Circle' was the first factory-women's club, and the *Lowell Offering* was the first magazine ever written exclusively by women.

"But it was too good to last. Industrial competition reached Lowell, and wages were reduced. In 1836 the girls struck against a wage cut. They marched through the streets in their white muslin dresses and green stockings, carrying green parasols, and singing. The strike was lost, and the industrial status of women in America rapidly declined." *

In 1930 Louis Adamic made a tour of New England, beginning with Lowell, to survey conditions there. He was interested in people, not in bloodless statistics, and his report on the New England mill towns provides a vivid picture of men and women experiencing the full force of the Depression.

LOUIS ADAMIC

NEW ENGLAND'S TRAGIC TOWNS†

ON THE train to Lowell, but a decade ago one of the most important cotton-textile centers in the United States, I sat next to a traveling salesman. He told me that six years ago he had worked in the office of a cotton mill in Lowell; now he lived in Chelsea.

"The 1930 census figures show the population of that city [Lowell] has gone down from 113,000 to around 100,000. And most of this decrease has occurred since 1927.

"Till recently no one dared to say out loud that things were on the decline. It was merely a sort of public secret for years that everything was not as it should be. The unemployed—thousands of them—walked around like ghosts (they still do; you'll see them) or were hiding away in their shacks and hall rooms."

* From "Women in Business," *Fortune,* September 1935.
† From Louis Adamic's *My America* (New York, Harper, 1938).

Until the mid-Twenties Lowell was a comparatively prosperous town. Not a few people there had a great deal of money, lived in fine houses, wore nice clothes, drove good cars. They were mostly business and professional folk and the better-paid mill employees. The general run of mill operatives, male and female, who formed numerically the largest group in town, the underdog class, earned less than twenty-five dollars a week when they worked full time, which barely enabled them to lead decent lives. By pinching they saved a little, but very little; a small percentage of them managed to acquire homes of their own.

Then, about five years ago, the mills began to shut down in Lowell. King Cotton was sick. With Coolidge Prosperity in full swing throughout the land, the people began to wear silk, imported from Japan, and other fine materials instead of cotton. There was still some demand for cotton goods, but only for the cheaper kind. Millowners were starting new mills in the South, where raw cotton was produced and, what was still more important to them, "the pore white trash" of Tennessee, Alabama and South Carolina provided cheaper labor than the Italian, Lithuanian and French-Canadian immigrants in New England. Also, there were no laws in the South, such as there were in New England, regulating the number of working hours and female and child labor.

In 1927 and 1928 Lowell practically ceased as a cotton-textile center. I found there eight enormous mills, all idle for years, dominating the town, each six or seven stories high and covering several blocks, with tall, unsmoking chimneys. Only here and there upon the lower floors a few hundred square feet were occupied by tiny industries, such as radio-assembly shops, which the desperate community, working through the Chamber of Commerce, had recently managed to lure to Lowell in an effort to create jobs for the thousands and thousands of former textile operatives who, caught by the circumstances of their lives, had not yet moved away. But these new industries in Lowell, lost in the immensities of the former cotton mills, were, of course, only a drop in the bucket so far as the local unemployment situation was concerned.

How many jobless people there were in Lowell who needed work desperately or urgently, nobody knew exactly. Labor officials told me that perhaps two thirds of the town's working population were idle or employed only part time. Not only textile workers were "out," but nearly two thirds of the organized building-trades craftsmen had had nothing to do for nearly two and a half years. Except for the new post office, there had been no new building in Lowell for more than three years.

The mayor and the other city officials had somewhat lower estimates of the extent of idleness in Lowell. Chester M. Runels, executive secretary of the Lowell Chamber of Commerce, said to me that he knew exactly how many jobless people there were in the city—"too damned many."

Bewilderment, perhaps, was the outstanding characteristic of the Lowell psychology. Mr. Runels confessed that he was spending sleepless nights trying to think of something—anything—that would put the city back on its feet industrially, but, in common with other leading Lowellites, remained only deeply perplexed. He was starting emergency measures to relieve "immediate distress," encouraging charity, trying to induce the better-to-do people in the community to renovate their homes before Christmas and otherwise "create" jobs for needy family men during the winter months. He realized, as he told me, that what Lowell needed was industries, for it was essentially an industrial city; it had started as a mill town and could continue only as an industrial community. But, obviously a very decent person, he was loath to try to lure manufacturers—with low rentals for floor space and cheap labor—from other towns and thus create unemployment elsewhere. Instead, he strove to "create" more new industries by urging local people with money to organize companies for the production of novelties and new commodities. But so far his success in this respect was meager. Several shoe companies had established themselves in Lowell since 1928, but civic and business leaders were frank in saying that they were "afraid of the shoe industry," because, with its cruelty to workers and its utter lack of organization, self-discipline and public conscience, the shoe industry (of which more later) was seldom, if ever, an asset to a community.

Charity, as one citizen remarked to me, was "the biggest industry in Lowell," and it promised to continue big for some time to come. I was told that the priest in charge of the Catholic charity organization and his two assistants were busy from twelve to fourteen hours daily investigating cases of poverty, collecting funds from the well-to-do, who still formed a rather numerous class in Lowell, and distributing what they collected. I was assured that the donations were spontaneous and liberal. There were other charitable agencies in the city, including a municipal welfare bureau, trying to eliminate so far as possible extreme hunger and suffering for want of clothing and fuel.

Business, obviously, was poor in Lowell. Every third or fourth store in the main streets was vacant. There were few "For Rent" signs in the windows, the proprietors figuring, I suppose, that it was no use putting them up. One sign read: "For Rent at Your Own Price."

I had a desolate feeling as I walked through some of the streets. There were rows of old wooden houses, unoccupied, uncared-for, their window-panes broken. Many of the tenanted houses in the working people's districts, evidently, had not been painted for years. I saw broken window-panes pasted over with paper, the residents, apparently, being too poor to replace them.

In the main business section, the five-and-ten-cent store seemed to be the only really busy place. A butcher told me that he sold few steaks and chops; most of the customers bought tripe, soup bones and the cheaper cuts of meat. He had ordered but few turkeys for Thanksgiving. Grocery and dry-goods prices were at least one-third lower in Lowell than in New York or Boston, but even so the stores were doing little business. Two merchants confessed they were operating at a loss; they were "caught"; people owed them money for years back, and they were hoping "things would pick up soon." Said one shopkeeper, "But I don't know how much longer I can hold out on hope."

A barber told me that people obviously were cutting their hair at home; several barbershops had gone out of business. A second barber, when I asked if many of his customers took hair tonic, said, "Hell, no!"— and proceeded to elaborate upon the tragedy of the barbering trade in Lowell.

I spoke with physicians. One admitted that he, like the other doctors in town, had difficulties in collecting his fees; perhaps more than half of his patients were "charity." A dentist informed me that the number of extractions, in proportion to other dental work that he performed, was increasing rapidly. "I suppose people haven't the money," he said, "to come for treatment before it's too late and the tooth has to be removed. Also, I imagine that improper or insufficient food the poorer people have been eating the last few years hastens the decay of teeth."

A neighborhood druggist, having nothing better to do, spoke to me for several hours. "Oh, quite a few working people in Lowell still have money," he said; "at least the number of bank accounts shows that, but they're holding onto it as if it was all there was in the world. Even some of the millworkers seem to have money saved up. How they managed to save anything is more than I know. Now, with the Depression they hold on to it. They're scared. They spend only for absolute necessities. They say, God knows how long the panic will last in Lowell. They're stuck in Lowell. They probably own a little property or have old parents who can't be moved. Some of those who were foot-loose back in 1928 and had a little money cleared out soon after the mills closed down for good. Some stayed, thinking the mills would open up again soon. They waited. Then it was too late for them to clear out. Now they're stuck. Their little savings, maybe, are all gone; and if not, since Wall Street went smash the rest of the country is not much better off than Lowell, and there's no use going elsehere. . . . Of course, I'd like nothing better than to sell out, even at a loss. In the last few years I've been making less than two and a half per cent on my investment. Next year I probably shan't make that much unless things pick up. But who's fool enough to buy me out? Besides, I'm married, kids are going to school, and people in the neighborhood owe me money; so what can I do but stick? If I were single, I'd probably just take my week's receipts, close up and go."

In Lowell I saw shabby men leaning against walls and lampposts, and standing on street corners singly or in twos or threes; pathetic, silent, middle-aged men in torn, frayed overcoats or even without overcoats, broken shoes on their feet (in a town manufacturing shoes!), slumped in postures of hopeless discontent, their faces sunken and their eyes shifty and bewildered—men who winced and jerked queerly when they noticed me looking at them and shuffled off uncertainly, wringing their hands in a mingling of vague desperation and of resentment at my gaze. I spoke or tried to speak with some of them, and I went into a few of the unemployed's homes in Lowell and heard and saw things which, if I described them, would make very melancholy reading.

But even so I was scarcely prepared for the painfully awry conditions that I found in Lawrence, once the leading wool and worsted city in the United States, a half hour's trolley ride from Lowell. According to the census, since 1920, or more exactly since 1927 or thereabouts, the population of Lawrence decreased from 94,270 to 84,949, or nearly 10 per cent.

The situation was different from that in Lowell, where, as I have stated, the cotton-textile industry had almost completely deserted the community and gone South. Most of the mills at Lawrence had not yet shut down. However, since 1926 they had operated very irregularly, giving for brief periods only part-time employment, and gradually decreasing the number of even part-time workers, for during the 1920s the wool, worsted and carpet industries had also been moving out of Massachusetts, where the law provided a maximum forty-eight-hour week for workers, and were starting mills in nearby Maine, New Hampshire and Rhode Island, where employers might work their people fifty-four hours a week, and in Connecticut, where they had a fifty-five-hour law. Another motive in the tendency of the textile interests to start new mills outside of Massachusetts was that in such old centers as Lowell, Lawrence, New Bedford and Maynard labor unions had become powerful, forcing up the wage scale. The mill-owners in Massachusetts realized that they had made a mistake in getting so many mills into a few towns close together. The labor agitators' work was easy when twenty or thirty thousand operatives were concentrated in one city. And the tendency now was not to build more than one small mill in any one town in Rhode Island, Connecticut, Maine or New Hampshire. The millowners figured that this diffusion would prevent "labor troubles."

Lawrence, with its tremendous mills, was a "mistake," which the mill-owners had been trying to rectify by operating the mills only a little more than was necessary to pay the overhead on the old mills, and thus killing the unions; for, when jobless or working only part time, workers cannot pay their union fees. The process of rectifying this "mistake" was still going on when I came. And it was a painful process to the people—especially the working people—of the city of Lawrence.

I happened to arrive before daybreak on a Monday morning and, walking about, saw hundreds of shabby, silent, hollow-eyed men and women, native and foreign-born, going toward the immense, dark mills. I discovered later that very few of them were going to work; most were seeking work. On Mondays they usually went to the mills to learn from the employment managers if any help would be needed during the week.

By eight o'clock the great majority of them were returning from the mills. Some had been told to come to work on Wednesday or Thursday or Friday; others, perhaps a majority of them, were told there was no work for them this week. Perhaps next week.

Women hurried home. Men stood on curbs, wretchedness inherent in their every action and aspect; penniless men, most of them without any intelligent, objective idea of what was happening to them, what was going on in Lawrence or in the textile industry. One of them said to me, "I don't know nothing, only that I have no job. No job—no job," he repeated in a shrill, half-hysterical voice.

I saw men standing on the sidewalks clapping their hands in a queer way, obviously just to be doing something. I saw men talking to themselves, walking around, stopping, looking into shop windows, walking again.

For several minutes I watched an elderly man who stood on a deserted corner near the enormous and idle Everett Mills in the posture of an undotted question mark. He did not see me. Every now and then he swung his arms, not because it was cold, but no doubt because he wanted activity other than walking around, which he probably had been doing for

years in a vain effort to get a job. He mumbled to himself. Then, suddenly, he stepped off the curb and picked up a long piece of string from
a pile of rubbish, and his big, work-eager hands began to work with it,
tying and untying feverishly. He worked with the string for several minutes.
Then he looked around and, seeing me, dropped the string, his haggard,
hollow face coloring a little, as though from a sense of guilt, or intense
embarrassment. He was shaken and confused and stood there for several
seconds, looking down at the rubbish heap, then up at me. His hands
finally dropped to his sides. Then his arms swung in a sort of idle reflex
motion and he turned, hesitated a while as if he did not know where to
go and finally shuffled off, flapping his arms. I noticed that his overcoat
was split in the back and that his heels were worn off completely.

The general aspect of Lawrence was not unlike that of Lowell: empty
stores—rows of shabby, unpainted, untended old houses—broken win-
dowpanes—no new buildings going up—people still moving out when
they could—and so on and on. In Lawrence, too, charity was one of the
main industries.

The Lithuanian priest, Father Juras, spoke to me for a couple of hours,
evidently glad of the chance to get things off his chest. "Yes, conditions
are bad," he said. "I don't know, I don't know. I can do so little. Many
of my people work only one or two days a week. They earn so little. I
hear that some workers in order to get and hold jobs must give a part of
their small earnings to unscrupulous mill bosses who have the power to
hire and fire them. . . . Mothers come to me and cry and say they have
no money to buy shoes for the children, and winter is here. We make
collections in the church, and I give them money for their children's shoes.
Not only for shoes, but for clothing, food and gas bills. Some of my people
don't work at all. For months and months—for years—no work. Some
have gone out of Lawrence, to the farms near-by, where they work just
for food and lodging. It is better than nothing. . . . No, very few become
Communists; almost none. Lithuanians are good, patient people. They suffer, but they don't know what is going to become of them. They come
to me and cry: What is going to happen to our children? One family I
know has lived on lentils, nothing but lentils, all this year. They can't
afford to buy bread. No work for them. The young people are restless.
They want money. They want to go to picture shows and dances. . . ."

He shook his head.

"Many of my people pay very little rent," he continued. "Some pay no
rent. The house owners don't throw them out. The tenants at least take
care of the houses. . . . Yes, some of the men drink. They're desperate. It

43

helps them to forget. But their characters degenerate. That is bad. They feel helpless: what's the use! I try to help. But—"

Again he shook his head.

The rector of one of the two French-Canadian parishes spoke to me similarly. "Oh, yes, we, too, have to buy shoes for children," he said. "We have a Catholic school here and we watch the children. If they need clothing, we give it to them. Many parents have nothing—no money, no work, or very little work. I have six priests in this parish assisting me. All day long they go around, from house to house, where we hear there is distress, and we help as much as we can. Our well-to-do parishioners are generous. Last Sunday we received three hundred dollars for the poor." He was unwilling to fix the blame upon the mills or any other factor in Lawrence. "I have come here only recently," he said. "I don't know whose fault this condition is. All I know is that things are terrible—no work for the people."

Speaking with the jobless, I noticed acute desperation. One man said to me, "You're from New York? Say, do you think there'll be a war soon? There was lots of work and high wages during the last war. Remember? Mills were going day and night."

Few of the unemployed in Lawrence—and elsewhere, for that matter —impressed me as competent people. They were willing, eager to work, but there was something dead in them, as from exhaustion or perhaps too much idleness; they lacked personal winsomeness or any power of demand. Lost, bewildered souls, victims in the pinch of the machine, victims of the 1920s' industrial-financial processes, of "rationalization" and speeding-up in the textile industry, victims of the greed for higher and higher profits on the part of the industrialists; victims of the country's incongruity. . . . The situation was infinitely pathetic, not to say appalling.

The Census Report showed that in the 1920s the population decline of New Bedford and Fall River, both cities with populations of over 100,000, was only 6.9 and 4.3 per cent, respectively; but the conditions in these towns were perhaps no better than in Lowell or Lawrence.

Fall River, one of the oldest mill towns in New England, was also practically dead as a textile center. Were I to describe its plight from the human point of view I should be only repeating, with slight changes, what I have said about the plight of Lowell and Lawrence. The immediate reason for Fall River's decline, however, was somewhat different. A former labor leader in Fall River said to me, without any attempt at hiding his bitterness, "The trouble with this place is that the machinery in all these big mills which you see is archaic. In some of them the equipment has not been replaced since the mills were built, thirty and forty years ago. Of course, they cannot compete in production efficiency with mills equipped with modern machines, each of which produces with the aid of a single worker more than twenty machines here used to produce with ten workers. But years ago most mills were tremendous money-makers. They paid dividends of as high as two and three hundred per cent. At the same time the wages were slavery wages. They employed children in their early teens and women, pregnant and otherwise. They worked them night and day, twelve and fourteen hours at a stretch. That was before Massachusetts legislated against such things. . . . It was a high-pressure 'racket,' cruel to the workers, cruel to the city of Fall River, suicidal for the mills. . . ."

New Bedford was a victim of a combination of circumstances. There was archaic machinery in some of the mills. New Bedford, too, was a "mistake"—like Lawrence—which was being rectified; the companies whose mills dominated New Bedford had also new mills in the neighboring states and in the South where laws allowed longer working hours and there were no labor unions.

I bought lunch for a jobless worker who told me he had not eaten a decent meal for months—"or maybe it's years. I'm losing track of time." He had a family of four. A brother of his in New Jersey, he told me, had recently killed his wife and child and committed suicide. "I don't blame 'im," he said. "I'd do the same; only I ain't got the guts. I'd have to kill four of 'em. And I couldn't . . . I couldn't. Christ, ain't it awful! . . . And suppose I do get a job soon. I am in debt hundreds of dollars and it'll take me years to pay it back. There's nobody I know in town who's ever had any money that I don't owe him some. We owe to the groceryman, butcher—everybody. You don't know what it means to have a wife and kids and no work and no money, and be in debt."

In Maynard, Massachusetts, the conditions were extremely chaotic, too, though—quantitatively, at least—not as tragic as in the larger towns. There is but one considerable mill in Maynard. Once it had employed 1,500 people; when I was there, two thirds were completely "out" and the rest worked only part time, earning from $8 to $9 a week. Approximately the same was true of Housatonic, another small mill town in Massachusetts which I visited.

I spent a few days in the Rhode Island mill towns—Manville, Woonsocket, Ashton, Berkley and Lawnsdale, not far from Providence; most of which have but one good-sized mill working part time. But those who worked there, while they worked, worked long hours for lower wages than similar workers received in Massachusetts. I saw bad working conditions —men and women and even boys and girls in their teens working fifty-four hours a week. I saw "speeding-up" and "stretching-out." I saw girls in one town, for instance, running thirty wide looms from before sunup till after sundown. In most Massachusetts towns, where the unions had some power, operatives ran on the average of only twenty looms eight hours a day, and even that was considered a great strain upon a person's energy and nerves.

And the average shoe-manufacturing town was no better than the average textile town in New England. Haverhill, Massachusetts, was one of the largest shoe centers in the country, with shoe-factory employees comprising four fifths of Haverhill's laboring men and women, and from the human point of view the situation was as appalling as in the textile towns. Things were further aggravated by a dispute between shoe manufacturers and the Shoe Workers' Protective Union, which included about half of the shoe people in town. Threats to remove their plants from Haverhill had been made by eight firms as the result of union opposition to contemplated wage cuts. The whole city was beside itself. People with whom I talked, including responsible public and semipublic officials, seemed unable to discuss the situation objectively. They talked incoherently, emotionally, about emergency measures to prevent suffering during the winter.

A public official who asked me not to quote him by name said to me, "You say the textile industry is stupid and chaotic. Well, it has nothing on the shoe industry. Here in Haverhill we have over thirty shoe factories. Most of them have been started by selfish little fellows with a few thousand dollars at their command. They rented a little floor space and then had the United Shoe Machinery Company lease to them machines which turn out shoes hand over fist. The manufacturers don't own the machinery; they pay royalties to the U.S.M. on every pair of shoes made. They get a shoe model that they think will sell and then they work day and night producing that model. When they think they have enough shoes manufactured they quit, and to hell with the workers, and to hell with Haverhill. Their most pressing problem then becomes to sell the shoes. And this goes on all over the country. The U.S.M. installs machinery almost anywhere. There are hundreds and hundreds of shoe manufacturers in New England and more elsewhere. The U.S.M. machinery has been working overtime; now there is overproduction. Now there's no work. And the workers who made millions of pairs of shoes did not make enough to have decent shoes on their own feet!"

But Haverhill, perhaps, was not the worst-hit town because of this chaotic overproduction and underpayment of workers in the shoe industry. In Lynn, Massachusetts, only about two thousand of the six thousand shoe workers were employed, full and part time. In Brockton and South Boston the production of working and jobless shoe people was approximately the same. In Manchester, New Hampshire, a worker, long out of a job, told me how, a month before, he had gone to New Haven, Connecticut, in search of work; how a policeman there arrested him for vagrancy, and how a judge threatened to jail him unless he left the city within thirty minutes.

Everywhere chaos and suffering because of stupid greed—because of no vision, no sense of social responsibility on the part of industry.

I describe the social-economic-industrial situation in these New England shoe and textile towns in such detail because what was true of them in 1928–30 became largely true by 1932 or 1933 of the entire United States —and for essentially the same reasons!

In my eleven days of traveling through New England I found but one busy, happy, prosperous town—Salem, Massachusetts, which impressed me as almost a complete antithesis of such places as Lowell, Lawrence, Fall River, Haverhill and Manchester. In comparison with these, Salem was a veritable boom town. In a population of about 40,000 only 600 were unemployed, most of them shoe workers. The stores and hotels in Salem were attractive, busy places. The homes were painted and the whole community had an aspect of well-being.

The reason for this happy status of Salem was mainly that the city had a great textile mill—the Pequot—whose management was intelligent and humane, trying with no small success to run its business not solely for its own immediate, narrow profit, but also for the benefit of its two thousand operatives and, through them, of Salem. The Pequot Mill workers' average weekly wage was around $34 for forty-eight hours—an amazing stipend for the textile industry. Their employment was steady; at least no one was laid off at a moment's notice, irrespective of his or her circumstances; for the Pequot management had tried in the past and continued in its efforts, to stabilize production as much as possible and plan ahead. The sanitary and safety appliances in the mill were the most modern. I inspected the mill and spoke with the workers and their union's leaders. Nowhere within the realm of the textile industry—and in very few other industries—were employees treated half so well as at Salem.

The result was that the relations between the management and the workers, all of whom were organized, were excellent, and that Pequot had a force of contented, healthy, efficient operatives who, individually and through their union, did everything possible to help the firm decrease the production costs. The textile workers' union at Salem was recognized by the Pequot people; indeed, the mill management and the union, headed by an intelligent labor leader, maintained a joint research bureau under the direction of an efficiency engineer, with the purpose of further decreasing the production costs, stabilizing production, and increasing the profits and wages as the operating costs were lowered in the mill.

In Pequot was a strong touch of industrial democracy. The employees did not live in constant fear of losing their jobs. When I was in Salem everybody there knew that the mills had enough work to run full time until the spring, and the workers were fairly sure that there would be work after that. In consequence, the people did not hesitate to spend their money. I saw mill girls come to work in the morning clad in raccoon coats, and in the evening I saw a group of them in evening gowns dining with boy friends at the Hawthorne Hotel. Naturally, then, Salem—in sharp distinction from Lowell, Lawrence, New Bedford and Fall River—was a pleasant, thriving town.

THE MINER'S ORDEAL

THE DEPRESSION was no novelty in the coal fields of America. The Twenties had seen a slight decline in the production of coal and a substantial decline in price. Bituminous production had gone down, between 1920 and 1929, by about 6 per cent, and prices by some 55 per cent. In 1932 production dropped by about 42 per cent from the 1929 figure (45 per cent from 1920), and prices fell by about 57 per cent from 1929 (81 per cent from 1920). This table tells the sad story:

BITUMINOUS COAL PRODUCTION

	Net Tonnage	Value
1920	568,666,000	$2,129,933,000
1929	534,988,000	952,781,000
1930	467,526,000	795,483,000
1931	382,089,000	588,895,000
1932	309,709,000	406,677,000

"The structure of the bituminous industry," one writer has noted, "was totally inadequate to meet the crisis. The horizon of the typical operator was fixed at the line of his own property. The consumers of coal, mainly the large steel, railroad and utility corporations, played the operators off against each other. Since labor constituted about two thirds of mining costs (and there was an enormous oversupply of labor), the operator passed on his falling prices in lower wages. Survival depended upon wiping out union wage scales and with them the union itself." * Indeed, one way of cutting wages where miners

* Irving Bernstein, *The Lean Years.*

were paid by the ton was the falsification of weights, and the miners were at the mercy of the checkweighman.

Throughout the Eastern coal-mining areas of Illinois, Kentucky, West Virginia, Ohio and Pennsylvania, the families of miners experienced unimaginable privation. In one community a teacher asked a little girl in her classroom whether she was ill. "No," said the child, "I'm all right. I'm just hungry." When the teacher suggested that she go home and eat something, the child replied, "I can't. This is my sister's day to eat."

In many mining towns a miner could buy only at the company store, where prices were usually higher than at outside markets. The miner often made his purchases against his next pay check, and regularly found himself, at payday, with little or no cash due him. There were other ways, too, by which the company would prevent the miner from buying elsewhere; generally it was the threat of dismissal, but in Harlan County, Kentucky, the miners frequently were paid in scrip, which was negotiable only at the company store. And from the Harlan County miner's pay envelope, according to a *Fortune* Magazine report, "the company deducted an average of $11.80 monthly for rent, medical attention, powder and caps and insurance. To pay this deduction, a man had to mine forty-five tons of coal a month, which meant he had to work nine days. Most of them worked a total of six days, and the result is a load of debt with no balance for food." *

There was little opportunity for the miners to change these conditions. A "troublemaker" could easily be replaced. Attempts at organization—by the United Mine Workers of America, the Progressive Mine Workers and, in Harlan County, the National Miners Union—were met with vigorous, often bloody, countermeasures by the companies.

IRVING BERNSTEIN

CATASTROPHE IN COAL†

In 1931 a Harlan miner wrote:

We are half fed because we can'nt feed ourselves and family's with what we make. And we can'nt go to a Cut rate Store and buy food because most all the company forbids such tradeing. If you got the cash. But now we have no cash. And the companies keeps their food stuffs at high prices at all time. So you can not clear enough to go anywhere. And if you do go some where and buy food you are subjects to be canned. . . .

We have been eating wild green. . . . Such as Polk salad. Violet tops, wild onions. forget me not wild lettuce and such weeds as cows eat as a cow wont eat a poison weeds. . . . Our family are in bad shake childrens need milk women need nurishments food shoes and dresses—that we cannot get. and there at least 10,000 hungry people in Harlan County daily. I know because I am one off them. . . . I would leave Harlan County if I had only $6 to send my wife and boy to Bristol, Va. and I could walk away—But I can't clear a dollar per month that why I am here. that why hundreds are here.

There was only the dim memory of a union in the Harlan field. The United Mine Workers, which had organized the region during World War I, was destroyed locally in the early Twenties. District 19, with jurisdiction over Harlan and Bell Counties, was a "paper" organization headed by William Turnblazer. Harlan had the reputation, richly deserved, of being "the toughest spot to unionize" in the United States. A Harlan operator put it succinctly: "We can't do business if they have unions." The mining companies and the public officials they controlled had no intention of yielding this distinction to another locality.

In February 1931, the Harlan employers cut wages 10 per cent. While

* "No One Has Starved," *Fortune,* September 1932.
† From Irving Bernstein's *The Lean Years* (Boston, Houghton Mifflin, 1960).

this was merely the latest in a long series of reductions, the reaction was unique. "We starve while we work; we might as well strike while we starve." The UMW staged a meeting at Pineville, the Harlan county seat, on March 1 at which Philip Murray exhorted 2,000 miners to join up. Many did. The Black Mountain Company retaliated by firing 175 of its men and the Black Star Company discharged 35. Evictions from company houses followed. Another meeting was held at La Follette three weeks later, addressed by Turnblazer and Congressman J. Will Taylor. They denounced the discriminatory discharges and evictions and urged the men to sign. Turnblazer promised that the UMW would provide food and money for a strike. Over 11,000 miners streamed into the union, and the mines shut down. Violence, endemic in the Kentucky mountains, soon appeared. The strikers, failing to receive food from the union, looted stores and gardens. Deputized mine guards physically assaulted the striking miners.

Near the town of Evarts on May 4 several carloads of deputies, carrying rifles and machine guns, engaged in pitched battle with about a score of armed miners. The Battle of Evarts lasted thirty minutes and at its end four men (three deputies and one miner) lay dead. An obscure strike in a remote mountain region suddenly erupted into nationwide prominence. Harlan County entered the national consciousness, like the name of the state in which it was situated, as "a dark and bloody ground."

Governor Flem D. Sampson was urged to send troops into Harlan. His agents first entered into an agreement with Turnblazer: the UMW would welcome the soldiers; food would be supplied; mine guards would be disarmed and their commissions as deputies revoked. The National Guard, 400 strong, arrived on May 6. The agreement was immediately repudiated. Union leaders were arrested, scabs, many of them Negroes, were imported, and mine guards retained their arms and commissions. In fact, on May 11, Sheriff J. H. Blair announced that he knew of no agreement and had no intention of relieving deputies. On May 16, Blair conducted a raid upon the offices of the UMW local in Evarts and uncovered evidence of IWW activity. Some of the members were Wobblies and they had applied for a charter in the Industrial Workers of the World. This allowed the enemies of the union to invoke Kentucky's criminal syndicalism law by claiming a conspiracy to overthrow the government. Further, twenty-eight UMW members were charged with first-degree murder for the death of a mine guard at the Battle of Evarts.

At this point the United Mine Workers quit. Turnblazer told the men that their strike was a "wildcat" and that they should return to work. The

UMW gave no reason, then or later, for the sharp reversal of policy. This failure gave apparent substance to the charge, repeatedly leveled by its enemies, that the union had "sold out" its Kentucky members. Whatever the merits of the accusation, there was abundant evidence that the cause was hopeless: the operators were relentless, the apparatus of the state was on their side, food and funds were virtually nonexistent, and economic conditions were desperate. The strike of the mountaineer coal diggers, which slowly petered out, was not a collective bargaining dispute: it was a revolt born of desperation and doomed to defeat.

Recognizing this, the Communist Party filled the vacuum UMW left. The attractions were irresistible; here, in fact, was the class war with capitalism Marx had predicted, with the state joined against the workers. The "reformist" trade union was bankrupt. In their present mood the miners, innocent of unionism and collective bargaining, to say nothing of political polemics, were readily manipulable. The Harlan murder trial before a prejudiced judge whose wife was a member of the Coal Operators Association (the people of Harlan, Judge David Crockett Jones declared, don't need "anyone from Russia or any warped twisted individuals from New York to tell us how to run our government") might be exploited as another Mooney-Billings or Sacco-Vanzetti case. The Party, sensitive to the charge of foreign influence, would speak for an impeccably "American" constituency: the Kentucky mountain folk were indubitably Anglo-Saxon, their pioneer ancestors had followed Daniel Boone through the Cumberland Gap, they spoke Elizabethan English, did square dances and sang old English ballads. American writers and intellectuals, by 1931 moving into the Communist Party and its environs in large numbers, could be counted on to dramatize the Harlan spectacle and to evoke national and even international sympathy. The Party considered Harlan, Malcolm Ross observed, as "one of those powder boxes where a well-placed fuse can blow a hole in the Capitalist System."

Dan Brooks, organizer for the leftist National Miners Union, arrived in Harlan on June 19 and was soon followed by Jessie Wakefield of the International Labor Defense, who took over legal and relief activities. Many of the miners were eager for any outside assistance regardless of source. The local union held a secret meeting on July 2 which voted to send delegates to the NMU convention in Pittsburgh in mid-July. The organization then came into the open. A picnic attended by 2,000 miners and their families was staged on July 26 and was followed by a state convention of 500 delegates at Wallins Creek on August 2.

Behind the NMU marched the writers and intellectuals, those estimable tourists Judge Jones called "snake doctors from New York." Early in November the Dreiser Committee made a widely publicized voyage to Harlan County. Theodore Dreiser was chairman of the National Committee for the Defense of Political Prisoners. In open telegrams he invited a number of prominent citizens—senators, businessmen, publishers, college presidents—to join the trip. Almost all refused. His group consisted mainly of writers—John Dos Passos, Sherwood Anderson, Charles Rumford Walker and Bruce Crawford, among others. Their results were published in a book, *Harlan Miners Speak*. Early in 1932 a committee of New York writers, including Waldo Frank, Edmund Wilson, Malcolm Cowley and Mary Heaton Vorse, descended upon Harlan with several truckloads of food and clothing. They were followed by a delegation of pastors and several groups of students. Finally, in May 1932, a committee of prominent attorneys made the trip under the sponsorship of the American Civil Liberties Union. It seemed that a writer or intellectual who failed to reach Harlan in 1931–32 was hardly worth his salt. The attendant publicity gave the county's name a certain stench in the national nostrils and helped to launch an investigation by the Senate Manufacturers Subcommittee in the spring of 1932.

Any disposition the operators may have had to abide by the rules evaporated with the arrival of the Communist union in the summer of 1931. They were no longer merely defending low wages, union-busting, and evictions; they now guarded the American Way of Life. This required the suppression of civil liberties by terror in Harlan and Bell Counties. According to Herbert Abel, the operators conducted

. . . a systematic unrelenting campaign. The forces of the coal guards roam the countryside at night, terrorizing the inhabitants. Meetings are broken up with tear-gas bombs, raids are conducted almost every night with their consequent toll of deaths, houses are broken into and property confiscated, the mails are tampered with, the slightest resistance is met with the force of guns.

Scores of people were arrested for criminal syndicalism. Visitors were made unwelcome. The Harlan County attorney notified Arthur Garfield Hays that his "godless, self-appointed, nondescript, iconoclastic minority of grandiloquent egotists" would be treated like "mad dogs." Outsiders were beaten, ridden out of the county and subjected to seizure of property. The operators called in a notorious gunman, Bill Randolph ("He's killed three or four men," one of his defenders admitted). Relief was denied to strikers. Herndon Evans, editor of the Pineville *Sun* and chairman of the local Red Cross, admitted that he checked with the employer to determine whether applicants were on strike. "We tell the men on strike that they'd better go back to work, even if there is water in the mines and conditions aren't what we'd like to have them."

The campaign was a spectacular success. By the end of 1931, the National Miners Union was smashed and the Harlan and Bell operators had achieved control over their workers. At this point the union performed an act of irresponsibility to its few remaining loyal members: NMU called a general strike for January 1, 1932. It proved a disaster. The union disappeared from Kentucky and its members were hounded out of the mines.

By the winter of '32–33, the coal industry was in a state of complete demoralization. Its condition called to mind the old western Pennsylvania story about the final day of a worked-out mine: The last grizzled miner placed the last lump of coal on the last worn-out pit car. He threw his battered broom and his rusty pick and shovel atop the load, and guessed at its weight. With the help of his faithful but ancient dog harnessed to the car (the mine mule had died) he laboriously dragged the load to the tottering old tipple and dumped it into the last railroad car below on the rusty siding. The tipple at that moment collapsed. The pit car dropped in a heap and fell to pieces. The old dog died. Since the grizzled old miner didn't know what else to do, he went on strike.

SIGNS OF CHANGE

ALTHOUGH, in general, the hard times of the early Thirties affected the living conditions of practically all Americans, for some the necessary adjustments were minor. Some families in the higher economic strata merely had to reduce the lavishness of their entertainment; others, on a slightly lower economic level, had to forego some of the luxuries of foreign travel, club memberships, or palatial domestic establishments. But the vast majority of those with jobs and regular incomes made their adjustments by finding more of their recreation in the home or where entertainment and sport were comparatively inexpensive or free.

Hobbies, like stamp collecting and jigsaw puzzles, and table games, like checkers and chess, achieved unprecedented popularity. But it was bridge that acquired by far the greatest number of devotees. In its new, more intricate form, contract, bridge absorbed the attention of people in all sections of the country. Proficiency at it became almost a social requisite—so much so that in 1931 the American public paid ten millions dollars for lessons.

The year before, it had been an outdoor recreation that established itself in comparable measure. In 1930, according to Frederick Lewis Allen, "the Department of Commerce had found at least one thoroughly prosperous business statistic to announce: there were almost 30,000 miniature golf courses in operation, representing an investment of $125,-000,000, and many of them were earning 300 per cent a month. If the American people were buying nothing else in the summer of 1930, they were at least buying the right to putt a golf ball over a surface of crushed cotton seed and through a tin pipe." *

Together with the change in recreational interests, there was a noticeable change in the public's attitude toward heroes of the day. As Allen put it, "the noble art of ballyhoo, which had flourished so successfully in the 1920s, had lost much of its vigor. Admiral Byrd's flight to the South Pole made him a hero second only to Lindbergh in the eyes of the country at large, but in the larger centers of population there was manifest a slight tendency to yawn; his exploit had been overpublicized, and heroism, however gallant, lost some of its spontaneous charm when it was subjected to scientific management and syndicated in daily dispatches. As for Shipwreck Kelly, premier flagpole sitter of the 1920s, he was reported to have descended from the summit of the Paramount Building in 1930 because no one seemed to be watching.

"There were other signs of change; some of them had begun long before the panic; others developed some time after it; but taken together they revealed striking alterations in the national temper and the ways of American life.

"One could hardly walk a block in any American city or town without noticing the women's clothes, for

* Frederick Lewis Allen, *Only Yesterday* (New York, Harper, 1931).

55

instance. The skirt length had come down with stock prices. Dresses for daytime wear were longer, if only by a few inches; evening dresses swept the ground. Defenders of the knee-length skirt had split the air with their protests, but the new styles had won out. Bobbed hair was progressively losing favor. Frills, ruffles and flounces were coming in again, and the corset manufacturers were once more learning to smile.

"The long skirts and draperies and white gloves of 1930 and 1931 were the outward signs of a subtle change in the relations between the sexes. No longer was it the American woman's dearest ambition to simulate a flat-breasted, spindle-legged, carefree, knowing adolescent in a long-waisted child's frock. The red-hot baby had gone out of style. Fashion advertisements in 1930 and 1931 depicted a different type, more graceful, more piquant, more subtly alluring; decorum and romance began to come once more within the range of possibilities.

"What the fashions suggested was borne out by a variety of other evidence. The revolution in manners and morals had at least reached an armistice.

"Not that there was any general return to the old conventions which had been overthrown in the 1920s. The freedom so desperately won by the flappers of the now graying 'younger generation' had not been lost—the people were pretty much bored with the whole idea.

"Robert Benchley expressed a widely prevalent opinion when he wrote in his dramatic page in *The New Yorker,* late in 1930, 'I am now definitely ready to announce that Sex, as a theatrical property, is as tiresome as the Old Mortgage, and that I don't want to hear it mentioned ever again.' " *

Despite Mr. Benchley's weariness with the subject, the cause of women's freedom had made substantial advances in the world of business and industry; by 1930 nearly eleven million women were working, and their purchasing power became a major factor in the production and merchandising programs of entire industries. In business offices, women had won virtually inviolable jurisdiction in typing, filing, stenographic and secretarial functions. In nursing, teaching and store clerking, too, women had achieved a majority.

The deepening Depression of the early Thirties whittled away some of the economic advantages that women had gained. Their average wages dropped steadily, and job opportunities became relatively scarce. In New York offices, for instance, women's salaries, which in 1931 ranged from $30 to $60, in 1936 ranged from $25 to $35. And in many places women found that marriage made them ineligible for employment; many municipal public-school systems, for instance, would not hire married women and would automatically dismiss teachers who did marry.

And yet, even during the Depression, women penetrated still further into occupational fields from which they once had been excluded. In 1933 President Roosevelt appointed the first woman Cabinet member in United States history—Frances Perkins, as Secretary of Labor—and the first woman diplomatic representative of this country—Ruth Bryan Owen Rohde, as Minister to Norway.

* Frederick Lewis Allen, *Only Yesterday.*

BASEBALL IN THE EARLY THIRTIES

DESPITE hard times, baseball, the great American pastime, continued to draw as many fans as ever. The excitement of the pennant race and the World Series helped divert the people from their troubles, at least temporarily. In 1932, Babe Ruth thrilled the country by a feat since become legendary, when, with two strikes on him in the third game of the World Series between the New York Yankees and the Chicago Cubs, he pointed in the direction of the center-field bleachers and hit a home run on the next pitch to that very spot.*

The decade had opened with two great performances in golf and horse racing: in 1930 Bobby Jones got his Grand Slam, winning both amateur and open golf championships in England and America; and in the same year, Gallant Fox, with Earl Sande up, took the Triple Crown, by winning the Kentucky Derby, the Preakness and the Belmont Stakes.

But it was baseball, year in, year out, that held the lion's share of the attention of the sports audience. Superstars like Babe Ruth, Dizzy Dean, Jimmy Foxx, Carl Hubbell, Lefty Grove, Joe DiMaggio and Bob Feller helped maintain an intense public interest in the game. In the early Thirties the cry was often heard, "Break up the Yankees!" or, "Break up the Athletics!" These two teams, with their star-studded rosters, had so dominated the American League that from 1926 through 1932 no other team in the league had been able to win a pennant.

Such prowess did not guarantee world championships, however; anything could happen in a World Series. In the 1930 Series the Athletics had beaten the St. Louis Cardinals of the National League, four out of six games; in the 1931 series the two teams met again, but this time something new had been added—a man by the name of Pepper Martin.

* Years later, Charley Root, the Cubs' pitcher in that incident, said that Ruth hadn't pointed anywhere but had merely held up one finger and called out to Root, "You still need one more, kid."

W. C. HEINZ

PEPPER MARTIN—THE
HAPPIEST HOOLIGAN*

WHEN the 1931 Series opened Pepper was just a 27-year-old rookie who'd been kicked around the minors for six years. When it closed he had 12 hits and five stolen bases, and the St. Louis Cardinals had licked Connie Mack's great Philadelphia Athletics. What the sports writers wrote then is still true today. In all the history of baseball no other ballplayer has ever come out of nowhere as suddenly and as sensationally.

Pepper had hit .300 in the regular season of '31, but when he broke loose in that Series he came as a complete surprise. The Athletics had just won their third pennant in a row and were going for their third straight win in the Series. They had Mickey Cochrane, one of the all-time great catchers, Jimmy Foxx, who ended up second only to Babe Ruth in home runs, and Al Simmons, who led the league in hitting that year with .390. Throwing for them they had George Earnshaw and Lefty Grove, who had led the league for three years and that season had a record of 31 and 4.

"How do you feel going into your first Series?" Frank Graham, who worked for the New York *Sun* then, said to Pepper just before they opened in St. Louis.

"Like a kid with a little red wagon," Pepper said. He took off his cap and scratched his head. "It seems a shame, though," he said. "Here I am, gettin' into a World Series in my first year as a regular. Think of all the great ballplayers who have been in the majors for years and never get into a World Series."

Think of all the great ballplayers who did get into a World Series, though, and never did what Pepper did. In the first game Grove beat the Cards, 6–2, but he didn't hold Pepper.

"When they raised that flag before the game and we stood at attention," Pepper said, "that silence was so strong it was noisy. I don't know how we got 'em out in that first inning, but when I came up there was two

* From *True* Magazine, October 1959.

men on and two out. I rubbed my hands and resorted to prayer. I said: 'God, be my helper.' "

"I guess He was," I said. *

"He was," Pepper said, nodding, "and that fast ball of Grove's, if you got ahold of it, it'd ring."

Pepper boomed a double off the right-field wall and drove in a run. He also got two singles and stole his first base. When the Cardinals won the second game, 2–0, Pepper got a double, a single and a walk off Earnshaw, stole second and third and scored both runs. By the time the Series moved to Philadelphia everyone in Shibe Park who hadn't seen the games in St. Louis wanted to see if Pepper was real.

"Which one," someone would say, "is he?"

"That one there," someone else would say, "with the dirty uniform."

"I must be warm-blooded," Martin says now, "because I'd always sweat a lot playin'. That's why I never wore slidin' pads. After a few minutes my uniform was wet, and then the dirt would stick to it."

Now when Pepper would get on base there'd be a hum in the stands. Then there'd be an eruption at first, the hum would rise in a roar and Pepper would be streaking for second, the dirt flying behind him. Mickey Cochrane would reach for the pitch-out, throw and there'd be a cloud of dust and Pepper, beak first, would be plowing into second on his belly. Then he'd get up with that big grin on his face, and even the Philadelphia fans would be standing and applauding.

"When I come up in that third game," Pepper says, "Grove said to me: 'You country --- -- - -----, I'm gonna throw this right through your head.' I said: 'You country --- -- - -----, you do that.' Cochrane had to laugh, and I hit the pitch out to the scoreboard in right center.

"You know, they blamed Cochrane for my stealin', but that wasn't right. It wasn't a question of me studyin' the motion of the pitchers, either. I guess it was the subconscious brain that told me to go. I only got the steal sign once in that Series, but you steal in the first ten steps, and I always knew I had the base stole about the time I got under way. Really, I felt sorry for Cochrane. Once he said to me: 'Don't you ever make an out?' "

Pepper got that double, a single and another stolen base in that game and the Cardinals won, 5–2. The next day Earnshaw beat them, 3–0, and gave up only two hits. It was Pepper who ruined the no-hitter. He got both hits and stole his fifth base.

"What's he hitting, George?" Connie Mack asked Earnshaw.

* Author Heinz talking; part of article was based on an interview with Martin in 1959.

"Everything I throw him," Earnshaw said.

"It got so," Pepper's wife says, "that when he'd come up I'd say: 'No. He's not due to get a hit again.' Then he'd get another hit, and finally I just broke down and cried."

That was in the fifth game. Pepper got a homer, two singles and a sacrifice fly and batted in four runs as the Cardinals won, 5–1. Frank Frisch was playing second base for the Cardinals then, and he still talks about that one.

"I can see it like it's yesterday," Frisch says. "In the sixth inning Pepper says to me: 'You get on, Frank, and I'll hit one nine miles.' I got a double, and damned if he didn't do it. He lined the first pitch into the left-field seats."

By now Pepper owned Philadelphia like he owned St. Louis. Crowds followed him wherever he went and waited for him in the lobby of the Ben Franklin Hotel and outside on the sidewalk for hours.

"Tell me, son," one old guy said to him, "where'd you learn to run like that?"

"Well, sir," Pepper said, scratching his head. "I guess I learned it out in Oklahoma. When you get to runnin' out there, there ain't nothin' to stop you."

When the teams left to finish the Series in St. Louis, the crowds mobbed the car Pepper was riding in and jammed traffic on Market Street. At Broad Street Station the cops had to clear a path, and Judge Kenesaw Mountain Landis, who was then Baseball Commissioner, walked up to Pepper and shook his hand.

"Young man," he said, "I'd give anything to change places with you tonight."

"Well," Pepper said, thinking, "it's agreeable to me, salaries and all."

"I don't believe you," Landis said.

Landis was making $65,000 a year and the Cardinals were paying Pepper $4,500. The A's shut Pepper out after that and won the sixth game, 8–1, but the Cards won the seventh, 4–2, with Pepper catching the last out, and he got $4,467.59 out of the winner's share. Then they paid him that $2,500 a week for the vaudeville tour, but after a month Pepper quit.

"I ain't no actor," Pepper said. "This is takin' money under false pretenses and practicin' deceit."

"It just amazed me," his wife says, "that all those people wanted just to *see* him that much."

When Pepper quit the tour he stopped in at St. Louis to see Branch

Rickey. Rickey was the general manager of the Cardinals, then, and he asked Pepper what he'd done with the $10,000.

"Why, I got it right here," Pepper said. "Can't you see all my pockets are bulgin'?"

"Judas Priest!" Rickey said. "Somebody'll rob you."

"No they won't," Pepper said.

Rickey made Pepper buy some bonds, but as soon as he got back to Oklahoma City he unloaded them and paid off the mortgage on his Dad's ranch and bought a home for himself and Ruby. Even if he'd carried the cash back in his kick, though, anyone who tried to lift it would have had to kill Pepper or he'd have been killed himself.

"Pepper Martin," Rickey once told Arthur Daley, of the New York *Times,* "is the most genuine person I've ever met in my life. There never was an ounce of pretense in the man. He was one hundred per cent in everything he did. When he fell in love he fell head over heels in love. If he wanted a new bird dog or a shotgun he bought it whether he could afford it or not. He went all out in everything, and that was why he was so great a ballplayer."

"I can't understand that about myself sometimes," Pepper says. "When I was about eighteen I run a motorcycle race with a fella in Oklahoma City. He had high handle bars and wore them glasses, and in those days I thought that was sissy. We started out by the Capitol and he got ahead of me. Then he slowed up, with a car in front of him and another comin' the other way, and I was about a hundred feet behind. I had mine opened up, and I went right between those two cars. It was so close that I had to turn my hands up on the handle grips to keep from gettin' scraped, but I beat him.

"With nothin' at stake but to win the race," Pepper says, thinking about it, "it was a crazy thing to do. I don't know why I'm like that."

When Rickey calls Pepper a great ballplayer, though, he's talking about something that doesn't show in the records. The records say that in thirteen seasons of playing the outfield and third base for the Cardinals, Pepper averaged .298. Three years he led the National League in stolen bases. In addition to hitting .500 and stealing those five bases in that '31 Series, he got eleven hits in the 1934 Series when St. Louis beat Detroit. But statistics are no way to measure Pepper Martin.

"Pepper," Ripper Collins says, "was the kind of a guy who would kill you with a slide just to get to the next base. If you survived he'd stay up all night nursing you back to health. Then, if the same situation came up again the next day, he'd do it again."

Rip played first base for the Cardinals and later for the Cubs and the Pirates. When he first showed up in a Cardinal camp, though, they tried him in left field.

"They warned me," he once told Frank Graham, "to look out for Martin. They told me never to try for a ball on the fringe of his territory and to keep out of his way if he came into mine, because I might be knocked down and trampled. They told me, too, that it wouldn't do any good to yell for a ball, because he wouldn't hear me.

"I played next to him for four days, being careful to keep from under his feet, and this day, after he'd run from center field into my territory and caught a ball, he discovered his shoe was untied. He threw the ball back to the infield, called time and then knelt and tied his shoe. I stood there, looking at him and he looked up and smiled and said: 'Hello, son. What's your name?' I said: 'Collins.' And he said: 'Collins, eh? When did you join us, today?' "

Rip Collins can tell stories about Pepper by the hour. One of them has to do with the time Bill Terry was playing first base and managing the Giants, and he and Rip met on the field.

"Terry," Rip says, "said to me: 'You don't know how lucky you are not having to play against that Martin. When he's running for first I can hear him coming like doom, and it scares me.' So a couple of years later I'm playing first for the Cubs and here comes Pepper running for first, and it scared me, too."

"I used to bring my knees up high," Pepper says. "I liked to get a good piece off the ground.

"I remember one day in St. Louis when the temperature was up over a hundred and it was too hot to take battin' practice. It was Ladies' Day and the ladies were just sittin' there without anything to amuse them and I felt sorry for them. I got some paper and went under the stands and found some wood. Then I got a blanket from the clubhouse and I built a fire in front of the dugout and sat down in front of it with the blanket around me. Then Diz and Rip Collins, they come out with blankets and sat down with me, and that amused the ladies."

Pepper's two big diversions, though, were his midget racer and his Mudcat Band. One winter, when he came into St. Louis to sign his contract, he saw some midget races at the Arena.

"When I seen 'em run," he says, "I wished I had one, and the next year I had one built. It cost me fifteen hundred dollars, and about every other week I had to send it to Milwaukee to get it fixed for fifty or a hundred dollars."

Lou Schneider, who won the Indianapolis 500 in 1931, drove for Pepper. The car was white—with "Martin Special," a ball bat and two cardinals painted in red on the side—and Schneider won a few races with it.

Once, in the clubhouse before a game, Frisch was giving the club a raking over when suddenly he ran out of words. "Why don't you -------s say something?" he said.

"Well, Frank," Pepper said, "what do you think? Should I paint my racin' car red instead of white?"

Another time, the Cards were opening a crucial series with the Pirates in St. Louis and Pepper missed batting practice. When he did come running into the clubhouse there was grease up to his elbows.

"Where you been?" Frisch said, starting on him.

"I'm sorry, Frank," Pepper said, "but I had a bet with a guy I could beat him in a two-mile race and he was late showin' up."

"That's great!" Frisch said. "We're tryin' to win a pennant and you're tryin' to win a racing bet. How much was the bet?"

"Two quarts of ice cream," Pepper said, "and I won, too."

"No," Frisch said, shaking his head. "We're not crazy. We're perfectly sane, all of us."

"The Dutchman," Dizzy Dean said to Pepper, "is goin' out of his mind."

ROBERT SMITH

THE GASHOUSE GANG,
THE DEANS, AND OTHER HEROES*

PEPPER MARTIN was a member of the Gashouse Gang, the 1934 St. Louis Cardinals, which was almost a reincarnation of the 1894 Baltimore Orioles. There was the same fiery team spirit, the same reliance on craft, teamwork and aggressive play, the same unified determination to keep umpires and opponents in their places.

Frank Frisch, the manager of the crew, was a graduate of the New York Giants, where he had been inoculated with the very virus of Mc-

* Excerpted from Robert Smith's *Baseball* (New York, Simon and Schuster, 1947).

Grawism. Leo Durocher, the shortstop, had earned the nickname Lippy from his own teammates when he was with Miller Huggins' New York Yankees; and he had got himself waived right out of the American League after two seasons. Dizzy Dean, of course, was no man to pull out of any sort of encounter, be it vocal or physical.

Jerome Herman Dean had been a raggedy little cotton picker when he should have been going to school; and when he should have been living in a secure home, running with playmates he had known since he could talk, he was traveling in a ramshackle car with his father and brothers from one backbreaking job to the next. The Army to him had been a refuge, where a kid could get regular meals, shoes, clean clothes and a proper bed to sleep on.

His ability with a baseball was the only thing Dean owned, when he was a kid (he was only nineteen when he signed first with Houston), that offered him a chance to vaunt himself on fairly equal terms with boys who had been to school, had known clean clothes and had taken meals for granted. His boasting, when he was breaking in to baseball, was almost hysterical—fantastic far beyond belief, haphazard to the point of sense-lessness. He gave himself two different names and three different birth-places in his eagerness to create a background and a personality that people would want to hear about. He contradicted himself, made promises he sincerely meant to keep and broke them immediately because he sincerely thought he was doing right to change his mind.

Steering him through this morass of adolescent antics were two people he had been lucky to meet: his wife, who was determined that her Dizzy was going to win the good things he deserved, and a newspaper writer named J. Roy Stockton, who realized how much ability the boy possessed and who owned the patience, the good nature and the human sympathy to see, through Dizzy's vainglorious babbling, the essential sweetness of the boy's nature.

For Dizzy Dean was not only the finest baseball pitcher of modern times, but an unusually intelligent boy with a great fondness for people, a sharp wit and, at the bottom of his heart, an honest desire to work his head off for the people who liked him.

In this era, between the end of the Hoover regime and the entry of the United States into the Second World War, there were several distinct types of successful professional ballplayers; and it is well to remember in judging them that practically all of them were still boys, many very poor boys, and that most of them had to grow up in the public prints, with each

64

silly boast, thoughtless threat and angry recrimination baked into hard type and left for the world to stare at.

Without his fiery speed ball and his sharp-breaking curve, Jerome Herman Dizzy Dean would have been just a goodhearted and unhappy little braggart, cheated by poverty of a chance to develop his better-than-average mind. As he grew older, he became somewhat shrewd about his own eccentricities and saw to it that his priceless publicity did not wither and die. But he learned, too, that just being Dizzy Dean out loud was not what made people love and admire him—that he had to work hard and win ball games. So he worked hard and won ball games; and people bought tooth paste carrying his name, paid money for his pictures, gave their kids clothing with his name inscribed, or fed them the breakfast food that the comic strips said Dizzy Dean consumed.

He was at his most attractive when he talked about his brother Paul (who was called "Daffy" only by the sports writers). Paul, three years younger than Jerome, had a lightning-fast ball and excellent control. His three-quarters overhand pitching motion was almost the duplicate of Dizzy's, but he did not have Dizzy's spectacular curve—or Dizzy's penchant for talking loudly, loosely and endlessly. Without his eccentric brother, he'd have been merely a very good pitcher. But to Dizzy he was "faster than me," "better than I ever was," and compared to Paul, said Dizzy, "I'm just a semipro." He saw to it that Paul got his rights, too. He even threatened a strike unless Paul's salary were increased. And Paul repaid his interest by returning the admiration sevenfold and sticking to Dizzy in whatever tempestuous stunt the older Dean felt he had to turn to.

When Dizzy went on strike against appearing in exhibition games or being shown off like a prize dog, Paul went on strike, too, and acted just as angry. When Dizzy repented and came back to work twice as hard, Paul too bore down and won a row of ball games.

Typical of Dizzy Dean's antics, which won him the dislike of a number of people who were not inclined to make allowances, was his childish bobbing of the ball up to Pittsburgh batters in a game where he thought the rest of the team wasn't trying. One of his most famous stunts—made more famous because he did it all over again in front of a photographer—was his tearing up two uniforms (Paul helped him) when Manager Frank Frisch suspended him and his brother after they had refused to take the field unless a fine were rescinded. Frisch kept both Deans out of the game after that, in spite of popular clamor, until Dizzy sought the aid of Landis. Landis, after hearing the story, told the Dean brothers quite frankly what a pair of spoiled kids they looked like. And Dizzy, swallowing his pride and his threats with dignity equal to Babe Ruth's, set to and pitched for Frisch some of the finest games of his career.

Dizzy was a good hitter. He loved baseball enough to play any position, and he knew enough about the game to have been valuable anywhere. But he was most valuable to his club in the pitching box. They got their money's worth from Dizzy, too. Not only did he pull countless customers in at the gate; with the aid of Paul, he pitched the Cardinals into a pennant they had practically abandoned hope of winning. That was the year he and Paul won forty-nine games between them. Toward the end of that season, one Dean or another was pitching almost every day.

To see Paul and Dizzy pitch a double-header was like seeing the same man do a perfect job twice. From the center-field bleachers it was not easy to tell them apart. They were built alike and were about the same size. Their motions were nearly identical, both smooth, almost effortless sweeps of the arm halfway between sidearm and overhand. To a batter, there was not much to choose between that streaking fast ball of Paul's and the crackling curve that Dizzy could pour in.

Dizzy shortened his own career by pitching when he had to favor a broken toe. The toe had been hurt when he was pitching his heart out in an all-star game. When his better nature was appealed to, Dizzy was as generous with his skill and strength as he was with his money. And with money he was another of those who "did not know the value of a dollar" —just as if a kid who had worked from dawn to dark for a grudging fifty cents did not know more about what money was and wasn't worth than any news writer alive.

Dizzy got into many a row, with his own teammates, with opponents, with newspapermen, and with the president of the league. He could take a licking with good grace, and he could dish one out. And when he locked horns with the president of the league, he did not exactly come in second. This last set-to came about because Dizzy, harried by a sudden new ruling which forced him to make a distinct pause after his pre-pitching stretch and before sending the ball to the plate, made extra-long pauses which delayed the game interminably. The umpire penalized him for this; and afterward Dizzy found occasion to declare publicly that Umpire George Barr and President Ford Frick were "a pair of crooks." Frick, he went on to say, was "our great little president—but a pain in the neck to me."

For this lèse-majesté, Frick suspended Dean and ordered him to New York. Dean denied making the remarks. A newspaper reporter insisted he had. Frick, who, like many other men, thought that a boy becomes a man when he gets a wad of money, insisted on a "written retraction." He wrote it and asked Dean to sign it. But there Dean balked. "I ain't signing nothing," he announced. And he did not sign it, either. Frick lifted the suspension, apparently realizing at last that you could no longer kick a man out of the game just for losing his temper at the boss.

Perhaps not the high point of his career, but certainly the episode that becomes him best, was his fulfillment of a promise to a hospital full of crippled kids to strike out Bill Terry, who was then playing manager of the Giants. The kids had assured Dizzy they would be listening to the radio account of the game, and Dizzy said he would, if possible, fan Terry with the bases full. In the ninth inning of the game next day, with two out and the Cardinals one run ahead, the first two men hit safely. The next man was Critz and after him came Terry. Critz got a base on balls. Dean walked down toward Terry and smiled. "I hate to do this, Bill," he said. "But I done promised some kids I'd fan you with the bases full. That's why I walked Critz."

Then Dizzy went back to the mound and poured this fast ball through for two quick strikes. With two strikes on a good hitter, the traditional— and safest—thing to do is to waste a ball, that is, give the batter a chance to hit a bad ball. But Dizzy fogged the next one, waist-high, across the center of the plate, and Terry just stared at it. That was strike three. Dizzy came chuckling in to the bench.

"Bill never figured I'd dare put that last one right through the middle," he explained.

Dizzy, when his arm was gone, managed to keep pitching for a time on his craft. And perhaps he could have held a baseball job for many years more, with his brains and hitting power. He chose, however, to accept an offer to broadcast baseball games over the radio.

There were other famous players who did their arguing with their fists: Tex Carleton, who once took a swing at the great Dizzy Dean himself; Showboat Ernie Orsatti; Wild Bill Hallahan; and K.O. DeLancey.

Their doings during the championship season of 1934, and particularly in Detroit in the World's Series, sharpened the public taste for vocal and physical aggressiveness on the ball diamond to such an extent that the results have never been properly measured.

The Gashouse Gang set upon umpires and upon fans with a ferocity and a unanimity that had not been seen since McGraw was still playing third. In squads of four and five they used to march out to shout into an umpire's face, unmindful of the fact that Commissioner Landis, following Ban Johnson's lead, was ever ready to back the dignity and security of league umpires with the full strength of his office. It cannot be said that their verbal assaults upon umpires were as well motivated as were those of the old-time "kickers." There were two and often three umpires in even the most ordinary game nowadays, and they were all men who had been trained for their positions by years of major-league baseball or of minor-league umpiring. They were alert, quick-witted and thoroughly honest members of an honorable profession. But Frisch knew that it helped team spirit and enraptured the customers if his gang yelled for every extra inch.

In the 1934 World's Series, the Gashouse Gang introduced to the whole nation an adjunct of professional ball which casual fans had never noticed—the art of bench jockeying, that is, digging vocal spurs into the personal sore spots of individual members of the opposing team. By their scholarly application of this talent they heated up opponents and fans until they finally boiled right over.

Detroit, that fall, when the World's Series began, was like an army camp. All normal commerce, all social activity, even the operations of the great newspapers, were either stalled or utterly unraveled. Clerks deserted their counters, mothers carried their hungering children to the ball park, workingmen stood idle in the street, trolleys neglected their schedules, salesmen forgot to make their rounds, businessmen shushed their customers, and office girls allowed correspondence to turn yellow in the sun. For the first time in twenty-five years Detroit had a World's Series in its home park, and the natives could not have been more stirred had they been called to repel an invasion from Mars. Every avenue and byway echoed with the blasts of street radios which promised great doings in the offing, reported the current play at the park, or repeated over and over again what had taken place just a few hours before.

There were three great heroes in the city then: Schoolboy Rowe, the enormous young hurler ("With a wind behind him," said Dizzy Dean, "he's pretty near as fast as Paul"); Manager Mickey Cochrane (Black Mike), a graduate of Connie Mack's Philadelphia Athletics, where he had become the greatest catcher of the day; and Hank Greenberg, the breathtakingly handsome first baseman who was threatening to push Babe Ruth right off the home-run throne.

Upon these three the brash St. Louis bench jockeys concentrated all their genius. Schoolboy Rowe, delighted to find himself able to face a radio microphone without swallowing his tongue, had concluded a broadcast with a gay little murmur to his wife, who was listening at home: "How'm I doing, Edna?" How many hundred times he must have wished he could have taken a broom and wiped those words away! For he could not make a move upon the diamond after that without a brassy chorus of "How'm I doing, Edna!" arising from the St. Louis bench amid hoarse cackles of sardonic merriment.

Some overwrought caption writer had seen fit to print a picture of Mickey Cochrane under the line OUR STRICKEN LEADER on a day when Mickey had been only mildly bruised. That particular phrase provided the St. Louis bench with a needle they must have stuck under Cochrane's skin a couple of thousand times.

Hank Greenberg reacted to his first World's Series with the tense excitement of most young and suddenly famous ballplayers. And the cries of the St. Louis players did not ease his tension. "Boy," yelled Dizzy Dean, "what makes you so white? You're trembling like a leaf! Must be you heard Old Diz is going to pin your ears back!"

On the field of play the Gashouse Gang implemented their vocal needling with plenty of rough base running; and they finally hit the jackpot when Joe Medwick, who is put together like a small brick building, slammed into Marvin Owen, the Detroit third baseman, and Owen retaliated by tagging him with force enough to leave a mark. The two men almost simultaneously began to slug at each other. And when, after the row had been quelled and the St. Louis inning completed, Medwick took his position in the outfield, the nearby fans greeted him with a shower of vegetables, worn-out fruit, sandwiches, boxes, pieces of chairs, and bottles —in fact, anything bruising they could set their hands to. Judge Landis, in the stands, finally decided that Medwick would have to be withdrawn.

It must not be thought that the Gashouse Gang was the first, the last, or the only team to instigate this wholesale participation by fans in the side issues of the game. In St. Louis there had been several instances of bottle throwing—one an almost fatal injury to Umpire Billy Evans. In the Twenties, Whitey Witt, then a New York outfielder, had been struck on the head and seriously hurt by a thrown bottle. McGraw's Giants, too, had undergone a shower of bottle in the same St. Louis park. Detroit fans in the Twenties, stirred to action by the exchange of obscenities, bean balls, and fisticuffs on the diamond, piled down into the fight to the number of many hundreds, bringing clubs made out of chairs to give the New York Yankees' Murderers' Row a little of their own medicine. And in the Yankee Stadium, not too long ago, fans heaved a gross or two of bottles at Umpire Rue because he had called a ball foul which might possibly have been fair.

But it was the Gashouse Gang and its eager publicists who began to make it clear that "color" in the form of rough talk and violence was as salable a commodity as eccentricity. In St. Louis, coupled with aggressive and winning baseball, it pulled in throngs so deep they had to sit on the grass.

Bench jockeying, of the type exemplified in that Detroit series, has always been a part of baseball, enjoyable to the players and even valuable in a way.

The accomplished bench jockey and his understudy, the loudmouthed man, take pains, however, to find the aspect of a man's personality or background which he can least bear to have discussed; and they harp on that with as much vulgarity and as little wit as they can manage.

But the public attitude toward baseball, through the Roosevelt era, was not entirely one of vaunting the loudmouth, the name-caller, and the picker of fights. Much was left of the sophisticated sentimentality of the late Twenties, when hero worship, both gay and solemn, colored the published annals of the game. As the Thirties grew older, however, and people in increasing numbers participated in the great mass movements—the NRA, the sit-down strikes, the new unions of employed and unemployed, the petitionings of Congress—they became less likely to be moved to tears by the story of the man who silently bled to death because "the show must go on" or so that fellow crooks rather than "coppers" should privately avenge his murder. Heroes now had to be of truly heroic size: not men who owed allegiance to a team, a private ethic, or the College Militant, but men who faced a whole world of enemies, with a town, a country, or even half a nation at their backs.

When Carl Hubbell, the New York Giants' lean pitcher, who was called "Long Pants" because of his habit of fastening his knee pants just above his ankles, struck out, as a representative of the National League in an all-star game, five in a row of the most murderous sluggers in the American League, you might have thought he had beat back with a rusty bayonet a squad of assassins come to do our President to death. There is no denying that Hubbell demonstrated unusual ability with a baseball. Using his famous "screwball" (the Mathewson fadeaway), he showed the most-talked-of hitters in the opposing league that there was more to the game than just slamming the horsehide sphere with all the strength in your back. But the tributes to his clear-eyed daring, his raw courage, his fierce heroism that echoed through many a parlor at broadcast time suggested he must have been bathed in blood.

In the seasons just preceding the Second World War, fans in many parts of the country used to lend themselves quite honestly to the delusion that the Browns, the Dodgers, the Pirates, or the Reds were championing them and their city against all who had conspired to keep the milk, the honey and the gold forever from there.

Other towns, while perhaps never so fervid, had their own heroes in this age. In Boston, I know, many boys felt about Wesley Ferrell—who used to throw his "nothing" ball down to his brother Rick while batter after batter waved vainly at it—the way they should have felt about their fathers. In the early part of the Depression period, the Braves' pitchers Lou Fette and Jim Turner, two "old men" (they were rookies, though in their thirties), brought solace to many a young fellow who was watching for the first gray whisker on his temple.

In Cincinnati young Johnny Vander Meer became the man most kids wanted to be when they grew up: he pitched two no-hit games in succession. Pitcher Bobo Newsom (called Bobo because he called everybody else Bobo) had a following in nearly every city in the country, for he played in almost every one, shuttling from majors to minors, from National to American Leagues, and from team to team in a manner never equaled. A few of the better folk found baseball reasonably attractive after blue-blooded young Charlie Devens, a star at Harvard, had put in a spell with the Yankees. In Washington and Chicago, Joe Kuhel was known as the ablest first baseman in the business; and Bill Jurges was another man who could have had a free drink in almost any Chicago bar when beer came back. New York kids grew to manhood and womanhood blindly admiring a quiet lad who had been a major leaguer since he was sixteen—Mel Ott, who finally became manager of the Giants.

For the fans who missed Babe Ruth—who had left baseball before the 1930s were out—the Yankees offered Joe DiMaggio, a lean, long-nosed center fielder from California. Joe, compared to Ruth, was like a ball-playing machine. He never seemed to excite himself at the bat. He swung smoothly and gracefully, with great precision and a tremendous follow-through. He was what is known as a wrist hitter, for he held his swing until the final instant, took almost no forward stride and then snapped the bat at the ball in a short swift arc. He was not a bad-ball hitter, was not given to striking out and never offered the appearance of either gaiety or anger, or tremendous effort. His smile was self-conscious, his manner withdrawn to the point of chill. He was interested in money—his own and other men's. He preferred the company of those who "counted" and had little time for small boys who wanted autographs. Like the majority of modern ballplayers, he was of a saving nature, never upset anyone with the size of his tips or the abandon of his spending, and sought out many devices for boosting his income off the field and on.

He was as accomplished on defense as he was at bat. He sped gracefully and easily across the green outfield, hardly seeming to lift his feet higher than the grasstops. Until he injured a shoulder, he sent long, low, almost geometrically perfect throws into the diamond. He was soft-spoken on and around the ball field and created no exciting stories for the press— except the wonders he worked at bat. His marriage to a showgirl and the subsequent rumors of divorce made a scattering of items for the Broadway columnists, but these were nothing to the fans. He held out frequently for higher pay, once hired a Broadway character to "manage" him, and made himself unpopular early in his career, with some fans and teammates, by missing, for one reason or another, part of the training and playing season.

DiMaggio set new records for consecutive hitting, and continued to blast the ball when he should have been laid up with a bad arm, a bad foot, or some more serious ailment.

MILDRED "BABE" DIDRIKSON ZAHARIAS

In 1950, an Associated Press poll declared Babe Didrikson the greatest all-around woman athlete of the first half of the twentieth century.

At the age of nineteen, she was a sensation in the 1932 Olympic Games at Los Angeles, winning the 80-meter hurdles and setting a new world record with the javelin throw, and she would have had at least a first-place tie in the high jump but for a judge's ruling against her style of jumping. Paul Gallico said she could also "play basketball, tennis, pool and billiards, swim, golf in the 80s, and throw a baseball and a football." One of her tricks was to go up to an opponent before a sports event and announce, "Ah'm gonna lick yuh tomorrow." She usually did.

Shortly after her Olympic success,

Miss Didrikson turned professional. In 1938 she married George Zaharias, a wrestler, and with his encouragement she became one of the country's top women golfers. She won the U.S. Women's Open golf championship three times and, after being reinstated as an amateur, was the first American to win the British Ladies golf championship.

Mrs. Zaharias was one of the most popular athletes of her day and an especial favorite of the press, for she made good copy. Her death in 1956 ended a career that spanned almost a quarter of a century, during which countless newspaper and magazine pieces were written about her. One of the very best of those is Paul Gallico's portrait of her at the 1932 Olympics.

PAUL GALLICO

THE TEXAS BABE*

During the recent Olympic games in Los Angeles, four of us, including Grantland Rice, played a game of golf at Brentwood with Mildred "Babe" Didrikson, the world's champion lady athlete. At the conclusion of the round, during which the Babe belted the ball consistently for 240 and 250 yards and sneaked long, easy irons up to the cup, there was a moment of slight embarrassment as we paid off our porters and settled petty bets. Nobody knew whether to invite the Babe into the men's locker room for

* From *Vanity Fair,* October 1932.

a bath and a drink, or whether to say, "Well, good-bye, kid, see you later."

Eventually, the Babe traipsed off with some of the women folk, but as we sat around in the locker room with towels around our haunches, clinking ice in tall glasses and telling lies, we missed her in a way. Up to the eighteenth green, she had been one of us—and better than most of us. The strange, nineteen-year-old girl-boy child would probably have been right at home there.

If one must be a Muscle Moll, and apparently this urge smolders in many a female chest—there were hundreds of them, the pick of the nations, at the Olympics—then I suppose the next thing is to be the best one in the world, the Muscle Moll to end all Muscle Molls, as it were. When a lady athlete can perform the feats that La Didrikson can, she begins to exercise a peculiar and mysterious fascination all her own.

Your deponent spent considerable time in the Chapman Park Hotel in Los Angeles, where the lady athletes of all nations were quartered, studying at close range the Muscle Molls, and I am still giving them to you, with the exception of three or four of the American girl swimmers and divers and the incomparable Didrikson. You can't have her. I like her. She's a champion. She is a champion of champions. She is unquestionably the greatest all-around athlete this country has ever produced. If she were a man—well, there never has been a man who could do half the things she can in sports, or do them as competently.

The Babe stands five feet seven inches in height. She weighs 126 pounds. She has greenish-blue eyes, an aquiline nose, a mop of brownish hair, close-cropped in back like a boy's, but worn floppy, and a little longer in front. Her mouth is large and thin-lipped. One of the girls on the swimming team said she had a mouth like a lizard's. The comparison is apt. There is light fuzz on her upper lip, her face, her neck. She has an enormous Adam's apple. Her legs are powerful and hirsute, with large, strong ankles. Her body is slim, compact, hard. She has the biceps of a village blacksmith. She is magnificently graceful. She looks like a boy. She is a splendid dancer. She would rather dance than do anything else. She plays, among other games, baseball, football, golf, basketball, polo, soccer, lacrosse and tennis. She was said to be entering the women's national golf tourney in Massachusetts. She is taking adagio dancing on the side. But darned if I know what makes her tick.

I went through the whole list of sports with her, trying to find something she couldn't do—fencing, bowling, skating, billiards, swimming, diving—she is an adept at all of them. Finally I said, "Great guns, Babe, isn't there anything you don't play?"

"Sure," she said—"Dolls."

There was no use asking her about boxing. We had already heard the two classic stories, and both verified. In high school she entered an amateur boxing tournament and flattened three bona fide males before they discovered what was going on. In Dallas, Texas, at some kind of athletic affair, someone suggested that she slip on a pair of 12-ounce mittens and spar with Babe Stribling, younger brother of Willie the Clutch.

She said, "I will if you can make him promise not to go easy with me." They sparred. Didrikson foot-feinted, showed Stribling her left and then banged him square on the potato with a right cross that split his mouth and brought the evening's entertainment to a charming conclusion.

She was introduced to Frank Craven in the lobby of the Chapman Park one evening, and golf was mentioned. The Babe was masticating some gum. Without breaking the beautiful rhythm of her jaws, Marvelous Mildred clouted Craven on the spine and offered to golf, wrestle, or fight him. Mr. Craven paled, coughed and retired.

Her first appearance in the Olympic games was in the javelin throw. Somebody said, "There's Babe!" I saw an individual who looked like a boy, dressed in a white track suit and shorts, with the red, white and blue diagonal band and the American shield on her chest, running across the field with fluent grace. Her short hair was flying in the breeze of her own speed. Her spear was poised. Diana! When she came to the scratch, she dropped her arm back and whipped it through the air, 143 feet, 4 inches. The old world's record for women was 132 feet, ⅞ inch. The javelin never did attain any height. It flew practically on a line. The Babe explained it, afterward. "It sliypped," she said in her husky drawl. "It sliypped outa mah hand. Ah'd a throwed it much further, if it hadn't sliypped."

It was just as well that it "sliypped." If it hadn't she would have killed six officials at the other end of the field with it.

There is nothing she cannot do in track and field athletics. She sprints, hurdles, broad jumps, high jumps, throws the javelin and discus and puts the shot. In the trials in Chicago she won eleven events. They permitted her to enter but three in the Olympics: the javelin, the 80-meter hurdles and the high jump. She set a world's record in the first two and was robbed of a third, in the jump, by an official.

But none of this explains her. Her parents are Norwegians, Ole and Hannah Didrikson. Her father was a ship's carpenter who came to Port Arthur, Texas, in 1900, where she was born, June 26, 1913. She remembers that she never cared to play with dolls but was always swiping her father's tools and driving nails into things. She has some brothers and a couple of sisters. Of her younger brother, she says that he will be a great all-around athlete. Asked whether her sisters did anything in sport, she hesitated a moment and then said, "Aw shoot, no. They caint do anythin'. They're sissies."

Girls and men who are not athletic are sissies to her. Her attitude toward her sister athletes is curiously aggressive. She went up to Helene Madison, the champion swimmer, in the lobby of the hotel one evening and said to her, "You're the swimmin' champion, ain't yuh?" Helene admitted it. "What's your time for the hundred?" Helene named it—the world's record. The Babe banged Helen on the shoulder. "I'll cut two seconds off that next year," she announced. The serious Madison nearly had a fit. The fancy divers *did* have a fit when Babe calmly announced to them that she could do a two and a half somersault, a dive that very few men do well.

The Los Angeles prints did not receive the Babe kindly. She was outspoken about her powers. For instance, she claimed an eighty-two and drives of 250 yards, after ten games of golf. Of course this was ridiculous. And so, to see for ourselves, we fixed up a golf date. It was the girl's eleventh game of golf. She turned up at the first tee with one of the finest golf swings we had ever seen. Her grip was wrong. But she whistled that clubhead through like a man. She was playing with borrowed clubs after a six months' layoff. When she came to the ninth tee she lashed a ball 260 yards. Grantland Rice said to Olin Dutra, who was standing on the tee, "Did you see that?" Olin replied, "I saw it, but I don't believe it." She played the second nine in 43.

There she was, striding down the fairway in an old pink dress (which she made herself), an Olympic "jumper," and a white hat with a red, white and blue band perched weirdly on the extreme top of her head. She would smack one down the middle of the fairway and say, "Boy, Ah sure hit that one. This is one game I sure would like to know how to play."

She is the same way in competition, eager to go and absolutely confident of her powers. In the high jump, she hardly waited for the official to get out of the way before she was running for the bar. In the 80-meter hurdles she broke once before the gun. Twice meant disqualification. So she sat in her toe holes and let the field get away, caught the leader by inches and broke the world's record.

The Babe was first discovered playing basketball in Houston, Texas, by Colonel M. J. McCombs, a former athlete himself. She came to Dallas to play on the basketball team of his insurance firm. He taught her to run, jump, throw weights and hurdle. The loyal Babe says, "Everybody's claiming how they coached me now. They's just one man coached me and that's Colonel McCombs."

Everybody in Los Angeles was talking about the Babe. Was she all boy? Or had she any feminine traits? She slaps men of short acquaintance on the back hard enough to jar them from head to foot and will roughhouse with anyone. But she saw a pair of shoes she liked in a shop window and bought six pairs because they had none like them in Dallas. She can swear like a man, ride horseback, shoot and play polo, but she came into the room of some of the American swimmers one afternoon, glowing, with a box under her arm. Clothes! New bathing suits! She spread them out on the bed. One of the bathing suits was scant and low-cut in the back. She said, "Boy, Ah guess I'll sure look pretty slick in that."

She told me she had two interests in life: (1) to crack every existing track record for women and crack them so that they would stay cracked, and (2) acquire a husband. I couldn't find out anything about the necessary qualifications for the latter, except that he mustn't be a sissy. Her travels in athletic competition have given her an age and poise far beyond her years. She never gets tired. The day she won the eleven events she admitted that she was a little tired at the end, but not very. She could have gone on.

A very paragon of Muscle Molls.

But not a very happy girl, I judge. She knows that she is not pretty, that she cannot compete with other girls in the very ancient and honored sport of man-trapping. She uses no cosmetics, creams or powders. But she competes with girls, fiercely and hungrily, at everything else.

Underneath, there dwells a child. A national celebrity at nineteen, interviewed, photographed, pursued by autograph pests, she shows flashes of wistfulness that are at times pathetic. There was a garden party at the hotel. The blond Georgia Coleman and Joan McSheehey, the lovely Eleanor Holm and one or two others of the American swimmers were clowning on the lawn with a group of the men athletes, swimmers and divers— young, good-looking kids. They were joining hands and dancing in gay, meaningless circles. The circles merged and became one large one that suddenly swept across the lawn to a shaded corner where stood the Babe in her blue track pajamas, with the shield of the United States on its breast.

Georgia Coleman broke the circle and ran over. "Come on, Babe," she coaxed. "Come on, get in here with us, we're having a Paul Jones."

Babe said, "Shoot, honey, ah caint! I'm competin' tomorrow. . . . Ah caint play tonight. . . ."

The circle formed again and went spinning around the lawn, a rim of young, laughing faces. The greatest woman athlete in the world stood on the outside, looking on.

QUEEN OF THE SKIES

THE Thirties would see undreamed-of expansion of aviation for travel and transportation. Until the decade began, most Americans who "went up" did so for the thrill, sight-seeing at the local airports and county fairs. At that time, there were many who believed the future of aviation was to be found in the development of the rigid airship, the dirigible.

During World War I, the Germans had used the dirigible effectively in air raids over England, where it proved to be a potent psychological weapon. Enthusiasts for air power not only emphasized the dirigible's weapon value, but predicted a great future for it in transportation.

The United States Navy's first dirigible, inflated with hydrogen, was constructed in England; while being tested for flight across the Atlantic, fire broke out and the ship went down. This accident put off acceptance of the ships in the United States until helium, a noninflammable gas, was put into use. In 1925, the first American-built dirigible, the *Shenandoah,* broke into three pieces, a victim of a line squall. But the Navy pushed forward; the Goodyear Company was put to work constructing the two largest airships to date—the *Akron* and the *Macon.*

The *Akron* was 785 feet long and, after being christened by Mrs. Herbert Hoover in 1931, began a series of shakedown cruises. In May 1932, the "Queen of the Skies" completed her first cross-country trip, arriving at the San Diego Naval Base. What happened at this attempted landing is told in the following article by John Toland, who goes on to give an account of the tragic end of this flying ship.

JOHN TOLAND

THE *AKRON* AND THREE
WHO CAME BACK*

AT 9:30 A.M. the "Queen of the Skies" descended through the thick fog bank, coming into the clear at 1,200 feet. Now the heat of the morning sun quickly expanded the helium, making the ship extremely buoyant. Four of the ship's propellers were inverted, like huge overhead fans, in

* From John Toland's *Ships in the Sky* (New York, Holt, 1957).

79

an effort to pull the *Akron* toward the ground. The power fought the buoyancy, but the dirigible stayed aloft. Since Lieutenant Commander Rosendahl, the ship's skipper, did not want to valve precious helium, the battle against buoyancy lasted many minutes.

It wasn't until eleven o'clock that the 400-foot trail ropes were dropped from the port and starboard sides of the nose, falling neatly between the two landing parties. To the surprise of those in the control car the landing crew merely stood watching the ropes instead of picking them up. Rosendahl looked at Lieutenant George Campbell. Both men knew that they were in for a rough landing. The crew was more inexperienced than they had feared.

Rosendahl made two more passes over the sandy field before the trail ropes were finally grabbed and attached to "spiders," ground lines fitted with wooden toggles. Each of the ground crew men hung onto a wooden toggle, while Peck shouted instructions frantically. The seven-eighths-inch steel mooring cable spun out of the nose of the ship and hit the ground. It was coupled to a ground cable leading to the top of the mooring mast. The winch wound slowly, dragging the reluctant ship down.

The heat of the ground now made the *Akron* even more buoyant. The nose bobbed up. Those men on the forward spiders were lifted slightly from the ground. Then the tail leaped up, almost standing the "Queen of the Skies" on her stubby nose.

Engine Number 8 sputtered. Mechanic Sid Hooper struggled to keep it going but it soon stopped: the steep angle had cut off the fuel. Emil Klaassen had the same trouble in engine room Number 4.

Rosendahl instantly gave orders to valve helium, but it was too late. The angle had automatically tripped the ballast bags and 3,000 pounds of water were dumped. All the engines had by this time rung up "stop." Rosendahl had to act quickly. "Cut the mooring cable!" he ordered. "Let everything go!"

The cable attached to the mast was released, and the two ground parties were told to let go. The *Akron* shot into the air with the long trail ropes dangling below.

From the hatch near Number 4 engine room, Mechanic Quinny Quernheim could see that the starboard trail rope was cleared. Then he noticed that there was a little cluster of men still clinging to the other rope. Fifty feet above ground a tiny figure dropped from the rope. At 100 feet, a second man slipped off the spiders even before the first one struck the ground.

Quernheim watched in horror as the second man hit and bounced.

Shakily he went into the engine room. His face was pale. "My God!" he said to his partner, Klaassen. "That kid smoked when he hit the ground!"

Others in the ship were watching the third man on the spiders. He appeared to be tangled in the web of lines several hundred feet below the ship. Rosendahl knew that if he tried to land the buoyant ship he would probably dash the man to death. He told the rudder man to head for the ocean where the air was smoother.

Two crews, under Lieutenants Roland Mayer and George Campbell, began to improvise rigs to transfer the trail line to the mooring winch so the ground crew man could be reeled to safety.

The *Akron* was now flying 2,000 feet above the Pacific. The stranded sailor, who was sitting astride a toggle, wrapped in a tangle of ropes, looked up. "Hey!" he called, "when the hell are you going to land me?"

An officer called encouragement through a megaphone, but the sailor below didn't seem to need it. He waved and then took off his white cap, stuffing it in his jumper. He didn't want to be read off for losing government property.

The men in the nose of the *Akron* were now trying to figure out a way to haul the sailor into the ship. The top twenty-five feet of the trail rope was one-inch cable—and wouldn't revolve around the drum of the mooring winch.

Boatswain's Mate Second Class Dick Deal volunteered to go down and tie a line below the steel cable section. Deal was slowly lowered out of the nose of the dirigible in a bosun's chair. As he swung dangerously, twenty-five feet below the bow platform, he grabbed at the swaying trail rope. Finally he reached it and, after fifteen minutes, tied a line to it. A few minutes later the steel cable section was cut off and the rope attached to the mooring winch. Then the sailor was hoisted up a few feet at a time.

After a tense hour and a half his head was level with the bow platform. Chief Arthur Carlson, a survivor of the *Shenandoah,* leaned down and grabbed the sailor. At last he was on the platform—safe. He was a rugged, rawboned young man of twenty-one and he was far less excited than those on the platform. He looked around curiously. He had never seen a dirigible this close before.

Captain Rosendahl came up to the young man. "Son," he said, "what do you think of your ride?"

The sailor, whose name was Bud Cowart, grinned. "Captain, that was a lily dilly!"

Young Cowart escaped without a scratch, but two others had died. The "Queen of the Skies" was now more than a jinx, she was a killer.

SKIES were overcast on the morning of April 3, 1933, at Lakehurst. Low clouds scudded across the field from the ocean. But despite the threat of bad weather, in Hangar Number 1 sailors and civilian workers were preparing the *Akron* for her fifty-ninth flight.

In the nearby Administration Building, just across Lansdowne Road, officers were anxiously looking out the windows of the commandant's office. One of the main missions of the flight was to calibrate radio direction-finding stations up in New England, the First Naval District. And work of this nature could not be accomplished unless the skies cleared.

A few minutes before eleven the phone in Commander Fred Berry's office rang. The commandant of the station talked a moment, and from the tone of his voice it was obvious that he was connected with Washington. Then he held out the phone to Commander Frank McCord, the *Akron's* new skipper. "The admiral wants to talk with you," said Berry.

McCord, a short, good-looking man, took the phone. He didn't have to be told who "the admiral" was. At Lakehurst there was only one admiral—William A. Moffett, Chief of the Bureau of Aeronautics and a staunch friend of the rigid dirigible.

While McCord was talking, his executive officer, Lieutenant Commander Herbert V. Wiley, went into the next room and called up the ship's aerologist. "What are the weather probabilities for the flight, Lieutenant?" he asked. Wiley was a big, solidly built man with a shock of shaggy gray hair and a ruddy face that was surprisingly young. With his deep, brooding eyes and broad, thoughtful forehead, he looked more like a philosopher than an airshipman—a philosopher with a barrel chest.

At the other end of the wire young Lieutenant Herbert Wescoat said the ship could be safely taken out of the hangar, but it would be definitely impossible to do any radio or compass work for at least another day.

Wiley quickly went back to the other room. In an undertone he told McCord the bad news. The *Akron's* captain repeated it to Moffett, then hung up. "The admiral," he said, "is coming up from Washington. He wants to fly with us, in spite of the weather."

Late that afternoon the office was crowded with those scheduled to make the evening flight. Admiral Moffett, accompanied by Commander Harry Cecil, had arrived from Washington, where everyone was still buzzing from the new President's stirring "nothing to fear but fear itself" speech. Besides Commander Berry, others who were going along for the ride that evening were A. F. Masury, a reserve Army colonel from the International Motor Company, and three junior officers from the station, who needed the flying time.

In spite of the threatening weather there was the usual preflight air of expectation and excitement, with a leavening of buffoonery and horseplay. For with Moffett present, the men knew the flight wouldn't be canceled unless a hurricane sprang up.

At 4:20 P.M. McCord and Wiley went to the station aerological office and examined the weather map made only twenty minutes before. The captain turned to his executive officer. "Cancel the airplane hook-on drill," he said. "But see if you can take aboard a training plane."

An hour and a half later the two men met again at the weather office. There was a light northeast wind and the temperature had fallen 20 degrees. Wiley phoned the hangar, ordered the Officer of the Deck to put 3,500 pounds of water ballast aboard.

Wiley, a meticulous airshipman who never left a thing to chance, then went to the great hangar himself. Finding the inside temperature even higher than he'd expected, he ordered additional ballast put aboard to compensate for the difference of 16 degrees between the hangar and outside. He walked out on the field and looked up. Thick balls of fog were rapidly forming.

By six o'clock the hangar was alive. Most of the crew men making the flight had already put their gear on the *Akron*—toilet articles, sleeping-bag liners, and heavy flying clothes. Now they were standing under the ship or loafing in one of the adjoining shops.

Chief Machinist George Walsh looked in the big mechanic shop. "Hey," he called to Mechanic Sid Hooper, "you don't have to make the trip. It's only a short hop. Get Anderson."

Hooper didn't care. He had logged plenty of hours, and Vic Anderson, the third man in Number 8 engine room, needed a qualifying hop for watch-stander. Hooper found Anderson in the crowd. The youngster was nervous with excitement as Hooper handed over his heavy, fur-lined gabardine flight jacket, skull-cap flight helmet lined with fur, and big sheepskin-lined flying boots. Then Hooper went to the front of the hangar to wait for his wife. She was coming to watch the ship take off—the first time he'd allowed it. Now he wouldn't even be aboard.

A few late-comers were on their way, driving over the dark, lonely roads lined with scrubby pines and dwarf oaks. Robert Copeland, chief radio operator, was being chauffeured by his wife. The misty, overcast weather made her nervous. For the tenth time she asked him how dangerous lightning was. Copeland, who had originally studied to be a missionary, laughed at her fears. "Lightning will go right through the propellers and won't hurt us," he insisted.

Two veterans of the *Shenandoah* were on the back road trom Lakewood. Henry Boswell still looked boyish and unsophisticated. The other man was Dick Deal, who had risked his life the year before to save Cowart in San Diego. He had been scheduled to make the last flight of the *Shenandoah,* but Ralph Joffray, who had relatives in St. Louis, had asked to take his place. Joffray had been at the wheel, next to Lansdowne, when the control car tore out of the *Shenandoah.* This last-minute change suggested to Dick's shipmates that he be called "Lucky" Deal. By a curious twist of fate, five years after the *Shenandoah* crash Deal had married Joffray's widow, the former Gertrude Matthews of Lakewood. At that moment she was at their home on Thirteenth Street in Lakewood, worrying about their hound bitch who was about to have puppies.

Fog thickened as their car crawled through a hollow. Both men had made many stormy trips but neither liked the look of the weather. Boswell, usually a lighthearted fellow, became somber as they neared Lakehurst. "I hope," he said, "they've got sense enough to cancel this flight."

At 6:25 P.M. the heavy hangar doors opened slowly. Fog curled in like smoke. The ship was walked out of the hangar at six forty-one. Seven minutes later the mobile mast had carried its burden to the center of the mooring circle. The temperature was 41 degrees.

Every man was at his landing station. Captain McCord stood at the port side of the control car, giving commands to Lieutenant George Calnan, in charge of ballast. Wiley was at the captain's right, conning the rudder man. Boswell was at the elevator wheel just behind Captain McCord. Admiral Moffet stood back out of the way next to Navigator Harold Mac-Lellan. The admiral watched the weighing-off operations with his usual absorption.

Copeland was in his radio shack, a tiny cabin above the control car. He looked out the window, trying to see his wife, who was standing in front of Hangar Number 1. But it was so dark and foggy that the great shed was only a formless mass. At the bow stood Dick Deal, and at the other end of the ship, almost a sixth of a mile away, Metalsmith Second Class Moody Irwin was at the emergency control station, in the forward section of the huge lower fin. It was a tiny room, just large enough for one man at the elevators and one at the rudder wheel. Irwin leaned out the port window. It was his job to release the X frames that supported the fin during handling operations. These X frames had been devised as insurance against a freak gust of wind.

In all there were seventy-six aboard the *Akron* that evening, including the Navy's Air Chief; the commandant of Lakehurst; Lieutenant Calnan, a former world's champion fencer; Lieutenant Wilfred Bushnell, the copilot of the American balloon that had won the Gordon Bennett Race over Switzerland the year before; five survivors of the *Shenandoah* crash, Boswell, Carlson, Quernheim, Shevlowitz and Russell; twenty-two-year-old John Weeks, who had just married without telling his mother; and a young sailor, Paul Hoover, who couldn't swim and had a morbid fear of water.

At seven twenty-eight the ship slowly left the ground, pushed up by four inverted propellers. In front of the hangar, Mechanic Sid Hooper, his wife, Mrs. Copeland and others—wives, friends, civilian workers—waved and shouted farewells that could not be heard. They watched the great ship disappear into the dense fog at 300 feet. Now only the dull roar of its motors could be heard.

A moment later the roar was heard by Norman Walker, who was driving his wife to Toms River. The veteran airshipman, the only American to live through the *ZR-2* (*R-38*) crash, tried to peer up through the thick fog. "I hope," he said jokingly, "that thing holds up."

Not a man aboard the *Akron* had the slightest feeling of apprehension. A few enlisted men did think it was damned foolishness to be setting out on a calibrating mission in a pea-soup fog. But they knew that Admiral Moffett would rather ride in a big rigid than eat; and it was easy to sympathize with him, feeling almost the same way themselves.

By now the ship was circling above the fog bank; the Naval Air Station was a dim glow 1,200 feet below. McCord realized that it would be too dangerous to bring any planes aboard, and at 7:39 P.M. he ordered Copeland to wire the station that planes weren't required. Since the fog extended over the ocean, McCord headed the ship west with only six motors running. He had decided to cruise inland where visibility was reported better. Then, when the coastal regions cleared, the ship would turn north to arrive, at seven the next morning, over Newport, Rhode Island.

"*Akron* flying Lakehurst to Philadelphia to Delaware Capes, thence along coast," wired Copeland at seven forty. It was the last clear message Lakehurst received from the ship.

Although the watch didn't change until eight o'clock, Metalsmith Moody Irwin decided to relieve his partner early. Irwin, a slender, thin-faced man of twenty-eight with a tiny mustache, walked up the port keel to frame 170 and took up his post in front of the telephone. Unlike the *Shenandoah*, the *Akron* had three keels, all V-shaped. One keel was near the top of the ship, running from bow to stern like a backbone. By means of this keel gas valves could now be inspected without going topside. The other two keels were near the bottom of the ship—one curving along the port side and the other along the starboard. Nine cross-walks connected the two lower keels, making the inside of the ship a complicated maze of tunnels.

The frames, like those of the *Shenandoah*, were numbered starting with the rudder. Engines Number 1 and 2 were at frame 57.5, 57.5 meters from the rudders; the airplane hangar ran from 123 to 147.5; the control car ladder was at 170; and the tip of the nose was 213.5. The frames aft of the rudder were given a minus designation: for example, the machine-gun nest at the extreme tail was —25.75. The cells were also numbered from the stern, running forward from cell 0 in the tail to cell 11 at the nose.

At eight o'clock Dick Deal took over the telephone watch on the starboard side of the ship. He hadn't been on duty more than ten minutes when a familiar, stocky figure came down the keel, heading for the officers' wardroom. It was Admiral Moffett. "Well, we're on our way!" said the admiral. He stopped and the two chatted for a few minutes. He and Deal had shared many flights and were old friends. Rank meant little to the Chief of the Bureau of Aeronautics. "These are my happiest hours," confided the admiral. "Nothing like being on board a dirigible!"

The admiral passed forward, and Deal looked out a window. Visibility had cleared; Philadelphia could be plainly seen. He looked at his watch. In forty-five minutes he was due to relieve Ralph Stine at the elevators.

In the blacked-out control car, Wiley decided to take a smoke. He walked back to the room, which also served as the officers' smoking room, in the after end of the car. Soon he noticed that the ship was moving faster. His curiosity aroused, he walked forward. He found that now eight engines were running at standard speed, and the ship had turned east.

In explanation McCord pointed to the south where lightning was flashing. At that moment Aerologist Wescoat reported that there had been thunderstorms over Washington at 7:00 P.M. Deal climbed into the car and took over the elevator wheel from Stine. McCord and Wiley stood by anxiously watching the lightning.

Wiley walked back to MacLellan's cubicle. "Where are we?" he asked. "We'll cross the coast at Atlantic City, I think," said the navigator.

They were again shrouded in fog. McCord told Deal to bring the ship down to 1,500 feet. Deal slowly lowered the *Akron*. At last the dull lights of a town could be seen through the mist. Lightning flashed again. It seemed to be only about twenty-five miles away. Rain began to strike the windows.

The captain ordered the course changed northeast.

"I think we'd better go west, sir," said Wiley tensely. Old airshipmen had a theory that, with such a storm approaching, the dirigible should be headed toward shore. But McCord shook his head. "No," he said pointing to the west. "I saw two flashes of lightning there."

At least a dozen men aboard the *Akron* that night knew that the ship should have turned west. But the captain, although he'd passed the airship pilot's course, had spent almost all his Navy time at sea, learning to be a master mariner.

Deal began to have trouble with the elevators. The air was smooth, but the buoyancy of the ship kept changing capriciously as the *Akron* bobbed in and out of the fog. Stine was called back to the control car to stand by in case Deal needed help.

At ten o'clock Deal was exhausted and glad to be relieved by Rufus "Red" Johnson.

"The ship's one and one-half degrees light, sir," Deal told Lieutenant Clendening, the Officer of the Deck. "Can I go up into the ship now, sir?"

"Stand by Johnson," replied Clendening. He had just seen two thunder-heads and was afraid the ship was in for some heavy weather.

MacLellan stuck his head out the navigator's cabin. "I think we're over Asbury Park, sir," he called to McCord.

The skipper nodded. Then he turned to Wiley, who was staring ahead at the turbulent skies. "I'm going up and take a look at the weather map," he said.

The lightning was now only a few miles off. Great, jagged bolts would strike horizontally and then be answered, a moment later, by vivid vertical flashes. But in spite of the lively electrical display the air was still calm and Johnson was having little trouble with the elevators.

Deal walked back to the navigator's room. Colonel Masury was seated at the port window, looking nervously out into the storm.

Suddenly thunder rumbled almost overhead. Long vertical bolts of lightning flashed on both sides of the ship, and the rain increased in force. The storm had caught up with them at last.

"It's pretty bad, isn't it?" the colonel said.

Deal tried to reassure Masury. "There's nothing to worry about, Colonel," he said. "We've been in worse electrical storms than this one." Lightning flashed, illuminating the colonel's drawn face. Deal wondered why older people, who had a lot less to live for, were always more frightened than the young. Deal peered forward. McCord, who had returned from the weather room, was anxiously looking out the starboard windows. Wiley looked out the port. Then the two officers silently changed positions.

87

"You should have been with us in the *Shenandoah*," said Deal to Masury. "The time we were coming from Buffalo back in nineteen twenty-four, the lightning was so bad over Wilkes-Barre that the control car seemed to be a ball of fire."

Masury found little reassurance in the story. "I'd just as soon not fly in a thunderstorm," he shouted above a resounding clap.

On the starboard side of the room MacLellan was dropping flares over the side to check his position. But the sea of fog below was too thick.

"Look!" cried Masury. He pointed down. "I can see lights on the ground!"

Deal looked out the port window. He saw the lights and called Mac-Lellan. The navigator joined them. After a moment he began to laugh.

"That's just the reflection of the light from the officers' quarters on the fog."

In the radio room above them, Copeland, fearing that the antenna might be hit by the lightning, had hauled it in. Anyway the radio had been useless the past hour because of the static.

Copeland nodded in greeting as Admiral Moffett clambered past his room and down the ladder into the control car. The radio man figured that the admiral had been wakened by the lightning.

When Moffett reached the bottom of the ladder he looked forward. There Wiley and McCord were changing positions rapidly, like dancers in a peculiar ballet.

Thunder crashed, as if announcing the admiral's entrance. "It's almost as bad as one we struck in Alabama," he said to no one in particular. His feet apart, he rode the easy roll of the ship. There was no nervousness on his face. The admiral was enjoying himself.

McCord told Wiley to go up and have a look at the weather map. The executive officer went aloft and found out from Wescoat that only about two thirds of a map had been received before the radio went off. Wiley examined the map fragment, shook his head dolefully and returned to the control car.

"What do you think, Commander?" McCord asked him.

"We certainly have a storm center down there, sir," answered Wiley. "It's something to play with."

"We'd better take her to sea," said McCord.

Again Wiley suggested heading west. But McCord had made up his mind. They would run east and then south to get ahead of the storm center.

The *Akron* headed out into the black skies over the Atlantic.

At 11:30 P.M. conditions were still normal in the ship. Deal was having coffee and a sandwich in the crew's mess hall above the airplane hangar, on the starboard side. He chatted with Chief Machinist Walsh for a few minutes. They agreed it was a sad night for flying. Then Walsh started on another inspection of his eight engines, and Deal strolled back to the starboard telephone at frame 170. Glancing out the window, he noticed lightning near the radio antenna. Copeland had just been given permission to lower one antenna fifteen feet, to the level of the bottom of the control car, so that he could try to get some weather information.

Lieutenant Calnan looked over Deal's shoulders. "Stand by the fire unit," he ordered, "in case anything catches fire."

Moody Irwin brushed by Calnan and started down the ladder to the control car. "I'm ready to relieve you, Red," he told elevator man Johnson a moment later.

"The ship's a little heavy," said Johnson, handing over the wheel. Because a "heavy" ship was inclined to climb, Irwin carried 5 degrees down elevator, which held the *Akron* at her given altitude, 1,600 feet. Ralph Stine, an expert elevator man, stood behind Irwin in case of an emergency.

The lightning was now flashing all around the ship, blinding Irwin for several seconds at a time. He found he was having more and more difficulty holding the tail up.

"She's tail-heavy," he called to Lieutenant Calnan.

Calnan immediately sent for Henry Boswell, the most experienced elevator man on the ship. In a minute Boswell was at the controls.

"Check on the slack adjusters and counterbalance springs," said Calnan. Boswell nodded. He made the adjustments, then turned the wheel back to Irwin.

The storm seemed to get worse, and McCord finally ordered the dirigible headed back for the coast. But Navigator MacLellan had no idea where they were. Not only had the tricky, veering winds muddled their bearing, but also one of McCord's orders had been misunderstood; when the captain had called for a 15-degree change in course, the helmsmen thought he'd said 50 degrees.

Copeland was still doing his best to reach the home radio station. At 11:45 P.M. Radioman Third Class Robert Hill, the Lakehurst operator on duty, heard the *Akron's* call, but the static was too heavy to read the message. Five minutes later an amateur radioman, Arthur Hullfish of 224 East Montgomery Avenue, Wildwood, New Jersey, thought he could hear someone trying to establish communications on short wave. He distinctly heard the call letters "NAL," but then the message was broken up by static.

At a few minutes before twelve, Hill heard another call from the *Akron*. Again the Lakehurst operator couldn't make sense out of the message. It was just about this time that the men in the *Akron's* control car sighted the Jersey coastline. Neither MacLellan nor McCord had figured that they were so close to land.

"One hundred twenty degrees compass!" ordered McCord quickly. For all he knew they might be heading straight for the Empire State Building.

The *Akron* turned slowly and headed back over the Atlantic. In a few minutes she was submerged in fog.

At twelve the watch changed. Tony Swidersky and Joe Zimkus relieved Irwin and Stine at the elevators. Irwin started wearily toward the galley for sandwiches and coffee before turning in.

Dick Deal headed for the enlisted men's smoking room, which was above the plane hangar on the port side. Stine was there. So was Elmer Fink, an engineer and the ship's comedian. The thunder was now rumbling louder than ever.

"That's beer kegs being rolled around!" said Elmer.

It was a legitimate topical joke—3.2 beer was to be legalized the next day—and Stine and Deal laughed. And they smoked contentedly as little Elmer, in rare form despite the storm, continued to entertain them. After a pleasant ten minutes the two elevator men left the smoking room.

"Bad night for airships," remarked Deal. "Good night." The men separated, each heading for his bunk. Deal went into a tiny, canvas-walled room. He sat on his bunk and took off his shoes. He'd already removed his heavy flying trousers in the smoking room, and he flopped on the bunk with his head toward the keel walkway. On either side of him were two empty bunks. They belonged to men who'd just come off duty and were in the galley having a midnight lunch.

The keel lights shone dully over his head as he lay back and listened to the roar of Number 8 engine. It was a pleasant, comforting sound. He wasn't very tired. He never was tired on the first night of a flight. He flopped over on his stomach, leaning on his elbows with his face resting in his hands. There was no use corking off until his shipmates got back from the mess hall.

Irwin was lying on his bunk a few yards forward. He was too tired to take off anything except his shoes. It'd been a rough watch.

In Wildwood, the storm rose to such intensity that Arthur Hullfish decided to disconnect the radio belonging to the people who lived on the other side of his house. He ran out into the storm. Over the crackle of lightning and the crash of thunder, he could hear the heavy boom of the surf 1,000 feet away. He looked out toward the Atlantic. It was blanketed with fog. Hullfish quickly unhooked the aerial and ran back into the house. He wanted to see if he could pick up those strange short-wave calls again.

At twenty minutes past midnight Admiral Moffett again came down from his cabin above the control car. Even an old seadog couldn't sleep through a storm so wild. He stood in the darkened control car watching every maneuver intently.

Young Joe Zimkus was spelling Swidersky at the elevators. But Tony, by far the more experienced man, stood watchfully behind Joe. McCord and Wiley were still peering out the front windows, trying to find a break in the storm. The control car began to jerk spasmodically. Deafening peals of thunder were now following almost instantly after the rips of lightning. It seemed to Wiley that the sky above was cracking in two. The screaming wind told him that they must be near the center of the storm itself.

Suddenly young Zimkus cried, "We're falling!"

The elevator wheel tore out of Joe's hands and began spinning. Zimkus stood transfixed and watched the wheel whirl madly. Swidersky pushed Zimkus aside, threw himself on the wheel. It tried to tear itself from his hands. Wiley grabbed two of the wheel's spokes. Together the two powerful men yanked the nose of the ship up.

"I got it, sir," said Swidersky a moment later. He was in a sweat.

Wiley looked at the altimeter. It read 1,100 feet and was sinking fast even though the ship was almost at an even keel.

"Should I drop ballast, Captain?" asked Wiley quietly.

"Yes," replied McCord, who had already rung up for more knots from the engines.

Wiley yanked at the toggles, emptying the service bags. The executive officer turned and looked at the altimeter again. They were down to 950 feet. But he knew that instrument was unreliable and could be off as much as several hundred feet. He reached up and pulled at the emergency toggles. Sixteen hundred pounds of water dumped out of frame 187. The needle on the altimeter wavered, stopped at 800 feet, and then began to shoot up almost as fast as it had fallen.

Wiley stood behind Swidersky, conning him cagily to reduce gradually the rate of rise. At 1,300 feet the executive officer tensed. "All right," he said. A moment later he saw that Swidersky had good control of the ship. "Now bring her up to 1,600 gradually, and then level off." Wiley stepped back a pace and began to breathe more normally. The crisis was over.

Inside the ship, Irwin had noticed the fall and rise. Several bunks aft, Deal had heard the telegraph ring in Number 8 engine room. Then he felt the ship surge forward with increased speed. After a few minutes he heard another ring in the engine room. The roar of Number 8 motor slacked off, and he knew they were back on standard speed.

Below them, the control car was swaying harder and faster than ever. Blinding flashes of lightning lit up the dark car, elongating the black figures of the men and distorting their faces weirdly. The ship was tossed up and down violently. Wiley knew they had finally hit the storm center.

"All hands to landing stations!" he called.

Although the rocking motion was less noticeable in the crew's sleeping quarters, which were near the ship's center of gravity, Deal wondered sleepily what the devil was going on. Leaning on one elbow he glanced up at Number 7 cell. It was surging and gasping like a creature in pain. It reminded him of one of those respiratory bladders attached to a patient during an operation. His drowsiness instantly disappeared. Something was happening. He rolled out of bed.

As Deal stood erect, the ship lurched sideways heavily, as if she had been hit by a big club. There was an alarming crackle overhead. He looked up. Girders 7 and 8 had snapped in two.

Irwin was half dozing when he heard a sound like the crack of a paper bag bursting. He looked up and saw that girder 7, the big longitudinal, had parted.

Up forward Chief Bosun's Mate Carl Dean was shouting, "All hands forward!"

The lurch almost knocked Wiley off his feet. The gust that had caused it was the most vicious he'd ever felt. As soon as he recovered his balance he saw that the lower rudder control rope had been carried away. He told the captain. Then he began unclutching the broken rudder control.

"She's falling," reported elevator man Swidersky with no emotion in his voice.

Captain McCord looked at the altimeter. The ship was falling fast—faster than the first time.

"Full speed!" he ordered. The engineering officer instantly rang up the eight engine rooms.

Just as Wiley finished unclutching the lower control, the upper control snapped. He could hear a high, shrill whine inside the ship. It sounded to him like sheaves carrying away. He knew the ship's structure had been damaged somewhere.

92

By this time Swidersky had the bow of the ship up almost 20 degrees in an effort to stop the fall. "Eight hundred feet!" he called.

There was no confusion in the control car as the ship plunged into blackness below. Lieutenant Calnan, who had appeared a moment after the landing station signal, was standing patiently by the ballast board. With both controls broken and useless, Wiley hung to the girder alongside the port window. He stared down fixedly, waiting for the water to loom into sight.

Arthur Hullfish was back at his short-wave set. Once again he picked up faint staccato signals. Then he began to hear plain language instead of meaningless code. Hullfish knew he'd cut in on a distress signal of some kind. Frantically he began to copy words. "Two bays [or guys] control broken—ship bad condition—heavy storm strong wind—going up now—[something] broken." Then only isolated words and short phrases could be heard. "Out—700 feet—nose—nose up—breaking center—run into something—crashing [or cracking]."

There were a few more signals, then dead air. Hullfish looked at his watch. It was 12:26 A.M. He studied the gibberish he'd written. It made no sense whatever. He decided to forget the whole thing.

When Deal had seen the girders snap, he decided to call the control car. But when the ship began falling rapidly by the tail he knew he should drop fuel tanks first. Looking up the keel, he saw a tank, suspended above the walkway, start to break loose. He hurried forward so he wouldn't be crushed. The gangway was now so sharply angled that he had to pull himself up girder by girder.

Irwin was ten yards behind Deal. He, too, saw the gas tank tilting crazily, and he scrambled up the steep catwalk. Passing the tank, he heard a shriek of metal as the after-suspension gave way. The 120-gallon tank crashed to the keel. It missed Irwin by inches, but in his rush to get forward he never saw it. He climbed to the telephone at frame 170.

Deal, who hadn't time to put on his shoes, was at frame 175 with half a dozen men. Chief Paul Jandick squeezed past him going aft. The others stood silently about, hanging onto girders for support. Girders were breaking and wires singing from strain. Though the lights were still glowing above the catwalk, everyone knew the ship was breaking up. Bill Russell, survivor of the *Shenandoah*, looked at Deal. Neither spoke. Chief Dean waited motionless.

Deal wondered whether they were over land or sea, and which would be worse for a crash. The men at 175 stared at each other and hoped for a little good luck.

Several miles away the German oil tanker *Phoebus,* out of New York and bound for Tampico, was fighting the heavy seas. Thirty-four-year-old Captain Karl Dalldorf had taken the mate's watch because he wanted to be on the bridge all through the storm. Then a flashing of lights appeared in the air off his bow. He had no idea what the lights were, but he was sure they weren't the Barnegat Inlet Light: he had just passed it a few miles back.

Now the lights seemed to be on or near the water. Dalldorf, figuring it was a plane crashing into the sea, instantly changed his course. The 9,226-ton, twin-screw motorship plowed through the twelve-foot waves full speed ahead.

Wiley, looking out the port window, could see nothing but fog below. Suddenly the choppy, wind-lashed sea appeared through a hole in the fog. "What's the altitude?" asked Wiley.

"Two hundred feet," answered Swidersky.

"Stand by to crash!" called Wiley. Since broken wires had ruined their regular telegraph system, he ordered the engineering officer to ring up the crash signal on the emergency bell-pull system. Just as the engine cars began repeating back the order, there was a heavy jolt. The tail, dragging far below the control car, had struck the ocean.

Lights went out all along both lower keels. Irwin jumped through the ship's outer covering. He plummeted through the criss-cross tangle of wires and out of the dirigible.

Ten yards forward, Deal felt icy water bursting through the keel at his feet. He had a horrible, panicky feeling. He and the others with him were caught inside a trap of metal and wires. There was still no sound from the men at frame 175. The *Akron* didn't carry life preservers. They all knew that it would soon be over.

Water flooded in over Deal's head. He felt his right leg being clutched and held by wires. He kicked frantically. He yanked at the wires. Somehow he got loose and shot to the surface of the water. The starboard side of the ship was drifting away from him.

Irwin struggled as the great hull of the *Akron* slowly rolled on top of him, pushing him below the waves. He jackknifed his legs until his feet were on the ship's structure. Then, his lungs bursting, he pushed off and dived as deep as he could. Moments later his head popped out of the water. He had barely cleared the sinking wreckage. He kicked off his low-cut crepe-soled shoes. It was easy because he had made a habit of leaving them untied when off duty. He took a deep breath and then, as he sank, started removing his bulky flying coat. Finally he got the coat off and shot to the surface again. Then he swam as hard as he could, away from the foundering ship and the undertow.

A few seconds after the crew's quarters were flooded, water rushed through the open port window of the control car, which was listing to starboard. The torrent picked up Wiley and carried him out the starboard window. He felt a mass of rubberized fabric on top of him and knew that he was being dragged down with the ship. He swam under water until his lungs seemed about to burst. Then he surfaced. Lightning flashed and, in the brief glow, he saw the dirigible, her bow pointed in the air, drifting away. He saw two lights on the stern section. Beyond were the lights of a vessel. Even farther off was a glare he thought came from Barnegat Lighthouse. Wiley swam toward the *Akron*.

Irwin was swimming away from the dirigible. He wasn't particularly afraid of drowning: he knew that they were near the Jersey coast, and he figured that if necessary he could swim to land. But he *was* afraid of sharks. He'd been afraid of them since he was a little boy. He kicked his feet frantically to scare them away. Looking around for something to help keep him afloat, he saw phosphorous flares blazing near the submerged control car. They had probably burst out of the locker in the navigator's room and ignited upon hitting the water. Finally he saw a fuel tank— perhaps the same one that had almost hit him a moment before the crash. It was bobbing like a giant cork twenty yards away. He struggled through the heavy seas toward it.

When at last he reached the 120-gallon tank, two men were already clinging to it. During the next flash of lightning he recognized Copeland, the radio operator, and Mechanic Lucius Rutan. Irwin grabbed onto the slippery tank with one hand and slowly took off everything but his underclothes. It wasn't until then that he realized how cold he was. Several hundred yards away he saw the "Queen of the Skies," her bow sticking out of the water like an inverted ice cream cone. A moment later, in another flash of lightning, he saw about a dozen men struggling in the water about fifty yards away. The sea was momentarily quiet, and the cries of the swimming men were faint and frightened. Irwin would never forget the sound of their cries.

Deal heard the cries for help all around him. But he couldn't help; he was hard put and lucky just to keep himself afloat. He figured that he'd been swimming about twenty minutes, and if he didn't find a piece of wood or floating debris he'd soon go under. A bolt of lightning lit up the great white-flecked swells. In the flash he saw several men floating by on a tank. Desperately he struck out for the tank, and he was tiring with each stroke. A few yards from it he reached the end of his endurance and started to go under. Then he felt himself being pulled. His hands hit metal. He hung onto the tank and took a deep breath.

"Who's here?" he asked.

"Irwin," said the man who had pulled him onto the tank.

Rutan didn't answer so Irwin added, "And Rutan."

The last man said, "This is Copeland."

Deal was hopeful for the first time since the crash. It was a good feeling to have company.

Wiley had heard the fading cries for help. He had found a board about three feet square, and when he saw a man struggling not far away he swam toward him. A wave tore the board from his frozen hands, and dragged him under. After he had fought his way to the surface again, he couldn't find the man who had cried out.

Wiley was now about 400 yards from the wallowing dirigible. The wind changed, and as the waves began hitting him squarely in the face, he realized that he didn't have a chance of swimming toward the ship. He wondered, without panic, how long a man could live in that icy, heaving sea. He knew he was in good condition; and if he budgeted his strength he had as good a chance for survival as anyone. So he swam easily, trying only to keep afloat.

The four men were having trouble hanging onto the bouncing fuel tank. Each big wave would sweep somebody off. Whenever Rutan was knocked off, he tried to climb on top of the tank; and each time the tank threatened to roll over. If it did, thought Deal, they'd all go under.

Then a wave tore Deal off the tank. As he swam back he noticed that the feed-pipe, which had connected with the main gas line, had snapped off.

"We've got to keep this feed-line above water!" he told the others. Should water flow into the broken pipe, the tank would fill up and sink. He clamped his hand over the jagged pipe to keep out the water.

"It's just a matter of time," said Deal encouragingly. "Somebody'll find us."

The men said nothing.

Irwin was no longer cold. In fact, he was beginning to feel pleasantly warm. His eyes started to close, and he realized with a start that he was freezing. Quickly he ducked his head under water to rouse himself. If he stopped fighting he'd be finished.

Deal was now at the other end of the tank. He reached across it with both hands. Irwin saw what he meant and clasped hands with him. The two men locked each other onto the bucking tank.

They'd been in the water over an hour.

Suddenly Deal shouted, "There's a ship!"

Irwin turned and looked. As the tank reached the crest of a wave, lightning ripped across the sky; and far away he saw the unreal outline of a ship.

Deal prayed that the ship would find them in the deep troughs and foaming water. He kept straining to follow the ship. One moment it would be riding high, the next it would plunge down and out of sight behind a great swell.

"It's just a matter of time," Deal kept repeating over and over.

A big wave smashed against the tank. Rutan slipped off. Slowly he sank. For a moment his hands writhed at the surface, then he was gone. No one could help him.

Now Deal could see a green light on the ship. He shouted. In a semi-delirium Irwin saw two green lights, though vaguely he knew there should be only one. Perhaps the second was the reflection in the water. Then he began to shout, too. Copeland remained silent, his teeth clenched, a look of helpless strain and fatigue on his face.

The ship's deck lights flashed on. Deal felt a surge of hope. Then the ship's whistle began blowing. That must mean, he thought, that they'd spotted the tank.

A wave broke Irwin and Deal apart, and both floundered in the water. Irwin grabbed wearily at the tank. "I can't hold out any longer!" he gasped.

"Hold on!" Deal cried. "We'll be all right in five minutes."

Wiley saw the lights, too, and he heard the continuous, plaintive cries of the men on the fuel tank. He still had nothing to cling to, but he had been swimming with as little effort as possible, riding each giant wave cautiously. The rescue ship was floating toward him, almost broadsides. Wiley swam toward it with strong strokes. In a minute a circular life buoy was tossed near his head. Wiley reached out and caught the buoy. He was hauled aboard the *Phoebus*.

As if in a dream Irwin saw a life buoy scaling toward him from the darkness. It flopped in the water ten yards away. He left the tank and swam lazily to the buoy. His arms and legs were heavy, lifeless. He wished he could go to sleep. As he was dozing off he hooked his right arm through the buoy. He grabbed his chest with his right hand, locking himself to the preserver. Then he lost consciousness. When sailors pulled him onto the *Phoebus* at 2:00 A.M. his fingernails were dug into his bleeding chest, and his eyes were closed. He was in a deep sleep.

Deal, still holding onto the tank, saw a group of sailors hauling Irwin aboard and another group lowering a lifeboat from the ship. Dim figures were struggling with tackle lines, and Deal figured something must have fouled. It seemed an hour before the boat was finally over the side. At last it hit the water and speared toward the tank.

At that moment a big life raft floated serenely by. It was the fourteen-man raft kept in the airplane hangar—the only raft on the *Akron*. It was empty. A moment later he imagined he saw somebody grab Copeland. Then he felt himself being lifted. Then everything blacked out.

After the four men were picked up, the two lifeboats of the *Phoebus* continued searching in the forty-five-mile-an-hour gale. Several men sank just before they could be reached. Mattresses and bits of wreckage covered the sea. No more survivors were found.

When Deal came to, he was in a bunk in a pitching stateroom. Packed around his naked body were whisky bottles filled with hot water. German seamen were vigorously rubbing his legs.

Deal was shivering so violently that he couldn't talk. A fifth of whisky stood on a chair next to his bed. He sat up, his teeth chattering. He grabbed the bottle with numbed, fumbling hands. He took big gulps of the whisky. The German sailors laughed, encouraging him with broad gestures to drink more. He finished the entire fifth. But it had no effect on him—except to make him feel warm inside at last.

"What ship are we on?" he asked.

A young sailor who had lived in New York four years told him that it was the *Phoebus*. They'd left New York late that afternoon and luckily had been blown a little off their course. Then the door opened and Commander Wiley walked in.

"How do you feel?" he asked Deal. There were deep hollows under Wiley's dark, sad eyes, but he was in good condition.

"O.K.," said Deal. "How many survivors are there, sir?"

Wiley hesitated. Then he said, "Not many, Deal."

In the adjoining stateroom Irwin came awake and immediately felt warmth on his stomach. He didn't know it came from a bottle filled with hot water. As soon as he opened his eyes, the chief engineer of the *Phoebus* boosted him to a sitting position. The German started pouring a tumbler of whisky down his throat. Irwin thought he was still in the ocean, imagined he was swallowing salt water. He moaned and struck the glass out of the German's hand. He clutched at the chief engineer's hat, tearing it apart with violent jerks. Then he lost consciousness.

When he opened his eyes again there was no one in the room. He didn't know where he was or what had happened to him. He figured he'd been knocked out in an accident. He lay back on the bunk for a few minutes trying to make sense out of vague memories. A few minutes later he sat up. Seeing a bottle of 5-Star Hennessy on a table across the room, he slowly slung his legs out of the bunk. (Actually, it was 3-Star—there has never been a 5-Star Hennessy.) He wanted a good, long drink. He put his feet on the floor and took a step. But his numb legs crumpled under him. He lay on the floor unable to move.

The fourth man—Copeland, who had almost become a missionary—never regained consciousness. Before the Germans could lay him in a bunk his life faded away. Only three of the *Akron's* complement of seventy-six were now alive.

The papers that evening were full of the tragedy. The nation was stunned. President Roosevelt said, "The loss of the *Akron* with its crew of gallant officers and men is a national disaster." Billy Mitchell sprang to the defense of the rigid dirigible. "They were helping to develop a defensive arm that still will be invaluable in the future," he declared. "We should not let an accident of this kind hold up our airship development. We must go forward."

Red-bearded Anton Heinen was also heard from. "There should be no whitewash of the *Akron* disaster," he said, "as there was of the *Shenandoah* tragedy."

By the end of the day few believed anyone else had survived the deadliest crash in the history of aviation. But at Lakehurst the women still kept vigil. They still scanned the dark, empty skies as if expecting the big ship to return any moment. Although all the workmen had left Hangar Number 1 long before, half a dozen automobiles still stood inside the vast, tomblike building. They belonged to members of the *Akron's* crew. Outside the hangar half a dozen dogs sat waiting.

The day after the crash the three weary survivors were flown to Washington to see the Secretary of the Navy. The next morning they were driven to the White House. Franklin D. Roosevelt insisted on taking time to talk with them.

"I'm thankful you're here," said the President. "Sit down and tell me all about it."

Wiley, in clipped tones, told of their crash and rescue. Deal, who wore tight-fitting civilian clothes, put in only a few words. Irwin said even less.

The President congratulated them on their narrow escape. Then, to relieve their tension, he told an amusing story of the inept Congressional investigation of the *Titanic* sinking. The President told them that many of the Congressmen involved thought that starboard meant the left side of a ship.

The three men laughed a little.

When Wiley praised the seamanship of the *Phoebus* crew, Roosevelt turned to his Assistant Secretary of the Navy, Henry Latrobe Roosevelt. "I shall personally write a letter to the captain and crew of that ship," he said, "and thank them for their gallant work."

A few days later Deal returned to Lakehurst and his greatest ordeal. He didn't know what to say to the widows. It would be especially hard with the wives of his old mates of the *Shenandoah*.

Irwin also had a hard chore. He felt he had to go to Seaside Park, New Jersey, to see the wife of his dead friend, Red Johnson. She was on the beach when he arrived. After they talked a minute about Red she started like a sleepwalker across the sand, tears pouring down her cheeks. To Irwin's horror she walked into the ocean. Before he could kick off his shoes and take off his pea jacket she had sunk out of sight.

Irwin dove in after her. He had a struggle bringing her back to the beach—she was bigger than he and she fought to stay in the sea.

That same day, not many miles away, the body of William Moffett, the airshipmen's favorite admiral, was washed ashore. The few who, like young Mrs. Anderson, still prayed for a miracle, knew at last it was the end of all hope.

SOME PRETTY EXPENSIVE SYSTEMS

As unemployment rose from four million in 1930, to eight million in 1931, to more than twelve million in 1932, "a gap had opened between the official mood in Washington and the human reality in city streets and in the countryside . . . between the presidential vision of accelerating private construction, mounting confidence, and the actuality of privation and fear." *

President Hoover had defined the function of government in 1931 as that of bringing about "a condition of affairs favorable to the beneficial development of private enterprise," and he insisted that the only *moral* way out of the Depression was by self-help. The people should find inspiration, furthermore, in the devotion of "great manufacturers, our railways, utilities, business houses and public officials."

The trouble was that the business leaders, who in the Twenties "had never had it so good," were unable to suggest a sound way out of the dilemma of unemployment; few of them appeared to believe they had any responsibility to the general welfare, and certainly they did not want the government to take any action. Henry Ford said, for instance, "government should stick to the strict function of governing . . . let them let business alone"; and "unemployment insurance would only insure that we would have unemployment."

The irony here was that while businessmen regarded federal aid in the form of relief to the unemployed "as spelling the end of the Republic," they did not object to federal aid to business.

What avenues of self-help were there? *Fortune* Magazine said, "The theory was that private charitable organizations and semipublic welfare groups, established to care for the old and the sick and the indigent, were capable of caring for the casualties of a world-wide economic disaster. In application, social agencies manned for the service of a few hundred families and city shelters set up to house and feed a handful of homeless men, were compelled by the brutal necessities of hunger to care for hundreds of thousands of families and whole armies of the displaced and jobless. And to depend for their resources upon the contributions of communities no longer able to contribute, and upon the irresolution and vacillation of state legislatures and municipal assemblies long since in the red on their annual budgets.

"The psychological consequence was even worse. Since the problem was never honestly attacked as a national problem and since the facts were never frankly faced, people came to believe that American unemployment was relatively unimportant. They saw little idleness and therefore believed there was little. It was possible to drive for blocks in

* From Arthur M. Schlesinger, Jr.'s *The Crisis of the Old Order* (Boston, Houghton Mifflin, 1957).

the usual shopping and residential districts of New York and Chicago without seeing a breadline. And for that reason, and because their newspapers played down the subject as an additional depressant in depressing times, and because they were bored with relief measures anyway, the great American public simply ignored the whole thing."

By 1932, only about 25 per cent of the unemployed were getting relief, and it was restricted primarily to food benefits. *Fortune* went on to say:

"Such is the problem created by three years of increasing unemployment and two years of hand-to-mouth relief: city after city attempting to feed a half or a third or a quarter of its citizens upon gifts made from the reduced earnings, or from taxes levied on the overappraised homes of the other half or two thirds or the other three quarters; city after city maintaining the lives but not the health of its unemployed on a survival ration; city after city where the whole mechanism of relief has failed or is about to fail or has survived only by abandoning a major part of its task; and beyond the cities the mill towns and the coal mines and the 'cropper farms where relief is merely a name.

"The Depression, along with its misery, produced its social curiosities, not the least of which was the wandering population it spilled upon the roads. Means of locomotion vary but the objective is always the same —somewhere else. There were the hitchhikers whose thumbs jerked on-ward along the American pike, and the number of spavined Fords dragging destitute families from town to town in search of a solvent relative or a generous friend.

"Dull mornings last winter, the sheriff of Miami, Florida, used to fill a truck with homeless men and run them up to the county line. Where the sheriff of Fort Lauderdale used to meet them and load them into a second truck and run them up to *his* county line. Where the sheriff of Saint Lucie's would meet them and load them into a third truck and run them up to *his* county line. Where the sheriff of Brevard County would *not* meet them. And whence they would trickle back down the roads to Miami. To repeat.

"It was a system. And it worked. The only trouble was that it worked too well. It kept the transients transient and it even increased the transient population in the process. But it got to be pretty expensive, one way or another, if you sat down and figured it all out—trucks and gas and time and a little coffee. . . ." *

About two million people were roaming the country—several hundred thousand of them were young people—looking for a job, hope, or anything that would suggest that life had not passed them by. The young traveled alone, or with one companion, and most of them wanted work. The following narrative by Eric Sevareid is not one of despair, as so many of their stories must have been. From it one can take a certain pride in the generation formed by these years.

* "No One Has Starved," *Fortune,* September 1932.

ERIC SEVAREID

HITCHHIKER*

AT TWENTY, the eye is sharp, perceptions are keen, and the heart is never again so warm. Every man one meets, the lowliest tramp, is alive and vibrant with personality, with meaning, with Self. The colors of the sky are brilliant, there is extraordinary beauty in a cowshed at sunrise, and in the warm night the clicking cadence of the freight car's wheels sends one easily to confident sleep with no more than an arm for pillow. I traveled alone; it is the right and only way. You do not have to talk if you would rather be silent; you can stop where you will, doze when you wish, and think your own thoughts. All that the eye sees, the mind registers, and the heart envelops is filtered by the screen of Yourself, untreated, unmodified by the conditioning presence of another being. There is no other way to find out the world and to touch the boundaries of your own limitations for finding out. I discovered all this—and America.

The grain was full and high in North Dakota, this place which I had never desired to see again. I had forgotten that the grain rose and settled with the undulating swell of the ocean, that the distant barn became a rising and falling ship on the rim of this sea, its cupola a mounted stack. I had forgotten that the clouds of summer were fat and laundered white and that small shadows moved over the surface of this inland ocean. I had forgotten the precision design of a furrowed field on a canvas so spacious that lines were long and clean and never crowded. I had forgotten how the rails were fixed to the earth, how they bent and fastened the world down at the far edge, where the curvature of the planet was apparent to the human eye. It was incredible, at first, to find that Velva was still there, every house intact. It had grown not older, but younger. The river had not yet reached the width I knew, and the great trees in our yard had begun all over again as saplings. All should have been in decay and ruin, dying and dead among weeds. Instead, all was green, pruned, and trimmed. There was concrete sidewalk over the coulee where there had been only a treacherous board; radio antennae had replaced the lightning

* From Eric Sevareid's *Not So Wild a Dream* (New York, Knopf, 1946).

103

rods upon the roofs; there were yellow parking signs where the hitching posts had stood, and gleaming Buicks had replaced the dusty buggies.

It was not by their faces that one knew them all, instantly and without mistake. Things fade from the retina of the eye's recollection, but there are sixth and seventh senses which retain it all. The faces were strange, but not what was *in* the faces. The special, strong, untransferable *feeling* of each was the same. It is by this that a child knows those around him, and through this mysterious medium it all comes back when he is grown.

A young man with whom I used to make a daily trade—his pony for my Ranger bicycle—drove me to Minot (the "Magic City") in his six-ton truck. He had a farm of his own now and he considered me with the faint condescension and suspicion with which men of property regard the unpropertied. I wandered into a park in the darkness and slept in a clump of brush, to be wakened in fright by fearful noises from what sounded like very large animals. They were. I was sleeping next to the bears' cage in the zoo. A telephone lineman drove me forty miles in his Ford half-truck, remained silent the whole distance, and uttered his first words when he invited me in to dinner with himself and his wife at his roadside shack. A young traveling salesman picked me up and drove me seven hundred miles into the heart of the vast Montana country, in a long limousine, the back of which was stacked with cases containing samples of his wares, which were ladies' underclothing. His extra suits, carefully pressed, hung on hangers in the car's interior. He wore dark sun-glasses and small, stiff collars which he changed twice a day. He worried about the manicured nails of his soft, white hands and talked constantly and confidently. He told me, repeatedly, that he had the world by the tail, and I believed him. "What you want to be a newspaper reporter for? Naw, naw, that's no good. I know some of them guys around the *Tribune* in Chicago. I can buy and sell any two of them guys. Naw, I got the racket. I can clean up two-three hundred a week, commissions alone, not counting the bonus. You gotta know how to go at these local yokels, gotta impress them —big car, swell clothes—gotta breeze in on them, talk fast, give 'em the idea you're in a rush and doing them a favor. Of course, my goods are straight, best that money can buy. Don't want to get mixed up in any cheap racket, then you can't go back a second time. I make it, but I spread it around. I ain't tight with it. Take the girls to the best spot in town, tip a lot. Never turned down a bum for a handout yet, pick up guys all the time on the road. Here. Here's five bucks. Go on, take it. Take it. I know you're broke. Take it. What's the diff? Lots of guys are broke." Unable to resist his sales technique, I took it, humbly.

He was an inland sailor, with a girl in every department store. For hours he discussed them—intimately—and I was fascinated and impressed by this insight into a life of irresponsible, sexual freedom which I had scarcely suspected. The one in Fargo he called "Silky," in homage to the texture of her skin, more particularly the skin of the small of her back. There was Margie in Minot, and somebody else in Great Falls whose private qualities and capacities are better left undetailed. He always wired ahead to these ladies to give them time to prepare for his coming. It never occurred to him that he might be disappointed, and, so far as I knew, he never was.

I watched him haggle with a granite-faced garage man for a tire. His complete, overriding confidence was remarkable, and I listened in mute, uneasy wonder. He got the tire at much below the asking price—something I knew I could never do. I felt sympathy for the garage man, but my friend and protector took the keenest pleasure in his victory. He hadn't cared about the price at all; it was the fun of the contest, the testing of his powers. I understood that here was a man who would never go hungry, who would always be able to take care of himself and his round little stomach at no matter what cost to those around him. It was my first acquaintance with the Wise Guy incarnate. I was to see them later, in many countries, where honest people starved, where honest men stole that their families might eat. But these, the Wise Guys of the world, the Slick Operators, never starved, never had to steal. War and the collapse of their countries, their society, scarcely touched them. They are an international breed, owing allegiance to no one, not even to one another. They manipulate currencies, they operate black markets; they live for money, and money seems to exist for them. It is the only reality in life to them, and they are contemptuous of anyone who does not share their knowledge, incredulous of those who do not share their belief. They are the outlaws of society, but they are not the hunted. They are, indeed, the hunters, the merciless hunters.

Helena was a sudden discovery, isolated, alone in a lost valley, connected with the world by the frail liaison of a highway, a thin white tape that disappeared in the distant hills, and a rail line, a silver wire that flashed its presence to the sun before vanishing in turn among the crags. Here I entered the Ford roadster of a pink, chubby man named Smith whose business it was to advertise the benefits of milk to the American people. He was on a leisurely survey of the American West, with an incidental aim. There was a girl living in Missoula. He had not seen her since their college days, eight years before. They had rarely corresponded. But he had decided, in those eight years of experience, that she was the only girl he wanted to marry. He wasn't sure, now, whether she was married or not. At Missoula I slept among the smells of unwashed bodies and disinfectant in the Salvation Army, while Smith went off to pay his visit of surprise. He picked me up in the morning and said, after a few miles: "She wasn't married—but she's going to be." He could not prevent happy smiles from breaking out on his cherubic face. "Like a goddam novel, isn't it?" he said. He drove me many hundreds of miles and we were briefly chagrined at parting, before the door of my uncle's house near Seattle. (My parents came from extremely large families, far scattered since, and I had the benefit of intimate staging points.)

For five dollars, one could ride a double-decker bus all the way from Seattle to northern California. I rode for twenty-four hours or more, stifled by day, shivering by night, sustained on the thick sandwiches prepared by a worried aunt. At Portland, a slim girl with unnatural blond hair and greasy lipstick climbed into the seat beside me. She carried only a hand-bag and wore only a set of green pajamas. At least to me they were pajamas; they may have been what we now call slacks. She was bound for San Francisco, or maybe Los Angeles, or maybe San Diego. She wasn't quite sure; it didn't matter. She chewed her gum, fiddled with her hand-bag, examined her eyebrows in the little mirror a half-dozen times, then peered over my shoulder. "Watcha reading?" I was trying, between head-aches, to understand an erudite article in *The Atlantic Monthly* on science and religion. "Jesus," she said, "you're pretty young to be a dope." She fidgeted awhile and offered: "What's the difference between a mountain goat and a soda jerk?" I did not know. "The soda jerk mucks around the fountain." She was something new; I did not know how to talk with her, and very soon she abandoned me for gayer company in the lower deck, a party of sailors from the *Pennsylvania,* whom she assisted with guitar, song, and flask throughout the night despite the timid protests of other, less enduring travelers. Undoubtedly the sailors solved the problem of her destination. She was a plain, honest whore, operating on her own. The Ritz hotels of the world are full of them, not so plain nor so honest; they do not wear green pajamas in public, and their jokes are slightly more subtle, but they travel by the same means, with the same happy indifference to the next destination.

I bathed in the brown, thick waters of the Sacramento River, slept under its willows, followed on foot the macadam road that wound through the vineyards, and crossed over the dreary wastes of lava rock, making for the purple mountains in the distance. At seven in the morning sweat blinded my eyes, the soles of my feet were burning, my tongue was swollen and parched. The nearest hummock shimmered and dissolved in a subaqueous world of refracted light. I became half-faint, stumbled frequently, lost sight of the mountains, and made my goal the next telephone pole, and the next, in whose six-inch shaft of shade I could lay my face. I was lying thus, when the first driver came along and took me on to Oroville. The rural postman's truck traversed the Feather River, where the gold had once been shoveled up like sand, mounted the Sierra heights, skirted a great hole in the side of the roadbed where a mountain lion had chosen to bury his kill, and deposited me a mile high, at the cabin of a certain Fitzgerald, fair-weather prospector, who surveyed my skinny frame with disappointed doubts in his narrowed eyes. But he kept me, all summer, and I earned my keep.

In those Depression years of the early Thirties, many men had drifted back into the high reaches of these mountains, and a minor resurgence of placer mining began. We were more like scavengers; some filtered and fingered through the piles of sand and stone, the "tailings" from earlier boom days when pressure hoses had washed away whole sides of mountains, leaving them bleached and scarified. Others, such as Fitzgerald and I, hopefully enlarged the abandoned beds of precipitous streams, heaved out endless blobs of the slabby clay in long-handled shovels, ran tons of the stuff over the washboard riffles of our wooden sluices. But, like our neighbors, we worked only four or five hours a day. The hope of finding gold, which almost none of us ever did, was more of an excuse to live in the hills where life was cheap, than anything else. There was a kind of mutual understanding among the men that they were there waiting until the unnatural economic troubles in San Francisco or Sacramento blew themselves out. They brewed beer and turned their sluice boxes into iceboxes where the bottles stood all day in the running water. If Big Foots at the Buster Brown Mine shot a deer one day, we would all gravitate over for a venison feast and would aid, without asking questions, in burying the bones, hide, and antlers so the game warden would find no evidence. Beer parties developed with spontaneity at this cabin, then at another—loud parties, attended frequently by large, blowsy middle-aged women who often arrived on the fenders of decrepit Ford cars which somehow bumped over the rutted trails. They had powerful voices, and an enormous capacity for beer, and spoke the four-letter words simply because they were ignorant of the politer synonyms. If one were not careful, he would experience a heavy, flabby, red arm on his neck, dragging him with astonishing power down upon a cot amid screams of delight from the assembly.

I was just "Slim," the newcomer, the tenderfoot, and fair game for all pranks. When the news somehow got out that I had been to college and had even written things for newspapers, the relationship became unnatural and they left me alone. In a way, it was relief; in a way, I regretted it. Few of the couples were married, which surprised me, since I believed "living in sin" was an exclusive indulgence of the rich.

It was mostly a world of men, of artisans. It did not seem to matter what they had been before—shipyard workers, printers, saloonkeepers— they all had an easy, instinctive comprehension of wood and iron, dynamite and cement, air currents, water pressures, the properties of ore, of soil and seed. They could make trees fall precisely where they wished, transform a motorcycle engine into a power saw, build a fireplace with no question of its failing to draw, produce a complicated plumbing system from a creek and a few lengths of pipe, worm a dog one hour, bake a chocolate cake the next, install a carburetor the next, and repair a gold watch in spare time. So easily, all this was done! None of them ever read a book of directions, studied a blueprint, or consulted with a colleague. They just did it, with leisurely, natural system, and it stayed done, it worked. None of them could have quoted a single law of physics or chemistry, and the words would have sounded like embarrassing nonsense to them anyway. Yet they understood, they *knew*, their *hands* knew. The world of the knowing hands, a world I could never enter—yet half my countrymen dwell in it always. A world of its own, inside America, from which we were to draw a host of sergeants and corporals to make an army work in a manner that was the envy and despair of the others—the British, the French, the Germans, the Russians, all the others.

I had to take these men on their own terms, try to communicate in their language, because they could not in mine. "Fitz" would bait me:

"Jesus H. Christ, don't hold that bit like it was a lily flower! Now turn it, turn it every time you hit it. Keep turning it. Now douse the rock, let the pieces run out. How far in does the dynamite have to go? How far in! Well, that beats me—and you one of them college boys. Jesus H. Christ, when I was your age I was bossing a gang of fourteen men. What in the name of Almighty God do they teach you in them colleges!"

But there were private moments that came frequently during the fresh morning hours of work, moments that never return to one in later years, of pleasure keen to the point of anguish. Fog would vanish, the mountain was unveiled and cleansed, and sweet, dank odors flowed out like per-fumed oils upon bright waters. The day sounds would begin: the shrill chippering of a squirrel overhead, the dull smacking of a woodpecker, and down in the valley the tinkle of a cowbell. Near the ditch, in a patch of saw grasses, little globules of dew gathered and dropped, gathered and dropped, like the ticking of sweat drops in the secret hair. The taste of salt was sharp in the corner of the mouth, and the wooden shovel had a good, grainy feel in the hand. In these moments the power of life exploded slowly through the veins, and one worked in a savage orgasm until exhaustion came.

By the end of summer Fitz noticed that I could swing up the leaden-heavy shovel with easier grace than he and could stand longer spells at the bucksaw than he. He said nothing, but the baiting ceased, and that was understood between us as the highest form of compliment. In September he drove me down to Quincy, still unable to make out a young man who offered to perform the most back-breaking labor for no return, even paying his share of the board. I left with a deeper chest, heavier shoulders, and a souvenir phial containing about eighty cents' worth of gold flecks in black dirt—all that our mine had produced.

I awoke before dawn from a bed among the damp weeds by the Union Pacific tracks at Sparks, the division point near Reno, and found an "empty" in the long freight train making up for the thirty-six-hour run across the Great American Desert to Salt Lake. I entered a new social dimension, the great underground world, peopled by tens of thousands of American men, women, and children, white, black, brown, and yellow, who inhabit the "jungle," eat from blackened tin cans, find warmth at night in the box cars, take the sun by day on the flat cars, steal one day, beg with cap in hand the next, fight with fists and often razors, hold sexual intercourse under a blanket in a dark corner of the crowded car, coagulate into pairs and gangs, then disintegrate again, wander from town to town, anxious for the next place, tired of it in a day, fretting to be gone again, happy only when the wheels are clicking under them, the telephone poles slipping by. Some were in honest search of work, but many were not. They had worked—once—but jobs did not last, pay was low, they had had to move on and on for new jobs, until finally it became easier just to move, to move for the moving. Perhaps this world has gone now; one never hears of it. Perhaps wartime prosperity has wiped it out; I do not know. In the Thirties it was a vast, submerged, secondary United States with its own categories of cities, advertised by its own kind of chambers of commerce, its own recognized leaders, its strong men and its recognized bad men, its ragged dowagers and grimy debutantes, and its own laws—such as they were—which dealt primarily with self-preservation. The true world of private enterprise and individual initiative. It will come back, unless America is very wise, but next time it may have lost its "picturesque" quality; they may not beg cap in hand; they may fight with something else but razors because they will know other weapons, and they may not confine their fighting to themselves.

There were strange men among them, remarkable men, unknown to the rest of America. No one has written the biography of Tex, King of Tramps, for example. I never saw him, but I knew there was an obsession in him not unlike Hitler's, a terrible straining of the ego to find expression— either that or he was a wandering imbecile having a glorious time. At least fifty times in the course of a couple of thousand miles I came across his insigne, his coat of arms: Tex—KT. You would find it carved on the wooden seat of a privy on the edge of a Nevada town, penciled on the wall of a shower room in a Salvation Army flophouse in Idaho, chalked on the iron side of a locomotive tender in South Dakota, painted in six-foot letters of red on a white cliffside high up in a Montana canyon. Men told me you found it from Maine to California, everywhere, printed, written, carved thousands of times in the course of what must have been fifteen or twenty years of wandering.

In the jungle, cities were judged and rated on the basis of their citizens' generosity with handouts and the temperament of the railway "deeks" who guard the freight yards. You did not, for example, attempt to travel through Cheyenne, Wyoming, if you had any alternative. You were apt to be chased from the yards there not only with clubs, which was fairly common, but with revolver shots, and it was a long walk to the next station. You traveled through a certain Idaho town only at careful intervals to avoid the monthly raid by the sheriff, who filled his jail with indigents, fed them on nineteen cents a day, and collected a dollar a day from the local government for each occupant. There was no rancor against the sheriff—he had to have his dodge, his racket, like everybody else—but you just avoided him, unless, of course, the weather was rugged and handouts were not forthcoming and you desired a month indoors with steady meals.

One of the most renowned and fearsome characters to dwellers in the jungle was Humpy Davis, railway dick at Harvey, North Dakota. He, it appeared, was a bearlike hunchback, who took a fiendish pride in his ability to clean out a crowded box car, singlehanded, in one minute flat. Normally he used a club, and the score of broken arms and heads was running extremely high, when a conclave of hoboes out in Vancouver decided that Humpy must be eliminated for the good of all concerned. They elected a tall Negro, famous for his marksmanship, to do the job.

110

News travels fast by the jungle grapevine. Humpy knew, and waited. One day he observed a Negro, alone, walking steadily toward him between the tracks. This was it. Humpy stood still, letting him come on. Suddenly the Negro stopped, swung up his hand, and fired. The legend relates that Humpy did not move, did not raise his arm. Instead, he shouted: "Shoot at my head, you black bastard, shoot at my head!" The assassin fired again. Humpy, unmoving, repeated his instruction. The Negro fired his six shots, yelled in astonishment and terror and, as he began to run, was brought down by a single shot. Humpy walked across the yards to a beer parlor, unbuttoned his shirt, and exhibited his bulletproof vest with six indentations over the heart so closely grouped that a coffee mug could cover them all. It is a favorite story in the jungle. If one doubts it, he is wise not to express his doubt.

My empty box car at Sparks rapidly filled, the train operators having deliberately left it open and vacant in order to avoid having the inevitable load of hoboes clambering around on top of the cars or clinging to the tender. All were bums by choice save one weather-beaten couple of advanced age who came from New Mexico. They had just lost their small farm and were looking for new opportunities. The man carried a great pack with a washboard strapped on it, while his wizened little wife held their scabby hound dog by a length of frayed clothesline. They represented Respectability among us, were accorded a whole corner to themselves and not included in the unending argument, jeering, boasting and scuffling.

I sat in the open doorway, swinging my legs in the sun, and listened to a youngster of sixteen. He was well built, with a remarkably attractive, open face, which had a way of slipping quickly into a sneer, becoming then almost sinister. He was boasting of his racket, and I was failing to understand. Finally he took out a crumpled sheet of paper. I read: "For services rendered, I have delivered the following articles to——— [the boy]." Then came a list including watch, fountain pen, set of evening clothes, silver-backed hairbrushes, and so on. "That was in Frisco last month," the boy explained. "I work fast. I find the café where the queers go, mix in with the bunch that looks richest, go home with one of them, and before I get through with him he's given me everything he owns and the written statement. I'm a minor. It's a criminal offense. But he can't do a thing about it, not a thing." He discussed it openly, casually, as if he were boasting of his prowess at baseball. I had only the vaguest notion of what homosexuality was all about, had never been acquainted with anyone I knew to be abnormal in this way, and rather imagined it was something confined to certain boys' schools in England and the Bohemian quarters of Paris. Suddenly it was all around me. I noticed men with glazed, slightly bulging eyes and uncertain voices who traveled in company with boys in their teens. The men were referred to as "wolves" (long before that word became slang for Casanovas of normal physiology). A Negro boy named Freddie, no more than fourteen, joined our group one day. He was complaining loudly about the perfidy of a white man who had picked him up while he had been hitchhiking the evening before. "Offered me a quarter if he could ——, then he wouldn't give me the quarter, the skunk. Kicked me out of his car. But I slammed a rock through his back window, the bastard," Freddie finished boastfully, and was rewarded by general acknowledgment that it had served the so-and-so right. All this told so naturally, as if it were an open, common matter understood and accepted by everyone. Except for me, apparently it was.

Freddie was very nearly the cause of my death one night. We had reassembled in the box car after a brief foray through a bleak Nevada hamlet, and now, as the train rumbled through the night, we squatted around a small fire in the middle of the car floor, exchanging tidbits. Freddie was missing; somebody thought he had caught the train at the other end, and when we heard a banging on the roof we knew he had, and that he had run over the tops, leaping in the darkness from car to car. Somebody slid the big door wide open, and we heard Freddie yell: "Grab my legs, I'm coming down." We looked at one another. There was silence for a moment. A man said: "How about you, Slim? You got long arms." I had no choice of action. I stood by the door, while a chain of three or four men fastened themselves to one of my legs. The wind blew in my face. The train was racketing along a narrow bridge over a dark canyon. Suddenly there were Freddie's dangling feet, then his legs, swinging in close, then away again as the box car tilted, then close again. I grabbed them, felt myself being torn out of the car, then was toppled over backwards, on top of the human chain, Freddie on top of me. Except for a moment, ten years later, when I found myself at the door of a plunging airplane, trying to jump, I have never known a greater terror. Freddie had stolen a bottle of cherry brandy. He was the hero of the evening, and we ate, drank, and sang to the accompaniment of a harmonica until long after midnight.

I was traveling with two boys of seventeen, bound like myself for Minneapolis where they had recently been suspended from high school for unauthorized absences. We had made a secret pact: they did the begging for food (at which they were expert) and, whenever there was no time to beg or the fruits were meager, I would buy food for the three of us from my

112

store of six or eight dollars which was tied in a handkerchief and secured out of sight inside my belt. (Murder for much less than that was a commonplace in the jungle.) One night we sat by the rails of the "Oregon Short Line," next to the water tank on the outskirts of Ogden, Utah, where we knew our train would pause. We were after the manifest, the "hot shot" —a sealed, nonstop freight train, representing to this social dimension what the Century does to another. We became aware that an enormous Negro was standing a few feet away. He said: "Good evening," sat down beside us, and chewed on a straw. Eventually he said: "Catching the hot shot?" I said we were. Finally: "Rode it once myself. Long, cold ride. Get mighty hungry." More silence and then he said casually: "Tell you what. One you boys want to walk over to my house, have my wife fix up a few sandwiches for you." I got up and said that was kind of him and that I would go along. My companions said nothing.

We walked along a narrow road, bordered by weeds and ditches. He seemed to be in no hurry and said nothing. I was worried about missing the train and asked him where his house was. "See that light?" he answered. The light appeared to be at least a half-mile away. We walked on, and it began to seem very strange to me. Why should a Negro, obviously poor, go so much out of his way to aid three young white tramps? I was becoming very uneasy, trying to think of some way to withdraw, when the man turned abruptly, walked across a plank over the ditch, and halted by a clump of willows. "Come here a minute, Slim," he said.

My throat had become suddenly dry and I could not answer. He called in a soft tone two or three times: "Come here—got something to show you." All manner of ideas flashed through my head. Did he know about my money and intend to murder me for it? Had he some grisly object there he wanted me to carry away on the train?

He walked deliberately back and stood towering over me so close I could smell his breath. "Want to make a quarter, Slim?" he said softly, coaxingly.

My voice returned enough for me to say in what I hoped were even tones that I couldn't do anything for him. I turned and began to walk back down the dark roadway, the hair on the back of my neck tickling, expecting something to strike me at any moment. Then two figures stepped from the ditch and stood there, waiting, in my path. My heart beat faster, but my head got very cool. I had walked into a trap and was about to be "rolled." I kept on, approached them, lifted my hands over my head, and said in an abnormally confident voice: "All right. You can have anything I have on me."

113

One of them said: "For Christ sakes, Slim, what do you think you're doing?"

My two loyal, very wise companions had followed us. They got out their knives and wanted to attack the Negro, but let themselves be dissuaded. They scolded me at length for being so dumb that I hadn't recognized a queer, and I had nothing to say. My hands shook for an hour afterwards.

There were glorious days of sunshine, days when we stretched out nude on a flat car cooled by chunks of ice someone tossed down from the "reefer" adjoining, days when we swung our legs idly and yelled to the girls working in the passing fields, days when we abandoned the trains and swam naked in deep mountain pools of cold, clear water. In the night there was hazard and danger, always. There was a midnight halt while the train reorganized at a sleeping Montana division point on the Milwaukee line. The hoboes gather in a hamburger shop, the only concern still open for business. It was a cold night. With their pennies and nickels the tramps provided themselves with thick mugs of coffee. I ordered sandwiches for myself and my companions. Then to my horror I discovered I had only a five-dollar bill. I passed it over the fake marble counter to the waiter as surreptitiously as I could, and no one noticed. But Montana is a silver state, and the waiter returned with four heavy, gleaming silver dollars in his hand. He did not put them in my anxiously outthrust palm but proceeded to drop them, ringing, clattering on the counter, one at a time. I was conscious that the sounds of eating and drinking around me had ceased and that every eye had turned in my direction. I stuffed them in my pocket and we rose, leaving our food unfinished, sauntered out the door and then ran with all our strength to the train. We hurried along from car to car, scrambling, panting, until we found one with the door unlocked. It was half-filled with lumber. We climbed in, shifted the boards until we had made a hole, then pulled them over us. As the train began its slow, jerking start we heard boots scuffing the boards above our heads. Later we could catch a few words. The voices we recognized as belonging to two of the more evil-looking tramps of the earlier evening. They were talking about the kids with the silver dollars. The voices ceased after a time, and we drifted to uneasy, uncomfortable sleep. In the morning the men were gone.

I arrived at my father's house with my face black from the coal dust of a locomotive tender—my berth during the final roaring, kaleidoscopic night of clinging to a passenger express.

DOWN AND OUT AT ANACOSTIA

WAS there anyone who believed it was necessary to take action?

The critics of American business seemed as unprepared as the businessmen themselves. Labor leaders were befuddled—with two exceptions: John L. Lewis of the United Mine Workers and Sidney Hillman of the Amalgamated Clothing Workers, both of whom felt the government must assume leadership to cure the sick economy.

While the Administration stood foursquare against taking initiative, the Congress seemed to be in a state of paralysis, unable to create, let alone pass, any helpful legislation. One Senator had shown a persistent concern with the business cycle, the labor movement and other facets of the industrial society—Robert F. Wagner of New York. There were a few others—La Follette of Wisconsin, Norris of Nebraska and Hugo Black of Alabama, for instance— who believed in relief and who offered programs; but it was Wagner who proved the rallying voice in 1932, as he would in later years.

In February 1932 the Reconstruction Finance Corporation had been organized to make loans to banks, railroads and insurance companies. But later that year it was disclosed that more than half of the 126 million dollars distributed had gone to three large banks.

"We shall help the railroad; we shall help the financial institutions; and I agree that we should," said Senator Wagner. "But is there any reason why we should not likewise extend a helping hand to that forlorn American, in every village and every city of the United States, who has been without wages since 1929?"

Finally, in July 1932, the Emergency Relief and Construction Act established an RFC fund of 300 million dollars for loans to the states, but President Hoover cautioned the states not to call on the money "except in absolute need."

Still there were no signs of serious revolt in the people. They were sad and defeated, not rebellious.

A qualifying footnote to such a generalization was the increase in shipments of gold beyond our shores by some of the wealthy in the country who wished to avoid paying taxes. Colonel Robert R. McCormick, publisher of the Chicago *Tribune,* carried on a campaign to get people to pay their full taxes, while at the same time, in his own tax report, he listed his personal property as being little more than $25,-000, on which he paid a tax of about $1,500. Samuel Insull, one of the country's biggest speculators in the world of finance, was indicted for embezzling funds, but not before he fled the country.

There had been isolated strikes and a few hunger marches on local and state seats of government; not until summer of 1932 was there an incident big enough to focus the country's attention on growing resentments. A group of World War I veterans called on the government for immediate payment of their bonus for services in the war, a payment not scheduled to be made until 1945. At the time, the Patman bill, which provided for immediate payment, was before the Congress.

The proposal caught fire. Fifteen thousand veterans, some with wives and children, arrived in Washington in late spring of 1932 and camped on the Anacostia mud flats, to lobby for the passage of the bill. On June 16, the Patman bill was defeated. Five thousand veterans left Washington, but the remainder simply waited on the flats. Congress voted money to pay their fares home, and then adjourned. Still, the veterans did not stir, their leaders exhorting them to hold fast.

MACARTHUR, EISENHOWER
AND PATTON VERSUS THE VETS

THE Hoover Administration had chosen to ignore the "invaders" and some people suggested the whole thing was a Communist plot, even though the veterans behaved in an orderly fashion. Not until an accident set off a scuffle between the police and the veterans, did the government take a step. Then Hoover ordered General Douglas MacArthur, Chief of the Army, to evacuate the veterans and their families.

MacArthur is said to have excused the unnecessary brusqueness of the evacuation by suggesting that a mob was about to seize control of the government.

The veterans were undoubtedly a source of embarrassment to the President but they had been unarmed, and this cavalier handling of down-and-out Americans seemed to many to be further proof of the government's callous unconcern for the plight of the people.

In *The Lean Years,* Irving Bernstein has provided a description of this unusual military operation:

"The armed forces that gathered in the vicinity of the White House consisted of four troops of cavalry, four companies of infantry, a mounted machine-gun squadron, and six whippet tanks. MacArthur himself was in command. At his side was his aide, Major Dwight D. Eisenhower, and one of his officers was the dashing George S. Patton, Jr.

The operation was delayed an hour while an orderly rushed across the Potomac to Fort Myer for Mac-Arthur's tunic, service stripes, sharpshooter medal, and English whipcord breeches.

"He then led the troops in dramatic display down Pennsylvania Avenue before a huge crowd, arriving at the troubled area at 4:45 P.M. 'We are going to break the back of the B.E.F.' [Bonus Expeditionary Force], MacArthur told Glassford [Superintendent of Washington Police]. The soldiers, using tear gas, quickly cleared the old buildings and set them on fire. By 7:15, all the encampments within the city had been evacuated and burned.

"MacArthur then sent his forces across the Anacostia bridge. Thousands of veterans, their wives, and children fled before the advancing soldiers. The troops attacked with tear gas and set fire to a number of huts. There was virtually no resistance. The veterans then spread the conflagration. By morning Anacostia was a smoldering ruin.

"The military operation was carried out swiftly and efficiently. Total casualties, including those in the earlier fracas, were two veterans shot to death, an eleven-week baby in grave condition (he later died), an eight-year-old boy partially blinded by gas, two policemen with fractured skulls, a bystander shot through the shoulder, a veteran's ear severed by cavalry saber, a veteran stabbed in the hip by a bayonet, more than a dozen persons injured by bricks and clubs, and over 1,000 gassed. Property damage of value was slight, perhaps the most important loss being twenty old sycamores and elms seared by flames near the Pennsylvania Avenue encampment."

Thus was the "invasion" of Washington repulsed. How the Bonus Army was then dispersed is told in the following selection.

MALCOLM COWLEY

THE FLIGHT OF
THE BONUS ARMY*

WHEN the veterans of the Bonus Army first tried to escape, they found that the bridges into Virginia were barred by soldiers and the Maryland roads blocked against them by state troopers. They wandered from street to street or sat in ragged groups, the men exhausted, the women with wet handkerchiefs laid over their smarting eyes, the children waking from sleep to cough and whimper from the tear gas in their lungs. The flames behind them were climbing into the night sky. About four in the morning, as rain began to fall, they were allowed to cross the border into Maryland, on condition that they move as rapidly as possible into another state.

The veterans were expected to disperse to their homes—but most of them had no homes, and they felt that their only safety lay in sticking together. Somehow the rumor passed from group to group that the mayor of Johnstown had invited them to his city. And they cried, as they rode toward Pennsylvania or marched in the dawn twilight along the highways, "On to Johnstown."

Their shanties and tents had been burned, their personal property destroyed, except for the few belongings they could carry on their backs; many of their families were separated, wives from husbands, children from parents. Knowing all this, they still did not appreciate the extent of their losses. Two days before, they had regarded themselves, and thought the country regarded them, as heroes trying to collect a debt

* From *The New Republic*, Aug. 17, 1932.

long overdue. They had boasted about their months or years of service, their medals, their wounds, their patriotism in driving the Reds out of their camp; they had nailed an American flag to every hut. When threatened with forcible eviction, they answered that no American soldier would touch them: hadn't a detachment of Marines (consisting, some said, of twenty-five or thirty men, though others claimed there were two whole companies) thrown down its arms and refused to march against them? But the infantry, last night, had driven them out like so many vermin. Mr. Hoover had announced that "after months of patient indulgence, the government met overt lawlessness as it always must be met if the cherished processes of self-government are to be preserved." Mr. Hoover and his subordinates, in their eagerness to justify his action, were about to claim that the veterans were Red radicals, that they were the dregs of the population, that most of them had criminal records and, as a final insult, that half of them weren't veterans at all.

They would soon discover the effect of these official libels. At Somerset, on the Lincoln Highway, some of them asked for food. "We can't give you any," said a spokesman for the businessmen. "The President says that you're rebels—don't you understand? You're all outlaws now." A veteran's wife and children were refused admission to a hotel, even though they offered to pay for a room in advance. At Johnstown, the wealthier citizens were dismayed to hear of their arrival. Possibly half the workmen in the city were unemployed; a fifth or a sixth of the population was in need of charity. Ten thousand hungry people were a threat in themselves, but the editor of the Johnstown *Tribune* was about to conjure up new terrors. He wrote:

Johnstown faces a crisis. It must prepare to protect itself from the Bonus Army concentrating here at the invitation of Mayor Eddie McCloskey. . . .

In any group of the size of the Bonus Army, made up of men gathered from all parts of the country, without discipline, without effective leadership in a crisis, without any attempt on the part of those leaders to check up the previous records of the individuals who compose it, there is certain to be a mixture of undesirables—thieves, plug-uglies, degenerates. . . . The community must protect itself from the criminal fringe of the invaders.

Booster clubs, community organizations of every sort, volunteer organizations if no sectional group is available, should get together in extraordinary sessions and organize to protect property, women and possibly life.

It is no time for halfway measures. . . .

The heroes of 1918, now metamorphosed into "thieves, plug-uglies, degenerates," were preparing to gather in the outskirts of the city, in the camp site offered them at Ideal Park. And the leading citizens, aided by the state police, were planning to use any means short of violence to keep them from reaching it. Mr. Hoover's proclamation had done its work.

At Jennerstown is a barracks of the Pennsylvania State Police, looking for all the world like a fashionable roadhouse. In front of the barracks is a traffic light. The road ahead leads westward over Laurel Hill and Chestnut Ridge; the right-hand road leads nineteen miles northward into Johnstown. It was the task of state troopers to keep the Bonus Army moving west over the mountains, toward Ligonier and the Ohio border.

In half an hour on Saturday morning, I saw more than a thousand veterans pass through Jennerstown—that is, more than fifty trucks bearing an average of twenty men apiece. Later I was told that the procession continued at irregular intervals until Sunday evening. The troopers would wait at the intersection, twenty men on their motorcycles like a school of swift gray sharks, till they heard that a convoy was approaching; then they would dart off to meet it in a cloud of dust and blue gasoline smoke, with their hats cutting the air like so many fins. One of the troopers stayed behind to manipulate the traffic light. As the trucks came nearer, he would throw a switch that changed it into a mere yellow blinker, so that all of them could shoot past the intersection without slackening speed. They were full of ragged men, kneeling, standing unsteadily, clinging to the sideboards; there was no room to sit down. Behind each truck rode a trooper, and there were half a dozen others mingled with the crowd that watched from in front of a filling station.

The contrast between these homeless veterans, hatless, coatless, unshaven, half-starved—most of them hadn't eaten or slept for thirty-six hours, a few hadn't had so much as a drink of water—and the sleekly uniformed, smug, well-nourished troopers who were herding them past their destination, produced a sharp effect on the crowd of backwoods farmers, who otherwise cared little about the Bonus March.

"Hey, buddies," they shouted, "turn right, turn right. Johnstown"—pointing northward—"Johnstown." The hungry men smiled and waved at them uncomprehendingly.

But a few had seen that something was wrong, that they were being carried beyond their meeting place. They tried to pass the word from truck to truck, above the roar of the motors. As they went bowling through the level village street, there was no way of escape; but just beyond Jennerstown, the road climbs steeply up Laurel Hill; the drivers shifted into second gear—and promptly lost half their passengers. The others, those who received no warning or let themselves be cowed by the troopers, were carried westward. The following week I met a New York veteran who hadn't escaped from the convoy till it passed the Ohio line. A Negro from Washington, a resident of the city for thirty years—he wasn't a bonus marcher at all, but made the mistake of walking through Anacostia in his shirt sleeves—was arrested, piled into a truck, and carried all the way to Indianapolis before he managed to tell his story to a reporter.

As for the veterans who escaped at Jennerstown, they lay by the road-side utterly exhausted. Their leaders had been arrested, dispersed, or else had betrayed them; their strength had been gnawed away by hunger or lack of sleep; they hoped to reunite and recuperate in a new camp, but how to reach it they did not know. For perhaps twenty minutes, they dozed there hopelessly. Then—and I was a witness of this phenomenon— a new leader would stand forth from the ranks. He would stop a motorist, learn the road to Johnstown, call the men together, give them their instructions—and the whole group would suddenly obey a self-imposed discipline. As they turned northward at the Jennerstown traffic light, one of them would shout, "We're going back!" and perhaps half a dozen would mumble in lower voices, "We're gonna get guns and go back to Washington."

Mile after mile we passed the ragged line as we too drove northward to the camp at Ideal Park. We were carrying two of the veterans, chosen from a group of three hundred by a quick informal vote of their comrades. One was a man gassed in the Argonne and tear-gassed at Anacostia; he breathed with an effort, as if each breath would be his last. The other was a man with family troubles; he had lost his wife and six children during the retreat from Camp Marks and hoped to find them in Johnstown. He talked about his service in France, his three medals, which he refused to wear, his wounds, his five years in a government hospital. "If they gave me a job," he said, "I wouldn't care about the bonus."

The sick man, as we passed one group of veterans after another, pointed northward and said in an almost inaudible voice, "This way, comrades, this way. Comrades, this way," till his head fell back and he lapsed into a feverish sleep.

It seemed the ragged line would never end. Here the marchers were stumbling under the weight of their suitcases and blanket rolls, here they were clustered round a farmhouse pump, here a white man was sharing the burden of a crippled Negro, here white and Negro together were snoring in a patch of shade. The road curled downward into the valley where Johnstown swelters between steep hills. On either side of us were fields of golden grain, cut and stacked for the threshers; a moment later we were winding through a forest. It was a landscape not unlike the high

121

hills north of the River Aisne. In that other country, fifteen years before, I had seen gaunt men coming out of the trenches half-dead with fatigue, bending under the weight of their equipment. The men on the Johnstown road that day were older, shabbier, but somehow more impressive: they were volunteers, fighting a war of their own. "And don't forget it, buddy," one of them shouted as the car slowed down, "we've enlisted for the duration."

At Ideal Park, where the new camp was being pitched, there was the same determination, combined with a hysteria caused by sudden relief from tension. A tall man with a tear-streaked face was marching up and down. "I used to be a hundred-percenter," he said, "but now I'm a Red radical. I had an American flag, but the damned tin soldiers burned it. Now I don't ever want to see a flag again. Give me a gun and I'll go back to Washington."—"That's right, buddy," said a woman looking up from her two babies, who lay on a dirty quilt in the sun. A cloud of flies hovered above them. Another man was reading the editorial page of a Johnstown paper. He shouted, "Let them come here and mow us down with machine guns. We won't move this time."—"That's right, buddy," said the woman again. A haggard face—eyes bloodshot, skin pasty white under a three days' beard—suddenly appeared at the window of our car. "Hoover must die," said the face ominously. "You know what this means?" a man shouted from the other side. "This means revolution."—"Yes, you're damned right it means revolution."

But a thousand homeless veterans, or fifty thousand, don't make a revolution. This threat would pass and be forgotten, like the other threat that was only half concealed in the Johnstown editorial. Next day the bonus leaders would come, the slick guys in leather puttees; they would make a few speeches and everything would be smoothed over. They would talk of founding a new Fascist order of Khaki Shirts, but this threat, too, can be disregarded: a Fascist movement, to succeed in this country, must come from the middle classes and be respectable. No, if any revolution results from the flight of the Bonus Army, it will come from a different source, from the government itself. The army in time of peace, at the national capital, has been used against unarmed citizens—and this, with all it threatens for the future, is a revolution in itself.

ELECTION YEAR—1932

PERHAPS the people themselves were not ready for radical leadership, but the plain fact was that even if they had been, none of the radical or the old reform parties had anything attractive to offer. But the people would be given a chance to express their feelings in the forthcoming election. Cracks were beginning to appear in the composure of some of the nation's leaders. Said Senator David A. Reed in 1932, "I do not often envy other countries their governments, but I say that if this country ever needed a Mussolini it needs one now."

President Hoover was nominated by the Republicans to run again; the Democrats nominated the Governor of New York, Franklin D. Roosevelt. Some of the liberal commentators of the day thought Roosevelt was too weak and vacillating. His record in Albany had been good on welfare and conservation, but his co-operation with the Seabury investigation of corruption in New York City had left something to be desired. Consequently, no one could forecast just what Roosevelt had in mind when, in his acceptance speech at the convention in Chicago, he spoke of establishing a "new deal" for the people.

In the months that followed Roosevelt's nomination, he consulted frequently with a group of advisers, which was called his "brain trust"—men like Moley, Tugwell, Rosenman and Berle. They were as much concerned with the economic and social dilemmas of the time as were the politicians; and, well versed in political theory and economic philosophy, unhampered by traditional ideas of the market place, they were not afraid to advise experiment.

One of the main questions to be settled was how big a role the federal government should assume in planning and, in particular, just how much control it should exercise in making decisions "to promote the general welfare" of the people. Roosevelt made his position clear: businessmen "had to assume the responsibility which went with power; when they failed, the government must be swift to protect the public interest."

The Republicans abhorred government "interference" and insisted that the country would right itself eventually if it was just let alone. Roosevelt and his advisers observed that this policy had had no noticeable effect in arresting the downward trend of the economy and that active measures were necessary—tougher regulatory policies for business, more social planning, sounder practices for banking, plus keeping the budget balanced (no one had the courage to declare against this—in public, at least); all these came under debate within the "brain trust."

THE CAMPAIGN

In campaigning for the election, Roosevelt made a good impression upon the public, but the people made just as strong an impression on him. "For Roosevelt," Arthur Schlesinger says, "the faces before him were an unforgettable experience—the great mass of Missourians under the lights before the Capitol at Jefferson City, the Kansans listening patiently in the hot sun at Topeka, the Nebraska farmers in the red glow of sunset at McCook, the stricken but dauntless miners of Butte.

" 'I have looked into the faces of thousands of Americans,' Roosevelt told a friend. "They have the frightened look of lost children.' Roosevelt himself, endlessly watching out of train windows, from the back seat of automobiles, from the platform of the crowded auditoriums, smiling, waving his battered Italian felt hat, seemed to gather new strength from the people." *

Hoover's campaign was received with a mixture of approval and hostility. The people held him respon-sible for the bad times. The President could not believe the government deserved such ill feeling, and he campaigned hard, charging that Roosevelt's New Deal ideas would bankrupt the country and vitiate the very foundations of the American government.

On Election Day the American people went Democratic: Roosevelt polled 22,809,638 votes to Hoover's 15,758,901.

Roosevelt announced his Cabinet members soon afterward; among them were Cordell Hull, as Secretary of State, and Frances Perkins, as Secretary of Labor, the first woman Cabinet member.

Before the inauguration, efforts were made to bring Hoover and Roosevelt together to discuss mutual action to arrest the ever-deepening crisis, but their personalities and their philosophies were too far apart for them to find common ground.

ARTHUR M. SCHLESINGER, JR.

THE INAUGURAL†

THE WHITE HOUSE, midnight, Friday, March 3, 1933. Across the country the banks of the nation had gradually shuttered their windows and locked their doors. The very machinery of the American economy seemed to be coming to a stop. The rich and fertile nation, overflowing with natural wealth in its fields and forests and mines, equipped with unsurpassed technology, endowed with boundless resources in its men and women, lay stricken. "We are at the end of our rope," the weary President at last said,

---

* Arthur M. Schlesinger, Jr., *The Crisis of the Old Order.*
† From Arthur M. Schlesinger, Jr.'s *The Crisis of the Old Order* (Boston, Houghton Mifflin, 1957).

as the striking clock announced the day of his retirement. "There is nothing more we can do."

Saturday, March 4, dawned gray and bleak. Heavy winter clouds hung over the city. A chill northwest wind brought brief gusts of rain. The darkness of the day intensified the mood of helplessness. "A sense of depression had settled over the capital," reported the New York *Times,* "so that it could be felt." In the late morning, people began to gather for the noon ceremonies, drawn, it would seem, by curiosity as much as by hope. Nearly one hundred thousand assembled in the grounds before the Capitol, standing in quiet groups, sitting on benches, watching from rooftops. Some climbed the bare, sleet-hung trees. As they waited, they murmured among themselves. "What are those things that look like little cages?" one asked. "Machine guns," replied a woman with a nervous giggle. "The atmosphere which surrounded the change of government in the United States," wrote Arthur Krock, "was comparable to that which might be found in a beleaguered capital in wartime." The colorless light of the cast-iron skies, the numb faces of the crowd, created almost an air of fantasy. Only the Capitol seemed real, etched like a steel engraving against the dark clouds.

On the drive from the White House to the Capitol, the retiring President, his eyes lowered, his expression downcast, did not try to hide his feelings. The nation which had helped him rise from a poor Iowa farm to wealth and power, which he had repaid with high-minded and unstinted service, had rejected him. "Democracy is not a polite employer," Herbert Hoover later wrote. "The only way out of elective office is to get sick or die or get kicked out."

It was customary for the retiring President to ask his successor for dinner on the night of the third of March; but Hoover had declined to issue the usual invitation. At length, the White House usher insisted that the President-elect must be given the opportunity to pay his respects. Instead of the traditional dinner, a tea was arranged for the afternoon of the third. It had been a strained occasion in the Red Room, complicated by fruitless last-minute discussions about the banking crisis. Finally the President-elect, recognizing that Hoover was not in the mood to complete the round of protocol, politely suggested that the President need not return the visit. Hoover looked his successor in the eye. "Mr. Roosevelt," he said coldly, "when you are in Washington as long as I have been, you will learn that the President of the United States calls on nobody." Franklin Delano Roosevelt, hurrying his family from the room, returned to the Mayflower Hotel visibly annoyed. "It was . . ." a close friend later reported, "one of the few times I have ever seen him really angry."

Now Hoover sat motionless and unheeding as the car moved through crowded streets toward the Capitol. Doubtless he assumed the occasional cheers from the packed sidewalks were for Roosevelt and so not his to acknowledge. But for Roosevelt, sitting beside him in the open car, these last moments belonged to the retiring President; it was not for the President-elect to respond to the faint applause. On they drove in uncomfortable silence. Passing the new Commerce Building on Constitution Avenue, Roosevelt hoped that at least this sight might tempt the former Secretary of Commerce into an exchange of amiabilities. When a friendly remark produced only an unintelligible murmur in reply, the President-elect suddenly felt that the two men could not ride on forever like graven images. Turning, he began to smile to the men and women along the street and to wave his top hat. Hoover rode on, his face heavy and expressionless.

The fog of despair hung over the land. The images of a nation as it approached zero hour: the well-groomed men, baffled and impotent in their double-breasted suits before the Senate committee; the confusion and dismay in the business office and the university; the fear in the country club; the angry men marching in the silent street; the scramble for the rotting garbage in the dump; the sweet milk trickling down the dusty road; the noose dangling over the barn door; the raw northwest wind blasting its way across Capitol plaza.

In the Capitol, the President-elect waited in the Military Affairs Committee Room. Sober and white-faced, he sat in silence, glancing at the manuscript of his inaugural address. Huey Long, the senator from Louisiana, glimpsed him and started to sweep into the room; then paused at the threshold and tiptoed away. Ten minutes before noon Roosevelt started down the corridor toward the Senate, only to be stopped. "All right," he said, "we'll go back and wait some more." When the moment arrived, he was to ride in his wheelchair to the east door; then walk thirty-five yards to the speaker's stand.

A few moments before, in the Senate Chamber, the new Vice-President, John Nance Garner of Texas, had taken his oath of office. There followed a rush from the Senate to the inaugural stand outside. The mass of people, swarming into the narrow exit from the east doors of the Capitol, blocked the runway. In a moment the congestion was hopeless. Garner and the retiring Vice-President, Charles Curtis of Kansas, had meanwhile reached the stand. The Texan, with no overcoat, shivered in the harsh wind; he borrowed a muffler and wrapped it around his neck. Near him Curtis disappeared into the depth of his fur coat, looking steadily at the floor, apparently lost in memory. Gradually, invited guests began to force their way through the jam: members of the new Cabinet, half a dozen senators, the new President's wife, his mother, his tall sons. Eventually Charles Evans Hughes, the Chief Justice of the United States, made his appearance, erect and stately, a black silk skullcap on his head, his white beard stirred by the wind and his black robe fluttering about his legs. In a leather-upholstered chair to the left of the lectern sat Herbert Hoover.

The tension in the crowd mounted steadily with the delay. Presently a Supreme Court attendant arrived bearing the family Bible of the Roosevelts. Then, at last, the bugle sounded; and Franklin Delano Roosevelt, intensely pale, leaning on the arm of his eldest son James, walked slowly up the maroon-carpeted ramp. The Marine Band, in its scarlet jackets and blue trousers, finished the last bars of "Hail to the Chief." There was a con-vulsive stir in the crowd, spread over forty acres of park and pavement; then cheers and applause. Mrs. Woodrow Wilson waved a handkerchief. Bernard Baruch leaped upon a bench and swung his black silk hat. Josephus Daniels, the new President's old chief, his eyes wet with tears, pounded vigorously with his cane. A few rays of sunshine broke for a moment through the slate clouds upon the inaugural stand.

The Chief Justice read the oath with dignity and power. Instead of returning the customary "I do," Roosevelt repeated the full oath. ("I am glad," Hughes had written when the President-elect suggested this. ". . . I think the repetition is the more dignified and appropriate course.") The family Bible lay open to the thirteenth chapter of the First Corinthians. "For now we see through a glass, darkly; but then face to face: now I know in part; but then shall I know even as also I am known. And now abideth faith, hope, charity, these three; but the greatest of these *is* charity."

Six days before, Roosevelt in his Hyde Park study, writing with pencil on a lined, legal-sized yellow pad, had made a draft of his inaugural ad-dress. Waiting in the Senate committee room on inauguration day, he added a new opening sentence to his reading copy: "This is a day of consecra-tion." But, as the great crowd quieted down, the solemnity of the occasion surged over him; he said, in ringing tones, "This is a day of national consecration."

Across the country millions clustered around radio sets. The new Presi-dent stood bareheaded and unsmiling, his hands gripping the lectern. The moment had come, he said, to speak the truth, the whole truth, frankly and boldly. "Let me assert my firm belief that the only thing we have to fear is fear itself—nameless, unreasoning, unjustified terror which paralyzes needed efforts to convert retreat into advance." The speaker flung back his head. "In every dark hour of our national life a leadership of frankness and vigor has met with that understanding and support of the people themselves which is essential to victory."

The bounty of nature, he continued, was undiminished. "Plenty is at our doorstep, but a generous use of it languishes in the very sight of the supply." Why? Because the rulers of the exchange of mankind's goods "have failed through their own stubbornness and their own incompetence, have admitted their failure, and have abdicated. . . . They have no vision, and when there is no vision the people perish. The money changers have fled from their high seats in the temple of our civilization." The crowd delivered itself of its first great applause. "There must be an end," Roosevelt went on, "to a conduct in banking and in business which too often has given to a sacred trust the likeness of callous and selfish wrongdoing." Again the crowd shouted.

"This Nation asks for action, and action now. . . . We must act and act quickly. . . . We must move as a trained and loyal army willing to sacrifice for the good of a common discipline, because without such discipline no progress is made, no leadership becomes effective." "It may be," he said, "that an unprecedented demand and need for undelayed action may call for temporary departure from that normal balance of public procedure." If Congress should fail to enact the necessary measures, if the emergency were still critical, then, added Roosevelt solemnly, "I shall ask the Congress for the one remaining instrument to meet the crisis—broad Executive power to wage a war against the emergency, as great as the power that would be given to me if we were in fact invaded by a foreign foe." The crowd thundered approval in a long, continuing demonstration—the loudest applause of the day.

Roosevelt—"his face still so grim," reported Arthur Krock, "as to seem unfamiliar to those who have long known him"—did not acknowledge the applause. Nor, indeed, did all share the enthusiasm. Some who watched the handsome head and heard the cultivated voice mistrusted what lay behind the charm and the rhetoric. "I was thoroughly scared," the retiring Secretary of State, Henry L. Stimson, wrote in his diary. ". . . Like most of his past speeches, it was full of weasel words and would let him do about what he wanted to." Edmund Wilson, covering the inaugural for the *New Republic,* saw "the old unctuousness, the old pulpit vagueness," the echoes of Woodrow Wilson's eloquence without Wilson's glow of life behind them. "The thing that emerges most clearly," wrote Wilson, "is the warning of a dictatorship."

But the unsmiling President showed no evidence of doubt. "We do not distrust the future of essential democracy," he said in summation. "The people of the United States have not failed. In their need they have registered a mandate that they want direct, vigorous action. They have asked for discipline and direction under leadership. They have made me the present instrument of their wishes. In the spirit of the gift I take it." Herbert Hoover stared at the ground.

The high clear note of the cavalry bugles announced the inaugural parade. Franklin Roosevelt, in the presidential car, waved greetings to the crowd along the way—men and women now curiously awakened from apathy and daze. The horsemen wheeled into line, and the parade began.

In Washington the weather remained cold and gray. Across the land the fog began to lift.

WILLIAM MANCHESTER

THE GREAT BANK HOLIDAY*

IT IS SLIGHTLY more than a quarter century since panic closed America's banks—since that improbable month when Norman Vincent Peale denounced capitalists, John D. Rockefeller ran out of dimes, Macy's announced that demanding cash from its customers would be unpatriotic, and what were then known as step-ins were solemnly accepted as legal tender in Madison Square Garden.

Even then it had an air of fantasy, and was quickly forgotten, just as it had been unforeseen during the lame-duck winter of 1932–33 which led to it. And yet there had been omens of the panic. There was, for example, the jigsaw-puzzle craze, which reached its crest at the very moment America was plunging into the terminal trough of the Depression. During that winter some 6,000,000 puzzles were sold, and in retrospect the significance of the vogue seems painfully clear. It was a time of searching for elusive answers in politics and economics. The jigsaw turned out puzzles a man at least could solve.

In Detroit the weekend of February 11–12 newsstands enjoyed a heavy sale of 500-piece (*Lincoln*) puzzles. They were tough to do. Thousands of automotive workers were still frowning over card tables Monday night as their children, huddled by radios, hoarded the currency of the young— Ralston box tops, Ovaltine seals, Rice Krispies labels, Tastyeast wrappers. None of the puzzle workers, of course, suspected that very soon American parents would be reduced to even stranger exchange. But the time was at hand, and for Detroit it was the very next day, St. Valentine's Day, 1933.

President Hoover was singing his swan song over the networks at ten o'clock that evening before the Republican National Committee. Among those not listening was the Democratic Governor of Michigan, William A. Comstock. It was nothing personal. At three o'clock that afternoon he had received an urgent telephone request to join a conference of bankers in downtown Detroit, and he had been there ever since. Detroit's Union Guardian Trust Company was in straits. If it failed it probably would take every other bank in the city with it, and the bankers were asking Com-

* From *Holiday*, February 1960.

stock to declare a banking moratorium throughout Michigan. At midnight he agreed, drove to the state capital at Lansing and issued a proclamation closing the state's 550 banks. He called it a holiday.

The idea was not new. For more than a year the nation's harassed business community had been begging for breathers, and in two states, Nevada and Louisiana, it actually had been given them. Nevada, however, had a population of only 91,000, and Louisiana's moratorium covered just one weekend. Michigan, on the other hand, was the heart of the automotive industry. Its citizens, moreover, were depleted of cash after the long weekend and unprepared for Comstock's valentine. The proclamation was too late for the regular editions of the morning papers; extras greeted workers arriving downtown with the news that they were cut off with whatever cash they had in their their pockets. In some cases this was almost nothing, but there was no hysteria, no gathering in front of the closed banks. The general mood was casual, even gay. After all, it *was* a holiday.

To be sure, it was awkward. Many of the newsboys peddling the extras were obliged to sell on credit. Those who did collect coins found themselves hailed by cruising merchants waving bills and pleading for change. A few storekeepers, unable to locate silver, had to close their stores; those who sought relief in Windsor, Ontario, were coldly told their checks would be accepted "subject to collection," and under the phony holiday air there was a feeling of uneasiness about the value of what currency there was. The Dow Chemical Company of Midland began coining magnesium into "Dowmetal Money," with an arbitrary value of twenty cents—the first of a series of substitutes which were to plague the economy for a month.

Still, there were reassuring signs. Merchants talked of organizing a change bureau. Milk companies promised to continue deliveries. Before noon a shipment of gold estimated at $20,000,000 was flown from Federal Reserve coffers in Chicago, and that night another $5,000,000 arrived from Washington to meet money orders and Postal Savings withdrawals. Surely, everyone said, the bronze doors would yawn wide the next day. Wags told other wags the story of the man who had to call his wife, couldn't cash a bill, and borrowed a nickel from an apple seller on Woodward Avenue. "Brother," the optimists sang blithely, "can you spare a dime?" And in Dearborn, Henry Ford heard the piping voices of two hundred children chant, "When the bough breaks, the cradle will fall."

But the doors didn't yawn. Later in the week they were held slightly ajar—depositors could withdraw five per cent of their accounts. It wasn't enough even to meet local payrolls. Detroit's Colonial Department Store, frankly resorting to barter, offered dresses for salted Saginaw herring, suits

131

for livestock, assorted merchandise for eggs and honey. By the following week jokes were discarded. The holiday had been extended.

Michigan's plight had been aggravated by plunging real-estate values, but the Depression was nationwide. Since the crash of 1929 more than 5,500 American banks had failed, and the public, understandably, was edgy. It responded by hoarding. Gold was vanishing from vaults at the rate of $20,000,000 a day, and depositors who couldn't get metal were taking paper, so that the government was called upon to expand its currency at the very time the gold on which it was based was disappearing.

Bank panics are always suicidal. In 1933, however, the situation had been complicated by three years of deflation. Even the soundest institutions held mortgages and securities which had fallen to a fraction of their former value. The nation's 18,569 banks had about $6,000,000,000 in cash to meet $41,000,000,000 in deposits, and bankers who were forced to sell mortgages or securities to raise cash would suffer heavy losses. President Hoover was trying everything he could think of to turn the tide— R.F.C. loans to banks, debtor relief, higher duties on Jap sneakers and Czech rubbers—but nothing seemed to work.

Now Michigan had fallen. Abruptly the daily outflow of gold from the rest of the country's banks jumped to $37,000,000; currency withdrawals to $122,000,000. Banks everywhere were swarming with wild-eyed depositors taking out cash—in the Bronx a young mother rented her baby, at twenty-five cents a trip, to women who used it to claim preference at the head of bank lines; and the week of February 20 in Maryland the Baltimore Trust Company paid out $13,000,000, nearly half of it on Friday. Late Friday night Governor Albert C. Ritchie declared a three-day holiday for the state's two hundred banks. The second state had collapsed.

Responsible men were making a painfully self-conscious effort to keep their heads. The Detroit *News* commented, "It is an experience we shall have to look back upon, and no doubt grin over," and the Baltimore *Sun* said cheerily, "Life . . . will be filled with pleasant and unpleasant things as it was before. And it will have the additional advantage that everybody will have something to talk about."

The president of the Baltimore Association of Commerce saw no reason why business should not continue as usual; the Bureau of Internal Revenue issued a stern reminder that income taxes were due in two weeks.

Nothing from Hyde Park dispelled the illusion of unreality. Indeed, the pixie mood of the press seemed superbly matched by President-elect Roosevelt's selection of a man to be Secretary of the Treasury, a puckish little

railway-equipment manufacturer who wore a gray toupee, loved puns, collected five-dollar gold pieces, and spent his leisure time composing on a
guitar. A week later, when the new administration took office, the country
was to know another William H. Woodin—hard-driving, ingenious—but on
the eve of office his most striking achievement known to the public was the
composition of a song for children:

> *Let us be like bluebirds,*
> *Happy all day long*
> *Forgetting all our troubles in*
> *A sunny song.*

In Indianapolis and Akron that Sunday, February 26, banks announced that withdrawals would be limited to five per cent of balances.
During the night institutions in a dozen other Ohio cities fell into line,
and on Monday—as flames gutted the Berlin Reichstag and Japanese
troops marched into a Manchurian blizzard—the number grew to one
hundred. Across the river from Cincinnati, five Covington, Kentucky,
banks adopted similar restrictions. Monday evening Governor Gifford
Pinchot of Pennsylvania signed a bill permitting individual institutions to
close at will, and Thomas W. Lamont informed Hyde Park that in the
view of J. P. Morgan, "the emergency could not be greater."

It could be, and soon was. By Wednesday, frantic governors had declared bank holidays in seventeen states. Pinchot acted so hurriedly he
had to watch the inauguration five days later with only ninety-five cents in
his pocket. Governor Allen of Louisiana, on the other hand, openly withdrew his expense money for Washington and then entrained, leaving behind
his dictated proclamation closing all banks.

It was on Wednesday, March 1, that the President-elect—who, Arthur
Krock reported, was being asked by responsible men to assume power *now*
—drove to his Manhattan home at 49 East Sixty-fifth Street and went into
conference with Woodin. They did not emerge until Thursday afternoon,
when, preceded by the screaming sirens of twenty motorcycles, they raced
down Fifth Avenue and turned west toward the river. During the morning
a light snow had sifted over the city. New Yorkers stood silently in it,
staring at the cavalcade. Outside Radio City Music Hall, King Kong, enjoying his first Manhattan run, leered toothily. In the Hudson the French
Line steamer *Paris* lay quietly at berth, her cargo space reserved—though
no one in the party knew it yet—for $9,000,000 in fleeing gold. On the
other side of the river a special B. & O. train was waiting, and all that
afternoon, talking now with Woodin of banks, now with Farley of religion,

Franklin Roosevelt thundered through a cold fog, toward Washington.

It was sleeting when they reached Union Station. In the Presidential Suite of the Mayflower Hotel a sheaf of telegrams awaited Roosevelt: banks were closed, or closing, in twenty-one states and the District of Columbia, and Federal Reserve figures showed the week's gold loss to be $226,000,-000. He was scarcely unpacked when Woodin drew him aside. Secretary of the Treasury Ogden Mills and Eugene Meyer, of the Federal Reserve Board, had telephoned to suggest a proclamation closing all banks. President Hoover felt less drastic action, under the Trading-with-the-Enemy Act of 1917, would do. Roosevelt's approval was solicited, but he, still declining to act until he had the authority, refused to advise anyone. Fair skies had been forecast for Saturday's inauguration, but now the barometer was falling.

The last page of the New York *Times* of Friday, March 3, carried an ad depicting "John Doe" and "Jane Doe" acclaiming the "Good Work" of the Bowery Savings Bank. Presumably its purpose was to hearten depositors. It failed. By noon long lines of New Yorkers had formed opposite Grand Central Station and were filing into the world's largest private savings bank, demanding cash. By 3 P.M. the Bowery closed its doors, with a huge crowd still unpaid. At the same hour Governor Henry Horner of Illinois sat in the Federal Reserve Bank of Chicago, plucking nervously at his mustache, reading figures which showed that Chicago banks had paid out $350,000,000 in two weeks. After seventeen days in the hinterland, the storm was hammering at the nation's two financial strongholds.

That morning Miss Catherine Shea, a messenger for the Treasury Department, had brought Herbert Hoover his last $500 pay check. He had received it with a semblance of cheer; reports reaching him before noon suggested that the panic was lessening. After lunch, however, it became clear that this was only an illusion. Minnesota and Kansas were gone. North Carolina and Virginia were going.

In Washington the National Symphony Orchestra had scheduled as its first number that evening a composition by the incoming Secretary of the Treasury. Woodin had reserved a box, but wasn't in it. He was in the Presidential Suite with Roosevelt, Raymond Moley, Cordell Hull and Jesse Jones, debating the wisdom of a nationwide bank moratorium, while in the White House the same question engaged Hoover, Mills and Meyer. Hoover called Roosevelt twice, to compare notes. Thomas Lamont, who was at the New York Reserve Bank with sixteen other bankers, telephoned the Mayflower. Daniel Ellis Woodhull, president of the American Bank-note Company, was with them and was prepared to print scrip, but the bankers didn't feel this was necessary; they were sure they could stay open.

At 1 A.M. Roosevelt suggested to Hoover that they turn in and get some sleep. They did. And as they slept, their advisers decided everything for them.

Moley, stepping from the elevator into the Mayflower lobby, found Woodin waiting for him. "This thing is very bad," Woodin said wearily. "Will you come over to the Treasury with me? We'll see if we can give those fellows a hand."

At the Treasury were Mills and Meyer, back from the White House, A. A. Ballantine, Mills's Undersecretary, and F. G. Awalt, his Acting Comptroller. Before them lay the latest bleak Federal Reserve figures. During the last two days, $500,000,000 had been drained from the nation's banks. They were convinced that the New York bankers did not understand the immensity of the disaster, and must be protected. Governor Herbert Lehman, who had canceled his trip to the inauguration at 11 P.M., awaited the decision of the Lamont group. Mills and Woodin agreed that regardless of what the bankers decided Lehman must be persuaded to close New York's banks, and that Horner must also declare a moratorium for Illinois.

At 1:45 A.M. Horner's hotel telephone jangled—his groggy bankers were ready to capitulate. He taxied to meet them, and together they held a telephone conference with Lehman and the Treasury. At 2 A.M. he proclaimed his holiday. The sixteen New York bankers, meanwhile, piled into five limousines and drove to Lehman's home, where arguments continued. Moley, spent, fell asleep in Mills's office. Finally, at 4:20 A.M. the Governor of New York had reached his decision.

Woodin shook Moley. "It's all right, Ray. Let's go now. Lehman's agreed."

Hoover was told at 6 A.M. "We are at the end of our rope," he said. "There is nothing more we can do."

On Saturday, March 4—the day Franklin Roosevelt took office and Howard Scott, technocrat, was formally declared bankrupt—inauguration visitors in Washington found this notice posted over hotel counters:

Members find it necessary that, due to unsettled banking conditions throughout the country, checks on out-of-town banks cannot be accepted.

THE WASHINGTON HOTEL ASSOCIATION

The financial heart of the country had ceased to beat. Banking in every state was wholly or partly suspended. Flags flew in Wall Street, honoring the inauguration, but the Stock Exchange was closed, and so, for the first time in eighty-five years, was the Chicago Board of Trade. By 10 A.M. Woodhull's presses were roaring, turning out $250,000,000 in scrip for the New York Clearing House.

In Washington, the sky was the color of slate. Money worries had kept half the anticipated crowd at home; Vice-President Garner wore a borrowed muffler; Woodin, unable to reach his seat, perched on a railing with a cameraman; and during his address Roosevelt, uncovered and coatless, braced himself in the chill wind.

"President Hoover, Mr. Chief Justice, my friends . . ."

He was flaying the money-changers, gone from the temple. Later it occurred to some that his speech had political implications, but actually it was mild abuse. That weekend—Norman Vincent Peale, no revolutionary, demanded from his Fifth Avenue pulpit the following morning that the bankers and corporation heads get down on their knees before God and confess their sins. Yet the fact is that the Treasury, at least, had never been freer of politics. Awalt, the Republican Acting Comptroller, was working on under the Democrats, his uncut hair hanging over his ears. Ballantine, the G.O.P. Undersecretary of the Treasury, was drafting Roosevelt's first fireside chat on the banks. And Mills's invocation of the Trading-with-the-Enemy Act, originally written for Hoover, was issued by Roosevelt Sunday night.

His cigarette holder atilt, the new President declared the next four days a holiday for all banks and empowered Woodin to make exceptions. An embargo was declared on the export of gold—the *Paris* sailed without her precious cargo. Congress was being called into special session on Thursday, when emergency legislation would be ready. Meanwhile the people of the United States would have to manage without money-changers.

How was it done? A great deal depended on who you were—and where you were. As a rule, the farther a man was from home, the greater his plight. If you were in Havana, you found that Cuba had declared its own holiday. In Cairo you were offered seventeen piasters to the dollar—the previous day's rate had been twenty-eight—and in Montreal your dollar dropped thirty-five cents in value overnight. Traveling salesmen had to hitchhike—one, in New York, hawked his shoe samples in a hotel lobby to earn his fare home. Ten New Yorkers stranded in Chicago were sent home in a bus by their hotel.

In Reno that week, fewer than a half-dozen court cases were filed each day; women had court costs and fees, but lacked funds for train tickets. Miami was in an uproar—the American Express Company declared a fifty-dollar limit on the cashing of its checks there Monday as five thousand tanned visitors lined up. Pasadena's exclusive Huntington Hotel printed scrip for stranded millionaires; among these seen in the lobby queue were Edward Bausch, of Bausch and Lomb; Sir Montagu Allan; and Prince Erik of Denmark. In Washington, Cordell Hull's first official chore was to deal with enraged diplomats, who argued that their money was entitled to diplomatic immunity from sequestration. He held them off—their plight was no worse than that of many an American alone in a strange city where his credit meant nothing. In New York a drunken Hawaiian entertainer killed his partner for accepting a check. As Prince Mike Romanoff, the noted impostor, noted piously, "A great many people's checks are now as good as a great many others."

At home Americans struggled along with varying success, depending upon the length of local holidays. Detroit, in its fourth week of moratorium, was suffering. Two thirds of the city's 1,400 laborers had been unable to raise anything on their pay checks, and several fainted on the job from hunger before emergency food cards were issued. Merchants estimated their business at 60 to 70 per cent below normal, restaurant cash registers were crammed with signed lunch checks, and doctors, unable to get gasoline, had to restrict their calls. In Springfield, Massachusetts, on the other hand, a newspaper survey showed that the average citizen had $18.23 cash—in trousers, purses, teapots and baby banks—when the city's banks closed on Inauguration Day.

In such communities the problem was not cash, but change. Many a man was walking the streets with a full wallet, unable to buy cigarettes, ride a bus, or use a pay telephone, because no one would break his bills. As early as Saturday, March 4, New York suburbanites began redeeming their commutation tickets to obtain silver. That night a crowd flourishing $100, $500 and even $1,000 bills formed in Pennsylvania Station—buying tickets to Newark.

Automats were invaded by women in mink who got twenty nickels change for dollar bills and left without eating anything, subways by men in Homburgs who had never ridden a subway and didn't intend to start now. Clerks, watching their stocks of coins shrink, became wary. On Lexington Avenue a man with a fifty-dollar bill tried to buy $3.52 in shaving supplies; he was advised to grow a beard. The Commodore Hotel turned away a changeless man with a $30,000 certified check. Hotel managers sent bellhops to churches to exchange bills for silver. Churches, however, were having their own difficulties; even the devout were close-fisted that March 5. One Methodist minister in New York advised his congregation to keep its silver; another solicited an offering of IOU's.

As the week wore on the shortage of change became crippling. On Monday storekeepers in Elgin, Illinois, learned that a sixteen-year-old boy had saved 11,357 pennies toward his college education, and within an hour they had his home surrounded. There weren't many such caches, however; by Wednesday even the eleemosynary Mr. Rockefeller had run out of dimes and had to give his caddie a whole buck. About the only people with fluid currency were the Alaskans, who were using gold dust, and bootleggers.

Credit indeed, was the only solution to the holiday, as smart retailers had realized at the beginning. "If I try to get all my cash I shall certainly make matters worse," declared Jesse Isidor Straus, president of R. H. Macy & Company, which normally dealt only in hard money. "Use your charge account at Lord & Taylor!" "Use your credit!" cried newspaper ads. "Do not declare a moratorium on your appetite," advertised the Hollywood Cabaret Restaurant. And in Texas, pharmacists accepted IOU's for prescriptions. Gimbel's extended credit to patrons of its restaurant, and taxi dancers in Manhattan's Roseland Dance Hall accepted IOU's—from men who could produce bankbooks.

Harry Staton, manager of the Herald Tribune Syndicate, was in California when the banks closed there. They kept on closing ahead of him, but he returned to New York on ten dollars, signing his name all the way. When he visited a gambling casino, the manager agreed to give him chips on credit, but warned that he would be paid in chips if he won. In Florida, two race tracks folded. More significant to the economy were the steel industry, whose orders hit a new low; the real-estate business, which was paralyzed; and the automotive industry, some of whose plants were forced to close. Barbershops and railroads reported sharp declines. Hollywood was near ruin—box-office receipts dropped 45 per cent, and every studio shut down. King Kong went into his second week at Radio City, but he was snarling at empty houses.

Where credit failed, people fell back on barter or improvised scrip. During the first week of the new administration, stamps, phone slugs, Canadian dollars, Mexican pesos and street-car tickets were used for currency. Mormons in Salt Lake City designed a paper money that could be used locally; the Greenwich Village Mutual Exchange issued $1,000 in tokens to member businesses; in Princeton the *Princetonian* printed twenty-five-cent scrip notes for students, to be redeemed when the banks reopened. A Wisconsin wrestler signed a contract to perform for a can of tomatoes and a peck of potatoes; an Ashtabula newspaper offered free ads in exchange for produce; and a New York state senator arrived in Albany with twelve dozen eggs and a side of pork to see him through the week.

The most spectacular experiment in barter was conducted by the New York *Daily News,* which was sponsoring the semifinals of the Golden Gloves tournament in Madison Square Garden. The price of seats was fifty cents, but any article worth that amount was accepted as admission, provided the five-cent amusement tax was paid. An appraiser was engaged, who inspected, during the evening, frankfurters, mattresses, hats, shoes, overcoats, fish, noodles, nightgowns, steaks, spark plugs, cameras, sweaters, canned goods, sacks of potatoes, golf knickers, mechanics' tools and foot balm. A boy presented his New Testament, a girl her step-ins. The items most frequently offered were jigsaw puzzles.

Nearly everyone assumed the holiday would end with the formal adoption of scrip—local currencies, managed by states, cities and individual firms. Atlanta, Richmond, Mattituck, Long Island, and Knoxville, of all places, were already on the stuff; before the week of March 6 was out Nashville would have $1,000,000 in circulation; Philadelphia, $8,000,000. The Louisville *Courier-Journal* was paying its employees in private scrip. More than a hundred communities were having notes printed, including Chicago, Boston, Providence, New Haven, Detroit and New York. Governor Lehman had appointed Al Smith chairman of an Emergency Certificate Corporation, and tellers' cages were being constructed in the New York Clearing House to distribute rainbow-colored bills ranging in value from one dollar to fifty dollars. In Nutley, New Jersey, a safety-paper company which had been working three days a week for months went on three shifts, turning out six tons of scrip for Wisconsin and Tennessee.

To Secretary of the Treasury Woodin, however, the thought of state and municipal currencies and company certificates floating around the country was appalling and at breakfast on Tuesday, March 7, he told Moley that he had been up half the night, brooding over alternatives. Scrip wasn't needed, he had decided. "We can issue currency against the sound assets of the banks," he said. "It won't frighten people. It won't look like stage money. It'll be money that looks like money." There was nothing to lose. After all, he said publicly, "We're on the bottom. We're not going any lower."

Working endlessly in his Carlton Hotel suite with Carter Glass, Woodin met Thursday's legislative deadline. As congressmen filed into the special session the finished bill was handed to the clerk—"My name's Bill, and I'm finished, too," Woodin muttered—and was read aloud. Few representatives heard it above the hubbub. They had no copies of their own—there had been no time to print them; even the copy given the clerk bore last-minute changes scribbled in pencil. In thirty-eight minutes they whooped it through while Eleanor Roosevelt sat knitting in the gallery like a benign Madame Defarge, counting votes. Then they crowded into the Senate chamber to hear Glass explain just what it was they had done.

The little Virginian backed it, though he acknowledged there were parts which shocked him. It was, in fact, a shocking measure, ratifying all acts "heretofore *or hereinafter* taken" by the President and the Secretary of the Treasury. It provided prison terms for hoarders, "conservators" rather than receivers for weak banks—a euphemistic triumph almost as great as "holiday"—and authorized the issuance of $2,000,000,000 in new currency based on bank assets. At 8:36 P.M. a rumpled Roosevelt signed it in the White House library, surrounded by unpacked books and pictures from Hyde Park. That evening the Bureau of Engraving and Printing recruited 375 new workers. The official printing presses of the United States finally were going into action.

All that night and the next the lights of the Bureau twinkled across the tidal basin. There was no time to engrave new dies—plates bearing the imprint "Series of 1929" were pressed into service. There wasn't even an opportunity to acquire facsimile signatures of two officials from each of the twelve Federal Reserve banks; signatures were taken from files in the district and sent by messenger to the American Type Foundry in Jersey City, where logotypes were cut. Early Saturday morning planes began taking off from Washington bearing bales of cash. The first were delivered to New York's Federal Reserve bank shortly before noon. Transfer to member banks began immediately.

The real trick was prying open the rigid fists of hoarders, who in one week had taken 15 per cent of the nation's currency out of circulation. Even a bewitched Congress couldn't make the penal clauses apply to hoarding that already had taken place, and so the government turned to the spur of publicity. On Wednesday, March 8, the Federal Reserve Board announced that its banks would prepare lists of persons who had withdrawn gold since February 1 and who failed to bring it back by March 13, the following Monday. Newspapers had scarcely appeared with this announcement before bank switchboards were jammed. Anonymous callers wanted to know what would be done with the names, what it was all about. The replies were ominously vague. Callers were told only that if they had gold and wanted to return it, the banks would open for them, and newspapermen would be kept out of lobbies.

In the next few hours thousands of mattresses were torn open, cans dug up, hidden boxes brought forth. Banks everywhere reported long queues, reminiscent of the preceding week's panic but comprised this time of men and women carrying Gladstones and briefcases. In Cleveland $300,000 was deposited that day; in Minneapolis, $182,000. Thursday, the day Woodin's bill was cheered through Congress, Cleveland took in $500,000, Philadelphia $700,000, Richmond $163,000. The real flood of double eagles, however, was in New York, which, despite a fifty-six-mile gale—which tore loose the stitching in a woman's petticoat and sent a sheaf of gold certificates scudding across Sixth Avenue—banked $30,-000,000 that day. One man brought in $700,000; one firm, whose identity remains a secret, delivered $6,000,000 in bullion to the Federal Reserve Bank.

Encouraged, the bank extended its order on Friday, asking for reports covering withdrawals of the past two years. The widened hunt brought bigger game; the nation's gold supply rose dramatically. By 9:30 A.M., when the Federal Reserve Bank of New York opened, there was a line of 1,000 people, their pockets and luggage sagging with gold. An hour later, the crowd had grown to 1,500. Filing through the grilled gates, the depositors filled out deposit slips, presented the same bags and rolled paper stacks they had withdrawn, and waited while the money was counted. When the bank closed at 5 P.M., two hours late, 4,000 people had passed in and out.

The flow continued, uninterrupted, on Saturday, enhanced in Wilmington by a twenty-year collection of gold pieces turned in by Irenée du Pont. By that night, Federal Reserve banks had recovered $300,000,000 in gold and gold certificates—enough to support $750,000,000 additional circulation. Even before the planes took off with new bank notes, Woodin had permitted individual savings banks to dole out ten dollars to each depositor. Business began to stir, and not all the money was spent for necessities. In Boston Saturday afternoon a *Herald* reporter found several hundred women crowded around five counters in a bargain basement buying jigsaw puzzles.

Roosevelt extended the national moratorium while the Treasury separated strong banks from the weak. After the passage of Thursday's bill Woodin invited applications for permission to reopen; actual openings would start Monday. It was the next week that killed Woodin—he was under a doctor's care before it was over, and in his grave the following

141

year. Yet despite his heroic effort, the staggering task of examining 18,000 institutions would have been impossible without the technical knowledge of the Republicans, who stayed at their desks. Awalt, in the first few days, returned home only to shower and change his clothes; James Douglas, who had been assistant secretary under Mills, served as the contact man with the twelve Federal Reserve Banks, forty state banking departments, and clearinghouses everywhere. In the whirlwind tempers were short, but did not follow party lines. "We were," Moley later recalled, "just a bunch of men trying to save the banking system."

In New York on Monday, all but nine national banks were allowed to reopen; in Philadelphia, all but six. At the end of the week 13,500—75 per cent—of the country's banks were back in business, and the sweet notes of gongs again were heard in stock exchanges. Price rises on the Chicago Board of Trade strained at the legal limit, and in New York stocks jumped 15 per cent. We have John T. Flynn's word for it that the New York ticker clicked off the message, "Happy Days Are Here Again."

Of course they weren't really. One dollar in every ten was tied up in frozen deposits on March 14—when the Bureau of Internal Revenue finally agreed to give income-tax payers sixteen days grace—and as late as October the government still was trying to reorganize 376 banks. But the panic had been ended without currency chaos or nationalization of the banks. Undoubtedly the medicine had been strong; the inflationary movement, once started, was irresistible; in April America left the gold standard. The months that followed saw an entirely new concept of the economy developed in the NRA, AAA, CCC, the Federal Securities Act, the Stock Exchange Act, and, in 1935, the Public Utility Holding Company Act. The power of the bankers had been irrevocably broken.

It was in Roanoke, Virginia, that J. P. Morgan was discovered during the holiday on his annual automobile trip south. He was shy as ever, and declined comment on the Depression. He did, however, remark that he was glad the morning's fog was lifting.

"I like to read the signs along the road," he said.

THE HUNDRED DAYS

THE Roosevelt Administration wasted no time in tackling the many problems that lay before the country. Once the bank holiday had been declared by the new President, Congress was convened and a flood of legislation was swiftly enacted. The first bill, the Emergency Banking Act, was whipped through both houses and signed by Roosevelt at the White House in a matter of just eight hours. This bill declared the bank holiday at an end, and set forth regulations for new transactions.

During the Hundred Days, the period of the special Congressional session which terminated on June 15, 1933, the following legislation was enacted:

March 9—the Emergency Banking Act

March 20—the Economy Act

March 31—creation of the Civilian Conservation Corps

April 19—abandonment of the gold standard

May 12—the Federal Emergency Relief Act

May 12—the Agricultural Adjustment Act

May 12—the Emergency Farm Mortgage Act, for the refinancing of farm mortgages

May 18—the Tennessee Valley Authority Act, setting up a system of dams on the Tennessee River to produce electrical power and sell it to consumers

May 27—the Truth-in-Securities Act, necessitating full disclosure of facts in all stock issues

June 5—cancellation of the gold clause in public and private contracts

June 13—the Home Owners' Loan Act, to refinance home mortgages

June 16—the National Industrial Recovery Act, instituting a system of industrial self-government under federal supervision, and \$3.3 billion public works program

June 16—the Glass-Steagall Banking Act, separation of commercial and investment banking, and guaranteeing all bank deposits

June 16—the Farm Credit Act, reorganization of agricultural credit

June 16—the Railroad Co-ordination Act*

In addition to helping formulate the new legislation, President Roosevelt delivered speeches, initiated informal press conferences, held his Cabinet meetings, and set up the new machinery for his Administration, which seemed to be galloping off in all directions at once. He was making such an impact upon the country, the press and even the business world, that Secretary Ickes said, "It's more than a New Deal, it's a New World; people feel free again, they can breathe naturally. It's like quitting a morgue for the open woods."

One of the first critical problems to be dealt with by the New Deal was relief of the unemployed.

* As listed in Arthur M. Schlesinger, Jr.'s *The Coming of the New Deal.*

ARTHUR M. SCHLESINGER, JR.

THE RISE OF FEDERAL RELIEF*

THE NEW DEAL thus launched in 1933 a series of experiments in agricultural, industrial, commercial, and monetary policy. These programs
were addressed both to the immediate task of recovery and to the larger
task of reconstruction. Yet they could not, in the best of circumstances, be
expected to take effect overnight. There remained in the meantime the
problem of the millions of men and women who had no work and could
find none. No one knows how many there were on Inauguration Day—
at least 12 to 15 million, over a quarter of the labor force—subsisting
wanly and desperately on relief. How to keep these people going until
jobs were available again?

Most people close to the subject had long since concluded that the only
hope was a federal program. During the short session before Inauguration,
a parade of experts—social workers, municipal officials, representatives of
charities—came to Washington to testify for Senator Costigan's federal relief bill. None spoke more authoritatively than Harry L. Hopkins, head
of Franklin Roosevelt's Temporary Emergency Relief Administration in
New York. Hopkins dismissed the idea of loans to penniless states as un-
realistic and called for a federal welfare agency—not a banking agency,
like RFC—to make direct grants to states for relief purposes.

Hopkins had already made the same points in a letter to the President-
elect in December 1932. But in the early weeks of 1933 the banking and
agricultural crises shouldered the relief problem out of Roosevelt's attention. Unable to get through to the President, Hopkins turned to his former
Albany colleague, Frances Perkins. Accompanied by William Hodson, a
veteran social worker and director of the Welfare Council of New York
City, he met Miss Perkins at the crowded Women's University Club on a
March evening. The only place they could find to talk was a cramped space
under the stairs. There Hopkins and Hodson tersely laid out a federal
relief program. Miss Perkins, impressed by the precision of their knowledge, got them an appointment with the President.

* From Arthur M. Schlesinger, Jr.'s *The Coming of the New Deal* (Boston, Houghton
Mifflin, 1959).

Other members of the Administration were arguing for action. Even John Garner spoke up one day: "When we were campaigning," he said, "we sort of made promises that we would do something for the poorer kind of people, and I think we have to do something for them." Roosevelt agreed, and on March 21, 1933, sent a message to Congress requesting the establishment of the office of Federal Relief Administrator. At the same time, he called in Costigan, La Follette, and Wagner and asked them to draw up a bill.

The bill proposed a Federal Emergency Relief Administration with $500 million for grants-in-aid to states. It produced some violent reactions. "I can hardly find parliamentary language," said Simeon D. Fess of Ohio, "to describe the statement that the States and cities cannot take care of conditions in which they find themselves but must come to the Federal Government for aid." "Is there anything left of our Federal system?" asked John B. Hollister of Ohio. "It is socialism," said Robert Luce of Massachusetts, adding with his scholarly meticulousness, "Whether it is communism or not I do not know." "God save the people of the United States," said C. L. Beedy of Maine. These were minority views. The bill passed the Senate on March 30 by a vote of 55 to 17 and the House three weeks later by 326 to 42.

Roosevelt quickly decided on Hopkins as head of the new agency. He had a little trouble with Governor Lehman of New York, who was disinclined to let Hopkins go. Finally on May 19, Hopkins telegraphed Lehman: PRESIDENT STATES HE WAS WIRING YOU AND WANTS ME TO REPORT TO HIM MONDAY MORNING. Lehman wired Roosevelt in anguish: YOU HAVE THE ENTIRE COUNTRY FROM WHICH TO MAKE CHOICE. But Roosevelt knew what he wanted. On May 22, 1933, Harry Hopkins went to Washington.

Hopkins was a lean, loose-limbed, disheveled man, with sharp features and dark, sardonic eyes. He talked quickly and cockily, out of the side of his mouth; his manner was brusque and almost studiously irreverent; his language, concise, pungent, and often profane. "He gives off," noted one observer, "a suggestion of quick cigarettes, thinning hair, dandruff, brief sarcasm, fraying suits of clothes, and a wholly understandable preoccupation." He was at his best under pressure. Wearing what friends described as his hell's-bells or you-can't-put-that-over-on-me expression, he would screw up his face and fire a volley of short, sharp questions until he had slashed through to the heart of a problem. Understanding what had to be done, he wasted no time in formalities, but assumed responsibility, gave orders, and acted. He expended nervous energy carelessly and restored it by chain-smoking and by drinking cup after cup of black coffee. Beneath his air of insouciance and cynicism, he had a buoyant—almost gay—conviction that all walls would fall before the man of resource and decision. And underneath the hard-boiled pose, there lay a surprising quick sensitivity to human moods and relationships.

Action was instantaneous. Before evening on the second day, Hopkins had thrown together a staff, begun the collection of information, alerted forty-eight state governors to set up state organizations, and sent emergency aid to seven states. He warned his staff that he would soon be the most unpopular man in America: he planned to keep reminding the nation of unemployment and poverty, "and they won't want to hear it." Still, for all his forebodings, he set to work with aplomb.

The Federal Emergency Relief Administration did not deal directly with relief applicants. It made grants to local public agencies. Half of its $500 million was to be assigned on a matching basis—one dollar of federal funds for every three dollars of state money spent for relief during the three months preceding. The other half was to go where need was urgent and the matching requirement could not be met. Exhorting, cajoling, scolding, threatening, Hopkins and a small field staff used their power to pump new life into the faltering state agencies. Where a local organization seemed hopelessly incompetent, Hopkins asked the governor to make the necessary changes. Most of the time, his evident disinterestedness won co-operation. In a few cases, FERA had to go into the state and appoint its own administration. Hopkins remained profoundly convinced of the values of decentralization. He kept his Washington staff small and gave great responsibility to state administrators, while at the same time holding them as well as he could to the national mark.

The critical problem of relief, as he saw it, was preserving the morale of people forced to live by government handouts. Men and women who lacked jobs for reasons far beyond their own control should not, Hopkins believed, be made to feel like paupers; it was necessary not just to feed them but to maintain their self-respect. "I don't think anybody can go year after year, month after month, accepting relief without affecting his character in some way unfavorably," he wrote in June 1933. "It is probably going to undermine the independence of hundreds of thousands of families. . . . I look upon this as a great disaster and wish to handle it as such."

A measure of degradation in relief seemed inescapable. Since limited funds had to go as far as possible, it was essential that no one obtain relief who could get along without it. Thus FERA could not escape the means test. Investigation was left to local case workers, who could presumably conduct it with least humiliation to the applicant. Once need was established, the problem became the form in which relief was to be granted. Some states had set up special commissaries where reliefers could go for food. This was a cheap enough form of relief; but Hopkins, feeling that it portended a ghetto for the unemployed, liquidated the commissary system as fast as he could. The grocery order removed those on relief less from normal society. Still, it placed the family under a paternalism, compelling them to buy what the nutritionists decided they needed. Hopkins much preferred giving straight cash, even if the reliefer used it for tobacco or liquor; on the whole, he felt, more damage was done to the human spirit by loss of choice than by loss of vitamins.

Basically, however, Hopkins objected to direct relief in any form. Keeping able-bodied men in idleness, he believed, could not help but corrode morale. In 1932 the mayor of Toledo, Ohio, said: "I have seen thousands of these defeated, discouraged, hopeless men and women, cringing and fawning as they come to ask for public aid. It is a spectacle of national degeneration." It was this which Hopkins wanted to avoid in demanding a more creative response to the catastrophe. Instead of putting the unemployed on the dole, why not offer the weekly government check in exchange for labor performed for the public welfare? Work relief, Hopkins said, "preserves a man's morale. It saves his skill. It gives him a chance to do something socially useful." Of course, it would cost more than the dole. But the advocates of economy in relief, Hopkins said, never counted in the cost of depriving citizens of "their sense of independence and strength and their sense of individual destiny."

Although FERA, thrown so suddenly into the breach, could not escape direct relief as its main instrument, a wide variety of work relief projects were devised under Hopkins' relentless prodding. Thus teachers on relief rolls were assigned to country schools which would otherwise have had to close their doors; by December 1933, about 13,000 teachers, paid from relief funds, were holding classes in rural areas. FERA too had a special program to take care of transients—the thousands of jobless men roaming the country in search of work and hope. There were provisions for drought relief, and for grants to local self-help and barter associations. Hopkins invited experiment, calling on state administrators to show "imagination." Some local organizations remained resistant. This was partly because of the added expense of work relief, partly because of the

147

added administrative difficulties. And often, when they tried it, the projects were ill-conceived and unconvincing.

As the fourth winter of the depression approached, new unrest stirred among the jobless. According to a *Fortune* report, men and women on relief "do not like the dole. They are almost unanimous in demanding *work*." Radicals and Communists were tireless in exploiting disappointments and grievances. In August 1933 several thousand members of the Ohio Unemployed League marched on the State House at Columbus. "We must take control of the government," shouted Louis Budenz, one of the agitators, "and establish a workers and farmers republic." Was it safe to try and negotiate the winter of 1933–34 on the direct relief basis? It seemed more and more evident that a new and better federal effort would be necessary to meet the winter's challenge.

Hopkins, in Chicago on a field trip late in October, pondered the next step. His staff wanted him to make an all-out fight for a federal works program. Hopkins agreed in principle. But he was not sure he could sell the idea at the White House, and he was disturbed by the threat of labor opposition. In his Pullman drawing room between Chicago and Kansas City (where he was to confer with the Federal Re-employment Director of Missouri, Judge Harry S. Truman), Hopkins brooded over the problem. In Kansas City he received word from Aubrey Williams, a top FERA aide, that Samuel Gompers himself had once favored a works program, a fact which might turn aside labor objections. Encouraged, Hopkins called Washington and asked for a White House appointment.

Hopkins outlined his scheme at lunch with the President on the day of his return. Roosevelt asked how many jobs he thought he could provide. Hopkins answered four million, if he could get enough money. Roosevelt, thinking aloud, remarked that Ickes' Public Works Administration was slow in getting under way; perhaps Hopkins could get funds out of the PWA appropriations. Indeed, the whole effort might be conceived as a means of tiding the unemployed over one more winter, by which time PWA could begin to take up the slack.

This was the beginning of the Civil Works Administration. By November 15, Hopkins announced his objective: "the employment of four million by December 15, 1933." He set himself a prodigious job. Though CWA, unlike FERA, was empowered to operate works projects directly, Hopkins had no planning staff, no shelf of light public works, no formulated program. CWA jobs, moreover, had to be easy to learn and short in duration; winter weather limited the type of project available; necessary tools were in short supply. Yet Hopkins, always at his best when confronted by impossibilities, allowed nothing to get in the way of rapid expansion. He immediately converted much of his FERA staff to CWA and adopted the existing state relief organizations as CWA's local arms. Project ideas, generated in the atmosphere of pressure, came both down from Washington and up from the field. Hopkins missed his first target date—by December 14, there were only 2,610,451 on CWA rolls—but by the middle of January he was well over the 4,000,000 mark.

CWA tackled a tremendous variety of jobs. At its peak, it had about 400,000 projects in operation. About a third of CWA personnel worked on roads and highways. In the three and a half months of CWA's existence, they built or improved about 500,000 miles of secondary roads. Next in importance came schools—40,000 built or improved, with 50,000 teachers employed in country schools or in city adult education, and large numbers of playgrounds developed. CWA gave the nation nearly 500 airports and improved 500 more. It developed parks, cleared waterways, fought insect pests, dug swimming pools and sewers. Three thousand writers and artists found CWA employment utilizing their own skills. ("Hell!" said Hopkins. "They've got to eat just like other people.") Above all, it supplied work to four million Americans who would otherwise have festered in humiliation and idleness.

Of course, Hopkins paid a price for speed. In money, the cost was considerable—in the end, nearly a billion dollars. And there were administrative lapses too which Hopkins characteristically exposed before his critics could discover them. In January 1934, he lashed out at evidence of political interference and graft in CWA operations. "I never anticipated anything of the kind," he told newspapermen. "I suppose I'm naïve and unsophisticated, but that's the truth. I didn't, and I feel very badly about it." He ordered investigations, shook up incompetent or tainted state organizations and began to bring in Army officers to strengthen the program against corruption.

Lieutenant Colonel John C. H. Lee, a stern West Point engineer assigned to study CWA for the War Department, watched Hopkins' unorthodox methods with astonished admiration. "Mr. Hopkins' loose fluidity of organization," he concluded, "was justified by the results achieved. It enabled him to engage for employment in two months nearly as many persons as were enlisted and called to the colors during our year and a half of World War mobilization, and to disburse to them, weekly, a higher average rate of wage than Army or Navy pay." CWA, Lee said, reached every county and town in the United States in a period of two months during one of the most severe winters on record.

The accomplishments of the CWA were possible through the arduous efforts of the young Administrator and the group of able young assistants which he has assembled and inspired. They have worked daily long into the night with a morale easily comparable to that of a war emergency. These assistants address Mr. Hopkins fondly as "Harry." There is no rigidity or formality in their staff conferences with him, yet he holds their respect, confidence and seemingly whole-souled co-operation.

As for the reliefers themselves, FERA field investigators like Lorena Hickok and Martha Gellhorn provided graphic reports of their condition. Poignant images spilled out of these documents—the cry in September 1933 in Pennsylvania, "Our children must have shoes, or they can't go to school"; the Catholic priest in Scottville, Pennsylvania, begging for medical supplies to keep his people alive; the little boy in Houston, Texas, who refused to go to school wearing trousers of black-and-white-striped ticking because everyone would know his family was on relief; the man in Camden, New Jersey, explaining that he went to bed around seven at night "because that way you get the day over with quicker"; the South Dakota farm wife who had a recipe for soup made from Russian thistles—"It don't taste so bad, only it ain't very filling"; the sixteen-year-old girl keeping house for her family in a dark tobacco barn in Wilson County, North Carolina, the place scrubbed spotlessly clean, the girl saying sadly, "Seems like we just keep goin' lower and lower"; pinned on her bosom, as one wears a brooch, was a 1932 campaign button, a profile of Franklin Roosevelt.

In 1933 Lorena Hickok noticed evidences of Communist activity. "They are very, very busy," she wrote from Aberdeen, South Dakota, in November, "getting right down among the farmers and working like beavers." In Pennsylvania the unemployed, she felt, were "right on the edge"; "it wouldn't take much to make Communists out of them." Martha Gellhorn, moving around the country a year later, found less organized protest. The idolatry of Roosevelt, she thought, was taking the spirit out of opposition. "The problem," she wrote Hopkins, "is not one of fighting off a 'red menace' . . . but of fighting off hopelessness; despair; a dangerous feeling of helplessness and dependence." Everywhere there seemed a spreading listlessness, a whipped feeling like the hitchhiker who said to Theodore Dreiser, "I'm going downhill. I'm going to hell, really. I don't care as much as I used to." Miss Gellhorn was disturbed most of all by this smell of defeat: "I find them all in the same shape—fear, fear driving them into a state of semicollapse; cracking nerves; and an overpowering terror of the future . . . each family in its own miserable home going to pieces."

The relief rolls were changing in character. First, there had been the unemployables; then had come the working-class unemployed; but now, increasingly, white-collar workers, their savings exhausted by four years of depression, their scruples conquered by want, their self-respect eroded by fear, were going on relief. They hated it, but in the end they saw no alternative. "I simply had to murder my pride," an engineer told Lorena Hickok. "We'd lived on bread and water three weeks before I could make myself do it." "It took me a month," said a lumberman. "I used to go down there every day or so and walk past the place again and again. I just couldn't make myself go in." And with white-collar relief there came new tensions. Above all, the compulsion to cling to some semblance at least of past ways of life complicated relationships with the relief administration. "We can provide overalls, but not tailored business suits," said Miss Hickok. "We can't keep those white collars laundered."

FERA and CWA had at least kept conditions from becoming worse. On the whole, there was less revolt, less starvation, and less Communism than might have been expected. As Hugh Charles Boyle, the Roman Catholic Bishop of Pittsburgh, told Lorena Hickok, "Inadequate though it may be, the emergency unemployment relief has been and is the most stabilizing force we have. . . . The Federal Government will have to put up the money, or—well, God help us all!" And CWA, because it provided work, was received by the unemployed—or at least by those who could get on its rolls—with special gratitude. Miss Hickok was in Iowa on the first CWA pay day. "And did they want to work?" she wrote Hopkins. "In Sioux City they actually had fist fights over shovels!" "It was pathetic to watch some of the reactions," reported a CWA administrator. "I saw a few cases leave the office actually weeping for sheer happiness."

Still, Hopkins's view was that federal relief was doing only a minimal job. "We have never given adequate relief," he said in 1936. Many social workers and public officials agreed. Thus Lawrence F. Quigley, mayor of Chelsea, Massachusetts, wrote Hopkins in January 1934 that only 155 people in his town could get CWA jobs; another 2000 were congregating sullenly in City Hall; "a spark might change them into a mob." "I believe," said Mayor Quigley, "that the Federal Government, once having acknowledged its responsibility by giving jobs merely for the sake of a job, must now put every unemployed man to work doing the most useful task that can be found for him. . . . If some such remedial measure is not immediately adopted I make bold to predict fundamental and sweeping changes in the structure of our government before the end of the present year."

This was one view. Other Americans believed that any national relief program at all was too much. As the economic situation began to improve in 1934, some of this opinion began to be vocal. When someone asked him about the homeless boys riding the rails in search of employment, Henry Ford said equably, "Why, it's the best education in the world for those boys, that traveling around. They get more experience in a few months than they would in years at school." Even a liberal businessman like Robert E. Wood of Sears, Roebuck could identify relief as the New Deal's "one serious mistake." "While it is probably true that we cannot allow everyone to starve (although I personally disagree with this philosophy and the philosophy of the city social worker)," Wood wrote, "we should tighten up relief all along the line, and if relief is to be given it must be on a bare subsistence allowance." Winthrop Aldrich of the Chase National Bank called for the elimination of work relief. Lincoln Colcord, reporting to Hopkins in 1934 on talks with businessmen, summed up business opinion as one of opposition to work relief, not only because of its cost but because all work projects—even ditch digging—were deemed competitive with private industry.

There was considerable resentment too in farm areas, especially in the South. Planters complained that relief made it impossible to get cheap Negro farm labor. "I wouldn't plow nobody's mule from sunrise to sunset for 50 cents per day," as one aggrieved farmer wrote to Governor Eugene Talmadge of Georgia, "when I could get $1.30 for pretending to work on a DITCH." (Talmadge forwarded this letter to Roosevelt, who dictated a biting reply. "I take it, from your sending the letter of the gentleman from Smithville to me," the President said, "that you approve of paying farm labor 40 to 50 cents per day." Figuring in the seasonal character of the employment, Roosevelt reckoned this to be $60 to $75 a year. "Somehow I cannot get it into my head that wages on such a scale make possible a reasonable American standard of living." On reflection, Roosevelt decided to send the letter under Hopkins's signature.)

Most pervasive of all was the feeling that the whole theory of federal relief was incompatible with American individualism. Much of this concern was doubtless the rationalization of objections to high taxes, to high wages, and to any increase in federal power; but much too reflected authentic anxieties over what dependence on government handouts might do to the American people. "Our present efforts in the direction of relief," wrote the banker Frank A. Vanderlip in a statement repeated ten thousand times by business leaders in these years, "have broken down self-reliance and industry. I profoundly believe that society does not owe every man a living."

It was easy to ridicule such arguments. When Hoover attacked federal aid to the unemployed for weakening the "moral fiber" of the people, Harold Ickes retorted that Hoover as President had not hesitated "to weaken the moral fiber of banks and insurance companies and manufacturing and industrial enterprises" by handing them millions of dollars. Hoover's policies no doubt justified Ickes's retort. Yet the issue raised by conservatives was a real one. Hopkins himself worried about moral effects: that, of course, was why he preferred to offer the unemployed jobs rather than the dole. Lorena Hickok was alarmed when she heard little boys in Salt Lake City boasting about whose father had been on relief longer. Some people on relief, she commented sorrowfully, became "gimmies"; "the more you do for people, the more they demand." Social workers said, "They are beginning to regard CWA as their due—[they feel] that the Government actually owes it to them. And they want more." Some projects were themselves too obviously sham to help the morale of either the workers or the public. The term "boondoggling" arose to describe the most futile of the leaf-raking or ditch-digging efforts.

TOO MUCH, TOO SOON

THE opponents of the New Deal didn't waste any time; relief measures had been barely started when newspaper editorial writers, political cartoonists and satirists swung into action, writing off the whole idea as a "sinful" waste of the taxpayer's dollar. Frank Sullivan's "cliché expert," Mr. Arbuthnot, exemplifies the old-line conservative's reaction to relief, and the whole New Deal, in the following excerpt from a fictional dialogue.

Q: Do you mean "orgy of spending?"

A: That's just the phrase I was searching for. You know how it's all going to end up?

Q: How?

A: Inflation. We're going to have the worst inflation in this country you ever saw. These taxes. Twenty-five cents out of every dollar goes for taxes. . . . Now, you take relief. I certainly think it's all right to help people who deserve help, but I don't believe in all this coddling. . . . The trouble with half the people on relief is they don't *want* to work. You can't tell me that most of these people can't find work. If a man wants a job bad enough he'll find one all right. . . .

Q: What about the WPA, Mr. Arbuthnot?

A: Oh, the shovel brigade. I'm against the WPA and the PWA and all this alphabet-soup stuff. Say, speaking of the WPA, did you hear the one about the WPA worker and King Solomon? Why is a WPA worker like King Solomon?

Q: I heard it. Now then—

A: Because he takes his pick and goes to bed.*

The Hundred Days legislation had hardly got on the books when *Vanity Fair* published the following spoof of relief measures.

JOHN RIDDELL

HOW TO RELIEVE EVERYBODY†

EVER since I can remember (which is about the day before yesterday), the newspapers have been filled with columns and columns of figures, statements and statistics explaining the latest Government plans for Farm

* Frank Sullivan, *A Pearl in Every Oyster* (Boston, Little, Brown, 1938).
† Condensed from *Vanity Fair,* August 1933.

Relief. We have read about the Debenture Plan, the Equalization Fee Plan, the Voluntary Allotment Plan, and the Plan Against Surplus Production. After studying all these Plans to relieve the Farmer, therefore, I have finally put forth my own Plan, whish is known as the Plan to Relieve People Who Have to Read All These Plans. Personally, I feel a little relieved already.

Before I go into this particular Plan of mine and explore its possibilities, armed only with a flashlight and a ball of twine, I think I should attempt first to explain the whole Farm Problem in such a way as to confuse everybody even further about it, if possible; and in order to mix up the reader completely I should like to offer the following simple illustration of just what is meant by Farm Relief.

For example, let us say that Mr. A., a farmer, has just raised a parsnip. Nobody wants a parsnip, least of all Mr. A.; and so the Government steps in and offers Mr. A. five dollars if he will take his parsnip somewhere and get rid of it. Mr. A. gets rid of the parsnip and spends the five dollars for parsnip seeds, with which he raises one hundred more parsnips. He gets rid of these parsnips to the Government for five hundred dollars; and with this five hundred dollars he goes into the parsnip business on a large scale, raising millions of parsnips and getting rid of them to the Government at five dollars a parsnip. Thus Mr. A. is relieved because he raises parsnips, everybody else is relieved because he gets rid of them again, and the Government is relieved in time of all the money in the Treasury. This is known, roughly, as Farm Relief.

I have devised my own Farm Relief Plan, which contains several handy methods designed especially to cut down this surplus production as far as possible. For example:

CUTWORMS

One suggestion for limiting production would be to include a few high-grade cutworms henceforth in every package of seed sent out by Our Congressmen in Washington. (In certain sections of the country, boll weevils, corn-borers or Japanese beetles could be substituted.) By sowing these busy little worms in his garden, the Farmer would soon find his entire production was being cut in half, usually right at the roots.

SUBSTITUTING SOMETHING ELSE FOR "SEED"

One reason the Farmer produces too much wheat or cotton is because he sows wheat-seeds and cotton-seeds, which grow up to be wheat or cotton. A second suggestion for limiting production, therefore, would be to sow things in the garden which would *not* grow up to be wheat or cotton, such as china cup-handles, rusty nails, suspender buttons, or old galoshes.

SUBSTITUTING SOMETHING ELSE FOR "SOIL"

For that matter, production may also be curtailed considerably by removing the "soil" or "dirt" in which these seeds flourish, and substituting something else in which they will *not* grow, such as a solid cement walk or an old mattress. A good substitute for soil consists of two parts gravel, equal parts of crushed brick, large pebbles and sand, one part ground glass, and just a dash of soapy water from the kitchen window.

WEEDS

In weeding the Farmer could cut down his surplus production considerably if he would pull up the plants, and leave the weeds.

FORECLOSURES

If all these other methods of limiting production fail to work, however, we can always fall back on the sure plan of having the banks foreclose all the farm-mortgages which they hold. Once we get the bankers to take over the farms in this country and run them the way they ran their banks, we won't need to worry about surplus production. They'll have every farm closed in a week.

In the meantime, besides cutting down surplus production, my Farm Bill goes ahead at the same time and increases public demand for what the Farmer *does* produce. In other words, according to my plan, the Farmer not only produces nothing at all, but in addition he gets a much better price for it. This is accomplished by the simple principle known as Rotation of Crops.

Rotation of Crops consists of planting all the different crops which a Farmer might raise—i.e., oats, peas, lima beans and corn (succotash), squash, pumpkins, apples, cider, or hooked rugs—on the different levels of a large machine built like a Ferris Wheel, and then rotating the crops slowly in front of the consumer. The moment the consumer shows the least bit of interest in one of the crops, such as radishes, the Farmer presses a button and the wheel turns, elevating the level with the radishes up into the air, just out of the consumer's reach. This teases the consumer, and he wants the radishes more than ever. By rotating his radish crop two or three times before the consumer's nose, the Farmer will soon have the harassed radish-lover completely in his power, and not only can he get any price he wants for his radishes, but in addition can probably palm off a few old beets or turnips as well.

Unfortunately, there is one angle of the Farm Adjustment Act which has never been made very clear, and that is the leasing proposal. According to this suggestion, the Government will go out with a lot of money (all those billions and billions of dollars which have been lying around for years just gathering dust) and rent out of bearing all the poor lands and surplus farms. These leased farms would then be posted by the Government as officially "out of production," and thereafter any ear of corn or spear of wheat poking above the surface in the spring would be arrested on sight.

One method of putting this land to use would be to cut it up into small portable sections, and ship it to the larger cities to use for parking spaces.

Another use for this surplus land would be to turn it over to the public for peasant-dancing. There is almost no peasant-dancing going on in this country today, and this would be a very good chance to get it started. In every news-reel that I have seen for the last year, there has always been a scene showing Bavarian peasants or Tyrolean peasants wearing short pants and little hats with feathers in them, stamping up and down and snapping their fingers and occasionally shouting "Hey!"

Last but not least, our Farm Bill must solve the problem of how to persuade the farmers to *accept* all this money which the Government wants to pay them. Judging from the attitude of our agricultural experts, the American farmer is a highly sensitive creature, whose pride would be cut to the quick if the Government simply went out and handed him this money as a gift. In fact, the whole purpose of the Farm Bill seems to be to attempt to disguise this gift to the farmer under vague and elaborate terms such as the Debenture Plan or the Voluntary Allotment Plan or the Equalization Fee Plan. Working on this theory, therefore, my own Farm Bill has devised several further methods of tricking the Farmer into accepting money from the Government without embarrassing him, let alone the Government:

1. Put the money in a colored Easter Egg and leave it on his doorstep some night.

2. Bury the money at various points about his farm—under the gatepost, behind the barn, or in his mattress—and then write the Farmer an anonymous letter telling him where it is hidden. The Farmer will enter into the spirit of the treasure-hunt, and he will not know where the money is coming from. (Inasmuch as the Government won't know either, this will make it unanimous.)

3. If these methods fail, the agricultural expert can put on a false

157

mustache and tell the Farmer that he is a long-lost uncle named Abner and that he has just decided to leave the Farmer his entire fortune in his will.

4. Give the money to the Farmer as a prize for making the largest number of words out of the sentence: "Everybody loves the Farmer."

5. Put the money in a bank, and then make the Farmer president of the bank. In this way, the Farmer will find himself taking the money out of force of habit.

In this way the Farmer will be persuaded sooner or later to accept this money which we are all trying so hard to give him. In the course of time the Government doubtless will manage to turn over all the money in the Treasury to the Farmer. Thus the Farmer will have all the money in the country. Then it will be up to him to pass a *Non*-Farm Relief Bill, to relieve everybody else.

ARTHUR M. SCHLESINGER, JR.

MORE ON THE RISE
OF FEDERAL RELIEF*

YET WHAT was the answer? Hopkins and the Administration considered relief of some sort inevitable; the alternative was revolution. If this were the case, work relief seemed the form most compatible with self-respect and individualism. And the argument for work relief was more compelling in 1933–34 than it might be later. At a time when morale was low and before other spending programs were showing results, an emergency works program could have marked stimulative effect, both economically and psychologically.

For their part, the businessmen had no clear alternative to present. Some doubtless wished to abolish relief altogether. But few were prepared to avow this as their objective. This left most in the unsatisfying position of deploring the moral consequences of relief while advocating the form of relief which by their own theory was morally most deleterious—the cash handout, the detested dole. This contradiction did not, however, notably restrain many from doing all they could to forestall a works program.

Work relief really presupposed a national effort, since forty-eight separate works programs were inconceivable. Consequently returning relief to the states would effectively doom the works idea. And it would save money over-all; since state governments could not create the market for their own securities, the resources available to them for relief were limited. Best of all, such a policy would diminish the power of the national government. So the restoration of relief to the local communities became the key conservative issue. In December 1934, for example, a group of business leaders meeting at White Sulphur Springs under Chamber of Commerce and N.A.M. auspices, demanded that the states take over relief. But when *Today* Magazine wired state governors asking them what they thought about this proposal, only one of the thirty-seven replying—Gene Talmadge —agreed. Thirty-three said that their states had already reached the limit of their contributions.

* From Arthur M. Schlesinger, Jr.'s *The Coming of the New Deal* (Boston, Houghton Mifflin, 1959).

The fiscal point was only one of the arguments for federal relief. Many observers in addition considered a national program better proof against waste and graft. "Turning federal funds over to the states for administration," as Senator James F. Byrnes of South Carolina put it, "would mean more politics instead of less politics in administration." "If the relief system were not centralized where centralization is necessary," said the political writers Joseph Alsop and Turner Catledge in *The Saturday Evening Post,* "the inevitable result would be the greatest pork-barrel riot Congress has ever seen."

Still, some wanted a pork-barrel riot. Others wanted to kill work relief. Others wistfully hoped that defederalization might bring on a new access of local responsibility. And so a debate began which continued through the rest of the decade.

The first phase of the debate boiled up over the extension of CWA in January and February 1934. Criticism of CWA had been muted at first— a fact plausibly explained by Al Smith in December 1933 on the ground that "no sane local official who has hung up an empty stocking over the municipal fireplace is going to shoot Santa Claus just before a hard Christmas." (The embattled Hopkins replied with feeling, "The hell they won't. Santa Claus really needs a bullet-proof vest.") But the charges of waste and corruption—despite the fact that Hopkins was the first to reveal them—strengthened the hands of those who had disliked the works program all along. More important, Roosevelt, under pressure from southern Democrats and from his Director of the Budget, Lewis Douglas, was beginning to feel that the expensive CWA operation must end for the sake of the budget.

Hopkins, and most social workers and liberal Democrats, disagreed with this decision. So too did many Republicans; Governor Alfred M. Landon of Kansas, for example, wrote Roosevelt, "This civil-works program is one of the soundest, most constructive policies of your administration, and I cannot urge too strongly its continuance." To the left of the New Deal, Norman Thomas organized a march on Washington to protest against termination. In a single week nearly 60,000 letters and wires deluged the CWA office and the White House. CWA workers engaged in strikes and demonstrations. Yet, once the President had made his decision, Hopkins accepted it and, with his usual brusque efficiency, destroyed the organization he had so brilliantly built up. Roosevelt, in the atmosphere of neurotic administrators weeping on all available shoulders—the Johnsons, Richbergs, Peeks, Hulls—was grateful for Hopkins's uncomplaining loyalty.

What remained of CWA was transferred to the Emergency Work Relief Program of FERA, though work relief continued here only in diminished form. Where CWA had offered jobs at regular wages both to reliefers and to jobless persons who, for whatever reason—probably pride—had refused to go on relief rolls, FERA had to confine itself to those on relief and pay them only substandard wages; and, where CWA had planned and operated its own projects, FERA could finance only state activities. FERA nonetheless carried on substantial parts of the CWA program, including the white-collar projects.

In addition, FERA developed new programs of its own during 1934. An experiment of special interest was the Federal Surplus Relief Corporation, first conceived in the fall of 1933 as a means of circumventing the irony whereby crops piled up in the countryside while the cities went hungry. "Will you and Peek and Harry Hopkins," Roosevelt wrote Henry Wallace in September, "have a talk and possibly prepare a plan for purchase of surplus commodities such as butter, cheese, condensed milk, hog products and flour, to meet relief needs during the course of the winter?" Jerome Frank proposed doing it through an independent corporation; and, starting in December, the Federal Surplus Relief Corporation began to acquire surplus commodities with the double purpose of helping the farmer by removing price-depressing stocks from the market and of helping the unemployed by giving him food. The Corporation began with pork from the martyred pigs and soon moved from food to surplus cotton, blankets, and even coal.

As FSRC operations expanded in 1934, some businessmen began to charge it with the sin of competing with private enterprise. When FSRC purchased cotton and sent it to FERA workrooms to be made into mattresses for the unemployed, the mattress manufacturers erupted in indignation; nor were they satisfied by FERA's demonstration that the mattresses went only to people who, because they had no money, could not possibly subtract from the mattress market. The drought of 1934 intensified both FSRC activities and business criticism. Taking over cattle which otherwise would have perished uselessly in the drought areas, FSRC proposed that they be converted into canned beef and shoes for men and women on relief. These plans provoked a storm of denunciation. Shoe manufacturers virtuously refused to rent the government the necessary machinery. Such adverse reaction restricted the scope of FSRC activities. In the two years before it was transferred to AAA in 1935, the total value of surplus commodities which FSRC was permitted to distribute amounted to only about 265 million dollars.

FERA's support of self-help production roused equally strong business resentment. The self-help movement had sprung up spontaneously in the early Depression. People who had no money could still work, and it seemed logical to some to try to trade what they could make for what they needed. In time, it began to seem similarly logical for state governments to provide facilities to enable the unemployed to manufacture things necessary for their own subsistence. FERA was consequently authorized by Congress to make capital grants to states to promote the "barter of goods and services."

In June 1934 the State Relief Commission of Ohio set up the Ohio Relief Production Units, Incorporated; and in a few months the state leased a dozen factories, in which unemployed men and women made dresses, overalls, furniture, and stoves for their own use or for exchange with relief agencies in other states. Half a dozen more states were similarly preparing to bring together idle labor and idle factories (often mattress factories or canning plants) to produce for the unemployed. It was estimated in the summer of 1934 that probably 50,000 families through the nation were members of self-help groups, some organized privately, some under state sponsorship. In the fall, these production projects accounted for 15 per cent of the employment under the Emergency Work Relief Program.

As these programs developed, however, the phrase "production-for-use" began to acquire sinister connotations. The impression grew in business circles that the self-help program was the entering wedge of socialism. The "Ohio Plan" was suspicious enough; and when Upton Sinclair, running for governor in California, envisaged production-for-use by the unemployed as the nucleus for a radical reconstruction of the economy, reaction was vigorous and unequivocal. FERA, because of business hostility, could grant in two years only a little more than three million dollars to self-help co-operatives (this figure does not, however, include the rather more significant support production-for-use received in the works programs). By 1935 the production-for-use and the self-help programs were both on their way out. (Only the President himself remained interested as when, confronted with new supplies of electric power from the new federal dams, he asked Ickes and Hopkins in the spring of 1935 to consider the government's going into the business of producing aluminum, nickel, or magnesium with unemployed labor.)

FERA's Rural Rehabilitation Division was charged with the responsibility of relief on the countryside. Its most useful efforts went to what was known as "rehabilitation in place"—that is, loans to farm families for seed, fertilizer, livestock, or farm tools. It also engaged less profitably in attempts

162

to set up rural communities, based on Roosevelt's old dream of decentralized industry and subsistence homesteads. Eventually these activities were absorbed by the Resettlement Administration in 1935. The Transient Division of FERA continued through 1934 to deal with the still large numbers of men on the road; this program disappeared in 1935.

Some of FERA's most striking successes were in particular localities. Thus imaginative FERA leadership saved Key West, Florida, from decay and probable extinction. In 1934 two-thirds of the inhabitants of Key West were on relief. The town government was bankrupt, and local services had wholly broken down, leaving the streets cluttered with garbage and rubbish. J. F. Stone, Jr., the regional FERA administrator, persuaded the governor of Florida to declare a state of "civil emergency," under which municipal powers in Key West were to be delegated to the Florida Emergency Relief Administration. It was an act of dubious legality, but it was enough. The Key West Volunteer Work Corps was then organized to clean up the streets and beaches; houses were painted and renovated, hotels reopened, an air service subsidized (by FERA funds), a federal art project set up, the FERA Marimba Band formed—and Key West entered a new, profitable and perhaps ultimately even more ruinous phase as a resort town.

Following the demobilization of CWA, FERA in 1934 resumed its efforts to hold the relief line, at the same time continuing under Hopkins's driving leadership to diversify and improve the quality of its projects. If much of FERA activity at this point had the air of marking time, it was because the relief picture could not be clear until the Public Works Administration swung into full operation.

THE NEW DEAL—JUNIOR DIVISION

OF ALL the legislation of the early days of the New Deal, the law which created the Civilian Conservation Corps probably was most directly and completely the brain child of President Roosevelt. For more than twenty years the conservation of natural resources had been for him a subject of special interest; and in the particular problem of reforestation as a method of land conservation he was an expert, with a background of personal experience as well as governmental program. In 1932, as Governor of New York State, he had put 10,000 unemployed to work on reforestation projects. Years before that, he had given over many acres on his Hyde Park estate to trees in order to renew the land, so that, as he once explained it, his great-grandchildren would be able to farm the land as productively as it had been farmed in the nineteenth century.

In his acceptance speech at the 1932 National Convention, Roosevelt had spoken of putting a million unemployed to work in the forests of the nation; and it was to this idea that he turned, after his inauguration, immediately after the more urgent banking crisis was brought under control. He had the assistance of several experts and advisers in formulating the organizational details, but it was substantially his idea that was offered to Congress in a message less than three weeks after he became President. Public opinion was not overwhelmingly favorable when the measure came up for hearings in Congress. Some influential people, including members of the President's Cabinet, thought that the organizing of large groups of unemployed and probably embittered young men might lead to armed rebellion. The labor movement feared the regimentation of labor and a depressing effect on wages. Observers on the Right saw the specter of communism, and those on the Left saw the threat of fascism. Nevertheless, under the sponsorship mainly of Senator Robert F. Wagner, of New York, the bill authorizing the establishment of the CCC became law on March 31, 1933.

The CCC was placed under the jurisdiction of the Labor Department, which quickly set up its apparatus for administering and recruiting. The War Department mobilized regular and reserve officers to operate the camps.

Enlistment in the CCC was limited to single men between the ages of eighteen and twenty-five, from families that were on relief; and it was, of course, voluntary. Everywhere, the recruiting personnel found eligible young men eager to join the organization, especially after the earliest joiners began to write home about their experience.

"By the middle of June," Arthur Schlesinger says, "1,300 camps were established; by the end of July over 300,000 boys were in the woods. They discharged a thousand conservation tasks which had gone too long unperformed. They planted trees, made reservoirs and fish ponds, built check dams, dug diversion ditches, raised bridges and fire towers, fought blister rust and pine-twig blight and the Dutch elm disease, restored historic battlefields, cleared beaches and camping grounds, and in a multitude of ways protected and improved parks, forests, watersheds and recreational areas.

"They did more, of course, than reclaim and develop natural resources. They reclaimed and developed themselves. They came from large cities and from small towns, from slum street corners and from hobo jungles, from the roads and the rails and from nowhere. One out of every ten or eleven was a Negro. Some had never seen mountains before, had never waded in running brooks or slept in the open air. Boys from the East Side of New York found themselves in Glacier Park, boys from New Jersey at Mount Hood in Oregon, boys from Texas in Wyoming. Their muscles hardened, their bodies filled out, their self-respect returned. They learned trades; more important, they learned about America, and they learned about other Americans." *

A monthly wage of thirty dollars was given each enrollee, part of which was a family allotment, and a green uniform was worn in winter, olive-drab in the summer. From 1933 through 1941, some 2,750,000 recruits served in the CCC. Because

* From *The Coming of the New Deal.*

the per-capita cost was about $1,075 per year, the CCC could be said to be one of the more expensive forms of relief, but this cost was more than offset by the gains in conservation, as well as the preservation of the health of America's young men.

A second major youth program was the National Youth Administration, begun in June 1935. At the height of its effectiveness, the NYA had enrolled more than 600,000 boys and girls between the ages of sixteen and twenty-five. At least seven eighths of the enrolled were given student aid to enable them to finish high school or college. The remainder were given aid in part-time employment out of school—lettering signs, sewing, soil-erosion control, et cetera. Many critics charged that the NYA was inefficiently managed and leaned too far to the left politically; its success depended largely on local administration, and with only the small appropriations granted under the NYA there was undoubtedly a tendency to boondoggle.

But if you were young and a member of a depression family in the early Thirties, the CCC and the NYA restored hope and a faith in the future. An instance of this is provided in the following first-person narrative of a young Negro CCC enrollee as transcribed by two writers on a WPA (Works Progress Administration) project.

NELLIE G. TOLER AND JAMES R. ASWELL

WEARY WILLIE*

MILLARD KETCHUM had just come in from his day's work in the field. He was still in his blue CCC work uniform. "This is better clothes than I ever had at home," he said, "before I got to the CCC. You see, at home they was so many of us, we couldn't have much clothes to wear and in summer time we jist didn't wear no shoes, and no shirts much, nor nothing else much.

"Let me git you some where to set if you want to talk a while. Hey, Sarge! kin I git a few minutes off to talk here to this lady here? Okay, Sarge."

When asked about his family, he said, "Well, my mama she come from Bundy County. She was a Dunlap. My papa, he come from Chester County, over here nigh Henderson. They live at Zama now and been there about two year. I ain't got so big a family to keep up, not so big as lots of the boys has. I jist got five brothers and one sister. I'm the oldest and I ain't but nineteen year old.

"My brothers, they's named Winston Gormer, Jim Ables, Luther Crocker, Ray Slowey, and Jonathan Junior. My sister she's named Pearlie Jo and she's thirteen.

"We's farmers and renters. Ain't ever owned no home as yet. We lives at Zama now with a Mr. Lew Truitt. We've got two big houses on each side of us and they's shore pretty, too. We ain't got so big a house to live in—jist a small house, but my mother she's a good housekeeper and keeps everything spick and span. Ain't much trouble, you know, with a little house to keep it clean. We ain't got so much in it neither. Jist enough to make it comfortable for us. We got plenty of beds, though, arn bedstids, and all. You know jist like most any pore farmer's got, but enough to do us all.

"I ain't never been much to school. Jist went to the second grade, that's all, excepting what I learned here in the CCC. I could have gone, I guess, but for some reason didn't keer nothing about it. Jist didn't want to go.

* From *These Are Our Lives* (Chapel Hill, North Carolina University Press, 1939).

I would have went if I wanted to. They didn't make me not go. We jist didn't none of us go. I got one brother that went to the second grade, too, and my sister she went to the first. Then she quit. We jist wasn't a family that like school.

"I quit that old second grade when I was fourteen. I left home and went to work. Been on my own ever since. I went down here to Woolard and went to work on a farm. The man he was sick and not able to work and had to have somebody to help him. That's why I got to work so long, and even got the job at all. Got twenty dollars a month."

I asked. "Would you go on to school and finish now if you had the chance?"

"Don't know whether I could or not. I would really like to learn." He flushed and scowled. "The boys they make fun of us when we can't read the funnies nor nothing. I look at pictures in books, and things like that in the recreation hall, so they won't laugh at me. I wish I had gone on to school now and would go as far as I could if I git the chance. Guess I couldn't git much learning now though, could I? I'm too old most to learn now."

I asked if he wanted to stay with the CCC.

"Yes'm, as long as I kin, because I git plenty to eat here. I didn't always at home, not the same kind of stuff, anyhow. Guess we had plenty, such as it was, at home, but it jist wasn't good like this, nor enough of it for the kind it was. I git to go more, git to see more. I'm learning too. I watch the others, and then, I have more clothes and can keep cleaner too.

"You see where we is at home they don't go to school. None of them has gone any since they moved to Rivers County. They's three at home now to go to school, but they ain't went none and guess they won't ever. I got higher'n any of 'em. My littlest brother, he three year old now. I git thirty dollars a month and send twenty-two of it home to them. They need it! My papa he don't make enough to do for all, jist renting and farming like he does.

"You see, my pap drinks some. Not all the time, but he gits drunk at times, and that makes it hard on mama. I got drunk a few times. First time I jist all at once didn't know what was wrong. I jist couldn't walk, so I set down and went to sleep. I don't drink now. I quit since I got in the C's which I've been in nineteen months now.

"I ain't never voted yet. Ain't old enough and don't think I will till I git old enough, neither. My papa, he's a 'Publican, but I'm going to be a Democrat myself. He don't vote in every election neither. But I'm going to when I git old enough. I'll take them all in as they come.

167

"Do I go to church?

"Well, no'm. Not now. But while in the C's I do. The chaplain preaches to us two times a month, and I like to hear him. He makes tears come in my eyes, too. I quit drinking all on account of him. I'm a good boy now. I don't go to church at town much because I'm afraid they'll laugh at me. My mother she's a Baptist, but I jist go to any of them. I always give some money when I have it to give.

"Down home it's different. I've rambled all over that place and they ain't got no churches down there. I been there two years and ain't ever seen no church yet. Some of my little brothers ain't never seen no church yet.

"No'm. Ain't ever been sick to speak of. Ain't never had nothing but measles and 'pendicitis and had them both in Camp and got my bills paid. If I'd been at home, I wouldn't had no operation, couldn't have paid for it. I skipped all other sorts of being sick. I ain't never had pneumonia sickness yet. I jist about got all the doctor bills at home paid up now because I sent my whole check home and done without going to shows or smoking and everything to git them all paid up. The family's sick lots."

"Are you ever homesick?"

"Yes, heck! I have enough to eat, but by gosh, when the rest gits to raising cane to go home, sometimes it makes me homesick, too. I don't git there much because I can't pay my way. I like to see my mother though. You see, at home we have peas with bugs and weevils in them. We have sweet potatoes and I don't like peas, and sometimes we have pudding and meat when Mama has time to make pudding for us.

"You ought to go to my house some time. We got a pump, and the water ain't much good. But Mom she's clean. They jist don't make them no cleaner than my ma. And I got a girl at home. She jist lives half a mile of me. We go walking every time I go home, because we ain't got no car. We go boat riding sometimes, but I don't like swimming. I can't swim and, anyway, I don't want to see my girl in swimming and nearly naked like most of them goes. I ain't going in for anybody looking like that. I kissed her last time I was home, but didn't do that till after dark. I ain't never asked no girls here at Belgrade to go with me nowhere. I'm afraid they won't. Anyhow, I'm going to marry some day when I git a good job to keep her up. It would be too many children to keep up on what I make now. Mama needs what I make for the ones at home."

"What does your father do?"

"Blame if I know. Nothing. Jist sets around the house after he gits off work at night. You see, he farms. After the crop is laid by, he don't do nothing much. Jist sets around. He might go out to the stores some. They's three or four little stores around there, about half a mile apart. He won't let me go off in a car. I went riding in an auto one time with my girl and a whole lot of us. It runned off in a ditch and I ain't got in none of them no more. I jist ain't going no more. I'm afraid.

"I git up about five in the morning, eat breakfast, go to morning classes, then go to the field. I don't work nearly so hard in this as I do in the field at home. I git to be with lots of boys that I wouldn't at home. They help me lots, show me how to do things I wouldn't have never knowed about. I like all my bosses and I like all the fellers. They tease me sometimes, but they like me, too.

"They call me Weary Willie. I guess it's because I look so sleepy-headed. I go to the shows some and I guess I make much as I need. I spend every blame penny I git my fingers on. I get eight dollars a month to spend. I sure do run through with it. Bet I could spend twenty dollars without half trying."

ON A TRAIN TO MEMPHIS

IF THE CCC had been in existence as early as 1931, could there ever have been a Scottsboro Case? It's an interesting speculation.

The nine Scottsboro boys were marked by the Depression, members of that army of 200,000 roving the country; with perhaps another fifty to sixty young people, they were hoboing on a freight train bound for Memphis.

It was March 25, 1931—their last day of freedom for several years; almost twenty years would go by before the last one, Andrew Wright, gained his release.

SCOTTSBORO BOYS*

1931

March 24—Two white girls, Victoria Price and Ruby Bates, from Huntsville, Alabama, hobo their way to Chattanooga and stay there overnight.

March 25—They return on a freight train leaving Chattanooga for Alabama. On the train are a number of Negro and white boys who engage in a fight, the white boys being thrown off the train. Alleged rape of the two girls by the Negro boys follows. When the train pulls into Paint Rock, Alabama, at 1:30 P.M. nine Negro boys, aged thirteen to twenty, are arrested and locked up at Scottsboro, the county seat. Victoria Price and Ruby Bates are examined by doctors that afternoon.

The attitude of the community becomes so threatening that the governor calls out the militia late that night.

March 26—The Negro boys are taken to Gadsden, Alabama, under military protection.

March 31—The grand jury, called into session at Scottsboro the previous day, indicts the nine boys for rape.

April 6-9—The boys are tried at Scottsboro and all are convicted except

* Abstracted, by the editor, from Dr. Allan K. Chalmers' *They Shall Be Free* (Garden City, N. Y., Doubleday, 1951).

Roy Wright, in whose case the jury disagreed. All are sentenced to death. The boys were represented by a white attorney from Chattanooga, one Stephen Reddy, retained by a local ministers' association, and local lawyers appointed by the court.

April–May—Atttorneys for the International Labor Defense and the National Association for the Advancement of Colored People enter the case. George W. Chamlee of Chattanooga, former county solicitor general, is retained by some of the defendants.

June 22—Motion for a new trial is argued by J. R. Brodsky of the ILD and is denied.

July 10—Executions for this day are postponed pending appeals to higher courts.

July 1931–March 1932—Protests from all over the world are registered by radicals, labor unions, important personages, ministers, et cetera.

1932

March 24—The Alabama State Supreme Court affirms the conviction of seven defendants but reverses the conviction of Eugene Williams on the ground that he was a minor and as such could not be tried in the Circuit Court until after a hearing in the Juvenile Court. The court denies a rehearing on April 9.

April 27—Ada Wright, mother of Andrew and Roy Wright, sails for Europe with J. L. Engdahl, general secretary of the ILD, to address meetings in many countries.

July 3—150,000 German workers fill the Lustgarten in Berlin to hear Mrs. Wright plead for the lives of her sons and the other defendants.

According to Dr. Chalmers, Mother Wright's trip to twenty-eight foreign countries was so successful that the Communist ILD arranged for at least eight other "Mother Wrights" to appear simultaneously in widely scattered parts of the world. Nobody knows accurately how much money the Communists raised for the Scottsboro Case. Some have estimated as high as a million dollars. According to Dr. Chalmers, a reasonable estimate of ILD expenditures during the years they were actively engaged in the case was in the neighborhood of 50–60,000 dollars. The ILD gets credit for organizing the defense of the boys in the early years and maintaining the early fight, but because of the clumsiness of some of their work, suspicions were aroused that the Communists had hold of such a good thing they weren't in a hurry to let it go.

October 10—The appeal to the United States Supreme Court is argued by Walter H. Pollak, retained by the ILD.

November 7—The United States Supreme Court reverses the conviction of the seven defendants on the ground that appointment of counsel appearing for them in the original trial at Scottsboro was inadequate and ineffective and violative of their constitutional rights. A new trial is ordered.

1933

January 5—Ruby Bates, at Huntsville, Alabama, writes a letter to a boy friend denying that the Negro youths attacked her. Local police secure the note.

January 23—The ILD secures a court order to photostat the Ruby Bates letter for use as defense evidence.

At Birmingham, Judge M. P. McCoy hears a writ of habeas corpus asking for the release of Roy Wright, still held in jail though unsentenced.

January 30—Writ is dismissed. Roy Wright is still held.

March 13—Samuel S. Leibowitz, New York criminal lawyer, is retained by the ILD.

March 27—The case of Haywood Patterson, the oldest defendant, is separated from the others by the State of Alabama, and he is placed on trial at Decatur.

April 9—Patterson is convicted and the jury imposes the death penalty. (He was defended by Leibowitz, J. R. Brodsky and G. W. Chamlee, all retained by the ILD. Ruby Bates appeared at the trial and reversed her previous testimony, denying that the boys committed rape on her or Victoria Price. Her story is challenged by Victoria Price who maintains her original testimony.)

April 16—J. R. Brodsky files with Judge Horton a motion for a new trial for Haywood Patterson on the ground that the conviction was against the weight of evidence.

April 28—The Scottsboro boys protest ill treatment in Jefferson County jail, in Birmingham, with a hunger strike.

June 1—Judge Horton orders two of the boys under sixteen years of age to be transferred to the Juvenile Court.

June 22—Judge Horton grants the motion for a new trial of Haywood Patterson and sets aside the conviction with a lengthy opinion reviewing the case and concluding that the conviction was not justified by the evidence.

172

November–December—Haywood Patterson, on trial for the third time, from November 20 to December 1, before Judge W. W. Callahan at Decatur, is convicted and again the jury imposes the death penalty. Clarence Norris, another defendant, is put on trial immediately after and is similarly convicted after a week. Both boys are represented by Leibowitz, Brodsky and Chamlee.

1934

February 24—Motions for a new trial are denied by Judge Callahan.

May 1934–January 1935—The Alabama Supreme Court again affirms the convictions; in November petitions are filed in the United States Supreme Court for review of both convictions.

1935

January–February—The United States Supreme Court on January 7 grants petitions for review, and the appeals are argued on February 15–18 before the Court by Leibowitz and Walter H. Pollak.

April 1—The Supreme Court reverses the convictions of both boys on the ground that Negroes were excluded from the panels of grand and petit jurors which indicted and tried the boys.

May 1—New warrants are sworn out by Victoria Price, the only complaining witness since the withdrawal of Ruby Bates from the prosecution.

November 13—The grand jury at Scottsboro returns new indictments for rape against all the boys *including the two transferred to the Juvenile Court.*

December—The Scottsboro Defense Committee is formed, composed of all agencies co-operating in the defense: the ILD, the NAACP, the American Civil Liberties Union, the Methodist Federation for Social Service, the League for Industrial Democracy, and the Church League for Industrial Democracy (Episcopal).

The head of the new Defense Committee was Dr. Allan K. Chalmers of the New York Broadway Tabernacle Church and from this point on the tide begins to turn ever so slightly in favor of the boys. As soon as the Committee was functioning, it had a neuropsychiatric case study made of each of the boys. The following is an excerpt of a "stream of talk" report on one of the boys. (Remember they had now been in prison for five to six years.)

"While out in the street I suffered with asthma. Some nights I can't catch my breath. This steel and concrete just kills me. No outlet, no exercise, no window in front of my cell; some nights I just can't get my breath. I have a hurting in my right side and my left side of my head. When I lay down I just can't catch my breath—all stove up. Would like to know the cause of that.

"How is my mind, Doc? I know I done lost my health. My health ain't so good. Then to some things I can remember just as good and then some I am forgetful. Like I know what year I was born in but I just couldn't think of it just now. Doc! I tell you the truth I am just lucky to be living. I know you hate to hear the truth, but I just as soon be dead at times as be living. It seems that they like to pick at me. I ain't done nothing and I can't understand what I am in solitary for.

"Been in solitary a year the twenty-fourth of this month and every doctor in the U.S. knows that as long as I been in here I ain't in good condition. Every now and then a pain hits me back of my head. I can't understand. I feel like I am not going to get up or get out of here anyway. I'm in here on a frame-up, Doc, I just got to say I think I am doing well to keep the mind I got now. Can't get no exercise, no outlet, go up to take a bath and right back. Don't never get out.

"I'm going to hold up as long as I can."

The Committee hired a local lawyer from Huntsville, the accusing girls' home town, to assist Leibowitz and to reduce some of the hostility that prevented Leibowitz from obtaining his usual success with such cases. Leibowitz had attempted to handle the Scottsboro boys' defense without reference to or consideration of Southern prejudices, and Southern hostility was fierce. By January 23, Patterson was convicted for the fourth time, but instead of the death sentence, he was sentenced to seventy-five years' imprisonment.

Dr. Chalmers now formed a local committee in Alabama to help with the fight. Eventually forty-nine Alabama citizens, white and colored, subscribed to the work and helped form a common ground for sympathy and help from other Southerners.

The "leniency" of Patterson's seventy-five-year sentence distressed the prosecution, and the state began to look for ways to get a compromise. Dr. Chalmers was told, "Plead the boys guilty and they'll get only seven years," which would have let them out of jail very soon.

Dr. Chalmers personally rejected such an arrangement, but for the boys' sake he suggested the prosecution put the proposition up to them directly.

It was then revealed the proposal had already been made to the boys, but none believed it was on the level. Finally, Dr. Chalmers agreed to confirm the proposal to the boys as being an honest one, but he was prepared to advise them against acceptance.

He described his visit to Andy Wright; all the boys had been in solitary for four months, which meant each spent his time in a room little more than the size of a nine-by-six rug. A shelf bed folded against the wall. Once a week they were taken out, given a shower and allowed to walk for thirty minutes along an empty corridor.

He greeted Wright, told him of the progress that had been made in the formation of the committee, and then he said, "The authorities have promised that if you plead guilty you can go free. But you are not guilty. You are under no obligation. . . . I'll stick with you as long as we live, but I must be honest with you—I don't know when we'll get you out."

Wright clutched the bars, his face up against them. He said, "Doc, I'll rot here till I die before I'll say I did something I didn't do just to get out."

That summed up the boys' opinion, and Dr. Chalmers did not even bother to communicate their decision to the prosecution. But other attempts by the prosecution to make deals continued.

1937

June 14—Alabama State Supreme Court confirms Patterson's fourth sentence.

July 15—Clarence Norris, convicted for the third time, receives the death sentence.

July 22—Andrew Wright convicted, receives sentence of ninety-nine years.

July 24—Charles Weems tried, convicted, receives seventy-five-year sentence.

July 24—Ozie Powell pleads guilty to a charge of assault with intent to murder and is sentenced to twenty years in jail. (After the January 1936 trial, Powell had slashed a man while in a Sheriff's car being taken back to prison; Powell was shot and permanently injured.) The rape charge against Powell and four others is dropped. Roy Wright, Olen Montgomery, Eugene Williams and Willie Roberson are freed. The other defendants are returned to prison.

December—An interview is held with Governor Graves of Alabama by Dr. Edmonds of Birmingham, chairman of the Alabama Scottsboro Defense Committee, Grover Hall, editor of the Montgomery *Advertiser,* and Dr. Chalmers. At the end of that conference the Governor freely states his intention of releasing the boys as soon as the cases are out of the hands of the judiciary. In the following months Governor Graves continues to make plans to assist in the boys' release via parole before the end of his term, December 31, 1938.

In late October, however, former Senator Heflin, of Alabama, began to pressure the Governor against the release, and the Governor then began to employ delaying tactics. The Committee sought the help of President Roosevelt, who invited Governor Graves to visit him at Warm Springs, Georgia. The Governor, who had great admiration for the President, ducked the meeting. According to Mrs. Roosevelt, the President then sent him a strong letter urging him to live up to his promises to release the boys. To no avail. Graves was told by Heflin and other Alabama political figures that "if he were to go through with his original plans, he was through politically, and he found himself unable to stand up to that."

In December, Dr. Chalmers released, with the backing of the Committee, a pamphlet, "A Record of a Broken Promise." He was fully aware that such a denunciation was a "luxury" but it did bring about a change in the attitude of the press of Alabama, which now swung in behind the Committee's efforts. The new governor wanted no part of the case, but now the Parole Board seemed to offer some hope; when, in March 1940, the case was taken up before that body, the board was "favorably inclined," but they decided nothing could be done "for the present."

Dr. Chalmers and the Committee were discouraged, but through Grover Hall they approached the Parole Board with the suggestion that one of the boys be paroled in his care so that rehabilitation could be begun as an example to those in the nation who were still aroused at the endless frustrations in the freeing of the remaining boys. The Parole Board (the Alabama State Board of Pardons and Paroles) reported to Mr. Hall, the go-between, that they had made their decision and that was that.

When an interview was finally granted to Dr. Chalmers, he was forced to wait in the outer office for nearly three hours. He said, "I never knew during this time what reception I would receive. The polite hostility with which I was finally met was not encouraging. The crux of the conference may be summed up in the words of one of the Board members. He was angry as he leaned forward and said vigorously: 'Dr. Chalmers, we have made our decision and you must abide by it.' He pounded the table when he said 'must.'

" 'Judge,' I answered quietly, 'you are a teacher in a Bible School, aren't you?'

" 'Why, yes,' he answered, startled at this sudden mention of things sacred.

" 'I am a minister of that same gospel,' I continued. 'In the Bible from which you teach, and from which I preach, there is a text referring to the fact that man may be judged by the words, "whatsoever you would that others do unto you, do you even so unto them." If I were the chairman of your defense committee if ever you were in trouble, would you want me to accept the decision of the authorities no matter how vigorously they made it?'

"He looked at me soberly and then said, 'No, I wouldn't.'

" 'That is the reason,' I answered, 'why I cannot accept your decision as final.'

" 'Our decision will stand for now,' he said, smiling for the first time. 'But we'll be glad to see you whenever you want to come back.' "

Finally, in November 1943, Charlie Weems was released, and in 1944, Andrew Wright and Clarence Norris, and in 1946, Ozie Powell. Wright was back in prison soon after his first parole, because of a fist fight and his leaving the state of Alabama. But he went back to prison voluntarily, knowing at the time that his being wanted jeopardized the others' chances of getting out.

1948

July 17—Haywood Patterson escapes from prison for the second time. His stay at Kilby has been full of misery and cruelty. He reaches Dr. Chalmers and asks for help. He is given it, but told to make a new life where he is not known. The FBI checks Dr. Chalmers regularly but Patterson remains at large for two years. Then his book, *Scottsboro Boy,* is published, and the FBI catches him outside the Detroit office of the Civil Rights Congress. But Governor G. Mennen Williams refuses to allow the State of Alabama to extradite Patterson and the matter drops right there. Patterson, after eighteen years in prison, is free.

There remains only Andrew Wright.

1950

June 9—The Associated Press reports that Andy Wright left prison on parole today "with no hard feelings toward anyone." Thirty-eight years old, he says, "I'm not mad because the girl lied about me. If she's still living, I feel sorry for her because I don't guess she sleeps much at night."

His release has been in jeopardy right up until the last minute because Patterson's book was a savage denunciation of the people and the system which is the Alabama prison administration.

Andrew Wright's first letter to Dr. Chalmers, after his release, is short but eloquent:

"Doc, when are you coming to see me. I feel like a rabbit in a strange wood."

"NEW YORK, NEW YORK, WHAT A HELL OF A TOWN!"

In New York City, one of the country's greatest public servants, Fiorello H. La Guardia, a Republican, was elected mayor in 1933. The city had suffered the agonies of the Depression, and the corrupt political machine of Tammany Hall must have seemed even more distasteful to New Yorkers when the Seabury investigation disclosed that Tammany politicians had milked appropriations for building and construction, had accepted bribes from organized crime, had corrupted the courts, all during the height of the Depression. If ever a city needed an honest administrator to "throw the rascals out," New York City did.

The following selection is from the affectionate memoir by Ernest Cuneo, La Guardia's onetime law clerk.

ERNEST CUNEO

LIFE WITH FIORELLO*

FIORELLO's campaign [for Congress, in 1932] had for me an epic quality of almost Homeric proportions. He made it seem that way. He dramatized every instant of it. He was the dauntless captain of a gallant, horribly beleaguered ship, and though we yawed on the very brink of eternity, because of his supreme skill and courage we did not go under.

My services in the campaign were assumed. Bundles of ordered campaign literature arrived, and I signed for some. Fiorello told me not to do that because money was very limited; everything had to be checked in a central place. Otherwise, diversity of control would result in our buying things we couldn't pay for. He also told me that if I signed for anything I'd be liable, which was something to think about, too. It made me feel very uneasy, however, to see him concern himself about a $68 order when he was fighting for his political life.

* From Ernest Cuneo's *Life with Fiorello* (New York, Macmillan, 1955).

Then Fiorello told me that in the campaign I was to be a speaker. Speaking on street corners is certainly nothing new in political campaigns. In fact, street-corner stumping sounded a little unattractive intrinsically, and I wondered if I might not be getting some kind of brush-off.

I asked him what he wanted me to talk about and he seemed a little surprised, and said, why, anything I pleased. The implication was that I was thoroughly conversant with the situation and could play the whole thing by ear. I was pleased.

The Twentieth District ran from about 100th Street to somewhere up around 120th, and from Lexington Avenue over to the East River. Its heart was 116th Street. It encompassed at that time a large Italian and a considerable Puerto Rican population. It included many huge tenements, where yellow lights shone dimly from the backs of long dark corridors deep within. The black store windows of small ventures which had gone under stared out onto the shabby streets like empty eyeball sockets.

But though the backdrop was depressing, the people weren't. Their economic situation generally was bad, of course, but the average person seemed not nearly so wretched as those who had gone downtown to seek out Fiorello for personal help. In fact, the people in that area gave the impression of throbbing life. They were active, determined not simply to survive but to go on loving life itself. Kids ran in droves. Tolerant, amiable, good-natured mothers looked on with the air of having completed self-evident, all-fulfilling missions in life. Pushcart transactions were at once traditional ceremonies and enjoyable battles of wits.

The next evening I climbed into the back of a big delivery truck equipped with a movable loudspeaker and ordinary wooden benches along the sides. There were a couple of other people already there. Bunting festooned the outsides, and pictures of Fiorello with Republican eagles, and his own symbol, the Liberty Bell, at the four corners completed the *décor*. A small group cheered as we drove off. The truck jounced downtown a few blocks, where a very large crowd was awaiting us. Our truck went slowly through the crowd, turned into a sidestreet, and stopped. The tailgate was let down, and the microphone was moved to the very end of the truck. All was ready. The crowd eddied up to the very edge of the tailgate; the street was packed with people on all sides of us.

I sat on the bench, reviewing my notes, as things got under way. I remember the purplish arc lights, and the shadow of a wire in front of it swinging back and forth like a pendulum. I wasn't nearly as nervous as I thought I'd be. I heard myself described as a distinguished young visitor

180

who was thoroughly familiar with all of the grave national problems of the day and who enjoyed the confidence of our great leader, Fiorello H. La Guardia, short cheer, your mike. I grabbed it and started to talk.

It was generally agreed in newspaper circles that La Guardia and Bob La Follette had the most informed, socially conscious electorates in the country. It was an education to me, during that campaign, to see the concentrated attention which was bestowed on every speaker. There was no nonsense about the content of speeches. They could not be general: the sense of the meeting was that either you had something to say or you hadn't. The red carpet that might have been laid out for you could be snapped out from under your feet at any moment if you failed to live up to your billing.

I opened up on the City Trust, as I had planned. I had intended merely to outline it in general, but I found such rapport that I was able to go into it in detail. From the record, I named the names and charged the crimes. The Democratic leaders were heavily involved, and I cited chapter and verse. The obvious conclusion I hammered home: Who could be found to oppose the election of La Guardia, save those content to send a thief to office? "Thief" is as strong a word in Harlem as anywhere else. I was greatly satisfied with the reception I received.

Later that evening, back at headquarters, some men came over and asked me if I didn't think the only way out of the transit problem was receivership for the city subways and eventual municipal ownership. I said I wasn't sure, that I hadn't looked that far into it. Another group asked me if I didn't think the Federal Reserve should make risky equity loans direct, as a pump primer; I said I did. There were a half-dozen questions which indicated that many of those present were at least as familiar with government finance as most Congressmen, and certainly more knowledgeable than I.

When I saw Fiorello the next day, I could tell he was not pleased. "Ernest," he asked, almost plaintively, "what the hell did you do up there last night?" He pushed his glasses up on his forehead.

"Nothing," I said. "I just attacked the City Trust banditry, that's all."

Fiorello sighed. "Now They will be pouring money in there to beat me." He looked both gloomy and nettled.

"Who?" I asked in amazement. "Who'll pour in money against you because of *my* speech?"

"Why, Wall Street, the Big Banks." He made a sweeping gesture. "They were fighting me generally, but now it's personal. The Big Banks have

181

done the same damn' things as the City Trust, and now you've gone and frightened them at just the wrong time. Money will *pour* in against me. Well, it can't be helped now."

I just couldn't picture the Boards of Directors of the big banks downtown scurrying into executive session because of an obscure speech by a law clerk on a street corner in Harlem. I said as much. Fiorello shook his head. "No," he said, "the Democratic leaders are probably downtown right now, collecting thousands." I had mad visions of fleets of armored cars rushing gold bullion uptown posthaste, with Morgan and Aldrich wringing their hands and praying it was enough. It was, I thought, too silly for words. Yet the idea was enormously flattering. I felt like a young Disraeli, regretful that his first speech had upset the balance of power in Europe but determined to be resolute about it all. "Well," I soothed, "let's wait and see."

Presumably the Money Barons refused to be stampeded into parting with their cash, because nothing was ever heard of it again. I decided, however, to concentrate thereafter on Fiorello's voting record and his Congressional leadership. There was material enough there, Heaven knew, because Fiorello had taken a position on practically every bill before Congress during his tenure of office.

The speakers were eventually assigned to specific trucks, and the trucks made specific stops. Most of the speaking took place between 8:00 and 10:30 P.M. Fiorello himself would often speak at the final gathering of the evening, and he drew immense crowds. He was eloquent, factual, and sincere; he always ended on a fighting note, and he had them with him all the way. Our "enemies" deliberately scheduled a meeting one night for the same time and place as a meeting we had announced, at which Fiorello was slated to speak. Fiorello got there early and climbed up on the truck with us. A large crowd of La Guardia supporters was on hand. Sure enough, as the appointed hour drew near, a huge mob of people accompanied by a band could be heard coming up the avenue. Our opponents stopped about a block from the edge of our crowd. Between the two groups stood one lone policeman. Suddenly both crowds became absolutely silent. They faced each other like two shaggy, unfriendly animals.

"Ernest," said Fiorello, very quietly, "go and tell that cop we were here first and we're staying. Tell him," he said, "that if the Law can't protect us, we can protect ourselves." I rose to go, but he caught me by the sleeve and added: "Get tough with him. And if you have to hit him, don't hesitate."

182

My stomach muscles froze. "You mean *hit* the *cop*?" I bleated unbelievingly.

"Yes," said Fiorello. "Punch him in the eye if he tries to finagle us."

There is an old superstition among newsmen that it is very bad luck indeed to sock a New York cop, and I had seen strong evidence, as an ex-reporter myself, in support of it. But down I clambered from the truck and made my way through the crowd; or rather, a way opened for me. I passed the outer fringe of our followers with all the enthusiasm of a space cadet leaving the earth's gravitational field in a faulty rocket. I advanced on the cop, thinking we two were like Sohrab and Rustum meeting between the opposing lines. Just before I reached him, I looked back at Fiorello under the arc light, and he nodded his head vigorously by way of reassurance. I straightened my shoulders, walked the rest of the way, and aggressively stuck out my jaw.

"Listen," I snarled. "La Guardia says we were here first and we're gonna stay here. If you can't enforce the law, we'll do it for you."

He was a bulky young Irishman, about my age. He poked his face right into mine.

"*You* listen," he said. "I got eyes. Tell him to keep his shirt on. And I don't need no help from nobody." He turned on his heel, faced the other crowd, and moving his arms as if he were shooing chickens, he started walking toward them. "Beat it," he said to them. "Go on, beat it." They hesitated for a moment, then broke. A couple of blocks away, their band struck up and they all marched off. I was dizzy with relief. There was no question about it: Fiorello would have resorted to violence then and there had it been necessary.

An elderly lady came into the office one afternoon, apparently a shopkeeper of small means. She was on a mysterious errand; she said she wanted to give the money, *this time*, to Mr. La Guardia himself. "*This time?*" frowned Fiorello. "Show her in."

She explained to him that one of our ward leaders had asked her for twenty-five dollars for a secret La Guardia campaign fund, and she had given him fifteen dollars. The balance, she had made up her mind, she would hand to Fiorello himself, to be sure he got it. Fiorello called in one of the girls, and the woman told her story while it was taken down. La Guardia explained to her that he wanted to keep our records straight. It was immediately typed up, and La Guardia read it to her. He told her if what she had said was true, he would like her to sign it. She signed. Then

Fiorello phoned the Police Commissioner and asked him to investigate. The Commissioner apparently asked why, because Fiorello barked, "Because there's a chance one of *my* leaders may be a crook!" That, I thought, took real political guts.

Toward the end of the campaign I was having an early dinner down at the Little Venice with some friends one night when the headwaiter came over with a message: Mr. La Guardia wanted me uptown right away. I said to tell him I'd be along as soon as I finished eating. The captain came back and said it was urgent, that I was to leave immediately. With the air of a Foreign Secretary being called away from his house guests by a fussy Prime Minister, I excused myself. The deferential captain hurried me into my coat. I felt like Sheridan hurrying up to Winchester. The spirit of the Alamo and the Relief of Lucknow pervaded me. To the Rescue! I arrived at headquarters, and half a dozen people said in hushed voices, "The Major wants you." It was like walking through a verbal arch of crossed swords: "The Major wants you."

The Major greeted me with a hearty "Ah!" as if my arrival meant he could stop worrying. He quickly motioned me into a huddle. I knew I was the envy of all.

"Ernest," he whispered, "they're going to pull the fire alarm when I speak tonight." He drew back as if aghast at the terrible secret he had just imparted to me, and his expression suggested that I too must be confounded by such a diabolical plot. I couldn't imagine what this had to do with me and my mad dash uptown. I had expected that Fiorello was at least going to seek a temporary injunction against the United States Navy, or some such outlandish dramatic move that would rock the nation back on its heels.

"Why," I said absently, "they'll never get away with it."

This was greeted with vociferous enthusiasm by Fiorello. He clapped me heartily on the back. "Attaboy!" he said. "Get right over there."

"Get over where?" I asked, completely bewildered.

"Over to the fire alarm box," he said, "and punch anybody in the eye who comes near it!"

My Foreign Secretarial robes slid from my shoulders to the floor in an untidy heap. Visions of the Alamo and Lucknow dimmed. I wasn't even a bodyguard, I reflected; I was a bouncer. "Wait a minute," I said. "Suppose there *is* a fire? *Then* what do I do?"

"There won't be any," he assured me impatiently. "There hasn't been one in that vicinity for fifty years. Hurry up, now. Get going!"

I made my way outside, running a gauntlet of eager questions, but I just held up one hand and shook my head: Atlas staggering under the secret burden of the world. But to myself I thought bitterly, Big Deal for a Big Shot. I perspired with humiliation: if anybody were to find out the real reason why I had been called, I'd never live it down.

I took up my lonely vigil by the fire alarm box, feeling definitely sub-human. To make matters worse, one of those cold autumn rains began to fall with a quiet, discouraging persistence.

About nine-thirty a cab drew up in the drizzle. The door flew open and a cheerful voice called out: "Hey, Mr. President! Come on, get in. He's not speaking tonight after all." With cheerful malice, it added, "Never mind; 'they also serve who only stand and wait.' "

Fiorello was a dynamo throughout the campaign—absolutely tireless. People waited to see him in long lines, and he saw every one of them. He kept tabs on the smallest detail, but could switch from a trivial registry question to a fiery speech concerning basic issues on no notice at all. He was everywhere at once, encouraging, strengthening, and inspiring us all.

In the last days before the election he told me that I was to function as a Deputy Attorney General of New York. Each side was allowed a few to patrol the election. I went downtown and was sworn in. The night before election I will never forget. Fiorello sent for me and we went off by ourselves behind a big screen. His powerful jaw was set. He said, "Ernest, what are you going to do if they try to steal the election tomorrow?" His eyes glittered with a thousand lights, like the hard, cold glitter in the eyes of a poised black panther. I was almost hypnotized; I know I had difficulty swallowing before I could speak.

"Listen, Major," I said. "I took an oath and I'll live up to it. I know a crime when I see one. Nobody has to tell me what to do!"

"What will you do?" he persisted.

"I'll arrest them," I said angrily, "or get killed trying to."

He put his hand on my arm. "No," he said, "we don't want arrests; we want votes. If they rush the machine, knock them away from it. Then cast as many votes for me as they stole. You hear? Vote until they knock you out! Tomorrow," he continued, "I've given you a post of honor. Ernest, it's dangerous." I was about to deprecate this when he said slowly: "They might shoot you. You could be killed."

Well, that's just dandy, I thought; from baby carriages on the bean to bullets in the chest. "For God's sake, then, give me a gun!"

"No," Fiorello said deliberately, "you can't have a gun. I'd sooner see you dead than tried for murder."

185

"Well, *I* wouldn't," I assured him. "I want a gun."

"No," he said firmly and soothingly, as to a child, "you can't have a gun. And," he added sharply, "I don't want you to get one anywhere else. You hear? If you don't want to go, you don't have to, but you can't take a gun. Understand?" He must have been reading my mind; I had been thinking, Why ask him? Somewhere I'd get a pistol that night. Now that was out. I promised I wouldn't get a gun, and we parted.

But I got sorer and sorer the more I thought about it. I tried to catch his eye, but he evaded me. I went over later in the evening and tapped him on the shoulder. "No gun," he said levelly, without even looking at me, and went right on talking to the person he was with.

Fiorello's climactic speech that night was unforgettable. The finale of every La Guardia campaign was a great ceremony. It always took place at his Lucky Corner, 116th and Lexington. Thousands of people were on hand, a moving demonstration of faith by people who regarded Fiorello not only as their own champion, but as the champion of humanity as a whole. There was almost a religious fervor about it. Fiorello spoke, and his soul was in every word. Never had his integrity, all his gifts, found better expression. He was a charging lion. As he concluded, a searchlight played down on him from somewhere above. And at the end the tumult of the crowd was such as must have toppled the walls of Jericho.

I slept very little that night. I just lay in bed and stared at the ceiling of my darkened room. It was unthinkable that Fiorello would send me into a gun fight without a gun. I tried to believe it was just like the night before a big game, but that wasn't true. Noel Coward once described his sensations before an opening—as though his stomach were a paper bag with a sparrow fluttering inside. But my stomach seemed to have shriveled to a hard, wrinkled walnut. Dawn came at last and I got ready to go uptown. The polls opened at 6:00 A.M. I ate no breakfast because I had read somewhere that if you were shot the difference between life and death could be the presence of food in your stomach. The theory was that the food poisoned the wound. I didn't believe it, but I was taking no chances.

I arrived at my assigned location at 5:45. There was already a short line of voters outside. I noticed a little boy playing with a hoop by the door, and I thought it was a hell of an hour for a kid to be up. The polling place was a long store with windows on both side of the entrance. The registration books were to the right as you entered, and the voting booths were further back and on the left, over against the wall. Near the window to the right of the door stood three young seminary students, representing the Honest Ballot League, as I recall. The inspectors were already seated. Two policemen in bull harness were at their stations near the curtained voting booths.

So was our opponent's man, a little older than I, and about my size. I took off my topcoat and hung it up.

The voting started. The first voter came in, checked with the inspectors, and entered the booth. The opposition man brazenly moved the curtain aside with his hand and peered in. I challenged the vote at once and told the cops to make an arrest. They suggested that I just take it easy. The Tammany man walked out with the voter. I followed. I told the three young clerics to stand by, there was going to be trouble. I went outside and discovered my adversary passing down the line, openly handing out money from a large roll of bills.

By this time the second voter had completed inspector's check and was going into the booth. Back came the Tammany man and again he poked his head inside the curtain. And again I challenged the vote, with the same negative results.

A third man came in, checked, stepped into the booth. As the Tammany man raised the curtain to watch the vote, I belted him on the jaw with everything I had. He went flying into the machine and collapsed to the floor. All hell broke loose. The two cops jumped me, and I locked with one of them. We scuffled and cuffed, and the cop yelled that I was under arrest. I said *he* was. Neither cop, I noticed, went for his gun; in fact, the other cop was now engaged in picking up the fallen man. With the heightened perception one tends to have in moments of crisis, I saw that the young clerics were praying and that the little boy outside was jumping excitedly up and down and waving his hat.

The cop and I had just broken apart, still arresting each other, when a huge limousine hurtled to a screaming stop at the curb. Men tumbled out of it and came running into the store. This is it, I thought. I just stood there, waiting for the bullets. I felt naked, and my arms were going up and down in short jerks like a pawing bear. "Now and at the hour of our death, Amen," came fleetingly to mind from out of my childhood. It was all over in seconds. In all, seven men rushed in, their right hands in their pockets. *But* they wore great big La Guardia buttons in their lapels! They formed a semicircle around me, facing the cops, and just stood there, crouched. Not a word. I regained my voice, and from behind my barrier I told the cop again that those first three votes were challenged. He said he'd heard me the first time. The fellow I had hit was on his feet now, and the second cop was helping him wash his face at a sink at the back of the store.

Now another black car roared up and out jumped Fiorello. He apparently knew all about what had happened because he burst in shouting, "Attaboy, Ernest, give 'em hell!" He tongue-lashed the cops and said they'd go to prison if there was any more nonsense. He said they'd date time for the rest of their lives from the second anything funny happened there again. I saw that the La Guardia men were leaving, and I asked one of them in a low voice where they were from.

He whispered: "Friends of Fiorello. Amalgamated Clothing Workers of America."

Fiorello looked around defiantly and then motioned for me to leave with him. We got into the car. "There won't be any more trouble there," he said. Then, "Are you all right?" I started to say that of course I was all right, but instead I broke into a torrent of tears. I was as surprised as Fiorello. He said what was I crying for, I had done fine. For a moment or two I couldn't stop. I had seen football players cry in the dressing room after a tough game, and it isn't exactly crying so much as a release of tension, but I had never been affected that way before. Fiorello gazed out of the window while I pulled myself together, and for the rest of the ride he was gruffly kind.

He was right; there was no more trouble that day. The fellow I had hit was gone when I went back in the afternoon, but he soon reappeared. It was awkward at first, but it seemed to me that he was actually trying to be friendly. He smiled, and I went over and said I was sorry that I had had to belt him. He said to forget it, it was all part of the game. He stuck out his hand and I shook it.

Fiorello carried that particular precinct by less than fifty votes. But it was obvious that over-all it was a Democratic landslide from Buffalo to the Battery. By eleven, we knew the bad news. Fiorello had lost a very close race.

I felt terrible. We walked up the dark street together. At the corner he stopped. "Well, Ernest," he said, "we did our damnedest. And you can't do better than that. Now go home and get some rest." I told him I didn't want to, but he ordered me to go. I didn't know what to do. I wanted desperately to help him. I went on down the block alone and crossed the street. Then I looked back. He was talking to some people who had come along. They parted and he walked on by himself. I followed him, keeping well back on the opposite side of the street, hoping something would occur to me to do, but nothing did. He climbed the steps to his house and walked in, closing the door gently behind him. I never felt so miserable in my life as I did standing there on that street. I don't know how long it was before I turned and started the long walk home.

Within a month after his defeat, Fiorello was busy regaining lost ground. Postcard invitations were sent to a special list of people known to be actively interested in better government for New York City, and a meeting was held in Town Hall. An audience of over five hundred showed up and warmly applauded Fiorello's calm, cool speech. In the main they were old faithfuls—the hard nucleus of Fiorello's support. As had happened in the past, Fiorello was down to base strength, laying careful foundations for a new edifice to be built on the ruins of an old defeat.

However careful or logical his plans may have been, his immediate future was to be shaped by a seemingly unrelated series of events which he could not possibly have anticipated. This chancy chain of events began four years before with a gambling game and a pistol shot. It is not too extravagant to borrow a page from history by saying that this was a shot heard eventually round the world, for it had a direct bearing on the subsequent election of two men to the highest elective office in the land. The figurative ricochet of this bullet radically changed the complexion of party politics in New York City and in Albany; and at least the echo of the explosion rang through the corridors of the White House.

The gentleman on the receiving end of the literal bullet was, of course, Arnold Rothstein, banker to the underworld, one of the most verminous characters that ever infested New York City. One October evening in 1928, two notorious big-shot gamblers, "Titanic" Thompson and "Nigger Nate" Raymond, anxious for some action, invited Arnold Rothstein to participate in a game of High Spade. The evening's diversion was expensive for Rothstein; he lost $340,000. He resolved this dilemma in characteristic fashion: he welshed. But this proved even more expensive. On a Saturday night early in November, he received, while dining at Lindy's, another cordial invitation, this time from gambler George Mc-Manus, to attend a floating crap game at the Park Central Hotel, a few blocks north. Rothstein bustled out, his sporting blood aroused. At 11:10 P.M. Mr. Rothstein was found at the service entrance of said hospice, his right side punctured by a .38 bullet, a wound of which he subsequently died at Polyclinic Hospital on the following Tuesday. On his deathbed Rothstein had only enough strength to caution his friends and well-wishers everywhere, including his lawyer, to keep their mouths shut; and, having completed his last furtive act, he died, thereby performing the one act of public service ever connected with his name.

In the meantime thirty-five New York City detectives were halfheartedly going through the motions of finding out who did the shooting. The murderer was never caught.

Up to the day of his timely demise, Rothstein had always made it a point to know the price of every corrupt official in the city, and always had the money to pay it. He knew to a penny the market on lost souls, from rigged security operators and horse race fixers down to what a Bowery bum would do for the glass of rotgut whisky that was killing him. And Rothstein traded on it all. If Rothstein alive had been an unsavory article, Rothstein dead was a calamity. His activities had not been limited to the dregs of society; on the contrary, certain of his dealings had involved some very eminent citizens indeed. The publication of his records might make for embarrassment, it was felt. Not to put too fine a point on it, City Hall was in an uproar. Mayor Walker was unhappy and upset.

After the killing the police went to Rothstein's fortress home and seized his voluminous files. A judge ordered that they be put in the custody of a Tammany district leader—for "safekeeping." Although it took two trucks to move them, the trustee shortly reported to the court that they had been stolen, and the court solemnly accepted this explanation.

But at least one record actually was missing, for in 1929, when he went down to crushing defeat in the mayoralty race against Jimmy Walker, Fiorello produced it. It was the record of a loan of $19,940 from Rothstein to a pitiful excuse of a magistrate named Albert Vitale, of the Bronx. That was the touch-off match to the powder train which was to blow the old Tammany Hall to smithereens forever.

There were two Democrats in New York State who bore no more love for Tammany than Fiorello did. One was the distinguished Judge Samuel Seabury, who had been done out of the Governorship by the Wigwam in 1916; the other was Franklin D. Roosevelt, whose first act in public life fifteen years before had been to stamp on Tammany's toes for opposing his election as State Senator. The paths of Fiorello, Seabury, and Roosevelt were to converge with effects important to the nation's history. The man who brought them together was Adolf A. Berle, Jr., Professor of Corporate Finance at Columbia University. In 1928, however, no one of the men involved had any more notion that this would occur than Arnold Rothstein himself, laid out in Brooklyn in his pine box, for once in a game he couldn't fix.

190

The Appellate Division named Judge Seabury to investigate the Magistrates' courts. It was open knowledge at the time that magistrates' appointments were sold to loyal and zealous ward heelers. Some of the magistrates really represented a family enterprise. All relatives who had two dimes to rub together went into the pool, the family had the honor of including a judge in their number, and everyone sat back for dividends. The caliber of this bench can be imagined, but not described.

Seabury went after his quarry cautiously, even though he had the backing of the press. It is a phenomenon of all investigations that the "breaks" come in the form of volunteer witnesses once the investigations are announced. The Magistrates' courts investigation went true to form. One night there walked into the New York *Daily News* office a desperately ill little pimp by the name of Chile Acuna. Acuna said he was tired of framing innocent women for the Vice Squad and helping to railroad them before crooked magistrates. A pimp is not the world's most reliable witness, and the *News* checked carefully. What they found disgusted a city which was used to stenches: one woman magistrate had actually doctored the court records in her zeal to protect the police-vice ring. Innocent women had been framed, all right, and by the dozen.

This set off a second investigation: the Hofstadter Committee to investigate corruption in New York City, with, again, the implacable Sam Seabury as its counsel.

Mayor Walker tried to wisecrack it out of existence. He paraded across the line of fire with leers and knowing winks to vociferous if cynical applause; but when he was in complete command of his faculties—which was seldom in those later days—the strain made his skin look like old parchment. From Washington, Fiorello threw what assistance he could to Seabury; but there was a game of far larger stakes developing, and no one knew it more than the agile incumbent at Albany, Governor Franklin D. Roosevelt.

Roosevelt certainly loved Tammany no better than did La Guardia or Seabury, but, unlike them, he needed the Hall badly. He was an all-out candidate for the Presidency and, if he got it, a hands-down choice to win. Now Roosevelt was in a dilemma. Every bit of the shocking evidence Seabury was unearthing made headlines across the nation. Tammany, an absolute necessity to Roosevelt until his nomination, would be a millstone around his neck west of the Hudson once he had it. With his usual perfect timing, however, F.D.R. pulled the neatest political trick of the year, and it landed him squarely in the center ring of the Big Top for two performances and a double encore.

Meanwhile, Seabury had assembled a highly competent staff of accountants and lawyers and told them to see what they could find. To no one's surprise, they found plenty. The various machine leaders had large amounts of money, the explanation of which convulsed the nation with hoots of angry laughter. Wonderful Damon Runyonesque characters were uncovered: Tin Box Farley (no relation to James, of course) whose only explanation for his funds was that he had simply found them in his little tin box; the fifty-four starving McQuades who were the ridiculous excuse offered by that rascal for his bulging deposit box; and mighty Jimmy Hines, caught far up the creek, not only without a paddle, but in the same boat with the master gangster Dutch Schultz. The Board of Standards and Appeals, which had jurisdiction of zoning and building permits, was exposed as a million-dollar-a-year racket, but only after Tammany had challenged Seabury's subpoena up to the Court of Appeals and lost.

The contest had all the drama and violence of a heavyweight championship fight. Crafty old Judge Seabury kept boring in with heavy body punches, and the Democratic Party winced as far north as Albany when his crashing right landed on its soft underbelly, Tammany. There was no doubt as to what Seabury's knockout blow was to be. He had, in the parlance of the fight game, telegraphed his punch: it was going to be a crushing overhand right, tagged for the political glass jaw of one James J. Walker.

The Seabury technique was coldly methodical. It took time, but under the paralyzing body blows of exposure after exposure Tammany was at last brought to bay, breathing heavily and badly hurt. The trail of blood left by the dying Rothstein led straight to the paths of corruption within the city machine, and those paths were narrowing rapidly in the direction of the back door of the Wigwam. All at once it was too late for Jimmy's fancy footwork; he was going down for the full count unless saved by the referee—i.e., Governor Roosevelt.

In desperation, Tammany went into a clinch. It hung on with the claim of constitutional privilege and the rule applying to burden of proof in a criminal case. Seabury had proved big, unexplained, and inexplicable bank accounts, but he still had to prove, and beyond a reasonable doubt, that these sums actually represented graft in order to make a case.

As 1932 rolled in, Governor Roosevelt viewed the untidy New York scene with absolutely unmixed emotions: everyone knew he was out for himself. He preferred to remain 150 miles north, in Albany, away from the furious scuffle in progress, and thus avoid the consequences of any wild swings. For Seabury's sake he deplored, and for Tammany's he demurred, an elegant exhibition on the high wire if there ever was one.

But ringwise Sam Seabury knew that F.D.R. was in a tough spot, and he decided to capitalize on it. He suddenly declared that he was not conducting a criminal trial, but a legislative inquiry, thereby taking off his back the heavy burden of proof. He stated that the proof he had was not intended for a Grand Jury action: it was meant for Governor Roosevelt, and he laid it at Roosevelt's feet, thereby making himself the most unwelcome visitor in the Upper Hudson Valley since Gentleman Johnny Burgoyne.

The nation held its breath; it looked as if the New York Governor was cornered. A rapid look at the spring calendar—instead of the issues— quickly decided the man on the high wire. F.D.R. simply had to have Tammany support for the convention, still three months away. To the amazement of all, and the admiration of many, he resoundingly denounced graft and corruption in general, but ruled that Seabury had failed to make a case in particular. Tammany breathed a sigh of relief heard across the nation. With this heartening demonstration of party regularity in the face of tremendous pressure, the big city machines of Jersey City, Chicago, Kansas City, and New Orleans took a more kindly view of the Squire of Hyde Park. Which only goes to prove how little politicians know about politics. Jim Farley took planes, trains, and busses to the far hinterlands and ultimately piloted F.D.R. through to the nomination for the Presidency at Chicago. With that accomplished F.D.R. lost no time in letting it be known that the Tammany millstone around his neck would shortly find itself at the bottom of the sea. Everybody understood this but the Wigwam, which, in its innocence, was apparently unable to comprehend such a fast double play.

Immediately after the convention, Seabury examined Walker, and then renewed his attack at Albany. In brief, Seabury stated that there were large, unexplained amounts of money in the hands of public officials, and that he wanted another ruling from the Governor: though not enough to convict, were they not enough to remove? Fiorello also pressed the point. He sent me chasing for statements by Presidents Grover Cleveland and Theodore Roosevelt and, backed by them, he submitted that a public office was a public trust, and what did Governor Roosevelt intend to do about it all? F.D.R., the marvel of the high wire, was waiting for just this cue. With a great flip, he described a complete arc and a full about-face, declared that public office was *indeed* the highest of trusts, and descended gracefully to his waiting Admiral's cape as Commander-in-Chief, which he never thereafter doffed. His feat left Tammany holding the bag, in fact a lot of little black ones, which contained one-way tickets to Sing Sing. Only Roosevelt could have managed the stunt, and it was a question as to which he had more of—skill or brass.

Fiorello and I were at the intersection of Seventh Avenue and 47th Street when the news trucks came tearing into Times Square and the newsboys started shouting "Extra!" I ran over and got a paper with the headline "Roosevelt Sustains Seabury," and the subhead "Rules Public Officials Must Explain Private Funds." Fiorello scanned it and said very solemnly, "Ernest, this is a great day for our country."

Before the ink was dry on the extra, Jimmy Walker's sponge came sailing into the ring in the form of a one-sentence letter to the City Clerk: "I hereby resign as Mayor of New York City, James J. Walker." The Walker-La Guardia political duel was ended.

When the Lame Duck Congress opened, F.D.R., through Adolf Berle, Jr., made Fiorello his spokesman for certain legislation. Oddly enough, Fiorello became the savior of the railroads he so ardently disliked by jamming through the Railroad Bankruptcy and Reorganization bill. Far closer to his heart was the Farm and Home Mortgage Relief bill. And together Fiorello and Berle patterned the legislation that resulted in the famed "77B" of the Federal Bankruptcy Act, providing for an extension of private credit obligations under supervision of the court. Altogether, it was perhaps the most active Lame Duck session in the nation's history. As the time came for Fiorello to step down and for F.D.R. to step up, the two men knew they had much in common, including one trustworthy friend in Berle.

During this period Judge Seabury kept slugging away. His revelations were such that the new Democratic Governor of New York, Herbert Lehman, a man of absolute personal honor, decided to appoint a Special District Attorney for New York County. The Seabury exposures had made corruption not a party issue, but a public cause. Governor Lehman, as a mark of his integrity, picked a man of the opposite party to root out and prosecute all civic irregularity. He was as honest as he was cold. Thomas E. Dewey was to go on to Albany three times as Governor and he stopped twice at the very threshold of the White House. These things aside, he would still be remembered as the man who broke the hold of the Lepke, Luciano and Dutch Schultz gangs.

Fiorello was out and F.D.R. was in as the jockeying for the New York mayoralty race began in the spring of 1933. Early in May, Fiorello urged an anti-Tammany ticket to be headed by Al Smith, with Socialist Norman Thomas for Aldermanic President and Bob Moses for Comptroller. These nominations were duly made, with the fullest knowledge on Fiorello's part that none of the men named could possibly accept them. Fiorello, however, indicated that he stood ready to save the situation; if Al Smith wouldn't head the ticket, he, Fiorello, would.

A number of independent groups started a "Stop La Guardia" movement, working toward a joint ticket with the Republicans. It didn't look too good for Fiorello as the climax approached in late July. But Berle had arranged a series of private conferences between Seabury and Fiorello, as a result of which Seabury agreed to cast for Fiorello. When the showdown occurred early in August at the City Club, Berle and Seabury carried all before them. Fiorello came out of it with the Republican and Fusion nominations. It looked to be another rough, tough battle.

Fiorello adopted as his campaign song "Who's Afraid of the Big Bad Wolf," and the interminable tootling in the streets had people ready to start screaming. Overnight, however, it became "The Battle Hymn of the Republic," and the most fervid crusade in New York City's history was under way. The final lines seemed drawn.

But they weren't. The new man in the White House had a few ideas of his own. Without a word of warning, F.D.R. had Boss Ed Flynn of the Bronx split the Democratic ticket by nominating Joe McKee on a Recovery platform against the bumbling Tammany candidate, John O'Brien. At the same time, F.D.R. sent Berle to Cooper Union with a public White House repudiation of McKee! Roosevelt nominated McKee through Flynn and then denied him support through Berle—thus splitting the Democratic ticket. To nominate and then repudiate while allowing the nomination to stand is one for the books. It was. The books at final audit read: La Guardia—858,000; McKee—604,000; O'Brien—586,000.

Fiorello entered City Hall straight down the middle of F.D.R.'s split ticket. It was one of the nattiest double plays on file. Up in the Bronx and down on Fourteenth Street they still call it a double cross. Though the debate raged as to whether the President had pitched a ball or a strike, all were agreed that Fiorello was very nimble on the bases. Well, you have to be to steal home.

In Judge Samuel Seabury's home at exactly midnight on January 1, 1934, Fiorello H. La Guardia took the oath of office, administered by Supreme Court Justice Philip J. McCook, as Mayor of New York City. At exactly one minute after midnight, he ordered the arrest of the most notorious gangster in town—Lucky Luciano. His take-off next morning was jet-propelled, and the momentum never let up until he stepped out of office twelve years later. He would dictate to secretaries in relays for at least twelve hours every day. No longer a legislator who had to persuade and negotiate, he now had what amounted to virtual dictatorship within his domain, and he pushed his prerogatives to the limit. When his labors ended, he had greatly altered the face of the city, from its charter to its highways, from its hospitals to its high schools. The outpouring of his prodigious energies was strictly in line with the convictions he had always held. He set about realizing his theories at boiler-works tempo.

At the end of his first six months, he rendered a report to the people. Among other things, 400 new playgrounds had been opened in that period and the city had begun to distribute milk, at cost, to the poorer sections. The hospital system was completely revised; so was the setup of the Health Department. All sorts of food-market racketeers were on the run. Almost every department had felt his none too gentle hand, and had heard during surprise visits harsh demands for greater economy and efficiency. Remarkably, though, considering all these new departures, he had wiped out the budget deficits; and the city bonds, which were at 78 when he took office, were now over par. The bankers had enough confidence in him to give him an interest rate of ¾ of 1 per cent, whereas historically Tammany had had to pay 4 per cent. Adolf Berle deserves much of the credit for this. One of Fiorello's first official acts was to appoint Berle City Chamberlain, with instructions to put the city's financial house in order.

Fiorello's fiscal policies were a pride and a joy to him. Public utilities found themselves the recipient of a brand-new tax, and had their old ones lifted. Since, under the law, they are entitled to a fair return, however, it was also something of a consumer's sales tax for all the fanfare. But it paid off, and along with the cutting of nonperforming officeholders, the city treasury soon began to show color in its cheeks—or, if you prefer, its checks. New Deal money flowed into the city. Berle continued on as a White House financial adviser, and the two Chief Almoners, Ickes and Hopkins, were old friends of Fiorello's. It was a source of immeasurable relief in the Capital to be able to make large grants, knowing that under Fiorello's gimlet eye every dime would go for its designated purpose. Federal aid, of course, did a lot to lift the strain on the local treasury, but there was no doubt, in any event, that the city's credit was sound.

When the time came for Fiorello to refund some long-time obligations, he thought it would be a novel idea to get the money from the R.F.C. The R.F.C. politely declined. The banks thereupon upped their interest rate to 4½ per cent. Fiorello at once threatened to go around the country selling his own bonds in key cities. It never came to that, however, because a compromise was finally reached. During the hassle one of Fiorello's young socialite secretaries sought to act as mediator. He remarked that he thought he could smooth the whole thing out: by a strange coincidence he was spending the weekend with the opposition's leading investment banker. "Don't apologize," snapped Fiorello. "A lot of young men aren't particular where they sleep around on weekends!"

From the first, Fiorello dropped in on municipal lodginghouses unannounced, taking his place in the lines, to see how the luckless were being treated. With the plight of the city's unemployed uppermost in his mind, he spent much time and thought in preparing a request for a record-breaking relief budget. Typically, he left as little to chance as possible.

He completed his careful preparations for the presentation of his relief budget and then rolled up his sleeves. Anticipating the constitutional issue, he declared that all lawyers were semicolon boys—that they had retarded civilization more than cancer and smallpox combined. He had determined to press for an over-all of about three billion dollars. He called to the first public hearing the chairman of the board of the largest bank in the city, intending to bait him into some sort of "Let-'em-eat-cake" remark. Aggressively, he asked the banker how much money he thought it would take to keep his fellow citizens from starvation. The banker, tipped off as to Fiorello's three billion estimate, calmly stated that it might run to six billions, and Fiorello's sails flapped feebly and hung slack. The expected opposition developed from the political quarter. As Fiorello started to read his findings, he was interrupted by an alderman who declared that relief money was already being misdirected. The alderman had documentary evidence, sworn affidavits, no less, proving that prostitutes were receiving relief money. He demanded that the practice be stopped, and that the budget be curtailed to the extent that these women were included. Fiorello bent upon the alderman his best busy-browed glare. "I thought that question was settled two thousand years ago, but I see I was wrong. Mr. Sergeant-at-Arms," he thundered, "clear the room! Clear the room—so this big bum can throw the first stone!"

As had been widely predicted, Fiorello's activities as Mayor were consistent with all his previous views. He continued to go down the line for Labor with a capital L; in any given dispute he did exactly what might have been expected of him, though theoretically his was now an impartial position. All of his craft, and he was a very crafty man indeed, was employed for the benefit of working people. With the power of City Hall behind it, his opinion very frequently was decisive. It all came under the head of ministerial prerogative, but the ruthlessness with which it was applied left no doubt as to his personal bias or the inevitable result of any given issue. At one point all the waiters in the city went out on strike. Their strike may or may not have been doing too well. At any rate, the city's hotels and larger restaurants managed to carry on—that is, until Fiorello entered the scene. What he did was classically simple: under the Health Law the city could inspect anyone handling food at any time. Fiorello, without warning, chose the height of the evening dinner hour to order a health inspection of all the scab waiters on duty, thus paralyzing service. The managements didn't like the findings either: several waiters were found to be suffering from contagious diseases. The inspections ceased as soon as an agreement with the regular waiters was reached, which was very shortly. The Building and Fire departments were preparing to make elaborate inspections when the managements came to terms.

At another time girl laundry workers went on strike. They were badly underpaid, and their working conditions were very poor. Hearkening back to the sweatshop era, and Fiorello's part in the fight against them, it was no surprise that as Mayor he would be their vigorous champion. Under the guise of keeping order, he practically blockaded the laundries with squads of police. The laundry owners went to City Hall to protest. Fiorello received them with elaborate courtesy and listened most patiently to their complaint. That alone should have put them on their guard, but it didn't. They told him that he was interfering in a labor dispute, and that the city was supposed to be neutral. Fiorello heartily agreed. The labor-union leader tried to say something, but Fiorello told him to shut up. Fiorello then turned to the spokesman of the laundry owners and asked him if he had an application to make. The spokesman swept himself firmly into the saddle of Fiorello's Trojan horse by repeating that his sole desire was to have the city remain neutral. Fiorello asked that this request be made in writing. The laundry owners hastily complied with a written request that the city withdraw all support from either side. As soon as it was handed to him, Fiorello announced that the application was granted, and that the city henceforth would be absolutely neutral. Thereupon he picked up the telephone, called the Water Department, and blandly ordered the Water Commissioner to turn off the water in all laundries, since the city was neutral in the fight. The laundry owners collapsed on the spot.

Fiorello ran true to form in his ideal of public service, too. He expected to be besieged by officeseekers, and, to a degree, he was. But he disposed of this problem at once. Immediately after his election, he addressed his entire campaign headquarters force. He said, in a very few sentences, that a Cause, not a man, had succeeded; and now he had been elected the Chief Magistrate of the city. "My first qualification for this great office," he declared, "is my monumental personal ingratitude!" There was disgruntlement, of course, and even a few heartbreaks, but Fiorello never swerved from his position: he got the best people he could for the jobs at hand, especially the top ones. Some of his highest appointments went to men outside the city, a new precedent which caused much wailing and gnashing of teeth. But Fiorello maintained that he hired a man on his abilities and not on the basis of where he slept at night. He felt the strain, however. He told Adolf Berle one evening that he'd like to be able to say "yes" to everything which was asked of him, but that he had taken an oath of office which he intended to honor. "The devil," said Fiorello, "is easy to identify. He appears as your best friend when you're terribly tired and makes a very reasonable request which you know you shouldn't grant."

After he got settled in, Fiorello was practically his own Police Commissioner. As an ex-Commanding Officer, he knew that nothing goes down to the ranks faster than the disposition of the command tent. He used to say that any variation at the center made for terrific wobbles around the circumference. He also believed that the most sensitive department in the city was the Police, so there was little astonishment in his insistence of City Hall support for honest cops. Very early in his administration, a physician who was a casual personal acquaintance got a ticket for illegal parking. The doctor forcefully told the young patrolman that the ticket was inacceptable, whereupon the boy arrested him and brought him to the station house. The physician afterward went down to City Hall in person to report this grievous wrong. Fiorello called the station house and asked to speak to the young patrolman. The captain of the precinct, who by this time had heard all the details, came on instead and was all apologies. He explained to the Mayor that the arresting officer was a rookie cop who just hadn't known any better. Fiorello, of course, hit the ceiling. "He's a better cop than you are," he raged, "and I called him up to tell him I was sending him a box of cigars. He's the kind of cop I want—and you're not!" The rookie got his cigars, delivered significantly by the Mayor's car, and Fiorello very nearly broke his superior. This story ran through the department like wildfire.

General O'Ryan, the Police Commissioner, was a stickler for form, and he and the Mayor did not get on any too well. One bitter February day, when the city was in the grip of one of the worst cold waves on record, O'Ryan issued an order stating that policemen must wear their coats in summer. The Mayor at once issued countermanding orders. The freezing city roared with laughter at this battle over what uniform would be worn in sweltering July. Trivial though the incident was, it resulted in O'Ryan's eventual resignation, which had long been brewing. Fiorello was not displeased; and it was fitting that the situation had come to a head over a quarrel relating to the comfort and well-being of the rank and file, whom Fiorello was always to defend at the expense, if necessary, of his own top brass.

A story once went the rounds to the effect that Police Commissioner Valentine, O'Ryan's successor, had put a bodyguard on Fiorello without his knowledge. A couple of detectives were established in an apartment near his with orders to keep a protective eye on him. Fiorello found out about it somehow and hit the roof. He summoned the detectives to his office. "Very well," he said, "at the expense of the *taxpayers* you're protecting me. Where was I last night at eight-thirty?" They didn't know. "I was hiding out," Fiorello told them acidly, "in a front box at the opera. Five thousand other people knew where I was, but not you two. I guess you must be the same detectives that looked for Dutch Schultz."

Savage is the word for Fiorello's feeling about gangsters. His instructions to the Police Department were, in effect, Be sure you've got the right man, then give him the works. This ruthless point of view exercised several civil liberties groups, and protests were lodged regarding irregular police procedure. Fiorello once called Valentine over to City Hall to face one such group. "Louie," he said, "these people claim you violate the Constitution." "So do the gangsters," said Valentine. Fiorello nodded, much pleased, and dismissed the petitioners forthwith.

There is no doubt that Fiorello did in fact go far beyond constitutional limitations in his unremitting war on gangsterism. Inside or outside the legal framework, however, he never deviated an inch. When it became common knowledge that a notorious criminal by the name of Terranova was in effect barred from New York by an order for his detainment at the city limits, a delegation of liberals protested. Their argument was that if every mayor did the same it could become an arbitrary injustice that would put a stop to freedom of movement in the United States. "You're absolutely correct," Fiorello told the body; and, turning to his Police Commissioner, he added: "Terranova has a perfect right to come into New York City. Let him come in, by all means! *Wait until he gets to 125th Street—and then go to work on him.*"

His standards for police action were almost the same as for an armed reconnaissance patrol in time of war. One time a thug had got the drop on a Jersey City cop, and at pistol point the patrolman had yielded up his own weapon. Mayor Hague of Jersey City condoned it; he said the cop had had no alternative to surrendering his pistol. Fiorello at once issued an order to New York's Finest that this philosophy was not in their tradition —that they should yield their lives before yielding their guns. He said he expected them to shoot it out under any and all circumstances. It was what Fiorello would have done himself if he were a cop. The order made me think of his scathing attack on Dutch Schultz in 1931. The gangster numbered among his friends powerful Bronx officials and even sported a deputy sheriff's badge. The papers blazoned Fiorello's disparaging remarks, and there was muttering to the effect that the outspoken Congressman was a candidate for a bullet. I felt a little alarm, and one night, after a particularly blistering attack on New York judges who had gangster pals, I insisted on walking home with him. He wanted to know why. I didn't want to tell him, but he pressed me and I finally said I was afraid he might get shot at. He looked very tired. Then he brightened up and said, "Oh, well, a bullet in the head is a good way to die."

By and large, though, Fiorello thoroughly enjoyed himself as Mayor. His office gave him plenty of opportunity to indulge his fondness for the spotlight. Leading a contingent of New York policemen in a Washington, D.C., parade was a routine gratification, but conducting the combined Police and Sanitation departments' bands to a capacity Carnegie Hall audience was meat and drink. The city was virtually tied up for days as its two key departments braced themselves for the ordeal. Everybody was afraid that Fiorello the Conductor might let loose on them as Fiorello the Mayor. The stage manager of this stupendous spectacle took no chances and went down to City Hall for final instructions. He asked Fiorello how he wanted the spotlights used. "Shall I play them on you as you come down the aisle, and follow you right up to the podium, Mr. Mayor?"

"Hell, no!" said Fiorello. "Just treat me like Toscanini!"

THE NOBLE EXPERIMENT

THE story of Prohibition belongs mostly to the Twenties; but the excesses, the contradictions, the failure of that "experiment noble in motive" came to their natural conclusion in the Thirties.

The excesses—in the evolution of a multibillion-dollar industry outside the law and against the law— reached their greatest heights in the early Thirties; and everywhere the public saw the criminal manifestations.

The contradictions—in the almost universal use of the liquor that the Eighteenth Amendment had supposedly banished—were everywhere apparent; everywhere the "best people" enjoyed liquor, seemingly without fear of censure. The speakeasy, operating outside the law through undercover payments to local law-enforcement officers, had taken on a peculiar glamour for its customers; and the man who had "his own bootlegger" achieved a special status in the eyes of his fellow citizens.

The failure—in that the law had become the supporting props of a criminal industry; that it had been largely annulled in most aspects; and that it had become an enormously expensive "nonlaw" to enforce—had become inescapable to the vast majority of Americans.

The over-all question of Prohibition was explored and re-explored in countless forums. Proponents invoked the authority and wisdom of the Scriptures and presented sociological statistics. Opponents cited criminological statistics and invoked the Articles of the Constitution. But nowhere was there an acknowledged consensus.

By 1932, an election year, forces were set in motion to roll back the Eighteenth Amendment. The Democrats—the "wet" party—agreed at their national convention to include within their platform a plank that called for repeal. Roosevelt made reference to it in the course of his campaign, and it was one of the issues on which the electorate voted.

However, in February 1933, before Roosevelt's inaugural, the lame-duck Congress approved the submission of the Twenty-first Amendment to the states for ratification.

In the selection which follows, Frederick Lewis Allen tells us what happened when the thirty-sixth state ratified the Amendment that abolished Prohibition—and ended an era.

FREDERICK LEWIS ALLEN

REPEAL*

AT THIRTY-TWO and a half minutes past three (Mountain Time) in the afternoon of the fifth of December, 1933, the roll call in the ratification convention in Utah was completed, and Utah became the thirty-sixth state to ratify the Twenty-first Amendment to the Constitution, repealing the Prohibition Amendment. A telegram went off to Washington, and presently the Acting Secretary of State and the President declared that Prohibition was at an end, after a reign of nearly fourteen years.

Crowds of men and women thronged the hotels and restaurants waiting for the word to come through that the lid was off, and when at last it did, drank happily to the new era of legal liquor. They thronged, too, to those urban speakeasies which had succeeded in getting licenses, and remarked how readily the front door swung open wide at the touch of the doorbell. But the celebration of the coming of repeal was no riot, if only because in most places the supply of liquor was speedily exhausted: it took time for the processes of distribution to get into motion. And as for the processes of legal manufacture—which for distilled liquors are supposed to include a long period of aging—these were so unready that an anomalous situation developed. The available liquor was mostly in the hands of bootleggers; even the legal liquor was mostly immature. Among the people who, during the first days and months of repeal, rejoiced in at last being able to take a respectable drink of "good liquor" instead of depending upon "this boot-leg stuff," thousands were consuming whisky which consisted simply of alcohol acceptably tinted and flavored. To a public whose taste had been conditioned for years by bootleg liquor, good bush needed no wine.

Drinking, to be sure, did not become legal everywhere. Eight states remained dry—all of them Southern except North Dakota, Kansas, and Oklahoma. (These states received—at least in the years immediately following repeal—very little assistance from the federal government in protecting their aridity.) Fifteen states made the selling of liquor a state monopoly—though seven of these permitted private sale under varying regulations,

* From Frederick Lewis Allen's *Since Yesterday* (New York, Harper, 1940).

most of which, in a determined effort to prevent "the return of the saloon," forbade perpendicular drinking and insisted—at least for a time—that drinkers be seated at restaurant tables.

Despite these qualifications, the change in the American mores which began in 1933 was tremendous.

Hotels and restaurants blossomed with cocktail lounges and taprooms and bars, replete with chromium fittings, mirrors, bright-colored modern furniture, Venetian blinds, bartenders taken over from the speakeasies, and bartenders who for years had been serving at the oyster bar or waiting on table, and, now, restored to their youthful occupation, persuaded the management to put on the wine list such half-forgotten triumphs of their ancient skill as Bronx and Jack Rose cocktails. So little building had been going on during the Depression that the architects and decorators had had almost no chance for years to try out the new principles of functional design and bright color and simplified furniture; now at last they had it, in the designing of cocktail lounges—with the odd result that throughout the nineteen-thirties most Americans instinctively associated modernist decoration with eating and drinking.

Hotels in cities which in days gone by would have frowned upon the very notion of a night club now somewhat hesitantly opened night clubs with floor shows—and found they were a howling success. Neat new liquor stores opened—in some States operated by government authority, in others under private ownership. It took some time for customers to realize that it was no longer necessary for a man carrying home a package of rum to act the part of a man carrying home a shoe box; and in some towns where the dry sentiment was still strong, there were men who continued to patronize bootleggers rather than subject themselves to the embarrassment of walking into the state liquor shop.

Whether there was more drinking after repeal than before cannot be determined statistically, owing to the obvious fact that the illicit sale of liquor was not measured. The consensus would seem to be that drinking pretty surely increased during the first year or two and probably increased in quantity thereafter, but that on the whole it decreased in stridency.

One change was manifest; there was more mixed drinking than ever, just as there was more smoking by both sexes. (In the six years from 1930 to 1936 the production of cigarettes went up from 123 billion to 158 billion, while the production of cigars decreased a little.) On the whole, men and women were spending more of their time in one another's company and less of their time segregated from one another. Perhaps it was not an altogether unrelated fact that most men's clubs were still somewhat anxiously seeking members throughout the nineteen-thirties and that many of the lodges were in dire straits. Was it not possible to infer that the male sex, for one, was enjoying mixed company too well to want very urgently to get away from it? Possibly the cause of feminism was triumphing in a way which the earnest suffragists of a generation before would never have expected—and at which they might have been dismayed.

And what became of the bootleggers? Some of them went into the legitimate liquor business or other legitimate occupations, some of them went into business rackets and gambling rackets, some joined the ranks of the unemployed—and a large number of them went right on bootlegging. For one of the most curious facts about the postrepeal situation was that the manufacture and smuggling and wholesaling of illicit liquor continued in great volume. The federal government and the states, in their zeal to acquire revenue from the sale of liquor, had clapped upon it such high taxes that the inducement to dodge them was great. Year after year the Internal Revenue agents continued to seize and destroy stills at the rate of something like 15,000 a year, and straightway new ones sprang up. In his report for the fiscal year ending June 30, 1938, the Commissioner of Internal Revenue, reporting that only 11,407 stills had been seized, noted, "This is the first year since the enactment of the Twenty-first Amendment that there has been a decline in illicit distillery seizures." Likewise rum-running—or, to be more accurate, the smuggling of alcohol—continued to provide a headache for the customs officers and the Coast Guard; in February 1935, more than a year after repeal, the Coast Guard found twenty-two foreign vessels lying at sea *at one time* beyond our customs waters, waiting for a chance to sneak in.

THE WORST CRIME OF ALL

KIDNAPINGS increased at an alarming rate in the early Thirties. In Chicago alone, police recorded two hundred kidnapings in 1930 and 1931, with ransom payments amounting to two million dollars.

In 1932 the Lindbergh kidnaping shocked the nation and an aroused Congress enacted a law prescribing graded penalties, including execution, for abductions across state lines. Thereafter if a kidnaping was classed as a federal offense the F.B.I. was automatically brought into the case.

The FBI compiled a formidable record; from 1932 to 1937 they solved all but one of the kidnaping cases in which they had performed investigative work. The Lindbergh case was solved, and the death sentence was meted out as punishment. Such achievements discouraged would-be kidnapers, and by the end of the decade this crime was almost a rarity.

In the two selections that follow, Frederick Lewis Allen and Stanley Walker review, from different angles, the most celebrated—and consequential—kidnaping in our criminal annals.

FREDERICK LEWIS ALLEN

THE LINDBERGH CASE*

ON THE EVENING of the first of March 1932, an event took place which instantly thrust everything else, even the grim processes of Depression, into the background of American thought. The baby son of Colonel and Mrs. Charles A. Lindbergh was kidnaped—taken out of his bed in a second-story room of the new house at Hopewell, New Jersey, never to be seen again alive.

Since Lindbergh's flight to Paris nearly five years before, he had occupied a unique and unprecedented position in American life. Admired almost to the point of worship by millions of people, he was an uncrowned prince; and although he fiercely shunned publicity, everything he did was so inevitably news that the harder he tried to dodge the limelight, the more

* From Frederick Lewis Allen's *Since Yesterday* (New York, Harper, 1940).

surely it pursued him. His new house at Hopewell, remote and surrounded by woods, had been built largely as a retreat in which the Lindberghs could be at peace from an intrusive world.

And now, suddenly, this peace was shattered. Within a few hours of the discovery that the Lindbergh baby's bed was empty—the blankets still held in place by their safety pins—a swarm of police and newspaper men had reached the house and were trampling about the muddy grounds, obliterating clues. And when the news broke in the next morning's newspapers, the American people went into a long paroxysm of excitement.

More police and reporters arrived; the nearest railroad station was transformed into a newspaper headquarters; news from Hopewell crowded everything else to the back pages of the papers; President Hoover issued a statement, the governor of New Jersey held police conferences, anti-kidnaping bills were prepared by legislators in several states, the New York *Times* reported the receipt on a single day of 3,331 telephone calls asking for the latest news. Bishop Manning of New York sent his clergy a special prayer for immediate use, declaring, "In a case like this we cannot wait till Sunday." William Green asked members of the American Federation of Labor to aid in the hunt for the criminal. Commander Evangeline Booth urged all commanding officers of the Salvation Army to help, and referred to "the miraculous accomplishments with which God has honored our movement along these very lines through our lost and found bureau." Clergymen of three denominations prayed over the radio for the baby's deliverance. Wild rumors went about. Babies resembling the Lindbergh child were reported seen in automobiles all over the country. The proprietor of a cigar store in Jersey City brought the police on the run by reporting that he had heard a man in a telephone booth say something that sounded like a kidnaper's message. And the Lindberghs received endless letters of advice and suggestion—the total running, in a few weeks, to one hundred thousand.

From day to day the drama of the search went on—the Lindberghs offering immunity to the kidnaper in a signed statement, giving out the pathetic details of the baby's accustomed diet, asking two racketeering bootleggers named Spitale and Bitz to serve as intermediaries with the underworld; and soon the chief actors in the Hopewell drama became as familiar to the American newspaper-reading public as if the whole country had been engaged in reading the same detective story. Mr. and Mrs. Oliver Whateley, the butler and his wife; Betty Gow, the nurse; Arthur Johnson, her sailor friend; Colonel Schwarzkopf of the New Jersey State Police; Violet Sharpe, the maid at the Morrows' house, who committed suicide;

and Dr. John F. Condon ("Jafsie"), the old gentleman in the Bronx who made the first personal contact with the kidnaper—these men and women became the subjects of endless conjectures and theorizings. When a stranger asked one, "Have they found the baby?" there was never an instant's doubt as to what baby was meant, whether the question was asked in New Jersey or in Oregon. One would hear a hotel elevator man saying out of the blue, to an ascending guest, "Well, I believe it was an inside job"— to which the guest would reply heatedly, "Nonsense, it was that gang in Detroit." If the American people had needed to have their minds taken off the Depression, the kidnaping had briefly done it.

On March 8, a week after the crime, old Dr. Condon—college lecturer and welfare worker in "the most beautiful borough in the world," as he called the Bronx—conceived the odd idea of putting an advertisement in the Bronx *Home News,* to the effect that he would be glad to serve as an intermediary for the return of the Lindbergh child. The next day he received a letter, misspelled in an odd Germanic way, containing an enclosure addressed to Colonel Lindbergh. He called up the house at Hopewell, was asked to open the enclosure, described some curious markings on it, and at once was asked to come and see Colonel Lindbergh—for those markings were identical with the code symbols on a ransom note which had been left on the window sill of the baby's room! On March 12, Dr. Condon received a note which told him to go to a hot-dog stand at the end of the Jerome Avenue elevated railroad. He found there a note directing him to the entrance of Woodlawn Cemetery. He presently saw a man in the shrubbery of the cemetery, and he went with this man to a bench near by, where they sat and talked. The kidnaper had a German or Scandinavian accent, called himself "John," and said he was only one of a gang.

Further negotiations—which left no doubt that "John" was indeed the kidnaper, or one of the kidnapers—led to the payment of $50,000 in bills to "John" by Dr. Condon (accompanied by Colonel Lindbergh) in St. Raymond's Cemetery in the Bronx on April 2—whereupon "John" handed Dr. Condon a note which said that the baby would be found safe on a "boad" (meaning *boat*) near Gay Head on Martha's Vineyard. The Colonel made two flights there by plane and found no "boad"; clearly the information given was false.

Then on the evening of May 12, 1932, about six weeks after the kidnaping, the newsboys chanted extras in the streets once more: the child's body had been found by chance in a thicket near a road five and a half miles from the Lindbergh place. Whether he had been killed deliberately or accidentally would never be known; in any event, the kidpaper had chosen that spot to half-bury the little body.

"BABY DEAD" announced the tabloid headlines: those two words sufficed.

A great many Americans whose memories of other events of the decade are vague can recall just where and under what circumstances they first heard that piece of news.

The story seemed to have reached its end, but still the reverberations of horror continued. Soon it was clear, not only that the kidnaper had added the cruelty of Lindbergh's hopeless search by plane to the barbarity of the original crime; not only that Gaston B. Means had wangled $100,000 out of Mrs. McLean of Washington on the criminally false pretense that he could get the child back; but also that John Hughes Curtis of Norfolk, Virginia, who had induced Colonel Lindbergh to go out on a boat in Chesapeake Bay to make contact with the kidnapers, had concocted—for whatever reason—one of the most contemptible hoaxes ever conceived. These revelations, coming on top of the shock of seeing the Lindberghs forced to deal with representatives of the underworld (as if the underworld were quite beyond the law), brought thunders of dismay from preachers, orators, editorial-writers, columnists: there was something very rotten indeed in the State of Denmark. And the tragic sense that things were awry was deepened.

There the Lindbergh case rested in 1932. But we must go ahead of our history to recount the sequel. It came over twenty-eight months later, on September 19, 1934, when the kidnaper was arrested. Ironically, one of the things which facilitated his capture was that in the meantime the New Deal had come in, the United States had gone off the gold standard, and the gold certificates which had been handed over to the kidnaper had become noticeable rarities.

The kidnaper proved to be not a member of the organized underworld but a lone criminal—a fugitive felon from Germany, illegally in the United States—one Bruno Richard Hauptmann. He was arrested in the Bronx, was tried at the beginning of 1935 at the Hunterdon County Court House at Flemington, New Jersey, was convicted, and—after an unsuccessful appeal and a delay brought about by the inexplicable unwillingness of Goveror Harold Hoffman of New Jersey to believe in his guilt—was electrocuted on April 3, 1936.

The evidence against Hauptmann was overwhelming. Leaving aside the possibly debatable identifications of him and other dubious bits of evidence, consider these items alone: 1. Hauptmann lived in the Bronx, where

209

Dr. Condon's advertisement had appeared, where Dr. Condon had met "John" and where "John" had received the ransom money. 2. The numbers of the ransom bills had been recorded: many of these bills had been passed in parts of New York City accessible to a resident of the Bronx; it was the passing of one by Hauptmann in a Bronx garage which led to his arrest. 3. When arrested, Hauptmann had a $20 ransom bill on his person. 4. No less than $14,600 in ransom bills was found secreted in his garage. 5. He was a German, his tricks of speech corresponded roughly to those in the ransom letters, he had once used in an account book the spelling "boad," and he used other misspellings and foreign locutions like those in the ransom notes. 6. His handwriting was similar to those in the notes. 7. He had had no regular means of support after March 1, 1932, but had nevertheless spent money freely and had had a brokerage account of some dimensions (with which he was quite unsuccessful). 8. His story of how he got his money, through an alleged partnership in a fur business with one Frisch, and how he kept it in a shoe box on a shelf, was vague and unconvincing. 9. Furthermore, the kidnaper had left behind, at Hopewell, a ladder of odd construction. An expert from the Department of Agriculture, Arthur Koehler, not only found, from the sort of wood used in the making of this ladder and from peculiarities in its cutting, that it had been a part of a shipment to a Bronx firm, but also that irregularities in the planing of it corresponded to irregularities in a plane in Hauptmann's possession. 10. Finally, one piece of the wood used in the ladder fitted precisely a piece missing from a floor board in Hauptmann's attic, even the old nail holes in it matching to a fraction of an inch!

STANLEY WALKER

THE JUDGING OF HAUPTMANN*

THE trial of Bruno Richard Hauptmann, for the murder of the Lindbergh baby, which began in Flemington, New Jersey, in the first part of January 1935, was so spectacular, so bizarre, that in restrospect it seems almost incredible that things could have happened as they did. Everything conspired to make the trial dramatic. In its bare, simple outlines the case had

* From Stanley Walker's *Mrs. Astor's Horse* (New York, Stokes, 1935).

all the ingredients of a starkly realistic mystery story. But that was not enough. It remained for the press, the radio, the officials and the spectators to make of it a fantastic extravaganza.

The 300 or more reporters covering the trial filed more than 10,000,000 words. Foreign correspondents sent hundreds of thousands of words by radio, cable and mail. Many radio stations were busy broadcasting transcripts of the testimony. In addition, news commentators and extralegal authorities discussed all aspects of the case. Hearst's New York *Journal,* which was instrumental in employing defense counsel, and which paid the wife of Hauptmann $25 a week, had thirty reporters and a posse of photographers on the scene. The New York *Times* devoted more space to the trial than the other papers, simply because it had more room. It was, surely, the trial of the century.

One of the unforgettable characters of the trial was Edward J. Reilly, a criminal lawyer from Brooklyn, who had been retained as chief of defense counsel. Known as the "Bull of Brooklyn," Reilly had a long, successful record of defending criminals. His strength in his home county usually lay in political pull, oratory or convenient witnesses. As soon as he took over the defense of Hauptmann he began issuing statements. There were, he said, new witnesses. He knew who did the kidnaping. He knew many dark secrets. The forces of the prosecution, headed by David Wilentz, Attorney General of New Jersey, began answering Reilly, and this interchange continued up to the start of the trial.

The sideshow motif became evident early. Sheriff John H. Curtiss, of Hunterdon County, a fat man who came from New England, perceived almost immediately that he could make a good thing out of the trial. His first move was to keep the minions of Mayor Frank Hague of Jersey City out of the scheme. Mr. Hague is a man of considerable dignity, but some of his "boys" have a habit of "muscling in" on important trials, no matter in what part of New Jersey they are held. A committee of reporters, with one of the Hague men at the head, set out for Flemington to discuss seating arrangements. When they arrived, Sheriff Curtiss eyed the Hague fixer with contempt. After some blustering the Hague man departed, leaving the Sheriff in complete power.

The Sheriff informed each reporter, when he came to get tickets for his paper, that there would be a $10 tax on main floor seats and a $5 fee for balcony seats. Most of the reporters paid it, knowing that they could put the item on their expense accounts. But one young fellow from the New York *World-Telegram* telephoned his office before paying; the editor, in crusading mood that morning, ordered a story on the Sheriff's fee-fixing.

Then the fun began. The Board of Freeholders, all Democrats, announced an investigation of the Sheriff, who was a Republican. The Sheriff explained that he was only trying to save the county a little money, and that the "contributions" were merely to meet the cost of installing benches and a temporary press table. He offered free seats to the *World-Telegram*. The reporters, realizing that they would have to keep on good terms with the Sheriff for many weeks, let the matter drop.

Afterward the Sheriff was more cautious. A third person, connected with a telegraph company, could get anyone a ticket for a price. Even Mrs. Ogden L. Mills, wife of the former Secretary of the Treasury, had to pay to get in. Tickets could be obtained for $10, $5, a pint of good bonded rye, or a box of cigars. The Sheriff smoked cigars. Tickets were good for one session only; the reporters were lucky to have received season passes for $10 each. A ticket, of course, did not guarantee a seat. Many paying customers saw the show from the aisles, radiators and window sills. Panes of several windows were broken by eager spectators, adding a pleasant tinkle of falling glass to the regular trial noises.

On one occasion a woman drove up in front of the courthouse in a Rolls-Royce. Her uniformed chauffeur leaped out and open the door. The woman, wrapped in mink, stepped out and drew from her pocketbook a $100 bill, which she waved, announcing in a loud, clear voice that she would give all of it for a ticket. She got the ticket.

The first to realize the possibilities in the housing situation was Bert Pedrick, owner of Flemington's only hotel, a ramshackle three-story wooden building. He bought up options on most of the rooms available in the town. He paid the owners $1 a night and charged newspaper men $5 a day for room and board. After the trial Bert paid off the mortgage on the hotel and bought a new sedan.

Everybody in town was out to make money. The Women's Exchange, where homemade pastries, breads and rolls were brought by matrons during normal times for sale to their sisters, emerged as a tearoom. The Methodist Episcopal Church became a luncheon spot, with women from the auxiliary serving meals. This enterprise was subsidized by the state, which fed all its witnesses and officers there. After the trial the church bought a new organ. An evangelist from the Middle West saw an opportunity to save some souls while the trial was in progress. The Reverend J. Fred Bindenberger of Flemington liked the idea and promised the sky pilot his church. Other pastors objected. A compromise was reached under which the visitor agreed not to mention the Hauptmann trial in his exhortations. The revival was a failure.

The souvenir salesmen overran the place. One enterprising fellow made up a batch of miniature ladders. They were simple affairs, about eight inches long and two inches wide, the pine in them being of cigar box thickness. These miniatures were handed out to salesmen, who went about shouting that it was possible to purchase "exact duplicates" of the famous ladder used in the kidnaping for twenty-five cents. The ladders differed greatly from the principal exhibit in the case, but the buyers didn't mind. The ladders sold. One young man, highly excited, bought a ladder and tied it to his lapel with a red ribbon. He said to his companions:

"I'm going to leave it on too, by God! I'll march in on Gertie with it. Then won't she kick herself when she sees what she missed. The double-crossing bitch!"

A man with a metal press did a fair sort of business. He set up for business on the porch of the hotel. He had constructed a die depicting the Hunterdon County courthouse, surrounded by the legend, "Hauptmann Trial, Flemington, N. J." On the stand beside the press lay several hundred bright new pennies and several fine strips of copper. By running the copper strips through the press, together with the pennies, he turned out Lincoln heads backed by the courthouse and the legend. The pieces sold for five cents each, three for a dime.

The Flemington pottery turned out a set of book ends on which the courthouse appeared. These bits of clay were bought by the more wealthy visitors and today serve as parlor exhibits in many a home. A quick-sketch artist turned out portraits of Hauptmann and other principals of the trial by the dozen; post cards with scenes of Flemington were sold at five cents each; pictures of the jury ranged from a dime to twenty-five cents. The higher-priced jury pictures were "suitable for framing."

Boys from the high school made pocket money running copy for reporters. They had managed to get days off from school. These sharp lads hit upon a scheme of financing their yearbook. The town was overrun with autograph seekers. One day several of the boys appeared in the bar of the hotel with a large drawing board. They went from reporter to reporter and asked for autographs for the yearbook. It seemed that the book was to be dedicated to the reporters who covered the trial. As each man jotted down his name, he was asked for a contribution of twenty-five cents. The reporters didn't feel they could refuse. The boys also got signatures of most of the principals except Colonel Lindbergh and Hauptmann. A week later there was offered for sale at twenty-five cents each, copies of the sheet with the autographs, headed by the inscription, "The Trial of the Century." The youth of Flemington made a lot of money.

The crowds of curious were bad enough on weekdays, but on Sundays they were worse. After the first Sunday, when visitors stole everything in the courthouse they could get their hands on, the Sheriff wanted to close the place on Sundays, but the American Legion and the Kiwanis and Rotary Clubs volunteered to supply guards who would not only stop souvenir hunters but would answer the questions of the sightseers. When the visitors began arriving the second Sunday they found huge placards scattered about the courtroom. Over the chair of the defendant was the sign, "Hauptmann." Likewise there were signs indicating where the judge and jury sat, the witness chair, Colonel Lindbergh's chair, and the spot where Walter Winchell usually kept himself. The crowds were especially eager to see Mrs. Hauptmann and her little son. Every time the two appeared on the street, the crowd would rush for them. Somehow the sightseers seemed to find it astonishing that the child should appear as a pleasant-faced, chubby baby rather than as some sort of monster. Reilly wanted to have the baby brought into the courtroom, but Justice Trenchard, presiding, refused to allow it. Nevertheless, the jury got several glimpses of the child.

A man who got relatively little attention during the trial was Warden Harry O. McCrae, who guarded Hauptmann. Of course he got a few cigars now and then for divulging how Hauptmann had slept, or what he ate, but that was about all he got during the trial. Later, however, it developed that McCrae also had entered into the spirit of the thing. Because the officials feared that Hauptmann might attempt suicide if allowed to eat with ordinary knives and forks, he was forced to use paper utensils. The warden supplied this equipment, but when Hauptmann had finished eating, the warden hid the utensils in a little basket under his desk. After the trial he handed out paper spoons, forks and plates to any friends who happened to call—each and every one of them guaranteed to have been used by none other than Bruno Richard Hauptmann.

The macabre spectacle finally came to an end. The most dismal scene of all was the courtroom from the time the jury went out until it returned with the verdict of guilty. Justice Trenchard left the bench and went to his chambers to read. Attorney General Wilentz sat in the jury box. Reilly was in the witness chair. The floor was strewn with papers, cigarette stubs and remnants of sandwiches. Some, with paper bags in their hands, ate sandwiches and cakes and drank coffee, milk or applejack. The more sportive element played games of checkers and tick-tack-toe. Some of the journalists started a dice game in Justice Trenchard's library without his knowledge. Soon reporters, radio men, stenographers, lawyers and Broadway hangers-on were trying their luck. One man won $200 on two passes. A member of the defense counsel collected $75 and said, "That's more than I earned during the whole trial." At this point Justice Trenchard left his chambers and started for the library to get a book. The players, however, were warned. They quickly hid the dice and money and when the old justice entered the library he saw an unusually studious group of young men, all poring over law books. As soon as the justice left, the game was resumed.

Meanwhile, Wilentz, sitting in the jury box, amused his listeners with such jests as, "This is where I should have been in the first place." Reilly, in the witness chair, burlesqued the testimony of state's witnesses. He shot questions at himself, then pretended to be too deaf to hear them. He would cup his hand to his ear and say, "What was that? What? Repeat the question." Reilly is known far and wide as a card, and his barroom stories and repartee were among the most engaging aspects of the Flemington period. Before the jury came in Reilly and a woman reporter stood up in front of the judge's bench and sang "When Irish Eyes Are Smiling."

As soon as the jury had found Hauptmann guilty its members were besought by agents to go on the stage. The foreman was offered $800 a week and the other members $500 a week each. Some of them considered it seriously. So far had the carnival spirit run that many persons could see no impropriety in the jury going on the stage. This attitude was expressed by County Judge Adam O. Robbins, who had relinquished his post in order that Justice Trenchard might sit at the trial. Asked what he thought of the jury accepting the offer, he said:

"Couldn't blame them if they did. You don't make that much farming in a lifetime. Nope, I think it might be a good idea."

The vaudeville scheme collapsed, but the members of the jury did write (or rather, had ghostwritten) articles in which they discussed the trial. They also wrote a book, each contributing a chapter. These twelve men and women had become so impressed with their importance that they found it difficult after the trial to return to their ordinary tasks.

American newspapers were criticized because of the sensational fashion in which the trial was handled. There were many astounding excesses, violations of ethical canons, double-crossings by reporters and officeholders, and an unbelievable amount of trickery. Indeed, sound films of the trial were taken surreptitiously during the first few days, shown at a few theaters, and then suppressed. Undoubtedly the press and the radio people overstepped all limits of dignity, but they were not alone. The lawyers in some respects were worse. And there was printed during the trial a long, learned discussion of the evidence in the New York *Law Journal,* the official law periodical of the First Judicial Department of New York. This article discussed the evidence editorially as it had developed thus far, and pointed out that some of the testimony given was hardly credible. Many old-fashioned lawyers were perturbed at this.

It is difficult to see what could have been done to make the trial a model of decorum. It was too big, and the interest was too great. Justice Trenchard was not to blame; indeed, he did the best he could in a trying situation.

Two exhibits in the life of Flemington deserve mention. One was the menu devised by the owner of a hash house several doors from the hotel. The proprietor was not getting as much business as he had hoped for. His itinerant chef suggested a novel way of getting customers. One morning a sandwich board appeared in front of the place. It was headed "Trial Lunch." Some of the items were: "Writers' cramp soup, 10¢"; "Lindbergh steak, 50¢"; "Hauptmann beans, 35¢"; "Trenchard roast with Bruno gravy, 40¢"; "Jafsie chops, 50¢"; "Jury pie, 10¢"; "Reilly pudding, 20¢"; "Press custard, 10¢; and "Photog's ice cream, 10¢."

Another exhibit is a song sung around the bars, the hotel and the rooming houses of Flemington. It is a parody of the old German "Schnitzelbank" song, long a favorite in the beer halls. It is entitled "Du Schoene Hauptmann Trial," and goes as follows:

DU SCHOENE HAUPTMANN TRIAL

Ist das nicht ein dowel pin?
Ja, das ist ein dowel pin,
Fitted das nicht nicely in?
Ja, es fitted nicely in.
Dowel pin, etc.

THEY CALLED IT BANKBUSTING

IN THE early Thirties, individual desperadoes achieved national notoriety as never before; their exploits were front-page stories in the press and their relative "popularity" was determined by the order in which their names appeared in the FBI's list of Public Enemies. They were not members of the organized city gangs that ran the rackets and levied "protection" taxes on small businessmen, as did the Capone gang, for instance. With hard times upon them, these modern Jesse Jameses simply decided to take money from banks, killing in cold blood when anyone got in their way. This was outlawry in its oldest form.

At times the press and a willing public seemed to create a spirit of Roman holiday around these manhunts; the very names of some of the criminals suggest the publicity man—"Pretty-Boy" Floyd, bank robber and killer; "Baby-Face" Nelson, bank robber, kidnaper and killer; "Machine-Gun" Kelly and his whole family, kidnapers; Clyde Barrow and his gun-moll, Bonnie Parker, killers and hold-up specialists; and the most publicized of them all, John Dillinger, bank robber and killer. The Dillinger manhunt was followed so avidly that when he was slain the whole country appeared to have experienced a kind of emotional catharsis.

Until 1933 a state line was the bankbuster's best friend. If he managed to get away from the scene of the crime and into a neighboring state, he was relatively safe from apprehension. There was little effective co-operation among the separate state police departments, and no central clearinghouse for the co-ordination of activities. The Seventy-third Congress, however, passed some twenty anticrime laws, including one that reorganized the Federal Bureau of Investigation, to provide for the apprehension and prosecution of interstate criminals. With such organization on the side of the law, the "percentage" in favor of the roving desperado was reduced. And with the centralization of responsibility for the pursuit of fugitives, the opportunities for flamboyant enterprise in the newspaper coverage of such man hunts disappeared. The heyday of the bankbuster was over, but it had been an exciting time while it lasted.

A L A N H Y N D

DILLINGER*

JULY 1933

THE time bomb that was to terrorize the Middle West began ticking a few minutes after eleven o'clock one morning early in July 1933. John Dillinger, Jr., twenty-nine years old, fresh from a nine-year stretch in the Indiana state penitentiary at Michigan City, had returned to his father's scraggly ten-acre produce farm outside Mooresville. His father, a small, stoop-shouldered man in his middle sixties, was standing near the water pump, thumbs hitched in his patched overalls.

A truculent fellow, John Dillinger was five feet eleven, weighed 170, and had reddish-brown hair, yellowish-brown eyes and a tight, mean mouth. In the months that lay ahead Dillinger's features, scowling from newspaper front pages, were to become familiar the length and breadth of the land.

"Hello, Pa," Dillinger said.

Old John didn't answer, just nodded.

"What's wrong, Pa?"

"It's your mother."

Up on the second floor, a worn woman lay panting on a four-poster. She was John Dillinger's stepmother—the only person for whom he had ever developed a genuine affection. She barely managed a smile. Before the sun went down that afternoon, she died.

That night, after the undertaker had called for the body, Dillinger sat with his father in the kitchen. "What was wrong with Ma?" he asked. "You never told me about her while I was away."

"It was her heart," said old John. "Her heart went bad after the banks."

Old John had lost his savings in a bank. The mortgage people now were threatening to foreclose on his farm. Savings banks all over America had failed during John Dillinger's last months in prison.

Next day, Dillinger went into Indianapolis, sixteen miles away, and walked into an employment agency.

"I'd like to get a job as a machinist," said Dillinger.

* Condensed from *True* Magazine, September 1956.

"How much experience have you had?" the interviewer asked him.

"A couple of years."

"Where?"

Dillinger cleared his throat and looked at his feet.

"I said, where have you had your experience?" the other insisted earnestly.

"Well, it's like this. I've been in prison. But—"

The man shook his head. "Not a chance," he said. "Employers aren't hiring ex-convicts. Jobs are too scarce. Sorry."

Dillinger got the same brush-off at other employment agencies. He checked the newspapers, but there were no ads for machinists.

Dillinger thought about the shirt factory in the penitentiary at Michigan City, where he had spent five of his sentence years. He thought of the four men—Pierpont, Hamilton, Makley and Clark—who'd been his closest friends while he was in prison. . . .

A few days later, John Dillinger walked into a rooming house on the South Side of Chicago and called on Homer Van Meter. Little Homer stood just five feet, one inch high. Twenty-six years old, he looked eighteen, with a round boyish face, guileless blue eyes and soft brown hair. As ex-cons, unable to get work, Dillinger and Van Meter were starting with a lot in common.

Dillinger was full of plans. "We could make an awful lot of money holding up banks. Me and you and a couple of other fellows could get together and make a nice living. You only got the cops to think about when you rob a bank, and cops ain't very smart. The people who work in the banks have got a lot of relations who lost money in banks. I'll bet some of the people who work in banks would be glad to see us. And anyway, it ain't their money."

AUGUST 1933

One afternoon early in August, Dillinger and Van Meter went to Wrigley Field to see the Chicago Cubs. This was the year that Bill Terry's New York Giants were to cop the pennant and beat Joe Cronin's Washington Senators in the World Series. Dillinger and Van Meter settled themselves in the grandstand along the third-base line and drank Cokes and munched hot dogs. What he was plotting, as he sat there with Van Meter, one eye on the ball game, was to spring his four old friends—Hamilton, Pierpont, Clark and Makley—from Michigan City.

"What we could do," Dillinger decided, "is put some guns in a crate of that thread they ship to the prison shirt factory. I've got a contact in that thread factory outside Indianapolis. Harry always opens the crates. I think I'll drop him a note."

A few days later in the prison shirt factory, Harry Pierpont (doing twenty years for armed robbery) opened a crate of thread and got the note. Dillinger was shipping in a load of guns and ammunition; Harry should stand by for a crate with a few splashes of black paint under the address lettering.

Pierpont passed the news along to an armed-robbery specialist named Harry Makley. Makley, in turn, told John Hamilton—a square-faced thirty-eight-year-old murderer known as Three-Finger Jack because he had lost the middle finger on his trigger hand in a Chicago gun fight. Dillinger's fourth friend who got the message that day was Russell Clark.

Dillinger went to a hot-car dealer in Chicago and bought a black Ford sedan, paying for it with cash.

Late one dark, sticky night, the third week in August, Dillinger was up on the loading platform of the thread factory doctoring up a crate of thread. He put in some guns, some ammunition and an envelope containing $1,000 in cash. Then he nailed it up and splashed some black paint under the address lettering.

SEPTEMBER 1933

A few minutes before noon on September 4, Dillinger and Van Meter drove into Indianapolis, got out of the black Ford and strolled casually into the State Bank in the heart of Indianapolis. There were six tellers' windows and the desks of three officers behind a mahogany railing out on the floor.

Dillinger and Van Meter stood at a counter facing the tellers' cages. Dillinger made a rough sketch of the premises on a deposit slip.

"I don't like the great big windows in this place," he told Homer. "People on the street can look right in and see everything. I'm going outside. You go over to one of the tellers and get a bill changed and while you're doing it act tired and yawn and stretch your hands over your head."

When Van Meter returned, Dillinger said, "I could see your hands. We got to make sure nobody puts their hands in the air when we hold up this place."

Dillinger spent the rest of the day cruising around downtown Indianapolis. He made notes of the distances between blocks—down to a tenth of a mile—how long it took traffic lights to change, how heavy the traffic was on certain streets and various crossings.

The nearest police station was five blocks from the State Bank. Dillinger, driving at normal speed over the distance, estimated that it would take the cops at least a minute and a half to reach the bank. So he put a time limit on the job—ninety seconds from the time he walked in until he ran out. He figured it would take the cops ten seconds at least to get into action.

A ten-second jump was all Dillinger asked for. By virtue of his study of the traffic conditions and his souped-up car, he could move in and out of downtown Indianapolis at least as fast as any pursuer. And if worse came to worst, he could always shoot his way out.

At four minutes after one the afternoon of September 5, Matt Leach * got a flash from the Indianapolis police. Two armed men had walked into the State Bank at one o'clock sharp. The taller of the two had announced a holdup but warned everybody not to put their hands in the air. While his companion covered everybody, the tall one forced one of the bank officers to take him behind the cages. There, he scooped up fistfuls of bills. Every few seconds he glanced at his watch and called to his companion: "Thirty seconds . . . twenty seconds . . . two seconds!" Then: "Let's go!"

Matt Leach quickly identified Dillinger and Van Meter. Through his experience as a municipal cop in Gary, Leach had established several solid contacts in the underworld. He couldn't get a line on little Homer but from a stool pigeon he learned that Dillinger was hiding out in Dayton, Ohio, in the apartment of a sister of one of his four pals in Michigan City.

Acting on Leach's tip, the Dayton cops hung around the apartment house and pounced on the unsuspecting Dillinger, taking him without a struggle. Dillinger, viewing his capture philosophically, grinned at his captors. "All right," he said. "You've won this hand. But you can bet I'll win the next one."

News of Dillinger's capture was soon buzzing over the grapevine at Michigan State [Penitentiary]. On the morning of the twenty-sixth Dillinger's four friends—Pierpont, Hamilton, Makley and Clark—equipped with the stuff he had smuggled in to them, overpowered two guards and a visiting sheriff and used them as hostages on a break.

At a few minutes after eleven o'clock that night the four escapees barged into a little gospel mission just off Fountain Square in Indianapolis. The intruders stripped four derelicts and changed from their prison clothes. In a few minutes Dillinger's four friends were barreling through the moonless countryside, planning to spring Dillinger from jail. One bad turn deserved another.

* Captain Leach was operating head of the Indiana State Police.

OCTOBER 1933

Sixteen nights after the Michigan City break, Pierpont, Makley, Clark and Hamilton drew up in front of the jail in Lima. Dressed in new suits and wearing snap-brim hats, the four walked into the warden's office.

"Who's in charge here?" asked Pierpont, the cruel one.

"I am," said Sheriff Jesse Barber.

"We're deputies from Michigan City," said Pierpont. "We've come to take Dillinger back to the penitentiary."

"I'll have to see your credentials," said the sheriff.

Pierpont reached toward his inside jacket pocket, drew a gun and emptied it at the sheriff—the first murder of the Dillinger mob.

When the sheriff's wife and a deputy came running in, the four outlaws grabbed them, herded them into a cell and slammed the door shut. With the sheriff's key Pierpont then freed Dillinger.

Shortly after midnight they pulled up to a darkened farmhouse that was not wired for a telephone.

Through an unlocked back door, Dillinger went inside. A dog sprang at him. He fired once and killed the animal.

A light went on in the house. The five intruders heard footsteps approaching. Presently a figure came into the kitchen. Dillinger snapped on the light and leveled his gun at the man in the doorway—a middle-aged farmer in bare feet and nightshirt.

"How many people in this house?" asked Dillinger.

"Just my wife," said the terrorized farmer, "and my two sons."

"How old are your sons?" asked Dillinger.

"Seventeen and eighteen."

"Get them down here. And your wife, too. I'm hungry."

Next morning, Dillinger sat in the parlor, listening to radio news flashes about the murder of the sheriff and the hunt for the killers. His four pals had split up to cover the family; the farmer and the sons were out in the fields as usual, not daring to tell.

Posses were scouring the countryside for Dillinger and the men who had sprung him, with orders to shoot on sight. Every so often one of the four others would come in and ask Dillinger what the news was.

"Everything's all right," Dillinger reported. "We'll just stay here until we can move."

Late in the afternoon, he decided they could safely get to Pierpont's mother's farm near Leipsic, about ten miles away. "We can dig a cave under the barn and stay there in case the cops do come around."

Mother Pierpont, a wrinkled old crone who spent most of her time sitting in a rocker in the parlor, smoking a corncob pipe, was not surprised to see them.

"Hello, son," she said to Harry. "What did you have to go and kill that sheriff for? Now, everybody'll be after you, so be careful."

The boys worked through the night, fashioning a cave under the barn floor. They scattered the dirt in the fields so it wouldn't attract attention. By morning, with Ma covering up the boards on top with straw, the five fugitives were safely hidden in the cave.

That very afternoon, Matt Leach, acting on a hunch, visited Ma Pierpont's place. First thing he did was to check the barn. Noticing the pile of hay over the cave, he gave it a few jabs with a pitchfork. But Matt jabbed horizontally, not vertically, and hit the straw, not the camouflaging floor boards.

Mother Pierpont kept the boys in food and reading matter, and one day Dillinger spotted a newspaper item.

"Listen to this! The cops in Peru, Indiana, just laid in a new stock of machine guns and ammunition to make things hot for us." He grinned. "We could sure use some machine guns and ammunition. . . . "

Next day, Homer Van Meter, who had been lying low in Chicago, appeared at the Pierpont farm.

"How'd you know where we were?" Dillinger asked.

"Instinct," said Homer.

"You're just in time," said Dillinger. "I got a job for you in Peru."

Dillinger, Van Meter and Pierpont arrived in Peru late at night. Van Meter, coached by Dillinger, went into the police station and palmed himself off to the lone man on duty as a writer for a detective magazine.

"I want to write up a story about how you are protecting your community," little Homer said.

The cop showed Homer the new arsenal.

"You on duty here alone?" asked Homer.

"Yeah," answered the unsuspecting cop. "I get relieved at eleven o'clock."

At half past ten Pierpont walked into the station and asked the cop directions to Indianapolis. As the cop got up from his desk, Pierpont grabbed him. Dillinger appeared and helped Pierpont lock the cop in a cell. Then they cleaned out the police station and drove off with all the guns and ammunition.

Dillinger now went off alone on a reconnoitering tour. He spotted just what he was after in the town of Greencastle, some forty miles southwest of Indianapolis—the National Savings and Trust Company, a compact red-brick building right across the street from the courthouse. Putting on a pair of dark glasses, Dillinger went in and drew a sketch of the interior layout.

Two days later, Dillinger returned to Greencastle with Van Meter and Pierpont. He assigned little Homer to remain in the car, which was parked down the street from the bank, and make note of how many people went in and out. He and Pierpont strolled around town, looking over traffic conditions. Dillinger, on this second visit, noticed that there was more activity around the bank than he ordinarily cared for; too many people lounging around the courthouse. Nonetheless, the plum looked too ripe not to be plucked.

Back in the cave, at Mother Pierpont's farm, Dillinger and the others tossed the problem around. How could they pull a job with so many people looking on?

Dillinger finally got an idea. "We'll make believe we're movie people making a movie. We can rob that bank and everybody who sees it will just think we're making a movie."

The rehearsal, entered into by the boys with all the enthusiasm of amateurs getting set to stage a high-school play, had Makley standing in front of an imaginary jug with a make-believe camera and tripod and wearing his cap turned backward. Hamilton, who was to be attired in white shirt, open at the neck, and puttees, was carrying a director's megaphone. Little Homer, the assistant director, was standing by while Clark, the assistant cameraman, was carefully measuring the distance between the camera and the entrance of the repository of concentrated wealth.

A couple of imaginary people were to wander over from the courthouse and ask the boys what was going on. "We're from Paramount Pictures," little Homer was to explain. "We're shooting a scene of a couple of bank bandits escaping."

Dillinger and Pierpont, wearing yellowish make-up, and carrying machine guns, were then to appear and, on directions from Hamilton, go inside the bank.

The holdup accomplished, everybody was to be off in a car, in a cloud of dust, before anybody on the outside realized that the caper had been real instead of make-believe.

Something changed John's mind, though. Then, on the morning of the twenty-third, the boys pulled just another routine robbery—for them. They took to the hills with $74,382.14.

NOVEMBER 1933

Early in November, four months after he had begun operations, John Dillinger was wanted by two states and by the government of the United States. Ohio wanted him to take up where he had left off in Lima. Matt Leach wanted him for bank hold-ups in Daleville, Rockville, Indianapolis and Greencastle. The FBI wanted him for the Indianapolis and Greencastle heists, because the banks in those cities were national institutions.

The four bank jobs so far had yielded a total of slightly more than $127,000, of which Dillinger, after splitting with his co-workers, had kept roughly one fourth, or more than thirty grand. At the going rate for machinists, he had made as much in four months as he would have made as a machinist in twenty years.

Dillinger decided to make Chicago his headquarters. In addition to being big, Chicago had other advantages. Its police department was honeycombed by crooked cops who, should they be lucky enough to spot him, could be bought off.

Unable to trust anybody but himself, Dillinger wondered where to keep his wealth. He had no faith in banks, and he could not carry the money around with him.

Finally, under a variety of aliases, John rented about a dozen mail boxes in post-office substations around Chicago. He stuck about $20,000 in envelopes, and mailed the money to himself. Then he mailed all the box keys, except one, to one of the boxes. He went to a shoemaker and had him insert the key to the master box between layers of leather in one of his shoes. He retained more than $10,000 in cash, which he carried around with him for emergencies.

Assuming the name of Jack Lawrence, John moved into a semirespectable rooming house on the North Side. The other members of the gang—Pierpont, Hamilton, Makley, Clark and Van Meter, whose faces were totally unfamiliar to the average cop—were scattered in other rooming houses in the immediate neighborhood.

DECEMBER 1933

In the first week of December, Dillinger and Makley happened to notice a bank that was, surprisingly, both open and closed. The Unity Trust and Savings on West North Avenue had recently gone out of business, but a sign in the front window proclaimed that a room in the rear, used exclusively for safe-deposit boxes, was still open for business.

John went in. The safe-deposit room was in the rear, and Dillinger saw that there was just one attendant on duty, an elderly man.

Dillinger came out and told Makley to go in to the safe-deposit room and pose as a salesman of burglar alarms. Charlie was to find out if the place was wired for sound. In a few minutes Mackley reported back. The room wasn't wired. There was no electrical alarm system to thwart an assault on the place.

Dillinger got the boys together.

It was during that conference that Dillinger conceived something new in lookouts—a fake Santa Claus. Since Christmas was coming on, Makley, the fat one, was to dress himself up as Santa Claus, complete with pot and bell, and station himself outside the bank building. The fraudulent Kris Kringle was to keep an eye on things while the robbery was in progress. If anybody tried to enter the bank, Makley was to divert them by volunteering the information: "They closed early in there this afternoon. They'll be open at nine in the morning."

At one o'clock on the slate-gray afternoon of December 13, the caper got under way. Dillinger, carrying a suitcase, arrived and dropped a coin in Santa's pot. "Everything clear?" he asked Makley.

Charlie nodded. "Nobody's inside but the attendant."

John went inside, removed the sign from the window, and waited for his co-workers. Three-Finger Hamilton, Pierpont, Van Meter and Clark appeared within two minutes. All but little Homer went back to the safe-deposit room. Van Meter remained in the bank proper to act as a liaison between the boys in back and the Santa Claus out front.

The back room was a bare, stuffy, windowless affair, with only the one door. All four walls were lined with steel safe-deposit boxes. The attendant —a man named Johnston—sat at an oak desk in the far corner of the room, facing the door. He was quickly bound and gagged and Dillinger took his place at the desk.

Dillinger took a portable radio out of the suitcase, and tuned in on the police frequency. Pierpont and Hamilton got out an acetylene torch and began to work on the safe-deposit boxes. Grimly efficient, they had a whole row of the boxes open in less than fifteen minutes. Dillinger examined the contents. He had developed a good eye for what was negotiable and what wasn't. The valuable stuff he put in the suitcase.

At a few minutes after two, an elderly gentleman who had got by the outside boys ambled into the back room. "What's going on here?" he snapped.

"What's your box number, dad?" asked Dillinger, friendly but business-like.

"Five hundred and three. Why?"

Dillinger asked Hamilton if he had come to Box 503.

"We're just opening that row now," said Hamilton, not even turning around to look at the depositor.

"Just stand over here in the corner, dad," said Dillinger, tying up the old man.

At a quarter to three, Pierpont and Hamilton had torched their way into about three hundred boxes. Dillinger had collected more than $70,000 in cash and about $150,000 in negotiable bonds.

At five minutes before three o'clock—the hour a signal would go off if the bound-up attendant didn't punch in—the boys packed up and left. They departed the premises one by one, split up and walked casually out of sight, Dillinger carrying the suitcase.

The caper in the safe-deposit room caused quite a furor in Chicago. Matt Leach quickly identified the culprits and kept pestering the Chicago cops to flush them. Late one afternoon, when the dusk was thickening, a detective recognized Three-Finger Jack on the street. But Three-Finger Jack saw the cop first and murdered him on the spot.

The murder made things too hot even for Dillinger. He decided to go to Florida with a woman he'd picked up—Evelyn Frechette—Makley, Pierpont, Clark and three ladies of casual morals whom the latter three had acquired. Three-Finger Jack was to lie low until things quieted down. Little Homer was to make a business trip through the Middle West, looking for new banks to bust.

Criminals on the lam, Dillinger had learned, usually traveled in high-powered cars by night. "We'll go in secondhand Fords," Dillinger said, "and we'll travel in the daytime."

The eight travelers, riding in two Ford sedans, arrived in Daytona Beach a few days before Christmas. Makley, cast by Dillinger in the role of a Wall Street broker, went to a real-estate office and rented a seventeen-room house on the waterfront. It was quiet on the waterfront in late December and the boys had nothing to do except lie around.

There they were, then, with no money worries, with no work crying to be done, and with their physical wants taken care of. And were they happy? You bet they were.

But finally Pierpont and Makley, the frisky ones, began to crave action.

227

Their share of the loot was burning holes in their pockets. They went into Daytona Beach and bought Cadillac roadsters, paying cash.

On New Year's Eve, Evelyn Frechette appeared wearing a slinky black evening gown. She asked Dillinger, "What are we goin' to do tonight? It's New Year's Eve, you know, Johnnie."

"Nothin'," said Dillinger. "We're stayin' right here."

Pierpont and Makley felt like getting drunk. Dillinger, who never drank, decided it might be fun to try some liquor.

Along toward midnight, the four boys and the four girls were out on the veranda, feeling no pain. Pierpont, hunched over the balustrade, was looking out at the water. The tide was coming in and the whitecaps, visible in the moonlight, were big and loud. He thought it would be fine sport to shoot at the whitecaps. Dillinger, feeling his liquor, agreed. So Harry went inside and brought out three machine guns. The boys waited for midnight. Then, when they heard the whistles blowing, they emptied the machine guns at the whitecaps. A neighbor, hearing the racket, called the cops.

When Pierpont saw a prowl car pulling up in front of the house, he said to Dillinger, "It's the cops. Let's kill the bastards!"

Dillinger, suddenly regaining sobriety, vetoed the suggestion. "I'll take the guns inside," he told Pierpont and Fat Charlie. "Just tell the cops you're sorry you made so much noise. And be real nice about it, too."

JANUARY 1934

Everybody slept until noon New Year's Day. The girls made scrambled eggs and coffee. Dillinger, settling himself in a big chair, began to leaf through a local newspaper that Makley had brought home the previous day. Suddenly, he stiffened. "Hey, Pierpont," he yelled. Pierpont came in from another room. "Look at this in the paper here!" said Dillinger. He pointed to a photograph of a man sitting at the wheel of a white Cadillac roadster.

Dillinger was furious. "You stupid fool! I ought to blow your brains out." Pierpont had actually posed in his new Cadillac for the publicity-conscious dealer who had sold it to him.

"Matt Leach reads every paper printed and he'll see that picture," Dillinger said. He turned to the hallway leading upstairs. "Hey, Evelyn!" he yelled. "Pack up right away. We got to get out of here quick!"

Dillinger decided not to stay with Makley, Pierpont, Clark and their molls. He and Evelyn drove west to Nebraska, then turned around and headed back east. On the way back Dillinger dropped several taunting postal cards to Matt Leach. Every card said the same thing:

Having wonderful time. Wish
you were here.
JOHN DILLINGER

Leach knew the cards were genuine because the handwriting matched with authentic Dillinger penmanship. The postmarks on the cards indicated that John was traveling from west to east. Leach deduced that Dillinger was using the cards as a red herring and after mailing the last card he would turn around and head west.

But John did no such thing. He kept going straight to Chicago, landing there the second week in January. Pierpont, Makley and Clark had meantime gone to Tucson, Arizona, because Evelyn had told John that Tucson was a nice place and thought they should eventually go there. One attractive feature of Tucson was its proximity to the Mexican border. If things got too hot, Dillinger planned to go there with his girl.

Settled in Chicago, Dillinger contacted Three-Finger Jack, who had been lying low after murdering the detective, and little Homer, who had been off on a scouting trip. Little Homer told John that there was a bank in East Chicago, Indiana, that was just begging to be taken.

Dillinger rubbed his hands together. "In Indiana, eh. Won't Matt Leach be surprised if I hit his territory again!"

Arriving in East Chicago with Three-Finger Jack and little Homer, John made a tour of the downtown district. The First National Bank and Trust Company was a handsome, two-story marble building that accommodated, on each side of the entrance, a drugstore and a dime store. The traffic in front of the bank was quite heavy. There was a cop on the beat —a fellow named O'Malley—whose movements, Dillinger noted, seemed to be erratic.

Until now, it had never occurred to Dillinger to wear a bulletproof vest. But, with the instinct that some criminals have, he decided to equip himself with one for the East Chicago job. He sent little Homer, the innocent-looking errand boy, to Chicago to buy one.

Dillinger and Hamilton were to go into the bank at 11 A.M. sharp and spend exactly four minutes inside. Little Homer was to remain outside to keep an eye on things.

The day of the robbery, Dillinger's souped-up Ford pulled to a stop in front of the bank. Dillinger and Hamilton, carrying machine guns in two suitcases, walked inside. They laid the suitcases on a counter reserved for customers, and casually extracted the machine guns.

"Keep your hands at your sides!" Dillinger told the dozen customers and the bank help. Hamilton kept an eye on everybody, while Dillinger went behind the cages and scooped up stacks of bills. He lined his pockets with more than $40,000 in fives and tens.

Dillinger's four minutes were just about up when Van Meter popped in, jerking his thumb in the direction of the door. Dillinger came out from behind the cages to cope with the emergency.

Patrolman O'Malley walked in. As O'Malley drew his service revolver, Dillinger raised his machine gun. The machine gun jammed. Three-Finger Jack couldn't help out because he was standing directly behind Dillinger, and little Homer was unarmed.

Everybody dropped to the floor except the three outlaws and the cop. O'Malley emptied his service revolver at Dillinger. John's hunch about that bulletproof vest paid off.

The last of O'Malley's bullets had just bounced off Dillinger's vest when John got his gun going. Grinning, he practically cut Patrolman O'Malley in half. Fifteen seconds after the murder he and Hamilton and Van Meter were driving off.

A few hours later, Matt Leach exhibited a stack of rogues-gallery pictures around the East Chicago bank and got positive identifications on Dillinger, Hamilton and little Homer.

Van Meter and Three-Finger Jack blew to the wilds of Wisconsin. Dillinger, with Evelyn, ran for Tucson. There, at the Congress Hotel, he joined Pierpont, Makley and Clark.

On the night of January 23, they all gathered in Dillinger's room on the second floor of the Congress Hotel in Tucson for a little game of poker. Considering how well fixed they were, they played for comparatively small stakes. The game had hardly got underway when Dillinger, dealing, began to sniff the air. "I thought I smelled smoke," he said.

A minute or so later, Clark, who seldom said anything, spoke up. "Damn, it's awful hot in here."

Pierpont went and opened the door. A tongue of flame licked at him. "Christ!" yelled Pierpont, "this place's on fire!"

The boys and Evelyn got out, though, and holed up in rooming places around town. Somebody, however, had gotten a good look at Dillinger at the time of the fire and when the delayed take set in, the hunt was on. Evelyn went back to the Midwest, safely, but Pierpont, Makley and Clark were picked up, one by one, without a struggle. And then one night Dillinger, with his guard down, got out of his car after a little drive somewhere and, going into his hide-out, walked into a nest of gun muzzles and gave up without a word.

Thirty-six hours after the capture, Matt Leach walked into the jail at Tucson and faced John Dillinger for the second time.

"Hello, copper," said Dillinger, grinning. "Did you get all the cards I sent you?"

"Yes, Johnnie," answered Leach.

"What's on your mind, copper?"

"To get you back to Indiana to stand trial for the murder of that policeman in East Chicago. And your three friends are going back to Ohio for murder."

Dillinger was still grinning on the train rolling eastward. "There ain't a jail in this whole country strong enough to hold me," he told Matt Leach.

"We'll hold you in Crown Point, Johnnie," Leach replied.

When Dillinger, now coming into his own as a celebrity, got off the train with Leach at Chicago, the press was there in force, aiming questions and cameras at the outlaw as if he were a movie star. A fat woman with stringy reddish hair shouted: "Oh, Johnnie, I want to marry you!" Dillinger just grinned.

At Crown Point, Leach and two other cops drove up to the county jail with Dillinger and turned him over to the sheriff. The sheriff was a woman—Lillian Holley—who had succeeded her husband when a crazed murderer had shot him to death.

The cameramen wanted more pictures. They had no sooner begun to scream for their shots than the prosecutor of Lake County—a local politician named Bob Estill—got into the act.

Acme News Pictures got Sheriff Holley, Prosecutor Estill and Dillinger together and had a little chat with them. "The three of you line up," he said. "You stand on the left there, Mrs. Holley, and you stand next to her, Mr. Estill. You stand next to the prosecutor, Johnnie."

The photographer grew thoughtful. "Suppose," he said to the prosecutor, "you put your arm around Johnnie's shoulder. You, Johnnie, you rest your arm on the prosecutor's shoulder—just to show there's no hard feelings." The prosecutor and the outlaw followed instructions and the picture was snapped.

That picture was to have political repercussions for months afterward —the prosecutor posed as being palsy-walsy with the country's Number One criminal while the woman sheriff smiled on benignly.

FEBRUARY 1934

Dillinger was in the county jail in Crown Point, Indiana, awaiting trial for the murder of the cop during the bank holdup in East Chicago.

Mrs. Holley, the lady sheriff, had put on twenty extra outside guards—ten by day and ten by night. They patrolled outside the jail, carrying machine guns. But in her elaborate precautions, Sheriff Holley overlooked one thing—Dillinger's cunning.

When the lights were out one night, Dillinger wrote a letter of instructions to Homer Van Meter. Next day he slipped it to a prisoner who was being released. When Van Meter received the letter, which had been addressed to a hot letter drop in Chicago, he got busy following Dillinger's instructions.

Van Meter sat down and wrote a batch of letters, signing himself "Taxpayer," and mailed them from Crown Point. The letters, addressed to the local newspaper and to the city fathers, all struck one note: Taxpayers' money was being squandered on all those unnecessary guards around a stout jail.

One of the letters to the newspaper editor was published in the paper. The paper, impressed by the letters, ran an editorial suggesting that the outside guards around the jail were now unnecessary. The city fathers, impressed by the paper's stand, and fearing to run afoul of public sentiment, quickly disposed of the extra guards.

Now Dillinger addressed himself to the second half of the problem—the fact that the warden and his deputies came into the exercise area armed. One morning, while Warden Lou Baker was unlocking Dillinger's cell, Dillinger asked, "Warden, ain't you afraid that somebody might take your gun off you when you come in here?"

The idea struck the warden like a ton of bricks; he had never considered the possibility. He promptly dumped the problem in the lap of the lady sheriff. She then issued an order that neither the warden nor any of his deputies were to go into the exercise area carrying arms so long as John Dillinger was in residence. Thus, before the month of February was over, John Dillinger had removed the guards from the outside of the jail and disarmed those on the inside.

Sometime that February—probably during the last week—John Dillinger came into possession of a gun. . . .

MARCH 1934

At a few minutes after nine o'clock on the morning of Saturday, March 3, Warden Baker entered the exercise area and let Dillinger out of his cell. Baker was just inserting a key in another cell when Dillinger stepped up behind him and jabbed the gun in his back.

"Don't turn around, Warden," said Dillinger. "Just do as I say and you'll stay alive."

"All right, Johnnie. All right. What do you want me to do?"

"Call Blunk in here."

Ernest Blunk, the jail's fingerprint expert, came in, to be surprised by the gun in Dillinger's hand.

"Throw me your keys, Warden," Dillinger told Baker. He locked the warden and the fingerprint expert into his cell, where they stood meekly.

Dillinger, having learned the layout of the jail building and the location and the movements and the names of all the jailers, told Warden Baker to summon the others, one by one. There were five other special guards in the building. After leaving their arms outside the exercise area, they came in, singly. As each man entered, Dillinger locked him in the cell. In ten minutes he had the seven men locked up.

Half an hour later, Dillinger was far out in the open country.

The ticking of the time bomb was growing louder. . . .

Three nights after his break from Crown Point, Dillinger drove alone into Lima, Ohio, in a stolen car. He parked the car two blocks from the jail there. He pulled his hat down over his eyes, put on a pair of horn-rim glasses, and ambled through the darkness toward the jail. He walked to the edge of a flood of light illuminating the building. There was a crowd around the jail and the area was electric with excitement.

Dillinger eased himself into the edge of the crowd. "What's all the excitement about?" he asked.

"They're afraid that man Dillinger is goin' to come here and get his friends out," a woman told him.

"Is that so," said Dillinger.

"But he'll never do it," said the woman. "Why, they got a hundred guards around the place. National Guards, too."

Dillinger was considering trying the same stunt in St. Paul that had worked so successfully in Crown Point—drawing all those guards off. But Leach found out about those spurious "Taxpayer" letters. Getting hold of one, he'd had the handwriting analyzed. It was Homer Van Meter's writing. Leach not only tipped Lima off to watch out for such letters but broke the story in the papers.

Dillinger went to Chicago and contacted Evelyn Frechette. Then, he summoned Homer Van Meter and Three-Finger Jack Hamilton and the three of them roared through Indiana and Ohio, knocking over six banks in eight days for a total score of $103,000. He took his loot—one third —and mailed it to one of his post-office boxes in Chicago.

Matt Leach, at the State House in Indianapolis, was growing desperate. Governor McNutt was putting the pressure on him and the newspapers were putting the pressure on McNutt.

The Hoosier outlaw now had a hold on the imagination of the entire country. Practically every detective in the Middle West was carrying a rogues-gallery shot of John. Dillinger's likeness, pasted up inside the cages of banks, scowled down at the tellers. Bank tellers in Indiana and Illinois got jittery every time a strange man sauntered up to the windows. Some tellers, spotting somebody who aroused their suspicions, instinctively pressed alarm buttons. One day, the Chicago police rushed to eight different banks on false alarms.

The latest news about John—usually a baseless rumor of some kind—came out of radio loudspeakers. As the month of March drew to a close, the Hoosier outlaw's notoriety had spread across the Atlantic. The London *Times* and the Manchester *Guardian* were asking their correspondents in this country for all the news on Dillinger.

Newspaper offices around the country were being bombarded with tips, some sincere, others by practical jokers, that Dillinger was here, there, everywhere. With the exception of the Lindbergh baby kidnaping two years previously, no police case in the annals of American crime has ever stimulated the volume of tips that poured in while John Dillinger was at large. The Chicago *Tribune*, tongue in cheek, mirrored conditions this way:

Mr. Dillinger was seen yesterday looking over the new spring gloves in a State Street store in Chicago; negotiating for a 12-cylinder car in Springfield, Ill.; buying a half dozen sassy cravats in Omaha, Neb.; bargaining for a suburban bungalow at his home town of Mooresville, Ind., and shaking hands with old friends; drinking a glass of soda water in a drug store in Charleston, S.C.; and strolling down Broadway swinging a Malacca cane in New York. He also bought a fishing rod in a sporting goods store in Montreal and gave a dinner at a hotel in Yucatan, Mex. But, anyhow, Mr. Dillinger seems to have kept very carefully out of London, Berlin, Rome, Moscow and Vienna. Or at least if he did go to those places yesterday he was traveling incog.

The Detroit *Free Press,* taking the stand that things had gone far enough, addressed an editorial to J. Edgar Hoover, angrily ordering him to bring in the outlaw. The London *Daily Telegraph* inquired on its front page: "What Is Happening in America?" The Governor of Indiana, who since boyhood had nursed an ambition to be President, wondered how he could ever go to the voters and ask to run the country, when his own State Police couldn't run an outlaw to the ground.

MAY 1934

J. Edgar Hoover, tight-lipped and unsmiling, saw to it that the heat did not lessen in intensity when the not-so-merry month of May rolled around. Hoover continued to beseech the public to keep shooting in tips.

Evelyn Frechette was picked off a Chicago street and given a jail term for harboring a fugitive. Makley and Pierpont, found guilty of murdering the sheriff in Lima, were sentenced to the electric chair. Clark got off with life.

Dillinger began to feel very sorry for himself. His world was rapidly shrinking. He decided to hide out in Skid Row in Chicago. Not even the G men or Matt Leach would think to look for him and Hamilton and little Homer there.

Skid Row, only a few minutes by taxi from Chicago's Gold Coast, was a derelicts' purgatory. Here, from all corners of the land, came men with broken lives to find surcease in the "smoke" that retailed for as little as a nickel a shot. Detectives seldom thought to hunt down anybody in Skid Row. The reason was simple. The men who populated Skid Row were so far gone physically, mentally and morally that they didn't have what it took to commit nickel stick-ups, let alone a high-class job.

Dillinger and his pals were lying in a quarter flophouse one rainy afternoon when Dillinger fell to contemplating Hamilton's missing finger. "Be sure and keep that hand in your pocket when you're outside," Dillinger suggested.

Hamilton in turn suggested that Dillinger keep his face well hidden. "Every flatfoot in the country could probably draw a picture of you from memory," he said. "Them FBI passed around millions."

Dillinger didn't answer. But he grew very thoughtful. In a little while he said, "You fellows stay here—right in this flophouse here. I'm goin' away."

"For how long?" asked Van Meter.

"A few weeks."

JUNE 1934

Early one afternoon, the first week in June, John Dillinger returned to the flophouse. Three-Finger and little Homer were sitting at a smoke-stained table playing cards. Dillinger walked up to the table and stood behind Hamilton, facing Van Meter. Although both players had noticed Dillinger, neither paid any attention to him, marking him down as a kibitzer.

Van Meter looked up at Dillinger again. His eyes lighted up. "Look who's standin' behind you!" he told Three-Finger.

Hamilton studied Dillinger a few hot moments. "Well, I'll be a son-of-a-bitch! I wouldn't of known you."

Dillinger's hair was not auburn but jet black. He had grown a small bushy mustache. His eyebrows had been thinned. And he was wearing silver-rimmed eyeglasses.

"You look a lot younger, Johnnie," said Van Meter. "At least ten years younger."

Dillinger had been in a private hospital where a gangster physician had given him a face lift.

JULY 1934

When the month of July dawned, John Dillinger had a premonition of death. He was all alone now. Homer Van Meter, taking a walk one night, had been picked up by the cops. Three-Finger Jack Hamilton, sauntering out of the Skid Row joint for a breath of air, had been shot down in the street.

Dillinger left Skid Row, drew all his money out of his post-office boxes and carried it around with him. He got into a black Ford sedan and began to drive through the Indiana countryside, traveling by night, sleeping by day.

Early in July, Dillinger pulled into a gas station in southern Indiana to get the tank filled up. Just as he was leaving, he caught the attendant looking at him. He knew the attendant had recognized him. He was about to reach for his gun when two other cars pulled into the station. John drove off, certain he would be followed. The roadblocks would be up in a matter of minutes.

He turned in at a farm and knocked on the door. An old lady answered. "Who lives here with you?" asked Dillinger.

"Nobody, son," said the old lady, not recognizing John. "I'm a widow woman. I live alone."

"Mother," said Dillinger, pressing ten ten-dollar bills in the old lady's hand, "I need help. I want you to hide me. And if anybody comes looking for me you ain't seen me. Understand?"

"Yes, I understand." The old lady counted the money. "Why," she said, "you're John Dillinger!"

"That's right, Mother. I'm John Dillinger."

"Why," said the old lady, "you're not really bad at all, giving a poor woman like me money like this."

Next night, after Dillinger left, the old lady told her neighbors all about him. The papers got the story. A Robin Hood legend, phony as it was, began to attach itself to Dillinger.

On the tenth day of July, John Dillinger drew up to his father's farm outside Mooresville. It was noon and the sun was baking the dry brown fields. Old John Dillinger, working a tomato patch near the weather-beaten house, looked up at the car and squinted in disbelief. "Johnnie," he said, "it ain't safe for you to come here."

"I can take care of myself," said Dillinger. "I just wanted to see you."

The old man nodded toward the homestead. "We'll go inside."

"No. Let's walk in the fields. I want to walk in the fields."

"But somebody might drive by and see you, Johnnie."

Dillinger half laughed. "Nobody'd think of lookin' for me here, Pop."

The elder Dillinger peered into his son's face. "You look different. I can't say just why, but you ain't the same."

"It's this mustache, Pop."

"No, Johnnie. It's somethin' about the eyes."

Dillinger didn't answer. He took his father by the arm and walked into the fields. "I won't be seein' you again, Pop," Dillinger said. "Somethin' tells me that."

"Don't say that, Johnnie, I don't like it."

Seven nights later, on July 8, John Dillinger walked into a lunch wagon on the South Side of Chicago. "Coffee," he said to the waitress. "With cream and sugar." As he drank the coffee, Dillinger kept looking at the waitress, who was busy serving customers. She was blond and had a hard, pretty face. "Gimme another cup," said Dillinger.

Three quarters of an hour later, when Dillinger was ordering his fifth cup of coffee, the girl said to him, "You sure drink an awful lot of that stuff."

Dillinger glanced at a big wall clock; it was ten-forty. "What time do you get through?"

The girl smiled. "I get relieved in twenty minutes. Why?"

"I thought I'd take you home."

The blonde looked him over. "Okay, Buster."

Her name was Pauline Hamilton. She led Dillinger to a frame house a block and a half from the lunch wagon. They went up two flights of stairs to a small flat that smelled of good cooking. "Anybody home?" she called out.

"I'm in here readin'," came a voice from a bedroom.

"Come on out, Ann," said the blonde. "I want you to meet somebody." Turning to Dillinger, the blonde asked, "What did you say your name was?"

"Lawrence," replied Dillinger. "Jack Lawrence."

"What do you do for a livin', Jack?"

"Salesman."

A compact, square-faced woman of middle age, swathed in a fancy blue satin dressing gown, appeared in the doorway. "This is Ann," Pauline told Dillinger. "Ann Sage. She used to run a place in East Chicago. I worked for her, only we got closed up."

Ann Sage crossed in front of Dillinger and sat on a red plush sofa. "What's your name?" she asked Dillinger. "I don't think I got your name."

"Lawrence. Jack Lawrence."

"You new in Chicago?"

"Yeah. Just visitin'."

"We want to use the bedroom, Ann," said Pauline.

"Go right ahead," said Ann, picking up a magazine.

Next morning, over coffee in the kitchen, Ann Sage said to Pauline Hamilton, "That fellow you had here last night, I can't get him out of my mind."

"Why?"

"If he didn't have that mustache, and if he had big bushy eyebrows instead of them thin ones, I'd swear it was John Dillinger."

Next night, when Pauline walked into the flat with Dillinger, Ann Sage went out of her way to be nice to him.

The next day, Ann Sage walked into police headquarters in East Chicago and sought out Detective Martin Zarkovitch, a hard-faced man who was a good friend of hers. The friendship between Zarkovitch and Ann Sage had remained undisturbed despite the fact that the Sage woman had been closed up three times by the East Chicago police as the madam of a house of ill fame. Ann Sage was, as a matter of fact, in very hot official water that day when she went to East Chicago to talk to her detective friend. Miss Sage was a citizen of Romania and, under the law, was subject to deportation as a thrice-guilty lawbreaker.

"I think I know where John Dillinger is," Ann Sage said to Detective Zarkovitch.

"You don't say!" said Zarkovitch. "Where!"

"He's come to my flat twice now to see Polly Hamilton. He was there last night and night before last. And he'll probably be there again tonight."

The detective leaned across his desk. "You sure about this, Ann?"

Ann Sage was absolutely sure. Dillinger had grown a mustache and had

had his eyebrows thinned. But there were other things about Lawrence that checked with the known facts about Dillinger. Lawrence didn't smoke, drink or swear. His speech was definitely that of a Hoosier. And he was flashing a big roll of bills. No, there was no doubt that Jack Lawrence was John Dillinger.

At the very hour Ann Sage was sitting in the office of Detective Zarkovitch, Matt Leach entered the Chicago field offices of the FBI. He was ushered into the office of Melvin Purvis, the special agent in charge of the Chicago field office.

"I was wondering," Leach began, "if you had any line on Dillinger."

"No," said Purvis, "I wish we had. But we haven't the slightest idea where he is."

"No leads at all, huh?"

"Yes, we get leads. But every time we run them down we find they're false."

The next morning Melvin Purvis had two visitors—Ann Sage and Detective Zarkovitch. Ann Sage told Purvis she thought she could lead him to Dillinger, but she wanted to make a deal: if the FBI would pull strings in Washington with the Immigration Department to wash out that deportation rap, she'd put the finger on Dillinger. Purvis said he couldn't make a deal even if he wanted to; the FBI and the Immigration Department weren't that close to each other.

"All right," said the madam, "I won't put the finger on Dillinger."

Purvis said coldly, "If you don't, I'll arrest you for harboring a fugitive."

Purvis wanted to know where Dillinger lived. Ann Sage didn't know. Dillinger had never volunteered the information, and she had been too cagey to ask. Well, then, when was Dillinger expected at her flat again? Dillinger was coming the following night, Sunday, July 21. What time? About seven o'clock. Fine, said Purvis. He and several of his men would plant themselves in Ann Sage's apartment and surprise Dillinger when he came in.

Ann Sage shook her head. "Like hell you will," she said. She didn't want to have any part in the actual capture. She didn't want any publicity. What with trying to beat a deportation rap, it wouldn't look very good to have the papers come out and say that Dillinger had been visiting a girl friend in her apartment. No, Purvis would have to think of something else.

"Well then," said the G man, "when Dillinger comes to your place tomorrow night we'll take him in the street before he goes in."

Ann Sage, who was more or less in a position to call the shots, was against that, too. "I'll tell you what," she said to Purvis. "I think maybe I can talk Dillinger into going to the movies. *Manhattan Melodrama* is playing at the Biograph. Clark Gable's in it, and Dillinger's nuts about Clark Gable." The Biograph Theater, a neighborhood movie house, was less than two blocks from Ann Sage's apartment.

That was the plot, then: Ann Sage and Pauline Hamilton were to go to the Biograph Theater with Dillinger. He was not to be taken until after he came out of the theater and the G men could move in on him.

At a few minutes after nine o'clock on the night of July 22, 1934, John Dillinger sat in the fifteenth row of the Biograph Theater, between Ann Sage and Pauline Hamilton. Up on the screen, the picture was ending. Clark Gable, in the role of Blackie Gallagher, a gangster in *Manhattan Melodrama*, had been convicted of murder and was leaving his cell in death row to walk the last mile to the electric chair. "Die the way you've lived," Gable was saying to his cellmates as he started on the last mile. "That's the way to take it."

Dillinger, his gaze glued to the screen, didn't move a muscle.

The picture ended and the house lights went up. Dillinger walked up the aisle first, Polly Hamilton behind him and the Sage woman, dressed in a bright-orange-colored dress, behind Polly. G men, planted in the audience, spotted the madam's bright dress and fell in behind her. Several moviegoers brushed right up against John Dillinger as he made his way up the aisle, but they were too preoccupied by what had happened to the fictional killer on the screen to give a real killer a second look.

Outside, Melvin Purvis and twenty-two G men, sitting in parked automobiles, were straining their eyes for some sign of Dillinger or a signal from an agent emerging from the theater. It was Purvis who spotted Dillinger. "There he is . . . right behind Ann Sage!"

"Some picture," Dillinger was saying to Pauline Hamilton. "That Clark Gable sure is some actor." On one side of the Biograph Theater was an alley that had led to the theater's stage entrance when the place had played live attractions. Dillinger and his two companions had to pass the alley on their way back to the apartment. As Dillinger approached the alley, three G men were close behind him. The idea was to sneak up behind him and grab him before he could reach for his gun.

Dillinger was talking about the picture as he reached the mouth of the alley. Apparently he had addressed a remark to either Ann Sage or the Hamilton girl and was expecting an answer. None was forthcoming. He looked to the right. The Hamilton girl was not there. He turned quickly to the left. Ann Sage was not there.

With the instinct of an animal, John Dillinger knew he had been ambushed. He never stopped to look behind him. He just knew. He ducked into the alley and began to run.

He hadn't gone ten feet when the G men began to blaze away. That was all there was to it. John Dillinger was hit so fast and so often that he probably never even felt any pain.

THOSE WERE THE DAYS

REMEMBER how important a nickel was in the Thirties? A five-cent piece, the twentieth part of a dollar, purchased many things and many services. If you were a child and wanted to buy the biggest and best candy bar, a nickel would do the job. To get from the Bronx to the Battery by subway in New York, it took just a nickel. A local telephone call could be made by depositing only a nickel. Could Horn & Hardart have thrived without the stream of nickels passing through the glass windows in the Automat? And what about the cup of coffee, and the weekly magazines such as *The Saturday Evening Post, Collier's, Liberty*—just five cents. The juke box began to hum when the nickel dropped in, and the one-armed bandit (slot machine) earned fortunes, in nickels, for organized crime.

Let us assume, then, that it was a solid underpinning of daily business. In deep Depression, when any and all kinds of nostrums were proposed to cure the economy, someone might have decided that the ubiquitous five-cent piece was behind our troubles, and then decided on a program of action. The Great Nickel Panic didn't happen, but, believe it or not, there were even *crazier* schemes proposed for ending our troubles.

CREIGHTON PEET

THE GREAT NICKEL PANIC*

ONE AFTERNOON late in the spring, John B. Rutherford, billionaire and philanthropist, decided that the civilization extant in New York in the year 1931 was so excessively unsatisfactory as to require changing. The city was too large, traffic was very trying and life was not the simple, leisurely thing it should be. For one thing people were always taking subways and "L's," thereby getting themselves into the most outrageous and unpleasant crowds. For another thing telephones were forever ringing and taking the minds of the citizenry off the thinking of great thoughts. Again, such institutions as soda fountains and automats were rushing all the leisure and

* From *Vanity Fair,* September 1931.

242

fine flavor out of eating. In fact, this machine age thing had gone far enough.

For fully fifteen minutes the famous Rutherford mind revolved about the project of altering the current state of affairs, and at the end of that time Rutherford pressed a few mother-of-pearl buttons on his desk, calling in a selected assortment of private secretaries. In the following five minutes commands and instructions calculated to completely paralyze the more objectionable aspects of city life were given, and the secretaries set about their duties.

All modern life, reasoned the great philanthropist, depended upon the use of the nickel, or five-cent piece. Remove the nickel and life would eventually be forced to assume a more leisurely pace. It would take time, of course, to absorb all the nickels in circulation, but old Rutherford's patience was as unlimited as his vast fortune.

Two hundred actors out of work—men and women of all ages and types, and all sworn to the strictest secrecy—were engaged to go about the city collecting nickels. They were specifically instructed never to go to banks and ask for nickels in quantities. They were to take only such nickels as they received when asking for them. One day a worker would get nickels in automats, drugstores and cigar stores ("to 'phone") on the west side of Broadway, and the following day he would make a visit to the uptown local stations of the east side subway. A couple of weeks later he or she would attend to the drug and cigar stores on the east side of Broadway. Nothing was hit-or-miss. The campaign was executed with military precision, and every ten days each worker evolved a new disguise.

Four delivery trucks were fitted up and chastely inscribed AMERICAN SERVICE CORP., and set to patrol such well-traveled thoroughfares as Broadway, Seventh Avenue and Thirty-fourth Street. Whenever a worker spied one of these trucks parked for a few moments at the curb, he would climb up beside the driver and, after giving the password, he would be allowed to crawl through a small door into the interior of the truck. Here sat an accountant who exchanged twelve dollars for every ten dollars' worth of nickels produced. Some collectors were able to gather as many as a thousand coins a day, but the average haul was about five hundred. After dark, the trucks slipped, one by one, into the private driveway of the old Rutherford mansion on Fifth Avenue, the big gates were closed, and more sacks of nickels were noiselessly dumped into an unused cellar. Within a week the pile was as high as a man's head, and Rutherford ordered another storeroom cleared of old trunks and boxes.

It was fully three weeks before any public notice was taken of the short-

243

age of nickels. By this time 2,100,000 subway fares had been salted away in the cavernous Rutherford cellars. By the end of the fourth week, when 2,800,000 nickels had been withdrawn from circulation, the public at large became suddenly and acutely aware that something was wrong with the economic world. Lines at subway change booths trebled in length, and each patron was allowed but one nickel at a time. Elevateds, surface cars, and some bus and ferry lines were slowed up considerably, and officials were losing much sleep trying to think of some way out of their difficulties. The telephone company was simply miserable, for it turned out that a lot of nickels, burning holes in people's pockets, were the cause of a tremendous number of phone calls. When nickels became difficult to find, or a call could only be made with a dime or a quarter, a lot of girls were left sitting all alone by the telephone, with nothing at all to keep them from reading good books.

The attitude of the press to the nickel shortage was at first frivolous. Columnists and cartoonists had quite a bit of fun with people who stayed home from work because they couldn't find a nickel to get down town with, and for some weeks city desks refused to take anything as trivial as a nickel shortage seriously. Who would hoard nickels, and why? Besides, there were so many millions of nickels about that no matter how many were lost or confiscated, there would always be enough to carry on business. . . .

But this optimistic attitude was suddenly altered on Friday of the fifth week of the Rutherford secret crusade. By this time some 3,360,000 nickels were lying in the vaults of the old Fifth Avenue mansion. On the evening of this day, rush hour crowds, furious at the long queues waiting at the subway change booths at Grand Central, pushed aside the guards, jumped over turnstiles, and forced open the emergency exists. The following day similar riots occurred in several other subway stations. The telephone company was facing a crisis in its affairs, and the Automat people were forced to close down all but the cafeteria sections of their high-speed restaurants. The same day advertisers were thrown into a panic by the news that The Saturday Evening Post, Liberty, and Collier's were dropping circulation heavily, and that the sales of five-cent candy bars were shrinking. You could, of course, buy two things costing five cents each by using a dime, or give a quarter in payment and receive two dimes in exchange, but an amazing number of people wanted to buy just one single five-cent article, and unable to do so, discovered that they hadn't really needed it at all.

Needless to say, the Rutherford agents had begun to have as much trouble finding nickels as anyone else, and even by patronizing the nickel scalpers outside the subway stations who sold two or three nickels for a quarter, they were often unable to find more than a thousand or so coins a day. By the end of old Rutherford's eighth week of crusading, 4,475,000 nickels had been withdrawn from use, and both city and Federal detectives were working on what the newspapers, now alarmed, referred to as the NICKEL PANIC and the FIVE-CENT MYSTERY. The directors of subways and other public utilities, unable to wait till the mints could issue extra coins, tried manufacturing slugs or counters, until it was discovered that fully as many bogus coins as they were making were being stamped out and sold in sacks, a dollar for a hundred. After a week this plan was abandoned, no more slugs were issued, and many of the makers of the fake counters were caught and prosecuted.

The end of the ninth week found 4,975,000 nickels out of circulation. At this time the Rutherford agents decided to exercise more caution in the collections. The agents made up sacks of nickels in distant apartments and hotel rooms and smuggled them into the Rutherford mansion in boxes of groceries, cases of liquor and other commonplace containers.

But it was not until twelve weeks after the work had started that old Rutherford's scheme showed any signs of success. A man named Smith, living on West 178th Street, announced that he was tired of the city's toil and strife and that existence must certainly be more pleasant out in the country where there were no subways, very few telephones, and where nickels were but an unpleasant memory. The newspapers got wind of Mr. Smith's ideas and printed big stories of his plan to take his family to the country and live the simple life. The following day eighty-seven more families announced that they were going back to their home towns, and the Real Estate board was pulling out its hair in large fistfuls. By the end of the week three thousand apartments were deserted, leases were but an idle jest, and some twelve thousand men, women and children had left the city. By the end of the seventeenth week thousands of "permanent" New Yorkers had gone to live in the country.

Old Rutherford was feeling pretty happy about things and pretty proud of himself as a public benefactor, when the papers joyfully announced that the U. S. mints, working overtime, were producing five million new nickels, one million of which were to be placed in circulation immediately. For a while things looked bleak for old Rutherford. People stopped moving out of town, the subways began to clog up again, and the whole plan began to look like a failure. But this setback was only temporary. On the eighteenth week the Rutherford collections jumped from a trifling 3,000 coins to 190,000, and a few days later it was obvious to everybody that the same mysterious agency which had swallowed all the previous nickels was fast making way with the new coins.

This news alarmed the civic authorities, and a mass meeting of the great men of the city was called to decide on a course of action. Foremost among the speakers was old Rutherford himself. He even mustered up a few tears for the occasion, and spoke touchingly of the wheels of progress, mass production, the majestic Hudson, and his early New York ancestors.

By the twenty-second week of the great crusade 6,682,000 nickels were safely hidden away and nearly a million people had left the city. About forty collectors were still on the job, but they were resorting to the most elaborate devices to escape suspicion.

Old John B. Rutherford had taken the curse of hurry from the greatest city in the world. He was a benefactor, an unsung hero. The following spring trees were replanted in Park Avenue, the elevated line discontinued running trains and planted flowers and vines in boxes along the tracks, and a thousand extra benches were ordered by the park commission. Business had more or less disintegrated, it was true, but life had at last become endurable for all those who were forced to remain in the city. People grew little gardens on the setbacks of their apartment houses, and a few years later such things as canned vegetables were unknown. The telephone rang so seldom that its sound became as welcome as the spring sunshine. Couples who had never even dreamt of such things had babies, and business slackened so much that even on a weekday you could see the sun just as plain as plain. The millennium, in fact, had arrived.

THE SYNDICATE

WITH THE onset of the Depression, there were fewer customers who could afford bootleg liquor. The repeal of the Eighteenth Amendment reduced the take of organized crime even further. The take from gambling, prostitution and narcotics may not have decreased, but the loss of illegal liquor sales prompted the gang overlords to move into the labor unions. They invaded the unions through transportation, a key operation in industry. By 1932, it was said that in Chicago Al Capone controlled two thirds of the unions or at least collected tribute from them; such trades as cleaning, barbering, baking and paving were under the thumb of gangsters.

In Detroit, the Purple Gang muscled into cleaning and dyeing, coal and the building trades, according to Irving Bernstein. In Cleveland, the undertaking business was taken over by the rackets, and New York was probably as racket-ridden as any other city. But it was not until the close of the decade that the extent of organized crime was made known to the public, in all its sordid details and subhuman riffraff, revealing a country-wide network, with a board of directors—the Syndicate. "To insure their organization, one and all concentrated on developing connections, on municipal, state and national levels. The cartel is so finely organized that it can swing elections in many places—and regardless of which political party holds the reins." *

One of its most ruthless arms, uncovered in investigations in the Thirties, was a group of murderers located in Brooklyn, known as Murder, Incorporated. Its members were employed to kill anyone standing in the way of "business."

BURTON B. TURKUS AND SID FEDER

THE ALMOST-ASSASSINATION
OF THOMAS E. DEWEY†

No ONE expected Dutch Schultz was ever coming back when he took off running at the start of 1933, about a step and a half in front of the Internal Revenue men.

* Turkus and Feder, *Murder, Inc.*
† From Turkus and Feder's *Murder, Inc.* (New York, Farrar, Straus, & Young, 1951).

The Dutchman had tried everything before he took flight. No amount of pressure from his political connections, however, had been able to soften Uncle Sam. After all, Schultz's income then was something more than just loose change. His return from beer alone, from 1929 through 1931, was a matter of $481,000, with all overhead paid. Then there were such other remunerative grabs as the protection racket and the numbers.

Even Dutch's sincerest supporters could see only certain conviction and a long stretch as guest of the government, if he so much as poked his face out of his hole. Gangland didn't especially care. When the boss mobsters voted the national Syndicate into existence in 1934, the absent Dutch was not wanted. He was isolationist—antagonistic to the new aim toward amalgamation. The bosses knew that, at heart, he was a mad dog whose maniacal outbursts and twitching trigger finger would get everyone associated with him into serious trouble sooner or later.

For most of his thirty-three years, he had been that way—this hoodlum scion of a Bronx saloonkeeper and a pious, patient woman whose great grief it was that the son she adored turned out as he did. Born Arthur Flegenheimer, he had a brief exposure to education in P. S. 12, where the principal was Dr. J. F. Condon, who was to achieve international notoriety as the "Jafsie" ransom man of the Lindbergh baby kidnaping.

At seventeen, Arthur was already serving fifteen months for burglary. When he emerged, his playmates nicknamed him Dutch Schultz, after an infamous member of the old Frog Hollow Gang of the Bronx. He began to put together a gang of his own. Notable among his early hired hands was Joey Rao, whose police record went back to 1920. It included sixteen arrests, and convictions for burglary and felonious assault. Once, while spending some time in New York City's House of Correction on Welfare Island, Rao was the "prisoner boss," in connection with such items as kangaroo justice and distribution of drugs.

In recent years, Rao suddenly acquired entrée to many and unexpected places. In November of 1950, a probe of politico-crime tie-ups was launched in New York, after Samuel Kantor, a district leader, charged that "underworld characters are exerting influence on City Hall." Almost the first names to pop up were Joey Rao and his brother-in-law, Joe Stracci, who is more notorious as Joe Stretch.

The probe uncovered a drive by Tammany Hall to oust former General Sessions Court Judge Francis X. Mancuso from his post as Democratic leader of the 16th Assembly District. For this purpose, a meeting of election captains, district leaders and officials of prominence in Tammany Hall and in the city government was held next door to Rao's home in

East Harlem. The District Attorney [Frank S. Hogan] described the meeting as a "gangster-controlled" political session. He said that Rao and Stretch showed up at the meeting and "laid down the law in strong-arm language."

"The presence of Rao and Stracci," declared Hogan, "had the same effect as if they had leveled a gun at the heads of the persons at the meeting."

Rao's explanation was novel, anyway. "I went over and looked into the house because I thought it was a crap game," he reported innocently. "It was a political meeting. So, I ain't interested . . . I go home."

For Dutch Schultz, back in the late Twenties and early Thirties, Rao advanced to the post of manager of Harlem for slot machines. Dutch had aligned himself with leading moguls of the one-armed bandits—Dandy Phil Kastel, the bucket-shop impresario, and Phil's boss, Frank Costello.

As Repeal neared, Schultz moved into the restaurant racket, snatched control of a window cleaners' union and grabbed the $20,000,000 numbers racket in Harlem. The profit in a single numbers bank ran as high as $4,000 in one week. He had a stable of prize fighters, raced his own horses and owned pieces of various night clubs. His gang of gunmen was the envy of mobdom.

When it came to principle, Dutch hit new lows, even for a mobster. He was a cheating guy always. His beer was the worst. His liquor was cut horribly. Even the 1,000-to-1 odds against the player in the numbers game didn't satisfy him. He hired Abbadabba Berman, a mathematical wizard, to make it absolutely foolproof—for Schultz. The daily winning number was based on the total of mutuel odds at certain race tracks such as Coney Island, in Cincinnati, and Tropical Park, in Florida, both racket-controlled then, and the New Orleans track, in which Mayor Robert Maestri, who was Huey Long's political heir, had more than a passing interest. Abbadabba was a human comptometer, and was able to rig the final odds so that it would bring out the most lightly played policy number for that day. It mulcted the players of millions.

Now, there has always been a suspicion that something more than just the insane Schultz violence was behind his omission from the national Syndicate. Dutch's comparatively new restaurant racket, which had mushroomed into a $2,000,000 annual extortion, caught the eye of Louis Buchalter, known as Lepke—an eye easily caught by profitable "gimmicks" in industrial extortion. With the explosive hoodlum left out of the cartel, Lepke could embrace this racket without violating Syndicate law against muscling. He simply moved in and took over while Schultz was in flight. Nor was Lepke the only one who made hay while the Dutchman had his back turned. Charley Lucky's Unione did the same with a major portion of the lush Harlem numbers banks Dutch had developed.

"He won't be back, anyway," was the gangland excuse.

The bosses also summoned Bo Weinberg, whom Dutch had named acting commander in chief of his crack cadre of killers.

"You deliver the mob to us, and we'll take care of you," they suggested persuasively. "The Dutchman ain't coming back, ever."

Bo was not only a good gunman; he was an adroit businessman. There would be little percentage in holding out for something as nebulous as the return of Schultz. Nor did it smack of sharp business to buck the Syndicate. The moguls just reached out and took what they wanted, anyway. Bo made a wholesale delivery of the troop. The torpedoes were adopted en masse, and spread among the Syndicate's various subsidiary branches. The annexation of the Schultz empire was then complete.

And then—Dutch beat the rap!

From the moment he had started his flight, his former associates had buried the Dutchman. The interment turned out now to have been grossly exaggerated.

For a while it had looked very bad. However, with Dutch safely out of sight, his lawyers had continued plugging away. Their chief goal was to defeat the government's demand to try him (as, if and when he exposed himself) in metropolitan New York, where his reputation and record would be a serious handicap with any jury. In spite of the government's determined efforts, the attorneys finally succeeded in winning a change of venue. When he came out of hiding, the trial would be taken upstate, to Syracuse, where Dutch Schultz was a name known only through the newspapers.

With that guarantee, the Dutchman emerged after eighteen months under cover. Out on bail pending trial, the conniving mobster moved into Syracuse early, and craftily set out to achieve a notoriety completely new and different from that to which he was accustomed. He did a great deal of socializing with the townsfolk. He took up charity—making sure that word of his noble gestures reached the newspapers, so the citizens who might serve on the jury would be apprised of what a lovely fellow he really was. The result was that, when the trial was held, Schultz escaped, temporarily anyway, on a hung jury—a disagreement.

Much to his satisfaction, the retrial was moved, thanks to his lawyers' efforts, even farther upstate—to the tiny border town of Malone. Once more, Schultz arrived early, and slyly plotted his defense. He spent money all around the place. He sent gifts to hospitalized children. He entertained expansively and expensively. He was, as a result, thought of most sympathetically among the citizenry of Malone. And the jury acquitted him. It drew a blistering denunciation from Judge Frederick Bryant.

"The verdict was dictated by other considerations than the evidence," the jurist charged.

Dutch dropped out of the clouds on the mob. No one, however, was particularly perturbed. The Syndicate was a going concern by then. New York still had a number of embarrassing matters to take up with him. So, the Dutchman had to settle in Newark, New Jersey. He called in Bo Weinberg immediately, and demanded an accounting of his staff.

Bo was forthright and no longer in awe at talking up to the boss. He advised his deposed employer it would not be healthy to try a comeback in the New York rackets. Perhaps he was too blunt. At any rate, that turned out to be Bo's last recorded appearance. The better gangland society has always maintained, over its teacups, that he got a gift of a cement overcoat shortly thereafter, and that he is still wearing it—on the bottom of the East River.

It was soon clear to the Dutchman that, during his vacation, a new era in gangdom had risen, based on an organized, concretely knit front. No single mob could crack it. Schultz could no more blast this efficient system out of his way than he could recoup the empire it had purloined from him. As touchy a torpedo as he was, Dutch still was not sufficiently bereft of his reason to try it. There was enough room left, anyway, for him to maneuver. He was able to save some of his numbers, and he managed to dig up assorted action in New Jersey without drawing rude stares from Longy Zwillman.

He had no particular financial worries, anyway. Dutch's personal bankroll was estimated in the millions—sometimes as high as seven million dollars.

Early in 1935, a Manhattan grand jury was investigating the numbers racket in New York, when some shenanigans began to take place.

An assistant District Attorney had been presenting the evidence—and doing an excellent job that was rapidly nearing indictments against "important" people. Suddenly, the assistant D. A. was called off the case. In his place, the District Attorney, personally, appeared. At once the investigation began to sag badly. The District Attorney then was William C. Dodge. Later, it was to be revealed that Dodge's election campaign had enjoyed contributions of some $30,000 from Dutch Schultz's organization.

The grand jury took the bit in its teeth. It demanded removal of the District Attorney from the investigation on the ground that he was not supplying the evidence it wanted. It became, in fact, one of the few "runaway" grand juries in New York history. (Grand jurors rarely realize they have the power to order before them any witnesses they wish to hear and to pursue any inquiry they deem necessary. Both the District Attorney and the court are subservient to the grand jury. Actually, a "runaway" jury is nothing more than a jury aware of its authority—especially when a prosecutor is unaware of his obligations.)

The grand jury that ran away in 1935 demanded that Dodge be superseded by a special prosecutor who would really dig into the rackets. The suggestion was made that the appointment go to a young lawyer named Thomas E. Dewey, who had compiled a hard-hitting record in the Federal Attorney's office. Immediately there were indications that Dewey would not be welcomed in certain quarters. The newspapers, however, picked up the jury's demands, and Governor Herbert Lehman designated Dewey, in a wide-sweeping mandate, to delve into the rackets in New York City.

Excitable even when normal, Dutch blew up completely at this. He got his current lawyer on the telephone.

"Hey, mouthpiece," he bellowed, "what does the word nemesis mean?"

"Why, Arthur," replied the attorney, who insisted on complete formality with his client at all times, "it means a hoodoo, a jinx."

"Just what I thought," Schultz nodded dolefully as he hung up.

It affected him most morbidly. Night after night, he wept in his cups about it.

"That Dewey," he would moan. "He is my nemesis."

Dutch had something there, at that. As an assistant Federal Attorney, Dewey had obtained the indictment for income-tax evasion which had started all of Schultz's woes. Now the same Dewey was looking into the numbers, which was one of the very few lines of business Dutch had left. For many days, The Dutchman brooded. The mad dog began to froth; the nemesis became an obsession. One night, it got him.

"Dewey's gotta go," Schultz slammed the table and screamed. "He has gotta be hit in the head."

In the old days, such a pronunciamento would have had an official ring to it. Now, though, it was no longer the ultimatum of the Boss with one hundred of the top triggermen of the era to back his play. Now he was just one gangster—and at the fringe of the cartel, at that. However, Dutch was not the only mobster who wanted Dewey removed. Others—accredited members of the Syndicate—felt his elimination was called for; but for business, rather than personal reasons. That made it a subject for the board of governors, like any murder matter involving intermob affairs. A meeting was called in New York to consider the case. Schultz was so beside himself that he slipped over from his home base in Newark, despite the standing order for his arrest on sight if he ever set foot in Manhattan. Although not part of the cartel, he was permitted to sit in as an interested party in a similar line of business.

Following protocol and procedure very carefully, the new democratic order limited discussion to the question of whether Dewey should be stopped and if so, the extent of the stopping. This was not a meeting held in desperation or dread. The bosses sat down as coolly and methodically as any board of directors considering important business policy. These gang lords had seen investigations come and go. No one was panicky. In fact, no one—except Schultz—was even very excited. Everyone had his say.

There was no unanimity of judgment at the conclave. The division of opinion ranged from outright assassination of the prosecutor as the sound means of ending the investigation, all the way to, "forget about him." The discussion dragged on. Finally, some of the wiser heads felt more time should be taken to weigh so important a problem. After all, murdering a prosecutor was not just any mob job. Eventually, in order to allow for profound thought, it was decided to adjourn for one week, and meet again.

"But suppose next week we vote to take him?" interposed the single-track-minded Dutchman. "We should be ready to do the job quick."

That was logical. It would be wise to blueprint in advance the mechanical details of so delicate a matter, in the event the ultimate decision favored assassination. The directorate agreed to have Dewey cased between sessions. His movements, his comings and his goings (and his stops) were to be thoroughly checked and clocked. All necessary details for the execution were to be prepared. It was Murder, Inc.'s customary painstaking and studied preparation, by which risks of failure due to carelessness were eliminated.

Obviously, this assignment would require utmost subtlety and finesse. The job was, in fact, so top priority that no less an individual than Albert Anastasia, czar of the Brooklyn waterfront and boss of the Syndicate's newly added death squad, was proposed as the ideal man to do the casing and take charge of preparatory details, such as the getaway car and murder weapons. No one opposed the nomination. It was an important piece of work and required an important man. Albert A. was important enough to be officially described as "the overlord of organized crime" in Brooklyn.

In those days, Dewey never moved without his two bodyguards. The caser would have to be especially adroit to avoid attaching suspicion to himself. Someone got the idea for the perfect subterfuge. A child was borrowed from a friend to accompany the caser. What could be less sinister than a devoted father romping with his offspring?

For four straight mornings, this "proud parent," with his decoy child pedaling a velocipede, took up an innocent stand in front of Dewey's apartment building. Each morning, they were already there when the prosecutor and his guards emerged. It must have been a fine show of parental devotion to Dewey and his companions—this man willing to rise early enough to spend a bit of time with his heir before heading off for the daily toil.

For the inoffensive "father," the setup was ideal. Given four mornings of uninterrupted observation, he noted that Dewey's daily routine followed a pattern. The prosecutor and his guards left the apartment at practically the same minute each day. They headed for the same drugstore a couple of blocks away. There, the guards took up a stand outside the door, while Dewey went inside. He remained for several minutes, then reappeared, and the trio would be off.

The pharmacist could hardly be suspicious of the proud parent and his child who dropped in on two different mornings just after Mr. Dewey left. The man was very disarming; seemed interested, mostly, in seeing that the tot did not ride his tricycle into a floor display of beauty soap. It was no trouble for the man to learn that the prosecutor's regular stop in the drugstore was to make the first phone call to his office each day. Later, when someone mentioned it, Dewey recalled that morning call.

"I did not want to disturb Mrs. Dewey by using the phone in our room at the apartment so early," he explained. Besides, it was very likely that his home phone was tapped, once his probe began.

By the fourth morning, the caser felt he had established that Dewey's actions were regular habit. The prosecutor could be counted on to do the same thing every day. Meantime, the other necessary details were being handled with the same efficiency. From a public garage, the Brownsville troop stole a black four-door sedan, especially selected for inconspicuous color and high-speed power. This would be the getaway car for the killer, if the decision was to proceed with the assassination. The car was stored carefully away in a prepared "drop," to remain under cover until needed. License plates were stolen from another car, and transferred to the "hot," or stolen, vehicle, completing the almost impenetrable disguise. Guns for the job were secured by rifling one of a number of crates of weapons, waiting on a pier for shipment to some European government. Even if their absence were eventually noted—which was unlikely—it would be months, and thousands of miles, away.

Not even that insurance satisfied the combination's sticklers, however. The guns were also specially treated. The usual precaution against tracing a pistol is to file off the numbers. Crime-fighting science has discovered, though, that the metal beneath the number on a weapon is compressed when the numerals are stamped in. Thus, when the number is simply filed away, an application of acid—nitric or hydrochloric—will bring out the ghostlike imprint of the figures. The Brooklyn hoods, well aware of this, had a gunsmith who could circumvent it. He merely gouged out the metal completely—and an acid bath produced nothing but blank steel. Finally, the business end of each weapon was threaded so that silencers could be attached. With that flourish, everything was ready to carry out the mandate, if the decision of the adjourned meeting of the board of governors dictated the assassination of Dewey.

The report of the caser showed exactly how it would be done. On the day selected, the gunman would get to the drugstore a few minutes before the regular time for Dewey's arrival. He would be inside and waiting and the bodyguards, who always remained outside, would not know there was a stranger even in the neighborhood. Keeping his back to Dewey, the trigger-man would be "buying" a tube of toothpaste or a box of cornplasters, or something, until the prosecutor went into the phone booth, as usual.

"Dewey'll be a sitting duck in there," it was pointed out.

Out would come the gun—equipped with silencer. That was a must. The flat crack of the silencer would never carry enough to be audible to the guards through the closed door of the store, above the street noises. The assassin would turn and blast Dewey, cornered there in the booth. The druggist would be drilled where he stood, behind the counter. There would be no outcry, no sound of gunfire, no alarm—and no identification later.

Having completed the contract, the killer would ease out. The guards, having heard nothing, would barely look his way as he ambled past. Casually, he would turn the corner to the waiting getaway car, which he would abandon with the untraceable guns wherever convenient. Before the bodyguards grew perturbed enough to investigate, there would be ample time for a smooth, easy disappearance.

All of this was before the board of governors as the adjourned meeting opened. Dutch Schultz was on hand again, as anxious as ever for the elimination of his nemesis. The debate was resumed. However, this time the Syndicate's cooler heads dominated. The new-order mob moguls balanced the necessity for any killing against the consequences it might stir up. Besides, Lepke and Lucky Luciano were firmly convinced they knew the technique with which to meet the danger that threatened.

"All investigations collapse when no witnesses are around," argued the czar of industrial extortion. Lepke always maintained the same philosophy. He had learned it through probe after probe that had died slow deaths in the past.

"We are bombproof when all the right people are out of the way," he pointed out. "We get them out of the way now—then this investigation collapses, too."

Lepke's logic was deadly. Under our system of jurisprudence, witnesses before a grand jury must make out a prima facie case of crime before law enforcement can secure an indictment. Without the essential witnesses, a prosecutor cannot muster such a case.

The other directors of crime respected Lepke's judgment. His record was excellent. On the basis of his "success" alone, he must have the right answers.

"Besides," both he and Lucky propounded another powerful point, "the best Dewey can do is try to go after the New York rackets; he can't touch anything outside of New York."

No one in the Syndicate could ignore as particularly pertinent a consideration as that. Dewey was bound to Manhattan by jurisdictional limits. The take from the New York rackets was important, but it was a drop compared to the businesses the cartel was operating across the nation. And assassinating a prosecutor would stir up such righteous indignation throughout the country that it could very well dam up the financial flood from the lucrative rackets in all other places.

"If we knock him off," cautioned another of the gang lords in support of this view, "even the Federals will jump on the rackets. We'll be chased out of the country."

The proposed assassination, then, was potentially disastrous enough to blow up the entire national empire of crime. Sacrificing the whole chain-store system to halt an as yet embryonic threat solely against New York was not sound business. That was the main concern of the directors: good business. They saw the light. Lepke's sage and forceful persuasion, backed by Lucky, won out. They took a vote, and the directors decided to permit Dewey to live.

The decision was not unanimous. Dutch Schultz did not approve. Nor did Gurrah, Lepke's snarling partner. This might have been expected. Of the entire group, these were the two strong arms famed for doing most of their thinking with their muscles. All the rest, however, turned thumbs down on the idea of murdering the special prosecutor. They were not inspired by any humanitarian motives. The executives of national crime spared Dewey's life solely for the sake of—national crime.

Dutch Schultz was of that era and ilk of power-mad paranoiacs so pampered and fawned upon by favor-seeking punks that they came to believe their orders were royal decrees and their wishes ordained commandments.

Dutch was neither satisfied nor happy with the edict sparing Dewey's life. He made no secret about it.

"I still say he ought to be hit," the mad dog barked defiantly. "And if nobody else is gonna do it, I'm gonna hit him myself."

Anyway, he contemplated, it would be a shame to waste all that valuable data gathered by the "proud parent."

"That drugstore phone booth is a natural," thought the outlaw hoodlum. So, in defiance of the board of governors, Schultz set out to murder Dewey on his own—using the very scheme the board had discarded. It looked foolproof.

Dutch Schultz was a blowhard. Like all blowhards, he talked too much. He couldn't keep this one to himself. To an associate, he whispered that he was not only going to do it—but he even said when. He boasted that he was going to get the big rackets-buster in forty-eight hours!

No such startling undertaking could be kept off the grapevine for long. Anyone who heard such a whisper must realize it was guilty knowledge, much too hot to keep. In short order, the Syndicate buzzed with the report that the Dutchman was going to "take" Dewey on his own. The gang lords were shocked—not so much at the assassination plot as at the defy.

"That Dutchman is just daffy enough to do it, too," Lepke warned the others. "This is no good."

Obviously, Schultz's insane plot would bring on the cartel the entire heat of the Law that the leaders had always avoided. It would wreck the rackets and launch the biggest war on crime in history. Or, as one informer told us:

"They got scared that rubbing out Dewey would hit them where it hurt the most—in their pocketbooks."

Having ordained that Dewey should live, the chiefs of crime now had to insure his life. And since Dutch was rushing the demise of his nemesis, the insuring would have to be done in a hurry. The fact that Schultz was plotting to defy Syndicate decree for personal reasons made this a matter of prime importance. It was especially significant in that this was the first real challenge to and test of Syndicate law.

The directors discussed it—and ruled that the Dutchman himself must die to guarantee Dewey's life. The mob actually ordained that it would rub out a mobster—to save a prosecutor!

Schultz was a veteran of gang gun fights, tough to corner. Over in Newark, his guard was always up. For public appearances, his favorite spot was the Palace Chophouse in downtown Newark, and things were so arranged there that he could transact business and social obligations in a sort of back-room niche, easily guarded at its one entrance.

This was a special job; it would take special men. Without a word of palaver on personnel, each of the bosses immediately picked, mentally, the exact men called for. Lepke had two operatives on his staff made to order for it. Lepke knew it, too. He designated both for this all-important mission —"Charlie the Bug" Workman, one of gangland's most deadly executioners, and Mendy Weiss, a hulking, snarling murderer with a touch of directional ability.

Mendy was a strangler and a strong-arm veteran of the labor wars. He was an operational boss on Lepke's staff—although perhaps not quite as important as he liked to have others believe. He fancied getups like one flashy all-green outfit that practically blinded an entire courtroom one day. It was Mendy who reveled as acting boss when Lepke was in hiding in 1939, and ordered murder done as far away as California.

Bug Workman, one of the most valuable gunmen in the entire underworld, was a curly-haired completely casual killer, custom-tailored from head to foot. Because of his ability at assassination, his place in gangdom was high, for a gunman. Although not a member of the directorate, he sat in council chamber with the executives and did only important work for the boss. Detectives called him the Powerhouse. When it came to doing a job of slaying, gang style, the Bug was practically a mob all by himself.

"A guy has to be a bug to do what Charlie does," his admiring gunmates used to say, shaking their heads in awe over the score of contracts he had handled.

For the Dutch Schultz expedition, a third party would be needed, someone who knew his way around Newark to pilot the getaway car for the two New Yorkers. The story is that this third man was supplied by the Jersey mob, and was especially familiar with the best routes. He is identified to this day only as Piggy; there are, however, suspicions as to who he is.

On the night of October 23, 1935, one of the hundreds of cars rolling through the Holland Tunnel, outbound from New York, was an inconspicuous black sedan, carrying three inconspicuous-appearing men. Their talk was equally inconspicuous, idle chatter of fights and baseball and maybe a bit of politics, like any three men thrown together in an automobile.

Their mission, however, was not so innocuous. They were on their way to beat a deadline—on assassination. Dutch Schultz was just thirty-six hours away from murdering Thomas E. Dewey, special rackets prosecutor, and the trio had strict orders from the overloads of the underworld to stop the Dutchman—for keeps!

The car slid swiftly through the aromas from the slaughterhouses and glue works which make automobiling across the Jersey meadows more comfortable with the windows rolled up, even on hot days. In Newark, Piggy, the driver, found the Palace Chophouse easily enough. They pulled up in front of the place not long after ten o'clock.

Mendy was designated as "cover" for the getaway. He stayed at the door. Piggy, as wheelman, remained in the car, ready to pull away. Charlie the Bug barged right into the place.

There was a bar in the long front room, and beyond it this sort of backroom niche, which the Dutchman used as a combination office and cozy nook. The "finger" had reported that Dutch would be there that night.

The Bug strolled the length of the bar, breezily and completely carefree, like a man on his way to the free-lunch counter in the better days. Just off the end of the bar was the men's room. Workman flipped open the door to it. Even the bold Bug would not overlook an uncovered quarter, from which a flanking attack might be launched. Inside, a fellow, his back to the door, was washing his hands. Something about him looked familiar.

"One of the bodyguards, I guess," thought Workman. And he pulled out his pistol and fired. The handwasher toppled without even turning off the faucet.

The Bug, gun ready, now advanced on the boys in the back room. The bar had emptied in a hurry. The bartender, with admirable presence of mind, disappeared behind the mahogany. A World War I veteran, he knew the advantages of defilade under fire.

In the rear room sat three Schultz aides. A business meeting had been in progress. Before them, papers were piled on the table—apparently the monthly accounting of Dutch's enterprises. One strip of adding-machine tape carried a long list of figures, among them entries of $313,711.99 and $236,295.95. Obviously, the Dutchman had reorganized well. The three lieutenants, however, were no longer interested in financial statements. As Workman appeared, they opened fire. The Bug fired back. He kept banging away, and pretty soon, Lulu Rosenkrantz, who was Dutch's chauffeur and bodyguard, and Ab (Misfit) Landau, one of his torpedoes, and Abba-dabba Berman, the human comptometer who fixed the daily number, were all dead.

Workman was troubled, though, as he retired once more to the empty bar. The word had been that Dutch was to be there. The Bug had not seen Schultz. And there was no one else in sight.

"Funny," thought the Bug. "The Dutchman ought to be around. I got to take him."

Then, it dawned on him:

"Why, sure . . . that guy in the toilet. No wonder he looked familiar."

He was right. The man in the men's room had been Dutch Schultz. The first to go had been the mob magnate whose extermination the Syndicate had ordered to save the life of a law-enforcement officer. Almost simultane-ously with the realization, a recollection hit Charlie the Bug of an incident in the Dutchman's life which is legend among New York's police. One June night in 1931, Dutch and his torpedo, Danny Iamascia, had just slipped out of Schultz's hideout on upper Fifth Avenue when they noted two vague figures detach themselves from the shadow of a building across the street.

"The Mick," snapped Schultz in warning, presuming they were repre-sentatives of his sworn enemy, Vincent Coll, the maddest mobster New York ever saw. Dutch and Danny went for their guns. The two figures made no threatening move, though, until the hoodlum and his stooge started shooting. For, the two figures were not the Mad Mick's men. They were Detectives Julius Salke and Steve DiRosa. The battle did not last long. Detective Salke put a bullet through Iamascia. Dutch, seeing his triggerman fall, threw his own gun away and started running. Detective DiRosa could have shot him right then. Instead, he took off after the speeding Schultz, caught him in a matter of yards and dropped him with a superb bit of tackling.

The police legend is that Dutch reached into his pocket after his arrest, brought out all the cash he had on him and offered it as a bribe for his release. And all the cash he had on him was a mere $18,600! The officer was so incensed at the bribe attempt, the legend runs, that he roared, "You miserable bum, I'll shove that dough down your throat." And, the legend concludes, the officer had the Dutchman down and had one end of this king-size roll of bills in the Dutchman's mouth, and was doing just that, when a fellow officer persuaded him it was not a nice way to treat money.

All of this ran through Charlie the Bug's mind as he stood in the middle of that Newark saloon that night in 1935, with Dutch on the toilet floor, mortally wounded. Now it may have dawned on him that all the pistol-popping was going to bring a lot of curious policemen rapidly. But the threat was not nearly strong enough to outweigh the possibility—and the hope—that maybe lightning could strike twice in the same place. Back into the gents' room barged the Bug, and he gave Dutch's pockets a thorough and total frisk. He never mentioned to anyone afterward whether it proved worth while.

Mendy was supposed to be at the door of the chophouse covering the getaway when Charlie the Bug started out, leaving Dutch Schultz and his trio of hired hands fatally wounded. But Mendy was not there.

The Bug did not think that was right. Suppose he had needed cover for his escape. Outside, there was no Piggy at the wheel of the getaway car, either. In fact, there was no getaway car. And right then was neither the time nor the place to be on foot in Newark, in the vicinity of the Palace Chophouse.

The hue and cry was going up all over the neighborhood by now—and no wonder, with all that gunfire. The Bug could see any number of curious citizens bearing down rapidly, from all directions. He slid into an alley, and from there he had to dash across back yards, slip through vacant lots and leap over fences, before he finally made his getaway back to New York. Those guys, he pondered in annoyance, must have run out on him. What irked the Bug was that they had taken the car with them. Not only did he have to run practically all the way home, but it had made him late for a date, besides. Charlie the Bug was fit to be tied.

The incident raised hob in the underworld. Mendy and Piggy had a lot of explaining to do—especially Mendy, because he was a staff gunman. Under the Syndicate's law, abandoning a post and a mobmate, while on organization business, is fatal. Not even the fact that he was a trusted lieutenant of the mighty Lepke could ease Mendy out of this one. Unless he had a perfect explanation, the bull-shouldered strangler would have to stand trial before the kangaroo court.

The supreme court of crime was made ready for Mendy. The mere fact that he was not there when the Bug came out of the chophouse made it an open-and-shut case. The situation looked bad. Mendy foresaw his danger, and immediately reported his side to his boss, in a desperate move to avoid a trial. Surprisingly, he maintained that he had definitely remained at his post until the contract was all finished. The bulky badman admitted he wasn't at the chophouse door when Workman finally came through it. That, however, was no contradiction, he held.

"I claim," Mendy concluded, "that hitting the Dutchman was mob business, and I stayed there till it was over. But then the Bug went back in the toilet to give the Dutchman a 'heist.' I claim that was not mob business any more—that was personal business."

That being the case, Mendy maintained, he had a perfect right to depart forthwith, before the Law arrived, and to take Piggy and the getaway car with him. On a point of law, the Bug's act was simply *ultra vires*—it was not in furtherance of the purposes for which the corporate mission was organized.

There was no argument against such logic. Not even the Bug would dispute the point. Mendy was discharged without even standing trial.

Dutch Schultz did not bow out immediately the night Bug Workman blew a big hole in him with his .45.

The dying Dutchman lingered, in fact, for close to twenty-four hours, with Police Stenographer John Long glued to his bedside in a Newark hospital, shorthanding his every gasp, and Police Sergeant Luke Conlon asking him questions in his few conscious moments. Mostly, though, it was delirious babbling, interspersed with an occasional lucid word or phrase or paragraph, as Schultz struggled for life. For only about two hours, on the afternoon following the shooting, did any of his garbled ramblings have any coherency at all.

Apparently the violent gangster never knew what hit him, there in the men's room of the saloon. At least, that was the impression he left in the brief chances Sergeant Conlon had to put any questions to him through his coma.

Q—What did they shoot you for?
A—I don't know, sir . . . honest . . . I don't even know who was with me, honestly . . . I went to the toilet . . . I was in the toilet. When I reached the can, the boy came at me.
Q—The big fellow gave it to you?
A—Yes . . . he gave it to me.
Q—Do you know who this big fellow was?
A—No.

Once, in reply to another query about who shot him, the writhing hoodlum groaned:

"The boss himself."

Both FBI agents and police investigators grabbed at the babbled phrase as pointing directly to Lucky Luciano. Wasn't Lucky head of Unione Siciliano, they reasoned? Wasn't the head of Unione always known as the Boss?

Later, The Dutchman brought in another name, and sent the investigators off on another tangent:

Q—What did the big fellow shoot you for?
A—Him . . . John? . . . Over a million—five million dollars.

"John," FBI and police figured, could be Johnny Torrio, the sharp little gangster who had turned Chicago over to Al Capone. No one knew then, of course, that he had given gangland the recipe for national organization. In fact, no one even dreamed a national organization existed. But they did know that in underworld stature, John was a "big fellow." As for the "five million dollars," that probably was Dutch's estimate of his loss through the mob's snatch of his rackets.

Mostly, Schultz just lay there gasping and raving. From his wandering snatches came few, if any, pieces to fit the puzzle.

"If we wanted to break the ring . . . no, please . . . I get a month," he stammered once, through teeth clenched with pain. And again, "My gilt-edge stuff . . . and those dirty rats have tuned in."

And still again, "No . . . no . . . there are only ten of us and there are ten million of you fighting somewhere. . . . So get your onions up and we will throw up the truce flag."

The thread through all this was that the muscling of his rich rackets by Lepke and Lucky preyed on Schultz's distorted brain. The "I get a month" may have referred to a time limit given him by the Syndicate to clear up his business. He may have tried to get paid off—"get your onions up"—for agreeing to pull out of the rackets entirely.

Later, there was:

"Please crack down on the Chinaman's friends."

One of Dutch's bitter enemies was Charles Sherman, a Waxey Gordon strong-arm and narcotics executive known to the underworld as the China-man, or Chink. Schultz's "crack-down" request was followed to the letter within a couple of months, incidentally. Sherman's body was found buried in quicklime on the Sullivan County farm of Jack Drucker, a Brooklyn boy who was Murder, Inc.'s Sullivan County manager for a time. It was Drucker who carried an ice pick, the night one Walter Sage was stabbed to death and dropped into a lake with a slot machine tied around his neck.

Off and on during that twenty-four hours on his deathbed, Schultz stammered parts of other names that only added to the mystery.

"Now listen, Phil . . . Fun is fun . . . What happened to the other sixteen?" was one bit of incoherency. Phil, in this case, could have meant Dandy Phil Kastel, Frank Costello's general field manager (then and now), with whom Schultz had been in deals over slot machines.

He failed to mention his wife directly at any time, but at one point, a request to "get the doll a roofing" was taken as a plea to his mobmates, in his delirium, to see that she was cared for. His wife, however, never saw any of his millions. Dutch's pals and underlings, who were generally understood to be holding his money for him (since he never did trust banks), demonstrated exactly how much honor there is among thieves by making off with his fortune as soon as his trigger was no longer there to defend it.

On the other hand, there were half a dozen occasions when he cried out for "mama." Once, toward the very end, tossing with pain, he sobbed:

"Mother is the best bet . . . And don't let Satan draw you too fast."

Perhaps the quiet, churchgoing woman who tried so hard to make her son respectable could take some solace, at last, from that.

The most puzzling development of the Dutchman's last hours, however —even more puzzling than trying to make sense out of his deathbed delirium—were the antics and verbal ambulations of his twenty-one-year-old, hatcheck-girl wife, Frances.

Frances has frequently been pictured, and especially in one recently published book, as a shy, shrinking violet, brought up on that block of West Forty-seventh Street which Damon Runyon dubbed Dream Street. The romance of Frances and the cheating, conniving criminal flowered in a couple of hours one night in a restaurant on Dream Street where she was a combination hatcheck-cigarette girl. Dutch came into the place and promptly went "on the make" for her. Sweet Frances would have nothing to do with this miserable plug-ugly—for at least an hour after she first set eyes on him. Then he told her he was *the* Dutch Schultz. From that moment, it was a beautiful romance.

The day after Dutch was shot, Deputy Police Chief John Haller of Newark, plunging into the investigation, thought he ought to ask her a few questions. That was only natural. Frances told him, explained the deputy chief with a mystified air, that the wedlock joining her and her mobster mate operated under a "legal contract." The usual satisfactory results were achieved evidently. The legal contract had produced two children.

Deputy Chief Haller said that, at first, Frances told him she had not been near the Palace Chophouse the night the love of her life was murdered. Then police had an employe confront her, and the employe said, sure, she was there only two hours before the fireworks.

Frances, the deputy chief stated, now did a neat verbal flip-flop. She explained that she had left Dutch two days before, had gone to New York and had stayed there until the evening of the shooting. On the murder night, she stopped in to see Dutch at the saloon about eight-thirty, on her return from her New York visit. She refused to tell the police official, he said, with whom she had stayed in New York for those two days and two nights, or whom she had seen there. She left the chophouse on the murder night, after visiting with Dutch for about half an hour, and she went to a nearby movie.

"I got out about eleven o'clock, and there was a crowd in front of the tavern [chophouse]," the deputy chief quoted her. "I thought it was a saloon raid, so I walked right by."

She walked to the tube station, and took a train back to New York, evidently preferring the bright lights of Manhattan, at that moment, to the company of the mobster with whom she shared such a great and abiding love that it was written about in books, like Romeo and Juliet. Reaching New York about midnight, she bought a newspaper. It was then she learned that the "saloon raid" actually had been the slaughter of her husband and his chums.

Did Frances now hurry back to Newark to be at the bedside of her mate, who was near death? Did she run—her pure little heart thumping in panic —to the nearest phone to try to learn the very latest word of his condition? Deputy Chief Haller said she told him she went in the opposite direction, to the apartment she maintained in Jackson Heights—a short subway trip to Long Island—and she went to sleep. Some time the following afternoon, Frances finally got back to Newark.

This was all very interesting, the deputy chief agreed. It left him still wondering, however, who had fingered Dutch; who had let the mob know that he would be in the chophouse that night when the killers arrived?

Not long after Dutch Schultz ended up in the gents' room, Kid Twist Reles gave a party at his home. It was a strictly social evening—no business. (No one to be shot, slugged or strangled, that is.)

A lot of the boys were there, relaxing from the everyday toil. It was noted, though, that Charlie the Bug Workman was not getting into the swing of things as merrily as the rest, and this was surprising. As the evening wore on, the curly-haired hoodlum loosened up some. Finally, he leaned forward in his easy chair and brought his pet peeve onto the floor. He hadn't believed Mendy's excuse.

"Nice thing, huh," he was hurt and bitter. "Here I go on a job with two guys and they're supposed to be good. I do all the work. That's okay. But these two bums run out on me. You know what those bums did? . . . That Mendy and Piggy—they 'pigged' it!"

And out popped the story. It showed how worked up the Bug really was, when he got as eloquent as that. It was the costliest conversation of his life. Two of his listeners were his host, Kid Twist, and Allie Tannenbaum—who was called Tick-Tock by the mob because he talked with the easy regularity of a clock at work. Of course, the Kid, being an individual who got around in the gang, already knew many of the details from other sources.

And when the Kid began to sing for us that Good Friday night five years later, he included the story of the Dutch Schultz slaughter, and the Bug's bitter and voluble monologue at the party. Only then did the startling motive for the quadruple blood bath come out for the first time anywhere, except in the innermost sanctums of crime.

As might have been expected, the assassination of the Dutchman had stirred up all manner of furore. For five years, the possible motives advanced had almost outnumbered the suspects.

When Reles talked and the "inside" cracked, the actual reason finally leaked through gangland's forbidding silence. The mad-dog Dutchman was hit, not by a New York mob, but by a national syndicate. He was hit, not because he stood in the way of the rackets—the mob already had taken over his major operations—but simply because he insisted on murdering Dewey in defiance of this syndicate, and the gang lords believed that would hurt their business. Only then did it come to light: Thomas E. Dewey had been within thirty-six hours of never living to be almost President of the United States and a three-time Governor of New York State!

A long time later, I related the story to Dewey. I was tremendously impressed by his obvious personal courage. Through all the details, step by step, he said not a word, gave never a sign of the slightest shock at learning he was mere hours away from certain death. But when I mentioned the baby on the velocipede—the decoy for the man casing him— Dewey's eyes widened a fraction. It was a barely perceptible flicker; hardly any motion at all. It gave me the idea, though, that he had recalled the tot—and its "proud parent."

And what ironical justice developed! Organized crime had saved Dewey's life in 1935. Four years later, Dewey dealt organized crime the most severe blow it ever had been hit up to that time. He convicted Lucky for his rackets and Lepke for industrial extortion. And Lepke and Lucky had led the campaign to save him, when Dutch wanted him murdered.

It took four more years for the touch that rounded it all out. Then, Lepke, doomed for murder in our Brooklyn probe, made one last desperate plea for executive clemency. That is a right enjoyed by every man, even a Lepke, under American justice.

Nine years before, Lepke had the life-or-death say over Thomas E. Dewey—and Lepke had said life. Now Lepke was begging for his own life for the crimes he had committed. And the man who now had the life-or-death say over Lepke was—the very same Thomas E. Dewey!

WILLIAM MCFEE

THE *MORRO CASTLE* FIRE*

SATURDAY, September 8, 1934, was a blustery autumn day along the Atlantic coast. There was some rain, the leaves were falling, and so was the barometer. It was the kind of day on shore which indicates dirty weather at sea. September is the hurricane month.

Three days earlier, September 5, the *Morro Castle*, of the Ward Line, sailed from Havana on her homeward run to New York. September 8, in a storm of wind and rain, she was three miles east of Barnegat, heading for the Ambrose Channel, where she would pick up her pilot. It was nearly three o'clock in the morning. Her 318 passengers and most of her crew of 231 men and women were asleep.

The usual Friday night conviviality, the "farewell dinner," the paper hats and toy balloons, the drinking, dancing, and love-making, the traditional culmination of a pleasure cruise in the West Indies, had been clouded by an unusual event. Captain R. Willmott was taken ill at dinner and died within a few hours.

It was a grave psychological strain for the chief officer, Mr. William F. Warms, who had come off watch at eight o'clock. He was about to turn in, for he had a strenuous day ahead of him in New York, when he made the discovery. To find his captain dead in his bunk, to face the sudden responsibility of taking over the command of the ship, would impose a burden on the strongest of men.

Mr. Warms, moreover, had another anxiety.

The gap between chief officer and master of any ship is wide enough, but in this particular case much of the executive authority usually assumed by a chief officer by custom and tradition had been retained by the dead captain. We have to keep this in mind when we come to the actions of Captain Warms, suddenly confronted with the most terrifying emergency to be faced by the master of a vessel crowded with helpless, sleeping passengers.

At five minutes to three Mr. Hackney, acting second officer, saw smoke issuing from the stokehole fiddley. He called down from the bridge to the

* From "The Peculiar Fate of the *Morro Castle*," in *The Aspirin Age* (New York, Simon and Schuster, 1949).

engine room to know "if there was a fire in the engine room." Cadet Engineer William F. Tripp, an eighteen-year-old Massachusetts Institute of Technology student, who was on duty near the telegraph and telephone, for they were about to pick up the pilot, replied in the negative. He knew of no fire. This is a highly important detail which, for some reason, was not emphasized by the experts. One minute later, at 2:56, Mr. Hackney pulled the fire alarm, which would be relayed all over the ship.

By this time, of course, Captain Warms was on the bridge. Accepting the above official record, confirmed by Mr. Tripp's log sheet, we face the extraordinary facts that (1) some eighteen minutes elapsed before the captain ordered a radio call for assistance; (2) the radio operator, Mr. Rogers, whose cabin, fifty feet aft of the navigating bridge, was on fire, sent three times to ask for instructions; (3) other ships near by saw the fire and sent calls before the *Morro Castle* call went out; (4) the ship was kept at nineteen knots, into a twenty-mile wind, in darkness, pouring rain, and pounding seas, before being stopped.

By that time, around half past three, the fire had made such headway that the ship's upper structure, from the forward funnel to the mizzenmast, which rose abaft the deck ballroom and the veranda, was a furnace. The passengers were crowding to the tourist section of the ship, right on the stern rails, on B and C decks. They were pouring through the passageways. Some, who were later seen at portholes, screaming for help, had been trapped in their cabins and were to die horribly there. Six young ladies, who had been carried by stewardesses from the bar to their cabins at the end of the evening's festivities, were not seen again. Some, of course, probably less fuddled, more athletic, and more enterprising, squirmed their way through their portholes and dropped into the sea, and were lucky enough to be picked up by the boats.

Most of the passengers, however, suddenly awakened by the raucous loud-speakers, frightened by the roaring of the flames and the running of men who had lost their wits and had no one to command them, surged aft through the smoke-filled passages. In such a case the word "panic" is inadequate. It conveys nothing of the actuality. These people, running through corridors of a burning ship, half-clothed and many of them half-demented, were in a bad way. When they came out on the after rail it was raining in torrents. There was no light save the lurid flames leaping at them from the superstructure. Below them was the dark turbulence of the sea, dotted with crying people in life belts, calling to the boats dimly seen, standing off fearfully from the heat of the burning ship. Desperation came to these people, and a measure of courage too. Down they went, jumping, or sliding down ropes, and, being inexpert at such business, scorching their soft hands, so that some of them were forever incapacitated for their professional work. There were many women there too, and they threw off their flimsy shoes by the rail, discarding their lipsticks and compacts, their lighters and cigarettes and girdles, as though, when faced with the final, grim, eternal verities of the sea, they instinctively abandoned the nonessentials.

WARREN R. MOULTON

RESCUE AT SEA*

(A Coast Guardsman's Story of the Morro Castle)

I WAS called at midnight September 8 to go on patrol two and a half miles north. I left the station at 12:10 A.M., noting the barometer was falling as I went out. Wind was northeast, sky overcast, weather thickening fast. Marked increase in wind with high surf rolling in, which indicated heavy weather off shore. Some lightning and thunder for about ten minutes at 1:50 A.M., followed by heavy rain squalls, and fog banks. All boats close in running for harbor.

When I got off watch at 4 A.M. I heard the lookout man telling the skipper that he had seen either a boat on fire or distress signals. The man off patrol and I both looked out to sea, but it was so thick we could see nothing. As I went down I heard the skipper sending a call to all stations, and reporting to the commander of this district that he was going to try to get out to sea, but did not think that any of our boats would make it on account of the bar. I did not think so either.

Five of us, all told, started in the surf boat. As we left the dock, the skipper hollered to another member of the crew to bring out the station Pickett boat just as soon as it was light enough to get her out. He did not think she could make it at that time. She is about forty-eight feet long and a mighty fine sea boat, with a very poor engine in her, plenty of power when the damn thing runs, which is not any too often.

We managed to get across the bar and for the next seven or eight miles

* From The New Republic, Oct. 31, 1934.

we had an awful fight, until we were within half a mile of the burning ship. Then we ran into something I never want to see or hear of again. The ocean was fairly lit up by the light of the burning ship, and the water was simply alive with screaming men and women. We stopped, and it very nearly spelled the end of us and a great many others, for so many grabbed the boat at once that we were nearly capsized and sunk. I do not know how many minutes we stopped, but certainly not more than five, and I heard the skipper bellowing at me to go ahead on her. I got her under way and for the next half-mile there was a fight on that I will never forget. Every sea broke over us, washing us from stem to stern. The crew did all they could to keep others off, and prevent our running over someone in the water; the skipper was at the tiller, I at the engine controls. The water was so deep that my hands on the gas throttle were covered. All around, ahead, on each side and astern, were men and women, all excited, a few with their hands stretched out toward us, calling for help; and we, already overloaded, unable to help at all. The rain beat down, the spray flew, and the way those upturned faces looked as they rose on the crest of a wave with the firelight flickering on them was awful. This lasted for about half a mile, then we were abreast of the burning ship and no one in the water to be run down.

There was nothing to do now but keep the boat headed into the sea, every wave breaking over us, for the next two and a half or three miles to the *Andrea F. Luckenbach,* the only steamer there at the time. We managed to crowd a little more speed on. Just as day was breaking we drew up to the *Luckenbach*'s Jacob's-ladders. I looked at our cargo for the first time; women back of me in the stern piled three deep, men and women over the engine box, cordwood fashion, all alive. Just how many there were I do not know, for we had our hands full to get them aboard the ship and keep our boat from being smashed alongside.

As soon as the last passenger was off and aboard ship, our skipper went aboard to get the master to move in closer to the *Morro Castle* so as to be more help to us. Later he did. We started back for another load. Before we got back to the burning ship two more steamers had arrived and put out lifeboats; I do not know how many, but quite a few. Most of them were heavily loaded then, but a few were not, and these were either hauling people out of the water or doing all in their power to draw up to the stern of the *Morro Castle*, where there must have been two hundred people crowded, either along the deck rail, in the water, or hanging by ropes over the stern. We stopped and loaded with women, all women, except three men who were just about gone, right alongside of us.

We went to the nearest ship, the *Empress of Bermuda,* British register, just as quickly as we could. We could not get our load of passengers aboard as no one would throw us a line to hold on to, and they kept the ship's head too much in the wind to give us a good lee so as to enable the women to make the Jacob's-ladder hanging over the side. Finally we had to leave the ship and run over to the *City of Savannah* and put them off. Those fellows and the captain really gave us wonderful help. The minute we were alongside they threw us a line both forward and aft to make fast to before the boat even lost headway. They opened one of their cargo ports and lowered ropes to tie around the women and men who could not climb the ladder.

When we got rid of the next load the ship's lifeboats had gotten the last of the passengers and crew who were aft on the *Morro Castle* and in the water around her. There were about a dozen men on the forward deck, which was not on fire at that time. We tried to get them, but the captain and the rest of the crew refused to leave.

Up to this time there had been no other Coast Guard boats on the scene, just us, in a little twenty-six-foot boat. We made a circle around the *Morro Castle* to see if we had missed anyone, and found the chief wireless operator hanging on the forward boat tackle block. This was on the weather side, and every time a sea came he would go completely out of sight. We had a time getting him aboard without getting busted ourselves.

Along about now the Pickett boat from our station drew up alongside the *Luckenbach* with one of her lifeboats in tow. They had picked it up drifting toward shore, overloaded, with the crew unable to handle her on account of the high seas that were running. The crew was completely played out when they took them in tow. I have since heard there were fifty people on that boat.

By now our gas was getting low. We started to the leeward to take a look at the inlet to see if we could possibly get in. When we were about two and a half miles from the *Morro Castle,* we saw two ship's lifeboats bob up away off on our starboard, but could not make out what they were doing, as it was raining so hard. They seemed to be drifting helplessly toward the breakers, about half a mile inshore. When we were within about a hundred yards of the first boat we saw a girl throw up her hands just a little way from us. We went to her and just as we got her on board, the rain slacked; as we rose on top of a sea, as far as we could see the ocean was dotted with both living and dead.

We were but a few minutes in getting a load of the living, took the lifeboat in tow, and started for the *City of Savannah,* two and a half miles to the windward. The boat we had in tow was one of hers.

On the way we saw our Pickett boat and signaled them to go to the assistance of the other lifeboat. After years, it seemed to me, we reached the *Savannah* and were unloaded in a hurry by her crew, as we were all just about done in by now. As soon as we unloaded, we went back to where the Pickett boat and lifeboat were last seen. The lifeboat was gone, and the Pickett was there rolling helplessly, about to be capsized by each sea. We ran down by them and hollered to know what the trouble was. They said their engine had stopped and they had gotten a fishing boat to take the lifeboat with them. Even if we had had the power to take the Pickett in tow, we could not have done it, as our gas was getting low. We decided the only thing to do was for me to board the Pickett and see if I could get her engines to running. The regular engineer was not on board, he having gone on liberty before the fire started. I got aboard her some way, and straightened up to take a look around. I saw a dead woman lying across the stern, dead lying on top of the cabin; the port side of the deck and cabin were red, dripping blood. In the after cabin were the most forlorn men and women I have ever seen, and all with hardly a rag on. Bilge matter was on the after-cabin floor and in the engine room forward, and everywhere one of the worst smells I have ever smelt where they had vomited. A fish factory is cologne compared to the smell on that boat.

One of the boys was on the stern in his underwear, trying to get the rest of his clothes on. I did not know the reason at the time, but have since heard from the crew that he deserves a lot of credit, which he is not getting. When the engine stopped on them, they were trying to come up to three women with life preservers on; he went overboard and managed to pull them close enough for the rest to get them on board. His name is Monroe Wilson of Marshalburg, North Carolina.

I managed to get the engine running after a while. How long I was, I do not know, nor how close we were to the breakers when we got started, as we could not see very far on account of the heavy rain. Judging from the way the sea was running, it could not have been far. We ran around after that for a while, but could find nothing but dead with life preservers on. We picked up a few of them, but it was such a job to get them on board and they would soon be on the beach anyway. The fellow in charge thought it best to get those in the cabin to a doctor, and leave those already dead alone. Shank River Inlet Bar was out of the question by now, as it was a great deal rougher than when we came out that morning. We thought of Sandy Hook, but it was twenty-five miles up the beach, and from the pounding the old boat was getting we were all doubtful whether she would stand it long enough to make it, even if the engine did not fail, and I was pretty certain it would, as the lubricating-oil pressure had dropped from forty-five pounds to fifteen, on account of gasoline's getting in when they were trying to start it before I got there. I said to go in Manasquan Inlet, which was about five miles from us, but he said he had never been there and did not know the way. I told him I had been there once and thought I could go again, so he gave her up to me and we made it some time that evening.

How many we pulled out of the water, I don't know. I kept count up to fifty-six, the skipper says one hundred and sixteen in all.

STANLEY WALKER

MORRO CASTLE AFTERMATH*

ONE HUNDRED THIRTY-SEVEN persons lost their lives. From four o'clock in the morning until long after nightfall, New Jersey residents of communities along the shore dropped their normal occupations to aid in rescue work.

The burning hulk, known to contain many charred bodies, broke loose from the cutter that was towing her at six-thirty in the evening and wallowed to a shallow berth less than forty yards from the Convention Hall at Asbury Park.

The next day, Sunday, crowds estimated at from 125,000 to 250,000 flocked to Asbury Park to see the burning ship. The majority came by automobile, jamming traffic in almost endless snarls. In New York 2,038 persons took advantage of the special half-price, one-day excursion run offered by the Pennsylvania Railroad. From various parts of New Jersey the Central Railroad hauled an additional 1,058 sightseers to Asbury Park at bargain rates. Philadelphia also sent excursion trains.

It was the largest crowd in any one day in the history of the resort. Local businessmen, from hot dog venders to hotel proprietors, saw their

* From Stanley Walker's *Mrs. Astor's Horse* (New York, Stokes, 1935).

chances for money. The beach where the smoldering liner lay was, of course, the center of interest.

Many spectators seemed to share the opinion of a fat woman who, after sitting for hours on the damp sand, explained to the girl beside her, "Yeah, I'm tired all right, but I ain't going to see nothing like this for a long time." On the boardwalk the man with the telescope, who usually made a bare living charging ten cents to look at the moon or passing vessels, did a thriving business in views of the *Morro Castle* at twenty-five cents a look.

Soon the officials of Asbury Park realized that they had stumbled on pay dirt. Very early a project was on foot to rope off the beach and boardwalk for one hundred yards to the north and south of the Convention Hall and to charge twenty-five cents for the privilege of a good look.

By Monday, September 10, there were stories around that there had been looting on the *Morro Castle*, and the governor sent two hundred soldiers from Fort Hancock. They were immediately put to work by Asbury Park officials directing traffic. Among the loot from the ship were supposed to have been purses, wallets, jewelry, luggage and passengers' clothing.

On Monday afternoon the City Council of Asbury Park by a vote of three to one decided to take over the *Morro Castle* as a permanent tourist attraction.

But there was an unforeseen joker in the "happy improvement plan." When the city fathers claimed the *Morro Castle* they did not know that she carried a cargo of green hides. When the wind blew in from the sea, the stench of scorched and rotting hides nauseated the citizens. Even the boardwalk concessionaires, known as men of exceptionally strong stomachs, turned a bit queasy and went around with pained, baffled expressions. Soon the whole town was tired of the *Morro Castle*. One official, however, still had faith. He sent squads of men aboard the ship to remove the cause of the odor, but not all of his policemen and firemen and all their chloride of lime could stop that all-pervading odor.

The city officials and the Chamber of Commerce, panicky now, begged the salvagers to take the nasty thing away. But the perverse ship remained stuck in the sands for many months. It was not until one chilly morning in March 1935 that the salvage tugs gently nosed the old hulk into deep water and started her on her last voyage to New York and the scrap heap.

THE MAGNIFICENT PUBLIC WORKS

THE Public Works Administration, organized in June 1933, was a part of the grand plan of attack on unemployment, and with its help large-scale undertakings such as TVA and the Grand Coulee Dam were begun, as well as smaller projects such as schools, highways, sewage systems, bridges and the like. The Agency was slow to get off the ground but the Chairman of the Public Works Board, Harold Ickes, was to become acclaimed for incorruptibility, not speed. With the tremendous funds at his disposal, he wanted to avoid scandal at any cost.

The PWA could loan or make outright grants of money to states and public organizations to begin their own construction work; the agency could use its money for its own projects; and it could loan money to private corporations. In addition, the PWA went to work for the Navy, constructing aircraft carriers—the *Yorktown* and *Enterprise* —cruisers, destroyers and submarines.

Such public works, while attacked by conservatives all over the country, were, under Secretary Ickes, honestly operated for the public good. Ickes was not going to "hire men to chase tumbleweeds on windy days."

Conversely, conservatives among the businessmen were apt to find it easy to accept government money to complete private business operations—the Pennsylvania Railroad, for instance, accepted 80 million dollars as a loan to electrify its road between New York and Washington. The Triborough Bridge in New York City was finished with PWA funds after private investors and banks refused to buy bonds for its completion; and PWA money was put up to hasten the completion of Boulder Dam, later christened Hoover Dam—there had been an appropriation under Hoover to begin work on this dam near Las Vegas, Nevada, on the Colorado River. Hoover Dam was the first of the magnificent achievements completed in the Thirties to meet the need for better conservation of the country's resources.

BRUCE BLIVEN

BOULDER DAM*

WHEN I crossed southern Colorado from east to west, my train, dropping several thousand feet from the top of the transcontinental divide in the course of a few miles, wound downward through a canyon beside the bed of an insignificant, an inconsequential river, trickling along in an amiable and unimportant way. Days later and hundreds of miles distant I met the same river again, now become the lordly Colorado, whose course, carved at one point through a vertical mile of colored rock, provides the Grand Canyon, the most awesome single spectacle in the whole world—the Colorado, which in flood has in the past wreaked incalculable damage but will never do so again, will on the contrary be of tremendous usefulness to that part of the human anthill which lies within a vast circle whose central point is a few hundred miles from the river's mouth in the Lower California Gulf.

What Hath Man Wrought.—You reach Boulder Dam by automobile from Las Vegas, Nevada (of which more in a moment). For two thirds of its length the road runs straight across the semidesert upland through sparse and stunted vegetation; then you twist upward and to the left amid barren small hills. You pass a barrier where a uniformed representative of Uncle Sam looks you over (and politely turns you back if you happen to be unemployed and looking for work), and in a twinkling here you are in Boulder City. A few years ago this was bare desert, without a tree or a teaspoonful of water; now it is a pleasant community of curving boulevards along the hillsides, bastard-Mediterranean architecture, green lawns, palms and bright flower beds. The men who are making the dam live here in big air-cooled dormitories, traveling to and from the dam itself, a few miles away, in huge buses. As many as 5,000 persons have been employed simultaneously, though with the end of the job perhaps only eighteen months away the number is now reduced. The men work in three shifts—day, swing and graveyard; they eat in a huge restaurant whose staff

* From *The New Republic,* Dec. 11, 1935.

tosses off lightly the task of preparing up to 10,000 "sit down" meals and 5,000 box lunches every day.

The work is exceedingly hard, often dangerous, and not particularly well paid; the average payroll works out at about $35 per week per person, which, in view of the many highly skilled men who get more than this, means that large numbers get less. Nevertheless, in several ways the workers here have had unusually good conditions—including the air-cooled sleeping rooms in a climate where the summer temperature often goes above 120 degrees (I have seen it myself at 127). The men's living quarters reminded me strongly of conditions in an average dormitory for men in a Western college; and when I mentioned this I was told that in fact a large proportion of the workers had been college men who, because of the vagaries of our economic system, had been unable to get jobs more appropriate to their training.

Thumbing the Nose at Mother Nature.—Up still higher into the hills, a few miles on winding mountain roads; a long and sharp descent with a hairpin turn, and here you are, a quarter of a mile downstream from the dam. At this spot a few years ago the river roared and hissed at the bottom of a deep notch cut between ugly, tumbled, black hills, with hardly a blade of vegetation on their sharp-edged shoulders of volcanic material. Men came and clambered over the rocks, squinted far down at the green and white water against the black, deeply shadowed walls, and this is what they have done: they have built vast tunnels through the canyon walls, paralleling the course of the mighty stream; they have turned the water out of its bed; in that dry bed they have constructed by far the largest dam on earth, six hundred feet through at the base and towering almost two thirds as high as the Empire State Building. Upstream from that dam is now accumulating a lake which will take ten years to fill. It will then be 115 miles long, 8 miles wide at its widest point, and it will contain enough water to cover all of New York State to a depth of one foot. If by some miracle of nature the river itself were to disappear from the face of the earth, its mighty current would continue to sweep onward at the normal volume for *two years* before this lake would be exhausted.

What you see as you come around that hairpin turn is a vast wall of new gray-white concrete, curved in a beautiful bow with its arch upstream for strength. Just beyond it are four concrete towers which look "modern" because they are functional—two on either side of the dam, close inshore —the intake towers through which will pass the water for the hydroelectric plant. That plant will lie nestled against the downstream side of the dam, a U-shaped structure which in fact will be twenty stories high but will, I should say, look like a pygmy beside the flank of that incredible man-made mountain. At present, the floor of the canyon below the dam is the usual appalling litter that goes with big construction—temporary roads, wooden scaffolding, a tangle of power cables. Even from our height, a little below the top of the dam itself, the workers moving about amid their rubbish heaps seem incredibly small and weak; the mind refuses to grasp the fact that these tiny dolls and others like them have actually turned aside the river, built that vast cliff of concrete, chiseled and blasted out all these roads, many of them cut into the very face of the cliff, bored the mighty tunnels through which the entire river is now racing silently, far below our feet in the bowels of the hill.

Abstractedly, as we see huge cages move out on cables strung across the canyon, and then descend 700 feet with their massive cargoes, we hear the Voice of Explanation in our ears: The purposes of Boulder Dam are flood control, irrigation, silt control, water supply and electricity. The new aqueduct, many miles downstream, will carry one billion gallons of water per day to Los Angeles, a distance of 239 miles, over desert and through mountains, lifting it a quarter of a mile, by means of pumping stations, in the process. Still farther downstream, a new irrigation canal will carry water to 1,000,000 acres and ultimately to 500,000 more. In addition, flood danger will be eliminated from another vast area. The dam, when completed, will have a maximum electric capacity four times that of Niagara, three times that of Muscle Shoals, two and one-half times that of the great Russian dam which was once called Dnieprostroy. The sale of electricity and water should pay the expense of construction within about fifty years (the aqueduct will cost some $60,000,000 more than the dam itself, and is next only to the Panama Canal among the great projects of the modern world).

The dam is by far the largest single piece of masonry ever attempted. It weighs 6,000,000 tons, and if this were poured in a cube, it would cover a square block and rise higher than the Empire State Building. Because of the heat engendered in pouring, the dam would take a hundred years to cool, if left to itself. To hasten the process, more than 500 miles of tubing have been built into the structure, through which ice water circulates from a plant capable of turning out 1,000 tons of ice every twenty-four hours (compare that with your electric refrigerator). This dam, which is being built by a combination of private companies, was first tailor-made in the Denver offices of the Reclamation Service, where the plans were all drawn. The actual construction, of course, was mostly done on the spot. Before construction could begin, a branch railroad had to be built thirty-three miles in length; many miles of first-class highway were constructed and, oddly enough, a power-line 222 miles long was strung to bring electricity, for the building job, to the place which will ultimately produce the world's largest supply of it.

The top of the dam is broad enough for a roadway, and is already used for that purpose. Eventually, the main highway between Chicago and Los Angeles will go through here and tin-can tourists rattling along at fifty miles an hour toward the Coast will glance down casually at the lake on the right, the river resuming its flow on the left. Probably few of them will ponder very much about 6,000,000 hours of heartbreaking, risky work performed here by steel-helmeted men in overalls, who, the task completed, will have gone their anonymous way toward the next job.

Worm's-Eye View.—My friend Buddy the chauffeur, tearing down a winding mountain road, deposes and says:

The brakes on this car are all shot. Hope you don't mind? I can most always hold her by going into second gear.

Sure, I worked on the dam. Say, everybody around here has taken a crack at it one time or another, or anyhow tried to. Men came here from pretty near everywheres, 'specially a couple years ago when it was just getting started. Lots of them were hired, and then got in the cage for their first trip down. You seen it: the cage goes out over the canyon, 700 feet high and then in the middle it goes on down. Lots of men couldn't stand it. They'd hang onto the cage and ride back up on the first trip and quit right there.

Good many men been killed here. What do you expect? It's dangerous work. Don't know exactly how many, but it must be close to 200. Quite a lot of them fell. A fellow was running the hoist that pulls the cage up and down on the cables. One time he was bringing up a cage with three men in it, and when it got to the top he forgot to pull the lever. The hoist wheels went on turning, the cable raveled out, and the cage dropped. Sure, all killed. Did they fire the hoistman? Say, they never caught him to fire him. Anybody that gets in an accident like that, he lights out for all hell and you never see him again.

Used to be a cable bridge across the river—also 700 feet up. Floor was two planks, each twelve inches wide, no handrail, or nothing. Many a man come here, took one look at that bridge and quit. Sometimes somebody would start across, standing up, of course, and leaning against the wind. Then he'd look down, or get thinking about it, and lose his nerve. He'd drop to all fours, hugging them planks, and crawl off an inch at a time. When two of you met, walking from opposite sides, you'd take hold of hands, swing out and past each other, straighten up and let go of hands again. One fellow got scared in the middle of the swing, and the other man fell. After that they strung another cable for a sort of handrail. Wasn't much good, though; kept hitting you in the leg as you walked and you'd come off of there all black and blue.

A fellow was sitting in a painter's chair, hung down over the side of the dam, 'bout twenty-five feet from the top. He looked up and seen a man slip and come down, over the edge. Son of a gun if he didn't kick the face of the dam, swing out and catch the guy right in the air. Saved his life. Tore his coat though. And then the man he caught turned out to be a supervisor. Son of a gun!

It's funny about them hoistmen. Even when they are just running a cage out and down, up and in, they differ a lot. You'd get so you'd know who was at the levers, just from his style. You seen them big buckets to carry wet concrete; did you notice how the whole bottom opens out to let the stuff through? Course, when she empties, the bucket jumps up a little with the weight off. This fellow Smitty, now, he could jerk the lever so when she bounced, she come up twenty-five feet. Nobody else could do it. He could unload ten buckets to anybody else's nine, right along. The other men said it was the helpers he had, but Smitty said No, they could give him any helpers they wanted, and he'd still beat them. Did, too.

Well, I missed that truck. Guess you thought I was going to hit, didn't you? I'll have to have somebody look at these brakes and see if they can't be fixed.

Wide-open Town.—So far as anyone can discern from casual observation, the only occupations of Las Vegas, Nevada, are drinking, gambling and prostitution. They must do something else there, but if so it is not discernible to the innocent tourist's eye. Probably the dam, with up to 5,000 men, mostly single, has helped, though old inhabitants tell me that Las Vegas has always been one of the most wide-open towns in a wide-open state. It is a bit startling, at first, to walk down the main street at 11 A.M. and see in almost every block one or more gambling houses, doors open to every passerby, crowded with men and women, old and young, playing Keno, roulette, poker, shooting craps, or betting on horse races, described by a raucous-voiced gentleman who gets his facts by direct wire from the track. Las Vegas' Painted Ladies go in for raspberry-colored sailor pants, coral-tinted blouses and high-heeled slippers; their faces, beneath the metallic-looking orange rouge which is universal in the Southwest, are haggard and burned like the faces of all desert people. Every second or third man you meet has had about three drinks too many, and is glad of it.

281

The ladies, as always, drink less or hold it better, and obligingly help keep their gen'l'men friends from rolling into the gutters.

Perhaps I had better break down and confess that going in for sin in a Big Way, as Las Vegas does, seems to me a pretty awful spectacle. It is carrying over the habits of the old West into an era of long-distance buses, radio sets and ubiquitous Ford V-8s. The cowhand or miner who once got to town on an occasional Saturday night now can, and apparently does, come in and raise hell any odd Tuesday morning that he feels like it, and whatever glamour there once was to the business of buying excitement has departed. (A Western friend to whom I said this, replied: "You're just kidding yourself. There never was any glamour, except in Wild West novels.")

Probably I am being both unfair and sentimental, but I found myself making comparisons between Boulder City and Las Vegas, to the disadvantage of the latter. Boulder City was built and is still largely controlled by the federal government, and it has none of the things of which its rival has so many too many. Even if you assume that Las Vegas is Boulder City's necessary slum, you still can't help feeling that in this place private industry shows itself in one of its less savory forms.

(Las Vegas Chamber of Commerce: Please don't write.)

THE PEOPLE, YES

ONCE the government had pushed through programs to help the poor and distressed, it was still not always easy to see that they actually got their benefits. For example, the sharecroppers or tenant farmers in the South gained very little from the Agricultural Adjustment Administration. They existed in a semifeudal state, dependent upon their landlords for food, shelter and clothing, and while their plight had been a national disgrace for years, the landlords were not about to give up their economic advantages that came from exploiting such cheap labor. Also, these poor souls were the first to suffer when the government's crop and acreage reduction measures went into effect.

In 1936, the Secretary of Agriculture, Henry Wallace, having returned from a trip through the cotton states from Arkansas to the East Coast, declared he had never seen, even among the peasants of Europe, such poverty as existed throughout the sharecropper belt. Through the AAA and the Resettlement Administration, efforts were made to deal with the problem but progress was slow.

In some cases, the 'cropper families piled into their old rattletrap cars, if they owned such, and set off for the Far West, in hope of getting work as fruit and vegetable pickers. These migrant workers, their ranks swollen by displaced farmers from the dust-bowl areas, inevitably created new social problems wherever they went. And as migrant workers, they were outside the reach of the AAA.

Just getting work was not enough; after years of hard times, a feeling of security about the future was important too. Thousands of workers flocked to the huge construction jobs, but how were they to live when their part of the work was completed?

These, and many other questions as to the way people were existing in the changing times, needed to be answered. Writers like Erskine Caldwell, James Agee, Benjamin Appel, Nathan Asch, and others, moved out into the heartland to talk with the people and write about them. In the case of Nathan Asch, he simply got aboard a Greyhound bus one day in 1936 and started across country.

NATHAN ASCH

IN SEARCH OF AMERICA*

I WALKED along the street in Texarkana, Texas, where Louisiana, Arkansas and Texas almost make a corner, and I wondered how I could get to live a week with a sharecropper family. I had crossed Arkansas and come here because I wanted to see the most isolated, the deepest cotton country, untouched by the world and not knowing the outside world. Probably I should have gone back to Alabama, but I had heard that of late years cotton had been grown each year further westward, until now Texas was the great cotton state.

But where was I to go? How does one look for a sharecropper's shack? Where does one find the impudence to step off the road, and enter a home and demand shelter there? There are highways that leave Texarkana and go off in every direction; which highway to take? And where does one stop?

I stood and I watched a young man with blond hair and red face look at his car—it had Minnesota plates—and sadly shake his head. I asked what was wrong.

He said, "The axle's broken."

I offered to help him push it to a garage. He said, "What's the use? I can't buy another axle."

I said, "You're a long way from home."

He said, "I've just got enough money to buy gasoline home. I better get a bus ticket instead."

I said, "Let's go and have a glass of beer."

His name was Peder, and he and his brother had a small farm in northern Minnesota. They couldn't get back what they put into wheat, and it didn't pay for them to raise hogs. They had a few cows and a lot of hens; and there was just enough work for one, so they took turns, one staying at home and the other traveling all about the country.

Peder said, "I've been just about everywhere, and I guess I've stopped now."

I asked him how much would a new axle cost, and he told me. I said, "Have you seen how the sharecroppers live?"

* From Nathan Asch's *The Road* (New York, Norton, 1937).

He said, "They live terrible."

"Let's really find out how they live," I suggested. "What they eat and how they sleep, and what they talk about."

He said, "All right. We're bad enough up in Minnesota, but I'll be ashamed to look these people in the face."

We put in a new axle and we got a map, but all we could see were names of towns and of roads. We asked a man at a filling station.

He looked at us strangely but he said, "It's all cotton around here. You go down by the Red River and you'll see nothing but farms."

We drove east out of town on a United States highway, and then it became just a country road. It was too early for plowing, and in the fields there was nothing but stubble. Alongside the road there were tumbled-down shacks.

Peder asked if I wanted to stop. I said No. Let's go on for a while. Down below us was Red River, but first we came to Garland, Arkansas. It was the meanest town that I have ever seen. No city slum, no suburb, no condemned row of tenements ever had a more wretched appearance. With one exception there wasn't a house that was painted, a house that was whole, that had a whole roof, that was not on the verge of collapse. With but that one exception there was not a house that could be called a house. There was no glass in the windows, no doors that had hinges, no wall without a yawning crack. The exception was the church, which was new, and the minister's house. There must have been a thousand people who lived in Garland, Arkansas, but these white and black creatures wore clothes that could not be said to have ever had color or no patches, or been sold new in a store. This was not in the bleak, hopeless Ozarks, it was in rich cotton country; and about a half mile beyond, down by the toll bridge, there was a newly built filling station, and the attendant and a man in breeches and boots were admiring a brand-new automobile. I asked Peder to stop.

We got out of our car and we strolled toward the two men and we stood admiring the beautiful car. I asked the man in boots if the car was his. He smiled Yes.

I asked, "You farm around here?"

He said Yes, he had about four hundred acres.

I asked, "How many tenants have you got?"

He said he didn't know yet. Last year he'd had thirty families, but he said he was considering not having any tenants this year. He was playing around with the idea of having nothing but day labor.

I asked, "Where are the families from last year?"

285

He said, "Oh, I let them stay on through the winter."

I asked how did he think they had lived on through winter; it didn't seem to me that the heat would stay in with all the holes in the walls.

He said, "Those sons of bitches can live through anything. They've got hides like hogs."

I asked if he didn't think it would increase the value of the land if the improvements on it were weathertight, were in habitable condition?

"No," he said. "Anybody who'd do that would be crazy. He'd be laughed at. Two years ago I had one of those brain storms. I built a new outhouse for each tenant shack. Do you know what those bastards did? The first cold spell, and they knocked down the outhouses and they burnt them for fuel."

"Where can they get fuel?"

"They can buy it. I sell it."

We got back in the car and Peder asked, Where now? I suggested we get on a side road. We drove almost down to Red River, and then turned off on a dirt road.

I said, "What do you think of this for an idea: 'The worse you exploit somebody, the worse you hate him.' You have to. Your conscience wouldn't let you alone."

Peder said, "If I was his tenant I'd shoot him."

We saw a sign, "Lost Prairie—1 mile." We saw a man walking down the road and we gave him a ride. He wore overalls and half of his face was covered by a birth mark. We asked him if he lived in the neighborhood. He said he was a renter. Where did he rent? Well, he didn't rent nowhere right now. The doctor in Texarkana who owned the land he lived on had hired day labor. Sometimes he got day work in the fields.

"How much do you get?"

"Anywheres from fifty to sixty cents a day."

"How many hours do you work?"

"From dark to dark."

We drove along, then the man said he was home. We asked if we could meet his wife, and he took us inside. The shack had four walls, with newspapers stuck in the cracks, and two beds and a stove and a packing box at which the wife was standing and ironing. Two children were in school, and the eldest boy was out rabbit hunting. "Maybe he'll bring us a rabbit." Peder and I sat on a bed and we smoked cigarettes. The wife kept on ironing, then she stopped and straightened her back.

The man said, "Her back gives her misery."

286

I asked why she didn't go to the doctor that owned the land they lived on.

The man said, "He charges two dollars." Then he lost his temper and shouted at his wife, "Why don't you stop ironing?"

She turned to us. "The children have to look clean or they won't let them in school."

The man muttered, "School!"

The woman said, "If they get an education, it's something nobody can take away from them. I'll keep them in school if I have to die for it."

Peder said, "Why don't you do something about it? Why don't you and your friends get guns and go on the towns?"

The man shook his head. "Well, by God. Something will have to happen pretty soon."

We left. We drove on; that whole country must have been called Lost Prairie, because there was no town on the road.

We came to a shack that was leaning on piles, elevated from the ground, and seeming as if it had to collapse the next moment. There were two Negro children lying on the side of the road; a Negro woman and man sat on the threshold. The man held a twig in his hand. We got out of the car and came toward the house; and the man smiled pleasantly at us.

We said we were from the North; we had been driving around and were talking to people and asking them questions. Could we ask him some questions?

Again he smiled nicely and said, "Sure enough. You want to know the truth and we'll give you the truth."

For the last six years he had been renting eleven acres from the lawyer in Texarkana. It was the time of the year to discuss the renting, but the lawyer had not come; each year he was late; he wanted to scare them into buying a mule. Each year they refused, and the lawyer threatened to stop renting to them. He wanted a hundred and sixty dollars for it, but "it can't be a good mule if he's so anxious to sell it."

The woman said, "If we had money, we'd buy a cow with it."

We asked if we could go inside their home. They nodded "Of course."

There were two rooms; the room they slept in and the room where they cooked. An opening in the wall was the entrance, there was no frame to it, no place for a door. Inside the room there was a mattress on the floor, and that was all. In the inner room there was a stove and an oil lamp and a packing box. That was all in that house. There were no beds, no second mattress for the children, no table, no dresser, no chairs, no mirror; there was no closet; there were no clothes in that house. In the room where they cooked there hung from a nail a side of bacon, they said from a hog they had killed last fall. And the place was a sieve; light could be seen through the four walls and the ceiling.

Peder and I did not look at each other, and we came down from the house, and I said, "I don't see how you people can live."

The Negro said, "We don't live here. We're just here."

I said, "How can he demand a hundred and sixty dollars? Where would you get a hundred and sixty dollars?"

"He'd take it off our share in the fall."

"What is your share in the fall?"

The man didn't know. The reason there was no meal in the house was that until the shares were agreed the storekeeper would not give them credit. Whatever they bought through the summer he put into the book; and in the fall the lawyer settled out of their share. Last fall there was enough left to buy the children a pretty for Christmas.

We left that house and we drove on to another house; and this one had a real door, and I knocked on it; and the door opened, and inside the room was papered with old newspapers. The people living there had a sense of decoration, and the newspapers had been cut into patterns of print and pasted on the walls with frills and with curls. There was a place on the floor where a fire was burning and three Negro women sat around the fire.

They were suspicious of me and remained silent. I tried to explain. In faraway New York City there was a newspaper interested in how they lived. I would write stories about them.

They said they couldn't afford it. I said it would cost them nothing. I would just talk to them and then write about them. They didn't believe me. They didn't believe anybody wrote pieces for nothing. I went back to the car and there was the Negro man talking to Peder. He too was suspicious.

I said, "We're your friends. We can't stand to see how you live. We're going to write about it; we're going to make people so mad they'll have to do something about it."

I took his hand and I pressed it. He pulled it away.

He said, "I was trained by Southern white folks, and I know my place. Maybe if I had been trained up North, I'd have been different. But I'm here. And I know my place and I keep it."

He went back to the house with the paper inside, and we drove on. We stopped at other houses and we saw the same picture and heard the same story. It was the time for renting; and the planters were trying to get advantageous shares; and they were considering abandoning the share system altogether; and hiring day labor to work from dark to dark at fifty to sixty cents for the day. We asked the people what they would do, and we were told: "We don't know what we'll do."

It was in Oklahoma that I went inside the dust storm that for three weeks obscured the sun and made everything, food, water, even the air taken into the lungs, taste gritty. It blew into the eyes, underneath the collar; undressing, there were specks of dust inside the buttonholes; in the morning it had gathered like fine snow along the window ledge; it penetrated even more; it seeped along the wiring of the house; and along the edges of the door button there was a brown dusty stain. Sometimes it did not blow; it stood between the buildings, dulling them, and dulling the mind, making thoughts oppressive, giving the city a mood of foggy melancholy. As in a disaster one only thought of dust, one saw it, felt it, tasted it and lost his sense of smell. In the country, the road, the ditches, the fields, the grass, the plants, even the sky above, everything was covered by the dust; cattle stood head down, immovable, not tasting the gritty leaves; automobiles went slowly; and when even the road was obscured from the driver's vision and all the world, everything that one could possibly see was just a brownness, one had to stop and wait.

Until I had gone over the crest of mountains in Wyoming, the dust was always there. Everything I thought was complicated by the thought of dust; in everything I ate I tasted dust. It was the last thing before I fell asleep, and the first thing with consciousness at waking. I missed Oklahoma City, because arriving in the morning after a sleepless night on the bus, and looking at the choking morning town, I couldn't bear to enter it. I went on in the bus. The thought of air became precious; the memory of pleasant mornings in New England, of plants that were green, of dew on leaves, of the sun brightly rising in a sky that was clear, was so sweet that I half lay on the bounding seat in the grimy bus and daydreamed of it. It became something that had perhaps never happened; something in a life so far in the past it was a previous life. Everyone in the bus seemed dejected, and even the usually squirming children did not squirm now. They sprawled on their seats and whimpered.

Now the dust was lighter; we could see outlines of objects through it, even a quarter of a mile away. The bus had left the flatness of western Oklahoma and had ridden into the Panhandle of Texas, also flat and ever stretching. We were passing wheat land from which the storm had stripped away the top soil, cattle land deposited with dust and ruined as range, and oil three thousand feet below, safe from the elements and with gas pressure waiting to push it to the surface.

We came near Borger; everywhere in the haze we saw camps of sheds with black enormous columns rising from them, and then as the wind again rose, the columns wavered, diffused, sprawled; we approached them, entered them, and were blind as in a night that had no moon to light it. The driver must have guessed the straightness of the road, because we couldn't see our hands laid on our laps; and as we left the blackness into comparative clearness of the dusty air, we saw the cement road was as black as pitch, where previously the wind had played the black stuff on it. Carbon black plants, someone in the bus explained; from millions of badly lighted wicks burning natural gas, soot was deposited, nine tenths of it wasted to dirty the Panhandle air, and what had been retained on slowly revolving cylinders was scraped off; the carbon black, the smallest-particled substance that man knew, invisible even in the microscope, was used in the making of high-speed printing ink.

It was a waste of precious natural gas; in the Panhandle they said that enough natural gas was wasted, in one field alone, to light all of Chicago, with the rest of Illinois. And it wasn't only partially wasted, as in the smudge of making carbon black; at night driving through the range the world was a fantastic night scene of gas-burning flambeaux, illuminating the waste land even through the dust. Almost everywhere there was a derrick, and near it a pipe stuck out of the ground, a tremendous lighted torch, throwing off and consuming gas from the sands below. It was a waste of gas; and it was indirectly ruinous, because the pressure needed to bring oil to the surface was slowly weakening, fading. But what could you do, they said shrugging, when below all that country was the sea of oil and the atmosphere of gas, and it belonged to anyone that could drill to it, that could get to it first? Why should anyone save gas, never to be replaced, when by wasting untold millions of cubic feet of it, he could get a few barrels of oil that he could sell? Even the great oil companies that to keep on existing had to conserve what was down below, even they wasted oil and gas, because they had to compete with other oil companies and had to get the stuff quickly to the ground.

I had a letter for Jim Bailey, a drilling contractor in Pampa. He lived in the hotel where the oil men stayed, and there I found him, ready to go to bed after a hard day's work, with a bottle of bourbon. He was kind; everyone was kind; everyone welcomed a stranger just off the bus, did not ask him questions, made him feel at home; within half an hour there were five men in leather jackets in the room, looking at their glasses and telling stories of the old boom days before the great oil companies had grabbed off all the possible oil-bearing lands. The telephone rang, and Jim Bailey answered it and listened to it and then pulled off his pajamas and pulled on his pants. His crew had broken off a drilling bit three thousand feet below, and the drilling was held up; the hole that had cost thousands, that had taken weeks of endless pounding by the cable tools in the effort to reach the sands below, was lost for good, and he was maybe ruined, unless the bit was fished out and brought back to the surface.

I drove with him through darkness, spotted by the flambeaux burning gas away, past ghostly operating derricks silently pumping oil, past rotary drilling outfits, the whole illuminated derrick shaking as the pile whirled crazily into the hole; off the main highway and through more darkness to the silent, lighted derrick with the crew standing helpless waiting for the boss. Soon the bull wheel spun, and the drilling line descended with the fishing tool, and for hours they fished, as blindly as one does fish, only deeper, over three thousand feet. The drilling line rose time and time again, pushing to the surface nostril-tickling gas, spilling oil over the derrick floor and over us. The donkey engine again rotated its elbows, again the line quickly descended with another tool. I set myself into a derrick strut and I fell asleep; and woke hours later, in the grayness of a Panhandle dawn, with nothing getting lighter as the dust still permeated the entire world. I was tired from the endless traveling, shaking in the bus, no relief from dust in my lungs. And still they were fishing for the broken bit; and someone took me to the hotel in Pampa; and, rested now, twenty-four hours later, I came back to the derrick, and they were still fishing. Jim Bailey, foul now with all the oil on him and a two days' growth of beard, was drinking coffee from a thermos bottle, and beneath his leather jacket the edge of his silk pajama top was still sticking out.

I was walking in the hazy evening along Larimer Street in Denver, hearing music playing and voices through the suddenly opened doors of the Mexican cafés and trying to decide to go into one; then with the noise torn off by the doors again closing, hesitantly going on—when through one of the doors two girls came out and almost fell on me. They were Mexicans; one of them was drunk and asked me if I would buy them wine. We went inside the crowded smoky room; three men sat on chairs and played nostalgic Mexican music; two fat cops, giants among the Mexican boys and girls, walked up and down the room and stood over tables and stared; the dancers and the drinkers, Spanish eyes set in Indian faces, with strong hook noses, high cheekbones, and always even on overalls and cheapest dresses a touch of color, tried to dance and drink, and make believe the police were not in the room, watching them, determined to find trouble.

The two girls led me to a booth and sat themselves and ordered red wine; they drank one glass of wine and then ordered another; and then drank that, and the drunker one of the two said she wanted to dance. I said I didn't want to dance. She said I had to.

I asked the other one, "What's the matter with her?"

She said, "She's in love."

And then I looked up and there was a young fellow with black polished hair looking as if he wished he had a knife.

I rose from my seat and went up to him, and I took his hand and I said, "Look, there's an extra place in our booth and I wish you'd take it."

He said, "Who are you?"

I said, "I'm nobody at all. Just a man from the East."

Suspiciously, he went with me. I ordered more wine, and I acted as if I were terribly interested in the other girl.

I asked her, "What's wrong with them? Why don't they get married?"

She said, "They haven't got no kids."

I said, "What?"

"They can't get a contract," she said, "if they don't have no kids."

I asked for explanations. All these Mexicans worked in the sugar-beet fields in northern Colorado. During the winter they lived in colonies on relief; and in the spring when the time came to make an agreement with the growers for work in the fields, the contract unit was a family, a father, mother and their children. I said I thought that child labor was forbidden; I thought there had been an agreement made.

She said, "Well, maybe there is. All I know is that when beet-picking time comes around they close all the schools, and if you're young and ain't had no time to get kids of your own, you don't get no contract."

I said, "Why don't you people do something about it?"

The boy who was in love shrugged his shoulders. "They say all the time if you don't make a contract, if you don't get off relief, they'll ship you back to Mexico."

I asked, "How old were you when you came?"

"I was born here. They can't deport me."

But the girl who was in love had been five years old when her family had been brought over to work in the beet fields. The next year she had

292

picked beets and had continued ever since. Now she was drunk. And she wanted to dance.

I said, "You two dance. But I want to talk to some of your friends."

He brought some friends over, and the cops came, too.

One of the cops wanted to know, "What's going on around here?"

I rose, and I took my credentials from my pocket.

The cop said, "You mind coming out with us?"

I went out with them. We walked to the corner of the block we were on, and the cop said, "Buddy, you don't want no trouble. And we don't want no trouble. Why don't you go home?"

I asked, "Are you going to run me in?"

He said No, he wasn't. But I was not going back into the Mexican café. He added, "Why don't you be a good fellow and go home?"

Chiver, Aragon and I got into the old dilapidated sedan and started off for northern Colorado. The sedan had been on the go for weeks in other parts of Colorado, and Chiver had tried to sleep in it, had lived in it, had stood on its uncertain top and made speeches to the assembled beet workers. His eyes were red with tiredness, his hands were not steady, and he almost fell asleep in the Denver traffic. Aragon must have been tired too; he had hitchhiked from the North the night before, had reported to his office and had been told to find Chiver coming from the South and to start out again. It must have been the Indian blood in him that made his eyes seem inscrutable, that prevented me in the following two days from guessing Aragon's feelings.

To me, everything about Aragon was amazing; this man whose face was of red copper, whose head was like an eagle's, whose shoulders were so wide that when he spread his arms to prove a spoken point he looked like an eagle with the wings outstretched, who had broad hands and enormous body, had the most musical voice I have ever heard and spoke correct and unaccented English. Look at him and he was a big red Indian, but speak to him and you heard old Spain. He was well read, and though Chiver had been a year to college, Aragon could outargue him on every necessary subject and decide the point and act on it; and though Chiver was the leader of this expedition it was Aragon that led, and Aragon that kept Chiver to the chosen line and called him down when Chiver enthusiastically and devil-take-the-consequences got off the line.

Aragon was a peon and the son of a peon, while Chiver's father had been a beet grower and Chiver himself had grown sixty acres of beets until

293

two years before, and had kept Mexican families on his own farm and had paid them what other growers paid. But the combination of the sugar company and the current times had proved too much; he had been sold out; his wife was on relief; and Chiver was organizing the sugar-beet workers; Aragon was organizing too. They were going into northern Colorado, to visit the colonies of Mexicans and to try by some means to organize them into a common front against the growers.

Yet the growers were as much victims of the situation as the Mexican workers were. The growers did not buy new automobiles as did the planters in the cotton country. When in the fall the price was paid for the delivered beets and divided among the grower and the Mexican, the Mexican got almost nothing, but the grower after he had paid the interest on the mortgage on his house and land, after he had paid for seed and the interest on the loan for seed, did not get anything either. He owned the house he lived in and the land he planted, but the bank in which the mortgage on these chattels lay was controlled by the sugar company, and the company set the price for beets, arbitrarily, without the semblance of an open market, of competition. He could accept the price that was offered by this one company, or his beets could rot.

And all the stories that for years had appeared in the newspapers of the nation describing the awful living standards of sugar workers of other nations and begging for a protective tariff, all these stories were misleading, were lying stories, because when lawyers for the sugar company elected to the United States Senate had finally succeeded in getting the protection, and incidentally ruined the economy of Cuba, the living standards in the sugar country did not rise, the difference between the world price and the American price for sugar was transformed not into increased education, better homes and more nourishing food, but into dividends for the sugar company; and in the blackest year of the Depression, when world trade was paralyzed and profits did not exist, the sugar company, protected by the tariff and profiting from the living standards it had imposed on both growers and workers, made profits of nine millions of dollars.

In the beet industry a lot of work was needed in the fields, and all this work had to be done in the summer months. The grower himself in the spring drilled the land with seed, but when the fourth leaf appeared, and beets had to be blocked, then thinned, hoed, topped, and later in the summer pulled to be trucked to the factories nearby, no natives in America wanted to do this sunburnt, aching work. Years ago Mexican families had been recruited from Mexico, shipped up north in trucks; during the season they lived right in the fields, in shacks, sometimes in wagons to be pulled right to the edge of work so as not to waste time; and when the summer was over they had to leave the shacks and wagons and live in colonies in towns and wait till the following spring. Relief was only an innovation. Up till two years ago six in a family together earned less than three hundred dollars a year, and when they returned to winter quarters with what was left after the storekeepers had been paid, they were forced to pay rent by the same sugar company which also owned the colony they lived in. When relief was introduced the Mexicans were well used to living on almost nothing. And when this year, squeezed by the company, the growers tried in turn to squeeze the Mexicans, by offering them contracts that would pay less even than in previous years, many Mexicans refused. Spontaneous strikes broke out in sugar counties.

And now the announcement had come that those who refused to accept the contracts would be taken off relief and would be deported.

Chiver and Aragon were to visit the colonies in Weld County, richest in all of Colorado, and were to get the Mexicans together at mass meetings and find out if the sporadic strikes and the refusal to accept new contracts would make it possible to organize all the beet workers into one large sugar union that could make itself, they hoped, as strong as the sugar company. The problem was to find the colonies in each town they came to, to get inside of them without the officials of the sugar company knowing, to hold meetings, to organize local unions, to have representatives appointed from each district who could later meet and work out the proposed union's program. The problem further was to convince the terrified Mexicans that beets always would be grown, and that even if the sugar company were to disappear, they, the Mexicans, could not be made to disappear; their work was needed, and whatever happened they would not be deported.

The little car arrived in Brighton, Colorado, and there were natives and Mexicans walking along the street, and we drove to where there were still more Mexican faces, in front of a poolroom, and Aragon got off and talked in Spanish to some boys. He came back.

"They've got a hall somewhere in the colony," he said. "But they don't know if we can get it for a meeting. Let's go down there."

We turned off the main street and the cement highway, got onto a dirt road, passed a polling place (there seemed to be a local election being held that day and a crowd of citizens was there). We drove past progressively poorer houses, a railroad spur and a factory, past the breathless sour smell of old beet pulp, to a place that looked like an empty yard in spite of shacks crazily leaning over it. We talked to a little boy and to a Mexican lady and then Aragon disappeared.

When he came back he said, "They want a dollar for the meeting hall, and they want to know what we want it for. And they look as if they were going to telephone to somebody. We'll hold the meeting in the vacant lot."

We drove back to town and to the pool hall, went inside and Aragon asked for quiet and told everybody in Spanish to come to the vacant lot. In the street he told little boys to summon their fathers. We drove again to the vacant lot and waited.

There was the wall of a house facing where we were and as the Mexicans arrived they went up to the wall and sat on the ground against it and did not look at us nor at each other but rolled cigarettes and waited. When about thirty had arrived Aragon stood before them and spoke to them in Spanish. I did not understand what he said, and they did not seem to listen, but looked at the ground and smoked cigarettes. At first they were in a line before him; then the pattern changed, he was like a star in the half-crescent of a moon; his voice did not change, they did not seem to listen, but soon he was in the center of a circle; though they looked away, they were all around him. I never saw brighter eyes nor more immovable faces; I never knew less of what went on in the minds of people I was watching than when I watched these Mexicans' faces as they listened to Aragon. Then he stopped and Chiver spoke, in English. Chiver told them about the other meetings he had been to, in the South; he said they had been enthusiastic meetings; he said the beet workers in southern Wyoming, in Nebraska, in western Kansas all were organizing, all were going to stand together strong against the growers.

He said, "Once the beet plants are peering out of the ground they can't do a thing without us. But we can do a lot. We can force them to do whatever we want to. And if they don't listen, do you know what we can do? We can go at night, with hoes; five hundred hoes in the dead of night can do an awful lot of damage to a beet field."

The Mexicans weren't listening. Those that were sitting rose; quietly, with no change of expression they drifted, one by one, away. We got back into the car.

Aragon said to Chiver, "You'll never be anything but a bankrupt beet grower, trying to revenge yourself on other beet growers. If I ever again hear you say anything about hoes, I'll smash you in the face."

I didn't hear Chiver speak again, and I never understood what Aragon said, but I felt between him and the other Mexicans a sort of silent understanding. I seemed to feel what he said more in the pauses between his words, in the silence which he, a man not really fitted for speech but more for doing, needed to arrange his thoughts.

We drove on, and we spent that night in Johnston, Colorado. The colony there looked more like an imaginary colony. There was a whitewashed wall and inside there were little whitewashed houses, looking like hives in a bee colony, and really not much larger than bee hives, having only one room. Aragon knew a man who lived in one of the houses, and while word was being sent to the workers to come together, the lady of the house dished food out of a pot that stood on a brazier, while little Mexican girls stood shyly in the doorway and watched us, eyes shining.

It is hard to describe how little this house was, because there were two beds in it, and there was a dresser, and there was the brazier where they cooked, and there was room to stand between the beds, but the whole room was not ten feet square, and in this room lived a family of nine. It was clean, walls whitewashed, curling curtains in the windows, and holy pictures on the walls. And the beds were covered with embroidered spreads, and on one of the beds there lay a little naked baby with a teething ring in the mouth, and on the other were two older children, that looked like twins, asleep. And into this room, now crowded, perhaps fifteen men came in to hear Aragon speak; and after he had spoken they organized a local of the beet workers' union and elected a secretary. It was all done so quietly that the twins never woke.

I spent that night with a motherless family, the children sighing in their sleep, and the father in the morning clumsily feeding canned milk to the youngest child; Chiver and Aragon slept elsewhere, and in the morning we drove to Fort Collins.

It is a larger city. The meeting was held in a lodge hall, two American flags crossed over the speaker's table. When we arrived, we drove through the Mexican streets, and, modern Paul Reveres, we called out whenever we saw a Mexican going by:

"Come on at once to the meeting hall."

There were about three hundred people there when Aragon started to speak. The night before in the two preceding towns the workers all seemed more Spanish in appearance, with little shaven mustaches and long sideburns. Here they were Indians, the faces incredibly red, with bold high cheekbones. They were the faces that one sees on the Indian pennies, in portraits of old Indian warriors. The eyes were not the piercing Spanish eyes, but covered with some inner-looking film, and dull. They sat, tremendous men, like sculptured statues, and heard. And when the time came, they rose and they told their names, and when these had been written down, they clumsily made their crosses.

The reception girl asked, "Is there anything I can do?"

I said, "I'd like to see the manager of the lumber company. I just came from New York. . . ."

"Oh, you're from New York. Just a minute." She pressed a switch, and she said something into the receiver. "You go right in," she told me.

I went into a room where there were many maps, and there a man sat at a desk and nodded to me.

I said, "I'm from New York. I've been traveling all over the country trying to find out what makes things run."

"What makes them run?" he asked.

I said, "I don't know. And the further I'm traveling the less I'm finding out."

"Well, sit down," he said. "What can I do for you?"

I said, "For instance, the lumber industry. I want to get a picture of it. Nobody in the East knows anything about it."

He said, "It's a pretty big industry. We're just one company, but we hire ten thousand men."

"I want to live for a while with the loggers in a lumber camp. I could stay around Tacoma and talk to the men out of work. But I don't want to do that. I want to watch them working," I said.

"And you want to write about it?" he asked.

I said, "Yes."

He thought a moment, then he said, "All right. We're not ashamed of our company."

The following day, the purchasing agent who was returning to head-quarters and I drove about sixty miles away from Tacoma and arrived at dusk at the company town, a large office building and company store, little houses for the married men, larger homes for the purchasing agent and the superintendent, and a long row of bunkhouses for the single men. The purchasing agent was hungry, and he drove me toward the office, went inside and brought me a check for tomorrow's breakfast, yelled once or twice, "Bull cook!" got no answer, told me, "You'll find the bull cook somewhere around, and tell him to give you a bed for the night"; and then the purchasing agent went home to supper. It was getting dark, I walked up and down the porch and smoked cigarettes. I had no idea what a bull cook was, but I yelled the words "Bull cook!" just like the purchasing agent.

A little fat man appeared. He wore a skullcap on his head, and he asked me what the hell I wanted. I wanted to know if he was the bull cook, and he said, "God damn it, yes!"

I showed him the check and demanded a bed. He took me toward the bunkhouses and opened one door, and said, "You sleep in that bed. Nobody's using it tonight."

The bull cook disappeared. It was night now and he hadn't even shown me where the washroom was. There were some old newspapers lying in the corner. I took off my clothes and got into bed, and read the old newspapers to forget my hunger. Then I tried to sleep.

It was dark yet when the whistle blew, but I was ready for breakfast, and ate as much as anyone else did. Then I was told to wait for Number 4. I went out to the track and saw logging trains go by, and then an engine came with a sign Number 4. I got into the caboose with three other men, and we started for the camps in the mountains. We rode over narrow trestle bridges, past logged-off, burned-off land, and we turned past a spot where I was told a year before an engine had fallen and killed its crew and still lay, red now with rust, past logs that had rolled off the cars and rotted black in the ditches, up to siding 8. I was to live at camp 2, and I had to wait for Number 110 to get me. Number 4 rolled away, and I waited, near a telephone booth, all alone in the world, and then I saw an engine coming nearer with the sign Number 110. It didn't stop, it just slowed down a little, and I jumped on the steps, holding on with one hand, my bag in the other. That was how I got to camp 2.

The city shoes were the worst part of the stay, because I could scarcely walk in the woods with them on. I stumbled on the stones, and then I tried to walk on the ties; and everywhere I heard axes hitting into wood, and was certain I had now arrived, and I would see men working around a curve. Finally I saw the smoking top of the giant skidder. I saw a section gang working on the grade. I had arrived.

There were about a hundred men flipping the claws of the skyline tight over the logs, watching the great logs suddenly lifted into air, dangling; and then, a lever pushed forward at the track below, the logs rushed down the skyline, down the hill, not like great hulks weighing many tons but like fragile twigs, hitting a huge tree in the way of the skidline and smashing it out of the way, down, down, where they were lowered at the track, where the loaders' claws seized them, lifted them, dexterously placed them on the railroad cars.

I climbed up the tremendous skidder, the world's largest piece of movable machinery, set on four flatcars, and sat with the operator and watched his hand move forward and, gesture multiplied a million times by power, a mile up the hill, at the other end of the steel-cabled skidline, a log was lifted and began rushing down. The other day the cable had snapped and like a mile-long snake had twisted below, cutting off whole trees and killing a man. I watched the loaders riding on the logs, and as these were set down on the cars the loaders jumped up to avoid the shock.

It was three days before I understood the various divisions of work, all the operations from the moment the boss faller marked a tree to fall, to the time when the loaded train chug-chugged up the grade. But by the time I left I could have probably done the simpler work, like loading, or perhaps helped with oiling of the skidder. The skilled work—falling, buck-ing, marking—I could not have done for years, especially falling, because you almost have to be born a faller to become one; and you usually have to have a brother about your size to be your partner.

I left the roadbed and carefully stepped on a fallen hemlock, walked down it in my city shoes, afraid of stepping on a piece of loose bark that, more slippery than a banana peel, would send me flying into the brush. There was over a hundred feet of this log and then I jumped on a Douglas fir and walked down it, to where I joined the two Bottleson brothers, Big Quart and Little Quart. Little Quart set the head of his axe against an enormous cedar, pointing the way it would fall, hung the oil bottle on, and began knocking off the bark. Big Quart joined him. His axe swung inside of his wrist and hit the naked wood, chipping off a piece. The brothers made the cut—Big Quart and Little Quart, then one and two— even and so smooth it was almost polished out. On opposite sides they made a hole in the bark and set their shaking stands, stepped on them, set the saw opposite the cut, and swung easily this way and that way and in and out in elbowed rhythm. They let me try to saw. They told me to exert no effort, to swing the saw as you would swing a baby, as softly, and themselves they did it, I felt, as tenderly, and to one to the other, oiling it constantly. They took the saw out, and set a wedge in the cut; they hit the wedge with a hammer—one—two—three; they lifted the tremendous tree a small bit of an inch; waited. The tiniest crack was heard. They shouted, jumped. The cedar stood still. Then it leaned—like a swan diver spread itself very slowly down—and fell—crashed—smashed—breaking it-self in two. A tree had been in the way; it had snapped off that tree. It had shaken the side of the entire hill.

At four-thirty they heard Number 110 coming down the grade and knocked off work; Big Quart picked up the lunch boxes and the heavy wedges; Little Quart threw the saw upon his shoulders making it dance.

The bucker had finished sawing a log across, and joined the brothers, and together they stepped uphill on the fallen hemlock, walking easily in their calk-bottomed boots.

On the track, the loggers were climbing into the ancient coach, behind Number 110, falling into the plush, torn, oil-filthy seats, staring at the fresh stickers that asked them to join the lumber workers' federation, that had been mysteriously pasted on each glass pane somewhere through the day. They half lay, and steam rose out of their clothes. They were too lazy to light cigarettes.

"Oh, for Mae West," somebody called out.

Everybody smiled.

"Oh, for a Turkish bath and a glass of beer."

Slowly they passed the lunch boxes to be piled up forward.

"Look at this damned thing," said one they called San Quentin Joe. "Why can't I get a thermos that doesn't leak? I want some coffee, too."

Somebody suggested, "Thow it out of the window."

"I'd like to," said San Quentin Joe, "throw it the fifteen miles straight down to headquarters, so it will smash against the purchasing agent's head."

"Pipe down, Joe," whispered the other. "I'll bet there's a stool pigeon around."

San Quentin Joe slowly stood in the aisle, turned around and announced in a loud voice, "Listen, stool. I've served time, and I'll serve time again. You tell that purchasing agent if he ever comes to camp 2, I'll cut him into pieces and make him over again."

After supper we went to the bunkhouses, and it seemed to me everything was too quiet. Men lay on their bunks and read magazines. I asked if that was all they did. I was told these were the married men, who had to save their money. Some others were in Bunkhouse 9.

I went to 9. I slid back the door; and there were about twenty men sitting on the bunks, watching, and in the center of the room, on the table covered with a blanket, there was a poker game going on. I joined the game. They were the wildest crew I'd ever played with. It was table stakes, and they thought nothing of putting twenty dollars on an ace in the hole, twenty dollars it had taken them weeks to save, and which they were going to spend on a wild weekend on the Seattle skid road. Sometimes they won and their imaginations soared, and again they lost and went to sit on the bunks and to watch, forced now to remain in the camp for many weeks to come.

I was returning to my bunkhouse that night, and one of the loggers suggested I go with him. He took me to another car; there half of the men in camp were listening to a union organizer. And he had not ridden up on trains as I had. There was no transportation for an organizer. He had walked up the hill along railroad ties, hiding each time a logging train went by. If the timekeeper had found him, he'd have been beaten up. They listened to him urging them to support the federation; and when at eight forty-five the lights flickered, warning us that in fifteen minutes all lights would be out, the organizer had the signed slips in his pocket and had disappeared in the mountain night, to somehow find his way back to the road fifteen miles below.

But I saw them also when they didn't work. They had a five-day week, and Friday night the camp would be empty; they would be with their families, or dead drunk in a hotel with a two-dollar whore; or they would be laid off, on the skid road in Tacoma, in Seattle, in Spokane.

I saw these towns at the height of the season, when millions of feet of rough lumber were shipped every day to Japan, to Australia, to South America, to Europe; when other millions of feet were cut into planks and made into chairs and sent to every town in the Union; when lumber companies operated at capacities; and still the skid road in Seattle was black with unemployed loggers on relief, on the soup line, in shelters. I saw the pitiful dime shows, where not only ancient pictures were shown, but the piano played, and a line of unbeautiful girls, dressed in dirty rompers, kicked their ungraceful legs not very high. And the men didn't watch them. Their eyes were not alive. They slept, or if they didn't sleep their minds were fogged with hunger, no home, nothing to live for, no tomorrow to expect. Somehow they had gotten a dime, and they were better off than were those with empty pockets outside in the rain.

The night I stayed in a flophouse I couldn't bear to breathe through my nose, and I couldn't bear to look at the other men on the mattresses about me. I was there to see them and see how they lived, but I didn't care if I missed this sight, because if I stayed there another hour I didn't want to live. The lights were out, except in the hall, and I lay on my arms behind me, and I closed my eyes and I closed my mind. And then I began to hear that these men sleeping were beginning to breathe in and out together, as if they somehow had become one homeless unemployed, as if all this breathing in and out together had become one gigantic sigh. I rose, and put on my shoes, and I walked out into the rain, and in doorways lay these men's future, lay what they would become: junk, with still beating arteries, huddled in doorways.

It wasn't the purchasing agent the men hated so much. It was the fact that the pay was small, and the week had been shortened to five working days, and the season was short, only a few months, and there were too many loggers for the work to be done, and there was no other work to be done; and they hated the fact that for the moment they were working, were eating, were sleeping in beds; but soon, as inexorably as death, a notice would come from the Tacoma office through the purchasing agent, through the timekeeper, that the season was ended, that they were to be laid off, that they had better prepare for the Seattle skidline.

Six months before there had been no Coulee City, Washington, nor Grand Coulee, Washington, nor Mason City, Washington. There had been, since the earth first formed, a flatness made by lava, through which from off the mountains flowed the Columbia River. A glacier inched down from the north, and with it crept rocks and gravel, and for a million years the river dug another bed in lava. The glacier disappeared, the river swung back to its earlier course, and left the weird Grand Coulee, a valley in the lava, a fifty-mile-long trench, miles wide, with walls a thousand feet high. The walls were dark, streaked with green and red, and in some crevasses there grew a little bit of grass. But the world at this place was volcanic dead world, until word came that the Grand Coulee was to be dammed off, turned into a great irrigating ditch, and the dam itself would create more electric power than could be made by any other dam in North America, or maybe in the world.

It was eighty years since first this thought had come of damming the Columbia River waters and transforming the million acres of volcanic-ash-topped desert into farming land, and it might have taken another eighty years before the thought was realized in digging; only in the Pacific Northwest there were too many people out of work, and to take up the slack the federal government was creating work and had set aside millions for this digging project. Almost all the men chosen to work on the dam would be the unemployed and taken off relief.

Experts came, surveyed and drafted and blueprinted; builders came and put up the company town for three thousand men—so many dormitories, two men to a room, so many houses for the married men, a store of such a size with furniture to sell and clothes and groceries, a movie house, a jail, a beauty parlor for the women folks, a bank if you wanted to save your money; and on the other side of the proposed dam wall there also grew up the town of Grand Coulee, Washington, for those who didn't want to save their money, with beer parlor, saloons, gambling joints and whore-houses. When I got to the Grand Coulee Dam, operations had not started very long before, but there were almost ten thousand people in that former waste; and in Coulee City, which was neither company town nor night town, I met a man who had five thousand dollars and was going to build a restaurant and grill, and he told me:

"In business you can't be afraid. You've got to spend money to make it."

The proposed irrigation of the Columbia River basin was a relief proj-ect, but you'd think the place was a boom town. Speculators had gotten hold of land along the highway leading to Grand Coulee, and as the bus drove along walls eaten away by millions of years of water, suddenly there was a proposed townsite. Somebody had put up the sign, Grand Coulee, in tall letters; underneath, in smaller letters, Good Water, Business and Resi-dential Sites, Acreage; had measured off imaginary plots of land and stuck in small stakes marked Bank, Hardware Store, Garage; a little further off on more empty land there were the words Residential Section; and there was absolutely nothing there but these signs and basalt rock and high coulee walls. And in Coulee City men stood before offices marked Real Estate, and sauntered over toward any car that stopped and asked people to think of the home of their dreams and said this place was it.

The combined companies that had contracted to put up the power plant and the first unit of the dam really surpassed magnificence when they built the company town. The little rooms were neat, the showers clean and of the latest type, the glorified store had as many counters as a department store, the recreation hall was lined by a long copper-covered bar; there were pin games standing around the hall, there were card tables, and pool tables and a candy counter. The dining hall shone like an elegant restaurant in New York; and the kitchen looked like a laboratory, with most modern equipment; there was a special machine for taking tendons out of chicken thighs, and there was a special room for making ice cream.

The combined companies had not been afraid to spend money. But then there was no reason to be afraid when they had a contract with the federal government, when they were assured that their dormitories and their elegant dining hall would be filled for years; when every pin game, and every ticket the man sold in their movie house was bringing back money they had paid out as wages. They could give nourishing food and have clean linen on the workers' beds; they were taking back in the form of pay for room and board more than half of the twenty dollars weekly wage they paid. And the men who worked with a shovel eight hours day outside in the coulee, married men whose families had been for years on relief, who had lost homes and had had to give up their insurance policies, whose children needed to have their teeth repaired, and needed shoes for school in the Northwest winter, these men ate well; but now that they had jobs and had been taken off the odious relief, they could send their families less each week in cash than they had received on relief.

And there again I saw how people hate the people they rob. I was in the office of the combined companies, and I said I would like to visit the night town of Grand Coulee. Everyone was horrified; everyone warned me against going. I was told, "They hate people that wear white collars and shirts. They take their meanness out in drink there; and when they're drunk they're dangerous; they'll think nothing of smashing you in the jaw, or of stabbing you."

I went there at night, and I was scared. There were no lights on the one street of Grand Coulee; but light came out of the saloon windows and fell on the wooden planks and threw shadows on the overalled men that stood on the street. They stared at me, and I walked nervously, trying not to meet their eyes. I heard voices shouting in a place called Black Mack's, and I forced myself to enter. There were perhaps fifty men there all drinking beer and all gathered around a blond woman who was playing the piano. I stood and I listened to drunks trying to sing. I began to notice one was staring at me, and I felt cold and did not look at him. I tried to keep on listening to the singing, and I tried to edge out of the place. But the man came toward me as I was trying to get out. He put his hand out and stopped me and said:

"Let's have a beer."

I said, "O.K. Let's have it on me."

He said, "If you don't have it on me, I'll cut your heart out."

We had a beer on him. Then on me. Some others joined in and everybody drank and everybody paid. We became friendly. They asked me since I had a home what did I want to come to this hellhole for. I told them.

The man who had wanted to cut out my heart said, "Come on outside."

Outside, beyond the few lights around us and the string of flares in the Coulee, lighting up the construction, everything was dark. No one lived a mile, nor fifty miles away. There was no light in the sky, there was no wind where we stood. There was nothing except the badly used piano inside, and drunks singing.

The man said, "I didn't want to tell you in there, but I'm a poet."

I said, "Yes?"

"Yes," he said, "I'm alone a lot. And I get to thinking about things. It comes out in words, sort of."

"Could I read it?"

"It's for nobody to read." He hesitated. "I do it for myself."

"I'd like to see it," I said.

He was shy. "No. It would be too much like showing my insides. I guess not. Let's go in and have another beer."

SECURITY AT ANY COST

MANY PEOPLE became disheartened when, after two or three years of the New Deal, Utopia was not at hand. This mood made them peculiarly more susceptible to political demagogues and political "prophets" than they had been even in the earlier hopeless days of the Depression. H. G. Wells said, "The New Deal has not gone far enough fast enough for them, and that is what the shouting is about."

Thousands upon thousands of Americans turned to the nostrums of the Catholic "radio priest," Father Coughlin, to the panaceas of Dr. Francis Townsend, with his Old Age Pension Plan, and to the Share-the-Wealth plan of Senator Huey Long.

Dixon Wecter said, "Whatever evil they did, these salesmen of panaceas, even the most cold-blooded and cynical of them, helped in their fashion to hasten the adoption of social security."

Nobody knows just how far Huey Long might have traveled along the road to fascism. His activities won him many loyal followers, but also earned him the bitter resentment of many others, even in his home state of Louisiana. Hodding Carter, an anti-Long newspaperman in Hammond, knew what it was to fight the Kingfish head on. He now publishes a newspaper in Greenville, Mississippi, but he didn't leave Louisiana until after Long's death.

HODDING CARTER

HUEY LONG:
AMERICAN DICTATOR *

FOR newspapermen, those were Gargantuan, memorable days. You stood beside his hotel dining table, as he slopped up great tablespoonfuls of cereal with a sidewinding sweep or tore broiled chicken to pieces with his fingers, and you jotted down the incessant harangues against the lying newspapers, the city machine, and the battered enemy politicians, while the bodyguards glowered protectively near by. You didn't like him, if only because the slugging of newspapermen didn't seem justifiable even for vote

* Condensed from *The Aspirin Age*, ed. Isabel Leighton (New York, Simon and Schuster, 1949).

getting, and especially when the strong-arming became personal. You were chased by militiamen across the parade grounds of Jackson Barracks in New Orleans and held a prisoner after you had sneaked in to discover whether the Governor was calling out the troops on the eve of the Senatorial election—in which the Governor was a candidate.

In a corridor of the garish Roosevelt Hotel, managed by an oily former shoe clerk who was now his paymaster and treasurer, you watched a fellow reporter being hustled out of the Governor's suite. Inside the suite the reporter had struck the Governor in retaliation for being cursed, and the Governor had struck back, but only after his bodyguards had pinioned his attacker.

You interviewed him after he had precipitated a silly international incident by receiving a German admiral in disheveled green pajamas, and you laughed in spite of yourself at his shrewdly appealing account of his gaucherie. You heard a pale-faced man, thrust before a microphone, identify himself as Sam Irby, who had been kidnaped by state police on the eve of an election because he had threatened to tell what he knew about his daughter and the Governor, who employed her as his secretary. And after Irby had told who he was, in front of the microphone in the hotel headquarters, you marveled at his exoneration of the Governor, and speculated upon the reasons therefor.

Afterward, in the corridor, a fellow reporter was to have a gun thrust into his stomach as he sought to enter the elevator on which the mysterious Mr. Irby was being whisked away.

And then you testified in United States District Court that a telegram, also absolving the Governor and purportedly coming from the mother of another kidnaping victim—the secretary's ex-husband—was signed with the name she had borne before her second marriage. Counterfeit, neither pure nor simple, was this telegram which you had seen and read on a speaker's stand in New Orleans on one of the last heated nights before election. And so, endlessly, through brawling campaigns, brawling legislative sessions, brawls . . .

By the spring of 1935, Huey Long owned Louisiana. And in that spring another and lesser man, except for his honesty, gave a fey, lonely warning.

The Louisiana legislature had granted Senator Long, through his administrative and judicial proxies, incontestable control of all elections, including the appointment of commissions, the power to disqualify unfriendly voters, and the privilege of padding the voting lists wherever and whenever necessary. Already he possessed the courts, the municipal police forces, the schoolteachers, the taxing authorities, the Governor, the state government, even the banks. Now, the vote itself.

And Mason Spencer, an unimportant, honest man, rose in the legislature and said this:

> When this ugly thing is boiled down in its own juices, it disenfranchises the white people of Louisiana. I am not gifted with second sight. Nor did I see a spot of blood on the moon last night. But I can see blood on the polished floor of this Capitol. For if you ride this thing through, you will travel with the white horse of death. White men have ever made poor slaves.

Representative Spencer was a better prophet than historian. In September of that year, the Capitol's marble floors were soiled with blood. Huey Long's blood, and the blood of the quiet, studious young doctor who shot him.

But the prophet of tragedy had overlooked the history of his state. Most Louisianans had been docile political slaves for years. Few knew enough about their state to recognize this almost uninterrupted and hitherto gently managed servitude. Nor was it something which those who did know want to be bruited about.

Louisiana politics from the Purchase until the Civil War was a story of genteel corruption, of steady political degeneration, of venality, of a studied neglect of civic advancement. Reconstruction further debilitated self-government; and where Reconstruction ended, rule under the gold-directed manipulation of the Louisiana Lottery began. At the beginning of the twentieth century, Louisianans could count on the fingers of one hand those major public servants who in all Louisiana history had been honest and progressive, active in behalf of the small people, and given to implementing campaign promises with administrative performance. This is not to say that all were politically immoral or amoral, though most of them were. They resembled atavistic mastodons, towering above and unknowingly becoming trapped in a surging human slough. In this they were not unlike their fellow politicians elsewhere. The difference was that Louisiana had been so very safe for the mastodons.

Such was the political Louisiana in which Huey Pierce Long was born in 1893, in impoverished Winn Parish in north Louisiana, a breeding ground of economic and political dissenters. His background was tailor-made for a politician. A log cabin, albeit a substantial one, was his birthplace. His father was a farmer of small means but with considerable ambition, who managed to send six of his nine children—but not Huey—to college.

Young Huey hated both farm work and conformity. In high school he discovered his talent for spell-binding oratory, and the power of a vocabulary enriched by Biblical allusion and directness, acquired naturally in a devout Baptist home. This gift was useful in school politics, and soon thereafter in the art of the traveling salesman, an occupation which he chose upon graduation because his father was not able to send him, the eighth child, to college.

The years between his graduation and his becoming a member of the Louisiana bar at twenty-one tested to the limit his extraordinary physical energy and driving mental discipline—the only discipline which he ever perfected himself. He married before he reached the voting age, and supported himself and his wife by peddling Cottolene, a cooking compound, throughout north Louisiana, meeting thereby and making friends of many farm folk who were to become the core of his political organization. He attended Oklahoma University Law School for one tempestuous term. Then, incredibly, he completed the three-year law course at Tulane University in eight months and, securing a special examination from the Louisiana Supreme Court, became a lawyer at twenty-one. No other student at Tulane has ever matched this record.

As Huey Long put it in his autobiography, he "came out of that courtroom running for office."

He hung out his shingle in Winnfield, county seat of Winn Parish. And here he received his first lessons in an economic-social philosophy that would later burgeon into a gaudy national movement. His first benefactor in Winnfield was a state senator named Harper, a prosperous man for the locality, but a "radical" who proposed a redistribution of national income as the only cure-all for the country's ills. During the First World War, Harper published a pamphlet calling for conscription of the nation's wealth as well as its manpower. A federal grand jury indicted him. He was defended by his young disciple, Huey, who was deferred in the draft because he had a wife and child. (Huey also tried to gain exemption as a public official. He was a notary public.) Huey, through questionable strategy, won Harper's acquittal.

Most of his other early cases were minor ones, the only kind available to a beginner in a crowded profession. But at twenty-four Huey sought the one state office open to one of his age, a state railroad commissionership. The Railroad Commission was Louisiana's three-man utilities regulating body. He won. In the campaign he gained another ally, an older Winnfield man named O. K. Allen, who lent him five hundred dollars to help finance his campaign. Later, when Long was elected United States Senator, he rewarded O. K. by making him his Governor, stooge, and errand boy.

As Railroad Commissioner, Huey was something uncomfortably new and strange. Some regarded him as a radical menace; others saw only a coarse publicity-seeking clown, a thickening, comical-looking youngster with a face that was a puffy caricature of a cherub, with its dimpled chin, snub nose, and unruly, curling reddish hair. But among the masses there were multiplying thousands who saw a champion, a new Great Commoner. He damned and insulted Bigness in all its Louisiana manifestations: Standard Oil, the state's dominant and frequently domineering industry; the large corporations; the corporation lawyers. He clamored for a common-carrier pipeline law—Standard had denied the use of its own to the independents, among them a company in which Huey owned stock—and for a higher severance tax on oil. He won a telephone rate reduction.

In 1920 he supported, for Governor, John M. Parker, a onetime Bull Moose, because he believed the comparatively liberal Parker would deal strongly with Standard Oil. But Parker, to Huey's thinking, was too lenient after he became Governor. Huey broke with him, was indicted and convicted of libeling the Governor, and was fined a dollar and given a thirty-day suspended sentence. He refused to pay the fine, so the judge and opposing counsel made up the dollar themselves.

But he was winning friends and influencing voters. In 1924, at the height of the bitter Klan fight in Louisiana, Huey Long, now thirty, announced for Governor. He tried to go down the middle on the Klan issue. He almost succeeded. Before Election Day he predicted that he would win if rain didn't keep the mud-farmers away from the polls. It rained. Yet, in a three-cornered race, he polled seventy-three thousand votes against eighty-four thousand and eighty-one thousand for the other two candidates. His day had not yet dawned. But already the uneasy feeling had arisen among his opponents that he would be unbeatable the next time.

From 1925 to 1928 Huey mended political fences, kept himself in the headlines, and built up a large and lucrative practice as attorney for some of the vested interests against which he ranted. He explained it in his autobiography this way: "When the millionaires and corporations fell out with each other, I was able to accept highly remunerative employment from one of the powerful to fight several others who were even more

311

powerful. I made some big fees with which I built a modern house in the best residential section of Shreveport at a cost of forty thousand dollars." There were other and less charitable explanations of his affluence.

The 1928 campaign was more like a cyclonic disturbance than another three-way race for the governorship. Huey was probably the most indefatigable campaigner and best catch-as-catch-can stumper the demagogically fertile South has yet produced. He belabored and promised and defamed, speaking in the harsh, bitter language of the poor man, eighteen and twenty hours a day. His promises were bright ones, long overdue: good roads for the farmer, lower utility rates, free bridges, free schoolbooks. He mixed filthy imputations with rhapsodic pleading. Beneath the erroneously named Evangeline oak, he drove his program home to openmouthed, whooping Cajuns:

And it is here that Evangeline waited for her lover Gabriel who never came. This oak is an immortal spot, made so by Longfellow's poem. But Evangeline is not the only one who has waited here in disappointment. Where are the schools that you have waited for your children to have that have never come? Where are the roads and the highways that you spent your money to build, that are no nearer now than ever before? Where are the institutions to care for the sick and disabled? Evangeline wept bitter tears in her disappointment. But they lasted through only one lifetime. Your tears in this country, around this oak, have lasted for generations. Give me the chance to dry the tears of those who still weep here.

No rain fell on Election Day this time. The evil city, New Orleans, again rejected him, but Catholic and Protestant farmers united to give him a lead, though not a clear majority. His two opponents wouldn't join forces; and at thirty-five Huey Long sat in the Governor's chair that he was to transform into a throne. Louisiana's poor whites had come into their own. "Every man a king, but no man wears a crown," Huey's campaign banners had proclaimed. No man, that is, but Huey himself. And already he was boasting, "I'm going to be President someday."

The campaign had been only a movie trailer, teasingly heralding what was to come. Long summarily discharged every state jobholder under executive control who had not actively supported him. Loyal lads from the bayous and burnt stump lands began to replace the town and city slickers. Lacking a majority at the first session of the legislature, he swapped patronage for concessions, and in both House and Senate placed his own men in the chair. The legislature approved his proposal for a thirty-million-dollar bond issue to provide farm roads, increased hospital and other institutional support, and free schoolbooks, levying a severance tax and higher gasoline taxes to pay for the program. Behind Huey were the people, and the people wanted these things.

And with the people behind him, Huey expanded ominously. Defying rule and convention, he personally directed strategy from the floors of the House and Senate. Once he bragged that he was the state constitution now, and again that he had bought a legislator like a sack of potatoes. He coerced banks which hesitated to make the state a tide-over loan. When the legality of his free textbook law was challenged because it included parochial schools among the recipients, he argued his own case before the United States Supreme Court and won brilliantly. Without constitutional authority, he ordered the state militia into the unfriendly, wide-open parishes adjoining New Orleans, and closed the casinos until the gamblers co-operated.

All this was shocking enough to those Louisianians who favorably recalled less troublesome days and ways. But when Huey summoned the legislature into special session to enact a five-cent occupational tax on oil to aid "the sick, the halt, the blind, and the children," all hell broke loose. A barrel-house free-for-all took place on the floor of the House when Long's Speaker, smelling impeachment in the air, declared the House adjourned *sine die*. Bloody-faced legislators groped blindly for assailants who had struck them from behind. Men were felled by inkwells, canes, bare fists. A protesting representative hopped from desk to desk like a mountain goat, vainly trying to reach the Speaker and wreak personal vengeance on him. Men were cursing, screaming, some sobbing in anger.

The next day the Speaker decided that the House had not adjourned, and the House proceeded to impeach Huey Long. The charges ranged from the grave to the ridiculous. Huey had sought to bribe legislators. He had plotted the murder of an opposition Senator. He had misused, misapplied, and misappropriated state funds. He had squandered monies allocated to a national governors' conference in New Orleans on a riotous, bosomy party, testimony concerning which left some governors red-faced. He had acted unbecomingly in public places, even to the extent of getting cockeyed drunk. Without authority he had ordered the classical old Governor's Mansion torn down to make way for a new one. He habitually used unquotable profanity, required signed, undated resignations from his political appointees, made illegal loans. The House impeached.

Huey fought back with promises, intimidation, and circulars, distributed by the hundreds of thousands by state employees to the faithful. Again he barnstormed Louisiana. His primary targets, not altogether without justification, were Standard Oil, the newspapers—particularly the New Orleans newspapers—and the old political guard.

To most of the state it looked as if Huey was finished. Then, dramatically, he produced a round robin, signed by fifteen senators, who declared that no matter what evidence was submitted to the Senate they would not vote to convict the Governor because they believed the charges against him were invalid. The number was one more than enough to prevent the two-thirds majority necessary for conviction. The deserving fifteen reaped earthly rewards, and never again was Huey in dire political danger.

From this fiasco emerged the dictator, vindictive and intent upon a domination that could not again be challenged. No holds had been barred by either side in the impeachment fight. From now on there were to be no holds except those in which Huey was master. The impeachment fight technique would be improved upon later, but never radically altered. Frighten the wavering legislator by appealing over his head to the voters. Woo him with certain gratuities to be arranged on the side. What was the legislature, anyway? Just a hodgepodge of ward heelers from New Orleans, a scattering of lawyers, a couple of wagonfuls of simple-minded and simpleton farmers, most of them alike in that they had a price. Own them. Fashion them into a ready blade with which to carve empire.

Louisiana's frightened, vengeful Governor surrounded himself with a half-dozen gun-ready, slugging bodyguards. He established a weekly newspaper, the *Louisiana Progress,* staffed it principally with skillful, conscienceless young newspapermen, and sicked it on his enemies. State employees found it good insurance to subscribe to the *Progress,* the number of subscriptions depending upon the size of their salaries, but with a minimum of ten to be sold, eaten, or used as wallpaper. No opponent big enough to be worthy of notice escaped its libeling. The voters of the nation's most illiterate state could understand its cartoon obscenities even when they couldn't spell out the text.

The public-works program went into high gear. The Depression was rocking Louisiana. Public works meant needed jobs. And the administration could count on at least five votes for each employee; the votes of the aunts and uncles and cousins and wives and children of jobholders who made it clear to their relatives that their fifteen to thirty dollars a week was secure only so long as they could prove their loyalty with political performance.

The first program was followed by a second and more ambitious one: a sixty-eight-million-dollar highway construction project, a five-million-dollar skyscraper capitol, and another twenty million dollars in assorted projects, all to be financed by an additional three-cent hike in the gasoline tax. With a year and a half yet to serve as Governor, and with the opposition organizing against the program, Huey decided to run for the United States Senate with the state program as his platform.

The use of the sound truck and the financial strangulation of the enemy city of New Orleans were the principal innovations of the campaign. Conservative, goateed, seventy-year-old Joseph Ransdall, the incumbent whom Huey dubbed "Feather Duster," burbled unavailingly. Huey won hands down; and when his inimical Lieutenant Governor claimed the Governorship because of Long's election to the Senate, Huey called out the state police and the National Guard, read the Lieutenant Governor out of office, and put in the president *pro tempore* of the Senate as acting Governor. He designated his old benefactor, O. K. Allen of Winnfield, as the apostolic choice for the next full term.

Meanwhile he concocted what might have been a good if desperate expedient for the cotton South. With Biblical precedent to back him up, he proposed that in protest against ruinous five-cent cotton the South should let its cotton fields lie fallow for a year. But Huey managed to insult Texas, the South's principal cotton producer, and the Texas legislature, thumbing its nose at "the arrogant jackass who brays from Louisiana . . . ignoramus, buffoon, meddler, and liar," would have none of the plan. So it died.

The wider horizon beckoned. In January 1932, the Kingfish from Louisiana breezed into Washington. For the next three and one-half years he performed simultaneously in two rings of a dazzling political circus, the capital of Louisiana and the capital of the nation. He soon broke with President Roosevelt, each sensing in the other a challenge, and from the Senate floor ridiculed "Prince Franklin, Knight of the Nourmahal," and his New Deal, unconcernedly violating the Senate's rules of personal decorum by lampooning such Administration stalwarts as Carter Glass, Henry Wallace (Lord Corn Wallace), Ickes (the Chicago Chinch Bug), Hugh Johnson (Sitting Bull), Joe Robinson, and Pat Harrison. No Senator could match him in debate or in monopolizing the front page. Day after day Huey made news. Sometimes amusing news, as in the controversy over whether corn bread should be dunked or crumbled in turnip-greens pot-likker. Sometimes bad news for Huey, as when an unidentified guest at a Sands Point, Long Island, club resented with hammering fists the Kingfish's impatient and misdirected attempt to make use of a urinal before the other had moved aside. On another occasion his national and state prestige sagged momentarily when the Old Regular machine in New Orleans rebelled, returned its mayor, T. Semmes Walmsley, to office, and Walmsley followed up his victory by journeying to Washington and waiting around unavailingly to thrash the well-guarded "yellow coward."

In 1934 Long formalized the program which he hoped would eventually win him the Presidency. The hazy concept of a national redistribution of wealth, presented fifteen years before by the obscure state Senator from Winn Parish, took definable shape in a national "Share Our Wealth" organization. No dues were necessary. Huey produced the expense money as easily as the nation disgorged the followers, both by the hundreds of thousands. No matter that the Share Our Wealth program was demonstrably impracticable as presented. It *was* believable: a limitation of fortunes to $5,000,000; an annual income minimum of $2,000 to $2,500 and a maximum of $1,800,000; a homestead grant of $6,000 for every family; free education from kindergarten through college; bonuses for veterans; old-age pensions, radios, automobiles, an abundance of cheap food through governmental purchase and storage of surpluses. The Share Our Wealth members had their own catchy song, "Every Man a King," their own newspaper, the mudslinging *Louisiana Progress*, expanded now to the *American Progress*.

The movement was nothing less than a new political party, heir to the yearnings and frustrations of the Populists, the Whiskey Rebels, the Know-Nothings, the Free Silverites, of all the have-nots of capitalism. Almost singlehanded, Long won the election of Hattie Caraway of Arkansas to her deceased husband's Senate seat. The Share Our Wealth clubs began cutting across old lines in Mississippi, Alabama, Georgia. The New Deal became worried and began to use its Louisiana patronage accordingly.

By legislative action Long made sure that no federal relief money could be obtained by any Louisiana municipality or county except with the approval and supervision of an agency of his own. The administration retaliated by withholding PWA project funds. Revenue agents roved through Louisiana from 1932 until long after Long's death, and with eventually decisive results. A Senatorial committee timorously held hearings in New Orleans relative to the corruption which accompanied the election to the Senate of a Long ally, John Overton; and, after being defied, browbeaten, and ridiculed by Huey and his jibing lieutenants, exonerated Overton with a weak-kneed finding that he "had not personally participated in or instigated any fraud."

As the Share Our Wealth chorus swelled, Huey, like a wise military tactician, took care to protect his rear. In a spectacular, degenerative series of special sessions in 1934 and 1935, his legislature reduced Louisianians almost literally to the status of Indian wards. Together with this final elimination of the actualities of democratic self-government—to the unconcern of a majority of the unconsulted electorate—came new benefits: homestead tax exemption, theoretically up to two thousand dollars; abolition of the one-dollar poll tax; a debt moratorium act; and new taxes—an income tax, a public utilities receipts tax, an attempted "two cents a lie" tax on the advertising receipts of the larger newspapers, which the United States Supreme Court pronounced unconstitutional.

Perhaps it seems inconceivable that any legislature, no matter how great the material rewards for its complaisant majority, could have so completely surrendered a people's political powers and economic and personal safety to one man. But Louisiana's legislature did. Administration-designated election supervisors were given the sole right of selecting voting commissioners, sole custody over the ballot boxes themselves, and the privilege of designating as many "special deputies" as might be necessary to guard the polls. Huey's figurehead Governor, O. K. Allen, was given the power to call out the militia whenever he—or Huey—wished. The Governor could —and did—expand the state police force into a swarm of private agents, some uniformed and some not, their number and the identity of the ununiformed alike a secret. The State Attorney General was empowered to supersede any district attorney in any trial. The State Tax Commission was given the right to change any city or county tax assessment, so that a misbehaving corporation or individual might know just who held the economic stranglehold. An ironically designated civil service board was created, with appointive control over all fire and police chiefs, and a school budget committee with the right to review the appointments of every schoolteacher and school employee. The Governor was even enabled to replace the entire city administration of Alexandria, a recalcitrant municipality in which Huey had once been rotten-egged. There were other repressive measures, many others. But these are sufficient to indicate what had happened to self-government in Louisiana.

It is perhaps a corollary that in the last year of his life Long became obsessed with a fear of assassination. He increased his armed bodyguard, and took other unusual precautions to insure his personal safety. In July 1935, he charged on the floor of the Senate that enemies had planned his death with "one man, one gun, and one bullet" as the medium, and with the promise of a Presidential pardon as the slayer's reward. This plot, he said, was hatched in a New Orleans hotel at a gathering of his enemies.

317

A dictograph, concealed in the meeting room, had recorded the murderous conversation. I was at that meeting. It was a caucus of die-hard oppositionists, dolefully trying to decide what to do for the next state campaign. And the "plotting" was limited to such hopefully expressed comments as "Good God, I wish somebody would kill the son of a bitch."

And somebody did. That July, the white horse of death, foreseen by Mason Spencer earlier in the year, was but two months distant. On the night of September 8, a slender, bespectacled man in a white suit stepped from behind a marble pillar in the capitol as Long, accompanied by his closest aides and bodyguard, hurried to the Governor's office. Dr. Carl Austin Weiss, the man in the white suit, drew a small pistol and fired once. Seconds later, the assassin lay dead, his body and head riddled by sixty-one shots. Huey Long staggered away with one bullet wound, perhaps a second, in his stomach. Thirty hours later he died.

The ghost is not yet laid, although Huey Long is dead these many long years. Nor will it be for many years to come. For this hideous thing that we remember as the roughshod reign of the Kingfish was not hideous in its beginnings. Whether or not Huey Long himself was ever sincere in his protestations for the poor and downtrodden is, basically, beside the point. For he led a social-economic revolution in Louisiana; and after his death the entire South was debated ground.

It was not his political genius and ruthlessness alone that made him possible. There were two other factors equally important.

The first factor was that, after two hundred years, the people of Louisiana were ready and waiting for a messiah who would translate their needs into accomplishments. Theirs was the ground swell of the little people, a people undisturbed by his tactics as long as they got the roads, the free bridges, the hospitals, the free schoolbooks, the public works; as long as the men whom he pilloried and broke and banished were identified with the leaders of the past, bumbling representatives of an indifferent, negative ruling class. The little people shrugged at graft because of their certainty that there always had been graft of a kind. This time, whatever the politicians skimmed off the top, they were getting theirs too. And they were getting something else. Revenge. A fantastic vengeance upon the Sodom and Gomorrah that was called New Orleans. A squaring of accounts with the big shots, the Standard Oil and the bankers, the big planters, the entrenched interests everywhere. Huey Long was in the image of these little people. He talked their language. He had lived their

318

lives. He had taken them up to the mountaintop and shown them the world which the meek would inherit.

The second factor was the make-up of the forces actively opposed to Long. His disunited enemies had difficulty from beginning to end to maintain an alliance that had its base in military necessity alone. We were strange bedfellows: cynical spoils politicians of the Old Regular ring in New Orleans; ardent, idealistic New Dealers; inept leaders of the country parishes, turned out in short grass; nonpolitical gentility awakened from their slumbers by rude knocking; the hitherto secure representatives of Big Business; honestly disturbed, solid bourgeoisie. Our combined cries for good government made a dissonant chorus. Huey bowled us over like tenpins, with rare misses, from the time of the failure of the impeachment proceedings to his assassination.

Looking back, I know now that part of our failure arose from an unwillingness to approve any Long-sponsored proposal for change, regardless of its merits. We offered none of our own except a plea for democratic rule, and that sounded hollow in contrast. Yet, at the end, it became the one thing of importance to Louisiana.

And Long triumphed over men far wiser politically than we. President Roosevelt and his pulse-feeler, Jim Farley, became uneasy about Long's threat soon after the Share Our Wealth movement overran the borders of Louisiana. On the Senate floor he made the most adroit, belligerent, and fluent opponent look and sound like a political freshman.

Even had Huey Long relied only upon his mesmeric appeal to Louisiana's masses and his ability to make promised delivery of the material things those masses wanted, it is probable that he could have dominated his state as completely and for at least as long as he did. But he was not content to rely upon these weapons alone. His compelling lust for power as such—a primary, animating force in his political life—and the intense vindictiveness which from the start characterized his public career lured him to a morally indefensible position.

When impeachment seemed a certainty in those early months as Governor, he simply bought and paid for enough legislators "like sacks of potatoes" to prevent the majority vote necessary for conviction. From then on, Long bought those whom he needed and could buy, and crushed those who had no purchase price or whose price was too high.

Nor was the control of a governor, a majority of legislators, a court majority enough. It should be repeated that no public officeholder, no teacher, no fire chief or fireman, no police chief or policeman, no day laborer on state projects held his job except in fee simple to the machine. Except among the political jobholders, he used this economic power sparingly. Yet even private citizens made their living by his sufferance. Long could have taxed to extinction any business, large or small, and business knew it. Men could be—and were—arrested by unidentified men, the members of his secret police, held incommunicado, tried, and found guilty on trumped-up charges. A majority of the State Supreme Court became unabashedly his. Through his State Printing Board he cracked an economic whip over the rural and small-town press, lashing all but a few into sullen silence. A thug, making a premeditated skull-crushing attack upon a Long opponent, could draw from his pocket in court a pre-signed pardon from the figurehead Governor. Entire city administrations could be removed, not by the electorate but by legislative action.

In the end, these things indirectly destroyed Huey Long himself. There are many conflicting tales as to why and how he was killed. This much is a certainty: His assassination was not plotted. It is not probable that Dr. Weiss went to the capitol the night of September 8, 1935, deliberately to kill Long. But he must have intended to protest a grave injury, the double-barreled kind of injury Long delighted in inflicting. Dr. Weiss's father-in-law, an implacable enemy of Long, had been gerrymandered out of his judgeship. Two of the judge's daughters had been dismissed from their teaching positions in further retaliation. And worse, Long had circulated noisome rumors about the family's ancestry.

Political punishment compounded with savage slander—an old, tested formula for reducing enemies to impotence. But this time the formula distilled a deadly reaction. Those who knew young Dr. Weiss best say that he could have sought Long only to protest verbally or with his fists this grave slander. They say that he could have drawn his gun only because the bodyguards threatened him. Few people in Louisiana believe that the full, true story has been told, for Long's henchmen were the only spectators. Perhaps the single bullet, fired from Weiss's small pistol, fatally wounded Long. Perhaps there was a second wound, as many Louisianians believe, caused by a ricocheting bullet from a bodyguard's gun. One bullet, two bullets. It is unimportant now; it was unimportant even then. Out of the terror he created, out of the driving passion to destroy other men, out of the futility that warped the minds of the Louisianians who opposed him, Huey Long himself forged the weapon which felled him.

AMATEURS—THERE AIN'T NONE

In the golden era of sports, the Twenties, when money was easy-come, easy-go, the ballyhoo whipped up for a Dempsey-Tunney world championship fight was almost a show in itself; the sports writers of the day contributed to the atmosphere by depicting the stars in hero-worshiping prose. Came the Thirties, and a lot of the hoopla faded away; in its wake, some of the golden figures in the sports world had a tarnished look about them. For one thing, it became increasingly clear that "amateur" was a meaningless term. Paul Gallico said, "We ask only one thing of an amateur, and that is that he doesn't let us catch him taking the dough."

For Gallico was incensed by the hypocrisy of the colleges, which paraded under the banner of amateurism, while they raked in larger and larger sums of money from the stadium crowds watching football, and surreptitiously arranged subsidies for their players. In 1938 he published *Farewell to Sport*, which announced his retirement as a sports writer and expressed his contempt for much of the sporting world. One of his most corrosive chapters dealt with Primo Carnera, onetime world's heavyweight champion.

PAUL GALLICO

PITY THE POOR GIANT*

There is probably no more scandalous, pitiful, incredible story in all the record of these last mad sports years than the tale of the living giant, a creature out of the legends of antiquity, who was made into a prizefighter. He was taught and trained by a wise, scheming little French boxing manager who had an Oxford University degree, and he was later acquired and developed into the heavyweight champion of the world by a group of American gangsters and mob men; then finally, when his usefulness as a meal ticket was outlived, he was discarded, in the most shameful chapter in all boxing.

This unfortunate pituitary case, who might have been Angoulaffre, or

* From Paul Gallico's *Farewell to Sport* (New York, Knopf, 1938).

321

Balan, or Fierabras, Gogmagog, or Gargantua himself, was a poor simple-minded peasant by the name of Primo Carnera, the first son of a stone-cutter of Sequals, Italy. He stood six feet seven inches in height, and weighed two hundred and sixty-eight pounds. He became the heavyweight champion, yet never in all his life was he ever anything more than a freak and a fourth-rater at prizefighting. He must have grossed more than two millions of dollars during the years [1930–1935] that he was being ex-hibited, and he hasn't a cent to show for it today.

There is no room here for more than a brief and hasty glance back over the implications of the tragedy of Primo Carnera. And yet I could not seem to take my leave from sports without it. The scene and the story still fascinate me, the sheer impudence of the men who handled the giant, their conscienceless cruelty, their complete depravity toward another hu-man being, the sure, cool manner in which they hoaxed hundreds of thousands of people. Poor Primo! A giant in stature and strength, a terrible figure of a man, with the might of ten men, he was a helpless lamb among wolves who used him until there was nothing more left to use, until the last possible penny had been squeezed from his big carcass, and then abandoned him. His last days in the United States were spent alone in a hospital. One leg was paralyzed, the result of beatings taken around the head. None of the carrion birds who had picked him clean ever came back to see him or to help him.

No one who was present in Madison Square Garden the night that Primo Carnera was first introduced to American audiences will ever forget him as he came bounding down the aisle from the dressing room and climbed into the ring. It was a masterpiece of stage management.

He wore black fighting trunks on the side of which was embroidered the head of a wild boar in red silk. He disdained the usual fighter's bath-robe and instead wore a sleeveless vest of a particularly hideous shade of green, and on his head a cap of the same shade, several sizes too large for him and with an enormous visor that made him look even larger than he was. Leon See, the Frenchman, then his manager, was a small man. The bucket-carriers and sponge-wielders were chosen for size too—di-minutive men; everything was done to increase the impression of Primo's size.

Carnera was the only giant I have ever seen who was well proportioned throughout his body for his height. His legs were massive and he was truly thewed like an oak. His waist was comparatively small and clean, but from it rose a torso like a Spanish hogshead from which sprouted two tremendous arms, the biceps of which stood out like grapefruit. His hands were like Virginia hams, and his fingers were ten thick red sausages.

His head was large, even for the size of his body, and looking at him you were immediately struck with his dreadful gummy mouth and sharp, irregular, snaggle teeth. His lips were inclined to be loose and flabby. He had a good nose and fine, kind brown eyes. But his legs looked even more enormous and treelike than they were, owing to the great blue bulging varicose veins that wandered down them on both sides and stuck out far enough so that you could have knocked them off with a baseball bat. His skin was brown and glistening and he invariably smelled of garlic.

This was the horror that came into the Madison Square Garden ring and sent a sincere shudder through the packed house. That is to say, he was horrible until he commenced to fight, when he became merely pitiful and an object demanding sympathy. Behind what passed for the wild battle blaze in his eyes and the dreadful gummy leer, emphasized by the size of the red rubber mouthpiece (tooth-protector) with which they provided him, there was nothing but bewilderment and complete helplessness. The truth was that, handicapped by rules and regulations, a sport he did not understand and was not temperamentally fitted for, and those silly brown leather bags laced to his fingers, never at any time could he fight a lick. His entire record, with a few exceptions, must be thrown out as one gigantic falsehood, staged and engineered, planned and executed by the men who had him in tow and who were building him up for the public as a man-killer and an invincible fighter.

But I think the most dreadful part of the story is that the poor floundering giant was duped along with the spectators. He was permitted, in fact encouraged, to believe that his silly pawings and pushings, when they connected, sent men staggering into unconsciousness and defeat. It was not until late in his career, when in spite of himself he learned something through sheer experience and number of fights, that he ever knocked anyone out on the level. But he never could fight, and never will. In spite of his great size and strength and his well-proportioned body, he remained nothing but a glandular freak who should have remained with the small French traveling circus from which Leon See took him.

This big, good-natured, docile man was exhibiting himself in a small wandering cirque in the south of France as a strong man and Greco-Roman wrestler, engaging all comers and local talent in the nightly show, having found that it paid him more and offered a better life than that of his chosen profession of mosaic worker. Here he was discovered by a former French boxing champion who signed him up and apprenticed him to one Monsieur Leon See to be taught the rudiments of *la boxe*. It is highly probable that the time spent as a wrestler set his muscles and prevented him from ever becoming a knockout puncher. But Monsieur Leon See was taking no chances. He taught and trained Carnera strictly as a defensive boxer.

Now, it must be understood that Leon See was one of the most intelligent, smart and wily men that ever turned a fighter loose from his corner. He was not much more scrupulous than the bevy of public enemies who eventually took Carnera away from him simply by muscling him, but he was much more farseeing and he had certain well-thought-out notions and theories about the ridiculous game of boxing. Among them was the excellent and sensible thought that the human head was never intended by nature to be punched, and that secondly, from the manner of its construction out of hundreds of tiny, delicately articulated bones, the closed fist was never meant to be one of man's most effective weapons. In this last idea, Monsieur See was not alone. The coterie of tough guys and mobsters who eventually relieved him of his interest in Carnera rarely used the fist, reckoning it, as did See, an inefficient weapon. The boys always favored the pistol or Roscoe, also known as the Difference, the Equalizer, the Rod, and the Heat.

See was a keen student of the human body—for a prizefight manager— and he knew something about men. He was aware that abnormalities of size were usually compensated for by weaknesses elsewhere. He found out —exactly how is not known—that Primo Carnera would never be able to absorb a hard punch to the chin. He may have had some secret rehearsal in a gymnasium somewhere in Paris and, having ordered some workaday heavyweight to clout Primo one just to see what would happen, saw that the giant came all undone, wobbled and collapsed. Be that as it may, Monsieur See knew. And never at any time while he was connected with Carnera would he permit anyone to punch Primo in the head—neither his sparring partners nor his opponents. Since both received their pay from practically the same source, this was not so difficult to arrange as might be imagined. But See also had something else. He was a Frenchman and so he had a heart. He loved big Carnera.

Years later See proved to be right. When Carnera through exigent circumstances was forced to fight without benefit of prearrangement, and the heavyweights began to sight along that big, protruding jaw of his and nail him for direct hits, he was slaughtered. He was brave and game and apparently could take punches to the body all the night long. But one hard, true tap on the chin and he fell down goggle-eyed. For a long time during the early years, however, nobody was permitted to hit him there, and Carnera himself began to think he was invincible.

Primo's first trip to the United States was arranged through an American contact man and importer of foreign fighting talent, a character from Tin-Ear Alley named Walter Friedman or, as Damon Runyon nicknamed him, Walter (Good-Time Charley) Friedman. See was smart enough to know that without an American "in," without cutting in an American manager, he would not get very far in America. What he was not quite smart enough to know was how deep his "in" took him, that the ramifications of Fried-man's business and other connections were to lead through some very tough and rapacious parties.

Carnera's first fight in New York involved him with a lanky Swede named Big Boy Peterson. In this fight poor Carnera was hardly able to get out of his own way and caused his opponent the most frightful embarrassment through not being able to strike a blow that looked sufficiently hard to enable him to keep his end of the bargain, if there was one. Eventually Peterson succumbed to a push as Carnera lumbered and floundered past him, and to make assurance doubly sure, the Swede hit himself a punch on the jaw as he went down. Someone had to hit him.

Now, this was a shameless swindle from start to finish, one way or another. If Peterson was making an honest effort to fight he never should have been permitted to enter the ring. The press unanimously announced beforehand that it would probably be a sell and a fake, and when it was over, suggested strongly that it had been. But it said so in a gay and light-hearted manner as though the whole thing were pretty funny (as indeed it was), and there was no one on the New York State Athletic Commission either sufficiently intelligent or courageous enough to throw Primo and his handlers and fixers right out of the ring and thence out of the country. The Peterson fight in Madison Square Garden, the stronghold of professional boxing, was a sort of a test case by the Carnera crowd to see how much they could get away with. On that score it was a clean-cut success. They found out that they could get away with anything. And so they proceeded to do just that. Primo's first American tour was organized, a tour that grossed something like $700,000, of which handsome piece of money Carnera received practically nothing. He was barnstormed across the country in the most cold-blooded, graceless, shameful series of fixed, bought, coerced, or plain out-and-out tank acts ever. If one of them was contested on its merits it was only because the opponent by no possible stretch of the imagination, or his own efforts could harm Carnera or even hit him.

Where the fight could not be bought—that is to say, where the fighter was unwilling to succumb to a tap on the elbow for a price—guns were produced by sinister strangers to threaten him, and where neither threats nor money were sufficient to bag the fight, he was crossed or tricked, as in the case of Bombo Chevalier, a big California Negro who was fascinated by the size of Carnera's chin, and nothing would do but he was going to hit it, just to see what would happen. Between rounds one of Chevalier's own attendants rubbed red pepper or some other inflammatory substance into his eyes so that he lost all interest in tapping anybody's chin.

In Newark, New Jersey, a Negro was visited in his dressing room before the bout by an unknown party not necessarily connected with Carnera's management, and was asked to inspect shooting irons, and in Philadelphia another Negro, Ace Clark, was amusing himself readying up Carnera for a knockout—he had already completely closed one of Primo's eyes—when somebody suggested he look down and see what the stranger beneath his corner was holding under his coat, and what caliber it was.

Every known build-up fighter was lined up for this tour, including faithful old hands like K. O. Christner, Chuck Wiggens, and poor Farmer Lodge. Political and gangster friends in the cities visited volunteered with their private heavyweights for quick splashes that might look well on the record books. It was all for the cause. The more money Carnera made, the more the boys would have to cut up amongst themselves. It was all just one big happy family. It seemed almost as though every scamp in the boxing game contributed his bit somehow to that Carnera build-up.

Friedman, as has been indicated, was the go-between, and although Leon See was quite capable of all the planning necessary to keep Carnera in the victory columns, nevertheless it would have been considered bad form, and downright dangerous, if See had not cut the local boys in. And, at that, I suspect the said local boys showed the amiable and gifted Frog a few things about building up a potential heavyweight champion that made the two Stribling fights arranged by Monsieur See, one in Paris and the other in London and both ending in fouls, look like Holy Gospel.

As adviser and codirector of this tour, Broadway Bill Duffy was cut in. Bill was then in the night-club and fight-managing business, but in his youth he had been convicted of a little alfresco burgling and had been sent away for a spell. He was still to achieve the highest pinnacle of fame that can come to an American—to be named a Public Enemy. It is a curious commentary upon the conduct of boxing around New York that Duffy was allowed to operate as a manager and a second when there was a rule on the books of the State Athletic Commission, if indeed it was not written directly into the boxing law, that no one ever convicted of a felony was to be eligible for any kind of license.

Duffy usually split even on things with his dearest friend, Owen Madden, better known as Owney, who had also been away for a time in connection with the demise of a policeman. Owney was out on parole at the time—he was sent back later—making beer (and very good beer it was, too) and acting as silent partner in the operation of a number of prizefighters. Also in this crowd was a charming but tough individual known as Big Frenchy De Mange who made news one evening by getting himself snatched and held for ransom by Mad Dog Vincent Coll. The Mad Dog was subsequently rubbed out in a West Side drugstore telephone booth. But the subject, after all, is Primo Carnera and not gangsters and racket men, though pretty soon it was all one subject and all one sweet and fragrant mess. The boys had their connections in every town. The Philadelphia underworld collaborated through the medium of the always friendly and helpful Maximilian Boo-Boo Hoff, and the same courtesies were extended all the way through to the Pacific Coast, where occurred the Bombo Chevalier incident, which was too nauseous even for the local commission there to stomach. There was an investigation resulting in the suspension of a few unimportant people. But Carnera and his swindle went merrily onwards.

And it continued until he won the heavyweight championship of the world by ostensibly knocking out Jack Sharkey, then world's champion, in the sixth round, with a right uppercut. I say ostensibly because nothing will ever convince me that that was an honest prizefight, contested on its merits.

Sharkey's reputation and the reputation of Fat John Buckley, his manager, were bad. Both had been involved in some curious ring encounters. The reputation of the Carnera entourage by the time the Sharkey fight came along, in 1933, was notorious, and the training camps of both gladiators were simply festering with mobsters and tough guys. Duffy, Madden, et Cie., were spread out all over Carnera's training quarters at Dr. Bier's Health Farm at Pompton Lakes, New Jersey. A traveling chapter of Detroit's famous Purple Gang hung out at Gus Wilson's for a while during Sharkey's rehearsals. Part of their business there was to muscle in on the concession of the fight pictures.

If that fight was on the level, it wasn't like either of the companies operating the two pugs. If it was honest, the only explanation was that the boys were going sissy. As far as Primo knew, the right uppercut with which he tagged Sharkey in the sixth round was enough to kill a steer. He had knocked out many men with the same punch. Now he was the heavyweight champion of the world, and even if he didn't have any money to show for it, Italy and Mussolini were going to be very pleased. I have often wondered how long he remained innocent, how long it was before he began to catch on.

For instance, it must have been a terrible surprise and considerable of an eye opener to Carnera the night he fought Tommy Loughran in Miami as heavyweight champion of the world. It was a no-decision match and a bad one for the gang to make, but they had to do something because they were desperate for money at the time. If the Sharkey fight was crooked, it is probable that the entire end of Primo's purse had to be paid over for the fix.

The Loughran fight had to go on the level because no one had ever managed to tamper with Loughran, and neither he nor his manager was afraid of guns. And Tommy had another curious and valuable protection. He was a good Catholic, and many priests were his friends. The gunmen were a little shy of those padres, who might usually be found in twos and threes at Tommy's home or his training camps. But the mob figured that with a hundred-pound advantage in weight Carnera could take care of Loughran, who was little more than a light heavyweight and never was a hard hitter. During the fight Carnera hit Loughran more than a dozen of the same uppercuts that had stretched Sharkey twitching on the canvas, and never even reddened Tommy's face. Loughran was a cream-puff puncher and yet he staggered Carnera several times with right hands and was himself never in any kind of danger from a punch. He merely got tired from having Carnera leaning on him for half an hour. If nothing else, that fight beneath the Miami moon exposed how incompetent Carnera was as a bruiser, and how utterly false were the stories about his invincibility, besides casting fresh suspicion upon his knockout of Sharkey. We had all seen Loughran put on the floor by a 175-pounder. If a man weighing around 280 pounds, as Primo did for that fight, hit him flush on the jaw and couldn't drop him, and yet had knocked out one of the cleverest heavyweights in the business, it wasn't hard to arrive at a conclusion. It was obvious that he was a phony and the first stiff-punching heavyweight who was leveling would knock him out.

Max Baer did it the very next summer. The following summer Joe Louis did it again, and then an almost unknown Negro heavyweight by the name of Leroy Haynes accomplished the feat for the third time. And that was the beginning of the end of Primo.

His lucrative campaigns and the winning of the heavyweight championship had enriched everyone connected with him except poor Primo, who saw very little of the money he earned. There were too many silent partners and "boys" who had little pieces of him. Monsieur See had long since been dispensed with and shipped back to France for his health; he had served his purpose. But it was an evil day for Carnera when they chased Leon back to Paris, for Leon never would have permitted anyone to belt Carnera on his vulnerable chin. As suggested, the little Frenchman had a love for the big fellow whom he had taught and trained and watched over so carefully. The Duffy crowd had no love for anything. Fighters' chins were made to be smacked and they might just as well get used to taking the punches there.

It seemed as though their power was beginning to lose some of its effectiveness, exhausted perhaps by its own virus and viciousness, shortly after they had made Carnera champion. Primo escaped to Italy with his title and nothing else and later returned here for the disastrous fight with Loughran under the guidance of a little Italian banker by the name of Luigi Soresi, who appeared to be genuinely trying to get and keep for poor Carnera some of the money he was making.

The by-products of the Miami affair were typical and pathetic. Duffy and company were living over a Miami night club in style and spending money like water—Primo's money. Carnera was relegated to a cheap cottage back of the town with a trainer. No one really looked after him. No one cared particularly whether he trained or not. He came into the ring against Loughran twenty pounds overweight. Shortly after that Duffy was clapped into the jug for a spell for some boyish pranks with his income tax, and from the cooler he wrote pleading letters at the time that Carnera was preparing to defend his title against Baer, maintaining that he was needed to guide, advise, and teach Primo, to prime him for the first serious defense of his title, and that he should be given furlough from quod to attend to this matter. Carnera vigorously denied that he needed him. He was only too delighted to have Duffy held in durance vile. Of course what was really killing Uncle Will was that he was where for the first time he couldn't get his fingers on a nice big slice of the sugar that big, stupid Wop would make for boxing Baer.

It is difficult to bag or fix a heavyweight championship prizefight, though it has been done. But in the postwar sports renaissance there was so much money at stake in a heavyweight championship fight that it took more cash than most could produce to purchase either champion or challenger. It stood to reason that if the champion figured to make a million dollars or more out of his title he wasn't going to sell out for any less. Too, the power of the gangs was weakening. Repeal dealt them a terrible blow and took away their chief source of revenue. Three or four years before, Carnera's title would have been safe because his handlers would not have accepted any challenger for the title unless he agreed to preserve the state of the champion's health throughout the encounter. And there were always ways and means of keeping a challenger from double-crossing.

But Duffy was in the sneezer, as the boys sometimes quaintly called the jailhouse, Carnera was broke and needed money. He could only get it by fighting Baer. And the Baer fight could not be fixed. Baer's reputation was good; at least, he had not been caught out in any shady fights. He was a powerful hitter and it was apparent that now at last the rest of us were going to be made privy to what it was that happened when Carnera was struck forcefully on the chin. We didn't have to wait long. He was knocked down three times in the first round, and lost his championship in the eleventh round on a technical knockout when he was helpless, having been knocked down a total of thirteen times during the ten and a half rounds.

Not, however, until he fought and was knocked out by Joe Louis was it apparent what a dreadful thing had been done to this great hulk of a man. Strange to feel pity and sympathy excited for one so gross and enormous and strong. But the outsizes of the world are not the happy men, and their bulk is often of little use or help to them. If anything, it is a handicap when up against the speed and timing and balance of a normal man. Carnera's great strength was practically useless to him in the ring. The hardest blow he could strike was little more than a push. True, if he caught you in a corner he could club you insensible, but no smart fighter is caught in corners, and the big man was never fast enough anyway to catch anyone but out-and-out tramps.

When he fought Joe Louis he was defensively but little better than he was the first time I saw him, which, as it happened, was not in Madison Square Garden, but in the smoky, stuffy, subterranean Salle Wagram, a little fight club in Paris where I happened to be one evening when Jeff Dickson was promoting a fight between Primo Carnera, who had then been fighting a little less than a year, and one Moise Bouquillon, a light heavy-weight who weighed 174 pounds. Monsieur See was experimenting a little with his giant. It was obvious that Bouquillon was going to be unable to hurt him very much, but what I noted that evening and never forgot was that the giant was likewise unable to hurt the little Frenchman. Curiously, that fight was almost an exact duplicate of the one that Carnera as champion later fought with Loughran. Walter (Good-Time Charley) Friedman was there too. Many years later he told me quite frankly: "Boy, was that a lousy break for us that you come walking into that Salle Wagram that night and see that the big guy can't punch! Just that night you hadda be there. Leon wanted to see if he could go ten rounds without falling down. And you hadda be there. We coulda got away with a lot more if you don't walk in there and write stories about how he can't punch."

Joe Louis slugged Carnera into bleating submission, cruelly and brutally. Handsome Uncle Will Duffy was back in his corner again, jawing angrily at him when he was led trembling and quivering back to his chair after the referee had saved him again, one side of his mouth smashed in, dazed and dripping blood. The very first right-hand punch Louis hit him broke Carnera's mouth and hurt him dreadfully.

Here, then, was the complete sell. He had nothing. His title was gone, his money squandered by the gang. And the one thing he thought he had, an unbeatable skill in defense and an irresistible crushing power in attack that no man living could withstand, never existed. It was a fable as legendary as the great giants of mythology that he resembled. The carrion birds that had fed upon this poor, big, dumb man had picked him clean. They had left him nothing, not even his pride and his self-respect, and that probably was the cruelest thing of all.

In his last fight, the one with Haynes, he was again severely beaten about the head. One of his legs refused to function. The fight was stopped. While he lay in the hospital in New York for treatment, as I have said, he lay alone.

I often wonder what that hulk of a man thinks today as he looks back over the manner in which he was swindled, tricked and cheated at every turn, as he recalls the great sums of money that he earned, all of it gone beyond recall. The world has no place for him, not even as a freak in a circus, from whence he emerged and where he might happily have spent his life and become prosperous. Because as a giant, a terror and a horror, he stands exposed as a poor, unwilling fraud who was no man-killer at all, but a rather helpless, sad creature who, when slugged by a 185-pound mortal, either toppled stricken to the floor or staggered about or bled or had to be saved from annihilation by a third man who obligingly stepped between him and his tormentors.

He was born far, far too late. He belonged to the twelfth or thirteenth century, when he would have been a man-at-arms and a famous fellow with mace and halberd, pike or bill. At least he would have fought nobly and to the limit of his great strength, properly armed, because Carnera was a courageous fellow to the limit of his endurance, game and a willing fighter when aroused. In those days he would have won honor afield and would have got himself decently killed, or, surviving, would have been retired by his feudal lord to round out his days and talk over the old brave fights.

Today there is nothing left for this man but reflection upon his humiliations. He was just a big sucker whom the wise guys took and trimmed. What an epitaph for one who came from the ancient and noble race of giants.

All this took place in our country, Anno Domini 1930–1935.

THE BROWN BOMBER

CAPTURING the crown in the heavyweight division was not so easy then as it is today; Joe Louis, for example, did not become champion until he had fought a number of contenders, several of whom had been champions. His fight with ex-champion Max Baer on October 9, 1935, would produce the first million-dollar gate of the Thirties. The previous June, Baer had lost his crown to James J. Braddock, a longshoreman who had been on the relief rolls a year before.

Braddock's underdog victory was immensely popular—a Depression victim had caught the brass ring to fame and glory; if he could do it, anybody might. Braddock would lose the crown to Louis in 1937, and the next year Louis would take his revenge on Max Schmeling (who in 1936 had administered the only defeat in Louis' record prior to his ill-advised emergence from retirement in 1950) by knocking the German out in the first round.

Boxing fans saw good matches in other fight divisions—middleweight, welterweight, lightweight, and light heavyweight—where such memorable fighters as Barney Ross, Tony Canzoneri, Henry Armstrong, Jimmy McLarnin and Maxie Rosenbloom earned followings.

But it was Louis, a lethal puncher with great skills in every department, who marks these years and compares favorably with the great fighters of the past.

JONATHAN MITCHELL

JOE LOUIS NEVER SMILES*

THESE people are here, 95,000 of them, because they have money. Down there on the field, men have paid $150 and more for a pair of tickets. Twenty thousand seats were stamped "ringside," and the customers out beyond third base were bilked. They should have known that Mike Jacobs, who is running this fight, is a smart man. No one can do anything to him because he has the support of Hearst.

It feels good to have money again. Everyone in this crowd has money. The people who were swindled by Jacobs can afford it. Happy days are here again. Of course, things aren't so good, with twenty million on relief.

* From *The New Republic,* Oct. 9, 1935.

A man can be fired, and next morning there are ten men in line waiting for his job. But the unemployed have been around for a long time. No one can expect us to sit home and be sympathetic indefinitely.

It is a cold, clear night. The Stadium rises steeply around one half of the field. The floodlights on its upper edge are directed on the field and the bleachers, and the Stadium itself is black except for a steady row of red exit signs. Almost the whole of the immense field is covered with chairs. Jacobs has pushed the customers so closely together that all that can be seen of them, under the floodlights, is their microscopic, bright faces. They form neat rows, divided into plots by the aisles, like commercial Dutch tulip beds. There are acres of them, shining pinkly. Men in white, with high cardboard signs in their caps, move gravely about selling pop, like gardeners. The ring is at second base, and the movie operators' metal cage, high on a pole, that you used to see at fights, is missing. The only movement comes from white tobacco smoke, rising in heavy waves. Through it you can see the American flags along the top of the Stadium, after the fashion of the opening verse of "The Star-Spangled Banner."

Near at hand the crowd is a respectable, bridge-playing one. About a fifth are Negroes, more carefully dressed and more mannerly than the whites. The little drunk with the long woolen muffler is certainly a Bronx dentist. He thinks correctly that the preliminary match now going on is poor, and keeps screaming, "Lousy." He brandishes a handful of crumpled bills, and will give odds to anyone. There seems to be something painful in his past that he would like to explain, but the woolen muffler keeps blowing in his face, and communication between him and us is eternally frustrated.

There is a stirring in the aisles near the ring. The people who amount to something, and who are bowed through the police lines outside the Stadium, are entering. There are five state governors, the Republican National Committee, important business figures and a large number of people whose press agents made them come so that their names would be in tomorrow's papers. Max Baer and his attendants are now at home plate. A dozen little pushing figures open up the crowd for him, and another dozen follow behind. Baer wears a white bathrobe and has his hands on the shoulders of the state trooper in front of him. He nods to his many friends. Joe Louis, with another state trooper and other attendants, pushes in from third base. We learn afterward that his bride, Marva Trotter, is in the first row in a bright-green dress and orchids. Louis seems to see no one.

334

The floodlights are extinguished. Nothing exists except the brightly glowing ring. That is old Joe Humphries being lifted through the ropes, the man who announced fights before the Depression. Since then he has been sick, and had a bad time. We have all been having a bad time, for that matter. Jack Dempsey squats in Baer's corner, but no one notices him. Humphries' assistant is bawling into the microphones: "Although Joe Louis is colored, he is a great fighter, in the class of Jack Johnson and the giants of the past." His voice fades away, and returns: "American sportsmanship, without regard to race, creed or color, is the talk of the world. Behave like gentlemen, whoever wins." Nearly two thousand police at the entrances of the Stadium are there to break up a possible race riot.

Baer has stripped. He has made a lot of money, Baer has. From all reports, he has spent a lot. He has played Broadway, Miami and the other hot spots. Why shouldn't he have done so? Joe Louis takes off his flashing silk bathrobe, blue with a vermilion lining. It is the only extravagant gesture he makes. For all his youth, he is thick under the jaws, thick around the waist. His face is earnest, thoughtful, unsmiling.

Max Baer hasn't been, I suppose, what you would call a good boy. Joe Louis has, though. This is his greatest advantage. He once was taken to a night club, and it is reported that within ten minutes he wanted to go home. He said he was sleepy. He is supposed to have saved his money. Louis' father died when he was only two years old, down in Alabama. Until she married again, his mother had a hard struggle to support the children, and they were very dear to her. Louis is fond of his mother. She is a Lily of the Valley at her church in Detroit, where the family now lives. The Lilies are having a supper, or some such event, in a few days. She wants him there, and he is going with his new wife.

We are too far away to hear the gong. They are out in the middle of the ring, with a stubby little man in a white sweater moving softly around them. Baer holds both hands, open, clumsily in front of him. Look at Joe Louis. He is leading with a straight left arm, his right hand before his face ready to block, and his right elbow tucked in to his ribs. That is scientific. That is what they teach in correspondence courses, or the night gymnasium classes of the Y.M.C.A. In the first thirty seconds, you can tell that he reeks of study, practice, study. Any romantic white person who believes that the Negro possesses a distinctive quality ought to see Louis. He suggests a gorilla or a jungle lion about as much as would an assistant professor at the Massachusetts Institute of Technology.

Baer stands flat-footed, with his great death-dealing right fist doubled by his side. He swings, and you can almost count three while the fist sails through the air. Louis moves sidewise and back, because he has been taught that if you move with a blow it can never hurt you. Baer's glove slides up the side of Louis' head harmlessly. He swings again and again, and, carefully and unhurriedly, Louis slips away. Look! Louis at last is going in. A left, a right and another left in close. Louis has pulled in his head, and, with both arms up before him, he looks like a brown crayfish. All you can see is the twitching of his shoulders. So incredibly fast he is that the blows themselves are almost invisible. His hands cannot possibly move more than a few inches. Look! Baer is backing into a neutral corner. Louis is raining down blows. Baer's nose spurts blood, his lower lip bleeds, his face is red pulp.

Baer must have meant something to many people. He made wisecracks and went to parties and was a harbinger of the return of the old days. He was Broadway, he was California and Florida, he represented the possession of money once more and spending it. This saddle-colored, dour-faced, tongue-tied, studious youth, who is punishing Baer, punishing him more cruelly than human flesh and bones can endure, what does he represent? Baer stands with his hands hanging at his sides. He is helpless. He cannot hit the dissolving form before him, and he has never learned to protect himself. He holds his fine head, with its sweep of tightly curled hair and its great, brooding nose, high above his torturer. Pride alone keeps his head up, pride that has no tangible justification whatever. It was the same pride that kept Colonel Baratieri at Adowa, twenty years before Joe Louis was born.

It is the first round, and the fight is as good as over. Maybe it was foolish to spend money going to a fight. There must be many people, even down there in the ringside seats, who couldn't afford to spend what they did on tickets. No one can be sure of his job with twenty million on relief. This is a crazy country, with people handing out a million dollars to Mike Jacobs and Hearst, while families right here in New York City are without enough to eat.

Round one is ended. Jack Dempsey vaults into the ring in a single, startling leap. Perhaps it is a trick. He must have vaulted from the ground to the edge of the ring platform, and from there into the ring itself. But from a distance, it seems one motion, and it is beautiful. Beside the man that Dempsey was, Baer and Louis and Schmeling are phonies. Nowadays everything, including men, is somehow different.

The next three rounds are slaughter. In the second, Baer makes a wild, swinging, purposeless attack. For probably fifteen seconds, he appears formidable, but his attack has no substance inside it. With the third round, he is beaten, but Louis does not rush in, as Dempsey would have, to kill. Deliberately he circles Baer, with his earnest, thoughtful face, seeking an opening through which to strike without possible risk of injury. He takes no chance of a last, desperate fling of Baer's prodigious right hand. He is a planner. He is a person who studies the basic aspects of a problem and formulates a program. Apparently his studies are satisfactory, for he carefully steps up and knocks Baer down twice. Baer is on the canvas when time is called. Dempsey slides across the ring, picks Baer up like a mother, fusses over him until the fourth, and final, round. Baer once more is down. When the stubby referee, swinging his arm, reaches seven, he tries to rouse himself. This turns out later to have been a fortunate gesture. The customers who suspected the honesty of the fight, and were unconvinced that a man could be half killed by fifty blows full on the jaw, were reassured as they watched Baer struggling to his feet. Had he been trying to throw the fight, they reasoned, he would have lain still. At the count of ten, Baer is on one knee, his swollen face wearing a comical expression of surprise.

The floodlights return us to time and space. Near at hand, there is remarkably little cheering, even from Negroes. They act as if, despite the police, they think it more prudent to restrain their feelings. There in the ring, placing his hand on Baer's shoulder in a stiff gesture, is the best fighter living, and the first Negro whose backers and trainer are men of his race. No white man shares in Louis' winnings. If the whites of the Boxing Commission will permit the match, he will be champion of the world.

All across the Stadium, the neat tulip beds are being broken up as tiny figures push into the aisles and toward the exits. A man with a small blond mustache is sobbing: "Maxie, why didn't you hit him?" Downtown in the Forties and Fifties, redecorated speakeasies will quickly be crammed to the doors and customers turned away. In Lenox Avenue in Harlem, Negroes will be tap-dancing from curb to curb, and singing: "The Baer goes over the mountain," and "Who won the fight?" Tomorrow the financial sections of the newspapers will report that business leaders regard the fight as final proof that the country's economic worries are past, and a comfortable and prosperous future is assured.

THE NEW LEISURE

MORE TIME TO PLAY

IN THE first years of the Depression, some businesses had cut working hours in order to spread employment and reduce pay checks; later, when the NRA (National Recovery Administration) codes, which had provided for a maximum forty-hour work week, failed to withstand court challenge, the five-day week was already well established in factory and business office. There was more free time.

War clouds over Europe discouraged overseas travel, and Americans turned to their homeland. Air travel expanded, the car trailer was developed, and trailer camps and roadside cabins (the motels of today) were built; public beaches and national and state parks were built in large numbers by the government's public-works projects. By the middle of the decade there were some thirty million people traveling around the country, visiting, vacationing by car.

People, as always, loved the new, the odd, the curious in their entertainment. The Thirties saw thousands of men and women crouched over bingo boards, teen-agers perched in trees vying for records for the longest roost, college boys swallowing goldfish and burying each other alive for kicks, and the chain-letter craze threatening to swamp the mails.

Baseball was still the great summer pastime, but American football, in the Thirties, became the biggest money-maker of all the sports. Professional football drew larger and larger gates after 1933 with end-of-season championship playoffs between East and West divisions of the National Football League. And college football saw a sudden mushrooming of postseason Bowl contests to compete with the famous annual Rose Bowl game.

In tennis, the United States finally won back the Davis Cup in 1937, only to lose it to Australia in 1939; the great players of the day were Ellsworth Vines and Don Budge, who in 1938 was the first player ever to hold the American, British, French and Australian singles titles.

And the same Associated Press poll that named Babe Didrikson an outstanding performer, also chose Jesse Owens as the top track performer in the first half of this century. Owens, a Negro, was the sensation of the 1936 Olympic Games at Berlin, winning the broad jump, the 100-meter and 200-meter runs, and sharing winning honors in the 400-meter relays. Hitler, furious at such a public setback to his Master Race propaganda, walked out of the stadium just before Owens was awarded his gold medals.

There were, indeed, many great sports heroes in the Thirties; at the same time, however, there was a tremendous increase of participation by many Americans in such "new" sports as bowling, skiing, softball, bicycling and golf—the opening of more and more public golf courses brought thousands of new golfers into the game. It was a time when more people seemed to want to get out to play, themselves, not just watch others.

CAFÉ SOCIETY

The leisure of the upper classes, too, was affected by the changing times. According to *Fortune* Magazine, "in the day of hunger marches and breadlines, the elaborate dinner dance seemed to the owners of most great houses vulgar if not dangerous ostentation." Society members began giving smaller dinners in public hotels or cafés; Prohibition had forced the upper classes to go out to find a drink, and "rising real-estate values drove them out of their old brownstone houses into apartments, reconciling them to standardized mass entertainment parallel with the new standardized mass housing. Then came the Depression, shrinking the inherited incomes, dealing a blow to the debutante ball that had been the old order's focal point, and making Dutch-treat dates conventional." *

Often, in the Thirties, the salaries of screen stars surpassed the Depression-shriveled incomes of the older invested fortunes. It was inevitable that screen personalities were sought after—they were already rubbing elbows in the cafés, and, of course, they also brought variety and excitement to the upper crust. "The old 400 was no longer an end in itself. This brought about a distinct change, in that the urbane man about town was supplanted by play-boys and professional extra men, and, together with this, the café society was taken over lock, stock and barrel by the women." *

Certainly society lost no glamour and gained heavily in publicity for itself. After all, stars' reputations were built on publicity and now with "so many faces and fortunes coming from the world of entertainment, society became more receptive to publicity—indeed, with a few exceptions, it was avid for favorable mention in the proper newspaper columns and magazines." *

Out of this new seeking for publicity were bred the special columnists whose business it was to become familiar with the chichi world, resulting in the society gossip column. Inevitably the columnist himself became sought after, to the extent that his appearance at social functions "threw the hostess into delirious joy." In this period Elsa Maxwell thrived; she was heard to say that "no party was ever more successful than the published accounts of it in the papers." †

NEWSPAPERS AND COMIC STRIPS

Perhaps newspapers had gained a certain new glamour in their attention to the antics of café society, but they were losing readers, who were turning to radio and the movies, both of which competed directly with news and entertainment features of the press. Only in the registering of independent opinion did some of the newspapers continue to maintain superiority over the other two media, which were harried respectively by advertising pressures and mass box-office standards.

The newspapers that survived the Depression did not lose much in individual circulations, but many others became victims of mergers with larger papers, or were casualties of the bad times. By the end of

* "The Yankee Doodle Salon," *Fortune,* December 1937.
† "The Yankee Doodle Salon."

the decade fewer than 125 cities had more than one newspaper ownership, and 2,000 weekly papers had dropped by the wayside.

News and picture magazines also ate into the available readership. As a consequence news space gave way to increased use of the news photograph and the comic strip. The comic strip was not new, but now there was a stronger emphasis on the adventure serial strip, a new phase of "entertainment"—just about the time the old cliff-hanger motion-picture serial was dying out.

Of the five most noted comic strips originating in the Thirties, one was strictly an adventure strip—Milton Caniff's "Terry and the Pirates"—and it spawned more variations and imitations than any other strip in history.

The other four also set styles: "Blondie," followed over the next twenty years by a half-dozen light-hearted family strips; "Dick Tracy," the first of many cops-and-robbers strips; "L'il Abner," from which came a few regional satires by Al Capp's imitators; and "Joe Palooka," father of the straight sports strip.

The Palooka strip suggested "the old wistful portrait of power that did not corrupt. Here were all the human virtues embodied in a man who, if he were not so pure, could become a menace to society, but who, being so pure, was the kind of idol an American invariably bowed to. Even the name Palooka was perfect." *

In "Blondie," the American husband and father was presented often as "downright incompetent, but his instincts are good." This strip had a fantastic success, running in over a thousand papers all over the world, and becoming the subject of a number of motion pictures and a television series. "Dagwood, the father, sustains a six-to-one ratio in defeats over victory, but those defeats spring from his good nature, and not from real deficiencies; he lacks a capacity for cruelty; once a man has padded a cave with evergreen boughs, brought home skins and meat, perpetuated his kind, he becomes a useless supernumerary, tolerated for his weaknesses and barely permitted to delude himself with the ludicrous notion that he is of value to society." *

In "L'il Abner," Capp supplied satirical exuberance. He loved to prick frauds, lance nerves, and perhaps more than any other humorist of his day, he is "bitterly resentful of the fact that Americans have become afraid to laugh at each other." *

Chester Gould, the creator of "Dick Tracy," was led to produce the strip because of the success of gangsterism in national crime, and "his anger was directed specifically at the laxity of the local police and the seeming impunity by which hoodlums operated." * The Dick Tracy strip had a real impact upon various institutions, not excluding the police departments.

Caniff's "Terry and the Pirates" first appeared in October 1934. And while other adventure strips were popular—"Tarzan," "Flash Gordon," "Prince Valiant," for example—it was Caniff who caught the "restless, adventuresome spirit of the times better than anyone." * When, eventually, ownership of "Terry" came into dispute, Caniff easily created a new strip of his own— "Steve Canyon."

* Stephen Becker, *Comic Art in America* (New York, Simon and Schuster, 1959).

JOKES, GAGS AND A BIT OF SATIRE

Advertisers began to sell their products through comic strips in the late Thirties—the comic strip was no longer just a collection of jokes, gags, or satirical whimsey; "the public wanted a reflection of the contemporary world." *

Some of the obvious targets of national humor either were missing or didn't catch on. The New Deal and events in Europe proved poor subjects for satire. *Vanity Fair* tried hard to needle the New Deal, but went out of business before the decade was over. The black-out gags of vaudeville and burlesque were not so popular, but the great underground of jokes and gags that pass from citizen to citizen rolled on. The nationally prominent were worked over—the President and Mrs. Roosevelt were the subject of thousands of stories, many of which were offensive; but it always seems to be open season on Presidents.

For a while a new magazine called *Ballyhoo* tried to leaven some of the "hard sell" of magazine and radio advertising by poking fun at the ad man's follies; *Ballyhoo* suggested their motto in the following rhyming nonsense:

> "Little drops of hooey
> Little grains of bunk
> Make the silly public
> Buy a lot of junk." †

And the *Ballyhoo* editors wrote a mock Ten Commandments, as from the advertiser to the consumer, the first commandment being:

"Thou shalt not have for thyself any unpleasant breath, any congested cough, any film on thy teeth, any athlete's foot, or the likeness of any disease that is in heaven above, or on the earth beneath, or in the waters under the earth."

The second commandment:

"Thou shalt not take the name of pink toothbrush in vain."

And so on until, by the tenth, the velvet glove was off:

"Thou *shalt* covet thy neighbor's car, and his radio, and his silverware, and his refrigerator, and everything that is his." †

The demagogues, the social prophets, the poor man in the street and the arrogant businessman, all got their lumps, but there was hardly any noticeable body of gags built up around them; chances are that no single individual or national incident appeared big enough to sustain the creative satisfactions of the jokesters.

Vaudeville had died, radio and the motion-picture comics seemed smothered in moth balls, unless they were working out sketches that fitted their public characters; the times perhaps demanded too much in dedication, and just possibly the people were still too much in a state of shock to appreciate real wit, even if there had been much in evidence. Great comedians such as the Marx Brothers, W. C. Fields, Bobby Clark, and even Chaplin, were at work, but their best work had been developed and polished in the great days of vaudeville.

Instead, a kind of foul-ball humor was popular, often indirect and whimsical—the shaggy-dog story, for instance.

"By the mid-'30s the shaggy-dog story ran a close second to the off-color story in oral acceptance.

---

* Stephen Becker, *Comic Art in America*.
† *Ballyhoo* Magazine.

Winchell, Lyons and other columnists began to reproduce more and more specimens, and *Esquire* and other magazines featured articles which were little more than collections of such jokes. They were still chiefly devoted to the nonsense of intoxicating rumhounds, rather than shaggy-dog stories really, but by the end of the decade only one in five of the animal characters was a dog. The others were horses, cats, pigeons, etc. Even among the dog stories the shaggy species was rare. The shaggy-dog story is really a counterpart of the fable, in that a fable has animals talking and acting like human beings for satirical purposes. Perhaps the most famous of all such is the tale of the horse that can pitch and field baseball superbly but, when asked by the manager if he can bat, replies, 'Who ever heard of a horse that can bat!'

"Or the horse that walked up to a bar and asked for a martini with a dash of horse-radish. The bartender mixes it and hands it over. The horse polishes it off, smacking his lips, saying, 'I suppose you think it's strange that I should ask for a martini with horse-radish.' 'Hell, no,' says the bartender, 'I like them that way myself.' " *

Then there was the "Knock-knock" story, still around today. A person would announce, "Knock-knock," and the listener was to respond, "Who's there?" "Freda." "Freda who?" "Freda you, but five dollars to anyone else." † Unquestionably, it was punning in its lowest form, and people winced as often as they laughed.

In the early Thirties, Americans were heard saying "check and double-check" from the Amos 'n' Andy show. Later, Joe Penner, a radio comedian, who had come out of burlesque, had us saying "Wanna buy a duck," and "Oh, you na-a-asty man"; and for some strange reason a lot of us were convulsed—for a while. And from the newsreels Lew Lehr provided "Monkeys is the cwaziest people."

A girl called her date "smooth," and an article of dress might be "neat." The teen-agers called each other "creeps" but a "killer-diller" might be anything "terrific." Admiring a dancing couple or a band's hot rhythm, one said they were "in the groove."

* Evan Esar's *The Humor of Humor* (New York, Horizon Press, 1952).
† Joke contributed by Walt Grove.

THE JOINT IS JUMPING

A JAZZ critic once wrote that no matter what distinctions are made between jazz and popular music, certain basic elements were common to all American music—a strong, swinging beat, supporting a rhythmically free, improvised melody, such melody stemming from a popular song. Furthermore, he was of the opinion that these qualities jelled best in the swing era, a time that provided just the right mold for all the previous variations of American music—blues, ragtime, brass band, et cetera. Whether one agrees with this or not, it is certain there has never been a response to popular music to equal America's enthusiasm for swing in the late Thirties.

Frederick Lewis Allen has written about a demonstration of that enthusiasm:

"One morning in the winter of 1937–38 a crowd began to gather outside the Paramount Theater in Times Square, New York, as soon as it was light. By 6 A.M. three thousand people were assembled in the otherwise empty streets—mostly high-school boys and girls in windbreakers and leather jackets. By 7:30 the crowd had so swelled that ten mounted policemen were sent from the West Forty-seventh Street Station to keep it under control. At eight o'clock the doors of the theater were carefully opened to admit 3,634 boys and girls; then the Fire Department ordered the doors closed, leaving two or three thousand youngsters out in the cold.

"Benny Goodman and his orchestra were opening an engagement at the Paramount.

"In the same year a Carnival of Swing was held at Randall's Island in New York with twenty-five bands present; over 23,000 jitterbugs listened for five hours and forty-five minutes with such uncontrollable enthusiasm that, as a reporter put it in the next morning's *Times*, the police and park officers had all they could do to protect the players from 'destruction by admiration.' " *

Many dancers were turning into listeners and it was easy to understand why. The music was generally recognized as something more than just dance music; it was "swing" and it was "hot jazz," and people were beginning to understand that the country had a great, though not so old, tradition in jazz music; people were writing about it, and more and more people were buying records and discussing the work of the performers. They had been going to the movie houses to see the bands perform in person, and they had also stayed home at night to listen to certain bands over the radio; and young people gathered wherever they could to appreciate the rhythm and the beat. I recall leaving a dance once, while in high school, to join a group around a car radio, where we stood around clapping hands to the beat of the Casa Loma band on the old "Camel Caravan" program, and exclaiming over the Clarence Hutchenrider riffs.

* Frederick Lewis Allen's *Since Yesterday*.

MARSHALL STEARNS

THE SWING ERA*

DURING THE "Swing Era," the greatest mass conversion in the history of jazz took place. For swing music was sold—as a new kind of music—from coast to coast, with all the high-pressure tactics of modern publicity. It was brought to the attention of the public in the press and at the movies, on the stage and in the ballroom, on the juke-box and over the radio. And it made converts for whom new words such as "jitterbugs" and "bobby-soxers" were coined. And again, because most of them were young and liked to dance, swing music lasted quite a while. In many ways it is still with us, although the fans are older.

Generally speaking, swing music was the answer to the American—and very human—love of bigness, for the formula of the big Harlem bands which had solved the difficult problem of how to assemble a large orchestra and still play hot jazz was adopted. At the same time, there was a real demand. With the repeal of Prohibition in 1933, jazz was brought out of the speakeasy. There was room to expand. The Depression was fading out as far as middle-class America was concerned, and a vociferous market sprang up among the college kids.

The "sweet" dance bands succeeded in building themselves up to nine men and a violinist without much trouble. They used stock arrangements that offered no creative problems. With little improvising and less rhythm, these orchestras (referred to as "mickey-mouse" bands by jazzmen) cheerfully churned out dance music that was melodious and did not interfere with the conversations of the patrons.

The big, sweet dance band was a profitable business. Where was the big, swinging dance band? As early as 1923, Fletcher Henderson had a band of ten musicians and ran head-on into the problem of making them play together as a team. With the aid of arrangers such as Don Redman, he gradually solved the problem. By 1926, Henderson led a truly swinging band of eleven jazzmen—a fact that can be documented by listening

* From Marshall Stearns's *The Story of Jazz* (New York, Oxford University Press, Inc., 1956).

344

to "The Stampede" (Col. 654). The band played regularly at the Roseland Ballroom on Broadway, where it became something of a legend among a few white musicians. White jazzmen in the Twenties marveled at the fire and guts of the Henderson band and copied what they could, but they considered much of the music clumsy and crude. The band, they said quite sincerely, played out of tune and the individual musicians were always hitting "clinkers" or wrong notes.

By European standards the white jazzmen were right. But the ears of most musicians are better educated today. What sounded rough and out-of-tune then sounds relaxed and swinging now. The jazzman's notion of the liberties that may be taken with the perfect pitch of European music has been steadily broadening toward a predictable goal—the freedom of the street cry and the field holler. Jazz that once sounded tortured has a habit of soon sounding tidy. Yet, in 1939, Benny Goodman still spoke of "digging" the music out of a Henderson arrangement. This attitude was both typical and honest. A few years before, Isham Jones had enthusiastically purchased Don Redman's arrangement of "Chant of the Weed," only to discover that his band couldn't play it.

Fletcher Henderson and his big band were not alone. Before the Twenties were over, Negro bands led by Chick Webb, Earl Hines, Cecil Scott, William McKinney, Charlie Johnson, Luis Russell and, of course, Duke Ellington were all playing a style in which the whole band swung together. And before 1935, when Goodman arrived, these bands were joined by Cab Calloway, Jimmie Lunceford, Teddy Hill, Les Hite, Andy Kirk, Don Redman and especially, Bennie Moten. This music was swinging, relaxed, powerful, but for the most part unheard.

The distinction between these colored bands and the Goodman band which started the swing craze is indicated by Goodman's own comment:

. . . that's why I am such a bug on accuracy in performance, about playing in tune, and with just the proper note values . . . in the written parts, I wanted it to sound as exact as the band possibly could make it.

Goodman stressed precision and the accurate pitch essential to European harmony, and worked unceasingly toward that goal.

There were at least two pioneering white bands preceding Goodman: The Dorsey Brothers and the Casa Loma band.

Jimmy and Tommy Dorsey had been making records under their own names with a variety of musicians as early as 1928. By 1934, they had a fairly stable band of their own with twelve musicians—two trumpets, three trombones, three saxes, and four rhythm. This is one saxophone short of the standard swing instrumentation. "We were trying to hit somewhere between Hal Kemp and the Casa Loma band," Tommy Dorsey once told me. Unfortunately, the arrangements now sound heavy and cluttered and the rhythm was almost of the "shuffle" variety.

The Casa Loma band from Detroit was a different story. With the same instrumentation as the Dorsey Brothers, but without the star soloists, the Casa Loma band adopted the arranged "riff" almost too wholeheartedly. With the skill and foresight of such arrangers as Southern-born-and-bred Gene Gifford, the band learned to read harmonized solos and play riffs, the brass and reed sections calling and responding to each other in a variety of ways. What is more, they learned to roll along together, generating considerable swing as a whole. (In the early Thirties, they recorded, first "White Jazz," then "Black Jazz," and Decca issued albums with the same titles, but not even the jazzmen saw anything unusual about it.) The Goldkette band and the Casa Loma band came from Detroit and played the same arrangements. "The Casa Loma band could swing more," Redman once told me, "perhaps because they were a great team without so many highly paid and temperamental stars."

How did the whole Casa Loma band learn to swing, using the call-and-response pattern between the sections? They must have had a collective ear that was relatively undisturbed by the so-called "crudities" in the music of the Fletcher Henderson band and others. Above all, their arranger, Gene Gifford, was no stranger to the blues and gospel singing of the Southwest, which he toured in his teens with the Bob Foster and Lloyd Williams bands. In this territory, the call-and-response pattern was standard for practically all music, and the swing formula for big bands was no novelty. In 1932, moreover, they could have heard the first outstanding recordings of a big, swinging band with the "five brass, four saxes, and four rhythm" that Benny Goodman later helped to standardize. These records were issued on Victor's popular series and stocked by record stores where white people traded: Bennie Moten's Kansas City band with Count Basie at the piano. And in the same year, this band played the Savoy Ballroom in New York and upset the jazz applecart. "The only time we were bothered," says Count Basie, "was when we played opposite a little guy named Chick Webb."

The Moten band raised the riff to a fine—and even improvised—art, while retaining the blazing solo work of top jazzmen, and frequently combined the best of both. The leaders of the brass and reed sections would invent a series of ascending riffs on the spur of the moment (i.e., a "head" arrangement) which the entire section would forthwith play.

346

The popularity of the Casa Loma band among the Eastern colleges was outstanding as early as 1931. And the Casa Loma band was Benny Goodman's model. Speaking of his booking agent and friend, Willard Alexander, who had just graduated from an Eastern college, Goodman writes:

Since the Casa Loma was so popular with the college kids, it was tough trying to sell a sweet band against them, and he had the idea of building up some young band that would go into the same field, playing the kind of music that the youngsters liked.

In 1936, the Goodman band took the place of the Casa Loma band on the well-paid "Camel Caravan" radio show.

In 1930 the average small-town white boy (especially on the East Coast) who loved jazz heard only the Casa Loma band. Virtually alone, they played swinging jazz—mixed with a large amount of engaging sweet music such as "Smoke Rings" and "In the Still of the Night"—on phonograph records, in ballrooms, and on the air. As the first big white band to swing, they had an enormous influence in the East, where it counted heavily at that time.

While the Casa Loma band was building up its college following, Goodman made a living playing club dates (one-night local engagements) and radio programs in the studios with big commercial orchestras led by B. A. Rolfe, Rubinoff, Al Goodman, or Johnny Green. Goodman had learned how to read music, swiftly and well, which meant more jobs. This did not endear him to his colleagues from Chicago who were inclined to sneer— and with some reason, considering the attitude of symphony men—at people who could read music. ("I can read them notes," cried Wingy Manone indignantly, "I just can't separate 'em—five flats look like a bunch of grapes to me.")

In 1933, Goodman met the resourceful critic, John Hammond. On a trip to England, Hammond had sold the idea of special hot-jazz recordings to a vice-president of the English Gramophone Company. Hammond promised to supervise the recordings himself and to feature the playing of Benny Goodman. At the time Hammond hadn't met Goodman, but he soon did and convinced him, too. What musicians should they hire? Hammond held out for Gene Krupa and Jack Teagarden, while insisting that a drummer who had played with Meyer Davis be dropped. Goodman insisted upon a heavy Arthur Schutt arrangement. They had to use a "society" tenor saxophonist because he was the local contractor who got the musicians together according to union regulations.

In those days, if a musician wanted to record a popular tune, the music publishers insisted that he use a "stock" arrangement, which would make the melody recognizable—and uninspired—wherever it was heard. He might be permitted to record a tune of his own, played hot if he signed away the rights to the recording supervisor. Pressure was sometimes exerted to make him play in a "corny," or old-fashioned, style which would be sure to sell. Goodman recorded "Shirt Tail Stomp" (Brun. 3975), for example, in a hillbilly style at the urging of record-company executives. When it was issued in 1928, Ted Lewis, whom Goodman burlesques on the record, liked it enough to offer him a job. The job helped pull Goodman though the Depression.

Hammond had insisted on special arrangements, however, and Goodman's first record for the English Gramophone Company—"I Got a Right to Sing the Blues" and "Ain'tcha Glad"—was a notable success in England. When the American record executives woke up and decided to issue it in the United States, only Hammond's violent objections kept them from coupling each side with a commercial number by Clyde McCoy or Harry Reser "to insure the recording's success." Goodman went on to make a series of recordings for Columbia at a new low of $100 a side, employing such musicians as Teddy Wilson and Coleman Hawkins and such singers as Billie Holiday, Jack Teagarden and Mildred Bailey.

As the series progressed, Goodman began to appreciate and employ first-rate Negro musicians. On this point, he is quite frank about the importance of Hammond's influence:

It was during these months, around the end of 1933 and the beginning of 1934, that I first began to make records with colored musicians. For this the responsibility must be given almost entirely to John Hammond, who really put me back in touch with the kind of music they could play . . . It just happened that in working along as I had during those seven or eight years, I had gotten out of touch with them. . . .

Later on, Benny Goodman broke the precedent against bands of mixed color—not without some difficulty—by employing Teddy Wilson at the Hotel Congress in Chicago.

By 1934, Goodman had his own orchestra and a job which paid less than scale at Billy Rose's Music Hall. An air-shot over WMCA, however, made new friends. Three months later "the mob found a cheaper band." Then came the big break. The National Biscuit Company was ready to launch its new Ritz cracker, and an advertising firm sold them the idea of a "Let's Dance" radio program with three bands: Xavier Cugat playing rhumbas, Kel Murray playing sweet dance music, and Benny Goodman playing a little more rhythmic jazz. The three bands alternated from 11 to 2 A.M. every Saturday night, and the program was carried by fifty-three stations from coast to coast.

The rumor of "kick-backs" still survives, but the biscuit company financed eight new arrangements of Goodman's choosing during the first thirteen weeks. His choice is revealing. With the constant prodding of Hammond, Goodman hired better hot-jazz men and went to Fletcher Henderson for his new arrangements. At this stage in the development of swing music, we can pinpoint certain musical relationships. Henderson sold Goodman arrangements that Henderson had been using for three to five years. It was Goodman's precise style of playing the arrangements that hit the great American public as something new and exciting.

The "Let's Dance" radio show, together with a series of recordings, began to build up a small but devoted following. "I had to do what I thought I was best at," says Goodman, "and just then it was having a hot band." From week to week, the band sounded better over the radio (at that, only every third number was played "hot"). But the general public was as yet untouched. MCA, the Music Corporation of America, persuaded by a young collegian in their employ, Willard Alexander, decided to book the Goodman band, much to the annoyance of most of the people at the agency. At the time MCA booked only sweet bands. They put Goodman into the Hotel Roosevelt in New York City, the home of Guy Lombardo. "Every time I looked around, on the night we opened," says Goodman, "one of the waiters or the captain would be motioning to us not to play so loud." The band was not a success.

In desperation, Alexander booked Goodman for a series of one-nighters, with a month stopover in Denver, to the West Coast where there seemed to be a little interest. The band worked its way out, playing in Pittsburgh, Columbus, Toledo, Lakeside (Michigan), Milwaukee, and then Denver— where Kay Kyser was pulling them in. The spot was called Elitch's Gardens and the owner phoned MCA at once, announcing that "the music was lousy and the leader was a pain in the neck," to quote Goodman himself. And business was terrible. By switching to stock arrangements, the band held the job but morale hit a new low.

The band's morale was still low after playing Salt Lake City and San Francisco. They recalled trumpeter Wingy Manone's observation: "Man, good jazz just can't make it over them tall Rockies." When they arrived at the Palomar Ballroom in Los Angeles, their new location for a month or so, the band became downright frightened. The ballroom had an enormous dance floor, plus a huge section with tables where food and liquor were noisily served. And they charged admission. For the first hour, the band played the sweeter tunes with the softer arrangements. Goodman was desperate:

If we had to flop, at least I'd do it in my own way, playing the kind of music I wanted to. For all I knew this might be our last night together, and we might as well have a good time of it while we had the chance.

I called out some of our big Fletcher arrangements for the next set, and the boys seemed to get the idea. From the moment I kicked them off, they dug in with some of the best playing I'd heard since we left New York. . . .

The first big roar from the crowd was one of the sweetest sounds I ever heard in my life. . . .

The Swing Era was born on the night of August 21, 1935.

The immediate reason for the sudden success of the Goodman band, according to Benny himself, is that "it was a dancing audience—that's why they went for it." Again, Goodman's phonograph records preceded the band's success, and disc jockeys had been playing some of the best of them. Further, the "Let's Dance" program hit Los Angeles between the hours of 7 and 11 P.M.—the time of maximum listening and the time when the teen-agers could hear it. They were still dancing the Lindy, and Goodman's music was just right for it. In a matter of months, the jitterbugs and bobby-soxers were dancing the Big Apple and the Shag—up and down the aisles of theaters, too—while the Goodman band played on. Above all, they were the first band to give the current hits of Tin-Pan Alley, such as "Goody Goody," for example, a jazz treatment which sold enormously.

If Benny Goodman became the "King of Swing" in 1935, reaping all the publicity and profits, the man behind the throne was Count Basie. For it was the Basie band that gave depth and momentum to the whole Swing Era while planting the seeds that later gave birth to bop and the "cool" school of jazz. In 1935, after the death of Bennie Moten, Bill Basie gradually built up his own band. He and his band were playing the Reno Club in Kansas City in 1936, when John Hammond heard them over experimental station W9XBY and alerted Benny Goodman and Willard Alexander of MCA.

The Basie band was scuffling. "It was a cracker town but a happy time," Basie recalls. At the Reno Club, imported Scotch was fifteen cents a shot, domestic ten cents, and a hot-dog stand was located next to the bar. "We played from nine o'clock in the evening to five or six the next morning, including the floor shows," says Basie, "and the boys in the band got eighteen dollars a week and I got twenty-one." When Buck Clayton joined on trumpet, the boys sacrificed twenty-five cents apiece and Clayton got two dollars a night. Down the street at the Sunset Club, boogie-woogie pianist Pete Johnson and blues-shouter Joe Turner (who made a great hit with rock and roll in 1954), were working for less. Actually, things weren't as bad as they seemed, because prices were low and tips from gangsters high.

MCA booked Basie for a trial run at the Grand Terrace Ballroom in Chicago. Nothing much happened. Then the band was brought to the Famous Door on New York's Fifty-second Street. The word got around fast. On the way to New York, Basie augmented his band from nine to fifteen men:

—I wanted my fifteen-piece band to work together just like those nine pieces did. I wanted fifteen men to think and play the same way. I wanted those four trumpets and three trombones to bite with real guts. BUT I wanted that bite to be just as tasty and subtle as if it were the three brass . . . I said that the minute the brass got out of hand and blared and screeched . . . there'd be some changes made.

The Famous Door was about the size of a large closet and, once inside, patrons found themselves sitting under the guns. When the band started to play, some listeners felt as if they were inside a loudspeaker-enclosure with the volume up. You either loved it or hated it—there was no middle ground—but to New York musicians the power and swing of the Basie band was a revelation.

Aided by the ground-breaking success of Benny Goodman and the astute managing of Willard Alexander, the Basie band with its more relaxed and powerful beat became an immediate and lasting success. "When we first came to New York we tried to experiment," drummer Jo Jones recalls, "so after a week of experimenting we found out that there was nothing old hat about what we had been doing." In a short time, Basie was influencing Goodman deeply. Goodman adopted Basie's numbers, such as "One O'Clock Jump" (which was the first Goodman recording to sell over a million), and then began to use Basie and some of his musicians on recordings. Fortunately, Basie had recorded his own version of "One O'Clock Jump" (in part, a riff taken from Redman's arrangement of "Six or Seven Times") about seven months earlier and, although it did not sell nearly as well, the original had wide distribution and musicians could hear and appreciate it.

The very birthplaces of the musicians associated with Basie made a roll call of the Southwest: Herschel Evans, Denton, Texas; Jimmy Rushing, Oklahoma City, Oklahoma; Buck Clayton, Parsons, Kansas; Jack Washington, Kansas City, Kansas; Oran "Hot Lips" Page, Dallas, Texas; Don

Byas, Muskogee, Oklahoma; Joe Keyes, Houston, Texas; Joe Turner, Kansas City, Missouri; Walter Page, Gallatin, Missouri; Eddie Durham, San Marcos, Texas; and Lester Young, Woodville, Mississippi.

The Basie band accomplished a revolution in jazz that we are still trying to estimate. Specfically, the Basie piano style, with its frequent openings for the bass fiddle, led to the de-emphasis of the left hand in modern jazz piano. The style of drummer Jo Jones, who rode the high-hat cymbal, left its mark on bop drummers. And the relaxed style of tenor saxophonist Lester Young helped to produce the "cool" school of jazz. A younger saxophonist, Dexter Gordon, says that he stopped playing after he heard Lester Young. "It was too much . . . I threw my horn away and didn't touch it for two years." Benny Goodman reacted differently: "This is the first time," he told John Hammond, "that I've ever heard a tenor sax played the way it should be and not overblown." (He swapped his clarinet for Young's tenor saxophone and, they say, sounded like Young for a whole evening.) Above all, the Basie band developed the use of the "head riff" (the improvised unison phrase, tossed back and forth by brass and reed sections) to the level of fine art. On a less evident but more important level than the Goodman band, the band of Count Basie underwrote the Swing Era. Goodman's "King Porter Stomp" was recorded in 1935, Bob Crosby's "Dixieland Shuffle" in 1936, Tommy Dorsey's "Marie" in 1937, Artie Shaw's "Begin the Beguine" in 1938, and Glenn Miller's "In the Mood" in 1939. (The importance of the disc jockey becomes evident.) The musical sources for many of these swing bands were documented, in part, by another band under the leadership of Charlie Barnet. He made a recording with "The Duke's Idea" on one side and "The Count's Idea" on the other (Bluebird 10453), paying homage to Duke Ellington and Count Basie. For the next ten years, swing music made big money and bandleaders became as popular—and as unpredictable—as movie stars.

LISTENING TO B.G.

In the fall of 1936, Otis Ferguson, an editor of *The New Republic,* had visited the Café Rouge, as it was then known, at the old Hotel Pennsylvania in New York City to listen to the Benny Goodman band. His description of the intense feelings one brought to listening to the good jazz of the day is inspired and lyrical but true.

OTIS FERGUSON

THE SPIRIT OF JAZZ*

Swing in, swing out, the band is up again and drawing the people out like the sun in the fable. With Krupa, Reuss (guitar) and the inspired quiet Stacey (piano) laying down a thick rhythmic base, it plays on through whatever songs are the demand of the day, making most of them sound like something. This is an organization in the line of the great jazz bands—Jean Goldkette, Fletcher Henderson, McKinney, Cotton Pickers, Ellington, Kirk, *et al.*—a little lighter than some of these but more beautifully rehearsed and economical, and with cleaner edges. The reed section, scored as such, is more prominent than in older hot bands, giving a fuller lyric quality; but the section (five men counting Goodman) has a hard skeleton of attack and swing that supports any relative lightness of brass. The band as a whole gets its lift from the rhythm men and the soloists as they take off; it is built from the ground rather than tailored.

The quartet, composed of Goodman, Gene Krupa, Teddy Wilson and Lionel Hampton, plays every night—clarinet, piano, vibraphone, drums—and they make music you would not believe. No arrangements, not a false note, one finishing his solo and dropping into background support, then the other, all adding inspiration until with some number like "Stomping at the Savoy" they get going too strong to quit—four choruses, someone starts up another, six, eight, and still someone starts—no two notes the same and no one note off the chord, the more they relax in the excitement

* From *The New Republic,* Dec. 30, 1936.

353

of it the more a natural genius in preselection becomes evident and the more indeed the melodic line becomes rigorously pure. This is really composition on the spot, with the spirit of jazz strongly over all of them but the iron laws of harmony and rhythm never lost sight of; and it is a collective thing, the most beautiful example of men working together to be seen in public today.

It isn't merely hell-for-leather either. Gene Krupa, a handsome madman over his drums, makes the rhythmic force and impetus of it visual, for his face and whole body are sensitive to each strong beat of the ensemble; and Hampton does somewhat the same for the line of melody, hanging solicitous over the vibraphone plates and exhorting them (Hmmm, Oh, Oh yah, Oh dear *hmmm*). But the depth of tone and feeling is mainly invisible, for they might play their number "Exactly Like You" enough to make people cry and there would be nothing of it seen except perhaps in the lines of feeling on Benny Goodman's face, the affable smile dropped as he follows the Wilson solo flight, eyes half-closed behind his glasses. There was a special feeling among them the first morning they recorded this piece, the ghost of the blues perhaps; and when the clarinet takes up you will hear the phrases fall as clear as rain, with a sustained glow of personal essence that starts where command of the instrument (the tension of mouth, delicate fingering, etc.) leaves off. Then Hampton sings a chorus, his vibrant hoarse voice and relaxed emphasis so appropriate to the general color; and when they take up again the instruments blend so perfectly as to be indistinguishable, singing in unison with a sweet breadth of tone that goes beyond the present place and time to some obscure source of feeling and native belief. The term swing—no more definable in words than the term poetry—is defined at its best in this piece, where the actual beats are lost sight of in the main effect, so that the inexorable and brute lift of the time signature as carried in Krupa's great drum seems fused in the harmony and melodic line of the song. And you may say of the excitement this thing starts in the blood only that these four men are quite simple and wonderful together, that they are truly swinging.

The quartet is a beautiful thing all through, really a labor of creative love, but it cannot last forever and as the band starts again you realize that even in jazz there are several kinds of musical appreciation. For if they'll agree to put on the "Bugle Call Rag" before the end of the evening I'll be willing to say there's nothing finer. There is some hidden lift to this old band standby, with its twenty quaint notes from the "Assembly" call dropping the barrier to a straight-out progression of simple chords—and they are off, riding it with collective assurance and fine spirit, the men in their sections, the sections balancing, the soloists dropping back with care for the total effect. The guests are presently banked in a half-moon around the stand, unable to be still through it or move away either; and as it builds to the final solid chords, Krupa becoming a man of subtle thunder and Benny lacing in phrases, the air is full of brass and of rhythms you can almost lean on. The music seems more than audible, rising and coming forward from the stand in banks of colors and shifting masses—not only the clangor in the ears but a visual picture of the intricate fitted spans, the breathless height and spring of a steel-bridge structure. And if you leave at the end, before the "Good-Bye" signature, you will seem to hear this great rattling march of the hobos through the taxis, lights and people, ringing under the low sky over Manhattan as if it were a strange high thing after all (which it is) and as if it came from the American ground under these buildings, roads and motorcars (which it did). And if you leave the band and quartet and piano of the Goodman show and still are no more than slightly amused, you may be sure that in the smug absence of your attention a native true spirit of music has been and gone, leaving a message for your grandchildren to study through their patient glasses.

LET'S DANCE

THERE WERE many other big bands, and they were eager to play hotel engagements—if the hotel had a direct wire for broadcasting over a radio station. Remember listening late at night to the bands at the Coconut Grove in Hollywood, the Glen Island Casino in Westchester, the College Inn at the Hotel Sherman in Chicago, or the dance music at the huge ballrooms in Chicago, the Trianon and Aragon?

A band's reputation could be made almost overnight by the jukebox, where a successful record sometimes was worth six solid months of radio exposure. Jukebox hit records helped to make the reputations of such bands as Artie Shaw's, Larry Clinton's, Tommy Dorsey's, and even Ozzie Nelson's.

In the early Thirties people had very little to celebrate; they felt vulnerable and, as much as anything, wanted to be soothed. One could take a date to the movies, or just stay home of an evening and dance to radio music, but there came a time when you wanted to get out and be with others. The big cities provided sporting events and the theater (if the prices weren't too steep for the pocketbook), but not the smaller communities. The big social events were apt to be the dances, especially if you were of high-school or college age. Until the jukebox took over later in the decade, a few live musicians were necessary to provide the music. All over the country, in the small towns, you might hear "Are you going to the dance?" and "Who're you taking?" in anticipation of the coming weekends and holidays.

And in the summer there were dances at the amusement parks, dance halls and roadhouses, on lakes, near beaches, with big dance floors that could hold hundreds of couples. It was not that these places did not exist in the Twenties (there are comparatively few today) but then there were more things to do and see, and there was more money for traveling.

A stag line was permissible, and often there was a dance program card on which to note the exchanges of partners. High-school gyms, town halls and such often doubled as dance floors, and frequently a dance would be scheduled as an afterpiece to a basketball game; the people were already there, and gas for the car didn't come cheap.

It seemed, too, that almost everybody attended the dances. More men danced, unconcerned with poor technique, and in the early years of the decade there were few obstreperous new dances to shame "the old folks" off the dance floor. When "jitterbugging" arrived with the Big Apple, Shag and Lindy Hop, later in the decade, it was every man for himself. By then, I suppose, we were beginning to believe the Depression was on its way out for most of us; we felt a sense of release, and welcomed the big bands and the new dances with an excitement and exuberance unmatched in the Twenties and the later decades. Wherever there was a patch of dance floor and a jukebox, in taverns, restaurants, roadhouses and even soda joints, young people took time to listen and dance to the latest records by Goodman, Glen Gray, Artie Shaw and others. If you couldn't get a date with your favorite girl, you settled for the fourth favorite so long as she liked to dance.

And if you wanted to learn the latest step in those days, you didn't go to Arthur Murray's; if you were lucky enough to be in New York City, you visited the temple of swing, the Savoy, up in Harlem.

OTIS FERGUSON

BREAKFAST DANCE, IN HARLEM*

THE PLACE is uptown, up the one and only Lenox Avenue, and you can dance from nine o'clock Saturday evening right through to eight o'clock Sunday morning. The breakfast dance, and swing it, men. On most nights, even most Saturday nights, there are two bands and the show is over at two or three. But tonight, one night out of every few weeks, breakfast is the limit, there are four bands in all and in short they will be able to serve it up as long as you can take it. If not longer.

It is a respectable place too. No barrelhouse, no basement creep-joint. A ballroom, in fact. Inside, up the wide flight of stairs after you have put up your seventy-five cents, the manager is nice enough and the people are nice enough, and there is no trouble. The long crowded bar at one end of the table space sells only beer (ten cents) and California wine (twenty cents a glass, out of gallon jugs). Some bring their own bottles of hard, but these can weave into the Gents, all in good time, and take care of whatever gets too much for them. There are two Gents, side by side. No trouble.

It is twelve o'clock and you can still get on the floor. The rain. The manager is very sad that people can still get on his floor. There should be more of a jam than on Ladies' Nights; but it drizzles badly and there is not more of a jam.

The hall must be seventy-five yards long by twenty-five wide, the ceiling and lights are low. In the few seconds between numbers, or in the minute when one band takes over from another, the place a rich babble, with "You saids" and "How come womans" and "Ain't that it thoughs." And

* From *The New Republic*, Feb. 12, 1936.

when the band gets pretty well into it, the whole enclosure, with all its people, beats like a drum and rises in steady time, like a ground swell.

Impossible to see everything at once. The bands; the people drinking, or half-asleep at tables over their beer, or promoting their private bit of business slapstick, romance; the musicians off duty, making horseplay or eating part of their supper with a sort of genial and quiet boisterousness.

"Doggone," says the one they call Choo, sitting like a four-poster, one of the first artists in this country on the tenor saxophone, "doggone, ain't no meat here *at* all. What that man mean, dishing me out this for charmaine?" Choo says, shoveling it in. And the dance floor is a hopeless intricate mass of flying ankles, swirls, stomps—really beautiful dancing. As dancing, superb. Everybody immensely noisy, sweating, full of spirits. Here today and here tomorrow too.

It is a strange sort of atmosphere. You cannot see everything at once but you can feel everything at once, a sort of unifying outflow of energy, you can almost see it burn. Its focal point is around the stand of rough and well-splintered wood, where the lights are and the music stands, and the bass drum spiked to the floor and the stringbass fixed in a socket and the big pianos with the keyboards worn like flights of old wooden stairs.

The single stand, for the two bands, is about sixty feet long, and narrow, down one side of the hall. It is the center of most of the light, but still dim enough. The wall behind it is painted into an extravagant blue background, and by means of trick spotlights thin clouds seem to be drawn across it perpetually, giving the effect of motion and smoke, and the bands play under that, dominating the hall and bearing down on it, inexorable, all steam and iron, like freight trains.

On the floor and at the tables and along the bar there are all the people, hundreds of them (fifteen-sixteen hundred on a capacity night maybe); and off toward one corner there is a row of hostesses, two bits for three dances; and there are rose-colored lights let into the ceiling and things going on everywhere. But the real life of the hall is over here on the stand, where the boys are lined up in two rows, stomping away and sweating their brass horns till the floor shakes, where the great moon of the sousaphone bell shines down on the dancers and the beat of guitar-piano-stringbass-drum nails all this lavish and terrific energy down to the simple restraints of a time signature. And when Teddy Hill's men begin swinging the last choruses of the specialty number "Christopher Colombo," with those driving brass figures and the reed section going down to give it body, the dancers forget dancing and flock around the stand ten deep, to register the time merely with their bones and muscles, standing there in one place with their heads back and letting it flow over them like water—invitation (and the waltz be damned) to blow the man down. The floor shakes and the place is a dynamo room, with the smoky air pushing up in steady waves, and swing it, men, get off, beat it out and in a word play that thing. It's a music deaf men could hear.

The spirit belongs as much to the place as to any particular music makers. Because this hall has something to it. Shadows maybe. The rafters have echoes of Fletcher Henderson's great swing band, and of Louis (the Reverend Satchelmouth) Armstrong, roaring through his fantastic horn, and of Mr. Ellington, the Duke, the Great Dusky, and of Cab Calloway, leading crazy man, who got his start here, of McKinney's Cotton Pickers and the Chocolate Dandies—and who not. Name a band, the manager says, you just go ahead name a band which I can tell you personally that band played here, including Paul Whiteman. There is something in the air here, a demand to be given something on the part of the people, that shapes matters, so that when a group needs to get really together and tightened up, this is where it books in.

But the spirit of all this is not just an urge to flash-bang-blare and shiver the windows. There are shrewdness and loving care going into this, and many subtleties. Not the usual fuss and gargle about art and the artist's line on war'n'fascism. Just so many of the boys apparently playing a job, playing a date, making a record for Victor, a tune for the networks or the dancers—talking about it among themselves with a peculiar reserve and modest dignity. Some of them, the best of them, burn themselves up to keep it strong and unspoiled, finely marked with the obscure beauty of their invention. The best of them would not be Lombardos, Duchins, Vallees, Reismans, even if they had the showmanship, brute luck and gall to do it. Here somehow a good tenor man can make a tone pattern that will have a dancing strength and freshness, the only one of its kind because it is made directly from his own command of an instrument, his own exuberance and sadness. Anything outside of this stern, continually inventive tradition (also to be found, shall we say, in Bach) and above all anything without this drive peculiar to the form, may be effective, tricky, may pay well. But it will be fake. It will lack the element of creation, and be fake. "Some of these tenor men," Choo says, off the stand again, "I see they go copying off Hawkins and them. Shuck. A man never get playing it really good till he putten something into it, you think? A man don't watch out, all he putten in is spit. I don't know, shuck. I work really hard trying to blow it out clean, like I can be proud of it, but a man playing around every night—shuck, I don't know . . ."

Having expressed it without saying it, or anything really, Choo breaks off in embarrassment. "Doggone this man," he says, "about this here no-good charmaine. If I eaten any meat here tonight I'll—"

But this part of it does not bother you at the time. It is three, four, five o'clock and nobody seems to know it. More people are asleep at the tables, fewer people are on the floor; but otherwise there is this same hot stuffy genial air, this same squandering of energy under the dim lights. Teddy Hill's boys have hung around a while, their spot having been taken over for the night, and dispersed in pairs and groups gradually, after observing the other man's music. And the dominant spirit of rhythm in the place is now Chick Webb, the old-timer, the little hunchback who sits bolstered up before his set of very elegant white traps, beating at them with a fierce tremendous love of the thing that sends a whole band, and gives the beat to the floor, which still shakes.

But this is Harlem. Down the stairs and outside, where the music is only a throb in the air, it is morning and already light enough to see that this is Harlem, a community. There are only a few people about—several coming out of the hall, carousing off to breakfast from the breakfast dance, several who have not been in the hall.

"Say Mac, how about a cigarette now," one of these latter says to me, stepping up as though he'd buy up the block in another minute, if the mood took him. "Guess I'd light up now, if you got a spare." He hasn't any matches either. "Well how is it up there?" he says. "Pretty crowded up there? Can't get on the damn floor I bet."

"It's pretty good—plenty of room though," I say.

"Pretty crowded though, ain't it? I figured you couldn't get on the floor, you know."

"Well, there's some there but there's plenty of room."

"Is that so? I figured it would be too crowded. . . ."

"Well say now," he says. He has made the touch for a smoke with no trouble. "You wouldn't be having a dime now, extra, I suppose? Just so's I can—well say Mac, thank *you*—so's I can get me some coffee. Funny about that. I figured it'd be too crowded up there, a guy couldn't get on the floor, you know?"

His line by now is obvious. The loud front, the wistfulness and poor pride behind it, the place not to his classy liking. He finishes the touch for the dime and waves me on my way regally. I'm to come look him up some time. Knows everybody up there. Sure. Come up some night, just mention his name. Fix me up with some nice girls too, sure.

The cuffs of his frayed cheap trousers walk jauntily off up the Avenue past rubbish and newspapers, dusty and rustling in the early morning, and off down a sidestreet of gray poor doorways, empty stores, pinched tenements. And it is not possible now to overlook where a breakfast dance ends and where it came from—the rags and mean tatters of Harlem, an American community bled dry. The thump of Chick Webb's drum is fainter in the open air, but to listen to the fine terrific beat of jazz from here is to recognize all at once another element, always present in the music but usually below its surface, most vivid in the blues (I woke up this mornin', I had to pawn my shoes). There is a gay abandon and all that, up the one and only Lenox Avenue; there are lights and people carrying on and what not. To be sure. And that is about the half of it. It is out of the lives of the people here that the music comes, and so if you will stand here you may suddenly feel it, the whole of it with undertones and overtones, its abandon and bitter sorrow.

THAT LUSH LIFE IN CELLULOID

LOTS OF US enjoyed our leisure at the movies. The experience of going was like an insidious candy we could never get quite enough of; the visit to the dark theater was an escape from the drab realities of Depression living, and we were entranced by the never-ending variety of stories. Hollywood, like Scheherazade in *The Thousand and One Nights*, supplied more the next night, and the next night after that.

Soon the distributors took away the comedies and short subjects, which many of us relished not only for the laughs but also for the anticipation they enabled us to feel before the big show. In their place we were given the double feature, which some of us enjoyed because it kept us in the theater twice as long. After a while we perceived that the double feature was also a device for dumping second-rate films on the public. But we still went—"hooked" by the habit—and the distributor, for his sins, was soon forced to accept the block-booking technique; to get the A picture, he had to accept a quota of B, C and Z products.

Three out of five people disliked the double feature; but a minority, it seems, was strong enough to force the program on the rest of us. While there may have been those who refused to have their hours raped by Hollywood fantasies, it was years before the rest of us got over the craving.

By the end of the decade there were between 52 million and 55 million attending the movies every week of the year. To the girl in the glass-enclosed cage (she started the gentle separation from reality) we handed over our hard-earned money—averaging, annually, five dollars a person or twenty-five dollars a family for the total population of the country (big money in those days, remember). There were more than 15,000 theaters to choose from, more movie houses than banks, twice as many as hotels and three times as many as department stores. If you didn't like the product, you must have been un-American—because the picture industry had a capital investment in the United States of two billion dollars.

Business looked good, right? as Mort Sahl would say today. Back in 1933, the theater owners thought it should be better. So they invented Bank Night and Dish Night, and Bingo, Keeno, Screeno and such games to go along with "our daily double." (Patrons of today, please note, when you complain about the popcorn and candy wrappers under foot.)

Not everyone swallowed Hollywood whole; some took offense. Ruth Suckow, writing in *Harper's* Magazine, objected to the Galatea machine which turned out the gods and goddesses:

"It would seem at times that this nation, losing the strong Puritan orthodoxy it brought to the new continent, yet still crude and young in the mass, has turned to the worship of those picture gods, real and yet unreal, common as life and yet

362

larger than life, known in minuter detail than next-door neighbors and yet shiningly remote, because they have come to represent certain national ideals reduced to the lowest common denominator. For that is what the screen does—it reduces while it magnifies, grinds down what it exalts into the typical.

"Motion pictures constitute the only art in which the players are actually able to see themselves. Nearly everybody prefers a flattering photograph." * After analyses of the stars of the day—Garbo, Gable, et cetera—she decided that "in spite of the skill that goes into the making of American motion pictures, they form an unconscious social document rather than an art." *

It is doubtful that, even though Miss Suckow was right about most of the product, anyone in Hollywood was one whit concerned; and anyway everyone was too busy making pictures for the double bills. Or making news—on the forty-second day of the bombardment of London, the London *Mirror* cabled its Hollywood correspondent for 280 words concerning Ann Sheridan's contract dispute with Warner's.

"No other community in America," Leo Rosten has said, "is reported upon each day so intensely, so insistently, and with such a deplorable premium on triviality.

. . . The sheer magnitude of this adoration invites awe. Each day, millions of men, women and children sit in the windowless temples of the screen to commune with their vicarious friends and lovers. Each night they read the newspaper pages (or the screen magazines) devoted to the stars and all their petty histories. Is it any wonder that one of the great appeals to the individual club member is 'Say, I could do that!'—no other industry presents so simple an invitation to the ego.

"It's one of the very few fields of enterprise left in America in which youth is promised high rewards, in which youth is, indeed, an advantage rather than a burden . . . and in which inexperience is of little account." The would-be movie star "needs no capital, no training, no skill." †

The industry flourished; in 1939 alone, Hollywood produced almost four hundred pictures. But did it produce anything that resembled art? Undoubtedly—Miss Suckow to the contrary—and if for no other reason than that a certain percentage derived from the nation's published fiction, was directed by brilliant men from the theater—and the motion picture world too—and that frequently excellent performances were given, even by some of those "gods and goddesses."

* "Hollywood Gods and Goddesses," *Harper's* Magazine, July 1936.
† Leo Rosten, *Hollywood* (New York, Harcourt, Brace, 1941).

ARTHUR KNIGHT

THE MOVIES*

THE SILENT FILM had created a world of persuasive reality despite the absence of voices and the verifying clangor of natural sound. Indeed, much of the art of the silent film lay in the invention of means to circumvent these artificial limitations. Then, suddenly, they were all removed, and the sounds of the real world became as much a part of the film as its sights. The public positively reveled in the new sensation, the opportunity to hear its favorite stars talking and singing, to hear the crack of a pistol, the roar of a motor or even the ring of a telephone. It was exactly like the first years of the movies all over again. Then, anything that moved was fascinating.

Many of the studio heads were quite willing to agree that talkies were simply a thing of the moment—but at the moment, they pointed out, it was the thing that the public wanted. Indeed, those producers who hesitated to bow to this obviously popular demand, preferring to hold off until the whole thing blew over, were soon out of business entirely. The public's enthusiasm for sound was so strong that attendance leaped from 60,00,000 paid admissions per week in 1927 to 110,000,000 in 1929. When the stock market crashed in the fall of 1929, the impetus provided by the introduction of sound proved strong enough to carry the industry safely through the first years of the Depression. By 1930 the silent film was a thing of the past, Charlie Chaplin's *City Lights* (1931) and the Flaherty-Murnau *Tabu* (1931) coming as last, lovely reminders of an art that was no more. By the start of the Thirties, in every film-producing nation the studios had converted to sound. It was to take them many a year, however, before they could regain the artistry and power of the best of the silent era.

In 1929, after little more than a year of talkies, *Variety* wryly reported, "Sound didn't do any more to the industry than turn it upside down, shake the entire bag of tricks from its pocket and advance Warner Brothers from the last place (among the film companies) to first in the league."

* Condensed from Arthur Knight's *The Liveliest Art* (New York, Macmillan, 1957).

The films had learned to talk, and talk was uppermost in everyone's mind. Script-writers who had trained themselves to think in terms of pictures gave way to playwrights who thought in terms of stage dialogue. Established directors were either replaced by directors from the New York stage or supplemented by special dialogue directors. Many a popular star—especially the European importees—suddenly found himself unemployed; while the Broadway stage was again swept clean to replace those actors whose foreign accents, faulty diction or bad voices the temperamental microphone rejected.

And then a new and imposing figure appeared in the studios, the sound expert. It was the sound expert who concealed the microphone in the vase of flowers on the boudoir table, who dictated where actors must stand in order to record properly, who decided where the camera must be placed in order to keep the microphone outside its field. He was the final arbiter on what could and what could not be done, and his word was law. The camera itself, now imprisoned within a soundproof booth, was robbed of all mobility. And the experts, concerned with nothing beyond the sound quality of the pictures they worked on, continually simplified their problems by insisting that scenes be played in corners, minimizing long shots for the more readily controllable close-up. In no time at all the techniques, the artistry that directors had acquired through years of silent films were cast aside and forgotten in the shadow of the microphone.

Sound gave the banks and the investment houses their first real hold upon the motion-picture industry. Every studio needed sound, and most of them also needed vast sums of new working capital to make the equipment purchases and studio alterations required to convert to sound. Both the equipment and the financing led ultimately to the same sources, to Western Electric, RCA and their affiliated banking houses. Soon their representatives were sitting on the boards of the motion-picture companies, making policy with—and sometimes in place of—the veteran showmen who had brought their studios from obscurity to world-wide prominence. They appointed the sound experts who dominated the studios through 1929 and 1930. These men knew only about acoustics and microphone characteristics. But because they had the backing of the people who were paying for it all, they often usurped the functions of both producer and director. As a result, a transition that would have been difficult in any case was made more difficult still. Producers whose main stock in trade was their knowledge of entertainment values suddenly found their hands tied. Directors who understood the necessity to keep the picture moving and alive found themselves arbitrarily overruled in favor of the microphone.

It is to the eternal credit of genuinely creative and courageous men like Ernst Lubitsch, Rouben Mamoulian, Lewis Milestone and King Vidor that they had the ingenuity and vitality to circumvent the experts and lift the new medium out of the rut of dully photographed plays and vaudeville routines into which it had fallen. They had no rules to go on, no precedents to quote. They had the opposition of the sound men to contend with, and the indisputable fact that at the box offices across the nation almost any film was making money as long as it talked. But these men sensed that talk alone was not enough, and that the public would soon tire of the novelty of sound for sound's sake and demand again to see a *movie*. It was their pioneer work that brought forth the techniques to make the movies move again.

Ernst Lubitsch, by 1929 the top director at Paramount, made the important discovery that a talking picture did not have to be *all* talking, nor did the sound track have to reproduce faithfully each sound on the set. In his first talkies, *The Love Parade* (1929) and *Monte Carlo* (1930), he included many passages that were shot without dialogue or any other synchronized sound. For these, he was able to bring the camera out of its soundproofed box and proceed in the old silent techniques, moving his camera freely, changing its position frequently. Music or effects were put in later. One of the high points of *The Love Parade* was a running gag with Maurice Chevalier telling a risqué joke to members of the court. Each time he approaches the tag line, his voice sinks to a confidential whisper, a door closes, or the camera leaps outside to view the effect of his story through a window. Audiences of 1929 were delighted to find a new element in the talkies—silence!

Lubitsch also knew how to use the sound camera to serious purpose. In *Broken Lullaby* (1932), his one dramatic film of this period, he emphasized its antiwar theme in many brilliantly conceived shots. The sights and sounds of an Armistice Day parade are glimpsed between the crutches of a one-legged soldier. Early in the film, while a minister is praying for peace, the camera in ironic counterpoint moves slowly down the center aisle of the cathedral, past row on row of kneeling officers, their spurs gleaming, their swords stiff by their sides. By shooting such sequences silent and adding the sound later, Lubitsch obtained not only greater freedom for his camera but the kind of control of the elements in his scene essential to artistic creation. The "Lubitsch touch," that sparkling combination of wit and irony already famous in the silent film, reached its fullest expression in his early talkies.

Meanwhile, King Vidor in his first talking picture, *Hallelujah!* (1929), explored the possibilities of the sound track to evoke mood and atmosphere. It was an all-Negro picture made, for the most part, in Memphis, Tennessee, and the swamps of Arkansas. The fact that the film was done largely on location, away from rigid studio supervision, gave Vidor an enviable amount of freedom for that time. Much of it he shot silent, later creating an impressionistic sound track for all but the direct dialogue passages. He showed that the source of a sound is less important than its quality, that sound can create an emotional aura about a scene quite independent of the words and faces of the actors. Lewis Milestone worked in much the same way in making his *All Quiet on the Western Front* (1930), photographing his scenes of troops on the march and in the trenches with a silent camera and adding in later the whine and crash of bombs, the clatter of small-arms fire and the shrieks and moans of the wounded and dying.

Postsynchronization became the first point of departure in the development of the new art.

The other was an improvement in the camera itself. During the first years of sound, the camera had been forced into a small soundproofed booth to keep the whir of its mechanism from reaching the sensitive, cranky microphone. During 1930, however, the cameras began to emerge from these boxes, enclosed now in soundproofed "blimps" which, while still cumbersome, permitted a far greater freedom of movement. It then became the director's problem to force the reluctant sound experts to give that new mobility full rein, to demand from them more flexible microphone setups. Before long, the stationary microphones were being replaced by mikes suspended on long booms that could be swung to follow the players anywhere.

Perhaps the first director to appreciate fully the implications of sound was the Frenchman René Clair. Originally opposed to the whole idea, he insisted on the predominant importance of the visual element, declaring that the sound film need not and should not be, to use his own term, "canned theater." He demonstrated to everyone's satisfaction that much of silent technique was still valid, that it was the image and not the word that kept the screen alive. Because René Clair had instinctively grasped this principle in his first three films, and turned them out with a flair and finish unmatched anywhere at the time, his pictures had a profound effect upon other directors. He had achieved what they were groping toward. He had brought back into films spontaneity, movement, rhythm.

Perhaps the leading director of dramatic films in this country to revolt against "canned theater" movies during the early years of sound was

Rouben Mamoulian—ironically, one of the many Broadway directors brought to the studios in 1929 specifically to make "canned theater." Despite his theater background, Mamoulian felt that the camera could and should move, appreciated the importance of the close-up for dramatic emphasis, fought against the prevalent notion that the source for every sound must be seen. For him, the camera was far more than a passive observer looking on while actors recited their lines—and the function of the director was more than merely helping the actors to say their lines better. He had to help the audience find what was dramatically significant in a scene, picking out what was important with his camera, making it seem fresh and illuminating through the imagination and inventiveness of his visuals.

By the time he made *Dr. Jekyll and Mr. Hyde* (1932), Mamoulian had full control of his new medium. From start to finish, it was a virtuoso work; almost every scene revealed the director's desire to break away from a literal use of the camera and a conventional use of sound. The entire first reel was shot in the first-person technique, the camera assuming the identity of Dr. Jekyll. From that position we see his hands as he plays the organ, the shadow of his head upon the music rack. When Jekyll is ready to go out, the butler hands hat, cloak and cane directly to the camera. After a carriage ride through the streets of London, it enters the doors of a medical school and passes on into the operating theater. Here a complete 360-degree turn around the hall brings the camera to rest for the first time upon the face of Dr. Jekyll (Fredric March). Quite apart from its indisputable pictorial effectiveness, this use of the subjective camera built a growing suspense, a curiosity about the appearance of the man we know will turn into the monstrous Hyde. The transformations themselves were ingeniously achieved upon the screen (Mamoulian has steadfastly refused to divulge the secret of his technique), accompanied by a vivid, synthetically created sound track built from exaggerated heart beats mingled with the reverberations of gongs played backwards, bells heard through echo chambers and completely artificial sounds created by photographing light frequencies directly onto the sound track. The recordists referred to it as "Mamoulian's stew," but it was probably the screen's first experiment with purely synthetic sound.

Outstanding for its understatement both of sound and visual was Mamoulian's handling of the scene in which Hyde murders Champagne Ivy (Miriam Hopkins). Hyde forces the thoroughly frightened girl to sing her pathetic music hall song. Suddenly he bends over her, passing completely out of the frame. For a long moment the shot reveals only the bedpost, a highly ornamental carving of the Goddess of Love. Then the singing stops abruptly, and Hyde's triumphant face rises once more into view. We need be shown no more.

Mamoulian's own films after *Love Me Tonight* are again indicative. *Song of Songs* (1933) with Marlene Dietrich, *Queen Christina* (1933) with Greta Garbo, *We Live Again* (1934) with Anna Sten had a visual beauty, a sensuous quality that often surmounted the banality of their scripts. Certain scenes—Garbo with the grapes in *Queen Christina* or the long tracking shot to the completely immobile close-up of Garbo that closes the film—linger in the mind as directorial touches that added cinematic life to stories that made their main points through dialogue. Certainly, Mamoulian's concern for the dramatic effect of his imagery made him the logical choice as the director of the first feature-length film shot in the improved, full-color Technicolor, *Becky Sharp* (1935). His handling of the great ball before the Battle of Waterloo with its artfully designed shifting patterns of color, its gay pastels mounting to a climax of blood-red cloaks disappearing into the darkness, reveals again his ability to work imaginatively with the raw materials of his art. And when in 1936 he turned once more to musical comedy in the satiric *Gay Desperado,* he showed that he was now able to move as lightly and freely in a realistic world of thieves and radios and high-powered motorcars as in the fantasy world of *Love Me Tonight*. Always the creative director, Mamoulian best exemplifies those talented men of the early Thirties who were consciously seeking to transform the talking picture into a genuinely cinematic art.

It was perhaps inevitable that, during the first hectic years of sound, the film cycles reappeared with renewed vigor. They seemed to chase each other across the screen, one right after the other—transcriptions of Broadway musicals, prison pictures, gangster pictures, newspaper pictures, backstage musicals. With the entire industry unsure of itself, any outstanding success was soon followed by the simultaneous release of literally dozens of other films on the same subject from every studio in Hollywood. Curiously enough, this had a salutary effect on the films themselves. The studios did not try merely to imitate what had gone before; they tried to make their films better than their competition. They tried to polish techniques and stories until their own efforts were more attractive, more effective, more "box office." The number of films in each cycle may have driven the moviegoer of the early Thirties almost out of his mind by making it seem that every new picture he went to was the one that he had seen the week before. But through these cycles the film forms were themselves able to develop characteristic styles and techniques, an increased mobility and cinematic power.

369

One of the first and most obvious fields for exploitation by the new sound camera was, of course, the Broadway musical. During 1929 and 1930, a great many of these made the transition to film—*The Vagabond King, The Desert Song, Rio Rita, Sunny, Golden Dawn, Gold Diggers of Broadway, Song of the Flame* . . . The list is endless. Actually, however, very little original thinking went into them. It was enough that they had popular titles, famous stars and familiar tunes. In 1930 Samuel Goldwyn brought to Hollywood a dance director from the New York stage, Busby Berkeley, to handle the musical numbers for *Whoopee,* starring Eddie Cantor. And things began to happen. Berkeley, one of the most original and daring of the directors in this field, saw no reason why the dances should be a mere reproduction of the stage originals. Not with a camera capable of taking scenes from any angle and any position. In *Whoopee* he carried his camera high up into the flies and shot straight down on the dance floor. In subsequent films, he photographed from below, from the sides, from above. For one astonishing moment in "The Shadow Waltz" from *Gold Diggers of 1933,* he tilted the camera at a 90-degree angle to the floor and photographed the girls mirrored in a lake, pirouetting down either side of the screen. Since such dance sequences were generally inserted into well-worn backstage stories, purists frequently pointed out that Berkeley's work was ridiculous, that his dances could never conceivably take place on any stage in the world. They were, of course, absolutely right. What they ignored was the fact that the story was merely an excuse for the production numbers, and that Berkeley was producing the purest combination of visual and sound that had yet come from the American studios. Berkeley's vogue was to be gradually superseded by the growing popularity of the more intimate style of dance films introduced by Fred Astaire and Ginger Rogers during the mid-Thirties.

The popular gangster films of the early Thirties—*Little Caesar* (1930), *The Public Enemy* (1931), *Scarface* (1932)—and the almost concurrent cycle of newspaper melodramas also did much to return to the screen some of its former mobility and vitality. Generally written directly for the screen, they eliminated the long, fragrant speeches of the legitimate theater in favor of such pungent phrases as "We're gonna take you for a ride"; "He got bumped off"; and "You can dish it out but you can't take it." In keeping with the tone of this dialogue, the editing was similarly taut and to the point. In a typical scene from *Little Caesar,* the gang is discussing the fate of one of its members:

"Eddie's turned yellow. He's goin' to rat on us."

"He can't get away with that."

"I just seen Eddie goin' into the church."

"Get Eddie," says Little Caesar. And the scene cuts abruptly to a church exterior, with Eddie coming down the steps. A long black car swings ominously into view; there is a burst of machine-gun fire and Eddie lies sprawling on the steps. Followed by a flat cut to the next scene, Eddie's funeral.

There was a speed, a vigor, a sense of the contemporaneous scene, a realism of character and incident about these films that was in sharp contrast to the talky problem plays that surrounded them. They had action, racy dialogue, the sharply naturalistic performances of people like James Cagney, Edward G. Robinson, Joan Blondell, Lee Tracy, Paul Muni and George Bancroft. They boasted that their incidents were based on fact, that their stories came from the headlines. And they excited audiences in ways that the drawing-room comedies, boudoir romances and static musical comedies did not. They were like a breath of fresh air sweeping through the heavily padded studios of the early sound era, blowing away some of the conventions, some of the stiffness that had crept into the medium with the advent of the microphone.

And directors—even directors who were not working on gangster films— responded to their tonic. In *The Front Page* (1931), one of the first and fastest of the newspaper cycle, Lewis Milestone solved the problem of translating the Hecht-MacArthur play into a film by keeping the camera almost constantly in motion, by cutting frequently and by staging the dialogue at breakneck speed. King Vidor, faced with much the same problem in bringing to the screen Elmer Rice's *Street Scene* (1931), used few moving camera shots but worked out a shooting script in which every single shot was taken from a fresh angle.

Nowhere were the dislocations caused by the addition of the sound track more apparent than in the field of film comedy; and yet here too a balance was soon reached that proved of value to film makers in all fields. Prior to the introduction of sound, of course, comedy had been almost entirely a visual medium, with emphasis on character and physical humor. Subtitles—especially those subtitles that introduced the various characters— might carry an occasional wisecrack. ("He had water on the brain. In the winter it froze and everything slipped his mind.") In the sophisticated or folksy comedies of the Twenties, there might even be a snappy retort. Will Rogers, for example, punctuated his silent comedies with typical Rogersisms—but, significantly, Rogers was never as popular on the silent screen as he was after sound came in. In sound, the humor shifted abruptly from visual to verbal, and a whole new crowd of comics—largely imported from the New York stage and from vaudeville—came clamoring through the studios. The Marx Brothers, Ed Wynn, Lou Holtz, Eddie Cantor, W. C. Fields, Jimmy Durante, Frank Morgan, Bobby Clark, Charlie Ruggles and, soon after, Bob Hope were all brought west because they could handle a humorous line or witty repartee. Keaton and Lloyd, Harry Langdon and Raymond Griffith drifted into either the obscurity of studio office jobs or complete retirement. At the same time, such relatively minor comics from the silent days as Laurel and Hardy, Edward Everett Horton and Joe E. Brown were suddenly boosted to stardom. They were stage trained. They could talk.

Typical was the case of Buster Keaton. At the close of the Twenties, he was M-G-M's highest-paid comedian. Early in the Thirties he was cast in a series of comedies with Jimmy Durante. Nominally, Keaton was the star; but whatever success the pictures scored was so clearly due to Durante that Keaton's contract was simply allowed to expire. He had established himself as a silent, frozen-faced comedian. Durante's natural style was volatile, explosive. It was Durante, not Keaton, that the talkies wanted.

Nor were all the stars of the stage completely at home on the talking screen. Ed Wynn's simple-minded funny man, Beatrice Lillie's cool sophistication, Fanny Brice's broad dialect humor and even broader bathos found scant acceptance outside New York. Even Eddie Cantor—successful in theater, radio and now television—was never as warmly received in the movies. Radio stars like Amos 'n' Andy, Jack Benny, Fred Allen and Kate Smith were notably unsuccessful when they tried the screen. The characters that had sparked the imagination of millions when heard in the living room never quite seemed to satisfy those same millions when they came to see them in the movie houses.

On the other hand, the Marx Brothers, W. C. Fields, Will Rogers, Bob Hope, Jimmy Durante and Marie Dressler—each had some special quality of voice and personality that found an immediate response in audiences around the world. Their humor was verbal, but it also had a strong visual quality. It is difficult to think of Will Rogers and Marie Dressler without recalling their shrugs and gesticulations, their special forms of mugging. Jimmy Durante is a veritable fury of activity, magnifying every emotion until it becomes a parody of itself. Bob Hope, with the smooth patina of years of vaudeville trouping, has a cock of the eye, a twist of the lip or a flip of the hand to accompany every line.

It is in the films of the Marx Brothers, however, and of W. C. Fields— and in such rare, offbeat items as *Million Dollar Legs* (1932), *Six of a Kind* (1934) and the Hope-Crosby *Road* series—that one finds the real flowering of comedy in the sound films. Indeed, the Marx Brothers presented a perfect filmic combination—the fast-talking Groucho, the silent, nimble-witted pantomime of Harpo, and Chico, the saturnine fall guy (with statesque Margaret Dumont generally around to play straight). Even though their very earliest films, *The Coconuts* (1929) and *Animal Crackers* (1930), were nothing more than crudely photographed versions of previous stage hits, the swiftness of the dialogue and Harpo's eloquent byplay all but concealed their technical deficiencies. Such a fantastic colloquy as the one from *Animal Crackers* in which Groucho and Chico discuss the mysterious disappearance of a valuable painting needs nothing beyond a sound track and a well-focused camera:

"We'll search every room in the house," says Groucho.

"What if it ain't in this house?" says Chico.

"Then we'll search the house next door."

"What if there ain't no house next door?"

"Then we'll build one," says Groucho—and the two immediately set about drawing up plans for building the house next door.

All their better pictures had similar sequences. In *Duck Soup* (1932) Groucho as the Prime Minister of Fredonia holds up a document and says to his assembled council, "Why, it's so simple a child of ten could understand it"; then, *sotto voce* to Chico, "Run out and find me a child of ten. I can't make heads or tails of it."

Just as in the gangster films, this dialogue had a racy fascination of its own. It was talk, true; but it was also more than talk. It had, in the most literal sense, a picturesque quality—a quality that was best conveyed by a wholly passive camera. But alternating with and counterbalancing all this dialogue were sequences of frantic activity and pure pantomime—the trick with the mirror in *Duck Soup*, with all three Marxes dressed as Groucho and circling suspiciously about one another; the travesty on opera in *A Night at the Opera* when Harpo inserts "Take Me Out to the Ball Game" into the orchestra's score for *Il Trovatore* and then runs amuck in the scenery; the inspired mayhem of the operating scene from *A Day at the Races*, with Groucho calling for X rays and Harpo and Chico rushing in with the evening papers.

As a team, the Marx Brothers achieved an almost perfect balance of sight and sound, marred only by the occasional *scènes obligatoires* of Harpo playing the harp and Chico the piano. (In one of their pictures Groucho, as if aware of the letdown in tempo, says directly to the audience, "Look, I have to stay here, but why don't you go out to the lobby for a smoke until this whole thing blows over?") Although directors invariably sought to enliven such sequences with trick shots of Chico at the keyboard, with close-ups of Harpo's unique fingering of his instrument, with zoom shots and striking angles, they were never able to force cinematic life into what remained essentially stagy performances. Apart from such moments, however, the skillful interplay of the Marx Brothers created a kind of humor that was ideally suited to the requirements of the sound camera.

If the Marxes provided perfect foils for one another, W. C. Fields was the perfect sound comedian in himself. The irascible, bumbling braggadocio that was his screen character was also, it would seem, his off-screen character as well. He was an unpredictable eccentric whose confirmed pessimism had been nourished by years of adversity. A lifetime of rigorous training as a juggler in circus and vaudeville had made his every gesture and movement a masterpiece of precise timing. The result was an incomparable blend of half-articulate howls of rage, mumbled bits of private philosophy ("No man who hates small dogs and children can be *all* bad"), and eloquent pantomime. Many of the best sight gags in his earlier pictures were developed from his old stage routines, such as the golfing scene with the bent clubs in *You're Telling Me* (1934), his attempts to sleep on a noisy back porch in *It's a Gift* (1934) and the hilariously crooked poker game in *Mississippi* (1935).

There was always an air of improvisation about a Fields picture, as if his comedy patter and throw-away lines had been caught almost by accident by the camera. One had the feeling that the next time the picture was run, they might not even be there! It gave his films the peculiar fascination of a newsreel, a one-time happening to a truly unique character. The pictures themselves were invariably abominably constructed, a hodgepodge of plot and gags that shot off in all directions. Indeed, his final film, *Never Give a Sucker an Even Break* (1941), almost defies description, its narrative has so many breaks and changes. But, like all the Fields films, it is full of the most inspired inanities—Fields diving out of an airplane after his whisky bottle and comparing an ordinary cigarette to the new king size as he plummets to earth, his running warfare with the formidable waitress at the local hash house. ("I did *not* say this meat was tough. I just said I didn't see the horse that usually stands outside.") And, as in all the Fields films, there were the familiar props—the agile cane, the straw hat that constantly popped out of his hands or flew off his head, the stump of a cigar that half concealed his more scurrilous oaths.

Fields wrote most of his own pictures, using such improbable noms de plume as Otis J. Cribblecoblis or Mahatma Kane Jeeves; probably no one else could have realized quite so well the picaresque qualities inherent in the character, or dreamed up the mass of petty harassments through which Fields fought his way with beady eye and wide-swinging cane. Like the Marx Brothers, like Will Rogers and Bob Hope, Fields' humor was verbal; but what gave it character and substance was the bulbous nose, the look of outraged dignity and larcenous innocence that accompanied everything he said or did.

The fact is that in the work of the best comedians of the Thirties the sound film was coming closer to striking a proper balance between its visual and aural elements. Much of this was instinctive, much was the result of happy accident; but also, out of the accumulating skill and experience of directors and technicians alike, a sure craftsmanship was emerging. And as accident gave way to method, so too did the flamboyant trickery of the early years of sound give way to style. In the series of Fred Astaire and Ginger Rogers musicals that brightened the mid-Thirties, for example, a camera technique was evolved that broke sharply with the exuberant, exhibitionistic patterns of the Busby Berkeley dances and permitted the closer integration of musical and story elements. The Astaire films were intimate, the dances coming not as interruptions but as extensions of the story. Astaire and Rogers danced because words alone could not convey their feelings.

At first, the problem of getting into the dance was often solved mechanically, with the awkward expedient of the song cue—a bit of dialogue incorporating the title of the number or explaining its presence in the picture ("Listen, dear, they're playing our song!"). Soon, however, the Astaire films were simply letting the music steal in under the dialogue without any attempt at explanation or excuse. The dancers respond to it, and the number is under way. And they utilized the camera's innate ability to cover great areas, to fall back as the dancers move forward, to cut nimbly from place to place.

After his first few pictures, Astaire began to direct as well as to choreograph his dance sequences, with notable success. He brought his camera increasingly into the play of the dance, judiciously placing it to provide a tight frame for his own solo work, pulling it back to create new dimensions for the ensembles, moving it freely to sustain at all times the line of the dance. It was an unobtrusive, discreet and beautifully functional use of the camera—and one that, for the first time, achieved the balance between camera, image and the sound track that is the true art of the sound film.

What the Astaire films reveal, with their grace and lightness and sureness of touch, is the approaching technical maturity of the American film

375

makers. From an overemphasis of sound, many had moved to the opposite extreme, to an overemphasis of the visual element. By the middle of the Thirties, a happier balance was being achieved. Directors no longer feared sound, nor did they try to conceal long dialogue passages behind a myriad of artificially created scenes. The better writers had long since discovered the difference between stage dialogue and talk on the screen while, at the top level, people like Dudley Nichols, Robert Riskin and Joseph Mankiewicz were writing with a strong awareness of the visual requirements of the medium as well. A whole corps of superbly trained cameramen— many of them, like James Wong Howe, Karl Freund and Arthur Edeson, with experience extending far back into the silent era—were fully prepared to transform their work into striking images. The sound engineers and technicians had, in a brief half-dozen years, supplied the studios with equipment that, for all its complexity, was incredibly flexible and allowed a maximum of control at every point; they stood ready to supply the director with virtually any effect he might request. As is always the case, masterpieces were few and far between. But the period of experimentation was over and the period of integration and consolidation could begin.

One of the first directors to achieve this integration in dramatic films was England's Alfred Hitchcock, whose mystery thrillers began to appear on American screens in 1935. Perhaps because the mystery form has always laid emphasis on visual shocks and surprises, the full extent of his contribution has been somewhat underestimated. Hitchcock did far more than simply bathe his stories in somber lighting and deep shadow to create in his audiences a dread of the unexpected. And also, it should be added, he did more than invent a series of brilliant, equally disquieting surprise effects on the sound track (although some, such as the woman's scream in *The 39 Steps* that merges with the shriek of a locomotive's whistle, have become classics in the field).

One has only to read through the first few pages of John Buchan's *The 39 Steps*, however, and compare the novel with Hitchcock's screen treatment of it to recognize his full stature. From Buchan's description of his hero wandering about London, looking in windows, stopping in bars, taking in a show, Hitchcock selected the one incident—scarcely more than a passing phrase—that lent itself best to dramatic screen treatment. He opens the film at a variety theater—something for the eye, something for the ear—and leads the narrative back there for the dramatic finale. Throughout the film the incidents are suggested by the novel rather than reproducing it scene for scene. Hitchcock, who has always worked on his own screenplays, prefers to invent around an idea, letting it develop in filmic terms rather than in terms of the novel or short story used as source material. His favorite device was the "magguffin," his own term to describe a visual or sound gimmick—a snatch of music, a man with a twitching eye, a ticking time bomb—that runs throughout the picture as a sinister leitmotif. In *The 39 Steps* this "magguffin" is a man with a missing finger. The key figure in the mysterious spy ring, he is wholly Hitchcock's invention: there is no counterpart for him in the original novel.

What contributed to the fascination of such vintage Hitchcocks as *The 39 Steps* (1935), *Secret Agent* (1935), *The Woman Alone* (1936), *The Girl Was Young* (1937), and *The Lady Vanishes* (1938) was his deliberate underplaying of climactic scenes. A woman staggers toward the camera and then, as she collapses, we see the hilt of the dagger in her back. A boy unwittingly carries a time bomb across London; we see him mount a bus and then, in long shot, the bus blows up. We are not shown the kidnaping of the old woman in *The Lady Vanishes*; we only know that suddenly in her place in the railway carriage has appeared a dreadful grim-faced substitute wearing her clothes and claiming to be Miss Froy. In *The Woman Alone*, while Sylvia Sidney is preparing to murder her husband in the shadowy movie house, on the sound track is heard the macabre refrain from Disney's cartoon *Who Killed Cock Robin?* There was a casual urbanity about Hitchcock's most carefully prepared moments, whether visual or aural, that quickly established his supremacy not only as a director of thrillers but as a master of the sound-film medium. His pictures, eagerly awaited during the late Thirties, led inevitably to a Hollywood contract. Although Hitchcock frankly admits that he is now doing what he calls "the commercial thing," few directors today can rival him in the grace and polish, the slick surface finish of his star-studded comedy melodramas.

Unquestionably the greatest single difficulty that faced the directors of the mid-Thirties was the problem of handling dialogue gracefully.

Before any approach could be successful, however, there had to be a drastic revision in the dialogue itself. The script writers, whether recruited from the theater, from radio, or from the silent movie, had to discover a truly filmic language, a language with a lively fascination of its own. Primarily, it was a dialogue that had to approximate more closely the patterns of ordinary speech than is either necessary—or desirable—on the stage or in literature. The theater demands a richness of verbal imagery to help cloak the immobile and restrictive nature of its settings. Stage dialogue is full of descriptions of off-stage events that must be reported because they cannot be shown. It is laced through with psychological insights into character and motivation that sound highly artificial in the movies.

Nor is the language of literature, particularly as discovered in the novel, any more suitable for direct filming (although there is growing evidence that many of today's writers have been strongly influenced in their conception of dialogue by repeated exposure to the motion picture). Ideally, no screen character can be permitted the paragraphs of introspective speeches that the protagonist of a novel so often indulges in. And certainly the long, discursive passages in which the author explores the ramifications of his theme—always one of the primary attractions of the novel form—defy translation into film in terms of dialogue.

Screen writers had to invent dialogue that was at once rich and colorful, pungent and amusing, but also stripped of inessentials. They had to learn not only what to say, but also how much could be left unsaid—how much could be left to the camera and the actor and the director to put on the screen through action and gesture or by implication. The script for a film is like an orchestral score. It is the conductor's interpretation of the music that finally brings it to life for the concert audience. It is the director's visualization of the script that creates the movie, blending dialogue with action to produce the most affecting combination of both.

The Informer demonstrated the advantages of a strong writer-director team, a collaboration that in John Ford and Dudley Nichols produced such memorable films as *The Lost Patrol* (1934), *The Plough and the Stars* (1936), *Stagecoach* (1939) and *The Long Voyage Home* (1940). Another outstanding writer-director team of the Thirties was Robert Riskin and Frank Capra. In such enormously popular comedies as *Lady for a Day* (1933), *It Happened One Night* (1934), *Mr. Deeds Goes to Town* (1936), *You Can't Take It With You* (1938) and *Mr. Smith Goes to Washington* (1939), Capra demonstrated his confidence in the ability of his colleague to write dialogue that held its own upon the screen by filming long passages without any change in camera position whatsoever. His special skill lay in re-creating the speed and humor of silent comedy in the sound medium, feeling out the subtle relationship between dialogue and camera, sensing when cutting or camera movement was required and when words alone could carry the momentum of his scene. If the talk was good, he reasoned, why try to hide it? A favorite technique of his was to start an extended dialogue passage with the camera some distance away from his principals, then slowly, almost imperceptibly, track in to a large two-shot, as if irresistibly drawn by his interest in what the people were saying.

In *It Happened One Night*, with entire sequences played within the confines of a bus or a small tourist cabin, Capra ingeniously contrived to keep his screen alive by scanning the faces of the passengers on the bus, or discovering his stars almost haphazardly among the people and the packages and seats that surrounded them. Only when the dialogue was important, when it bore significantly on the development of the story, did he move in for protracted close-ups. But these close-ups were completely functional: they emphasized the words. Capra sensed when he could count on Riskin's lines to carry a scene without additional visual pyrotechnics, when they could be shot with a static camera or when the full effectiveness of the scene required the extra mobility of the moving camera and staccato editing of silent days.

A particularly delightful sequence illustrates his ability to blend the two: Clark Gable and Claudette Colbert are sitting on a fence by the side of the road holding an animated conversation on the best way to thumb a ride from the passing cars; Capra filmed this entire scene in a single shot without moving his camera. But when Gable walks out to the road to demonstrate his hitchhiking methods (capped by Colbert's conclusive evidence that the knee is mightier than the thumb), Capra builds the scene from short snatches of pantomimed action brilliantly edited together— climaxed with an adroit montage in which a glimpse of Miss Colbert's leg brings a car to a screeching halt.

Capra was also among the first to perceive that the use of dialogue on the screen involved not only the preparation of a taut, vivid, idiomatic prose, but also a more specialized handling of the actors delivering that dialogue. And here was perhaps the final adjustment that directors had to make to sound. In silent days the director could (and often did) build a star's performance out of bits and pieces—a close-up of the actor, a reaction shot, an insert of an object or an image that underscored the emotional content of the scene. With sound, much of this "synthetic" kind of acting was automatically eliminated. Not only did the actors now have to speak their lines, but—as Al Jolson in *The Jazz Singer* so clearly revealed—the sound track itself produced a far greater awareness of their essential personality than the silent camera ever had. Voice, face, mannerisms and temperament were fused together by the sound camera to create that elusive, indefinable quality known as "box-office appeal." These were the elements that the actor brought to his part—along with whatever measure of talent he possessed.

More important than acting ability, however, was the photogenic magnetism of the star, around which the director could create a characterization. It was a quality which, when properly used, added its own dynamism to the film. And directors like Capra, Ford, George Cukor and William Wyler who gained the reputation of being "good with actors" were good because they knew how to fit their stars to their roles, and how to utilize their personalities to sustain the momentum of a scene.

Though American pictures are often casually dismissed as "escapist entertainment," the forms of that escape vary from era to era and have their own significance. The public did not suddenly demand "realistic" pictures, but it could no longer be amused by high society exchanging bons mots at the cocktail hour nor stirred by the matinee idols or pretty sopranos and impoverished young tenors. Sound had made possible a new degree of realism in motion pictures and when, late in 1930, Warner Brothers' *Little Caesar* brought throngs to the box office once more, the course was clear. What the public obviously wanted was a hard-hitting, naturalistic form of drama that took its themes from the headlines of the day.

The studios quickly brought to the screen not only a staggering succession of gangster pictures (fifty in 1931 alone!), but equally sensational exposés of rackets, political corruption, prison brutality, bank failures and newspaper scandal sheets. If there was any element of escapism in these films, it lay in their tendency to blame isolated individuals for what were in fact national problems. Audiences seemed to find some reassurance in the thought that everything could be solved by the jailing—or shooting—of a brutal warden, a hoodlum gangster or a power-hungry politician. In *The Big House* (1930), *Little Caesar* (1930), *The Front Page* (1931), *The Public Enemy* (1931), *The Secret Six* (1931) and many more, the public was given strong, unadulterated dramatizations of the stories behind the daily headlines. Often such films were cynical and cheap, but occasionally they proved to be sincere and perceptive investigations of evils and abuses aggravated by the Depression. Indeed, the facts revealed by *I Am a Fugitive from a Chain Gang* (1932), based on an actual case, were so shocking that an aroused public forced a reformation of the chain-gang system.

Not only did the many topical films of this era reflect their times, but even the Depression romances had a metallic twist. Their heroines—Constance Bennett, Tallulah Bankhead, Joan Crawford, Marlene Dietrich, Greta Garbo, Barbara Stanwyck—were frequently ladies who took to the streets or became rich men's mistresses in order to provide food for their babies, an education for their sisters or medicine for their husbands. Despite these sentimentalities, however, such films as *Susan Lenox* (1931), *Blonde Venus* (1932) and *Letty Lynton* (1932) were quite explicit in establishing the milieu of poverty that drove their heroines into a life of shame. Nor was it sheer coincidence that these virtuous prostitutes invariably encountered public enemies or crooked politicians in their rise from gutter to penthouse. In their own way, they were merely confirming the gangster theme that the only escape from Depression-bred despair was to live outside the law.

And the general public, if box-office returns are any index, not only condoned but applauded these fallen creatures, just as they were fascinated by the exploits of the gangsters and racketeers. The heroines may have sobbed a bit over their lost virginity, the Little Caesars may have ended up perforated by bullets, but while they lived there was a glamour and fascination to their lives that was in glaring contrast to the drab realities of 1931 and 1932.

Obviously, in making heroes of gangsters and heroines of prostitutes, the movie companies departed far from both the letter and the spirit of the Production Code they had so virtuously agreed to in the halcyon year of 1927. The Depression had produced a new world, a new morality— and the studios, in giving the public what it wanted, reflected the seamiest side of the picture with unprecedented accuracy. Far too accurately for some tastes. Letters of protest began to reach the studios and the Hays Office from all the more respectable elements in communities across the country. Church groups, women's clubs and patriotic associations passed resolutions condemning the industry. Editorials appeared in the newspapers and sermons were preached from pulpits denouncing the growing immorality of the movies, urging the film producers to assume a greater social responsibility for the pictures they were turning out, prodding local censorship boards to increased vigilance and more rigorous standards. *Scarface* (1932), for example, at once one of the best and most brutal of the gangster films, was held up for months until the producers inserted several placatory scenes showing an aroused citizenry demanding action against what the film's subtitle described as "the shame of a nation." Even with these additions, *Scarface* was severely censored in many communities, banned outright in others.

As a result of such efforts the films became, if not more moral, at least more moralizing. Sermons on civic responsibility became the price one had to pay for pictures that dealt realistically with the more sensational aspects of the social scene. Under the sustained pressure of the protest groups, the wave of gangster films began to subside. During 1933 it gradually merged into another cycle, with the FBI men and other law enforcers as the new heroes. Actually, the G men were simply gangsters in disguise, acting with as little concern for "due process" as the gangsters they were hunting. But official morality was once more being served.

With the election of Franklin D. Roosevelt and the prompt introduction of NRA relief measures and reforms early in 1933, a new note of optimism appeared both in the country and in its films. The musicals, which only a short time before had been singing "Brother, Can You Spare a Dime?" and "Ten Cents a Dance," were now shouting out that "Happy Days Are Here Again" or "Stand Up and Cheer"—"good times are here!" Indeed, the musical comedies reflected this new optimism not only in their songs but in their themes as well. Typical of the era were the plots of *Footlight Parade* (1933) and *100 Men and a Girl* (1937), in which groups of starving musicians, singers and dancers were rounded up by Dick Powell or Deanna Durbin and prodded into putting on a show. Their success provided employment and happiness for all. In much the same way, King Vidor's *Our Daily Bread* (1934) showed a heterogeneous band of unemployed city people finding their salvation by working together on a farm co-operative. "Back to the soil" was reiterated as the solution to urban hard times in such films as *Stranger's Return* (1933), *State Fair* (1933) and *As the Earth Turns* (1934).

In keeping with the reformist trend of the NRA period, the topical films, the exposés of rackets, corruption and abuses of power took a more positive stand. Prohibition and gangsterism, juvenile delinquency, strikebreaking and prison reform were problems that an enlightened citizenry could do something about, once the facts were brought to their attention. It was in this spirit that the studios—and especially Warner Brothers—put into production such frankly controversial pictures as *Wild Boys of the Road* (1933), *Massacre* (1933), *Black Fury* (1935) and *The Black Legion* (1936), such vigorously antilynch films as *Winterset* (1936), *Fury* (1936) and *They Won't Forget* (1937).

While the predominantly affirmative and constructive outlook of these films was encouraged by the growing liberalism of the era, it is also true that a new sense of caution and constraint was forced upon the industry by the formation of the Legion of Decency during 1933, set up to implement a new Production Code. Drawn up by Catholic churchmen and lay members, the new Code was a thorough revision of the original structures established by the Hays Office during the "flaming" Twenties—but this time reinforced by the power of the Church to bring economic reprisals against any studio that violated its rulings. Sex and crime had become so prevalent on the screen that when at last the Legion of Decency made its official appearance, in April of 1934, many of the Protestant denominations were ready to support it in its announced campaign to clean up the movies. The Code, with but few minor revisions, has remained in force ever since.

With the rise of the Legion, many of the crude excesses of the tough, realistic school of film making were quickly eliminated; but at the same time much of the forthright honesty of the period also disappeared from the screen as well. Mae West was an early victim. Her good-humored vulgarity and frank sexuality in films like *She Done Him Wrong* (1933) made her irresistible to the reformers. The biggest box-office draw of 1933–1934, she became a prime target for the outraged forces of decency. To conform to the new Production Code, her scripts were so bowdlerized that by 1936 the Mae West character had lost its sex and her films their appeal. Her few subsequent screen appearances consisted of innocuous parodies of her former roles in pictures like *My Little Chickadee* (1940) with W. C. Fields. To avoid a similar fate, James Cagney, Clark Gable and Edward G. Robinson, the movies' favorite gangsters of the early Thirties, found it expedient to diversify their roles and lead more virtuous screen lives.

The industry itself quite consciously began laying greater emphasis on purely escapist themes—big Westerns, costume dramas, historical films and adaptations of the classics. While treatment of the social scene was suffused with what Richard Griffith has aptly termed "the fantasy of good will," the feeling that if everyone were kind and generous to his fellow man, the Depression could soon be overcome. This idea found its fullest and most popular expression in Frank Capra's *Mr. Deeds Goes to Town* (1936). Gary Cooper, a youthful millionaire, decides to give away his inherited fortune to the unemployed after discovering that his business associates are all parasites and cheats. The fact that no real-life millionaire has ever distributed his fortune with such openhearted innocence in no way diminished the attractiveness of the idea.

Mr. Deeds was one in a long cycle of films appearing during the mid-Thirties that came to be called "screwball" comedies, pictures that did anything and everything for a laugh. But while the action in these films was always wildly at odds with any conventional response to a similar situation, most of them had as their point of departure the terrible realities of that period—unemployment, hunger and fear. In *My Man Godfrey* (1936), for example, William Powell plays one of the "*nouveaux* poor," a man ruined by the crash and reduced to living in the city dumps. Some scatterbrained socialites find him on a scavenger hunt and make him their butler. Because of his own experience with poverty, Godfrey is able to enlighten his employers and transform them into useful, social-minded citizens. In *Easy Living* (1937), Jean Arthur, an unemployed secretary, suddenly finds herself in possession of a priceless mink coat flung out the window by a millionaire in a moment of pique; her scathing denunciation of his thoughtlessness while others are starving was the high point of the picture. And yet both of these were presented—and taken—as comedies. As Lewis Jacobs has written, "If 'screwball' comedies successfully turned the world on its ear, that was perhaps the way it already looked to a Depression generation which felt cheated of its birthright and apprehensively faced further loss in the steady approach of war."

As the Thirties wore on, these growing tensions produced a notable series of films that rode the mounting wave of liberalism without recourse to either the "fantasy of good will" or "screwball" subterfuge. Labor unrest, slum housing, unemployment and dislocation aggravated by the dust storms of the mid-Thirties—all of these were put on the screen with a directness that stressed the social and economic sources of such hardships. There were sympathy for the common man and new hope for a better tomorrow. In place of the contrived and improbable "happy endings" of the Depression musicals and "back to the soil" films, there was now a forthright expression of belief in the inherent strength of democracy to bring about national recovery and a solution to these problems. Characteristically, when John Steinbeck's bitter novel *The Grapes of Wrath* was filmed by John Ford in 1939, the picture faithfully transmitted the shocking and desperate plight of California's migratory workers, but material in the book was freely transposed so that the film might end on a strong declaration of faith in the ability of the American people to win through.

A belief in the democratic way of life was also implicit in an impressive and highly popular series of biographies that appeared throughout the late Thirties. Some of these films—such as John Ford's *Young Mr. Lincoln* (1939) or *Abe Lincoln in Illinois* (1940)—turned to American heroes whose lives and principles exemplified the democratic tradition. Others depicted great artists, scientists and political leaders in their battle with the bigots and reactionaries of their day. The careers of such international figures as Louis Pasteur, Dr. Ehrlich, Madame Curie, Emile Zola and Benito Juárez were presented as thinly veiled sermons on behalf of democracy and enlightenment. *The Life of Emile Zola* (1937), for example, reached its climax in Zola's classic *"J'accuse"* defense of Captain Dreyfus, a scathing denunciation of anti-Semitism and intolerance in all its forms. Underlying all these films was the awareness that our cultural and intellectual freedom was a precious heritage that the growing forces of fascism both at home and abroad were threatening to destroy.

DISASTER IN THE FARM LANDS

OF ALL the nation's resources, the land in the Thirties was in the most critical condition. The prairies had been overgrazed, the trees which once held moisture in the earth had been cut and not replaced, and in many sections of the country the land was exhausted from over-cultivation. Replenishment was overdue, but in some areas man had waited too long.

The first blow fell only a few months after the President took office; in South Dakota, on Armistice Day, 1933, a great dust storm boiled up over the land—the first of many that would sweep the Great Plains from Texas to Canada.

"By midmorning a gale was blowing, cold and black. By noon it was blacker than night. It was a wall of dirt one's eyes could not penetrate, but it could penetrate the eyes and ears and nose . . . and the lungs until one coughed up black.

"People were afraid, because they had never seen anything like this before . . .

"When the wind died and the sun shone forth again, it was on a different world. There were no fields, only sand drifting into mounds and eddies that swirled in what was now but an autumn breeze. There was no longer a section-line road fifty feet from the front door. In the farmyard, fences, machinery, and trees were gone, buried. The roofs of sheds stuck out through drifts deeper than a man is tall." *

FREDERICK LEWIS ALLEN

WHEN THE FARMS BLEW AWAY†

THE GREAT black blizzard of November 11, 1933—which darkened the sky in Chicago the following day and as far east as Albany, New York, the day after that—was only a prelude to disaster. During 1934 and 1935 thousands of square miles were to be laid waste and their inhabitants set adrift upon desperate migrations across the land. There was a long story of human error behind it.

During the latter part of the nineteenth century the Great Plains—a region of light rainfall, of sun and high winds, of waving grasses—had

* R. D. Lusk, "The Life and Death of 470 Acres," *The Saturday Evening Post,* Aug. 13, 1938.
† Excerpted from Frederick Lewis Allen's *Since Yesterday.*

386

been the great cattle country of the nation: a vast open area, unfenced at first, where the cowboys tended the cattle-kings' herds. Before the end of the century this range had been badly damaged by overgrazing; then the land was invaded by homesteaders, who tried to wring a living from the semiarid soil. World War I brought a huge demand for wheat, and tractors for large-scale machine farming became available, and the Plains began to come into their own as a crop-producing country. The sod covering which had protected them was plowed up on the grand scale. A new power era had come, it was said, to revolutionize American agriculture; factory methods were being triumphantly applied to the land.

To be sure, there wasn't much rain. The mean annual rainfall was only between 10 and 20 inches on the Plains (as compared with, for example, 20 to 40 in the Mississippi Valley region, and 40 to 50 in the North Atlantic). But there was a pretty favorable series of years during the 1920s and the farmers were not much disturbed.

Nineteen-thirty was a bad year in parts of this territory; 1931 was worse in the Dakotas: 1932 was better. Then came 1933: it was a swinger, hot and dry. During that first summer of the New Deal, farmers in South Dakota were finding that they couldn't raise even enough corn to feed the livestock. In western Kansas not a drop of rain fell for months. Already the topsoil was blowing; there were places in Kansas where it was said that farmers had to excavate their tractors before they could begin to plow. That fall came the Armistice Day black blizzard.

During 1934 and 1935, the thermometer in Kansas stayed week after week at 108 or above, and the black storms raged again and again. The drought continued acute during much of 1936. Oklahoma farms became great dunes of shifting sand. Housewives in the drought belt kept oiled cloths on the window sills and between the upper and lower sashes of the windows, and some of them tried to seal up every aperture in their houses with the gummed paper strips used in wrapping parcels, yet still the choking dust filtered in and lay in ripples on the kitchen floor.

A farmer, sitting at his window during a dust storm, remarked that he was counting the Kansas farms as they came by.

Westward fled the refugees from this new Sahara. In 1934 and 1935 Californians became aware of an increasing influx into their state of families traveling in ancient jalopies; but for years the streams of humanity continued to run. They came along U.S. Highway 30 through the Idaho hills, along Highway 66 across New Mexico and Arizona, along the Old Spanish Trail through El Paso, along all the other westward trails. They came in decrepit, square-shouldered 1925 Dodges and 1927 La Salles; in battered 1923 Model-T Fords that looked like relics of some antique culture; in trucks piled high with mattresses and cooking utensils and children, with suitcases, jugs and sacks strapped to the running boards.

They left behind them a half-depopulated countryside. A survey of the farmhouses in seven counties of southeastern Colorado made in 1936 showed 2,878 houses still occupied, 2,811 abandoned; and there were also, in that area, 1,522 abandoned homesites. As these wanderers moved along the highways they became a part of a vast and confused migratory movement. When they camped by the wayside they might find themselves next to a family of evicted white Alabama sharecroppers who had been on the move for four years, snatching seasonal farm-labor jobs wherever they could through the Southwest; or next to tenant families from the Arkansas Delta who had been "tractored off" their land—expelled in order that the owner might consolidate two or three farms and operate them with tractors and day labor; or next to lone wanderers who had once held industrial jobs and had now for years been on relief or on the road—jumping freights, hitchhiking, panhandling, shunting back and forth across the countryside in the faint hope of a durable job. And when these varied streams of migrants reached the Coast they found themselves in desperate competition for jobs with individuals or families who for years had been "fruit tramps," moving northward each year with the harvests from the Imperial Valley in southern California to the Sacramento Valley or even to the apple-picking in the Yakima Valley in Washington.

Here in the land of promise, agriculture had long been partly industrialized. Huge farms were in the control of absentee owners or banks or corporations, and were accustomed to depend upon the labor of migratory "fruit tramps," who had formerly been mostly Mexicans, Japanese, and other foreigners, but now were increasingly Americans. Those laborers who were lucky enough to get jobs picking cotton or peas or fruit would be sheltered temporarily in camps consisting typically of frame cabins in rows, with a water line between every two rows; they were very likely to find in their cabin no stove, no cots, no water pail. Even the best of the camps offered a way of life strikingly different from that of the ruggedly individualist farmer of the American tradition, who owned his farm or else was preparing, by working as a resident "hired man," or by renting a farm, for the chance of ultimate ownership. These pickers were homeless, voteless nomads, unwanted anywhere save at the harvest season.

When wave after wave of the new migrants reached California, the labor market became glutted, earnings were low, and jobs became so scarce that groups of poverty-stricken families would be found squatting in makeshift Hoovervilles or bunking miserably in their awkward old Fords by the roadside. Being Americans of native stock and accustomed to independence, they took the meager wages and the humiliation bitterly, sought to organize, talked of striking, sometimes struck. At every such threat, something like panic seized the growers. If this new proletariat were permitted to organize, and were to strike at picking time, they might ruin the whole season's output of a perishable crop. There followed antipicketing ordinances; the spectacle of armed deputies dislodging the migrants from their pitiful camps; violence by bands of vigilantes, to whom these ragged families were not fellow citizens who had suffered in a great American disaster, but dirty, ignorant, superstitious outlanders, failures at life, easy dupes for "red" agitators. This engulfing tide of discontentment must be kept moving.

These unhappy wanderers of the West were only a small minority of the farmers of the United States.

The AAA [Agricultural Adjustment Administration] had begun the colossal task of making acreage-reduction agreements with millions of farmers in the hope of jacking up the prices of crops and thus restoring American agriculture to economic health. It made credit available to farmers and tried, through the Farm Mortgage Moratorium Act and other legislation, to free them of the immediate hazards of debt.

Farm prices rose. For example, the farmer who had received on the average only 33 cents a bushel for wheat in 1933 received 69 cents in 1934, 89 cents in 1935, 92 cents in 1936, $1.24 in 1937, and 88 cents in 1938. The cotton farmer who had received an average price of 5.6 cents a pound for his cotton in 1933 received between 10 and 13 cents during the next four years, and 7.9 cents in 1938. And certainly there was a general improvement in the condition of those farmers who owned their own farms—and lived outside the worst drought areas. There were gains in equipment and in comforts; more of these farms had electricity than in 1930, more had tractors and trucks, more had bathrooms, automobiles and radios. But this was not a complete picture of what had happened.

To begin with, quantities of farmers had lost their farms during the hideous early years of the Depression—lost them by reason of debt. These farms had mostly fallen into the hands of banks or insurance companies, or of small-town investors who had held the mortgages on them, or were being held by government bodies for nonpayment of taxes, or had been bought in at tax sales. As early as 1934, the National Resources Board stated that nearly 30 per cent of the total value of farm land in the West North Central States was owned by "creditor or government agencies which have been compelled to take over the property." At the small prairie city, the local representative of a big New York insurance company was a very busy man, supervising the management of tracts of property far and wide. In the callous old Wall Street phrase, the farms of the United States had been "passing into stronger hands"; and that meant that more and more of them, owned by people who did not live on them, were being operated by tenants.

For over half a century at least, farm tenancy had been on the increase in the United States. Back in 1880 only 25 per cent of American farms had been run by tenants. Slowly the percentage had increased; now, during the Depression, it reached 42. The growth of tenantry caused many misgivings. Tenants were not likely to put down roots, did not feel a full sense of responsibility for the land and equipment they used, were likely to let it deteriorate.

The passing of farms into "stronger hands" was accompanied by another change. More and more the farm owner, whether or not he operated his own farm, was coming to think of farming as a business. He was less likely to use his farm as a means of subsistence, more likely to use as much of it as possible for the growing of crops for sale.

In certain parts of the South and Southwest this trend toward mechanized farming took a form even more sinister; farm tenancy was becoming merely a way station on the road to farm industrialism. The tenants themselves were being eliminated. The AAA, strangely enough, was unwittingly assisting the process.

How easy for an owner of farm property, when the government offered him a check for reducing his acreage in production, to throw out some of his tenants or sharecroppers, buy a tractor with the check, and run his farm mechanically, with the aid of hired labor—not the sort of year-round hired labor which the old-time "hired man" had represented, but labor engaged only by the day when there happened to be work to be done.

Where did the displaced tenants go? Into the towns, some of them. In many rural areas, census figures showed an increased town population and simultaneously a depopulated countryside. Said the man at a gas station in a Texas town, "This relief is ruining the town. They come in from the country to get on relief." Some of them got jobs running tractors on other farms at $1.25 a day. Some went on to California—out of farming as a settled way of life into farming as big business dependent on a large, mobile supply of labor.

390

NEW WORLD A-COMIN'

PRESIDENT ROOSEVELT, in announcing his plan for the Tennessee Valley Authority, said it would have "the broadest duty of planning" for the good of everyone in the country. "This power development of war days leads logically to national planning for a complete river watershed involving many States and the future lives and welfare of millions. It touches and gives life to all forms of human concern."

And on the day the President signed the TVA bill, Senator Norris said, "It is emblematic of the dawning of that day when every rippling stream that flows down the mountainside and winds it way through the meadows to the sea shall be harnessed and made to work for the welfare and comfort of man."

Both men believed intensely in public power, and their eloquent words obviously were deeply felt; without their combined efforts one of the nation's greatest works would not have been accomplished. Perhaps it would not bring about a Utopia in the Tennessee Valley; neither would its success bring galloping socialism upon the country; but a most remarkable spirit of cooperation was evidenced once work had really begun in the Valley. In the words of Broadus Mitchell, "The TVA addressed itself to the greatest public-works project in history, with the engineer, the architect, the chemist and men of a score of other sciences commanded to lead the way. It was a union of heart and mind to restore what had been wasted. It was a social resurrection." *

DIXON WECTER

TVA†

FOR WHITE and black alike, the key to the South's economic welfare lay in using her natural resources with keener social intelligence. True, conservation was no novelty even in this prodigal, easygoing land. After the Civil War some South Carolinians had built up a modest but thriving industry in preparing phosphates for soil enrichment, and in 1918 Woodrow Wilson had caused the construction of a dam and two nitrate plants at Muscle Shoals on the Tennessee River in northern Alabama to make ex-

---

* Broadus Mitchell, *Depression Decade* (New York, Rinehart, 1947).
† Excerpted from Dixon Wecter's *The Age of the Great Depression.*

plosives and fertilizers for war and peace. Henry Ford and other industrialists long cast covetous eyes upon this development, and for years it
remained a bone of political contention. Meanwhile the Tennessee basin,
draining portions of seven Southern states, with a population of four and
a half million, continued like the rest of the South to denude its topsoil,
deny it replenishment and squander other resources like timber, minerals
and water power.

For this region, whose income and living standards were below the national average and even under the Southern median, a new destiny began
in May 1933. Thanks to a twelve-year battle waged by Senator George
W. Norris and other conservationists and to Roosevelt's conviction that
power resources belong to the people, the Tennessee Valley Authority was
created to promote flood control, navigation, electric-power production,
proper use of land and forest and "the economic and social well-being of
the people." The new agency was to deal with all natural resources as a
single big problem and make decisions without constant reference to
Washington. Interstate in character, it worked co-operatively with seven
state governments and scores of local ones. At last regional planning on a
large scale had been given the signal to go ahead.

Though the TVA could invoke the power of eminent domain in matters like flood control, the essence of its program affecting the people's
daily life was voluntary. Under a planning council six divisions—representing agriculture, forestry, industry, engineering and geology, land use,
social and economic aspects—maintained "demonstration units," which
became the chief means of individual persuasion. While still engaged in
building locks and dams and power plants, it began the retirement of
submarginal lands, soil conservation, afforestation, the introduction of
better farm machinery and the fostering of local manufactures, public
health and education.

The hill dweller of Tennessee, Alabama and North Carolina inclined
to stubbornness, conservatism, suspicion—the traits of ingrained sectional-
ism. In the lowlands a few oldsters at first avowed that, rather than move,
they would just sit in their rocking chairs till the water came up to drown
them. New-fangled methods of plowing and household gadgets also left
them dour. But as the program progressed—with vast works of concrete
and steel rising skyward and transmission wires spanning the valleys,
brown water turning deep blue, ragged hillsides changing into rich green—
inertia yielded to curiosity and then appreciation, with youth and the better
educated taking the lead. Sharecroppers, white and black, found jobs with
the TVA which gradually converted them into skilled craftsmen or me-

chanics; many were glad to exchange ramshackle cabins for the prefabricated workers' dwellings whose example began to raise housing standards in the Valley. Malaria control and the curbing of stream pollution enhanced regional health at the same time that the TVA health and safety department was supervising the medical needs of workers and setting a remarkable record of freedom from industrial accidents.

Instead of the capricious, destructive river and its tributaries of the old days, a chain of lakes presently stretched across the Valley, stocked with fish and offering nine thousand miles of shore line for recreation. A private organization called the Tennessee Valley Waterway Conference devised, with aid from TVA technical experts, a series of public-use terminals linking the railroads and truck highways with a navigable channel six hundred and fifty miles long.

Meanwhile the once backward region had become the second-largest producer of power in the United States, with municipalities and co-operatives in partnership with the TVA supplying electricity to consumers at three cents a kilowatt hour instead of ten. Responsibility for the distribution of this current fell largely to local boards made up of public-minded citizens. While home consumption of electricity for the nation increased 63 per cent between 1934 and 1942, that in the Tennessee Valley (beginning at 17 per cent below the national average) almost doubled. Freezing lockers, electric pumps, hay driers, motors to grind feed and cut wood—these were the sinews of new might, instruments for promoting agricultural efficiency and enhancing standards of living.

Although some branches of private industry, eager to sell more electric ranges and other appliances, rejoiced at these developments, the private purveyors of electric power abominated the new agency. Roosevelt's contention that TVA rates constituted "yardsticks so that the people of this country will know whether they are paying the proper price for electricity of all kinds" provided hot debate. Cost factors of the TVA could be figured variously—in terms, for example, of allocation between electric power, navigation and flood control, or of estimates for depreciation and amortization and the interest to be charged theoretically to the investment (since the TVA, financed largely by congressional appropriations, paid virtually no interest). Its bookkeeping was further complicated because it paid nothing for benefits provided by other federal services, such as materials and labor furnished by the WPA and Civilian Conservation Corps, workmen's compensation under the United States Employees' Compensation Commission, the franking privilege and low freight rates on land-grant railroads.

While its foes argued therefore that its rates did not cover true costs but flourished a yardstick as pliable as the "rubber dollar," its friends replied that TVA wholesale charges were actually high enough to cover all these disputed items, plus its payments to states and counties in lieu of property taxes of 12.5 per cent of gross revenues, roughly equivalent to taxes borne by private utilities. This issue, a matter of exhaustive congressional inquiry, was extremely complex. If, however, TVA rates failed to furnish an exact yardstick, they did serve to deflate excessive profits in the private-utility field, not only in the Tennessee Valley but through the nation. Thanks to this and other causes, the average residential rate for the whole country declined from 5.52 cents in 1933 to 3.67 in 1942.

For several years the TVA and local subsidiaries of Commonwealth and Southern, the chief utility corporation in this region, worked together in a precarious harness of enforced co-operation. But upon expiration in 1936 of the TVA's contracts to use private transmission lines, open war broke out, with the corporation's president Wendell Willkie leading the squadrons of private enterprise. A limited victory for the TVA, gained from a Supreme Court decision in 1936 holding that construction of the Wilson Dam was constitutional, was enormously re-enforced three years later when the tribunal ruled that private companies had no legal right to protection from TVA competition.

Through its power of appropriation Congress alone held a whip hand over this half-a-billion-dollar property. With a few notable exceptions, the majority of lawmakers acquiesced in the view of TVA Chairman David Lilienthal that "a river has no politics." Its personnel were chosen and promoted on the merit system under the TVA's exclusive responsibility, the sole instance of this method in the whole system of permanent federal agencies. Not only did the staff appear to be well insulated from political tampering but, in accord with the philosophy of regionalism, they represented a wide geographical selection, and were frequently loaned to junior projects, like the Northwest's Bonneville Dam or South Carolina's Santee-Cooper development.

The President and his National Resources Committee tended to stress the river valley as the unit of regional planning. On June 3, 1937, he recommended that Congress create six more projects, conceived at this stage, perhaps out of deference to congressional caution, less as "little TVA's" possessing executive authority than as planning boards.

In other respects as well, the conservation of the nation's natural resources under the second Roosevelt had gone forward even more swiftly than under the first.

FASHIONS—HIGH AND LOW

HOLLYWOOD STARS, from Shirley Temple to Greta Garbo, influenced the fashions of the day. In the past, new styles in clothes were often slow to take hold. Now, through newsreels and feature films, news of fashions quickly spread throughout the country. The manufacturer who thought small-town women did not know this year's styles from last was in trouble. "Previously," David Cohn says, "clothing merchants could trace the peregrinations of clothing styles as they slowly moved from Fifth Avenue down to Fourteenth Street, then to Main Street six to twelve months later. Now women wore the same style simultaneously, with variations brought about by cost and local divergencies of taste." *

This quick awareness encouraged acceptance of American designers, who previously had run a poor second to the French. Elizabeth Hawes opened the first all-American fashion show at Lord & Taylor's in New York City early in the decade, and helped the sale of her own originals, as well as other American designers, with her books about the fashion business.

Smart dressmakers began to give names to their dresses, as names are given to race horses, and the advertisers opened up full throttle. "The limits of the credulity of allegedly hardheaded women seeking youth and a fashionable figure have not been found. American women in 1935 in search of youthful bodies and slim, willowy figures continued to be of great comfort to the rubber planters of the world." *

The ideal girl of that year was Ginger Rogers, and this brought about the flat tummy, a slim young waist, and the realization of a corsetmaker's dream. Miss Rogers' slim lines and her glamorous costumes of the day influenced the production of corsets and allied garments to the tune of 67 million dollars. And the "slimming" of women forced closer-fitting and scantier undergarments.

There was a shift in the material used in women's undergarments from cotton to silk and rayon. In the Sears Roebuck catalogue, for instance, old-fashioned drawers were no longer advertised, and women were advised to wear Sears' "briefs —sleeker, smoother, skin-light, skin-tight!" The trend was helped by the success of the strip-teasers.

"One of the most successful [strippers] was Sally Rand, onetime leader in the Christian Endeavor Society from Kansas City, Missouri, whose bubble and fan dances at the World's Fair in Chicago, 1933, were so sensationally successful. Within a short time her earnings had jumped to $6,000 a week, which led her to observe that 'I never made any money until I took off my pants,' and to her confession that she was 'fanning her brother though college.' And children bounced their rubber balls to the rhyme,

* David L. Cohn, *The Good Old Days* (New York, Simon and Schuster, 1940).

"Sally Rand has lost her fan;
Give it back, you nasty man." *

Romance and youth were the stuff of women's fashions of the Thirties. The Sears catalogue confirmed it.

Moonlight Sonata—you, winsome and desirable in clouds of rayon net, your tiny waist sashed with whispering rayon taffeta.

Whispers in the Dark—you, pretty as a picture in a formal of celanese rayon ninon, agleam with rayon satin stripes. Proud puffed sleeves, softly shirred bodice, slashed in a V . . .*

And dresses were definitely designed for the young. Women, no matter what age, were willing to suffer any torture in the fitting salons, beauty parlors and even at the hands of the plastic surgeons: "Save the surface and you save all." *

Hairdos changed as well. By 1935 hardly a town in the United States was without at least one beauty parlor. With the development of the permanent wave, a regular visit to the hairdresser's was a matter of course.

"The American girl wanted her stockings sheerer and sheerer in transparency, and she was sold on the finest texture" * by endorsements by the Hollywood stars. At the beginning of the decade, American manufacturers were producing 300 million pairs of silk stockings annually, and the price per pair was approximately $1.50. By 1938 they were 91 cents. The price of raw silk had dropped, and technology had produced rayon. But there was a partial rollback of this "progress" in 1938 and 1939, when American women were asked to boycott silk, and to use cotton and lisle instead, as a protest against

Japan's invasion of China. Magazines and newspapers carried photographs of the American woman burning her silk stockings and flaunting her legs in lisle hosiery.

The girl of the Thirties began to show her curves again, to the satisfaction of men. Frederick Lewis Allen described her as "alert-looking rather than bored, with a pert, up-tilted nose and an agreeably intelligent expression; she appeared alive to what was going on around her, ready to make an effort to give the company a good time." And "the prevailing style of hairdress (a shoulder-length page-boy or curled bob) was likewise simple, and lovely. In the years to come it may be that one of the most charming recollections of the period was that of hatless girls striding along like young blond goddesses, their hair tossing behind them. One recalls the complaint of a young man that almost every girl appeared good-looking—from behind!" †

Dresses and skirts had dipped to as low as ten inches off the floor in the early Thirties, but began to creep upward as the decade went on, until they were worn just below the knee. Most women now wore painted fingernails, without complaint from husband or escort, who had fought the good fight when the style was first introduced at the beginning of the decade.

Men's clothing, as usual, suffered no dramatic change, but stiff collars, garters, vests, spats and such were discarded in the interest of economy. Trousers were worn long and baggy, and the jacket with a belted back was successful for several seasons.

* David Cohn, *The Good Old Days.*
† Frederick Lewis Allen, *Since Yesterday.*

In the higher circles of fashion and design, there was apt to be experiment and capriciousness, exhibiting a kind of perverse humor, but adding up to damn' little, according to Cecil Beaton.

CECIL BEATON

FASHION AND DESIGN*

WOMEN'S FASHIONS in the name of practicability comprised street suits of indeterminate shape and length, "formal" pajamas, tea gowns with horse halters around the neck, and the creations so un-Parisian in taste of Schiaparelli. Yet Schiap was in her own way something of a genius. She injected a healthy note into the Thirties, inventing her own particular form of ugliness, and salubriously shocking a great many people. With colors that were aggressive and even upsetting, including a particular puce she referred to as her "shocking pink," Schiap began her revolution.

She used rough-looking materials, oaten linens, pebbly crashes, and heavy crepes—put nylon and other new materials to good purposes, and used synthetic fabrics for her dresses. Mrs. Diana Vreeland of *Harper's Bazaar* once sent a Schiap dress to the cleaner's. The next day she received a telephone call informing her with regret that the dress had been put into the cleaning fluid and there was nothing left of it.

Schiap was the first dressmaker to travel extensively, and wherever she went she brought back representative clothes of that country. On holiday in Switzerland she would make a mental note of the ski instructor's clothes —on her return, women would be given thick jerseys with padded square shoulders.

At one moment in the late Thirties, this capricious designer fell under the surrealist influence. In her shop a shocking-pink sofa became a pair of lips. She often put women in apparently unfeminine clothes, going so far as to introduce bus-conductor outfits. One suit, decorated with closed bureau drawers, was inspired by Dali. By 1938 fashion had gone into such a state of decadence that it seemed surely a last warning before the tower of Babel fell.

The Thirties, from the point of view of the arts and fashion, strikes one

* Condensed from Cecil Beaton's *The Glass of Fashion* (Garden City, N. Y., Doubleday, 1954).

as being perhaps the least interesting in recent decades: heavy wrought-iron doors, Knole sofas, backs bound with bandages of metal galloon and their adjustable ends held insecurely by tasseled knobs, placed cater-corner in even the smallest rooms; cigarettes were kept in disemboweled books; lamp shades were made of old music parchment; almost anything could be given a pseudoantique look by the simple expedient of applying a coat of yellow varnish.

There were the Chicago World's Fair and the New York World's Fair, both heralding the beginning of the acceptance of modern architecture with its straight lines, plain materials and obviation of detail. Interior decorating then went modern with a vengeance. But the mass-produced modern furniture was to be as impersonal as anything that had ever been turned out at Grand Rapids.

Fashion photographers came into their own. [My] own pictures became more and more rococo: like the souls in torment in Bosch's Hell, ladies of the upper crust were to be seen in published photographs fighting their way out of a hatbox or breaking through a huge sheet of white paper or torn screen, as though emerging from a nightmare, as seen through a plate-glass window which had been daubed with whitewash. White-on-white paper was often used as the background with a sheath of whitened branches.

Perfectly normal ladies were pictured in extremes of peril with one arm covering the face or thrust forward in exaggerated perspective straight toward the camera. Backgrounds were often exaggerated and often tasteless. Some of this meretricious work was inspired by a literary approach. Mannequins dressed to kill would be photographed with smoking guns, and smart witnesses would appear in the "witness box." At this time much unrestrained activity was afoot in the fields of decoration—night clubs were done up as bird cages, baroque excesses in plasterwork were allied to the plush luxuries of late Victorianism. Magentas and pinks together with bright yellows were favorite colors. Depression life in the Thirties had its highlights. Art, especially under the influence of such painters as Dali, Picasso and Berard, was impinging very closely on fashion.

Perhaps no other person [than Greta Garbo] has had such an influence on the appearance of a whole generation, though in fact the owner of this face possesses other qualities that cannot be improvised or imitated. The whole secret of her appeal seems to lie in an elusive and haunting sensitivity. We find ripples of feeling appearing at the surface, coming from some deep and unknown source. Though Garbo has been credited with having little clothes sense and obviously has paid no attention to the rules of current fashion, she had an innate flair with what is fitting for her and she possessed a great natural taste, being capable of appraising good clothes as well as appreciating them. At the time of her Hollywood advent, film makers attempted to make Garbo conform to their patterns, frizzing her hair and dressing her in impossible trappings. But by degrees, as she gained more authority, Garbo was able to assert her instinct and bring her real beauty to the fore, previously lost behind the unreal human façade Hollywood had devised for her as another of its temptresses.

[It was one of the paradoxes of fashion] that a woman who has not possessed an evening dress for twenty years should emerge as one of the leading influences on style of her day. And what Garbo achieved in clothes has been reflected also in make-up. Before Garbo, women's faces were pink and white. But her very simple and sparing use of cosmetics altered the face of the fashionable woman. For a number of years she used no lipstick or powder. It had been customary for stage people to use blue paint on their eyelids, but Garbo, by drawing a black line to accentuate the upper eyelashes, brought the line of the lid back into vogue.

In retrospect, the Thirties fashions were dull . . . and foolishness was widespread: Dali on a hot summer's afternoon read a lecture on surrealism in a diver's suit.

But brilliant personalities and artists were not lacking. Even in a low-pressure period they will turn water into wine, dross into gold, mutton chops into hats and meretricious material into art.

GOING TO COLLEGE

A COLLEGE DEGREE in the Thirties was not quite the help it is today in getting a job. No matter how much education a college graduate had, he might consider himself lucky, in the early years of the decade especially, just to land one of those marginal selling jobs (no guaranteed salary, commission only).

There was a hell of a lot of waiting—waiting to get an education, waiting to find a job, waiting to get married—all of which depended upon obtaining the money. Some people hung around the colleges, afraid to leave. Arthur Miller says he knew graduate students "who lived in an abandoned house, with no electricity or heat, and never took the boardings off the windows for fear of discovery, and one of them had been around so long he had gone through every course in the Lit school, but Roman band instruments." *

The colleges themselves did not have it easy. Their endowments had fallen off, as had the interest on their investments, and enrollments were down, and not until the middle of the decade would they rise. Yet, reactionary voices protested the government's program of assistance to students, through the National Youth Administration and the Federal Emergency Relief Administration.

ARTHUR MILLER AT MICHIGAN

Years later, Arthur Miller observed that he had attended the University of Michigan with the help of the NYA, but that within two months after leaving school, in 1938, he was on relief. Nevertheless, his college years obviously meant a lot to him. He says, "I thought I had accomplished something. I knew at least how much I did not know. I had found many friends and had the respect of the ones who mattered to me. It had been a small world, gentler than the real one, but tough enough." *

"I loved the idea of being separated from the nation, because the spirit of the nation, like its soil, was being blown by crazy winds. Friends of mine in New York, one of them a *cum laude* from Columbia, were aspiring to the city fireman's exam; but in Ann Arbor I saw that if it came to the worst a man could live on nothing for a long time. I earned $15 a month for feeding a building full of mice—the National Youth Administration footing the bill—and out of it I paid $1.75 a week for my room and squeezed the rest for my Granger tobacco (two packs for thirteen cents), my books, laundry and movies. For my meals I washed dishes in the co-op cafeteria. My eyeglasses were supplied by the Health Service, and my teeth were fixed for the cost of materials. The girls paid for themselves, including the one I married.

"I do not know whether the same thing happened at Harvard or Columbia or Yale, but when I was at Ann Arbor I felt I was at home. My

* "University of Michigan," *Holiday,* December 1953.

400

friends were the sons of die-makers, farmers, ranchers, bankers, lawyers, doctors, clothing workers and unemployed relief recipients. They came from every part of the country and brought all their prejudices and special wisdoms. It was always so wonderful to get up in the morning. I recall going to hear Kagawa, the Japanese philosopher, and how, suddenly, half the audience stood up and walked out because he had used the word Manchukuo, which is Japanese, for the Chinese province of Manchuria. As I watched the Chinese students excitedly talking outside on the steps of Hill Auditorium, I felt something about the Japanese attack on China that I had not felt before.

"It was a time when the fraternities, like the football team, were losing their glamour. Life was too earnest. But I remember glancing with sadness at the photographs of Newman, Oosterbaan and the other gridiron heroes and secretly wishing that the gladiatorial age had not so completely disappeared. Instead, my generation thirsted for another kind of action, and we took great pleasure in the sit-down strikes that burst loose in Flint and Detroit, and we gasped when Roosevelt went over the line with the TVA, and we saw a new world coming every third morning, and some of the old residents thought we had gone stark raving mad.

"I tell you true, when I think of the Library I think of the sound of a stump speaker on the lawn outside because so many times I looked up from what I was reading to try to hear what issue they were debating now. The place was full of speeches, meetings and leaflets. It was jumping with Issues." *

YOUTH IN COLLEGE†

THE PRESENT-DAY *college generation is fatalistic.* Certain college presidents will deny this and they will be right in terms of sections of their own broods. But before any minute spectrum analysis is undertaken, the investigator is struck by the dominant and pervasive color of a generation that will not stick its neck out. It keeps its shirt on, its pants buttoned, its chin up, and its mouth shut. If we take the mean average to be the truth, it is a cautious, subdued, unadventurous generation, unwilling to storm heaven, afraid to make a fool of itself, unable to dramatize its predicament. It may be likened to a very intelligent turtle, skeptical of its biological

* "University of Michigan," *Holiday,* December 1953.
† Condensed from *Fortune,* June 1936. The magazine had conducted a poll of college youth in twenty-five American universities, and from the many interviews and questionnaires it attempted to ascertain the character of the composite college student.

inheritance, the shell, but determined not to be a bull, a bear, or a goat. The turtle has security and . . .

Security is the summum bonum *of the present college generation.* This may be convicting the average undergraduate of having good sense, yet security is usually thought of as the ideal of middle age. Yearners for security do not set foot on Everest or discover the Mountains of the Moon. They do not even defy the racketeers and start new wet-wash laundries. They want a haven in a . . .

Job that is guaranteed to be safe and permanent. The present-day average undergraduate is no chancy gambler. He doesn't expect to make much money. If the student decides on teaching or on a government job in the civil service, it is not only because he has ideals about molding the future generations or about helping his country. It is also because teaching and the civil service promise a relief from economic uncertainty. A professor's $5,000 per annum means—security. If the undergraduate selects a profession it is mainly because business seemingly does not offer opportunities for aggrandizement as it did in the golden Twenties. And if he does go into business he is perfectly willing to do what he is told without quibbling—and also without any attempt to force or insinuate his personality and values upon his superiors in the company that has employed him. He is, in brief, tractable corporation material. But are good corporation heads made out of tractable material? And if not, where are the future industrial and financial leaders coming from? Nice, decent, and willing boys may ultimately be a liability. Kingdoms often fall when they are in the hands of the epigoni.

We may have implied that it is an apathetic generation, but "passive" is an apter adjective. For, if one says to a young professor of economics, "You have a gutless gang of youngsters in your college," the professor will be perplexed. "Why, no," he will say, "the college boys of today are way ahead of those of ten years ago. They are much more interested in political and social questions. They know what is going on in the world. They read the papers intelligently. They take many more courses in economics and history and the social sciences." So another generalization may be set up. The undergraduate of today is . . .

Intellectually curious about the world. Does this contradict the passivity generalization? Seemingly, but when the inquiry is pressed one discovers that the impression of passivity and the impression of lively intellectual curiosity are two faces of the same coin. The answer one gets depends on what type of question is asked.

If one queries the average undergraduate about his chances for the future or if one talks with him about his ability to twist the world to his own desires, it is then that one will find him a fatalist—at least a stoic, at worst a whiner. Questions bearing on the personal equation bring out the facts that he doesn't think he will attain great heights in the world as it is constituted and that he doesn't think he can make that world over. He may deplore war, but he can't see himself thwarting the forces that make for war. Evidently he is a fit human paving stone for the juggernaut.

However, if one talks with the average undergraduate about the general *conditions* to be expected in the future, one will find oneself in the presence of a chatty, energetic, brightly curious young person. How can this be reconciled with the fatalism elicited by questions bearing on the personal equation? The answer is pat: a cautious, fatalistic person never moves into new country without first getting all the information he can about it. Our slave does not contemplate rebellion and a break for freedom; he merely wants to know the conditions of his servitude. Yet intellectual curiosity born of caution may, indeed, result in the crusades of tomorrow. At the moment the student sniffs the wind. He may be waiting to see how much life the business cycle—or series of business cycles— has in it. If jobs expand, the student will apparently go back to the *status quo ante* 1930. But it will be no complete spiritual reversion, for the student will have a background of political thinking that will forever prevent him from taking prosperity for granted. And if the prosperity fails to hold up . . .

The undergraduate will turn to new leaders. He is already doing so to some extent. The old-style campus big man no longer commands unqualified allegiance. The football star, the crew captain, the "muscular Christian" from the college Y.M.C.A., the smoothie from the big prep school who becomes track manager, the socially graceful prom leader—these still have honor and respect. But the intellectually curious person, who used to be considered queer or "wet" unless he had extraintellectual characteristics to recommend him, is climbing past the conventional big man. Englishmen, long accustomed to spotting future undersecretaries of the Foreign Office, future labor theoreticians, and even future Prime Ministers on visits to Cambridge or Oxford, have remarked on this mutation in American campus leadership and are inclined to set 1932 as the date at which the mutation became apparent.

This does not mean the colleges are becoming radicalized. Again it is important to emphasize, at least pro tem, the passive element. The new-style leader is more apt to demand courses in Communism, Fascism, and the works of Thomas Jefferson than he is to take a stand for or against a given type of social organization. The fact that students have been flocking to history, economics, and sociology courses does not mean that Leninism or Henry Georgeism is rampant under the elms. The new leaders limit intransigence to a demand for information. Tomorrow, if economic indexes turn downward, the demands may become more active in character. Meanwhile the student marks time and dallies with . . .

Culture and the Good Life. Unable to plot his future, the average undergraduate has turned to minor cultural and semicultural activities, in which there has been a great diffusion. Ping-pong, court tennis, squash rackets, rushing for the Berkshire snow train to get a weekend's practice in the telemark or slalom race, experiments with the Leica candid camera—the popularity of all such things is increasing by leaps and bounds. If it were not that they tend to displace a working direction, a major drive, in most instances, one might say that the Good Life had at least reached America. Yet the Good Life cannot be attained by making a cult of hobbies. The Good Life demands some animating . . .

Faith, with a dependent moral code. One might think that a lack of worldly faiths or an obscure terrestrial future could be counted upon to turn the undergraduate to thoughts of mystic matters. Yet—save for an occasional Buchmanite flurry—religion, as an institution, has taken a back seat. Too passive to be atheist, the undergraduate is vaguely deist. The girls' colleges show more religious hunger than the boys'.

Liquor and sex used to be part of the great triumvirate of campus topics that included religion. Today economics is to the fore as bull-session pabulum, with religion playing a minor role. Liquor as a conversational topic is passé. Less flamboyant drinking is the present-day rule; there is no prohibition law to defy, hence one can drink in peace. As for sex, it is, of course, still with us. But the campus takes it more casually than it did ten years ago. Sex is no longer news. And the fact that it is no longer news is news.

The family as such is no longer an object of derision, as it was in the early Twenties. Fathers and mothers are listened to once more, at least in the East and in the Middle West. (The Pacific Coast universities, which lag behind the colleges of the East, show less evidence of respect for parental dicta, but even on the coast the tide is beginning to turn.) Deference to the advice of father is part of the general yearning for security among the young. It is also part of a world hunger for certainty. And as the world wags, so wags the undergraduate.

THE CAMPUS WALKS AND TALKS

When the male undergraduate, 1936 model, gets up in the morning—at seven-thirty if he has early classes, at eight-thirty if not—he will, if he goes to a wealthy college, put on sloppy gray flannel bags and a tweed coat that is guaranteed to last for four years, or for the duration of the college course. The clothes, which represent an over-all investment of some $45, might be attributed by the cynical to a Depression fashion of imitating the proletariat. Economy in dress has cost Jack Feinstein and other college tailors many haggard nights. And when the undergraduate dashes quite bareheaded down the entry steps to breakfast, a recent rumor that some hat factories have shut down is readily credible.

Breakfast is a hurry-scurry matter of orange juice, eggs, toast, and coffee (the undergraduate has given up breakfasting on Coca-Cola), plus a quick glance at the college daily and an even quicker glance at some outside newspaper. This quick-flash gutting of the news is not limited to the sports page, for Hitler, Mussolini and Stalin have become quite as superficially exciting as the sports heroes.

After breakfast comes another dash, usually to classes. In some universities, however, compulsory chapel lingers on, at least for freshmen and sophomores. And in the colleges where the student is still fated to spend ten or fifteen minutes in putative worship, he does it with an air of extreme fatigue. The fatigue is so evident that when the enterprising editor of the *Daily Princetonian* recently assembled a Leica camera portfolio of typical worshipers—some half asleep, some tying shoes and neckties, some reading the New York *Herald Tribune,* some playing Salvo, some doing lessons, and some simply gawking at the rafters—it clinched the case against chapel with the Board of Trustees. By such persuasive methods has the undergraduate won his case against compulsory institutional religion in many of the universities.

The secular and contemporary orientation of the average undergraduate is apparent in the choice of courses to which he hurries after breakfast or chapel. He no longer preferably takes his scholastic eye opener with a professor who discourses on Platonism or "the best that has been thought and said" in the world's cultural history. Instead, he stampedes in preponderant droves to classes in the sciences, in sociology, in history, and in economics, and the teacher who does not illustrate a lecture with topical reference to the magazines and daily papers may be considered a dull fellow. If the student is pursuing culture, it is quite likely to be in a course on the contemporary novel that has been added to the curriculum at his own demand. Once the emphasis on history and the social sciences has been discounted, one is struck by the cultural diffusion represented by the choice of favorite subjects. Horticulture may appear on the elective schedule along with labor relations; ceramics and art interpretation may vie in popularity with a class in social-service work.

Since academic standards have been tightened up during the past decade, the average student who remains in college does some serious studying. Classroom horseplay still exists, and an antic student may try to snap a professor in action with a camera concealed by a couple of books, but there is less reading of *The Saturday Evening Post* in the back rows these days. Hence, the morning hours in college are largely devoted to constructive work. Around twelve o'clock comes a letdown that lasts well into the afternoon. The average undergraduate may turn up for lunch at his club or fraternity wearing an old sweater, if house rules made in a more formal day have been relaxed. He consumes large quantities of milk at lunch, and feels sleepy afterwards. When he gets up from the table it is to play pool, to read magazines, to listen to the radio—or to sit around and gas with his friends. If he is diligent about any particular line of work he may break the siesta tradition and bury himself in the library. But this is rare.

At three-thirty the tempo quickens. Today the typical undergraduate is a far healthier specimen than the one who tried to ruin himself before twenty-five in Charles Wertenbaker's 1928 college novel, *Boojum!*, and he may almost certainly be found on one of the playing fields by midafternoon. If he can't make a varsity squad he doesn't repine; he doesn't want to die of an athlete's heart any more than he wants to die of a drunkard's. But he likes to keep in mildly good shape and he goes in for a vast profusion of intramural games: touch football, softball, tennis, golf (it's more than your life is worth to walk across a college links), squash, handball, ping-pong (played vociferously), and scrub baseball. There are no special coaches for any of these sports, and no one cares greatly whether his side wins or loses. Lou Gehrig may make the "old college try" for an impossibly distant foul ball at the Yankee Stadium; but the old college try is absent from intramural athletics on the campus. The kids are out for mild fun, and they quit when they feel like it.

At six o'clock an infinitesimal number of undergraduates may serve cocktails (gin and lemon juice) in their rooms. But the typical student will go from his sports straight to dinner. After dinner there ensues a studious period for the majority, although on some nights the student will go to the movies. The Eastern undergraduate laughs derisively at the "collegiate" pictures produced by Hollywood directors who use the Pacific Coast campuses as location. (Anything that is "collegiate" is beneath the contempt of the Eastern collegians, in fact, and the campus sales of *College Humor* have dropped to almost nothing. Likewise the sale of banners, for which the student has no use. He prefers tasteful etchings in his room.)

When the movies are over, the prospective Phi Bete returns to work from his unwonted early evening relaxation. The college humorist goes off to adapt *The New Yorker* one-line joke (which has ousted the two-line joke except in jerkwater college weeklies) to the campus world, and the littérateur seeks solitude to blend the style of Hemingway with the influence of the *New Masses*. The less conscientious or ambitious student may play bridge (poker is only indulged in by a few "sports"), or he may go to the town taproom for a glass or two of beer and a bull session devoted to politics, sex, student personalities, and criticism of university policy. If he goes home to read, he will pick up Santayana's *The Last Puritan,* Vincent Sheean's *Personal History,* or some other national best seller. In F. Scott Fitzgerald's generation, student reading was often adventurously *sui generis.* It was the day of the campus popularity of the "quest book," which featured as its central character a Wellsian or a Compton Mackenzian young man in search of his soul. This type of book has ceased to be written. The modern blending of campus and national reading habits does not cover one item, an anonymous book called *The Psychology of Getting Grades,* which costs a dollar. This is unmentioned on the best-seller lists, but it is runner-up to Santayana on more than one campus. In it one can learn how to outguess the professor and even how to choose him before one has to outguess him.

Between ten-thirty and twelve-thirty the campus subsides into sleep. A few independent drunks, who care little for the Friday or Saturday night tradition, come roaring in at three, but the average undergraduate doesn't get tight until classes and study are over for the week. Weekends are not so frequent as they used to be, the obvious reason being that money has not been plentiful. But one doesn't have to go far away from college to drink. The stages of college inebriation are ranked as follows: high, tight, looping, stinking, plastered, out. Some would put tight after looping. But regardless of the grading of intermediate philological degrees of drunkenness, most of the drinking undergraduates think high is the desirable state of glow for a weekday night and even for the ordinary weekend. At spring house parties and at the football games the student can proceed to the tight and looping (or looping and tight) stages without causing any particular commotion.

When the college man meets the college girl, at the prom or the spring parties or in New York on a weekend, they dance very much as they danced some ten years ago. Those who would try to correlate styles in dancing with aspects of social change had better take warning from the fact that college dancing has passed arbitrarily back and forth between eras of high-speed jazz and the walking-talking-dancing slow movement of 1934. After the cheek-to-cheek business of the early Twenties came a variety of formations in which the girl's back was all but broken, with the lean-to formation winning the prize for most uncomfortable. Now, long after the demise of the jazz age, posteriors are back to a normal vertical, cheeks are back together, and the jazz tempo has been resumed. F. Scott Fitzgerald's Amory Blaine would still feel at home at a prom.

But it is doubtful that he would feel at home with the modern college girl if he came to know her away from the dance floor. Only girls referred to sarcastically as Midwestern sorority types dress up every day in a manner to suit Amory's Isabelles and Rosalinds. The typical Eastern college girl wears a tweed skirt and a sweater (probably knitted by herself) and low-heeled shoes. With no make-up and little lipstick, she presents a casual, even an untidy, appearance while on the campus. And the casualness is carried over into the girl's surface air of self-possession, which is unstudied.

The girl undergraduate gets up at eight, goes to classes conscientiously, and keeps her appointments with faculty people. At mealtime, and in between meals at the drugstores, where she eats a number of strange concoctions, she usually talks about what happens at school, and she may go on to discuss politics. Bull sessions on religion and sex are for more secluded moments. They are more frequent during freshman and sophomore years; upper-class girl students have too much work to do, have talked themselves out with their really good friends, and have discovered the advantages of getting enough sleep. Athletics do not bulk large in the girl student's life. She may do a little swimming, play a little tennis. A very few go in for golf. In the evening the girl student may go to the movies, but more often she retires to her room (she likes to live alone) or goes visiting. Late in the evening she makes tea (cocoa is no longer the midnight staple) and spreads some biscuits with jam. Although she is not allowed to smoke in her bedroom, the girl student consumes a large number of cigarettes during the day. In most ways she is behavioristically indistinguishable from many girls who don't go to college.

In the girls' colleges there is an inchoate hunger for religion or at least for philosophical certitude. But it is difficult to see much hope for institutional religion even among those who lust for certainty. God, to the undergraduate, is like the deity of the Unitarians—an "oblong blur."

So far as a moral code goes, the undergraduate, both male and female, seems to be fashioning one, without the aid of institutional religion. Ten years ago sexual promiscuity was either a fact or an idea that haunted the imagination. The backwash of war and the crumbling of the Victorian verities threw a generation into wild experiment or at least into lurid reading. Today the student takes sex more calmly, although on some male campuses, the sight of a pretty girl still provokes the usual scabrous ribaldry and cries of "fire, fire."

It is impossible to discover with any accuracy the actual sexual habits of a generation, but if the present-day undergraduate indulges in intercourse before marriage with any frequency he doesn't talk very much about it. Contraceptive knowledge is widespread, and the male undergraduate knows that contraceptive devices can be bought at filling stations. Hence, whether he uses his knowledge for practical purposes or whether he merely reassures himself for a distant future, a shadow has been lifted from his mind.

Fifteen years ago, when college girls sat up to the late hours of the night, they talked about careers and living their own lives. The trek to Greenwich Village was on. Today the prospect of marriage and children is popular again. Sixty per cent of the college girls and 50 per cent of the men would like to get married within a year or two after graduation, and 50 per cent of each sex would like to have children soon after marriage. On the subject of working wives, however, the divergence is sharp. For where only 15 per cent of the men think their future mates should hold paid jobs after marriage, 40 per cent of the girls look with favor upon continuing to work. Most girls are afraid of boredom; hence even if they have economic independence they want to be doing something. Forty per cent of the boys and 30 per cent of the girls consider two children per family the ideal number. Very few want no children at all; very few want more than four. Harvard, Princeton and Virginia, while not exactly for race suicide, have a low average desire of 2.8 children per male capita; Yale, "mother of men" and "mother of colleges," is considerably more philoprogenitive and desires an average of 3.2 offspring.

409

So far we have been considering the behavior and the sex mores of the animal. And in these respects there are some differences between this generation and its predecessor. But man is supposed to be a thinking animal, and the biggest difference between this generation and the one of the Twenties is in the subject that forms the content of its thought. That subject is the world crisis. Sometimes quite palpably, sometimes indefinably, it colors nearly everything the student does and says. Fear of the future and a vague sense of imminent frustration have taken the Fitzgeraldian cockiness out of the average undergraduate. If he drinks less and wenches less, it is because the stuff of the newspaper headlines is on his mind. A few have been enormously stimulated by the uncertainty of these years, but they are the exceptions. However, both the timid ones and the zestful ones have been mulling over the same social and economic problems. This mulling has not yet produced a definite youth movement, but the campus is a little—a very little—to the left of the country as a whole.

And because it is a little to the left, the Hearst newspapers have grown volubly excited about the "menace" of undergraduate radicalism. This excitement has resulted in considerable distortion of the truth. No ism has as yet altered the contours of the American university world. Undergraduate society is still shaped like a turnip. Liberals and democrats—or at least people who react favorably to the stimuli of liberal and democratic phrases —form the thick equatorial bulge of the turnip. These liberals and democrats are vaguely internationalist in their thinking; nationalism is out of fashion at the moment, for the student tends to identify it with imperialism and the suppression of alien populations.

At the taproot of the turnip is a numerically negligible group of Reds. The Fascist stem is even skinnier than the taproot. Announced conservatives make up a north temperate zone that is not quite as sizable as the south temperate zone of those vaguely interested in an ill-defined socialism. (When a Goucher girl says she is socialist it probably means that she has social good will, not that she is interested in the theories of Karl Marx.) Those who believe in the aristocratic principle balance the combined worshipers at Communist and Fascist shrines.

Curiosity about the conditions that will face the student after he has graduated has put new life into the arguments and attendance at many a campus political union. It was student curiosity that led to the widespread inflation of the sociology, history, and economics departments. But the increase in the number of instructors in the social sciences has not been sufficient to assuage the inquisitiveness of the thinking 5 or 10 per cent of the undergraduates. In many colleges—North Carolina, Minnesota,

Princeton, Yale and Dartmouth, to pick random examples—the cerebrating 5 to 10 per cent has, on its own initiative, invited guest speakers such as General Hugh S. Johnson, Harold Laski, Westbrook Pegler, Norman Thomas, Arthur Krock, Raymond Moley, George Soule, Jr., Fiorello La Guardia, Edmund Wilson, and Jouett Shouse. The inquisitive students are pretty much in the listening stage, and the question-and-answer periods that follow the speeches reveal more of a desire for information than any willingness to battle for or against specific ideas.

Although a nationwide college poll on Franklin D. Roosevelt would reveal more about sectional, class, and family backgrounds than about the political effect of university affiliation, the experimental ideas churned up by the New Deal propaganda have made a marked impress on the undergraduate mind. The New Deal has been dramatized so often as a youth movement that it has stimulated an interest in experimental government even among boys and girls who think Roosevelt is selling the country down the river. The young Republican who votes for Landon or whomsoever next fall will do so not for consciously reactionary motives, but with hopes that the Republican party will provide a liberalism in action that is less costly than the present Democratic brand. The thinking section of the undergraduate population definitely has its ear to the ground. And to some extent the impression of lassitude in the colleges springs paradoxically from the undergraduate eagerness to listen to propaganda for the new society. This propaganda, whether Communist, Fascist, or New Deal, continuously stresses the importance of state action, so quite naturally the listening student is apt to be left with the idea that he must sit around and wait for the Great White Father (or the Great Red Father) to give the nod.

Undoubtedly there is a good measure of lip service to liberalism among the undergraduates, but ten years ago there was not even lip service to any formulated political creed. When the Harvard *Lampoon* editors of 1935-36 apologized to the visiting Professor Laski for the attack made upon him by the 1919 editorial board in the days of the Boston police strike, they may have been indulging in an easy gesture. Yet the gesture is symbolic of the alteration that has come over the campus since the Twenties.

Of bona fide collectivist radicalism in the colleges there is at most only a chemical trace. There are, for example, some of the leaders of the American Student Union. This Union is the result of a merger of Socialist and Communist groups, but it has lost sectarian sharpness by its recent tactic of taking in liberals and progressives who are against war and Fascism but not necessarily for a socialistic organization of society.

411

Snobbery still prevails at Yale, Harvard and Princeton, though the girls' colleges no longer feel strongly about social prestige on the campus. At the wealthier men's liberal-arts colleges the campus is divided into the "white men" and the "black men." The black men are also known as "drips" and "meatballs." (Ten years ago the word was "wet smack"; twenty years ago, "the unwashed.")

Ten or twenty years ago campus snobbery often looked down upon the rough diamond who had brains. But the new orientation toward perplexing economic and political news has caused even the college snob to withdraw his objections to brains, which today need not be accompanied by social graces. Puzzled, unable to get satisfying answers from his teachers, the average student has ceased to regard the football star and the smoothie who qualifies for prom leader as the repositories of all virtue. The new orientation has produced a type of leader that contrasts vividly with the old-style campus headman. The Depression has brought the American college abreast of the English university at last, with the result that future administrators, politicos and thinkers can undoubtedly be spotted in sophomore year.

The shift in leadership is so clear and striking, so apparent in so many universities that it amounts to a structural change in the undergraduate world. The impact of the universal economic crisis on the campus obviously called forth the new leader. Hence referring to him as "English" is merely a way of explaining him by analogy, for he has, actually, sprung from the native soil. If a plateau of prosperity lies ahead for American business—and for the undergraduate who is seeking a job—the mutation will not have a mushroom growth in the near future. But it is undoubtedly here to stay: the fact that America has reached the end of pioneering and must henceforth grow intensively rather than extensively guarantees the new leader his niche and his influence.

A PRESIDENT WHO CARED

In 1933 the nation had witnessed an entirely new kind of leader as head of the government. John Gunther says that his best quality was his "extreme humanity." He defined humanity in terms of F.D.R.'s range from "amiability to compassion, from fertility in ideas to subtlety in personal relationships, from the happy expression of animal vitality to the deepest cognizance of suffering and primitive despair." *

He was a master politician, perhaps the best the country has ever had, and this was coupled with a great capacity to inspire idealism in people. Frances Perkins said that she and "everyone else came away from an interview with the President feeling better."

Furthermore, he was a President who was accessible to the people, not only to the members of his Administration but to the people at large. His oldest son, James, recalls F.D.R.'s policy:

"One of Father's first orders when he moved into the White House was symbolic of the New Deal's humanity. He circulated word to his staff, from the top secretaries to the telephone operators, that if persons in distress telephoned to appeal for help of any sort, they were not to be shut off but that someone was to talk with them. If a farmer in Iowa was about to have his mortgage foreclosed, if a homeowner in one of the big cities was about to lose his home, and they felt desperate enough about it to phone the White House, Father wanted help given them if a way possibly could be found; he was keenly cognizant of the suffering he had seen on his campaign trips.

"Many such calls were taken— sometimes by me, when I was in the White House, and occasionally by Mother. Often ways were found to cut red tape with some federal agency. After Father's death, Mother received letters from strangers, who told her how, in the dark Depression days, they telephoned their President and received aid." †

* John Gunther, *Roosevelt in Retrospect* (New York, Harper, 1950).
† James Roosevelt and Sidney Shalett, *Affectionately, FDR* (New York, Harcourt, Brace, 1960).

ARTHUR M. SCHLESINGER, JR.

F.D.R. AS PRESIDENT*

THE WHITE HOUSE routine had not altered much from 1933. The day still began for the President soon after eight o'clock with breakfast on a tray in his bedroom. Beside the narrow white iron bedstead was a plain white table, covered with telephone, pencils, memoranda, ash trays, cigarettes, nose drops and a glass of water. Ship prints and seascapes, old Roosevelt treasures, hung on the wall. Over the fireplace, on top of the marble mantelpiece with its grape carvings, was an assortment of family photographs, toy animals and whatever other mementos had caught the President's fancy. Like every room in any Roosevelt house, the presidential bedroom was hopelessly Victorian—old-fashioned and indiscriminate in its furnishings, cluttered in its *décor,* ugly and comfortable.

While breakfasting, the President looked rapidly through half a dozen leading newspapers, half of them bitterly critical of his administration (the New York *Herald Tribune,* the Washington *Times-Herald,* and the Chicago *Tribune*). He usually wore a sweater or cape, a dressing gown was too much trouble for a crippled man. The breakfast conferences of the Hundred Days were now pretty well abandoned, except in moments of emergency. Even Eleanor Roosevelt, pausing to see her husband on her way out, usually said no more than good morning; "he liked no conversation at this hour." The newspaper scanning was the first phase in Roosevelt's unceasing effort to get the feel of the government and the nation.

Between nine and nine-thirty his secretaries—Steve Early and Marvin McIntyre, with Louis Howe, until he became ill, and then usually Colonel Edwin M. Watson, better known as Pa, the President's military aide—came in to discuss the day's schedule. In the next half hour Roosevelt dressed and shaved. Often he combined this with business. Thus Harold Ickes:

When I got to his study, his valet ushered me into his bedroom, telling me that the President was shaving. He waved toward the bathroom and the President called out to me to come in. There he was, sitting before a mirror in front

* From Arthur M. Schlesinger, Jr.'s *The Coming of the New Deal* (Boston, Houghton Mifflin, 1959).

414

of the washstand, shaving. He invited me to sit on the toilet seat while we talked. When he was through shaving he was wheeled back to his room where he reclined on his bed while his valet proceeded to help him dress. . . . I was struck all over again with the unaffected simplicity and personal charm of the man. He was the President of the United States but he was also a plain human being, talking over with a friend matters of mutual interest while he shaved and dressed with the help of his valet. His disability didn't seem to concern him in the slightest degree or to disturb his urbanity.

Around ten-thirty he was ordinarily pushed in his wheelchair along the newly constructed ramps to the executive office in the west wing of the White House. Here, in the lovely oval room, he held his official appointments and spent most of his working day. The room had the usual Rooseveltian country-house informality. "You would think," said Emil Ludwig, "you were in the summer residence of the general manager of a steamship company, who has surrounded himself with mementos of the days when he was captain." On the wall hung Hudson River prints by Currier and Ives; ship models stood on the mantel: a litter of memoranda, government reports, books, toy pigs, donkeys and ship's rudders lay on his desk; on the floor, at the President's side, occasionally rising to be patted, were two fine Irish setters. The symbols of high office—the presidential flag, the Great Seal in the ceiling—were subdued and inconspicuous. Behind the President, light streamed softly in through great glass windows running down to the floor, and to the east, briefly glimpsed, were the quiet rose garden and the porticoes and the magnolia trees. In the commotion of Washington, this bright and open room had an astonishing serenity.

Most presidential appointments took place here in the two hours before lunch. The President aimed at seeing people at fifteen-minute intervals, but often fell behind, while visitors waited in the anteroom and McIntyre and Watson did their soft-spoken best to hurry things up. Lunch took place at his desk, with food served from a metal warming oven; it was often hash with a poached egg (when two eggs came, Roosevelt sometimes sent word to the housekeeper that this was a waste of food); lunch too was usually combined with business. In the afternoon there might be more appointments; then, about midafternoon, the President usually called in Grace Tully for an hour or two of dictation. About five o'clock during the first term, the office staff was briefly summoned for what he called "the children's hour," an interlude of relaxation and gossip. Soon after five-thirty, the office day ended; and the President took twenty minutes in the White House swimming pool, installed as a result of money raised in a campaign sponsored by the New York *Daily News*. Refreshed by exercise, the President prepared for dinner, ordinarily preceded by a martini or an old-fashioned. After dinner, he often went to his private study, a genial oval room on the second floor next to his bedroom, and dictated some more or read papers or held further conversations. Usually in bed before midnight, he quickly threw off the concerns of the day and in five minutes was deep in sleep. Unlike other Presidents, Roosevelt never allowed the Secret Service to lock the doors of his room at night.

Roosevelt's immediate staff was loyal and efficient. The longest in point of service, of course, was Louis Howe, who had worked for Roosevelt nearly a quarter of a century. Howe was only in his early sixties, but, frail and wizened, he was older than his years. His devotion to the President was more proprietary than ever, and his waspishness toward everyone else more insistent. But both Franklin and Eleanor Roosevelt cherished him. On certain matters, especially politics and patronage, Roosevelt continued greatly to value Howe's counsel; and on most matters he welcomed his opinions. "I am going to talk this over with Louis," he would say. "He has forty ideas a day and sometimes a few good ones." While the President often dodged Howe's advice, if he had to bypass his old friend he did so with incomparable tact.

As for Howe, he did not allow his protégé's eminence to constrain their relationship. Once McDuffie, the President's valet, brought him a message to which he replied snappishly, "Tell the President to go to hell." McDuffie, appalled, told his wife Lizzie, one of the White House maids, that he could not possibly deliver such a message to the President. Lizzie said she would fix it up; "Mr. President," she said, "Mr. Howe says that is a hell of a thing to do." The President laughed skeptically: "That isn't what Howe said, Lizzie. He told me to go to hell." Roosevelt's feeling toward Howe, as Richberg discerningly remarked, was that of a middle-aged son who still appreciated father's wisdom but was also impatient at father's efforts to keep him under parental guidance.

By the end of 1934, Howe's health, never good, grew steadily worse. He spent more and more of his time in his suite on the second floor of the White House. In February 1935 bronchial complications brought about a collapse. He was rushed to the Naval Hospital and put under an oxygen tent. Doctors despaired of him. "He seems to cling to life in the most astonishing manner," Eleanor Roosevelt wrote sadly to Molly Dewson, "but I am afraid it is the end." She underestimated his vitality. He rallied and, though he never left the hospital for long, he stayed alive another year. Much of this time he spent in bed, doubled up in an effort to reduce the pain; he let his beard grow into a straggling goatee which made his appearance more peculiar than ever. He continued to follow politics with sharp-eyed attention, sending out a flow of confusing directives to the National Committee and to Cabinet members. The Roosevelts visited him regularly. But he knew in his heart that he had not long to live. One day a friend told him that everyone counted on him for the 1936 campaign. "No," the old man said. "No, they'll have to run this campaign without me." He paused for a moment; then said, "Franklin's on his own now." In mid-April 1936, Louis Howe died.

Eleanor Roosevelt always felt that Howe's death left an irreparable gap in Franklin's life. Howe was almost alone, she believed, in being ready to follow through an argument with her husband, forcing him by peevish persistence to see unpleasant sides of an issue: "After Louis' death," she wrote, "Franklin frequently made his decisions without canvassing all sides of a question." Harold Ickes said the same thing: "Howe was the only one who dared to talk to him frankly and fearlessly. He not only could tell him what he believed to be the truth, but he could hang on like a pup to the root until he got results." Moreover, Howe unscrupulously organized campaigns to press his views; at his instigation, Eleanor Roosevelt, Farley, Ed Flynn and others would suddenly converge on the President and, as if by accident, make the same point. Eleanor Roosevelt felt in addition that her husband saw a better cross section of people and heard a greater variety of views when Howe was alive.

These things were probably true. Yet Howe's range was limited. "Louis knows nothing about economics," Roosevelt once said; in fact, he knew little of any aspect of public affairs, and was only vaguely aware what the New Deal was all about. Howe would have saved Roosevelt from mistakes in politics, but hardly from mistakes in policy. Still the subtraction of the most vehement nay-sayer from the entourage was certainly a misfortune.

Roosevelt had named Howe his Chief Secretary as a testimonial to his years of service. His other secretaries, Early and McIntyre, received the same salary as Howe and, as time went on, took over more and more of the day-to-day responsibility. Early, a tough, hard-driving, profane newspaperman just under fifty who had been for many years an ace for the Associated Press, had press relations as his main job. McIntyre, a gentle, agreeable man in his middle fifties, with a long and not especially distinguished background in newspaper work and public relations, was more or less in charge of political appointments (though, as in any Roosevelt operation, this seemed at times everybody's responsibility). Both Early and McIntyre were Southerners, Early from Virginia, McIntyre from Kentucky. Both had worked for Roosevelt in the 1920 vice-presidential campaign. Both were aggressively nonideological. Each preferred the political and business types with which they were familiar to the odd new breed of New Dealers; in McIntyre's case, an innocent fondness for the company of lobbyists was more than once a source of embarrassment to the White House. Both were loyal to Roosevelt rather than to his philosophy. But they kept out of policy questions and each strove to do as fair a job as possible.

Pa Watson, the military aide, who ran the general appointment schedule, was a more complex and subtle figure. An Alabaman in his early fifties who had been an aide to Wilson at Versailles, Watson was a man of winning personal charm. "I have never known anyone just like him," Ickes once said. ". . . He could be relied upon to keep us all in a mellow humor, and this without any effort on his part, but simply by being himself." People so adored the bubbling good nature that they sometimes missed the sophisticated awareness which lay beneath the quips and stories. Not a New Dealer, Watson had a greater understanding than Early and McIntyre of what the New Deal was about.

Of all the staff, Marguerite LeHand, the President's personal secretary, was undoubtedly closest to him and had most influence upon him. Missy was now in her late thirties, a tall, slender woman, prematurely gray, with a lovely face and attractive gray-blue eyes. She had worked for Roosevelt so long that she knew intimately his every expression and mood; his fondness for her was so great that he would listen to her as to few others on questions of appointments and even policy ("Mr. President, you really *must* do something about" so-and-so or such-and-such). She lived on the third floor of the White House and, when Eleanor Roosevelt was away, acted as White House hostess, inviting people who she thought might divert the President. Eleanor Roosevelt, while respecting Missy's abilities and understanding her value to her husband, felt that "occasionally her social contacts got mixed with her work and made it hard for her and others." People like Bill Bullitt and Tom Corcoran, she suggested, "exploited Missy's friendship" for their own purposes. But "though occasionally someone fooled her for a time, I always waited for enlightenment to come, with confidence born of long experience." Missy was pretty and gay and liked lively company; there can be no question that she brought an essential femininity as well as a sympathetic common sense into Roosevelt's life, and there is no evidence that she ever abused the affection and trust he reposed in her. An attack of rheumatic fever in 1926 had strained Missy's heart; and more and more of the office work, as, for example, taking dictation, fell to Grace Tully, another pretty and lively girl, who had worked for Roosevelt since the 1928 campaign. Both girls were Catholics, Miss LeHand of French, Miss Tully of Irish descent. They both cared deeply about the objectives of the New Deal. Both were exceptionally able and devoted women.

One other key White House figure was the executive clerk, Rudolph Forster, who had been there since the McKinley administration. His responsibility was the channeling of state papers, and he did this with an austere and frightening efficiency. For him the job was an end in itself; Presidents came and went, but papers went on forever. "You would be terrified," he once said to a Roosevelt assistant, "if you knew how little I care." (Yet even Forster, in the end, succumbed. In the 1944 campaign, as Roosevelt was leaving the White House on a political tour, Forster, with what Robert E. Sherwood described as "the air of one who was willfully breaking all of the Ten Commandments but prepared to take the consequences," shook the President's hand and wished him luck. Roosevelt, astonished and moved, said as the car drove away, "That's practically the first time in all these years that Rudolph has ever stepped out of character and spoken to me is if I were a human being instead of just another President.")

The next concentric circle beyond the White House staff in the President's constellation was the Cabinet. In the American system this had always been an ambiguous and unsatisfactory body. At the beginning of the republic, some conceived it as a sort of executive council. All grave and important matters, it was supposed, would be submitted to a Cabinet vote in which, as Jefferson put it, "the President counts himself but one." But Presidents, even Jefferson, recoiled from such a conception; and Jackson, in his general process of revolutionizing the Presidency, decisively redefined the relationship between the President and his Cabinet.

Jackson flatly declined, for example, to submit questions to vote. "I have accustomed myself to receive with respect the opinions of others," he said, "but always take the responsibility of deciding for myself." Lincoln, going even further, found Cabinet meetings so useless that he often avoided them and at one time seemed on the verge of doing away with them altogether. As for voting: "Ayes one, noes seven. The ayes have it" —or so the old story went. "There is really very little of a government here at this time so far as most of the Cabinet are concerned," complained Gideon Welles, Lincoln's Secretary of the Navy; "certainly but little consultation in this important period." Or again: "But little was before the Cabinet, which of late can hardly be called a council. Each Department conducts and manages its own affairs, informing the President to the extent it pleases." Theodore Roosevelt ignored his Cabinet on important issues. Woodrow Wilson did not even bother to discuss the sinking of the *Lusitania* or the declaration of war with it. "For some weeks," wrote his Secretary of the Interior, Franklin Lane, "we have spent our time at Cabinet meetings largely telling stories."

Roosevelt remained generally faithful to this tradition, though he made rather more effort than Lincoln or Wilson to recognize the Cabinet's existence. At first, he planned two Cabinet meetings a week on Tuesday and Friday afternoons. Effectively he had only one, however; the Tuesday meeting was first enlarged to include the heads of the emergency agencies and then dropped almost entirely. Sessions took place in an atmosphere of characteristic Roosevelt informality. The President ordinarily began with a recital of pleasantries, telling stories which tickled him or joshing Cabinet members about their latest appearances in the newspapers. Then he might throw out a problem for a generally rambling and inconclusive decision. Or, turning to the Secretary of State, he might say without ceremony, "Well, Cordell, what's on your mind today?" Then he would continue around the table in order of precedence.

The men—and one woman—sitting around the table were of varying qualities and abilities. They had conspicuously one thing in common—a high degree of personal rectitude. "For integrity and honesty of purpose," wrote Raymond Clapper after twenty years of covering Washington, "I'll put this Cabinet against any that has been in Washington since the war. It is one thing that does truly distinguish this group. There is not a shady one in the lot." Beyond that, the people around the table represented a variety of viewpoints and temperaments, held together only by a loyalty to, or at least a dependence on, the President. There was Garner (whom the President, to his later regret, invited to attend Cabinet meetings) with his complacent country sagacity; Hull, courteous and grave, always vigilant to defend his authority against real or fancied depredation; Henry Morgenthau, closest personally to the President, earnest, devoted, and demanding; the testy and aggressive Ickes; the preoccupied and thoughtful Wallace; Homer Cummings, bland, canny and unperturbed; Jesse Jones, wary and self-contained; the intelligent and articulate Miss Perkins (whose protracted discourses appeared to fascinate the President, but bored most of the others and at times enraged Ickes—"she talks in a perfect torrent, almost without pausing to take breath"); the amiable Farley, reacting only when politics came into the discussion—they were all forceful personalities, regarding each other with a show of conviviality which often only barely concealed depths of suspicion. For the most part, they chose problems of only middling—or else of highly general—significance to communicate to the group. This was partly because, in the inevitable jostling of bureaucracy, each felt that every man's hand was against him, and none wanted to expose vulnerabilities. It was also because the conviction grew that some members would "leak" tasty items—Garner to his cronies on the Hill, or Ickes to the columnist Drew Pearson. Questions that really troubled them they reserved for private discussion with the President afterward, a practice which Garner used to call "staying for prayer meeting." "Then you would stay behind," as Morgenthau described it, "and whisper in his ear and he would say yes or no."

The members of the Roosevelt Cabinet, as usual, suffered frustration and, as usual, thought their experience unique. In private, they echoed the familiar laments of Gideon Welles and Franklin Lane. "Only the barest routine matters were discussed," burst out Ickes in his diary after a meeting in 1935. "All of which leads me to set down what has been running in my mind for a long time, and that is just what use the Cabinet is under this administration. The cold fact is that on important matters we are seldom called upon for advice. We never discuss exhaustively any policy of government or question of political strategy. The President makes all of his own decisions. . . . As a matter of fact, I never think of bringing up even a serious departmental issue at Cabinet meetings." "It seemed to me," wrote William Phillips, sitting in occasionally for Hull, "that a great deal of time was wasted at Cabinet meetings and much of the talk was without any particular import." "The important things were never discussed at Cabinet," said Morgenthau. "The President treats them like children," Tugwell wrote in his diary, "and almost nothing of any importance was discussed."

The meetings evidently retained some obscure usefulness for the President. The reaction he got from this miscellany of administrators perhaps gave him some idea of the range of public opinion. It also helped him measure the capacity of his subordinates. Grace Tully reports, for example, that he preferred Henry Wallace's willingness to speak out on a wide variety of problems "to the reticence or indifference of some Cabinet members." But, like all strong presidents, Roosevelt regarded his Cabinet as a body of department heads, to be dealt with individually—or, sometimes, as a group of representative intelligent men, useful for a quick canvass of opinion—not as a council of constitutional advisers.

Beyond the Cabinet there stretched the Executive Branch of the government—an endless thicket of vested usage and vested interest, apportioned among a number of traditional jurisdictions, dominated by a number of traditional methods and objectives. This was, in the popular understanding, the government of the United States—the people and departments and agencies whose office it was to carry out the national laws and fulfill the national policies. The President had few more basic responsibilities than his supervision and operation of the machinery of government. Little fascinated Franklin Roosevelt more than the tasks of presidential administration. And in few things was he more generally reckoned a failure.

This verdict against Roosevelt derived ultimately from a philosophy of public administration—a philosophy held for many years after by Civil Service professionals, expounded in departments of political science, and commending itself plausibly to common sense. This school's faith was in logical organization of government, founded on rigid definitions of job and function and maintained by the sanctity of channels. Its weapons were the job description and the organization chart. Its unspoken assumption was that the problems of administration never change; and its consuming fear was improvisation, freewheeling or unpredictability—which is nearly to say creativity—in the administrative process. From this point of view, it need hardly be said, the Roosevelt government was a textbook case of poor administration. At one time or another, Roosevelt must surely have violated every rule in the sacred texts of the Bureau of the Budget.

And this conventional verdict found apparent support in much of the literature written by men who worked for Roosevelt. Though these reports differed on many other things, one thing on which they very often agreed was in their complaint about Roosevelt as an administrator. They agreed on one other thing too—the perspective from which they were written. Nearly all exhibited the problems of the Presidency from below—from the viewpoint of the subordinate rather than from that of the President. The picture created by this mass of individual stories, while vivid and overwhelming, was inevitably distorted and too often querulous. For no subordinate ever got what he wanted or thought he needed. In later years, George C. Marshall would talk of "localitis"—the conviction ardently held by every theater commander that the war was being won or lost in his own zone of responsibility, and that the withholding of whatever was necessary for local success was evidence of blindness, if not of imbecility, in the high command. "Localitis" in one form or another was the occupational disease of all subordinate officials; and, in a sense, it had to be, for each of them ought to demand everything he needed to do the best job he can. But "localitis" offered no solid ground for judgment of superiors, whose role it must inevitably be to frustrate the dreams of subordinates. The President occupied the apex of the pyramid of frustration. The essence of his job was to enforce priorities—and thereby to exasperate everybody. And, in Roosevelt's case, there is little left in the literature to emphasize the view from the summit, where any President had to make his decisions. As Grace Tully (whose book does something to redress the balance) commented on other memoirists, "None of them could know that for each minute they spent with the President he spent a hundred minutes by himself and a thousand more with scores of other people—to reject, improvise, weigh and match this against that until a decision was reached on a public policy."

The question remains whether the true test of an administrator may be, not his ability to design and respect organization charts, not his ability to keep within channels, but his ability to concert and release the energies of men for the attainment of public objectives. It might be argued that the essence of successful administration is: first, to acquire the ideas and information necessary for wise decisions; second, to maintain control over the actual making of the decisions; and, third, to mobilize men and women who can make the first two things possible—that is, who can provide effective ideas and information, and who can reliably put decisions into effect. It is conceivable that these things may be more important than preserving the chastity of administrative organization— that, indeed, an excessive insistence on the sacredness of channels and charts is likely to end in the stifling of imagination, the choking of vitality, and the deadening of creativity.

Franklin Roosevelt, at any rate, had some such philosophy of administration. The first task of an executive, as he evidently saw it, was to guarantee himself an effective flow of information and ideas. And Roosevelt's first insight—or, at least, his profound conviction—was that, for this purpose, the ordained channels, no matter how simply or how intricately designed, could never be enough. An executive relying on a single information system became inevitably the prisoner of that system. Roosevelt's persistent effort therefore was to check and balance information acquired through official channels by information acquired through a myriad of private, informal and unorthodox channels and espionage networks. At times, he seemed almost to pit his personal sources against his public sources. From the viewpoint of subordinates, this method was distracting when not positively demoralizing. But Roosevelt, with his voracity for facts and for ideas, required this approach to cross-check the official system and keep it alert as well as to assure himself the balanced and various product without which he could not comfortably reach decisions.

The official structure, of course, maintained a steady flow of intelligence. Roosevelt was, for a President, extraordinarily accessible. Almost a hundred persons could get through to him by telephone without stating their business to a secretary; and government officials with anything serious on their minds had little difficulty in getting appointments. In addition, he read an enormous number of official memoranda, State Department cables, and government reports, and always tried to glance at the *Congressional Record*. The flow was overwhelming, and he sought continually to make it manageable. "I learned a trick from Wilson," he remarked to Louis Brownlow. "He once told me: 'If you want your memoranda read, put it on one page.' So I, when I came here, issued a similar decree, if you want to call it that. But even at that I am now forced to handle, so the oldsters around tell me, approximately a hundred times as many papers as any of my predecessors." Certainly his subordinates paid little attention to the one-page rule.

What gave Roosevelt's administrative practice its distinctive quality was his systematic effort to augment the official intelligence. The clutter of newspapers on his bed each morning marked only the first stage in his battle for supplementary information. In this effort, reading was a useful but auxiliary weapon. Beyond government documents and newspapers, he read little. So far as current magazines were concerned, the President, according to Early, "sketches the field," whatever that meant. As for books, Roosevelt evidently read them only on holiday, and then not too seriously. When Frances Perkins sent him the Brookings study *America's Capacity to Produce*, he replied, "Many thanks. . . . I am taking it on the trip and will guarantee to browse through it but not of necessity to read every word!" On the whole, he preferred to acquire both information and ideas through conversation.

Many visitors, it is true, left Roosevelt with the impression that he had done all the talking. This was markedly less true, in his first term, however, than it would be later. Indeed, Henry Pringle, reporting the Washington view in 1934, wrote, "He is a little too willing to listen." And the complaint against Roosevelt's overtalking meant in some cases only that a visitor had run into a deliberate filibuster (thus William Randolph Hearst's baffled lament after a session with Roosevelt in 1933, "The President didn't give me a chance to make suggestions. He did all the talking"). "Words are a good enough barrage if you know how to use them," Roosevelt told one visitor. Like many talkers, moreover, Roosevelt absorbed attitudes and ideas by a mysterious osmosis on occasions when the visitor complained he hadn't got a word in edgewise.

Conversation gave him an indispensable means both of feeling out opinion and of clarifying his own ideas. He talked to everybody and about everything. His habits of conversation out of channels were sometimes disconcerting. He had little hesitation, if he heard of a bright man somewhere down the line in a department, about summoning him to the White House. Ickes complained bitterly in his diary about "what he does so frequently, namely, calling in members of my staff for consultation on Department matters, without consulting me or advising with me." And often he bewildered visitors by asking their views on matters outside their jurisdiction. "He had a great habit," said Jesse Jones, "of talking to one caller about the subject matter of his immediately preceding interview." "I would go to see the President about something," wrote James P. Warburg, "and the fellow who was there before me talking about cotton would be told by the President, 'Well, why don't you stay.' Before we were through the guy who was there talking about cotton was telling him what to do about gold." All this, irritating as it was to tidy minds, enlarged the variety of reactions available to him in areas where no one was infallible and any intelligent person might make a contribution.

Moreover, at this time, at least, conversation around him was unusually free and candid. Always sensitive to public criticism, Roosevelt could take a large measure of private disagreement. Moley describes him as "patient, amenable to advice, moderate and smilingly indifferent to criticism." "In those days," wrote Richberg, "he enjoyed the frankness and lack of deference with which the original 'brain trusters' and I discussed problems." When people disagreed, they said so plainly and at length. "I had numerous quarrels with him," wrote Ed Flynn, who once (in 1940) hung up on him in the midst of a phone conversation. "However, as with sincere friends, the quarrels never impaired our friendship."

In seeking information, Roosevelt took care not to confuse the capital with the nation. "Pay no attention to what people are saying in Washington," he once told Molly Dewson. "They are the last persons in the country to listen to." He loved going out to the country himself and got infinite stimulus from faces in crowds, from towns quietly glimpsed out of the windows of slow-moving trains, from chance conversations with ordinary people along the way. But polio and the Presidency limited his mobility. Instead, he had to urge others to get out of Washington. "Go and see what's happening," he told Tugwell. "See the end product of what we are doing. Talk to people; get the wind in your nose."

His first reliance was on his wife. From the first days after his disability, he trained her to do his looking for him. "That I became, as the years went by, a better and better reporter and a better and better observer," she later wrote, "was largely owing to the fact that Franklin's questions covered such a wide range. I found myself obliged to notice everything." While he sometimes doubted her judgment on policy and especially on timing, he had implicit faith in her observations. He would say at Cabinet, "My Missus says that they have typhoid fever in that district," or "My Missus says that people are working for wages way below the minimum set by NRA in the town she visited last week." "It was not unusual," said Grace Tully, "to hear him predicate an entire line of reasoning upon a statement that 'my Missus told me so and so.' " In addition, he liked detailed reports of the kind Lorena Hickok and Martha Gellhorn rendered on the situation of people on relief. And he listened with interest to any reasonably succinct account of human conditions anywhere.

Another great source of information was the mail. Five to eight thousand letters a day came normally to the White House; in times of anxiety, of course, many more. The mail was regularly analyzed in order to gauge fluctations in public sentiment. From time to time, the President himself called for a random selection of letters in order to renew his sense of contact with raw opinion. As the White House mail clerk later wrote, "Mr. Roosevelt always showed a keen interest in the mail and kept close watch on its trend."

In all these ways, Roosevelt amassed an astonishing quantity of miscellaneous information and ideas about the government and the country. "No President," wrote Alben Barkley, "has ever surpassed him in personal knowledge of the details of every department"; and he could have added that probably no President surpassed him in specific knowledge of the geography, topography and people of the nation. Roosevelt took inordinate pride in this mastery of detail and often displayed it at length when those around him wished to get down to business. But, at the same time, the information—and the pride in it—signified the extraordinary receptivity which was one of his primary characteristics.

This receptivity produced the complex of information systems by which he protected himself from White House insulation. It oriented the administrative machinery away from routine and toward innovation. It made possible the intellectual excitement of the New Deal; it helped provoke a tempest of competing ideas within government because everyone felt that ideas stood and fell at the White House on their merit, not on whether they arrived through the proper channels. Good ideas might pop up from anywhere. "You sometimes find something pretty good in the lunatic fringe," Roosevelt once told his press conference: after all, America today was remade by "a whole lot of things which in my boyhood were considered lunatic fringe." Anyone with new theories had a sense that they were worth developing because, if good, they would find their way to the center. Sometimes this caused problems: Roosevelt was occasionally sold on harebrained ideas which more orderly procedures would have screened out and which taxed responsible officials before he could be unsold. But, on balance, benefits far outweighed disadvantages. H. G. Wells, who saw in Roosevelt's union of openness of mind and resolution of will the realization of his old dream of the Open Conspiracy, wrote with admiration in 1934, "He is, as it were, a ganglion for reception, expression, transmission, combination and realization, which I take it, is exactly what a modern government ought to be."

If information was the first responsibility of the executive, the second was decision. American Presidents fall into two types: those who like to make decisions, and those who don't. One type designs an administrative system which brings decisions to him; the other, a system which keeps decisions away from him. The second technique, under its more mellifluous designation of "delegation of authority," is regarded with favor in the conventional theory of public administration. Yet, pressed very far, "delegation of authority" obviously strikes at the roots of the Presidency. One can delegate routine, but one cannot delegate any part of the serious presidential responsibility. The whole theory of the Constitution makes the Chief Executive, in the words of Andrew Jackson, "accountable at the bar of public opinion for every act of his Administration," and thus presumably accountable in his own conscience for its every large decision.

Roosevelt, in any case, was pre-eminently of the first type. He evidently felt that both the dignity of his office and the coherence of his administration required that the key decisions be made by him, and not by others before him. He took great pride, for example, in a calculation of Rudolph Forster's that he made at least thirty-five decisions to each one made by Calvin Coolidge. Given this conception of the Presidency, he deliberately organized—or disorganized—his system of command to insure that important decisions were passed on to the top. His favorite technique was to keep grants of authority incomplete, jurisdictions uncertain, charters overlapping. The result of this competitive theory of administration was often confusion and exasperation on the operating level; but no other method could so reliably insure that in a large bureaucracy filled with ambitious men eager for power the decisions, and the power to make them, would remain with the President. This was in part on Roosevelt's side an instinct for self-preservation; in part, too, the temperamental expression of a restless, curious, and untidy personality. Co-existence with disorder was almost the pattern of his life. From the day of his marriage, he had lived in a household of unresolved jurisdictions, and it had never occurred to him to try to settle lines finally as between mother and wife. As Assistant Secretary of the Navy, he had indulged happily in the kind of administrative freewheeling which he was not much concerned to penalize in others now. As his doctor once said, Roosevelt "loved to know everything that was going on and delighted to have a finger in every pie."

Once the opportunity for decision came safely into his orbit, the actual process of deciding was involved and inscrutable. As Tugwell once put it, "Franklin allowed no one to discover the governing principle." He evidently felt that clear-cut administrative decisions would work only if they expressed equally clear-cut realities of administrative competence and vigor. If they did not, if the balance of administrative power would not sustain the decision, then decision would only compound confusion and discredit government. And the actualities of administrative power were to be discovered, not by writing—or by reading—executive orders, but by apprehending through intuition a vast constellation of political forces. His complex administrative sensibility, infinitely subtle and sensitive, was forever weighing questions of personal force, of political timing, of congressional concern, of partisan benefit, of public interest. Situations had to be permitted to develop, to crystallize, to clarify; the competing forces had to vindicate themselves in the actual pull and tug of conflict; public opinion had to face the question, consider it, pronounce upon it—only then, at the long, frazzled end, would the President's intuitions consolidate and precipitate a result.

Though he enjoyed giving the impression of snap decisions, Roosevelt actually made few. The more serious complaint against him was his weakness for postponement. This protraction of decision often appeared a technique of evasion. And sometimes it was. But sometimes dilemmas did not seem so urgent from above as they seemed below—a proposition evidently proved when they evaporated after the passage of time. And Roosevelt, in any case, justified, or rationalized, delay in terms of his own sense of timing. He knew from hard experience that a person could not regain health in a day or year; and he had no reason to suppose that a nation would mend any more quickly. "He could watch with enormous patience as a situation developed," wrote his wife, "and would wait for exactly the right moment to act." When people pressed proposals on him, he often answered (as he did to Frank Walker in 1936), "You are absolutely right. . . . It is simply a question of time." The tragedy of the Presidency in his view was the impotence of the President. Abraham Lincoln, Roosevelt said, "was a sad man because he couldn't get it all at once. And nobody can." He was responding informally to an important young questioner. "Maybe you would make a much better President than I have. Maybe you will, some day. If you ever sit here, you will learn that you cannot, just by shouting from the housetops, get what you want all the time."

Yet his caution was always within an assumption of constant advance. "We must keep the sheer momentum from slacking up too much," he told Colonel House in 1934, "and I have no intention of relinquishing the offensive." Woodrow Wilson had given him a cyclical conception of social change in America. Roosevelt told Robert H. Jackson that he had once suggested that Wilson withhold part of his reform program for his second term. Wilson replied in substance: We do not know that there will be a second term, and, if there is, it will be less progressive and constructive than the first. American history shows that a reform administration comes to office only once in every twenty years, and that its forward impulse does not outlast one term. Even if the same party and persons remain in power, they become complacent in a second term. "What we do not accomplish in the first term is not likely to be accomplished at all." (When Roosevelt told this story to his press conference in the first year of his second term, he lengthened the period of possible accomplishment from four to eight years.)

This technique of protraction was often wildly irritating to his subordinates, enlisted passionately on one side or another of an argument and perceiving with invincible clarity the logic of one or another course. It was equally irritating to his opponents, who enjoyed the advantages of over-simplification which come from observation without responsibility. But the President's dilatory tactics were, in a sense, the means by which he absorbed country-wide conflict of pressures, of fears, of hopes. His intelligence was not analytical. He did not systematically assess pros and cons in his own mind. What for others might be an interior dialogue had to be externalized for Roosevelt; and it was externalized most conveniently by hearing strong exponents of divergent viewpoints. Listening amiably to all sides, watching the opposing views undergo the test of practice, digesting the evidence, he gradually felt his way toward a conclusion. And even this would not often be clear-cut. "He hated to make sharp decisions between conflicting claims for power among his subordinates," noted Francis Biddle, "and decided them, almost always, in a spirit of arbitration: each side should have part of the morsel." Quite often, he ordered the contestants to work out their own compromise, as in NRA and on farm policy. In this connection he liked to cite Al Smith: "He said if you can get the parties into one room with a big table and make them take their coats off and put their feet up on the table, and give each one of them a good cigar, you can always make them agree."

With the conclusion, however reached, a new phase began. When Garner once tried to argue after Roosevelt had made up his mind, the President said, "You tend to your office and I'll tend to mine." ("I didn't take offense at that," said Garner, "because he was right.") "You could fight with Roosevelt and argue with him up to a certain point," said Morgenthau, "—but at no time during his waking hours was he anything else but a ruler." Wayne Coy, who was a Roosevelt assistant for some years, observed that one could say exactly what one thought to Roosevelt, so long as he was saying only "in my judgment" or "I think." When he said "The President thinks," the time for discussion was over. To another assistant, James Rowe, who insisted that he should do something a particular way, Roosevelt said, "I do not have to do it your way and I will tell you the reason why. The reason is that, although they may have made a mistake, the people of the United States elected me President, not you."

Often he announced his decisions with bravado. He liked to tell advisers, "I'm going to spring a bombshell," and then startle them with novel pro-posals—or rather with proposals novel to them, not perhaps to another set of advisers. "He delights in surprises—clever, cunning and quick," said Hugh Johnson. "He likes to shock friends as well as enemies with some-thing they never expected." But he seems rarely to have supposed that any particular decision was in a final sense correct, or even terribly important. "I have no expectation of making a hit every time I come to bat. What I seek is the highest possible batting average." He remembered Theodore Roosevelt's saying to him, "If I can be right 75 per cent of the time I shall come up to the fullest measure of my hopes." "You'll have to learn that public life takes a lot of sweat," he told Tugwell, "but it doesn't need to worry you. You won't always be right, but you mustn't suffer from being wrong. That's what kills people like us." After all, Roosevelt said, suppose a truck driver were doing your job; 50 per cent of his decisions would be right on average. "You aren't a truck driver. You've had some preparation. Your percentage is bound to be higher." And he knew that the refusal to decide was itself a form of decision. "This is very bad," he said to Frances Perkins, "but one thing is sure. We have to do something. We have to do the best we know how to do at the moment." Then, after a pause: "If it doesn't turn out right, we can modify it as we go along."

This dislike of firm commitments, this belief in alternatives, further reduced the significance of any single decision. As Miss Perkins observed, "He rarely got himself sewed tight to a program from which there was no turning back." The very ambiguity of his scheme of organization—the overlapping jurisdictions and duplicated responsibilities—made flexibility easy. If things started to go bad, he could reshuffle people and functions with speed which would have been impossible in a government of clear-cut assignments and rigid chains of command. Under the competitive theory, he always retained room for administrative maneuver.

Only a man of limitless energy and resource could hold such a system together. Even Roosevelt at times was hard put to keep it from flying apart. But he did succeed, as no modern President has done, in concentrating the power of executive decision where the Constitution intended it should be. "I've never known any President," said W. M. Kiplinger, "who was as omnipresent as this Roosevelt." "Most people acting for Roosevelt were messenger boys," said Ed Flynn. "He really made his own decisions."

ELECTION YEAR—1936

AMERICANS soon had an opportunity to express their opinion of F.D.R. Nineteen thirty-six was an election year. To many people, so much had happened since March 1933, it was hard to remember the Presidency in the hands of anyone other than F.D.R. To most of us, there wasn't much doubt that Roosevelt would be re-elected. There was no one of any stature within the Democratic party to give him any real competition for the nomination. There were some disgruntled Democrats, such as Al Smith, who had turned against the New Deal and Roosevelt, but none of them presented a serious challenge.

The Republicans had a choice among former President Hoover, Senators Borah and Vandenberg, Colonel Frank Knox, publisher of the Chicago *Daily News,* and Governor Alf Landon of Kansas. Landon, not entering the primaries or really fighting for the nomination, won it quite easily; Knox was chosen as his running mate. Their slogans for the campaign were "Stop Roosevelt," and "The Holy Crusade for Liberty."

F.D.R. formally accepted the renomination by the Democrats in Philadelphia on June 27, and John Garner was chosen as his running mate again.

MARQUIS CHILDS

CAMPAIGN*

ONCE EVERY two or three decades comes an election that is for the party in power no more than a high-spirited picnic. Such was the campaign of 1936. If Mr. Roosevelt's political enemies had wanted to make it impossible for him to be defeated, they proceeded on exactly the right course. The background was the unbelievably inept Liberty League with its ermine-and-emeralds dinner at the Mayflower Hotel in Washington. Sage old Jack Garner said when it was all over that the Democratic party needn't have spent a cent, needn't have made a single speech. It was all done by an opposition that lacked any understanding of the temper of the American people.

From the beginning a buoyant sense of confidence ran through the

* From Marquis Childs's *I Write from Washington* (New York, Harper, 1942).

Democratic party. At Philadelphia in June the emirs and the pashas of the city machines gathered for what would be a roistering ratification meeting. They were all there—Hague of New Jersey, Kelly and Nash of Chicago, Pendergast of Missouri, Crump of Tennessee, and the lesser figures—to make as much noise as possible. They knew which side their political bread was buttered on. The vast expenditures of the New Deal had put into their hands power they had hitherto scarcely dreamed of.

A political convention, even when there is a real contest in sight, is a curious institution. This one was purely circus, a circus with only one act and that act a set piece out of the origins of American political history. Yet it took an orthodox five days padded with traditional gestures to build up to that ancient climax.

Spreading their tents, surrounded by their retinues, the emirs and the pashas were prepared to enjoy this comfortable occasion. In the Bellevue-Stratford, in the Ritz-Carlton, in the Benjamin Franklin, they set up headquarters where whisky and good will were dispensed with equal liberality. To fill in the dull hours they gossiped with each other, moving from one royal suite to another like reigning monarchs gathered for a coronation. They were formidable men. They controlled millions of votes and votes were power. You approached them with respect and caution.

In certain respects Tom Pendergast of Kansas City was the most formidable of them all. A thick, squat man with a head set solidly on a short bull neck, he moved with commanding dignity through crowded hotel lobbies. I had been assigned to do a roundup story on the bosses. "Let's get them all in," said O. K. Bovard, then managing editor of the *Post-Dispatch.* "Let's show what all this is based on." But I was to omit Pendergast who was to have special treatment from Spencer McCulloch of the St. Louis staff. There were several reasons why I was to leave out the Missouri boss, one of them being that Pendergast had sworn to knock me down on sight, and he was a man of his word.

That had come out of an encounter a year before. I had seen him off on the maiden crossing of the *Normandie,* it being one of his specialties to make the first eastward crossing on each new luxury liner. Hints of the scandal that was to dethrone him were already in the air and I followed him from his apartment in the Waldorf-Astoria Towers to the boat to ask some pointed questions. At the hotel he had been belligerent. "Yes, I told O'Malley to approve that insurance deal, and what're you going to do about it?" he growled.

At the boat it was different. For one thing I brought up to his suite Comte Bertrand de Jouvenel of *Paris-Soir* who was making the round trip on the great, gaudy new boat. Pendergast and the very blond Mrs. Pendergast were ensconced in the living room of their suite which was almost literally filled with flowers, orchids and lilies of the valley, expensive flowers. This was Pendergast, the Maharajah of Missouri, in all his glory.

Under Bertrand's suave, flattering manner, his charm turned on full force, they both expanded. De Jouvenel had come on board with a small trunk full of books on American politics. I had advised him to forget about them and concentrate during the four-day crossing on the massive little man who was in himself an encyclopedia of American political practice.

"I am told," said De Jouvenel, "that you are the ruler of Missouri, Mr. Pendergast. Can you tell me how it is that you do it?"

From an American, Pendergast might have taken the question as an effrontery, as *lèse majesté*. But this was a foreigner. You could see him turning it over in his mind.

"Well, I'll tell you how I do it," he said with a look of pride on his face. "It's a very simple thing when you come down to it. There's people that need things, lots of 'em, and I see to it that they get 'em. I go to my office on South Main Street in Kansas City at seven o'clock in the morning and I stay there when I'm in town till about six o'clock at night and during that time I see maybe two hundred, maybe three hundred people. One needs a half a ton of coal. Another woman's gotta get a job for her boy. I see to it that they get those things. That's all there is to it."

There was more in the same vein as the old man grew expansive. Set against the background of the orchids and the lilies of the valley, the amboina and macassar modern fittings of the B-deck suite, it made a wonderful story and I rushed off the boat just before sailing to write it. If he had seen it cold when he returned a few weeks later, Pendergast might have taken it in his stride. But one of his henchmen back in Missouri must have radioed to him the full text of the story. When I saw De Jouvenel in Paris some months later he told me that on the following morning while he was being shaved in the barbershop, Pendergast had descended on him, making wild and threatening gestures and brandishing a sheaf of radiograms. Poor Bertrand never quite understood the wrath of the ruler of Missouri. That was the reason I gave Boss Tom a wide berth at the Philadelphia convention.

There was as yet no sign of his dissolution. He was riding high and so were all the others. They had come into the promised land and they proposed to stay there; forever, if that were possible.

President Roosevelt arrived on a special train from Washington to be the star of that last and anticlimactic act. And so great was his histrionic ability, his sense of timing, his sense of crowd reaction, that he converted a foregone conclusion into something like a triumph. The crowd, a hundred thousand or more, stretched away into the darkness of Franklin Field, cheering wildly at each pause, as though the roar out of the warm, sticky night came from a single throat.

That was the beginning of a big succession of triumphs, of roaring crowds, of streets full of cheering people. The President himself could scarcely have had any illusions as to the outcome of the campaign. He is too shrewd a politician, too keen a judge of trends and tempers, to have failed to realize that it was a walkaway.

At Cleveland the Republicans had nominated Governor Alf Landon of Kansas, a pleasant, cheerful man who had been waiting in the proper expectant attitude for the lightning to strike. The truth was that the really ambitious men in the party, men like Vandenberg of Michigan, had ducked the nomination. They sensed that it spelt not merely defeat but disaster. The contest in Cleveland was almost as lame as the one at Philadelphia. There were men who wanted the honor but none with any weight. Landon, looking discomfited and out of place in the glare of the floodlights and the popping of the flash bulbs, was Hobson's choice.

President Roosevelt set out in early October on a major campaign tour that was to take him as far west as Sheridan, Wyoming. The atmosphere on the ten-car campaign train that rolled out of Union Station in Washington was a gala one. The President knew that he was going to like this expedition. His campaign technique had been perfected over the years until it was almost second nature with him. Moreover, he was to visit the fiefdoms of his chief lieutenants and he knew that everywhere a royal welcome was being prepared.

Perhaps no man in American political history had ever started on a campaign under a more fortunate augury. The city bosses were preparing to put on a kind of popularity contest, each one trying to outdo the other. Earlier in Jersey City, Mayor Hague had turned out the town and half the state in an imitation of a Roman triumph. From the moment that the procession of cars rolled out of the Holland Tunnel the thunder of bombs assaulted the ear, and the whole city under a cloudless blue sky seemed one mass of flag-waving humanity. Hague, an iron-jawed master of ceremonies, rode in the presidential car with the President to Hague's great public hospital and clinic in the center of the city that Hague regarded, with the simple possessive sense of a medieval baron, as his city.

The train rolled westward. Denver was big. St. Louis, on the return, was colossal. But it remained for Mayor Kelly in Chicago to put on an act that made everything else look like a halfhearted rehearsal. In the early evening the President rode for five miles in an open car through streets so crowded that only a narrow lane was left. In spite of the protests of the Secret Service, people had been allowed to swarm off the curbs and it was all that the motorcycle police could do to force a way through for the presidential cavalcade.

This was King Crowd. They were out to have a large time and they had it. Every kind of band—bagpipes, piano accordions, jazz, fife-and-drum, bugle corps—lined the narrow lane of humanity through which the presidential party passed. As the parade turned off Michigan Boulevard into West Madison Street the mass of people became denser and noisier. They shrieked from rooftops; they sang and danced; they leaned from tenement windows and loft windows to wave and shout. And all the time a rain of torn paper fluttered down, like gray snow in the half-lighted streets.

If King Crowd had its hero, it also had its hated and despised foe. Not the least remarkable thing about this extraordinary demonstration was the hostility shown toward the Chicago *Tribune,* and, in a lesser degree, toward William Randolph Hearst's Chicago *Herald-Examiner.* Because news photographers with their cameras clung to the outside of nearly every car, the crowd could spot the press. "Where's the *Tribune*?" "Down with the *Tribune*!" "To Hell with the *Tribune*!" These shouts were heard along the entire line of march but particularly in the slum areas on West Madison Street.

King Crowd in the streets was remarkable, but the real spectacle was at the stadium where the President was to deliver his address. The entire front of the great hulking building was illuminated with huge calcium flares that threw an eerie blue light for blocks around. As the presidential party arrived, earsplitting bombs burst overhead and the crowd, a hundred thousand strong, surged up in an almost irresistible tide. Sweating police struggled to keep a way clear so that the President's car could be driven into the stadium. When he appeared on the platform a blare of sound swept up and for a moment seemed to overwhelm him by its intensity. For once the composure of this master of crowds appeared shaken and it was not until he began to speak that he slipped into his customary confident manner.

In the course of this tremendous outpouring so well prepared by Mayor Kelly there was evident that iconology which was to manifest itself many times again. All along the line of march photographs and drawings of President Roosevelt were held up on sticks and poles, waved frantically as he passed. Back again on the campaign train the Secret Service men who had ridden on the running board of his car looked as though they had been through a football scrimmage, their clothes torn and bedraggled. They admitted it was the worst experience they had ever been through.

A campaign train is like nothing else under the sun. It is a transcontinental sound wagon, a glorified road company of the greatest show on earth, a traveling convention of politicians and minor prophets. Around the voice and the personality in the last car the whole machine revolves. Each climax is built up to his appearance. For the thirty or thirty-five reporters on the train, and especially for the press association men, it is a grueling, exhausting grind.

Yet it has its compensations. If there is a good crowd on board you can be sure of something diverting or something funny every minute of the day. The candidate himself is likely to supply a good many laughs. Roosevelt did this deliberately. He knew that back in the press car we were parodying the perfection of his technique. In the two dining cars were loud speakers, and for ordinary whistle stops most correspondents did not get off the train to go back to the rear platform but heard the speech via the loud speaker.

The little drama was almost always the same. When the microphones on the rear platform were switched on, after the train had ground to a stop, you could hear the murmur of the crowd, a vast buzzing noise, punctuated here and there by shrill cries and shouts. Then, as Roosevelt emerged from the door of the car onto the platform, on the arm of his son Jimmy or escorted, perhaps, by a local politician, the noise of the crowd would swell to a roar, here and there individual voices carrying over the roar, "We want Roosevelt," "We're for you, Mr. Roosevelt . . ." Customarily a local bigwig, the congressman from the district, or the governor, would gallop through a conventional introduction full of loud encomiums. Then the roar again, and Roosevelt waiting until it died down, his infallible sense of timing . . . "My friends, I'm happy to be here in ——. The last time I was here was ——. I see your —— looked excellent as I came along. . . ."

We back in the dining car knew this formula so well that someone would invariably supply a facetious name or a facetious date well in advance of the benign voice out of the loud speaker. Another device of the old master was to remind his audience that at some time in the past one or more of his relatives had been connected with local history, usually the settling of the place. It was difficult to believe that so many Roosevelts and Delanos could have been in so many different places.

The universe within a universe being drawn across the continent in slightly shabby Pullman cars was a center for ceaseless gossip and rumor. We had in the end car one of the most extraordinary figures of our time who was engaged in exhibiting himself to millions of people in the midst of that greatest of all American institutions, a presidential election. With him was his wife, herself no mean public figure. It was about these two that most of the gossip centered. We watched them lead their curious public lives and we speculated endlessly about their private lives. Every scrap of information, every rumor, every report, became a part of the legend of these two principals.

They were surrounded by lesser characters who took on importance and coloration from their proximity to the principals. Marvin McIntyre, wraith-like, his voice husky with fatigue, would play poker or bridge until five or six in the morning back in one of the press cars; then, cheerful as a cricket, would greet the local politicians who came on board at the first stop of the day. Judge Rosenman, the ubiquitous Sammy the Rose, was one of the speech writers on the train. Senator Wheeler of Montana, so soon to be an enemy, was part of the entourage for a time; he was afraid that Roosevelt was being too timid. Jimmy, the ebullient, the glad-faced, the smiling, the hand-shaking Jimmy, was on board and so was his wife, the gentle Betsy. This was an easy, comfortable family excursion.

The train wound back through the Middle West, through Michigan where in each industrial city thousands of men and women stood along the railroad tracks just to catch a glimpse of the President. But of course, said the wise old heads on the train, he would never carry Michigan. What was it they said about the visitation of politicians? People would come out to look certainly; they would come out to look at a dead whale on a flatcar. That was what the knowing correspondents said and we tended to agree with them. Look at the crowds that turned out to see Al Smith.

In Detroit, in Cadillac Square, was the same huge, yelling, roaring, almost uncontrollable crowd, or a Detroit version of it; the same struggling police lines, the same wild, frenzied cheering, the same smile from Roosevelt, the same easy, almost casual, wave of his hand. We were weary of crowds, we in the press cars. There had been no opportunity to service the Pullmans. Water flowed from the tap in trickles. The lights were a dim blur.

The contrast with Landon was painful. He had apparently never realized that campaigning in the era of the news reel and the radio calls for a technique as deliberate as that of a Hollywood star. You could be homely and homespun but if you didn't know how to put it across you looked merely inept and foolish. Landon was utterly unprepared for the fierce white light that beat on him after his nomination, just as he was unprepared to make the vital decisions that are called for each day in a national race.

Briefly, I was on the Landon train where the atmosphere was sober and uncertain. We went to Portland, Maine, for a fling at the Maine electorate just before Maine's presidential balloting (old saw: "As Maine goes, so goes the Nation"). I haven't the slightest recollection what Landon talked about. I only remember feeling pained at realizing how badly the Republicans managed these things. The rally was held in a baseball park outside of Portland and the speaker's stand had been constructed at what would be approximately center field. This left most of the audience, in the grandstand and the bleachers, removed by a considerable distance from the candidate. And about the time the speaker was to mount the rostrum a thick fog rolled in from the sea. Poor Landon might as well have been speaking from the bottom of the ocean for all the personal relationship he established with his listeners. As he began to speak, hedged in by a battery of microphones, two or three news photographers climbed a two by four not ten feet away and aimed at him. It wobbled uncertainly with their weight and Landon, glancing up from his manuscript, whispered several times audibly, "Get down from there, get down, I tell you!" He had the unhappy look of a man who has just taken his seat in the dental chair for what is certain to be a long and painful ordeal.

There were no amateurs in the Roosevelt camp. The President finished his strenuous tour in a warm glow of self-confidence, with the roars of the crowd still echoing from far out across America. It had been as successful as anyone had dared to hope and yet the strange thing was that, removed a little from the tumult and the shouting, it was difficult to realize why it had all happened. What made the enthusiasm of the tour seem all the more extraordinary was the fact that only by stretching the meaning of the phrase could Roosevelt's talks be called political speeches. They were more like the friendly sermons of a bishop come to make his quadrennial diocesan call. Bishop Roosevelt reported on the excellent state of health enjoyed throughout this vast diocese, particularly as compared with the miserable state that had prevailed before he took high office.

This was the central theme of almost every talk he made. The issues of the campaign and the policies to be followed in the future were touched upon only incidentally, if at all. The President promised crop insurance and crop control of some sort. He told the motor manufacturers that they must increase the annual wage paid to their workers through "planning." He said that work relief was important. But other than this he scarcely mentioned issues. And almost invariably he referred to his Republican opposition as one would speak of the forces of darkness, the embodiment of an almost abstract evil, and yet tolerantly as of an inevitable counterpoise to the good life for which he, the President, spoke. These forces of darkness had been beaten by the New Deal Saint George, and the President assumed in his talks that of course no one would be so deluded as to invite the dragon back again. Sometimes he asked the direct question of his audiences—do you want the powers of reaction in office again? Always a roaring chorus of noes came back.

For the last day or two Jim Farley joined the caravan. The meaning of the crowds and the cheers and the rain of torn-up telephone books had not escaped the big fellow. We sat with him in a drawing room on the last afternoon and talked it over. He was in a jovial mood. The big expanse of his bald head glistened and the tempo of his gum chewing was if anything faster than normal. Big Jim had worked hard for this. It was all over, he said. Nothing that the President could do or say in the two and a half weeks that remained could lose the election for him. The only question now was how large his majority would be, and although Farley had not yet got down to predicting states, he was certain that it would be large.

The Roosevelt campaign of that year was essentially Farley's kind of campaign. There were those within the Roosevelt inner circle who believed that issues should be discussed; the people should be educated on the big questions that the country faced. Henry Wallace was one of those who thought there should be more discussion of the state of the nation. But the practical politicians scoffed at such suggestions. A campaign, they said, was how you got elected. It had nothing to do with education. Hadn't the Republicans talked about the full dinner pail for forty years or more and got away with it four times out of five? This was Roosevelt prosperity, New Deal prosperity, and the Farleys in the party proposed to ride it through.

That was what Roosevelt did in the autumn of 1936. After the Middle West we went to New England. Same company, same show, same crowd. At Providence they swarmed like ants over the capitol plaza and the approaches to it. Boston Common just at dusk appeared to be packed solid with humanity. Motoring through Cambridge in the early darkness we heard a strange and alien sound. From the sons of Harvard on the curbstone came loud boos for that other son of Harvard in the front car. He was all those things the fathers of young Harvard men called him; a renegade, a traitor to his class.

We had been motoring since eight o'clock in the morning in a long furious procession that frequently got out of control of state police; fighting the crowds through mill towns all of the way. Yet the principal appeared as blithe and confident that evening before a huge crowd in Worcester as though it had been the first speech of the day instead of the twenty-first. We conceded that he could take it.

Curiosities were always turning up. In the course of that motor tour of New England a bland, supremely self-centered, young Englishman joined the party as a reporter, of sorts, to have a look at the quaint American system of electioneering. His name was Randolph Churchill and he was the son of a Tory politician named Winston Churchill. Young Randolph had inherited a generous share of his father's poise and self-assurance which American newspapermen found rather hard to take. On the train one night, the motoring over for the day, Heywood Broun put Churchill through a mild hazing, but so bland was this young aristocrat's exterior that it had no effect whatsoever. He was a little irritating and the next day the boys saw to it that as the hours wore on he was relegated to cars successively further back in the procession, until by midafternoon he might just as well not have been with the party at all.

This was one kind of campaigning. That same fall I was to see another kind. On orders from Bovard I sampled Norman Thomas's technique. If the Roosevelt campaign was almost straight showmanship of a very high order, the Thomas tour was a political Chautauqua. Norman and his courageous wife traveled without benefit of retinue, he in an upper berth, she in the lower. They traveled that way for weeks on end, Norman speaking from twelve to fourteen times a day, with a kind of endurance that only politicians must be endowed with. At each stop they would be met by earnest disciples who would take them in hand for the day's events. Often Thomas talked at schools and public forums, taking advantage of an audience wherever he could find one.

Almost invariably he gave them a rapid-fire harangue. The New Deal, built on the corrupt city machines, was no more suited to save the country than the reactionary G.O.P. They were both corrupt and dead, and only Socialism could save democracy, Thomas told his listeners, his voice growing hoarse, his talk sounding more like a scratchy phonograph record as he repeated it for the sixth or seventh time. His audiences were of course small. Six or seven hundred students or teachers, crowded into the auditorium of Antioch College at Yellow Springs, Ohio, was the high mark of a day of speechmaking in Ohio. Through the party organization and through the funds the party could command, through the prestige of his

441

high office and the magnetic appeal of his personality, Roosevelt reached millions directly and on the air while the Socialist, Norman Thomas, spoke to thousands.

In the closing days the President carried his campaign to Pennsylvania. Pennsylvania was considered a doubtful state. In Pennsylvania lived the Republican party's great angel, Joseph Pew of the Sun Oil Company, who was out to elect Landon at whatever cost. But the Democrats too had an angel in Pennsylvania. On the platform with Roosevelt at Harrisburg sat John L. Lewis. I seem to recall that he had a slightly possessive air as though this had been a *fête de Versailles* that he had ordered and paid for, as indeed he had. I am frank to add, however, that this may have been merely an interpretation read into that grim and mysterious physiognomy in the light of the later knowledge that its owner had given a half-million dollars out of the United Mine Workers' Treasury to the Democratic war chest. For that matter John L. Lewis always looks possessive, and with good reason, for he has made the largest trade-union in the United States his personal property. On the platform on that blowy day, with his miner cohorts in the crowd before him, John L. may well have dreamed dreams of imperial grandeur. This was Franklin Roosevelt's inning. John L. Lewis's would come next.

One of the extraordinary things about a political campaign is the way in which the partisans are able to hypnotize themselves. Anyone with the slightest knowledge of what the American people were saying and thinking could have known that Landon hadn't a Chinaman's chance. Yet he himself was persuaded of his victory and so were many of the people around him. Weren't the newspapers for him?

The Republicans in the closing week made stupid mistakes that I believe Landon would not have made if the ultimate decisions had not long since passed out of his reach. For one thing there were the pay-roll notices threatening workers with the loss of their jobs if Roosevelt should win. Similarly the Social Security pay-roll deductions were made to seem part of an evil conspiracy to curtail the average man's income. Anyone with ordinary political judgment should have known that that kind of thing would produce an effect exactly opposite from the one intended.

It gave Roosevelt a chance to end his campaign in a blaze of emotion. Landon had had a huge rally earlier in Madison Square Garden. Of necessity Roosevelt's meeting had to be half again as big and twice as loud— and it was. They hate me, said Franklin Roosevelt of the rich and the mighty, and I welcome their hatred. The packed Garden exploded in a steamy torrent of sound. Only in this last speech did the President open up the New Deal stops—housing, work relief, social security—promising that these gains would be held and new goals set.

On the night of the great victory the clan Roosevelt was gathered at Hyde Park. Forty-six states in the Roosevelt column, that was something that the simplest mind could understand. Even before midnight the wise-money boys were looking for a place in the Roosevelt van, repenting their sins of omission and commission. William Randolph Hearst telephoned from California to tell the ebullient Jimmy how astonished and happy he was that the man he had sought to defeat through every kind of editorial trick and incessant salvos of type a foot high was actually the choice of the American people and by so overwhelming a majority.

In this moment of triumph all the oddly assorted elements within the Democratic party sang hosannahs. The President in his campaign had covered them all in; no one had been excluded. And nothing had been altered by the great tide of votes rolled up by the personality and the voice and the hope they implied.

THE PRESS AND THE CAMPAIGN

Most of the press in the big cities was for Landon. Publisher William Randolph Hearst said: "I'll stake my reputation as a political prophet on Landon's victory," and ran editorials suggesting that the Communists were, under instructions from Moscow, going to vote for Roosevelt. This line of attack gathered momentum during the campaign.

And the news magazine the *Literary Digest* said, "Our poll indicates that Landon will win 32 states, 54 per cent of the popular vote and 370 electoral votes."

The New York *Times* stayed with Roosevelt, and among the small-circulation papers there was a standoff between Roosevelt and Landon. Among the columnists, Walter Lippmann was for Landon, Westbrook Pegler for F.D.R. And while the polls of Gallup and Roper began to register a swing to the Democrats, predicting a sizable victory, that "disturber of the peace," H. L. Mencken, the Baltimore *Evening Sun* columnist, announced, with customary boldness, "They can beat him [F.D.R.] with a Chinaman."

H. L. MENCKEN

THE CHOICE TOMORROW*

Nevertheless, and despite all Hell's angels, I shall vote for the Hon. Mr. Landon tomorrow. To a lifelong Democrat, of course, it will be something of a wrench. But it seems to me that the choice is one that genuine Democrats are almost bound to make. On the one side are all the basic principles of their party, handed down from its first days and tried over and over again in the fires of experience; on the other side is a gallimaufry of transparent quackeries, puerile in theory and dangerous in practice. To vote Democratic this year it is necessary, by an unhappy irony, to vote for a Republican. But to vote with the party is to vote for a gang of mountebanks who are no more Democrats than a turkey buzzard is an archangel.

This exchange of principles, with the party labels unchanged, is naturally confusing, but it is certainly not so confusing that it goes unpenetrated.

* From the Baltimore *Evening Sun,* Nov. 2, 1936, as reprinted in H. L. Mencken's *A Carnival of Buncombe* (Baltimore, Johns Hopkins Press, 1956).

Plenty of Republicans who believe sincerely in a strong federal government are going to vote tomorrow for the Hon. Mr. Roosevelt, and plenty of Democrats who believe sincerely in the autonomy of the states and a rigid limitation of the federal power are going to vote, as I shall, for the Hon. Mr. Landon. Whether the shift that confronts us will be permanent remains to be seen. But while it lasts it is manifestly very real, and those who let party loyalties blind them to its reality will be voting very foolishly.

The issue tends to be confused by a distrust of both presidential candidates, inevitable under the circumstances. There are those who believe that the Hon. Mr. Roosevelt, if he is re-elected, will abandon the socialistic folderol that he has been advocating since 1933 and go back to the traditional program of his party, and there are those who believe that the Hon. Mr. Landon, if elected, will quickly turn out to be only another Harding, Hoover or McKinley. Both notions, it seems to me, represent little more than a naïve sort of wishful thinking. Landon, I am convinced, will actually stay put, and so will Roosevelt. Roosevelt, to be sure, has flopped once, but he has now gone too far down his new road to turn back again.

The defense commonly made of him is that he confronted, in 1933, an unprecedented situation, and so had to resort to new and even revolutionary devices in dealing with it. There is no truth in either half of that theory. The situation that he confronted differed only quantitatively, and not at all qualitatively, from others that had been confronted in the past. And of all the devices he employed in dealing with it the only ones that really worked were those that had been tried before.

I am aware that there are many undoubtedly intelligent persons who believe otherwise. The fact, indeed, is not to be wondered at, for the intelligent, like the unintelligent, are responsive to propaganda, and all the propaganda since 1933 has been running one way. But it still remains historically true that all the major problems before the country when Hoover blew up were intrinsically simple and familiar ones, and it still remains true that those which were not tackled in tried and rational ways still remain unsolved.

All the rest was quackery pure and unadulterated. The situation of the country was exaggerated in precisely the same way that a quack doctor exaggerates the illness of his patient, and for exactly the same reason. And the showy and preposterous treatments that were whooped up had no more virtue in them, at bottom, than his pills and liniments. We then and there entered upon an era of quackery that yet afflicts and exhausts the country. We'll not get clear of it until all the quacks are thrown out.

Whether that will happen tomorrow I do not know. The probabilities, as anyone can see, are largely against it. But soon or late the business will have to be undertaken, and the longer it is delayed the more difficult it will become. For people in the mass soon grow used to anything, including even being swindled. There comes a time when the patter of the quack becomes as natural and as indubitable to their ears as the texts of Holy Writ, and when that time comes it is a dreadful job debamboozling them.

The *bona fides* of the Hon. Mr. Roosevelt was pretty generally assumed in the first days of his Presidentiad. He was, to be sure, excessively melodramatic, but observers remembered that he was a Roosevelt, and that a talent for drama was thus in his blood. Even his closing of the banks—in retrospect, a highly dubious measure—was accepted without serious protest, even by bankers. The NRA, when it was first announced, seemed a plausible if somewhat violent remedy for admitted evils, and most of his other devices of those days got the same tolerant reception.

But as his administration closed its first year, and he gradually extended and elaborated his program, it began to be evident that he was going far beyond the borders of the reasonable, and that the theory underlying some of his major operations, as it was expounded by his principal agents, was becoming increasingly fantastic and absurd. Bit by bit, the purpose of restoring the country to its normal manner and ease of life was submerged in the purpose of bringing in a brummage Utopia, fashioned in part out of the idiotic hallucinations of the cow states and in part out of the gaudy evangel of Moscow. And simultaneously, the welfare of the American people as a whole began to be forgotten in a special concern for special classes and categories of them, all of manifestly inferior status and all willing to vote right for goods in hand.

In brief, the New Deal became a political racket, and that is what it is today—that and nothing more. Its chief practical business is to search out groups that can be brought into the Hon. Jim Farley's machine by grants out of the public treasury, which is to say, out of the pockets of the rest of us. To serve that lofty end the national currency has been debased, the national credit has been imperiled and a crushing burden has been put on every man who wants to pay his own way in the world and asks only to be let alone. The excuse that a grave emergency justified such pillage is now abandoned. The emergency is past, but the pillage goes on.

At tomorrow's plebiscite this grandiose and excessively dangerous Tammanyizing of the country will come to judgment, with the chances, as I have said, in favor of its ratification. That it will be supported heartily by all its beneficiaries goes without saying. Every dole-bird in the country, of whatever sort, will certainly vote for it. It will get the suffrage of all the gimme pseudo-farmers in the Middle West, of all the half-witted share-croppers in the South, of all the professional uplifters and of all the job-holders on Farley's ever-swelling roll. It will be whooped up by every politician who lives and thrives by promising to turn loose A in B's corn-field. It will have the kindly aid of all other varieties of professional mes-siahs, ranging from the fantoddish prophets of millenniums to the down-right thieves.

Will there be enough of them to ratify it? Probably not. It will meet also some support by honest if deluded men and women. Thousands of them, I gather, are in the ranks of the labor organizations. They have been told that the New Deal saved them their jobs, which it didn't, and that it will prosper them hereafter, which it won't, and large numbers of them have believed. The actual fact is that they are not, and can never be, the beneficiaries of any such carnival of loot; they can only be its goats. In the long run the cost of the whole show will settle down upon them. In the long run every man and woman who works will have to pay for the upkeep of some Farley heeler who has been taught that working is foolish and unnecessary and even a shade immoral.

The Brain Trust brethren, of course, still promise that all the bills will be sent to the rich. Well, they were so sent in Russia, and paid in full. But when they had been paid, more money was still needed, and it is now being provided by the Russian workers. Living in filthy and miserable dens, and badly fed on poor and monotonous food, they labor under a brutal stretch-out system which yields them the equivalent of ten American dollars a month. That is what Utopia always comes to in the end.

THE NEW DEAL AND THE SUPREME COURT

TOWARD the middle of 1935 it seemed that the New Deal had won its fight against the Depression and that the Roosevelt reforms were now a permanent part of the country's laws. Business was good, industrial production was up, more people were working, more money was available for investment, stock prices were climbing and corporation dividends were increasing. Political pressures had abated, and everywhere people seemed to be settling back into their traditional attitude toward federal government as something to be debated more or less amiably around election time and then to be left to the politicians, something that one *should* know about but never finds the time to keep tabs on. Happy days were here again!

There were, of course, thunderings on the Right and rumblings on the Left; but in the main these manifestations were confined to relatively small groups—the rarefied circles of financial and industrial command on the one side, and the dedicated partisans of small, doctrinaire political movements on the other. Both sides found effective individual support in the various sectors of American life, but neither achieved any active mass following among the great body of the American people.

But the Roosevelt Administration soon found its whole legislative program threatened, from an area that had been considered almost negligible in the political life of the nation

—the federal courts, where a new kind of offensive was being launched against the New Deal. It was not, at first, the kind of action that made front-page headlines; it was, rather, a long series of undramatic little actions conducted according to rules that the ordinary citizens did not understand. But, in their possible consequences, these isolated actions were as important as a national election, for they were to determine whether the New Deal was constitutionally valid.

In 1935 and 1936 such actions in the federal district courts produced more than sixteen hundred injunctions restraining the executive branch of the government from enforcing the enactments of the legislative branch. Never before had the judiciary so freely overruled the Congress and the President; equally remarkable to informed observers was the number of sweeping denunciations of New Deal philosophy that accompanied the judges' decisions. Not surprisingly, therefore, the Administration saw substantial significance in the fact that of the more than 250 district court judges only about one fourth had been appointed by Democratic Presidents.

As the offensive grew, it developed a new technique by which New Deal representation in these cases was effectively eliminated. A corporation, for example, that might wish to have the government restrained from enforcing an onerous federal statute did not itself apply to the court for an injunction, but encouraged its stockholders to seek an injunction restraining the corporation from complying with the law's provisions, on the grounds—as before—that the provisions were unconstitutional.

Eventually, all of this litigation would be adjudged by the Supreme Court, and there the Administration soon found an almost equal readiness to nullify New Deal laws. In 1935 the Court vetoed the government's regulation of the petroleum industry and the National Industrial Recovery Act; in 1936 it invalidated the AAA crop control program and the Guffey Coal Act; and during this period it also ruled unconstitutional a number of state enactments relating to employment practices and social welfare.

To many observers the Court's decisions went far beyond the traditional limits observed by Supreme Court justices in the exercise of their right of judicial review. Critics of the Court pointed out inconsistencies, and even outright contradictions, in several decisions. New Deal partisans went further and charged that the Court had based their decisions on political bias rather than on strict interpretation of the Constitution. Roosevelt himself avoided the question of motivation, but complained that the judges were putting the country back into the "horse-and-buggy days."

Inevitably, some critics called into question the Court's authority to determine the constitutionality of Congressional or Presidential actions. And, indeed, the Constitution does not grant that power to the Supreme Court; but tradition and precedent have amply established it, and no one would seriously suggest that it

be taken away. Nevertheless, the proper limits to the exercise of that function had long been the subject of debate, much of it conducted by judges themselves who advocated most rigorous self-restraint.

Members of the Administration, however, were not encouraged by what they had seen of judicial self-restraint on the part of the conservative majority in the Court. They were well aware that the Constitution afforded Congress several methods of dealing with a frustrating Court. Through legislation the Court's right to rule on the constitutionality of federal legislation could be drastically curtailed; for the Constitution states that in all "the other Cases before mentioned"—that is, other than cases affecting ambassadors, other public ministers and consuls, and those in which a state is a party —"the supreme Court shall have appellate Jurisdiction, both as to Law and Fact, with such Exceptions, and under such Regulations as the Congress shall make."

Further, the Constitution does not say how many justices there may be in the Supreme Court; the Congress may determine that. And through the years the number of judges has several times been changed. In 1789, when the Court was established, the number was six; in 1807 it was raised to seven, in 1837 to nine, in 1863 to ten; in 1866 it was lowered to eight; and in 1869 it was raised to nine.

But a difficult problem remained: On what grounds could they persuade the Congress and the public to support any change in the Court? For some reason the charge that the judges had fallen behind the times did not seem adequate; something more concrete was desired. Advanced age might be an argument, for the judges ranged in age from sixty to seventy-nine in 1935—"nine old men," indeed. Unhappily for that argument, however, the oldest of them, Justice Brandeis, was one of the three judges who regularly sided with the liberal minority—himself and Justices Stone and Cardozo.

The argument that only two of the justices had been appointed by a Democratic President was even weaker, because one of the two was a member of the solid conservative bloc in the Court, while two Republican appointees—Justices Stone and Cardozo—were steadfast liberals.

For the purpose of an outright legislative move to curtail the power of the Court, the record of the Court's decisions might have furnished some support, for it shows, besides many inconsistencies and contradictions, many instances of decisions handed down on a vote of five to four—which opens the question whether the one judge who completed the majority was rightly given the power to determine the disposition of legislation that had been enacted by a large number of elected representatives of the people. But arguments like that are difficult at best; they require many steps in proving them, and Roosevelt knew that brevity is the key to success in public debate.

Roosevelt was not the first President to become embroiled in open dispute with the Supreme Court. Jefferson, Jackson, Lincoln, and Theodore Roosevelt, all had clashed with the Court. Franklin Roosevelt was well informed on the history of the problem that he faced. How he went about solving that problem is presented in the following selection, by James MacGregor Burns.

JAMES MACGREGOR BURNS

COURT PACKING: THE MISCALCULATED RISK*

WAS IT AN omen? The famous Roosevelt luck seemed to forsake the President on the January day in 1937 when he entered his second term. Bursts of cold rain soaked the gay inaugural decorations, furled the sodden flags around their staffs, and drenched dignitaries and spectators alike while they gathered below the Capitol rotunda. The rain drummed on the cellophane that covered Roosevelt's old family Bible, as he stood with upraised hand facing Chief Justice Hughes.

* From James MacGregor Burns's *The Lion and the Fox* (New York, Harcourt, Brace, 1956).

450

They eyed each other, the old judge, his wet whiskers quivering in the wind, the resolute President, jaw stuck out. Hughes read the oath with slow and rising emphasis as he came to the words "promise to support the Constitution of the United States." Roosevelt gave the words equal force as he repeated the oath. At this point, he said later, he wanted to cry out, "Yes, but it's the Constitution as *I* understand it, flexible enough to meet any new problem of democracy—not the kind of Constitution your Court has raised up as a barrier to progress and democracy."

The President turned to the rain-spattered pages of his inaugural address. "When four years ago we met to inaugurate a President, the Republic, single-minded in anxiety, stood in spirit here. We dedicated ourselves to the fulfillment of a vision—to speed the time when there would be for all the people that security and peace essential to the pursuit of happiness. We of the Republic pledged ourselves to drive from the temple of our ancient faith those who had profaned it; to end by action, tireless and unafraid, the stagnation and despair of that day. We did those first things first."

But the covenant "with ourselves" did not stop there. "Instinctively we recognized a deeper need—the need to find through government the instrument of our united purpose to solve for the individual the ever-rising problems of a complex civilization. Repeated attempts at their solution without the aid of government had left us baffled and bewildered. For, without that aid, we had been unable to create those moral controls over the services of science which are ncessary to make science a useful servant instead of a ruthless master of mankind. To do this we knew that we must find practical controls over blind economic forces and blindly selfish men."

The rain poured down, dripped off Roosevelt's bare head, dulled the cutting edge of some of his sentences. As the intricacies of human relationships increased, he said, so power to govern them also must increase— power to stop evil, power to do good. "The essential democracy of our Nation and the safety of our people depend not upon the absence of power, but upon lodging it with those whom the people can change or continue at stated intervals through an honest and free system of elections." Did the Chief Justice, sitting a few feet away on the President's right, catch the faint warning in the sentence?

The President was turning now to the future. "Shall we pause now and turn our back upon the road that lies ahead?" He looked at the crowd. "Many voices are heard as we face a great decision. Comfort says, 'Tarry a while.' Opportunism says, 'This is a good spot.' Timidity asks, 'How

451

difficult is the road ahead?' " The nation had come far since the days of stagnation. But dulled conscience, irresponsibility, and ruthless self-interest already were reappearing. Here was the challenge to American democracy:

"In this nation I see tens of millions of its citizens—a substantial part of its whole population—who at this very moment are denied the greater part of what the very lowest standards of today call the necessities of life.

"I see millions of families trying to live on incomes so meager that the pall of family disaster hangs over them day by day.

"I see millions whose daily lives in city and on farm continue under conditions labeled indecent by a so-called polite society half a century ago.

"I see millions denied education, recreation, and the opportunity to better their lot and the lot of their children.

"I see millions lacking the means to buy the products of farm and factory and by their poverty denying work and productiveness to many other millions.

"I see one-third of a nation ill-housed, ill-clad, ill-nourished.

"It is not in despair that I paint you that picture. I paint it for you in hope—because the Nation, seeing and understanding the injustice in it, proposes to paint it out. . . .

"To maintain a democracy of effort requires a vast amount of patience in dealing with differing methods, a vast amount of humility. But out of the confusion of many voices rises an understanding of dominant public need. Then political leadership can voice common ideals, and aid in their realization.

"In taking again the oath of office as President of the United States, I assume the solemn obligation of leading the American people forward along the road over which they have chosen to advance. . . ."

BOMBSHELL

Just two weeks later Roosevelt and Hughes faced each other once again— this time in the gracious, brilliantly lighted East Room of the White House. It was the President's annual dinner for the judiciary. At the center of the scene were the President, jauntily waving his cigarette holder to point up his stories, and the great jurist. Both were in a jovial mood; the talk ran fast and free. Around them were banked others of the nation's great— cabinet members, judges, senators, bankers, even the Gene Tunneys.

The jollity barely concealed a certain tension in the air. Key New Deal measures were crowding the Supreme Court's docket. Rumors were running through Washington that Roosevelt, armed with his huge popular

452

endorsement, was aiming some kind of attack on the Court. Besides the President, only a handful present knew the truth of the rumors. Watching Roosevelt and Hughes, Attorney General Cummings wished the secret were out. "I feel too much like a conspirator," he complained to Rosenman. Roosevelt, on the other hand, was probably savoring the irony of the moment. On the eve of a great battle the commander of one side was giving a banquet to his adversaries.

But the President was a bit nervous too. During the next two days he pored over his message to Congress, adding, erasing, shifting phrases and sentences. His main concern was to keep his plan secret; he had not told some of his closest aides. On February 4 he called an extraordinary meeting of Cabinet members and congressional leaders for the following day. Amazed White House stenographers were told to report at 6:30 the next morning to mimeograph documents for this meeting and for a press conference.

Next morning the Cabinet and congressmen waited wonderingly in the long, low-ceilinged Cabinet room. The President was quickly wheeled in. He called out cheery greetings, then turned directly to the business at hand. Announcing his intention to meet the challenge posed by the Court, he read excerpts from his message that would go to Congress in an hour.

Amid dead silence, he outlined his plan. For every Supreme Court justice who failed to quit the bench within six months after reaching seventy, the President would be empowered to appoint a new justice up to a total of six. The message to Congress talked much of judicial efficiency, congestion in the courts, the need for new blood, the problem of injunctions; and the President's bill involved new appointments at the district and circuit court level too. But the crux of the proposal leaped out from the long legal phrases—the power Roosevelt was asking to flank Hughes and his brethren with six New Deal justices.

The meeting was a study in mixed emotions. Ickes was elated that the President had moved at last. Cummings, twiddling his pince-nez with a slightly self-important air, was pleased to have long been a part of the unfolding drama. But the congressional delegation sat as if stunned. Garner and Rayburn said not a word. Robinson, deep concern written on his face, gave a feeble indication of approval. Henry Ashurst, chairman of the Senate Judiciary Committee, must have thought of his heated denial during the campaign that Roosevelt would try to pack the Court, but he loyally spoke out in support of the bill. Speaker Bankhead bore a poker face throughout.

There was virtually no discussion; the President solicited no opinions from his party's leadership. At the end he wheeled off to meet a waiting group of newspapermen. Over this session Roosevelt presided like an impresario. Again and again bursts of laughter punctuated his reading of his message to Congress, as he interpolated telling little points; the President threw his head back and joined in the laughter. Once again he demanded absolute secrecy until the message was released.

Driving back to Capitol Hill from the White House, Garner and his colleagues were still silent. Suddenly Hatton Sumners of Texas, chairman of the House Judiciary Committee, turned to the others. "Boys," he said, "here's where I cash in." The group took the news to Congress with them. By the time the message was read, the cloakrooms were filled with little knots of legislators asking one another, "What do you think of it?" In the first hours it seemed as though the proposal cut through each House, down the middle. Two sons of Texas signalized the extremes. In the House, New Deal Representative Maury Maverick grabbed a mimeographed copy of the bill, scribbled his name on it, and threw it into the bill hopper almost before the reading clerk was finished. In the Senate lobby Garner held his nose with one hand and vigorously shook his turned-down thumb.

A messenger hurried across the plaza to the Supreme Court building. Inside, the justices were hearing an argument. Only Brandeis had heard the news; just before the justices entered the Court, Corcoran, with Roosevelt's consent, had "crashed the sacred robing room" to tell him, and Brandeis had instantly expressed his disapproval. Now a page slipped through the draperies behind the dais and handed a paper to each justice. The attorney at bar, sensing the sudden tension on the bench, paused a moment. Hughes shifted restlessly in his chair, Van Devanter looked grim, Butler seemed to chuckle. But judicial mien quickly reappeared, and proceedings continued.

Blazing headlines carried the news to the people during the afternoon. Next morning, reading the newspapers in bed over his breakfast tray, the President was not surprised at the howls of anguish in the editorial columns. He had expected this; what he was banking on was the approval of the people. As it turned out, the proposal at the outset split the American people neatly in half. Could Roosevelt mobilize a popular majority behind his plan? Could he convert such a majority into congressional action?

The suddenness of Roosevelt's move, the obvious pleasure he found in presenting his handiwork, and the utter secrecy that surrounded its preparation all gave the impression of a proposal that had been hastily cooked up after the election. Actually Roosevelt had been considering judicial reform for over two years.

Even before the Court's all-out attack on the New Deal in 1935 Roosevelt was thinking of enlarging the Court to protect his legislation. That he would not brook judicial opposition on a crucial matter was apparent from the radio address to the nation he planned in the event that the Court found against him in the gold cases. Only the Court's slim vote in his favor turned him from defiance of the Court through presidential proclamation and an appeal to Congress. When the Court voided the NRA and other measures, the President's view that action must be taken steadily hardened.

But what to do? For a while Roosevelt had toyed with the idea of a constitutional amendment. Various types were possible: directly enlarging congressional authority in specific economic and social fields; granting Congress power to re-enact and thus "constitutionalize" a measure voided by the Court; requiring a six to three or even a seven to two vote in the Supreme Court to strike down an act of Congress; setting an age limit on judges or giving them terms instead of appointments for life. Eventually Roosevelt decided against the amendment method. At best it would take too long. More likely, an amendment, even if it won two-thirds majorities in House and Senate, would never hurdle the barriers carefully contrived by the framers of the Constitution—three-quarters of the state legislatures or of state conventions—especially since these assemblies tended to over-represent conservative, small-town interests and attitudes.

"Give me ten million dollars," the President said later, "and I can prevent any amendment to the Constitution from being ratified by the necessary number of states."

Could an act of Congress do the trick? A measure that directly challenged the High Court by trying to curb its power would probably be voided by the Court itself. There was another method, however, that seemed certainly constitutional because it was sanctioned by precedent. This was to enlarge the Court's membership, as previous presidents had done, by inducing Congress to authorize new appointments. At first, packing the Court seemed distasteful to the President, perhaps because the objective would be so transparent. But he kept returning to the idea. He was fascinated by a historical precedent—Asquith's and Lloyd George's threat through the King to pack the House of Lords with new Peers if that chamber refused to bow to the supremacy of the House of Commons.

Clearly the President feared a direct assault on the Court. Perhaps he sensed—as polls indicated—that in late 1935 most of the people opposed restriction on the Court's veto power. The Democratic platform of 1936 had come out only for some "clarifying amendment." During the campaign Hoover and others demanded that the President confirm or deny that he planned to pack the Court. Roosevelt not only ignored the specific question—as a seasoned campaigner would—but he skirted the whole problem of the Supreme Court. Doubtless his silence helped him roll up his great majority—but it also meant that he gained no explicit mandate to act on the Court.

At the first Cabinet meeting after the election Roosevelt raised the Court issue. He expected, he said with mock glumness, that McReynolds would still be on the bench at the age of one hundred and five. An appeal to the people might be necessary. The problem "must be faced," he wrote to Joseph Patterson of the New York *Daily News*. But how to face it? Before Roosevelt left on his cruise to South America, he set Cummings to work in Washington poring over a sheaf of plans for overcoming the nine old men—or at least five of them.

Mulling over various proposals one December morning, Cummings ran across a recommendation that Attorney General—now Justice—McReynolds had made in 1913 that when any federal judge, except Supreme Court justices, failed to retire at the age provided by law, the President should appoint another judge to preside over the Court and to hold precedence over the older one. Why not, thought Cummings, apply the idea to the Supreme Court?

"The answer to a maiden's prayer!" Roosevelt reportedly exclaimed when Cummings brought in his idea. And so it must have seemed. The plan was clearly constitutional. It was, compared with most of the other proposals, quite moderate in character, involving no change in the venerable system of checks and balances. Most important, the plan could be presented to the country as part of a broader program of reconstructing the whole federal judiciary in the name not of liberalism but of greater efficiency and expedition in the courts. And Roosevelt, with his penchant for personalizing the political opposition, must have delighted in the thought of hoisting McReynolds by his own petard.

All that remained was the matter of how to present the plan. Why did Roosevelt insist on almost conspiratorial secrecy? Why did he spring the plan suddenly on Robinson, who would have to manage the fight in the Senate; on Ashurst, who just before had hotly denied that Roosevelt had any plans for packing the Court, on his old progressive ally Norris, on Brandeis and Stone, on Rayburn and Garner, on Farley and Ickes, even on McIntyre and Early? Roosevelt explained to Farley that he feared premature disclosure by the press. This explanation is unconvincing.

Roosevelt was too astute a politician to think that secrecy was worth the price of excluding key leaders from the decision-making conferences. Moreover, Roosevelt himself had leaked the essence of the plan to a *Collier's* writer a few weeks before the announcement.

The explanation lies deeper—deep in Roosevelt's personality. He had won what he considered to be a personal election victory over the Old Guard. Now the Old Guard remained entrenched in the ramparts of the judiciary. The stage was set for a Rooseveltian onslaught against the citadel as exhilarating and triumphant as his rout of the Republicans. He set the stage with his old flair for timing and suspense. His final presentation combined in a curious fashion two Rooseveltian traits—his instinct for the dramatic and his instinct for the adroit and circuitous stratagem rather than the frontal assault.

Both instincts failed him. "Too clever—too damned clever," said one pro-New Deal newspaper. The President's liberal friends were disturbed. Some of them had hoped that Roosevelt would make a direct attack on the Court's conservative veto. Others used his disingenuousness as an excuse to desert the cause. Still others disagreed with his particular plan. Years before, Roosevelt had lamented that reform came slowly because liberals had such difficulty in agreeing on means. His words would fly back to mock him in 1937.

GUERRILLA WARFARE

Battle lines formed quickly but not in a way that was to Roosevelt's liking. He was not surprised that Republicans and conservative Democrats flared up in opposition. This was to be expected. But alarming reports reached the White House from the Senate. Two noted progressives, Burt Wheeler and Hiram Johnson, were opposed. So were Democrats Joseph O'Mahoney of Wyoming, Tom Connally of Texas, Bennett Clark of Missouri, Ed Burke of Nebraska, and a dozen others of the kind of men on whose loyalty the President had counted. And—worst blow of all—Norris. Although in the end he supported the bill, the old Nebraskan, within a few hours of Roosevelt's announcement, said quietly, "I am not in sympathy with the plan to enlarge the Supreme Court."

Something was happening to the Grand Coalition that had carried Roosevelt to his election triumph. Something was happening to the Republicans too. Knowing that their little band in Congress could not overcome the President in a straight party fight, they resolved to stay silent and let the Democrats fight one another. When Hoover, Landon, and other national leaders wanted to rush to the microphone and make the court plan a party issue, congressional Republicans McNary, Borah, and Van-denberg, acting quickly, headed them off. The Liberty League, moribund after November 1936, was silent. Roosevelt found himself aligned not against Republicans but against his own fellow partisans.

"What a grand fight it is going to be!" Roosevelt wrote Creel. "We need everything we have got to put in it!" To visitors he declared confidently that "the people are with me." Were they? Within a few days it was clear that the proposal had struck deep into the complex of American emotions. There was a crescendo of protest. The New York *Herald Tribune* gave seven of its eight front-page columns to the proposal. Patriotic groups moved quickly into action. New England town fathers called mass meetings. Bar associations met and denounced. Mail flooded congressional offices; some senators received over a thousand letters a day. What amazed congressmen was less the amount of opposition than the intensity of it. There was a pervasive element of fear—"fear of the unknown," columnist Raymond Clapper thought—and a deep reverence for the Supreme Court.

Many of the protestants cited their middle-class background, their little property holdings, their fear of labor and radical elements. Events helped sharpen these fears. During the early months of 1937 a rash of sit-down strikes broke out. The picture of grinning, insolent workers barricading factories against the owners was disturbing to people who wanted law and order, and a curious, emotional link was created in the conservative middle-class mind between the court plan and labor turbulence. For the first time, William Allen White wrote Norris, opposition to Roosevelt was coming "not from the plug hat section but from the grass roots."

The protest was not wholly spontaneous. Busily stoking the fires were Roosevelt's old friend Frank Gannett and other prominent conservatives. "Get busy fast!" Borah urged Gannett; the New York publisher put $49,-000 into the campaign and raised almost $150,000 more from several thousand contributors. Full-page advertisements blossomed in the newspapers; fervent oratory filled the air waves; speeches were franked by the tens of thousands through congressional offices and out to the country. And still the hand of Republican leaders was hardly visible.

One early effect of this surge of protest was to strip Roosevelt's proposal of its "efficiency" façade and to show it plainly as an attempt to liberalize the Court. Abruptly shifting his tactics, the President decided to wage his campaign squarely on this basic issue. And he resolved on a direct appeal to the country. "The source of criticism is concentrated," he wrote a friend late in February, "and I feel that as we get the story to the general public the whole matter will be given wide support."

Significantly, his first appeal was to his party. Addressing a resplendent Democratic victory dinner at the Mayflower Hotel on March 4, the President summoned his partisans to defend his proposal. Roosevelt seemed in the best of humor, but his voice was stern and commanding. He warned his party that it would celebrate victories in the future only if it kept faith with the majority that had elected it. "We gave warning last November that we had only just begun to fight. Did some people really believe we did not mean it? Well—I meant it, and you meant it."

A new crisis was at hand, the President asserted—a crisis different from but even graver than four years before. It was the ever-accelerating speed of social forces now gathering headway. The President dwelt at length on the fate of remedial measures at the hands of the courts. Then he brought his speech to a stunning climax:

"It will take courage to let our minds be bold and find the ways to meet the needs of the Nation. But for our Party, now as always, the counsel of courage is the counsel of wisdom.

"If we do not have the courage to lead the American people where they want to go, someone else will.

"Here is one-third of a Nation ill-nourished, ill-clad, ill-housed—NOW!

"Here are thousands upon thousands of farmers wondering whether next year's prices will meet their mortgage interest—NOW!

"Here are thousands upon thousands of men and women laboring for long hours in factories for inadequate pay—NOW!

"Here are thousands upon thousands of children who should be at school, working in mines and mills—NOW!

"Here are strikes more far-reaching than we have ever known, costing millions of dollars—NOW!

"Here are Spring floods threatening to roll again down our river valleys —NOW!

"Here is the Dust Bowl beginning to blow again—NOW!

"If we would keep faith with those who had faith in us, if we would make democracy succeed, I say we must act—NOW!"

The President's fireside chat a few days later was more pallid and more defensive. Again he dwelt on the conditions of four years before, the "quiet crisis" that faced the country, the failure of the Supreme Court to pull together with the other horses in the "three-horse team" of the national government. The Constitution must be saved from the Court, and the Court from itself. He directly met the charge of packing the Court by denying that he had any intention of appointing "spineless puppets." He explained at length why he had not chosen the amendment alternative. He pointed to his own record of devotion to civil and religious liberty.

"You who know me will accept my solemn assurance that in a world in which democracy is under attack, I seek to make American democracy succeed. You and I will do our part."

The President was not depending on oratory alone. From the outset a special White House staff, under Roosevelt's close direction, managed an aggressive campaign. They dispatched speakers to the country, channeled ideas and arguments to friendly legislators, and put pressure on senators hostile or silent on the measure. The form of this pressure was a subject of open wrangling among Democrats. At the very least, Corcoran and the other Administration agents put it up to senators in stiff terms to back up the President. Senators were tempted with new patronage arrangements and with federal projects for their states, and even with judicial appointments for themselves. Pressure was also brought to bear on a number of senators through Democratic organizations in their home states, including Chicago's Kelly-Nash machine and Pendergast's Kansas City organization. Some senators—certainly Robinson himself—could hardly forget that passage of the measure would mean that the President could allot six Supreme Court judgeships—the most highly prized appointive job in America.

Roosevelt's appeal to the people had some impact. Support for the plan reached its highest point in mid-March. But the actual deciding would be done on Capitol Hill, and here things were not going so well.

Roosevelt's aides were not operating on Capitol Hill with their usual efficiency. Part of the trouble was caused by James Roosevelt, whom his father had appointed as an assistant early in 1937. Eleanor Roosevelt, foreseeing the pressures amid which James would have to work, opposed the appointment, but her husband saw no reason why the fact that he was President should deprive him of his oldest son's help. Eleanor's doubts were vindicated. James made promises that seemed to have special authenticity but in fact did not; the efforts of the other aides on the Hill were undermined; and congressional friction and bitterness increased.

The senatorial opposition, on the other hand, was functioning with extraordinary skill and smoothness. The Republicans were still relatively quiet. On the Democratic side Carter Glass supplied the moral indignation and Wheeler and O'Mahoney the liberal veneer, while middle-of-the-road Democrats like Royal S. Copeland of New York, Frederick Van

Nuys of Indiana, and Connally furnished the anchor line of votes. Against them was aligned a solid core of New Dealers and a group of senators who went along with the bill largely out of personal loyalty to the President. A score of senators were—openly, at least—on the fence.

In mid-March the seat of battle shifted to the reverberant, multi-columned Senate caucus room, where the Judiciary Committee held hearings on the measure. Cummings led off for the Administration with a statement that reflected the President's original plea for a more efficient judiciary. He was followed by Assistant Attorney General Robert H. Jackson, who tried valiantly to bring the subject back to the issue of liberalizing the Court. Both were subjected to a barrage of unfriendly questions. So effective was the cross-examination that a dozen experts from the American Bar Association were rumored to be in Washington furnishing ammunition. Other Administration witnesses testified over the next ten days, including President Green of the A. F. of L., political scientists Edward S. Corwin and Charles Grove Haines, Editor Irving Brant of the St. Louis *Star-Times*. Then it was the opposition's turn.

Shrewdly handled, the congressional hearing can be a powerful weapon against the executive. Although not himself a member of the Judiciary Committee, Wheeler was ready, through his friends on the committee, to use it to turn the Administration's flank. A veteran of Montana's stormy politics, he was a man temperamentally at his best in opposition: tireless, vengeful, resourceful, and often choleric. Despite his protestations of love for the President, he had reason to feel disgruntled; an early and strenuous worker for Roosevelt's nomination, he had had little recognition, and he knew that he—who had been, after all, the Progressive party running mate of the great La Follette in 1924—had taken a more liberal position than the President on many relief and reform measures.

Wheeler opened the attack on the Court bill before the committee. Suddenly he produced the opposition's bombshell—a letter from Chief Justice Hughes showing categorically that the Supreme Court was abreast of its work and arguing that a larger Court would lower its efficiency. In the few minutes the letter took to read it made three things clear: that a coalition had been forged between the senatorial opposition and the politicians of the judiciary, who were quietly doing what they could against the plan; that this coalition was attacking Roosevelt on his weakest salient, his original charge of inefficiency; and that the political skill of Hughes himself had been thrown into the fight.

Outwardly Hughes had preserved his usual benignity in the face of the Court plan. "If they want me to preside over a convention," he said, "I can do it." But the old politician's fighting instincts were aroused. He wished to speak out—but how could he in the face of the restraints that tradition imposed on the Court? Roosevelt's use of the inefficiency argument gave him the perfect opportunity to attack the plan in the guise of supplying data. The Chief Justice was ready even to appear personally before the committee, but Brandeis objected, so a letter had to do. Working feverishly over a weekend to meet Wheeler's timetable, the Chief Justice turned the letter over to the Senator with a smile. "The baby is born."

Hughes's political leadership and shrewdness matched Roosevelt's. He had not been able, he informed the committee, to consult with every member of the Court, but he was confident that his letter was in accord with their views. Actually, at least one justice, Stone, resented Hughes's failure to consult him and disagreed with part of the letter. Perhaps the Chief Justice knew or suspected that Stone disparaged Hughes's reputation as a liberal Justice, that Stone, through Irving Brant of the St. Louis *Star-Times*, was letting his views be known to the White House. In any event, Hughes's strategy was perfectly executed.

Dismayed by Hughes's counterthrust, the Administration had to sit by idly while the committee heard witness after witness. For days on end their arguments against the President's plan filled the press and radio. Roosevelt hoped that "things would move faster from now on," as he wrote a friend, but the opposition saw the advantages of delay. To make matters worse, the Administration had no one on the committee with Borah's or Wheeler's or Connally's brilliance in cross-examination. Here, too, the President was paying a price for his secrecy; Senator Hugo Black, a tenacious and resourceful parliamentarian, had left the Judiciary Committee at the beginning of the year.

During the critical weeks of late March and early April popular support for the plan slowly, steadily ebbed away. The backing that Roosevelt aroused in his two speeches lacked stability and depth; it simply disintegrated as the long fight wore on. Much of the trouble lay in the deep fissures running through workers and farmers, the two great group interests that Roosevelt had counted on because of their unhappy experiences with the Court. The A. F. of L. was now locked in trench warfare with the C. I. O., and labor rallies organized by the Administration fell apart in the face of this split, local Democratic party quarrels, and general apathy. The farm organizations were not acting as though there had ever been an AAA decision. Leaders of the powerful Farm Bureau Federation were silent; the Grange was against the plan; and—worst of all—the Farmers Union was divided. Evidently the farm leaders were responding less to a sense of calculated self-interest than to the currents of feeling sweeping middle-class America: respect for the "vestal virgins of the court"; fear of labor turbulence; concern for law and order and property rights.

In this extremity Roosevelt turned to the Democratic party. Farley industriously toured the party circuit, trying to build grass fires behind lagging Democratic congressmen and vaguely threatening punishment to deserters. All in vain—on this issue the party lacked vigor and militance. Moreover, prominent Democratic leaders outside the Senate were decamping on the court issue. In the cabinet itself Hull was quietly hostile. In Roosevelt's own state his old comrade in arms Governor Lehman came out against the bill, and even Boss Flynn of the Bronx, the most stolid of party war horses, was opposed.

At the beginning of April the President was still optimistic. Corcoran, Pittman, La Follette, and others had been reporting enthusiastically on the chances of victory. When Senator Black warned him of the opposition's determination and tactics of delay, Roosevelt replied: "We'll smoke 'em out. If delay helps them, we must press for an early vote."

BREACHES IN THE GRAND COALITION

Roosevelt was wrong. By April the chances for the Court plan were almost nil. The President simply could not command the needed votes in either Senate or House. Then on April 12 came a clinching blow. In a tense, packed courtroom Hughes read the Supreme Court's judgment sustaining the Wagner Act.

If Roosevelt had been as acutely sensitive to political crosscurrents during this period as he usually was, the Court's shift would not have surprised him. A few weeks after the election, while Roosevelt and Cummings were leafing through Court plans, Roberts had told the Chief Justice privately that he would vote to sustain a Washington minimum-wage law and overturn a contrary decision of a few months back. Hughes was so pleased he almost hugged him. Final decision was delayed, however, because Stone was ill for some time, and because Hughes saw the disadvantages of appearing to yield before the Court-packing plan. By the end of March the time seemed ripe for the decision on this case and on three others favorable to the Administration. Still, these were only straws in the wind, and they had little effect on Roosevelt's plans. The Wagner Act decision two weeks later, however, showed the decisive alignment of Hughes and Roberts with the three liberals.

Once again the Chief Justice had outfoxed the President. How much he changed his technical position to meet the tactical needs of the hour is a subject of some dispute among constitutional experts. Certainly Hughes's position on the companion cases to the main case of April 12 seemed a long jump from some of his earlier judgments; on the other hand, the Chief Justice, like most politician-judges, had been flexible enough in his positions to make the jump possible. His new position was more important politically than legalistically. He had consolidated a majority of the Court behind him; he had taken the heart out of the President's argument; he had upheld a measure dear to labor and thus reduced even further its concern over the Court—and he had done all this without undue sacrifice of the Court's dignity.

Outwardly Roosevelt's reaction to the Court's move was gleeful. "I have been chortling all morning," he told reporters. "I have been having a perfectly grand time." He compared the *Herald Tribune*'s enthusiastic hailing of the decision with its approval two years before of the Liberty League lawyers' opinion against the constitutionality of the Wagner Act.

"Well, I have been having more fun!" Roosevelt went on amid repeated guffaws from the reporters. "And I haven't read the Washington *Post*, and I haven't got the Chicago *Tribune* yet. Or the Boston *Herald*. Today is a very, very happy day. . . ." He quoted with relish a remark a friend had made to him: the No Man's Land had been eliminated but "we are now in 'Roberts' Land.' "

Inwardly the President was more puzzled than pleased. Should he press on with the Court fight? He must have sensed immediately that Hughes had given the plan's chances a punishing blow; he had hoped for a complete veto of New Deal legislation so that the issue would be sharpened for the people. He soon learned, moreover, that Robinson and others of his lieutenants were talking compromise. "This bill's raising hell in the Senate," Robinson reportedly told a White House representative. "Now it's going to be worse than ever, but if the President wants to compromise, I can get him a couple of extra justices tomorrow." On the other hand, Robinson himself posed a problem. It had long been understood that the doughty Arkansan would receive the first vacant justiceship and thus fulfill a life ambition. But the Senator's appointment would clearly be a recognition of service to Roosevelt rather than a recognition of legal distinction or ingrained liberalism; once on the Court, moreover, Robinson might swing right. To offset this appointment there must be others.

Roosevelt had further reasons to stand pat on his proposal. He was now in the fight to the hilt, and compromise would be interpreted as defeat for him and victory for Wheeler and the other rebels. He still hankered for six of his own appointees—liberal-minded judges with whom he could establish friendly personal relations such as he had enjoyed with the state judges when he was governor. Crucial New Deal measures were still to come before the Court, and the justices might swing right again if the pistol at their head was unloaded. Finally, the President still thought that he could win. Had he not saved many a measure during the first term, when prospects looked bleak, simply by sticking to his guns?

So the order was full speed ahead. "We must keep up—and strengthen—the fight," the President wrote Congressman David Lewis. As if to flaunt his confidence over the outcome he made plans to fish in the Gulf of Mexico at the end of April. Roosevelt's manner was still buoyant.

"I am delighted to have your rural rhapsody of April twelfth and to know that the French Government has spring fever," he wrote on April 21 to Ambassador William C. Bullitt in Paris. "Spring has come to Washington also and even the Senators, who were biting each other over the Supreme Court, are saying 'Alphonse' and 'Gaston' to each other. . . .

"I, too, am influenced by this beautiful spring day. I haven't a care in the world which is going some for a President who is said by the newspapers to be a remorseless dictator driving his government into hopeless bankruptcy."

The Supreme Court turnabout marked a decisive shift in the character of the Court fight. No longer was the issue one of Roosevelt New Deal versus Old Guard Court. Now the fight lay between the President and Congress. When the Court upheld the Social Security Act a few weeks later, it served to take the Court as an institution even further out of the struggle. But not its members. In May and June, Hughes made speeches that were hardly veiled assaults on the Court proposal.

Roosevelt returned from his fishing in mid-May. He was in a militant mood. After talking with precinct committeemen during the train trip back, he told the Cabinet, he was as certain as ever that the people were still behind the bill. Democrats in Congress who opposed it, he added, might expect defeat at the polls. Roosevelt warned Garner privately that he, the President, had brought a lot of congressmen in on his coattails, and that he might openly oppose Democrats who were against the bill. He had Robinson and other leaders in, laughed off their fears, explained away the defections they gloomily reported, and sent them back to the battle.

That battle was still going badly. Shipstead came out against the bill, as did several other senators on whom Roosevelt was relying. Party leaders were warning of a deepening split among the Democrats. Even White

House assistants were losing confidence and counseling compromise. Other New Deal measures were being pulled down with the Court bill. Then, on May 18, the opposition played another card. Wheeler and Borah, knowing of Van Devanter's wish to retire, got word to the justice that a resignation timed to coincide with an expected vote by the Judiciary Committee against the Court bill would help the plan's opponents. For Wheeler knew what that vote would be. A few minutes after Roosevelt read Van Devanter's notice of retirement on the morning of May 18 and had written in longhand a cool but polite note of acceptance, the Senate Judiciary Committee met in executive session. After brushing aside several compromise measures it voted 10-8 that the President's bill "do not pass." The committee line-up symbolized the split in the ranks of the Grand Coalition: six Democrats of diverse ideological hues deserted the President.

Face to face with this deepening split, Roosevelt executed one of the rapid tactical shifts that so often threw his opponents off guard. He turned to the possibility of compromise. But his freedom of maneuver here was unhappily narrowed by a conjunction of circumstances that stemmed partly from sheer bad luck and partly from the way in which he had handled matters. Van Devanter's retirement not only knocked one more prop from under the President's plea for new blood on the Court; it also precipitated in acute form the old problem of rewarding Robinson with a justiceship without alienating the "true" liberals and making a mockery of Roosevelt's arguments for the bill. Within a few hours of Van Devanter's retirement, almost as if by plan, both opposition senators and supporters of the bill were crowding around Robinson's front-row desk in the Senate chamber, pumping his hand, calling him "Mr. Justice." The Senate was in effect nominating Robinson to fill the vacancy.

In this extremity Roosevelt turned to the direct person-to-person persuasion for which he had such a flair. Against the advice of Corcoran and Jackson, who wanted him to let the bill go over to another session or even to accept defeat and take the issue to the country, the President decided on a shrewd but risky tactical move. Through Farley he let it be known to Robinson that the Senator could expect to take Van Devanter's place. Then the President called Robinson in and agreed to accept a compromise on the bill, but he added that if there was a bride there must be bridesmaids. He asked Robinson to take full leadership of the fight for a compromise bill. The President was now seeking to turn the senatorial support for Robinson's appointment to his own advantage. If the senators wanted to help their old colleague, they would have to provide some extra appointments as well. The danger in the plan was that everything depended on Robinson.

And the President did not fully trust the majority leader. He complained to Ickes that Robinson had lost his punch, that there was no leadership in Congress. Speaker Bankhead was not strong in the House, he said, and Rayburn was so anxious to succeed to the speakership that he feared to offend anyone. The President was especially upset about Garner. Exclaiming that "my ears are buzzing and ringing," the Vice-President had left on a long-planned vacation in Texas just as the fight in the Senate was coming to a head. But the President never expressed his feelings directly to Garner. Instead, after the Vice-President had been away several weeks Roosevelt urged his return in a letter that offered every bait that might lure the sulking Texan. Knowing of Garner's fears about government spending and labor violence, and his old populist distrust of bankers, the President predicted a balanced budget for the coming year and declared that the public was "pretty sick of the extremists which exist both in the C.I.O. and some of the A.F. of L. unions and also of the extremists like Girdler and some of his associates backed by the Guarantee [sic] Trust Co., etc." Roosevelt ended his appeal on a personal note.

"And finally, just to clinch the argument for your return, I want to tell you again how much I miss you because of you, yourself, and also because of the great help that you have given and continue to give to the working out *peacefully* of a mass of problems greater than the Nation has ever had before." But the Vice-President stayed in Texas.

Garner's own sit-down strike signalized the state of the Democratic party. It was not the Court plan alone that was splitting apart the Grand Coalition. The attack on the plan served as a rallying cry for the conservatives who feared the rising tide of labor turbulence, for the "old" liberals who disliked the President's indirections and his personal handling of party matters, for New Deal liberals who prized orderly processes and constitutional traditions. Seeking to placate these elements Roosevelt, when asked about the deadlock between labor and management, said calculatedly, "A plague on both your houses." Lewis's howl of indignation and the icy silence of the party Old Guard indicated that in striving to veer between the various factions Roosevelt was keeping the warm support of none.

At the end of June Roosevelt tried another tack—and one that again illustrated his preference for direct personal handling of affairs. A grand political picnic was arranged at Jefferson Island in Chesapeake Bay, to which Democratic congressmen were invited. The plan was to submerge

467

intraparty bickering in three days of good fellowship. The President was at his best. Seated in an armchair under a big locust tree, he chatted congenially and drank beer with groups of shirt-sleeved legislators. He even allowed Martin Dies of Texas to induct him into the Demagogue's Club, involving a pledge to favor all spending bills and no tax bills, to do nothing to harm his chances for a third term, never to be consistent—and not to send controversial proposals to Congress.

In sharp contrast to this bucolic scene was the grim atmosphere of the Senate. There, day after day, Robinson was making the rounds of the Democrats, pleading with them to support his compromise plan. The new measure was mild enough, allowing the President to appoint only one coadjutor justice a year for any justice who had passed seventy-five and failed to retire. Even so, Robinson found it hard going, and often he had to resort to a personal plea to embarrassed senators for help in realizing his life ambition. When Robinson opened debate on the bill in the Senate he seemed to reporters, as he sawed the air with violent gestures and beat off his interrogators, like an aging bull tormented by the fast-moving picadors around him and stung by their *banderillas*. Day after day Robinson roared his arguments and threats at the opposition, meanwhile desperately counting and recounting the small majority he had lined up. But he had come to the end of his road. On the morning of July 14 he rose from his hotel bed, took one step, and fell dead, a copy of the *Congressional Record* in his hand.

The stroke that ruptured Robinson's heart ruptured as well the bonds of personal loyalty on which the majority leader had been depending for his compromise plan. There was a sudden rush away from the bill. Even as Robinson was buried in Little Rock the congressmen who had escorted the body out on the funeral train were busy sparring over the bill. On the train back to Washington, Garner, who had joined the delegation in Little Rock, went down the aisles systematically counting noses. On the morning of July 20 he reported to the President.

"How did you find the Court situation, Jack?" Roosevelt asked.

"Do you want it with the bark on or off, Cap'n?"

"The rough way," Roosevelt said with a laugh.

"All right. You are beat. You haven't got the votes."

NOT WITH A BANG BUT A WHIMPER

The end of the Court fight was anticlimactic. Roosevelt asked Garner to arrange the best compromise that he could. Whether the Vice-President tried to salvage something out of the bill or simply surrendered is shrouded in the obscure maneuvering of the last days. By now Congress was out-side anyone's control; "everything on the Hill seems to be at sixes and sevens," Ickes complained. Appropriately enough, the Judiciary Commit-tee served as executioner by offering a motion to recommit the Court bill. Only twenty senators voted against recommittal. A week later the Senate rushed through an emasculated bill, making minor reforms and improve-ments, which the President halfheartedly signed into law.

The last episodes of the Court fight were entangled with a struggle over the Democratic leadership in the Senate. Pat Harrison of Mississippi and Alben W. Barkley of Kentucky were vying for Robinson's mantle in one of those contests that become all the more bitter because they cleave the membership of an intimate club. The Court fight sharpened tempers of the opposing factions. Roosevelt was on good terms with both senators, but he had several reasons to prefer Barkley. The Kentuckian was a more reliable New Dealer and was personally more loyal to Roosevelt; he had, for example, given active support to the Court bill while Harrison was passive. And if Harrison won the position, he would probably have to vacate chairmanship of the Senate Finance Committee and this vital post would fall into the hands of a conservative Democrat.

Clearly Roosevelt had his preferences—but could he act upon them? Not if he was to follow the custom that forbids presidential interference in the Senate's internal affairs. Roosevelt's method of resolving this prob-lem was characteristic. Openly he took a neutral position; to be sure, he addressed a letter to "My Dear Alben" urging a continued fight for the principles of the Court bill, but Barkley's position as acting majority leader permitted this public show of friendship.

Privately the President was not neutral at all. A check showed that Senate Democrats were split almost evenly between the two candidates. Every vote would count. An obvious weak link in Harrison's ranks was Senator William H. Dietrich, who owed his Senate seat largely to Boss Ed Kelly of Chicago. Roosevelt asked Farley to telephone Kelly to use his influence with Dietrich. Farley refused on the grounds that he had prom-ised the principals that he would keep hands off. The President thereupon turned to Hopkins and Corcoran, who threw White House pressure on Dietrich and others. The Harrison forces mobilized pressure too. Senator Harry Truman, who had pledged his vote to Barkley, had to ask the Ken-tuckian to be released of his promise. Among the shifters was Dietrich—from Harrison to Barkley. Barkley's victory by one vote was an important victory for the President, but one that sharpened the ill temper of the Senate.

The Court fight over, Roosevelt sought to regain direction of his general legislative program. Congress, he told his Cabinet, must take responsibility for what was done and what was left undone. The President was especially concerned about the farm situation. If farm prices fell next year, he said, a good many Democrats would be defeated in the next election. While Roosevelt talked, Ickes scribbled on a piece of paper and passed it to Farley: "The President seems to be indulging in a curtain lecture for the benefit of the Vice-President."

Congress was still wallowing in confusion. Earlier in the session it had passed, under Roosevelt's proddings, several important bills. One of these was the Guffey-Vinson bituminous coal bill providing for governmental and private co-operation in marketing, price control, and trade practices. Others were a revised Neutrality Act and renewal of the Trade Agreements Act. Congress had also enacted the Farm Tenancy bill, authorizing federal loans to farm tenants, sharecroppers and laborers, to help them buy their own farms. This was work done, but it seemed strikingly small in the light of the President's broad challenge, in his inaugural, of "one third of a nation ill-housed, ill-clad, ill-nourished."

Could that challenge still be met? By the end of July five Administration measures awaited action in Congress: wages and hours, low-cost housing, executive reorganization, comprehensive farm program, and creation of seven regional agencies patterned somewhat after the TVA. When Congress adjourned late in August, only one of these measures had been made into law. This was the Wagner Housing bill. It was significant that this lone Administration victory was due far more to Wagner and an indefatigable group of public-housing enthusiasts and lobbyists than to the President. Roosevelt, to be sure, did help persuade a key chairman in the House to report the bill out of committee, but only after weeks of backing and filling in the White House.

Equally significant was the reason that the rest of Roosevelt's program failed. In part that failure stemmed from Roosevelt's original calculation that Court reform would have a better chance if other major bills were postponed in its behalf. Later he appeared to swing to the opposite view that at least one of the measures—wage-hour regulation—would be so popular that it would unify Democratic ranks split over Court reform. Both calculations proved wrong.

But there was a more important reason for Roosevelt's legislative difficulties—a reason that reflected the strategic weakness of his political position. The trouble was that the ample coalition that he had summoned to his personal support in November—and which had responded to that summons—was already falling apart.

The blocking of the wage-hour bill showed how extensive were the fractures in the coalition. When Senator Black introduced his proposed Fair Labor Standards Act late in May, Roosevelt vigorously urged passage. "We have promised it," he said. "We cannot stand still." Quickly the bill ran into snags. Southerners from low-wage states, including Harrison, deserted the President on the issue. Sharp differences developed among labor groups, not only between A. F. of L. and C.I.O. leaders but also within the two organizations. As if all this was not enough, a fight broke out between low-tariff and high-tariff Democrats over a protectionist clause in the bill. Pressure against the bill was put on Farley and Roosevelt through Democratic leaders in the South. After a struggle the bill passed the Senate, and by calling in President Green of the A.F. of L. and acceding to his major demands Roosevelt was able to ease the bill through the House Labor Committee. Then the bill stalled in the face of a coalition of Republicans and Southern Democrats on the Rules Committee. In vain Democratic leaders summoned a caucus to put force behind the bill; not enough Democrats showed up to make it an official caucus.

By mid-August the President was ready to give up the fight for the rest of his program. He decided to call Congress back in special session during the fall. Let the congressmen get back to their districts, he said, and they would return with a strengthened feeling for the New Deal.

But one task remained for the President before adjournment—and a most pleasant task. Van Devanter's seat on the Court was still open.

A pleasant task—but not an easy one. Roosevelt wanted a durable New Dealer, a relatively young man, either a Southerner or Westerner, and a competent lawyer, who at the same time would clear the Senate without difficulty. This last was the rub, for in the sweltering Washington heat the senators seemed to be more bitter and unpredictable than ever. For this reason the President leaned toward a New Deal Senator. He finally chose Black over other senatorial possibilities mainly because the Alabaman had gone down the line for Roosevelt's policies; the President felt drawn to Black also because he faced a hard battle for re-election and perhaps because Black had an only child suffering from deafness. While Roosevelt did not rate Black's legal talents very high, he was more concerned about seasoned liberalism than expertness. Despite some grumbling in the Senate, the usual clubby feeling prevailed, and after a brief debate Black was readily confirmed.

471

"So Hugo Black becomes a member of the Supreme Court of the United States while the economic royalists fume and squirm and the President rolls his tongue around in his cheek," Ickes crowed in his diary. The President was not to roll his tongue long. A week or so later, after Black had left for a vacation in Europe, a Pittsburgh newspaper produced categorical proof that the new Justice had been a member of the Ku Klux Klan. The rumors that Black had neither confirmed nor denied during the confirmation debate were true. The press exploded with shrill attacks on both Black and the President.

"I did not know that Black belonged to the Ku Klux Klan," Roosevelt said to a friend. "This is very serious." The President was deeply disturbed. He told reporters that nothing could be said until Black returned from Europe. Privately he did what he could. He asked Ickes to go to Borah and see if he would help out. Wheeler and others had been demanding that the President investigate Black, and Roosevelt particularly wanted Borah's backing for the proposition that the President had no right to make such an investigation. Borah fully agreed. By the time Black returned from Europe Roosevelt had left on a Western tour, and all eyes were on the justice.

Harried by reporters, Black turned to the radio and laid his case before perhaps fifty million people. He denounced intolerance, and pointed to his congressional record in defense of civil liberties. Then, in his soft, strained Southern voice he admitted that he had been a member of the Klan, but asserted that he had long ago dissociated himself from it. After referring again to his civil liberties record, he ended with a sad "good night."

And thus ended Roosevelt's battle against the Court.

Roosevelt's enemies could not help gloating. Surely the President had suffered a dizzy fall in the short span of six months. At the beginning of the year he had towered over the political scene, with his colossal vote of approval in November and with his huge majorities in Congress. Then he seemed invincible. Yet now he had been beaten.

Why had this political colossus stumbled and fallen? Roosevelt's critics were quick with an explanation: Pride goeth before a fall. Intoxicated with success, Roosevelt had recklessly attacked a venerable American institution. Overly sure of himself, he had made mistake after careless mistake. His potency had gone to his head. Learned pundits quoted Lord Acton: "Power tends to corrupt, and absolute power corrupts absolutely."

Was it really so simple? A closer look at the Court fight showed that the real story was much more complex than this morality tale suggested.

Roosevelt did not go about the job of Court reform recklessly. Quite the contrary—he struck at the Court only after a long period of waiting, and under what he considered to be the best possible conditions. His plan was not hastily conceived; he had searched through a variety of proposals to find one that would have a good chance of clearing Congress and at the same time achieve his purpose. Nor was his plan a radical one. Compared with some of the constitutional and legislative proposals of the day, it was mild indeed.

That Roosevelt's cocksureness led to mistake after mistake and thus defeated the plan was another explanation of the time—and one that was assiduously promoted by those who, like Hopkins and Ickes, had little to do with conducting the fight for the Court bill. Such a view fails to explain, among other things, why the remarkably astute Roosevelt of 1936 became the bungler of 1937. The theory that Roosevelt did not direct the fight personally and the mistakes were made by subordinates is incorrect; he was in command throughout. Much was made of Roosevelt's stubbornness in clinging to the original plan; but this stubbornness was precisely the quality that had saved measures in previous terms—when it had been called firmness or resoluteness. Certainly Roosevelt made mistakes in the Court fight, but so did his opponents.

All such explanations ignored the probability that the original Court plan never had a chance of passing. This was the crucial point. For—if the plan was indeed doomed from the start—the Court's switch and Van Devanter's resignation and Robinson's death became mere stages in the death of the bill rather than causes of that death.

That the Court bill probably never had a chance of passing seems now quite clear. Roosevelt's original proposal evidently never commanded a majority in the Senate. In the House it would have run up against the unyielding Sumners, and then against a conservative Rules Committee capable of blocking the bill for weeks. From the start Democratic leaders in the House were worried about the bill's prospects in that chamber. Robinson's compromise plan might have gone through the Senate if he had lived. More likely, though, it would have failed in the face of a dogged Senate filibuster, or later in the House.

Any kind of Court reform would have had hard going. The popular reverence for the Constitution, the conception of the Supreme Court as its guardian, the ability of the judges—especially Hughes—to counterattack in their own way, the deep-seated legal tradition in a Congress composed of a large number of lawyers—all these were obstacles. Yet there was tremendous support in Congress and in the country for curbing the

Court's excess. Undoubtedly some kind of moderate Court reform could have gone through.

The fatal weakness of Roosevelt's plan lay partly in its content and partly in the way it was proposed. The plan itself seemed an evasive, disingenuous way of meeting a clear-cut problem. It talked about judicial efficiency rather than ideology; it was aimed at immediate personalities on the Court rather than long-run problems posed by the Court. The manner of presentation—the surprise, Roosevelt's failure to pose the issue more concretely in the election, his obvious relish in the job, his unwillingness to ask his Cabinet and his congressional leaders for advice—alienated some potential supporters. More important, this method of presentation prevented Roosevelt from building a broad coalition behind the bill and ironing out multifarious tactical details before springing the attack— behind-the-scenes activities in which Roosevelt was highly adept.

That this masterly politician should make such errors even before his bill was born is explained partly by Roosevelt's personality, partly by his view of the political circumstances at the end of 1936.

Clearly Roosevelt had come to love—perhaps he had always loved— the drama, the suspense, the theatrical touches, and his own commanding role in projects that astonished the country and riled the enemy. But it was more than this. Roosevelt had fought the campaign on a highly personal basis. And he had built a winning coalition around himself—not the Democratic party, not the Democratic platform, not the liberal ideology— but around himself. He had won a stunning victory in spite of the doubters, the rebels, and the perfectionists. The master strokes in the campaign were largely of his own devising.

Roosevelt's handling of the Court fight was the logical extension of his presidential campaign. But now he met a new set of factors, and some of the old tricks did not work. Now he was trying to push a controversial bill through Congress, not win popular votes for himself as a beloved leader. He could not maneuver as he once had; victory depended on conciliating key congressmen and clearing labyrinthine channels. The Grand Coalition seemed to have shriveled away. With the President's blessing, Stanley High tried to activate the Good Neighbor League—it failed to respond. The mighty legions of farm and labor, so powerful in November, seemed to melt away in the spring. Roosevelt turned to the Democratic party; it was a scattered and disorganized army. He appealed for support on the basis of a "quiet crisis," but people saw no crisis. It was not March 1933.

The Black appointment repeated the whole problem in minor theme.

Here again Roosevelt consulted only with two or three persons, and not with his congressional leaders. It was well known on Capitol Hill that the Alabaman had had Klan connections, and as Ickes said after the sensation broke, the leaders could have helped protect the President if Roosevelt had let them in on the decision beforehand. As it was, Roosevelt had to take personal responsibility for a personal appointment. Black went on to make a distinguished record as a justice, especially in the field of civil liberties—but this could not help Roosevelt at the time.

All in all, the Court fight was a stunning defeat for the President. Whether or not it was a fatal or irretrievable one, however, depended on the events to follow. Two years later, with his eye on a string of pro-New Deal Court decisions, the President exulted that he had lost the battle but won the war. As matters turned out in Congress and party, it could better be said that he lost the battle, won the campaign, but lost the war.

THE C.I.O. TAKES THE OFFENSIVE

By 1935, workers in many parts of the country were persuaded, as never before, of the importance of solidarity. Unionization had brought substantial gains to garment workers, coal miners, and newspapermen. Furthermore, they undertook to exert political influence as a group; John L. Lewis and his United Mine Workers contributed a half-million dollars through Labor's Non-Partisan League to help re-elect F.D.R. and sustain the New Deal.

But Detroit, the home of the automobile, the greatest center of industry in the country, was virtually untouched by the rising tide of unionism. The American Federation of Labor, organized around the craft unions, had no place for the unskilled and semiskilled workers from the mass-production industries. In November 1935, eight unions, led by John L. Lewis, formed the Committee for Industrial Organization within the A. F. of L., for the express purpose of organizing these unskilled workers. The following year they were expelled from the A. F. of L.

The first target of the new C.I.O. was to be the steel industry in Pittsburgh, known as "Big Steel." A half-million dollars was allotted by the union to organize the steel workers. Surprisingly, the "Big Steel" companies decided not to fight the C.I.O.'s request to negotiate a contract, and the steel workers won wage increases, the eight-hour day, the forty-hour week, vacations with pay, and seniority rights. However, the "Little Steel" companies in Ohio and Illinois were another matter; last-ditch battles were fought over a period of four years before the unions gained recognition and a contract.

Meanwhile, in Detroit the United Automobile Workers Union, now affiliated with the C.I.O., was agitating to establish their right to organize and bargain. They, too, were faced with a formidable antagonist.

The General Motors management had been making plans to meet the threat of unionization; from January 1934 through July 1936 they had spent almost a million dollars in the employment of private detectives and company spies.

WORKING IN THE DETROIT AUTO PLANTS*

THE MASS production of automobiles for a long time has been the plati-tudinous symbol of American "progress," a word which is almost always associated with mobility alone.

Until the beginning of 1937, however, there was very little which resembled progress in the management-labor relations of our four-billion-dollar motor industry. The 433,000 men and 18,000 women employed in making passenger cars, trucks, hearses, tanks, station wagons, tractors, buses, taxicabs and ambulances faced, and in part still face, conditions more medieval than modern.

Despite the widely publicized five- and six-dollar-a-day minima, and hourly rates which, for a few, reached highs of $1.09, annual earnings of auto workers averaged less than $1,300 in the prosperity year of 1926 and less than $1,000 in the depression year of 1935. The feeling of insecurity generated by such incomes and by the irregular employment they reveal was described by an Italian punch-press operator named Rizzo:

I worka six years with this job, but all that time eight months is the longest I ever go steady in one year. For more than one year I only worka two or three days a week. Everybody say here, "Why don't you save when you worka?" But how can you save when you no worka steady? If I could get $5 a day all year, I could put this little pieca for the coal, this little pieca for the rent, this little pieca for the electric and maybe then I can putta this away for to save and know where I go. But now you work, you make something; you stop. You spend what you got save. You getta the debts. Then you get a job. You pay the debts. You save a little. You stop. And now I stop too long this time. Me, I don't drink. I stay home nights with the keeds.

Even so, the wages in motors are relatively good when compared with those paid elsewhere. On the other hand it takes all the makeshifts of a poverty more shabby than genteel to stretch them over the seasonal lay-offs to which the industry, by its own promotion of gadget consciousness and the annual model fetish, and its acute sensitivity to any rise or decline in national purchasing power, has become particularly prone.

However, it was not against the size of the pay envelope, per se, that General Motors workers staged a series of sit-downs at the end of 1936.

* From Herbert Harris' *American Labor* (New Haven, Yale University Press, 1938).

477

The cause for this spectacular strike, which lasted forty-four days, involving 40,000 workers directly and 110,000 indirectly, and paralyzed sixty plants of a giant corporation in fourteen different states, went deeper into the secret places of the psyche than the question of so much cash return for so much work done.

It expressed the pent-up resentments of men in revolt against being dehumanized, against being only a badge, a number, a robot in thrall to a vast and intricate succubus of machinery, draining them of energy, threatening to cast them on the scrap heap after a few short years. It reflected a long-simmering rebellion against humiliations inflicted by the impersonality of a great corporation which, no more callous than its rivals, sapped the health and vitality of its workers and then turned them over to the government to support as soon as approaching middle age began to diminish their usefulness.

Today [in 1938], for instance, motorcar manufacturers still lack, toward their workers, even that rudimentary sense of responsibility which prompts any dirt farmer to pasture a faithful horse; they remain indifferent to how fast the men wear out as long as there are others to replace them, and appear equally indifferent to the inadequacy of their buying power.

Inside vast oblong buildings of brick, glass, and stone, under the hot glare of arc lights, amid the whir and chug-chump of wheels, the automobile workers stand alongside great belt lines which move in front of them inexorably at the touch of a distant control button.

In the interior of a body plant, for example, at the far end of the belt, a new frame, a metal skeleton, bolt-sinewed, begins its journey. It reaches the first man who puts on a rim, goes to another who sets a fender, while underneath, men on their backs on little roller carts tighten axle bolts, each man doing the same thing, eyes fixed on the chassis, sweat rolling from his face, jaws clamped, lift, turn, screw, liftturnscrew, with the tempo often imperceptibly quickened, unable to leave the line to go to the toilet, to get a drink of water, hour on hour, with the straw boss warning step lively, you're slipping fella, with the fear of losing the job if you don't keep up, making you strain tired muscles till your own body is a single throbbing ache while the belt, detached as a river coursing between its banks, flows smoothly on.

In other departments, even in the assembly of standardized units for crankcases, radiators, cushions, such scenes constantly occur, especially at times of peak production, and are virtually the same whether the individual plant is owned by Ford, General Motors, or Chrysler, who between them control 93 per cent of the domestic business, or by independents like Nash,

Hudson, Packard, Studebaker, and Graham who divide the remaining 7 per cent of American auto sales.

When the shift is over the workers tumble half-dead with fatigue into buses, trolleys, or their own cars, mainly secondhand. Some acquire nervous twitchings popularly called "the shakes." They get home "too tired to do anything but eat and go to bed."* They are too all-in even to read the paper, or take in a movie with the wife, or shoot a game of pool with the boys, or play cards with friends.

"It takes your guts out, that line," and "The speed-up, that's the trouble," form the dual refrain of auto workers in Detroit, Flint, Hamtramck, Saginaw, Pontiac, and other Michigan communities.

In recent years the auto workers have been increasingly recruited from the hills of Tennessee and Kentucky and from the farms of Michigan and Ohio. Beginning in 1922 and tapering off in 1930, the migration of these men to Detroit and other towns accounted for forty-seven out of every one hundred automobile employees. During the same period an appreciable influx of Negroes from the South reached its apex in 1926 when nearly 10 per cent of all Ford employees were colored and assigned to the harder, heavier tasks such as "sanding" and "foundry work." Many of the workers, of course, are transients comprising the so-called "suitcase battalions" and "bundle brigades" who rush in at the first rumors of a busy season and largely vanish at the first signs of slackening schedules.

The young backwoods men and women who flocked to motordom's Mecca were lured by visions of what, by agricultural standards, was a Big Money paradise. Mainly of "good American stock," they tended to be as parochial as they were healthy and strong. They knew nothing of unionism, often regarded their jobs as temporary, as a means of "getting some money saved" and then buying a farm or opening a little business on their own. They were also unskilled, nor did they have to be otherwise. With the mounting mechanization of the industry, about 45 per cent of its jobs can be learned within two or three days; about 35 per cent within

---

* During the Flint sit-downs a group of women were interviewed at Cook's restaurant, commissary for the strikers. A dumpy, motherly woman of German descent, with straw-colored hair and pale-blue eyes, declared, "I'd like to shout from the housetops what the company's doing to our men. My husband, he's a torch solderer; they call 'em welders, but that's not what he is; he solders. You should see him come home at night, him and the rest of the men in the buses. So tired like they was dead, and irritable. My John's not like that. He's a good, kind man. But the children don't dare go near him, he's so nervous and his temper's bad. And then at night in bed, he shakes, his whole body, he shakes."

"Yes," chimed in her companion, a sharp-faced brunette, "they're not men any more if you know what I mean. They're not men. My husband he's only thirty, but to look at him you'd think he was fifty and all played out. And unless we have the union things will get worse."

a week; some 7 per cent within two weeks, and the remaining 13 per cent within a month to a year or longer.

The old-time craftsman's sense of creative satisfaction in the work of his hands is therefore a lost emotion for the majority of the industry's workers. They rarely see, or can recognize, the finished product to which they have contributed their own minute and regimented share. Often they handle only a part of a part of another part; for in this sphere the division of labor has attained a degree of specialization that is at once an engineering feat of a high order and an object lesson in how the technics of a civilization outstrip its ethics and its social values.

During the past two decades the industry's emphasis upon youth, with its greater speed and endurance, has kept displacing older employees at an ever-accelerating rate. In the Detroit region small-loan firms refuse to consider auto workers over forty as acceptable risks, despite the amazing number of hair-dyeing specialists who flourish in the vicinity; for to the auto worker the discovery of the first "silver threads" is perhaps even more tragic than the same discovery by the professional beauty.

But this disregard of seniority rights—rights which mean simply that the man longest on the job has a prior claim to it, especially at a time of rehiring after a slack season—is only one among many grievances plaguing the industry's labor since the end of the World War. Others include the "incentive" or bonus plan by which a group of workers, geared to the human metronome of the fastest among them, receive extra money for extra "lump" output. In this operation calculations for figuring the return of each worker are so abstruse that often they have no way of finding out how much they earn.

But more injurious to individual self-esteem on the job is the practice of espionage. In this the motor manufacturers were among the most conspicuous offenders until revelations of the LaFollette Senate subcommittee, investigating civil liberties, caused cancellation of many contracts with such private detective firms as the Pinkerton Agency to which General Motors, over a period of three years, paid $419,850, or Corporations Auxiliary which cost Chrysler $72,611 for 1935 alone.*

* There are 228 other detective agencies dispensing what is euphemistically named "industrial service." It is, of course, nice work if you can get it as the $50,000 and $60,000 a year salaries of executives in such concerns attest. Among certain legal theorists, the fact that American corporations have spent as much as $80,000,000 a year for this espionage activity would seem to call into question their right to remain incorporated under the laws of any state in the union. All the states—along with the Federal government—guarantee civil liberties, which have rarely been so flagrantly violated as in this setting of men to spy upon workers and "report" their efforts to form a union of their choice by exercising their constitutional rights of freedom of speech and of conscience.

Henry Ford, supreme individualist, who does his own financing and owns his own steel, cement, electric power and light, and assembly plants, his own coke ovens, and the like, also "rolls his own" in matters of espionage. He has hired Harry Bennett, an ex-sailor, ex-pugilist, to establish a spying and stool-pigeon system which works in the plant and also in large measure dominates the police and politics in Dearborn, Michigan. The favorite pursuit of Bennett and his boys is ganging up on union organizers, trying literally to beat them down, and otherwise forestall the coming of collective barganing to Ford's.

On May 26, 1937, for example, Walter Reuther and Richard Frankensteen, top officials of the United Automobile Workers, who had secured a city permit to distribute union leaflets to Ford workers as they changed shifts, took their places atop a street overpass debouching from one of the gates of the great River Rouge plant. Newsmen and photographers who had learned of their intention chatted with them for a moment and shot a few pictures. Suddenly, Frankensteen and Reuther and their companions observed that a crowd of some one hundred and fifty men had converged on an adjacent platform, and were lounging about. They had seemed to materialize as if in response to a signal. They definitely didn't appear to be workers, for, as Reuther later testified at a National Labor Relations Board hearing,

. . . they had no lunch baskets and wore no badges. . . . After the pictures were taken we were approached by some of these men on all sides. . . . One called out that we were on private property and to get the hell off of there. Frankensteen and I turned to get off the bridge in obedience to the command. I had hardly taken three steps when I was slugged on the back of the head. I tried to shield my face by crossing my arms. They pounded me over the head and body. . . . I was knocked to the ground and beaten. . . .

They picked me up and threw me bodily on the concrete floor of the platform. Then they kicked me again and again. They tried to tear my legs apart. Seven times they raised me off the concrete and threw me down on it. They pinned my arms and shot . . . jabs to my face. I was dragged to the stairway. I grabbed the railing and they wrenched me loose. I was thrown down the first flight of iron steps. Then they kicked me down the other two flights. . . .

Frankensteen was given a similar "workout" and one of his aides had his "innards smashed."

Whereas Ford's public-relations staff strove mightily to convey the impression that Frankensteen and Reuther had been repulsed by "loyal employees" incensed by union efforts to convert them, the testimony given by reporters and cameramen, along with Dr. Sanford of the Chicago Federation of Churches who happened to be on the scene, revealed that "thugs, hoodlums" and "brass-knuckle-men" of Bennett's "Ford Service" organization were responsible for this vicious attack.

Moreover, despite the fact that a Grand Jury has indicted the Ford Motor Company and members of Bennett's strong-arm squad for willful intent to do bodily harm, Bennett still retains his post as "personnel director" of the company and still boasts that if a Ford worker joins a union, he knows the particulars within twenty-four hours and has arranged for the man's discharge within forty-eight.

The general knowledge among auto workers that the man next to them on the line may be a secret agent, eager to amplify a kind word about unionism into a plot to "take over the factory" and impelled to make up lies out of whole cloth to justify his pay, freezes the warmth of normal human intercourse among men sharing a common enterprise.

Furthermore, under the division of executive authority that prevails in the industry, the foreman, who is management's surrogate, right on the job, exerts a tremendous power. He sometimes exacts tribute from the workers, allowing them to keep their jobs by kicking in so much a week, or "selling" the less strenuous assignments.

Early in 1933, goaded by wage cuts, layoffs, inhuman resort to the speed-up, workers began to walk out in a congeries of minor, intradepartment strikes that were yet portents of more to come. On September 22, the Mechanics Educational Society, an independent union which had enrolled nearly all of the industry's highly skilled tool and die makers, pulled out hundreds of its adherents in protest against incomes which had shrunk from an average of $2,717 in 1929 to $1,300 in 1933. In the Detroit region such "aristocrats" of labor, accompanied by many commoners, walked out at Buick, Chevrolet, A. and C. Spark Plug, Fisher Body, Cadillac, Dodge, Hudson, Plymouth, Packard, and extended their strike to Ford at Edgewater, New Jersey, and to Nash at Kenosha, Wisconsin.

Meantime the NRA codes for the motor industry were being formulated in the summer of 1933. The weather was hot, the atmosphere electric and the codes displayed both characteristics. They were transparently pro-employer—to such an extent, indeed, that it was the auto workers who first rechristened the NRA the "National Run Around."

Angered, the auto workers cast about for guidance toward unionism's goal. They had a confusion of choices. The I.W.W., the Socialist party, the Communist party, the American Industrial Association all entered the arena with at least paper organizations eager to enlist members. At last the

A. F. of L. itself yawned out of its somnolence, stretched, and stumbled into activity.

Its organizers, however, were largely men who had been graduated from the brown derby, "I'm tough, see, have a cigar, leave it all to me, boys" school of the old-time pot-bellied walking delegate. They were also hobbled at every step by the jurisdictional jealousies of the various crafts. Despite such handicaps, however, an estimated 210,000 auto workers more or less quietly joined the Federation's "federal unions."

But the new unionists were bewildered. They couldn't get their questions answered. They asked if they were going to become a nationwide industrial union, or whether they were to be kept waiting until the membership was subdivided into craft groups. Nobody seemed to know, least of all the field organizers. The A. F. of L. didn't know either. It was marking time, its most costly and colossal luxury from its earliest days.

Meanwhile, to forestall the growth of any genuine unionism and to comply with the letter, and not the intent, of the collective bargaining provisions in the NRA codes, the employers started to fashion "company" unions, often forcing men to join them on pain of forfeiting their jobs. Meanwhile, too, as the speed-up and longer hours for but slightly increased pay continued, the A. F. of L., prodded by rank-and-file insistence, set March 1934, as the date on which auto workers all over the country were to go on strike and with a single bold stroke end company unions and all the fraud and chicane they implied.

At President Roosevelt's request, however, this "threat to returning prosperity" was averted by Federation leaders and many long days of muddled mediation ensued. For a time, the inertia of the Automobile Labor Board, the craft squabbles within the A. F. of L., the organization conflicts outside of it, provoked an estimated 75,000 unionists into turning in or tearing up their union cards.

Elections held early in 1935 under the Board's auspices clearly reflected the prevailing temper of the nation's auto workers. Out of a total of 154,-780 ballots cast, 111,878 workers voted for "unaffiliated representation." In other words, the majority were so fed up with the clamors of competition for their allegiance that they didn't want any of the existing unions to act as their agents. Only 14,057 voted for the A. F. of L., 7,071 for other legitimate unions, and 21,774 for the company-run kind. Hundreds of thousands of workers refrained from thus registering their will, apparently in their discouragement believing even this gesture a waste of time.

Yet the deep desire to be unionized swirled like a strong current temporarily dammed up. The A. F. of L.'s federal locals had meanwhile begun banding together in what was, at first, a loose alliance under the name of the United Automobile Workers. It was directed by Francis J. Dillon, an A. F. of L. veteran business agent hand-picked by William Green against the majority votes of delegates to the U.A.W.'s convention at Detroit in August of 1935. The convention reluctantly agreed to permit Dillon to remain at the helm until an appeal citing his unfitness could be considered by the executive council of the A. F. of L. which was scheduled to convene at the Federation's own annual sessions in Atlantic City two months later.

But this appeal somehow was sidetracked in the tumult that surrounded the withdrawal of John L. Lewis and company from the A. F. of L. to form their Committee for Industrial Organization. In any event Green insisted on keeping Dillon in command of the United Automobile Workers, a tactical blunder of the first magnitude. For Dillon epitomized the old-fashioned approach to unionism adhered to by the more Victorian-minded craft leaders. On the other hand, the United Automobile Workers were more and more convinced that unionizing techniques devised for the nineteenth century were not applicable to the twentieth. In one of its earliest pamphlets, addressed to the worker, it declared, ". . . No man today is alone an automobile maker. You join with thousands of others in a collective productive effort. Does the manufacturer hire you, put you at a bench or forge, give you a heap of iron ore, a pile of cloth, a supply of raw rubber and a few sheets of glass, and then tell you to get to work and make automobiles individually? . . ."

Animated by this outlook, the auto workers in general were heartened by the creation of the C.I.O., founded as it was on the premise that either mass-production workers were to be organized, and speedily, or that "labor's voice" would soon be modulated down from at best a mild forte to a very soft and plaintive pianissimo, if it were to be heard at all.

Various other unions, such as the Coughlin-sponsored Automobile Industrial Workers Association and the Associated Automobile Workers of America, called the "Greer bunch" after the name of its principal, shared the affection of the U.A.W. for the industrial idea. All three groups began to talk about a fusion of forces, looking to the C.I.O. for guidance. They didn't get it, at first. The C.I.O. was already embroiled in fifty-seven different varieties of controversy and had to feel its way cautiously for some six or seven months. By the time Roosevelt was re-elected, however, it was sending scouts and advisers into Detroit to assist the U.A.W. in ousting

Dillon and hence to shatter A. F. of L. prestige and influence for many miles around.

In the spring of 1936 the U.A.W. supplanted him by electing Homer S. Martin as its president. He was thirty-four years old, a former minister emotionally identified with the underdog.

Late in December 1936, after a vigorous organizing campaign, the U.A.W. sent a letter to Mr. William S. Knudsen, then executive vice-president of General Motors, asking for a conference on the general subject of collective bargaining. The letter enumerated the auto workers' complaints and pointed out that local attempts to settle questions of wages, hours, and work conditions with branch officials had always arrived nowhere.

The company replied, through Mr. Knudsen, that it could not talk, and suggested that Martin and his followers seek adjustment of grievances with local plant managers. This was, in Martin's view, nonsense. The corporation's industrial relations policy was explicitly determined at the top and local administrators merely carried out the orders of their superiors.

"It's the merry run-around again," muttered U.A.W. members and in exasperation many of them spontaneously sat down in the Fisher Body Plant at Cleveland, Ohio, on December 28, 1936—ringing up the curtain upon the most spectacular and significant capital-labor drama of the post-crash period.

Next day the sit-down was extended to Fisher Body Plant No. 2 in Flint, Michigan, where the U.A.W. had submitted a sample contract to the plant manager with the request that he ponder its terms as the basis for future discussion. In reply he discharged five stanch unionists. Enraged by this "sock in the teeth," U.A.W. members and others also sat down. Next morning workers in Fisher Body Plant No. 1, also in Flint, heard the rumor that the company had begun to remove necessary tools and dies to weaker union places, to Pontiac, Michigan, and even to Atlanta, Georgia, to forestall production stoppages and to have the workers in these places break the Flint strike. In protest, U.A.W. men and their well-wishers sat down in Fisher Body Plant No. 1 with a gaiety that was later transformed into a grim tenacity of purpose, while the movement caromed to Anderson, Indiana, to Kansas City, Missouri, to Norwood, Ohio, and to Atlanta, Georgia, spreading from one General Motors plant to another throughout the country.

The high command of the C.I.O. which had recently annexed the United Automobile Workers was surprised and shaken by the sudden-

485

ness of this sit-down epidemic and would have preferred smallpox or something simple instead. From the standpoint of John L. Lewis and his aides, the timing of this strike in motors couldn't have been more maladroit. At the moment the C.I.O. was hurling nearly all of its new might in money and men into the Steel Workers Organizing Committee's drive on steel, proceeding on the theory that if this "most impregnable fortress of the open-shop" could be made to yield to the C.I.O.'s assault, the whole industrial salient could be more readily conquered. To Lewis, as to his Marshal Ney, Scotch-born Philip Murray, success or failure in unionizing steel was to be Austerlitz or Waterloo. They hadn't reckoned on any new major engagements on a new front.

Yet they were duty bound to send succor to Homer Martin and the U.A.W., which as a union was still very young. Its leaders were honest and intelligent but they by and large lacked experience in all the multifarious activity, from publicity releases to maintenance of morale, that any big strike entails. With misgivings, Lewis dispatched John Brophy, Director of Organization for the C.I.O., to U.A.W. headquarters in the Hoffman Building in Detroit as the herald of more reinforcements and supplies to come, and later wired the Flint sit-downers that the C.I.O. and its affiliates "pledge you complete and unanimous support in the conduct of the strike. . . . You men are undoubtedly carrying on through one of the most heroic battles that has ever been undertaken by strikers in an industrial dispute. The attention of the entire American public is focused upon you. . . ."

With the stubborn and desperate courage of men carrying the banners of a new crusade, the Flint sit-downers refused to be dislodged for weeks that stirred headline writers to new heights, editorial writers, columnists, and radio commentators to new hysterias, provided bitter debates in the Senate and House, and divided most of the population into two emotionally overstrung camps, warring over the subject of the strikers' favorite song:

> *When they tie a can to a union man,*
> *Sit-down! Sit-down!*
> *When they give him the sack, they'll take him back,*
> *Sit-down! Sit-down!*
>
> *When the speed-up comes, just twiddle your thumbs,*
> *Sit-down! Sit-down!*
> *When the boss won't talk, don't take a walk,*
> *Sit-down! Sit-down!*

BRUCE BLIVEN

STRIKE AT THE FLINT PLANT*

To GET INSIDE a plant while a sit-down is in progress is a hard job. On the day I entered Fisher Body No. 1, the strikers had been holding the fort for two weeks. In that time not a soul had entered the building without their consent, and very few under any circumstances. When our car pulled up at the curb before the big, modern structure, set back in a green lawn like a Middle Western high school, a reception committee of five or six sturdy men was waiting. They promptly searched our party, and the car, for weapons. Only when they had been reassured as to our identity were we allowed to go up the walk to the plant itself. All the doors had been shut and heavily barricaded, two weeks earlier. To get in, you climbed on a pile of packing boxes, and swung yourself over the lower third of a heavy window of steel and opaque glass, hinged horizontally at the top. On a platform just inside was another reception committee, friendly enough on the surface but with grim undertones in their voices as they checked over our credentials. During the whole period of the sit-down, nobody left or entered the plant without a pass, and without being searched on his way out and in.

The room in which we found ourselves was a vast oblong, used for building automobile bodies. A double line of these extended the length of the plant, close together, looking with their uniform gray color and their smooth and bulging contours a little like so many kneeling elephants, trunk to tail. As you went forward along the line, each of these bodies was a trifle closer to completion than the one behind it; those at the very end even had the colors they will bear when chassis, engine and wheels have been added and they are off to the road.

Fifteen hundred men had lived for two weeks in a building never intended to be lived in at all, yet the place was remarkably neat and tidy, at least as clean as it is under normal conditions. Beds were made up on the floor of each car, the seats being removed if necessary, and the members of the night shift of guards were sound asleep in the haphazard quarters. They had no weapons of any kind except braided leather billies im-

* From "Sitting Down in Flint," *The New Republic,* Jan. 27, 1937.

provised inside the plant after the sit-down had started. The guards off duty slept in their clothes, with these billies thrust into a pocket or, sometimes, loosely grasped in the sleeper's hand.

The degree of organization among these men was something to think about. An elected strike committee was in general control. Every man had specified duties, to be performed at specified hours. Meals were prepared with food brought by friends on the outside and passed in through a window, these meals being served in the plant cafeteria at stipulated hours. A barbershop was in operation in one of the rest rooms. Liquor was absolutely forbidden. An emergency post office was set up and there was a heavy movement of mail in both directions—all of it censored by a special committee.

For recreation, the men played cards or listened to the radio, or to a daily concert by the members of the workmen's band, who were staying in. Hundreds of friends and relatives of the strikers visited them every day. With characteristic Yankee ingenuity, the strikers had rigged up a loud-speaker system throughout the plant, with a microphone at the "main entrance." When a visitor called to see any given striker, he was paged over the loud-speaker system. When meetings of all the strikers (except the guards on duty) were held, the union leaders or the members of the strike committee also used a microphone, to make sure of being heard by their listeners, sitting on the floor in the odd bits of space not occupied by machines. I could not see—and I looked for it carefully—the slightest damage done anywhere to any property of the General Motors Corporation. The nearly completed car bodies, for example, were as clean as they would be in the salesroom, their glass and metal shining.

HERBERT HARRIS

SIT-DOWN AT GENERAL MOTORS*

THE "SIT-DOWN" which between September 1, 1936, and June 1, 1937, involved 484,711 American workers not only in motors but in rubber, steel, textiles, shipbuilding, subways, oil refining, shoes, newspaper publishing, baking, aircraft, and countless other manufacturing service and retail-

* From Herbert Harris' *American Labor* (New Haven, Yale University Press, 1938).

ing spheres, is a strike of a very special kind. Whereas in the everyday variety employees leave mill or mine or store or factory to picket outside their place of business, in the sit-down they remain inside at or near their usual posts but do no work. They just sit or stretch out on the floor or benches or loll around on their feet. And if a sit-down lasts long enough— dozens of them in mass-production plants last only a few minutes or a few hours—it becomes a stay-in, properly speaking, though the term "sit-down" is already a colloquialism used to describe this technique, per se, whatever its duration.

Its advantages are obvious. Police and militia can more easily disperse a picket line in the open than an "occupied" plant where windows may be barricaded and gates barred. "You can't ride a horse through a brick wall," remarked a grizzled old unionist in Detroit during the General Motors stay-ins. "With the sit-down today the boys don't have to put up with that, anyway."

Sit-down psychology differs profoundly from that of any other strike tactic. In the first place, the men stay together all the time instead of meeting irregularly at a hall or union headquarters or in the street. They talk, become better acquainted, generate feelings of unity and co-operation, "one for all, and all for one." In the second place, the sit-down gives the individual worker a new and rare sense of power—especially in highly mechanized industries where relatively few men can literally "tie up the works." Gongs go bonging, phones shrill, straw bosses storm, managers get flurried and mad and machinery is idle—all because of what he and his companions have done.

Contrary to popular impression, the sit-down is not an instrument designed and patented by the C.I.O., although its widespread use in this country happened to coincide with the high spots of the C.I.O.'s organizing campaign during 1936 and 1937 especially.

Len DeCaux, editor of the *Union News Service,* the movement's official news bureau, declared:

As a matter of fact the first experience of the C.I.O. with sit-downs was in discouraging them. This was in the Akron rubber industry, after the Goodyear strike. C.I.O. representatives cautioned . . . the new unionists against sit-downs on the ground that they should use such channels for negotiating grievances as the agreement provided.

And in supporting this general approach, John L. Lewis at about the same time announced that "the C.I.O. stands for punctilious observance of contracts, but we are not losing any sleep about strikes where employers refuse to recognize well-defined principles of collective bargaining. A

C.I.O. contract is adequate protection against sit-downs, lie-downs, or any other kind of strike."

Despite William Green's statement that "both personally and officially I disavow the sit-down strike as a part of the economic or organization policy of the A. F. of L.," numerous Federation unions, notably electricians, hotel and restaurant, theatrical and building service employees engaged in sit-downs to protect their wage scales and for other reasons. It is, furthermore, a tactic resorted to mainly in industries that have been, or are, vigorously anti-union. During the period previously mentioned, that from September 1, 1936, to June 1, 1937, which witnessed the greatest extent of sit-downing, motors—which had been historically open shop— had about a quarter of a million sitters; rubber, which for a generation has been a "No Man's Land" for unionism, had about forty-five thousand; and textiles, still a battleground for pro- and anti-union forces, had about twenty-five thousand. On the other hand, in coal mining, where the United Mine Workers is well established, there were only 270 workers who sought to use the sit-down, and none at all in the extremely well-organized men's clothing and women's wear trades.

The American sit-down, in short, affirms not the right to the factory (which is not operated but kept in a state of quiescence) but the right to the job, a "vested interest" in it, and the attempt to protect this work territory against the invasion of others, strikebreakers, pending the settlement of differences between labor and management. The sit-down does not challenge ownership of productive equipment; but it does challenge the privilege of the "employer," whether corporation or individual, to retain within his (or its) own hands the enormous powers over employees that result from the fact that most families of wage earners live from hand to mouth, through no fault of their own, and often are but a few days removed from starvation.

From the mists and fogs of emotion-charged words marking the discussion of the sit-down one clear question emerges: Is purely legal title to a producing property the only right that should be recognized in the American democracy?

In Flint, Michigan, the power of General Motors was arrayed against the implications of this view in a community where, out of 165,000 inhabitants, 50,000 depended directly upon the company for livelihoods gained from Buick, Chevrolet, and Fisher Body plants. Anti-sit-down sentiment, after the first days of the strike, was crystallized by an organization called the Flint Alliance. It was composed of "loyal employees," most of whom somehow contrived to resemble bar-flies and poolroom toughs from nearby

Detroit, a sprinkling of General Motors executives and subadministrators and people from its technical and commercial divisions, some local businessmen, and almost all the vigilante-minded personalities in the vicinity. The Alliance's propaganda was fabricated by the high-pressure, high-priced Floyd E. Williamson who, himself an "outsider" imported from Manhattan, based a large part of his anti-union blasts upon the "un-American activities" of "outside" organizers. As the sit-down progressed, Alliance spokesmen grew daily more vociferous in their demands for violence, some of them promising that soon law-and-order committees of indignant citizenry would forciby evict the sit-downers who by the thousand had dug in for a long siege.

To oust the strikers, General Motors had secured from Judge Edward Black an injunction which commanded them to vacate company property and also forbade picketing. Although he owned nearly $200,000 worth of General Motors stock, Judge Black considered himself sufficiently impartial to issue his edict, a belief not entirely in accord with the more commendable traditions of the American bench. When Sheriff Wolcott delivered the Black doument to the sit-downers he was jeered and good-naturedly told to go home. Meantime, company officials, both local and national, and U.A.W. and C.I.O. leaders were busy fencing, mustering all their skill for parry and riposte, all of them with an eye on the public gallery.

On January 12, the company shut off the heat in Fisher Body Plant No. 2, and its own gray-uniformed police, reinforced by regulars from the local Flint force, were instructed to prevent the shipment of food into the building. It was hoped that this "diet of cold and hunger" would break the morale of the sit-downers.

Inside the plant, the men missed their lunch, shivered, and grew restive at the prospect of being also deprived of their dinner. Shortly before seven o'clock that evening, a United Automobile Workers sound truck rolled up before the great rectangle of Fisher No. 2, with Victor Reuther, a top-notch organizer for the union, at the microphone. At first he politely asked the police, both public and private, for permission to have food sent in to the sit-downers from the union's kitchen. The metallic lungs of the amplifier lifted his voice high above the sounds of the street until everyone within a half-mile radius could hear his plea. The officers, both the gray and the blue, were mute. Reuther tried another tack. He appealed to them as workers, urging the necessity for co-operation among all kinds and degrees of labor. There was no response, save the cheers of the sit-downers. He then became more aggressive, assuring the officers that strikers outside the plant would get food to the sitters. Some fifteen minutes later a group of pickets carrying pails of coffee and cartons of buns, like an oversized backfield, starting on an end run, bowled over the police guarding the door to the plant and brought food to their famished friends.

At 8:45 some sixty policemen set upon pickets stationed at plant entrances, clubbed them with night-sticks, and drove them inside the building. A sergeant smashed a glass pane in one of the doors and thrust the nozzle of a tear-gas gun through the jagged space, pumping shells into the vast interior. Other officers fired buckshot into pickets and men clustered near the door, wounding fourteen who were later removed to the hospital.

The sit-downers replied to this attack with literally everything they had: coffee-mugs, pop-bottles, and steel automobile hinges weighing two pounds each. At the beginning of the battle, a clarion voice from the sound truck cried: "We wanted peace. General Motors chose war. Give it to 'em!" In the road strikers formed a phalanx around the sound truck, repelled all efforts of police to dismantle it, and overturned three police cars and another belonging to the sheriff.

At midnight the policemen closed in their ranks and, with guns cracking, tried to rush the main entrance, only to be met by a devastating stream of water from a big fire hose which, along with the steel-hinge missiles, compelled them to retreat and finally to abandon their assault. This affair was promptly named "The Battle of the Running Bulls."

The bloodshed of that night, and the fears of more violence to come, resulted in the appearance of 1,500 of Michigan's National Guardsmen in Flint. Acting under instructions from the cool-headed, humanitarian Governor Murphy who was valiantly seeking to settle the strike by pacific means, they managed on the whole to preserve order almost impartially.*

Meantime—after the strikers by a ruse had captured the crucial Chevrolet motor assembly plant No. 4, and John L. Lewis had called on President Roosevelt to intercede for them against the "economic royalists represented by General Motors and the Du Ponts," who had opposed his re-election with the same fervor that the auto workers had supported it; and after Washington conferences between Secretary of Labor Frances Perkins and Alfred P. Sloan, president, and William S. Knudsen, vice-president of the company, had produced mutual recriminations—General Motors obtained from Circuit Judge Paul V. Gadola a significant and sweeping court order. It directed the sit-downers to evacuate company-

---

* One major, however, confessed his bitter disappointment that he was unable to test the value of his pet idea, shooting vomiting gas into the sit-downers via the plants' ventilating systems.

owned plants under penalty of imprisonment for contempt of court and a fine of $15,000,000, the estimated value of the invested properties. Again Sheriff Wolcott served to mocking and derisive groups of determined men the order that set 3 P.M. on February 3 as the deadline for leaving the struck plants.

In reply the sit-downers sent telegrams to Governor Murphy. The message from Fisher Body Plant No. 1 read in part:

We the workers . . . have carried on a stay-in strike over a month in order to make General Motors Corporation obey the law and engage in collective bargaining. . . . Unarmed as we are, the introduction of the militia, sheriffs, or police with murderous weapons will mean a blood-bath of unarmed workers. . . . We have decided to stay. . . . We have no illusions about the sacrifices which this decision will entail. We fully expect that if a violent effort to oust us is made many of us will be killed, and we take this means of making it known to our wives, our children, to the people of the state of Michigan and the country that if this result follows from the attempt to eject us, you are the one who must be held responsible for our deaths.

The night before the "zero hour" day of February 3, the sit-downers, pallid under blazing arc lights, listened grimly to their radios, or played cards or parcheesi or checkers or dominoes, or tried to lose themselves in newspapers or magazines, or talked in subdued tones. Many were convinced that the morrow meant massacre. For defense against expected machine guns, inadequate clubs dangled from their belts. An air of almost Oriental passivity, as of men who wait in resignation for the beat of destiny's drum, hung over them. Their faces were stern and thoughtful, and few slept.

In the morning roads leading into Flint were filled with cars and trucks carrying union sympathizers from Akron, Lansing, Detroit and Toledo who by the thousand swarmed over the town and had to take over the direction of traffic themselves, for no policemen were in sight. The visitors moved toward the various sit-down plants, and only the women's emergency brigades, with their red and green berets, brought color to a somber procession that for weapons held pokers, broom handles and pieces of pipe.

While Flint's clocks ticked on toward the showdown hour of three in the afternoon, Governor Murphy in Detroit finally succeeded in arranging a conference between William S. Knudsen for the company and John L. Lewis for the United Automobile Workers. To Sheriff Wolcott, who had the duty of enforcing the Gadola eviction order, Governor Murphy wired that everything should be held in abeyance during the Knudsen-Lewis conversations; and the Sheriff, more than pleased to oblige, suddenly discovered that he lacked proper legal sanction, anyway, along with a sufficient force to carry out the Gadola edict, although the Flint Alliance and the company's legal staff in Flint assured him that they could together remedy both deficiencies.

When this turn of events was made known, sit-downers, pickets, and unionists from other cities made high holiday. Their violins, saxophones, banjos, cornets struck up hillbilly airs and square-dance tunes, and men and women swung partners joyously over the frozen lawns surrounding the various plants.

Next day the company complied with President Roosevelt's request that in the public interest its representatives should again meet with spokesmen of the strikers. A wearing week of conferences ensued between William S. Knudsen, G. Donaldson Brown and John Thomas Smith for General Motors, and John L. Lewis, Lee Pressman (general counsel for the C.I.O.), Homer Martin and Wyndham Mortimer for the strikers. Time after time only the moral strength and suasions of Governor Murphy, who presided over the negotiations, prevented their collapse, and cigarette and cigar ashes spilled over trays amid the temper-fraying clashes of strong wills and stronger wants.

Eight days later, the Governor, his face haggard with strain and lack of sleep, had the great personal triumph of seeing at long last a meeting of minds out of which came the agreement terminating one of the most important capital-labor disputes in recent times.

The contract signed by General Motors and the United Automobile Workers was a great step forward for unionism in motors and contained seven basic provisions: (1) recognition was to be granted to the U.A.W. for its members only, and not as sole collective bargaining agent; (2) straight seniority rules were to prevail after six months of service; (3) shop committees were to be set up to smooth out grievances on the job; (4) a survey of speed-up evils was to be made; (5) the forty-hour week was to continue in force; (6) time and a half for overtime was to prevail; (7) no discrimination was to be exercised against unionists, who could wear their union buttons and talk about their organization during lunch hours.

The union requests for a uniform minimum wage, affecting plants in all parts of the country, and for the thirty-hour week were both denied.

Primarily as the result of its sit-downers' forty-four-day defiance of General Motors, the United Automobile Workers (late in 1938) had some 370,000 dues-paying members out of an industry-wide maximum potential of 450,000. It is thus the third largest among the C.I.O. unions. It has collective bargaining agreements with all of the independents and with two of the Big Three, General Motors and Chrysler. Currently it is trying to unionize Ford* against an opposition as stubborn as a peasant's prejudice and as strong as a billion dollars.

The U.A.W. is doubly young—both in its short time of existence as a union and in its membership, since the industry still places a premium upon speed and endurance in its workers, attributes most generally found in men and women under forty, even under thirty-five. The union's maverick sit-downs, condemned by motor magnates and (some of them) by Martin himself, have derived from a new sense of liberation from oppression; from flawed methods of adjusting "line" and departmental grievances; from foreman-worker antagonisms that had been piling up for years and were often aggravated by both the self-assertion of the new unionists and the desire of the straw boss to show them that he was still top-dog. Many of the pettier officials, indeed, still believe it their purpose in life to bring obloquy upon the union whenever possible; and neither side has as yet been "educated up" to the patience and will to good will necessary for a harmonious management-union relationship.

* The union's campaign culminated in a contract signed in June 1941.—ED.

BOOKSELLING AND BEST SELLERS

In the Depression years millions of readers rediscovered the public library. Three to four million more people borrowed books in 1933 than in 1929, and the total circulation of library books increased nearly forty per cent. These same years saw the development of the private circulating library, where a book could be rented for three cents a day. To many readers the ownership of a new book had become an impracticable luxury.

In consequence, the sale of books to the general public amounted to 22 million dollars in 1933, about half of that in 1929. Cheap hard-cover reprints of best sellers found a ready market (successful paperback editions would not appear until 1939); book clubs offering selected new books at reduced prices began to flourish as more and more book buyers subscribed to the beneficent authority of the "library judges."

The desire to "escape" was clearly reflected in the general book buyer's choice. In the opinion of Frederick Lewis Allen, "*The Good Earth* by Pearl Buck, which led the fiction best-seller list in 1931 and 1932, probably had an additional appeal because it took readers away to China. The appearance of *The Fountain* by Charles Morgan, on the same list for 1932, may have been partly due to the fact that it told of a man who escaped from the outward world of ugly circumstance into a world of inward reflection." * The same might be said about the success of James

Hilton's *Lost Horizons*, which made the best-seller list in 1935. The historical novel too offered escape. *Anthony Adverse* by Hervey Allen led the best-seller lists of 1933 and 1934, while *Gone With the Wind* by Margaret Mitchell was number one in 1936 and 1937. *Northwest Passage* (1937) by Kenneth Roberts and *Drums Along the Mohawk* (1936) by Walter D. Edmonds were also long-lasting favorites.

During the same time, superb biographies were published—Carl Van Doren's *Benjamin Franklin*, Marquis James's *Andrew Jackson,* Carl Sandburg's *Lincoln*, Douglas Southall Freeman's *R. E. Lee,* to name but a few.

Guidebooks to personal success were popular: *Live Alone and Like It* by Marjorie Hillis, *Wake Up and Live* by Dorothea Brande, and *How to Win Friends and Influence People* by Dale Carnegie were huge successes.

Books by journalists reporting on conditions in Europe indicated a growing general interest in foreign lands. Among the best of these works were Vincent Sheean's *Personal History* (1935), Negley Farson's *Way of a Transgressor* (1936), John Gunther's *Inside Europe* (1936) and Pierre van Paassen's *Days of Our Years* (1939).

These titles are a sampling of the best sellers of the decade. What did the author have to look forward to in terms of income if he were lucky enough to get a best seller?

* Frederick Lewis Allen, *Since Yesterday.*

EDWARD WEEKS

HARD TIMES AND THE AUTHOR*

IN NORMAL times the financial status of our author admits of three levels.
At the top are a small group of what I might call literary magnates—
E. Phillips Oppenheim, Zane Grey, Mary Roberts Rinehart, Willa Cather,
Sinclair Lewis, Louis Bromfield, Kathleen Norris—each one of whom in
full production might earn in the neighborhood of $70,000 a year. A
fellow publisher has made a composite picture of the income of a popular
novelist whose new book has just sold 50,000 copies and who is eager to
pursue every offer. Before you read these figures, let me caution you that
mighty few moguls are capable of this earning power and still fewer of
them can maintain it for long.

Royalty at 15% of $2.50	$18,750
Motion picture rights	25,000
Sale of serial rights on next novel	15,000
Misc. short stories, all written but up to now rejected .	3,000
Contract for 6 short stories	6,000
Lectures (net)	2,500
Misc. rights (English, foreign, second serial)	2,500
Motion picture contract for editorial work for 10 weeks at $500 a week	5,000
	$77,750

I doubt if in any year as much as one per cent of the writing profession
is capable of reaching this maximum figure. In 1934 there were exactly
fifteen authors whose books sold 50,000 copies or more in the United
States.

On the plane next below will be found a group of well-known novelists
and short-story writers, authors of the best technical books and the standard juveniles, and a few exceptional biographers who with utmost industry
are able to average an earned income of between $10,000 and $15,000 a
year. They comprise perhaps 12 per cent of the writing profession.

By simple subtraction, 87 per cent of our army of writers are to be
found on the third and lowest plane. To put it generously, the annual

* Condensed from the *Atlantic Monthly,* May 1935.

proceeds of their writing range somewhere between $800 and $5,000. The Authors Guild puts their average earning in *good times* at $2,500 a year. Since many of them are people of maturity with families to support, it goes without saying that the members of this third estate must depend either upon private incomes or part-time jobs if their bills are to be met. For them literature is a poor staff and a not altogether reliable crutch.

The pinch of hard times was of course felt on each of these levels. The shrinkage of advertising and circulation compelled magazine editors to economize. That is to say, they reduced the size of their publications, they printed material they had paid for but never used; they bought, in short, about half as much new material as they had needed in the happy days. Magazine writers who had been living in assumed security suddenly realized that their markets were disappearing and—worse—that even when a sale was made they were likely to receive a price smaller by 50 per cent than what they had been accustomed to.

Meanwhile the book writers were facing their own particular grief. Readers were losing the habit of buying the many books they wanted; they had suddenly become price-conscious. They bought only the irresistible books; the others were borrowed from the public libraries or rented from the circulating libraries in the bookstores. The royalties of even the best established writers came down on the toboggan; the royalties of authors whose books customarily sold over 10,000 copies suddenly dropped 50 per cent below the 1929 return. The royalties of unestablished writers, by which I mean first novelists, young poets, beginning biographers, dwindled to the vanishing point. "Fewer and better books" was an ideal rule to enforce if booksellers and publishers were to survive. But, reduced to financial terms, it meant that mature authors had to tighten their belts and beginning authors had to surmount a higher wall than heretofore.

MAJOR NOVELISTS

How DID the Depression affect the serious writers of the period?

Many had left the United States in the Twenties because they could not do their best work in the boom atmosphere. Malcolm Cowley, writing in the *New Republic* in 1939, put it another way: The Thirties had brought a "sense of relief" to the writers, who "had been unhappy in the boom days, which were dominated by their enemies, the businessmen." Cowley went on to say:

"The Depression brought hundreds of writers home from Europe. Though their reason for returning was in many cases merely that their money had run out, they showed the usual tendency of writers to find historical motives. . . . They rediscovered America, in one book after another, and it was a different America from the country they had deserted early in the 1920s. To carry the process one step farther, European writers began to follow them westward, as political refugees or tourists, so that New York became a capital of world literature. Its importance began to be recognized abroad." *

Among the returning writers were three major novelists who, while primarily identified with the Twenties, would influence the new generation; they were F. Scott Fitzgerald, Ernest Hemingway and John Dos Passos.

FITZGERALD

Fitzgerald's influence was on the wane; the publication of his novel *Tender Is the Night* in 1936 received little attention, and many reviewers found it disappointing. Not until his death, and the posthumous publication of the unfinished *The Last Tycoon* in 1941, would his star begin to rise again. Fitzgerald's predilection for self-destruction was incompatible with the mood of the Thirties. Writers were inclined to be impatient with his asocial writings, and unsympathetic with his absorption with himself as an artist. Nevertheless, he was producing important work in this period, and must be considered part of it.

HEMINGWAY

When Hemingway went off to Europe in the early Twenties, he was seeking an environment of the greatest possible isolation, a condition he considered essential for the creative artist. This did not mean isolation in the physical sense, for he enjoyed relationships with other expatriates; rather he saw himself and the protagonists of his work as individuals who must stand apart from the society to which they belonged. Only by doing this could an individual be free to discover the true meaning of the self.

Maxwell Geismar believes Hemingway marks the end of the cult of the individual, which was an integral part of the lost-generation syndrome. The Depression forced writers, Hemingway included, out of isolation and made them aware, as Geismar says, of "the transience of our materialistic

* Malcolm Cowley, "A Farewell to the Thirties," *The New Republic,* Nov. 8, 1939.

power which they had felt so inimical to creative values."

Hemingway's novel *To Have and Have Not*, published in 1937, was set in a Florida resort town during the Depression and bore signs of his new concern with social problems. While it was not ranked with his best work, it was reviewed as part of the "social protest" fiction of the time. The turnabout in Hemingway was detected when, as Harry Morgan, the protagonist, lies dying at the end of the story, he says, "No matter how . . . a man ain't got no bloody . . . chance." And Hemingway adds, "It had taken him a long time to get it out and . . . all of his life to learn it."

Hemingway published only one novel in the Thirties, but he continued to write and publish superb short fiction, along with two nonfiction works—*The Green Hills of Africa* (1935) and *Death in the Afternoon* (1932).

It was Hemingway's style, however, rather than his social protest, which had a powerful influence upon other writers, from newspaper reporter to aspiring novelist. When they worked to simulate it, they usually ran aground, unable to equal the simplicity of expression that Hemingway had achieved only after years of struggle to make the words fit the experience. And while some writers, particularly the hard-boiled (which included John O'Hara and James M. Cain) managed to match its glittering surface, their work frequently bogged down in violence for its own sake.

DOS PASSOS

It is in the work of John Dos Passos that a connection can be found linking the writers of the Twenties and the writers of the Depression. Dos Passos shifted the focus away from the lonely individual to society itself; the dominant theme was not the failure of the individual but the failure of society to provide a healthy environment for the successful development of all human beings. In his trilogy, *U.S.A.*, Dos Passos was the first to combine in one huge orchestration all the manifestations of our modern industrial society.

By the use of certain technical devices, like the "Newsreels," the "Camera Eye," and "Biographies," he widened the scope of the novel. And yet, as Maxwell Geismar says, "though the exposition in *U.S.A.* was brilliant and its picture of American life was full and varied, the novelist's conclusion was simple, and not encouraging. Filled as the three volumes were with achievements of urban power, in the land of power, the 'Newsreels' became ever more sensational and chaotic, while the 'Biographies' of our national heroes formed only the record of their disinheritance [and] the 'Novels' recounted only the disintegration of these average lives, from the obscure merchant seaman Joe Williams to the publicity wizard J. Ward Moorehouse; and the reflections of the author in 'The Camera Eye' became in turn increasingly desolate. Thus the immense national energy which had built up such a remarkable society within so short a period had apparently become centrifugal: the elaborate system was shaking itself apart. In fact, just as each novel of the trilogy was better than its predecessor, each was more despairing." *

* From *Literary History of the United States* (New York, Macmillan, 1953).

Dos Passos wrote about the emptiness of the American success myth and the appeal of radicalism, but he overlooked the majority of Americans who are attracted to neither, who live between the two poles and give society its stable center. It is Geismar's observation that the characters in *U.S.A.* "are not in their entirety accurate historical creations but very often the symbols of a bleak and despairing view of life." For if they were accurate representations "there would be little value in the catharsis of social revolution . . . for such a revolution implies the freeing of human traits which the present social order is crushing. But in these American protagonists, what is there to free? Where are the little moments of human warmth, generosity, decency? If this is an accurate portrait of the race, then we may also say that the Capitalism which Dos Passos is attacking, if it is the cause of these social types, seems also to be their proper orbit." *

Nevertheless, *U.S.A.* was a landmark among the social novels that were written in the Thirties and its influence is still seen today in the work of many young writers.

FAULKNER

In the work of William Faulkner, concern about the individual's isolation is successfully blended with criticism of the industrial society. Of course, the society is one that is peculiar to the deep South. Within his imaginary county, Yoknapatawpha, he creates all life.

The Yoknapatawpha saga was begun with the novels *Sartoris* and *The Sound and the Fury*, both published in 1929; then followed *As I Lay Dying* (1930), *Sanctuary* (1931), *Light in August* (1932), *Absalom, Absalom!* (1936), and a collection of stories in *The Unvanquished* (1939). This alone represents an impressive production, but there were also two more volumes of stories, *These Thirteen* (1931) and *Dr. Martino* (1934), and two other novels, *Pylon* (1935) and *The Wild Palms* (1939), all unrelated to the saga.

According to Geismar, " 'Jefferson,' Mississippi, is the capital of this world which reaches backward in time to the origins of Southern culture and forward to the horrid prophecies of its extinction, and which ranges down in social strata from dying landed aristocracy, the Sartoris and Compson families, to the new commercial oligarchy of the Snopeses, down to the poor-white Bundrens of *As I Lay Dying*, to the pervert Popeye of *Sanctuary* and to the Negro Joe Christmas of *Light in August*, turned brute again by the society which had raised him from the animal.

"[It is in] these ancestral halls in which echo only the sobs of the possessed and demented . . . [that] Faulkner built his work on an even grander scale than Dos Passos. He related even his minor personages with one another, elaborated their genealogy from generation to generation, gave them a countryside: a deep land of Baptists, of brothels, of attic secrets, of swamps and shadows." †

If his writing was tortuous, and his characters sometimes grotesque, his work had qualities that are seldom found in the work of other writers. In Faulkner's world the reader will find a pervasive element

* Maxwell Geismar, *Writers in Crisis* (Boston, Houghton Mifflin, 1947).
† From *Literary History of the United States*.

of deep family affection and a range of sensitively shaded emotional relations between the very young and the old, both Negro and white. There is also a rare, wonderful backwoods humor, evident not only in the novels but also in the short stories.

Most readers reacted strongly to Faulkner's work (as they still do today), in admiration or complete rejection. The great cry against him was his lack of discipline and his constant experimentation. But he is the kind of author who writes only when moved by the inner voice, and probably he should then be judged, as Malcolm Cowley has said, as "an epic or bardic poet in prose, a creator of myths . . . [which] he weaves together into a legend of the South."

WOLFE

Thomas Wolfe was very early recognized as one of the important spokesmen of the younger generation. His four huge novels, more than a million words in length, may be considered a single work, a story of his life, thinly disguised as fiction. *Look Homeward, Angel* (1929), a family chronicle of the Gants, reviews the author's early years in North Carolina through the eyes of Eugene Gant. *Of Time and the River* (1935) tells of Eugene's years at Harvard, his return home at the time of his father's death, and his visit to Europe in the early years of Hitlerism. The posthumously published *The Web and the Rock* (1939) and *You Can't Go Home Again* (1940) continued the story (with the protagonist's name now changed to George Webber) almost to the point where, in real life, it was ended by the author's death in 1938.

"This huge novel," Geismar says, "multiformed and sometimes inchoate as it was, with its alterations, always in progress, formed a central document of the period. Just as Dos Passos reinvigorated the naturalistic novel by means of the symbolist techniques, so Wolfe regenerated the whole tradition of native realism through the electric charge of curiosity, of lyricism, of anger and protest, and perhaps even of pure excitement which he put into it." *

Many readers are irritated by Wolfe's overwriting, and his overdramatization of experience; others describe his writing as rich, sensuous rhetoric. F. Scott Fitzgerald was not of the latter group; he suggested that Wolfe could benefit from a consideration of Flaubert's concise style.

Wolfe's answer was a defense of the "putter-inner" as against the "taker-outers." "I want to be a better artist," he said. "I want to be a more selective artist . . . but Flaubert me no Flauberts, Bovary me no Bovarys. . . ." And he went on to defend his intense appetite for all experience. In the opinion of Frederick J. Hoffman, "He wished to make from quantity a qualitative assertion concerning the meaning of life in its American cultural setting."

But if his novels lacked artistic structure, to many readers the lyrical prose passages were filled with color and tone—in a day when other writers were pruning their works to the lean, hard sinews so popular with the hard-boiled school. And Wolfe's partisans were moved by his laments over the transience of joy and the brevity of the individual life in the infinite river of time.

Who, since Whitman, has cele-

* From *Literary History of the United States.*

brated the glamorous pageantry of America, who has so unblushingly cried out over the "everlasting, living dream"? "I think the true discovery of America is before us," Wolfe wrote. "I think the true fulfillment of our spirit, of our people, of our mighty and immortal land, is yet to come. I think the true discovery of our own democracy is still before us. And I think that all these things are certain as the morning, as inevitable as noon."

His faith in America did not derive merely from some mystical promise of our land. At the time of his death, he had begun to achieve, as Geismar says, "the merging of the artist with his material: humanity." Wolfe indicated that identification when he wrote, "Mankind was fashioned for eternity, but it is with present evils that he is now concerned. And the essence of all faith . . . for such a man as I, the essence of all religion for people of my belief, is that man's life can be, and will be, better."

FARRELL

To discover *Studs Lonigan* now is probably not the overwhelming experience it was for some of us in the Thirties. Here was another massive novel—this time a documentary of the spiritually impoverished in an Irish-Catholic section of Chicago—which shocked the reader with its unglossed picture of the drab and vicious underlife of our cities. *Studs Lonigan* is one of the most striking examples of Depression literature; it is a raw, bitter exposition of the failure of the important institutions—home, church, school and playground—in the education of young men. The street and the poolroom had become the potent educative factors,

and our awareness of tragedy was strong as we watched Studs fall victim to his environment.

Farrell is often compared with Dreiser, and it is not hard to draw a parallel between his Studs and Dreiser's Clyde in *An American Tragedy*. Alfred Kazin believes that the difference between the two writers is that Dreiser, despite his awkward style, manifested a deep sense of poetry, while Farrell, less sentient, demonstrated a "literalness of mind which showed all through the Depression literature in the surrender of imagination and in the attraction to pure force."

Farrell continued to write about his section of Chicago for most of the Thirties, bringing out such novels as *A World I Never Made* (1936) and *No Star Is Lost* (1938), which began a new series about Danny O'Neill, clearly patterned on the author himself. Eventually readers complained that his style was clumsy and that he was tone-deaf in his choice of words and rhythms. Perhaps if he had gone outside his South Side Chicago environment in search of fresh settings the critics might have dwelt less insistently on his style. At any rate, Farrell served an important purpose then, one that can still be appreciated today, by calling attention to the spirit-stifling misery and demoralizing meanness that pervades so much of lower-middle-class city life.

STEINBECK

John Steinbeck, author of the most popular novel about the Thirties, *The Grapes of Wrath* (1939), was born in California, went to college at Stanford, but did not stay long enough to get his degree; he worked as a carpenter, painter, newspaperman, ranch hand, and wrote his first novel, *Cup of Gold* (1929), about the pirate Henry Morgan.

For his second novel, *Pastures of Heaven* (1932), he chose his own California valley country as the setting for a loosely connected group of stories. Later, in *Tortilla Flat* (1935), he wrote with ironic humor of the *paisanos* who reject hard work and competition (capitalism) and live off the land or the sea—or off anyone they can.

In Dubious Battle (1936), a "proletarian" novel, told the story of a strike conducted by migrant fruit pickers. In the following year he brought out an entirely different kind of novel, *Of Mice and Men* (1937), about the strange companionship of the powerful but feeble-minded giant Lennie and his friend and protector George. The success of this book, Steinbeck's first best seller, was due, at least in part, to its being about men who desired no more than enough to eat and a place to sleep.

In 1939, *The Grapes of Wrath* was immediately acclaimed "a great novel." It sold more than 300,000 copies in its first year and continued a best seller into the following year. It told the story of an Oklahoma family, the Joads, who lost their tenant farm in the Dust Bowl and migrated to California in search of employment as itinerant farm workers. "Readers who had thought of migrant workers as so many negligible thousands on the road or at work in masses," Carl Van Doren said, "now suddenly realized that they were not that at all. The Joads might have been any ordinary farm family uprooted and turned out to

drift over the continent. This novel did more than any other Depression novel to revise the picture of America as Americans imagined it." *

The novel may have been a kind of social tract, as some reviewers said it was, but to many thousands of readers it was a moving experience, and Steinbeck's powerful indignation at the sight of human suffering found a warm response in their hearts.

THE NEXT IN LINE

There were many other novelists of the decade whose work was important and still is read today. Some of them have had a surprising influence on later writers. Witness, for example, the novels of Nathaniel West with their satirical observations of life in the Thirties, and Horace McCoy's short novel *They Shoot Horses, Don't They?* (1935) with its setting a marathon-dance contest—in France the existentialists call it "great."

In the opinion of some critics, the work of John O'Hara and Erskine Caldwell in the Thirties is still their best. O'Hara's *Appointment in Samarra* (1934) and *Butterfield 8* (1935) put him in the front rank of the "hard-boiled" school. Caldwell's *Tobacco Road* (1932) and *God's Little Acre* (1933), and his many short stories, showed a deep concern about the injustices experienced by the Southern sharecroppers, but he chose to deal with them ironically, combining a grim humor with outrageous situations.

Many other novels of the Thirties, and some collections of short stories, have come back into print, and have had wide circulation in paperback

* Carl Van Doren, *The American Novel* (New York, Macmillan, 1940).

editions. It is worth recalling some of them:

William Saroyan's early collections of short stories—*The Man on the Flying Trapeze* (1934), *Inhale, Exhale* (1936), *Love, Here Is My Hat* (1938), and *The Trouble with Tigers* (1938).

James M. Cain's slick, tough, immensely readable novels—*The Postman Always Rings Twice* (1934) and *Serenade* (1937).

Marjorie Kinnan Rawlings' novels of Florida backwoods people—*South Moon Under* (1933) and *The Yearling* (1938).

Richard Wright's *Uncle Tom's Children* (1936)—his best work, *Native Son,* which placed him among the great writers of his time, did not appear until 1940.

Jerome Weidman's novels of rapacious enterprise in the New York City clothing industry—*I Can Get It for You Wholesale* (1937) and its sequel *What's in It For Me* (1938).

John Marquand's *The Late George Apley* (1937) and *Wickford Point* (1939), both of which started a new career for him as a serious novelist after years of success as a writer for the popular magazines.

Katherine Anne Porter's two collections of stories—*Flowering Judas* (1931) and *Pale Horse, Pale Rider* (1939).

The Thirties also saw the emergence of James Gould Cozzens, Jesse Stuart and Conrad Richter, as important novelists. And, of course, those novelists with reputations already firmly established continued to publish throughout the decade— Elizabeth Madox Roberts, Thornton Wilder, Sinclair Lewis, Ellen Glasgow, Stephen Vincent Benét, and Robert Nathan, to mention a few.

THE WRITERS' PROJECT

AN ENORMOUS body of writing was produced between 1935 and 1939 under the auspices of the WPA's Federal Writers' Project. Over six thousand writers of all kinds produced 378 books and pamphlets. Major efforts were the guidebooks to states, cities and waterways.

"The WPA's Historical Records Survey, instituted in 1936," Dixon Wecter reported, "sent forth relief workers to take inventories of local public records stored in city hall cellars, courthouse garrets and library lofts, to index old newspaper files, to make abstracts of court cases wherein nuggets of local history were embedded, to examine business archives and church records and even to scrutinize moldering tombstones for vital statistics. The allied survey of federal archives combed the land for national administrative and historical documents. Luckily, the recent perfecting of microfilm rendered possible the photographic preservation of millions of pages crumbling into decay." *

Out of all this emerged an America hitherto unknown.

ROBERT CANTWELL

THE GUIDES†

IT IS doubtful if there has ever been assembled anywhere such a portrait, so laboriously and carefully documented, of such a fanciful, impulsive, childlike, absent-minded, capricious and ingenious people, or of a land in which so many prominent citizens built big houses (usually called someone's folly) that promptly fell into ruins when the owners backed inventions that didn't work.

There was unquestionably something secretive and mysterious about them, but it was counteracted by an odd, clownish, lunatic sense of humor —they composed irreverent jingles for their tombstones, made up jocular names for their villages and farms, and were continually deciding boundary

* Dixon Wecter, *The Age of the Great Depression.*
† Excerpted from Robert Cantwell's "America and the Writers' Project" in *The New Republic,* Apr. 28, 1939.

lines, the locations of county seats and the ownership of plantations by flipping a coin.

They were great builders of spite fences, spite churches, spite towns—their captains of industry even built spite railroads. The four hundred citizens of Ilo, Idaho, moved their whole town a mile and a half to set it up across the railroad tracks from another town and for thirty years refused to incorporate with it.

Scattered through these volumes are brief biographies of prominent, notorious, or merely eccentric individuals who once swung weight in their own communities and whose marks—whether they be the Shot Tower of old Dubuque, or the addresses of prominent prostitutes scratched on the transoms of New Orleans—still remain.

The Guides have no rigorous standards to determine inclusion; people are mentioned whether they succeeded or failed, whether their inventions worked or not, whether they won or lost their duels, made money inside or outside the law: the only test seems to be that some living evidence of their presence, if only a legend or the name of a street, still persists in their own towns.

How has it happened that nobody ever thought before to trace the careers of the vast majority who guessed wrong—the leading bankers who put their money in canals in 1840 and in Maine shipyards in 1856, who plunged on slaves in 1859, and bet that Florence, in Baboon Gulch, Idaho, would be the leading city of the state? What a fine group of far-sighted financiers have really turned up in the Guides! They bought lots in Indianola, Texas, and refused to let the railroad enter Cantwell's Bridge, Delaware; they invested in river steamers, stagecoach companies, pony expresses, whale fishing, or cannon-ball foundries, or like Captain Hauser of South Dakota shot foul gases into the air to bring on rain.

It is a grand, melancholy, formless democratic anthology of frustration and idiosyncrasy, a majestic roll call of national failure, a terrible and yet engaging corrective to the success stories that dominate our literature.

History in relation to place also has the effect of transforming the roles of the leading actors. You can read a dozen biographies of Grant and get less insight into his early career than is supplied by a history of Galena—no biography communicates the sense of the boom environment in which he functioned, or pits him so clearly against the hard-drinking, violent, amoral get-rich-quick world that formed his character. When you read Grant's biography in relation to his own development, you wonder why he lent himself to the schemes of speculators; when you consider it in relation to the history of Galena, you wonder how he could have been expected to do otherwise.

If [the Federal Writers' Project] continues,* if the state guides can be completed and organized nationally, if the state encyclopedias can be brought out in consistent forms, and if the material in the files can be segregated and indexed for historians—there can be no question of the Project's value. It will revolutionize the writing of American history and enormously influence the direction and character of our imaginative literature.

* It didn't; it ended June 30, 1939.—ED.

THEATER—THE FABULOUS INVALID

THE commercial theater, as represented on Broadway, was beset by economic trouble, as usual. Caught between rising unemployment and high prices at the box office, the independent producers could do very little about either; they contended that high prices were dictated by rigid charges for theater rental and by union-fixed salary levels for the actors and stagehands. Consequently, many erstwhile theatergoers, those who could not afford the standard prices of $2.20 and $1.10, no longer went to the plays.

As a result of competition from ever-increasing numbers of motion-picture houses, more and more theaters throughout the country had been forced to close their doors; vaudeville was a thing of the past, and its musicians and stagehands had swollen the ranks of the unemployed. Some of these people found work in Hollywood, but there the average employment for the 22,000 actors registered with casting agencies was only seventy days a year.

Help was forthcoming once the Works Progress Administration was established in 1935; one of its provisos was to qualify relief efforts by helping the "employables" to find work within their own skills or trades; to create jobs for theatrical workers, a system of regional theaters was organized under the Federal Theater, and funds appropriated to produce plays at small admission prices.

It was argued by many in the commercial theater that there were no people with talent on the relief rolls to act in government-produced plays. Time would prove them wrong.

The Federal Theater survived many attacks within Congress; on June 30, 1939, however, an amendment was added, as a sop to the critics of work relief, to the new WPA appropriations bill cutting off funds for the Theater Project.

Sometime later Miss Hallie Flanagan, former director of the project, received a telephone call from a Congressman. She expected that he wanted to offer his sympathy; instead he wanted to talk about the theater project in his state. She said, "But, Congressman, there is no Federal Theater. You voted it out of existence."

A stunned silence. Then, *"What?"*

"It was abolished on June 30 by Act of Congress."

Again, silence. Then a shocked and heavy voice said, "Was *that* the Federal Theater?"

HAROLD CLURMAN

THEATER GROUPS

THE GROUP THEATER *

RECENTLY, in his sumptuous apartment in Paris, Irwin Shaw, whose lyric, antiwar play *Bury the Dead* was first produced by one of the smaller theater groups in 1936, very nearly sighed as he remarked to his guests, "How exciting the theater was in the Thirties. We all thought of what we wanted to express and what had to be said rather than about success." That was very nearly the truth of the matter.

The Group Theater—which I founded together with Cheryl Crawford and Lee Strasberg—began its career on Broadway, where it remained for ten years. The Group was the "elder statesman" among the new organizations that gave the Thirties its particular theatrical character. But the Group did not represent Broadway any more than the Neighborhood Playhouse, the Provincetown Players, the early Theater Guild, the Civic Repertory Theater—organizations typical of the Twenties, whose houses were all south of Times Square—were off-Broadway enterprises in the sense that we think of such enterprises today. Even the younger, smaller, less enduring groups of the Thirties—the Theater Union, Theater Collective, Theater of Action—though they all functioned more or less in the vicinity of lower Manhattan, were not what we today consider off-Broadway operations. For though most of those brave bands were terribly poor—always on the verge of extinction—they were enormously ambitious. Ambition gave even the least valid of their productions a certain ardor and flare that communicated genuine excitement.

The ambition I speak of in the theater of the Thirties—whether physically on or off Broadway—was a moral, social, artistic ambition. When Stella and Luther Adler, J. Edward Bromberg, Morris Carnovsky, Margaret Barker, Franchot Tone, Mary Morris, Alexander Kirkland and others joined the Group Theater's acting company, they were already well known. They chose the Group, and in the main were loyal to it through thick and thin, because the Group's policy in plays, in acting technique, in organizational setup, in social seriousness, appealed to them as artists and

* From "Groups, Projects, Collectives," *Theatre Arts*, September 1960.

citizens. The Group—and most of the other organizations I have named—wanted to make the theater vitally expressive of the American scene, of the life of the times. They also hoped—this was especially the Group's aim—to develop actors as conscious artists, and eventually to produce new playwrights.

ODETS *

Although *Awake and Sing!* was a modest one-set play, Odets was unable to raise the money to produce it. Neither was I, when I addressed myself to backers interested in the "better things" in the theater. The play, which showed people grappling with the petty details that mess up their lives, seemed in script form to make an unpleasant, harsh impression. The pettiness and mess were more apparent than the play's tenderness and pathos.

I decided to appeal to Franchot Tone† in Hollywood. I called him by phone, and told him we needed five thousand dollars to produce Odets' play. He asked me to send a script on to him for reading. I promised to do so, but I insisted that he send the money without waiting for the script. Franchot laughed and agreed.

Though it is true that everything at this time was done *con amore*, a few trifling circumstances cast shadows to highlight the generally creative atmosphere of our work. During the first week of rehearsal J. Edward Bromberg asked if we could release him for an engagement in Hollywood, since his part in our play was only a secondary one. When I rejected the very thought of this, he said no more about it.

I was living with Odets on Horatio Street, and after rehearsal he kept me up nights to discuss the progress of the play. (We promised each other that if the play prospered, we would move to more respectable quarters.) I hardly slept at all. Because of overconcentration and the rapid pace of production—the play was rehearsed less than four weeks—I was in a state of almost complete exhaustion as opening night approached.

There were only nine members of the Group company in *Awake and Sing!* Most of the others were busy with rehearsals of *Waiting for Lefty* under the direction of Sanford Meisner and Clifford Odets. It was to be given at a benefit for the *New Theatre Magazine*, unofficial organ of the new insurgent movement in the theater.

Sunday night, January 5, 1935, at the old Civic Repertory Theater on Fourteenth Street, an event took place to be noted in the annals of the American theater. The evening had opened with a mildly amusing one-act

* From Harold Clurman's *The Fervent Years* (New York, Knopf, 1945).
† Franchot Tone had joined the Group Theater in its first year, 1931.

play by Paul Green. The audience, though attracted by the guest appearance of a good part of the Group company, had no idea of what was to follow.

The first scene of *Lefty* had not played two minutes when a shock of delighted recognition struck the audience like a tidal wave. Deep laughter, hot assent, a kind of joyous fervor seemed to sweep the audience toward the stage. The actors no longer performed; they were being carried along as if by an exultancy of communication such as I had never witnessed in the theater before. Audience and actors had become one. Line after line brought applause, whistles, bravos, and heartfelt shouts of kinship.

The taxi strike of February 1934 had been a minor incident in the labor crisis of this period. There were very few taxi drivers in that first audience, I am sure; very few indeed who had ever been directly connected with such an event as the union meeting that provided the play its pivotal situation. When the audience at the end of the play responded to the militant question from the stage: "Well, what's the answer?" with a spontaneous roar of "Strike! Strike!" it was something more than a tribute to the play's effectiveness, more even than a testimony of the audience's hunger for constructive social action. It was the birth cry of the Thirties. Our youth had found its voice. It was a call to join the good fight for a greater measure of life in a world free of economic fear, falsehood, and craven servitude to stupidity and greed. "Strike!" was *Lefty's* lyric message, not alone for a few extra pennies of wages or for shorter hours of work, strike for greater dignity, strike for a bolder humanity, strike for the full stature of man.

The audience, I say, was delirious. It stormed the stage, which I persuaded the stunned author to mount. People went from the theater dazed and happy: a new awareness and confidence had entered their lives.

A series of *Lefty* performances was given every Sunday thereafter at the Civic Repertory Theater—all of them benefits. Finally on February 10 the press was invited to see *Lefty*, given together with the Group's experimental sketches.

The reviewers liked *Lefty* very much. At this time, after the Theater Union had done three productions, and the Jewish workers' group known as Artef had won a degree of esoteric fame, one or two commentators noted that "the progress of the revolutionary drama in New York City during the last two seasons is the most recent development in the theater."

Awake and Sing!, which had been in rehearsal about ten days when *Lefty* was first presented, opened on February 19, 1935. It was accorded a very favorable but not sensational newspaper reception. In the New York *Times* Brooks Atkinson, after calling Odets the Group's "most congenial playwright," went on to say: "Although he is very much awake, he does not sing with the ease and clarity of a man who has mastered his score. Although his dialogue has uncommon strength, his drama in the first two acts is wanting in the ordinary fluidity of a play. . . . To this student of the arts *Awake and Sing!* is inexplicably deficient in plain theater emotion."

Awake and Sing! was written out of the distress of the 1932 Depression (not to mention Odets' whole youth). It was completed in 1933 and belatedly produced in 1935. Yet only when it was revived in 1939 did the same reviewer say: "When Clifford Odets's *Awake and Sing!* burst in the face of an unsuspecting public four years ago, some of the misanthropes complained that it was praised too highly. Misanthropes are always wrong. For it is plain after a glimpse of the revival last evening that *Awake and Sing!* cannot be praised too highly. . . . When it was first produced, it seemed febrile as a whole and dogmatic in conclusion. It does not seem so now; it seems thoroughly normal, reasonable, true."

Now when no one ever mentions the possibility or desirability of a repertory theater,* it might be pointed out that there can hardly be any true theater culture without it, since most judgments in the theater are as spotty and short-sighted as those Mr. Atkinson confessed. Indeed, the judgment of any work of art on the basis of a single hasty contact would be as frivolous as most theater opinion. And, since I have paused to make the point, I might add that only by constant repetition through the seasons did the plays of Chekhov become box-office in Russia.

A bit of loose talk about Chekhov's influence on Odets cropped up in some reviews. Odets knew very little of Chekhov's work at this time, but quite a lot about Lawson's *Success Story*, in which he had served as Luther Adler's understudy. It was Lawson's play that brought Odets an awareness of a new kind of theater dialogue. It was a compound of lofty moral feeling, anger and the feverish argot of the big city. It bespoke a warm heart, an outraged spirit and a rough tongue.

But the talk of Chekhov's influence on Odets' work was a minor note in the reception of his plays. Far more common was the bugaboo of Marxism or Communism. They constituted the specter that haunted the Thirties. Rumor on these subjects was so prevalent that it reached even the daily theatrical columns. One reviewer, for example, spoke of "the simplicity of his (Odets') communist panaceas." He preferred *Awake and Sing!* to *Lefty* because in the latter "one finds Mr. Odets working now as a party member."

The Left press at the time of Odets' first success granted his importance,

* Mr. Clurman was writing in 1945.—ED.

but was careful to make serious reservations about *Lefty*, spoke gingerly of *Awake and Sing!* (in the *New Masses*), and called it "a comedown for the Group Theater, an unimportant play whichever way you look at it," in the *Daily Worker*.

Odets became the central figure of the so-called Left movement in the theater. But the relation of his work to Marxism or Communism was of a special sort not to be understood in terms of glib political commentary. The Marxist drift of the Thirties no more "caused" *Lefty* or *Awake and Sing!* in January and February of 1935 than *Lefty* and *Awake and Sing!* caused the organization of the CIO in November of that year. All these phenomena, including also the NRA and the later acts of the New Deal (the National Labor Relations Act, and so on), were an outgrowth of and a response to a common dislocation that convulsed our whole society. They were all undoubtedly related, but they are by no means comprehensible if they are lumped together mechanically as if they were identical.

Odets' work from the beginning contained "a protest that is also prophecy." There was in it a fervor that derived from the hope and expectation of change and the desire for it. But there was rarely any expression of political consciousness in it, no deep commitment to a coherent philosophy of life, no pleading for a panacea. "A tendril of revolt" runs through all of Odets' work, but that is not the same thing as a consistent revolutionary conviction. Odets' work is not even proletarian in the sense that Gorky's work is. Rather is it profoundly of the lower middle class with all its vacillation, dual allegiance, fears, groping, self-distrust, dejection, spurts of energy, hosannas, vows of conversion, and prayers for release. The "enlightenment" of the Thirties, its effort to come to a clearer understanding of and control over the anarchy of our society, brought Odets a new mental perspective, but it is his emotional experience, not his thought, that gives his plays their special expressiveness and significance. His thought, the product chiefly of his four years with the Group and the new channels they led to, furnished Odets with the more conscious bits of his vocabulary, with an occasional epithet or slogan that were never fully integrated in his work. The feel of middle-class (and perhaps universal) disquiet in Odets' plays is sharp and specific; the ideas are general and hortatory. The Left movement provided Odets with a platform and a loud-speaker; the music that came through was that of a vast population of restive souls, unaware of its own mind, seeking help. To this Odets added the determination of youth. The quality of his plays is young, lyrical, yearning—as of someone on the threshold of life.

It was nonsense for the New York *Sun's* reviewer, in order to challenge the validity of *Lefty*, to check with a taxi driver on his average earnings. *Lefty* was not basically about the hackman's low wages, but about every impediment to that full life for which youth hungers. Hence the play's wide appeal.

Perhaps Odets privately harbored the belief that socialism offers the only solution for our social-economic problems. Perhaps his desire to share a comradely closeness to his fellow men might attract him to those who hoped to bring about a socialist society, but he must also have suspected that temperamentally he might prove a trial to any well-knit party. Instead of being an adherent of a fixed program, a disciplined devotee of a set strategy or system, Odets possessed a talent that always had an ambiguous character. If because of all this the regular press was misled into chatter about his "Marxism" while the Left press was frankly perplexed and troubled by him, it may also be guessed that Odets too was pretty much in the dark on this score.

On the one hand, Odets felt himself very close to the people—the great majority of Americans—even in his bent for the "good old theater"; on the other hand, his heart was always with the rebels. But who precisely were the rebels, and what did they demand of him? Those he knew were a small minority, and they marked out a line for him that he could not altogether accept. After the first flurry of Odets' success had passed, everyone discovered a "change" in him. The conventional reviewers were glad; the Left was disconcerted. But, in the sense they had in mind, both were wrong—Odets had not changed.

Perhaps the truth is that the vast majority, to which Odets felt he belonged as much as to any rebellious few, had not yet created for itself a cultural clarity or form, not to speak of other kinds of clarity or form—had not, for example, yet made for itself a theater in which he could function freely. Perhaps the "few" who often criticized him more harshly than anyone else did not know how much they had in common with those they professed to scorn.

Whatever later wisdom might declare, Odets in the spring of 1935 was the man of the hour. Theatrically speaking, the climax of the Odets vogue came with the production of *Lefty* as a regular show on Broadway.

Since *Lefty* was only an hour long, we had to have a companion piece to go with it. Odets himself supplied this by dramatizing a short story purporting to be a letter from Nazi Germany he had read in the *New Masses*. The play, written to order, was finished in less than a week. Cheryl Crawford directed it, and the setting was designed by an unofficial Group apprentice, Paul Morison, who had performed similar services for us at Green Mansions.

This twin bill opened at the Longacre Theater on March 26, 1935, at a price range from fifty cents to a dollar and a half—something of an innovation on Broadway.

In order not to disturb the casting of *Awake and Sing!*, all the actors not engaged in that play took over the production of *Lefty* and *Till the Day I Die*, which, incidentally, was one of the first serious anti-Nazi plays to reach the New York stage.

Odets himself played Dr. Benjamin in *Lefty* (originally played by Luther Adler), and on opening night his appearance was greeted by an ovation. This was the last acting assignment of his career. Lee Strasberg under an assumed name played a small part in the anti-Nazi play. In the new *Lefty* cast Elia Kazan, replacing Bromberg, was thunderously effective. Everyone was sure we had picked him off a taxi to play the part— our "discovery" from Constantinople, Williams College and Yale!

The new play was respectfully received though the New York *Times* reviewer thought: "If you want to register an emotional protest against Nazi policy, Mr. Odets requires that you join the Communist brethren"— a rather peculiar interpretation of a play that at most called for a united front against Nazism. But the plea for such a front in those days was chiefly associated with Communists.

The play actually was a rather old-fashioned piece of theater in a style that derived from the swell of Odets' sentiment, an unavowed inclination toward romantic drama, and a feeling for social currents. It was a little artificial, yet not without some qualities of youthful sweetness and idealism.

Awake and Sing! never made much money. Odets believed the failure of *Awake and Sing!* to become a box-office smash was due to the Group's lack of business ability. He was wrong; the play attracted an important but small part of the theatergoing public: those who bought the cheaper tickets. *Lefty* and *Till the Day I Die* were seen by a devoted and intelligent public still too small (and poor), alas, to furnish box-office comfort.

Yet, except for their bewildered backers, the plays were an enormous success. They were the talk of the town, the thing-to-see for all who wished to remain abreast of the times. If we hadn't known this through reviews, interviews, public clamor, and an excited correspondence, I at least should have guessed it by the constant buzzing of the phone in the University Place apartment I shared with Odets.

The lion hunters were on the trail. Actresses, publicists, bankers, novelists, editors, wanted to meet the boy wonder. There was a difference in his situation as compared to that of a young writer like Thomas Wolfe, who was similarly sought after on the publication of *Look Homeward, Angel*. The difference was that while Odets was regarded by many as the dramatic find of the day, he was in addition that new phenomenon, a radical, a revolutionary, a Red.

An interest in an important new playwright was altogether normal for people like Tallulah Bankhead, Ruth Gordon, Beatrice Lillie, Helen Hayes, Charles MacArthur, Clare Boothe (Luce). But when Bernard Baruch began to examine him, when Edna Ferber asked that he be invited to a party that she might simply "take a look" at him, when Walter Winchell sought him out to have him explain the meaning of Communism (only to decide that he preferred to get the information from the "top man," Stalin himself), we were confronted with a sign of the times as significant as it was comic.

Odets was in a whirl, pleasant at first no doubt, a little terrifying later. He bought himself more records and virtually doped himself with music. Little girls he had known in the days of our jaunts to Stewart's Cafeteria on Sheridan Square now approached him timidly (or suspiciously) and asked if they could still speak to him. This infuriated and bruised him. He began to feel rather shut off, isolated.

At the time *Awake and Sing!* was written, a Hollywood scout offered him $500 a week on the gold coast. Odets asked me if it wasn't "unrealistic" to refuse it. I replied that it wasn't, if for no other reason than that he would be offered more later. When, despite all the acclaim, his earnings were relatively modest, though greater than they had ever been before, his agent called to tell him that M-G-M was willing to go as high as $3,000 weekly, perhaps even higher. Like a conspirator he whispered that he might be willing to consider it.

I overheard this conversation and was troubled by it. When I was at sea on my way abroad in April, I wrote him a letter confessing my reaction. It was his duty to himself, to his colleagues, and to his audience to go on writing plays. The three first plays, and the recently completed *Paradise Lost*, were a mere beginning. Odets answered that he was happy I had written him as I did. Indeed such criticism as my letter implied was always welcomed by him: it made him feel responsible. In 1937, after the success of *Golden Boy*, when I wrote him a letter in which I was very severe with him for not making better use of his time than he was wont to do at such periods, he said to me: "I received your letter. I loved it."

Perhaps not all artists are so, but many flourish only when they feel a concern for their work that is eager, jealous, essential.

People from all over the country swarmed into our offices. They wanted to join us, they said, because they were in sympathy with our aims. It was often a rude shock to them when I pointed out that we were a theater, not a cult, and that talent was still the first requirement for work with us.

The actors were now riding the crest of the wave. I do not mean this in any material sense, since most of the Group had as vague an understanding of their own economic situation as I did. They never worried over money except when they were broke, in which case a few dollars in their pockets would make them feel affluent again. They were thriving with a sense of fulfillment, the feeling that they were part of the main current, which to an extent they had helped create.

Our activity was incessant. A few of our people made experimental films with Ralph Steiner. Others helped direct plays for new groups. Kazan, for example, did this for the Theater of Action, which produced *The Young Go First*, a play about the CCC camps. We arranged a symposium of lectures at the New School for Social Research. Lee Strasberg gave a course on stage direction at the Theater Collective School. At Mecca Temple Morris Carnovsky did a monologue by Odets called *I Can't Sleep*, one of the pages of Odets' work most significant for its indication of the source of his inspiration—the troubled conscience of the middle class in the Depression period. At the same time a playlet by Art Smith called *The Tide Rises* based on the San Francisco marine strike used the talents of the younger people in the Group and showed the Odets influence already at work.

New theater societies were being formed all over the country to give the three Odets plays. Group Theaters shot up like mushrooms: in Chicago, Hollywood, New Orleans, San Francisco. A Negro People's Theater was set up in Harlem to give *Lefty* under the direction of our own Bill Challee. All in all, *Lefty* was being done in some sixty towns which had never before witnessed a theatrical performance. Thirty-two cities were seeing the twin bill of *Lefty* and *Till the Day I Die* at the same time.

Even suppressions, bans, arrests on grounds of "unlawful assembly" or "profanity," served to increase the play's prestige. These occurred in Philadelphia, Boston, New Haven, Newark, Dorchester, Chelsea and Roxbury. On the West Coast Will Geer, managing a small enterprise that had announced *Till the Day I Die*, received a menacing note: "You know what we do to the enemies of the New Germany." He produced the play, and was severely beaten up by Bundist hoodlums. In New York Odets put an extra heavy lock on the door of our apartment.

From a political or sensational standpoint, all this came to a boil when Odets went down to Cuba as head of a committee to study labor and social conditions, with emphasis on the status of students under the reactionary Mendieta regime. The visit—under the auspices of the League of American Writers—was supposed to last two weeks. It lasted a few hours; on the arrival of the *S.S. Oriente* the entire committee, composed of timid little white-collar workers and teachers, were arrested as "agitators."

The story made the headlines. Telegrams of protest were sent, meetings held, petitions signed. When I heard that some of the Group actors had called a protest meeting for the acting profession and saw one of them haranguing the small audience, beer-hall fashion, I became almost as annoyed as I had been amused.

Odets had been chosen to head the committee because in six months he had become a name. To be used in this way flattered him and appealed to his Hugoesque imagination. He wrote a few amusing reports on the matter for the New York *Post*, made highly inflammatory statements, and sounded off generally like a gay hothead in the Parisian Forties of last century. He soon became bored with his own busyness, temperamentally foreign to his introverted nature.

Odets' plays aroused interest not only in theatrical and minor political circles but in the literary world generally. The book reviewers devoted columns to him: he was being read in the same spirit as were the novels of Dos Passos, James Farrell, Erskine Caldwell, John Steinbeck, Robert Cantwell and Thomas Wolfe. The Group as a whole drew strength from this graduation from Broadway onto the larger American scene. It also drew some false conclusions from it.

This became evident in its reaction to new plays—for example, *Winterset*. Maxwell Anderson was contemplating letting the Group, for which he had an abiding affection, produce the play if it would cast Burgess Meredith in the leading role. Despite interesting production possibilities and a fine basic theme, it left me rather cold. I could not make myself comfortable in its atmosphere of an "Elizabethan" East Side! But, considering the state of American drama, it was not a play to be dismissed lightly.

We decided, therefore, to read the play to our company. With the exception of two or three people the actors were more averse to the play than I. Though its theme was Justice and its idea sprang from a prolonged pondering on the historic Sacco-Vanzetti case, they felt no immediacy, no true life in the play, only a filtering of these matters through a sentimental literary imagination.

Lee Strasberg did not so much disagree with this reaction as he feared its consequences on the course of our development as a practical theater. Because he felt himself under a cloud at this time, he failed to fight for his opinion. Two years later, when I admitted to the company that we had made a mistake in not doing the play, for all our reservations, since the function of a producing organization cannot be equated with that of the critic in his chair, the company maintained the integrity of its character and expressed shock at my change of view.

Yet it must not be assumed from this that the actors had become altogether complacent because of their newly won acclaim. On the contrary, there was a strong urge to make further progress.

GROUPS *

I have not yet mentioned—except in passing—the extraordinary phenomenon of the Federal Theater, which began its career on October 1, 1935, only to end it because of political pressure on July 1, 1939. Under the direction of the doughty Hallie Flanagan, the Federal Theater Project was the first (so far, the only) nationwide government-sponsored theater in the United States. This project, born not out of a love or appreciation of the theater, but as part of the Works Progress Administration, which was established to give employment to needy people in socially useful jobs, made a contribution to our theater the significance of which has to this day not been fully recognized. For the Federal Theater, often harshly criticized by professional show folk and politicians who suspected it of being too useful to the Roosevelt administration, proved what might be accomplished in a creative sense by a government-promoted theater organization in the hands of devoted craftsmen.

"Aren't very many of the Federal Theater productions amateurish?" I was once asked at a lecture I gave at the time. My answer then—as it would be today—was: "Yes—and so are many Broadway productions." Though most of the Federal Theater personnel came from relief rolls, and nine out of ten dollars were spent for wages, the Federal Theater employed ten thousand people, operated theaters in forty states, published a nationally distributed theater magazine, conducted a research bureau serving not only its own theaters but twenty thousand schools, churches and community theaters throughout America, and played to audiences totaling millions.

* From "Groups, Projects, Collectives," *Theatre Arts*, September 1960.

The project invented the "Living Newspaper," a cinematic and journalistic type of production dealing with such subjects as agriculture, flood control and housing. *One Third of a Nation* (designed by Howard Bay) was in every respect a thrilling show, which attracted large audiences on Broadway at something like a dollar top.

It was in the Federal Theater that Orson Welles first displayed his lavish talent (with the Negro *Macbeth, Doctor Faustus* and *Horse Eats Hat*). Later, with the indispensable aid of John Houseman, he formed the Mercury Theater—the last of the outstanding ventures of the Thirties. The Mercury's first production, *Julius Caesar* (in which Martin Gabel, Joseph Cotten, Hiram Sherman and George Coulouris appeared, along with Welles himself), was an example of how gratifying the social enthusiasm of the Thirties could be when applied to Shakespeare.

The Federal Theater produced T. S. Eliot's *Murder in the Cathedral, The Swing Mikado,* a dramatization of Sinclair Lewis' *It Can't Happen Here,* the first American performance of Bernard Shaw's *On the Rocks* and Paul Green's *The Lost Colony.*

Perhaps the most succinct testimony to the swell of fervor the project aroused in the country was published in *Federal Theater Magazine,* written by a member of the audience: "We're a hundred thousand kids who never saw a play before. We're students in colleges, housewives in the Bronx, lumberjacks in Oregon, sharecroppers in Georgia. . . . We're the Caravan Theater in the parks, Shakespeare on a hillside, Gilbert and Sullivan on a lagoon, the circus under canvas, Toller on a truck. . . . We're the Living Newspaper; we're the Negro theater, the Yiddish theater and theaters throughout America playing not only in English but in French, German, Italian and Spanish; we're the file, we're the record, we're theater history."

The theater of the Thirties was often referred to as a "left theater," a "Roosevelt theater," a theater of "creeping socialism," or worse. The record shows that this was mostly eyewash. The theater then reflected what was going on in the world around it. What was going on affected everybody and resulted in many changes that are not only permanent but universally approved. The theater movement of the Thirties, often verbose, hotheaded, loudmouthed, bumptious and possibly "pretentious," did not produce Communism in our midst; it produced a creative ferment that is still the best part of whatever we have in our present strangulated and impractical theater.

WARD MOREHOUSE

THE PLAYS OF THE THIRTIES*

PLAY production in the 1930s shrank, dropping from an average of around 250 plays a season to about half of that total. Hollywood continued its merciless raids upon the Broadway scene, signing dramatists, actors, directors. Theater building in Manhattan came to an abrupt halt shortly before the decade arrived; there were empty playhouses from ocean to ocean as the great era of touring plays and stock productions began a steady decline; theaters in New York and elsewhere were demolished to make way for parking lots and garages, and many became movie houses. Vaudeville was near starvation (the Palace in New York changed its two-a-day policy in 1932, when it added films, and for much of the Thirties, films were the sole attraction there). Producers went broke, as did the actors (broker than usual), but there were no mass suicides.

The American dramatist revealed a consuming interest in a wide variety of subjects, and he did not hesitate to grapple with vital, contemporary issues. There was a trend toward the social-minded theater, and a widespread appreciation of nostalgia, which was revealed in such pieces as *One Sunday Afternoon, Ah, Wilderness!* and *The Star-Wagon*. The critics, taking themselves and their profession very seriously, started the New York Drama Critics' Circle. The organization actually came into being as a result of the disgust over the inane choice of Zoë Akins' *The Old Maid* for the Pulitzer prize of the season of 1934–35 in preference to Lillian Hellman's *The Children's Hour*.

Perhaps the leader of the new playwrights was the same Lillian Hellman, who first flashed into the town's consciousness with *The Children's Hour*, a sound and adult drama, and who was represented again later by *The Little Foxes*, a masterpiece of construction, which also was the first of her studies of predatory Southern families. Sidney Kingsley arrived on the scene with two resounding successes, the realistic *Men in White* and *Dead End*. Clifford Odets revealed a capacity for vivid characterization and flaming dialogue in *Awake and Sing!* and *Golden Boy*.

Among the established dramatists, Maxwell Anderson emerged as a one-man theater with the historical pieces *Elizabeth the Queen* and *Mary of*

* From "These Full Lean Years," *Theatre Arts*, September 1960.

Scotland; the political, and sharply satirical *Both Your Houses*, a Pulitzer prize winner; and the imaginative and poetic *Winterset* and *High Tor*, which won the first two best-play awards of the new Critics' Circle in successive seasons. Wit and urbanity went into S. N. Behrman's polished writing in *Biography* and *No Time for Comedy*. Eugene O'Neill contributed two vastly important—and highly interesting—works, *Mourning Becomes Electra* and *Ah, Wilderness!* There was unforgettable poignance in Thornton Wilder's *Our Town*, which deals with love and marriage, life and death in a small community in the long, long ago, and which has been recurrent in the theater, professional and amateur, ever since its première in 1938. The redoubtable Robert E. Sherwood had a productive time of it; his output ranged from the high comedy of *Reunion in Vienna* to the mingling of philosophy and melodrama of *The Petrified Forest* (written after a stay in Reno), to *Idiot's Delight*, with its prophecy of the approaching war, and to the exalted drama of *Abe Lincoln in Illinois*. Paul Osborn turned out a touching and whimsical theater piece, *On Borrowed Time*; Howard Lindsay and Russel Crouse achieved the long-run wonder of all time with *Life with Father*, dealing with the reminiscences of Clarence Day (the decade produced another marathon work in *Tobacco Road*); James Thurber and Elliott Nugent wrote a vastly entertaining comedy of college life, *The Male Animal*, and in 1939 the stocky, thick-browed and explosive William Saroyan, one of the newcomers, contributed that sensitive and observant—and funny—work, *The Time of Your Life*. The locale was a saloon; the characters were people who just drifted in. He won the award of the Critics' Circle and that of the Pulitzer committee, but resolutely returned the Pulitzer check for $1,000.

The decade was a romp for the playwriting team of George S. Kaufman and Moss Hart. They gave Broadway the hilarious *You Can't Take It with You, Once in a Lifetime, Merrily We Roll Along, I'd Rather Be Right, The Fabulous Invalid, The American Way* and *The Man Who Came to Dinner*. Josephine Hull, playing the unmethodical Mrs. Sycamore in *You Can't Take It with You*, who became a playwright because a typewriter was delivered at her home by mistake, was wonderful in that comedy, doing just about as much for it as the authors did.

The first Pulitzer prize winner of the Thirties, Marc Connelly's *The Green Pastures*, drew its material from Roark Bradford's *Ol' Man Adam and His Chillun*. It was performed for five years, in New York and on tour, yet Connelly had great trouble getting it produced at all; the script specified an all-Negro cast (his characters included De Lawd and the Angel Gabriel, Noah and the King of Babylon and Ol' King Pharaoh, the Stout

Angel and the Thin Angel and the Custard Maker and the children of the Heavenly Fish Fry).

The careers of some famous producers ended in the Thirties. David Belasco's fifty-year reign in New York came to a close with his death in 1931, during the run of his last offering, *Tonight or Never*, with Melvyn Douglas and Helen Gahagan. Florenz Ziegfeld died in 1932, though several editions of the *Follies* were presented later in the decade. And George M. Cohan, tired, confused and steadily losing interest, continued to act, but his producing and writing activity dwindled; he knew that he was on his way out. But Lee Shubert seemed ready to go on forever. He was still taking his daily sun-lamp treatments at the Astor barbershop, still reporting at his circular cubicle in the Shubert Theater building, and still staying up until 2 A.M. It was during the early Thirties that he said to me:

"The Shuberts have thirty-five theaters in New York and we have to keep getting plays into these theaters. We can't stop; we've got to go on always. We have seventeen hundred actors now working for us, and next season we'll have more. A man who produces hits must also have failures. I expect 10 per cent of my productions to be successful, 20 per cent to be moderately successful, and the rest unsuccessful. That's the average from season to season. The taste of the theatergoing public is now changing everywhere. There's a demand for class; the sensational type of play doesn't go any more."

Some others among the older managements were still in business. Sam H. Harris was very active, and so were John Golden, Arthur Hopkins, William A. Brady and Arch Selwyn. The Theater Guild was by now a well-established producer—and a leading one—along with Gilbert Miller, Herman Shumlin, George Abbott, Jed Harris, Richard Aldrich, Dwight Deere Wiman, Alfred de Liagre, Jr., and Brock Pemberton. The New York Theater now belonged to them, just as it had been the domain of Belasco and the others who were departing. I remember calling at the offices of George C. Tyler a few years before his death. He popped up from behind a battered roll-top desk, something that he must have had since he was starring William Hodge in *The Man from Home*. He was an aging, emaciated, self-pitying figure. "You've come to see me?" he said incredulously. "Why in the world would anybody want to come to see me?" He moved from his desk to a window overlooking Forty-second Street, once a great theatrical thoroughfare. "Just come here and see this awful street. It was so wonderful. Now it's cheap and tawdry and only half alive. What's happened to the theater I knew and loved? What's happened to all the world?"

What was happening was that the theater was shrinking, physically. Gone, too, were the stock companies from such strongholds as New Haven and Worcester, Newark and Washington, Pittsburgh and Atlanta. But the decade witnessed the rise of summer theaters as we know them today—package shows, touring stars (many of them cast off by Hollywood), apprentices, and schools for actors and technicians. In the second half of the Thirties there were thirty-odd legitimate playhouses in New York—a little more than half the total in the Twenties. But their marquees carried the names of some of the finest actors this country has known. The Thirties produced many newcomers who went on to fame. But there were also many well-established favorites among the roster of players, which included Alfred Lunt, Lynn Fontanne, Katharine Cornell, Helen Hayes, Ina Claire, Tallulah Bankhead, Gertrude Lawrence, Judith Anderson, Walter Huston, Noel Coward, Paul Muni, Ruth Gordon, Luther Adler, Eva Le Gallienne, Alice Brady, Leslie Howard, Josephine Hull, Monty Woolley, Raymond Massey, Jane Cowl, Lillian and Dorothy Gish, Howard Lindsay, Dorothy Stickney and George M. Cohan. And that's merely a cross section.

GUY BOLTON

THE MUSICALS*

IN RESPECT to musical comedy, there is a school of thought that maintains life began at '43, the year *Oklahoma!* was born. Without intending any reflection on that fine show, I would like to ask: In what way is it superior to the *Porgy and Bess* of 1935? Has it a better score? Is its artistry greater? Are its musical numbers more firmly integrated with the story? Are its characters more vivid, better drawn?

An outstanding difference between the musicals of yesterday and today is one of size. Small musicals like *Peggy-Ann, Music in the Air* and *Leave It to Jane* are gone, which seems to me a pity. Charm, which we, who wrote in the Twenties and Thirties, considered a prime essential, was easier to capture in the smaller dimension.

In the Thirties, air conditioning was not standard equipment in the musical theater, by any means, and runs were shorter. But there was talent.

* From "Musicals Too Were Memorable," *Theatre Arts,* September 1960.

Rodgers and Hart turned out some memorable shows: *On Your Toes*, *Babes in Arms*, *I'd Rather Be Right* (with George Kaufman and Moss Hart), *I Married an Angel* (their own long-run champion of the decade, with 338 performances) and *The Boys from Syracuse*. Good as their contribution was—and all of those musicals came within a three-year span: 1936–38—I think the palm should go to George Gershwin. In the Thirties he wrote the scores of *Girl Crazy* (1930), *Of Thee I Sing* (1931), the first musical to win the Pulitzer prize, and *Porgy and Bess*. Gershwin's remarkable range is illustrated by those three achievements. Among so-called light scores, I doubt that *Girl Crazy* has yet been beaten; in the field of near opera, *Porgy and Bess* is outstanding; the satire in *Of Thee I Sing* extends from lyrics to music, the recitatives being an amusing burlesque of grand opera (in such numbers as "I'm About to Be a Mother" and "Wintergreen for President," the music is as much a source of laughter as the words). Jerome Kern wrote two outstanding numbers, "All the Things You Are" (from *Very Warm for May*, 1939) and "Smoke Gets in Your Eyes" (*Roberta*, 1933), but the scores as such were no match for *Show Boat*, or his earlier musicals. Gershwin's *Girl Crazy*, presented at the Alvin Theater exactly one year after the historic Wall Street crash, introduced Ethel Merman to the New York stage; it also brought forward another newcomer, Ginger Rogers. With the exception of *Porgy and Bess*, this was Gershwin's top score. In general there was a greater emphasis on comedy in the musicals of the Thirties than there is in those of today. One sad and significant fact was the loss of houses for legitimate productions, a trend that worked a particular hardship on the musical stage.

The only notable change that has occurred since the Thirties involves the use of ballet and trained ballet dancers. The musicals of the Thirties may have been of lighter substance than those of today, but they followed the Gilbert and Sullivan tradition by aiming at satire more than do the current shows. Larry Hart, Rodgers' partner, was particularly gifted in this field, and the travesty of the New Deal, *I'd Rather Be Right*, provided him with an excellent subject for spoofing.

The one really memorable musical of 1934 was Cole Porter's *Anything Goes*. It ran for 420 Broadway performances. Cole's next show, *Leave It to Me* (1938), was a pasquinade dealing with the Soviet Union, a subject he tackled again, seventeen years later, in *Silk Stockings*. *Leave It to Me* is chiefly memorable as the show that introduced Mary Martin and "My Heart Belongs to Daddy." And the chorus included two young men named Van Johnson and Gene Kelly. Kelly's presence in a chorus illustrates a point in regard to the dancing ensemble of the Thirties. The dominant choreographer was Bob Alton; it was he who staged the numbers of *Leave It to Me* and *Anything Goes*, both of which were rightly famed for their work in that department. Alton had devised the idea of making up a chorus line of solo dancers who had not yet achieved solo rank. In that way he was able to bring individual artists forward to compete in succession, much in the manner of a challenge dance. Naturally such highly trained specialists could not be expected to be vocalists as well, so another troupe of specialists, trained singers, were engaged, the two groups taking the place of the largely untrained dancers-singers of the Twenties. Part harmony and special choral effects came into use, as a result, and such a division of the chorus was maintained through the years, though the present-day chorus members must have talent in more directions than ever before. Another requisite of pre-Alton days suffered to some degree when the new order arose in the Thirties; not all the trained vocalists were beauties. I remember Channing Pollock's somewhat acid comment: "The moment I looked at the chorus, I knew they could sing."

DANIEL BLUM

NEW FACES*

FEW PERSONS noticed a thin, freckled girl who played the maid in *A Month in the Country* at the Guild Theater (now the Anta) in the spring of 1930. The girl had graduated from Bryn Mawr, appeared with a Baltimore stock company, and had a few roles on Broadway, including the job of understudying Hope Williams in *Holiday*, before she was seen in the Turgenev play. But in the fall of that year, when the same girl supported Jane Cowl in *Art and Mrs. Bottle*, the critics tossed a few posies at Katharine Hepburn. Two years later she received greater acclaim in *The Warrior's Husband*; from that point she went on to stardom in Hollywood and has returned to the stage periodically.

Little mention is made of the appearance of Bob Hope in *Smiles* (1930) or *Ballyhoo of 1932*. But in 1933 he came into his own in *Roberta*. Playing supporting roles with Bob were George Murphy and Fred MacMurray. *Say When!* and an edition of the *Ziegfeld Follies* followed, and by 1936 Hope was starring in *Red, Hot and Blue*.

* From "New Faces Became Old Favorites," *Theatre Arts*, September 1960.

Another star of that show was Ethel Merman. Six years earlier she had left a stenographer's desk in Astoria to become an overnight sensation in *Girl Crazy*, singing "I Got Rhythm" and "Sam and Delilah." She popularized "Life Is Just a Bowl of Cherries" in *George White's Scandals* (1931), and "Eadie Was a Lady," "Rise 'n' Shine" and "You're An Old Smoothie" in *Take A Chance* (1932). Then came *Anything Goes*, two years later, and Merman more than had it made.

The program of *Forsaking All Others* (1933) lists "A Gentleman— Henry Fonda." The role was a walk-on. Prior to that he had gained experience with the Omaha Community Playhouse, spent several summer seasons with the University Players at West Falmouth, Cape Cod, and appeared in small parts in two New York productions, including *The Game of Love and Death*. In 1934 he was in the first *New Faces*. Success came in the same year with *The Farmer Takes a Wife*, in which he appeared with June Walker. A year later he was in Hollywood, making the film version, and he returned to Broadway once more during the decade— in *Blow Ye Winds*, a flop, in 1937. During his four years at Princeton, James Stewart was active in college theater (his tenor voice and his accordion playing won him great popularity in the Triangle Club). A summer season at West Falmouth girded him for storming producers' offices. When *Carry Nation* opened at the Biltmore Theater in New York on October 29, 1932, young Stewart was playing Constable Gano. It was his Broadway debut; the production ran seventeen performances. It was also the metropolitan bow for Joshua L. Logan, Mildred Natwick and Myron McCormick. Stewart's next role was the chauffeur in *Goodbye Again*. He appeared in *Spring in Autumn, All Good Americans, Yellow Jack, Divided by Three, Page Miss Glory* and *A Journey at Night*, and in 1935 he departed for the film capital.

Logan, McCormick, Miss Natwick and Margaret Sullavan, together with Stewart and Fonda, had all served their apprenticeships with the University Players at West Falmouth. Miss Sullavan made her first New York appearance in 1931 in *A Modern Virgin*. Four more flops followed, but the critics were much aware of this lovely girl with the throaty voice. In 1933 she replaced Marguerite Churchill in *Dinner at Eight*, and then went to Hollywood, returning to Broadway in 1936 as the star of *Stage Door*.

Josh Logan was not the only struggling actor of the Thirties who went on to success as a director. The Group Theater produced a number of others. Elia Kazan, Robert Lewis and Sanford Meisner were actors in such Group offerings as *Men in White, Waiting for Lefty, Till the Day I Die, Weep for the Virgins, Paradise Lost, The Case of Clyde Griffiths* and

Golden Boy. John Garfield was another who came to the fore with the Group in the mid-Thirties. During the same period, another noted play-wright-director, Garson Kanin, was a young actor in such George Abbott successes as *Three Men on a Horse* and *Boy Meets Girl.* Director Sidney Lumet was an eleven-year-old actor in *Dead End,* one of the dramatic hits of the decade. He was also in the Max Reinhardt production of *The Eternal Road* (1937), together with Kurt Kasznar and Lotte Lenya.

The Federal Theater Project of the WPA (1935-39) helped the careers of such then unknowns as Orson Welles, Joseph Cotten, Arlene Francis and Hiram Sherman. The last three appeared in the WPA pro-duction of *Horse Eats Hat* that Welles directed. The same actors were prominent in the brief but exciting career of the Mercury Theater, estab-lished in 1937 by Welles and John Houseman.

The first edition of the revue *New Faces,* which opened March 15, 1934, was a stepping stone for other young performers: Imogene Coca, Nancy Hamilton, Charles Walters, who has become a well-known film director, and Alan Handley, the television producer. And it helped to establish producer-talent-hunter Leonard Sillman and a show that has had three other successful editions through the years.

In 1934 the *Page Miss Glory* program had this entry: "Reporter from *The Telegram*—Betty Field." The part was a walk-on, and her New York debut. But soon George Abbott employed her in *Three Men on a Horse, Boy Meets Girl, Room Service* and *What a Life,* long-run hits, one and all.

José Ferrer was the Second Policeman in *A Slight Case of Murder* (1935). It was his first assignment on Broadway. By the end of the follow-ing year, he was given a paddle to wield in *Brother Rat,* another memora-ble Abbott farce comedy of the era. Eddie Albert was also in the cast.

In Montgomery Clift's first professional appearance on the New York stage, he was one of Thomas Mitchell's precocious brats in *Fly Away Home* (1935). The success he won served to break down the parental ob-jections to his going into the theater. *Jubilee, Yr. Obedient Husband, The Mother* and *Dame Nature* provided him with other juvenile roles for the next five years.

On November 9, 1938, the critics and the usual rude first-night audience gathered at the Imperial Theater to witness the opening of a musical, little knowing that they were about to witness theatrical history, but before the final curtain, the hit of the evening was a newcomer from Texas named Mary Martin, even though the cast included such veterans as Sophie Tucker, Victor Moore and William Gaxton. The Texas girl stopped the show—Cole Porter's *Leave It to Me*—with "My Heart Belongs to Daddy."

GUNS AND IDEALISTS

AMERICANS who sympathized with labor and the political Left were usually strongly anti-Fascist, and the Spanish Civil War aroused many of them to action. They pressed for help to the Loyalist government; they wrote letters, argued, and stirred up controversies to make others conscious of the significance of this struggle against the Fascists: here was an opportunity to stand fast against fascism, perhaps to halt the fateful tide toward war. Eventually, three thousand Americans went to Spain and took up arms against the Fascists. They wrote a page in our history quite unlike any other.

On July 17, 1936, several garrisons of the Spanish army in Spanish Morocco rose against the civil government. The coup might have been defeated if Mussolini had not immediately supplied the insurgents, led by Generalissimo Franco, with the necessary materiel for making war—planes, ammunition, and even troops. While the civil government and their faithful, to be known as the Loyalists, rallied a good deal of support, many of the Spanish institutions and organizations fought for themselves at first, and the resultant state of anarchy enabled Franco to move steadily through the country, sweeping up all opposition. In early November, he reached the outskirts of Madrid and here, with their backs to the wall, the Loyalists mustered a stubborn opposition.

Volunteers from many countries had arrived to fight against fascism and Franco. While they were small in number—never amounting to more than fifteen thousand men—they provided an inspiring and effective defense against Franco at the gates of Madrid. They were known as the International Brigades.

The Internationals were never a major force in the Loyalist armies—the Spaniards did most of the fighting on both sides. But they were often used as shock troops, which meant that their casualties were as high as 70 per cent.

Perhaps this was the first time since the Crusades that men all over the world felt a need to stand and fight for an ideal. Many volunteers were Communists, but even a Communist was under no compulsion to give his life for Spain. Idealism was a factor.

The largest nationality in the Brigades was the French, partly because of their proximity to Spain and partly because of an overwhelming sympathy many French had for the Loyalist cause. Americans began arriving in December, but did not go into action until February. By then there were enough for a battalion of 450, and they chose the name Abraham Lincoln Battalion. Later a second group called itself the George Washington Battalion.

The Americans were ill prepared for combat; the United States at that time did not have universal military training—one of the few countries at that time which did not. Supposedly they were to get three months' training at least, but they were placed in action too soon to receive it. Herbert L. Matthews, distinguished foreign correspondent of the New York *Times,* has described some of the action in which American volunteers were involved:

"In the middle of February when the rebel advance [Franco's men] seemed almost irresistible, the Lincoln Battalion, along with other fresh Internationals, were withdrawn from their training center and rushed into the line. On February 16, Americans took their places in the Fifteenth Brigade along with what was left of the English battalion that had fought since early November. . . .

"I used to go down to Morata, because the hub of the world struggle against fascism had temporarily been moved from the capital to that little town, for all the Internationals were there engaged in barring the way to Madrid once again. Both sides were locked in an immovable grip. The fiercest fighting occurred around Pingarron Hill, to the northwest of Morata. It was a dominant position which the rebels had occupied and fortified strongly and despite fierce exchanges they remained in possession of it. Pingarron Hill evidently weighed heavy on the stomach of the Loyalist general, and he determined to assault it.

"Bob Merriman, California teacher of economics, was ordered to take the Lincoln Battalion across an open terrain and over a preliminary rise 'at all costs.' The attack started shortly after dawn on February 27. The aerial bombardment was ineffectual, the artillery weak, and the tanks either refused or were not ready to go. But Merriman had his orders. At zero hour, as the men moved forward, he was wounded and an English officer with World War I experience took the first wave of Americans over himself, and gained the preliminary position with hardly the loss of a man. A Spanish battalion was on the right, and an English battalion to the right of the Spanish. The English drove forward well, but the Spanish held back. That meant catastrophe, for as the Americans came forward they met not only the fire from the positions ahead but a murderous crossfire from their right.

"The result was almost literally a massacre. Of the succeeding waves of Americans hardly any reached that first position. One hundred and twenty-seven men were killed and approximately 175 wounded. One American, Robert J. Raven, was wounded from two grenades, one of which mangled his feet while the other burst almost in his face. A nurse told him later that he was permanently blinded. He was silent for a moment. Then he said, 'I came to Spain prepared to give my life; I won't squeal because I've lost my eyes.' " *

The battalion was reduced to approximately 135 men but it stayed in the lines, where the men who lived soon learned how to take cover and perform the other rudimentary acts to save themselves in combat.

Later Matthews visited the area when there was a period of idleness and found the Americans playing ping-pong, baseball and so on to pass the time. They had dug in strongly now, and he was impressed with their trenches. He complimented a New York Irishman who said, "Sure, we aren't going to pay rent after this

---

* Herbert L. Matthews, *Two Wars and More to Come* (New York, Carrick & Evans, 1938).

war. We'll just build dugouts in Battery Park."
One of the American soldiers was

Alvah Bessie. He describes combat
in Spain, beginning with the movement up to the lines in March 1937.

ALVAH C. BESSIE

FIGHTING IN SPAIN*

TWO NIGHTS before, there had been a fiesta around a huge bonfire, and
singing and a cheap French champagne that tasted more like sour hard
cider, and there were *avellanos* to eat and shells to toss in the fire, and
there were speeches. Young girls had come up from Barcelona to visit us,
representatives of the Unified Socialist Youth, and though at that time we
knew little enough Spanish, one of them, a small, plain girl, was able to
fire us with immense enthusiasm. There was also a young man, every inch
a man, who had been impressed into Franco's army in the north and had
managed to escape to us with a Fiat machine gun and three other armed
men.

"We must be moving," the older men said, "When they throw a fiesta
for you, it never fails."

At five in the morning of the thirtieth we were up and lined up and
marched down toward the road, where there were cases and cases of unused Russian rifles, packed in grease. These were issued to the men, and
as we had no rags with which to clean them we tore wide strips off our
underwear, wiped barrel, stock and bolt, ran strips through the bore. My
rifle, whose metal work bore the stamp of the Russian Imperial Eagle, was
numbered 59034. Under the partly obliterated Imperial emblem was a new
stamp, the hammer and sickle of the Soviet Union.

There was no time to clean the arms adequately; we cleaned and wiped
them as we marched. We halted for a moment to receive little paper packs
of cartridges, 165 rounds a man, which the men stuffed in their pockets
or packed into their blanket rolls. We halted again to take on a load of
hand grenades, a modification of the World War Mills bomb, made of seg-
mented cast iron and provided with a lever and a pin. None of us had
ever tossed a live grenade. We went onto the main road and marched in
artillery formation on either side of the road, the scouts going ahead at

* Condensed from Alvah C. Bessie's *Men in Battle* (New York, Scribner, 1939).

the point and on the flanks, the main body moving slowly along. Every fifteen minutes there were "avion" warnings, and we scattered off the road into the ditches and the fields, lying on our faces till the whistle blew.

LATER

We had one section of Spanish boys attached to each company, and lying there in the line I caught a glimpse of one of them crawling through the underbrush, his mountainous pack-sack swaying like the howdah on an elephant's back. He came from behind me, and to the right and was crawling toward Tabb's machine-gun squad, saying, "I want to see the machine gun working." I heard Tabb shout to him to get down, that he was in the line of fire, but the boy kept coming at him, smiling, saying, "I want to see the machine gun," and then he rolled onto his side, his hands seeking his groin, shouting. "Mama mia! Ai! Mama mia!" Tabb's gun let a burst fly at the rough crest opposite, and I looked across and could see where the bullets hit the stone, but there were no men in sight.

I was sent on patrol alone, and when I got back the Spanish boy was still lying in front of our lines, groaning. Dick told me to get a stretcher-bearer and I went back down the hill, sweating and grunting to myself, but momentarily relieved by being out of the line of fire. Below, there was a first-aid man, but no stretcher-bearer was available and the *practicante* was reluctant to come back up the hill. "Bring him down," he said, and I said, "We can't you'll have to go up," and all the way back up the hill he kept saying, "Keep down, be careful, look out, the fire's pretty hot up here, where is he?" It got on my nerves and I felt good thinking of him alone out there, dressing the wound, while I could drop back behind the hill and sit down and light a cigarette.

When I got back, Dick said, "Look over there; there's a mountain. There are a lot of troops behind that hill, but we don't know who they are, ours or theirs. Go over and find out and try to get back by dark."

The body felt light; the head detached from the body; the feet a long way below and carrying the detached body along by their own independent effort.

There was a sniper who followed me along through the edge of the woods and across the open space, and I kept thinking, This is too close for comfort, you bastard; and then I entered the woods and promptly lost my way. (I wonder what it's like in Brooklyn now, I thought; and how much do they get on relief, and do the kids get enough orange juice and corn flakes and does she get enough to eat or does she scrimp on her own chow to line the kids' bellies?)

I looked back, but the hill on which the Battalion had taken up positions was hidden, and I stood there, thinking. When I left I was going due west into the sun, and the mountain was somewhat north of west, and now the sun is on my left when it should be on my right—and what is it like in Brooklyn? I sat down and rolled a cigarette. Letting my mind play with the compass directions, and then Luke Hinman came along. He was a Battalion scout and had given me a few simple lessons in scouting a few days before, and so I asked him about the directions watching his hard, kind face with the broken nose, the firm lips, the blue eyes. He didn't talk much.

Moving through the woods quietly with your rifle at the ready was good. Then I came across a guy we can call Hal, another Battalion scout, who was sitting in the woods, or rather lying on his back with his eyes closed. "What're you up to?" I asked; and he said, smiling, "I'm on patrol." So I moved on and found the hill and came cautiously behind it. There was another company of Lincolns there, the third. I started back through the woods and located Hal again, who was still lying on his back. "How's the patrol going?" I said, and he said, "Couldn't be better." Goldbrick was the word that came into my mind, and I laughed to myself as I went along, thinking would they shoot him for that if I said anything which I won't but would they?

On the hill behind ours I met Hank Wentworth. "Dick's worried about you," Hank said, "Where you been all this time?" "Well to tell you the truth," I said, "when I started out I saw the kitchen truck at Headquarters and I got something to eat." "What'd they have?" he said. "Nothing came up to the line yet." "Oh, salad, steak and rice and French fried potatoes and wine and cookies and nuts and coffee—" "No crap," Hank said.

Just before dark, Dick received a message from Battalion which read, "Advise that enemy is expected to attack on your right flank; place a light machine gun on your right with instructions not to fire till they are 50 meters from you." And because I'd been over the terrain he sent me out with Sid, who was Tabb's gunner, and kept Tabb, Johnson and Taubman on the hill.

Sid had received a glancing blow on the head earlier that afternoon, and he had a handkerchief around his forehead that kept slipping over his eyes as we doubled down the back side of our hill and along through the wood that bordered the olive field. He was short and slim. But a sniper had seen us moving and he followed us through the wood as we went ducking around and under the low spruces, getting caught in the brambles, and

534

scratching our hands and faces. I was praying for the sun to set but it was still high over the western hill.

When we reached the point where we would have to cross the open space, we looked at one another. There was Sid, small and scared, and the black, wet face of the the the Negro, Johnson (my God, I thought, he must be fifty years old) and Moish Taubman, who used to say he was the laziest man in the Battalion, but had guts of cast iron. We crouched near the opening, waiting for each other to suggest some way of getting across. The bullets were hissing high or cracking low, and Moish said, "That son of a bitch is going to hurt somebody if he ain't careful"; and Sid said to me, "You're stronger than I am, suppose you take the gun, and go across first."

I took the light machine gun in my arms like an infant and faced the hundred meters of ploughed earth ahead. I took a deep breath and crouching low, started to run. I was crouched too low, felt myself falling, stumbling, lifted my head and shoulders so I could take longer strides, and zigzagged stumbling over the heavy clods of earth, thinking, fifty meters is awful close; if we wait till they get that close . . . Dick had said, "Bring the gun back, and come back yourselves."

The fascist machine gun spoke and the dirt kicked up around me; I ran, seeing the little wooded clump ahead, wondering if the others were right behind. When I reached the wood I fell flat on the gun and dug my face into the hard ground. The machine-gun bullets were snarling overhead and I lay there waiting, counting in my head, one two three four five, holding my breath for them to stop. Twigs and leaves kept dropping, and looking behind I could see where the slugs were kicking up the dirt, whining off the stones like a plucked piano string. No one had followed, so I lay face downward on the gun. Then they came panting almost grunting with the effort, and threw themselves down all around. After a while the fascist gun stopped firing.

We sat in the heavy darkness, tending the gun that faced up the valley, waiting. For a time we whispered about the possibility of the Battalion moving off without us, but there was no reason for this; we had taken two hills that day and there was nothing to worry about. We scouted about individually in the dark. We couldn't smoke; we couldn't talk. We listened till our ears hurt and no one came.

"I'll lead the way back," Sid said, and started confidently off. "Wrong way," I said, but Sid didn't answer. "You're going the wrong way," I said, and Sid stopped, waited for me to come up close, then said, "I'm in command of this squad." "O.K.," I said, "but you're going the wrong way anyhow."

We picked our way up the side of a hill, slipping on the exposed stones, dead tired and aching with the long day's tension. Johnson was carrying the gun, moaning quietly to himself. When we reached a halt on the side of the hill, he said, "Comrade, this comrade says you're going the wrong way. He brought us here; maybe he ought to know the way back. Maybe you better let him take us back, comrade. I'm done in," he said and sat down with the gun cradled in his lap.

APRIL 1937—IN THE HILLS ABOVE TORTOSA

Below us there were hundreds of men from the British, the Canadian Battalions; a food truck had come up, and they were being fed. A new roadster drove around the hill and stopped near us, and two men got out we recognized. One was tall, thin, dressed in brown corduroy, wearing horn-shelled glasses. He had a long ascetic face, firm lips, a gloomy look about him. The other was taller, heavy, red-faced, one of the largest men you will see; he wore steel-rimmed glasses and a bushy mustache. Herbert Matthews of the New York *Times*, and Ernest Hemingway. We introduced ourselves and they asked questions. They had cigarettes; they gave us Lucky Strikes and Chesterfields.

Hemingway did not seem to be discouraged, but Matthews was. Hemingway said, Sure they would get to the sea, but that was nothing to worry about. It had been foreseen; it would be taken care of; methods had already been worked out for communication between Catalonia and the rest of Spain; by ship, by plane, everything would be all right. Roosevelt, he said, had made an unofficial offer—or so he had been told—to ship 200 planes to France, if France would ship them to Spain. That was one of the best things we had ever heard of Roosevelt, but where were they? The war will enter a new phase now, Hemingway said; the Government's resistance will redouble, the people of Spain and Catalonia were fighting mad; the political organizations and trade unions were rounding up new replacements; the people wanted to counterattack; in mid-March Barcelona had been bombed 18 times within 48 hours, and 1,300 had been killed, 2,000 wounded. The Pope expressed his horror and his Christian indignation. All over the world popular sentiment, for the Loyalists from the start, and despite floods of Catholic and fascist propaganda, was growing stronger with every defeat the Government had suffered. There were huge demonstrations in London, Paris, Prague, Moscow and New York; the decent people everywhere were putting pressure on their governments to come to the assistance of Spain, but what can the decent people do?

We began to be aware of exactly how bad the situation was. The Brigade had gone in with about 2,000 men, and come out with 1,300; the Lincoln Battalion went in with about 500, and now we had about 120. Most of those who had come up from Tarrazona with me for their first action were gone.

AUGUST 1937

There was still some light in the sky as we moved out of the rest camp under the olive trees along the narrow trail leading over the low hills toward Gandesa. Then we turned off the main road onto a goat path that led into the hills. For two and a half hours we bent to a forty-degree angle, twisting and turning, slipping and stumbling up the almost impassable way. There was one thought in our minds: It's going to be hell getting food, water and munitions up this hill; it's going to be tough for the wounded.

With the dawn we could really see what we had to work with; a bare mountainside thrust into the empty sky, facing a concealed enemy slightly below. All day, we waited in the heat; there was no water. Then water came up—water disinfected with iodine and mixed with Spanish cognac. A squadron of fascist planes came over and unloaded upon the men on our left.

LATER

It was bitter cold, and we lay on the bare rocks, waiting, waiting for what, we did not know. They were singing over on their hills, a weird Moorish song that curdled your blood and made your spine run cold.

We listened to them singing, and we watched the sudden moon come from behind the wet clouds and then disappear again. The wind came up and blew the clouds away and we lay strewn all over the hilltop like the dead, waiting.

Dawn came up through the heavy fog. Fog meant no airplanes, so we could relax. But by ten in the morning we could hear them, and Curtis, flat in the next hole, said, "Here they come." "Don't worry," I said. "There's no ceiling; they can't see through the fog"; and so we remained silent and listened to them droning and droning overhead. And then, suddenly, there was the familiar whistling and a load fell directly into the *barranco* behind the hill, across the way from us, and the earth rose under us and threw us off and we fell back again, our hands clasped over our heads, hearing the falling rocks and dirt, waiting to be hit, our ears ringing.

Later that day, the ceiling was unlimited, but there were no further planes; the afternoon grew deathly quiet and the heat grew intense, but nothing happened. No rifle fire, and no shelling. That was the end of our third day in that hole.

THE NEXT DAY

We were crouched in the shallow *refugios* alongside the cliff; I was lying on my back and Dick was catching a little sleep at my feet, with Archie behind him with Sans. It had just passed noon when they opened up, and from the start they had our range. We could count about seven batteries at work, all of them concentrated on our sector, that was no more than 500 yards wide. They came, you heard them from the start to the end, the three low harmless thumps of the faraway guns, then a brief silence, then a low hissing, growing crescendo into a riffling whistle (a scream if they were coming close), and then a deafening crash that reverberated between the two slopes that enclosed the *barranco* behind the hill.

"That was close," Curtis said. "They've got us spotted."

He was in the next hole with the telephonist, Felix. I turned onto my back, saw Aaron's automatic pistol tucked between the two rocks where I had put it.

I heard them coming again, and closed my eyes, put my arms over my face and waited. You felt nothing at such moments except a tightening of the belly, and you drew up your legs instinctively and then it was all over. There were occasional duds; occasionally a shell whistling close overhead would suddenly lose its twirling motion and, turning end over end, go scuffling through the air making a noise like a small boy blowing air between his lips. You wanted to laugh when you heard those.

From where I was lying, if I lifted my head, I could see the built-up parapets of the other men in the *plana mayor*, the stretcher-bearers, the barber, the quartermaster Lara. When the shells were coming they were nowhere to be seen; after they had landed and the shrapnel had stopped screeching and smacking at the stone, they all sat up, sticking their heads over the parapet as though they were puppets in a Punch and Judy show.

"What about it?" Archie yelled; and Dick shouted, "What about what?"

"We ought to be up in the line," the commissar said; then they both ducked, and the thing went off and deafened us and the stones fell in on us from where the shrapnel and concussion had chipped away the cliff.

There was a terrific tearing smash and everything was black and a voice was screaming, screaming. I went out for a moment and came to and put my hand on top of my head and looked at my hand, but there was no blood on it. It was difficult to see, the air was clogged with rock dust and smoke and the ringing was continuous and the voice kept screaming on a high note. Far away, I heard Dick say, "Who got it? You, Bess?" And I said, "I don't think so," and sat up.

The screaming came from behind me so I got up and looked, and there was Curtis, lying on his belly, his buttocks torn away, holding them with his hands, his face turned to me, dead white and powdered with rock dust, and his mouth open, his eyes looking at me, his mouth open screaming. I could not take my eyes away from his.

Felix lay behind Curtis, his legs bloody and his face still, and I climbed over the few stones that remained standing between us, and Felix said, "Take him first, he's worse." Curtis kept screaming although his mouth did not move, looking at me with his eyes wide and staring and I was saying, Take it easy take it easy take it easy, and suddenly it was good to be moving, good to be doing something instead of just lying there waiting for something to happen. I yelled for the *practicante,* but he was up in the lines; I yelled for a bandage and was handed a small one-inch roll that was worthless. I called the stretcher-bearers who came and we lifted Curtis out under the arms and knees, and they went away with him through the fire that was falling before us, behind us.

Felix's legs were badly torn and his foot was broken to bits, the bone stuck through the torn leather of his shoes. I gave him a cigarette and tried with my wet red hands to light it for him, succeeding after a time.

They were pounding the shallow lines on the hill crest; with artillery and antitank shells they were hammering away from left to right, and back again, and it hurt to watch; it hurt in much the same way that a sore knee hurts when you clumsily bang it again and again.

All day, hour after hour, they kept it up. They covered our parapets and every inch of the back side of the hill. They wanted by the sheer weight of their steel to blow us off that hill. The body was utterly exhausted and indifferent to conscious fear but straining to the snapping point. There was sweat, and there was internal pain.

It all seems very far away and meaningless, although you know the meaning or you would not be there; there is no immediate reality in this. You can think of Times Square with all its cars and all its people, and the focus narrows down and you can see their faces, ordinary commonplace faces like the faces you have known all your life, like the faces of the Spanish men and women and children you have seen in the cities and the small towns and the country, who are waiting back of the lines now, maybe reading a newspaper: our forces in the sector of X . . . repulsed, with heavy casualties. And what does it mean, tell me, and do you know? Faces, do they care about us over here? And do they even think of us with love? The women and the children and the men—do they know we are so far away from them and dying for them? Do they know this is their struggle too? There is no connection between the fact of war and people; not when you are in it. It seems to be something taking place upon another, insulated plane of existence that does not, while you live it, touch the people whom it really touches. You think of love.

For it is love alone that can, for even a moment of our time, give you the illusion that you are not alone, penetrate your loneliness and separate it from you for that moment. And you are afraid that you will die without that love; you are not just afraid to die. And this is the meaning of it all (the people's war); these men behind these fragile rocks, these men whose tender flesh is torn to pieces by the hot and ragged steel; they could not accept their death with such good grace if they did not love so deeply and so well—were not determined that love must come alive into the world. What other reason could there be for dying? What other reason for this blood upon your hands?

A CERTAIN KIND OF IDEALIST

A COOL reception awaited the Spanish Civil War veterans upon their return to America. They had gone to Spain despite official disapproval by the United States government, and some of its branches would give them a hard time for years to come. The State Department, for instance, refused to issue passports to Americans who had served with the Loyalists. A few years later, when the United States was arming for war, such Americans were considered poor risks at the induction centers; if you had fought in Spain, you were, *ipso facto*, a Communist.

Years later, at the time of the McCarthy hearings, Morris Ernst and David Loth wrote *Report on the American Communist*, in which they examined the "homogeneous" character of the Communist party member. It was their opinion that there was a strong strain of idealism in many of those interviewed, and that, in their way, they were "selfless, dedicated" people. The following story, told by a veteran of the Spanish Civil War, indicates that this very idealism was apt to be cynically exploited by the Communist party.

MORRIS ERNST AND DAVID LOTH

REPORT ON AN AMERICAN COMMUNIST*

"I JOINED the Communist party in the early Thirties. I was twenty-four at the time and worked for the federal government. Probably the thing that pushed me into the party was that I felt terribly guilty at being employed when there were so many unemployed.

"My difficulties with the party began when I went to Spain to fight with the Lincoln Brigade. The trouble probably started with the fact that I have a gift for languages. I learned to speak Spanish and to read it fluently in a fairly short time. As a result, I was able to read the Spanish papers and to talk to Spaniards.

"I began correcting my previous conception of the Spanish situation,

* From Ernst and Loth's *Report on the American Communist* (New York, Holt, 1952).

which I had gotten completely from the American Communist party. I learned, for example, that the Popular Front was a hoax. Nobody believed in it except schmoes who had never learned to read Spanish. I found that while the other groups in the Popular Front were adhering to its terms, the Communists were going right ahead and doing the very things they had agreed not to do which made the Popular Front possible. For example, none of the member organizations were supposed to recruit, proselytize, or use high-pressure tactics to win new members. The Communists were the only group which consistently violated this agreement. They viewed the Popular Front solely as an instrumentality, and used it accordingly. They gave lip service to the Popular Front idea and did just enough grandstand stuff to enable them to point with pride to their militant devotion to the Popular Front. The difference between what the party professed to do and what it really did made it pretty confusing for me for a while until the whole thing began to emerge in my own mind for what it was—probably one of the worst examples of organized large-scale hypocrisy in history.

"During this period when I was trying to sort things out in my own mind, I started getting in trouble at party meetings of the Brigade. I sounded off on a number of issues and rapidly became unpopular. Luckily I had a couple of old friends who had risen to important posts in the party who came to my defense when my deviationist attitude was reported, with reassurances that I was just a slightly crazy guy, not a disrupter or a spy. Dozens of boys in the Lincoln Brigade were executed for deviationist tendencies, sometimes on the pretext that they were deserters.

"When I got back to the United States in 1938, I was intellectually certain of where I stood with regard to the party. I didn't sever my connection, however, immediately in the sense of formally resigning. I just stopped going to meetings. The Friends of the Lincoln Brigade at that time had a tremendous amount of money at their disposal which was supposed to be used to help veterans. I made two speeches for them for which I was paid, but after that they obviously didn't trust me not to shoot my mouth off and didn't give me any more speaking engagements.

"After a few months I was notified to appear before the Control Commission. This was the disciplinary body which investigated grievances against members, carried on personnel investigations, and selected people for special duty or Comintern work. Notices to appear before the Commission were never sent out by mail, but by word of mouth. When the message reached you, you either kept the appointment or left town or just holed up and worried yourself to death, depending on what kind of a guy you were. I kept the appointment. I had no intention of making a big dramatic thing out of it and going into details of why I could no longer accept the party line. I just played indifferent. The man who interviewed me was very solicitous at first.

" 'What's the matter, comrade? Aren't you feeling well?'

"He said I was probably suffering from shell shock and offered to arrange for me to have a long vacation at Camp Kinderland, the party country resort. He held out the lure of possible re-employment by the party; I didn't have a job at the time. When none of this broke down the indifferent attitude I had assumed, he warned me that if I didn't pull myself together and start behaving properly, I would be expelled. Nobody had to explain to me what this involved. For people like me it meant complete ostracism and being cut off from all of the people who had been my friends. Even though I was sure where I stood in principle, I must admit this prospect gave me many hours of doubt as to what I should do. At some points I was almost convinced that the fault was with me, that it was my weakness not any defect in the party that was precipitating the break.

"The ostracism was as bad as my worst anticipations. Men I had lived with passed me on the street without speaking to me. Even a man whose life I had saved in Spain refused to talk to me. He had been wounded in battle, and I carried him to safety on my back for 15 kilometers from early morning to sunset, holding my pants up with one hand because I had used my belt as a tourniquet for his arm. The first time I met him on the street after my interview with the Commission, he passed me by. The second time, he couldn't stand it and asked me to have a cup of coffee with him. He justified himself by saying:

" 'I stick to the party.'

"Once that was off his chest, he never talked to me again. Things were so bad that I became suspicious of the few people who would still talk to me. I thought they had probably been assigned to keep tabs on me.

"Up to this point I had continued attending meetings of the Veterans of the Lincoln Brigade. While I still had no wish for an open clash with the party, I had not been able to sit quietly and watch the men who had fought fascism in Spain follow the pro-Fascist party line of neutrality toward the war in Europe. This was, of course, well before the invasion of Russia caused an overnight switch in the line.

"I suddenly found myself brought up on charges for expulsion from the Veterans of the Lincoln Brigade. To my astonishment I found my importance blown up to fantastic proportions. Earl Browder was the chief speaker against me. He called me the successor to Trotsky and described me as a cunning manipulator who had cultivated a bland exterior to cover up his devious and widespread machinations. The charges were seconded by John Gates, who delivered a speech reporting practically every word I had ever said during the years in Spain. He even had a detailed account of a meeting at which I had queried La Pasionaria's evaluation of a certain battle. [She was the fiery woman leader of Spanish Communists.] It was one of those damned petty semantic squabbles that people sometimes get into. But to hear Gates tell it, I was a disrupter whose object had been to lose the war in Spain. When I tried to speak in self-defense, I was physically escorted to the door."

A TURN FOR THE WORSE

By THE beginning of 1937, Americans felt they had left the Depression far behind them. The President, in his budget message in January, announced that the matter of continuing recovery in the economy could be safely turned over to the businessmen. The relief rolls were to be cut, and some of the Public Works projects would be reduced.

Even the budget might be balanced soon; the President made it clear, however, that the balancing of the budget would not be had at the expense of any needed relief measures.

Before the sound-money men in the country could clap hands, however, the economy suddenly took a nose dive in the fall of that year. Stock prices fell, until by March 1938, A. T. & T., which had been selling around $170 a share, was down to $110. What happened to the national recovery?

FREDERICK LEWIS ALLEN

RECESSION*

DURING the latter part of 1936 and the early part of 1937 there were sharp increases in the prices of goods. Business concerns had been accumulating big inventories. When the time came to sell these goods at retail to the public, the purchasing power to absorb them just wasn't there.

New investments had lagged; and what was more, the government spending campaign had been virtually halted; Secretary of the Treasury Henry Morgenthau had persuaded President Roosevelt to make a real attempt to balance the budget.

Result: the goods which were piled up on the shelves moved slowly. Businessmen became alarmed and cut production. Two million men were thrown out of work in the space of a few months—and became all the less able to buy what was for sale. Thus out of that apparently clear sky— no great speculative boom in stocks or real estate, no tightness in credit, no overexpansion of capacity for making capital goods (in fact, not nearly enough expansion)—came the Recession.

* From Frederick Lewis Allen's *Since Yesterday* (New York, Harper, 1940).

It brought its ironies. Precisely a year after the beginning of the great sit-down strikes in General Motors, the president of the corporation announced that about 30,000 production men were to be laid off immediately, and the remaining men would be reduced to a three-day week. What price CIO gains now?

Another irony was provided by the collapse of values on the New York Stock Exchange. On Tuesday, March 8, 1938, just as trading for the day was beginning, President Gay of the Exchange mounted the rostrum, and, as the gong rang to halt the brokers, read the amazing announcement that Richard Whitney and Company were suspended for "conduct inconsistent with just and equitable principles of trade." Whitney had been the leader of the Old Guard of the Exchange. With his downfall the last opposition to a reorganization of the Exchange crumbled—in accordance with the wishes of Chairman William O. Douglas of the Securities and Exchange Commission.

There was irony, too, in the earnest effort of Administration leaders to remain calm and hopeful-looking as they issued statements predicting an early upturn, while the economic landslide was roaring downhill. Hadn't there been another Administration, not so many years before, which they had ridiculed for doing much the same thing?

As the Recession deepened, there rose angry voices from the business community and the conservative press. The whole thing was the Administration's fault. This was a "Roosevelt Depression."

As 1937 turned into 1938 Roosevelt was still trying to balance the budget and to refrain from proposing measures which would frighten businessmen unduly, but slowly the Administration leaders were becoming convinced that no policy of retrenchment and appeasement would bear fruit.

All the while the New Dealers were urging a resumption of deficit spending, and on April 2—as things were getting worse and worse—the President threw in the sponge. At lunch on the train from Warm Springs to Washington he told Harry Hopkins and Aubrey Williams that he was ready to abandon the budget-balancing effort and go in for heavy spending again. On April 14 he went on the radio to explain that he was asking Congress to appropriate three billion dollars for relief, public works, housing, flood control, and other recovery efforts.

That spring the legislation went through Congress, and simultaneously business began to show faint signs of improvement. In the latter half of June the stock market sprang to life. Recovery began again.

But the Administration as a whole had been struck a very heavy blow by the Recession. Meeting a new economic crisis, it had disclosed itself as neither able to generate "confidence" in businessmen nor to concoct any new and effective measures of recovery. The best it could do was to take down from the shelf a bottle of medicine to which it had been addicted for years—pump-priming.

THE WRATHFUL ELEMENTS

IT WAS a rare year that at least one of the country's major rivers didn't reach flood crest and spill over on the land, creating havoc in the homes, and taking the lives of people who lived along its banks. Congress frequently passed flood control bills, but they were usually only stop-gap measures.

Finally, on June 22, 1936, Congress passed legislation which established an over-all national flood-control policy, and authorized construction of some two hundred control-works on the rivers. Before major progress was accomplished, however, the Ohio River went on a rampage in January 1937, which produced perhaps the worst flood damage in American history.

At Cincinnati the water rose almost eight feet higher than it had ever risen there before; at Louisville, almost seven feet higher. Nine hundred people lost their lives; five hundred thousand families were driven from their homes; and a month after the crisis almost three hundred thousand were still homeless.

"But these figures," Frederick Lewis Allen wrote, "give no impression whatever of what men and women experienced in each town during the latter days of January as the swirling waters rose till the Ohio seemed a great rushing muddy lake full of floating wreckage, and the cold rain drizzled inexorably down, and every stream added its swollen contribution to the torrent. Railroad tracks and roads washed away. Towns darkened as the electric-light plants were submerged. Business halted, food supplies stopped, fires raging out of control, disease threatening. The city of Portsmouth, Ohio, opening six great sewer valves and letting seven feet of water rush into its business district, lest its famous concrete flood wall be destroyed. Cincinnati giving City Manager Dykstra dictatorial powers. The radio being used to direct rescue work and issue warnings and instructions to the population as other means of communication failed: a calm voice at the microphone telling rescuers to row to such-and-such an address and take a family off the roof, to row somewhere else and help an old woman out of a second-story window. Breadlines. The Red Cross, the Coast Guard, the WPA aiding in the work of rescue and reorganization. Martial law. Churches above the water line being used as refuges. Mud everywhere, as the waters receded—mud and stench.

"Most dramatic of all, perhaps, the triumphant fight to save Cairo, Illinois: men piling more and more sandbags atop the levee, standing guard day and night, rushing to strengthen the wall of defense wherever it weakened, as the waters rose and rose—and did not quite break over." *

The only river in the East and Midwest areas of the nation that did not produce comparable damage was

* From Frederick Lewis Allen's *Since Yesterday.*

the Tennessee, now harnessed by the TVA.

The flood damage was barely cleared away, and the recession well on the way to being licked, when, in the fall of 1938, a hurricane suddenly struck the East Coast of the nation with savage force, killing 700 people, and destroying over two billion trees.

There was almost no warning—the present network of storm warnings did not exist then. People were caught in their beach houses and on vulnerable lowlands. Great South Bay was completely sucked dry by the vacuum created by the onrush of the first winds, and then when the tidal waves burst over Fire Island, hundreds of houses were smashed to kindling.

One woman hiding under her bed all night long looked out the window at daylight to observe she was now residing in the next town. And one family marooned on Fire Island clung to the stunted, gnarled beach trees the night through, watching the wind and waters wash away their house.

JOHN Q. STEWART

NEW ENGLAND HURRICANE*

NEWSPAPERS, especially outside New England, gave the stupendous hurricane of Wednesday, September 21, very inadequate treatment. For two or three days immediately following the disaster bits of it were front-page items, but the whole account was not available until the neurotic interests of editors had jumped to fresher happenings. Only in scattered fragments was the storm's story published at the time. The limitations imposed on reporting by excessive mania for speed never have been illustrated more emphatically.

The first hurried headlines the next morning, "Storm Hits Atlantic Coast," are about all that inattentive newspaper readers from New York City west are likely to remember of a catastrophe as dramatic and horrible as any ever accomplished by wind and sea and rain. Spectral fleets of aerial bombers over Czechoslovakia were made more real to the American public than the actual low-flying blasts of the typhoon.

"For twenty-five cents I'll listen to your story of the hurricane." A bored sandwich man is rumored to have paraded Boston Common with this sign. Yet no narrator would be able to supply him with an altogether complete and trustworthy description. History moved on September 21 too

* From *Harper's* Magazine, January 1939.

fast to follow across New England, and the telegraph lines in tatters went down behind her. The wind's destruction commenced about 2:30 P.M., along the south shore of Long Island, and ceased above the Canadian border after midnight. The disaster was threefold. Over sea beaches storm waves of the hurricane, few in number but towering as high as forty feet, swept everything away. Terrific winds carried destruction inland. Torrential rains swelled streams already flooding from earlier downpours.

Seven states, and the Province of Quebec, counted close to seven hundred fatalities. A seaboard as wealthy as any in the world, and its hinterland, heavily provided with telephones, radios, coast guards, and state police, felt the shock. There had been no warning worth the mentioning; telephones and coast guards were scarcely called to service. A sophisticated population died by hundreds with little or no knowledge of what raw shape of death this was which struck from the sky and the tide.

In the long and laudable annals of the government's weather forecasters that day's record makes what must be the sorriest page. Hindsight is easy. The routine responsibilities of the United States Weather Bureau are so important that criticism of the failure of this splendid body of men to rise to an unprecedented emergency is not altogether justified. Yet suppose that the broadcasting of adequate advance notice of storms had been the New York Stock Exchange's duty instead of the duty of a branch of the Federal Department of Agriculture! The outcry from Washington over the insufficiency of the warning which was given would have been immediate, bitter, and voluminous. Scores of previous lifesaving predictions of hurricanes along the sparsely populated Southern coasts would have been dismissed as insignificant.

Those storms which are the most terrible are brewed by salt air and sunshine, by the damp sea air and the warmth of the sun and the earth's turning. Hurricanes, the extreme violences to which the earth's atmosphere is subject, are formed in a narrow belt near the equator, the doldrums. There the air is the most stagnant on the planet. To the making of their vortical energies go thousands of billions of horsepower hours—tigerhours —of sunlight.

In different oceans these disturbances bear different local names, hurricanes, typhoons, willy-willies, cyclones. "Tropical cyclone" is the technical name. In the early morning of September 21, Long Island and New England, unaware of the danger, lay fully exposed in the probable path of a West Indian hurricane advancing off Cape Hatteras.

Northward that morning at forty-five miles an hour in the Atlantic the windless central hub of the whirling wind was approaching. It swept over the aroused sea and, successively, along the Carolinas, Virginia, Delaware, New Jersey barometers would dip and rise again as it passed. The Weather Bureau's routine observations at 8:30 A.M., E.D.S.T., alone ought to have been glaring warning. Already then the storm's circular isobars—or lines of equal barometric pressure—were sketched as lengthened into ovals with their long axes pointing north. During the preceding twelve hours, this weather map for Wednesday morning showed, the tropical cyclone as a whole had been moving at an average speed of thirty-five miles an hour. Continuation of the rapid advance was indicated, northward into a fatal barometric trough across New England between two high-pressure areas. The wind at Hatteras at 8:30 A.M. Wednesday was blowing from the northwest fifty miles an hour; and Cape Hatteras was scores of miles west of the hurricane's center on its less violent side. What if meteorological statistics of many years did indicate that September tropical cyclones in the north Atlantic, if they curve from Florida as this one did, nearly always curve again eastward and out to empty sea? This one's course eastward evidently would be blocked by that potent Nova Scotia high. Not for the hardy accustomed captains of the north Atlantic steamer lanes would be the task of dealing with this particular whirlwind.

The triangle of ocean from Long Island to Bermuda to Georgia bore few ships that day, or at any rate no radio officers who troubled to communicate, after early morning, wind speeds and barometer readings. Here was the Weather Bureau's undefended sector. A violent hurricane was known to be at large in it, but officialdom's undisturbed routines were not adjusted to disclose just where it headed. In the tropics these storms move more slowly than twenty miles an hour, but accelerated advances are not unusual in northern waters. Telephone lines south along the coast remained undamaged and available, but were apparently unused for the emergency assembling of weather data. Meteorology is not a very exact science; but to estimate from wind and barometer the approach of a hurricane center is an elementary exercise, and has long been an essential part of the training of navigators at sea.

In the northern hemisphere the winds blow round the center in the direction opposite to that which the hands of a huge clock lying on the ground would take. "Face the wind, then the center is to your right." The winds are strongest near the center and the barometric pressure is lowest there. Rising heated air accounts for that low, and the gyroscopic force of the earth's rotation starts the whirl. In the southern hemisphere it is always clockwise. The whole vortex, once formed, may travel for thousands of miles with unchanged structure. Air friction continually takes toll of its energy stored from the sun's evaporation of the sea, and forces the low-level winds to move inward to fill the central vacuum. Yet for a week or two the condensing water vapor of the rain releases power enough to maintain the reduced pressures at the center, and while that nuclear vacuum is maintained the rotating earth continues to urge the incoming winds around it. In this wise, long before James Watt, nature had harnessed steam.

Not until almost midafternoon September 21 did the rapid fall of barometers in New York City itself suggest to Weather Bureau officials cloistered in office buildings that the dreadful invader from the south had refused to follow precedent by recurving northeast to open sea. At 3 P.M. the warning went out from New York City that a hurricane center would pass over Long Island and Connecticut "late this afternoon or tonight, attended by shifting gales." Even this tardy notice was not adequately spread, and already the inner spirals of the wind were screaming against Long Island.

Days before, while the fledgling hurricane still was swooping northwestward from its nest in the doldrums, experienced Florida had battened down. But there were no preparations made Wednesday afternoon from Cape May to Maine. Dwellers in summer cottages and fishing settlements remained uninformed of peril until the unchained wind and sea informed them. Meteorology long has taught what the effects are when a hurricane crosses a coastline. For far too many people that afternoon the knowledge came too vividly and too late.

II

The breadth of the inner circle of devastating blasts was a hundred miles and more. From a stratosphere balloon poised precariously above the turmoil the murky winds would have been seen directed counterclockwise over the ground, around huge concentric curves within this circle. As the center moved north at fifty miles an hour across middle Long Island, the blow to the westward of the center was approximately from the north. To eastward it was from the south, and in that quadrant the hissing gales were ridden by steep "storm waves" from the Atlantic. Ahead the winds were roughly east, and they were west behind. The eastern half of this great anticlock was its "dangerous semicircle," where the northern advance of the hub added its speed to the far more rapid whirlings of the wheel. The western semicircle, which crossed New Jersey, eastern Pennsylvania, and eastern New York, was less destructive by much; for there the hub's northern speed subtracted from the southern rotation of the wheel. Even in a hurricane one hundred miles an hour is an important differential. Severe damage therefore principally was to the eastward of the hub's course. Next morning's weather chart would map the track of the center through New Haven, and just west of Hartford, over lower Vermont, and on toward Montreal. The worst damage did not extend much west of these points.

At 3:30 P.M., the Boston Weather Bureau issued a mild radio warning. It gave no indication that terror and death were beginning to blast the Long Island and Rhode Island and Cape Cod coasts. New Hampshire received no urgent word. There ought to have been steady repetition until radio masts went down, "Tell your neighbor—close your shutters—park your car away from trees—don't let the wind get in your house—tell your neighbor!"

In Randolph, in northern New Hampshire, we are nearly three hundred miles north-northeast of Long Island. High in the White Mountains, we can watch ebbs and flows of the clouds with a personal interest for which it appears bureaucratic routines are inadequate substitute. Already at 10:30 A.M. that Wednesday a marked change was evident in the character of the unpleasant weather which had prevailed since the previous Sunday. Several of us identified the new disturbance as probably a hurricane approaching from the south. We did not take it upon ourselves to communicate with Portland or Boston. We expected the developing storm to be an interesting but not a dangerous experience.

The temperature, for a September blow in northern New England, was ominously high, 64° at our altitude of 1,800 feet. The wind, from a little south of east, had a weight and a gustiness characteristic even of the outer circles of a tropical cyclone. Once known, such squalls are recognized again. We had had days of remarkable clarity: Sunday, Monday, and Tuesday, beneath low clouds the mountains had been curiously distinct whenever the unwelcome rains would cease. Hurricanes as a rule weaken rapidly over land. The vapory ground, sodden from a rainy summer, was ready to nourish this one as dreadfully as though New England had been the very Caribbean.

The development of the storm Wednesday morning and early afternoon at Randolph followed precisely standard textbook descriptions of the approach of a hurricane. The whipping raindrops were characteristically fine, like mist. The temperature held constant. The barometer fell slowly at first, but after 4 P.M. at 0.1 inch an hour. The wind then really began to build, and the rain slanted in blizzards. It seemed inconceivable that an intense disturbance should be coming, for there had been days' newspaper notice of the arrival of the almost worn-out hurricane of August 1933—but here it came.

"The center will pass attended by shifting gales." Northern New England was ignorant of this bland announcement. As night groped through the storm's twilight, catastrophic frenzy replaced our mountain air. Still the direction of the wind held to the south of east. At about 8:15 P.M. the barometer sharply stopped falling at 29.0 (corrected to sea level). Rapidly then the wind hauled round and soon the gale was tearing at the southern instead of the eastern shutters of our cottage. An amateur in meteorology knew by wind shift and barometer that the fearful anticlock whirl of the alien storm was rushing toward Canada with its hub passing to our south and west.

Out of the night's steady bellowing that one soon became unconscious of, every few minutes would rise a whine which demanded all attention as it drove directly at our thin south wooden walls and raved at every window crack. It seemed that the next gust or the next would breach our frail defenses. After 11:30 P.M. patches of stars appeared through thinning clouds; the wind rapidly lessened and, still strong and persistent, turned southwest. The barometer began rising as fast as it had fallen before, and it went to 29.5 by 7 A.M. Thursday as the never-so-welcome sun rose at its equinox in an almost cloudless sky. This had been no ordinary "equinoctial storm," but with New England casualness the inhabitants of the countryside set about removing its wreckage. The wind during the night had blown itself out at last in southern Quebec. Not for a day or two did we learn how comparatively fortunate our neighborhood had been.

The rapid northern advance of the storm had shortened its duration. Instead of the dozen hours of maximum tempest which Miami would have known, New England had but four or five. Only dwellers by salt water experienced the sea's unbelievable wildness, which across tropical islands is the gravest danger of these atmospheric vortices. The whole duration of the blow was perhaps twenty hours. The rain in Randolph was torrential between 4 and 6 P.M.; after that scarcely two more inches fell. The cyclone pressed at the heels of earlier heavy rains, and even without its deluge dangerous floods would have swept the lower river valleys.

III

Many of the most spectacular incidents of that afternoon and night in the northern hurricane's track will never be collected, for their central participants are dead. The danger of death brushed close to millions of others, how close we never shall know. New York City felt only the edge of the storm.

Along the New Jersey coast in mid-afternoon the barometer fell 0.4 inch in an hour as the center passed at sea. The wind there blew from the north during the early afternoon and then shifted toward west. Coast Guard stations appeared as uninformed as laymen. Over the sandspit which separates Barnegat Bay from the ocean, several gigantic waves reared in close succession about 5:30 P.M. They followed surf and high water which normally would have been accounted very violent. They were examples of the terrible "storm waves" which accompany hurricanes, and had been heaped up doubtless by the tempest's eastern semicircle, seventy-five miles or so offshore, when the blow was toward the coast. Reduced atmospheric pressure at the center may have helped form these waves. They hammered in at forty miles an hour against the opposing west winds of the western semicircle. They annihilated boardwalks and slapped debris against the sand dunes.

The south shore of Long Island and the exposed Connecticut and Rhode Island shores east of Montauk Point faced the full force of far stronger seas. Along these coasts beach after beach was scoured. At West Hampton, of thirty-room mansions no single vestige remained. Seventeen refugees huddled chest-deep in sea water on the second floor of one when the walls at last gave way. Survivors lost not only their houses; many lost houses and lots; for the beach was deeply channeled. In Suffolk County the reduction in assessed valuation of real estate is estimated at $50,000,000. Elaborate lawns a mile from the sea at Quogue were under breakers two feet high; a cottage washed across with ten people on its roof. Soon after 4 P.M. the eye, or center, was seen crossing Long Island there; for fifteen minutes the sky was blue, breezes were light, and people thought the storm had passed. While the center was approaching a barometer needle dipped toward 28 "like the second-hand of a watch."

Inland, at Wesleyan College in Middletown, Connecticut, the old stone tower of the chapel blew down after the audience had departed from the opening exercises of the term. A dozen of New England's beautiful campuses, and many more old village greens, were scarred with trees shattered or uprooted. Most buildings inland were undamaged, but where gusts were most turbulent windows were blown in, shingles were loosened, roofs were stripped off, barns rolled over. Slides blocked roads in the hills, and bursting dams ripped roads in the valleys. Gushing streams broke highway and railway bridges and poured down village streets. Mountain forests beloved of trampers and skiers underwent in four hours more damage than would have accumulated from the gales and freshets of a score of winters and springs. And in New London, Worcester, and Peterborough (New Hampshire), fires abetted the wind.

Long Island Sound was beaten to one unbroken sheet of foam. Both shores were invaded by wind-driven tides. A family who lived in Darien, Connecticut, caught by the gale on their schooner in the Sound, weathered it but found that the water had ruined their house on the shore. Along the mainland coasts from Stonington to Buzzards Bay, where Long Island no longer served as breakwater, the storm waves were murderous. Narragansett Bay suddenly flooded downtown Providence. People who watched the surf were snatched into the sea, even from behind the steering wheels of their cars. One fortunate family at Misquamicut, fleeing by automobile toward high ground at fifty miles an hour, barely outran the pursuing sea. From a hilltop house at Watch Hill a woman looked from her window and saw a giant wave approaching "like a fog bank coming fast." It came ahead of the wind; this was soon after 4 P.M., and three hours of horror followed. That house stood, but disintegrated leaves and grass covered it with gray-green paste.

When the water had receded, owners on lower ground at Watch Hill were unable to identify the sites where their houses had been. Among a crowd who innocently had dared the sea's edge there to gaze at the huge breakers, one young woman had the following experience. She saw that massive wave rushing in and knew that she would die; there was nothing to do. The impact threw her into the crossarms of a telephone pole, breaking her arm and injuring her leg. As the pole went down the whipping wire entangled her fast, and from afternoon until next morning she floated to a rescue across Little Narragansett Bay.

If this storm had struck before Labor Day, at the height of the seaside season, the list of the dead along these coasts might have exceeded the six thousand lost in the Galveston hurricane of 1900.

Widespread tragedy is never devoid of lighter accompaniment. A gentleman of Stockbridge, in the Berkshires, an ardent amateur of bad weather, was visiting in Florida; he wired his unsympathetic wife that he would lengthen his stay to see the hurricane. He missed it; his wife and children in Stockbridge had to leave their house by boat.

From the seacoast to the border, from western Maine to eastern New York, there was wicked damage to trees. As examples: of a grove of 40 noble white pines around a cottage on Lake Winnepesaukee, 39 are down, several across the cottage. Of 3,000 sugar maples in one planting in central Vermont, 100 were counted standing. In hilly country the damage was spotty, but nearly everywhere a fraction, negligible or tragic, of the trees are lying snapped off or uprooted. Natural forests of trees of all ages and sizes seem to have suffered less than plantings of identical trees.

Telephone, telegraph, and power lines were out of action for days. Even water mains were broken. Passengers along the New Haven's Shore Line two weeks after the disaster had to take to buses where the rails still failed. Some villages were without restoration of full mail service for eight days, whatever the proud inscription above the portals of New York City's central post office may proclaim. The Blue Hill Meteorological Observatory, near Boston, successfully measured winds flying 186 miles an hour.

IV

To the Northeast hurricanes no longer are an exotic and romantic phenomenon. From August to November is the season for West Indian hurricanes, and many have penetrated north before. Extensive lists given by Ivan Ray Tannehill, the marine meteorologist of the Weather Bureau, include the following since 1900 which reached New England: September 9, 1934; August 24, 1933; October 3, 1929; October 1, 1920; September 16, 1912; September 15, 1904; June 30, 1902. In most of these, however, winds in New England did not reach seventy-five miles an hour, which is the threshold of devastation—the number 12, or "hurricane," of the seaman's scale.

The combination of chances which made the storm of 1938 unusually severe undoubtedly will recur; although, it is to be hoped, not soon. There was comparable violence on September 3, 1821, along a path a few score miles west of 1938's. A little farther west, in September 1896, another remarkable hurricane spread havoc and death from Florida and Georgia north through amazed central Pennsylvania. Yet even in the most afflicted regions of the South, the probabilities have been stated as 20 to 1 against a destructive blow in any given year.

What were the factors which made the New England hurricane of 1938 so destructive? As regards loss of human life it stands apparently fourth among similar storms in the United States. As regards property damage— several hundred million dollars—it was far and away the worst in all history. No trustworthy explanation of its severity across New England can be given, but the following four factors were involved.

First, there was the unfortunate barometric high which for several days had been laggard east of Maine when it should have been rolling its hooped isobars across the Atlantic. (The expert meteorologist names these highs "extratropical anticyclones." Previous instances are on record of their apparent interference with the paths of tropical cyclones. The ordinary baro-metric low on our weather maps is an "extratropical cyclone"; usually it is a comparatively trifling disturbance.)

Second, this hurricane all along its path was a major one. It was of great intensity while still in southern waters, where the cruise liner *Carinthia* went through it on the Monday.

Third, the worst of the storm at many points along the northern coasts unluckily coincided with the local hour of high tide. With the moon only twenty-eight hours short of new, high tides that afternoon would normally have been greater than average. The exact configuration of a shoreline, as well as the state of the tide, always is important in determining how destructive the miscalled "tidal waves" become in hurricanes. Funnel-shaped harbors which lie open toward an oncoming blow offer a hazard especially serious. No mathematician can predict storm waves in detail, can integrate the sea's excitation by the swirls and vacuums of an advanc-ing whirlwind.

Finally, hurricanes require humid air for their sustenance, and it may have been the already soaking ground across New England which con-served this one's force to points so far inland.

Forecasting can save the lives of people and can effectively reduce the damage to property. But nothing in our power can save the trees in a hurricane—except hasty guy-wires rigged for tame trees here and there. There are residences in New England which three months ago were show-places for their trees and are now surrounded by stumps. Orchard trees are lying uprooted, pushed over from every point of the compass. Irre-placeable great trees with trunks four feet thick are down: birch, elm, oak, maple, spruce and pine. New England mourns for her trees; but with this solace: not all the resources of science could have saved them.

OLD-TIME RADIO

THE RADIO, with its tremendously varied "free" entertainment, seemed a wonderful investment in the Depression years. About 12 million sets were in operation in 1929. Between 1930 and 1932, 4 million sets were sold, and by the end of the decade 28 million homes were equipped. What other plaything took, daily, four and a half hours of a family's time—assuming the human ear was paying attention? (By the end of the Thirties most of us had discovered that little switch placed so conveniently in the inner ear, enabling us to escape the drone and rumble of the "hard sell," the newscaster, or just plain bad music.)

It is small comfort to the American public to recall that at the beginning of the Thirties the sales value of radio broadcasting was still considered a matter for argument. Sponsors were hesitant to utilize the hard sell. By 1932, with cutbacks in the sales of consumer goods, all pretense was dropped, and, led by George Washington Hill (bent on selling his cigars and Lucky Strike cigarettes, come hell or high water) the advertisers swallowed the medium whole. Product identification, when Ovaltine meant Little Orphan Annie and vice versa, was just around the corner.

Let's admit that the monster— many people called it that—was insidious in its daily impact; still, there were marvels here and there, particularly if you were young and impressionable. Nowadays it is fashionable to be nostalgic and sentimental about the old radio serials, and even about the old wooden console set—that rococo horror that dominated the living rooms of the 1930s.

In the beginning, it wasn't just the young who listened; the whole nation used to tune in every evening to hear Amos and Andy, and people would be heard saying the next day, "I'se regusted." Before the soaps and serials took over completely, there were some pretty amusing episodes in the lives of such as Lum and Abner, Vic and Sade, Myrt and Marge, and the Goldbergs. But who would have suspected, when G. Washington coffee introduced its genteel crime series based on the Sherlock Holmes cases, that we were in for a daily diet of mysterious murders.

But give radio its due. The fine thing about it, to quote Brock Brower, was that "the listener produced half the show right in his own head, taking his lead from a range of voices, a musical bridge, and a few sound effects." *

* "A Lament for Old-Time Radio," *Esquire,* April 1960.

FRANCIS CHASE, JR.

SOUND AND FURY*

THE WORD came from Washington. On Sunday, March 12, 1933—eight days after his inauguration—the President would speak. Reassuringly, he called it a "fireside chat." Americans turned on their radios and listened—sixty million hopeful, anxious Americans sat by their loud-speakers and listened. The White House announcer said, "Now, the President of the United States. . . ."

In simple language, the President explained the practices of banking, scored those few unscrupulous bankers who had gambled away other people's money, and explained his purposes in calling the national bank holiday. He ended with a plea for the confidence of the people.

For all practical purposes, that was the first broadcast from the White House. There had been other broadcasts originating there; even Calvin Coolidge had stood before the microphone and spoken to the people. But the people hadn't listened. The combination of a drab speaker and dull issues drove listeners to the livelier competition provided by "Amos 'n' Andy." Hoover didn't lack issues, but his total disregard of the human equation in talking before the microphone, the almost slide-rule precision and monotony of his talks, proved no listener magnet. In fact, during the period between 1929 and 1932, Hoover made ninety-five radio appearances—only nine less than Roosevelt made from 1932 to 1936. Few, if any, will recall the subject of one such talk.

Despite the President's gift for making complicated problems of government and economics understandable to the masses of listeners-in; despite the magnetism of his finely pitched radio voice, there were many who neither believed in his policies nor listened to his persuasive chats. The unfortunate thing then was that such opponents of the President's policies not only refused to listen to the President but they had no way of making their own views and policies known. Of course, they could buy time on the air; many stations would even give them time.

One night in the spring of 1934, after George V. Denny, Jr.—then assistant director of the League for Political Education—and a friend had been listening to a fireside chat, the friend told Denny of a neighbor who

* Excerpted from Francis Chase, Jr.'s *Sound and Fury* (New York, Harper, 1942).

refused to listen to anything Roosevelt had to say. Denny, upon consideration of that neighbor's attitude, together with the Fascist blasts against democratic processes and the growing belief among many Americans that democracy was a thing of the past, decided to convert this one man's intolerance into a bright sword unsheathed on behalf of a living democracy—the Town Meeting of the Air.

To Denny, would-be actor, the reasons for democracy's failure to function—as expressed in such acts of intolerance as refusal to hear the other side—stemmed first from a failure on the part of the nation's leaders, as a group, to dramatize their messages. In the second place, the spirit of fair play inherent in the American make-up was not being appealed to. The first program went on the air on May 30, 1935, over NBC, with Denny acting as moderator. The first subject was, "Which Way America—Fascism, Communism, Socialism or Democracy?"

The broadcast originated in the auditorium of New York's Town Hall, where some fifteen hundred could gather. Before the program, the audience was warmed to the discussion by an hour of free-for-all debate on the issue by the audience. A neat arrangement of portable microphones permitted people in all parts of the auditorium to take part in the discussion. The same system permitted them to question the speakers during the question period following the debate. The first broadcast—which went on the air without publicity—drew a response of three thousand letters. Town Meeting of the Air answered some of the arguments that radio was not free and that its stand on controversial discussion was a milk-and-water half measure. Town Meeting was built solely on controversy. It boasted an audience far in excess of the collective editorial pages of the American press at the time.

Ironically, one of the warmest discussions ever to find its way over Town Meeting—or any other—microphone was on the subject, "Do We Have a Free Press?" Frank E. Gannett, publisher of reactionary newspapers, defended the press; Harold L. Ickes continued his role as a press critic.

The American press is as free as it wishes to be (Ickes argued). So far as government control is concerned, the American press is free. . . . In fact, the American government annually pays an enormous subsidy to the press in the form of less-than-cost postage rates. . . .

Yet, while the American press is free as far as the government is concerned, it is nevertheless far from free. . . . Mr. Ickes then listed three accusations which, he maintained, the people level against the press:

First, the press has financial affiliations or is subject to financial pressure which limits its freedom. Second, it is subject to the influence of advertisers, causing omission, distortion or improper slanting of news and affecting its editorial opinions. Third, it is unfair to certain groups of citizens, especially workmen, whose interests conflict with those of the newspaper or its financial backers or advertisers.

Mr. Ickes then became specific. Town Meeting folk loved facts, and Ickes set out to show how Mr. Gannett's papers, in particular, were under such influence as he listed. He cited the Federal Trade Commission's investigation showing certain Gannett papers were largely financed by the International Paper and Power Company. He charged that such financing muzzled any free discussion by those papers of the power situation. He also pointed out the part Gannett's papers had played in opposing passage of the Pure Food and Drug Act, in 1933, when many of the large advertisers were against its enactment. For the third accusation, Mr. Ickes produced an article from a Gannett paper reporting a Town Meeting program a year before in which Gannett had engaged in debate with Edward O'Neal, of Illinois, a farm leader. The newspaper had a column and a half of Gannett's remarks but not a single reference to O'Neal.

Mr. Gannett's replies were largely in generalities, although he did assert that the financial arrangements for his newspapers were made with the International Paper Company, not International Paper and Power Company—a fact which Ickes, in rebuttal, denied. He dwelt upon the services of the press, accused Ickes of denouncing the press because the press had "defeated" the Roosevelt "court-packing" bill.

It was an Ickes night. No one ever captivated a Town Meeting audience with generalities, and the Secretary of the Interior came loaded with buckshot. Gannett seemed to have forgotten even his gun.

When the question period for the Gannett-Ickes debate opened, a man arose.

Why, Mr. Moderator, was your policy changed tonight to permit a personal attack on a speaker?

Mr. Denny: The policy wasn't changed. I want to make this perfectly clear: there is a difference between an attack made anonymously from the floor on an individual, and a speaker who is well known saying his say from the platform. The man attacked is right here on the platform and can answer back.

Woman: (To Mr. Gannett) Do you think that distortion of the facts is the privilege of a free press, as manifested during the campaign for the Presidency in 1936?

Mr. Gannett: I don't think any real newspaperman distorts the facts deliberately. There may be a misunderstanding of the facts. I don't know what you refer to by the distortion of the facts in 1936. Freedom of the press is freedom to print. You can print your paper and I can print one. Thank God, we have that privilege in America.

Man: (To Ickes) Did you come here tonight to discuss a free press or to reap vengeance on a newspaperman who happens to disagree with you?

Before Ickes could answer, Mr. Denny spoke: "Now you see, that is the difference between an anonymous attack from a man you don't know and an attack by Mr. Ickes on Mr. Gannett—who is here to answer whatever Mr. Ickes has to say. That is a personal question. Don't take advantage of the fair play you are granted here by asking questions like that."

Woman: (After an exchange between Ickes and Gannett) Couldn't we have peace in the family? Mr. Ickes and Mr. Gannett, both, couldn't we have peace in the family?

Mr. Ickes: If the lady wants peace, I wonder why she came here.

Mr. Gannett: Yes, we could have peace in the family if we all approved of Mr. Ickes' New Deal papers.

This is democracy in action. Town Meeting's microphones broadcast the words of the nation's leaders in many fields—Earl Browder, Communist candidate for President; Senator Taft, Senator Wheeler, John T. Flynn, Wendell Willkie, Mrs. Roosevelt, Dorothy Thompson, Max Lerner, Norman Thomas, to list a few.

Across the country, listening groups—gathering in CCC camps, in Y.M.C.A.s, in schools, colleges, private homes—used the Town Meeting program as a jumping off place for their own discussions.

At the beginning of the decade, radio, drawing more and more upon the type of act formerly found only in vaudeville, had made the entertainment circuits an economically unsound proposition. Advent of the Depression and the disappearance of spare change from American pockets, far from reviving variety, was like the final spade pat on vaudeville's grave. Variety houses across the land closed their doors, darkened the bright lights of their marquees while workmen moved in and almost overnight transformed them into movie palaces.

But vaudeville was to prove a lively corpse. Collapse of the variety circuits proved only that people, hard-pressed for the necessities of life, could no longer afford the luxury of touring troupes. Laughter was still desired and radio could provide it cheaply.

It was not a peculiar development in the history of radio, then, that its greatest strides forward were made during the very depths of depression when other, older industries were closing their doors and turning their employees over to relief agencies. In fact, the development of radio in a period when other business failures were creating widespread unemployment is one of the logical and wholly normal aspects of the industry. Radio, by 1930, had taken two important steps toward meeting the public demands upon it for morale-building divertisement.

In the first place, manufacturers of receiving sets had made radio accessible to all. By the turn of the decade, factories were turning out the most efficient receivers at prices 40 per cent under the 1925 level. Even for those still unable to afford ownership of a radio set, listening was not out of the question. Loud-speakers blared out the baseball games from almost every corner cigar store; they were to be found in hotel lobbies, and, after the establishment of the National Emergency Relief Administration, radios became standard equipment in relief shelters and transient camps.

But making radio accessible to all was but the first step in radio's march. With the possible audience enhanced by millions, producers in the radio field were faced with the problem of broadcasting a type of program that would attract listeners. The matter of programming was further intensified by the growth of competition, for by now, radio was thoroughly commercial with three out of five shows sponsored by outside concerns. Shrewdly, radio executives realized that laughter was the prime need of the moment, and vaudeville, like Lazarus, rose from its grave and laughed a long, contagious laugh. Names which had come to mean much in the world of variety—Edgar Bergen, Fred Allen, Jack Benny, Burns and Allen—began to mean much more in radio. Where before, Jack Benny—by strenuous trouping—might have played to two hundred thousand people in the course of a season, he now found himself playing to as many as ten million on a single Sunday evening. Major Bowes particularly captivated the public fancy during those early Depression years with one of the oldest of vaudeville stunts, built upon the Cinderella motif—the amateur show.

The pioneer spirit so largely responsible for vaudeville's transition from the stage to the microphone was, oddly enough, neither a Keith nor a Sarnoff, but a youth with no deep-set roots in either vaudeville or radio. Rudy Vallee not only pioneered the radio variety show, but brought to radio such careful production, such fine showmanship and originality in both idea and presentation, that he might well be considered radio's first important producer. Beside his production efforts, his crooning accomplishments paled into an infinitesimal insignificance.

Among the stars he led for the first time to a microphone were Beatrice Lillie, Ezra Stone, Edgar Bergen, Carmen Miranda, Eddie Cantor, Milton Berle, Phil Baker, Olsen and Johnson. Ideas first presented on his broadcasts have led to independent radio shows when other producers developed them to the logical conclusion for which Rudy had no time. Notable among these are the universally popular "Aldrich Family" and "We the People." It is unfortunate that the greatest talent finder yet produced by radio has never been able to hold onto talent. Mr. Vallee was a hard man to work for, perhaps because of his own burning ambition to be a great dramatic star. On the very Thursday in 1929 when the stock market began to have palpitations of the heart, Rudy started his weekly, hour-long broadcast for Standard Brands under the title, "The Fleischmann Hour." On his second program he interviewed the Grand Duchess Marie, of Russia, following up on subsequent broadcasts with interviews with Max Baer, La Guardia, Heywood Broun and other notables outside the entertainment world. Soon, other programs were following suit and presenting such dignitaries, so Rudy turned to unknowns who had enjoyed some great experience or performed some feat of valor. In a few weeks, people were saying, "I was on the Vallee program," much as they would wear a Carnegie Medal. Years later, "We the People" was built into a popular network show along exactly the same lines.

Soon, too, listeners learned to watch the Vallee broadcasts for fresh talent. His talent scouts were busy searching out-of-the-way places for fresh voices and acts; they listened to local stations in all parts of the country, held countless auditions and hardly a top-notch variety network broadcast is heard today which hasn't at least one Vallee find in its cast. But his contributions were not to variety alone. He brought such stars of the theater as Helen Hayes, Ethel Barrymore, Eva Le Gallienne and Walter Huston to the microphone, not in scenes from Broadway plays (as was the radio custom) but in short dramas written especially for broadcast.

Radio Public Entertainer Number One of the U.S.A. and its Number One Salesman was Jack Benny.

After the war, Jack had taken up vaudeville seriously, playing the fiddle less and less and talking more and more. It was a long, slow process of accumulating gags, eliminating those which didn't click, polishing up those that did. For six years, in whistle-stop towns, he used the same opening gag. He'd walk out on the stage and ask the orchestra leader how the show was.

"Fine up to now," the primed leader would reply.

"I'll fix that," was Jack's comeback.

By 1930, vaudeville was on the way out but Benny—to whom vaudeville was everything—stayed on until there just wasn't any more vaudeville. In February 1932, Ed Sullivan had Jack on his radio program as guest. The public response was fair, and he began to study radio technique and to alter his routine to fit it. In May 1932, Canada Dry sponsored him in a program which was not too successful. Chevrolet and General Tires each gave him a turn on the air, but not until 1934, when General Foods, makers of Jell-O, hired him, was Benny ready, and the upsweep in Jell-O sales was one of the miracles of radio.

Benny knows that the public will always laugh at the cocky smart aleck who gets it in the neck, so he's the smart aleck. You are glad to see him get his due, and yet, you feel sort of sorry for him. He might, but for the goodness of God, be you or me. It was life transformed into ether waves every Sunday night.

His jokes were planted so expertly that even a child could grasp them; his timing perfect; his supporting cast good, well-paid and happy.

But if Jack Benny's broadcasts were the results of careful blueprinting, those of his public enemy and private friend, Fred Allen, were anything but planned. Allen was a wry-faced fellow with the most apt and buoyant wit on the air. Jack Benny or Bob Hope might keep a corps of writers busy. Fred Allen wasn't too certain of what he would say until it popped out, and his show was resultantly spontaneous. His program was built around a "Town Hall" sequence, in which a hick-town show was presented. Fred—tobacco-chewing dealer in bowls of wisdom sprinkled liberally with Tabasco and garnished with gall—was the epitome of the small-town wit. He was a sharper, more pungent and biting edition of Will Rogers. One Wednesday night, after an Allen broadcast, Owen D. Young elbowed his way through the throng at NBC to get near the comic.

"I've been listening to your program for years," Young beamed, "and I've been lucky enough to be in your audience the last three broadcasts."

"Well, Mr. Young," said Allen, chewing away at his tobacco like a baseball player, "I can understand why a person might want to see one of my programs once, just for curiosity's sake. But anyone who could sit through it three times should see a phrenologist!"

But the man who made the most money out of radio variety was the gruff, acidulous Major Bowes. At a time when entertainment marts of New York were flooded with talent out of jobs; when one of the most overcrowded divisions of WPA was its theatrical project, Major Bowes was attracting hundreds of stage-struck youngsters to the metropolitan area with the promise of fame and fortune. "Around she goes," the Major used to chant over the air, "and where she stops, nobody knows." He was talking of the wheel of fortune, and certainly it was not the Major's fault if he was unable to deliver on the gilded promises it held out. Travelers along the highways in 1934 and 1935 became accustomed to the signs hitchhikers wore on their backs: "En route to New York to appear on Major Bowes' program."

Amateur shows have always had a wide public appeal, and Major Bowes became the fairy godfather to many a one-night Cinderella. Only, unlike Cinderella, there was no prince in most cases. As a matter of fact, a huge percentage of the Bowes amateurs weren't even amateurs, but professionals out of work. They were paid ten dollars if they were good enough to get on a broadcast (a figure far under the AFRA minimum for radio talent and far under the amount expended by shows like "We the People" on its guests) and a few of them managed to get into a Bowes vaudeville unit for a few weeks of touring at salaries in the neighborhood of fifty dollars per week. But Bowes's amateurs sold coffee for Chase and Sanborn and, later, automobiles for Chrysler. They made Major Bowes one of the richest men in radio with an average yearly income from broadcasts and his vaudeville troupes of a million dollars.

A program like Major Bowes's Amateur Hour wasn't the result of programming trends like the variety shows of Bob Hope, Jack Benny or Fred Allen. His Sunday morning program from the stage of the Capitol Theater, in New York City, had long been a favorite—and well-handled—program, and there has never been any question about Bowes' showmanship. The amateur show he started locally on WHN in 1934 evoked such tremendous response that NBC put it on the network. Murray Hill 8-9933 (the number where votes on the amateurs were received by a battery of telephone operators) became the most famous telephone number in the world. The Major Bowes Amateur Hour was something that just happened. Attempts to duplicate inevitably failed. Charlie McCarthy was another such novelty act and rash imitators of radio's Pinocchio have learned, to their sorrow, that Charlie isn't quintuplets. The same held true for the character of "Baby Snooks," created by Fanny Brice.

From a standpoint of real public interest and benefit, there were programs such as the NBC Symphony Orchestra, heard each Saturday night in presentations of the world's great music, an aggregation of America's finest musicians. These broadcasts had a tremendous role in making great classical music the peculiar property of any man owning a radio set. It was broadcast "in the public interest," undertaken weekly without commercial sponsorship by a group of radio stations which, in this way, repaid the people of America for the use of their ether waves.

Arturo Toscanini, its first conductor, was a musical perfectionist, a maestro with a fearful temper, an unfailing memory and the power to lash his musicians into frenzies of fine playing. For the services of this seventy-three-year-old musical genius, NBC dipped into its own pocket to the tune of $4,000 per broadcast plus the income tax payments due on that salary. Because Toscanini, more than most conductors, conducted with his hands and face—never with his body—guests (like the Will Hayses, the Gene Tunneys, the Fredric Marches, United States senators and congressmen and diplomats) used to come early to get seats close to the front where they might see his sometimes pleased, sometimes furious expression. Perspiration poured from his forehead during these broadcasts, dripped from the end of his nose until, at intermission, he would have to change clothes completely. Two broadcasters had the official NBC okay to run over their allotted time without being cut off the air—President Roosevelt and Toscanini.

CBS's comparable attraction was its weekly presentation of the New York Philharmonic Orchestra. The Metropolitan auditions were also broadcast, and over the networks and on local stations, more good music was made available to average Americans than an Italian or Viennese millionaire could hear in years.

But perhaps the best example of what radio was accomplishing in its efforts to make great music the everyday companion of the American listener was afforded by the Metropolitan Opera broadcasts.

At the end of the decade that hallowed sanctuary of culture, diamond necklaces and double chins was fighting for existence. A million dollars was needed to keep the monstrous house from becoming the dark habitat of memories instead of the world's finest voices. In desperation, its directors turned to American radio listeners who, for several years, had been receiving opera broadcasts each Saturday afternoon.

The difficulty in which the opera company found itself was due to its peculiar organization. The opera house itself was owned by a group known as the Metropolitan Opera and Real Estate Company. Operas, on the other hand, were produced by the Metropolitan Opera Association, a nonprofit corporation. Stockholders of the former company were the holders of swanky parterre boxes around the Golden Horseshoe which they accepted in lieu of cash rental payments on the opera house.

Most of these early stockholders were dead. Their stock had passed into the hands of estates, and these legal entities cared little for Bizet or Mozart. The Metropolitan Opera and Real Estate Company began to contemplate liquidation of its holdings and sale of the opera house. That, literally, would have set the opera out on the sidewalk.

The problem was put squarely up to the people, to the radio listeners in Sioux Falls and Oak Grove, in Omaha and Ogden. Could democracy support opera and did it want opera?

More than 150,000 contributions—many of them family contributions —were received. They amounted to almost a half million dollars. They were the small gifts of everyday listeners who had never sat in the Family Circle and peered down upon the great stage of the Met. What had really occurred—and radio was responsible—was a sort of revolution. Radio had given the opera, once the property of the elite, to the people; now the people were giving life to the opera, deserted by the elite.

Radio's big staple, the daytime serial, or soap opera, never had such troubles, for sponsors of programs aimed at selling merchandise to house-wives discovered that adding listeners' teardrops to the dishwater was a big business. Daytime serials became the biggest thing in radio, whether you considered them from a standpoint of broadcast time, expenditure of the advertising dollar, listening interest, or effectiveness in selling what the sponsor had to offer.

The average network station by the end of the decade devoted five hours—in fifteen-minute segments—to daytime serials designed to entice women to buy household items. They examined most phases of American life in which dramatic possibilities inhere. One serial dealt with an orphan-age, another with a woman member of Congress, another with a widowed mother seeking a place in the business world, et cetera. The only definite requirement was that it be deeply touching, that each sequel end with a suspenseful situation, that it sell products. The serial writers learned that tragic, heart-stirring events were more gripping than the joyful ones, and a day's listening to the soap operas gave one a distorted view that all is far from well with America and that happiness was an unknown blessing. Some of the most successful and longest-running were "Young Doctor Malone," "Women in White," "Guiding Light," and so on.

At about the same time the daytime serials were beginning to take hold, a different type of late afternoon and early evening serial was finding its way to the airways. These were the kid shows; and in those early years, they were almost entirely of the blood-and-thunder variety. Invariably, these broadcasts were sponsored by advertisers who had something to sell for the household. The psychology was: Sell the kids and let the kids sell their parents. The device employed most effectively was the give-away.

Cereals, dairy products, flashlights all used this type of program effectively. We all remember serials such as "Little Orphan Annie," "Gangbusters," "Jack Armstrong—All American Boy," "The Lone Ranger," and dozens of others. At the end of the show, the announcer would tell his audience that, with each box top or wrapper of a certain product sent in, the sender would receive a badge making him a full-fledged member of the So-and-so Club (linked to the program) or a mask or pocketknife, exact replicas of those used by the character in the serial. Here, again, the advertiser had uncovered an effective means of merchandising, and while kid shows, even at their commercial height, reached only a fractional part of the popularity enjoyed by daytime serials (in 1938, less than five million dollars was spent on such programs), still they were an important part of radio.

Important radio drama came into being only late in the Thirties with the arrival of Orson Welles, Arch Oboler, and Norman Corwin. Radio produced other dramas of course. Dropping the time consumed by daytime serials, approximately 20 per cent of broadcasting time during the earlier years was given over to broadcast drama, but it was of a cut-and-dried pattern. "First Nighter," a weekly show on which boy-meets-girl and boy-gets-girl fifty-two times a year, was also a part of the broadcasting pattern. It was on "First Nighter" that Don Ameche, radio's first matinee idol, achieved recognition. There were many such shows on the air, and for light listening, they served a good purpose. One of the earliest and most successful dramatic shows of this type to hit the air was Louella Parsons' "Hollywood Hotel." The best remembered, perhaps, was Cecil B. De Mille's "Lux Radio Theater."

Arch Oboler's contributions to radio drama were twofold. He was the first writer to successfully employ the stream-of-consciousness type of writing in radio dialogue, and he brought to the air a type of imagery, almost fantasy, with which he clothed even the most realistic themes. Many, since the advent of Oboler, felt that fantasy is perhaps the field to which radio drama may best adapt itself. Oboler, himself, is not one of these. Oboler's writings had a terrifically wide range, perhaps because all radio writers were only a hop, skip and jump ahead of the microphone, which consumed words unmercifully. It was Oboler who wrote the famous lines which caused Mae West's banishment from the air.

"It wasn't the lines," Oboler insisted, "which were bawdy, but her manner of giving them." Then he quoted the lines.

"I want something to happen, a little excitement—a little adventure. A girl's got to have a little fun once in a while. . . . There's no future under a fig tree.

"A couple of months of peace and security and a woman's bored all the way down to the bottom of her marriage certificate. . . . If trouble means something that makes you catch your breath—if trouble means something that makes your blood race through your veins like seltzer water —mmm, Adam, my man, give me trouble!"

Most radio writers and actors worked under a cloak of anonymity, and only occasionally would an Orson Welles or an Arch Oboler or a Norman Corwin come along to rise above that cloak and make a name important.

But the most important dramatic broadcast from an experimental standpoint was a radio show not dominated by any one individual but the Columbia Workshop, where any writer, actor, producer or director with the creative spark might find voice. The Workshop was started as a now-and-then proposition in 1936 and, two years later, had become such an important training station for talent and testing ground for new techniques that it became a regular sustaining feature of the network. The prime importance of this group is that its efforts were directed toward developing radio drama fashioned to the medium rather than the mere adaptation of plays and motion pictures.

Sound, for the Workshop producers and writers, was a special and unique medium of expression, and sound effects on their programs are a composition in their own right. Sound is used to promote thought and emotion and, used this way, may develop into an art quite apart from the field of music.

To the microphones of the Workshop came plays from the pens of William Saroyan and Archibald MacLeish, whose *The Fall of the City* was recognized by critics as one of the best things on radio. Other plays heard on the series include Lord Dunsany's *The Use of Man*; Irving Reis's (Reis was one of the founders and guiding lights of the group) *Meridian 7-1212*; *A Drink of Water*, by Wilbur Daniel Steele; a number of Ambrose Bierce's eerie short stories adapted to the microphone; and Dorothy Parker's *Apartment to Let*.

If the Workshop had made no contribution to dramatic art in broadcasting, its contributions in the field of sound effects would more than justify its existence. *The Fall of the City* was staged in a Los Angeles armory to effect the hollow, reverberating sound which conveys the feel of great space. In *Alice in Wonderland*, during the scene in which Alice fell down the rabbit hole, the hollow sound her voice would have in such a predicament was effected by placing a box over the actress' head. When a man was stabbed on *The Ghost of Benjamin Sweet,* the sound of the dagger striking home was obtained by striking a knife into a watermelon. For a hospital scene, a microphone was actually placed against a man's heart and amplified many times.

But the Workshop's contributions to broadcasting went beyond that. It was in the Workshop that young Orson Welles learned much of his technique for broadcasting, working with Reis and Robson and others who grew up with broadcasting. Here, too, Max Wylie, Douglas Coulter and Davidson Taylor—all important names in radio production—found an opportunity to test ideas which became broadcasting tenets. And while Columbia Workshop was a co-operative affair in which all voices were heard and heeded, it, too, developed dominating individualities at various stages of its growth. Perhaps Norman Corwin was its most important voice.

Corwin was essentially a poet, and his plays were written with a lyrical beauty few other radio writers achieved.

At CBS, Corwin originated, wrote and produced *Words Without Music,* but he didn't come into his own until his rhymed fantasy, *The Plot to Overthrow Christmas,* was aired on Christmas Day, 1938. Audience mail poured into the studio and Corwin was given a free hand to develop his dramatic offerings. Perhaps the best Corwin piece was *They Fly Through the Air with the Greatest of Ease*, which was inspired by Vittorio Mussolini's relish at seeing men and horses in Ethiopia blown up by bombs he dropped. A part of the opening narration follows:

> All right, so it is morning.
>
> It is morning on a level field, still wet with dew;
>
> A field once used for haying, flown over one time by birds going north or birds going south to build homes;
>
> A meadow mowed upon by men, buzzed in by bees, and lingered on by lovers in the moonlight.
>
> Here, where last year stood the windrows of the hay,
>
> Is now such an aviary of birds as God had never dreamed of when He made the skies.
>
> Look close and you will see one now.
>
> They are wheeling it out of the hangar,
>
> Carefully . . .

Easily the most sensational figure in radio drama was Orson Welles.

Here was the man who dressed Julius Caesar in a blue business suit, rewrote Shakespeare (for the WPA theater), and gave Broadway a modern treatise on Fascism which made money. Who, when the WPA authorities decided a half hour before curtain time that he could not put on a labor opera with a leftist tinge: *The Cradle Will Rock*—simply loaded the cast, and costumes, scenery and properties (which belonged to Uncle Sam), along with a piano, into a truck and found a new theater that same evening, and the audience following him like the Pied Piper to the new theater in high glee.

A short time later his Mercury group of players was given a regular Sunday night feature on CBS. It was here that he developed the first-person narrative device for bringing radio drama intimately into the home and, whenever he could, Welles himself served as narrator. Hadn't he got his training as the hideous and insidious laugh in "The Shadow," an earlier radio mystery show, and as a part-time performer on the "March of Time" show? All this served to provide a proper overture to his famous dramatization of H. G. Wells's novel *The War of the Worlds*, which threw the Eastern seaboard of the United States into a complete tizzy. To understand partially why the country reacted so frantically, it is necessary to examine the state of jitters the American public had undergone in the Munich crisis.

September 1938 found a world harassed by the most serious problem since Sarajevo. Radio listeners of the day still remember the twenty days leading to Munich. Those intimately associated with radio—and particularly those in the news departments of the great networks—will never forget them. For during that period, radio—as a news medium—came of age.

Technically, the industry had long been ready to perform the job which the Czech crisis precipitated. In the spring of 1938, the Columbia Broadcasting System, in order to give listeners a better and more intimate picture of the Austrian *Anschluss*, had set up what it called its "European Roundup." Representatives of CBS, as well as newspapermen, stationed in important European capitals, were thus permitted to talk directly with the American listening audience and give on-the-spot interpretations of world-shaking events as they were happening by short-wave radio.

In 1936, radio newsmen, with portable transmitters, had stood among the crowds keeping vigil outside Buckingham Palace to learn of the condition of King George V. When death came for the beloved monarch who had guided his people safely through World War I, NBC was first on the air with the tragic news.

Later, when Edward VIII chose "the woman I love" above the seat of the mighty, his abdication was an epochal event not only in its historical significance and deeply touching nuances, but also because it was the first time that any king, anywhere, had used radio to explain his action.

That year, radio had felt its way, too, amidst shellfire and rattle of machine guns in on-the-spot descriptions of battles being fought between Fascist and Loyalist forces in Spain's Civil War.

In such events as these, newsrooms of the large networks were being molded and tempered and formed. Men like Abe Schechter, NBC's special-events chief, and Paul White, of CBS, had built up their organizations until they covered the world as completely as the city staffs of large daily newspapers covered their own cities. These skilled observers, winnowed through a long trial-and-error process, sat close to their teletype machines on the morning of September 12, 1938, for confidential reports from networks correspondents abroad indicated that *der Tag* was close at hand.

On the surface, and to the average American listener, the stream of American life flowed smoothly enough. Only the Tuesday night before, America had thrilled to a new type of program—"Information Please." The ideal of the program was to stump a board of experts consisting of John Kieran, sports writer; F. P. Adams, conductor of the famous "Conning Tower" column; Oscar Levant, wisecracking musical genius. Learned Clifton Fadiman, literary critic of *The New Yorker* magazine, presided as master of ceremonies. The board—or their guest experts—strove to answer all questions submitted by listeners or pay a cash penalty. Among the program's first guests were Paul de Kruif, scientist-writer; Stuart Chase, economist and author; Marc Connelly, playwright; and John Gunther, journalist and international observer. More than sixty thousand listeners sent in questions for the "Information Please" experts to answer that first week.

But under the surface, dire events were already in the making. On the afternoon of September 12, at two-fifteen, announcers on the various networks interrupted the regularly scheduled programs to announce that the world-awaited talk on Germany's foreign policy to be delivered to the Nazi Congress at Nuremberg by Adolf Hitler was now to be broadcast.

Then, before a fervent assemblage of his followers, Adolf Hitler began, in his guttural, half-hysterical style, an address which was to launch the world upon twenty nerve-racking days, days in which the stream of events flowed from one climax on to another with such rapidity that even the winged words of radio had difficulty in keeping pace. For several months, Hitler's demands upon the Czechs for special rights and privileges for the

Sudeten German minority had been growing. Now, at Nuremberg, in terms which were unmistakable, the Chancellor was to tell the world his latest demands and leave no question of the fact that the full weight of the growing German military machine stood squarely behind each spoken word.

During these twenty days, in more than a thousand broadcasts from important world centers by more than two hundred newsmen, radio followed wherever the finger of history pointed. American listeners heard Adolf Hitler, Neville Chamberlain, Édouard Daladier, Benito Mussolini, Eduard Beneš. Across the troubled lands of Europe journeyed men with microphones—by train, plane, automobile, horse cart. Americans, for the first time, realized how close were London and Prague, Paris and Berlin. They could hear a man breathe in Rome and a paper rustle in Munich. They heard, during these twenty days, broadcasts from Geneva, Nuremberg, Trieste, Stratford-on-Avon, Warsaw, Budapest, Clydebank and Castel Gondolfo. From minute to minute, as the world waited for the armies of Europe to move, American listeners heard—and understood—the development of the growing crisis.

Until Munich, there had been only an apathetic interest in world affairs on the part of the American listening public and commercial sponsors for European broadcasts were unheard of.

After Munich, the networks had little trouble selling news programs to sponsors, but at the moment it is fairly well established that the networks and their associated stations undertook the tremendous task of placing the troubled world in a showcase for its listeners without any idea that, someday, their investment would pay big dividends.

It was four o'clock in the afternoon when Hitler finished speaking. At 4:05 P.M., a news commenator in CBS's New York studios took the air. His name was H. V. Kaltenborn, and while radio listeners up until now were familiar with his voice, perhaps with his name, this tall, dignified master linguist and ad-lib artist was seizing in his two big hands a priceless moment. During the next twenty days, he refused to leave the studio, cat-napping on hard lounges there, having his meals brought in to him, munching on cold sandwiches, sipping black coffee while he studied teletype messages, cables and talked by long-distance telephone across the ocean to CBS newsmen in Europe and Asia. When the twenty days were finished and the peace of Munich had descended upon a still half-trusting world, Kaltenborn's name was a household word throughout America.

Now, grasping the contents of Hitler's spoken words, with only five minutes in which to translate them from German and digest them, Kalten-born went on the air.

"Adolf Hitler has spoken [he told an America which had not yet had time to study and understand the meaning of the address], and the world has listened, because it feared that the speech might mean war. And it may mean war, but not immediate war. Certainly if there is one thing clear in what Hitler has said . . . it is that there is no immediate intention of forcing a crisis. There was nothing in his speech tantamount to an immediate ultimatum. There was in it—and through it—a very definite declaration that Germany would no longer tolerate the oppression, as he called it, of the Sudeten Germans in Czechoslovakia. . . . "

Other networks offered similar analyses following the Nuremberg address, but no other analyst of that period possessed the quick clarity, the easy, fluent manner of Kaltenborn in making complicated declarations—declarations perhaps purposely couched in vague and uncertain terms for the war of nerves Hitler was fighting—simple and understandable to the mass of listeners.

On the evening of September 12, radio's newsmen, speaking from foreign capitals, reported to the American public on reactions of the various peoples concerned. CBS's Ed Murrow, speaking from London, said:

"There is little indication that Herr Hitler's speech this evening has decreased tension here. However, once again the British have demonstrated their ability to fly into a great calm at a time of crisis. . . . Feeling is widespread that the British Government will urge Czechoslovakia to do everything short of dismembering the country to prevent war."

In Berlin, commentators unanimously pointed out that the Germans in the street awaited the speech of their Chancellor with as many fears as did the rest of the world. From Prague, Iowa-born William L Shirer, who had witnessed the Austrian *Anschluss,* told his listeners that President Beneš had listened to the address in the palace, the cabinet members in their private homes and that demonstrations by the Sudeten Germans had been mild, with no arrests, nobody hurt. John T. Whittaker, crack member of the Chicago *Daily News* foreign staff, gave the reaction of the French from Paris:

"When Frenchmen heard what Hitler said about Czechoslovakia's alleged brutality to the Sudeten German minority and about the alleged conspiracy of the democracies against Germany, they smiled. What interests Frenchmen is that, though it was a menacing and provocative speech, it was not precise. . . . "

But on September 13, events moved rapidly as if to counter these opinions. The Czech Government declared martial law in five Sudeten German towns. Fourteen minutes after the communiqué had been handed to American newsmen, American radio listeners knew of it. In London, Prime Minister Chamberlain called his Cabinet to Number Ten Downing Street for a conference. The Sudeten German party delivered an ultimatum to the Czech Government at 7:30 P.M. and twenty-six minutes after the document was delivered, Americans knew of it. The ultimatum demanded that martial law be lifted within six hours.

Late on the afternoon of September 14, with war seemingly minutes away and actual fighting going on in Czechoslovakia, the world was informed in a radio news flash that Prime Minister Chamberlain would fly to Germany next day for a personal interview with Adolf Hitler in a final effort to ward off a European war. Again radio was reporting—and first—a première performance. For the first time in history, the head of a great government would plead personally with another government's leader in a war crisis!

Just before entering the plane, Mr. Chamberlain gave a farewell message to the British people which, as was becoming habit now, was heard also on American radio.

"I am going to see the German Chancellor," he said, "because the situation seems to me one in which discussions between him and me may have a useful consequence and the Fuehrer's reply to my suggestion encourages me to hope that my visit to him will not be without results."

For the first time, Europe was close to America—minutes away. And America was relearning its geography at the loud-speaker (and through "crisis" maps provided by the networks upon request), studying again the history which, a few years back, seemed unimportant and remote. For the echoes of medieval history were still reverberating in the ether waves, and the yellowed pages of dusty tomes on high library shelves came vividly alive in all these broadcasts. The roots of what was happening now had been planted long years ago.

And then, as the affairs of the world reached a most crucial point, something happened to radio. Short-wave transmission, never as perfect or as certain as the ordinary frequencies, can be utterly inaudible when atmospheric conditions are not favorable. Between September 15 and September 30, frequent electric storms over the Atlantic caused such interference that broadcasts did not come through and radio's news departments were forced to rely upon the same overcrowded cables and telephone lines as the

577

newspapers for their news dispatches. This meant that radio, if the storms continued, would be only a short time ahead of the newspapers—the time it took newspapers to set type and print, to be exact.

In this situation, Jack Hartley, of the NBC news staff, ingeniously arranged a circuit for that network which completely confused its opposition for several days and resulted in NBC's scoring several notable beats. He had broadcasts sent to Capetown, South Africa; relayed from there to Buenos Aires, across the South Atlantic; and from Buenos Aires to New York, all by short-wave transmission. Broadcasts traveled three times as far as usual, but arrived only a few seconds later than if they had been sent directly from London or Berlin or Prague to New York.

Reports from Berchtesgaden, where Chamberlain and Hitler were meeting, were meager, trimmed by the fine hand of the German censor. Speculation and rumor—reported as such to listeners—took the place of fact. Then, dramatically, came the cold announcement that Chamberlain would return to London after only a few hours with Hitler. Experts guessed that Hitler's demands were more than Chamberlain could grant.

A reporter for the British Broadcasting Company, who was heard by rebroadcast over American networks at noon, September 16, described the return of Chamberlain to the airport at Heston.

Glancing around the field out in front of the airdrome building he said, "I see Lord Halifax standing there and the German Chargé d'Affaires, Dr. Cross, and a crowd of people talking animatedly down below me . . . and at last the aircraft comes into sight. Now she is right to the southerly side and she is swinging round and she'll come across another full circle of the airdrome and land to the west. It's a tremendously dramatic moment!"

Prime Minister Chamberlain, worn and tired and bearing the umbrella which had already become his peculiar mark, stepped down from the plane and spoke into a microphone.

"I have come back again, rather quicker than I expected," he said, in a weary voice. "Yesterday afternoon I had a long talk with Herr Hitler. It was a frank talk but a friendly one, and I feel satisfied now that each of us understands what is in the mind of the other. You won't, of course, expect me to discuss now what may be the results of that talk. . . . I am going to have another talk with Herr Hitler, only this time he has told me that it is his intention to come halfway to meet me. He wishes to spare an old man another such long journey."

History was being made within earshot of the loud-speaker, and loud-speakers had become standard equipment in almost every American home.

To bring through the air and across thousands of miles of ocean the sound of Europe tearing up her maps was not an easy task despite the facile way in which it seemed to be handled by those who listened in. In Prague, the lobby of the Ambassador Hotel, where diplomats and newsmen gathered, was an indescribable madhouse of rumor, tension and confusion. Radio reporters, with their engineers and technical aides close at hand and ready to go on the air at the drop of a hat—or an ultimatum—milled around, tried to get telephone calls through to the frontier, to Berlin, to the government offices in Prague, itself. One lone Czech switchboard girl bravely strove to keep track of a hundred placed calls.

The six-hour ultimatum given the Czech Government had almost run its course. At about ten o'clock, one of the American correspondents managed to get a call through to his office in Berlin. Nothing was known there of the ultimatum. The German Government was issuing no news at all. A few minutes later, word came through from the first of the correspondents who had rushed up to the Sudeten territory. He said that revolt had broken out there and that police and troops, with machine guns and hand grenades, were striving to keep order.

On one score, all newsmen in Czechoslovakia were agreed: the Czechs were determined to fight to preserve their democracy and, if it became necessary, they would sell their freedom dearly. But the decision taken in Czchoslovakia to fight seemed already to have been voided in London where Chamberlain and Daladier were meeting. Even as the Henlein ultimatum reached its expiration hour, a joint communiqué of the British and French Governments was flashed to the world from London.

"Britain and France have reached complete agreement with regard to a policy aimed at promoting a peaceful solution of the Czechoslovakian question."

The communiqué added that the two governments hoped that thereafter "it will be possible to consider a more general settlement of European peace."

For six days, American radio listeners had watched the crisis grow, were aware of all the fine nuances and shadings behind the verbal barrages laid down in this war of nerves. Informed as perhaps no other people have ever been in such a time of crisis, they realized that the communiqué meant that the allies were prepared to sacrifice Czechoslovakia to save themselves, if Hitler did not demand too much.

Three more tense days of waiting followed. Negotiations upon which the decision—peace or war—hung, took place behind closed doors at the Hotel Dreesen, in Godesberg, where Chamberlain and Hitler held their second meeting. And again their meeting was brought into the sharp focus of the world's eye by radio.

During these days, CBS added a new wrinkle to radio news coverage when it put the two-way conversation (used as an anniversary stunt by NBC three years before) to practical use. Kaltenborn would talk from New York with correspondents in the various world capitals, ask questions, receive answers—and both ends of the conversation were heard instantaneously by American listeners. Radio fans heard from the lips of those on the ground the thoughts and reactions of people who, a short year later, were to be shedding their blood in a bitter war.

Radio men speak of this period as "The Munich Crisis." But in reality, it was a series of crises with one following another in rapid procession. Expiration of the ultimatum and the joint Franco-British communiqué brought one crisis to an end and laid the groundwork for the next which, even now, brewed and boiled behind locked doors at Godesberg.

Then, on the evening of September 23, listeners heard these quiet but dangerous words in an announcement from Godesberg:

"Mr. Chamberlain went to pay a farewell call on Adolf Hitler at ten o'clock tonight, which is five-thirty by New York time. So far, there is no word as to what transpired at this visit. A report throughout Europe is that negotiations between Chamberlain and Hitler are definitely ended."

The following day, Mr. Chamberlain returned to London. War seemed inevitable, hours away, and from Washington, President Roosevelt sent a direct message to Adolf Hitler and President Beneš, of Czechoslovakia, appealing for peaceful negotiation.

On September 27, Kaltenborn informed listeners that Hitler had ordered full mobilization for the following day and that he stood ready to strike on October 1 unless Czechoslovakia acceded to his demands. In London, by the light of flares and automobile headlights, trenches were being dug in the parks. There was a tight, tired look about the eyes of Londoners, and gas masks were being issued by air-raid-precaution men.

Next morning, Mr. Chamberlain reported for the first time to Parliament on his negotiations with Hitler. A running account of his statement, as the words fell from his lips, was being transmitted to the American people by an observer from a vantage point in the House of Commons. And listeners may have noticed in the public speeches of diplomats during this period a quality which had never been contained in even the most important utterances of the past's great statesmen. With Chamberlain—as with Hitler, Mussolini and Beneš—was the certain knowledge that the words he spoke were being heard in all corners of the earth; and that men in high and low places, the peoples of the earth, were passing judgment upon him. His speech was a justification of his efforts, an attempt to show that he had sacrificed dignity in flying to Munich and again to Godesberg, but that no sacrifice was too great if peace could be preserved. It was a skillfully worded plea for the sympathy and support of a world he knew was hanging upon his every word.

Just as he reached the point in his address where he declared that, in spite of all he had been able to do, war seemed inevitable, Sir John Simon handed him a penciled note. Members of Parliament, newsmen, a world that was all but present in the vivid word pictures being painted for it, sensed the importance of the missive and waited breathlessly as he unfolded it and read.

It was an invitation from Hitler to attend a conference the following day in Munich at which representatives of England, Germany, France and Italy would try, by peaceful negotiation, to avert war. Czechoslovakia, the nation most concerned in the negotiations, was significantly omitted from the list of conferring nations.

A scene unprecedented in British Parliamentary history followed. Never before was there such a tumult in the House of Commons. Amid cheers, shouts, crying and waving of papers, Chamberlain, tears streaming down his cheeks, sat down.

The same thorough coverage which had marked earlier developments in the crisis continued at Munich with the teamwork of on-the-spot reporters feeding news to commentators drilled in condensing, clarifying and interpreting it for the mass mind.

Then, suddenly, word came that the conference was about to close and that a protocol had been signed by the four parties. Newsmen and radio men rushed to the hotels where the various delegations were staying to receive their press releases, American reporters going to the British delegation's headquarters. Prior to the breaking up of the conference, however, Jordan, NBC's European news chief, had spoken to Sir William Strang, of the British group, and arranged to receive whatever releases that group made. When word that the conference had broken up and that the Italian delegation was already rushing from the building to catch its train reached the newsmen, they rushed for their waiting cars.

But on the way out, Jordan saw Sir William on the pavement, noticed that Sir Horace Wilson, with Strang, carried prepared releases. He asked for his copy and Strang, taking one from Wilson, handed it to him. Back up the stairs at breakneck speed raced Jordan, but in the improvised broadcasting room, a new difficulty confronted him. The German radio official in charge did not believe that he had an official text of the agreement at first and, later, when he was convinced, didn't like the idea of Jordan broadcasting it to America before the German text had been released to German listeners.

Tearfully, Jordan pleaded; then he became angry and a fist fight almost ensued. But Jordan's eloquence finally won out and, eight minutes after the release had been handed him, it was being heard by American listeners. The NBC broadcast was forty-six minutes ahead of all competition, and listeners tuned to NBC stations knew of the end of the free democracy which was Czechoslovakia before many of the correspondents who were present in Munich!

Statesmen throughout the world hastened to pay tribute to the power of radio. They said that radio, by keeping the world so fully informed, had forced the choice of negotiation upon leaders, who, twenty years before, might well have chosen war.

The palms which were being hung upon radio, as a medium of public information, after Munich were merited, and the developments of the months following Munich and leading to the outbreak of World War II amply bear out this statement. Americans were the best-informed people in the world during those fateful twenty days. Americans knew every move that was made as it was made, enjoyed brilliant interpretations of these moves by students of government and economics and international affairs. But American radio is a competitive and free institution.

What happened abroad?

In England, during the crisis, a prominent magazine recommended that readers who wanted to know the truth about Czechoslovakia should tune to the short-wave broadcasts from American stations! When Winston Churchill wanted to talk about the crisis, the British Broadcasting Company refused to carry his speech, which was heard only in America. When Anthony Eden discussed the subject from London, an American network made his words heard all across America—but not one Englishman, unless tuned to an American station, could hear his voice.

How well the French radio acquainted its listeners with vital facts is best illustrated by an American exchange student at the Sorbonne who, leaving France at the height of the crisis and two days after almost complete mobilization had been ordered, had her first knowledge of the mobilization and the fact that France was on the verge of war after she boarded an American liner.

In Germany, listening to foreign broadcasts had long been a misdemeanor. Hitler's one-tube sets were designed to pick up local signals only, and German listeners heard Nazi party exhortations, tales of Germans being killed and maltreated in Sudetenland and emotional outbursts by Nazi bigwigs.

The twenty nerve-racking days just ended had evidenced the growth to mature stature of radio newscasting. The necessity of the moment had molded into a finely organized and supersensitive sounding board various processes which had been building over eighteen experimental years.

Two weeks after the peace of Munich, radio gave a laboratory demonstration of how heavy that peace hung over the heads of Americans who had followed it from beginning to end; and of how effective the new technique of news broadcasting had become. Orson Welles, youthful writer-producer-director of the Mercury Theater, presented his group in H. G. Wells's *The War of the Worlds,* on Sunday evening, October 30. And to make it vivid, he simulated a news broadcast.

JOHN HOUSEMAN

THE MEN FROM MARS*

RADIO WAR TERRORIZES U.S.—New York *Daily News,* October 31, 1938

Everybody was excited I felt as if I was going crazy and kept on saying what can we do what difference does it make whether we die sooner or later? We were holding each other. Everything seemed unimportant in the face of death. I was afraid to die, just kept on listening.—*A listener*

Nothing about the broadcast was in the least credible.—Dorothy Thompson

THE SHOW came off. There is no doubt about that. It set out to dramatize, in terms of popular apprehension, an attempted invasion of our world by hostile forces from the planet Mars. It succeeded. Of the several million American citizens who, on the evening of October 30, 1938, milled about the streets, clung sobbing to one another or drove wildly in all directions to avoid asphyxiation and flaming death, approximately one-half were in

* From *Harper's* Magazine, December 1948.

terror of Martians—not of Germans, Japanese or unknown enemies—but, specifically, of Martians. Later, when the excitement was over and the shadow of the gallows had lifted, some of us were inclined to take credit for more deliberate and premeditated villainy than we deserved. The truth is that at the time, nobody was more surprised than we were. In fact, one of the most remarkable things about the broadcast was the quite haphazard nature of its birth.

In October 1938, the Mercury Theater, of which Orson Welles and I were the founding partners, had been in existence for less than a year. Our first Broadway season had been shatteringly successful—*Julius Caesar, The Cradle Will Rock, Shoemaker's Holiday,* and *Heartbreak House* in the order of their appearance. In April, Orson, in a straggly white beard, made the cover of *Time* Magazine. In June, the Columbia Broadcasting System offered him a radio show—The Mercury Theater on the Air, a series of classic dramatizations in the first person singular with Orson as master of ceremonies, star, narrator, writer, director and producer. He accepted. So, now, in addition to an empty theater, a movie in progress, two plays in rehearsal, and all seven of the chronicle plays of William Shakespeare in preparation, we had a radio show.

We opened on July 11. Among our first thirteen shows were *Treasure Island, 39 Steps, Abraham Lincoln, Three Short Stories* (by Saki, Sherwood Anderson, and Carl Ewald), *Jane Eyre, Julius Caesar* (with running commentary by Kaltenborn out of Plutarch), and *The Man Who Was Thursday.* Our second series, in the fall, began with Booth Tarkington's *Seventeen, Around the World in Eighty Days,* and *Oliver Twist.* Our fifth show was to be *Life with Father.* Our fourth was *The War of the Worlds.*

No one, as I remember, was very enthusiastic about it. But it seemed good programming, between the terrors of Dickens' London slums, and the charm of Clarence Day's New York in the Nineties, to throw in something of a contrasting and pseudoscientific nature. We thought of Shiel's *Purple Cloud,* Conan Doyle's *Lost World,* and several others before we settled on H. G. Wells's twenty-year-old novel, which neither of us, as it turned out later, remembered at all clearly. It is just possible that neither of us had ever read it.

II

Those were our golden days of unsponsored radio. We had no advertising agency to harass us, no client to cut our withers. Partly because we were perpetually overworked and partly because that was the way we did things at the Mercury, we never seemed to get more than a single jump ahead of ourselves. Shows were created week after week under conditions of soul- and health-destroying pressure. On the whole they were good shows. And we *did* develop a system—of sorts.

It worked as follows: I was editor of the series. With Welles, I chose the shows and then laid them out. The writing, most of it, was done by Howard Koch—earnest, spindly, six-foot-two—a Westchester lawyer turned playwright. To write the first draft of an hour's radio script took him about five days, working about fifteen hours a day. Our associate producer was Paul Stewart, a Broadway actor turned director. His function was to put the broadcast through its first paces and preliminary rehearsals. Every Thursday, musicless and with rudimentary sound effects, a wax record of the show was cut. From this record, played back later that night, Orson would give us his reactions and revisions. In the next thirty-six hours the script would be reshaped and rewritten, sometimes drastically. Saturday afternoon there was another rehearsal, with sound—with or without Welles. It was not until the last day that Orson really took over.

Sundays, at eight, we went on the air. Beginning in the early afternoon— when Bernard Herrmann arrived with his orchestra of twenty-seven high-grade symphony players—two simultaneous dramas were regularly unfolded in the stale, tense air of Studio Number One: the minor drama of the current show and the major drama of Orson's Gargantuan struggle to get it on. Sweating, howling, disheveled, and single-handed he wrestled with Chaos and Time—always conveying an effect of being alone, traduced by his collaborators, surrounded by treachery, ignorance, sloth, indifference, incompetence and—more often than not—downright sabotage! Every Sunday it was touch and go. As the hands of the clock moved relentlessly toward air time the crisis grew more extreme, the peril more desperate. Often violence broke out. Scripts flew through the air, doors were slammed, batons smashed. Scheduled for six—but usually nearer seven—there was a dress rehearsal, a thing of wild improvisations and irrevocable disaster. (One show was found to be twenty-one minutes overlength, another fourteen and one half minutes short.)

After that, with only a few minutes to go, there was a final frenzy of correction and reparation, of utter confusion and absolute horror, aggravated by the gobbling of sandwiches and the bolting of oversized milk shakes. By now it was less than a minute to air time. . . .

At that instant, quite regularly week after week—with not one second to spare . . . the titanic buffoonery stopped. Suddenly out of chaos, the show emerged—delicately poised, meticulously executed, precise as clockwork, and smooth as satin. And above us all, like a rainbow over storm clouds,

stood Orson on his podium, sonorous and heroic, a leader of men surrounded by his band of loyal followers; a giant in action, serene and ra-
diant with the joy of a hard battle bravely fought—a great victory snatched
from the jaws of disaster.

In later years, when the Men from Mars had passed into history, there
was some bickering among members of the Mercury as to who, exactly,
had contributed precisely what, to that particular evening's entertainment.
The truth is that a number of us made a number of essential and incalculable contributions to the broadcast. (Who can accurately assess, for instance,
the part played by Johnny Dietz's perfect engineering, in keeping unbroken
the shifting illusion of imperfect reality? How much did the original old
H. G. Wells, who noisily repudiated us, have to do with it? Or the second
assistant sound man? Or individual actors? Or Dr. Goebbels? Or Charlie
McCarthy?) Orson Welles had virtually nothing to do with the writing of
the script and less than usual to do with its preliminary rehearsals. Yet first
and last it was his creation. If there had been a lynching that night, it is
Welles the outraged populace would have strung up—and rightly so. Orson
was the Mercury. *The War of the Worlds,* like everything we did, was his
show.

Actually, it was a narrow squeak. Those Men from Mars barely escaped
being stillborn. Tuesday afternoon—five days before the show—Howard
Koch telephoned. He was in deep distress. After three days of slaving on
H. G. Wells's scientific fantasy he was ready to give up. Under no circumstances, he declared, could it be made interesting or in any way credible
to modern American ears. Koch was not given to habitual alarmism. To
confirm his fears, Annie, our secretary, came to the phone. She was an
acid and emphatic girl from Smith College with fine blond hair, who
smelled of fading spring flowers. "You can't do it!" she whined. "Those
old Martians are just a lot of nonsense. It's all too silly! We're going to
make fools of ourselves! Absolute fools!"

For some reason which I do not clearly remember our only possible
alternative for that week was a dreary one—*Lorna Doone.* I tried to reach
Welles. He was at the theater and wouldn't come to the phone.

The reason he wouldn't come to the phone was that he was in his
thirty-sixth successive hour of dress-rehearsing *Danton's Death,* a beautiful, fragmentary play by Georg Buechner out of which Max Reinhardt, in
an augmented form, had made a successful mass-spectacle in the Twenties.
Not to be outdone, Orson had glued seventeen hundred masks on to the
back wall of the Mercury Theater, and ripped out the entire stage. Day
after day actors fell headlong into the rat-ridden basement, leaped on and

586

off erratically moving elevators, and chanted the "Carmagnole" in chorus under the supervision of Marc Blitzstein.

Unable to reach Welles, I called Koch back. I was severe. I taxed him with defeatism. I gave him false comfort. I promised to come up and help. When I finally got there—around two the next morning—things were better. He was beginning to have fun laying waste the State of New Jersey. Annie had stopped grinding her teeth. We worked all night and through the next day. Wednesday at sunset the script was finished.

Thursday, as usual, Paul Stewart rehearsed the show, then made a record. We listened to it rather gloomily, long after midnight in Orson's room at the St. Regis, sitting on the floor because all the chairs were covered with coils of unrolled and unedited film. We agreed it was a dull show. We all felt its only chance of coming off lay in emphasizing its newscast style— its simultaneous, eyewitness quality.

All night we sat up, spicing the script with circumstantial allusions and authentic detail. Friday afternoon it went over to CBS to be passed by the network censor. Certain name alterations were requested. Under protest and with a deep sense of grievance we changed the Hotel Biltmore to a nonexistent Park Plaza, Trans-America to Intercontinent, the Columbia Broadcasting Building to Broadcasting Building. Then the script went over to mimeograph and we went to bed. We had done our best and, after all, a show is just a show. . . .

Saturday afternoon Paul Stewart rehearsed with sound effects but without Welles. He worked for a long time on the crowd scenes, the roar of cannon echoing in the Watchung Hills and the sound of New York Harbor as the ships with the last remaining survivors put out to sea.

Around six we left the studio. Orson, phoning from the theater a few minutes later to find out how things were going, was told by one of the CBS sound men, who had stayed behind to pack up his equipment, that it was not one of our better shows. Confidentially, the man opined, it just didn't come off. Twenty-seven hours later, quite a few of his employers would have found themselves a good deal happier if he had turned out to be right.

III

On Sunday, October 30, at 8:00 P.M., E.S.T., in a studio littered with coffee cartons and sandwich paper, Orson swallowed a second container of pineapple juice, put on his earphones, raised his long white fingers and threw the cue for the Mercury theme—the Tchaikovsky Piano Concerto in B Flat Minor #1. After the music dipped, there were routine introductions—then the announcement that a dramatization of H. G. Wells's famous novel, *The War of the Worlds,* was about to be performed. Around 8:01 Orson began to speak, as follows:

WELLES

We know now that in the early years of the twentieth century this world was being watched closely by intelligences greater than man's and yet as mortal as his own. We know now that as human beings busied themselves about their various concerns they were scrutinized and studied, perhaps almost as narrowly as a man with a microscope might scrutinize the transient creatures that swarm and multiply in a drop of water. With infinite complacence people went to and fro over the earth about their little affairs, serene in the assurance of their dominion over this small spinning fragment of solar driftwood which by chance or design man has inherited out of the dark mystery of Time and Space. Yet across an immense ethereal gulf minds that are to our minds as ours are to the beasts in the jungle, intellects vast, cool, and unsympathetic regarded this earth with envious eyes and slowly and surely drew their plans against us. In the thirty-ninth year of the twentieth century came the great disillusionment.

It was near the end of October. Business was better. The war scare was over. More men were back at work. Sales were picking up. On this particular evening, October 30, the Crossley service estimated that thirty-two million people were listening in on their radios. . . .

Neatly, without perceptible transition, he was followed on the air by an anonymous announcer caught in a routine bulletin:

ANNOUNCER

. . . for the next twenty-four hours not much change in temperature. A slight atmospheric disturbance of undetermined origin is reported over Nova Scotia, causing a low pressure area to move down rather rapidly over the northeastern states, bringing a forecast of rain, accompanied by winds of light gale force. Maximum temperature 66; minimum 48. This weather report comes to you from the Government Weather Bureau. . . . We now take you to the Meridian Room in the Hotel Park Plaza in downtown New York, where you will be entertained by the music of Ramon Raquello and his orchestra.

At which cue, Bernard Herrmann led the massed men of the CBS house orchestra in a thunderous rendition of "La Cumparsita." The entire hoax might well have exploded there and then—but for the fact that hardly anyone was listening. They were being entertained by Charlie McCarthy—then at the height of his success.

The Crossley census, taken about a week before the broadcast, had given us 3.6 per cent of the listening audience to Edgar Bergen's 34.7 per cent. What the Crossley Institute (that hireling of the advertising agencies) deliberately ignored, was the healthy American habit of dial-twisting. On that particular evening, Edgar Bergen in the person of Charlie McCarthy temporarily left the air about 8:12 P.M., E.S.T., yielding place to a new and not very popular singer. At that point, and during the following minutes, a large number of listeners started twisting their dials in search of other entertainment. Many of them turned to us—and when they did, they stayed put! For by this time the mysterious meteorite had fallen at Grovers Mill in New Jersey, the Martians had begun to show their foul leathery heads above the ground, and the New Jersey State Police were racing to the spot. Within a few minutes people all over the United States were praying, crying, fleeing frantically to escape death from the Martians. Some remembered to rescue loved ones, others telephoned farewells or warnings, hurried to inform neighbors, sought information from newspapers or radio stations, summoned ambulances and police cars.

The reaction was strongest at points nearest the tragedy—in Newark, New Jersey, in a single block, more than twenty families rushed out of their houses with wet handkerchiefs and towels over their faces. Some began moving household furniture. Police switchboards were flooded with calls inquiring, "Shall I close my windows?" "Have the police any extra gas masks?" Police found one family waiting in the yard with wet cloths on faces contorted with hysteria. As one woman reported later:

I was terribly frightened. I wanted to pack and take my child in my arms, gather up my friends and get in the car and just go north as far as we could. But what I did was just sit by one window, praying, listening, and scared stiff, and my husband by the other sniffling and looking out to see if people were running. . . .

In New York hundreds of people on Riverside Drive left their homes ready for flight. Bus terminals were crowded. A woman calling up the Dixie Bus Terminal for information said impatiently, "Hurry, please, the world is coming to an end and I have a lot to do."

In the parlor churches of Harlem evening service became "end of the world" prayer meetings. Many turned to God in that moment:

I held a crucifix in my hand and prayed while looking out of my open window for falling meteors. . . . When the monsters were wading across the Hudson River and coming into New York, I wanted to run up on my roof to see what they looked like, but I couldn't leave my radio while it was telling me of their whereabouts.

Aunt Grace began to pray with Uncle Henry. Lily got sick to her stomach. I don't know what I did exactly but I know I prayed harder and more earnestly than ever before. Just as soon as we were convinced that this thing was real, how petty all things on this earth seemed; how soon we put our trust in God!

The panic moved upstate. One man called up the Mt. Vernon Police

Headquarters to find out "where the forty policemen were killed." Another took time out to philosophize:

I thought the whole human race was going to be wiped out—that seemed more important than the fact that we were going to die. It seemed awful that everything that had been worked on for years was going to be lost forever.

In Rhode Island weeping and hysterical women swamped the switchboard of the Providence *Journal* for details of the massacre, and officials of the electric light company received a score of calls urging them to turn off all lights so that the city would be safe from the enemy. The Boston *Globe* received a call from one woman "who could see the fire." A man in Pittsburgh hurried home in the midst of the broadcast and found his wife in the bathroom, a bottle of poison in her hand, screaming, "I'd rather die this way than that." In Minneapolis a woman ran into church screaming, "New York destroyed this is the end of the world. You might as well go home to die I just heard it on the radio."

The Kansas City Bureau of the Associated Press received inquiries about the "meteors" from Los Angeles; Salt Lake City; Beaumont, Texas; and St. Joseph, Missouri. In San Francisco the general impression of listeners seemed to be that an overwhelming force had invaded the United States from the air—was in process of destroying New York and threatening to move westward. "My God," roared an inquirer into a telephone, "where can I volunteer my services, we've got to stop this awful thing!"

As far south as Birmingham, Alabama, people gathered in churches and prayed. On the campus of a Southeastern college—

The girls in the sorority houses and dormitories huddled around their radios trembling and weeping in each other's arms. They separated themselves from their friends only to take their turn at the telephones to make long distance calls to their parents, saying goodbye for what they thought might be the last time. . . .

There are hundreds of such bits of testimony, gathered from coast to coast.

IV

At least one book* and quite a pile of sociological literature has appeared on the subject of "The invasion from Mars." Many theories have been put forward to explain the "tidal wave" of panic that swept the nation. I know of two factors that largely contributed to the broadcast's extraordinarily violent effect. First, its historical timing. It came within thirty-five days of the Munich crisis. For weeks, the American people had been hanging on

---

* *The Invasion from Mars* by Hadley Cantril, Princeton University Press, from which many of the above quotations were taken.

their radios, getting most of their news no longer from the press, but over the air. A new technique of "on-the-spot" reporting had been developed and eagerly accepted by an anxious and news-hungry world. The Mercury Theater on the Air by faithfully copying every detail of the new technique —including its imperfections—found an already enervated audience ready to accept its wildest fantasies. The second factor was the show's sheer technical brilliance. To this day it is impossible to sit in a room and hear the scratched, worn, off-the-air recording of the broadcast without feeling in the back of your neck some slight draft left over from that great wind of terror that swept the nation. Even with the element of credibility totally removed it remains a surprisingly frightening show.

Radio drama was taken seriously in the Thirties—before the Quiz and the Giveaway became the lords of the air. In the work of such directors as Reis, Corwin, Fickett, Welles, Robson, Spier and Oboler there was an eager, excited drive to get the most out of this new, all too rapidly freezing medium. But what happened that Sunday, up on the twentieth floor of the CBS building, was something quite special. Beginning around two, when the show started to take shape under Orson's hands, a strange fever seemed to invade the studio—part childish mischief, part professional zeal.

First to feel it were the actors. I remember Frank Readick (who played the part of Carl Phillips, the network's special reporter) going down to the record library and digging up the Morrison recording of the explosion of the Hindenburg at Lakehurst. This is a classic reportage—one of those wonderful, unpredictable accidents of eyewitness description. The broadcaster is casually describing a routine landing of the giant gasbag. Suddenly he sees something. A flash of flame! An instant later the whole thing explodes. It takes him time—a full second—to react at all. Then seconds more of sputtering ejaculations before he can make the adjustment between brain and tongue. He starts to describe the terrible things he sees—the writhing human figures twisting and squirming as they fall from the white burning wreckage. He stops, fumbles, vomits, then quickly continues. Readick played the record to himself, over and over. Then, re-creating the emotion in his own terms, he described the Martian meteorite as he saw it lying inert and harmless in a field at Grovers Mills, lit up by the headlights of a hundred cars—the coppery cylinder suddenly opening, revealing the leathery tentacles and the terrible pale-eyed faces of the Martians within. As they begin to emerge he freezes, unable to translate his vision into words; he fumbles, retches—and then after a second continues.

A few moments later Carl Phillips lay dead, tumbling over the microphone in his fall—one of the first victims of the Martian Ray. There followed a moment of absolute silence—an eternity of waiting. Then, without warning, the network's emergency fill-in was heard—somewhere in a quiet studio, a piano, close on mike, playing "Clair de Lune," soft and sweet as honey, for many seconds, while the fate of the universe hung in the balance. Finally it was interrupted by the manly reassuring voice of Brigadier General Montgomery Smith, Commander of the New Jersey State Militia, speaking from Trenton, and placing "the counties of Mercer and Middlesex as far west as Princeton and east to Jamesburg" under Martial Law! Tension—release—then renewed tension. For soon after that came an eyewitness account of the fatal battle of the Watchung Hills; and then, once again, that lone piano was heard—now a symbol of terror, shattering the dead air with its ominous tinkle. As it played, on and on, its effect became increasingly sinister—a thin band of suspense stretched almost beyond endurance.

That piano was the neatest trick of the show—a fine specimen of the theatrical "retard," boldly conceived and exploited to the full. It was one of the many devices with which Welles succeeded in compelling not merely the attention, but also the belief of his invisible audience. *The War of the Worlds* was a magic act, one of the world's greatest, and Orson was just the man to bring it off.

For Welles is at heart a magician whose particular talent lies not so much in his creative imagination (which is considerable) as in his proven ability to stretch the familiar elements of theatrical effect far beyond their normal point of tension. For this reason his productions require more elaborate preparation and more perfect execution than most. At that—like all complicated magic tricks—they remain, till the last moment, in a state of precarious balance. When they come off, they give—by virtue of the unusually high intensity—an impression of great brilliance and power; when they fail—when something in their balance goes wrong or the original structure proves to have been unsound—they provoke, among their audience, a particularly violent reaction of unease and revulsion. Welles's flops are louder than other men's. The Mars broadcast was one of his unqualified successes.

Among the columnists and public figures who discussed the affair during the next few days (some praising us for the public service we had rendered, some condemning us as sinister scoundrels) the most general reaction was one of amazement at the "incredible stupidity" and "gullibility" of the American public, who had accepted as real, in this single broadcast, incidents which in actual fact would have taken days or even weeks to occur. "Nothing about the broadcast," wrote Dorothy Thompson with her usual

Martians, tall as skyscrapers, were astride the Pulaski Highway preparatory to wading the Hudson River. To us in the studio the show seemed to be progressing splendidly—how splendidly Davidson Taylor had just learned outside. For several minutes now, a kind of madness had seemed to be sweeping the continent—somehow connected with our show. The CBS switchboards had been swamped into uselessness but from outside sources vague rumors were coming in of deaths and suicides and panic injuries.

Taylor had requests to interrupt the show immediately with an explanatory station-announcement. By now the Martians were across the Hudson and gas was blanketing the city. The end was near. We were less than a minute from the Station Break. The organ was allowed to swirl out under the slackening fingers of its failing organist and Ray Collins, superb as the "last announcer," choked heroically to death on the roof of Broadcasting Building. The boats were all whistling for a while as the last of the refugees perished in New York Harbor. Finally, as they died away, an amateur short-wave operator was heard, from heaven knows where, weakly reaching out for human companionship across the empty world:

> 2X2L Calling CQ
> 2X2L Calling CQ
> 2X2L Calling CQ
> Isn't there anyone on the air?
> Isn't there anyone?

Five seconds of absolute silence. Then, shattering the reality of World's End—the Announcer's voice was heard, suave and bright:

ANNOUNCER

You are listening to the CBS presentation of Orson Welles and the Mercury Theater on the Air in an original dramatization of *The War of the Worlds*, by H. G. Wells. The performance will continue after a brief intermission.

The second part of the show was extremely well written and most sensitively played—but nobody heard it. It recounted the adventures of a lone survivor, with interesting observations on the nature of human society; it described the eventual death of the Martian Invaders, slain—"after all man's defenses had failed by the humblest thing that God in his wisdom had put upon this earth"—by bacteriological action; it told of the rebuilding of a brave new world. After a stirring musical finale, Welles, in his own person, delivered a charming informal little speech about Halloween, which it happened to be.

I remember, during the playing of the final theme, the phone starting to ring in the control room and a shrill voice through the receiver announcing itself as belonging to the mayor of some Midwestern city, one of the big ones. He is screaming for Welles. Choking with fury, he reports mobs in the streets of his city, women and children huddled in the churches, violence and looting. If, as he now learns, the whole thing is nothing but a crummy joke—then he, personally, is coming up to New York to punch the author of it on the nose! Orson hangs up quickly. For we are off the air now and the studio door bursts open. The following hours are a nightmare. The building is suddenly full of people and dark blue uniforms. We are hurried out of the studio, downstairs, into a back office. Here we sit incommunicado while network employees are busily collecting, destroying, or locking up all scripts and records of the broadcast. Then the press is let loose upon us, ravening for horror. How many deaths have *we* heard of? (Implying they know of thousands.) What do *we* know of the fatal stampede in a Jersey hall? (Implying it is one of many.) What traffic deaths? (The ditches must be choked with corpses.) The suicides? (Haven't you heard about the one on Riverside Drive?) It is all quite vague in my memory and quite terrible.

Hours later, instead of arresting us, they let us out a back way. We scurry down to the theater like hunted animals to their hole. It is surprising to see life going on as usual in the midnight streets, cars stopping for traffic, people walking. At the Mercury the company is still stoically rehearsing—falling downstairs and singing the "Carmagnole." Welles goes up on stage, where photographers, lying in wait, catch him with his eyes raised up to heaven, his arms outstretched in an attitude of crucifixion. Thus he appeared in a tabloid that morning over the caption, "I Didn't Know What I Was DOING!" The New York *Times* quoted him as saying, "I don't think we will choose anything like this again."

We were on the front page for two days. Having had to bow to radio as a news source during the Munich crisis, the press was now only too eager to expose the perilous irresponsibilities of the new medium. Orson was their whipping boy. They quizzed and badgered him. Condemnatory editorials were delivered by our press-clipping bureau in bushel baskets. There was talk, for a while, of criminal action.

Then gradually, after about two weeks, the excitement subsided. By then it had been discovered that the casualties were not as numerous or as serious as had at first been supposed. One young woman had fallen and broken her arm running downstairs. Later the Federal Communications Commission held some hearings and passed some regulations. The Columbia Broadcasting System made a public apology. With that the offical aspects of the incident were closed.

As to the Mercury—our new play, *Danton's Death,* finally opened after five postponements. Not even our fantastic publicity was able to offset its generally unfavorable notices. On the other hand, that same week the Mercury Theater on the Air was signed up by Campbell Soups at a most lavish figure.

Of the suits that were brought against us—amounting to over three quarters of a million dollars for damages, injuries, miscarriages and distresses of various kinds—none was substantiated or legally proved. We did settle one claim, however, against the advice of our lawyers. It was the particularly affecting case of a man in Massachusetts, who wrote:

"I thought the best thing to do was to go away. So I took three dollars twenty-five cents out of my savings and bought a ticket. After I had gone sixty miles I knew it was a play. Now I don't have money left for the shoes I was saving up for. Will you please have someone send me a pair of black shoes size 9B!"

We did.

NO RISKS, NO COMMITMENTS

THE POSITION of the United States in world power politics in the 1930s was not one of leadership, as it is to-day; there was plenty of opportunity to influence the squabbling countries in Europe, but F.D.R.'s attitude was apt to be "watch and worry." Personally, F.D.R. was intensely interested but, as James MacGregor Burns says, he was "unwilling to throw his weight into the balance, [he] was still confined to a policy of pinpricks and righteous protest. No risks, no commitments, was the motto of the White House." *

In Burns's judgment, F.D.R. had opportunities to reorient the people's fear of war and "direct it toward internationalist policies" rather than allow the drift to continue toward isolationism.

But as one remembers the state of the country at the time, with its neutrality debates and pacifist sentiment, it is doubtful that public opinion could have been changed substan-

tially. In 1937 over a half-million college students reputedly signed a pledge not to support the United States in the event of war. And in a poll taken in the same year, nineteen out of twenty people answered "No" to the question, Should the U.S. enter another war?

Also, one is apt to forget the national distaste, prevalent at that time, for military spending. According to Fortune, the United States Army on June 30, 1935, consisted of "165,000 men, 67 generals, enough rifles for one regiment, and a handful of effective tanks." † Next year the Army's plans for expansion via new equipment were limited to purchasing another 1,870 rifles.

It all seems like a bad dream now; but to the men who would have to fight the delaying actions in the Pacific in 1941 and 1942, the American people must have seemed the prize idiots of all time.

How did we get that way?

DEXTER PERKINS

THE RELUCTANT WORLD POWER‡

THERE HAVE BEEN periods in the history of the United States when foreign policy occupied a subordinate place, but the age of Roosevelt was not one of them. Withdrawal or participation—that was the choice confronting the

* J. M. Burns's *The Lion and the Fox.*
† "Who's in the Army Now?" *Fortune,* October 1935.
‡ Condensed from Dexter Perkins' *The New Age of Franklin Roosevelt* (Chicago, University of Chicago Press, 1957).

American people. They began by wishing to evade all responsibility for the world outside their borders. They ended by accepting responsibility as a major world power. The America of 1933 turned in on itself. The story of this change is central and fundamental to an understanding of the times.

We begin with what has been called American isolationism, but behind the conduct of nations, as behind the conduct of individuals, lies an emotional state, which, as a rule, transcends the logical processes by which it is justified. To put the matter another way, the mood of a nation is often as important as its opinions; public sentiment is often as important as public judgment.

There were many reasons why the United States should be isolationist in 1933. The Great Depression itself was the best of all reasons. Confronting the most serious problems of internal adjustment that they had ever faced, the American people were reluctant to project their gaze beyond the seas. It was easier to ignore overseas events because, of all the great nations, America had the most naïve view of the role of force in international affairs. The nation had risen to greatness without engaging in large-scale war, and "power politics" in the European sense had played very little part in the process. Without experience in this field, Americans viewed the competitions of Europe as a sinister game which they neither desired nor felt compelled to play. Moreover, the experience of intervention in World War I had not been a particularly enheartening one. The generation most influential politically in the Thirties had seen the idealistic program of Woodrow Wilson roughly handled at Paris; it had seen selfishness supplant altruism; and it had seen, just as President Roosevelt entered office, the nations of the Old World repudiate their indebtedness to the United States. Had Americans crossed the seas in 1917 and 1918, given money and blood for the relief of Europe from German oppression, only to come to this result? The complaint could be, and was, pushed further. Since scapegoats are always useful in this world, it was easy to believe, as President Hoover believed, that America would have emerged much sooner from the Depression if it had not been for the European economic crisis of 1931, if the wrangling nations of the Old World had not deepened their own economic difficulties by political rivalries, if they had not intensified their own misery by folly and the game of power. And, on top of all this, there subsisted, as there still subsists today, the notion that there is something unique about the political and economic order of the United States and that only contamination could come from closer association with the wicked world outside American borders.

In his inaugural address President Roosevelt had defined his foreign policy as the policy of the "good neighbor." The phrase was meant to have a universal and not a restricted geographical application, but it was so pat a description of his course of action in the Western Hemisphere that it soon became closely identified with that area. Here, as in other matters, Roosevelt sensed the public mood and translated it into action.

In his policy toward Latin America Roosevelt was much assisted by his two principal aides in the field of foreign affairs. Cordell Hull, the Secretary of State from 1933 to 1944, was precisely the kind of man to become enthusiastic over the good-neighbor policy. There have been few secretaries of state so prone to think in abstract principles, so attached to broad formulas of action, so persistent in expressing American policy in terms of aspirations and ideals. Possibly this was so because his grasp of facts and his experience were limited when he came to office. Moreover, Hull had been a devoted follower of Woodrow Wilson. Despite Wilson's lapses from idealism in his dealings with the republics to the south, the spirit of his diplomacy had often reflected that regard for the rights of other states which was to become an essential element in the diplomacy of the new Administration. Hull found in his memories of the past a strong support for the policies which he was to put into action.

But another figure strongly influenced the development of United States relations with Latin America. Sumner Wells, the Under-Secretary of State, had been, long before 1933, a sturdy opponent of the interventions in the Caribbean. At a time when interest in Latin-American affairs was at a somewhat low ebb among professional diplomats, he had made a specialty of these matters and had been chief of the Latin-American Affairs Division of the Department of State in 1921-22. He had gone to the same private school as the President, and to the same university as well. More sophisticated than Hull, closer to Roosevelt personally, ambitious and vigorous, he was a person to be reckoned with even at the outset, when he was only an assistant secretary. And though he and Hull were frequently to be at swords' points in the ten years of their association, though the President's habit of bypassing the Secretary of State was to introduce a painful element into the relations of Hull and Welles, each supplemented the other in our dealings with the republics to the south. Welles knew much more than Hull; but Hull, as a veteran politician and a former congressman and senator, was better qualified to translate the policy of the Administration into terms that could be understood and appreciated on Capitol Hill.

What was the essence of the good-neighbor policy? The root principle was the principle of noninterference in the affairs of independent states. It would, however, have been one thing to enunciate this principle in general terms; it was an entirely different matter to incorporate it in a formal diplomatic document. The Latin-American states had clamored for such a commitment at the Pan-American conference at Havana in 1928; and it had needed all the lawyerlike ability and diplomatic skill of Charles Evans Hughes to stave off action. But at the conference of Montevideo in 1933 and again at Buenos Aires in 1936, Secretary Hull gave them what they asked for. His manners and methods in dealing with the sometimes sticky pride of Latin-American diplomats were widely applauded; even the vainest of foreign ministers, Saavedra Lamas of Argentina, succumbed to his homely charm; and at home the Secretary had the satisfaction of seeing the agreements that he signed ratified unanimously by the Senate. Moreover, the United States gave early proof of its sincerity. In spite of great temptation, on account of the large American interests involved, it made no move toward intervention when a somewhat radical regime arose in Cuba; and, in 1934, when that regime was succeeded by a more conservative one, the United States agreed to the abrogation of the Platt amendment by which, as far back as 1901, it had reserved the right to intervene in the affairs of the island. In 1934 came the evacuation of Haiti and the departure of the last of the marines from the soil of any independent state. In 1936 an agreement with Panama ended American tutelage of that republic.

A second principle of the good-neighbor policy was inter-American co-operation. At Buenos Aires the nations of the New World (Argentina reluctantly consenting) agreed to consult together in the event of an international war "which might menace the peace of the American hemisphere." Two years later machinery was provided to carry this pledge into effect, and on this second occasion, at Lima, a resounding declaration of American principles was adopted.

A third aspect of the good-neighbor policy was the lowering of trade barriers. This was a favorite idea of Secretary Hull. Unsuccessful in imposing it on the President in 1933, Hull continued to press for action, and the result was the Reciprocal Trade Agreement Act of 1934 which authorized a 50 per cent reduction of tariff duties by presidential action in understandings with other states. To such a country as Cuba, heavily dependent on the American market, this was a decided boon.

Finally, the good-neighbor policy was characterized by a remarkable tolerance toward the economic policies of the Latin-American republics. The Administration stood aloof from the controversies raised by the defaults of many of these republics on their debts, and it pursued a most restrained policy when they handled American interests roughly. When, for example, the Bolivian government expropriated the holdings of the Standard Oil Company in Bolivia, the State Department raised no great protest. And when, in a measure much more far-reaching in effect, the Mexican government followed the same course, no particular outcry came from Washington, though a very limited settlement of American claims was made in 1940. When America entered the war in 1941, it was to reap its rewards in the remarkable solidarity of the American states.

The successes of American policy toward Latin America were hardly matched either in Asia or in Europe. In our outstanding controversy with Japan the President could hardly retreat from the position assumed by his predecessor, namely, that the United States would not recognize the new situation created by the Japanese occupation of Manchuria. But neither could he take positive action of any kind. The country was in no mood for a policy of adventure, and Roosevelt reflected the mood.

The temper of American opinion with regard to the Far East in these years was shown by the strong desire manifested in Congress to get out of the Philippines. It was in consonance with American promises and American ideals that the islands should some day receive their independence, but the movement in this direction in the Thirties was motivated by no such lofty conceptions. A combination of interests, especially the beet-sugar interests, which suffered from Filipino competition, and of isolationists who hoped for an abdication of responsibility in the Far East was responsible for the bill that passed Congress in 1934. In the course of the debate the argument was frequently used that the islands represented a dangerous commitment on which the American taxpayer would never be willing to make good. The independence measure provided for the withdrawal of the United States from its military bases at the end of ten years and left for future discussion the question of naval bases. In the meantime Congress neglected the defenses of Guam, the island outpost in the Pacific.

The Administration by no means entirely consented to the course of events in the Orient. Hull, according to his custom, addressed numerous moral homilies to the Japanese government, which, however eloquent, changed not a tittle the actual posture of affairs. The President sought ever larger and larger appropriations for the Navy, and by 1936–37 and 1937–38 these had become the greatest in history. In the fall of 1937, moreover, he sought to arouse American opinion. Speaking in the Middle West, in the midst of the region most isolationist in sentiment, he declared that "peace-loving nations" must "make a concerted effort in opposition to those violations of treaties and those ignorings of humane instincts which are today creating a state of international anarchy and instability from which there is no escape through mere isolation or neutrality." War, he went on to argue, must be quarantined like an epidemic disease. But it is no exaggeration to say that the speech fell flat, and the President himself seemed to skate away from any concrete application of his formula when press correspondents sought to elicit further information as to his intentions.

If it was not easy to rouse the American public where flagrant aggression had already taken place and where the interests of the United States were clearly menaced, it is not surprising that the Roosevelt Administration made no great effort to shape its European policy along lines of co-operative effort. Both in the field of armaments and in the field of economic policy, the President and his advisers were powerless to check the ominous course of events.

In the matter of armaments the situation was this. For some time Germany, disarmed by the treaty of Versailles, had been clamoring for the lifting of the restrictions on its armed forces. A conference had been convened in 1932 and was again in session in the spring of 1933. The French, justly suspicious of the great power across the Rhine, and especially of the new Reich of Adolf Hitler, wished some kind of guaranty against aggression in exchange for a grant of permission to the Germans to expand their military establishment. But such a guaranty was impossible for the United States to give. The utmost that the President could do was to declare, through his special representative Norman Davis, that in case the League of Nations applied sanctions against Germany, the United States would not interfere with such sanctions. Such a statement was pitifully inadequate to meet the situation. When, shortly after the Roosevelt offer, Germany abandoned the conference and a few months later withdrew from the League, it was clear that a new period of arms competition was at hand. The most farsighted observers already saw the dangers in the path ahead.

In March 1934, the magazine *Fortune* published a sensational article on the armaments business. Most of what it had to say concerned the tie-up between European arms manufacturers and politicians, often an unpleasant story. But the activity of the American steel companies at the Geneva naval conference of 1927 was also recalled. Hard on the appearance of this article the Senate voted to investigate the arms traffic. By a curious mental operation on the part of Senator Pittman, who was the chairman of the Foreign Affairs Committee, Senator Nye of North Dakota, a Republican of distinctly isolationist slant, was chosen to direct the inquiry. The chief investigator and informal counsel for the committee was Stephen Raushenbush, and under his spur the investigation went far beyond its original purpose. The policies of the Woodrow Wilson Administration were sharply criticized, and the thesis that American entry into the war was the work of wicked Wall Street bankers, aided and abetted by sinister arms barons, gained headway accordingly with American public opinion. The thesis, it is worthwhile to remark, was unsound. But in public affairs it is not the accuracy but the force of a belief that counts, and there can be little doubt that the tide was running strongly toward revisionism in 1934 and 1935.

In such circumstances Congress reacted in vigorous fashion to the drift of public opinion. Cordell Hull, with his Wilsonian background, was by no means enthusiastic about what began to be called "neutrality legislation," but President Roosevelt, opportunist politician that he often was, made no attempt to stem the developing movement. The first discussions turned on an embargo against the munitions traffic in time of war. Such an embargo, framed in absolute terms, was sure to benefit the most heavily armed and therefore, in all probability, the aggressor nation, and it would run squarely athwart any coercive action by the League of Nations against a law-breaking state. In the House these considerations had weight, and the imposition of the embargo was left to the discretion of the President, but the Senate took the bit in its teeth, and, in its final form, the arms legislation left no choice to the executive but to apply the prohibition on arms export to all nations at war without distinction. The President, aware of the strength of congressional feeling, signed the law with a commentary on its provisions and the expression of a hope that "more permanent legislation might provide for greater flexibility." He was later very much to regret his action.

The temper of Congress in the session of 1935 was demonstrated in another fashion. For a period of more than a decade the question of American adhesion to the protocol setting up the World Court had been much discussed. Nothing could have been more innocent than this proposal; for the court was a court of voluntary jurisdiction, and action on the protocol did not bind the United States to submit any specific question whatsoever to the international tribunal. Yet, from its first appearance in 1923, the court issue seemed to rouse substantial opposition. The court judges were elected by League machinery, and to the foes of the League, including such powerful senators as Borah, this alone was enough to condemn the whole idea. In 1926 the Senate had ratified the protocol but with reservations that proved distasteful to the many nations who had accepted the court. Painful negotiation followed on the reservations, and, when accord was reached, long delay followed on that accord. It was not until the spring of 1935 that the new agreement came before the Senate for ratification. And then occurred a most astounding phenomenon. A flood of protests swept into Washington, spearheaded by the nationalistic publisher William

Randolph Hearst and by Father Coughlin. Some 200,000 telegrams came to senators in a few days—40,000 in a single day—all of them expressing bitter opposition to the court. In the face of such a demonstration the Senate capitulated. The protocol failed of ratification by a vote of 52 to 36. Very rarely has a vote been accompanied by so much unreason.

Throughout the debate on the court the President had maintained an indifferent attitude. He had no mind to breast the tide of sentiment; the vote on the subject only confirmed the Administration in its extremely cautious attitude with regard to the whole problem of neutrality. This circumspection was soon to be demonstrated in a matter of far greater significance.

The League of Nations had been powerless to check the aggression of Japan. In 1935 and 1936 it was to be put to a new test. The Italian dictator Benito Mussolini had for some time coveted Ethiopia. Five days after the Italian troops crossed the frontier, the League Council found by a unanimous vote that Italy had violated the Covenant and committed an act of aggression. On November 18 the members of the League, acting with extraordinary accord, declared an arms embargo, an embargo on credits, a ban on Italian imports, and a partial ban on exports. But there was a serious weakness in its operations. The most vital of all exports to Italy was oil. And this the Italians were allowed to continue to buy from the outside world. Moreover, in the face of threat of war, the League leaders began to take fright. The League never did muster its courage to carry through a decisive program, and in due course the movement for sanctions collapsed. The Emperor of Ethiopia, the unfortunate Haile Selassie, was compelled to bow before the power of the new Rome.

What was the attitude of the Roosevelt Administration during the course of these events? It is fair to say that it was less co-operative, so far as the League was concerned, than the attitude of Secretary Stimson in 1931. "With the isolationist sentiment so strong," says Secretary Hull in his memoirs, "it was impossible to join any League body considering sanctions. I preferred that any action we took should be entirely independent and not even seem to be suggested by the League." This attitude was maintained throughout the whole Ethiopian imbroglio, and it was approved by the President himself.

In the United States the breakdown of sanctions confirmed the isolationists in their point of view. Congress in 1936 enacted further neutrality legislation which, in addition to its embargo provisions, forbade the extending of loans to belligerents. When civil war broke out in Spain in the summer of 1936, the same formula was applied. The prevailing philosophy that the way to avoid war was to refuse to assist either of the belligerents was futile and even dangerous. In the case of an international war, as we have said, it would mean strengthening the aggressor against his victim, and in a civil war it tended to encourage revolt against an established government by denying arms to constituted authority. But the majorities in favor of this course were overwhelming, and the President hesitated to put his prestige to the test by vetoing such legislation.

The tide of sentiment represented by the Neutrality Acts did not cease to flow in 1936, but in 1937 and 1938 there were some signs, though only slight, of a reaction. When the national legislature set about framing a permanent statute in the first of these years, conflicting points of view were evident. Apart from the fact that the restriction on trade militated against a victim of aggression, there was the fact that commerce in time of war might be of great benefit to the United States and that to cut it off entirely might work serious damage to the national economy. A certain ambivalence was evident in the action of Congress. In pursuance of its objective of preventing (on the basis of American experience in the last war) involvement in the next one, the new legislation made it mandatory for the President to warn Americans off belligerent merchant ships. But with regard to trade, it was finally decided that the middle course was to permit belligerents to buy in the American market, provided that they paid in cash and carried away their purchases in their own vessels. The list of commodities to which this provision was to apply was to be fixed by the President himself.

There was to be a final expression of the isolationist philosophy in 1938. The most extraordinary of all proposals of this extraordinary epoch is what came to be known as the Ludlow amendment to the Constitution. This amendment, introduced by an Indiana congressman, provided that the United States could enter a war only after a national referendum. The American people, faced perhaps by some instant danger, were supposed to debate the issue in every part of the land, expose their divisions to the possible enemy, and fracture their national unity in time of peril by sharp and perhaps bitter discussion. Moreover, if such a measure were not dangerous, it would prove to be futile. For as the history of the United States demonstrates, the actual declaration of war usually follows protracted negotiation which, under our constitutional forms, is in the hands of the President. Wars do not come about suddenly. A long train of events makes up the issues on which the final decision depends. A wise President will be guided by public opinion in determining these issues, but the nation will doubtless in the future, as in the past, wish to sustain the Chief Executive.

Nevertheless, the idea contained in the Ludlow amendment had much support. A public opinion poll showed that 75 per cent of those questioned were in favor of the principle in 1935, 68 per cent in 1938. When the issue was brought to the floor of the House in the latter year, it was clear that a great parliamentary battle impended. The President spoke out against the proposal; so, too, did the Secretary of State. When the vote was taken, the count stood 209 in the affirmative and 188 in the negative (a two-thirds vote being required). Three out of every four Republicans had been recorded as in favor of this remarkable measure, and three out of every eight Democrats had taken the same position.

The Ludlow amendment represents the isolationist sentiment in its most extreme form. It was based on distrust of the executive, on a conception of foreign policy which would have accentuated internal division and made effective action impossible, on that kind of fear of war which encourages others to war. It was the high-water mark of the movement of American withdrawal. But before many months had gone by, the scene shifted drastically, and a new era arrived. Events in Europe set the stage for great changes in the orientation of American diplomacy.

THE DECLINE OF TIN PAN ALLEY

DORON K. ANTRIM, writing about Tin Pan Alley in *Scribner's* Magazine in 1936, charged that "the major music publishers are now subsidiaries of the motion-picture companies; and 80 per cent of the popular songs turned out today are written for pictures. The leading song writers are in Hollywood under contract, or are free-lancing there.

"Since the advent of radio the sale of sheet music has steadily declined. Prior to 1925, the life of a hit song was sixteen months, with a total sale of slightly over a million copies. Since 1931, a song is considered good if it keeps on top for three months with a total sale of around 230,000. The publishers have other sources of revenue—such as the royalties paid for performing rights (via ASCAP)—but more and more songs must come from the mill in view of the short life of each song.

"The new output runs mostly to smartness and sophistication. Mabel, who used to play the sweet simplicities of the bicycle era on the upright piano, would experience difficulties negotiating the modern, tricky harmonies and rhythms; songs are not written for Mabel any more. They are fashioned for the singing stars in films, such as Bing Crosby and Grace Moore, according to their styles, likes and dislikes." *

Record sales had followed much the same dismal declining sales curve as sheet music, but when the record player was attached to an electrical motor early in the decade, sales began to increase again. Records were played in the juke boxes and over radio. Then we had the "Lucky Strike Hit Parade." When a song made the list of the ten most popular in the nation, it was played over and over again, week after week, *ad nauseam,* until mercifully it fell out of favor with the public.

In contrast to songwriting today, the Thirties was surely a rich period. Lots of songs written then are still being heard today.

SONGS OF THE THIRTIES†

1930

THE Gershwin brothers wrote music for two Broadway musicals, *Strike Up the Band* and *Girl Crazy,* from which "The Man I Love," "I Got Rhythm," "Embraceable You," and "Bidin' My Time" were hits. In the first *Little Show,* two outstanding

* "Tin Pan Alley," *Scribner's,* February 1936.
† Song titles from Sigmund Spaeth's *A History of Popular Music in America* (New York, Random House, 1948).

608

show tunes were "Body and Soul" and "Something to Remember You By." Other hits from Broadway were "Cheerful Little Earful" and "Would You Like to Take a Walk" from *Sweet and Low*, and, from less memorable offerings, Rodgers and Hart gave us "Ten Cents a Dance," and Cole Porter, "Love for Sale."

From the movies came "Three Little Words" and "It Happened in Monterey."

From Tin Pan Alley, "Time On My Hands," "You're Driving Me Crazy," "The Waltz You Saved for Me" (Wayne King's theme song) and "Bye Bye Blues." Two flamboyant numbers were "The Peanut Vendor" and "Around the Corner."

1931

The Broadway musical *Of Thee I Sing* provided "Wintergreen for President," and *The Band Wagon* gave us "Dancing in the Dark"; Rodgers and Hart were again represented with "I've Got Five Dollars" from *America's Sweetheart*. Earl Carroll's *Vanities* gave us "Goodnight, Sweetheart," and George White's *Scandals* had "Life Is Just a Bowl of Cherries," "That's Why Darkies Are Born," and "My Song." Billy Rose was co-composer of a great hit in "I Found a Million Dollar Baby."

Successful pop tunes were "Mama Don't Want No Peas and Rice and Cocoanut Oil," "All of Me," "I Love a Parade," "Sweet and Lovely," and "River, Stay Way From My Door." Also "As Time Goes By," the song that would be rediscovered by Dooley Wilson in the motion picture *Casablanca* in 1943. And the song Eddie Cantor helped make famous: "Now's the Time to Fall in Love (Potatoes Are Cheaper)"; plus "Who's Your Little Whoozis" and " 'Swonderful."

1932

The decade's best-remembered song (and perhaps least played these days) was "Brother, Can You Spare a Dime?"

Ethel Merman in *Take a Chance* introduced "Eadie Was a Lady" and "You're an Old Smoothie." Cole Porter wrote "Night and Day" for *Gay Divorcee*.

The film *Forty-second Street* supplied "Shuffle Off to Buffalo" and "You're Getting to be a Habit With Me"; and Rodgers and Hart wrote "Mimi" for *Love Me Tonight*.

Two memorable pop tunes were "Shanty in Old Shanty Town" and "I Cover the Waterfront."

1933

The popular stage musical, *Roberta*, gave us "Smoke Gets in Your Eyes" and "Yesterday," by Jerome Kern.

The movies had the catchy tune "Carioca" in *Flying Down to Rio*, "We're in the Money" and "Did You Ever See a Dream Walking?" in *Gold Diggers of 1933*, and "Temptation," from *Going Hollywood*.

Big hits from Tin Pan Alley were "The Last Round-up," by Billy Hill, and later in the year "The Old Spinning Wheel," both of which had gone begging for publishers for years; plus Hoagy Carmichael's "Lazybones," Rodgers and Hart's "Lover," and Harold Arlen's "Stormy Weather."

1934

From Broadway, Cole Porter's "I Get a Kick Out of You" and "You're the Top" out of *Anything Goes*. Also, from other shows, "Wagon Wheels" and "Swing Low, Sweet Chariot."

Hollywood provided "Little Man, You've Had a Busy Day," "Love in

Bloom," "June in January," "The Continental," "Stay as Sweet as You Are" and "Two Cigarettes in the Dark"; also "Cocktails for Two" and "All I Do Is Dream of You."

Memorable pop tunes were Duke Ellington's "Solitude"; and "Moonglow," "The Object of My Affection," and "Easy Come, Easy Go."

1935

This year was graced with Gershwin's great musical *Porgy and Bess* and its wonderful songs—"Summertime," "I Got Plenty of Nuttin'," "It Ain't Necessarily So" and "Bess, You Is My Woman."

And Cole Porter in *Jubilee* gave us "Begin the Beguine" and "Just One of Those Things."

In Hollywood, Irving Berlin's first movie score for *Top Hat* provided "Cheek to Cheek," "Isn't This a Lovely Day," and "Top Hat, White Tie, and Tails"; the film *Every Night at Eight* had "I'm in the Mood for Love"; and "Paris in the Spring" came from the film with the same name.

Pop tunes were "Red Sails in the Sunset," "When I Grow Too Old to Dream," "Deep Purple," "You Are My Lucky Star" and Ellington's "In a Sentimental Mood." The wackiest song of the year, and maybe any other, was "The Music Goes Round and Round."

1936

Cole Porter wrote "I've Got You under My Skin" and "It's De-Lovely" for Fred Astaire's film *Born to Dance* and Ethel Merman's Broadway musical *Red, Hot and Blue*, respectively. Rodgers and Hart had "There's a Small Hotel" in the Broadway production *On Your Toes*, and Jerome

Kern, writing for the motion pictures, contributed "A Fine Romance" and "The Way You Look Tonight" to the film *Swing Time*. Bing Crosby sang "Pennies from Heaven" in the film of the same name, and Johnny Mercer satirized Western songs with "I'm an Old Cowhand." And Berlin wrote "I'm Putting All My Eggs in One Basket," "Let Yourself Go" and "Let's Face the Music and Dance" for the film *Follow the Fleet*.

Pop tunes were "Is It True What They Say about Dixie?" "It's a Sin to Tell a Lie," "Christopher Columbus," "Say Si Si," "Shoe Shine Boy," "I've Got a Feelin' You're Foolin'" and "Goody! Goody!"

1937

Rodgers and Hart wrote "The Lady Is a Tramp," "Where or When?" and "Johnny One-Note" for *Babes in Arms*, a Broadway musical.

Cole Porter supplied "In the Still of the Night" and "Rosalie" for the film *Rosalie*; Hollywood also gave us "That Old Feeling," "September in the Rain" and "Once in a While"; Bing Crosby introduced "Sweet Leilani" in the film *Waikiki Wedding*. And Irving Berlin's most memorable for the year was "I've Got My Love to Keep Me Warm."

Two crazy pop tunes were "Dipsy Doodle," by Larry Clinton, the bandleader, and "The Merry-Go-Round Broke Down"; Maxine Sullivan made "Loch Lomond" popular all over again. And Johnny Mercer's "Bob White (Whatcha Gonna Swing Tonight?)" was recorded by Bing Crosby and Connie Boswell, a rhythmic catchy tune. Last but not least were two songs, "Once in a While" and "Nice Work if You Can Get It," the last by the Gershwin brothers.

1938

The "Hit Parade" on radio could bring even an old song back to popularity, and this year saw the following revivals: "Little Sir Echo," "A Tisket, A Tasket" "Penny Serenade" and "Ti Pi Tin."

Rodgers and Hart had three shows playing simultaneously on Broadway: *I'd Rather Be Right*; *I Married an Angel*, with a title song of the same name; and *The Boys from Syracuse*, out of which came "This Can't Be Love" and "Sing for Your Supper."

In Hollywood, out of *The Big Broadcast of 1938*, we had "Thanks for the Memory." Walt Disney's *Snow White* had "Whistle While You Work," "Heigh Ho" and "Some Day My Prince Will Come"—all popular hits. Johnny Mercer wrote a couple of catchy tunes—"Jeepers Creepers (Where'd You Get Those Peep-

ers?)" and "You Must Have Been a Beautiful Baby."

The far-out tune for the year was Slam Stewart's "Flat Foot Floogey with the Floy Floy."

1939

From Broadway shows, we heard "I Didn't Know What Time It Was" by Rodgers and Hart from *Too Many Girls*, and Jerome Kern's "All the Things You Are" from *Very Warm for May*.

The pop songs of the year included "The Beer Barrel Polka," Johnny Mercer's "And the Angels Sing," Hoagy Carmichael's "I Get Along Without You Very Well," Saxie Dowell's "Three Little Fishes," and "I'll Never Smile Again," "The Hut Sut Song," "Sunrise Serenade," "South of the Border," "Scatterbrain," "Stairway to the Stars," "Wishing" and "If I Didn't Care."

THE MARVELS OF ADVERTISING

In 1936 J. P. Morgan told the press that if "you destroy the leisure class, you destroy civilization. By the leisure class, I mean the families who employ one servant—twenty-five to thirty million families." Hardly were the words out of his mouth, when the housewives pounced on him to prove that he must have got his ideas of American domesticity from Hollywood. In the 1930 census there were fewer than thirty million families in the country, and fewer than two million servants to attend them.

While Mr. Morgan obviously had been misinformed, there was no doubt that millions of mechanical servants and labor-saving devices were available for the home: canning, baking, dressmaking, ironing, cleaning, lighting, heating, laundry, refrigeration—hardly any phase of home life was unaffected. Surely the salesman must be given his credit, and his ally the advertiser. If the advertising world ever should run out of products to plug, we can all be sure that in their genius they will invent others. As David Cohn says, "By 1930 all the common ills of the body, such as body odor, bad breath, dandruff, and so on, had in fact been spoken for by a group of powerful concerns; for other aspiring manufacturers there remained only the opportunity of inventing new ones. Up to this point the public had accepted the advertising of hitherto unmentionable products designed to remedy unmentionable ills, and— wouldn't you know it?—by 1939, imaginative copy writers were inventing scores of new ills, and advertising the products to cure them." *

Listed below are some of the plagues which America saw itself confronted with in the pages of newspapers and magazines:

> Underarm Offense
> Pendulosis
> Undie Odor
> Paralyzed Pores
> Colon Collapse
> Ashtray Breath
> Office Hips
> Athlete's Foot

Early in the decade two monitors for the public good, Arthur Kallet and F. J. Schlink, armed with evidence from organizations devoted to research among consumers, published a book, *100,000,000 Guinea Pigs*, which took out after the advertisers, the food and drug industries, and even government agencies. They named names and set off charges against nationally advertised products such as mouth washes, antiseptic solutions, and tooth pastes, proclaiming them too feeble to justify the extravagant claims in their advertising; bran cereals touted for "roughage" were, they stated, too rough for sensitive intestines; and the amounts of sulfur dioxide used in preserving dried fruits were, according to their findings, dangerously above the maximum limit set by

* David L. Cohn, *The Good Old Days* (New York, Simon and Schuster, 1940).

the Food and Drug Administration. This kind of exposé, along with other efforts, put pressure on the businessmen of the day to tone down (temporarily, at least) some of their reckless claims.

DIXON WECTER

THE CONSUMER AND SCIENCE*

A STRIKING paradox lay in the contrast between the acute health-consciousness of the American people—mirrored in advertising, syndicated medical-advice columns, radio talks on hygiene, the huge drug-counter traffic and myriad symptoms of faddism—and the government's traditional timidity or parsimony in approaching public health.

The deepening of the Depression worsened conditions. In 1932–1933, for example, investigations showed that the highest sickness rate occurred among wage-earning families which had suffered abrupt losses in income and living standards, while in general it stood about forty per cent higher among the jobless than among the full-time employed. Childhood and youth naturally remained the principal victims, and in these years undoubtedly were sown many of the causes that led to the rejection in 1940–1941 by Army medical examiners of almost half the first two million registrants examined under selective service.

In February 1938, Senator Robert F. Wagner introduced a national health bill, proposing grants-in-aid to states to foster either tax-supported systems of general medical care or combinations of public medicine with universal health insurance. Meeting inflexible opposition from the American Medical Association, it failed of passage, even though a Gallup poll found a majority of doctors favorable to schemes of voluntary health insurance and Surgeon General Thomas Parran in July publicly observed that "at the present time people in general are beginning to take it for granted that an equal opportunity for health is a basic American right."

Short of compulsion, the putting of medical and hospital costs on an insurance basis was indeed the innovation which the Thirties brought to several million families, chiefly with modest incomes. Just as medical centers and private-group clinics were a prime development of the previous

* Excerpted from Dixon Wecter's *The Age of the Great Depression* (New York, Macmillan, 1948).

period, so that of the new decade was the group-health association and the hospitalization plan. By 1938 the plan had spread to about sixty cities, enrolling some three million subscribers.

The Twenties had brought extraordinary blatancy and meretriciousness to advertising, and one of the Depression's early effects upon many manufacturers was to promote the substitution of smaller containers, looser packing, subnormal weight, misbranding and inferior materials. With the consumer impelled as never before to spend his dollar advantageously, a profusion of books like Arthur Kallet and Frederick J. Schlink's *100,000,-000 Guinea Pigs* appeared to warn him of pitfalls. American Medical Association committees spearheaded reform in the drug market, while its committee on foods, created in 1929, awarded grudgingly its seal of approval, rejecting two out of every three products submitted and insisting upon revised labels and deflated advertising claims for most of the remainder.

The New Deal also took a hand in the matter. Besides short-lived efforts under the NRA, it set up the AAA's Consumers' Counsel, which in partnership with the Bureau of Agricultural Economics, Bureau of Home Economics and Bureau of Labor Statistics, inaugurated a biweekly bulletin called the *Consumer's Guide*. In addition, the Federal Trade Commission from 1934 onward obliged many advertisers to correct errors and temper the exuberance of their claims, and the Wheeler-Lea Act in 1938 considerably strengthened such controls. Meanwhile demands increased for a sweeping modernization of the Pure Food and Drug Act of 1906, notably after the death of over seventy users of an "Elixir Sulfanilamide" purveyed by a drug company. Despite apathy by the press and open hostility from many commercial concerns, but under urgent pressure from women's organizations, the Food, Drug and Cosmetic Act of June 24, 1938, scrapped obsolete legislation and widened the domain of federal authority, requiring adequate testing of new drugs before their introduction to the market, sharply defining adulteration and misbranding, and prohibiting deceptions effected by containers and labels.

If the consumer had the cash or credit, he could buy more commodities —for health, efficiency, convenience and luxury—than any earlier American had been able to command. Multiplying the marvels of synthetic chemistry, industrial research poured forth a stream of new attractive wares at low cost. Between 1920 and 1940 the number of industrial-research laboratories grew from three hundred to more than two thousand, the scientists and technical experts they employed from six thousand to sixty, with General Electric, Du Pont, Radio Corporation of America, and Westinghouse setting the pace. The miracles of applied chemistry shielded several big concerns from the worst consequences of the Depression, notably the Du Ponts, who embarked upon a sales campaign for the nonporous envelope called cellophane. The results were so successful that the public began to buy its prunes and caramels and cigarettes thus encased. The same concern pioneered a synthetic rubber under the name "duprene," utilizing a process devised by Dr. J. A. Nieuwland, announced in 1931. Its importance became evident ten years later when Japan sought to retaliate upon American oil and metal embargoes by choking off the flow of natural rubber across the Pacific.

In the novel field of chemurgy, which early caught the eye of Henry Ford as well as the Du Ponts, farm products ranging from soybeans to skim milk were converted into plastics, and in 1939 Congress subsidized regional laboratories for further research. From such materials as camphor, carbon, alcohol, urea, asbestos and formaldehyde still other synthetics were achieved. Nylon, a polyamide fiber made from coal, air and water, was introduced to an appreciative feminine public in 1939–1940, while coarser fibers of the same product went into toothbrushes. Plywood, fibers made from cellulose, and new steels containing molybdenum, vanadium, nickel, chromium and tungsten proved of immediate industrial and future military importance. Pyralin, fabrikoid, plexiglas, plastecele, lucite and vinylite were other innovations. Within a short space it dawned upon the average person that wonderful new substances now composed the fountain pen with which he wrote, the radio cabinet at his bedside, the sponge in his bathroom, the wheel by which he steered his car, his wife's dresses, and the motion-picture film which they saw projected on the screen. And, thanks to imaginative designers like Norman Bel Geddes, many such products tended to greater functionalism, beauty and clarity of color.

In the mid-Thirties the process of cracking heavy oils, after extraction of gas and gasoline, added millions of barrels of fuel for consumers' use as well as raw materials for industrial alcohol, lacquers, plastics and synthetic rubber. As still another aspect of laboratory conservation, polymerization, a technique causing combustible gases to combine into gasoline molecules, promised eventually to add nine billion gallons of gasoline to the nation's annual output.

Machines serving to replace man's senses, including the ability to gauge form and size and weight and to test pressure and temperature, were joined in 1930 by the first commercially practicable photoelectric cell. This Aladdin's lamp of modern science could see better and farther than the human eye, without error, fatigue or color blindness. It proved itself an incomparable servant for sorting articles, matching hues, counting passing objects, regulating light, automatically leveling elevators at floor stops, opening doors and guarding gates and prison walls.

In practical acoustics the radio telephone attained its majority, its use on planes and ships presaging the "walkie-talkie" of approaching war days. In 1937 the coaxial cable entered commercial use: a single wire by means of the crystal wave filter and the vacuum tube could now carry two hundred and forty simultaneous conversations.

New processes also affected eating habits. The commercial adoption in 1930 of solid carbon dioxide ("dry ice") made possible vastly longer shipments of fresh edibles by land and sea, for its gradual release of carbon-dioxide gas killed or checked bacterial growth. The extremely rapid freezing of foods, preserving them with their natural flavors, had been devised in 1925 by Clarence Birdseye, and the method, bought by General Foods, was introduced to the retail trade in 1930. Four years later ten million pounds of such frozen foods as peas, corn, berries, oysters and other perishables were being sold. By the end of the decade the costs of refrigeration had been reduced by over three fourths, and though prices still remained higher than for fresh foodstuffs, the volume had grown to two hundred million pounds.

Even more sweeping developments in the American dietary came from physiological and medical research concerning vitamins. These investigations had begun before the First World War, but the modest total of forty-seven papers published on that topic in 1911 had grown to fifteen hundred annually by 1930. Knowledge advanced swiftly in regard to vitamin complexes, relations of vitamins to each other and to hormones, and their general effect upon metabolism, health, susceptibility to disease and longevity. The nature of vitamin A remained largely a mystery until the important work done in 1929 by Yale's M. D. Tyson and Arthur H. Smith; in the next year its plant source was identified with the pigment carotin. Vitamins A and B_1 were synthesized in 1936 and, largely through the researches of the Texan Tom D. Spies, nicotinic acid within the B_2 complex was discovered to be the cure for the Southern poor whites' scourge, pellagra. In 1937 Edward A. Doisy of St. Louis isolated vitamin K from alfalfa, and shortly afterward showed its potency in checking hemorrhage. On the other hand, these years brought into use the drug heparin, having precisely the opposite effect, and in the latter Thirties this anticoagulant began to be employed with marked success in preventing thrombosis and in treating bacterial heart disease.

The publicity about vitamins helped to modify certain culinary practices. Housewives learned not to keep fresh foods too long before consumption as well as not to boil vegetables excessively and then throw out the water; increasing use of the pressure cooker was thought to preserve vitamins; and more vegetables were served raw than ever before.

Physiology and medicine also recorded other important advances. Greatest was the discovery of sulfa drugs, particularly sulfanilamide, sulfapyridine and sulfathiazole. Pioneered in Germany, they were perfected and applied to new uses in the United States.

The widespread use by hospitals of desiccated blood plasma, perfected about 1940, held immense significance for the future. Rapid gains occurred in the thoracic field. In 1930, for example, the artificial lung was invented, enabling those with paralyzed chest muscles to survive, and new surgical techniques rendered it possible to remove an entire lung to check cancerous growth.

Along the borders of physiology and psychiatry occurred certain fruitful developments, such as the adoption in 1937 of the insulin-shock treatment for schizophrenia.

Such innovations as air-conditioning equipment, plastics, prefabricated houses, the photoelectric cell, synthetic rubber, television, gasoline from coal, et cetera, made it plain that, during the time when millions vainly sought work and hosts of factories rusted in idleness, technology had marched sturdily forward. In 1937 twenty per cent more goods and services could be produced than in 1929, with no additions to the labor force, and one engineer reckoned that something less than a twenty-four-hour work week could be made to serve all American productive needs. A Gallup poll in June 1939, asking those on relief, "What do you blame for the present unemployment in this country?" reported that the largest percentage said, "machines taking the place of men"—a reason both dispassionate and intelligent.

Some of these marvels of technology were displayed by the three great fairs of these years. Chicago's "Century of Progress" drew about ten million admissions in its first season in 1933. Unlike her glorification of Old World Culture in the exposition of forty years earlier, this occasion featured native achievements in invention and engineering, and its Hall of Science drew the largest number of visitors. The summer of 1939, febrile last season before the catastrophe of the Second World War, saw parallel exhibitions on opposite shores of the continent, with railways taking advantage of the circumstance by offering excursion rates to "See Two World's Fairs." San Francisco's Golden Gate Exposition, true to its architectural motif drawn from pre-Columbian and Spanish America, tended somewhat to play down modernism and technology save for the most ambitious floodlighting in color ever attempted and a lavish aeronautical display.

Bigger and more catholic was New York's "World of Tomorrow," its emblem of trylon and perisphere (a spire rising from the globe) symbolizing "the theme of social reconstruction." Its twenty-nine million admissions in 1939, including the King and Queen of England on an unprecedented good-will tour, saw the début of fluorescent lighting on a large scale, radio broadcasting of facsimile newspapers and a ten-million-volt lightning bolt discharged at intervals "to show how man has chained the forces of nature." The "Town of Tomorrow," bristling with innovations in housing, and the "Electrified Farm," revealing the wonders of hydroponics (the soilless cultivation of plants), attracted millions. Foreign nations occupied twenty-two variegated pavilions flanking the Court of Peace, with Nazi Germany conspicuously missing. Czechoslovakia, her independence lately destroyed, attempted nevertheless to carry on; Italy featured a gigantic waterfall and Japan a Shinto shrine enclosing a replica of the Liberty Bell made of eleven thousand cultured pearls and four hundred diamonds; while over the Soviet building the colossal figure of a worker towered into the sky holding aloft the Red Star. It was indeed the World of Tomorrow in parables and ironies. But, whatever political allegories might have been fancied beneath the show, the triumph of technology stood clearly forth, with some forecast of its still unwritten and perhaps incalculable effect upon the fate of modern man.

"MAYBE YOU CAN EXPLAIN IT TO ME"

GREAT STRIDES had been made in science and medicine, and in other vital areas of the physical world. But men did not seem to know enough about how to live with each other compatibly. There was still poverty —the President announced toward the end of the decade that one third of the nation was still ill-housed, ill-clad, and ill-nourished. For instance, there were still a million-odd migrant farm workers; listen to one of them speaking to a *Fortune* writer in 1939:

"Mister, you been to college, you learned things there—maybe you can tell me what's to become of us. You see, back in Oklahoma we had a farm. There's me and the three kids and the old lady and my mother. We got along, yea, and then things started to happen. First came the Depression and we couldn't get nothin' for our crops. Make maybe two hundred dollars a year. Course the farm started to go downhill—to dry up—and fust thing I knowed the whole blamed farm had dried up and blown away. Course, it weren't quite as quick as all that. There were a couple of years when we tried mighty hard. Didn't eat much those years.

"Well, come '35 it weren't no use trying any longer so we just packed up and pulled out. Came out here cause we hear you could make fair money harvesting crops. And ya know we did make fair money the fust year. Ya see the kids are twelve, fourteen, and fifteen years old so all of us can work except my maw—when there's work to be got. Well, we picked peas in the Imperial and Santa Maria, potatoes at Stockton, and grapes at Napa. We made high as seventeen, eighteen dollars a day. Course it costs a lot to move around and there was a time when we couldn't get no work, but we done purty good. Then last year we made the same places but it weren't no good. They didn't pay so good last year. Cut from thirty-five to twenty-five cents an hour and piece work was lower. We got by, though. But, God, Mister, what's going to happen to us this year? Here it is March and I only worked about two weeks so far. I tried every place and everybody but it weren't no good. People has kept comin' in here so now there's six for every job—and darn few jobs. See that sign? Says forty-five cents for picking a hundred pounds o' cotton. Know how long it takes to pick a hundred pounds o' cotton down here? Well, it takes just about a whole day. You know you can't feed a family o' six on forty-five cents a day. It ain't my fault, is it? Jees, I worked hard since I was a kid. I allus done what I thought was right, and I think I know right from wrong. I allus tried to teach my kids right from wrong. But I'm beginnin' to wonder. I don't know what to do. There's nothin' back in Oklahoma for us to go to and now there's nothin' here. Somehow somethin' don't seem right—I want to work and I can't—I want to bring up my kids decent. You been to college, Mister, maybe you can explain it to me." *

And there was the festering cancer of race prejudice. Anti-semitism was already somewhat diminished when the trauma of Nazism roused peo- ple against its evils. Fissures were also beginning to appear in the old, hardened attitudes of white toward Negro Americans. And behind every little victory were individuals who would rally to the cause of free men regardless of color or creed.

WALTER WHITE

MARIAN ANDERSON AND THE D.A.R.†

On an early spring afternoon in Washington in March 1939 a vivacious, auburn-haired Washington newspaper correspondent, Mary Johnston, excitedly called me out of the Senate gallery, where I was listening to another filibuster. She had just come from an interview with the president of the Daughters of the American Revolution, Mrs. Henry M. Robert, Jr., who had bluntly told Miss Johnston that neither Marian Anderson nor any other Negro artist would be permitted to appear in Constitution Hall. Indignant at this lily-white policy, Miss Johnston wanted me to give her a statement which she could use in a story.

I had watched Miss Anderson's struggle against poverty and prejudice with more than ordinary interest. Following the success of Roland Hayes, she gave a recital in New York's Town Hall in 1925 which might better have been postponed a year or so. That evening Marian sang badly, though those who have listened to her in later years will find difficulty in believing that anyone with so great a voice could ever sing other than perfectly. Perhaps her performance that evening was due to stage fright. Some believe that the fault was due to the voice teacher with whom she was studying. He was a devotee of the *bel canto* school, and had attempted to raise Marian's voice a full octave. The New York critics that next day were harsh, even bitter. Most of them recognized the existence of a great voice, but some of them pontifically declared that it had been ruined.

Marian was so heartbroken that she vowed never to sing again. Some

* "I Wonder Where We Can Go Now," *Fortune*, April 1939.
† From Walter White's *A Man Called White* (New York, Viking, 1948).

months later the N.A.A.C.P. was holding its annual conference in Phila-delphia. Roland Hayes was to be presented with the Spingarn Medal and the presentation was to be made by the provost of the University of Pennsylvania, the scholarly and eloquent Josiah H. Penniman. Harry T. Burleigh, the famous composer and baritone of New York's St. George's and Temple Emanu-El, was scheduled to accept the medal for Roland *in absentia*, as Roland was then on a concert tour in Europe. We invited Marian to sing, but received a flat refusal. It took long persuasion to induce her to change her mind. But on Spingarn Medal night in crowded Wither-spoon Hall she sang superbly and was forced to give encore after encore and then to take curtain call after curtain call. When at last the applause had subsided and the ordeal ended, Marian burst into tears and exclaimed, "Thank God! I've got my faith again!"

Now I welcomed Mary Johnston's suggestion, but pointed out that no one would be surprised to learn that I was indignant at the action of the D.A.R., and suggested that we get statements instead from some of Miss Anderson's famous fellow artists.

Mary agreed. Utilizing one of the high window sills of the Senate gallery as a desk, we drafted a telegram and compiled a list of distinguished musi-cians whom we would telegraph for comments. With gratifying speed the replies poured in from Lawrence Tibbett, Leopold Stokowski, Walter Damrosch, Kirsten Flagstad, Geraldine Farrar, and others, all praising Miss Anderson as a great artist and expressing indignation and almost disbelief that the D.A.R. had taken the action we had reported.

On my return to New York, I found Sam Hurok, Miss Anderson's manager, as indignant as I have ever known him to be. He proposed that attention be focused on the bigotry of the Daughters of the American Revolution by asking Miss Anderson to sing an open-air, free concert in Washington.

The idea was exciting. The most logical place was the Lincoln Memorial. Mr. Hurok agreed, and asked Gerald Goode to go to Washington with me to see if arrangements could be made. Virginia-born Oscar Chapman, Assistant Secretary of the Interior, with characteristic intelligence was enormously enthusiastic. He made an immediate appointment with Harold Ickes, Secretary of the Interior and throughout his life an unequivocal battler for justice to the Negro. Mr. Ickes was equally excited over the prospect of such a demonstration of democracy. President Roosevelt was leaving that afternoon for Warm Springs. But Mr. Ickes would not let him leave until the President had permitted him to come to the White House to tell the story. Hearing it, the President gave his approval and told Mr. Ickes to provide whatever facilities were necessary to make the concert the greatest event of its kind ever held.

The engagement for which the Daughters of the American Revolution had refused the use of Constitution Hall had been arranged by Howard University. Since the university was dependent for support upon congressional appropriations, Mr. Hurok did not want to involve it in a protest which might have widespread repercussions. He therefore made a proposal which was more difficult to turn down than any other I have received in all the years of my connection with the Association. He suggested that the Lincoln Memorial concert be under the auspices of the N.A.A.C.P. It would have meant publicity for the Association which could not have been bought for many tens of thousands of dollars.

But there was a broader issue involved than publicity. Because the N.A.A.C.P. is known as a fighting propaganda agency, its sponsorship of the concert might have created the impression that propaganda for the Negro was the objective instead of the emphasizing of a principle. I, therefore, proposed that the concert be given under the most distinguished and nonpartisan auspices possible—namely, a sponsoring committee on which would be asked to serve such persons as members of the Cabinet and the Supreme Court, senators, congressmen, editors, artists, and others who believed that art should know no color line.

It was natural that we should think instantly of Mrs. Eleanor Roosevelt as chairman of such a sponsoring committee. She had invited me to her apartment in New York a few days before to ask my advice on her resigning from the D.A.R. in protest against the treatment accorded Miss Anderson. She had resigned, and this focused world-wide attention on the episode. However, I did not feel that Mrs. Roosevelt should put herself on the spot, particularly since reactionaries in the South were already pillorying her for her attitude on the Negro.

I therefore went to Mrs. Caroline O'Day, Congresswoman-at-large from New York State, whose Southern birth in Savannah, Georgia, and whose standing and integrity were such as to make her the next logical choice as chairman of the sponsoring committee. Mrs. O'Day enthusiastically accepted the chairmanship and turned over all the facilities of her office to us for use in sending telegraphic invitations to those selected to be asked to serve on the sponsoring committee.

A few politically minded individuals—chiefly in Congress—were cagey. Some had their secretaries wire that the invitations would be "brought to the attention" of their employers. A few sought refuge in excuses like "my position makes it unwise for me to participate in controversial issues of this character." But the overwhelming majority of those invited accepted membership with promptness and enthusiasm. Justices of the Supreme Court, top-flight artists of world reputation, writers, diplomats, Cabinet officers, congressmen and senators, men and women of lesser renown, agreed to serve and thereby express their admiration for Miss Anderson and their indignation at the cavalier treatment the D.A.R. had given her. Seldom in history had a more distinguished group of Americans rallied to affirmation of democracy.

Among the sponsors were Mrs. Franklin D. Roosevelt and many other nationally and internationally known figures.

I drove down to Washington on Easter Eve. The weather was crisp and cold but heavy with the promise of approaching spring. However, as I approached Washington sleet began to fall. With it fell my hopes. I went to bed low in spirits because of the snow piling up on the streets outside. Weeks of thought and all our hard work seemed about to be thwarted by nature. I was almost afraid to look out of the window when I awoke early the next morning. I shouted with happiness to see the sun.

The concert was scheduled to begin at five o'clock. We drove to the Lincoln Memorial, approaching it from the rear. We had to park the car blocks away because every available place near by had already been pre-empted. What a sight greeted us when we came around to the front of the Memorial! Every one of the several hundred chairs which had been placed on the lower platform was occupied. Seldom in the history even of Washington had a more distinguished group of sponsors been gathered. But much more important to us was the audience itself. Seventy-five thousand white and colored Americans not only from Washington but from cities, towns and villages within a radius of hundreds of miles had gathered at the Memorial of the Great Emancipator to hear a singer of whom Toscanini had said: "A voice like yours comes but once in a century."

No member of that audience will ever forget the sight of Miss Anderson emerging from a small anteroom beside Gaudens' statue of Lincoln. She was apparently calm, but those of us who knew her were aware of the great perturbation beneath her serene exterior. On her right was gentle Georgia-born Caroline O'Day. On her left was Virginia-born Oscar Chapman. A tremendous wave of applause rose from the vast throng, which was silenced only when Miss Anderson gently raised her hand to ask that the concert be permitted to begin. Amplifiers poured out the thunderous chords of the opening bars of "America." Clasping her hands before her Miss Anderson poured out in her superb voice "sweet land of liberty" almost as though it was a prayer.

As the last notes of "Nobody Knows the Trouble I've Seen" faded away the spell was broken by the rush of the audience toward Miss Anderson, which almost threatened tragedy. Oscar Chapman plowed through the crowd and directed me to the microphone to plead with them not to create a panic. As I did so, but with indifferent success, a single figure caught my eye in the mass of people below which seemed one of the most important and touching symbols of the occasion. It was a slender black girl dressed in somewhat too garishly hued Easter finery. Hers was not the face of one who had been the beneficiary of much education or opportunity. Her hands were particularly noticeable as she thrust them forward and upward, trying desperately, though she was some distance away from Miss Anderson, to touch the singer. They were hands which despite their youth had known only the dreary work of manual labor. Tears streamed down the girl's dark face. Her hat was askew, but in her eyes flamed hope bordering on ecstasy. Life which had been none too easy for her now held out greater hope because one who was also colored and who, like herself, had known poverty, privation and prejudice, had, by her genius, gone a long way toward conquering bigotry. If Marian Anderson could do it, the girl's eyes seemed to say, then I can, too.

THE NATION'S HEARTBEAT WAS NEVER
MORE LOUD AND CLEAR

WITH so much still to be done, there was to be no opportunity for the government and the people to work together to finish the job: war was to come some months later.

Those who have written about the Thirties end their narratives usually with the solemn announcement of imminent war. But war is neither an end nor a beginning; after the war, even bigger chores faced America. The international scene absorbed our attention before we could turn to our own problems.

The work was still there to be done, as we see clearly in this year, 1961—in conservation, better regulatory practices for business and labor, fairer taxation, integration— a list as long as one's arm.

Perhaps what had happened to America in the Thirties made it easier for us to understand the crises, the catastrophes and plain human suffering in other parts of the world; and, I hope, now in our own country.

I like to believe, as does Frank Brookhouser, "that in the Thirties, despite their troubles and their tragedies, the men, women and children in America loved more strongly, felt more deeply, generated more warmth, and held more compassion for their fellow men than ever in our history, before or since.

"The people had more character.

"It was, granted, a grim and heartbreaking period in many ways. But the people triumphed over the loss and the disappointment and the suffering and the heartache. And never was the nation's heartbeat more loud and clear." *

* Frank Brookhouser, *These Were Our Years* (Garden City, N. Y., Doubleday, 1959).

ABOUT THE EDITOR

DON CONGDON *spent his early years in Pennsylvania in a coal-mining valley near Butler, and later went to high school in a chair-factory town near Erie. He came to New York in 1935, where he found work as messenger in a literary agency. Later he was an Associate Fiction Editor at* Collier's *Magazine and an Editor at Simon and Schuster. For the past fourteen years he has been an associate in the Harold Matson Company, an agency handling the work of some of America's most distinguished authors.*

Mr. Congdon has edited several other anthologies, among them The Wild Sweet Wine, Stories for the Dead of Night, *and two volumes on World War II,* Combat: European Theatre *and* Combat: Pacific Theatre.